THEORY *in* SOCIAL *and* CULTURAL ANTHROPOLOGY

AN ENCYCLOPEDIA

THEORY *in* SOCIAL *and* CULTURAL ANTHROPOLOGY

AN ENCYCLOPEDIA

EDITORS

R. Jon McGee
Richard L. Warms

Texas State University

1

SAGE reference

Los Angeles | London | New Delhi
Singapore | Washington DC

⑤SAGE reference

Los Angeles | London | New Delhi
Singapore | Washington DC

FOR INFORMATION:

SAGE Publications, Inc.
2455 Teller Road
Thousand Oaks, California 91320
E-mail: order@sagepub.com

SAGE Publications Ltd.
1 Oliver's Yard
55 City Road
London, EC1Y 1SP
United Kingdom

SAGE Publications India Pvt. Ltd.
B 1/I 1 Mohan Cooperative Industrial Area
Mathura Road, New Delhi 110 044
India

SAGE Publications Asia-Pacific Pte. Ltd.
3 Church Street
#10-04 Samsung Hub
Singapore 049483

Acquisitions Editor: Jim Brace-Thompson
Developmental Editor: Sanford J. Robinson
Production Editor: Jane Haenel
Reference Systems Manager: Leticia Gutierrez
Reference Systems Coordinators: Laura Notton and
    Anna Villasenor
Copy Editors: QuADS
Typesetter: Hurix Systems Pvt. Ltd.
Proofreader: Susan Schon
Indexer: Jeanne Busemeyer
Cover Designer: Glenn Vogel
Marketing Manager: Carmel Schrire

Printed in the United States of America.

Library of Congress Cataloging-in-Publication Data

Theory in social and cultural anthropology : an encyclopedia / edited
by R. Jon McGee and Richard L. Warms, Texas State University.

pages cm

Includes bibliographical references and index.

ISBN 978-1-4129-9963-2 (hardcover)

1. Ethnology—Encyclopedias. I. McGee, R. Jon, 1955–

GN307.T54 2013
306.03—dc23

2013016332

13 14 15 16 17 10 9 8 7 6 5 4 3 2 1

Contents

List of Entries

Reader's Guide

American Anthropologists and Anthropology

Abu-Lughod, Lila
American Anthropological Association
American Museum of Natural History
Applied Anthropology
Benedict, Ruth F.
Binford, Lewis R.
Bloomfield, Leonard
Boas, Franz
Bohannan, Paul
Burke, Kenneth
Butler, Judith
Carneiro, Robert L.
Chicago World's Columbian Exposition (1893)
Chodorow, Nancy
Chomsky, Noam
Clifford, James
Columbia University
Culture Area Approach
Du Bois, W. E. B.
DuBois, Cora
Dundes, Alan
Fischer, Michael
Foster, George M.
Fried, Morton
Geertz, Clifford
Goffman, Erving
Goldenweiser, Alexander A.
Goodenough, Ward H.
Greenberg, Joseph
Gumperz, John J.
Hall, Edward T.
Hallowell, A. Irving
Harris, Marvin
Herskovitz, Melville
Hurston, Zora Neale
Hymes, Dell
Jameson, Fredric

Kardiner, Abram
Kluckhohn, Clyde
Kroeber, Alfred L.
Labov, William
Lamphere, Louise
Leacock, Eleanor
LeVine, Robert
Lewis, Oscar
Linton, Ralph
Lounsbury, Floyd
Lowie, Robert
Marcus, George
Mead, George Herbert
Mead, Margaret
Mintz, Sidney
Morgan, Lewis Henry
Murdock, George Peter
Nader, Laura
Nash, June
Ortner, Sherry
Parsons, Elsie C.
Parsons, Talcott
Pike, Kenneth
Rabinow, Paul
Radin, Paul
Rappaport, Roy
Redfield, Robert
Rockefeller Foundation
Rosaldo, Michelle Zimbalist
Rosaldo, Renato
Sahlins, Marshall
Sanday, Peggy Reeves
Sapir, Edward
Scheper-Hughes, Nancy
Schneider, David M.
Service, Elman R.
Smithsonian Institution
Spiro, Melford
Steward, Julian
Swadesh, Morris

Tax, Sol
Tedlock, Barbara and Dennis
Tyler, Stephen A.
University of California, Berkeley
University of Michigan
Vayda, Andrew P.
Veblen, Thorstein B.
Wagley, Charles
Wallace, Anthony F. C.
Wallerstein, Immanuel
Wenner-Gren Foundation
White, Leslie
Whorf, Benjamin Lee
Wilson, Edward O.
Wolf, Eric

Biological and/or Social Evolutionary Perspective

Bastian, Adolf
Carneiro, Robert L.
Comparative Method
Condorcet, Jean-Antoine Nicolas de Caritat
Cultural Transmission
Darwin, Charles
Dawkins, Richard
Ethology, Human
Evolutionary Anthropology
Evolutionary Psychology
Freud, Sigmund
Fried, Morton
Gene-Culture Coevolution
Human Behavioral Ecology
Human Universals
Lubbock, John
Maine, Henry James
Malthus, Thomas R.
McLennan, John
Morgan, Lewis Henry
Müller, Max
Murdock, George Peter
Pitt Rivers, Augustus Henry Lane Fox
Service, Elman R.
Smith, Grafton Elliot
Spencer, Herbert
Sperber, Dan
Spiro, Melford
Steward, Julian
Tylor, Edward Burnett
Wallace, Alfred R.

Westermarck, Edward
White, Leslie
Wilson, Edward O.
Wittfogel, Karl

British and Commonwealth

Bailey, Frederick G.
Bateson, Gregory
Cambridge University
Darwin, Charles
Dawkins, Richard
Douglas, Mary
Evans-Pritchard, E. E.
Ferguson, Adam
Firth, Raymond
Fortes, Meyer
Fortune, Reo
Frazer, James G.
Gluckman, Max
Goody, Jack
Great Exhibition of 1851 (Crystal Palace)
Haddon, Alfred C.
Harvey, David
Hobbes, Thomas
Hocart, Arthur M.
Kuper, Hilda B.
Leach, Edmund
Lienhardt, Godfrey
London School of Economics
Lubbock, John
Maine, Henry James
Mair, Lucy
Malinowski, Bronisław
Malthus, Thomas R.
Manchester School
McLennan, John
Needham, Rodney
Oxford University
Pitt Rivers, Augustus Henry Lane Fox
Radcliffe-Brown, A. R.
Rhodes-Livingstone Institute
Richards, Audrey
Rivers, W. H. R.
Royal Anthropological Institute
Schapera, Isaac
Seligman, Charles Gabriel
Smith, Adam
Smith, Grafton Elliot
Smith, Neil

Godelier, Maurice
Gramsci, Antonio
Harris, Marvin
Herskovits, Melville
Human Behavioral Ecology
Leacock, Eleanor
Mair, Lucy
Malinowski, Bronisław
Malthus, Thomas R.
Marx, Karl
Marxist Anthropology
Material Production, Theories of
Mauss, Marcel
Meillassoux, Claude
Mintz, Sidney
Morgan, Lewis Henry
Nash, June
Polanyi, Karl
Political Economy
Rappaport, Roy
Rational Choice Theory
Richards, Audrey
Sahlins, Marshall
Sanday, Peggy Reeves
Scheper Hughes, Nancy
Service, Elman R.
Smith, Adam
Smith, Neil
Steward, Julian
Structural Marxism
Sustainability
Systems Theory
Tax, Sol
Vayda, Andrew P.
Veblen, Thorstein B.
Wagley, Charles
Wallerstein, Immanuel
Weber, Max
White, Leslie
Wittfogel, Karl
Wolf, Eric
World-Systems Theory

Ethnography

Abu-Lughod, Lila
Asad, Talal
Bailey, Frederick G.
Barth, Fredrik
Bateson, Gregory
Benedict, Ruth F.

Boas, Franz
Bohannan, Paul
Douglas, Mary
DuBois, Cora
Dumont, Louis
Evans-Pritchard, E. E.
Face-to-Face Interaction
Firth, Raymond
Fortes, Meyer
Fortune, Reo
Foster, George M.
Frobenius, Leo
Geertz, Clifford
Gluckman, Max
Godelier, Maurice
Goldenweiser, Alexander A.
Goody, Jack
Griaule, Marcel
Haddon, Alfred C.
Hallowell, A. Irving
Herskovits, Melville
Hocart, Arthur M.
Hurston, Zora Neale
Kluckhohn, Clyde
Kroeber, Alfred L.
Kuper, Hilda B.
Lafitau, Joseph-François
Leach, Edmund
Lévi-Strauss, Claude
Lewis, Oscar
Lienhardt, Godfrey
Lowie, Robert
Mair, Lucy
Malinowski, Bronisław
Mead, Margaret
Murdock, George Peter
Parsons, Elsie C.
Radin, Paul
Redfield, Robert
Richards, Audrey
Rosaldo, Michelle Zimbalist
Rosaldo, Renato
Sanday, Peggy Reeves
Schapera, Isaac
Scheper Hughes, Nancy
Seligman, Charles Gabriel
Spencer, Walter Baldwin, and
   Francis James Gillen
Spiro, Melford
Srinivas, M. N.

French

Alliance-Descent Debate
Althusser, Louis
Barthes, Roland
Bataille, Georges
Baudrillard, Jean
Bloch, Maurice
Bourdieu, Pierre
Comte, Auguste
Condorcet, Jean-Antoine Nicolas de Caritat
Deleuze, Gilles, and Félix Guattari
Derrida, Jacques
Dumont, Louis
Durkheim, Émile
Foucault, Michel
Geffray, Christian
Gennep, Arnold van
Girard, René
Godelier, Maurice
Griaule, Marcel
Hertz, Robert
Institut d'Ethnologie (Paris)
Lacan, Jacques
Lafitau, Joseph-François
L'Année Sociologique
Latour, Bruno
Lévi-Strauss, Claude
Lévy-Bruhl, Lucien
Lyotard, Jean-François
Mauss, Marcel
Meillassoux, Claude
Montesquieu, Comte de
Musée de l'Homme
Rivet, Paul
Rouch, Jean
Rousseau, Jean-Jacques
Sperber, Dan
Voltaire

Gender

Abu-Lughod, Lila
Alliance-Descent Debate
Butler, Judith
Childhood
Chodorow, Nancy
Cultural Transmission
Feminist Anthropology
Gender and Anthropology
Godelier, Maurice

Hurston, Zora Neale
Lacan, Jacques
Lamphere, Louise
Leacock, Eleanor
Material Production, Theories of
Mauss, Marcel
Mead, Margaret
Nash, June
Ortner, Sherry
Parsons, Elsie C.
Queer Theory
Race
Religion
Richards, Audrey
Rosaldo, Michelle Zimbalist
Sanday, Peggy Reeves
Scheper-Hughes, Nancy
Strathern, Marilyn
Subaltern Studies
Veblen, Thorstein B.
Wolf, Eric

German

Bachofen, Johann J.
Bastian, Adolf
Benjamin, Walter
Frankfurt School
Frobenius, Leo
Gadamer, Hans-Georg
Graebner, Fritz
Habermas, Jürgen
Hegel, Georg W. F.
Husserl, Edmund
Marx, Karl
Müller, Max
Simmel, Georg
Weber, Max
Wittfogel, Karl
Wundt, Wilhelm

Globalization

Abu-Lughod, Lila
Anderson, Benedict
Appadurai, Arjun
Applied Anthropology
Area Studies
Asad, Talal
Barth, Fredrik
Critical Theory

Dependency Theory
Economic Anthropology
Fanon, Frantz
Globalization Theory
Harvey, David
Jameson, Fredric
Lamphere, Louise
Marx, Karl
Marxist Anthropology
Mintz, Sidney
Mobility
Nash, June
Nationalism; Transnationalism
Polanyi, Karl
Political Economy
Postcolonial theory
Race
Sahlins, Marshall
Said, Edward
Scapes
Scheper-Hughes, Nancy
Smith, Neil
Subaltern Studies
Tambiah, Stanley
Urban Studies
Wagley, Charles
Wallerstein, Immanuel
Wolf, Eric
World-Systems Theory

Linguistics

Bakhtin, Mikhail M.
Barthes, Roland
Bloomfield, Leonard
Chomsky, Noam
Comparative Linguistics
Descriptive Linguistics
Ethnography of Speaking
Face-to-Face Interaction
Generative Grammar
Goodenough, Ward H.
Greenberg, Joseph
Gumperz, John J.
Hymes, Dell
Jakobson, Roman O.
Labov, William
Lounsbury, Floyd
Müller, Max
Pike, Kenneth

Prague School of Linguistics
Rivet, Paul
Sapir, Edward
Sapir-Whorf Hypothesis and Neo-Whorfianism
Saussure, Ferdinand de
Semiotics
Sociolinguistics
Swadesh, Morris
Whorf, Benjamin Lee

Literary and Interpretive Perspective

Abu-Lughod, Lila
Bailey, Frederick G.
Bataille, Georges
Benjamin, Walter
Boas, Franz
Burke, Kenneth
Clifford, James
Deleuze, Gilles, and Félix Guattari
Derrida, Jacques
Douglas, Mary
Du Bois, W. E. B.
Evans-Pritchard, E. E.
Fortes, Meyer
Foster, George M.
Foucault, Michel
Frankfurt School
Frazer, James G.
Frobenius, Leo
Geertz, Clifford
Geffray, Christian
Gennep, Arnold van
Gluckman, Max
Goldenweiser, Alexander A.
Goody, Jack
Graebner, Fritz
Griaule, Marcel
Hallowell, A. Irving
Humanistic Anthropology
Hurston, Zora Neale
Hymes, Dell
Jameson, Fredric
Kluckhohn, Clyde
Kroeber, Alfred L.
Kuper, Hilda B.
Leach, Edmund
Lévi-Strauss, Claude
Lewis, Oscar
Lienhardt, Godfrey

Lounsbury, Floyd
Lowie, Robert
Müller, Max
Nader, Laura
Needham, Rodney
Neo-Boasianism
Ortner, Sherry
Phenomenology
Postmodernism
Practice Theory
Rabinow, Paul
Radcliffe-Brown, A. R.
Radin, Paul
Redfield, Robert
Rouch, Jean
Sahlins, Marshall
Said, Edward
Sapir, Edward
Schneider, David M.
Semiotics
Smith, William Robertson
Srinivas, M. N.
Strathern, Marilyn
Symbolic and Interpretive Anthropology
Symbolic Interactionism
Tambiah, Stanley
Tedlock, Barbara and Dennis
Thick Description
Turner, Victor W.
Voltaire
Wallace, Anthony F. C.
Wilson, Monica

Marxist and Neo-Marxist Perspective

Althusser, Louis
Bakhtin, Mikhail M.
Baudrillard, Jean
Benjamin, Walter
Bloch, Maurice
Bourdieu, Pierre
Critical Theory
Dependency Theory
Fanon, Frantz
Frankfurt School
Godelier, Maurice
Gramsci, Antonio
Harvey, David
Jameson, Fredric
Lacan, Jacques

Latour, Bruno
Leacock, Eleanor
Lyotard, Jean-François
Marx, Karl
Marxist Anthropology
Material Production, Theories of
Meillassoux, Claude
Mintz, Sidney
Smith, Neil
Structural Marxism
Wallerstein, Immanuel
White, Leslie
Wittfogel, Karl
Wolf, Eric

Nineteenth Century and Earlier

Animism, Animatism
Aristotle
Bachofen, Johann J.
Bastian, Adolf
Comparative Method
Comte, Auguste
Condorcet, Jean-Antoine
    Nicolas de Caritat
Darwin, Charles
Ferguson, Adam
Frazer, James G.
Great Exhibition of 1851
    (Crystal Palace)
Haddon, Alfred C.
Hegel, Georg W. F.
Hobbes, Thomas
Lafitau, Joseph-François
Lubbock, John
Maine, Henry James
Malthus, Thomas R.
Marx, Karl
McLennan, John
Montesquieu, Comte de
Morgan, Lewis Henry
Müller, Max
Nineteenth-Century Evolutionary
    Anthropology
Pitt Rivers, Augustus Henry Lane Fox
Plato
Rousseau, Jean-Jacques
Smith, Adam
Smith, William Robertson
Spencer, Herbert

Torres Straits Expedition
Tylor, Edward Burnett
Voltaire
Wallace, Alfred R.
Wundt, Wilhelm

Other National Traditions

Anderson, Benedict
Appadurai, Arjun
Asad, Talal
Bakhtin, Mikhail M.
Barth, Fredrik
Fanon, Frantz
Freud, Sigmund
Gramsci, Antonio
Jakobson, Roman O.
Polanyi, Karl
Popper, Karl
Prague School of Linguistics
Róheim, Géza
Said, Edward
Saussure, Ferdinand de
Soviet Anthropology
Srinivas, M. N.
Tambiah, Stanley
Westermarck, Edward
Wittgenstein, Ludwig

Philosophers and Philosophies

Aristotle
Bakhtin, Mikhail M.
Barthes, Roland
Bataille, Georges
Baudrillard, Jean
Burke, Kenneth
Comte, Auguste
Deleuze, Gilles, and Félix Guattari
Derrida, Jacques
Gadamer, Hans-Georg
Habermas, Jürgen
Hegel, Georg W. F.
Hobbes, Thomas
Husserl, Edmund
Latour, Bruno
Lyotard, Jean-François
Marx, Karl
Mead, George Herbert
Montesquieu, Comte de

Plato
Popper, Karl
Rousseau, Jean-Jacques
Simmel, Georg
Smith, Adam
Spencer, Herbert
Utilitarianism
Veblen, Thorstein B.
Voltaire
Weber, Max
Wittgenstein, Ludwig

Postmodern Perspective

Abu-Lughod, Lila
Anderson, Benedict
Asad, Talal
Autoethnography
Barth, Fredrik
Barthes, Roland
Baudrillard, Jean
Bourdieu, Pierre
Burke, Kenneth
Clifford, James
Critical Theory
Deconstruction
Deleuze, Gilles, and Félix
    Guattari
Derrida, Jacques
Discourse Theory
Fischer, Michael
Foucault, Michel
Geertz, Clifford
Girard, René
Jameson, Fredric
Lacan, Jacques
Latour, Bruno
Lyotard, Jean-François
Marcus, George
Postmodernism
Poststructuralism
Practice Theory
Rabinow, Paul
Rosaldo, Renato
Said, Edward
Scapes
Scheper-Hughes, Nancy
Strathern, Marilyn
Tedlock, Barbara and Dennis
Tyler, Stephen A.

Psychological and Sociological Perspective

Bateson, Gregory
Benedict, Ruth
Chodorow, Nancy
DuBois, Cora
Dumont, Louis
Dundes, Alan
Durkheim, Émile
Fanon, Frantz
Fortune, Reo
Freud, Sigmund
Girard, René
Goffman, Erving
Hall, Edward T.
Hertz, Robert
Kardiner, Abram
Lacan, Jacques
L'Année Sociologique
LeVine, Robert
Lévy-Bruhl, Lucien
Linton, Ralph
Malinowski, Bronisław
Mauss, Marcel
Mead, Margaret
Parsons, Talcott
Rivers, W. H. R.
Róheim, Géza
Weber, Max
Westermarck, Edward
Wundt, Wilhelm

Theoretical Approaches

Alliance-Descent Debate
Cognitive Anthropology
Comparative Linguistics
Critical Theory
Cultural Ecology
Cultural Materialism
Culture and Personality
Culture Area Approach
Dependency Theory
Diffusionism, Hyperdiffusionism, *Kulturkreise*
Discourse Theory
Economic Anthropology
Ethnohistory
Ethnoscience; New Ethnography
Ethology, Human
Evolutionary Anthropology

Evolutionary Psychology
Face-to-Face Interaction
Feminist Anthropology
Game Theory
Gene-Culture Coevolution
Globalization Theory
Hermeneutics
Historical Particularism
Human Behavioral Ecology
Human Universals
Marxist Anthropology
Material Production, Theories of
Neo-Boasianism
Neo-Kantianism
Network Theory/Social Network Analysis
Nineteenth-Century Evolutionary Anthropology
Phenomenology
Political Economy
Postcolonial Theory
Postmodernism
Poststructuralism
Practice Theory
Psychological Anthropology
Queer Theory
Rational Choice Theory
Semiotics
Social Constructionism
Sociolinguistics
Structural Functionalism
Structural Marxism
Structuralism
Subaltern Studies
Symbolic and Interpretive Anthropology
Symbolic Interactionism
Systems Theory
World-Systems Theory

Theorists

Abu-Lughod, Lila
Althusser, Louis
Anderson, Benedict
Appadurai, Arjun
Asad, Talal
Bachofen, Johann J.
Bailey, Frederick G.
Bakhtin, Mikhail M.
Barth, Fredrik
Barthes, Roland
Bastian, Adolf

Bataille, Georges
Bateson, Gregory
Baudrillard, Jean
Benedict, Ruth F.
Benjamin, Walter
Binford, Lewis R.
Bloch, Maurice
Bloomfield, Leonard
Boas, Franz
Bohannan, Paul
Bourdieu, Pierre
Burke, Kenneth
Butler, Judith
Carneiro, Robert L.
Chodorow, Nancy
Chomsky, Noam
Clifford, James
Comte, Auguste
Condorcet, Jean-Antoine Nicolas de Caritat
Darwin, Charles
Dawkins, Richard
Deleuze, Gilles, and Félix Guattari
Derrida, Jacques
Douglas, Mary
Du Bois, W. E. B
DuBois, Cora
Dumont, Louis
Dundes, Alan
Durkheim, Émile
Evans-Pritchard, E. E.
Fanon, Frantz
Ferguson, Adam
Firth, Raymond
Fischer, Michael
Fortes, Meyer
Fortune, Reo
Foster, George M.
Foucault, Michel
Frazer, James G.
Freud, Sigmund
Fried, Morton
Gadamer, Hans-Georg
Geertz, Clifford
Geffray, Christian
Gennep, Arnold van
Girard, René
Gluckman, Max
Godelier, Maurice
Goffman, Erving
Goldenweiser, Alexander A.

Goodenough, Ward H.
Goody, Jack
Graebner, Fritz
Gramsci, Antonio
Greenberg, Joseph
Griaule, Marcel
Gumperz, John J.
Habermas, Jürgen
Haddon, Alfred C.
Hall, Edward T.
Hallowell, A. Irving
Harris, Marvin
Harvey, David
Hegel, Georg W. F.
Herskovits, Melville
Hertz, Robert
Hobbes, Thomas
Hocart, Arthur M.
Hurston, Zora Neale
Husserl, Edmund
Hymes, Dell
Jakobson, Roman O.
Jameson, Fredric
Kardiner, Abram
Kluckhohn, Clyde
Kroeber, Alfred L.
Kuper, Hilda B.
Labov, William
Lacan, Jacques
Lafitau, Joseph-François
Lamphere, Louise
Latour, Bruno
Leach, Edmund
Leacock, Eleanor
LeVine, Robert
Lévi-Strauss, Claude
Lévy-Bruhl, Lucien
Lewis, Oscar
Lienhardt, Godfrey
Linton, Ralph
Lounsbury, Floyd
Lowie, Robert
Lubbock, John
Lyotard, Jean-François
Maine, Henry James
Mair, Lucy
Malinowski, Bronisław
Malthus, Thomas R.
Marcus, George
Marx, Karl

About the Editors

R. Jon McGee received his PhD from Rice University in 1983. He is currently Professor of Anthropology at Texas State University, where he has taught since 1985. His research has focused generally on anthropological theory and the anthropology of religion. More specifically, he has conducted extensive studies on the religion, language, and culture of the Lacandon Maya. Among the many books he has written or edited are *Watching Lacandon Maya Lives* (Allyn & Bacon) and *Life, Ritual and Religion Among the Lacandon Maya* (Wadsworth). With Richard L. Warms, he is coauthor of *Anthropological Theory: An Introductory History* (McGraw-Hill), now in its fifth edition; and with Warms and James Garber, of *Sacred Realms: Readings in the Anthropology of Religion*, now in its second edition (Oxford University Press). McGee also leads an annual summer study abroad program in Canterbury, England.

Richard L. Warms received his PhD from Syracuse University in 1987 and is currently Professor of Anthropology at Texas State University, where he has taught since 1988. His research has focused on the history of anthropological theory, on commerce, religion, and ethnic identity in West Africa, and on African veterans of French colonial armed forces. With Jon McGee, he is coauthor of *Anthropological Theory: An Introductory History* (McGraw-Hill), now in its fifth edition; and with McGee and James Garber, of *Sacred Realms: Readings in the Anthropology of Religion*, now in its second edition (Oxford University Press). With Serena Nanda, he has coauthored the best-selling textbooks *Cultural Anthropology*, now in its eleventh edition, and *Culture Counts*, now in its third edition (Cengage Learning).

Contributors

Patricio N. Abinales
University of Hawai'i, Manoa

Abigail E. Adams
Central Connecticut State University

Augustine Agwuele
Texas State University

N. J. Allen
Institute of Social and Cultural Anthropology, University of Oxford

Lars Allolio-Näcke
University of Erlangen, Nuremberg

Michael Angrosino
University of South Florida

Rina Arya
University of Wolverhamptom

Florence E. Babb
University of Florida

William W. Baden
Indiana University–Purdue University, Fort Wayne

Liza Bakewell
Brown University

Daniela S. Barberis
Shimer College

Jerome H. Barkow
Dalhousie University

Stanley R. Barrett
University of Guelph

Ira Bashkow
University of Virginia

Kara Becker
Reed College

Joshua A. Bell
National Museum of Natural History, Smithsonian Institution

Janet E. Benson
Kansas State University

Amy Bentley
New York University

Cato Berg
University of Bergen

Laurent Berger
École des Hautes Études en Sciences Sociales, Paris, and Laboratoire d'Anthropologie Sociale, Collège de France

Magdalena Bielenia-Grajewska
University of Gdansk, Poland, and International School for Advanced Studies (SISSA), Italy

Stephen P. Borgatti
University of Kentucky

Dominic Boyer
Rice University

Daniel R. Braun
Princeton University

Simon J. Bronner
Pennsylvania State University

Cecil H. Brown
Northern Illinois University

Donald E. Brown
University of California, Santa Barbara

Julie K. Brown
National Museum of American History, Smithsonian Institution

Ian Buchanan
University of Wollongong

Morgan Buck
City University of New York Graduate Center

Allan Burns
University of Florida

Julia Cassaniti
Stanford University

William Chapman
University of Hawai'i, Manoa

Christopher Chase-Dunn
University of California, Riverside

Sally Cole
Concordia University

Gene Cooper
University of Southern California

Jeremy Coote
University of Oxford

Raymond Corbey
Leiden University

William Croft
University of New Mexico

Lee Cronk
Rutgers University

Jonathan Culp
University of Dallas

Talia Dan-Cohen
Washington University St. Louis

Eliza Jane Darling
Independent Scholar

Regna Darnell
University of Western Ontario

Veena Das
Johns Hopkins University

Rosa De Jorio
University of North Florida

Thérèse A. de Vet
University of Arizona

Mathieu Deflem
University of South Carolina

Daniela di Piramo
Griffith University

Lise M. Dobrin
University of Virginia

Virginia R. Dominguez
University of Illinois, Urbana-Champaign

Susan Drucker-Brown
Cambridge University

Alessandro Duranti
University of California, Los Angeles

Libuše Dušková
Charles University

Ute Eickelkamp
University of Sydney

Omnia El Shakry
University of California, Davis

Justin A. Elardo
Portland Community College

Alexei Elfimov
Institute of Ethnology and Anthropology, Russian Academy of Sciences

Thomas Hylland Eriksen
University of Oslo

Gillian Feeley-Harnik
University of Michigan

Richard Feinberg
Kent State University

Pamela L. Feldman-Savelsberg
Carleton College

Chris Fleming
University of Western Sydney

James J. Fox
Australian National University

Alex François
Le Centre national de la recherche scientifique

Elliot Fratkin
Smith College

Jonathan Friedman
University of California, San Diego

Gérald Gaillard
Universite des Sciences et techniques deLille 1

Jean-Claude Galey
École des Hautes Études en Sciences Sociales

Chris Garces
Cornell University

María Luz García
University of Kentucky

Robert Owen Gardner
Linfield College

Dustin Bradley Garlitz
University of South Florida

Volney P. Gay
Vanderbilt University

Haidy Geismar
New York University

David N. Gellner
Institute of Social and Cultural Anthropology, University of Oxford

Jerry Gershenhorn
North Carolina Central University

Frederic W. Gleach
Cornell University

Zoltan Gluck
City University of New York Graduate Center

Donna M. Goldstein
University of Colorado, Boulder

Alex Golub
University of Hawai'i, Manoa

Robert Gordon
University of Vermont

Anthony Grant
Edge Hill University

Travis J. Grosser
University of Kentucky

Gregory S. Gullette
Santa Clara University

Jane I. Guyer
Johns Hopkins University

Hans Peter Hahn
Goethe Universitat Frankfurt Am Main

Thomas D. Hall
Depauw University

Edmund T. Hamann
University of Nebraska, Lincoln

Richard Handler
University of Virginia

Michele Hanks
Case Western Reserve University

F. Allan Hanson
University of Kansas

Michael E. Harkin
University of Wyoming

Anthony Kwame Harrison
Virginia Tech

Faye V. Harrison
University of Florida

Keith Hart
University of Pretoria

Thomas N. Headland
SIL International

Anita Herle
University of Cambridge

Jacob R. Hickman
*Brigham Young
University*

Mathieu Hilgers
*Universite Libre de
Bruxelles*

Lawrence A. Hirschfeld
*New School for Social
Research*

Brian A. Hoey
Marshall University

Hiroko Inoue
*University of California,
Riverside*

Gwyneira Isaac
Smithsonian Institution

Cindy Isenhour
Centre College

Ira Jacknis
*University of California,
Berkeley*

Wendy James
Oxford University

Daniel Ezra Johnson
Lancaster University

Michelle C. Johnson
Bucknell University

Ana M. Juárez
Texas State University

Don Kalb
*Central European
University*

Sergei Kan
Dartmouth College

Malav Kanuga
*City University of New York
Graduate Center*

Martha Kaplan
Vassar College

Tim Kaposy
George Mason University

Frédéric Keck
*Centre National de la
Recherche Scientifique*

Ian Keen
*Australian National
University*

Alice Beck Kehoe
*University of Wisconsin,
Milwaukee*

Robert V. Kemper
Southern Methodist University

Jeremy R. Kendal
Durham University

Virginia Kerns
College of William and Mary

R. S. Khare
University of Virginia

Robert D. King
University of Texas

Frederick Klaits
*University at Buffalo, State
University of New York*

Bruce M. Knauft
Emory University

Conrad Phillip Kottak
University of Michigan

Sina Lucia Kottmann
Martin Luther University

Udo Krautwurst
*University of Prince Edward
Island*

Shepard Krech III
Brown University

Jens Kreinath
Wichita State University

David B. Kronenfeld
*University of California,
Riverside*

Paul V. Kroskrity
*University of California,
Los Angeles*

Donald V. Kurtz
*University of Texas, San
Antonio*

Darrell La Lone
DePauw University

Olli Lagerspetz
Åbo Akademi University

Michael Lambek
University of Toronto

Frederick P. Lampe
Northern Arizona University

J. Stephen Lansing
University of Arizona

Andrew Lass
Mount Holyoke College

Robert Launay
Northwestern University

Christine Laurière
*École des Hautes Études en
Sciences Sociales*

Daniel Law
Vanderbilt University

Murray J. Leaf
University of Texas, Dallas

John Leavitt
Université de Montréal

Winnie Lem
Trent University

Rebecca J. Lester
*Washington University
St. Louis*

James W. Lett
Indian River State College

Herbert S. Lewis
*University of Wisconsin,
Madison*

Victor Lidz
Drexel College of Medicine

Debra Lieberman
University of Miami

Thomas Looser
New York University

Mazyar Lotfalian
University of California, Irvine

Tommy Lee Lott
San Jose State University

Ian Lowrie
Rice University

Scott A. Lukas
Lake Tahoe Community College

Nancy Lutkehaus
University of Southern California

Wendy Luttrell
City University of New York Graduate Center

Michael E. Lynch
Cornell University

Andrew Lyons
Wilfrid Laurier University

Harriet D. Lyons
University of Waterloo

Judith Macdonald
University of Waikato

Thomas Malm
Lund University

Marc Manganaro
Gonzaga University

Maxine L. Margolis
University of Florida

Jonathan Marks
University of North Carolina, Charlotte

Jocelyn Marrow
Stanford University

Keir Martin
University of Manchester

Richard Joseph Martin
Princeton University

Bill Maurer
University of California, Irvine

Stephen McFarland
City University of New York Graduate Center

R. Jon McGee
Texas State University

Eric McGuckin
Sonoma State University

Elizabeth Mertz
American Bar Foundation, University of Wisconsin Law School

Lisa R. Messeri
University of Pennsylvania

Dale E. Miller
Old Dominion University

Dan E. Miller
University of Dayton

David Mills
University of Oxford

John H. Moore
University of Florida

Mary H. Moran
Colgate University

John Morton
La Trobe University

Muhammad Aurang Zeb Mughal
Durham University, UK

Serena Nanda
City University of New York

Edmund Neill
University of Oxford

Isak Niehaus
Brunel University

Charles W. Nuckolls
Brigham Young University

Stephen Nugent
Goldsmiths, University of London

Elisabeth Oberzaucher
University of Vienna

Rick O'Gorman
University of Essex

Sean O'Neill
University of Oklahoma

Jürgen van Oorschot
University of Erlangen-Nuremberg

Andrew Orta
University of Illinois, Urbana-Champaign

Alan J. Osborn
University of Nebraska

Keith F. Otterbein
University at Buffalo, State University of New York

Richard Pace
Middle Tennessee State University

Sam Pack
Kenyon College

Karthik Panchanathan
University of Missouri

Robert Parkin
Institute of Social and Cultural Anthropology, University of Oxford

Alejandro I. Paz
University of Toronto

William J. Peace
Independent Scholar

Eric J. Pedersen
University of Miami

Peter N. Peregrine
Lawrence University

Daniel Peretti
Indiana University

Alison Petch
*Pitt Rivers Museum,
    University of Oxford*

Maja Petrović-Šteger
University of Cambridge

Josipa G. Petrunic
University of Toronto

Paul Petzschmann
Carlton College

Anastasia Piliavsky
King's College, Cambridge

Sidney Plotkin
Vassar College

Maïa Ponsonnet
*Centre de Recherche
    et de Documentation
    sur l'Oc, Australian
    National University*

David H. Price
St. Martin's University

Naomi Quinn
Duke University

Sadiah Qureshi
University of Birmingham

Nigel Rapport
University of St. Andrews

Douglas Raybeck
Hamilton College

Deborah Reed-Danahay
*University at Buffalo,
    State University of
    New York*

Luke Rendell
University of St. Andrews

Camille Robcis
Cornell University

Stuart Rockefeller
Columbia University

Lars Rodseth
Syracuse University

Noel B. Salazar
University of Leuven

John A. Saliba
University of Detroit Mercy

Mahir Şaul
University of Illinois

Jane Schneider
*City University of New York
    Graduate Center*

Helen B. Schwartzman
Northwestern University

Robert Segal
University of Aberdeen

Ullica Segerstrale
*Illinois Institute of
    Technology*

David Shankland
*Royal Anthropological
    Institute*

Hidetada Shimizu
Northern Illinois University

Moshe Shokeid
Tel Aviv University

Samuel J. Sholtis
Pennsylvania State University

Amy Shuman
The Ohio State University

Salma Siddique
Edinburgh Napier University

Jack Sidnell
University of Toronto

Sydel Silverman
Wenner-Gren Foundation

Kimberly Eison Simmons
University of South Carolina

Adam Smith
University of Miami

Charles H. Smith
Western Kentucky University

Eric Alden Smith
University of Washington

Richard G. Smith
Swansea University

Claudio Sopranzetti
Harvard University

Graham St John
University of Queensland

Justin Stagl
Universität Salzburg

Anthony Stavrianakis
*University of California,
    Berkeley*

Paul Stoller
West Chester University

Ted Stolze
Cerritos College

H. Stephen Straight
*Binghamton University,
    State University of
    New York*

Marilyn Strathern
Cambridge University

Claudia Strauss
Pitzer College

Pauline Turner Strong
University of Texas, Austin

Thomas Strong
*National University of Ireland,
    Maynooth*

Constance R. Sutton
New York University

Raja Swamy
University of Arkansas

Arpad Szakolczai
University College, Cork

Stephanie Takaragawa
Chapman University

Barbara Tedlock
*University at Buffalo, State
    University of New York*

C. Jason Throop
*University of California, Los
    Angeles*

Bram Tucker
University of Georgia

Greg Urban
University of Pennsylvania

John van Willigen
University of Kentucky

Ulrich Veit
University of Leipzig

Elaine W. Vine
Victoria University of Wellington

Bradley B. Walters
Mount Allison University

Huon Wardle
University of St Andrews

Richard L. Warms
Texas State University

Alisse Waterston
City University of New York

Jack Russell Weinstein
University of North Dakota

Cameron Wesson
Lehigh University

Clifford Wilcox
Independent Scholar

Rafael Wittek
University of Groningen

Todd Wolfson
Rutgers University

Robert E. Wood
University of Dallas

Kevin A. Yelvington
*University of
    South Florida*

Katharine Young
*University of
    California, Berkeley*

Michael W. Young
*Australian National
    University*

Virginia Heyer Young
University of Virginia

Juwen Zhang
Willamette University

Introduction

Social and cultural anthropology are concerned with understanding the cultures, societies, and behaviors of people around the world. Typically social or cultural anthropologists study the behavior, beliefs, history, and lifestyles of people in other cultures or subcultures. However, the approaches anthropologists take are as diverse as the people who are studied. This encyclopedia summarizes some of the essential ideas, lives, and works of many of the key people who have built or had a major impact on the disciplines of social and cultural anthropology over the last several hundred years. Anthropological theory is of critical significance because it helps us think about who and what we are as human beings. At its most basic level, anthropology challenges us all to understand our own and other societies and cultures in the world. This encyclopedia highlights many of the ways that anthropologists have sought to do this.

Why an Encyclopedia of Social and Cultural Theory?

Theory is an essential component of social science in general and of anthropology in particular. Anthropologists collect data through fieldwork, but both the data they choose to collect and their interpretations of it are driven by their theoretical perspectives, whether these theories are held implicitly or explicitly. Theories are the tools that anthropologists use to explain what they observe and sort information they believe is significant from that which they think less important. For example, an anthropologist who takes a materialist perspective may focus on production technologies and their relation to the distribution of power within a society. An anthropologist who takes an interpretive perspective is more likely, however, to focus on the ways in which people understand their world and their position within it. The materialist might collect data about economic flows and manufacturing or farming techniques.

The interpretivist might study a symbolic system, religious ritual, or artistic expression. The most important data for the one may be virtually irrelevant to the other.

In the last half century, understanding theory in anthropology has become both increasingly important and increasingly difficult. It has become important as anthropologists have more frequently considered the nature of anthropological knowledge and debated the importance of different, often mutually exclusive understandings of culture. It has become increasingly difficult as the number of theoretical trends within the discipline has increased and as many of these have developed specialized vocabularies that are opaque to outsiders. Although almost all anthropologists have well-developed understandings of some theoretical positions, few are masters of all. This encyclopedia is intended to serve as a guide to critical theoretical positions and their most important exponents. It presents state-of-the-art entries that are detailed and informative enough for professional anthropologists but are written in language that is accessible to undergraduates. The entries present the critical aspects of the thinking of major theorists and schools of thought and place both theories and theorists in historical context. Although encyclopedia entries are certainly no substitute for detailed study, the entries presented here allow readers to access the most pertinent facets of anthropological theory and provide information that is authoritative but avoids the simplistic formulations often found in reference works.

Although this is an encyclopedia of theory in social and cultural anthropology, anthropologists have always freely borrowed ideas from each other and from other disciplines. An understanding of critical aspects of philosophy, sociology, history, literary criticism, psychology, biology, and other fields has become essential to an informed reading of much of current day anthropology. As you will see, these volumes include essays about many scholars who did not consider themselves anthropologists but who had an important influence on the development of anthropological theory.

At some level, all theory in social cultural anthropology, whether written in the eighteenth century or the twenty-first, addresses basic issues of how humans understand each other and the world around us. As you read multiple entries in these volumes you'll quickly come to understand that anthropological theory is not a more or less consistent body of information that can be reduced to a series of rules about why and how to do anthropology. Instead, anthropological theory is a body of more-or-less irreconcilable ideas about humans and their social, cultural, and physical worlds. Both in the past and in the current day, anthropological theorists have disagreed about virtually everything: from what anthropologists should study, to the ways in which they should study it, and what the goals of such studies should be. Herein lies the joy and the passion of anthropological theory: to engage in studying, thinking about, and writing anthropological theory is to join a centuries-old debate. It is to engage with and grapple with scholars from the classical world to the present day. It is to walk in the company of Kant and Boas, of Husserl, Foucault, and Geertz. On the one hand, this debate is truly hopeless: it is extremely unlikely that the diverse intellectual strands that make up anthropology will ever coalesce into a single authoritative "unified field" theory of anthropology. On the other, the debate has been enormously productive, generating new ways to think about ourselves and others; new ways to understand the world. It is also profoundly important. Although the ideas discussed in these volumes may at times seem extraordinarily abstract, even obtuse, they have practical consequences. The ways in which we understand the logic of, the motivations for, and the results of human social and cultural behavior has a deep influence not only on our daily behavior toward others, but on the ways that groups and nations treat their own members, wield power, exchange goods and information, write laws, conduct international relations, and make art.

Creating the Encyclopedia

With more than 300 entries by over 250 authors in more than a dozen nations, this encyclopedia covers the most influential theories and scholars in the history of anthropology. The list of entries selected for the encyclopedia was chosen by an international editorial board from diverse backgrounds within social and cultural anthropology. Many took time from their own work in places like India and Bali to guide us in the selection of entry topics. The theoretical entries have been written by leading experts in the field. Many biographical entries are authored by former students of the men and women who are the subjects of the entries. Almost all authors have previously published, often extensively, on the topics they were assigned for this work. We are profoundly pleased and grateful to present here new works by some of the best known anthropologists working today including Florence Babb, Donald Brown, Christopher Chase-Dunn, Sally Cole, Lee Cronk, Regna Darnell, Veena Das, Alessandro Duranti, Jonathan Friedman, Jane Guyer, Allan Hanson, Faye Harrison, Keith Hart, Wendy James, Bruce Knauft, Conrad Kottak, Stephen Lansing, Herbert Lewis, Nancy Lutkehaus, Andrew and Harriet Lyons, Jonathan Marks, Serena Nanda, Keith Otterbein, Robert Parkin, Peter Peregrine, David Price, Naomi Quinn, Moshe Shokeid, Sydel Silverman, Paul Stoller, Marilyn Strathern, Claudia Strauss, Barbara Tedlock, Greg Urban and many, many others who are equally illustrious.

The entries were chosen by McGee, Warms, and the editorial board. As the project progressed we often wished for the space to add many more entries. We apologize in advance for important theories and theorists we've missed but also acknowledge that any encyclopedia will be incomplete, not least because theory itself is growing, changing, and being reimagined. Entries are listed in alphabetical order and range in length from under 1,000 to more than 5,000 words. The lengths of the entries were determined following a rubric provided by SAGE and with extensive advice from the members of the editorial board. Each entry opens with a concise statement of the importance of its subject. In cases where the topic is a person, critical biographical details are discussed. Essays close with a brief recapitulation of the general contribution of the subject to anthropology. Essays are accompanied by a list of cross-references that direct readers to other related entries in the encyclopedia, and a list of suggested readings. These readings were selected by entry authors to guide readers to further works that will provide them with a deeper understanding and appreciation for the entry topics.

Acknowledgments

Although Warms and McGee are the authors of several textbooks, including a book on sociocultural theory, this is the biggest project either of us has worked on. A project of this magnitude cannot be completed without the guidance and assistance of a great many people. First we would like to acknowledge the guidance of Jim Brace-Thompson, Senior Editor at SAGE, who first approached us with this project and provided initial guidance in its planning. We are also indebted to Sanford Robinson, Senior Developmental Editor at SAGE, who provided us with timely assistance, answers to questions, and project schedules that he helped make sure we kept. We also must thank Laura Notton, Reference Systems Coordinator, and Leticia Gutierrez, Reference Systems Manager, for their invaluable technical assistance guiding all contributors through the Sage Reference Tracking System that made a project of this size possible. We would also like to thank our Production Editor, Jane Haenel, who is one of the most organized people we have ever worked with. Finally, and most importantly, we would like to thank the hundreds of colleagues around the world who contributed entries, helped us find authors for entries, provided critical reviews, and answered questions of all types. All graciously shared their time and knowledge with us. We have been humbled by the generosity and the depth and breadth of knowledge of our colleagues around the world. We set out to edit a reference work for students of social and cultural anthropology and ended up becoming students again ourselves.

R. Jon McGee
Richard L. Warms
Texas State University

Abu-Lughod, Lila

Lila Abu-Lughod, a prominent and prolific American anthropologist, has been a leading figure in the field of Middle East anthropology and in women and gender studies. Trained in anthropology, first at Carleton College and then at Harvard University, her writings have been strongly focused on in-depth ethnographic research, theoretical innovation, and attentiveness to the craft of writing. Widely read both within and outside of Middle East studies as an exemplar of engaged and feminist ethnography, the corpus of her works includes three single-authored ethnographies, *Veiled Sentiments: Honor and Poetry in a Bedouin Society* (1986), *Writing Women's Worlds: Bedouin Stories* (1993), and *Dramas of Nationhood: The Politics of Television in Egypt* (2004), in addition to numerous edited volumes. Her ethnographies, in particular, have focused on marginalized or subaltern communities, such as the Awlad 'Ali Bedouin of Egypt and rural Upper Egyptians, all the while remaining attuned to gender inequities.

Critical Contributions to Anthropology

Culture, Ideology, and Discourse

Abu-Lughod's first two ethnographies, *Veiled Sentiments* and *Writing Women's Worlds*, focused on the Bedouin community of the Awlad 'Ali, who reside in Egypt's western desert along a coastal strip on the northern edge of the Libyan Desert, and concentrated on women's worlds. Both ethnographies exhibited an extreme sensitivity to the dynamics between the anthropologist and the host community, not just in the well-worn concern for power imbalances but also in the focus on the dynamics of the intersubjective encounter between the researcher and her anthropological subject. Thus, she recounts her initial introduction to the community both as a guest and as a daughter accompanied by her father, an academic and social scientist, the late Ibrahim Abu-Lughod, an introduction that greatly facilitated her place in the Bedouin community as an adoptive daughter. Such narrative retellings are indicative of her concern for positionality, a lesson she both draws from and imbues with feminism. Indeed, in her interaction with the Awlad 'Ali, she refers to her situation as that of a "halfie," half-Arab and half-American, and to the insider-outsider status this bestowed on her, thereby avoiding the reification of the self/other distinction so common to reflexive anthropology.

The central question that animated *Veiled Sentiments* was the relationship between Bedouin poetic discourse and the discourse of ordinary life. Focusing on the *ghinnawas* or lyric poems of the Awlad 'Ali, she analyzed the disjuncture between the dominant cultural ideology of honor and the emotive poetic discourse of sentiment to explore the relationship between ideology and human experience. Rather than view the disjuncture as indicative of a separation between an ideological or sociocultural self and an emotively expressed "real self," she framed poetry and ordinary discourse as existing side by side in juxtaposition, the former as a shadow commentary on the latter. Poetic discourse, which often expressed vulnerability and other socially devalued sentiments, thus functioned as a culturally sanctioned dissident discourse and was itself a declaration of autonomy from the system. Theoretically, what *Veiled Sentiments* accomplished was a more nuanced and less reconciled view of culture and of the relationship between ideology and experience. In contrast to the ethnographic work of Clifford Geertz, which tended to view culture as a unified coherent whole that could be read as a text, or the work of Pierre Bourdieu, which presented a totalizing view of culture as superstructural ideology, Abu-Lughod's work remained ever attuned to contradictions and ambiguities and the coexistence of contradictory discourses, in keeping with the work of Michel Foucault.

The Politics of Knowledge and Representation

Abu-Lughod has been extremely attentive to the politics of scholarship, and this was especially reflected in the experimental ethnographic form of *Writing Women's Worlds*. In that ethnography, each chapter heading marked an anthropological theme on women and the Arab world, such as patrilineality, polygyny, and honor and shame, while each chapter deconstructed these concepts as part of the project of writing *against* culture. By writing against the culture concept, she sought to work against the tendency of social science scholars to generalize by destabilizing the idea of cultures as ahistorical wholes and critiquing the anthropological overinvestment in ethnographic typification and otherness. It must be noted that she did not destabilize these conventions simply by avoiding them. Thus, in discussing the concept of honor among the Awlad 'Ali, she viewed it not as the sole purview of men but rather as a moral ideal for both men and women. In sum, rather than emphasize holism and coherence, her subsequent narratives focused on individuals, mobilizing what she felicitously termed a *tactical humanism*. In the motivated tellings and partial perspectives of her storytellers, the reader emerged with a distinct sense of the everyday fabric and quality of "life as lived." In this, her consummate abilities as a storyteller echoed the narrative craft of her ethnographic protagonists.

This theme of writing against culture reverberated in her third ethnography, *Dramas of Nationhood*, in which she turned to that quintessential icon of modernity, television. Television as an ethnographic object was instructive, as it enabled a rethinking of the complexities of nationalism in a late-20th-century context, while refracting everyday life as portrayed in the ever-ubiquitous television serials and as inhabited by its viewers. Moving beyond Benedict Anderson's notion of the nation as an imagined community, she explored the fault lines and frictions of nationalism, its social inequalities as manifested in hegemonic cultural forms, while arguing that the nation-state remains a powerful frame of reference. This methodologically sophisticated multisited and multilevel ethnography included an examination of the elite cultural producers of Egypt's television serials and the subaltern audiences, in both rural Upper Egypt and Cairo, who watch them. Significantly, it was not a literary but an ethnographic and social analysis that took media content and textual analysis seriously.

Thus, in all three of her ethnographies Abu-Lughod has returned to an issue she raised in her groundbreaking 1989 article "Zones of Theory in the Anthropology of the Arab World," namely, the prevalence of theoretical metonyms in the study of the Arab world, clustered around segmentary lineage theory, harem theory, and Islam. Through her own scholarship, she has greatly augmented this theorizing by writing against the "culture concept" and by engaging with topics previously thought to be of little import in the study of the Arab world, namely, the anthropology of emotions and the study of mass media and national politics. Throughout this work, she has sought to situate cultural forms within their larger historical and sociopolitical contexts, without dispensing with the thick description and the anthropological endeavor to capture the poetics of everyday life.

Omnia El Shakry

See also Anderson, Benedict; Autoethnography; Bourdieu, Pierre; Foucault, Michel; Geertz, Clifford; Gender and Anthropology; Postcolonial Theory

Further Readings

Abu-Lughod, L. (1986). *Veiled sentiments: Honor and poetry in a Bedouin society*. Berkeley: University of California Press.

———. (1989). Zones of theory in the anthropology of the Arab world. *Annual Review of Anthropology, 18*, 267–306.

———. (1993). *Writing women's worlds: Bedouin stories*. Berkeley: University of California Press.

———. (Ed.). (1998). *Remaking women: Feminism and modernity in the Middle East.* Princeton, NJ: Princeton University Press.

———. (2004). *Dramas of nationhood: The politics of television in Egypt.* Chicago, IL: University of Chicago Press.

ACTION ANTHROPOLOGY

See Applied Anthropology

ALLIANCE THEORY

See Alliance-Descent Debate

ALLIANCE-DESCENT DEBATE

The alliance-descent debate was concerned with the relation between kinship and social organization. It was one of two prominent theoretical developments in the 1960s and 1970s that significantly discouraged anthropological interest in kinship analysis.

Origin of the Name

The contrast between alliance theory and descent theory was first offered by Louis Dumont in 1961 to characterize an argument that had been going on for 4 years between E. R. Leach (alliance) and Meyer Fortes and others (descent). Dumont described alliance as the structural theory of kinship; descent was defined as the theory of lineage or political systems. In a 1971 monograph, Dumont described descent theory more fully as the English theory of groups by filiation that had developed from A. R. Radcliffe-Brown and E. E. Evans-Pritchard through Fortes and Jack Goody, as against the theory of Claude Lévi-Strauss, which was oriented toward marriage alliance, as the latter was accepted, critiqued, and stated more generally by Leach and Rodney Needham.

Dumont recognized that the two theories did not fully exclude one another. Alliance theory was a better fit for South Asian ethnography; descent theory better described African social organization. So he described them as "mid-abstract." In fact, neither was a single theory but rather a cluster of claims.

Some were complementary, while others were opposed. Topics at issue ran from the interpretation of the rule that one should marry one's mother's brother's daughter to the general goal of social theory and the nature of objectivity.

Descent Theory

Descent theory as represented by Radcliffe-Brown, Evans-Pritchard, Fortes, and Goody combined a conception of the goal of social analysis drawn from French social positivism with a conception of objectivity drawn from logical positivism. The goal was to describe each society as a "total system" of corporate groups that determined individual behavior. The idea of objectivity was that an objective explanation had to refer to things that were "concrete" in some definite, material, sense. It could not refer to thought, which is subjective.

Radcliffe-Brown's first major work was an extensive monograph on the Andaman Islanders. It reassessed an earlier study by E. H. Man and focused entirely on beliefs and ceremonies, not social organization. Radcliffe-Brown announced his characteristic theoretical orientation only in the Preface, which he wrote years after the original study. Subsequently, however, he sought to apply it to a wide range of topics that ultimately figured in the alliance-descent arguments, including the mother's brother's relation, joking relationships, and kinship terminologies.

In Africa, Evans-Pritchard, Fortes, and Goody applied the same philosophical assumptions to what were commonly described as "segmentary societies." Since these involved a hierarchy of social units from tribe through clan, lineage, and household, they were more readily seen as total-system accounts. Relations between individuals were seen as determined by the corporate groups they were members of. Marital relations were relevant but not central. Rather, what was most important was the definition and juridical character of whatever groups held land or the material artifacts that were involved in the control of land, such as houses, cattle, and tools. Since these were descent groups, it was reasonable to call this perspective descent theory.

As a model for social analysis, in general, many ethnologists saw such accounts as artificially seeking to "objectivize" what was often subjective, intersubjective, or conceptual. Since the 1980s, this approach has been replaced in African ethnography by various social constructionist perspectives focusing on colonialism and postcolonialism.

Alliance Theory

In contrast to the efforts in descent theory to describe social organization as "concrete," alliance theorists commended their approach as "idealistic." This meant two different things. First, it was more explicitly concerned with symbols and meanings. Second, it self-consciously drew on the tradition of philosophical idealism for its epistemology. Lévi-Strauss's basic explanatory mechanism was not the assignment of people to material objects in physical space but "certain fundamental structures of the human mind."

Alliance theory began in 1949 with the publication of Lévi-Strauss's *Les Structures Elémentaires de la Parenté*. An English translation was published in 1969 under the editorship of Rodney Needham as *The Elementary Structures of Kinship*. The argument was clearly intended to update and supersede Émile Durkheim's *Elementary Forms of the Religious Life*. Both claimed to describe the simplest form of society, and both held that it was a total system of solitary kinship groups linked to one another by marriage and sharing an all-encompassing worldview. But Durkheim's argument was evolutionary: The elementary form was also the first form. This is no longer believable. Lévi-Strauss did not argue

that the elementary forms were the original forms of society but rather that they were the "basic units."

The elementary form of kinship, for Lévi-Strauss, was prescriptive matrilateral cross-cousin marriage (mother's brother's daughter [MBD] marriage). "Prescriptive" means that the choice of a spouse is absolutely specified in terms of a kinship category, in contrast to systems that are "preferential." Figure 1 represents the logic of the MBD prescription.

A triangle indicates a male, a circle a female, a line a connection by descent, and an equals symbol a connection by marriage. The lettered columns represent lineal descent groups. It does not matter whether succession is through males or females. Either way, every male marries his MBD.

With MBD marriage, there can be regular cycles of "marriage in a circle" for all the lineal groups or any subset, and the system will be self-replicating. Moreover, since women are always part of a larger flow of female goods balanced by a flow of male goods going the opposite way, the result is a cycle of "prestations" linking all the groups in the society. The logic is not the same for patrilateral cross-cousin marriage (father's sister's daughter [FSD] marriage), in which a male chooses a wife from among his father's sister's daughters. Here, the women would go one way in one generation and the opposite way in the next. So there would not be a flow of prestations throughout the society but only back-and-forth exchanges of the same prestations between the same groups.

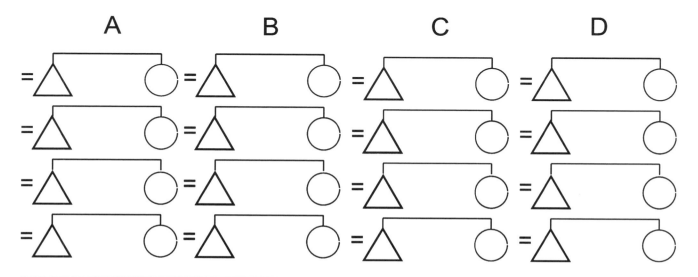

Figure 1 Logic of MBD Marriage
Note: MBD = mother's brother's daughter.

MBD marriage rules occur in a wide variety of historically unrelated societies. Unilateral FSD marriage is rare or nonexistent, depending on how tightly one defines it. Lévi-Strauss argued that the reason for this is that MBD marriage produced an "organic" social structure that was integrated and stable. FSD marriage, in contrast, produces a structure that is inherently fragmented.

An ethnographic problem with the idea of marriage in a circle is that actual MBD marriage systems often associate wife-giving status with a difference in social rank. Logically, this should create anomalies at the ends of the cycles. If wife givers are different in rank from wife takers and men of Lineage A take wives from Lineage B, and if men of Lineage B, in turn, take wives from Lineage C, then men of Lineage C should not take wives from Lineage A. But a man of Lineage C has to have a wife, and often does take a wife from A. The explanation was that while the cycle would be triadic in such a case, the relationship that it is based on is dyadic. Wife givers are separate from wife takers for any one group, and that is what matters. This dyadic opposition reflects a fundamental proclivity of the human mind, and it is the combination of the MBD logic and dyadic thought that provides the total social analysis.

As the alliance-descent argument was expanded by Leach, Dumont, Needham, and others, the list of anthropologists who disagreed in one or another expanded well beyond those who supported "descent theory" as Dumont had originally described it. So while the "alliance" side of the debate continued to be fairly well defined, the anti-alliance side became increasingly heterogeneous.

The Expanded Argument: From Fortes to Homans and Schneider

Some parts of alliance theory were readily accepted by other anthropologists, and some were not. The main controversies concerned the characterization of marriage patterns in terms of exchanges of wives by men, the association with dyadic ideational systems, and the claim that such dyadic systems reflected a fundamental proclivity of the human mind.

Lévi-Strauss also did not produce a comprehensive description of a community with the kind of "organic" unity that, as his theory said, MBD marriage gave rise to. There were no descriptions of such a community by others either for Lévi-Strauss

to cite. This was a serious defect, which subsequent proponents tried to overcome.

In 1951, Leach argued for structural analysis in Lévi-Strauss's sense in the "The Structural Implications of Matrilateral Cross-Cousin Marriage." This compared the social structures of the Kariera, Kachin, and Trobriand as variations on the logic of mother's brother's marriage but did not claim to provide a "total" societal analysis. Leach repeated the structural analysis in *Political Systems of Highland Burma* in 1954, but while his analysis of the marriage system was straightforward, he had a great deal of trouble with the larger society it should have structured. People did not report just one such larger system but three, which were very different from one another: Kachin Gumsa, Kachin Gumlao, and Shan. So the systems could not possibly have been the kinds of all-encompassing wholes that people were "in," as both Lévi-Strauss and his descent theory opponents imagined. One cannot be "in" three separate "total" structures at once. They could only have been cultural models that people used. Yet Leach did not conclude that the positivist goal of total-system analysis should be rejected. He concluded only that theory was necessarily different from description and that there should be more recognition of change.

A very different difficulty was raised by George Homans and David Schneider's 1955 *Marriage, Authority, and Final Cause*. Their argument was psychological, a cross-cultural variant of the Oedipus complex. They argued that in cultures where the father was the warm and supportive parent and the mother's brother was the harsh disciplinarian, boys would be sentimentally inclined to seek their wives through father's sisters and avoid relations through mother's brothers. This would happen with matrilineal descent, where the boy would be the heir of his mother's brother rather than of his own father. It followed that among societies with unilineal descent and unilateral marriage rules, one should expect MBD marriage where the descent rule was patrilineal and FSD marriage where it was matrilineal. Homans and Schneider located 33 societies with unilineal descent and unilateral marriage rules, of which 6 did not conform to the prediction. Two had FSD marriage and patrilineal succession, and 4 had MBD marriage and matrilineal succession. They then refined their original hypothesis to make the predictive factor not the system of inheritance but the location of the *potestas*, "disciplinary power." This left only one possibly anomalous case. It followed, they argued, that Lévi-Strauss's theory was superfluous. Furthermore, it was an appeal to final causes. It assigned the cause of the marriage choice to a future condition, in this case social integration. Real causes can only be "efficient causes." They also asked what kind of efficient cause would have been consistent with Lévi-Strauss's argument if he had proposed one. Their answer was rational purpose: Members of a society rationally or consciously arrange their organization to bring about successful evolutionary adaptation. They rejected this idea on the ground that people consider their own interests, not the interest of the society at large.

Reviews of *Marriage, Authority, and Final Cause* were generally favorable, although Fred Eggan noted that it seemed to have not fully appreciated Lévi-Strauss's explanation of the inherent conflict between FSD marriage and system integration, and he observed that there were no "fully functioning" systems of patrilateral cross-cousin marriage. A review by Rodney Needham conceded that Homans and Schneider had established the connection between potestality and MBD marriage "beyond a doubt," but it entirely rejected their criticism of Lévi-Strauss.

Needham followed with *Structure and Sentiment: A Test Case in Social Anthropology* (1962). About two thirds was a rebuttal of *Marriage, Authority, and Final Cause*. One third was the "test case," restating an analysis of Purum society that Needham had first published in 1958.

Needham argued that Homans and Schneider misunderstood Lévi-Strauss's argument, including the basic distinction between prescriptive and preferential marriage and the fact that Lévi-Strauss's analysis applied to lineal descent groups, not individualized genealogical relationships. Second, they also misunderstood much of the ethnography. And third, Needham argued that Lévi-Strauss's argument was not a final-cause argument, nor was Homans and Schneider's an efficient-cause argument. Instead, he argued, Lévi-Strauss's argument was structural while Homans and Schneider's was psychological, and psychological arguments were illegitimate.

Needham's Purum analysis utilized a 1945 monograph by Tarak Chandra Das. The Purum are culturally related to the Kachin. They numbered 303 people living in four villages. Das described them as organized into four patrilineal "sibs" that crosscut the four villages. Men married women from the sib of their MBD and did not marry women from their FSD. Das also described a series of rituals, including weddings and funerals, that displayed the status of a man, described by the kin term *apu*. The high status of the *apu* was symbolized in these rituals by the lower status of a group of relatives termed *maksas* and *ningans*, who always served rice beer and cooked pig. *Ningan* is a reciprocal female consanguine of *apu*, and *maksa* is her husband. So the exact glosses of these terms are important. The genealogical relations referred to as *apu* included mother's brother and mother's father, which was consistent with Lévi-Strauss's theory. However, they also included father's father and father's father's father, which contradicted the theory and which Needham did not mention. Das also explicitly described *ningans* as "married daughters of the patriline" (not of the sib), which Needham also does not mention. Needham interpreted all ceremonies with the *maksas* and *ningans* as involving prestations between sibs in exchange for wives, male goods for female goods, in a total system of triadic marriage cycles unified by the dyadic *maksa-apu* relation. Das makes it clear that the groups of *maksas* and *ningans* form only in relation to the *apu* as an individual, and the group dissolves on his death.

Most responses to Needham focused on the ways the actual Purum marriage patterns departed from the supposed MBD rule. Schneider, however, responded with a critical review of the entire alliance-descent debate, titled "Some Muddles in the Models, or How the System Really Works." He pointed out numerous problems of arbitrary interpretation on both sides and argued that neither Needham nor anyone else had provided a convincing test case because the theories were too muddled to admit of one, although alliance theory seemed to do a better job of recognizing the importance of symbolism. He also rejected "total-system models" in favor of "partial-system models." General interest in the debate ended soon thereafter.

Conclusion

Kinship systems involve ideas, organizations of many kinds, rituals, ideologies, mythologies, and sentiments. Alliance theory and descent theory each focused on just one aspect and claimed that it determined the rest.

When their arguments failed, some of the participants blamed the failure on kinship itself. In 1971, Needham argued that the term *kinship* had no meaning. In 1972, Schneider argued that kinship was a nonsubject. Yet anthropologists continue to study it, and several recent approaches have been much cleaner and better grounded empirically than any argument in the alliance-descent debate. For a recent assessment that relates the alliance-descent issues to more recent approaches, see especially Richard Feinberg and Martin Ottenheimer's *The Cultural Analysis of Kinship*.

Murray J. Leaf

See also Dumont, Louis; Godelier, Maurice; Lévi-Strauss, Claude; Needham, Rodney; Radcliffe-Brown, A. R.; Schneider, David M.

Further Readings

Barnes, R. H. (2006). Maurice Godelier and the metamorphosis of kinship: A review essay. *Comparative Studies in Society and History, 48*(2), 326–358.

Feinberg, R., & Ottenheimer, M. (Eds.). (2001). *The cultural analysis of kinship: The legacy of David M. Schneider*. Urbana: University of Illinois Press.

Fortes, M. (1972). Kinship and the social order: Current anthropology book review. *Current Anthropology, 13*(2), 285–296.

Leaf, M. J. (2006). Experimental analysis of kinship. *Ethnology, 45,* 305–330.

Schneider, D. (1965). Some muddles in the models. In M. Banton (Ed.), *The relevance of models for social anthropology*. New York, NY: Taplinger.

ALTHUSSER, LOUIS

Louis Althusser (1918–1990), a French Marxist philosopher, was a major intellectual figure during the 1960s and 1970s and significantly influenced the rereading of Marx and the development of a distinctive critical approach to Marxist theory and practice.

Biography and Major Works

Louis Althusser was born in 1918 in the city of Birmandreïs, a suburb of Algiers, Algeria. His father, Charles-Joseph Althusser, was a banker, and his mother, Lucienne Marthe Berger, was a schoolteacher and a devout Catholic.

Althusser lived in Algeria until 1930, when his father was reassigned to Marseilles, France. While living in Marseilles, Althusser studied at the Lycée Saint-Charles. In 1936, his family moved to Lyon, where Althusser attended the Lycée du Parc and prepared for the national entrance exam to the prestigious École Normale Supérieure (ENS). He joined the Catholic youth movement in 1937.

Althusser was successful in his 1939 ENS admissions exams but was called up for military service before the start of the academic year. In June 1940, he was captured by the Germans and spent the rest of the war in a prisoner-of-war camp in Schleswig-Holstein, Germany. This experience contributed to his loss of religious faith, his political development as a communist, and the onset of his lifelong struggles with clinical depression.

After the war ended, in October 1945 Althusser returned to the ENS but struggled to readjust to academic life after a 6-year interruption in his studies; he began to suffer from depression and was admitted to a psychiatric hospital. While convalescing in a small town in the French Alps, Althusser eventually completed his studies and received a Diplôme d'études supérieures for his thesis on Hegel, written under the direction of the notable philosopher Gaston Bachelard.

In 1946, Althusser had struck up a close friendship with Jacques Martin, a translator of Hegel, who later committed suicide and to whom Althusser's book *For Marx* is movingly dedicated. Under Martin's influence, Althusser had begun to read Hegel seriously. At the ENS, Althusser also befriended the young philosophers Michel Foucault, Jean-Toussaint Desanti, and Tran Duc Thao. He played an active role among progressive Catholic youth and helped organize the student union.

Most significantly, in 1946 Althusser met Hélène Legotien (née Rytman), who was 8 years his senior and a communist dissident. Hélène had taken part in the French Resistance and later became a distinguished sociologist. She and Althusser became lifelong companions and eventually got married in 1976.

In 1948, Althusser joined—and never left—the French Communist Party (*Parti Communiste Français*, PCF). He also passed his *agrégation*, a competitive examination (in which he ranked first in the written and second in the oral components) that provided him a license to teach philosophy in French secondary schools. However, Althusser instead accepted a position at the ENS of *agrégé-répétiteur* or, in the student slang, *caïman*. As *caïman*, he helped prepare students for the *agrégation*, and he remained in this position until 1980. In addition to his regular duties as a philosophy tutor, Althusser had a profound influence at the ENS because of his ability to organize official conferences and guest lectures by important figures in France such as Jacques Lacan, Gilles Deleuze, and Michel Foucault.

When his seminal works *For Marx* and *Reading Capital* were published in 1965, Althusser was thrust from a previously marginal position in the PCF into a position of being one of the party's leading public intellectuals.

In 1956, at the Twentieth Party Congress of the Communist Party of the Soviet Union, First Secretary Nikita Khrushchev had given a famous speech in which he denounced and criticized crimes committed by his predecessor Joseph Stalin and initiated a process of "de-Stalinization." For many Marxists, including Eric Fromm, Jean-Paul Sartre, and the PCF's leading theoretician Roger Garaudy, this provided an opportunity to rediscover the humanist roots of Marx's thought and to engage in a fruitful dialogue with non-Marxists. Althusser, however, opposed this trend, defended a "theoretical anti-humanism," and sympathized with criticisms made by the Chinese Communist Party—but he was careful not to identify himself openly with Maoism.

Although many of his students were involved in the tumultuous events of May–June 1968, Althusser himself was not supportive. As a result, he was rebuked by some of his former supporters, notably the philosopher Jacques Rancière. In response, Althusser engaged in a searching "self-criticism."

By the mid-1970s, Althusser and his supporters publicly contested the PCF's leadership over matters such as the contemporary relevance of the Marxist notion of the "dictatorship of the Proletariat." This struggle ultimately resulted in the publication in 1978 of his pointed challenge: *What Must Change in the Party.*

In 1975, Althusser defended a Doctorat d'État thesis for his published body of work, at the Université de Picardie, which later appeared in English as "Is It Simple to Be a Marxist in Philosophy?" (Althusser 2011, pp. 203–240).

Althusser's life took a tragic turn in November 1980 when, in a delusional state, he strangled his wife, Hélène, to death. After a lengthy psychiatric examination, Althusser was declared unfit to stand trial and committed to the Sainte-Anne psychiatric hospital. He was also compelled by the ENS administration to retire.

Until 1983, Althusser lived in various public and private clinics in the Paris area, initially under administrative detention, then as a voluntary patient, and finally, from 1984 to 1986, at some distance from the ENS, at an apartment in the north of Paris. Treated by various doctors, he was regularly visited by close friends. Althusser died on October 22, 1990, of a heart attack at the age of 72 at the Denis Forestier Geriatric Center.

Critical Contributions to Marxism

During the 1950s, Althusser gradually abandoned his youthful philosophical and political orientations. The high point of his writing during this period of rupture with the official Stalinist Marxism, to which he had been introduced in the PCF, was a short book on the 18th-century French political theorist Montesquieu, which appeared in 1959. In 1960, Althusser also translated, edited, and published a collection of writings by Ludwig Feuerbach, the 19th-century German materialist philosopher, who was a crucial philosophical influence on the early Marx and Engels.

Althusser's mature works include *For Marx* and *Reading Capital*, both of which appeared in 1965. The former is a collection of essays in which Althusser—borrowing a term from Bachelard—famously argued that there exists an "epistemological break" between Marx's early and his later "mature" writings. The latter collective work gathered seminar presentations given by Althusser and his students as they engaged in a detailed philosophical rereading of Marx's *Capital*. In *For Marx* and *Reading Capital*, Althusser argued that the works of the young Marx were largely confined to the categories of German philosophy and classical political economy, but with *The German Ideology* (1845), there was a profound shift toward a fundamentally different "problematic." Although Marx himself never fully grasped this theoretical reorientation, Althusser sought to reveal it by means of a careful and sensitive "symptomatic reading."

Other significant texts by Althusser during his mature period were his 1967 lecture series on "Philosophy and the Spontaneous Philosophy of the

Scientists" (Althusser, 2011, pp. 69–165) and his 1968 lecture "Lenin and Philosophy" (Althusser, 2011, pp. 167–202). In these lectures, Althusser broke with what he called his earlier "theoreticism" and advanced a new, practical conception of philosophy as the representation of class struggle in theory. Althusser's rethinking of philosophy as a dialectical struggle of idealist and materialist "tendencies" stimulated creative research and publications by his associates, such as Pierre Macherey, Pierre Raymond, and Dominique Lecourt.

In his highly influential 1969 essay "Ideology and Ideological State Apparatuses" (excerpted from a longer manuscript that was only posthumously published and has not yet been translated into English: *Sur la reproduction* [On Reproduction]), Althusser sought to reframe Marx's account of ideology not as a set of false beliefs but as a complex, and contradictory, assemblage of social practices through which every individual is transformed into a "subject" (Althusser, 2008, pp. 1–60). In other words, individuals do not originate as, but become, self-conscious and responsible agents through the interplay of a wide variety of "ideological state apparatuses," such as family, mass media, religious organizations, and especially the educational system. There is no single ideological state apparatus that produces in us the belief that we are self-conscious, responsible agents. Instead, we derive this belief in the course of learning what it means to fulfill the role of a parent, child, teacher, student, administrator, worker, citizen, religious believer, and so forth. Althusser never underestimated the significance of what he called the "repressive state apparatus," whose underlying violence is supplemented by the everyday social reproduction carried out by ideological practices. Nor did he deny the possibility of resistance to dominant ideologies through the establishment of counterideologies.

In the late 1970s and early 1980s, Althusser entered the final phase of his intellectual development. He acknowledged a "crisis of Marxism," rejected all orthodox versions of dialectical materialism as a broad worldview, and pursued instead what he called a "philosophy for Marxism," to be situated within what he variously called a "philosophy of the encounter" or "aleatory materialism" (Althusser, 2006). Although this later material is fragmentary, it makes explicit certain themes that were already implicit in Althusser's mature writings of the 1960s.

Althusser contended that there is a long materialist countertendency in the history of philosophy—which is predominately idealist—that has run its course through philosophers who are otherwise as different as Epicurus, Machiavelli, Spinoza, Hobbes, Rousseau, Marx, Heidegger, Wittgenstein, Foucault, Derrida, and Deleuze.

Influence on Anthropology

Althusser's direct contributions to anthropology were limited (see Resch, 1993, pp. 111–135). However, an interesting, but only posthumously published, text is "On Lévi-Strauss" (Althusser, 2003, pp. 19–32), which was originally written as a long critical letter that began to circulate widely during 1966. Although Althusser offered a few favorable remarks on Lévi-Strauss and his scientific approach, the bulk of the letter criticized not just "structuralist anthropology" but anthropology itself. According to Althusser, Lévi-Strauss misunderstood Marx, was guilty of methodological formalism, and wrongly conceived of "primitive societies" as existing outside history—as primitive, not simply in a relative but in an absolute or "originary" sense. From a Marxist perspective, however, there can be no such originary societies but only historical social formations. Althusser argued that Lévi-Strauss did not adequately understand the concept of a "mode of production" and, as a result, failed to grasp that kinship structures are relations of production that operate only within a given mode of production. The anthropologist Emannuel Terray acknowledged "On Lévi-Strauss" in his book *Marxism and "Primitive" Societies* (1972), which was originally published in a series edited by Althusser. The latter had initially proposed to include "On Lévi-Strauss" as an appendix to Terray's book, which, however, ultimately appeared without it.

Althusser's Legacy

Althusser was a central figure in the post–World War II renewal of Marxist economics, social theory, philosophy, and cultural studies. He drew from a wide variety of non-Marxist sources—Spinoza, Rousseau, and Montesquieu, the philosophy of science, and psychoanalysis—as well as from key thinkers in the classical Marxist tradition, such as Lenin and Gramsci, to move away from the intellectual isolation of Stalinist-influenced "official" Marxism.

Although commonly referred to as a "structural" Marxist, Althusser was in fact highly critical of most aspects of structuralism (see Montag, 2013).

Althusser's work has enjoyed multidisciplinary influence. His effort to reconstruct historical materialism was a stimulus for Anglophone analytic philosophers such as G. A. Cohen and Andrew Levine. His emphases on contradiction, immanent causality, and overdetermination have appeared in the analyses of social class developed by Nicos Poulantzas, Erik Olin Wright, and Richard Wolff and Stephen Resnick. Althusser's reformulation of the Marxist theory of ideology has been the point of departure for Judith Butler in gender studies, Slavoj Žižek in politics, and Michael Sprinker and Terry Eagleton in literary and cultural theory. Althusser's work has influenced new materialist approaches to biblical scholarship and innovative Latin American directions in "liberation theology." Finally, Althusser has inspired two generations of scholarship on the 17th-century philosopher Baruch Spinoza, by writers such as Étienne Balibar, Pierre Macherey, Pierre-François Moreau, and André Tosel.

Althusser's work has been criticized in various ways, perhaps most famously by his former student Jacques Rancière, the Polish philosopher Leszek Kołakowski, and the British historian E. P. Thompson. All disputed what they regarded as Althusser's wrong-headed scientific aspirations and his failure to break theoretically and politically with Stalinism. What is striking in such objections, however, was their reliance on summary or paraphrase and avoidance of close, contextualized readings of Althusser's works and their historical development. Indeed, these often strident criticisms appear today to be superficial and dated, especially in light of the posthumous publication of numerous texts—especially those concerning aleatory materialism—that have stimulated an international resurgence of interest in Althusser's thought, which is likely to continue for many years to come (see Diefenbach et al., 2012).

Ted Stolze

See also Barthes, Roland; Deleuze, Gilles, and Félix Guattari; Foucault, Michel; Gramsci, Antonio; Lacan, Jacques; Lévi-Strauss, Claude; Marx, Karl; Marxist Anthropology; Poststructuralism; Structural Marxism

Further Readings

Althusser, L. (2003). *The humanist controversy and other writings (1966–67)* (F. Matheron, Ed., G. M. Goshgarian, Trans.). New York, NY: Verso.

——. (2005). *For Marx* (B. Brewster, Trans.). New York, NY: Verso. (Original work published 1969)

——. (2006). *Philosophy of the encounter: Later writings, 1978–87* (F. Matheron & O. Corpet, Eds., G. M. Goshgarian, Trans.). New York, NY: Verso.

——. (2008). *On ideology.* New York, NY: Verso.

——. (2011). *Philosophy and the spontaneous philosophy of the scientists* (G. Elliott, Ed.). New York, NY: Verso.

Althusser, L., & Balibar, É. (2009). *Reading capital* (B. Brewster, Trans.). New York, NY: Verso. (Original work published 1970)

Diefenbach, K., Farris, S. R., Kirn, G., & Thomas, P. (2012). *Encountering Althusser: Politics and materialism in contemporary radical thought.* New York, NY: Bloomsbury Academic.

Elliott, G. (2009). *Althusser: The detour of theory.* Chicago, IL: Haymarket Books.

Montag, W. (2013). *Althusser and his contemporaries: Philosophy's perpetual war.* Durham, NC: Duke University Press.

Resch, R. P. (1992). *Althusser and the renewal of Marxist social theory.* Berkeley: University of California Press.

Terray, E. (1972). *Marxism and "primitive societies": Two studies* (M. Klopper, Trans.). New York, NY: Monthly Review Press.

Website

Décalages: An Althusser Studies Journal: http://scholar.oxy.edu/decalages/

AMERICAN ANTHROPOLOGICAL ASSOCIATION

The American Anthropological Association (AAA) is the largest association of anthropologists in the world. Its membership includes professional and student anthropologists from the United States and abroad, both academic anthropologists and applied or practicing anthropologists. While anthropologists and social scientists recognize the successes of the AAA in representing anthropology to the media and the government, it is also important to note that the AAA has played a significant role in shaping anthropological theory. Over the years, the AAA has

(a) defined the scope of professionalism; (b) provided a vital space to foster, perform, and enact anthropological identities; and (c) offered explicit valuation of good anthropological scholarship in the forms of prizes, awards, and fellowships. In each of these endeavors, the AAA's approach to anthropology has been marked by a commitment to intellectual and geographic holism, including work in four broad areas of anthropology identified throughout much of U.S. anthropological history as "the four subfields" of anthropology (archaeological anthropology, biological/physical anthropology, linguistic anthropology, and sociocultural anthropology/ethnology). Through its actual organization, large and small conferences, and policies and practices, the AAA has demonstrated an ideological commitment to research, teaching, and writing, and engagement with all of humanity's past and present. This "big tent" approach has practical implications for the practice of the profession, especially in the United States, but it is useful as well to note that it rests on a particular conception of the field of anthropology that has developed over the years in the United States.

Professionalism: Defining Anthropology as an Expert Domain

Since its founding in 1902, the AAA has been instrumental in defining anthropology as an academic discipline characterized by theoretical rigor, academic research, and writing. Prior to 1902, there were numerous other organizations dedicated to anthropology in the United States, such as the Anthropological Club of New York and the Women's Anthropological Society of America. These clubs and societies, however, were far from uniform in their goals or practices, and many consisted largely of amateurs and enthusiasts. The tension between amateur and expert anthropologists came to a head during the founding of the AAA in the first few years of the 20th century. At that time, William John McGee, a self-trained ethnologist who led the U.S. Bureau of American Ethnology, and Franz Boas, an academically trained anthropologist, engaged in a series of heated debates and political maneuverings to determine the nature of membership in the nascent society. McGee favored an inclusive model that incorporated amateurs and enthusiasts, while Boas preferred a far more exclusive one. Although Boas's model never entirely succeeded, professional/expert

anthropologists became the primary force and face of the emerging AAA.

The common factors binding AAA members together were training and expertise rather than geographical focus or subdisciplinary orientation. Despite their disagreement over the emphasis to be placed on training and expertise, McGee and Boas shared an inclusive understanding of anthropology as a discipline that encompassed archaeological, physical, linguistic, and ethnologic research. Indeed, in 1904, they explicitly stated that the AAA was dedicated to the biological, linguistic, archaeological, and ethnological components of humanity. This early commitment to four subfields of anthropology has remained a persistent component of the AAA's organizational contribution to anthropology. Few anthropologists personally engage in research encompassing the four named subfields as seamlessly as earlier anthropologists such as Boas did, yet the AAA remains organizationally dedicated to including each vein of research.

Conferences

The AAA and its 38 current sections organize and host 7–10 conferences each year, ranging from a few dozen participants to some 6,500. Best known are the megaconferences known as the annual meetings of the American Anthropological Association. These meetings act as opportunities for anthropologists to present their research, meet other anthropologists, and learn about the AAA's plans and business. While some researchers have questioned the scholarly merit of academic conferences, noting that they rarely result in peer-reviewed publications, these conferences play an important role in fostering and developing theory, nonetheless. As many scholars have noted, academic conferences constitute a performative space in which researchers enact their professional identities and new members are socialized into disciplinary norms of professional behavior. The organization and content of the meetings reveal the tacit intellectual values and disciplinary commitments of the AAA. The AAA meetings have historically included research papers and reports from each of anthropology's subfields. Increasingly, over the past few decades, they have also included films and other audiovisual presentations and, more recently, poster sessions. This act of inclusion alone speaks to the role of the AAA in fostering a disciplinary commitment to theoretical holism.

Of course, size matters. In the early years of the AAA, the annual meeting occurred over the course of a day, and all anthropologists present were able to attend all papers since it was held in a single room. For example, 42 people attended the 41st annual meetings, which were held at the Cosmos Club in Washington, D.C., in December 1942. By the 1961 annual meeting, attendance had grown to 1,117 people. This bred a sharp awareness of the new trends and developments across the subfields. Indeed, in her 1967 AAA presidential address, Frederica de Laguna reminisced about this time, when anthropologists would listen to all papers regardless of area of knowledge, subfield, or geographic base. By 1967, the AAA membership and scale of the annual meetings had grown enough to make such intimacy impossible. She noted that as the discipline grew, and journals and more specialized anthropological communities proliferated, such collectivity became impossible, yet, importantly, she implored the membership of AAA to retain their commitment to disciplinary holism.

Today the AAA meetings are far larger than they were in the 1960s and apparently growing. For years attracting some 4,500–5,000 participants, the meetings reached 6,000 in 2010 in New Orleans and more than 6,500 in 2011 in Montreal. Featuring at least 300 panels over a 5-day period, plus films, posters, as well as distinguished lectures and business, board, and committee meetings of multiple sorts, the annual meetings enact the "big tent" approach and the AAA's continued effort to be there for all anthropologists and to represent the entire field. Papers are included from each subfield of the discipline, and individual panels may include anthropologists from each of the subfields. Although social/cultural anthropologists (and newer configurations such as medical anthropologists) attend in larger numbers than archaeological and biological anthropologists, the AAA continues to promote, and stress its commitment to, the inclusion of all types of anthropologists. Despite the increased specialization among anthropological subfields in recent decades, the AAA Annual Meeting serves symbolically and practically as a site where anthropologists experience and celebrate the breadth of the discipline.

In relatively recent years, the annual meetings of the AAA have featured particular themes as an overarching form of meeting organization intended to foster collaboration across differences. With the growth of the discipline and increased specialization, it became more important and useful by the mid-1980s to have themes capable of uniting varying interests. This is especially apparent in the two themes for the 1984 annual meeting: "Biocultural Dimensions of Anthropology" and "Economic and Social Roles for Anthropologists in the 1980s." A major reorganization of the AAA had just taken place, driven by the need to maintain its tax-exempt status in the eyes of the U.S. government, and organizations that had maintained their separate legal standing had chosen to strengthen the AAA by fully joining it. Official AAA meeting themes helped signal the desire to proclaim and embrace the "big tent" approach quite openly, so it was not a surprise when Lynne Goldstein, the 1984 program chair, noted that she intended the themes for the 1984 AAA annual meeting to cut across boundaries within and beyond anthropology. More recent past themes have persisted in showing inclusiveness. They have included "Precarious Planet: Earth and Human Landscape" (1993), "The Public Face of Anthropology" (2000), and "Traces, Tidemarks, and Legacies" (2011), to name only a few. The themes of past meetings share a broadness intended to invite and foster interdisciplinary collaboration across subfields. Here, again, the AAA's commitment to disciplinary holism is apparent.

Geographic and topical openness remain the hallmarks of AAA's conception of anthropology and, hence, of theory in anthropology. For example, AAA sections focusing on particular areas of research or approaches to research, teaching, engagement, or analysis, such as the Society for Medical Anthropology or the Association for Feminist Anthropology, organize panels that typically include presentations drawing on research conducted in different regions, countries, or cultural groups. It is not uncommon to observe a panel with papers focusing on Latin America, Europe, and Asia. While such combinations are unlikely to surprise anthropologists, they reveal a persistent and ongoing disciplinary commitment. Indeed, the construction of the AAA annual meetings emphasizes the need to engage in comparison, even if individual anthropologists work in only one area or with a named group of people. Participants are surrounded by anthropological work on multiple issues based on research in places beyond their own experience or expertise. They may mostly attend certain panels or spend time informally talking with anthropologists whose work most closely resembles their own, but they will still be surrounded by many other anthropologists. Tacitly reinforcing the notion that all of humanity, past and present, deserves anthropological attention, the AAA's annual meetings are officially open to all theoretical persuasions and orientations. Yet this commitment is, in itself, a theoretical position and arguably the central theoretical contribution of the AAA.

Of course, in its official openness to all types of anthropological work, the AAA has also acknowledged, enabled, and at times fostered direct debate on timely questions of method, ethics, human rights, or theory. For example, in 1988, the General Anthropology Division hosted an often cited debate on the history of emics and etics between Kenneth Pike and Marvin Harris, well-known supporters of these two positions, and the numerous citations that followed show a broad level of anthropological engagement in matters of method, theory, and ethics. Over the past decade, discussions and debates about ethics in anthropology have grown in number and substance, as have arguments about advocacy, human rights, anthropologists in the military, and public engagement. Most recently, discussion about anthropology as science, or anthropology and its relationship to science, began online after the 2010 AAA Annual Meeting held in New Orleans, continued in both new and traditional media, was included in issues of *Anthropology News*, and was given space on the conference program of the 2011 AAA Annual Meeting in Montreal.

Presidential Addresses

AAA presidential addresses offer other revealing glimpses of the AAA's theoretical commitments. Over the years, AAA presidents have been markedly concerned with (a) disciplinary holism and (b) the ability of anthropologists to communicate anthropological understandings to a broader public. Some, like Louise Lamphere and Virginia Dominguez, have tried to call internal professional attention to areas of unfortunate inattention, or even tacit exclusion, in U.S. anthropological practice, including within the AAA.

Published presidential addresses show that many AAA presidents have been concerned with the nature and tenor of collaboration within anthropology, both among anthropology's named subfields and across geographic areas of expertise. Many

AAA presidents have reiterated de Laguna's urge to maintain the discipline's commitment to a holistic approach to the field. For instance, in the mid-1990s, Annette Weiner implored anthropologists to collaborate among the four subfields as a key part of their work. Anxiety about disciplinary fragmentation has not been limited to the (perceived) widening of the gap between archaeological anthropology, biological anthropology, linguistic anthropology, and sociocultural anthropology; it has also included regional foci. For instance, in his 1965 address, Alexander Spoehr worried that anthropologists' geographical and topical research was dividing them, and he reminded AAA members that cross-cultural comparison had to be the central feature of the discipline. AAA presidents' regular calls for disciplinary holism reveal a persistent dedication to the idea that anthropology is, and ought to be, a collaborative, cross-cultural, and cross-subfield discipline. They also, however, reveal concern that such collaboration happens less and less.

Past AAA presidential addresses also reveal a persistent concern about the relationship between anthropologists and the wider public. Some demonstrate a concern that the broader conditions of academic labor will negatively affect or curtail anthropological scholarship. For example, Don Brenneis's 2004 address examined the rise of private capital and managerialist ideologies in the academy and their potential consequences for anthropological scholarship, while James Peacock worried in 1995 about the persistent sense that anthropology was a noncore field that might eventually disappear from U.S. universities.

The addresses also reveal an ongoing belief that anthropological theorizing is important not just to anthropologists but to the broader public as well. Presidents such as Walter Goldschmidt, James Peacock, and Leslie White have all considered research and writing strategies to help anthropologists better communicate their ideas to the public and foster public interest in anthropology. These concerns demonstrate the degree to which the AAA sees anthropology as developing ideas that should be shared with the broader public.

Prizes

Scholars have argued that the awarding of prizes by academic and literary societies plays an important role in the disciplining and bounding of a field, and the AAA is a good example of that. The AAA awards a number of prizes to anthropologists for their scholarship, commitment to the discipline, and public outreach. In so doing, the AAA reveals its commitment to excellence across a number of professional arenas and its openness to work drawing on a range of theoretical paradigms. While the awarding of prizes to colleagues known for advancement of particular theoretical paradigms periodically raises eyebrows in certain parts of the broad membership and profession, it is interesting to note that multiple awards exist and winners can represent significantly different, even competing, theoretical paradigms in anthropology.

The AAA's own awards committee handles nominations for some AAA awards, works with certain AAA units to process and give AAA awards, and selects winners of a number of prizes presented by the sitting AAA president each year at the AAA awards ceremony. These now include the David M. Schneider Award, the AAA Minority Dissertation Fellowship, the Franz Boas Award for Exemplary Service to Anthropology, the Anthropology in Media Award, and the Alfred Vincent Kidder Award for Eminence in the Field of American Archaeology, to name but a few. It is noteworthy that many AAA prizes focus on anthropologists' contributions to the public, whether in awareness, preventive action, or applied research.

Interestingly, these awards cut across subfields, demonstrating that these values are common denominators capable of uniting scholars across subfield orientations. In addition, most of the formal sections of the AAA also award prizes of their own, and these too reflect an emphasis on quality and excellence in more specialized areas but usually likewise stress anthropological research based on participant observation, engagement with past and present scholarly communities, readability, and past or potential influence. Examples include prizes given by the Society for Cultural Anthropology, the Society for the Anthropology of Europe, the Society for Medical Anthropology, the American Ethnological Society, and the Society for Psychological Anthropology, just to name a few.

Policy

A recurrent theme through much of the history of anthropology in the United States (and, therefore, the AAA) is how anthropologists should best communicate their ideas to the broader public, influence public debate and discussion, and even engage with U.S. government policies and practices. Formal AAA resolutions and executive board motions have over the years condemned military activity, which is seen as contrary to the anthropological appreciation for social, cultural, linguistic, and historical diversity; anti-immigration legislation, seen as targeting ethnic and racial minorities; the exploitation of groups seen as geopolitically vulnerable; and systemic discriminatory practices both in the United States and elsewhere. Some resolutions have addressed practices outside the United States, although most have concentrated on U.S. actions and anthropologists' responses to those actions.

Over the years, the AAA has also made a point of advocating for anthropology with all known public and private funding agencies. Most significant here is the AAA's efforts to protect (and increase) funding for anthropology within the U.S. National Science Foundation, the U.S. National Endowment for the Humanities, the U.S. National Institutes of Health, and the large U.S.-based foundations. In its actions, the AAA leadership and staff clearly view some anthropological work as more humanistic than scientific, other work as more scientific than humanistic, and still other work as squarely within the arena of applied medical research. Arguably, the AAA then takes the stance that anthropology as a discipline spans the full range of knowledge-based professions located in higher education and research and that individual practitioners (and segments of the profession) are both grounded in anthropology and able to work collaboratively and substantively with colleagues and professionals outside of anthropology—crossing disciplinary lines with relative ease.

Internal Groupings and Sections

Fragmentation and unity are evident as well in the very structure of the AAA, including in its publications program. In 1984, following a proposal from the Board and a general vote, the AAA was restructured to resemble the organization it is today. The reorganization entailed the creation of sections dedicated to archaeology, linguistic anthropology, biological anthropology, practicing anthropology, and general anthropology, while also allowing for the possibility that new interest groups and sections would emerge in the future. Many have. The AAA is currently divided into 38 sections and just under 10 interest groups, and altogether, the AAA (and its sections) publishes nearly two dozen academic journals, annuals, and substantive newsletters. Many of the sections are thematically oriented, others are geographically oriented, and some are demographically, socially, or institutionally oriented. Their membership ranges in size from around 2,000 to around 200.

The AAA publishes six quarterly scholarly journals and multiple journals published two to three times each year. The oldest and best known is the *American Anthropologist*, often referred to as the flagship journal of the discipline (at least in the United States) and committed to publishing across all fields and subfields of the profession. That breadth of commitment is interestingly not present in most of the AAA's other journals, even the other prestigious quarterlies—the *American Ethnologist*, the *Medical Anthropological Quarterly, Cultural Anthropology, Ethos: The Journal of the Society for Psychological Anthropology*, and the *Anthropology and Education Quarterly*—all of which welcome manuscripts that advance anthropological research and thinking regardless of an author's training but not an author's type of work. Together, AAA's journals cover a great many topics and concerns but tend to do so as a stable of journals rather than as individual journals. This pattern parallels the "big tent" approach of the AAA as a whole—its commitment to intellectual diversity within the profession just as much as to human diversity overall.

Virginia R. Dominguez and Michele Hanks

Further Readings

Darnell, R., & Gleach, F. (2002). *Celebrating a century of the American Anthropological Association: Presidential portraits.* Lincoln: University of Nebraska Press and the American Anthropological Association.

Engle, K. (2001). From skepticism to embrace: Human rights and the American Anthropological Association from 1947–1999. *Human Rights Quarterly, 23,* 536–559.

Lewis, H. S. (2009). The radical transformation of anthropology: History seen through the annual meetings of the American Anthropological Association, 1955–2005. *Histories of Anthropology Annual, 5,* 200–228.

Stocking, G. W. (1960). Franz Boas and the founding of the American Anthropological Association. *American Anthropologist, 62,* 1–17.

AMERICAN MUSEUM OF NATURAL HISTORY

The anthropology department at the American Museum of Natural History (AMNH) is one of the oldest, largest, and most important such departments in America. The museum itself achieved prominence at a time when the dominant institutional home of American anthropology was in museums, and during its long history, the anthropology department has made many critical contributions to sociocultural theory or ethnology (an older term still used in museums). Its greatest period of national influence came during the years when the department was chaired by Franz Boas and Clark Wissler, ca. 1895–1920. Its centrality to the discipline has declined since then due to factors internal to the museum as well as to the changing institutional context of American anthropology.

The Early Years (1869–1894)

Founded in 1869, the AMNH is one of the several museums in New York City characterized by joint ownership and control: The city owns the land and its building and supplies operating funds, and a private board of trustees owns the collections and is responsible for curators and scientific staff.

Although the department was not formally established until 1873, the museum held anthropological collections from the beginning. However, unlike Harvard's Peabody Museum and the Smithsonian, the anthropology department at AMNH was not a leader in the early years of the field in America. While the accumulation of collections was largely haphazard, some outstanding artifacts were acquired during these years, most especially from the Tlingit and other Northwest Coast peoples, purchased from the naval officer and amateur ethnologist George T. Emmons.

The Franz Boas Years (1894–1905)

The professional importance of the department effectively dates to 1894, with the appointment of Frederic W. Putnam (1839–1915) to lead the department. Serving simultaneously as director and professor of anthropology at Harvard's Peabody Museum, Putnam resigned from the American Museum in

1903. Following an initiative fostered by the museum's president Morris K. Jesup, Putnam based the department's collections and displays on expeditions carried out by museum scientists. In New York, Putnam focused on archaeology, especially in the American Southwest and Mexico.

Franz Boas (1858–1942) was hired by the museum in 1895, first to curate a diorama based on his previous fieldwork in British Columbia, and then as curator of North American ethnology from 1896 to 1905. Boas, a German immigrant, was famed for his reorientation of American anthropology. His theories of cultural relativism supplanted the then dominant theories of social evolutionism. Many of the theoretical innovations associated with Boas—for example, the geographic distribution of culture traits or the separation of race, language, and culture—were first worked out in Boas's own museum practice.

As always, but especially important during these years, private donors were responsible for the funding of field expeditions, most notably the president, Morris K. Jesup (Northwest Coast and Plains), the brothers B. Talbot Hyde and Frederick E. Hyde Jr. (Southwest), Archer M. Huntington (Southwest), and the Duc de Loubat (Mexico).

Boas was director of the influential Jesup expedition to the Northwest Coast and Siberia (1897–1902). While ostensibly predicated on tracing the peopling of the Americas, the expedition is now valued for its fundamental collecting and ethnographies and for exploring the role of the geographical distribution of culture traits. Boas, however, was never able to write a final, summary volume.

During his tenure, Boas made an attempt to extend the scope of the department beyond the Americas by including Siberia on the Jesup expedition and by beginning an Asian initiative with Berthold Laufer, who collected in Siberia for the Jesup—along with Vladimir Jochelson and Vladimir Bogoras—and then in China (1901–1904); but he found little support for this program.

The exhibit halls were arranged principally by subdiscipline (but combined for the Southwest and Mesoamerica, and South America), and then by region, with a focus on North American ethnology, the main interest of Boas and Wissler. Boas derived this geographical schema—which contrasted with the typological displays of the Smithsonian—from both of his museum mentors, Adolf Bastian and Frederic

Putnam. In turn, his regional approaches became the norm in American anthropology museums.

Franz Boas also established the department's close relationship with Columbia University, which, through ups and downs, has remained to the present day. The great shift of the dominant institutional home of American anthropology from museums to universities, which occurred in the early 20th century, was symbolized by Boas's departure for Columbia in 1905.

The Clark Wissler Years (1905–1945)

Although not as renowned as his predecessor, Clark Wissler (1870–1947) was chair of the anthropology department for a much longer period (retiring in 1942), an important period of accomplishment and transition. Wissler certainly had a greater impact within the museum and a significant, although largely unacknowledged, one on the discipline at large.

As an ethnographer, Wissler is best known for his work among the Blackfoot as well as for the more general ethnographic survey of the Plains that he supervised. Wissler's greatest theoretical contribution generated by the survey was the salience of environmental factors in the formation of culture areas, but he also formulated the age-area concept as a basis for historical reconstruction. Although he derived his basic methodologies from the Jesup expedition, Wissler, unlike Boas, was able to effectively systematize them.

Robert H. Lowie (1883–1957), another Boas student, was a curator at the museum from 1909 to 1921. Known for his work with the Crow people of Montana and many other groups of western America, he also curated the museum's first halls for Africa, the Philippines, and Oceania. Lowie made important theoretical contributions to the study of social organization.

The Huntington expedition to the Southwest (1909–1922) innovatively combined archaeology and ethnology. Wissler was able to expand the expedition's scope beyond collecting to a double theoretical focus: (1) kinship and social organization and (2) the formulation of a regional chronology (based on stratigraphic excavations by Nels Nelson, pottery seriation by Alfred Kroeber, and tree-ring dating).

After Boas, Margaret Mead (1901–1978) was the most famous anthropologist ever associated with the museum. Serving as curator of Pacific ethnology from 1926 until 1969, she did important ethnographic research in the South Pacific (especially Samoa, the Admiralty Islands, New Guinea, and Bali). Mead, however, spent relatively little time with museums and material culture. Instead, she used her position as an independent base for her extensive research, writing, and lecturing. Mead was noted for her work on culture and personality, culture change, visual anthropology, and the general role of anthropology in American society.

During the 1920s, the importance of the department declined, at least in sociocultural anthropology, as curators left and were not replaced. By 1930, Mead and Wissler were the only ethnologists, and Wissler spent much of his time with administration. These personnel shifts coincided with a general stasis of the department's exhibits, which lasted until the early 1960s. Anthropology during the Wissler years was circumscribed by the museum's administration. The museum's president, Henry Fairfield Osborn, had little use for anthropology. A vertebrate paleontologist as well as a member of New York's social elite, Osborn collaborated with the museum's trustee Madison Grant, a leading eugenicist, to minimize the anthropological focus of the museum. Following Wissler as departmental chair, the physical anthropologist Harry L. Shapiro served for nearly 3 decades (1942–1970). During his tenure, he continued to emphasize archaeology as well as his own subdiscipline. Although he developed several innovative plans for comparative exhibits, Shapiro was unable to realize these due to the museum's continuing financial problems.

A Period of Transition (1945–1970)

After the challenge of the Depression and World War II, it took a while for the department to recover. Wissler's curatorial successor, Harry Tschopik, responsible for both North and South American ethnology, died prematurely, serving only from 1947 to 1956. However, paralleling the national trends, the Department of Anthropology underwent a revival in the 1960s. With an expanding economy and the Cold War support for science education, the museum was able to hire several new curators and began to renovate most of its exhibitions in advance of its centennial in 1969.

Stanley A. Freed (b. 1927) served as curator of North American ethnology from 1960 until 1999.

While he curated new exhibits for the Eastern Indians, the Plains, and the Eskimos, most of his research has been done in India; Freed is noted for his empiricism and wide-ranging ethnography. As one of the founders of the Council for Museum Anthropology, he was also active in the revival of museum anthropology in America.

Robert L. Carneiro (b. 1927) was the curator for South American ethnology from 1957 to 2010. Having trained with Leslie White at the University of Michigan, Carneiro is known for his contributions to materialist anthropology, especially cultural ecology, cultural neo-evolutionism, and the processes of state formation.

A much more humanistic kind of anthropology was represented by Colin Turnbull (1924–1994), an Oxford-trained African curator who served the museum from 1959 through 1969. Like Mead, Turnbull was a popular writer. His fieldwork with the Mbuti pygmies of the Congo resulted in *The Forest People* (1961), and his experiences with the Ik of Uganda are described in *The Mountain People* (1972).

Recent Years (1970–Present)

The role of sociocultural theory in the department has been revived since the 1970s, accompanied by a gradual diminution of the traditional museum functions of collection and exhibition. In this period, the department revived its program in Old World ethnology by appointing a long-term curator for Africa, Enid Schildkrout (curator, 1973–2005), and its first full-time curator in Asian ethnology, Laurel Kendall (curator, 1983–present). Schildkrout focused on the art of Central Africa, ethnicity and Islam in Ghana, and women and children in Nigeria. Kendall has worked mainly in Korea and more recently in Vietnam, contributing to the study of shamanism and culture change.

Since 2001, Peter M. Whitely has been the curator of North American ethnology, noted for his work on Hopi social structure and history. During the 1990s and the early 20th century, the curatorial positions in Africa and Oceania have changed frequently.

Since the passing of the national repatriation legislation in 1990, the museum has developed better relations with the Native American community. The museum organized a series of innovative exhibits focusing on the historicity of the museum collections: Carolyn Gilman and Mary Jane Schneider on Gilbert Wilson's Hidatsa collections (1987), Schildkrout on the Congo (1990), and Aldona Jonaitis, an art historian and former museum vice president, on the potlatch of the Kwakw*aka*'wakw of British Columbia (1991).

Following the lengthy tenures of Franz Boas, Clark Wissler, and Harry Shapiro as departmental chairs, the museum has introduced a system of revolving and limited chairmanships. Anthropology has not been as favored as some other departments, such as paleontology and astronomy, with the notable exception of the repeated renewal of the Human Evolution Hall. The department has expanded its ties to local universities, with a joint graduate program in museum anthropology at Columbia University and relations with the departments of anthropology and museum studies at New York University and, more recently, at the Bard Graduate Center.

Legacy

As in many museums, there has been a great deal of curatorial stability at AMNH. The curators, who often serve for several decades, are treated like academic faculty. With the freedom to choose their own topics of research, their research often has no clear relation to museums or material culture. Nevertheless, curators at the AMNH are among the leaders in their field. Coupled with its great historical legacy, the anthropology department of the AMNH remains important to the discipline in America.

Ira Jacknis

See also Boas, Franz; Carneiro, Robert L.; Columbia University; Lowie, Robert; Mead, Margaret; Smithsonian Institution

Further Readings

Freed, S. A. (2012). *Anthropology unmasked: Museums, science, and politics in New York City: Vol. 1. The Putnam-Boas era.* Wilmington, OH: Orange Frazer Press.

———. (2012). *Anthropology unmasked: Museums, science, and politics in New York City: Vol. 2. The Wissler years.* Wilmington, OH: Orange Frazer Press.

Hellman, G. (1969). *Bankers, bones, and beetles: The first century of the American Museum of Natural History.* Garden City, NY: Natural History Press.

Jacknis, I. (1985). Franz Boas and exhibits: On the limitations of the museum method of anthropology. In G. W. Stocking (Ed.), *History of anthropology: Vol. 3. Objects and others: Essays on museums and material culture* (pp. 75–111). Madison: University of Wisconsin Press.

Jonaitis, A. (1988). *From the land of the totem poles: The Northwest Coast Indian art collection at the American Museum of Natural History.* New York, NY: American Museum of Natural History.

Kennedy, J. M. (1968*). Philanthropy and science in New York City: The American Museum of Natural History, 1868–1968* (Unpublished doctoral dissertation). Yale University, New Haven, CT.

Regal, B. (2002). *Henry Fairfield Osborn: Race, and the search for the origins of man.* Aldershot, UK: Ashgate.

Weitzner, B. (1952). *A year by year summary of the Department of Anthropology, 1871–1952* [Manuscript]. Department of Anthropology Archives, American Museum of Natural History.

ANDERSON, BENEDICT

Benedict R. O'Gorman Anderson (1936–) is Aaron L. Binenkorb Professor Emeritus of International Studies, Government, and Asian Studies at Cornell University. He is best known for his book *Imagined Communities: Reflections on the Origins of Nationalism* (IC), which was published in 1983, revised, republished twice (1991 and 2006), and translated into 31 languages, most recently Thai. IC explores the relationship between technology, capitalism, and the role of languages in the birth of the nationalist imagination. The book has likewise introduced concepts that are now part of the social science and humanities lexicon: nationalism as imagined instead of invented; the contradictory nature of print capitalism, or the growth and marketing of indigenous newspapers; the modularity of the nationalist imagination and the ease with which it can be pirated; and the intimate and unbreakable links between nationalism and internationalism.

Indeed, IC's longevity has a lot to do with how these themes remain unchallenged. (The initial commentaries came mainly from literary criticism and anthropology, followed by sociology and history. Anderson's discipline, political science, was the last to recognize the book's significance.) The continuing engagements with the book by different scholars coming from disparate disciplines and fields could be said to constitute a narrative in itself and remain ongoing. This essay, however, focuses more on topics that have received lesser attention and the accompanying methodologies mustered by Anderson.

The first has to do with comparison. Although Anderson's formal training is in comparative politics, his way of looking at societies emphasizes differences rather than similitudes. This *negative comparison* (Anderson's term), as he suggested in an acceptance speech after being awarded the Albert O. Hirschman Prize for innovative cross-disciplinary studies by the American Social Science Research Council in 2011, is "not scalar, [does] not rotate around well-known norms, and [asks] questions that a good deal of political science is not well equipped to answer." It asks the question "what if" and "demands the help of many different sources and outlooks as well as languages." The results are a series of remarkably different ways of looking at the world.

Second, Anderson deftly shifts the centers of analyses away from where the prevailing scholarship expected these would be located, toward the margins, and then turns these into powerful hubs from which fundamental rethinking and reconsideration of the existing theory could be made. IC's bibliography is a good example of this. It confers equal status on Third World and Western sources. The French author Ernest Renan's *Qu'est-ce qu'une nation?* (1882) shares the limelight with Filipino José Rizal's two novels, *Noli Me Tangere* (Touch Me Not, published 5 years after Renan's) and *El Filibusterismo* (*The Subversive*, 1891), both groundbreaking texts on the rise of nationalism in the colonial world.

Official nationalism—a term borrowed from the historian Hugh Seton-Watson to describe reactionary attempts to expropriate nationalism, eliminate its progressive soul, and turn it into a state project—need not only be associated with philosophers like Carl Schmitt, who supported Nazi Germany. It would have found similar explanations among those supporting the monarchs and militaries of Japan and Thailand. And to make things more interesting and controversial, the chapter "Creole Pioneers" challenges the notion, popular especially among political scientists, that the critical ideas of nationalism came from Europe and argues that it was in the colonies—in North and South America as well as Asia—that the nationalist imagination developed.

Third, Anderson's unusual approach is made possible because of his extraordinary flair for languages and his extensive fieldwork. He learned some German and Russian in high school and was formally schooled in Latin, French, and Greek at Cambridge. At Cornell, where he studied under the eminent Southeast Asianist George McTurnan Kahin and where he subsequently taught after completing his dissertation, he added—with variations in fluency—Bahasa Indonesia, Filipino (Tagalog), Javanese, Thai, Dutch, and Spanish. In today's academic world, language learning is often narrowed as much as possible to one's favored region and/or country. Rarely does one learn other languages that may initially be tangential to one's concerns.

Beyond these formal languages Anderson taught himself the argot of the streets. He learned *prokem*, the language of Indonesian thieves, through his conversations with old communists who had shared jail cells with the former. In the Philippines, his encounters with street-smart teenagers enabled him to learn *Tondo Tagalog*, the Filipino spoken in the poor areas, and the lingo of the *bakla* (Filipino gays). Daily conversations in Thailand made him aware of *pasaa wairun* (teenager language), *pasaa tamluat* (police argot), and *pasaa nakleng* (the language of goons and local thugs).

His knowledge of language was made possible by his extensive fieldwork experience dating back to Indonesia under President Sukarno's "guided democracy" of 1957–1966, the democratic interregnum in Thailand in the early 1970s, and the post-Marcos period in the Philippines. Even though he was banned from entering Indonesia by that country's military government for 25 years, Anderson has spent more time in Southeast Asia than most of his colleagues and his cohort group.

Linguistic synchronicity with ordinary people and frequent sojourns in his countries of study (along with his long-term stay in Thailand) explain the ease with which Anderson combines literature, history, and ethnography with his formal training in political science and affinity toward (structural) Marxism. IC and works less well-known outside Southeast Asian studies—notably *Language and Power: Exploring Political Cultures in Indonesia*; *In the Mirror: Literature and Politics in Siam in the American Era*; *Why Counting Counts: A Study of Forms and Consciousness and Problems of Language in the Noli Me Tangere and El Filibusterismo*; and, of late, *The Fate of Rural Hell: Asceticism and Desire in Buddhist Thailand*—are fine examples of a fieldwork-driven, multidisciplinary approach. Like the sources he cites and the languages he deploys, one finds in Anderson's works literary allusions weaving themselves seamlessly into historical exegeses and the argot of political science, comparative sociology, and economics.

This idiosyncratic methodology—negative comparisons; centering marginal zones like colonies and peripheries while showing how often the purported centers of modernity and progress can become parochial; complementing comparative ethnography with Marxist structuralism; and blending language, literature, history, and sociology—is what makes Anderson's writings extremely attractive as well as challenging to scholars and public intellectuals. It is also what underpins the durability of his ideas and analyses.

Patricio N. Abinales

See also Abu-Lughod, Lila; Appadurai, Arjun; Nationalism, Transnationalism; Postcolonial Theory; Subaltern Studies

Further Readings

Anderson, B. (1965). *Mythology and the tolerance of the Javanese.* Ithaca, NY: Cornell Southeast Asia Program.

_____ (with Mendiones, R.). (1985). *Literature and politics in Siam in the American era.* Ithaca, NY: Cornell Southeast Asia Program.

_____. (1990). *Language and power: Exploring political cultures in Indonesia.* Ithaca, NY: Cornell University.

_____. (1998). *The spectre of comparison: Nationalism, Southeast Asia, and the world.* New York, NY: Verso.

_____. (2006). *Imagined communities: Reflections on the origins of nationalism* (Rev. ed.). New York, NY: Verso.

_____. (2007). *Under three flags: Anarchism and the anti-colonial imagination.* New York, NY: Verso.

_____. (2009). *Why counting counts: A study of forms and consciousness and problems of language in the Noli Me Tangere and El Filibusterismo.* Quezon City, Philippines: Ateneo de Manila University Press.

_____. (2012). *The fate of rural hell: Asceticism and desire in Buddhist Thailand.* Kolkatta, India: Seagull Books.

Cheah, P., & Culler, J. (Eds.). *Grounds of comparison: Around the work of Benedict Anderson.* London, UK: Routledge.

Kahin, A. R., & Siegel, J. T. (Eds.). (2003). *Southeast Asia over three generations: Essays presented to Benedict R. O'G. Anderson.* Ithaca, NY: Cornell Southeast Asia Program.

Animism, Animatism

The words *animism* and *animatism* are derived from the Latin word *anima*, which has a variety of meanings, including "air" or "wind," the "vital principle of life," and "soul" or "spirit." In anthropological, sociological, and religious literature, they are used to refer especially to those ancient (primitive) religious systems in which the belief that natural phenomena, animals, and all living things, including human beings, have a spiritual life force is central to a culture's worldview. In animism, everything is animated by personal "spirits," while in animatism all objects and beings are imbued with an impersonal power, often referred to as "mana."

The word *animism* was adopted by E. B. Tylor in *The Origins of Culture*, while animatism was coined later by R. R. Marett in *The Threshold of Religion*. Both anthropologists used the terms to explain the origin of religion and to describe the first stage in its development. Tylor argued that the first humans, reflecting on their dreams, concluded that souls or spirits pervaded all nature; Marett postulated that there was an earlier stage in the history of religion, a kind of "prereligion," which he labeled *preanimism* or *animatism*. While Tylor's theory assumed that human beings thought that everything in nature, especially living beings, had an individual "soul" or "anima," Marett insisted that this "anima" was neither an individualized power nor a separate entity but was rather some sort of impersonal force that could be controlled. From these early stages, both anthropologists developed elaborate theories of the development of religion in line with the then current theories of evolution.

Critique of Tylor and Marett

The theory of Tylor in particular influenced Western scholarship for three quarters of a century but, together with Marett's, has been largely abandoned. Criticisms of both Tylor's and Marett's views have come from both philosophers and social scientists. One of the most comprehensive critical overviews is that of the late anthropologist E. E. Evans-Pritchard, who in his work *Theories of Primitive Religions* referred to the many theories of the origin of religion as "just-so theories" that cannot be proved or disproved. The historian Kees Bolle remarked that these theories tend to reveal the mental attitudes of the researcher rather than the mentality of those being studied. Both Tylor's and Marett's theories postulated that the first human beings, whom they called "primitives" or "savages," were intellectually inferior and/or infantile and hence their deductions were either illusionary and/or the result of a not fully developed mind.

But while the theories of the origins of religion are no longer tenable and have been relegated to historical interest both in the social sciences and in the field of religious studies, the concept of animism as formulated by Tylor is still in use in anthropological textbooks, in ethnological studies, and in encyclopedias of religion and has become part of the English vocabulary. *Merriam-Webster's Collegiate Dictionary*, for example, defines *animism* as follows: "1: a doctrine that the vital principle of organic development is immaterial spirit; 2: attribution of conscious life to objects in and phenomena of nature or to inanimate objects; 3: belief in the existence of spirits separable from bodies."

Rethinking Tylor

Recently, several anthropologists have been rethinking Tylor's theory, questioning previous understandings of it, expanding on it, and rebutting the arguments that have been brought against it. Stewart Guthrie, for example, is still interested in the origins of religion, but, unlike Tylor, he stresses cognition, rather than experience, and even suggests that animals themselves can be said to be animists. Martin Stringer, on the other hand, reinterprets Tylor's *Primitive Culture* and concludes that he is not really proposing a theory of origins but rather offering a "plausible explanation" of the data he had amassed with great care. Moreover, he argues that Tylor's emphasis is not on "animism" as the primal religion but rather on the different elements of religious beliefs that are of the same kind in all levels of culture. Springer refocuses the reading of Tylor on myth and maintains that Tylor is interested in myth not because it shows how early humans thought but rather because it reveals the structure of the human mind. Nurit Bird-David takes a cognitive approach and reformulates animism as a "relational epistemology." She argues that the universal tendency to imbue things with a soul or spirit is brought about by cognitive skills, which humans acquire socially. For her, animism is not a religion but rather a way of relating to the nonhuman world.

Most scholars have affirmed that animism as a belief system is present in most societies. Tylor himself saw an affinity between the animism in early societies and the spiritualism of his era. Others have seen it as a natural religious form that is still manifest in current religious trends, like the New Age Movement. Contemporary Paganism has also been linked to animism. Graham Harvey, for instance, has pointed out that many Pagans describe themselves as animists and see animism as the theoretical background for environmental activism.

While Marett's view of religion and his formulation of animatism seem to have been relegated to the annals of history, Tylor's reflections on animism have continued to stimulate scholarly discussions. And some contemporary men and women have incorporated the concept of animism in their religious worldview.

John A. Saliba

See also Comparative Method; Evans-Pritchard, E. E.; Myth, Theories of; Religion; Tylor, Edward Burnett

Further Readings

Bird-Davis, N. (1999). "Animism" revisited: Personhood, environment, and relational epistemology. In Culture: A second chance? [Special issue]. *Current Anthropology, 40*(S1), S67–S91.

Bolle, K. W. (2005). Animism and animatism. In S. Young (Ed.), *Encyclopedia of religion* (2nd ed., pp. 362–368). Detroit, MI: Gale.

Guthrie, S. (2002). Animal animism: Evolution roots of religious cognition. In I. Pyysiainen & V. Anttonen (Eds.), *Current approaches in the cognitive science of religion*. London, UK: Continuum.

Harvey, G. (2009). Animist paganism. In M. Pizza & J. R. Lewis (Eds.), *Handbook of contemporary paganism* (pp. 393–411). Leiden, Netherlands: Brill.

Stringer, M. G. (1999). Rethinking animism: Thoughts from the infancy of our discipline. *Journal of the Royal Anthropological Institute, 5*, 541–555.

Anthropological Society of London

See Royal Anthropological Institute

APPADURAI, ARJUN

Arjun Appadurai (1949–) is an anthropologist whose writings, editorial work, and collaborative projects have had a major impact on conversations in the social sciences about globalization, nation-states, commodities, identity, and civil society. His work has played an important role in anthropology's growing engagement with talk about large-scale, even global social phenomena. Currently, he is Goddard Professor of Media, Culture, and Communication at New York University.

Born in 1949 in Bombay (now Mumbai), Maharashtra, India, Appadurai was educated at the elite Elphinstone College; he then studied in Brandeis University, where he received his BA in 1970. He went on to study with the Committee on Social Thought at the University of Chicago, where he received his MA (1973) and his PhD (1976), for a dissertation on the Parthasarathi Temple in Madras (now Chennai), Tamil Nadu. In the same year, he took a job teaching anthropology at the University of Pennsylvania. In 1986, he edited and wrote the introduction for *The Social Life of Things*, a collection of articles on material culture. Two years later, he and his late wife Carol Breckenridge founded *Public Culture*, a cross-disciplinary journal of cultural criticism. He left Pennsylvania for the University of Chicago in 1992, where he was the founding director of the Chicago Humanities Institute and director of the Globalization Project. While at Chicago, he published *Modernity at Large*, a collection of his own essays on globalization and nationalism, and later edited a book, *Globalization*, to which he contributed an important article; during this time, he also cofounded the Interdisciplinary Network on Globalization, a scholarly collaborative project. In 2001, he founded PUKAR (Partners for Urban Knowledge, Action, and Research) in Mumbai, a research collective dedicated to doing research in support of disenfranchised groups dealing with issues of urbanization and globalization. He moved to Yale University in 2002, where he was director of the Cities and Globalization Initiative, and in 2004, he became the Provost of The New School, where he also held the John Dewey Distinguished Professorship in the Social Sciences. In 2006, he published *Fear of Small Numbers*, a study of the connection between globalization, nationalism, and ethnic violence. He left The New School in 2008, taking up his current position at New York University. His most recent collection of articles, *The Future as Cultural Fact*, appeared in 2013. Appadurai has received numerous awards and honors, and lectures frequently throughout the world.

Contributions to Anthropology

In his introduction to *The Social Life of Things*, Appadurai adopted some positions that have had long-lasting impacts on how anthropologists think about commodities and that informed his later work on globalization. He drew on Georg Simmel and on Jean Baudrillard to develop a post-Marxist and post-Maussian perspective on commodities, arguing that the value of goods arises from the way they circulate. In addition, he introduced the concept that goods may be transformed as carriers of value as they move among different "regimes of value," or social conjunctures that value objects in different terms (e.g., as a commodity, heirloom, gift, or sacred object).

Appadurai's most far-reaching influence has been on thought about globalization, due primarily to a series of articles he wrote from the late 1980s to the mid-1990s and that were collected in his book *Modernity at Large*, notably "Disjuncture and Difference in the Global Cultural Economy," "Global Ethnoscapes: Notes and Queries for a Transnational Anthropology," and "The Production of Locality." Adapting Benedict Anderson's work on the centrality of collective imagination to nation-states, he argues that imagination underlies not only nations but all sorts of shared worlds of meaning and action. Cultural imaginaries are increasingly unconstrained by the logic imposed by nation-states, and the imaginaries associated with various realms of activity may not be isomorphic but disjunctive. The persistent disjunction among imaginative realms, he argues, is a defining characteristic of globalization.

This decentered, imagination-based model of globalization gives Appadurai a way to discuss what he calls "alternative modernities": the recognition that modernization is not a uniform process identical with progress or Westernization. On the one hand, power and cultural influence are no longer imposed on global peripheries by the traditional modernizing centers. For example, to people in Irian Jaya, it is the ways of Indonesia, more than America, that represent modernity and threaten to replace local mores. At the same time, the people once seen as recipients of Western cultural and political influence are increasingly able to indigenize outside influences in areas as varied as music, political ideology, technology, and even science. Where modernity was once seen as a threat to all sorts of local traditions, now, Appadurai claims, it increasingly offers freedom from the constraints of nationalism and offers the material for creative improvisation.

As an alternative to a state-based, center-periphery model of global order, Appadurai proposes that we look at the world in terms of the interaction and disjunctures among what he calls the "five dimensions of global flows": *ethnoscapes, technoscapes, financescapes, mediascapes,* and *ideoscapes.* Modeled on "landscape," these terms denote the ways in which *flows* of people, technology, money, media images, and political ideas are increasingly unconstrained by national policies or spaces; they are *deterritorialized.* For instance, today many people, due to massive migration and other forms of population movement, are members of ethnic groups that are no longer contained, or even defined, by an actual or potential national territory. At the same time, the complex ethnic worlds created by mass migration are in part products of the mobility of capital, and their cultural implications would be very different in the absence of the global distribution of media images. Yet the imaginaries projected by the financial world (financescapes) do not align with those articulated by the movement of populations and the politics of identity and belonging (ethnoscapes) or by the mediascapes of Hollywood, let alone Bollywood. The substance of these *scapes* is not only objective materials and relations but also their imagining; like landscapes, they are views of a part of the world and are organized in part through the gaze that beholds them. Appadurai is often credited with a major role in making possible discussion of globalization as a cultural, not just a political and economic, phenomenon. The notion of *public culture,* which he developed along with Breckenridge and fomented through the eponymous journal, was important here, signaling a concept of culture that was not attached to bounded communities, be they villages, tribes, or nations.

One of Appadurai's signature positions is skepticism, even antagonism, to the modern nation-state, and the sort of bounded territoriality that it embodies and propagates. Much of his work on globalization can be understood as the construction of a vocabulary for understanding identity, community, and the production of value that does not rely on the nation-state's spatial imagination. He regards the nation-state's claims to primordiality as a major source of ethnic violence. This critique of the nation-state leads to his skepticism of spatial analysis in general. In the Bergsonian tradition, he strongly distinguishes the spatial and temporal dimensions of social life, privileging the latter over the former. Here, he draws (at times obscurely) on the work of Gilles Deleuze, in particular his use of the terms *deterritorialization* and *flow.* Along with Manuel Castells and Ulf Hannerz, Appadurai played a leading role in the introduction of this last term into discussions of globalization. For Appadurai, ours is a "world of flows," which is to say that lived reality is constituted not by things and places but by the incessant movement of people, goods, information, and technology. The various scapes can be understood as articulations of "flows" of people, money, goods, images, and ideas. This in turn means that the supposedly traditional anthropological conception of culture and identity, as grounded in and defined by places, stands revealed as a colonialist imposition of the spatial logic of the nation-state. In Appadurai's view, community and identity (as well as commodities) are *deterritorialized,* which is to say that they are produced and experienced translocally and cannot be identified with any given place or territory. In a similar vein, Appadurai develops the terms *locality* and *context* into ways to understand the processes whereby people and communities are produced that do not depend on place or other spatializing concepts.

Appadurai is unusual in the extent to which his impact on anthropology and beyond has arisen from his work as an editor and collaborator. Two of his major publications are edited volumes, the journal he cofounded has proven hugely influential, and he has organized multiple cross-disciplinary centers and scholarly collaboratives. This aspect of his work is entirely consistent with the claim he made in the influential essay "Globalization and the Research Imagination" (which appeared in *Globalization*) that what determines whether and how subaltern people will be able to benefit from scholarly research is not primarily the issue of what is studied but of how the production and distribution of knowledge are organized. This analysis has also led him to an increasing interest in civil society organizations as a means by which the disenfranchised can attain agency in a globalizing world.

Critical Responses

One indication of the impact Appadurai's work has had on how social scientists think about globalization is the way other scholars have developed alternative approaches in part by critiquing his work; his writings and vocabulary have become defining features of the intellectual terrain, in relation to which others can locate themselves. Perhaps the most common caveat is that he neglects the evidence that many of the patterns of mobility and long-distance connection that we now associate with globalization have existed for decades, if not for centuries. A complementary complaint is that he puts too much weight on anthropology's past dependence on restrictive notions of the local and on its ahistoricism, ignoring, for instance, the centrality of diffusion to Boasian theories of culture.

Many social scientists reject Appadurai's turn away from place as a key element of social reality, particularly as this approach is manifested in the Deleuzian terminology of *flow* and *deterritorialization*. Others have been critical of the way he deploys the term *flow*, arguing that the concept tends to mask the agency of individuals and small-scale social formations in favor of the large-scale formations.

The articles in *Modernity at Large* have been criticized as suffering from an idealized vision of globalization: variously as being too blithe about colonized peoples' abilities to resist and reinterpret global economic and cultural forces, as waxing too enthusiastic about the emancipatory potential of capitalist globalization, and as exaggerating the decline of nation-states in the face of globalization. Appadurai claims some of these criticisms as a motivation behind writing *Fear of Small Numbers*, in which he explores interethnic violence as one of the darker aspects of globalization, even while extending his critique of the nation-state.

Other critics contend that Appadurai is vague about the theoretical significance of his arguments and often unclear about what theory he is drawing on. A related concern is that he bases his globalization work on very little ethnographic or other empirical information and that he offers little clarity as to how it might be developed into a research project. Andrew Jones, for instance, argues that putative global flows are likely impossible to measure and claims that neither Appadurai nor any of his readers has tried to develop the terminology of scapes into a real model of how global flows work.

These last caveats reflect Appadurai's chosen discursive genre: Even more than Clifford Geertz, Appadurai is an essayist. After his early ethnographic work, he adopted a style that is not strictly theoretical yet not ethnographic, or even heavily empirical, but characterized by relatively short pieces that articulate a synthetic vision of apparently disparate phenomena. His style has been called prophetic, and much of the influence of his writings is due to his ability to evoke new paradigms of thought in a highly sophisticated yet clear, even inspiring, fashion. These interventions have proven extremely fruitful in advancing and molding various anthropological conversations.

Stuart Rockefeller

See also Anderson, Benedict; Baudrillard, Jean; Deleuze, Gilles, and Félix Guattari; Globalization Theory; Scapes; Simmel, Georg

Further Readings

Appadurai, A. (1981). *Worship and conflict under colonial rule: A South Indian case*. Cambridge, UK: Cambridge University Press.

———. (1992). Introduction: Commodities and the politics of value. In A. Appadurai (Ed.), *The social life of things: Commodities in cultural perspective* (pp. 3–63). Cambridge, UK: Cambridge University Press.

———. (Ed.). (1992). *The social life of things: Commodities in cultural perspective*. Cambridge, UK: Cambridge University Press.

———. (1996). *Modernity at large: Cultural dimensions of globalization*. Minneapolis: University of Minnesota Press.

———. (2002). *Globalization*. Durham, NC: Duke University Press.

———. (2002). Grassroots globalization and the research imagination. In A. Appadurai (Ed.), *Globalization* (pp. 1–21). Durham, NC: Duke University Press.

———. (2006). *Fear of small numbers: An essay on the geography of anger*. Durham, NC: Duke University Press.

———. (2013). *The future as cultural fact: Essays on the global condition*. New York, NY: Verso.

Jones, A. (2010). *Globalization: Key thinkers*. Cambridge, MA: Polity Press.

Rockefeller, S. (2011). Flow. *Current Anthropology, 54*(4), 557–578.

Sen, A. (2010). Review of *Fear of small numbers: An essay on the geography of anger*. *Journal of the Royal Anthropological Institute (N.S.), 16*, 439–440.

APPLIED ANTHROPOLOGY

Although applied anthropology has a variety of meanings, generally the term refers to what professionally trained anthropologists do when they are involved in solving practical or policy problems found in society at large. This problem solving can be done either indirectly in support of an agency or sometimes directly. This is accomplished mostly through research and by direct involvement in the policy formation process or direct action, usually as an employee of a client organization on a contract or a direct-hire basis. The client organizations include not-for-profit agencies, governmental organizations, educational institutions, and business firms. In contrast to general anthropologists, their emphasis is not on the production of cultural description or theory for its own sake, although this may be incidental to their work. The primary goal of applied anthropology is to have an impact outside the discipline itself. Applied anthropology occurs in all the four subfields of anthropology (i.e., sociocultural, biological, archaeological, and linguistic anthropology). Marietta Baba, among others, has advocated that application and practice be regarded as a fifth subfield of the discipline.

When viewed in the most general terms, the phrase *applied anthropology* includes a wide variety of activities covered by what anthropologists have called practicing anthropology, public anthropology, advocacy anthropology, collaborative anthropology, cultural brokerage, and action anthropology. That said, it is not uncommon for some to contrast the idea of applied anthropology with the content associated with these other terms. For example, practicing anthropology is presented by some as an artifact of one's employment status apart from being a faculty member of a college or university and applied anthropology as a label that is appropriate for what certain kinds of academically employed anthropologists do. The term *practitioner* is often used to depict someone who is not a higher education institution faculty member but uses anthropological concepts and methods as an important basis for their work. In actual practice, these terminological contrasts do not hold up very well in reality. Also the self-labeling used may relate to cohort effects rather than specific differences in career orientation or strategy. That is, to an extent it depends on where and when you were "imprinted."

Certainly research services are an important component of applied anthropology as it is more common for applied anthropologists to be involved in research rather than direct action or policy making. The research tools of the applied anthropologist are similar to those found in general anthropology but are often supplemented by research practices that include rapid survey or assessment methods or the research methods structured by specific agency policies and requirements. Many applied anthropologists make use of quantitative methods. Associated with applied anthropology's research program is the goal of having an impact through one's research. This need goes far beyond publication in disciplinary journals to include multifaceted interaction with both community and agencies. As Barbara Rylko-Bauer and John van Willigen point out, effectiveness as an applied anthropologist requires the development of a complex of knowledge utilization strategies. In addition to being a researcher, applied anthropologists may engage in many other roles. These include evaluator, impact assessor, needs assessor, planner, advocate, trainer, expert witness, administrator, as well as others. With some exceptions, these roles are not consistently addressed in the existing training opportunities for application and practice.

History

Historically, the relationship between applied and general anthropology reflects the tension between the academic world and the practical world within which the applied anthropologist works. The term *applied anthropology* was first used in print in 1906 by C. H. Read and referred to an elite university program for training colonial administrators at Oxford University in Great Britain. Clearly, the need for trained applied anthropologists to serve the colonial administration helped create a funding base for one of the elite academic departments that continues to serve as the backbone of British academic anthropology today. In the United States, the Bureau of American Ethnology was created in the early 1880s as a policy research organization primarily dealing with the administrative-cum-military conflicts the United States had with Native Americans. The Bureau referred to this policy research as applied ethnology. The Bureau of American Ethnology quickly devolved into an apolitical, basic ethnographic research organization, eventually merging, in 1965, with the Department of Anthropology of the Smithsonian Institution. The point is that the earliest academic and research organizations in the United States and Great Britain were organized to serve the goal of application.

From these early developments, applied anthropology grew in the United States because of federal government programs associated with Franklin D. Roosevelt's New Deal in the 1930s. Many anthropologists became federal employees in the era of the Great Depression. Employment of applied anthropologists also increased during World War II. During that war, in the United States, almost all professionally trained anthropologists were working as applied anthropologists, some in uniform. These employment opportunities led to a professional awareness of common interests in application that led to the organization of the Society for Applied Anthropology in 1941. Following the war, there was an increase in college enrollments, which resulted in exponential growth in the number of academic positions, and interest in applied anthropology waned. However, concern for applied anthropology began to increase in the late 1960s with the increase in the supply of trained anthropologists and decreases in the academic job market. Starting at this time, a number of departments started graduate programs specifically focused on careers outside academic institutions.

Applied Anthropology in the Discipline

Clearly, applied anthropologists have had considerable impact on the development of the discipline, although, as Rylko-Bauer, Merrill Singer, and van Willigen point out, this impact is muted in the historical record. This muting is probably caused by the relatively low prestige of applied work compared with academic scholarship. Nevertheless, there have been significant impacts. As stated earlier, the potential for concrete application of anthropological research has always provided a rationale for funding academic departments and basic research organizations. Another important impact is that applied anthropologists have pioneered many areas of anthropological research. Early work in medical anthropology, legal and political anthropology, urban anthropology, population anthropology, and nutritional anthropology was stimulated by the need for application. Without the incentive associated with the needs of policymakers and administrators, these important topical areas would not have existed. Interestingly, work in these topical areas was often criticized as nonanthropological at the onset but has become mainstream today. A third area is that application contributed to the development of methods, especially through research practices such as various rapid assessment practices.

Domains of Application

Applied cultural anthropologists work in a wide array of fields, such as health and medicine, business, aging, agriculture, education, evaluation, agricultural development, nutrition, environment, cultural resource management, historic preservation, social work, and community development, among others. Those trained in archaeology work in cultural resource management. Some biological applied anthropologists are forensic scientists or experts in skeletal biology, among other areas. Within these contexts, effective applied anthropologists require the development of in-depth knowledge beyond what is usually associated with basic disciplinary training. Mastery of this field includes knowledge of the legal context of work in the area, the theory and methods of other kinds of practitioners in related areas, the domain-relevant scholarly literature beyond the anthropological work specific to the area, and its organizational structure.

Training Requirements

Effective preparation for a career in applied cultural anthropology includes substantial training in both qualitative and quantitative research methods. This includes survey methods and statistics as well as the ethnographic skills typically associated with research in cultural anthropology. These should be supplemented with preparation in research design and proposal development.

Unfortunately, many graduate departments do not offer an adequate course of study in research methods. Beyond a broad knowledge of research practices, applied anthropologists also make use of collaborative research and action strategies. These include approaches from within the discipline, such as action anthropology, collaborative anthropology, and empowerment evaluation, as well as approaches developed outside the discipline, such as action research, participatory action research, conscientization (Freirean method), community-based social marketing, and the other community-based approaches to action. While these modes of operation are thought of as being from outside the discipline, they are all congruent with the concepts valued by anthropologists and have strong family resemblances to anthropology. Careful consideration of the history of these extradisciplinary approaches usually shows that anthropological ideas and anthropologists have influenced their development. Furthermore, it is essential to experience and have the capacity to work in multidisciplinary teams and in various applied work settings, such as public agencies, nongovernmental organizations, or consulting firms. For this reason, field placements associated with practice or internships are important in the training process.

Role of Theory

The role of theory in applied anthropology is quite different from its role in general anthropology. While theorizing or theory production is not the primary task, it is an essential component of the process of application. Theory is required to function in the realm of application. Theory is a mechanism for the extension of observation and serves as the basis for understanding what is going on that is essential for acting in applied situations. That said, there is a strong tendency toward theoretical eclecticism. Simply put, there is much use of theory and concepts from other disciplines. Furthermore, there is an emphasis on theory and concepts that can be acted on rather than those on the cutting edge of disciplinary theoretical discourses. Theory is a tool rather than a product. There is some irony there because the work of applied anthropologists has great potential for the production of theory. The reason for this potential is that often the work of the applied anthropologist takes the form of natural experiments

that allow one to test interpretations or hypotheses about reality. This may include theoretical interpretations that are derived from the direct experience of the work itself, not in the sense of testing theory. At a basic level, the methods of theorizing in basic anthropology and applied anthropology follow similar intellectual methodological processes, in which observations are used to derive concepts and theories about reality. They differ in that basic research is referenced to truthful depictions of that reality, whereas applied work is more referenced to effectiveness rather than truth. What is now a foundation principle in applied anthropology is that practical problem-solving work with a community is more likely to proceed effectively if it is based on extensive collaboration between the practitioner and members of the community. This conception is important because it allows the applied anthropologist to be effective.

Organizations

The professional association most directly associated with applied anthropology is the Society for Applied Anthropology (SfAA). The SfAA serves applied anthropology and its members through an annual meeting and through the journal *Human Organization*, the career-focused publication *Practicing Anthropology*, and its *Newsletter*. Interestingly, the SfAA published what seems to be the first "ethics statement" by an anthropological learned society in 1949 under the leadership of Margaret Mead. Other organizations that serve the associational needs of applied anthropologists include the National Association for the Practice of Anthropology, which is a section of the disciplinary apex organization; the American Anthropological Association; and a number of regional or local practitioner organizations, such as the Washington Association of Professional Anthropologists, the Southern California Applied Anthropology Network, the Chicago Association of Practicing Anthropologists, and the High Plains Society for Applied Anthropology, among others. Organizations of local practitioners serve to provide a support group for maintaining the skills and knowledge of the discipline as well as a context for career development and job hunting. The Washington Association of Professional Anthropologists and the High Plains group are especially robust. The Washington Association of Professional Anthropologists serves the discipline by sponsoring the biennial Praxis Awards to recognize effective projects of practice and application, besides having a more locally focused program. High Plains supports the discipline through the publication of its journal *The Applied Anthropologist*, as well as by organizing an annual meeting and retreat. All the applied anthropology–oriented organizations have very prostudent programs. SfAA offers reduced dues rates for students as well as subsidies for student participation in annual meetings.

John van Willigen

See also Critical Theory; Dependency Theory; Foster, George M.; Mair, Lucy; Mead, Margaret; Oxford University; Royal Anthropological Institute; Tax, Sol

Further Readings

Baba, M. L. (1994). The fifth subdiscipline: Anthropological practice and the future of anthropology. *Human Organization, 53*(2), 174–186.

———. (1998). Theories of practice in anthropology: A critical appraisal. In C. Hill & M. Baba (Eds.), *The unity of theory and practice in anthropology: Rebuilding a fractured synthesis* (pp. 17–44). Washington, DC: National Association for the Practice of Anthropology.

Kedia, S., & van Willigen, J. (2005). *Applied anthropology: Domains of application.* Westport, CT: Praeger.

Read, C. H. (1906). Anthropology at the universities. *Man, 38,* 56–59.

Russell, B. H. (2011). *Research methods in anthropology* (5th ed.). Walnut Valley, CA: Altamira Press.

Rylko-Bauer, B., Singer, M., & van Willigen, J. (2006). Reclaiming applied anthropology: Its past, present, and future. *American Anthropologist, 108*(1), 178–190.

Rylko-Bauer, B., & van Willigen, J. (1993). A framework for conducting utilization-focused policy research in anthropology. In D. M. Fetterman (Ed.), *Speaking the language of power: Communication, collaboration, and advocacy.* Washington, DC: Falmer Press.

van Willigen, J. (2002). *Applied anthropology: An introduction* (3rd ed.). Westport, CT: Bergin & Garvey.

AREA STUDIES

Area studies is an interdisciplinary effort to develop knowledge of different world regions, typically from a vantage point situated, implicitly or explicitly, outside those regions. There are a variety of area studies configurations specific to distinct national academic traditions. Similarly, the history of specific regional studies within any given national academic context varies. Finally, the significance of area studies for the various core disciplines (anthropology, history, political science, etc.) is different for each discipline. This entry focuses primarily on area studies in the United States, emphasizing the period since the Second World War, when the trajectories of the various area studies projects came into closer institutional coordination. The focus here is on both the role of anthropology within area studies and the implications of changes in area studies for theory in anthropology.

Background

The study of different world areas includes distinct genealogies reflecting distinct historical circumstances. Latin American area studies in the U.S. context, for instance, dates to the turn of the 20th century. Its foundations reflect the emerging hemispheric ambitions of the United States within the long arc of the Monroe Doctrine (1823), the Spanish-American War (1898), and the "Good Neighbor Policy" of the 1930s. However, the various area studies stories in the United States converged during and after the Second World War through a set of efforts by the federal government and private agencies to encourage the systematic study of world areas for purposes framed explicitly as deriving from national strategic interests.

Beginning in the 1940s, through academic conferences, commissioned publications, and funding for new academic programs, foundations such as Ford, Rockefeller, Carnegie, and the Social Science Research Council sought to identify a new task for research in the social sciences and humanities in the United States. The call to develop international knowledge of the world was in part a response to a growing recognition of the United States as a "world power," for which continued and increasing international engagement would be inevitable. The postwar period, of course, was also the dawn of the Cold War, and the impetus to develop international knowledge was at the same time a strategic effort to learn more about the Soviet Union and about the terrain thought to be at stake in the Cold War, the newly conceived "Third World."

These strategic ambitions were also modular and modernist: aligning the study of different world regions as tokens of a single type and endorsing the promise of increasingly perfect knowledge of different areas and the challenges they faced and posed through the interdisciplinary coordination of specialist research. Earlier efforts, such as those of the the American Universities Field Staff, which sought to enlist the experience of country specialists to brief U.S. business faculty and managers, or Ruth Benedict's work on Japan for the War Department, offer a hint of the ethos of the time regarding the strategic use of knowledge of other places and the modernist faith in the possibility of decoding the secrets of the life ways of other cultures. The postwar period took this to another level, culminating in Title VI of the National Defense Education Act of 1958 (later continued as Title VI of the Higher Education Act of 1965). The Title VI, or National Resource Center, program linked the production of specialist knowledge of other world areas with the systematic production of area specialists, funding area centers in a range of research universities across the country through periodic multiyear grant cycles. Alongside the Title VI programs were a set of other federally funded initiatives—such as Fulbright-Hays (1961) and the International Research and Exchanges Board (1968)—promoting international expertise by supporting research and study-abroad opportunities for faculty and students.

Institutionalization

The area centers established by this postwar institutionalization of area studies focused on a standardized suite of salient world regions and comprised an equally standardized suite of disciplinary specialists from anthropology, history, languages and literature, political science, and so on. Area studies training stressed fluency in local languages and fieldwork experience in-country. One component of the National Resource Center (NRC) initiative is the FLAS (Foreign Language and Area Studies) program supporting instruction in "less commonly taught languages" deemed to be in the strategic interests of the United States. This combined focus on language and culture was especially congenial to the methods of anthropology, and anthropologists such as Julian Steward, Charles Wagley, Wendell Bennett, and Clyde Kluckhohn played key roles in

a number of the founding studies and conferences that gave shape to the area studies initiative. The prominence of anthropologists in this project also built on a midcentury enthusiasm for the concept of culture, which served both as a framework for marking difference in increasingly spatialized ways and as a promise of the possibility of understanding and assimilation through an extension of the sort of melting pot experience that had only recently come to shape American national self-consciousness.

This moment of "modern" area studies entailed a set of assumptions about the world and about knowledge production. At the core of these was a taxonomic claim that the world could be decomposed into a set of regions and that those regions were at once distinct enough from one another and each internally similar so as to warrant their development as discrete objects of expertise. The rationale for this division of the world—the histories that shaped the conditions that made regional claims plausible—was not absent from area studies scholarship. However, the divisions and not their production were the starting point of the area studies model, and this facilitated some streams of scholarship focused rather insularly on a particular region as an object of study coherent unto itself. Another powerful dimension of the institutionalized area studies project is the largely implicit assumption that the areas of area studies are all "other" to the United States. Despite the recognition in some of the founding documents of the area studies era that the United States is itself a world area, as it was institutionalized, areas studies fostered a vantage on the world looking out from the United States. Funding priorities of the Title VI programs discouraged research focused on migration to the United States as well as other phenomena blurring the distinctions between the West and other parts of the world. In these regards, area studies constituted a worldview, indeed, a worldview with funding, and as such it had a strong impact on the constitution of anthropology departments and other programs making up the core interdisciplinary area studies team. Anthropology departments founded or expanded during the postwar period were often shaped by the accumulation of faculty positions defined by their regional expertise; the map with stickpins marking the regional coverage of a department is a potent icon of this era.

The strategic Cold War context of the institutionalization of area studies in the United States also created political entailments for the project.

This cut both ways. On the one hand, much as the Office of Strategic Studies recruited social scientists during the Second World War, intelligence agencies were connected to the work of some area centers during the Cold War period. At the same time, regionally focused scholarship sometimes became the *object* of investigations by federal agencies concerned about the content and political sympathies of teaching and scholarship on, for instance, the Soviet Union, China, or Latin America. The first comprehensive code of ethics adopted by the American Anthropological Association in 1971 was spurred in part by the complex politics of area studies in the 1960s, as some anthropologists were connected to U.S. counterinsurgency efforts in Vietnam, Latin America, and other parts of the world.

A Critical Turn

The 1970s marked the start of a more critical turn in anthropological theory and practice, with important implications for area studies. As anthropologists came increasingly to critique static models of societies studied in isolation, the bounded, place-based, and essentialist character of area studies was called into question. As anthropologists wrestled with the implications of the colonial history and power dynamics of anthropological research and sought new models of collaborative knowledge production, the Western vantage of area studies and the close connection between the area studies project and the strategic interests of the U.S. government discredited it in the eyes of many scholars. As a growing number of anthropologists turned from community-based research to examine migrant and diasporic populations and ethnic groups in the United States, the limitations of the area studies model became increasingly apparent. And as the globalization of cultural phenomena came, by the 1990s, to be seen as among the most pressing questions for anthropological theory and practice, area studies seemed a pre-Copernican model of scholarship, better suited to a world that, if it ever existed, had now been essentially eclipsed.

Alongside a set of influential critiques of modernist midcentury anthropological theory and practice and a growing set of anthropological scholarship focused on globalization came a sustained critique of area studies over the 1980s and 1990s. In a world increasingly cast as "flat" and without borders, where the significance of national boundaries was being questioned and where the constitution of area studies scholarship was itself an object of study, the project of area studies was cast as a Tylorian survival—having outlived the era in which it once made sense. The apparent end of the Cold War in 1989 further marked an epochal shift, rendering area studies obsolete.

Area Studies for the 21st Century

However, the past decade has been marked by something of a renaissance of regionalism and a complex new dawn of area studies. This was impelled in part by the attacks of September 11, 2001, and a heightened sense of the strategic importance of cultural, linguistic, and contextual knowledge of a range of places around the world. New counterinsurgency models, including the U.S. Military's "Human Terrain System Program," have similarly sought to link regionally specific social science knowledge with military activities, embroiling anthropologists and other scholars once again in sharp debates about the politics and ethics of knowledge production. Somewhat less controversially, the Title VI program has expanded, beginning in 1988, with the addition of Centers for International Business Education and Research to the National Resource Center program. Guidelines from recent Title VI funding rounds make it clear that the transfer of area knowledge to professional fields in universities is a priority of the program, reflecting renewed strategic concerns with the international and global context of business competitiveness.

For anthropology, this long arc of the area studies project makes area studies an important reference point—good to think for contemporary anthropological theory. Area research was always an implicit theory of the nature of global interconnections; that was the foundation of the strategic utility of area studies. That the global ecumene announced in the late 20th century has not come to pass, that regional units continue to matter, offers an important insight into the texture of globalization, where global processes, local specificities, and the continuing production of local and regional differences within global contexts are interlocked topics of investigation for anthropologists today. Similarly, as the discipline of anthropology is increasingly focused on defining a public or engaged anthropology and exploring the application of anthropological knowledge to "real world" issues, the history of area studies offers cautionary and exemplary lessons. The current return of regional scholarship presents an opportunity to redefine the role of anthropology as part of an interdisciplinary social scientific engagement with policy and practice in the world. Finally, the institutional format of area studies served as a channel for collaborations between the United States and international scholars. At a time of growing awareness of the importance of a "world anthropology" incorporating research questions generated from an inclusive range of global positions, area studies and the regionally focused international professional social networks it gave rise to may be an important setting for future directions in anthropology as a global endeavor.

Andrew Orta

See also American Anthropological Association; Applied Anthropology; Benedict, Ruth F.; Globalization Theory; Kluckhohn, Clyde; Modernism; Steward, Julian

Further Readings

Alvarez, S. E., Arias, A., & Hale, C. R. (2011). Re-visioning Latin American studies. *Cultural Anthropology, 26*(2), 225–246.

Bennett, W. C. (1951). *Area studies in American universities.* New York, NY: Social Science Research Council.

Cahnman, W. (1948). Outline of a theory of area studies. *Annals of the Association of American Geographers, 38*(4), 233–243.

Escobar, A. (1995). *Encountering development.* Princeton, NJ: University of Princeton Press.

Hall, R. B. (1949). *Area studies: With special reference to their implications for research in the social sciences.* New York, NY: Social Science Research Council.

Hegeman, S. (1999). *Patterns for America: Modernism and the concept of culture.* Princeton, NJ: Princeton University Press.

Miyoshi, M., & Harootunian, H. D. (Eds.). (2002). *Learning places: The afterlives of area studies.* Durham, NC: Duke University Press.

Pletsch, C. (1981). The three worlds, or the division of social scientific labor, circa 1950–1975. *Comparative Studies in Society and History, 23,* 565–590.

Rafael, V. (1994). The culture of area studies in the United States. *Social Text, 41,* 91–111.

Steward, J. H. (1950). *Area research: Theory and practice.* New York, NY: Social Science Research Council.

Szanton, D. (2004). *The politics of knowledge: Area studies and the disciplines.* Berkeley: University of California Press.

Wagley, C. (1948). *Area research and training: A conference report on the study of world areas.* New York, NY: Social Science Research Council.

ARISTOTLE

Aristotle (384–322 BCE) was born in Macedonia. His father was a physician at the Court of Alexander the Great's grandfather, and Aristotle himself became tutor to Alexander. He dedicated himself to the careful study of nature, aided by the specimens Alexander sent back to him during his widespread military conquests. Of him, Charles Darwin said, "Linnaeus and Cuvier were my gods; but they were as schoolboys compared to Aristotle."

For 20 years, he studied at Plato's Academy. He developed the formal logic presupposed by mathematics and turned more toward nature, systematically carving out the spaces for the major fields of intellectual inquiry: physics, psychobiology, astronomy, ethics-politics, and metaphysics. Aristotle is known to have written some 200 treatises, of which, unfortunately, only 41 survive.

Philosophical Anthropology

In his psychobiological treatise *On the Soul,* Aristotle presented the theoretical understanding of the specimens Alexander had gathered. He distinguished three types of life, hierarchically arranged in the structure of the human being and found separately in different species: the *nutritive* level by which the organism grew, sustained itself, and provided organs for the next level, the *sentient,* which, in turn, provided material for the *intellectual* level, which disengages universal types from the sensory instances in the environment and thus grounds ordinary language and the various sciences.

Organisms involve four causal factors: (1) the materials that compose them; (2) the structure that organizes them; (3) the efficient causality that generated, built, and sustained them; (4) and the ends each of the organs served. Full maturity, the overall end of organic functioning, is indicated by the ability to reproduce. This fourth cause is the *teleological* or goal-oriented cause. The formal principle is the *psyche*. It is the formal, efficient, and final cause of life-forms that works materials into an integrally functioning whole. Aristotle defines it as "the first act of a body furnished with organs." "First act" indicates the type of organism and its basic powers. The second act is the movement of the powers from potency to act in development and adult functioning.

The development of *animal* forms involves organs for sentient awareness. Each sense is differentiated by the features of things manifest to awareness: color, sound, smell, flavor, and tactile features. The common root of these senses is a center, aware of itself through its appetites, that synthesizes the various features in a *phantasm*, or mode of appearance of the differing types to the perceiver. The goal of the synthesis is to present opportunities and threats in the environment for organic flourishing.

Human awareness presupposes both organic and sentient functions but rises above them to apprehend the universal form that Plato called the *eidos*, whose place is in the mind. The senses present the individual and actual; the intellect presents the universal and potential. The intellect has a receptive facet in relation to phantasms and an active facet, the *nous poietikos* through which the sensory is raised to the level of universality. Through both senses and intellect, human awareness is "in a way, all things," oriented toward the cosmic Whole. From this height, Aristotle turns to locomotion and ends with touch, for the point of intellectual activity is to be actively engaged with a world of physical things.

Ethico-Political Theory

Aristotle examined more than 100 examples of constitutions for which he developed a normative ethico-political structure. His ethics was the first part of the *Politics*, his most extensive reflections on human social life. Indeed, all human study is subsumed under the art of politics, which orders individuals and communities toward the good life. He considered several variants of monarchy, aristocracy, democracy, oligarchy, and tyranny and examined what tends to preserve and to destroy them. Description is in the service of the normative: the determination of what is the best constitution absolutely and what is best under various circumstances.

The *Politics* begins with an ideal-typical account of human sociopolitical evolution. According to Aristotle, human beings are both naturally social and naturally political. Human sociality is rooted in the fact that humans are not naturally self-sufficient but are naturally driven to form communities to meet their needs; they are innately gregarious, and they are rational or speech-using animals. Communities are thus based, not merely on instinct or desire, but more importantly on shared understanding—especially of what is good or bad, just or unjust, as embodied in social customs, laws, and constitutional forms.

Human sociopolitical development occurs in three stages: the household, the village, and the *polis* or city. The later stages subsume the prior. Thus, a village is a multitude of households, and a city comprises households and villages. The household (a family and its slaves and dependents) exists to meet the need for material preservation and reproduction. Villages are assemblages of families (often with a common ancestry) that exist to meet unspecified "nondaily needs." The city is an assemblage of households and villages, organized under a ruling body and capable of complete "self-sufficiency." Only in the city are human communities capable (in principle) of meeting all natural human needs. Although the city comes into existence for the sake of living, it stays in existence for the sake of living well.

While every good city must provide military security and material sufficiency, its proper end is the cultivation of virtue. Aristotle usually has in mind prudence, temperance, courage, and justice as the primary virtues. A life of virtue is the highest end for the city because it is the highest end for human beings. The fostering of virtue comes through the influence of unwritten customs and promulgated laws that encourage good habits. Because most human beings can only come to virtue through good, publicly enforced habits, it is the duty of the city to enforce such habits. The best constitution for a city then would be an aristocracy, where the wealthy, the educated, and the virtuous few rule the community through law. In this way, the naturally superior, who are most capable of contributing to the proper end of the city (virtue) are given power, proportional to their abilities, to further the common good. However, although virtue *ought* to be the end of the city, almost no existing city consistently attends to this goal, and a genuine aristocracy (where virtue counts for more than wealth or family connections) is exceedingly rare.

Besides his analysis of politics proper, there is Aristotle's analysis of the household, comprising the relations of husband and wife, parents and children, and master and slaves. Aristotle gives a normative account of each of these relations, where authority is rooted in the relation of natural superior to natural inferior. Thus, Aristotle stands near the origins of the way of thinking that justifies various social hierarchies because they reflect natural hierarchies. However, social hierarchies are criticized when they do *not* reflect natural ones. Thus, although Aristotle defends patriarchy and slavery, he sets clear limits to the authority of the superior in both relations.

This patriarchal view of the family considers the father as naturally superior to his children and his wife, rightfully exercising authority over them. However, patriarchy is not unqualified. Every natural community, based on natural needs, is good for all members. In the case of the family, patriarchal authority carries with it the responsibility of seeing to the good of the wife and children, their material security, and their education in virtue. Thus, in his rule over his household, a man must always rule with a view to the cultivation of virtue in those he rules. Hence, Aristotle pointedly criticizes non-Greeks for treating their wives as slaves. Though the natural authority of men over women is never explicitly questioned, a true husband would rule over his wife by persuasion and common understanding.

Aristotle notoriously offers a qualified defense of slavery but only insofar as it is "according to nature." This occurs when the enslaved person is capable of following commands and doing chores but is mentally deficient insofar as he is incapable of guiding his own affairs and thus requires a master. Here, slavery is good for both master and slave, and the hierarchy involved corresponds to a natural hierarchy of intellect. But slavery is not according to nature if the enslaved person is capable of responsible freedom. Then slavery rests on violence and law rather than nature, good for the master but not for the slave. Most slaves in Aristotle's time were not "natural" in this sense. However, Aristotle never condemns the slavery around him, and he appears to endorse the enslaving of non-Greeks, since barbarians were considered to be naturally fit for slavery. This may not have been Aristotle's considered

opinion, since enslavement of Asian barbarians was due to their lack of courage and not to mental deficiency. Furthermore, Aristotle praises the "barbarian" city of Carthage as one of the three best governed in his time. In sum, Aristotle neither decisively condemns nor decisively endorses the slavery of his time.

Robert E. Wood and Jonathan Culp

See also Habitus; Hegel, Georg W. F.; Hermeneutics; Hobbes, Thomas; Montesquieu, Comte de; Neo-Kantianism; Plato; Sapir-Whorf Hypothesis and Neo-Whorfianism

Further Readings

Barnes, J. (Ed.). (1984). *The complete works of Aristotle*. Princeton, NJ: Princeton University Press.
———. (Ed.). (1995). *Cambridge companion to Aristotle*. Cambridge, UK: Cambridge University Press.
Shields, C. (2007). *Aristotle*. London, UK: Routledge.

ASAD, TALAL

Talal Asad (1933–) is a social anthropologist and social theorist at the City University of New York. He has made major theoretical contributions to the study of Christianity and Islam, postcolonialism, secularism, and forms of violence under modernity.

This entry discusses three critical areas of Asad's contribution to anthropology:

1. *The artifacts of anthropology:* How anthropological theories and methods have produced the very objects they set out to discover

2. *Categories of modernity and other forms of reason:* The ways in which we can critique the categories of thought that are taken for granted under modernity by bringing other modes of reasoning into our apparatus of thinking

3. *Tradition and genealogy:* The methods by which the past might be rearranged in relation to the competing concepts of tradition and genealogy

A critical underlying method that joins these three issues is that of finding the right distance and scale at which objects might be apprehended or disclosed.

The Artifacts of Anthropology

A critical contribution of Asad to anthropological rethinking of its own apparatus was to show that the methodological instruments for collecting data in anthropology, such as recording of genealogies and tracking kinship relations, could themselves produce or change the objects of investigation. Thus, he showed that within the pastoral ecology of the Kababish Arabs he studied for his doctoral dissertation, the techniques of investigation made lineages appear to have much greater solidity than they possessed in reality. He then theorized that it was the complex conditions created by colonialism that had allowed certain strategically placed individuals and groups within the colonized societies to claim a new relation to history that had, in turn, been crucial in generating categories for rendering colonized societies knowable.

Following Michel Foucault, Asad's work has helped redefine our understanding of power, shifting the focus from the regulative aspects of power to its constitutive aspects. For example, in his analysis of the disciplines in medieval Christianity, Asad shows that power is not simply the means to impose one's will on another, as Max Weber had conceived it, but rather that it is a potential, the ability to *enact* something. Later, Asad came to think of power as "inner binding"; it emanated not only from outside but also from a willingness by subjects to be reshaped by authoritative discourses of the tradition to which they had voluntarily bound themselves.

Asad is probably most famous for his questioning of the concept of religion as a universal category. In his second book, *Genealogies of Religion*, he offered a sustained critique of Clifford Geertz's famous but somewhat glib formulation of religion as a "model *of* and a model *for* reality." Instead, Asad shows systematically how religion as a category emerged within modern Christianity by the imperative to identify and define practices that were encountered in other places as "religion" and by the gradual shift to "belief" as the defining element of a religion. Marshaling evidence from the particular and the concrete, he demonstrated how the idea of religion as a universal category emerged in early-modern Christianity and the concomitant shift to defining religions in terms of meaning and symbols rather than the cultivation of bodily dispositions.

In contrast to Geertz and many others, Asad does not think of discourse, first, as a system of meanings to which use (or metapragmatics) is then added, but rather, after Ludwig Wittgenstein, he thinks of body and language, and meaning and use, as constitutive of each other. Thus, he is more attuned to thinking of the individual as embedded in traditions, which form dispositions—the inner binding through which authoritative discourses are able to perform transformative work on individuals in reorganizing desires, passions, and memories.

Asad's critique of religion as a universal category is not an attempt to claim that no such thing as religion exists outside the Christian world (that would be patently nonsensical) but to show that apparently innocent-sounding ideas in anthropology, such as the definition of religion as affirming some aspect of reality (a model of reality), coincided neatly with missionary attempts to judge other people's practices as either "religion" or mere "superstition"—the former being attuned to a true Christian reality while the latter was to be condemned for affirming a false reality as evident in idolatry and superstition. Although Asad has mainly demonstrated the process wherein categories of one religion are generalized to create concepts that claim universality within the context of Christianity, he allows for the possibility that one could see different configurations of knowledge and power, say in Islam's rendering of itself as the final revelation that seals off the possibility of future prophecy or Hinduism's notion that the other religions can be assimilated within its theory of time as moving on a downward spiral. The student of any particular religion, he argues, must begin by unpacking the comprehensive concept, which he or she translates as "religion," into the heterogeneous elements that can be placed within a historical trajectory.

Categories of Modernity and Other Forms of Reason

Many scholars have seen Asad as primarily a critic of modernity, with its imperatives of sovereign, freely choosing individuals and the rearrangement of the private and public domains through notions of secularism and application of deliberative reasoning in the public sphere. In fact, Asad is much more interested in exploring the historical conditions that enabled the constellation of ideas and practices that constitute secularism. His most important move is to think of secularism, in his book *Formations of the Secular*, as emerging differently in different parts of Europe and the United States. What we have under the rubric of secularism, he contends, is not a single structure of signification but developments with historical breaks—a constant sliding of categories of religion and categories of secularism that come to define not only the structure of law but also the sensorial regimes through which a new kind of "common sense" is generated. Thus, for instance, Asad examines questions such as the constitution of the secular body, the picture of the "human" that underlies the discourse on human rights, and why modern sensibilities are horrified by a suicide bombing but not by the horrors inflicted by cluster bombing. In each case, he shows that there are specific modes of reasoning particular to modernity that are taken to be universal but that attention to breaks in history as well as to reasoning on these very questions from within other traditions destabilizes our commonsense conceptions of these issues. For example, it is taken for granted in discourses of modernity (whether philosophical, therapeutic, or popular) that all human beings want to avoid pain and increase pleasure. From this perspective, practices such as those of medieval monks who submitted their bodies to punishment in order to cultivate humility or Islamic warriors who seek martyrdom might appear to be cases of individual or cultural pathology. Yet a different theory of the person or the cultivation of the self might regard the acceptance of such pain as a voluntary binding to a tradition. Asad also draws attention to the contradictory attitudes to pain in secular regimes, which might declare the self-inflicted pain of medieval monks or Shia mourners as pathological but the pain of sadomasochism as an expression of freely chosen sexuality. The fundamental point in all these cases is Asad's ethical sensibility that no single form of life might be said to have a purchase over history.

Tradition and Genealogy

The idea of tradition animates much of Asad's work despite his early fascination with the work of Karl Marx and of Louis Althusser. Asad does not conceive of tradition either as one term in the tradition/modernity dichotomy or as primarily an intellectual lineage to which one owes allegiance. What interests him is the way individuals come to embody traditions through bodily dispositions, on the one hand, and submission to authoritative discourses by allowing themselves to be shaped by the disciplines that are instituted within the tradition, on the other. Tradition then is not so much about arguments or worldviews but about reshaping or reorganizing the desires of individuals. This conception of tradition allows Asad to think of his work as incorporating both the concept of tradition as inheritance and an application of the concept of genealogy through the concentration on discipline. He has applied this double notion to particular religions, namely, Christianity and Islam; to secularism and the constitution of modernity; and to anthropology as a disciplinary formation.

The conjoining of the concepts of tradition and genealogy is important because that is what allows Asad to critique the textualization of practices as well as the simultaneous elevation of meaning as the defining concept through which culture can be comprehended. In other words, Asad contests the notion that culture is like a text and that living entails first deciphering the meaning of the symbols through which culture is constituted and *then* acting in accordance with these meanings. He avers that this is a misleading picture of how human beings inhabit their worlds as beings steeped in history. While foregrounding the historical in his analysis, Asad deepens the idea of history by placing it within the larger problematic of how different societies relate to their past. He renders change through the imagery of glacial shifts, showing how slow shifts in subjectivities, and the accumulated weight of small changes, add up to create change. Asad does not deny the importance of large cataclysmic events but cultivates his own disciplinary practices to track these slow shifts by which the taken-for-granted assumptions about modernity and secularism come to define contemporary times. All through his writing, it is clear that the modern West is the main protagonist of his story, and he tells a compelling story about it by showing us its impact on all others. Like in a Henry James plot, where we learn about the protagonist by learning about the ripples and storms her character creates in all others around her, so might we learn about the West through the ripples created by colonialism and other forms of Western domination in the rest of the world.

A distinctive feature of Asad's methodology is the way in which he finds the right scale and distance for constituting his theoretical objects. Thus, for instance, to show that secularism does not pertain only to official policies of managing religious difference or the institution of new laws but implies changes in sensory regimes in the constitution of the subject, Asad needs to take the timescale through which slow shifts in subjectivities can be discerned with regard to our commonsense assumptions about pain. Like Foucault, Asad's thinking is constituted both through focalization of experience and its dispersal over time and space—a process that requires not only the right scale on which phenomena can be studied but also the right distance from what is being observed. Largeness or smallness of scale here is not a matter of simply multiplying a smaller scale to yield a larger one but of constituting the object through a language particular to each scale of the phenomenon.

Veena Das

See also Althusser, Louis; Foucault, Michel; Geertz, Clifford; Postcolonial Theory; Wittgenstein, Ludwig

Further Readings

Asad, T. (1970). *The Kababish Arabs: Power, authority, and consent in a nomadic tribe*. London, UK: Hurst.

———. (Ed.). (1973). *Anthropology and the colonial encounter*. London, UK: Ithaca Press.

———. (1993). *Genealogies of religion: Discipline and reasons of power in Christianity and Islam*. Baltimore, MD: Johns Hopkins University Press.

———. (2003). *Formations of the secular: Christianity, Islam, modernity*. Stanford, CA: Stanford University Press.

———. (2007). *On suicide bombing*. New York, NY: Columbia University Press.

Foucault, M. (1980). *Power/knowledge: Selected interviews and other writings, 1972–1977*. New York, NY: Random House.

Geertz, C. (1973). *The interpretation of cultures*. New York, NY: Basic Books.

Scott, D., & Hirschkind, C. (Ed.). (2006). *Powers of the secular modern: Talal Asad and his interlocutors*. Stanford, CA: Stanford University Press.

AUTOETHNOGRAPHY

Autoethnography is a qualitative research and writing methodology that incorporates the self-conscious voice of the researcher in the course of producing and representing ethnographic fieldwork and writing. The term *autoethnography* signals key aspects of the method, that which is personal to the researcher ("auto") and that which relates to a larger cultural or social group ("ethno"), and the ways in which these aspects are historicized, theorized, interpreted, and depicted ("graphy"). Autoethnography brings to the fore the emotional, intellectual, and social positionality of the ethnographer. In doing so, it directs theoretical attention to historically constituted subjectivities, cultural meanings, and social dynamics. It also raises important ontological, epistemological, and ethical questions about authoritative knowledge and anthropology's historical and contemporaneous role as a colonialist or neocolonialist, exploitative enterprise. The term, and practice of, autoethnography has given legitimacy and helped institutionalize alternative forms of ethnographic research and writing, including life histories and personal narratives.

This essay offers a brief history of autoethnography, its key proponents, and examples of autoethnographic texts. It also outlines major problems with the approach and highlights the method's potential for knowledge production.

Roots of Autoethnography

Autoethnography opens up an epistemological space to question the assumptions that underlie normative social science frames, explanations, understandings, and representations. Directly or indirectly inspired by the reflexive turn in anthropology, postcolonial and feminist studies, and other related disciplines (cultural studies, memory studies, and sociology), autoethnography emerged in the late 1980s and early 1990s. Some of its main proponents are Deborah Reed-Danahay, Carolyn Ellis, and Arthur Bochner. Autoethnography encourages the articulation of the self and personal reflection as an anthropological project, allowing for new ways of reading and writing ethnography and for considering the worlds within which ethnographers and cultural others are situated. Autoethnography emerges from and builds on the critique of empiricism that emerged in the late 1960s from postcolonial and feminist political projects and critiques of hegemonic models such as positivist science, value-free social science, and White, Western, male frames and representations. The postmodern effort to deconstruct established paradigms has led to new recognitions of earlier forms of what we might now call autoethnographic writing and encouraged new forms of ethnographic research, writing, and representation. In anthropology, the relationships among writers, readers, and subjects were no longer assumed but were problematized. Autoethnography came of age in this context.

Autoethnography privileges process and dynamic interaction as a means toward understanding and insight. It resists accommodating to a prescriptive mode of gathering and presenting ethnographic information and is uninterested in discovering universal truths. As such, there is no formula for "doing" autoethnography other than the presence of the ethnographic self in some way, the acknowledgment of the subjective, even emotional aspects of the enterprise, and the open acceptance of alternative narrative forms or experimental writing. The genre of autoethnography helps facilitate recognition of formerly marginalized scholarship and encourages scholars to break free from the constraints of standardized methods. Thus, there are multiple examples of works that may be classified in the genre, ranging from classics such as Zora Neale Hurston's *Dust Tracks on a Road* and Paul Friedrich's *The Princes of Naranja: An Essay in Anthrohistorical Method* to more recent efforts such as Ruth Behar's *Crossing the Border With Esperanza*, Carolyn Ellis's *The Ethnographic I*, and Christopher Poulos's *Accidental Ethnography: An Inquiry Into Family Secrecy*.

Contributions and Critiques

The past several decades have seen the publication of new, innovative ethnographies that are more reflexive, more engaging, and accessible to wider audiences than was the case with traditional, canonized anthropological writing. Autoethnography is open to a broad range of research objectives and techniques, narrative strategies, and even contributions by scholars from disciplines outside anthropology (e.g., communications, education). However, the very openness that is characteristic of the approach makes it difficult to locate specific works in the genre and threatens to dilute its meaning. As a result, there are new efforts to define subgenres within the category "autoethnography" (e.g., analytic autoethnography, subjectivist experiential autoethnographic writing, and postmodern/poststructuralist autoethnography"), though this endeavor does not necessarily address the core problem. Critics also raise questions about the potential in indigenous or native ethnographies to essentialize one's own culture. For

the method as a whole, questions remain as to how to assess the validity, reliability, and generalizability of findings. The greatest critical challenge facing autoethnography is the tendency among its practitioners to be or appear to be excessively self-centered and to write stories that too easily lapse into solipsism. Autoethnography is vulnerable to the charge of failing to adequately draw relevance to larger social, cultural, and political and theoretical issues.

Autoethnography's great contribution is in liberating social scientists from the constraints of traditional scholarly dictates. It has helped usher in the personal, the emotional, and the reflexive "I" in ethnographic encounters, whether in familiar places (at home; among one's own group) or in the traditional settings of anthropological research (away; among an "other" group). As such, autoethnography provides an important corrective to positivist models of research and writing and offers an honest appraisal of how knowledge gets produced. The challenge in autoethnography is to balance that honesty by presenting relevant and adequate information while refraining from irrelevant and excessive self-disclosure. Nevertheless, autoethnography encourages anthropologists to confront the silences and secrets concealed beneath the generalizations associated with traditional ethnographic practice. In doing so, it has the potential to contribute to the production of nuanced and politically informed knowledge that extends beyond scholar-readers to reach broader audiences.

Alisse Waterston

See also Abu-Lughod, Lila; Biography/Life Writing; Fanon, Frantz; Native Anthropology, Native Anthropologist; Postmodernism; Subjectivity

Further Readings

Buzard, J. (2003). On ethnographic authority. *Yale Journal of Criticism, 16*(1), 61–91.

Chang, H. (2008). *Autoethnography as method*. Walnut Creek, CA: Left Coast Press.

Ellis, C., Adams, T. E., & Bochner, A. P. (2011). Autoethnography: An overview. *Historical Social Research, 36*(4), 273–290.

McLean, A., & Leibing, A. (Eds.). (2007). *The shadow side of fieldwork: Exploring the blurred borders between ethnography and life*. Malden, MA: Blackwell.

Reed-Danahay, D. (1997). *Auto/ethnography: Rewriting the self and the social*. Oxford, UK: Berg.

B

BACHOFEN, JOHANN J.

Johann Jakob Bachofen (1815–1887) was the scion of a very wealthy patrician family of Basel, Switzerland. On his return to Basel in 1841, after brilliant studies in law and archaeology abroad, an equally brilliant career seemed to open up for him. He was within a short time elected to the Great Council and to the chair of Roman Law at the university and was also appointed judge of the Court of Appeal. Yet this was a time of political unrest for Switzerland. After a fierce and sometimes violent struggle between the democratic and conservative factions, Switzerland got a modern constitution in 1847, which turned the ancient federation of almost independent city-states into a federal state according to the pattern of the United States. Bachofen owed his early advancement to the hopes the conservative faction had pinned on him. Yet he turned out to be a diehard, unable to compromise. He despised his fellow patricians for their concessions to the liberal zeitgeist. After short incumbencies, he resigned his political mandate and his chair. He retained the judgeship, then an honorary part-time place in Basel, until 1866, when on his marriage to a lady of equal station, he finally retired to a life of scholarly leisure.

After the defeat of his faction, Bachofen abandoned his legal studies, which had brought him wide acclaim and calls to other universities, which he refused. Instead, he turned to archaeological studies, which were being increasingly seen as eccentric. He rejected the current method of philological source criticism as the worship of the letter in place of the spirit and stubbornly followed the guidance of the Romantic archaeologists Friedrich Creuzer and Joseph Görres, whose methods had focused on the interpretation of symbolism. He spent 20 years traveling all over Europe, visiting archaeological sites and museum objects and reading all extant classical sources. After this, he recommenced his best known work, and the one for which he is famous in anthropology. *Das Mutterrecht* (*Mother Right*) appeared in 1861. In more than 1,000 pages, it explored the earliest stages of religion, culture, and society. It identified the struggle between a female and a male principle as the moving force in life. The female principle predominated in the early stages of history, as it predominates in the early life of every human being. Yet, according to Bachofen, this predominance is not destined to last. It is superseded in the end by the male principle. The bulk of the book deals with myths and social institutions of preclassical antiquity, scrutinizing them for traces of an earlier predominance of women. It is not well organized and sometimes makes for dry reading. Yet this is occasionally relieved by flashes of insight clothed in forceful, compelling language.

This coexistence of two styles is not the least among Bachofen's attractions. It points to struggles within the breast of this staid and pious Calvinist. On the surface, he expounds a doctrine of progress, of the spiritualization of female earthiness by the dynamics of the male principle. Nevertheless, his most glowing and heartfelt passages evoke a lost paradise under the care of the mothers. Bachofen seems to regard the male principle as unstable, tending toward artificial construction, which withers away when losing contact with the female side. However, he does not spell this out. He had joined the Pythagorean-Neoplatonist-Gnostic tradition, which is reticent about its innermost thought. Thus, his book leaves plenty of scope for interpretation. Its main argument was summarized by Adrien Turel in 1939:

1st stage, mother right I ("hetaerism"): no marriage, sexual love, *ius naturale* ("natural law")—preculture, prehistory—food gathering—anarchy—cult of the earth—primitive fullness—symbolism

1st transition: abuse of women—reaction of female piety against male brutality

2nd stage, mother right II ("gynaecocracy"): marriage under female ascendancy, maternal love, *ius civile* ("civil law")—culture, prehistory—agriculture and handicrafts—tribal communities and city-states—cult of the moon and the night—preference for the left side—mythology

2nd transition: oppression of men ("amazonism")—male reaction by means of all-male, nonkin organizations—orgiastic ("Dionysian") religiosity

3rd stage, "father right": marriage under male ascendancy, paternal love, *ius civile* ("civil law")—culture, history—agriculture and industrialism—states and empires—cult of the sun and the day—preference for the right side—rational discourse—restrained ("Apollonian") religiosity.

Thus, Bachofen's plan looks like one of the three-stages schemes common in 19th-century evolutionary thought. Yet in examining his private papers, it is evident that he also contemplated a third transition and a fourth state. This third transition would lead via the contemporary triumph of liberalism and materialism and the concurrent desiccation of religiosity to imperialism, to revolutions, and finally to anarchy. What the fourth state would be Bachofen never spelled out. It could be either the end of mankind or its reinvigoration.

In his later years, Bachofen found a disciple in Alexis Giraud-Teulon, through whom he influenced "matriarchal theories" in anthropology, in particular those of John Ferguson McLennan and Lewis Henry Morgan. He corresponded with Morgan and studied anthropological literature (*Antiquarische Briefe* [Rare Letters], 1880–1886). Today, he is recognized, together with Joseph-François Lafitau, as the discoverer of the cluster of women-centered institutions

and myths called the "matrilinear complex." However, this is no longer regarded as a general stage of evolution. The "patriarchal theory" of Sir Henry Maine, which accounts for matrilineality as a special development connected with elementary forms of agriculture, prevails in modern anthropology. The "matriarchal theory" lingers on in feminism.

Giraud-Teulon was also read by Friedrich Engels and Sigmund Freud, and thereby, Bachofen influenced both Marxism and psychoanalysis. In Germany, after the defeat in World War I, a host of intellectuals and artists, neo-Pagans, and anti-Semites turned to Bachofen for spiritual and stylistic guidance. The best known figure in this "Bachofen renaissance" is the philosopher-psychologist Ludwig Klages. The same spiritual and stylistic influence was also visible in the area of feminism. Some feminist authors still believe in a matriarchal epoch in human history. Others make as much as they can of matrilineality. Yet Bachofen's importance for the feminist movement transcends such rather shaky historical constructions. His is the first theory that interpreted all history and society through the opposition of the sexes. He therefore can be seen as the Marx of feminism.

Justin Stagl

See also Freud, Sigmund; McLennan, John; Morgan, Lewis Henry

Further Readings

Bachofens, J. J. (1943–1967). *Gesammelte werke* [Collected works] (Vols. 1–10; Karl Meuli, Ed.). Basel, Switzerland: B. Schwabe.

———. (1967). *Myth, religion, and mother right: Selected writings of J. J. Bachofen* (R. Manheim, Trans.). Princeton, NJ: Princeton University Press.

Hildebrandt, H.-J. (1988). *Johann Jakob Bachofen: Die primar und sekundar literatur—mit einem anhang zum gegenwartigen stand der matriarchatsfrage* [Johann Jakob Bachofen: A bibliography of the primary and secondary literature—with an appendix on the present state of the matriarchal question]. Aachen, Germany: Dietrich Reimer.

Stagl, J. (1989). Notes on Johann Jakob Bachofen's *Mother Right* and its consequences. *Philosophy of the Social Sciences, 19*, 145–156.

Turel, A. (1939). *Bachofen-Freud: Zur emanzipation des mannes vom reich der mütter* [Bachofen-Freud: The emancipation of man from the realm of mothers]. Bern, Switzerland: Huber.

BAILEY, FREDERICK G.

Frederick G. Bailey (1924–) launched his career with the publication of three splendid monographs based on his research in India in the 1950s. Over the decades, he published 15 additional books and 40 scholarly papers and emerged as one of the outstanding political anthropologists of his era.

Born into a lower-middle-class family in Liverpool, Bailey was awarded an Open Scholarship to study Classics at Oxford in 1942, where he became aware that (like the Beatles) he spoke a working-class dialect called "Scouse." The Second World War was then in full swing, and in 1943, he joined the British army, resuming his studies at Oxford in 1946. After graduating with an MA and BLitt in 1950, he enrolled as a doctoral candidate in social anthropology under the supervision of Max Gluckman at Manchester University, at the time probably the leading center of anthropology in Britain. He received his PhD in 1955 and joined the faculty of the School of Oriental and African Studies at the University of London. In 1964, he founded the anthropology program at the University of Sussex. In 1971, he accepted a professorship at the University of California at San Diego, where as emeritus professor he has continued to produce influential books at a remarkable pace.

Bailey's work can be divided into three categories: the early Indian phase, his theoretical volumes, and his eventual turn toward anthropology at home. Probably the best known of the Indian monographs is *Tribe, Caste and Nation* (1960). This was a challenging project because it dealt with caste competition across an entire region. To cope methodologically, Bailey organized the study around 38 pivotal disputes, which he argued were "diagnostic" of the causes and directions of social change. The author's rich data revealed how ambitious individuals advanced their interests by manipulating the rival political structures of tribe, caste, and the modern state.

If the three Indian monographs made Bailey's name as a gifted ethnographer, his next book, *Stratagems and Spoils* (1969), confirmed his stature as an innovative theoretician. Drawing on the work of several prominent predecessors, such as Fredrik Barth, Edmund Leach, Raymond Firth, and Bronisław Malinowski, Bailey sketched out the essence of what became known as the transactional,

interactional, or processual model, sometimes also called action or agency theory. This new perspective, set in a broad and imaginative comparative framework, amounted to a massive attack on structural functionalism. Rather than assuming a close correspondence between the normative order and behavioral patterns, as Émile Durkheim had done, it painted a picture of inconsistent and contradictory norms and of choice-making individuals manipulating the norms and deviating from them in the pursuit of self-interest. As Bailey put it, in everyday life, most of us thread our way between the rules of society, seeking the most advantageous route.

In *Stratagems and Spoils*, Bailey distinguishes between normative and pragmatic rules. Normative rules are formal or ideal rules, guides to how we ought to behave. Pragmatic rules consist of the tactics and strategies that reflect actual behavior. Bailey's argument that human interaction is dominated by pragmatic rules is consistent with one of his most significant generalizations: Whether the focus is on politics or some other dimension of social life, an examination of institutionalized roles and formal rules will only afford a partial explanation because the causal core of human interaction is embedded in the informal realm.

Stratagems and Spoils has been criticized for promoting a cynical view of the human condition, but it also has been praised as the contemporary version of Machiavelli's *The Prince*. With its rejection of the rule-bound robot associated with structural functionalism, and its portrayal of social life as messy and constantly in flux, the transactional model has impressed many anthropologists as the field-worker's perspective par excellence.

Morality and Expediency (1977), an expanded version of the Louis Henry Morgan Lectures delivered at the University of Rochester in 1975, is Bailey's first major publication based on research in his own society. It really does represent anthropology at home because its subject matter is the politics of university life, especially in Britain and the United States. This book tracks the behavior of the self-interested, manipulative actor portrayed in *Stratagems and Spoils* into even murkier corners. The focus of *Morality and Expediency* is on the unprincipled side of human interaction, on "institutionalized facades, make-believe and pretence, lies and hypocrisy," on what "every public figure pretends does not exist."

Bailey's analysis of how decisions are made in committees, which as subsections of the bureaucracy should be (but are not) governed entirely by rationality and impersonality, and his imaginative reduction of the political machinations of his colleagues to 10 analytic constructs called *masks*, are worth the price of admission; indeed, the book as a whole provides a remarkable insight into the workings of universities that may well be generalized to other types of formal organizations. Yet *Morality and Expediency* did not have the same impact on the discipline as his previous books, and the reason is not difficult to discern. Anthropology at home still plays second fiddle to the discipline's historical focus on so-called exotic societies.

Over the years, Bailey has modified his position regarding some of the fundamental issues in the discipline, the obvious example being the shift from the focus on social structure in the Indian monographs to the transactional model in *Stratagems and Spoils*. In his early work, the basic methodological unit was the observable event or act; eventually, he began to assign analytic priority to ideas, to what goes on in people's heads and how it influences behavior. In a more recent study, *Treasons, Stratagems and Spoils* (2001), room is made for emotion, spontaneity, and duty alongside rational calculation and self-interest. As Bailey's conception of the actor and the social realm became more complex, his faith in underlying order, and thus in science, might have been eroded. Yet he never rejected the comparative method, nor did he disavow one of his most inspiring claims: Beneath the veneer of cultural variation, political activity everywhere, whether in tribal, peasant, or industrial societies, exhibits a common set of principles.

Stanley R. Barrett

See also Barth, Fredrik; Firth, Raymond; Gluckman, Max; Leach, Edmund; Manchester School

Further Readings

Barth, F. (1959). *Political leadership among Swat Pathans* (London School of Economics Monographs on Social Anthropology, No. 19). London, UK: Athlone Press.

Boissevain, J. (1974). *Friends of friends*. Oxford, UK: Basil Blackwell.

Fortes, M., & Evans-Pritchard, E. E. (Eds.). (1967). *African political systems*. London, UK: Oxford University Press. (Original work published 1940)

Kurtz, D. V. (2001). *Political anthropology: Paradigms and power*. Boulder, CO: Westview Press.

Leach, E. R. (1965). *Political systems of highland Burma*. Boston, MA: Beacon Press. (Original work published 1954)

BAKHTIN, MIKHAIL M.

Mikhail Mikhailovitch Bakhtin (1895–1975), the Russian literary critic, semiotician, and philosopher, is widely recognized as one of the central figures in social theory, and his influence has been felt in fields as diverse as anthropology, history, psychology, sociology, communications, rhetoric, comparative literature, and the philosophy of language.

Early Life: The Russian Revolution and the Bakhtin Circle

Born into an aristocratic family in Orel, Russia, at the end of the 19th century, Bakhtin came to champion those who were less fortunate than himself, always maintaining a sense of the broad scope of human life as he undertook his many theoretical projects. Coming of age at the time of the Russian Revolution, he attended the University of Saint Petersburg during the First World War, where he specialized in the study of classical literature and philosophy, while maintaining a lifelong interest in language and politics.

During the 1920s, Bakhtin came into contact with fellow intellectuals Valentin Voloshinov and Pavel Medvedev, now known collectively as the Bakhtin Circle, who were working as instructors for the People's Educational Department in Vitebsk. In time, they came to share a deep commitment to the philosophy of language as a key to social interaction, human psychology, and larger political processes. Though some have credited the works published under Voloshinov's name to Bakhtin as the sole author, it now appears that the influence may have been mutual. In contrast to the structural linguistics of the time, as exemplified by the writings of Ferdinand de Saussure, Bakhtin and his colleagues maintained that language was first and foremost a product of social interaction. This sense of language was often lost when studying formal features such as phonology or syntax in isolation, following the model of examining the records of dead languages (like Latin) with no living speakers. In looking closely at the social foundations of language,

Bakhtin identified a short list of major philosophical principles that are now standard in the social sciences and humanities, including dialogism, voice, heteroglossia, ideology, speech genres, the utterance, polyphony, double-voiced discourse, intertextuality, the chronotope, and the carnival.

The Dialogic Principle (or Dialogism)

A central image that recurs throughout Bakhtin's work is that of the simple act of engaging in face-to-face dialogue. Throughout his vast corpus of theoretical writings, this fundamental human context of communication was never far from view—an image that appears even in one of his first essays, "The Author as Hero in Aesthetic Activity," originally written in the 1920s. By starting with this basic image of the face-to-face encounter, Bakhtin was able to confront the profound asymmetry of communication, given that each person in an exchange inherently sees things from a very different point of view, literally seeing what is behind the other person's head or, more generally, what the other person may not even begin to see because it is beyond his or her direct experience. For Bakhtin, dialogue does not imply a conversation among equals but refers simply to the social nature of speaking, where one "aims" one's word at an audience, even in situations where there are substantial differences in power—where one party refuses to listen. Thus, for Bakhtin, communication is a double-sided act and the audience holds as much power as the author when it comes to shaping the meaning of a text.

In the *Dialogic Imagination* (1981), Bakhtin establishes a general case for a principle of *dialogism*, which captures the sense in which language emerges from the inherently social process of aiming one's words at an audience. This principle applies even to cases of *inner dialogue*, where one responds to oneself while thinking or where the author gauges the potential reactions of some imagined audience, not yet present. As a general process, the dialogical principle can even be extended to more remote cases, such as the extended "dialogue" between authors writing at different times—a concept now known as *intertextuality* among Bakhtinian scholars such as Julia Kristeva.

The Place of Ideologies in Society

Another central idea for Bakhtin was the concept of *ideology*, which was inspired by the works of Karl Marx, particularly Marx's emphasis on the false consciousness of the proletariat, who accepted a religious worldview that kept them from seeing the conditions of their oppression. From these political and religious roots, Bakhtin extended Marx's concept of ideology to encompass any "system of ideas" that served as a basis for arriving at a shared understanding—from scientists and their models to authors and their distinctive visions. In this way, Bakhtin observed, social interaction is necessarily charged with ideology, since a backdrop of common assumptions is a precondition for engaging in communication—even if these views are challenged and refined in the course of an exchange. This image of ideologies entering into conflict sets the stage for one of the maxims of Bakhtinian studies—the idea that dialog is *unfinalizable*, given that communication is fundamentally about the exchange of opposing points of view, which can never be fully resolved.

Utterance, Voice, and Double-Voiced Discourse

Staying close to the interactive source of discourse, the *utterance* occupied a place of central importance in social theory for Bakhtin—as an instantiation of language use, or a given person's *word*, as it is embedded in a particular context, including the submerged ideologies used by the actors to interpret those words. Thus, a simple color word like "black" or "white" can take on racial overtones and even incite a riot when uttered in an ideologically charged moment, such as a rally. A closely related concept is that of *voice*, or variable ability to be heard when communicating, based on the speaker's relationship to the audience, including the actor's power or lack thereof. Both concepts—utterance and voice—flow from the dialogical principle, given that the word is embedded in social interaction and charged with ideologies. In *Problems of Dostoevsky's Poetics* (1983), Bakhtin introduces the concept of *double-voiced discourse*, where a person speaks through someone else's words—as an author imbues the speech of a character with intentions of his or her own.

Speech Genres

Just as recognizable ideologies and voices permeate spoken discourse, utterance is composed of familiar *speech genres*, based on expectations for the structure and style of the utterance. This principle is developed in *Speech Genres and Other Late*

Essays (1986). Though derived from literary studies, which is filled with genres like epic poetry or political satire, Bakhtin saw this general concept as one of the organizing principles of all discourse, where one encounters relatively stable expectations regarding the character of a narrative, from greetings to conversations, oratory, storytelling, or sung performance. The concept has been especially influential among anthropologists and folklorists, such as Richard Bauman, who specialize in oral performances, framed by local standards, where organizing principles may include expectations concerning the pace, length, and tone of delivery, as well as the nature of the participation.

Heteroglossia

Given that speech emerges from social actors, each with their own intentions and distinct points of view, Bakhtin argued that language itself embodies inherent diversity at every level of structure and practice. Among Bakhtinian scholars, this principle is known as *heteroglossia* (a translation from the Russian *raznorečie*), or the internal diversity of all languages, which can be illustrated in terms of their many dialects, registers, and speech genres, each reflecting a segment of society, from class to ethnicity to the professions and age grades. While recognizing that the opposite, *monoglossic* trend is often at work, given the prevalence of efforts to enforce standards in language, Bakhtin is optimistic that diversity will prevail, in accordance with the dialogic principle. Drawing on the language of physics, he compared the monoglossic trend to a *centripetal force*, based on efforts to move toward a common center; similarly, he compared the heteroglossic trend to a *centrifugal force*, with a movement away from the standardization, toward internal diversity. With these two forces present, everyday speech becomes the site where these competing forces collide, with *heteroglossia*, or internal diversity, often winning out—as a by-product of the dialogical nature of language.

For Bakhtin, tensions are present at every level of language and society, starting with the word, which can convey multiple ideologies while simultaneously appearing neutral (such as "black" or "white"). In a similar way, even the individual becomes a site where this social diversity plays out, given that we all "live in a world of others' words." Thus, even when listening to a single person speaking, we hear echoes of other voices, including multiple dialects, speech genres, and ideological constructs. The same is true of texts, where these multiple voices become central to the task of alternating between characters—as Bakhtin observed in *Problems of Dostoevsky's Poetics*, where he praised Dostoevsky for writing *polyphonic* novels, with a range of voices. In this sense, perceptive novelists and ethnographers alike strive to capture a sense of ideological diversity, not assuming, as was the trend in Saussurean structuralism, that language (or culture) is uniform.

The Carnival

Nowhere does the clash of ideologies stand in greater relief than in Bakhtin's extended examination of the *carnival*, which he explores through the lens of medieval literature, in *Rabelais and His World* (1965), rather than confronting 20th-century political struggles head-on. There, beyond the direct control of governing bodies, subversive folk genres flourish and rise up to contest official hegemony, which often includes the appearance of the grotesque, to offset the everyday disciplines imposed by standards of piety or etiquette. Bakhtin's fascination with the carnival—and the *carnivalesque*—has been influential among anthropologists who study counterhegemonic movements as well as the classic rituals of inversion widely described in ethnographic writings.

The Chronotope

As a literary theorist, Bakhtin originated many concepts that dealt with the contours of the social imagination, or the way the audience comes to picture a similar mental image when in the presence of a narrator, such as a novelist, poet, or speaker. Even here, Bakhtin identified dialogical principles, such as the *chronotope*, or the relationship between space and time in imagination, given that these dimensions enter into a kind of dialogue in consciousness. The concept was inspired by a lecture Bakhtin attended on the four-dimensional space-time of Einstein's physics, which Bakthin applied to the philosophy of language, like the centripetal and centrifugal forces of ideology. Bakhtin recognized that authors often vary the ratio of space and time in crafting a story line, making time stand still, perhaps, or using space itself to measure the flow of time as the plot progresses. In early Greek romance novels, such as

An Ethiopian Tale, Bakhtin noted, there is almost an empty quality to the adventure time: Things happen, and time progresses, but without any movement in physical space and without any profound changes to the personalities of the characters. Bakhtin's concept of the chronotope has become a powerful trope for anchoring social events in a sense of socially constructed space and time, as told in narrative.

Broader Impact

Bakhtin's writings on the philosophy of language have had an enormous impact on the social sciences and humanities since his death in 1975—ironically achieving international acclaim after their author's life of relative obscurity. Since the rise of the postmodern critique in the 1980s, ethnographers have been influenced by the principles of *polyphony* and *heteroglossia*, striving to write works that capture a sense of diversity rather than uniformity in society. Performance theorists, in folklore, linguistics, ethnomusicology, and expressive culture, have found a central place for concepts like *speech genres, voice,* and *intertextuality* in their work. Linguistic anthropology has also been transformed by the pervasive use of the *dialogical principle* and the close examination of *ideologies* in language use, alongside now common tropes like *double-voiced* discourse and the *chronotope*. Though Bakhtin was almost silenced by Stalin for his religious views and political dissent, his voice continues to resonate with scholars in a wide range of fields, including major figures like Michael Siverstein and Jane Hill, among linguistic anthropologists, and Richard Bauman and James Clifford, among the theorists of cultural anthropology.

Sean O'Neill

See also Marx, Karl; Saussure, Ferdinand de; Sociolinguistics; Structuralism

Further Readings

Bakhtin, M. M. (1981). *The dialogic imagination: Four essays* (M. Holquist, Ed.; C. Emerson & M. Holquist, Trans.). Austin: University of Texas Press.

——. (1984). *Problems of Dostoevsky's poetics* (C. Emerson, Ed. & Trans.). Minneapolis: University of Minnesota Press. (Original work published 1929)

——. (1984). *Rabelais and his world* (H. Iswolsky, Trans.). Bloomington: Indiana University Press. (Original work published 1965)

——. (1986). *Speech genres and other late essays* (C. Emerson & M. Holquist, Eds.; V. K. McGee, Trans.). Austin: University of Texas Press.

——. (1990). *Art and answerability: Early philosophical essays by M. M. Bakhtin* (M. Holquist & V. Liapunov, Eds.; V. Liapunov, Trans.). Austin: University of Texas Press.

——. (1993). *Toward a philosophy of the act* (V. Liapunov & M. Holquist, Eds.; V. Liapunov, Trans.). Austin: University of Texas Press.

Morris, P. (Ed.). (1994). *The Bakhtin reader: Selected writings of Bakhtin, Medvedev, and Voloshinov* (with a glossary by G. Roberts). London, UK: Edward Arnold.

Volosinov, V. N. (1986). *Marxism and the philosophy of language* (L. Matejka & I. R. Titunik, Trans.). Cambridge, MA: Harvard University Press. (Original work published 1929)

BARTH, FREDRIK

Fredrik Barth is a Norwegian social anthropologist, born in 1928 and educated at Chicago and Cambridge Universities. He was originally a student of Raymond Firth and Edmund Leach, and he maintained a long-term friendship with Leach, who is acknowledged as a reader of several of his manuscripts. Barth was successful in founding a modern Norwegian anthropological tradition during the 1960s, which continues today, with emphasis on intensive fieldwork and the study of social organization. Barth's legacy includes research on pastoralists (herders) like the Kurds and Pathans (Pashtuns), who are very much in the news today; but he has also worked in a wide variety of other cultures. Barth is perhaps best known for his path-breaking approach to ethnicity in the introduction to the edited volume *Ethnic Groups and Boundaries*. Later, in a departure from his earlier focus on the political and social organization of groups in the Middle East and Pakistan, Barth turned to the study of knowledge in a nonliterate society. He undertook intensive fieldwork in an isolated New Guinea group to produce *Ritual and Knowledge Among the Baktaman of New Guinea,* a complex analysis of male initiation; this was later followed by comparative research on interior New Guinea groups. Barth and his wife, Unni Wikan, also an anthropologist, produced complementary volumes on the Omani trading town of Sohar. Barth also published a fascinating autobiography of the ruler of a Pathan kingdom in northwest Pakistan, *The Last Wali of Swat*. Barth's most recent fieldwork in Bali and Bhutan attempted a new approach to the study of complex societies.

Continuities and Changes Over Time in Barth's Theoretical Focus

Barth's early work, in the 1950s and 1960s, is similar in some ways to much of British social anthropology of the time: The author emphasizes social organization rather than culture; analyzes kinship systems, household forms, and political organization; and says little about history or the relation of groups to colonial authorities or newly independent states. Also, contrary to the expectations of research today, description and analysis are almost entirely from the male point of view. This is not surprising, for a variety of reasons, including cultural limits on the interaction of male researchers with women in Islamic societies. Barth is, however, very concerned with processes, particularly actors' decision-making processes, in contrast to other social anthropologists of the 1950s and 1960s, who emphasized group behavior. For Barth, social life consists largely of transactions between individuals seeking to further their interests through strategic choices, an approach known as *transactionalism*. Barth feels that a focus on the individual level can help anthropologists understand change in social systems. Earlier social anthropologists, according to Barth, had placed too much emphasis on how societies were maintained, which seemed to leave little room for the study of change. Barth views individuals as constantly adapting to both physical and social environments, a perspective basic to his approach to ethnicity in *Ethnic Groups and Boundaries*.

In Barth's introduction to *Ethnic Groups and Boundaries*, the outcome of a symposium for Scandinavian social anthropologists at the University of Bergen in 1967, he poses the problem of explaining ethnic group persistence. Until then, most anthropologists had assumed that distinct cultures were simply the product of social and geographic isolation. But Barth argues that boundary maintenance must be *explained* rather than taken for granted. Different ethnic groups may share cultural features, while boundaries do not disappear when people cross them: for example, when a child adopted from a foreign group or a household cannot maintain a

certain way of life and "drops out" to join another population. Important relationships may also exist between members of different ethnic groups, such as trade partners. Barth wants to observe the processes that create and maintain boundaries. His main point is that the relation between "ethnic group" and "culture" is not as obvious as we often assume. Ethnic boundaries are maintained using only a few cultural markers, and tracing the history of an ethnic group is not the same as describing the history of its culture. Cultural details change over time, but the particular type of social organization he calls the "ethnic group" persists. To use an American example, the Cheyenne of 1850 and the Cheyenne of the 21st century are culturally very different, but the Cheyenne *identity* has endured over time.

According to Barth, ethnic groups are a form of social organization based on self-identification and identification by others. Identity is indicated by cultural signs like language and dress and by loyalty to particular values, but the only cultural markers that matter are those that are significant to the actors themselves. To consider another person a member of one's own ethnic group involves common understandings about evaluation. Individuals are judged, and are willing to be judged, by agreed-on standards if they want to be considered members of a particular ethnic group.

Barth considers the circumstances under which ethnic distinctions emerge. First, population groups must develop that see themselves, and are seen by others, as distinct. Second, people must accept the idea that these categories should be judged by different standards. The greater the difference in values, the more limited the interaction between ethnic groups. In terms of ecology, the groups may control different niches or territories or be closely interdependent, but usually, the situation is a complex one.

Systems of stratification may or may not involve ethnic groups. If the groups are characterized by differences in the control of assets, then they make up a stratified multiethnic system. Barth considers the Indian caste system a special case, since caste boundaries are defined by ethnic criteria like marriage customs, funeral rituals, and polluting occupations. Ethnic group identity is conditional on performance, which often requires assets; in a stratified system, differences in access to assets (e.g., land) maintain the system.

In explaining why people change their ethnic identities, Barth argues that self-identity is a key component of ethnic identity, and if people cannot meet the performance expectations of their ethnic group, they may attempt to enter another one rather than face humiliation. Barth feels that a certain amount of variation and ambiguity should be expected in social life. He rejects the "ideal versus real" dichotomy, often used by anthropologists to discuss discrepancies between values and behavior, arguing that values become visible only through action. In spite of this normal variation, people try to keep their conventional stereotypes of ethnicity in everyday interactions, since they are useful in making sense out of experience and in relating to others.

Barth's comments on cultural contact and change are particularly interesting because they foreshadow much anthropological work of the past 4 decades. By the late 1960s, anthropologists could no longer treat non-Western societies as if they were isolated and unchanging. Western goods and institutions were spreading around the world, and colonial powers had been replaced by independent governments. Even though cultural differences have been reduced, Barth warns that ethnicity may still be important and boundary-maintaining processes will continue to operate. Barth examines the strategies of influential elites, members of ethnic groups in multiethnic states: These strategies include "passing" into industrial society, the acceptance of minority status while minimizing or hiding cultural differences, and emphasizing ethnic identity to create new movements. The political use of ethnicity is very common in today's world, and Barth sees it as just another way of making cultural differences relevant. Barth warns against the tendency of some anthropologists to take for granted the peaceful conditions that often obtained in societies under colonial rule. Life in many settings was previously less secure, and insecurity itself would have limited relations between groups due to fear and lack of opportunity for interaction. Following Barth, anthropologists have increasingly turned to the study of ethnic groups in multiethnic societies, and often to research on the politics of ethnicity, as states have universally imposed their rule on local populations. Barth feels that a focus on individual decision making can help one understand the processes of change in a way that more traditional social anthropology, with its emphasis on the stability of groups, cannot.

Because of the importance of the Pathan material in Barth's writings, this group is worth discussing in

some detail. The Pathans, or Pashtuns, are a large ethnic group found in Afghanistan and western Pakistan, organized patrilineally (with group membership traced through males from a male ancestor) and spread over an ecologically diverse region. Barth examines the processes of boundary maintenance and political organization among Pathans in several early writings. His account deals specifically with so-called traditional organization rather than a change taking place at the time of his fieldwork (1954). In his chapter in *Ethnic Groups and Boundaries*, Barth describes three major institutions central to Pathan identity: (1) *melmastia* (hospitality), (2) *jirga* (councils and involvement in public affairs), and (3) *purdah* (female seclusion). In the ideal setting, special men's houses exist where leaders can demonstrate hospitality and create followings; councils allow men who are supposed to be independent equals to make group decisions; and the separation of men and women allows men to *appear* to act independently of women. (In reality, of course, men and women depend on each other, as they do elsewhere.)

Unlike Pathans, the Baluch, on the southern border of Pathan territory, try to absorb people from other groups as commoners under subchiefs and chiefs. If Pathans have to leave their own society due to war, crime, or loss of herds, they can join the Baluch, but they must do so as clients and are not allowed to speak in council. Loss of independence is considered a failure among Pathans but not among Baluch; therefore, people lose their Pathan identity and become Baluch. In western Pathan country, by way of contrast, where Pathans settle among the Persian-speaking Hazara in Afghanistan, the newcomers can become rich landowners and patrons. However, if they lose their land, they can be denied rights as Pathans; this is also true of the Swat in northwest Pakistan. On the Indus plain in Pakistan, where the centralized government discourages independence and aggression, they become Panjabis. In the far northwest, where poorer agricultural yields make it impossible to maintain men's houses, with their associated hospitality, Pathans become Kohistani. In all these cases, Barth stresses individual *choice* of identity, a recurring theme throughout his work.

In an earlier article on Pathans, "Segmentary Opposition and the Theory of Games: A Study of Pathan Organization," and in his influential *Political Leadership Among Swat Pathans*, Barth analyzes the Pathan political organization from the viewpoint of individual strategic choices. As mentioned above, Pathans reckon kinship through patrilineal descent. However, closely related people (fathers and sons, and brothers) are rivals for land and power; Pathan leaders therefore try to build up a following of distant or nonrelated men to support them in disputes over land and other matters. Pathan politics is summed up in the saying (actually used by Pathans), "The enemy of my enemy is my friend." As a result of these struggles, the whole Swat Valley of Pakistan was divided into two different political blocs at the time of Barth's fieldwork. His argument, then, is that individual strategies based on self-interest actually *create* what earlier social anthropologists called the social structure.

Following the production of *Ethnic Groups and Boundaries*, Barth's research changed as he explored different topics and new areas of the world. His post-1960s work can be characterized as a striving to keep up with current trends in theory and to analyze more and more complex situations. In his next major research, Barth turned to the study of meaning, or rather, as he prefers it, "knowledge," since it is easier to show how information is transmitted and exchanged than it is to show the same for "meaning." Wanting to experience a society completely different from anything he had previously known, he moved his field research to Papua New Guinea. His book based on this research, *Ritual and Knowledge Among the Baktaman of New Guinea*, has the theoretical goal of analyzing ritual as a type of communication and as a way of thought. He sees ritual as embodying a tradition of knowledge and a particular worldview and wants to know what information is needed to participate in it. Barth's methodology, which is by no means easy to achieve, is to focus on what an initiate learns step by step, in this case by participating himself as much as possible in seven stages of male initiation. Because each stage reveals new information kept secret from all but the appropriate initiates (and all women), the meaning of rituals, artifacts, certain colors, sacred animals, and so on, varies greatly from person to person and is sometimes at risk of being lost altogether. A particular ritual like the rite of sacrifice can be viewed as a transaction between the one conducting the sacrifice and the god, but it signifies other things at the same time; to understand its "meaning," we must view it holistically, in all its aspects. Barth

categorically rejects the structuralist methodology of the 1970s, particularly that of Claude Lévi-Strauss, in which folk categories of the natural world are taken to reflect "native" thought about social categories. He criticizes this approach for its lack of fit with the real world, its inability to prove or disprove claims of fact, and its failure to ask whether the people involved have ever actually thought this way. Barth argues that it is simplistic to assume that religion consists of a neat, logical package of folk categories, ritual, and indigenous thought. He prefers to see cultural creativity at work, as people use familiar animals or objects as metaphors in ritual; that is, meaning is derived from the analogy between a symbol and what it symbolizes. Ritual events must be seen in context, and what people say about their purpose is important. Rather than impose his own logical structure on events, Barth takes pains to present the understandings of informants as carefully as possible, even to the point of avoiding questions that would introduce an outsider's perspective. Barth suggests that "native explanations" in anthropology are often just a product of the anthropologist's own curious mind.

During the 1980s and 1990s, Barth's research ranged from the Middle East and Pakistan back to New Guinea and then to Bali and Bhutan. His book on Sohar, an old trading community in Oman on the east coast of the Arabian Peninsula, both describes life in the town and attempts to explain how cultural pluralism—that is, a situation where a society contains multiple ethnic groups—is maintained. Together with his later fieldwork in Bali, it marks a turn in his research toward the challenge of describing and analyzing the culture of complex societies with a variety of religious traditions and ethnic groups. A major problem in the case of Sohar is determining the "parts" or groups that, for social anthropologists, are supposed to make up the social structure. Barth feels that the town cannot easily be described in terms of kinship groups, class, or even ethnic groups, which come and go. Returning to the level of the individual, he sees "structure" in values and ideas about interpersonal relationships. Ultimately, Sohar's cultural pluralism is based on tolerance, embodied in rules and institutions that allow diversity to flourish. *Balinese Worlds* (1993) attempts to describe and analyze a complex society and culture with ancient traditions of knowledge (Islam and Balinese Hinduism) and daunting local variation. Again, Barth argues that order is based on processes, that multiple realities exist (variation in occupation, traditions, historical context, statuses, etc.), and that anthropologists should not expect to find a neat, coherent whole.

Barth's transactional approach has been criticized by a variety of researchers. At one time it was considered an exciting new perspective because it promised a way of understanding how societies change, which early social anthropology did not. However, objections quickly arose. For one thing, it is not always clear that people have a choice. Also, their behavior may not always be rational, and they may not realize its implications. Barth views social structure as emergent, the result of many individual decisions; but most anthropologists today would argue that social systems have their own powerful limiting and even determining effects on individuals. Still, though later anthropologists gave relatively more importance to the very real constraints of society, by the 1980s, "practice theory" was reworking some of Barth's central points: the individual as strategic decision maker and his or her role in change. Because of Barth's work, in the work of others, anthropology is better equipped today to analyze a rapidly transforming and highly diverse world.

Janet E. Benson

See also Firth, Raymond; Leach, Edmund; Practice Theory; Structural Functionalism; Structuralism

Further Readings

Anderson, R. (2005). *Interview with Fredrik Barth*. Cambridge, UK: University of Cambridge. Retrieved from sms.cam.ac.uk/media/1112380

Barth, F. (1959). *Political leadership among Swat Pathans* (London School of Economics Monographs on Social Anthropology, No. 19). London, UK: Athlone Press.

———. (1959). Segmentary opposition and the theory of games: A study of Pathan organization. *Journal of the Royal Anthropological Institute, 89*(1), 5–21.

———. (1961). *Nomads of south Persia: The Basseri Tribe of the Khamseh Confederacy*. Oslo, Norway: Oslo University Press.

———. (1964). *Models of social organization* (Occasional Papers, No. 23). London, UK: Royal Anthropological Institute.

———. (1969). *Ethnic groups and boundaries*. Oslo, Norway: Oslo University Press.

———. (1975). *Ritual and knowledge among the Baktaman of New Guinea*. Oslo, Norway: Oslo University Press.

———. (1983). *Sohar: Culture and society in an Omani town*. Baltimore, MD: Johns Hopkins University Press.

———. (1985). *The last Wali of Swat*. Oslo, Norway: Oslo University Press.

———. (1993). *Balinese worlds*. Chicago, IL: University of Chicago Press.

———. (2007). Overview: Sixty years in anthropology. *Annual Review of Anthropology, 36*, 1–16.

Sperschneider, W. (1999). *Fredrik Barth: From fieldwork to theory* [DVD]. Gottingen, Germany: IWF Knowledge and Media and the Danish Film Institute Workshop.

BARTHES, ROLAND

Roland Barthes (1915–1980) was a unique, idiosyncratic, and, at times, contradictory thinker, who was nonetheless deeply influential in the formation of trends central to postwar social sciences and humanities. Especially for the trajectory of anthropology and social theory, his most lasting and important legacy may derive from the ways in which he put the field of semiology into practice. The themes and tensions seen in his writings on semiology, however, carry through much of his quite diverse career.

Biography and Major Works

Barthes was born in 1915 in the provincial town of Cherbourg, France. His father, a naval officer, was killed in battle when Barthes was only 1 year old, and he and his mother moved first to Bayonne and then to Paris, where Barthes attended secondary school. Viewed as a student with promise, Barthes spent his twenties studying for a license in classical letters at the Sorbonne; he then went on to earn degrees in philology and Greek tragedy. He also suffered from serious bouts of tuberculosis, which twice necessitated stays in a sanatorium and hindered his procurement of a stable academic teaching position. Barthes continued to write in the 1930s and 1940s, while taking occasional teaching roles in Biarritz, Bayonne, Paris, Romania, and Egypt. By 1952, Barthes found a permanent position at the Centre National de la Recherche Scientifique, and in 1960, he took on a directorship of studies at the École Practique des Hautes Études; finally, from

1976 to 1980, he was chair of Literary Semiology at the Collège de France; he also held an invited position at Johns Hopkins University. Barthes died in 1980 after being struck by a car.

Barthes kept an early distance from more orthodox institutional placements for intellectual reasons as well as practical ones. He was nondisciplinary as much as he was interdisciplinary in his thought. His preference for short essays, too, was part of his refusal of any "doctrinal" approach, and he denied having any audience in mind at all for any of his writing. Over the course of his career, Barthes wrote on literature for a variety of academic, popular, and political contexts (he was an influential contributor to the journal *Tel Quel*), but he also studied and wrote works of sociology; he held teaching positions at some of the world's best universities; but he also wrote for the underground wartime resistance newspaper *Combat* and founded his own theatrical group.

If Barthes is thus difficult to classify in terms of discipline, he is often more simply framed as a formative figure in the development of both structuralism and poststructuralism: He has been labeled as one of the seminal "gang of four" of structuralism, which also included Claude Lévi-Strauss, Jacques Lacan, and Michel Foucault, and along with Lacan and Foucault is also then typically associated with the emergence of poststructuralism. This biographical narrative of a general shift from structuralism to poststructuralism is ultimately a simplification. If anything, Barthes might more productively be read as working through an ongoing tension between structuralist understandings of social life as a set of underlying systems of relation and a materialist emphasis on social forces that can ultimately be explained as outcomes of political-economic conditions.

Barthes is perhaps most clearly and rigorously structuralist in the *Elements of Semiology* (1964); much of it reads like classic linguistic structuralism. Barthes draws heavily on Ferdinand Saussure's formulation of the sign as made up of signifiers and signifieds, systematically related into a larger order. And while Barthes placed real emphasis on the notion that structuralism implied a diachronic level of connection between elements of meaning, he argued in *Elements of Semiology* that the corpus of signs one analyzes should as much as possible be a synchronic set—a purely synchronic cross section

of history. This looks a lot like the static, subject-less structuralism for which even Lévi-Strauss was criticized. But there are hints of critique within *Elements of Sociology*, too. Barthes, for example, raises the possibility that systems of meaning can have their own "controlling groups," or social spheres of influence, that have greater sway in forming a discursive system—with the implication that while all structures of meaning are collective, there might be hierarchies of production and control. One can begin to see, in other words, a notion of agency and social critique.

The most important shift away from neutral structuralism, however, lies in Barthes's turn to an emphasis on connotation within signifying systems. In Barthes's scheme (drawing loosely on the work of the Danish linguist Louis Hjelmslev), connotation is like a second-tier system of signs, built on top of our everyday meanings. This is important because, it seems, the first order of signs is where history, knowledge, and culture enter; connotation, on the other hand, helps naturalize those signs as beyond culture or history. Thus, connotation is where Barthes locates ideology.

With this, Barthes returns the study of signs, and structuralism, to social, historical, and political relevance. In effect, cultures are understood *as* ideologies, which are historically specific formations that nonetheless work to naturalize the systems of meaning on which they are built. This is quite far from the universal, ahistorical structures of human mentality that Lévi-Strauss eventually described, and from structural anthropologists' general aversion to looking closely at societies undergoing radical change. Barthes may have thought it appropriate to focus on synchronic slices of historical moments, but these *were* nonetheless historical moments that he was getting at.

In *Elements of Semiology*, it is never quite clear how the analyst is able to critique or objectively stand apart from these ideologies—whether structuralist analysis in itself, for instance, can objectively penetrate the naturalizing effects of connotation. In an essay written just a year earlier ("The Structuralist Activity," 1963), Barthes somewhat strikingly argued that structural man *is* a real thing, but only for a specific historical moment (so structuralism is appropriate only as a particular stage in the history of method). As he put it, structural man at once helps create the idea of an abstracted system of signs, even while also revealing the functioning of that system—showing how signs do get naturalized and abstracted from history. Structural man has his place, therefore, and helps build a new language of criticism, but this is only one possible (and necessary) language of criticism, so once it has served its role, another will emerge. This too shifts the very idea of structuralism away from the universal role of the analyst indicated by Lévi-Strauss's approach. It also begins to show the ways in which Barthes looked for real material grounds for social analysis and historical critique while yet embracing what might be thought of as a more poststructuralist view that life (and therefore criticism) is made up of an open and changing plurality of views.

Empire of Signs (1968) can be read as the most poststructuralist of Barthes's books. It is of course about a real place, written during and after his trip to Japan. Numbers of anthropologists have taken it to be an accurately descriptive work on Japan. But Barthes also defined it as a fantasy about a system of signs *he* called Japan. In many ways, this system of signs is a vision of poststructuralism. Where elsewhere Barthes had said that difference arises out of distance from a center (or a general equivalent that gives central order to things), in this case he says that there is no center at all; Japan is therefore made up of empty signs. The analysis or interpretation of these signs is thus necessarily more uncertain.

This is a radicalization of Barthes's turn away from the idea of an author. Where at other points Barthes was more interested in the ways in which cultural systems ideologically imprisoned specific meanings, here his emphasis turned to the ways in which one might imagine a creative and productive relation to all signs, without being tied to prior certainties.

This might be called poststructuralism, but it is the type that sees signs as almost infinitely polysemic and open to new possibilities (signs as positively "disseminating" meaning rather than relationally pulling themselves apart). This, of course, would return agency to the idea of structural meaning in a strong way (presumably, everybody could find their own "Japan"). It is also a poststructuralism that anthropology never fully embraced.

Barthes's "empty signs" are not, however, postmodernist. For him, Japan may be composed of empty signs, but these signs nonetheless are real and there is still a real place that Barthes was reacting to.

Rather than arguing for a sign that had lost its referent, or lost its real (he has been read this way, too), Barthes instead was attempting to return to a kind of materiality of the sign. No longer interested in the meaning behind signs or objects, he was by this time more focused on objectness. In Japan, he found not just different meanings for objects but a different kind of object—what he called the "Japanese thing." The Japanese "object" was different because of context (e.g., the flexible space of a Japanese house), but this also meant that the very materiality of a "Japanese thing" was more open-ended and flexible. In these latter considerations, Barthes might be located with more recent trends toward radical empiricism, and the interest in emergent singularities that have been invoked by theorists as diverse as Gilles Deleuze and Alain Badiou.

On the one hand, then, Japan is a real site of difference for Barthes in more typically anthropological ways. It is also utopic. Barthes truly found a different kind of cultural language there, but he was also creating a polemic; Japan embodied the ideal opposition to the fixed meanings of Western bourgeois culture (it is almost as if Barthes was setting up two fundamentally different poles of culture and sign in general). Difference, for Barthes, thus emerges in part out of real, material, ethnographic contact with different languages, and different worlds, but also in part out of an oppositional relation.

Arguably, Barthes's most clearly articulated analyses, with greatest ongoing importance for anthropology, are already articulated in the brief essays on mythology written during the 1950s (compiled as *Mythologies*, 1957). A case for the openness of the sign is already made here, and for an interest in signs and meanings more generally, but Barthes clearly and consistently also desires to get back to the surface of social materiality. The images Barthes gives us in *Mythologies* are fragments, both in the sense of material positivities, material embodiments of mass cultural life—a plastic toy, for example, or a popular wrestler—and as fragments that (as with Benjamin) hold and reveal a whole world of relations. As he uncovers the historical specificity of these, he shows mythology to be in this case a fully modern construct (it is a mythology of mid-20th-century modernity). And myths are ideologies in the fundamental sense of laying out the structures by which we pursue our lives—somewhat like Geertz's idea of culture as a story we tell ourselves about ourselves, but closer to

Althusser's vision of ideology as the real, practical "imaginary" relation we have to the world. Modern myths are thus both the means by which our culture "captures" us into a determined, closed set of meanings and the material site of critique and change.

Contribution to Anthropology

As much as any writer of his time, Barthes in many ways laid out the groundwork for an anthropology of modern life. At a time when mass culture was concretizing itself as a new order of culture more generally, Barthes provided the means by which to analyze the objects—neither just visual nor just linguistic—that animate mass culture and the large-scale societies of which mass culture is a part. Even in his more text-based studies, Barthes remained a sociological thinker, and yet he never formalized his views into the kind of dogmatic approach that often came to define the field of cultural studies. These traits may allow for the ongoing influence of Barthes within the social sciences, as mass culture continues to evolve into new forms.

Thomas Looser

See also Althusser, Louis; Benjamin, Walter; Deleuze, Gilles, and Félix Guattari; Foucault, Michel; Lacan, Jacques; Lévi-Strauss, Claude; Saussure, Ferdinand de; Semiotics; Structuralism

Further Readings

Barthes, R. (1967). *Elements of semiology* (A. Lavers & C. Smith, Trans.). London, UK: Jonathan Cape. (Original work published 1964)

———. (1967). *Writing degree zero* (A. Lavers & C. Smith, Trans.). London, UK: Jonathan Cape.

———. (1972). *Mythologies* (A. Lavers, Trans.). New York, NY: Hill & Wang. (Original work published 1957)

———. (1975). *S/Z* (R. Miller, Trans.). New York, NY: Hill & Wang.

———. (1977). *Image music text* (S. Heath, Trans.). New York, NY: Hill & Wang.

———. (1982). *Empire of signs* (R. Howard, Trans.). New York, NY: Hill & Wang. (Original work published 1968)

———. (1986). *Grain of the voice* (L. Coverdale, Trans.). New York, NY: Hill & Wang.

Knight, D. (Ed.). (2000). *Critical essays on Roland Barthes.* New York, NY: G. K. Hall.

BASTIAN, ADOLF

Philipp Wilhelm Adolf Bastian (1826–1905) was a lifelong world traveler, undertaking a total of nine voyages throughout the world. In the 1860s, Bastian single-handedly founded German anthropology as an academic discipline. He held the first professorship in ethnology and founded a professional organization and a publication venue, both of which still exist today. Additionally, he established the Royal Ethnological Museum in Berlin, gathering on his own most of its collection during his voyages. In light of this, Bastian founded ethnology on the basis of the analysis of empirical material as a key to understanding social thoughts and human cultures. His analyses of these were built around his ideas about the psychic unity of humankind.

Life

Bastian was born in Bremen, Germany, on June 26, 1826. He was the second oldest of nine children of Friedericke Augusta Christine Krafft and Hermann Theodor Bastian, who had inherited the trading ship company J. W. Bastian & Sons from his father. Adolf Bastian was the only one of his siblings who received higher education, preparing him for his academic career. First Bastian graduated in 1845 from the School of Scholars (Gelehrten Schule), where he studied Latin, Greek, Hebrew, French, and English. Then, he received his first academic training in law at the University of Heidelberg. From 1847 on, he studied natural sciences and medicine at the universities of Berlin, Jena, Würzburg, and Prague, completing in 1850 his studies in Würzburg with a state examination and a doctorate in medicine.

In the same year, Bastian made his first world voyage, serving as a ship's physician. Using the contacts of his father's trading company, he first went to the Americas and South Asia. From there he continued his voyage to the South Seas, Australia, and around Africa. The 8 years of his first voyage initiated Bastian's lifelong passion for other cultures, determining his plans to pursue a career in ethnology. His first major publication, *Der Mensch in der Geschichte: Zur Begründung einer Psychologischen Weltanschauung* (The Human in History: The Foundation of a Psychological World View, 1860), gave a comprehensive theoretical account synthesizing the major insights gained on his first voyage. This book was the first anthropological account based on a thorough description of different cultures and witnessed through firsthand observations, establishing Bastian as an astute observer. Between 1861 and 1865, he made his second voyage to South and East Asia, where he engaged in the study of Buddhism. Subsequently, he returned to Bremen by crossing through Mongolia and Siberia. This voyage laid the foundation for the five volumes of *Die Völker des Östlichen Asiens: Studien und Reisen* (The People of East Asia: Studies and Voyages, 1866–1871).

After moving to Berlin in 1867, Bastian obtained his habilitation (an advanced academic degree) from the Friedrich-Wilhelm University with a thesis on history and geography, which qualified him for a tenured position in ethnology, to which he was appointed in 1868. At that time, he became president of the Gesellschaft für Erdkunde (Geographical Society). One year later, Bastian established with Rudolph Virchow the Berliner Gesellschaft für Anthropologie, Ethnologie und Urgeschichte (Berlin Society for Anthropology, Ethnology, and Prehistory) and cofounded the *Zeitschrift für Ethnologie* (Journal of Ethnology) as its publication organ. At that time, Bastian also became assistant to the director of the ethnological department of the Royal Museum in Berlin. From June to December 1873, he made his third voyage, which took him to the Loango coast (today, the Republic of the Congo). During his fourth voyage, to South and Central America, Bastian acquired large archaeological collections and excavated mummies at Ancón in Peru. This voyage provided the foundation for his major book *Die Culturländer des Alten America* (The Cultural Lands of Ancient America, 1879). In 1876, he was appointed director of the ethnological and prehistorical collection of the Royal Museum of Berlin, and 2 years later, he became executive board member of the Deutsche Afrikanische Gesellschaft (German African Society). On his fifth voyage, between 1878 and 1880, Bastian went to Persia, India, Indonesia, Australia, and Oceania and continued his travels with a trip to North and Central America.

Bastian's voyages provided him with the experiences of different cultures that laid the groundwork of his theoretical approach to ethnology, a field of research focusing on cross-cultural comparison

for the pursuit of general knowledge. In 1881, Bastian published his most important work, *Der Völkergedanke im Aufbau Einer Wissenschaft vom Menschen und seine Begründung auf Ethnologischen Sammlungen* (The Folk Ideas in Building a Science of Man and Their Grounding in Ethnological Collections). In 1886, he became the general director of the Königliches Museum für Völkerkunde (Royal Ethnological Museum). From 1889 to 1891, Bastian conducted his sixth voyage, which took him to Russia, Asia Minor, Egypt, and East Africa. From there he departed to India, Australia, and Oceania.

After his 70th birthday, Bastian concentrated on the study of Buddhism and organized his subsequent voyages accordingly. His seventh voyage from 1896 to 1898 took him to Java, Bali, and Lombok and his eighth voyage from 1901 to 1903, to India and Ceylon. At the age of 77, he made his ninth and last voyage, which took him to the West Indies to investigate a cave on a prehistoric site in Jamaica while pursuing further travels to Venezuela and Trinidad. On February 3, 1905, Bastian died after a brief illness in Port of Spain, Trinidad, and was buried there; his remains were later transferred back to Berlin to the graveyard in Berlin-Schöneberg.

Work

Bastian's work evolved around many integrally related topics and has many facets. The following account focuses on his program of ethnology as a science based on inductive methods, his concept of the psychic unity of humankind and his notions of elementary and folk ideas, his cross-cultural comparison of ethnographic collections, and his concepts of geographic regions and provinces.

Ethnology as a Science and the Method of Inductive Reasoning

Bastian founded ethnology as a natural science. Presuming positivism as a scientific paradigm, he expected to derive universal scientific laws from his collections of ethnographic material. To ensure the empirical foundation of ethnology as a science, Bastian used quantitative methods to establish what he called a thought statistic (*Gedankenstatistik*). This thought statistic could be launched by collecting cultural artifacts, including myths and folktales, as expressions of social thoughts. He saw the purpose of ethnology primarily grounded in the collection of ethnographic data and aimed at cross-cultural comparison. To achieve this, he used what he conceived as a method of "logical arithmetic," which served as a mathematical model of inductive reasoning.

In his academic program, he distinguished between anthropology, ethnology, and ethnography. He confined anthropology to the study of the biological and physical foundation of humankind, and he defined ethnology as the study of human culture and society. In contrast to ethnology, ethnography is defined as the descriptive and most detailed account of a single culture. In so doing, Bastian primarily stressed the methodological independence of ethnology as an academic discipline, considering ethnography as an integral part of it. The paradigmatic method employed in ethnology was psychology, which allowed him to study the social thoughts (Gesellschaftsgedanken) of different ethnic groups from their point of view. Bastian applied psychological methods to the study of cultures to prove what he called the psychic unity of humankind.

Psychic Unity of Mankind and the Distinction Between Elementary Idea and Folk Idea

For Bastian, ethnology is first and foremost the study of the social thoughts of ethnic groups as they manifest in folk traditions. Bastian urged that these social thoughts be studied with respect to the total environment of an ethnic group, leading to the comprehension of the local psychic perspective. Within this theoretical framework, Bastian studied humans as social beings and conceived all kinds of cultural phenomena, material or immaterial, as collective ideas that can be studied as cultural forms, being manifestations of the psychic unity of humankind (psychische einheit der menschheit). Bastian viewed all cultural phenomena therefore as products of the human mind, which is socially shaped by collectively shared thoughts. His theory of psychic unity proposed that the same dispositions can be found in all humans across cultures. That is to say, for Bastian, all humans have the same capabilities and dispositions in adapting to their respective environments. By employing inductive methods, he searched for universal features of humankind that could be found in all cultures, despite the variations and differences of cultures.

Bastian divided human social thought into two categories: (1) elementary ideas and (2) folk ideas.

Elementary ideas (Elementargedanken) are common to all cultures, whereas folk ideas (Völkergedanken) are the manifestations of elementary ideas in individual cultures. For example, according to Bastian, the incest taboo is an elementary idea found in all cultures. However, the particular form it takes, which may depend on specific social rules, is a folk idea. Although all societies attempt to classify social relations, which is an elementary idea, the ways in which age, gender, and other roles are classified are particular to individual cultures and are therefore folk ideas. Although Bastian aimed to establish his notion of the psychic unity of humankind as based on these elementary ideas, he argued that folk ideas emerge out of the elementary ideas due to geographic and historic factors like climate, disasters, cultural contacts, or wars, to which people adapt differently in different geographical regions and periods of time.

Ethnographic Data Collections and Cross-Cultural Comparison

Bastian was the first anthropologist to leave his armchair with the purpose of collecting data firsthand and establishing a scientific program on the basis of ethnographic fieldwork. He saw a long-term study of a single ethnic community that produced a written ethnography as desirable, but he made no such studies. Driven by the fear that cultures would vanish instantly after contact, Bastian collected as much data as possible, practicing so-called salvage ethnography with the aim of assembling a comprehensive inventory of social thoughts. Bastian's collections were compendious since he hoped not only to establish a universal archive of humanity, including all forms of folk ideas, but also to discover universal laws to determine the elementary ideas. Bastian hoped to demonstrate the psychic unity of humankind by finding parallels in the viewpoints of the natives of many different places.

The theory of the psychic unity of humankind was based on the massive collection of ethnographic material. As the ethnographic museum collection rapidly increased with each voyage, Bastian needed to systematize and classify it. Applying methods of inductive reasoning, the cultural artifacts were classified into ethnological types on the basis of cross-cultural comparison and conceived as elementary ideas. Avoiding the preexisting evolutionary classification systems, he took the geographic region as the foundational unit to serve as a criterion for his categorization of ethnographic material.

Theory of Geographic Regions and Provinces

Although Bastian chiefly intended to show the psychic unity of humankind, he was also interested in explaining the reasons for the differences among cultures and considered history and geography for these explanations. For this purpose, he gave priority to the investigation of cultural techniques leading to survival and adaptation in different environments. The determination of these factors was foundational for Bastian's theory of geographical regions and cultural evolution, which helped explain the differences in languages and ideologies across cultures. In this sense, Bastian drafted one of the first maps of geographical regions and provinces.

Bastian claimed that the evolution of cultures within a geographic region was based on climate, environment, and history. This included the study of local developments and the historical processes unique to each geographic region prior to European contact. He argued that geographic regions were relatively independent of one another. Although Bastian assumed interethnic contact zones, he emphasized independent development and stressed that historical processes play a more important role in the formation of geographic regions than does contact with other cultures. To further refine his ideas, Bastian introduced the notion of the geographic province to delineate cultural circles, units that were bigger than geographic regions and allowed him to account for the possible contact zones through exchange, trade, and migration.

Contribution to Anthropology

Despite the often incomprehensible style of his later writings, Bastian gained worldwide recognition through his vast collections and extensive publications (about 10,000 total pages). His ethnographic accounts were frequently quoted by Victorian anthropologists like Edward B. Tylor and James G. Frazer. In the later stages of his career, he fought bitterly with Ernst Haeckel about evolution and with Friedrich Ratzel about the theoretical foundations of diffusion and acculturation. Among his students were Karl von der Steinen, Albert Grünwedel, and Felix von Luschan; the last was the teacher of Fritz Graebner and Leo Frobenius. Bastian had a considerable impact on the South American research of Karl Theodor Preuss and Paul Ehrenreich. Moreover, his influence on Franz Boas's notion of historical particularism was substantial and sustainable; Boas received his training mainly under the guidance of Bastian, working closely with him at the Royal Ethnological Museum. Bastian's approach to the fields of study, including physical anthropology, archaeology, and prehistory, as well as ethnology and ethnography, with a recognition of the importance of language, prefigured Boas's idea of the four-field approach in the foundation of American anthropology.

Jens Kreinath

See also Boas, Franz; Frazer, James G.; Historical Particularism; Tylor, Edward Burnett

Further Readings

Bastian, A. (1860). *Der mensch in der geschichte: Zur begründung einer psychologischen weltanschauung* [The human in history: The foundation of a psychological world view] (3 vols.). Leipzig, Germany: Verlag von Otto Wigand.

———. (1871). *Beiträge zur ethnologie* [Contributions to ethnology]. Berlin, Germany: Wiegandt und Hempel.

———. (1881). *Der völkergedanke im aufbau einer wissenschaft vom menschen und seine begründung auf ethnologischen sammlungen* [The folk ideas in building a science of man and their grounding in ethnological collections]. Berlin, Germany: Verlag von Ferdinand Dümmler.

———. (1884). *Allgemeine grundzüge der ethnologie: Prolegomena zur begründung einer naturwissenschaftlichen psychologie auf dem material des völkergedankens* [General principles of ethnology: Prolegomena to the foundation of a scientific psychology on the material of folk ideas]. Berlin, Germany: D. Reimer.

Fischer, M., Bolz, P., & Kamel, S. (2007). *Adolf Bastian and his universal archive of humanity: The origins of German anthropology.* New York, NY: G. Olms.

Köpping, K.-P. (1983). *Adolf Bastian and the psychic unity of mankind: The foundations of anthropology in nineteenth century Germany.* New York, NY: University of Queensland Press.

Preuss, K. T. (1926). Adolf Bastian und die heutige völkerkunde: Zum gedächtnis seines hunderjährigen geburtstages am 26 Juni 1926 [Adolf Bastian and the modern ethnology: In memory of his birthday on June 26, 1926]. *Baessler-Archiv, 10,* 2–15.

Tylor, E. B. (1905). Professor Adolf Bastian: Born June 26, 1826; died February 3, 1905. *Man, 5,* 138–143.

BATAILLE, GEORGES

Georges Bataille (1897–1962) was an essayist and novelist who had an eclectic outlook and wrote on different subject areas, including art history, theology, anthropology, and economics. He is regarded as a philosopher of transgression who explored the consequences of thinking about the extreme. He has exerted an influence on poststructuralist thinking, including the work of Jacques Derrida, Michel Foucault, Jean Baudrillard, Roland Barthes, and Julia Kristeva, and on avant-garde publications such as *Tel Quel.*

Born in Billom, Puy-de-Dôme, to secular parents, Bataille initially wanted to be a priest and converted to Catholicism in 1914, which he later renounced in 1920. In 1918, he began training at the École des Chartes in Paris to become a medievalist librarian. In 1922, he gained a position at the Bibliothèque Nationale in Paris, where he worked until he resigned because of ill health (tuberculosis) in 1942. Seven years later, he resumed work as a librarian at Carpentras (1949–1951) and Orleans (1951–1961).

It is difficult to categorize Bataille's writings because he was interested in different areas of thought and worked across disciplines. However, his writings revealed certain preoccupations that were central to his thought. These included the concepts of the sacred and transgression. He was interested in exploring the limits and boundaries of social, anthropological, and economic systems, thereby moving beyond order, normalcy, and the profane into the exuberance of the sacred and the sovereign. Bataille proposed that it was in extreme states beyond the limit that opposites meet and that life opens up onto an experience of death and nothingness. This was explored in different works, such as the post-Marxist *The Accursed Share* (1949), which discusses the economics of exuberance, and *Eroticism* (1957), which examines the centrality of death in human experience.

In the formation of his thinking, Bataille was influenced by various philosophers, including Hegel, Nietzsche, and Sade. He attended Alexander Kojève's seminars on Hegel's philosophy (from 1932 to 1933); wrote a tribute to Nietzsche in the form of his book *On Nietzsche* (1945) and a volume of Nietzschean maxims, *Mémorandum* (1945); and identified with the Marquis de Sade's interpretations of eroticism, which exceeded the boundaries of normalcy, strove toward a sense of freedom that was unrestrained by law and morality, and emphasized the importance of violence, criminality, and transgression in their formulation. Another key influence was Marcel Mauss's notion of *The Gift* (1923), which examined the potlatch festival—which involved the ritual of gift giving that focused on expenditure and exchange—and formed the basis of Bataille's unconventional theory of economics, which emphasized excess over acquisition.

Bataille was also the pseudonymous author of erotic novels, including *Story of the Eye* (1928) and *Madame Edwarda* (1941), which are regarded as fictional studies of transgression. The inclusion of nonfictional elements in his novels, namely the preface and critical essays in *Story of the Eye* and the preface in *Madame Edwarda,* connects these projects to his central preoccupation with *jouissance* (which means a bliss without limits) and explores modes of communication that exceed language.

In addition to his writings, Bataille also remained active in a host of different political organizations, especially in the lead-up to the Second World War. He was associated in 1924 with the surrealists, together with figures such as Michel Leiris, but was later excluded from the International Surrealist Exhibition by André Breton, who (in his *Second Manifesto of Surrealism*) denounced him as excremental because of his preoccupation with the ignoble. He was the de facto editor of *Documents,* an art and ethnographic maverick journal that explored non-Western culture and that collapsed the distinction between high and low culture. The journal, which ran for 15 issues from 1929 until 1931, espoused the Bataillean notion of base materialism, which was a radical materialism that interrogated the bodily and formless origin of organic forms, thus undercutting the idealism of formalistic surrealism and the purity of modernism. Bataille was particularly drawn to aspects of the body that were commonly hidden from the public gaze, such as orifices, and discussed how these were channels to sacred expression.

In the 1930s, Bataille advocated an anti-Stalinist Marxism, which he expressed in his contributions to various journals, such as *La Critique Sociale*. In 1935, he founded the political group Contre-Attaque, which presented an antifascist stance to the Popular Front and united the intellectual community. The group was short-lived and dissolved in 1936. That year, Bataille established *Acéphale*, a review and a secret society that aimed to exercise the workings of the sacred through ritual transgression. This was followed by the formation of the College of Sociology, which he cofounded with Michel Leiris and Roger Caillois. The group, which brought together intellectuals such as Alexandre Kojève and Jean Wahl, explored their views on the Durkheimian sacred, the role of violence, and the formation of community. With the advent of the war, Bataille's thinking shifted from the outer manifestations of the sacred in everyday life to a more internalized experience of the sacred in *Inner Experience* (1943). In 1946, Bataille founded the anti-existentialist journal *Critique*.

During his lifetime, Bataille was a contradictory figure whose public persona as a librarian contrasted with his virulent and obsessive mental states. Since his death, he has enjoyed a revival in critical and cultural theory because of the 12-volume publication of his *Oeuvres Complètes* (Complete Works, 1971–1988) and translations of his works into English. Furthermore, the interdisciplinary nature of his work lends itself to art criticism, sociology, cultural studies, and theology and has established him as a key thinker of the 20th century.

Rina Arya

See also Barthes, Roland; Baudrillard, Jean; Derrida, Jacques; Foucault, Michel; Hegel, Georg W. F.; Mauss, Marcel

Further Readings

Botting, F., & Wilson, S. (1997). *The Bataille reader*. Oxford, UK: Blackwell.

———. (1998). *Bataille: A critical reader*. Oxford, UK: Blackwell, 1998.

Surya, M. (2002). *Georges Bataille: An intellectual biography* (K. Fijalkowski & M. Richardson, Trans.). London, UK: Verso Books.

BATESON, GREGORY

Gregory Bateson (1904–1980) was a multifaceted scholar who embraced fields as diverse as anthropology, linguistics, semiotics, systems theory, and cybernetics. He was an original thinker whose work influenced the growing environmental movement of his day, contributed to the emergence of new fields of investigation, and continues to exert an influence in a variety of disciplines, including ecological and environmental anthropology.

Life and Work

Bateson was born on May 9, 1904, in Cambridgeshire, England, as the third son of Beatrice Durham and the distinguished geneticist William Bateson. Bateson studied biology with a focus on zoology and natural history at St. John's College at Cambridge. After completing his BA in 1925, he visited the Galapagos Islands. Bateson began studying anthropology at Cambridge after being introduced to Alfred Haddon in 1926. In January 1927, he went for ethnographic fieldwork to New Guinea. Due to problems of communicating and interacting with the local people, Bateson left the field after a year. He returned to Australia and taught Pacific languages for a semester at the University of Sydney under Alfred R. Radcliffe-Brown. In February 1929, Bateson became interested in the Iatmul on a trip to the Sepik River in New Guinea. He conducted a year of fieldwork there with Haddon and Radcliffe-Brown as advisors.

In 1931, Bateson became a fellow of St. John's College, where he received funding for his ongoing research on the Iatmul. On his return to New Guinea, he met Reo F. Fortune and Margaret Mead, who were conducting fieldwork on a tribe on Manus Island. Bateson's extended conversations with them influenced his theoretical approach and subsequent analysis of his ethnographic data; even though he was supervised by Radcliffe-Brown and Malinowski, his thesis became a methodological criticism of functionalist theory. In January 1936, Bateson completed his study *Naven*. In the same year, Bateson and Mead married and started conducting their collaborative fieldwork in Bali. During the first 2 months, they coproduced the film *Trance and Dance in Bali,* before they moved to Bajoeng Gede, where they carried out extensive fieldwork on child-rearing practices, using film and photography as their primary research tools. As the world turned toward war in 1938, Bateson and Mead left Bali to return to New Guinea. After another year, they left for New York, with Mead already pregnant with their first and only daughter, Mary Catherine Bateson. During the subsequent years, Bateson continued working with Mead on previously collected Bali material.

In the 1940s, Bateson developed an interest in the study of system theory and cybernetics after being invited by Robert Wiener to attend the conferences of the Josiah Macy Jr. Foundation. In collaboration with Wiener and Mead, Bateson elaborated on the application of cybernetics to the social and behavioral sciences. At this time, Bateson was also involved in founding the Institute of Cultural Studies, which facilitated anthropological research on national character, including on Germany and Japan. In this context, Bateson carried out research on the Nazi propaganda film *Hitlerjunge Quex* (Hitler Youth Quex). In 1943, he started working for the Office of Strategic Services and spent about 20 months in Ceylon, India, and China; he also investigated the impact of a Japanese radio station on Burma and Thailand.

In the fall of 1947 and spring of 1948, Bateson taught first at the New School of Social Research in New York and then at Harvard University. In late 1949, after being divorced from Mead, Bateson moved to Palo Alto, California. He taught medical anthropology on a 2-year appointment at the Langley Porter Neuropsychiatric Clinic in San Francisco. This allowed him to study psychiatric communication in an ethnographic context by using mathematical theories of communication and language. In 1950, Bateson accepted a visiting professorship in anthropology at Stanford University, with main institutional ties to the Veterans Administration Hospital. During that time, he started his communication research on alcoholism and schizophrenic behavior with residents of the hospital.

In 1952, Bateson extended his research interests to the play behavior of otters at the Fleischhacker Zoo in San Francisco. Subsequently, he received a grant from the Rockefeller Foundation on the Paradoxes of Abstraction in Communication, which became a major point of departure for his subsequent

contribution to anthropological theory. He proposed a theory of play that addresses the different levels of abstraction involved in human and animal communication. In 1956, Bateson started filming forms of nonverbal communication, with a focus on schizophrenic behavior among children. Examining schizophrenia as a learned behavior in processes of family communication, Bateson focused on the principles of family organization, using game theories as his major paradigm. Supported by numerous grants, he continued to study animal behavior in the hope of integrating the patterns of dolphin ethology into the study of patterns in human social interaction.

Bateson elaborated on the idea of an "ecology of mind," reflecting his doubts about the reductionisms of the natural sciences while advocating a holistic and integrative approach. In 1968, he organized a conference of the Wenner-Gren Foundation on the Effects of Conscious Purpose on Human Adaptation. In 1970, he also gave the honorary Alfred Korzybski memorial lecture in New York, titled "Form, Substance, and Difference," where he proposed a new scientific paradigm: the science of metacommunication. Stimulated by its success, Bateson put together an anthology of his lifework, titled *Steps to an Ecology of Mind.* With its publication in 1972, Bateson received worldwide recognition and exerted a wider impact on the environmental movements of his time.

In 1973, Bateson became affiliated with Kresge College at the University of California, Santa Cruz. There he held a lectureship to explore innovative research with a focus on human relational approaches to ecology. During this time, the journal *CoEvolution* was founded to honor his work. In 1975, he revisited his field study on Balinese trance for a special issue of *Ethos* in honor of Mead's work, whom he met with in March 1976 to continue their conversation on visual methods in cultural anthropology. During that time, Bateson became a fellow of the American Academy of Sciences and was appointed to the Board of Regents of the University of California. In his subsequent book, *Mind and Nature: A Necessary Unity* (1979), Bateson aimed to elaborate his ideas on the coevolution of natural and cultural processes. Mary Catherine Bateson helped him finalize the manuscript after he was diagnosed with cancer. Bateson died on July 4, 1980, at the age of 76, at the guesthouse of the Zen Center in San Francisco.

Work

The work of Bateson is highly original, although the thematic fields it addresses may appear unrelated. His impact on anthropological theory is not readily identifiable because his most original ideas were often articulated in abstract terms and published in places where they could not immediately be recognized as part of the anthropological endeavor. Bateson's legacy lies in the formation of new analytical concepts and theoretical approaches. While his early work in New Guinea was dedicated to the study of the dynamics of cultural change, which he called schismogenesis, his subsequent work in Bali focused on nonverbal communication, leading him to theorize about play, framing, and forms of metacommunication. His idea of the ecology of mind was elaborated on the application of cybernetics to the study of social systems and expanded on related notions of feedback processes and the double bind, a situation in which a person cannot succeed or win no matter what he or she does.

Schismogenesis and the Dynamics of Cultural Change

In his first and only ethnographic study, *Naven*, Bateson conceptualized individual behavior and social structure in Iatmul culture as a dynamic system based on interdependent and mutually reinforcing relationships. Bateson rejected reductionism and avoided deducing individual behavior from social structure or inducing social structure from individual behavior. He conceived both individual behavior and social structure as embedded in mutual relationships and viewed social interactions as leading toward a provisional equilibrium of social relationships that always has the potential for immediate change. Bateson conceptualized the dynamics in social relations in terms of *schismogenesis*, the process of differentiation in social groups resulting from continuous interactions. Bateson conceived the formation of social structure and the configuration of social relations as emerging from social interactions.

Bateson understood schismogenesis as a conceptual scheme for analyzing cultural change, suggesting that anthropologists should not limit the study of cultural change to effects that are determined by external factors. He argued that the analysis of change within a single culture required the examination of cases of contact between different groups within the culture and that age, sex, social status, and kinship were key markers of different group membership. He considered the possible resolution of disturbances resulting from the interaction of different groups as a merely temporary equilibrium in an ongoing chain of reactions to reactions. In this way, he understood social structure as always having an inherently temporal dimension.

Bateson proposed that the outcome of disturbances in social relations was either complementary or symmetrical schismogenesis, the former resulting in unequal and the latter resulting in equal relationships of the social groups involved. In the complementary form of schismogenesis, two groups mutually provoke and reinforce reactions with each other. The inequalities in gender relations, parent-children relations, or class struggle are examples of mutually reinforcing patterns of dominant-submissive behavior. In the symmetrical form of schismogenesis, the interaction of the groups provokes similar forms of behavior. Some examples are arms races, public contests, or sporting events. Both forms of schismogenesis lead to a temporary balance through the subordination or competition of the groups involved, but they can also lead to conflict, fissures, and sometimes disastrous outcomes.

Framing, Play, and Metacommunication

Based on his research on nonverbal communication in child-rearing practices and his visual material on rituals of spirit possession in Bali, Bateson proposed a systematic approach to the study of personality and culture. In this context, he also inquired into the formation of moral behavior and national ethos by taking theories of frustration and aggression as a reference point for studying the cultural formation of ethos. Subsequently, he utilized these theoretical insights to develop his theory of framing, play, and metacommunication. In his 1955 article "A Theory of Play and Fantasy," he introduced the notion of framing as a form of metacommunication and addressed "framing" as a marker in social interaction that nonverbally changes the meaning and context of social interaction, as exemplified in the distinction between play and nonplay. The messages communicated within the play frame are metacommunicative and have a different meaning from those communicated outside the frame.

Bateson theorized that metacommunication was about social relations. Metacommunicative statements establish the relationship between interacting persons. The main feature with which Bateson distinguished communication from meta-communication was the difference between sign and signal that, he proposed, was recognizable in non-verbal communication. While Bateson conceived signs as unintentional and involuntary and therefore indexical (indicating some state of affairs), he defined signals as intentionally and voluntarily used and therefore conventional. The difference between the sign and the signal can be exemplified by the distinction between a twitch of an eyelid and a wink, the former being unintentional, while the latter may carry a clear message. This difference between sign and signal, according to Bateson, coincided with the evolution of human communication. Working on the hypothesis that metacommunication is integral to the growth of the human species prior to language, Bateson studied primate behavior at San Francisco's Fleishhacker Zoo in 1952. This research provided him with evidence that the predominant ways in which primates recognize the difference between signs and signals is play. Bateson took this ability to make such distinctions as a precondition for the differentiation of levels of abstraction in human communication.

Bateson conceived of play as a metacommunicative phenomenon of its own kind, bringing to the fore categorically different levels of abstraction established through the play frame. He argued that play involves forms of metacommunication through which organisms differentiate between play and nonplay. The distinction between sign and signal in metacommunication is exemplified by different types of messages transmitted in play behavior: (1) messages used as signs to express moods, (2) messages used as signals to simulate moods, and (3) messages used to distinguish between the first two types of message. For Bateson, the metacommunicative message, like "This is play," is of the last type, allowing the distinction between expression (i.e., the twitch or bite as a sign) and simulation (i.e., the wink or play-ful nip as a signal). These different messages are pertinent to play between, for example, children who pretend to act as parents or dogs who pretend to fight. The ability to perceive the difference between play and nonplay leads to higher levels of abstraction consisting of the metacommunicative message "This is play." Bateson perceived play as a form of learning that leads to higher levels of abstraction.

Using threat, theatrical behavior, and deceit as examples of metacommunication, Bateson argued that play implies a peculiar form of metacommunication. In framing, the metacommunicative message sets up hierarchical relationships between different levels of abstraction. Irony, teasing, or joking relationships may serve as further examples for the different frames of reference used in play behavior, where the interactive sequences of actions transmit signals that are "similar" to but "fundamentally different" from those they usually denote. Because the play frame transmits metacommunicative statements on different levels of abstraction, the respective frame creates the self-referential paradox. For Bateson, the message "This is play" is paradoxical because it is a negative statement that itself contains a negative metastatement. The metacommunicative message transmitted applies to different categorical orders depending on whether it is transmitted from inside or outside the frame. These statements are self-reflexive and context dependent as they refer back to the position from which they are made and exclude the possibility that they can transmit metacommunicative statements independent of the frame.

Cybernetics, Feedback Processes, and the Double Bind

Bateson elaborated on forms of metacommunication in relation to theories of codification and abstraction. He primarily used cybernetics and system theories to develop a theoretical model to distinguish between different forms of codification in animal and human communication. Employing mathematical information theory and cybernetics, Bateson furthered a framework that allowed him to conceptualize the self-referential paradoxes in metacommunication. Although *cybernetics*, coined after a Greek term, broadly refers to various kinds of automatic control systems, Bateson was particularly interested in its application to the social sciences and the evolution and forms of animal and human communication. He conceived of cybernetic circuits primarily as systems of communication. Such systems of communication respond to the information they receive from their environment. Bateson employed cybernetic models in the codification and transmission of information. Such information makes a difference between the real and the ideal state of affairs and transforms the system of communication by adjusting to the difference between the real and the ideal state. As a result, the process of communication between the real and the ideal leads to a temporary homeostasis, or the steady state.

Elaborating on the cybernetic insights as proposed by Wiener, Bateson analyzed systems of nonverbal communication within the framework of positive and negative feedback by applying them to situations of social interactions. Positive feedback refers to messages that communicate change, whereas negative feedback refers to messages that communicate control. In this respect, the cybernetic model stipulates the explanation of transformation in terms of serial and reciprocal cause-and-effect chains. Bateson argued that forms of metacommunication occur in organisms that are capable of establishing a higher level of abstraction by giving negative feedback to their immediate environments through means of control or self-regulation. The metacommunicative message establishes the rules that govern the subsequent behavior of the participants, and negative feedback means the enforcement of changes in social relationships.

In using his ethnographic material from New Guinea and Bali and expanding his concept of schismogenesis, Bateson further elaborated on the cybernetic model. His main contribution is his theory of the double bind as a way to explore forms of systemically distorted forms of communication and interaction. According to Bateson, the double bind can be explained in reference to misled forms of learning, namely to distinguish different levels of abstraction. Bateson defined double bind as a sequence of messages, in which the messages communicated lead to a paradox where the verbal message contradicts the nonverbally communicated message and where the one who is in a subordinate position can only lose. In his research on schizophrenia, the codification of a message is altered, and the form of learning is distorted, leading to an inability to discriminate different contextual cues, because what is said persistently contradicts what is done. In the study of alcoholism, Bateson exemplified his insights in the alcoholics' unwillingness to acknowledge the fact that they are alcoholics.

Contribution to Anthropology

Bateson's contribution to anthropology and his impact on the formation of theoretical approaches to anthropology have been significant, and his form of engagement in using system theory and cybernetics for analyzing cultural practices has proven fruitful. The most important contributions of Bateson can be seen in his theory of framing as well as his contribution to the study of play as forms of metacommunication. His studies in nonverbal communication led to the field of kinesics and proxemics, and symbolic interaction, as the studies of Ray Birdwhistell and Erving Goffman demonstrate. His considerations of play had a significant impact on the formation of ritual theories as proposed by Roy Rappaport, Don Handelman, and Michael Houseman.

Bateson had also a more direct impact on anthropological research, inspiring Clifford Geertz's system-theoretical approach to religion and culture as related to the study of Balinese rituals, and laid some theoretical groundwork for Geertz's method of thick description. Steven Feld and Deborah Tannen adopted Bateson's theory of schismogenesis for the anthropological study of ethnomusicology and sociolinguistics, and Rene Girard used Bateson's notion of the double bind in his theory of sacrifice. Bateson's use of film and photography helped facilitate the methodological enhancement of visual anthropology, and his impact can be seen in the work of Maya Deren and Jean Rouch and their participatory approach to visual anthropology. Besides that, Bateson's approach to the ecology of mind had a lasting impact on ecological and environmental anthropology that approaches ecology from system theory.

Jens Kreinath

See also Culture and Personality; Geertz, Clifford; Malinowski, Bronisław; Mead, Margaret; Radcliffe-Brown, A. R.; Rappaport, Roy; Visual Anthropology

Further Readings

Bateson, G. (1936). *Naven: A survey of the problems suggested by a composite picture of the culture of a New Guinea tribe drawn from three points of view.* Cambridge, UK: Cambridge University Press.

———. (1979). *Mind and nature: A necessary unity.* New York, NY: Dutton.

Bateson, G., & Bateson, M. C. (1987). *Angels fear: Towards an epistemology of the sacred.* New York, NY: Macmillan.

Bateson, G., & Mead, M. (1942). *Balinese character: A photographic analysis.* New York, NY: New York Academy of Sciences.

Handelman, D. (1979). Is *Naven* ludic? Paradox and the communication of identity. *Social Analysis, 1,* 177–191.

Harries-Jones, P. (1995). *A recursive vision: Ecological understanding and Gregory Bateson.* Toronto, Ontario, Canada: University of Toronto Press.

Heims, S. J. (1977). Gregory Bateson and the mathematicians: From interdisciplinary interaction to societal functions. *Journal of the History of the Behavioral Sciences, 13,* 141–158.

Houseman, M., & Severi, C. (1998). *Naven, or, the other self: A relational approach to ritual action* (Studies in the History of Religions). Leiden, Netherlands: Brill.

Kreinath, J. (2012). *Naven,* moebius strip, and random fractal dynamics: Reframing Bateson's play frame and the use of mathematical models for the study of ritual. *Journal of Ritual Studies, 26*(2), 39–64.

Levy, R. L., & Rappaport, R. R. (1982). Gregory Bateson 1904–1980. *American Anthropologist, 84*(2), 379–394.

Lipset, D. (1980). *Gregory Bateson: The legacy of a scientist.* Englewood Cliffs, NJ: Prentice Hall.

Marcus, G. E. (1985). A timely rereading of *Naven:* Gregory Bateson as oracular essayist. *Representations, 12,* 66–82.

Nuckolls, C. W. (1995). The misplaced legacy of Gregory Bateson: Toward a cultural dialectic of knowledge and desire. *Cultural Anthropology, 10*(3), 367–394.

BAUDRILLARD, JEAN

Jean Baudrillard (1929–2007), French philosopher, lapsed sociologist, critic of modernism and postmodernism, photographer, and public intellectual, was one of the founders of poststructuralism.

Baudrillard was born in the cathedral town of Reims, a major city to the northeast of Paris, in July 1929; he died on March 6, 2007, in Paris at the age of 77. In his youth, Baudrillard was interested in poetry (see *L'Ange du Stuc* [The Stucco Angel], published in 1978, a collection of his poems from the 1950s) and a science of the imaginary known as pataphysics (to which he had been introduced by one of his schoolteachers—see *Pataphysics* [2005]). Both interests influenced his subsequent writing and his philosophy throughout his adult life. However, it was his interest in German language and culture that he was to pursue in his undergraduate studies at the Sorbonne in Paris.

After graduation, Baudrillard began, in 1956, to teach German and sociology at a secondary school,

during which time he also completed, in 1966, his doctorate at the University of Paris X-Nanterre. Indeed, it was in the 1960s that Baudrillard began to meaningfully participate in French intellectual life by, among other things, writing literary reviews of fiction by Uwe Johnson, Italo Calvino, and William Styron for Jean-Paul Sartre's *Les Temps Modernes* (Modern Times) and translating from German to French, between 1956 and 1969, works by several major figures—Bertolt Brecht, Peter Weiss, Wilhelm E. Mühlmann, Karl Marx, and Friedrich Engels—on the intellectual left.

After defending his doctoral thesis in March 1966, Baudrillard taught sociology at the University of Paris X-Nanterre and was involved—alongside his mentor, the urban sociologist Henri Lefebvre—in supporting the Movement du 22 Mars at Nanterre, which sparked the events of May 1968 that erupted in Paris and across France. It was in 1968 that Baudrillard published his doctoral thesis as his first book, *The System of Objects,* a text that was followed up, over (and beyond) his lifetime, by the publication of more than 50 books, hundreds of articles, and dozens of interviews the style, content, and translation of which led him to be fêted both in France and across the world for his conceptual inventiveness and audacity.

Major Works

Overviews of Baudrillard's many writings typically discuss them in a chronological fashion, seeking to explain the evolution of his ideas over time as one narrative—most commonly by erroneously dividing his writings into two periods to describe an "early, Marxist Baudrillard" and a "later, postmodern Baudrillard." However, this is not the way to grasp the dual topology of Baudrillard's oeuvre, into which his major (and minor, for that matter) works must be located to be properly understood. In 1987, Baudrillard revealed that his corpus of writings should be understood as a "double spiral," a Möbius strip that traces not only the destruction of symbolic orders (primordial cultures) by semiotic ones (modern cultures) but also how the symbolic (ambivalence) cannot be completely erased by the signs and simulations (equivalence) that constitute modernity, precisely because the fundamental and radical form of modern cultures is ultimately still that of challenge and potlatch: the negation and sacrifice of value. Thus, while Baudrillard's many publications are all concerned with both condition (semiotic) and critique (symbolic), some of his works are predominantly concerned with theorizing the dominant semiotic order—a form of organization of opposed terms between which a dialectic can be established to create an irreversible, linear, and unidirectional system—while others are focused on the symbolic order—an alternative form of organization based on a circular form, a circuit, and reversibility, which has no separate terms and therefore calls into question the idea of value and the supposed dialectic that underpins all market societies.

The semiotic spiral—the mediatization and virtualization of modern capitalist societies—is explained across Baudrillard's oeuvre as the "code of social standing" in *The System of Objects* (1968); as the "code" in *The Consumer Society* (1970); as "sign value" in *For a Critique of the Political Economy of the Sign* (1972); as the "structural law of value" in *Symbolic Exchange and Death* (1976); as "hyperreality" in *Simulacra and Simulation* (1981); as the "vanishing point" in his experiential account of *America* (1986); as the "nonevent" and the "end of history" in *The Gulf War Did Not Take Place* (1991) and *The Illusion of the End and Events on Strike* (1992), respectively; as *The Perfect Crime* (1995); as "cloning" in *The Vital Illusion* (2000); as "virtual reality" in *Screened Out* (2000); and as "integral reality" in *The Intelligence of Evil or the Lucidity Pact* (2004) and *Why Hasn't Everything Already Disappeared?* (2007). In contrast, the symbolic spiral as critique and as a challenge to the semiotic order is similarly theorized across his works, predominantly as "symbolic exchange" in *Symbolic Exchange and Death* (1976); as *Seduction* (1979); as the "fatal" and "reversibility" in *Fatal Strategies* (1983); as "doubling" in *Suite Vénitienne/Please Follow Me* (1983); as *Impossible Exchange* (1999); as the "hostage" beyond the normal rules of exchange in *The Gulf War Did Not Take Place* (1991); and as "terrorism" in *The Spirit of Terrorism and Requiem for The Twin Towers* (2002). Thus, the overall shape of Baudrillard's oeuvre as a "double spiral" needs to be understood not only as a reaction to the failures of May 1968—and Baudrillard's subsequent rejection of Marxism (see *The Mirror of Production*, 1975) as no more than a simulacrum of capitalism—but

also as the eclipse of critical theory and sociology by fatal theory and anthropology as the basis for truly radical anticapitalist thought.

Baudrillard and Anthropology

The influence of anthropological theory and the study of indigenous "primitive" societies on Baudrillard's thought is particularly marked with regard to his conceptualization of symbolic exchange (1976) as a critique against the "perfection" of modern capitalism as hyperreal, as an integral or absolute reality where all illusion—evil, negativity, death, and so on—has been expurgated in the perfect crime of transforming the world into a simulacrum of limitless exchange.

Symbolic exchange as anthropology understands it (compare the work of the psychoanalyst Jacques Lacan on the "symbolic") is fundamental to Baudrillard's philosophy and oeuvre, serving as the basis for his critique of the disappearance of illusion in capitalist societies and cultures, which, through mass consumerism and the transition of the commodity into the commodity-sign, have been transformed into totalizing hyperrealities. Symbolic exchange was first explicitly presented as exterior to the commodity-sign or "code" in Baudrillard's third book, *For a Critique of the Political Economy of the Sign* (1972), before subsequently becoming the central theme and theorization of his fifth book—widely regarded as his *chef d'oeuvre*—just a few years later, *Symbolic Exchange and Death* (1976).

Baudrillard's understanding of the practice of symbolic exchange is shaped by his reading of anthropological studies on the gift and gift exchange in primordial—so-called primitive—societies, where gift exchange is understood to be central to social life. Specifically, Baudrillard's usage of symbolic exchange draws on anthropological theory—especially the work of Émile Durkheim, Marcel Mauss, Georges Bataille, and Bronisław Malinowski—and its studies of the circulation of gifts and countergifts in tribal societies—the potlatch and the Kula—as sumptuary and noneconomic, and thus beyond the use, exchange, and sign values of the commodity-sign that governs exchange in modern societies. Indeed, it is clear that Baudrillard's critique of contemporary societies and cultures is founded on abandoning sociology, which he considers, like Marxism, to be trapped in the "real" (the semiotic order)—see *In the Shadow of the Silent Majorities or the End of the Social* (1978)—in favor of an anthropological framework that offers an oppositional stance to commodity exchange, which, while perhaps utopian, has nevertheless been a living practice in other cultures.

Symbolic exchange is important for Baudrillard because it describes how gift giving in tribal societies is obligatory, ritualistic, and therefore reversible. That is to say that, while the giving of a gift creates empowerment through obligation and debt, any notion of power or accumulation is consequently undone by the countergift. Thus, Baudrillard is interested in how forms of symbolic exchange haunt contemporary societies, which are beholden not only to accumulation through commodity exchange but also to a "structural law of value" in general—a system of equivalence—that permeates beyond the economy. Indeed, while symbolic exchange is posited as an alternative to accumulative economic exchange whereby gift and countergift forge a more profound relation between participants, it is also Baudrillard's argument that symbolic exchange is, in fact, everywhere today because capitalist economic exchange would not be possible without a symbolic order that goes beyond the rational commerce of things or bodies.

Baudrillard's Legacy

Anthropology, among many other things, was influential in the development of Baudrillard's thought, especially in the 1970s when he was formulating his conceptualization of symbolic exchange as the opposite of commodity exchange. However, although there has been considerable exegesis of Baudrillard's works, especially of those published before the turn of the millennium, commentators have overwhelmingly focused on discussing Baudrillard's theorization of the semiotic through notions such as simulation and hyperreality (often to incorrectly label him as a "postmodernist"). The anthropological basis of Baudrillard's parallel focus on the symbolic throughout his oeuvre has been relatively ignored in comparison. Not only has a detailed study of Baudrillard's debts to anthropology not been undertaken but also far too little attention in general has been given to Baudrillard's attempts throughout his writings to bring into play that which the virtualization of the

world has attempted to disavow and displace: symbolic exchange, seduction, reversibility, catastrophe, fatality, absolute evil, impossible exchange, the irreducible, and the singular, to mention just a few.

Richard G. Smith

See also Bataille, Georges; Durkheim, Émile; Lacan, Jacques; Malinowski, Bronisław; Marx, Karl; Mauss, Marcel

Further Readings

Baudrillard, J. (1993). *Symbolic exchange and death.* London, UK: Sage. (Original work published 1976)

Clarke, D. B., Doel, M. A., Merrin, W., & Smith, R. G. (Eds.). (2009). *Jean Baudrillard: Fatal theories.* London, UK: Routledge.

Gane, M. (1991). *Baudrillard: Critical and fatal theory.* London, UK: Routledge.

Hefner, R. (1977). Baudrillard's noble anthropology: The image of symbolic exchange in political economy. *SubStance, 17,* 105–113.

Lane, R. J. (2000). *Jean Baudrillard.* London, UK: Routledge.

Smith, R. G. (Ed.). (2010). *The Baudrillard dictionary.* Edinburgh, UK: Edinburgh University Press.

Smith, R. G., Clarke, D. B., & Doel, M. A. (2011). Baudrillard redux [Special issue]. *Cultural Politics, 7* (3), 325–476.

BENEDICT, RUTH F.

Ruth Benedict's first book, *Patterns of Culture* (1934), deeply influenced all the social sciences. The book argued that culture members integrated their shared customs and values, and psychological dispositions into a configuration, a pattern. Her book also argued for cultural relativism—that is, the equal valuing of all cultural patterns. These themes were from the great storehouse of Franz Boas, her teacher and later her senior colleague in the Department of Anthropology at Columbia University. To her selection and elaboration of Boas's themes, she added ideas from psychiatry.

Benedict next turned to the investigation of cultures that had diversity in patterning, and to a new problem, the morality of societies. This work was interrupted by widespread concern about German racism and conquests in the late 1930s.

She responded with a book to combat racism, coauthored with Gene Weltfish, *Race: Science and Culture* (1940). When the United States entered the war, she was recruited, along with many other social scientists, to study the expected behaviors of enemy and allied nations. In the analysis of these modern-state societies with concepts worked out in the study of tribal societies, Benedict developed new formulations for the relation of the individual to culture. These were employed in her third and last book, *The Chrysanthemum and the Sword* (1946), which described Japanese culture as highly integrated yet offering diverse avenues of life. Two years later, in a peak of new activity, Benedict died suddenly of a heart attack at age 61.

Early Life and Work

Ruth Fulton was born in 1887 to a schoolteacher mother and a physician father. After growing up on her grandparents' farm in upstate New York and graduating from Vassar College, she turned to writing poetry and biographies of 19th-century feminists. She married Stanley Benedict, a professor of biochemistry at Cornell University Medical School. At age 33, she began studying anthropology at Columbia University with Franz Boas. His earlier students Alfred Kroeber, Robert Lowie, and Edward Sapir were only several years older than Benedict but had become, by the time she entered anthropology, influential in broadly developing Boas's paradigm. Benedict brought new ideas and was soon critiquing their work and rivaling it. Her early interest was in the psychological aspects of religious practices. She first compared vision experiences in "The Vision in Plains Culture" (1922) and next wrote "The Concept of the Guardian Spirit in North America" (1923), which was her PhD dissertation. Both were based on fieldwork and on a culling of the extensive ethnographic literature. Benedict did fieldwork in, and published on, four Southwest Indian tribes, Pima, Zuni, and, more briefly, Serrano and Cochiti. In 1928, 1932, and 1934, she published three articles foreshadowing her new approach, which she would soon elaborate in *Patterns of Culture*. Between 1930 and 1934, she also wrote seven entries for the *Encyclopedia of Social Science*—Animism, Child Marriage, Dress, Folklore, Magic, Myth, and Ritual—showing her engagement with traditional areas of ethnography. Boas liked her work and hired

her to teach in the graduate department at Columbia as soon as she completed her dissertation.

Patterns of Culture (1934) was written for a broad academic and general audience. This book described the cultural configuration, pattern of ideas, social organization, customs, and behaviors in three tribal societies and argued that the configuration shaped personality. The three societies described were the Zuni Pueblo Indians, the Kwakiutl of the northwest coast of Canada, and the island horticultural community of Dobu in Melanesia. Benedict wrote that the Zuni enacted and affirmed their gods' calendrical control of nature through traditional dances and ceremonies and enacted their cooperative kinship and community codes of an orderly and interwoven social structure. In strong contrast, Kwakiutl clan chiefs, bolstered by their kinspeople's high productivity of foods and arts, contested and shamed each other in lavish competitive gift giving; and their shamans, for their part, challenged their gods' supposed control of nature. In their less highly organized society, Dobuans practiced magic to protect their crops and their lives from the thefts and poisoning they believed their neighbors and kinsmen would inflict on them, while at the same time keeping a quiet balance of wariness and caution. Benedict saw each cultural pattern as an integrated whole. Tribal members behaved and believed, for the most part, within their cultural pattern. It shaped their psychic self, except for a few "misfits" always to be found in any culture, yet managing to live within ongoing practices. These misfits were of particular interest to Benedict because they showed the boundaries of each culture's ideas. The elements of the culture were selected by the group piece after piece, gradually integrating and reinforcing the pattern and eliminating discordant elements.

In *Patterns of Culture*, Benedict characterized Zuni culture as Apollonian in contrast to neighboring Plains Indian cultures, which she described as Dionysian, and she wrote that the Kwakiutl were megalomaniacal and the Dobuans were paranoid. She also wrote that culture was "personality writ large." This phrase and the designations of culture types were often taken to signify her whole meaning, by both critics and admirers, inviting nonengagement with the book's analytic depth. She did not again write these phrases or similar labeling of cultures. She commented in a letter to Margaret Mead that Raymond Firth, the noted British anthropologist, had written a very satisfactory review of my book. . . . His criticisms were ones I myself feel to the full— "tabloid" naming of cultures, animistic phrasings of how culture acts—though he mentions that I call attention to these phrases as verbal devices. (February 14, 1936, Mead Papers S5, Library of Congress)

Patterns of Culture made the idea of cultural diversity attractive to a Western-centered academic establishment. It became the subject of debates about the relativity of cultures, the integration of cultures, and the relation of personality to social analysis, retaining centrality in these arguments for at least a decade, and George Stocking may be correct in writing that it remained the most influential anthropological book for more than 3 decades.

Benedict's Elaborations on Her First Book

The widespread discussions of *Patterns of Culture* were for the most part strongly positive. A principal criticism was that she had misrepresented the Zuni by overlooking discordant elements, but this was shown to be incorrect and valid only for the neighboring Hopi pueblo Indians. During these discussions, she turned to deeper inquiries into two of the fundamental points of the book, one of which concerned variation in the degree of consistency in culture, which she discussed in her 1938 article "Continuities and Discontinuities in Cultural Conditioning." This point may have been inspired by Margaret Mead's fieldwork in Manus, New Guinea. Mead had been Benedict's student, and Benedict greatly admired her innovative and extensive fieldwork. In Manus culture, children were entirely exempt from the sorcery-driven culture of adulthood and learned none of its anxieties. Benedict took as examples of discontinuity not this case but the many societies with age grades. Each age grade—starting usually in late childhood, and graduating to youth, to warrior, to tribal elder—held ceremonies that taught initiates its new requirements, its privileges, and its secret knowledge. Even with radically different behavior requirements, from industry, to aggression, to sacred leadership, over a lifetime, most preliterate societies conducted their members successfully through the changes.

Benedict's second addendum to *Patterns of Culture* turned to research on the opposite side of the coin of relativity—that is, its nonjudgmental stance. In granting respect to any and all cultural arrangements, the concept of cultural relativity logically requires tolerance of many societies which caused suffering to those who had to live within them. For example, some hierarchical societies deprived subordinate members of a sense of worth. By no means did all hierarchies do so: Polynesian, African, and Polish hierarchical cultures each had its particular form of reciprocal behavioral obligations between aristocrats and commoners. An example of culture imposing anxiety was the belief in rampant sorcery in several North American Indian cultures, along with the absence of institutions to control sorcerers. Several more highly organized African societies, she wrote, brought sorcerers into courts and forced confessions. Benedict thought that extensive study of the ethnographic record could show which aspects of cultures supported and benefited their members and which caused a sense of repression, fear, or other detrimental effects that the society did not constructively cope with. She worked out comparisons of these factors in several cultures already well described in the ethnographic literature in these dimensions, making her comparisons in articles in *Frontiers of Democracy* (1941, Volume 7, pp. 110–112), *American Scholar* (1942, Volume 11, pp. 243–248), and *Atlantic Monthly* (1942, Volume 169, pp. 756–763) and in unpublished lectures of the same period, which are now accessible in her archived works at Vassar College. The social condition elaborated most she called "a sense of being free." She did not write of freedom itself, which is difficult to define in social dimensions given the ubiquitous constraints of social life. A "sense of being free," she wrote, could be achieved in many diverse types of society. Indeed, democracy, often characteristic of small societies, was not a guarantee of a sense of freedom if the society lacked institutions to control an internal aggressor. A level of institutionally developed social control was necessary to generate and protect the sense of being free.

Benedict's writings on the protections of freedom and security long predated the current related research topic, violations of human rights, and her method differed from the particularistic approach taken currently. Her research was comparative and universalistic, and more distanced from policy. It would be a good framework for the particularistic studies.

National Cultures

In the early 1940s debates about postwar political policies, Benedict began thinking in terms of national cultures. She warned against trying to democratize Eurasian countries because they typically had effective local governance exercised by clan leaders and supported by strong clan loyalty, institutions that could effectively resist intrusion from national-level organization. North Atlantic political institutions for achieving national policies by means of majority and minority negotiation and compromise, in contrast, were not challenged by strong community organization as in many Eurasian societies. Benedict's examples of the Eurasian pattern were from ethnographies of Chinese counties, where the system extended to quite large units, from Indian and Polish villages, and from the traditional Russian *Mir*, or village council. The Eurasian pattern is evident currently in tribal activism in Middle Eastern conflicts. Here again, her thinking was broadly comparativist and holistic. It was presented in an article in *Annals of the American Academy of Political and Social Sciences* in 1943.

Before World War II, the fields later called area studies and national culture hardly existed, and they were created as disciplines of research largely by the wartime need for information about enemy and allied cultures. Engagement with allies required more knowledge about their mores, and enemy cultures had to be understood to propagandize, conquer, and occupy them and to design workable military government during occupation. The Office of War Information (OWI) assigned Ruth Benedict to research reports on the local customs of Germans, Italians, and Netherlanders. She was assigned larger scale studies of Romania and Thailand. Her major assignment was Japanese culture. Her library sources were histories, ethnographies, folklore collections, literary works, and traveler's accounts. A rich resource in the literature on these European and Asian societies was collections of their proverbs, a folk form found widely in Old World cultures. Wartime allowed no fieldwork, the usual tool of the anthropologist, because of travel restrictions and the urgency for analysis. However, Benedict interviewed nationals of these countries who were living in the United States, and she was credited especially for insights from her Japanese American interviewees.

In her analysis and advice, Benedict argued for retaining the office of emperor as a locus of stability in Japanese society. She showed how their culture honor bound all Japanese in duty to their parents and beyond them to the emperor, and thus knit together the hierarchical social fabric. The emperorship was a deeply embedded institution in the culture, integrated into local social structures and customs as well as in people's sense of duty. Militarism had been a late imposition on it, not an outgrowth. Retention of the office of the emperor was a position many other influential advisers shared, and it became the basis of the U.S. government's eventual surrender and occupation policies.

She published her final OWI report on Japan as *The Chrysanthemum and the Sword* (1946), adding explanations for general readers about the circumstances of her research and prospects for constructive American Japanese relations. The book was quickly translated into Japanese and was widely admired as self-revelatory in Japan. It helped correct American public opinion about "our erstwhile enemy" and about Japanese Americans, whose civil liberties had been violated by rounding them up in internment camps during the war.

Benedict's depiction of Japan showed a high degree of cultural and social integration in a large nation. Nations had been little analyzed anthropologically, but deep integration was not thought expectable in them. Her study was important in this respect and also in being a refinement of her ideas about the relation of individuals to culture. It presented a new model of the "self" in culture. She found that after fulfilling their duty to the emperor and to their parents, and after the heavy obligation of "clearing one's name" from insult, Japanese persons could move on to other "circles" of behavior of enjoyable experience. Japanese childhood was outside the adult obligations, was a time for exuberance and free expression, and set a model for later behavior—"getting the taste out of life," a phrase used by the Japanese. This image of an individual savoring the culture's pleasures after fulfilling obligations described a "self" who learns culture but also uses culture and may manipulate it for benefits, not the earlier idea of culturally imprinted selves. This image could have been cited as a model for the developments of the idea of self that became common in the 1980s and 1990s, but Benedict's model was seldom noted. Furthermore, her analytic use of childhood illustrates a significant difference from many psychological anthropologists: Childhood in Japan, and in Thailand and Romania, cultures she also analyzed for OWI, was a period in a structured life cycle rather than a set of determinative experiences.

Postwar Work

After the focus on political and social values employed in OWI objectives, Benedict next turned to America. She saw deep egalitarianism, not just in the Bill of Rights, but originating in colonists' flight from rigid class systems in Europe to become egalitarian homesteaders here and their reining in of local governmental interference in defense of their independence. Later immigrants used the "liberty and opportunity" deriving from egalitarianism as a means to achievement and to becoming equal Americans. But this young democracy had problems too: "Intolerance of cultural pluralism" was one. Furthermore, children had to learn to act with initiative and independence to become achievers, yet they could not learn these qualities in childhood, when they had to accept the authority and moral judgments of parents. Women had greater freedom than in any other culture, partly because the nuclear family was unencumbered by wider kin ties and so mobile as to seldom have kinsmen nearby. But with such freedom, women neglected potentially useful community roles. This, along with the weakness of local government, meant that constructive social change was not undertaken. In this wide open system, secret societies and, later, interest groups promoted their own benefits and were hard to rein in. Benedict wrote elaborations of these points for diverse forums, including the *Saturday Review of Literature* (1948, Volume 31, Issue 52, pp. 5, 26–28), a proposed Grolier Press encyclopedia that never came to publication for lack of funding in the postwar slump of 1946–1948, and in a paper delivered to a Columbia University faculty symposium in 1948.

In addition to these writings, and to resuming teaching in 1946, she undertook directing a large project, Research in Contemporary Cultures, funded by the Department of Naval Research. In this project, she and numerous colleagues applied Benedict's and her colleagues' methods of analysis to six cultures: Russia, Czechoslovakia, France, East European Jews, China, and Syria. In addition to these two full-time jobs, she addressed several academic conferences in significant papers that are preserved in her archives. She also outlined for her publisher a book to include her Romanian and Thai analyses as well as the very interesting findings already emerging in Research in Contemporary Cultures. At this peak of activity, Ruth Benedict died. Research

in Contemporary Cultures had been in full swing for a year and a half under her direction. The work was funded for 3 more years, and numerous project papers were brought to publication.

In her first book, Ruth Benedict had described three cultures that were highly integrated. She acknowledged that this degree of integration was not usual, and she studied cultures that had diverse themes, showing how they could also integrate their more diverse experiences. The integration of ideas and customs was always her cue in analyzing cultural patterns. Overall, she thought of societies as bounded wholes more than many anthropologists did. After her first book, most of her work attempted to bring insights to postwar world problems. She had great hopes for the United Nations and went so far as to write, in a 1942 issue of the *American Scholar*, that the United Nations should have an army and all member nations should disarm and support its negotiating and armed apparatus. She was both an idealist and an acute analyst.

Virginia Heyer Young

See also Boas, Franz; Kroeber, Alfred L.; Lowie, Robert; Mead, Margaret; Psychological Anthropology; Sapir, Edward

Further Readings

Benedict, R. (1934). *Patterns of culture.* New York, NY: Houghton Mifflin.

Benedict, R. (1946). *The chrysanthemum and the sword: Patterns of Japanese culture.* Boston, MA: Houghton Mifflin.

Caffrey, M. M. (1989). *Ruth Benedict: Stranger in this land.* Austin: University of Texas Press.

Kent, P. (1996). Misconceived configurations of Ruth Benedict. *Japan Review, 7,* 33–60.

———. (1999). Japanese perceptions of *The Chrysanthemum and the Sword. Dialectical Anthropology, 24*(2), 181–192.

Mead, M. (1959). *An anthropologist at work: The writings of Ruth Benedict.* Boston, MA: Houghton Mifflin.

———. (1974). *Ruth Benedict.* New York, NY: Columbia University Press.

Modell, J. S. (1983). *Ruth Benedict: Patterns of a life.* Philadelphia: University of Pennsylvania Press.

Young, V. H. (2005). *Ruth Benedict: Beyond relativity, beyond pattern.* Lincoln: University of Nebraska Press.

BENJAMIN, WALTER

Walter Benjamin's contribution to the discipline of anthropology is perhaps, given the content and scope of this volume, comparatively large. This is not because Benjamin (1892–1940) was an anthropologist by training or by academic association in any recognizable way, nor is it because his *Gesammelte Schriften* (*Collected Writings*, 1972–1989) addresses the profession of anthropology in any systematic, historical, critical, or even occasional way. Rather, following his own characterization of the work of the 19th-century French poet Charles Baudelaire, we might say that Benjamin preserves the incognito of his own anthropological project so keenly as to render its influence at once everywhere and nowhere at all. Benjamin's enormous body of work takes seriously the etymological meaning of the term *anthropology*: the study of the human in its species being. Indeed, Benjamin's disciplinary contributions might be more readily observed in the fields of literary study and literary theory, media studies, philosophy of language, Jewish theology, or architectural theory, fields in which his work is routinely cited. However, his theories of modernity, his analysis of technology's relation to art and culture, and his contribution to the history of the senses take the emic view of collective life. Benjamin's idiosyncratically conjunctivist methods are meant to picture life under conditions of capitalism from the vantage of a participant observer.

Born on July 15th, 1892, into an assimilated German Jewish family, Walter Bendix Schönflies Benjamin enjoyed the privileges of a fin-de-siècle bourgeois Berlin family lifestyle. Benjamin's father, Emil, a businessman, and mother, Pauline Schönflies, the descendant of a merchant family of the Rhineland, came from relative affluence. The young Benjamin, an invalid and an unremarkable student, attended the Prussian-style gymnasium Kaiser-Friedrich-Schule in the Charlottenburg district of Berlin. In 1904, at the age of 12, Benjamin's parents removed him from school due to his continuing poor health. The mature critic would reflect on this period of quarantine with a sense of wonder and terror in his *Berliner Kindheit um neunzehnhundert* (*Berlin Childhood Around 1900*), published posthumously in 1950. Subsequently, Benjamin spent 2 years attending a rural boarding school) in Thuringia, central Germany. He returned to the Kaiser-Friedrich-Schule and earned his *Abitur* (high school certificate) in 1912. In April of the same year, Benjamin began his studies at the University of Freiburg. There, he would receive his early training in German literary study, psychology, and philosophy. Later, during his studies at the University of Munich, among the Marburg school of neo-Kantian philosophers, Benjamin would develop an interest in Husserl's phenomenological program, philosophy's claims to science, and the study of formal logic, interests that, along with his participation in Germany's national youth movement, would cast a great influence on his early writings.

The Anthropology of Language

Perhaps the most recognizable connections to anthropology, at least in its early disciplinary history, are developed in an unexpected place, Benjamin's language theory. The 1916 text *Über Sprache überhaupt und über die Sprache des Menschen* (On Language as Such and on the Language of Men), written during a course of study with the philologist and scholar of Andean art Walter Lehman, offers the most comprehensive account of the origin of language as it relates to the divine acts of naming in Genesis, the cultural conventions of early Judaism, and the animistic beliefs of primitive cultures. Benjamin suggests that "language as such" does not serve an agenda of rational communication: Rather, it communicates, and can only communicate, itself. The formulation is no less striking than it is obvious: Man must transmit language to himself. Indeed, the persistence of "languages of man" bears perpetual witness to a fact of "language as such." Linguistic being is in this way made to coincide with species being: "Language as such" names nothing other than this tradition, a language that no one *speaks* per se and yet is *spoken* everywhere. That "language as such" is conceived of as a tradition means that generations of speakers must each pass through the alembic of acquisition. In a suite of essays, "Doctrine of the Similar" and "On the Mimetic Faculty," Benjamin develops in detail the nature of this passage. Following the intuitions of Lucien Lévy-Bruhl's *Les fonctions mentales dans les societes inférieures* (*How Natives Think*), Benjamin turns to primitive forms of ritual, dance, and play, and early-childhood forms of imitation to better understand how man first did, and continues to, acquire language. It is in this pursuit of nonlinguistic modes of being and behavior that Benjamin discovers a strikingly original onomatopoetic relation to the world; the language of man, Benjamin asserts, translates natural, spontaneous, and magical signs into those that are repeatable, conventional, and arbitrary. Indeed, the language of man renews the primitive act of interpreting and imitating nature, only now by a set of codes that render it the mimesis of something entirely nonsensual. This original insight is communicated across a range of contexts that exceed its linguistic source. Indeed, the hermeneutical analysis to which Benjamin submits a whole variety of cultural phenomena might be described as an effort to discern the secrets of their fundamentally obscure presentation.

The Concept of History

The majority of Benjamin's wildly diverse writings saw publication only in posthumous form: first, in the incomplete edition of his *Schriften* (*Writings*, 1955) and, later, in the influential collection *Illuminationen: Ausgewählte Schriften* (1961), translated into English by Harry Zohn and published with an introduction by Hannah Arendt as *Illuminations: Reflections and Essays* in 1968. Benjamin's acclaim as a major intellectual of the 20th century was, likewise, only really achieved posthumously. Theodor Adorno's edition of the collected writings helped bring to Benjamin some of the recognition his work now enjoys, but his infamous failure to obtain an academic position, and later his piecemeal work for Frankfurt's Institute for Social Research, rendered marginal his contributions to the intellectual program of the Weimar republic and the Marxist theory of culture for which the Frankfurt school would become known.

Indeed, in 1926, early in his own career, Max Horkheimer, soon to be chair of Frankfurt's department of social philosophy, was asked by the professor of aesthetics, Hans Cornelius, to review the young Benjamin's *Habilitationsschrift* (the second dissertation, which qualifies one for academic appointment in Germany), *Ursprung des deutschen Trauerspiels* (published 2 years later, in 1928, and translated into English as *The Origin of German Tragic Drama* in 1977). Horkheimer read the document but refused to give it a positive recommendation. In a historical irony that Benjamin no doubt would have enjoyed,

the spurned text would come to be considered one of his most important contributions to literary study. The book offered a theory of the baroque German *play of mourning* and its relation to the figure of allegory, a symbolic mode in which, as Benjamin suggests, "any person, any object, any relationship can mean absolutely anything else." The study examines the representations of this original undecidability as they are played out by a genre that, distinct from tragedy, offers no necessary resolution to the conflicts it stages. Rather, *Trauerspeil*'s characters wander the densely bureaucratic labyrinth of its productions with but only the faintest hope of an end.

Benjamin (2004) says in a later essay derived from the Trauerspiel book, *Trauerspiel und Tragödie* (Play of Mourning and Tragedy), "Historical time is infinite in every direction and unfulfilled in every moment. This means we cannot conceive of a single empirical event that bears a necessary relation to the time of its occurrence" (p. 55).

The same can be said of artifacts of culture and, in particular, works of art. The consequences of this insight for the practice of criticism are extraordinary. Benjamin at once affirms the necessity of exploring the historical forces and networks in which works of art are composed and yet simultaneously suggests that contextual analysis can never exhaust or give any total meaning to its objects, simply because it could never determine what counts as their "particular historical situation." The infinite task of criticism is then to discover the elements of the new, the *Wahrheitsgehalt* ("truth content"), as they repeat and reformulate themselves across texts in subtle variations. The *Trauerspiel* book constitutes perhaps the most dramatic example of this thesis. Its epistemo-critical prologue, written after the study had been completed, reflects on the historical alignment of the 17th and 20th centuries. The critical reading of this set of historical plays, Benjamin claims, should reveal features of our own social and political situation, otherwise entirely opaque to us moderns. The functionaries and sovereigns in the world of the *Trauerspiel* are and are not our own allegorical doubles. We recognize in them the lineaments of our own existence, as if such a future nested intentionally in the plays themselves.

Literature and Media

With the scholarly climate too conservative for his radical thought, and the world of academic appointment closed after the rejection of his habilitation, Benjamin sunk into a deep depression. The would-be scholar, who was susceptible to lengthy bouts of melancholy throughout his life, spent the winter of 1928 traveling in Russia. The trip yielded the impressionistic essay "Moskau" (Moscow) and other fragments that dramatize the experience of a tourist who could neither speak the language of the city nor interpret its social semiotics.

Alienation and marginality would become central themes in Benjamin's work, along with the consideration of forgotten, deserted, or otherwise unvalued cultural phenomena: including children's books (of which he was an avid collector), defunct optical technologies, and the products of American mass culture. In the discards of Europe, Benjamin discerned the faintly utopian promise of another mode of life beyond the current, depraved state of capitalist development. The fragmentary, seemingly ad hoc manner of composition that would become a signature style of Benjamin's later writing was meant to yield up the flashes of this general insight in truly surprising ways. Perhaps the most accomplished example of this sort of prose collage is Benjamin's book *Einbahnstrasse* (*One Way Street*, 1979), published in the same year as the essay "Moskau." The text, remarkable for its promiscuity of range (it offers acute analyses of topics like the cultural history of German inflation and the detective genre in American letters), attempted to introduce its audience to a new kind of reading experience, less linear than compositional—a practice that must take its bearings from the work's own difficult, antisequential format. In this way, *Einbahnstrasse* takes up a central imperative of Benjamin's career, the innervation and recalibration of the human sensorium, the reconfiguration of its ways of interpreting the world.

The mid-1920s through the early 1930s were enormously productive for Benjamin. In addition to major essays on a range of German authors, from Karl Kraus to Franz Kafka, Benjamin undertook a series of studies in modern and contemporary French literature. This work included a translation of Charles Baudelaire's poem cycle *Tableaux Parisiens*, published with the remarkable essay "Die Aufgabe des Uberstzers" ("The Task of the Translator") as its preface in 1923; an unfinished translation of the first two volumes of Marcel Proust's *In Search of Lost Time*; and essays on French surrealism. He also published, in 1931, "Eine kleine Geschichte der Photographie" (A Little History of Photography).

The essay at once gives an overview of the generic and technical histories of the medium. Benjamin relates the art form to the collective impulses and procedures of archivization, memorialization, and reproduction and to the contingency of detail that always permeates any such efforts. But Benjamin does not rest there. Indeed, he argues that the medium furnishes us with an *Optisch-Unbewußt* ("optical unconscious"); that is, it frames and brings to light the heretofore inaccessible image worlds that dwell in the smallest features of our experience.

By 1933, Benjamin had begun to write in an adjunct capacity for the Frankfurt Institut für Sozialforschung (Institute for Social Research), which, along with its principal members, Horkheimer and Adorno, had officially relocated to New York to escape the hostile political climate that had emerged in the wake of Hitler's election to chancellor of Germany. One of Benjamin's earlier studies of French literature, "Zum gegenwärten gesellschaftlichen Standort des französischen Schriftstellers" (The Present Social Situation of the French Writer), written in 1934, appeared in the institute's principal organ, *Zeitschrift für Sozialforschung*, along with two of his most important essays, "Das Kunstwerk im Zeitalter seiner technischen Reproduziertbarkeit" and "Eduard Fuchs, der Sammler und der Historiker" (The Work of Art in the Age of Its Technological Reproducibility and Eduard Fuchs, Collector and Historian, respectively). In 1935, Benjamin became the journal's official "Paris Correspondent for French Literature," a position that defrayed some of the costs of his exile in France and provided him with a venue for his work.

Indeed, Benjamin spent most of the period between 1935 and 1940 in exile in Paris, attending to his massive, and ultimately unfinished, research project, *Das Passagen Werk* (The Arcades Project). The work was to be an extensive montage of high-capitalist culture, which took its principle of composition from the great steel and glass arcades of 19th-century commercial Paris. At the center of the work were Benjamin's studies of the ur-modernist poet Charles Baudelaire. What Baudelaire's poems ask in their splenetic mode—and Benjamin's work as a whole might be said to ask in an even more extreme fashion—is "What can culture do?" "How can it even survive?" "Why make art in such depraved circumstances?" and "What might a tolerable life be?" The social types who give voice to these questions, and for whom Benjamin is perhaps best known, the *flaneur*, the sandwich man, the whore, and the gambler, find their fullest articulations in the major work on Baudelaire: "The Paris of the Second Empire in Baudelaire," "Central Park," and *Charles Baudelaire: Ein Lyriker im Zeitalter des Hochkapitalismus* (Charles Baudelaire: A Lyric Poet in the Age of High Capitalism). The anthropology of this work, we might say, consists in Benjamin's imperative to treat his own moment as something no less strange, barbaric, or primitive than his object of historical analysis, the continua of the 19th and 20th centuries, the capitals of France and of Germany.

In June 1940, Nazi forces occupied Paris. Benajmin and his sister escaped to Lourdes, where they made preparations, with the help of Horkheimer and the Frankfurt cum New York Institute, to obtain a visa for emigration to the United States. Benjamin, however, never made it safely out of France. Having failed to obtain a visa in Marseille, from where he was to cross the Pyrenees into Spanish territory, Benjamin attempted to cross the border illegally. On September 25, 1940, the group of refugees with whom he was traveling discovered that the Spanish border town of Port Bou, where they were set to cross into safety, had been closed just days earlier. Fearing extradition to Germany by the French collaborationist authorities and internment in a concentration camp, Benjamin took the lethal dose of morphine he had been carrying with him for emergency use. He died the next morning, September 26, 1940. Soon after his death, the Port Bou border was reopened, and European refugees from the Nazi campaign were once more permitted to cross into Spain.

The great unfinished Arcades Project, entrusted to the French philosopher and librarian Georges Bataille by Benjamin before he fled Paris, to be hidden away in the recesses of the Bibliothèque Nationale, memorializes a set of long-standing concerns for the anthropological: man's particular, historical, and species life. The project's final, fragmentary form at once gives expression to the radical aesthetic intentions of Benjamin's work, to his effort to defamiliarize and resensitize the phenomenology of modernity, and to the dangerous, interruptive, and exigent circumstances of his own life.

Daniel R. Braun

See also Critical Theory; Cultural Materialism; Modernism; Phenomenology; Semiotics

Further Readings

Benjamin, A., & Osborne, P. (Ed.). (1994). *Walter Benjamin's philosophy: Destruction and experience.* New York, NY: Routledge.

Benjamin, W. (2004). *Selected writings: Vol. 1. 1913–1926* (M. W. Jennings & M. Bullock, Eds.). Boston, MA: Harvard University Press.

Ferris, D. (Ed.). (1996). *Walter Benjamin: Theoretical questions.* Stanford, CA: Stanford University Press.

Jennings, M. (1987). *Dialectical images: Walter Benjamin's theory of literary criticism.* Ithaca, NY: Cornell University Press.

Menninghaus, W. (1980). *Walter Benjamins theorie der sprachmagie* [Walter Benjamin's theory of linguistic magic]. Frankfurt on the Main, Germany: Suhrkamp.

Nägele, R. (Ed.). (1988). *Benjamin's ground: New readings of Walter Benjamin.* Detroit, MI: Wayne State University Press.

Nordquist, J. (1989). *Walter Benjamin: A bibliography.* Santa Cruz, CA: Reference and Research Service.

Redslob, B. (1992). *Auswahlbibliographie* [Selective bibliography]. In U. Steiner (Ed.), *Walter Benjamin 1892–1940* (pp. 401–422). Bern, Switzerland: Lang.

Richter, G. (2000). *Walter Benjamin and the corpus of autobiography.* Detroit, MI: Wayne State University Press.

Special Benjamin issues: *New German Critique, 17* (1979); *34* (1985); *39* (1986); and *48* (1989)

BINFORD, LEWIS R.

Lewis Roberts Binford (1931–2011) was perhaps best known for his profound impact on the discipline of archaeology. He played a key role in the transformation of archaeology from a particularistic study of select artifacts and human constructions to a holistic and scientific examination of past human behavior. Binford's epistemological approach essentially expanded the scope of social and cultural anthropological theory to encompass the entire span of human evolution. In fact, a portion of his archaeological research examined the very origins of "culture" itself. The following discussion, however, focuses primarily on his contributions to anthropological theory.

Biography and Definitive Works

Binford was born in Norfolk, Virginia, in 1931. During the Depression, he spent many hours hunting, fishing, and canoeing with his father in the Dismal Swamp near Norfolk. It was here that he learned about the wildlife, archaeology, and Native American history of this diverse region. Binford started college at Virginia Polytechnic Institute before enlisting in the U.S. Army. He was assigned to an army language school in California, where he completed an intensive course in Japanese. He then served as an interpreter in Japan and was assigned to work alongside several anthropologists who were involved in a large resettlement program on the Ryukyu Islands. Through this experience, Binford became interested in anthropology and archaeology. He went on to work in Okinawa, coordinating the remuneration of local communities, studying traditional house construction, and carrying out "rescue archaeology," when he assisted in relocating tombs that were being moved for military construction.

After his discharge, Binford completed college at the University of North Carolina (BA in 1957) and went on to pursue graduate studies at the University of Michigan (MA in 1958 and PhD in 1964). After completing his degree, Binford went on to have a distinguished teaching career at numerous universities, including the University of Michigan (1960–1961), the University of Chicago (1961–1965), the University of California–Santa Barbara (1965–1966), the University of California–Los Angeles (1966–1968), the University of New Mexico (1968–1991), and Southern Methodist University (1991–2003). While at the University of Chicago, Binford assembled his first cadre of graduate students, including Mel Aikens, Les Freeman, James Hill, Kent Flannery, Richard Gould, Bill Longacre, Tom Lynch, Christopher Peebles, Bob Whallon, Henry Wright, and others. Binford ultimately served as dissertation advisor for more than 79 students. His epistemological perspective and the results of his research are presented in 23 authored and coedited books and monographs, as well as in 141 journal articles, book chapters, reviews, and comments.

Two of his earliest publications, *Archaeology as Anthropology* (1962) and *Archaeological Perspectives* (1966), laid the groundwork for reorienting American archaeology and the discipline of archaeology in general. Binford forcefully argued that archaeologists should abandon the idealist concept of culture based on "shared ideas, norms, and traditions." He chose to adopt the anthropologist Leslie White's view that culture was a nongenetic means of responding to the challenges posed by both the biophysical and the social environment. White had also emphasized the thermodynamic, systemic nature of culture and the significance of energy capture for understanding cultural evolution and complexity. Binford saw that this perspective possessed considerable explanatory power and would serve anthropological archaeology quite well.

Previously, archaeologists and other social scientists had assumed that much of the past was unknowable. Binford, on the other hand, argued enthusiastically that all cultures are systems within which food getting, technology, social and political organization, trade, religion, and ideology are all intricately interconnected. Change within any one subsystem reverberates through all of the other, interrelated subsystems. Given this view, artifacts and associated materials could then be seen as the material correlates of a full range of past human activities. The major challenge that then confronted all archaeologists was to utilize the static remains that exist in the present to evaluate their arguments about the behavioral dynamics of past societies.

Theoretical Contributions to Anthropology

During the 1960s, American archaeology began to undergo a fundamental shift. The traditional working definition of culture and the "space-time" taxonomic systems for ordering archaeological information were recognized as inadequate. Archaeology, at this point, was like a language with an ever-expanding vocabulary but without a grammar! A significant paradigm shift was required to make more effective, and more productive, the use of archaeological "facts." It was time for a new synthesis, and Binford led the charge.

Binford's first major step toward building anthropological theory and reshaping American archaeology was his doctoral research. His dissertation, *Archaeological and Ethnohistorical Investigations of Cultural Diversity and Progressive Development Among Aboriginal Cultures of Coastal Virginia and North Carolina* (1964), focused on the South Atlantic Slope Culture area defined by the anthropologist A. E. Kroeber in 1939. This region lay between the Blue Ridge Mountains and the coastal plains and had been occupied historically by the Nottaway, Powhatan, Nansemond, Chowan, Tuscarora, and Meherrin. This culture area was both culturally and ecologically diverse. Native populations made use of a variety of food-getting technologies to obtain their food by means of hunting, gathering, fishing, and cultivating domestic crops. These Native American groups were also organized into a diverse array of sociopolitical systems.

Binford set out to make use of historical records and on-the-ground reconnaissance in order to identify archaeological sites that could be linked reliably to known tribal or ethnic groups in the region. The methodology is known as the *direct historical approach*. His ultimate goal was to study Native American cultural complexity and its causal linkages to the productivity of natural food resources such as plants, deer, bear, and migratory or anadramous fish throughout the piedmont region. This approach reflects a significant departure from the idealist view of culture (i.e., ideas drive and shape behavior) used by both anthropologists and archaeologists at that time because it causally linked the variation in biotic variables to the levels of complexity in cultural systems recorded in historic documents. Binford then used rich ethnohistorical literature to develop quantitative measures of cultural complexity based on tribal territory size, population density and distribution, settlement types and patterns, and degree of subsistence specialization. He found, for example, that the numbers of status positions as well as the population densities within these societies were highly correlated with fishing efficiency (the numbers of fish caught with devices and nets). Furthermore, Binford found that the Powhatan, who were characterized by the most complex sociocultural organization, had established clusters of villages and hamlets within the productive transition zone between freshwater and brackish-water habitats.

Much of Binford's research and writing to follow were devoted to constructing the epistemology and methodology for anthropological archaeology. He proceeded to develop research methods for archaeologists, involving statistical analyses, sampling, site survey and research designs, actualistic or experimental studies, and ethnoarchaeology (archaeologists studying the material remains generated by contemporary groups). It was also during this time that Binford began to give greater attention to the

philosophy of science and to deal with questions like "How do archaeologists know what they know?" and "How do they gain greater confidence in our knowledge about the past?" Binford cautioned, for example, that archaeologists must make careful use of ethnographic information and analogies. Once formal similarities are recognized between certain archaeological observations and relevant ethnographic records, archaeologists should then deduce a series of interrelated hypotheses that can be tested using archaeological data. In addition, archaeologists should expect to find patterns of past human behavior that are not represented by ethnographic analogs. During the 1970s, Binford began a long-term ethnoarchaeological study of caribou exploitation among the Nunamiut Eskimo of the Brooks Range in northern Alaska. One of the ultimate goals of this field research was to understand the behavioral dynamics that generated bone assemblages in the archaeological record. This investigation is also a very significant contribution to the anthropology of Arctic hunters. It provides invaluable insights into the exigencies of human adaptation to extreme environmental conditions, and it isolates the underlying reasons why a given behavioral strategy is employed in a given situation. Should caribou be butchered to derive select anatomical parts, or should the hunters strive to make use of the entire animal? What anatomical elements of the caribou provide the greatest amount of fat and therefore the greatest number of food calories? Under what environmental conditions do hunter-gatherers implement food storage? These are anthropological insights that are frequently not documented in traditional ethnographies.

In 2001, Binford published a major synthesis of his global study of hunter-gatherers, titled *Constructing Frames of Reference: An Analytical Method for Archaeological Theory Building Using Ethnographic and Environmental Data Sets*. This monumental study mirrors the general questions and rudimentary methods utilized in his dissertation nearly 4 decades earlier. Yet this research was conducted on a global scale, and it involved analyses of a comprehensive, comparative database, including 339 hunter-gatherer groups from the Americas, Greenland, Africa, India, Siberia, Japan, Southeast Asia, and Australia. These contemporary ethnographic cases were used to project estimates of population size and density for major biomes throughout the world. He concluded that the earth could have supported about 7 million hunter-gatherers prior to the appearance of farming and herding. Binford then constructed a "terrestrial model" that utilized measures of plant and animal productivity to calculate independent estimates of population sizes and densities for any given location on the earth. Additionally, 15 variables related to demography, subsistence, group size, and mobility derived from the historical and anthropological variables were, in turn, analyzed in relation to a diverse array of climatic and ecological variables (e.g., latitude, longitude, mean annual temperature and bio-temperature, mean annual rainfall, net annual plant productivity, and water balance). These variables had been calculated for 1,429 weather stations around the world.

Binford utilized the terrestrial model to generate 21 "empirical generalizations" about hunter-gatherer adaptations. Yet it should be emphasized that the relevance of the variables initially used by Binford was grounded in ecological and anthropological theory. He found, for example, that sedentary groups do not rely on terrestrial game animals. This is understandable given the high energetic costs of meat transport in the absence of dogs, sleds, watercraft, or horses. He was then in a position to generate expectations about resource intensification and transitions from preferred ungulate hunting to more intensive food-getting strategies based on plant gathering and processing, aquatic resources, plant cultivation, or pastoralism. By extension, Binford's terrestrial hunter-gatherer model possesses sufficient power to explain behavioral shifts toward other food-getting strategies.

Conclusions

Binford challenged anthropologists and archaeologists to expand the scope of their research, to develop more rigorous methodologies for data collection and analysis, and to think more critically. Science is a marathon without a finish line. Our understanding of past and present human behavior and cultural systems does not come easily. Social scientists can produce reliable knowledge by means of an iterative process that involves generating, testing, and refining (or rejecting) explanatory models. These models are, then, combined to construct scientific theories. The robust consequences of these theories are then continually scrutinized and evaluated. Binford continually made use of the complex web of what we know to define better what we do not understand about

the external world. He demonstrated how social scientists should make use of models and theories to identify productive anthropological and archaeological research questions, to construct causal arguments, and to evaluate those arguments by means of rigorous, structured observation and analysis. And he reminded us later in his life that theory building is not for the timid or faint of heart.

Alan J. Osborn

See also Cultural Ecology; Sahlins, Marshall; Steward, Julian; White, Leslie

Further Readings

Binford, L. R. (1980). Willow smoke and dogs' tails: Hunter-gatherer settlement systems and archaeological site formation. *American Antiquity, 45,* 4–20.
———. (1983). *In pursuit of the past: Decoding the archaeological record.* London, UK: Thames & Hudson.
———. (2004). Beliefs about death, behavior, and mortuary practices among hunter-gatherers. In J. F. Cherry, C. Scarre, & S. Shennan (Eds.), *Explaining social change: Studies in honour of Colin Renfrew* (pp. 1–15). Cambridge, UK: University of Cambridge.
———. (2004). Niche: A productive guide for use in the analysis of cultural complexity. In A. Johnson (Ed.), *Processual archaeology: Exploring analytical strategies, frames of reference, and culture process* (pp. 297–314). Westport, CT: Praeger.
Johnson, A. L. (Ed.). (2004). *Processual archaeology: Exploring analytical strategies, frames of reference, and culture process.* Westport, CT: Praeger.
Meltzer, D. J. (2011). *Lewis Roberts Binford, 1931–2011: A biographical memoir.* Washington, DC: National Academy of Sciences.

BIOGRAPHY/LIFE WRITING

Among other forms of life writing—autobiography, autoethnography, personal narratives, and life histories—biography (*bios graphia*) has long been a key method in writing anthropology. Biography examines the relationship between life and theory, the intersections of ideas with lives. Sources include letters, diaries, memoirs, field notes, and ethnographic writing. Biography also incorporates an oral dimension: conversations with the subject and with others about the subject to record memories and anecdotes.

Biography explores anthropology's foundational ideas through case studies of individual lives, situating them in broad historical currents and cultural movements. Franz Boas's discovery of the paradox of human sameness amid the plurality of cultures has, for example, been biographically traced to his personal experiences—of Inuit communality, of 19th-century German anti-Semitism, of American anti-immigration—and linked to his affinity for the aesthetics and politics of Romanticism and his revolt against Enlightenment universalism. Virginia Kerns, in her biography of Julian Steward, uncovered the roots of Steward's theory of the patrilineal band—as the primordial unit of human social organization—in his autobiographical memory of adolescence as a member of a band of boys at the Deep Springs Valley residential school in the California desert, a masculine sociality he reproduced in the student circles of male veterans who dominated post–World War II American universities. Pierre Bourdieu's theory of habitus and his idea of reflexivity have been biographically traced, through his own autobiographical writing, to his experiences of culture and class as his life trajectory took him from rural France, to postcolonial Algeria, to the Paris academy.

The biographical method illuminates anthropological thought and practice through its application not only to central figures in the discipline but also to those who led careers at its margins. Examples here are studies of the work of scholars such as Arnold Van Gennep and Ruth Landes. Van Gennep's idea of rites of passage is central in anthropology, but he remained self-employed outside the discipline; Landes, whose early-20th-century experiments in autoethnographic writing were at the time critiqued as unscientific, may now be seen as a pioneer of the self-reflexivity that has become an expected component of ethnography since the 1980s. Biography of lives lived on the edges of anthropology reveals ways in which professionalizing anthropology in the university created a canon of thought through processes of inclusion and exclusion. Boas and Ruth Benedict, based at Columbia University, strategically expanded the influence of Boasian anthropology by selecting their students' dissertation topics and placing the students at key institutions on graduation—Alfred Kroeber at Berkeley, for example. Biographical research documents how anthropologists located at those universities that train cohorts of PhD students have also played determining roles in the directions the anthropological canon has taken.

Biography and nation is another important intersection. Nancy Lutkehaus's biographical study of Margaret Mead as an American icon analyzes the central themes of Mead's writing—nurture and nature, the search for a better life—as reflections of 20th-century American values. Biographical writing by indigenous anthropologists and by anthropologists in Brazil, Mexico, Japan, India, and elsewhere further reveals the role national and/or postcolonial locations play in defining anthropology and sparks debate about the possibility of world anthropology or other anthropologies.

Gender and biography intersect in anthropology. Career stability makes building a personal archive possible. More men than women anthropologists have held secure academic positions, and wives have often worked as assistants, editors, and managers of archives, creating more extensive primary sources for future biographers of male anthropologists. Mead's curation of Benedict's archive (and of her own) is an exception. Feminist scholars have consciously chosen to work with the fragmented assemblages of women's biographical materials, analyzing those fragments as autobiographical.

Anthropology's central method—participant observation—is itself a biographical experience. Anthropologists record moments of epiphany during fieldwork in memoirs, diaries, fiction, and ethnography. In a diary kept during 1883–1884, the year he lived with Inuit on Baffin Island, Boas marveled at the "civilized" communal sharing of meat after the hunt, behavior that in his view contradicted the then prevailing ideas of primitivism and cultural evolution. Raymond Firth's extensive ethnographic record based on long-term fieldwork in Tikopia traces his move to humanism away from Malinowskian functionalism. Biography also reveals how autobiographical experience may overrule empirical evidence: Kerns writes that although Steward was never able to find the patrilineal band in field research, his autobiographical memory led him to continue to argue its centrality in the history of human social organization.

Life writing through the "life history" method has also long been a feature of ethnography. Boas established the recording of oral narratives of Native American elders as a central method in both field research and writing. Life histories remained important throughout 20th-century anthropology. Examples include Sidney Mintz's biography of a Puerto Rican migrant worker, Oscar Lewis's life histories of Mexican families, and Ruth Behar's life of a Mexican market woman. Barbara Myerhoff pioneered dialogical life writing, intertwining her telling of the life of a Jewish American immigrant tailor with reflections about her own relationship to Judaism. To write about the lives of Yukon aboriginal women, Julie Cruikshank experimented with writing oral forms of storytelling. Serving as scribes of marginalized lives, Nancy Scheper-Hughes has narrated the lives of mothers in a Brazilian shantytown who delay bonding with newborns, and Philippe Bourgois has recorded the narratives of crack dealers in Harlem.

Finally, the critical reflexivity of postcolonial anthropology has renewed interest in biography. To transcend self/other dichotomies, phenomenological approaches focus on lived experience, and ethnography locates once others as subjects—placing anthropologists in relation to, not outside, their object of study. In the 21st century, as anthropology seeks new knowledge through collaboration and cotheorizing, life writing as reflexive practice is key to its realization.

Sally Cole

See also Autoethnography; Boas, Franz; Bourdieu, Pierre; Firth, Raymond; Mead, Margaret; Mintz, Sidney; Scheper-Hughes, Nancy; Steward, Julian

Further Readings

Cole, S. (2003). *Ruth Landes: A life in anthropology.* Lincoln: University of Nebraska Press.

Gordon, R., Lyons, A. P., & Lyons, H. D. (Eds.). (2011). *Fifty key anthropologists.* London, UK: Routledge.

Kerns, V. (2003). *Scenes from the high desert: Julian Steward's life and theory.* Urbana: University of Illinois Press.

Lutkehaus, N. C. (2008). *Margaret Mead: The making of an American icon.* Princeton, NJ: Princeton University Press.

BLOCH, MAURICE

Maurice Bloch (1939–) has worked mainly in religion, rituals, power, cognition, and economic exchange. He is among the pioneers of the French Marxist tradition in British anthropology.

Biography and Major Works

Bloch was born in 1939 in Caen, France. He had a mixed family background as his great-grandfather was a miller from Lorraine while his grandmother's family were Sephardic Jews, originally from Portugal, who lived in Bordeaux. His mother's mother was a niece of Émile Durkheim as well as a first cousin of Marcel Mauss. Bloch had a chance to meet Mauss near the end of Mauss's life. During World War II, Bloch's father was arrested and killed by the Nazis, and his mother, a marine biologist, was held in Auschwitz along with other scientists and forced to do laboratory research for the Nazis. Bloch was protected by one of his father's friends during this period. After the war, his mother married John S. Kennedy, a British biologist.

Bloch attended Lycée Carnot in Paris but moved to Britain at the age of 11 along with his parents and joined the Perse School in Cambridge. At the Perse, he was inspired by his history teacher John Tanfield and by Douglas Brown, who taught him English literature. He also developed an interest in classical music, with Olivier Messiaen and Benjamin Britten being among his favorites. He entered the London School of Economics to study anthropology as an undergraduate, where he was inclined toward Maurice Freedman and Burton Benedict, who worked on the cultures of China, and Mauritius and Seychelles, respectively. During this period, he was also inspired by Mary Douglas at University College London and Adrian Mayer at the School of Oriental and African Studies, where he had gone to study linguistics. In addition to academics, he also acted in plays, usually French, at the university. Bloch was also involved in politics during his time at university, supporting the anticolonial struggles in Algeria, India, and China. After completing his undergraduate studies in 1961, he went to France to oppose the Algerian and Vietnam wars.

Bloch attended Cambridge University for his PhD, initially working with Meyer Fortes and the French anthropologist Germaine Dieterlen. Bloch was interested in working in India due to his earlier inspiration from Adrian Mayer's work, but his funding required that he work in Africa, and he decided to work in Madagascar. He conducted his field research in Madagascar from 1964 to 1966. Initially, Bloch carried out his research under the supervision of Audrey Richards, who had experience working with sub-Saharan African communities. At a later stage, he was supervised by Stanley Jeyaraja Tambiah, a specialist on Thailand and Sri Lanka. Bloch also had a chance to discuss his work with other pioneering social anthropologists at Cambridge like Edmund Leach and Raymond Firth. Caroline Humphrey, Marilyn Strathern, Andrew Strathern, Adam Kuper, Jim Faris, and Jonathan Parry were among his fellow PhD students.

Bloch completed his PhD in 1967. His doctoral thesis, *The Significance of Tombs and Ancestral Villages for Merina Social Organization*, focused on the tombs and kinship organization in Madagascar and was later published by Seminar Press as *Placing the Dead: Tombs, Ancestral Villages and Kinship Organization in Madagascar*. He was a lecturer at the University of Wales, Swansea, in 1967 and 1968, but in 1969, he accepted a lectureship at the London School of Economics, where his colleagues were Maurice Freedman, Lucy Mair, Jean La Fontaine, Ioan Lewis, and Peter Loizos. Bloch developed friendships with Alfred Gell and Olivia Harris, who were graduate students at the LSE at that time. In 1970, Bloch moved to the University of California at Berkeley, where he became interested in the work of linguists and of philosophers such as John Searle, leading him to study cognitive sciences. Not comfortable in the United States because of his Marxist links in France, Bloch returned to the LSE, where he continued to work on language and cognition. His article "Symbols, Song, Dance and Features of Articulation" (1974), on the criticism of semantics, has been widely read.

Bloch returned to Berkeley in 1974–1975, where he was influenced by cognitive anthropologists such as George Lakoff and Paul Kay. He was visiting professor at the Johns Hopkins University in Baltimore and the New School for Social Research in New York, but since 1976, his career has been almost entirely at the LSE, where he was promoted to Reader in 1976. Bloch has also taught and has been an occasional visiting professor at Paris West University Nanterre La Défense, University of Stockholm, and National Ethnology Museum of Japan, among others. He was appointed as full professor at the LSE in 1983 and elected a fellow of the British Academy in 1990.

Currently, Bloch is emeritus professor at the LSE and an associate member of the Institut Jean Nicod of the École Normale Supérieure in Paris. In addition to the many students he has supervised, his writings have been translated into at least 12 different languages.

Critical Contributions to Anthropology

Bloch has published books in both French and English and more than 100 articles relating to ritual, power, kinship, economics, religion, and money.

French Marxism and Structuralism in British Anthropology

Although Bloch was educated in the British anthropological traditions, he has long been connected with French Marxist movements. On the one hand, he was interested in the structuralism of Claude Lévi-Strauss, while on the other, he was influenced by several French Marxist writers with whom he had personal relations, including Maurice Godelier and Emmanuel Terray. Bloch organized a session at the conference of the Association of Social Anthropologists in 1973, in which French Marxists and British anthropologists discussed various theoretical interests. He tried to use the approaches of Marxist anthropology and Lévi-Strauss's structuralism alongside the then dominant paradigms in Britain, like methodological individualism and structural functionalism. The influence of Lévi-Strauss is particularly strong in *Placing the Dead*, where Bloch interpreted kinship organization as a schema of elementary structures. Anthropologists have different responses toward Marxism and Marxist analyses depending on the traditions they were trained in or the communities they have been working with, as Bloch demonstrated in his detailed description of Marxist analysis, *Marxist Analyses and Social Anthropology* (1975), and in *Marxism and Anthropology: The History of a Relationship* (1983). Marxist tradition was declining in France when Bloch was initially working through a French Marxist approach in British anthropology. However, Bloch persisted in a Marxist approach in his work on the representation of money and economic exchange, particularly in his book *Money and the Morality of Exchange*, coedited with Jonathan Parry, and the article "Zafimaniry Debt and Credit."

Ritual and Power in Madagascar

Bloch worked with two communities in Madagascar: a rice cultivating peasant community in central Imerina and the forest people of Zafimaniry. In *Placing the Dead: Tombs, Ancestral Villages and Kinship Organization in Madagascar*, Bloch presented the reinterpretive power of rituals in relation to ancestral tombs in central Imerina. Later in 1983, in *Death and the Regeneration of Life*, a volume of essays he coedited with Jonathan Parry, he discusses the role of women in funerary practices, in particular the dominant role of women in mourning and death rituals. Although Bloch worked on various topics ranging from linguistics to cognition and from money to morality, the study of rituals, religion, and power has been the focus of most of his works. In *From Blessing to Violence: History and Ideology in the Circumcision Ritual of the Merina of Madagascar* (1986), Bloch offered a concrete and influential neo-Marxist theory of ritual and power. He describes that, on the one hand, the circumcision ritual starts with blessings from God but ends with symbolic and physical violence and, on the other, at times, it symbolizes the mystic transmission of the moral identity from the descent group and then is used to legitimize and celebrate the dominance of one group of Merina over other Merina or non-Merina groups. He developed this theory further in *Ritual, History and Power: Selected Papers in Anthropology* (1989). As a further development in his approach toward ritual and violence, he synthesized a radical theory of religion in *Prey Into Hunter: The Politics of Religious Experience* in 1992, interpreting rituals as a denial of the transience of life and human institutions through sacrifice. Bloch published several articles, like "'Eating' Young Men Among the Zafimaniry," to further explain his ideas on power, rituals, and violence.

Bloch continuously used a historical approach of studying rituals and religion. In his article "Why Religion Is Nothing Special but Is Central" (2008), Bloch challenged the popular notion in anthropology that religion evolved as it promoted social bonding. He, instead, stressed that the development of brain architecture and power to imagine nonexistent things and beings transformed the nature of society, including religion. His stance was debated in anthropological as well as other intellectual spheres, since many anthropologists have been stressing the evolution of religion alongside technological or cultural development primarily for social bonding.

Cognition, Memory, and Culture

Bloch developed an interest in studying language and cognition at a very early stage during the time he spent at Berkeley. In that era, due to the works of scholars such as George Lakoff and Noam Chomsky, new dimensions in linguistics and cognitive psychology were being studied. Bloch's interest in child development also drew him closer to psychologists like Susan Carey, Dan Sperber, and Paul Harris. Bloch wrote *Political Language, Oratory, and Traditional Society* in 1975, which is considered one of the landmark books on political language in non-Western cultures.

Many anthropologists focus on the role of culture in studying language, while psychologists give primary importance to cognition and memory. Bloch, however, tried to balance the role in both disciplines of culture and cognition in understanding language. He has dealt with memory and cognition from a variety of theoretical and methodological perspectives. In "The Past and the Present in the Present" (1977), Bloch examined the cultural as well as the cognitive aspects of language while studying the temporal expressions of memory. In 1991, in "Language, Anthropology, and Cognitive Science," he advocated interdisciplinary approaches in the social and cognitive sciences. *Essays on Cultural Transmission* (2005) was another provocative work because of its call for a partnership between anthropology and cognitive psychology. In his recent works, like *The Blob* (2011) and *Reconciling Social Science and Cognitive Science Notions of the "Self"* (2010), Bloch reasserted this position. Bloch's approach, particularly in the studies of rituals, language, and cognition, has had a continuing influence in different domains of anthropological queries.

Muhammad Aurang Zeb Mughal

See also Cambridge University; Cognitive Anthropology; Godelier, Maurice; Lévi-Strauss, Claude; London School of Economics; Marxist Anthropology; Structuralism

Further Readings

Bloch, M. Interview by Alan Macfarlane on 29th May 2008 (S. Harrison, Ed.). DSpace at Cambridge,

University of Cambridge. Retrieved from http://www
.dspace.cam.ac.uk/bitstream/1810/198365/1/bloch.txt

Boden, M. A. (2006). *Mind as machine: A history of cognitive science* (Vol. 2, p. 526). Oxford, UK: Clarendon Press.

Houtman, G. (1988). Interview with Maurice Bloch. *Anthropology Today, 4*(1), 18–21.

Kaaristo, M. (2008). The reluctant anthropologist: An interview with Maurice Bloch. *Eurozine*. Retrieved from http://www.eurozine.com/articles/2008–02–28-bloch-en.html

Kuper, A. (1983). *Anthropology and anthropologists: The modern British school.* London, UK: Routledge & Kegan Paul.

BLOOMFIELD, LEONARD

Leonard Bloomfield (1887–1949) was an American pioneer of structural linguistics. Bloomfield came from a high-achieving intellectual family of Austrian Jewish origin and grew up in the hotel business. He was educated at Harvard and first specialized in Germanic languages, writing about Germanic secondary ablaut for his PhD. He continued to work on these topics through his career, teaching German at the University of Illinois, later teaching Germanic philology at Ohio State University and the University of Chicago, sometimes writing articles in German, and writing a textbook of Dutch (Bloomfield, 1944). He was later to turn his flair for practical linguistics to the U.S. war effort, producing a textbook and a grammatical sketch of Russian for the Army Specialist Training Program. He taught for most of his career at the University of Chicago, moving to Yale as Sterling Professor in 1940. Bloomfield wrote the *Call,* the academic proclamation that led to the founding of the Linguistic Society of America in 1925, publishing the first article in its journal *Language*. A paralyzing stroke in 1946 ended his career; and he died in New Haven, Connecticut, in 1949. His student Bernard Bloch published Bloomfield's obituary in the journal *Language* in 1949.

Cautious, reserved, uncharismatic but kindly (and with a whimsical and occasionally scabrous sense of humor), Bloomfield made quiet but massive contributions to general linguistics, and Austronesian and Americanist linguistics, all written in immediately comprehensible prose. His work in general linguistics includes two introductions to the field, *An Introduction to the Study of Language,* published in 1914, and the much longer *Language,* published in 1933; the latter work is still in print, and its account of processes in historical linguistics was long taken as the best introduction to the field. Bloomfield's earlier work reflects his interest in the psychological theories of Wilhelm Wundt; his later philosophical position was less dogmatic, and he showed much interest in behaviorism as posited by A. P. Weiss. Bloomfield's cautiousness about describing the semantics or system of meaning of a language with the same degree of scientific rigor as its grammatical structure was often misunderstood by critics as perpetuating an antimentalist view of language, in which semantics was excluded. This was not the case. He spent much time putting his ideas to practical effect, employing linguistic methods in attempts to enable English-speaking children to learn to read effectively.

His Austronesian works are few, principally comprising some work on Ilocano of the northern Philippines and a collection of texts, with grammatical description and glossary, of Manila Tagalog. Like the Ilocano sketch, this was based on fieldwork with a consultant, in this latter case a trainee architect at the University of Chicago, who dictated these texts to Bloomfield, and it achieves the linguistic ideal of descriptive adequacy because the use and sense of every form found in the text is accounted for and every feature of the grammar of the language attested in the text is explained. As a model of descriptive work, it has few equals.

From the 1920s, Bloomfield did much work on the Algonquian languages of Canada and the Great Lakes, producing an impressive collection of work, including texts, grammar, and dictionary materials, on Menominee, the Native American language once spoken around Elkhart Lake, Wisconsin, where he had grown up (until then it had barely been documented). His major work on this subject is *The Menomini Language,* which was published in 1962, 13 years after his death. Bloomfield also visited Saskatchewan, collecting two volumes of texts of Plains Cree, which he published in 1934. His 1958 study of an idiolect of eastern Ojibwe, *Eastern Ojibwa: Grammatical Sketch, Texts and Word List,* ranks with his Tagalog work as an intellectual accomplishment of high descriptive adequacy. Bloomfield also did secondary work on the conservative Algonquian language Fox (Mesquakie), from the analysis of texts collected by Truman Michelson, and he later reconstructed much of the Proto-Algonquian language's sound system and morphological structure, although his construction of a Proto-Central Algonquian language, including Ojibwe, Cree, Fox, Nenominee, and Potawatomi (and Miami-Illinois and Shawnee), has not withstood the test of time.

Bloomfield's best work tends to be of considerable length, and much of this appeared posthumously or is still only accessible through the Human Relations Area Files. Charles Hockett, Bloomfield's literary executor and fellow Algonquianist, produced an anthology of his work in 1970, which contained most of the important short pieces but omitted much good work (e.g., almost all his Austronesian work). This was often due to its bulk, though the anthology's contents show Bloomfield as deeply humane. In 1990, Robert Hall also published an interesting volume about Bloomfield and his achievements, including memoirs by former students and colleagues and younger scholars in his specialty areas. His collected works remain to be assembled under one imprint.

Bloomfield's main contribution is the scientific systematization of linguistic study and the presentation of rigorous models for linguistic description, from phonetics and phonology to syntactic and sociolinguistic matters; his writings, especially his 1933 volume *Language*, provided the means with which to study linguistics (both descriptive linguistics and topics in more strongly historical, sociological, and psychological aspects of the field, and as a scientific subject at the university level). The Bloomfield Prize recognizes especially great achievements in linguistics.

Anthony Grant

See also Wundt, Wilhelm

Further Readings

Bloomfield, L. (1914). *An introduction to the study of language.* New York, NY: Holt.
———. (1917). *Tagalog texts with grammatical analysis* (Vol. 3, Pts. 2–4). Urbana: University of Illinois Press.
———. (1933). *Language.* New York, NY: Holt.
———. (1934). *Plains Cree texts* (Vol. 16). New York, NY: Stechert.
———. (1942). Outline of Ilocano syntax. *Language, 18,* 193–200.
———. (1946). Algonquian. In C. Osgood (Ed.), *Linguistic structures of Native America* (pp. 85–129). New York, NY: Viking Fund.
———. (1958). *Eastern Ojibwa: Grammatical sketch, texts, and word list.* Ann Arbor: University of Michigan Press.
———. (1962). *The Menomini language.* New Haven, CT: Yale University Press.
Hall, R. A., Jr. (Ed.). (1990). *Leonard Bloomfield: A life for language.* Amsterdam, Netherlands: Benjamins.
Hockett, C. F. (Ed.). (1970). *A Leonard Bloomfield anthology.* Bloomington: Indiana University Press.

BOAS, FRANZ

Franz Boas (1858–1942), the German-born American anthropologist, was the predominant intellectual and organizing figure in the professionalization of anthropology in the United States in the late 19th and early 20th centuries. His efforts throughout a long lifetime gave American anthropology its shape and character. Boas arrived in the United States from Germany before there were anthropology departments or PhD degrees anywhere in the world; and through his research, writings, organizing and editorial activities, and training of generations of students, he created the field as it existed throughout most of the 20th century. He was also the leading moral figure in anthropology and its public face until his death in December 1942.

Biography

Franz Boas was born in Minden, Germany, in 1858, into a Jewish family influenced by the *Haskalah* movement, or the Jewish Enlightenment. Without denying their Jewish identity, such families abandoned most of the practices and beliefs of Judaism to become secular and "free-thinking" Germans. Young Franz was brought up in an atmosphere of science, art, and liberal politics; his feminist mother founded the first kindergarten in their hometown and was associated with political radicals.

From his childhood, Franz Boas had an insatiable appetite for learning—not only for all the sciences and mathematics but for philosophy, literature, folklore, geography, and cultural history as well. After graduation from Gymnasium, he attended the universities of Heidelberg, Bonn, and Kiel, where many of his teachers were among the world leaders in their fields. He completed his PhD in physics in 1881 with a dissertation in psychophysics (the forerunner of experimental psychology) titled "A Contribution to the Perception of the Color of Water."

After 6 months of compulsory military service, during which time he published seven scientific papers, Franz Boas turned in a new direction, undertaking a hazardous expedition almost single-handedly to Baffinland to study the Eskimos (Inuit) and their harsh environment. Geography and ethnography had long been among his interests; when he was 13 years old, he wrote of his desire to do research in "all the unknown lands" to know the customs and habits of the peoples there. Boas intended to study the relationship of a people who were as dependent on their natural environment as the Eskimos. During the year 1883–1884 on Baffin Island, he carried out research in geography, cartography, hydrology, meteorology, ethnography, and linguistics, and in 1888, he published one of the first scientific ethnographies, *The Central Eskimo*. As Cole noted in his 1983 article on Boas's diary from his Baffin Island work, for Boas, perhaps the most significant results of his experience among the Inuit were his realization of the common humanity and intelligence of his hosts, the *strengthening* (his word) of his view of the relativity of all culture, and his recognition "that the evil as well as the value of a person lies in the cultivation of the heart which I find or do not find here just as much as amongst us."

Boas returned confirmed in his belief that to serve humanity a man had to work to promote the truth and that science would be his way to the truth.

During the year 1885–1886, Boas completed the rigorous qualifications for a full-time academic position in geography at the University of Berlin, and he studied physical anthropology with Germany's leading physician-pathologist-proto-anthropologist, Rudolf Virchow, whose ideas and character greatly influenced Boas. Other important influences on Boas's ideas about race, culture, and language were Theodor Waitz, Moritz Lazarus, and Hermann Steinthal. He also worked as an assistant curator and studied ethnography with Germany's leading ethnologist, Adolf Bastian, at the Royal Ethnographic Museum. At the museum, he was inspired by what he learned of Northwest Coast culture, and he spent time with nine Bella Coola Indians who were visiting Berlin with a Wild West show, demonstrating aspects of their culture. During the summer of 1886, he began his lifelong field research with the native peoples of the Canadian Pacific Northwest.

In 1887, Boas married Marie Krackowizer, who had grown up in New York, and made the decision to immigrate to the United States. He was discouraged by Germany's rigid academic system and disaffected with the illiberal and anti-Semitic political climate there, and he believed that in America he would be freer, both politically and academically, to seek the truth as he understood it.

His first job in the United States, in 1887–1888, was as an associate editor of the new journal of the American Association for the Advancement of Science, which gave him an excellent platform for the publication of many short articles that displayed his depth and range as a scientist. From 1889 to 1892, he taught at Clark University, established 2 years before as a research institution. Although Boas and eight other distinguished faculty members resigned because of a dispute with the university's founder, during his brief stay at Clark, he was able carry out pioneering research in physical anthropology and publish a great deal of material from his Northwest Coast fieldwork. From 1892 to 1894, he served as "chief assistant" anthropologist for the World's Columbian Exposition in Chicago and helped establish anthropology at the new Chicago Natural History Museum (later the Field Museum).

In 1896, Boas began work at the American Museum of Natural History and teaching physical anthropology at Columbia University. While at the museum, he continued his pioneering work on the "life group," full-size dioramas representing people in action, and he conceived, organized, and directed the Jesup North Pacific Expedition, whose purpose was to explore the relationships between peoples and cultures of Siberia and their connection to the Native American cultures on the American side of the Bering Strait. Boas resigned his position at the American Museum in 1905, but he continued his career at Columbia University, where he had become professor of anthropology in 1899. Franz Boas formally retired from Columbia in 1936 but was active in anthropology and as a social and political critic until his death from a heart attack in the Columbia University faculty dining room on December 21, 1942.

Critical Contributions to Anthropology

Franz Boas arrived in the United States at a crucial moment, just as specialized scientific disciplines and societies were being formed, when generalist amateurs who ranged over various fields were increasingly being supplanted by scientists and scholars trained in specialized disciplines. Prior to this time, research into American Indian cultures, languages, and archaeology was the province of devoted amateurs. The physical anthropology of that era was primarily concerned with proving polygenesis and the inferiority of "the Negro" and was based on the ideas of a physician (Samuel George Morton) and a geologist (Louis Agassiz). Boas, however, had the benefit of specialized training and experience in human geography, ethnography, anthropometry, and other aspects of physical anthropology in Germany, whose science was much admired at that time. For Boas, the subject matter of anthropology included all human social life around the world and throughout time. With his background, he was uniquely placed to contribute to all aspects of the developing "four-field" approach in American anthropology, uniting cultural and physical anthropology, and linguistics and prehistoric archaeology into one program for the study of humanity.

Cultural Evolutionism and Race

Two major ideas dominated social thought when Boas arrived in America: (1) cultural evolutionism and (2) racial determinism. Evolutionary thought, following Lewis Henry Morgan, E. B. Tylor, and Herbert Spencer, viewed human history as the unfolding of an inevitable process of progressive development from simple to complex manifestations of culture. Accordingly, peoples could be ranked depending on where they were thought to fall on this great ladder of advancement. The idea was favored by both the political left and the political right: Karl Marx and Friedrich Engels interpreted this as a promise of a still more advanced future of egalitarian communism, while for the Social Darwinists and the prophets of colonialism and unrestricted capitalism, it proved that the wealthy and the powerful were in their positions by natural right as representatives of the most advanced stage of civilization.

Racial determinism was founded on the belief that cultural, historical, moral, and behavioral differences could be explained by heredity and that there were fixed biological entities called "races" that could be ranked as higher and lower on the scale of evolution. Generally, these rankings fit very nicely with those of the evolutionists, to the disadvantage of the poor, the colonized, and especially the peoples they called "Negroes." Franz Boas questioned both of these hegemonic paradigms, and in

1911, he published *The Mind of Primitive Man*, the single most important work for those who disagreed with evolutionism and racial determinism. This book gave a scientific basis to those who questioned those dominant ideas.

Attacking both paradigms on many fronts, Boas offered evidence that the culture of a people did not depend on their biology, that a simple culture did not mean simple minds, and that all humans are basically equal in their mental powers. He demonstrated that there was no inherent connection between a feature like skin color and a particular type of culture but that the culture of a people depended on multiple factors, including its natural environment, its location relative to that of other cultures as a source of new ideas and resources, and the accidents of individual innovations and creative reinterpretations of borrowed ideas throughout its history. Above all, he argued that cultures and learned behaviors are not functions of biology but depend on the complex past histories of peoples. Boas's arguments were consonant with his own values: his fervent belief in equality, the imperative to treat individuals according to their own qualities and not as members of a class to which they are assigned, and his insistence that one should avoid an exaggerated opinion of one's own culture and consider other cultures objectively. The implications of the arguments and demonstrations in that book for the new science of anthropology in the United States are incalculable.

Culture, Ethnography, and Psychology

Boas put the notion of culture and cultures at the center of American anthropology. He located culture within communities, lived and acted out by individuals in groups. Beyond his concern with the history and development of cultures, however, he emphasized the individuals who lived within these systems and the conscious and unconscious impact of their cultures on their psychology. Franz Boas's approach to the study of a culture is exemplified by his work with the indigenous peoples of the Northwest Coast, especially those he called the "Kwakiutl" (today they are known as the Kwakwa'wakw). He made 12 field trips to the area between 1886 and 1931. Because of the brevity of many of his summer visits and because so much of the "traditional" culture had already been abandoned, less of the material was collected through participant observation than through interviews with informants. From this research came an enormous volume of publications reporting on Boas's experiences at feasts, ceremonies, potlatches, and interviews. However, Boas also published many texts in the languages of each of the peoples (Kwakwa'wakw, Tsimshian, Bella Coola, Chinook, Bella Bella, etc.), with translations. These were mostly collected by Indian collaborators, then edited and published by Boas as part of his effort to capture for posterity everything of the language and culture that was available before it was lost forever. He hoped to present "the culture as it appears to the Indian himself," his "world view."

Boas contended that the habits and patterns of behavior imbibed by an individual from his or her culturally constructed childhood and environment became largely unconscious. Speakers of a language are usually not aware of the rules and peculiarities of their speech, and so it is with members of a culture; we frequently act automatically in conformity with tradition. Anyone, even trained anthropologists, may have strong emotions and irrational reactions when confronted with another culture. Boas hoped to avoid the unconscious subjective views of the ethnographer by having the Indians record their own texts. (Pursuing this method, Boas trained and worked with a number of Indians, including his third PhD student, William Jones, and Ella Deloria.)

Boas gave anthropology its picture of the Kwakiutl, their potlatch, and the wealth of their ceremonial and material life. Today, more than a century later, the Kwakwa'wakw are proudly undertaking a reconstruction of their old culture, drawing in large measure on the materials that Boas and his Indian collaborators made available through their linguistic and ethnographic research.

The Study of Languages and Linguistics

From his first published piece in *Science* in 1886 until his last completed manuscripts 56 years later, Boas was concerned with documenting American Indian languages. Many Indian languages were on the verge of extinction, and he worked tirelessly to have them recorded, training his students and Indian collaborators to collect language materials. He spent much of his life seeking funds for researchers and publishing the results of their work and was the moving force behind the *Handbook of American Indian Languages* and a founder and editor of the *International Journal of American Linguistics.*

His importance for linguistics more generally went far beyond these efforts, especially for the study of unwritten languages.

Boas's aim was to present these languages from the point of view of their speakers and to avoid analyses of them based on the categories of Indo-European or other classical languages. While discerning that all languages are built on the same general principles, he taught that each language had its own distinctive ways of looking at the world. (This is the same principle that Boas preached to his students regarding other aspects of the cultures.) His work ranged widely over the problems of language, and it also led to the study of phonetics by his student Edward Sapir, and the founders of structural linguistics built on his work on morphology.

Physical Anthropology

Boas made vital contributions to the related question of "race" and human variation, to studies of growth, and to research on hereditary and environmental influences on humans. Boas found the physical anthropology of his day to be little more than static taxonomy, anthropometrics, and speculation about race and character, but he left it as the modern study of human biology. His work lay behind the development of "the new physical anthropology" in the late 1940s.

Boas has been wrongly accused of insisting on the primacy of environment in an effort to discredit heredity as a factor in human behavior, well-being, and achievement. On the contrary, he repeatedly proposed and carried out studies seeking to determine to what extent and under what circumstances both heredity and environment operated and what was the relation between the two in various circumstances. He and his students made studies of human growth, intergenerational modifications of form, the impact of interbreeding, the plasticity of the human body under different environmental conditions, and so on.

Growth and Change

In 1890, Boas started the first longitudinal study of growth in America, measuring schoolchildren in Worcester, Massachusetts. The implications of this research were far-reaching, both methodologically and in substance. His work produced the first growth standards for height and weight for American children, and he introduced the notion of "tempo of growth"—showing that individuals vary in their *pace* of physical and mental development, slow at first and faster later, or vice versa, and partly dependent on environment as well as heredity. Focusing on the matter of pace, he introduced the terms *advanced* and *retarded* in place of *bright* and *dull*.

In 1908, Boas began a massive study of recent immigrants to New York City and their children, undertaken for the U.S. Immigration Commission. He and his assistants took measurements of stature, weight, length and breadth of heads (cephalic index), and facial index for 18,000 individuals. While they found some differences in stature and weight to the advantage of the American-born children—what might be expected from better nutrition and conditions in the new country—the finding with the greatest impact was that there was some tendency for the American-born children to differ slightly but definitely in head shape from their parents. The cephalic index had previously been considered both stable and a reliable marker of "race"—a vital factor in classification and the historic tracing of peoples. The finding that the cephalic index could respond to environmental differences, that there is a degree of plasticity in the expression of this trait, had a powerful impact on the field of physical anthropology and its position on race.

Race

Franz Boas is the most influential figure in the history of the debate over racial determinism and its inevitable accompaniment, racism. Although he began his work on human variation before the rediscovery of Gregor Mendel's research into genetics, using new measurements and observations, the biostatistical methods that he had developed, and his ability to rethink old problems, he stated a number of propositions that contradicted the tenets of the racial determinists. The fundamental elements of his critique were presented in *The Mind of Primitive Man* in 1911. Boas did not argue outright that "races" do not exist—which is the present consensus among physical anthropologists—instead he had a dynamic populational view, focusing on individuals and family lines and their histories, which contradicted the traditional static view. By insisting that "race," language, and culture are three distinct phenomena,

varying independently, he clarified many aspects of cultural history and made a convincing case that "race" cannot be correlated with historical success. Following various lines of evidence, Boas declared that there was no convincing evidence that differences in the mental behavior of people were due to physical differences. Boas inspired and guided the work of the social psychologist Otto Klineberg, whose research challenged the validity of intelligence quotient and other tests meant to prove the inferiority of Negroes and others. The findings of Boas and his followers directly countered the claims of the racial determinists, who rightly saw the Boasians as their most significant opponents. To some extent, this is still true in the 21st century.

The Influence of Franz Boas

Boas's influence and leadership were manifest as early as the 1890s through his research, publishing, editing, and organizing (associations, publications, and research projects), but once he began training doctoral students at Columbia University, he became central to the developing discipline. By 1920, 13 students of cultural anthropology and linguistics had received doctorates under Boas at Columbia, while the other seven PhDs in these fields in the United States at that time were deeply influenced by him. (Harvard had been producing PhDs in archaeology and physical anthropology since 1894.) His first Columbia PhD was A. L. Kroeber in 1901, and his last students got their doctoral degrees in 1940. Many of his students went on to be leaders in the field themselves, a number of them founding departments of anthropology at leading universities. His early PhDs included the most important figures in the intellectual development of cultural anthropology: A. L. Kroeber, Frank Speck (Pennsylvania degree), Robert H. Lowie, Edward Sapir, Alexander Goldenweiser, Paul Radin, Fay-Cooper Cole, and Leslie Spier. Students of a later generation included Ruth Benedict, Margaret Mead, Melville J. Herskovits, Gladys Reichard, Ruth Bunzel, Melville Jacobs, Ashley Montagu, and Ruth Landes. From 1914 onward, more than half of his students who were granted PhDs were women. His international reach was great as well. Among other activities, he spent the year 1911–1912 in Mexico helping establish the basis for stratigraphic work in archaeology in the country, working with Manuel Gamio, and he was an important influence on Gilberto Freyre, one of Brazil's most influential social theorists and intellectuals.

Boas was a political activist until his dying day, speaking out and organizing for freedom of thought and speech and the rights of individuals and groups. He fought prejudice, racism, and chauvinism wherever he encountered it, even at considerable personal cost and despite reprisals against his department. Many of the students who were attracted to him at Columbia had the same values, and this imparted to Columbian anthropology—and to some extent American anthropology—a distinctly liberal stance.

The author of six books and more than 700 monographs, articles, and other published pieces, Franz Boas touched every aspect of anthropology; his range of interests and expertise was enormous, and his legacy is anthropology as it exists in the United States—even with all of the changes in the field since his death. He was recognized and honored throughout the world for his scientific contributions; and although he and his work have often been challenged, his legacy is currently being rediscovered with a new appreciation early in the 21st century.

Herbert S. Lewis

See also American Museum of Natural History; Bastian, Adolf; Benedict, Ruth F.; Columbia University; Mead, Margaret; Morgan, Lewis Henry; Sapir, Edward; Spencer, Herbert; Tylor, Edward Burnett

Further Readings

Boas, F. (1888). *The central Eskimo*. Part of the sixth annual report of the Bureau of Ethnology, Smithsonian Institution, Washington, DC.

———. (1911). *The mind of primitive man*. New York, NY: Macmillan.

———. (1928). *Anthropology and modern life*. New York, NY: W. W. Norton.

———. (1940). *Race, language and culture*. New York, NY: Free Press.

———. (1966). *Kwakiutl ethnography* (H. Codere, Ed.). Chicago, IL: University of Chicago Oewaa.

Cole, D. (1983). "The value of a person lies in his Herzensbildung": Franz Boas' letter-diary, 1883–1884. In G. W. Stocking (Ed.), *Observers observed: Essays on ethnographic fieldwork* (pp. 13–52). Madison: University of Wisconsin Press.

———. (1999). *Franz Boas: The early years, 1858–1906*. Seattle: University of Washington Press.

Goldschmidt, W. (Ed.). (1959). *The anthropology of Franz Boas* (Memoir No. 89). Menasha, WI: American Anthropological Association.

Lewis, H. S. (2001). Boas, Darwin, science, and anthropology. *Current Anthropology, 42*, 381–406.

———. (2001). The passion of Franz Boas. *The American Anthropologist, 103*, 447–467.

Stocking, G. W., Jr. (1968). *Race, culture, and evolution: Essays in the history of anthropology*. New York, NY: Free Press.

———. (Ed.). (1974). *The shaping of American anthropology, 1883–1911. A Franz Boas reader*. New York, NY: Basic Books.

BOHANNAN, PAUL

Paul Bohannan (1920–2007), a prodigious representative of post–World War II anthropology, created, jointly with Laura Bohannan, an ethnographic corpus on the Tiv of central Nigeria that stands out as a unique achievement. The Bohannans conducted their Nigerian fieldwork between 1949 and 1953. Paul published in 1954 a description of Tiv farm life and in 1957 *Justice and Judgment Among the Tiv*, which is discussed below. With Laura Bohannan, he published *The Tiv of Central Nigeria*, five source books on Tiv religion and three source books on Tiv ethnography for the Human Relations Area Files, and *Tiv Economy*. In 1955, the Bohannans went for a second period of fieldwork among the Bantu Baluiya of western Kenya, an outcome of which was one of the four chapters Paul wrote in a book he edited in 1968, *African Homicide and Suicide*. From the 1960s through the 1990s, Paul Bohannan published several popular textbooks and edited or coedited high-profile volumes. This entry focuses on the areas of economic and legal anthropology, where Paul Bohannan exerted his greatest influence, although he also contributed theoretical ideas on religion, warfare, African homicide and suicide, and divorce in the United States.

In economic anthropology, Bohannan is known for the notion of "spheres of exchange." In two articles (published in 1955 and 1959), he explained that before the colonial period, Tiv exchanges fell into three categories. The first included locally produced foodstuffs, small livestock, household utensils, tools, and raw materials, all normally bartered in market-places. The second consisted of cattle, slaves, brass rods, and a locally woven cloth. The third had a single item, rights in marriageable young women, because the giving of a bride could only be compensated by the return of another marriageable woman to her guardian.

The first article was "Principles of Exchange and Investment." Tiv men strove to convert subsistence goods to higher category wealth and were scornful of a person rich in food and livestock but unable to turn them into prestige valuables, but these very values made conversions difficult. Those who converted down, meaning from prestige goods to food, had to invoke catastrophic circumstances or the need to help kinsmen to explain their actions and avoid humiliation. People converted up with the ultimate aim of accumulating dependents and power.

The term *spheres of exchange* was adopted from Raymond Firth's 1939 book on Tikopia, an island in the Pacific Ocean (precedents are W. E. Armstrong's description of Rossel Island shells as nonconvertible exchange media and Bronisław Malinowski's contrast between Trobriand food exchanges and the reciprocal gifting of *kula* valuables). Although the Pacific islands had nothing like the trade and currency traditions of the African savanna, Bohannan followed Firth closely, save for accentuating "marriageable girls," which for Firth was only a tentative category. He also elaborated on the ranking of the spheres, which became an indirect expression of the competitive ambitions of Tiv men. Bohannan presented the spheres model as his own "systematization" but consistent with the Tiv covert ideology; even so, generations of Africanists not familiar with economic anthropology or Pacific ethnography believed that the Tiv thought explicitly in terms of spheres of exchange as delineated by Bohannan and searched for similar kinds of thinking elsewhere in Africa.

Bohannan's second paper focused on money and introduced *special purpose money*, a term that Karl Polanyi had borrowed from brokerage firms' practices to explain aspects of ancient Babylonian economy in a 1957 coedited book. In some societies of antiquity, Polanyi wrote, money could be used only to pay taxes or in noncommercial obligations such as blood compensation or bride wealth; or one kind of money served to make such payments and another kind to buy and sell stuff in the marketplace;

or things were valued in a notional money that did not exist physically, while actual transactions took the form of barter. Polanyi argued that currencies such as these, fulfilling only one function, differ fundamentally from that found in our monetary system; the impression that these remote societies had a commercial life like ours is an illusion, because with no "general purpose money" economic integration could only be achieved by political decisions. Bohannan now reasoned that Tiv brass rods, which were exchanged against all other goods within the second sphere but not very frequently against food, should be considered more like special-purpose money. He thus modified Polanyi's idea of "special purpose," which was connected to the functions of money and not to the range of goods it could buy. According to Bohannan, Tiv economy was "multicentric" in the sense that barriers to exchange insulated different sectors from feedback effects. In the 20th century, however, colonial administration had introduced European coins and the obligation to pay taxes in them, and new commodities that could not be assigned to any sphere had flooded the markets. Women and junior men sold crops to outside merchants and used the proceeds to purchase local and imported goods. The administration also intervened to ban bride exchanges, encouraging instead the payment of bride wealth, which junior men favored. These developments had eroded the sphere boundaries and dissolved the multicentric economy, a source of great worry to community elders. The notion of spheres of exchange became one of the organizing principles in the book *Tiv Economy*, which Laura and Paul Bohannan coauthored in 1968.

D. C. Dorward and J. H. Latham, historians of Nigeria, criticized this abridged account of economic history that Bohannan provided. It was also said that it misleads about the precolonial West African savanna economy, which was one of the most monetized in the premodern world and made room for strong drives to self-actualize, as evident from subsequent ethnographies of Nigeria and prefigured also in the Bohannans' own. But those who popularized Bohannan's ideas should share the blame; reduced to caricature and reproduced endlessly as a textbook vignette, Bohannan's spheres of exchange were distorted beyond recognition to suggest almost the opposite of what he had meant by them.

In the 1960s, Bohannan, along with fellow economist at Northwestern George Dalton, became known as a promoter of Polanyi's ideas and, in the great rift that divided economic anthropology, a prominent substantivist. Their collaboration produced a book called *Markets in Africa*, which included 28 essays by acclaimed anthropologists. The introduction stressed, following a lead by Polanyi, that the marketplaces observed in many parts of Africa did not indicate a market principle–based economy. In those markets, women traded small amounts of perishables, or people sold one thing only to buy another, while households produced the bulk of their subsistence; more substantial exchanges materialized as gifts or obligations; land was allocated within household and kinship groups; and a king could administer trade in valuables. If these marketplaces manifested fluctuating prices and the play of supply and demand, these reflected only temporary scarcities and had no bearing on production decisions. Land and labor were not sold, and the market process did not serve to allocate resources, as it did in commercial economies. It is unclear how much these sound comparative economic systems ideas (which Polanyi highlighted in polemics against Central European opponents who were hostile to government regulation and planning) were understood among other substantivist or formalist anthropologists, mostly trained in the empiricist Boasian tradition. The downside was that these ideas downplayed, once again, West African long-distance trade connections to the Mediterranean and, from the 16th century onward, to the Atlantic. The introduction provided a typology for nonmodern economies: marketless (the Pacific), peripheral market (much of precolonial Africa), and peasant, where export crops sales had become indispensable for farmers, forcing other changes (20th-century colonial situations).

Bohannan's legal anthropology was built on litigation cases in Native Authority courts, which the British had introduced in their African colonies and on which the discipline of legal anthropology flourished in the United Kingdom and the United States. Bohannan aimed to understand Tiv ways of looking at disputes and their settlement, their "folk theory," which differs from "law," the folk theory of the Western world. He presented his project as the translation of Tiv categories of thought and action into those of the English language, to allow readers to make sense of them. But the influence of linguistic philosophers at Oxford, where he was trained, added a level of subtlety to his idea of "translation,"

and Bohannan set forth something more complicated than simple juxtaposition. First of all, not all Tiv notions are articulated or even "conscious"; the anthropologist needs to make explicit what was not said, discover premises, deduce ideas from behavior, and sometimes construct elaborate representations that hopefully correspond to Tiv agency but that were not verbally communicated by them. This "folk model" is a product of ethnographic theory, not a plain transcription of observations. Second, the English terms that are solicited for this task come loaded with meanings deposited by European institutions and culture history, which the anthropologist needs to strip away, or at least make manifest, in order to convey the Tiv mindset rather than distort it with unwarranted projections. This necessitates a double movement: As Tiv principles are interpreted, English legal terms also need to be explicated with an eye toward Tiv institutions. Bohannan conceived of a comparative jurisprudence, which would be based on the work of scholarly predecessors and remain distinct from the English folk model of law; Tiv material could illuminate analytic comparisons to build such a comparative discipline, but the idea remained embryonic in his writing.

Native Authority courts were a colonial innovation. Tiv built them into their culture by using the framework and vocabulary of *jir*, proceedings among kinsmen. Bohannan arranged his cases to explain how a complaint is brought; the behavior of defendants, judges, and witnesses; and how settlements were reached. He privileged Tiv expressions, because the language in which the process is conducted is key to the folk system. Bohannan also discussed substantive law as applied to marriage and debt. Tiv courts did not proceed by reference to a set of distinct rules and precedents. The Tiv also did not distinguish between tort, contract, and property, treating them all as forms of debt. Decisions depended on what was right in particular cases, to counteract the damage done by the breach of proper behavior. The plaintiff could also resort to self-help, and occasionally court settlements allowed for that. Yet the *jir* restored social relations, whereas in former days, self-enforcement could lead to revenge, which is not a jural mechanism. Tiv also sought redress by composing scandalous songs about a wrongdoer, which then turned into a contest and, in former times, often ended in a violent showdown between two groups.

Bohannan last presented proceedings that he called "moots," where neighbors and kinsmen decided disputes following death, illness, or an evil omen within the group under the guidance of community elders. These involved a different idiom and a set of images from Native court disputes. Eliciting the cosmology and mystical human agency underlying these proceedings, Bohannan rose to the summit of his ethnographic powers. The reparative actions following a moot were not secular but ritual, made to stand for many individual corrections of social relations.

Both court cases and moots made communities run smoothly. Bohannan displayed little interest in social alignments and causes, or in the conflicts that generated the cases he studied. His analyses open with the plaintiff bringing a grievance, the eruption of disorder, and end when the disturbance abates, at least temporarily, with the judges' settlement or the ritual concluding a moot. Durkheimian interest in cohesion subtends the analysis.

The term *folk system* perhaps conceals difficulties in Bohannan's work. Like the Tiv, most Euro-Americans do not distinguish between tort and crime; lawyers' language differs from common English speech; the boundary between lawyers' categories and comparative jurisprudence remains elusive. Max Gluckman complained that Bohannan's emphasis on Tiv culture made their proceedings look too different. On the one hand, a legal expert could identify many categories of action in Tiv proceedings that they do not recognize, as is true of British and American publics. On the other, Edmund Leach had already indicated that among the Kachin of Burma as well, "debt" subsumed multiple social relations; furthermore, the connection between debt and other social obligations survives also in some expressions of the English language.

Elsewhere, Bohannan generalized about law. Social institutions involve norms everywhere, but only some societies restate these norms as rules intended for a special institution that applies justice. When such a legal institution exists, trouble situations are disengaged from their social matrix and brought to the court to be handled according to this body of rules. Where "law" exists as a separate body, it can modify other social institutions because it can be out of phase with them, either because it lags behind changes in customs or because it is used for innovating. Bohannan noted, as did other legal anthropologists, that Tiv court cases did not end with a verdict but with compromise, where parties concurred in the principles and provisions of the settlement. Multicentric situations with multiple judges, moots, contests, oracles, and self-help lead not to neat systems of law and formal *corpus juris* but to less precise restatements of norms. Bohannan's legal anthropology does point to generalizations beyond the rich description of Tiv culture, although perhaps not as boldly as his economic anthropology.

Mahir Şaul

See also Durkheim, Émile; Firth, Raymond; Gluckman, Max; Polanyi, Karl

Further Readings

Bohannan, L., & Bohannan, P. (1968). *Tiv economy.* Evanston, IL: Northwestern University Press.

Bohannan, P. (1957). *Justice and judgment among the Tiv.* London, UK: Oxford University Press.

———. (1965). The differing realms of the law. *American Anthropologist, 67*(6, Pt. 2), 33–42.

Bohannan, P., & Dalton, G. (Eds.). (1962). *Markets in Africa.* Evanston, IL: Northwestern University Press.

BOURDIEU, PIERRE

With more than 35 books and a considerable number of scientific papers to his credit, Pierre Bourdieu (1930–2002) is regarded as one of the most important social scientists of the 20th century. His key concepts (habitus, field, capital, symbolic violence) and his analyses have had a decisive impact on all disciplines in the humanities and the social sciences.

Brief Biography

Pierre Bourdieu grew up in a small village in a remote area of southern France (Béarn). The son of a post office clerk, he was first sent to high school in the closest city and then to Paris to study philosophy at the renowned École Normale Supérieure. Coming from a lower class background, during his school trajectory, Bourdieu was subjected to "symbolic violence" that deeply affected his perception of social life and later his work, as he explained in his "non-autobiography." He did military service in Algeria for 2 years and then taught for another

2 years (1958–1960) at the University of Algiers, where he was engaged in an empirical study of labor, economy, and social change in Algerian society. This period inspired several books on Algeria and numerous case studies, subsequently integrated into his more general and seminal works. Returning to France in 1960, Bourdieu was assistant to the philosopher and sociologist Raymond Aron until 1964, when he was briefly an assistant professor at the University of Lille and then at the École Pratique des Hautes Études, where he became the youngest director of studies since the school's founding.

On his return to France, Bourdieu took his own childhood village in Béarn as an object of study and analyzed the restructuring of the peasantry. He showed that the transformation of the system of matrimonial exchanges resulted from a restructuring of society around the opposition between the outlying villages (*hameaux*) and the central township (*bourg*), which progressively acquires a monopoly of urban functions. Right from these early works, in his analyses of the peasantry, Bourdieu brings to light the impact of changes in sociological configurations on the techniques of the body (*hexis)* and on perception.

At the same time, Bourdieu embarked on a long-term reflection on culture, education, and inequalities that stresses the weight of social and cultural inequalities in educational systems. These inequalities enable the most privileged to reproduce their positions at the top of the hierarchy and block the social mobility of the most underprivileged. These works brought him to public attention, especially after the widespread protest movements of 1968.

In 1981, after the publication of two major works, *Distinction: A Social Critique of the Judgment of Taste* and *The Logic of Practice*, Bourdieu was appointed to a chair at the Collège de France, the country's most prestigious research institution. He carried on his research there for 20 years. In the 1990s, Bourdieu spoke out strongly and conspicuously against the ravages of neoliberalism and the erosion of the welfare state. Throughout his career, Bourdieu deployed very effective strategies to diffuse his works. He edited a collection for Editions de Minuit from 1964, then for Editions du Seuil in 1992. In 1975, he founded his own journal, *Actes de la Recherche en Science Sociales*, which stood apart from other academic journals in its format and layout, and in 1995, he created his own publishing house, Raisons d'Agir. He also edited a number of works that aimed to give an accessible overview of his work and gathered a large team of collaborators, who continue to develop his arguments in the most varied areas. Bourdieu died in 2002.

Empirical Diversity and Theoretical Unity

The extreme diversity of the objects of Bourdieu's empirical research, ranging from the peasant world to education, culture, science, and politics, finds its unity in a theoretical system that has had a decisive impact on the social sciences and has contributed to the exceptional productivity of its author. This theoretical elaboration was built up, on the one hand, through ethnographic fieldwork, participant observation, surveys through questionnaires, and statistical analysis, and, on the other, through rigorous discussions with many disciplines—mainly anthropology, sociology, philosophy, linguistics, history, and literature. Bourdieu was also remarkable for his great capacity to synthesize, putting forward a coherent combination of the contributions of a wide range of authors—often regarded as incompatible—and striving to move beyond a series of canonical oppositions (subjectivism/objectivism, micro/macro, etc.). His theoretical model is characterized by its epistemological foundations, the praxeological approach, and the articulation of two main concepts—*habitus* and *field*—and many auxiliary concepts including participant objectivation, symbolic violence, *doxa* cultural capital, and *hysteresis*.

Epistemology, Reflexivity, and Method

Bourdieu's work contains a considerable number of methodological and epistemological reflections. Drawing on the philosopher Gaston Bachelard, he declares that the sociological object must be built up through a succession of three epistemological acts. It must be *won* against common sense and the illusion of immediate knowledge, *constructed* rationally and through an adequate theoretical apparatus, and *confirmed* in experience—that is, tested against reality. To this end, scientific practice, like all practice, must be objectified by scientific analysis. The reflexive return to the tools of analysis is a precondition for scientific knowledge. To achieve this break with common sense, according to Bourdieu, the researcher must perform a twofold objectivation: (1) objectivation of the social conditions of production of the researcher—of his trajectory and the configuration and functioning of the field in which his work is embedded and the fields that influence his work—and (2) objectivation of his own work of objectivation—of the hidden interests invested in it and the profits they promise. This *participant objectivation* has also a profoundly political and liberatory aim, since the only true freedom is in the knowledge of constraints.

This epistemological vigilance at the heart of the work of inquiry is accompanied by the theoretical ambition of moving beyond the oppositions that structure the social sciences. According to Bourdieu, three main types of theoretical knowledge have been developed to study the social world. The first is phenomenological knowledge, which, as he conceives it, is a set of primary experiences of the social world. For Bourdieu, the problem with the phenomenological perspective (i.e., ethnomethodology or symbolic interactionism) is that it sets up no critical distance either from its own conditions of possibility or from the presuppositions that underlie the intuitive and spontaneous apprehension of the social world that it delivers. Second, objectivist knowledge starts out from the presupposition that the truth of the social world is not accessible from a primary, phenomenological experience and endeavors to construct the objective relations that structure representations and practices. Structuralism is a particular form of this second mode of theoretical knowledge. Bourdieu retains from it, essentially, the determination to break with native theories and above all with a substantialist mode of thought in favor of a *relational thinking* by which he intends to grasp each element analyzed by considering the system of relations within which it takes place and from which its meaning derives. However, this mode of knowledge is also limited, since by inquiring into the conditions of possibility of phenomenological knowledge, it moves away from primary experience. Objectivism proves incapable of developing a theory of practical knowledge of the social world, because it apprehends practices from outside without trying to reconstruct their generative principle. The third mode of theoretical knowledge, the praxeological mode (from *praxis* and *logos*) moves beyond these limits. It aims to grasp the dialectical relations between the objective structures and the structured dispositions that internalize these structures, actualize them, and contribute to their reproduction.

The praxeological mode of knowledge subsumes the objectivist approach by inquiring into the conditions of possibility of primary experience and by considering that the scientific object is *constructed*—but goes beyond it by giving its full weight to that experience. It aims to escape the opposition between objectivism and subjectivism by addressing practices and their mode of production through the dialectical, interdependent relationship between subjective and objective structures.

The Dispositionalist Approach and Habitus

To grasp practices and the unity of their diversity from a praxeological standpoint, Bourdieu mobilizes a concept that derives from a long philosophical tradition but that he makes profoundly sociological: the *habitus*. According to Bourdieu, the habitus is a system of transposable and durable dispositions: "structured structures predisposed to function as structuring structures." Habitus is the principle of the generation of practices and representations. It works as a matrix of perceptions, appreciations, and actions that integrates past experiences and lead agents to develop a regular and regulated behavior without being the result of obedience to rules. The habitus shapes not only a "predisposition," a "tendency," a "propensity," or an "inclination" to act but also a *conatus*, an agent's tendency to persist in his social being because he perceives the world through a system of dispositions—in other words, a set of schemes of perception, appreciation, and action that result from his socialization and that he transposes analogically from one experience to another. Habitus constitutes a generative principle that shapes a regulated improvisation that bears within it a *telos*, a finality, and an *amor fati*, the "love of destiny" that often leads individuals to act in conformity with the economy of the system of constraints and demands of which their dispositions are the product and to "make a virtue of necessity," in other words, to convert constraint into desire.

The dispositionalist theory is a theory of practice, and as such Bourdieu used it to study many objects. For example, he shows the importance of the system of dispositions and therefore the weight of social origin in educational choices, in the capacity to succeed in one's studies or to grasp the implicit principles that govern the production of teachers' judgments. Social inequalities have all the more impact when they are masked by the ideology of taste, of the natural gift (the prodigy, precocity), or of the vocation, which presents social differences as natural differences. The dispositionalist approach brings to light the weight of social differences in the appropriation of academic culture. Social origin plays a decisive role in the acquisition of the codes that make it possible to appreciate encoded works, such as works of art, and thus to succeed in the educational system. Inequality in access to legitimate culture led Bourdieu to study the symbolic dimension of relations of domination. The concept of *symbolic violence* designates the imposition of a cultural arbitrariness (i.e., the teacher's discourse) in the name of a social legitimacy (i.e., his or her status) that masks the power relations on which it is based (i.e., the asymmetrical relationship between teacher and pupil).

The habitus is a system of dispositions produced by internalization of the objective conditions. In so far as the members of the same class share their class experiences and situations, they will have distinctive habitus and lifestyles, which Bourdieu describes in particular in *Distinction: A Social Critique of the Judgement of Taste* (1979). This major work reexamines the Kantian question of the faculty of judging to build up a radical critique of modern esthetics by showing the weight of socialization in the development of the judgment of taste. The spontaneity of such judgments creates the illusion that they spring from free choice and often leads to denial of their social character. Developing a genetic structuralism that aims to analyze the genesis of mental structures and the genesis of social structures and their relations, Bourdieu shows that oppositions in cultural matters reappear at all levels of social life: in food, cosmetics and dress, musical preferences, interior decoration, and so on. These oppositions make it possible to establish emic systems of classification and to show that "taste classifies and it classifies the classifier." The agent's esthetic disposition constitutes the expression of a social position in relation to other positions in the social space. Tastes are the expression of a social difference, referring to an "art of living" that presents social differences as natural difference.

The strength of the dispositionalist analysis is in showing that the most spontaneous or involuntary behaviors, like the most considered behaviors, spring from a matrix of representations and practices that constitutes a system of durable, transposable dispositions acquired by an individual in the course of his socialization. Some socializing agencies exert a decisive influence on this process of incorporation, in particular the family, the school, the state, and the autonomized domains of activity that Bourdieu calls fields.

The Social Space and Social Fields

The singularity of social trajectories, experiences, and their chronology particularizes individuals. Each individual system of individual dispositions constitutes a structural variant of the others, but sociological analysis also establishes that a set of agents placed in similar conditions of existence that imposes a similar type of socialization produce homogeneous systems of dispositions that generate more or less similar practices, a set of common properties, and unquestioned shared beliefs (*doxa*) expressed into a lifestyle and a class habitus. Class habitus is produced through the internalization of the conditioning induced by a class social condition. So there is a correspondence between the objective divisions of the social world, the social structures and the mental structures that agents mobilize to act in a world structured in this way.

The correspondence between social structures and mental structures comes through the mediation of symbolic systems. On the basis of an analysis of French society, Bourdieu described a topology of the social space structured by classes and class relations. He retains from Marx the idea that the distribution of capital defines objective positions, but he expands the notion of capital by considering, in addition to its economic aspect, social, cultural, and symbolic dimensions. For Bourdieu, position in the class structure is therefore not limited to the position occupied in the relations of economic production. From Weber, he retains the idea that membership of a status group, and the lifestyle that this membership implies, affects the class situation. The lifestyle associated with a class conditions its symbolic status.

According to Bourdieu, in France, the social space is marked by a distribution of economic capital symmetrical but opposite to the distribution of cultural capital. Thus, for the upper and middle classes, the distribution is chiastic: Those richer in economic capital are poorer in cultural capital, and vice versa. On the basis of this distribution of capital, Bourdieu reconstructs the positions of groups and individuals in social space. These positions are established according to the volume of their capital and the structure of this capital, mainly the relative weights of economic and cultural capital. The latter is composed of objectivated properties (possession of goods and objects), incorporated properties (dispositions, schemes of perception and action, savoir faire, and competences), and institutionalized properties (qualifications, titles, and marks of recognition). The distribution of capital in its various forms determines the structure of positions in the social space with which lifestyles are associated.

Capital volume and structure determine the amplitude of the trajectories possible for an agent. A seemingly miraculous adjustment often leads agents to occupy a place that seems made for them. The homogeneity of the dispositions associated with a position and the coincidence of dispositions with positions result from the socializing mechanisms that, from primary socialization, orient agents toward positions adjusted in advance to them and for which they are themselves adapted. Nonetheless, this preestablished harmony is epistemic, and at the empirical level, it is often subject to many micro maladjustments. In practice, many discrepancies cause the adjustment of dispositions and positions to be less than entirely successful. Bourdieu noted the social suffering that could arise from substantial discrepancies, the sense of being "out of place," the effects of the progressive disjuncture between dispositions and positions that were initially aligned, the lags between settled dispositions and changing objective structures (*hysteresis*), or the tensions resulting from dispositions capable of entering into mutual contradiction (*cleft habitus*).

Within the social space, Bourdieu distinguishes autonomized domains of activity, which he calls fields (the political, literary, scientific, journalistic fields, etc.). The growing differentiation of the domains of human activity that accompanies the modernization of societies engenders the creation of social spaces endowed with a legitimacy and a functioning of their own. The theory of fields belongs to the development of a long tradition of analysis of the process of modernization and explicitly refers to Durkheim as regards the historical constitution and autonomization of fields, to Marx for the interpretation of the effects of this autonomization, and to Weber for the construction of the autonomy of a field or its internal struggles.

Like the habitus, for Bourdieu, the concept of the field is also a means of clarifying an epistemological and theoretical position that seeks to move beyond the classic oppositions that structure the social sciences. One of his objectives was to escape from the forced choice between internal interpretation and external explanation prevalent in sociology, which flows, in part, from the opposition between the phenomenological approach and the objectivist approach. The first of these privileges the internal coherence of the object studied, independently of its insertion in a precise social context. External explanation, for its part, characterizes representations and practices only by relating them to an overall system of relations within which they fulfill specific functions that transcend individual intentions. The theory of social fields constitutes a new way to move beyond the limits of each of these levels of analysis by articulating them. It is based on a relational epistemology that underlies the whole of Bourdieu's work: "The real is relational"; in other words, social interaction is constituted as a space of relationships that give things their properties (rather than things having properties in and by themselves).

A field responds to rules of functioning and institutions that are specific to it and that define the relations among the agents who compose it. Each field has rules of its own, but beyond the variations that distinguish each of the fields and their specific rules of functioning, it is possible to bring to light the invariants that shape and structure them. Bourdieu applied, developed, and nurtured his theory, confronting it with a multiplicity of apparently unrelated domains united only by the fact of their being specialized: religion, education, science, culture, the economy, fashion, bureaucracy, law, politics, journalism, power, and so forth.

A field is a space of relative positions within which actors and groups think, act, and take a place (*position*). Beyond their differences, agents are bound by a common *doxa*, a set of shared and unquestioned beliefs, specific to the field. Agents' positions within the field are defined by the volume and structure of their capital (including the form of capital specific to the field). In taking their "positions," persons and groups pursue interests linked to their field positions, which may consist in preserving or transforming the position they occupy and the resources associated with it. What is ultimately at stake in the struggles is the maintenance or transformation of the social structures and/or the structures of the field, the orders of legitimacy that prevail there. The principle of correspondence or homology between social structures and symbolic structures and the many phenomena of reproduction that Bourdieu describes have often led his work to be used to explain permanence and reproduction. However, the theory of fields offers useful theoretical tools and rich empirical descriptions for observing and analyzing social change, at three levels in particular: (1) that of the genesis of a domain of activity as it grows in autonomy, (2) that of the relations between more or less autonomous domains and their relationship with the state, and (3) that of the internal functioning of such domains, notably the revolutions in the field.

In the course of studies devoted to particular domains and more general formulations, the fields became more refined. However, Bourdieu's death left his work on fields unfinished and did not give him the opportunity to clarify the imprecisions, modifications, or contradictions in the uses he made of it.

Public Commitment

This overview would be incomplete without mention of Bourdieu's political and social commitment and in particular his public interventions in the 1990s. Denouncing the sufferings induced by condition and position, supporting the movement of the unemployed in France in 1995, pointing out the collusion between the field of power and the journalistic field, and condemning neoliberalism, Bourdieu placed himself on the left of the left. He engaged in reflection on the role and place of intellectuals in public debate. He remained convinced that the freedom of agents will come through knowledge.

Bourdieu fought for the constitution of a "collective intellectual," produced in particular through the grouping of specific intellectuals in networks capable of forming a critical mass and creating "the social conditions for the collective production of realistic utopias." The collective intellectual transcends the opposition between pure science and committed science. It should be able to organize collective research and stimulate and produce new forms of action, mobilization, and joint projects. Around the journal *Liber: Revue internationale des livres*, Bourdieu invited researchers, and also artists and writers, to overcome their internal boundaries and enter into

interaction with other domains of activity in order to promote a "scholarship with commitment."

Mathieu Hilgers

See also Critical Theory; Habitus; Social Constructionism; Structuralism

Further Readings

Bourdieu, P. (1977). *Outline of a theory of practice.* Cambridge, UK: Cambridge University Press.
———. (with Passeron, J.-C.). (1977). *Reproduction in education, society and culture.* London, UK: Sage.
———. (1984). *Distinction: A social critique of the judgement of taste.* Boston, MA: Harvard University Press.
———. (1987). *Questions of sociology.* Middletown, CT: Wesleyan University Press.
———. (1990). *In other words. Essays towards a reflexive sociology.* Stanford, CA: Stanford University Press.
———. (1990). *The logic of practice.* Stanford, CA: Stanford University Press.
———. (1991). *Language and symbolic power.* Cambridge, UK: Polity.
———. (with Wacquant, J. D.). (1992). *An invitation to reflexive sociology.* Chicago, IL: University of Chicago Press.
———. (1996). *The rules of art: Genesis and structure of the literary field.* Stanford, CA: Stanford University Press.
———. (1999). *Pascalian meditations.* Stanford, CA: Stanford University Press.

BURKE, KENNETH

Kenneth Burke (1897–1993) was an American social and literary theorist who began his career as a novelist, poet, and music critic.

Biography and Scholarly Career

Kenneth Burke's career did not follow a traditional academic path. After a brief undergraduate period at Ohio State and Columbia, he left academia to devote his energies to writing in the bohemian subculture of Greenwich Village. After working as a translator, magazine editor, and music critic, and producing several works of literature, Burke turned his attention to the philosophical study of language and the literary form. He served as a visiting or part-time professor, including positions at the University of Chicago, Harvard, The New School for Social Research, and Bennington College (Vermont), where he spent most of his teaching and writing life. Burke raised three daughters, one of whom was the Marxist-feminist anthropologist Eleanor Leacock (1922–1987).

Theoretical Contributions to Anthropology

Burke's broad, cross-disciplinary approach, and idiosyncratic rhetorical style makes his scholarly work difficult to categorize, but his legacy is far-reaching. In anthropology, his work is especially relevant to the fields of symbolic and interpretive anthropology, sociolinguistics, and performance studies. His most notable theoretical influence can be seen through the work of Clifford Geertz, Victor Turner, and Erving Goffman, among various others. Burke appeared to be equally influenced by anthropology, as he frequently references Bronisław Malinowski, Franz Boas, and Margaret Mead while integrating anthropological studies of ritual, magic, religion, and sacrifice throughout his writing. Following is a brief summary of his major contributions to anthropological theory.

Definition of Man

In his famous essay "Definition of Man," found in his *Language as Symbolic Action: Essays on Life, Literature, and Method*, Burke creates a definition of man (sic) as first and foremost the "symbol using animal." In his definition, the first clause identifies humans' capacity for symbolic action as distinct from the mere "motion" of nonhuman animals. This distinction highlights humans' unique capacity to use, reflect on, and generate new symbols while misusing (and often abusing) these symbols and their meanings in the process. Through his concept of the *negative*, Burke draws our attention to the moralizing capacity of language. He argues that the idea of "not something" is a purely human construction absent from the natural world. Through the symbolically constructed concepts of "not" and "thou shalt not," the negative allows for the formation of hierarchies and stratified forms of social order. Additionally, humans' capacity to use symbols allows us to transcend the conditions of our basic survival by making a largely taken-for-granted "second nature." In the last clause, Burke points out that an honorific search for worldly perfection is an underlying motive of human action, though often falling victim to the ironies and dichotomies of imperfection implied by its search.

Language as Symbolic Action

As his career progressed, Burke devoted considerable energy to examining the power of language and literature to shape attitudes and direct human behavior. He expanded his analysis beyond the literary text to explore how language functioned to frame social experience by drawing examples and data from fields as diverse as psychology, economics, politics, sociology, anthropology, and biology. He viewed language not simply as a tool for communication but as a dramatic and dynamic social process that constitutes purposeful social action.

In developing his constructivist approach, Burke explains how language works to filter and frame our experience. Through his concept of *terministic screens*, Burke demonstrates how words have a way of both revealing and concealing aspects of our reality, thus shaping the frameworks through which we make meaning and act in the world. Humans tend to interpret the world through the lens of their particular symbol systems. Burke reminds us, however, that while our terminologies provide a way of seeing the world, they also create a way of *not* seeing.

Burke developed this insight into a critical method he called *perspective by incongruity*. Using this method, the writer, rhetorician, or social or literary critic can force new interpretations by pairing seemingly incongruous or incompatible words, concepts, or ideas. For example, Burke used Thornstein Vebelin's notion of "trained incapacity" to illustrate how a person's training and education can create a certain blindness. This "verbal atom cracking" uncovers the multiple meanings, interests, and voices operating below the surface of our communication and illuminates the give-and-take of situated social action.

Because of the multiple meanings conveyed through our symbol systems, Burke argued, language is never neutral. Words carry the weight of their past and present uses, users, contexts, and connotations and therefore contribute dramatic tension to any interpretation. Despite the best intentions of the author to "fix" meaning in a particular choice of words, their relationship and proximity to other words, including their dialectical opposites, give rise to novel and often conflicting meanings.

Rhetoric

Burke's rhetorical theory provides an understanding of how power operates in and through language to create action and human cooperation. In *A Rhetoric of Motives* (1945), his definition of rhetoric moves beyond the ancient art of persuasion to focus on the concept of *identification*. Identification implies the process of both naming something and bringing people or things together through a shared interest, or "substance." Individuals create identification through a strategic use of a language of shared values, meanings, connotations, or attitudes about the world. While rhetoric can unite individuals symbolically, as a dialectical term, identification implies its opposite, division. Just as language can unite people by creating a rhetorical "us," it simultaneously generates a division by creating a necessary "them" or "other."

Dramatism

Burke did not simply view drama as a useful metaphor for understanding social life. He viewed social life as inherently dramatic. His theoretical system, *dramatism*, provides a complex and critical method to uncover the motives, attitudes, and relationships of power that underlie all symbolic interaction, and therefore all human relationships. For Burke, "motives" represent the linguistic springboards for action and provide "shorthand terms for situations," thereby providing valuable empirical data. Examining people's accounts of behavior provides rich "vocabularies of motive," illuminating the various ways individuals frame and understand situated social action.

In his *A Grammar of Motives* (1945), Burke explains his dramatistic *pentad*, a method used to analyze and uncover human motives in the language of art, literature, politics, or social interaction. He divides social action into five essential parts: *act*, *scene*, *agent*, *agency*, and *purpose* (he also adds attitude, which refers to an incipient or latent act). By examining the language operating in a given situation, the pentad helps us discover the relationships or the "ratios" between the *what*, *where*, *who*, *for what*, and *why* of a symbolic act. Through pentadic analysis, one can analyze these relationships or "ratios" by focusing on the clustering of key terms. For example, a *scene-act ratio* may examine the background setting of an act to explain the act itself,

or how the act itself might suggest why it appeared in a particular situated context.

Robert Owen Gardner

See also Sociolinguistics; Symbolic and Interpretive Anthropology; Symbolic Interactionism

Further Readings

Burke, K. (1945). *A grammar of motives*. Berkeley: University of California Press. (Reprinted in 1969)

———. (1950). *A rhetoric of motives*. Berkeley: University of California Press. (Reprinted in 1969)

———. (1966). *Language as symbolic action: Essays on life, literature, and method*. Berkeley: University of California Press.

Gusfield, J. R. (Ed.). (1989). *Kenneth Burke: On symbols and society*. Chicago, IL: University of Chicago Press.

Overington, M. (1977). Kenneth Burke and the method of dramatism. *Theory and Society, 4,* 131–156.

Rueckert, W. H. (1982). *Kenneth Burke and the drama of human relations* (2nd ed.). Berkeley: University of California Press.

BUTLER, JUDITH

Judith Butler (b. 1956) is a U.S. philosopher and critical theorist. She received her BA and PhD degrees in philosophy from Yale University and has taught at several U.S. universities, principally at the University of California, Berkeley, where she has been a professor in the Department of Rhetoric from 1993 to the present.

Butler rose to international prominence following the 1990 publication of her book *Gender Trouble: Feminism and the Subversion of Identity*, which synthesized a new language and analysis for understanding gender and sexuality as socially constituted, contingent, and contestable phenomena. Her theory of "gender performativity" influenced developments in feminist politics and theory in the 1990s and onward, and it came to be a touchstone for the then nascent field of "queer theory," an area of inquiry focused principally on critiques of coercive social norms related to sexual practice and personhood. She has published prolifically in areas related to the philosophy of language and hate speech laws; the cultural construction of the body; sovereign violence and the politics of grief; secularism; U.S. foreign policy in the 2000s; the legal framings of kinship and marriage; and more. Known for dense and careful scholarship, Butler has been an outspoken activist as well, lending her support to gay and lesbian causes, antiracist actions, contestations of neoliberal market fundamentalism, and critiques of state-sponsored violence in the Middle East and elsewhere.

Theory of Gender Performativity

Butler's work has always gestured toward anthropological theory. In developing her theory of gender performativity, she drew substantially on the work of Claude Lévi-Strauss (even while criticizing his structuralist account of meaning and the putative inevitability of heterosexuality in his analyses of kinship), as well as on Mary Douglas's analysis of body symbolism in varied sociocultural orders; Gayle Rubin, Esther Newton, Clifford Geertz, and other anthropologists are also cited. Butler's theory of gender performativity is meant to unsettle (to "trouble") various kinds of essentialism that have, in her view, dogged feminist analyses. Even while showing that gender could be various and that gender asymmetries in society were not inevitable byproducts of sexual inequalities in nature, Butler felt that feminist scholarship sometimes reified a unitary notion of "woman" or "the feminine," often in an attempt to recuperate these as against the social orders in which they were marginalized. For example, when accounts of the "social construction of gender" refer to cultural meanings layered "on top" of naturally sexed bodies, they assume what they need to explain: the way sexed bodies are rendered intelligible through the gendered grid that creates (interprets and interpellates) them. Categories of "woman" and "man" are not the cultural construction of "female" and "male." Rather, binary gender, and the compulsory heterosexuality it supports and necessitates, constitutes the sexes as discrete and disguises itself in so doing. Sex appears to stand before gender, even though it is gender that has created sex.

To understand this process, Butler draws on the philosophy of language, in particular the notion of the "performative" speech act, extending this theoretical construct as a powerful metaphor for how persons and relations are brought into being in a general sense. A performative in speech act theory is that which enacts what it says: most classically, and tellingly, the pronouncements of the marriage ceremony. The statement "I now pronounce you man and wife" creates the marriage in the act of saying. Crucially, in Butler's analysis, the performative gains its constitutive force only by re-creating and complying with prior instances of iteration. These instances accumulate into discursive conventions that authorize some statements (and the persons making them) to designate what is true, or even what simply is, to the extent that they conform to standards of intelligibility (e.g., norms).

By analogy, gender is performative insofar as it consists in accumulated acts that "cite" culturally conventional forms of conduct associated with men and women. In Butler's account, people do not "express" their genders when they act in the world; rather, their actions in the world create genders, through a kind of citational practice. If genders do not underlie (and thereby account for) the acts that instance them but instead are constituted by those very acts (acts such as particular forms of sexual practice or the sexed aesthetics of bodily comportment), it follows that the acting subject itself cannot be seen to stand apart from these forms of conduct either. Indeed, gender is coercive in society precisely in the way in which the "self" can be intelligible as an acting subject or a social person only to the extent that it conforms to the norms and forms of conventional gender identities. An ungendered person seems to be unthinkable, or in Butler's terms, impossible to perform. Butler's critique however suggests that the coherence of selves and sexes that culturally conventional appearances of accumulated acts attain is an illusion aiding and abetting hegemony, or gender inequality.

However, if the normative force of "gender" coerces conduct, it is not therefore uncontestable. Precisely because gender is elicited through citation (rather than expression), precisely because gender occurs in time as a residue of repeated acts of bodily style or comportment, its "necessity" is negotiable. Repetition in time opens the possibility for deformation, for what Butler calls "resignification"— performances that, in citing differently the conventions they enact, thereby expose their contingent character and in fact begin to change them. The political import of this theory is that gender is contestable because it is citational; Butler's is concomitantly a politics of the parodic.

Drawing on theories of language, discourse, psychoanalysis, and phenomenology, and often basing her accounts of the cultural "scripting" of gender in readings of literature (e.g., the writing of Willa Cather, Antigone), Butler's rhetorical emphasis on "performance" is understandable. But it has also persistently led to some misreadings and misunderstandings, above all to the misconception, which Butler had suggested, that all gender is "drag," a kind of costume or ornament that subjects adorn as they go through life. Gender, especially as it is linked to sexual norms, is in her view a form of coercive social reproduction; gender is one way in which the historically contingent and the socially varied come to appear necessary, natural, and therefore normative. In this sense, Butler's notion of gender performance bears fruitful comparison to the anthropological accounts of practice that gained prominence throughout the 1970s; if Butler had perhaps adopted a language of "practice," she might have avoided accusations that her theory was a voluntarist account of gender construction or a dematerialized critique of its politics.

In fact, Butler's notion of performativity is very close in conception to the idea of "practice" as adumbrated by anthropologists in the 1970s and 1980s, that is, as historically determined and culturally meaningful social action that brings subjects into being even as subjects are the instruments of its "logic" (e.g., Pierre Bourdieu, 1977, *Outline of a Theory of Practice*). Moreover, Butler's emphasis on "intersectionality"—the ways in which gender, sexuality, race, class, and so on must be understood together—resonates strongly with practice theory's accounts of society's mutually ramifying forms of hierarchy, and above all with its analysis of society as a pervasive system of domination. Finally, Butler's emphasis on "parody" and "resignification" bears fruitful comparison to the notion of "tactics" in practice theory, and its emphasis on the strategic negotiation of social structure in action. Most especially in Butler's emphasis on the socially constituted body as the site for the reproduction of schemas of perception and action, and in her critique of structuralist accounts of meaning, her work might have drawn more directly on practice theory; yet this is a possibility that remained largely unrealized in Butler's work and in derivatives thereof, as noted by Didier Eribon in *Insult and the Making of the Gay Self* (2004).

Alongside its unacknowledged resonances with practice theory, Butler's work bears fruitful comparison to a number of anthropological debates with which it was roughly coeval. In particular, within feminist anthropology, Butler's critique of both essentialism and social constructionism recalls Marilyn Strathern's rethinking of the presuppositions of feminist accounts of gender inequality across cultures in *The Gender of the Gift* (1988).

Style, Identity, and Abjection

These resonances notwithstanding, the anthropological reception of Butler has been patchy, in part because Butler's own use of anthropological theory has been patchy. Her influence is most pronounced in anthropological accounts of gender and sexuality. However, anthropologists have been more likely to quibble with some of the implications or intimations of Butler's work than to adopt a theory of gender performativity whole cloth. Anthropologists and others have suggested that Butler's critique of a self-authoring subject that stands before or outside the norms and forms that govern its intelligibility, and therefore constrain (and create) its possibilities for action, has sometimes been undermined by its own language. For example, in describing performativity as the citational reinscription of social convention through "stylized performance," Butler's reliance on theatrical metaphors belies a principal orientation to the constraints that coercive gender norms place on individuals. If gender is created through "style" (cultural convention), Butler's work sometimes gives the impression that gender is simply about style— the aesthetic or the formal, especially as these shape personal comportment. This tendency is most visible in her evident admiration for the ways the drag queens of gay culture ironize the putative certainties of gender and sex. In Butler's writing, gender often appears only as "style," as the formal or aesthetic shaping of efficacious social action.

Her critiques of the notion of an internally coherent and perduring "identity" notwithstanding, critics argued that her work is principally about the stultifying effects gender norms place on the creative self-expression of individuals, though Butler herself has had to correct this impression, especially in her 1997 work *The Psychic Life of Power*. Her critics have concomitantly suggested that the parodic politics of the performative that Butler theorizes inevitably seems to sideline questions of material inequality, or the empirical asymmetries characterizing relations between actually existing men and women. The shortcomings of Butler's language may be an artifact of its reliance principally on high theory (philosophy, critical theory, and psychoanalysis). Though amenable and open to anthropological work, Butler has mostly read rapidly through its empirical (ethnographic) basis to divine its theoretical insights. This is most pointed in the way she has largely avoided reading and writing about contemporary ethnographic work on non-normative gender and sexuality.

Criticisms of an overemphasis on language, on comportment and personal gender expression, and so on, notwithstanding, the evolution of Butler's work has more and more made explicit the stakes of her critique. Beyond her work on gender, Butler has criticized the ways in which sociocultural orders render some forms of life "thinkable," indeed "livable," and have relegated other forms of life to the unthinkable, and therefore "abject" (a term she mainly borrows from Julia Kristeva and that she used more frequently following the publication of her 1993 work *Bodies That Matter: On the Discursive Limits of "Sex"*).

Butler has thus focused her work more centrally on the forms through which some people and relations are "abjected" in hegemonic sociocultural orders. This abjection is most visible when some losses of life are grievable both personally and collectively, whereas others have been rendered ungrievable. They are ungrievable because they are fundamentally illegible (invisible) or unintelligible. These would include all those forms of non-normative sexuality or gender that are subject to pervasive forms of symbolic and social violence, whether that violence consists of hate crimes (physical assault, everyday epithet) or in the violence attendant on epidemics that may motivate little in the way of social concern (AIDS).

Extending this line of thinking, from 2001 onward, Butler has been concerned to understand the sociocultural logic underlying the collateral damage visited on populations that are subject to forms of state violence. In *Precarious Life: The Powers of Mourning and Violence* (2004), Butler asks, "Why are some lives (in rich and powerful countries, e.g., the United States) grieved when they are lost, while the killing that is done in the names of those lives remains invisible (as in the case of victims of the ongoing U.S. drone attacks in the Middle East)?" In bringing her account of the cultural constitution of the body round to the question of the very value of life itself, Butler has shown that her work has always been about the most intractable and important, indeed the most troubling, dynamics that characterize contemporary social life.

Thomas Strong

See also Feminist Anthropology; Poststructuralism; Practice Theory; Queer Theory

Further Readings

Butler, J. (1990). *Gender trouble: Feminism and the subversion of identity*. New York, NY: Routledge.

———. (1993). Critically queer. *GLQ: A Journal of Lesbian and Gay Studies, 1*(1), 17–32.

———. (1997). *The psychic life of power: Theories in subjection*. Palo Alto, CA: Stanford University Press.

———. (2004). *Precarious life: The powers of mourning and violence*. London, UK: Verso.

Eribon, D. (2004). *Insult and the making of the gay self*. Durham, NC: Duke University Press.

Mahmood, S. (2004). *Politics of piety: The Islamic revival and the feminist subject*. Princeton, NJ: Princeton University Press.

Strathern, M. (1988). *The gender of the gift: Problems with women and problems with society in Melanesia*. Berkeley: University of California Press.

CAMBRIDGE UNIVERSITY

A major U.K. university, widely known for its formative contributions to the British School of Social Anthropology in the 20th century, Cambridge has a long history of training practicing anthropologists.

The University and the Department

Cambridge University, founded in 1309, today combines two institutional elements. Departments (amalgamated into faculties) are teaching and research establishments supported by the state and its research councils; colleges are independently governed teaching and residential establishments with private as well as state funding. Relations between them fluctuated considerably over the 20th century. It was as a collegiate university that Cambridge nourished three early scholars who, apart from Robertson Smith, each put their stamp on anthropology: James George Frazer (Trinity College), W. H. R. Rivers (St Johns), and Rivers's student Radcliffe-Brown (Trinity) were primarily supported by college positions. St Johns later funded Gregory Bateson's first fieldwork. However, departments, regulated by the university's educational boards, were essential for attracting a critical mass of students. Here, Cambridge was slow to recognize anthropology.

This did not prevent collaborative research: Witness the second Cambridge Torres Straits expedition (1898), which, with Frazer's support, included two experimental psychologists, William McDougall and Charles Samuel Myers, and their teacher W. H. R. Rivers, and a physician, Charles Gabriel Seligman, who were all converted by their experience. The one who did the most to give anthropology at Cambridge a departmental presence had been its leader, Alfred Cort Haddon.

From ad hoc teaching in comparative anatomy and physical anthropology, Haddon became university lecturer in ethnology in 1900 (with crucial financial support from a fellowship at Christ's College), for a long time the only such post at Cambridge. (Rivers held a university position in experimental psychology; like Frazer, he lectured intermittently in ethnology.) No other full-time staff was appointed until the late 1920s. A university chair of social anthropology was created in 1932, its foundation funding coming through Trinity College from Frazer's associate, William Wyse. Appointed to the William Wyse chair were T. C. Hodson (1933–1936), J. H. Hutton (1936–1950), Meyer Fortes (1950–1973), Jack Goody (1973–1984), Ernest Gellner (1984–1992), Marilyn Strathern (1993–2008), Henrietta Moore (2008–). "Social anthropology" had been the rubric under which Rivers taught and which Radcliffe-Brown promoted as the comparative study of institutions.

When a Board of Anthropological Studies was created in 1904 for a postgraduate program, it drew in lecturers from archaeology, physical (now biological) anthropology, the Museum of Archaeology and Ethnology (later, Archaeology and Anthropology), Anglo-Saxon, Assyriology, and Egyptology, as well as ethnology; an undergraduate program mooted in 1913 was delayed by the war. The subsequent Board of Archaeological and

Anthropological Studies set the tone for several decades, with archaeology and the two anthropologies, social and biological, acting as a single department, but in 1970 each became an autonomous department within what was now a wider Faculty of Archaeology and Anthropology. The faculty was administratively reorganized as a single department again in 2010, the three subdisciplines now being divisions within it. In U.K. terms, the Social Anthropology Division is medium sized; in 2012, there were 18 core teaching/research staff (university and college), although the larger community included another 35 social anthropologists resident in Cambridge.

The Cambridge system focuses on the individual supervision of undergraduates as well as postgraduates; while many Cambridge BAs go on to do further studies elsewhere, before a master's became a requirement, undergraduates could proceed directly to the PhD. (Since the Cambridge MA originates in a BA, present-day master's degrees are known as MPhil.) Between 1933 and 1993, Cambridge PhDs—some with Cambridge first degrees, others from elsewhere—included Ray Abrahams, Debbora Battaglia, Marcus Banks, Fredrik Barth, Geoffrey Benjamin, Nurit Bird-David, Maurice Bloch, Barbara Bodenhorn, Lynne Brydon, Susan Drucker Brown, Anthony Carter, Jeremy Eades, Colin Filer, Derek Freeman, Takeo Funabiki, Esther Goody, Jack Goody, Kathleen Gough, Sarah Green, Ralph Grillo, Stephen Gudeman, Chris Hann, Keith Hart, Paul Henley, Polly Hill, Steven Hooper, Stephen Hugh Jones, Caroline Humphrey, Tim Ingold, Michael Jackson, Elizabeth Kennedy, Christopher Fuller, Heonik Kwon, Adam Kuper, James Laidlaw, Jean La Fontaine, Robert Launay, Peter Lawrence, Tanya Luhrmann, Henrietta Moore, Martha Mundy, Colin Murray, Christine Oppong, Jonathan Parry, Peter Rigby, Enid Schildkrout, Paul Sant-Cassia, Paul Sillitoe, Raymond Smith, David Sneath, Derrick Stenning, Roderick Stirrat, Andrew Strathern, Gillian Tett, Maya Unnithan, Michel Verdon, Piers Vitebsky, Monica Wilson, Peter Wade, Wiliam Watson, Harvey Whitehouse, James Woodburn, Nur Yalman, David Zeitlyn, and many others. It has been computed that at the end of the 20th century (1999), 24% of academic anthropologists employed in British departments had received their postgraduate training at Cambridge, the highest proportion of any U.K. university.

Three temporal-spatial horizons are of note:

1. *1898 to the late 1920s:* Research in Oceania led to a small stream of Melanesianist students, and also arguably a paradigm for emergent anthropological professionalism (solving a puzzle in kinship terminology).

2. *1950 to the late 1970s:* The turn to Africa, begun elsewhere in the 1930s, was consolidated through a cohort of West and East Africanists and their several students. The African Studies Centre, first under Audrey Richards, dates from this time.

3. *1990 onward:* South Asia long had a presence; Central and East Asia came into its own with an explicit focus on Mongolia, and its Russian and Chinese neighbors, institutionally recognized in the Mongolian and Inner Asia Studies Unit, founded by Caroline Humphrey with Urgunge Onon in 1986. Regionalism had once been controversial (Fortes apparently regarding himself an "anthropologist," not an "Africanist"), but the unit is an important focus for scholars from these areas.

Present-day undergraduate teaching at Cambridge takes such areas as opportunities for intense scrutiny, crosscutting them with theoretical developments in, for example, art, ethical systems, gender relations, globalization, law and the state, medicine and science, and world religions.

Major Theoretical Orientations

Anthropology did not develop at Cambridge in isolation from the London School of Economics, Manchester, Oxford, and University College London. Tracing its distinctive contributions forms but one thread among many.

Comparative Method and Fieldwork

Two concepts deployed by Frazer and Haddon became absorbed into the later self-definition of British social anthropology, although with radically different connotations. With the unit of knowledge a "custom," Frazer's *comparative method* consisted of classifying customs—whether burial rules or kin terms—by the (remote) inspection of similarities and differences. Haddon took this in another direction; the ecology of a region and data treated as a related set revealed development between types. Introducing the concept of *fieldwork* from biology (his expedition colleagues were "field anthropologists"), he had hopes for a Cambridge school of ethnology defined by "the intensive study of limited areas." The fieldwork that had been an implicit adjunct to Frazer's enquiries came to be an explicit focus, posing different problems. Fieldworkers entered into relationships with people, which is why Rivers recommended long-term stay, although present-day understandings of "intensive fieldwork" had to wait until Bronisław Malinowski.

In Haddon's Cambridge, training was given to probationers in the colonial civil service about to be thrown "into the field"; such "practical anthropology" was later of particular interest to Richards. Debate can still be generated over the theoretical status of fieldwork carried out under conditions of colonization.

British Social Anthropology: Defining Social Structure

Intensive fieldwork was a necessary but not sufficient condition for the theorizing that characterised British social anthropology in the mid-20th century. With a tension between holistic and systematic schema, laying out a structural basis for social life realized a Durkheimian vision of "society." Kinship systems (see the entry on Lewis Henry Morgan) provided the defining momentum. Whatever one thinks of the scholarly genealogy for the "British style of structural anthropology" that Fortes proposed, linking himself to Morgan via Rivers and Radcliffe-Brown (and Robert Lowie), the period following his appointment endorsed a strong model of societal structure that was equally strongly opposed (see the next section). Alongside building up a body of research students, significance has been put on Fortes's bringing to Cambridge a particular kind of seminar culture; certainly, the role that open controversy played in the theoretical development of the 1950s and 1960s cannot be overestimated. The previous 25 years, during which anthropology at Oxford came to rival that at the London School of Economics, are generally regarded as a period of doldrums for Cambridge. This was to change.

Fortes's genealogy, traced long after his own foundational work at the London School of Economics and Oxford, linked two Cambridge figures. Rivers's interpretation of kinship as a "principle of social organization" arose from the "genealogical method," a tool intended to provide an accurate record of interpersonal relationships that yielded all kinds of information on social life, including how certain relations were valued over others. Radcliffe-Brown's structuralist theorizing was to develop its own trajectory, entailing an idea of social order as a system, with kinship structures exemplifying how people regulate their relations to one another.

This later model became taken for granted; collaboration between Fortes and E. E. Evans-Pritchard, especially in the new ethnography of political systems (1940), threw up the role played in certain polities by "segmentary lineages." If kinship and society sometimes seemed coterminous, elsewhere descent groups took their place in Fortes's analytical distinction between political-jural and domestic-familial domains. (The term *kinship* might encompass both or be restricted to the latter.) Social structure understood in terms of social order allowed colonial subjects their own quasi-legal forms. If structure was the subject of study, its key analytic was relations. The study of kinship afforded insight into fine discriminations in behavior and practice that had major structural consequences. At Cambridge, this theoretical emphasis lay alongside a detailed focus on familial dynamics. The *Developmental Cycle in Domestic Groups* (1958), edited by Jack Goody, was the first of a new Cambridge series of papers. Goody's comparative approach to inheritance and succession stimulated the examination of corporate descent groups as property-holding entities.

Alternative Anthropologies

When modeling becomes explicit, questions arise about the interests at stake, the relationship between anthropological and folk models, and what is happening "on the ground." This became the empiricist terrain to which Edmund Leach, appointed a lecturer in 1953, brought a sceptical anthropology derived from his Burmese observations, and a semiotic/transformational one developed from his interest in mathematics (and subsequent reading of Claude Lévi-Strauss and Roman Jakobson). The fieldwork he carried out from Cambridge was the vehicle for one among many attacks on descent theory, open debate with Fortes making a heady intellectual cocktail for students. The challenge of an Asiatic perspective was underlined by Stanley Tambiah's appointment in 1964.

Fortes himself dealt with anomalies and contradictions in the descent group paradigm; Leach's assault raised quite different foundations for the study of social life (not equitable in any simple way with "alliance theory"; see the entries on descent theory and alliance theory). All this laid the ground in Cambridge for receiving theories originating in the general rejuvenation of Marxism and the rise of feminist anthropology in the 1970–1980s.

Internal debate was never all-consuming. Leach stimulated interest in the broad field of religion and ritual, alongside innovative approaches to economic anthropology. He also gave the discipline unprecedented exposure in his public broadcasts (the BBC *Reith Lectures*), addressing himself to big themes and a broad audience. Over his long writing career, Goody, who preferred the term *comparative sociology* to *anthropology*, has ranged across a vast interdisciplinary literature to answer world-scale questions about social transformation, challenging many myths about the West's uniqueness. His successor, the social philosopher/philosophical sociologist Ernest Gellner, brought in the whole sweep of civilization and modernity, to which Alan Macfarlane was already making his own historical-anthropological contribution.

World Affairs

When interests become explicit, so does the ethnographer's role; an implicit assumption about the international nature of anthropology turns into a substantive topic. Flatten the relationship between observer and observed, and an encompassing "world" comes into view. As elsewhere, Cambridge social anthropology has been drawn into world affairs, where the theoretical driver is comprehension of the complexities and specificities of life as it is lived under conditions assembled by global interests, new knowledge practices, burgeoning religions, political-economic disenfranchisement, environmental and other disasters, and unprecedented forms of citizenship.

A long-standing Cambridge contribution has come through the study of societies under socialist and post-socialist regimes (especially by Caroline Humphrey and her many students), where part of the strength has been the coherence of comparative interests

shared with national scholars. "Collaborative anthropology" is a description of contemporary anthropological practice, as well as the rubric under which a second Cambridge chair (established in 2005–2006) was initially held by Humphrey.

Marilyn Strathern

See also Barth, Fredrik; Bateson; Gregory; Bloch, Maurice; Comparative Method; Evans-Pritchard, E. E.; Fortes, Meyer; Frazer, James G.; Goody, Jack; Haddon, Alfred C.; Leach, Edmund; London School of Economics; Manchester School; Oxford University; Radcliffe-Brown, A. R.; Richards, Audrey; Seligman, Charles Gabriel; Smith, William Robertson; Strathern, Marilyn; Tambiah, Stanley; Wilson, Monica

Further Readings

Goody, J. R. (1995). *The expansive moment: Anthropology in Britain and Africa 1918–1970.* Cambridge, UK: Cambridge University Press.
Kuper, A. (1996). *Anthropology and anthropologists: The modern British school* (3rd ed.). London, UK: Routledge.
Spencer, J. (2000). British social anthropology: A retrospective. *Annual Review of Anthropology, 29,* 1–24.

CARNEIRO, ROBERT L.

Robert Leonard Carneiro, an American anthropologist, is best known for his contributions to scientific theories of the state and evolutionary perspectives in anthropology. His theoretical writings are based on comparative-historical data covering extremely long periods of time and involving a multitude of societies from across the world and are additionally supported by his own fieldwork among the Kuikuru of Brazil, the Amahuaca of Peru, and the Yanomamö of Venezuela.

Carneiro was born in New York City on June 4, 1927. He studied at the University of Michigan, where he received a BA in political science (1949) and an MA (1952) and PhD in anthropology (1957), the latter on the basis of a dissertation that offered an ecological study of the subsistence economy of the Kuikuru Indians. Carneiro completed his doctoral work under the supervision of the noted anthropologist Leslie White, whose evolutionary perspective greatly influenced Carneiro's thinking.

After a 1-year stay at the University of Wisconsin, Carneiro moved to the American Museum of Natural History, where he has been employed as curator since 1957. He presently serves as curator emeritus and professor emeritus of anthropology. Carneiro has additionally taught as visiting and adjunct professor at various universities. In the realm of anthropological theory, Carneiro is best known for his innovative theory of the state and his defense of evolutionism in the anthropological study of culture.

Carneiro's theory of the state was first published in the journal *Science* in 1970 and has since been refined, though not substantially altered, in additional writings. The theory holds that warfare directed at the conquest of land will lead to the formation of states under three material circumstances. First, the ecological condition of *environmental* circumscription has to be met so that the availability of agricultural land is confined. As additional land becomes unavailable due to environmental constraints (such as high mountains or broad waterways that cannot be traversed with available technologies), warfare will ensue, resulting in the conquest of accessible land and bringing about the political subjugation of once autonomous groups. Thus, there occurs a gradual formation of ever-growing unified political communities, which eventually reach the level of large and highly centralized states. Second, warfare will bring about state formation as *resource concentration* occurs, in which case, the availability of food is restricted, again bringing about war and political subjugation. Third, *social* circumscription refers to the fact that population pressure—that is, the density of a population relative to the available land—can reach a point whereby warfare will ensue as a result of a quest for territorial expansion. States grow in size by unifying once autonomous, smaller political communities until the point where they reach other large states—formed under similar conditions—and state borders among them are established.

Carneiro's interest in state formation is part of a more comprehensive interest in evolutionism and the need to develop a scientific theory of culture, especially to explain the development from relatively small-scale and autonomous communities (e.g., bands, villages) to more complex communities (e.g., chiefdoms) and large and highly differentiated societies (e.g., states, empires). Carneiro's interests are

thereby radically scientific in seeking to develop theories that can account for the variation in evolutionary development by identifying relevant conditions in the social and natural environment. His interests are fundamentally oriented toward developing a very general theory of culture. This ambition already formed the foundation of Carneiro's theory of state formation, which seeks to account for the formation of states in light of the observation that states of comparable degrees of complexity have evolved across the world at different periods of time. For Carniero, the development of complex political systems is of special relevance because the process mostly took place over the past 10,000 years after a period of about 2 million years of human existence when all social life was concentrated in autonomous bands and villages.

Methodologically, Carneiro attempts to uncover regularities in the evolution of culture by means of scaling the order in which certain traits of development have emerged over time, thereby relying on available archaeological and ethnographic data. These traits can be of various kinds, such as political, economic, legal, and symbolic, developing at various points over long periods of historical time. Carneiro thereby defends a unilinear perspective of evolution that seeks to establish general patterns (laws) of cultural development. Formulating an explanation for uncovered patterns of cultural evolution, Carneiro holds on to the idea of causation and places central importance on nonvoluntaristic explanations of warfare, which dispense with any factors related to the human will and instead emphasize materialist causes, especially ecology and demography, while minimizing any influence of myth, ideology, and other systems of ideas.

Developing his perspective on evolution, Carneiro has also contributed to theoretical discussions about other evolutionist perspectives on culture and society to highlight the variations, limitations, and strengths of various modes of evolutionary thinking. He has particularly contributed to the understanding and continued relevance of classical thinkers such as Herbert Spencer, Edward Tylor, and Lewis Morgan, as well as modern scholars, most notably Leslie White as well as Elman Service and Marvin Harris. Carneiro's discussions are not mere metatheoretical excursions but form a necessary component to delineate his particular perspective of evolutionism and to defend evolutionist anthropology in general from currents in anthropological theorizing that seek to dispense with the need for a general theory, especially under the influence of cultural relativism, historicism, and postmodernism.

The work of Carneiro enjoys considerable influence in the field of anthropology and beyond. Despite having elicited criticisms and surely not being considered the one final chapter in theoretical work on state formation, Carneiro's theory of the state is arguably the best known and most influential theory of the state developed in the social sciences. Carneiro's contributions to evolutionism in anthropology, which are generally of a more recent date, are as yet somewhat less known, though they can serve as an important antidote, among other perspectives, against the humanistic and antiscientific currents that occasionally mark the discipline of anthropology.

Mathieu Deflem

See also Cultural Materialism; Evolutionary Anthropology; Spencer, Herbert; Tylor, Edward Burnett; White, Leslie

Further Readings

Carneiro, R. L. (1970). A theory of the origin of the state. *Science, 169,* 733–738.

———. (2003). *Evolutionism in cultural anthropology: A critical history.* Boulder, CO: Westview Press.

———. (2010). *The evolution of the human mind: From supernaturalism to naturalism. An anthropological perspective.* New York, NY: Eliot Werner.

CHICAGO WORLD'S COLUMBIAN EXPOSITION (1893)

The 1893 World's Columbian Exposition was held in Chicago from May to October; it occupied 686 acres of land, and its estimated 65,000 exhibits attracted more than 21,480,000 paying visitors. The fact that the event fell between the financial panic of 1893 and the Pullman strike of 1894 indicates the unsettled character of the period and the artificiality of the vision of unity the event embodied. International expositions were, as Burton Benedict has argued, mammoth rituals in which all kinds of power relations were expressed, and the 1893 Chicago Exposition was no exception. Each of the various exposition exhibition sites illustrated a particular dimension of how anthropology was understood and practiced in this period.

The exhibits in the exposition's uniquely named Anthropological Building mirrored the important transition in anthropology occurring in this period, when traditional ethnology was refashioning itself into a broader, academic, multifaceted endeavor with the appropriation of scientific tools and pervasive collecting activities. Located in the southeast section of the exposition, the building was specifically named by Frederick Ward Putnam, who was in charge of the official Department M (Ethnology), and encompassed both historical archaeology and traditional ethnology as well as the newer work in physical anthropology. This diversity reflected how Putnam, as curator of Harvard University's Peabody Museum and Anthropology Department, and his exposition assistant, Dr. Franz Boas, understood the newer integrative processes involved in anthropology in this period.

Among the Anthropological Building's exhibits were artifacts, casts, and models made from a series of special ethnographic research projects directed by Putnam in the United States (Ohio, New Jersey) as well as in Mexico, Central and South America, and Northwest coast (under Franz Boas). Putnam had been able to finance these research projects with the use of exposition funds beginning in 1891. Alongside these collections were a diverse range of independently submitted exhibits from various individuals and state agencies, which, although their labeling and presentation were uneven, represented a cross section of collecting activities across the country.

On the upper-gallery level of the Anthropological Building, the physical anthropology section, under Boas's direction, was organized in a series of three laboratory spaces. Physical Anthropology occupied three rooms, the first showing the latest tools for recording, testing, and calculating physical information on large groups of people, including the results of Boas's recent measurement surveys of 17,000 North American Indians and 90,000 schoolchildren. Adjacent to these rooms was the Neurological Laboratory, supervised by the Chicago neurologist Henry H. Donaldson. On display were a series of models and casts of human brains and those of lower animals, showing brain structures, localization of functions, and modes of preservation. The next two rooms were of the Psychological Laboratory, managed by Professor Joseph Jastrow (Wisconsin), which showed various experimental psychology tests and instruments for the study of touch, color, and hearing and the recording and timing of reflexes. A separate room provided space where on-site anthropometric measurement and psychophysical data from volunteer exposition visitors were taken.

Just outside the Anthropological Building stood the monumental reconstructed replicas made from original molds of five key Mesoamerican archaeological ruins, including Uxmal and Labná in the Yucatán. Adjacent to these were a series of traditional American Indian homes and native encampments, including the bark longhouse of the Iroquois, the birch bark of the Penobscot Indians of Maine, and the skin-covered teepee of the Plains Indians. Beside the plank-covered house and totem columns of the Northwest Coast Indians of British Columbia (arranged for by Franz Boas), the Kwakiutl Indians from Vancouver Island performed their illusionist stage-crafted dances and ceremonial performances for the exposition spectators.

A distance beyond these outdoor traditional American Indian encampments was the modest display of the U.S. government's Bureau of American Indian Affairs. Its model schoolhouse display was initially created to stand for the future of Native American Indians rather than their past, featuring students from various boarding schools throughout the country, who were expected to perform their regular classroom activities before an audience of exposition visitors. This effort was both chronically underfunded compared with the Anthropological Building and undermined by disagreements with officials of the Carlisle Indian School, who had more ambitious goals of their own. Its presence, however, dramatized the tension between the well-supported efforts and growing popularity of academic anthropology and the official government policies of cultural and social assimilation for native populations.

On the famed mile-long thoroughfare of Midway Plaisance on the exposition's opposite northwest section, visitors encountered various national groups in their respective displays. Within this informal, confusing atmosphere of voyeuristic entertainment, brusque commercialism, and high-pitched popularization, the traditional cultural boundaries between spectators and ethnic groups were temporarily erased. These experiences and the daily parades by Dahomeyans, Samoans, Arabs, Sioux Indians, and camel-riding Egyptians from their respective village displays, however, accelerated the solidifying of ethnic biases and cultural stereotyping implicit in the tactics of displays of living people within this kind of artificial setting.

Finally, the powerful role of museum-based anthropology was on show in the official exposition exhibits of the Smithsonian Institution in the U.S. Government Building, centrally located in the exposition. Here, the work of the U.S. National Museum's Ethnology Division (under Otis T. Mason) and the Bureau of American Ethnology (under John Wesley Powell) was on view. Powell's linguistic map of North American tribes had provided the nexus for the selection of representative native groups for display. In addition to the display of well-documented artifacts, there were a series of life-size glass-cased manikins designed by Frank Hamilton Cushing that included female Navaho weavers, Zuni pottery makers, and a Hopi basket maker. With their accurate environmental settings and realistic poses, the idea of the "life group" was a substantial visual and technical exhibit innovation over the more static presentations of evolutionary artifact sequencing used previously, and it provided an important precedent for subsequent museum exhibit–making methodology.

Finally, the International Congress on Anthropology, held in conjunction with the 1893 Chicago Exposition from August 28 to September 2 ensured a powerful platform and attendance by leaders in academic and museum anthropology with the subsequent publication of their papers. In addition, a number of exhibits and collections from the Anthropological Building were later transferred to the newly created Field Columbia Museum (name changed to Field Museum of Natural History in 1905), originally housed in the Fine Arts Building after the close of the exposition. Although Frederick Putnam had expected to be named director of the new museum and Franz Boas served as curator for 2 years following the exposition, the directorship instead went to Frederick J. V. Skiff, previously in charge of the mining exhibits at the 1893 Chicago Exposition.

Julie K. Brown

See also Boas, Franz; Culture Area Approach; Great Exhibition of 1851 (Crystal Palace); Nineteenth-Century Evolutionary Anthropology; Race

Further Readings

Benedict, B., & Lowie, R. H. (1983). *The anthropology of world's fairs: San Francisco's Panama Pacific International Exposition of 1915.* Berkeley, CA: Scolar Press.

Brown, J. K. (1994). *Contesting images: Photography and the world's Columbian exposition.* Tucson: University of Arizona Press.

Hinsley, C. M. (1991). The world as marketplace: Commodification of the exotic at the world's Columbian exposition, 1893. In I. Karp & S. Lavine (Eds.), *Exhibiting cultures: The poetics and politics of museum display* (pp. 344–365). Washington, DC: Smithsonian Institution Press.

Jacknis, I. (1991). Northwest coast Indian culture and the world's Columbian exposition. In D. H. Thomas (Ed.), *The Spanish borderlands in Pan-American perspective* (pp. 91–117). Washington, DC: Smithsonian Institution Press.

Rydell, R. W. (1984). *All the world's a fair: Visions of empire at American international expositions, 1876–1916.* Chicago, IL: University of Chicago Press.

Trennert, R. A., Jr. (1987). Selling Indian education at world's fairs and expositions, 1893–1904. *American Indian Quarterly, 11*(3), 203–230.

CHILDHOOD

For most of the 20th century, anthropologists relied on theories from psychiatry and psychology to set the frameworks and questions for their studies of children, childhood, and socialization. Margaret Mead demonstrated this approach in her early work by calling for anthropologists to use their field sites as laboratories for putting Western theories of child training and personality development to the ethnographic test. Her overall goal was to demonstrate the malleability of human nature by showing that "cultural rhythms" were stronger than "physiological rhythms." Mead used her research in Samoa to challenge the theories of G. Stanley Hall, who assumed that adolescents everywhere experienced their stage of life as a time of storm and stress. Similarly, her fieldwork among the Manus in Papua

New Guinea was, in part, designed to investigate whether animistic thought in children was due to their intellectual immaturity, as Jean Piaget had argued, or was determined more by their sociocultural context. Not surprisingly, Mead suggested that her research proved that it was the latter. However, even while calling for critiques of Western theories of child development, Mead incorporated some of these models into her own studies, as she did using Erik H. Erikson's theories of psychosexual development as a way to interpret the research she conducted with Gregory Bateson on Balinese childhood. Only later in the 20th century did anthropologists begin to break away from the frameworks established by psychologists, as they turned their attention to more explicit models of language and communication as well as to social theorists such as Pierre Bourdieu, Michel Foucault, and Anthony Giddens. This important shift in orientation situates children within the micro- and macrolevel sociocultural and political economic processes that shape, and in turn are shaped by, the localized patterns of interaction that play such an important role in the lives of children everywhere.

Culture and Personality

From 1930 to 1960, the approach known as "culture and personality" dominated research on children and childhood in anthropology. The research questions in this field were generated by the psychological theories in vogue at the time, and this was the case whether anthropologists were seeking to "prove" or "disprove" these theories. There was great interest in examining the relationships between particular societal types (e.g., hunters and gatherers vs. agricultural groups), specific child-rearing patterns (e.g., toilet training, or the presence or absence of initiation ceremonies), and the formation of behavioral and personality characteristics believed to be typical of individuals in a particular culture. In the 1950s, a landmark project, known as the Six Cultures Study, was formulated and led by John Whiting and Irvin L. Child. The goal of this study was to collect comparative ethnographic information that would make it possible to test specific hypotheses derived from a psychocultural model of child rearing that posited causal relationships between economic/ecological and sociopolitical systems, child-rearing practices and the development of specific child and adult personality types. Research was conducted in six different areas of the world: Okinawa, India, the Philippines, Mexico, Kenya, and the United States. Not surprisingly, this study generated a large amount of data that has enabled researchers to look at a variety of issues, such as differences across societies in terms of training for responsibility or expectations for obedience, socialization for aggression, or the effect of schools on children's behavior. Unfortunately, there are a number of limitations to this material, especially because of the somewhat narrow focus on a predetermined set of "behavioral systems" (e.g., succorance, nurturance, self-reliance, and achievement) coupled with questionable assumptions about cultures as uniform and homogeneous entities. In addition, researchers were operating with a theory of language that conceptualized it as a *tool* for communicating, gathering, and extracting information but, in itself, playing no role in the constitution of this information.

The Interactional Turn

A turn toward a more explicit study of language and communication occurred in the 1960s and 1970s with the development of "ethnography of speaking" studies, especially as inspired by the work of Dell Hymes and John Gumperz. This approach opened up new theories and methods for studying children and socialization processes as illustrated by the work of Elinor Ochs, Bambi Schieffelin, and Jenny Cook-Gumperz, among others. Central to these studies was the collection and analysis of richly detailed interactions between children and their caregivers and children and their peers. The important role of language in constituting social and cognitive worlds led to studies of language acquisition and language socialization across multiple cultures. A range of issues overlooked by culture and personality researchers emerged in these studies. Most important, instead of taking the existence of a "social world" for granted, these studies started with questions about how social worlds are constructed out of everyday talk and interactional routines. By paying attention to the role of everyday discourse in the production of these social worlds, researchers were also able to understand and examine the interpretive processes participants themselves used to make sense of their interactions.

During this same time period, researchers in sociology, in the field known as ethnomethodology, were asking similar questions and also developing important critiques of the "developmental perspective" as applied to the study of children. In an important, but neglected, article from 1973, Robert W. Mackay argued that this developmental model views children as "incomplete beings"— immature, acultural, asocial, and incompetent individuals—who must be "filled up" by proper guidance and child-training practices. Similarly, in 1976, Matthew Speier called attention to the way these kinds of assumptions represent the "adult ideological viewpoint" that, he suggested, is embedded in almost all theories of child development. Understanding the role that a researcher's own folk model of childhood may play in the development of specific theories of socialization is now an important component of anthropological theorizing, but at that time, the influence of these ideologies was not widely recognized.

This work in the 1970s and 1980s is especially significant because it prefigured a series of publications, all of which surprisingly appeared in the same year (1990), that had a transformative effect on anthropological and sociological theorizing about children and childhood. Three books in particular illustrate this break with the previous theoretical models that had mostly dominated researchers' thinking about children and childhood. The important book *Constructing and Reconstructing Childhood: Contemporary Issues in the Sociological Study of Childhood*, edited by Allison James and Alan Prout, is significant because of its argument, as is evident in the title, that childhood is a social construction that must always be considered in relation to specific historical and cultural contexts. Equally important are two ethnographies that appeared at the same time: Bambi Schieffelin's *The Give and Take of Everyday Life*, reporting on her fieldwork examining the language socialization of Kaluli children in Papua New Guinea, and Marjorie Harness Goodwin's *He-Said-She-Said: Talk as Social Organization Among Black Children*, based on research conducted in an African American neighborhood in Southwest Philadelphia.

Most significantly, the James and Prout volume presents a sustained challenge to the dominant account of children in the research literature that conceptualizes development as a natural, continuous, and directional process that manifests itself in an orderly sequence of stages. In their words, the standard model of development

> is essentially an evolutionary model: the child developing into an adult represents a progression from simplicity to complexity of thought, from irrational to rational behavior. . . . Children's activities—their language, play and interactions—are significant as symbolic markers of developmental progress. (Prout & James, 1990, pp. 10–11)

This model of unilineal stages of development naturally unfolding in a predetermined sequence is very familiar to anthropologists as it replicates assumptions embedded in the models of human evolution put forward by scholars such as E. B. Tylor and Lewis Henry Morgan in the early years of the discipline. In part, this was the model that Mead was questioning in her early work, and it supports an ideology of childhood that is not attentive to social and cultural variation because the focus is on "childhood" as a natural, biological, and universal period of life. What makes this an especially powerful and effective ideology is that it appears as if it is *not* an ideology at all—because, of course, it is natural, inevitable, and universal.

The ethnographies by Schieffelin and Goodwin show us how important it is to examine the diversity that exists both within as well as across groups in terms of socialization practices and interactional routines. In *He-Said-She-Said*, Goodwin uses detailed transcriptions of interactions to illustrate how "situated activities" (e.g., "telling stories") shape the ways participants, who in her case varied by age and gender, are oriented toward each other, and the particular forms of speech and interaction that this produces. An earlier study by Shirley Brice Heath (*Ways With Words: Language, Life and Work in Communities and Classrooms*, 1983) demonstrated the importance of recognizing differences across race, class, geographic region, and social setting (e.g., classrooms in schools or family interactions at home) in examining patterns of language use across three different communities in the Piedmont Carolinas in the United States. These studies illustrate the ways richly detailed ethnographies can challenge the ongoing tendency to interpret differences in language use and literacy practices as deficiency, deficiencies that are almost always located *in* the child or *in* the child's family.

Globalizing Childhood

The studies from the 1990s discussed here also ushered in another transformation in anthropologists' theorizing about children and childhood. Here, the focus was not on microlevel interactions but rather on research examining the relationships between the child, the state, and global economic and political forces. In the mid-1990s, researchers such as Sharon Stephens and Nancy Scheper-Hughes began to argue for the importance of considering children and childhood within the context of global political-economic transformations. This challenge to place children in the context of "world systems" has been taken up by many researchers in the 21st century who are examining how children are affected by shifting labor markets; migration and immigration patterns; health crises such as the HIV/AIDS epidemic as well as endemic health problems associated with poverty and hunger, wars, and political turmoil; natural disasters and forced relocations; and the influence of global media and markets and technologies such as the Internet.

The Anthropology of Childhood

It may be too soon to articulate a specific "anthropological" theory of children and childhood, but the parameters of the one that is currently taking shape would certainly include the following assumptions. First and foremost is the view that children are active (not passive) participants in social life and, as actors, they both shape and are shaped by the opportunities and constraints they confront (which are themselves shaped by gender, age, class, and race/ethnicity differences). Instead of viewing socialization processes as hierarchical and centered on the ways adults "train" or "rear" children, socialization is seen as a process of give-and-take (negotiation and interpretation) between children and adults as well as between children and other children. At the same time, there is a recognition that children can only be understood in relation to the broader social, political, and economic contexts that impinge on their lives, but now researchers are not just concerned with the effects of these global forces on children but also with how children understand, adapt to, challenge, and even change these processes. The influence of what is often referred to as a practice-theoretical perspective makes understanding the relationship between agency and structure a central goal of research studies, and with this, as has already been discussed, attention is focused on the role and influence of specific practices or routines in a child's life while at the same time attention is drawn to issues of power and authority and the way cultural systems are produced and reproduced.

This approach presents researchers with a model that eschews either/or arguments (*it's nature, no it's nurture; it's micro processes, no it's macro processes*) and instead highlights the advantage that anthropology has always had, which is to recognize and celebrate the value of bringing multiple perspectives to bear on a specific topic without assuming that there will ultimately be "one truth." There is also the important acknowledgment that anthropologists, just like children, are not "acultural" and therefore are likely to be influenced by their own ideologies of childhood and that as researchers we need to be aware of how these ideologies may influence the development of specific theoretical models.

What is particularly exciting about this framework is that it is stimulating and supporting research on children in all of the subfields of anthropology. New attention to the study of children by archaeologists is providing much greater depth to our understanding of the role of children in historic and prehistoric societies (an especially important topic to pursue since archaeologists have suggested that children constituted more than 50% of prehistoric populations). Cultural and linguistic anthropologists are developing innovative frameworks for linking micro- and macrolevel studies, while biological anthropologists are combining research that is sensitive to cultural, political, and economic contexts with methodologies that enable researchers to examine changing biological processes in relation to changing environments. All of these studies are generating new topics for analysis (e.g., the biology of inequality) as well as challenging taken-for-granted assumptions about children's behavior (e.g., the idea that children "naturally" play in gender-segregated groups).

In this brief essay, what may fairly be seen as two important shifts in the discipline have been sketched: one is topical and the other theoretical. In the first case, it is exciting to see how the anthropology of children has moved out of the margins and is now recognized as an important topic for understanding the diversity of cultures around the world and across time. The second change is the one documented here: namely, the shift from relying on the theoretical frameworks of psychology and psychiatry to the development of a perspective stimulated by work in sociology but also uniquely anthropological in its comparative focus and integration of perspectives from archaeology and biological, cultural, linguistic, and applied research on children. Given these two important shifts in the discipline, perhaps it is now time to say that theories of childhood have finally "come of age" in anthropology.

Helen B. Schwartzman

See also Bourdieu, Pierre; Culture and Personality; Ethnography of Speaking; Foucault, Michel; Hymes, Dell; Mead, Margaret; Scheper-Hughes, Nancy

Further Readings

Goodwin, M. H. (1990). *He-said-she-said: Talk as social organization among Black children*. Bloomington: Indiana University Press.

James, A., & Prout, A. (Eds.). (1990). *Constructing and reconstructing childhood: Contemporary issues in the sociological study of childhood*. London, UK: Falmer Press.

Miller, P. J., Fung, H., Lin, S., Chen, E. C-H., & Boldt, B. R. (2012). How socialization happens on the ground: Narrative practices as alternate socializing pathways in Taiwanese and European-American families. *Monographs of the Society for Research in Child Development, 77*, 1–140.

Montgomery, H. (2009). *An introduction to childhood: Anthropological perspectives on children's lives*. Chichester, UK: Wiley-Blackwell.

Schieffelin, B. B. (1990). *The give and take of everyday life: Language socialization of Kaluli children*. Cambridge, UK: Cambridge University Press.

Schwartzman, H. B. (Ed.). (2001). *Children and anthropology: Perspectives for the 21st century*. Westport, CT: Bergin & Garvey.

CHODOROW, NANCY

Nancy Chodorow (1944–) is an internationally acclaimed feminist theorist, sociologist, and psychoanalyst. The impact of her work crosses the boundaries of social science and the humanities. Chodorow studied anthropology at Radcliffe College (1966), received her PhD in sociology from Brandeis University (1975), and later trained as a clinical psychoanalyst at the San Francisco Psychoanalytic Institute. Her melding of these disciplines is unique, as is her theory building, which over the years has shaped key developments in feminist theory, gender studies, psychoanalysis, psychological anthropology, and psychoanalytic practice. Chodorow is regarded as a founding scholar of second-wave feminist theory based on her groundbreaking book *The Reproduction of Mothering* (1978), an account that set the stage for a new psychology of gender. Although she first made her mark in gender studies, Chodorow's enduring contribution is her complex understanding of individual subjectivity, whether she is writing about social theory, gender inequality, sexual identity, mother-child bonds, psychoanalytic theory and practice, or clinical and ethnographic encounters. Although she is perhaps best known for *The Reproduction of Mothering*, it is her book *The Power of Feelings* (1999) that has most relevance for the field of anthropology.

The Power of Feelings develops the idea that people are shaped not only by outside forces (culture, power, and discourse) but also by forces within. By providing clinically informed examples, she elaborates and extends the claims made by psychoanalytic anthropologists about the intermingling of cultural and psychic forces as constituting human subjectivity and agency in the world—that we make the world and we are made by the world.

Chodorow argues that individual feelings, fantasies, and unconscious conflicts are bound up in but not reducible to cultural mandates about gender and sexuality and that efforts to explain gendered patterns in psychological life need not be at odds with what she calls clinical individuality. In *Individualizing Gender and Sexuality: Theory and Practice* (2012), Chodorow charts the development of her thinking and her stance toward theory building and clinical treatment as dependent on close listening to individuals who have distinctive, rich inner worlds and who live in a particular place and at particular historical moments in time.

The seeds of her focus on the individual subjective experience of gender and sexuality are found in *Reproduction of Mothering*, where she challenged two key notions: first, that there is a generic mother-child relationship and, second, that boys and girls learn to take on masculine or feminine traits by imitating others or because they are forced to do so. Instead, borrowing from object relations theory, she argued that early mother-child relationships of attachment and separation result in distinct gendered identities and personalities. She claimed that whereas girls establish their sense of self in connection with their female caregivers, boys establish their sense of self through separation. Girls' sense of self and identity is continuous with this early feminine identification, while boys must secure their masculine identity by rejecting or repressing what is feminine in themselves as well as by denigrating it in women. This fraught feature of masculine identification, achieved through a break in connection between self and (m)other, proved especially useful to feminist theorists who sought to account for the persistence of men's derogation and domination of women. Meanwhile, Chodorow noted that feminine identity is more continuous and complete than masculine identity but it too is fraught with boundary confusion. Rather than defining the self in opposition, women generally tend to arrive at a sense of themselves in relation to others. This emblematic feature of femininity can be self-sabotaging, and women may fail to claim enough autonomy or agency. Chodorow's revaluation of mother-daughter relations and connectedness rather than separation became the springboard for decades of research on girls' and women's development. Her insights about the fragility of masculinity also paved the way for new approaches in "masculinity studies" and understandings about homophobia and men and violence.

By suggesting that women's experience of mothering boy children is distinct from their experiences mothering girl children, Chodorow made the topic of maternal subjectivity a cornerstone of feminist theorizing. Given that Western idealizations of motherhood deny other parts of women's lives and identities in favor of their children's (insatiable) needs, this feature of her work on mothers as subjects rather than objects in relation to their children helped redefine debates on women, motherhood, and work. Chodorow's insistence that women bring distinctive desires, meanings, and motives to their experiences of mothering and sense of themselves in relation to their children (including generational, cultural, race, and class distinctions) challenged universalist theories of mother and child development. Her 1982 essay with Susan Contratto, *The Fantasy of the Perfect Mother*, set the stage for feminist inquiry into the cultural specificities of motherhood as an ideology, cultural practice, and personal experience.

Another facet of Chodorow's work has featured the role of relational family dynamics and early gender identifications in shaping adult sexual lives. Joining other psychoanalysts, Chodorow expands on Freud's legacy, particularly his *Three Essays on the Theory of Sexuality* (1905), to argue that sexuality is far more complicated and comprises more than one's choice of sexual object. In her 1994 book, *Femininities, Masculinities, Sexualities: Freud and Beyond*, she argues that like gender identity, sexual identity is highly individual, conflict-ridden, and constructed as a "compromise formation" between what is culturally and psychologically posed in binary terms ("heterosexuality vs. homosexuality," "masculinity vs. femininity," "activity vs. passivity"). Again, she identifies universal elements of sexuality that are taken up and combined by individuals in unique, idiosyncratic, and nonsingular ways, including one's experiential sense of one's own body, such as pleasure and arousal; one's internal world and mental representations about self in relation to the other; one's sense of feminine and masculine identity; one's sense of adequacy or conflict about one's sexual desire; and one's personal sexual fantasies (often filtered but not determined by culture).

Chodorow's contribution to psychoanalysis also crosses the usual disciplinary boundaries. She has added to the sociology and history of psychoanalysis as a field through her work on the lives of women analysts across generations. The clinical dimension of Chodorow's work has focused on the subjectivity of both client and clinician and the formative role that transference and countertransference plays. All the while, her persistent search is to identify patterns in how individuals make meaning, thus enriching our understanding of the powerful links between psyche and culture.

Wendy Luttrell

See also Feminist Anthropology; Freud, Sigmund; Psychological Anthropology

Further Readings

Chodorow, N. (1989). *Feminism and psychoanalytic theory*. Cambridge, UK: Polity Press.

———. (1989). Seventies questions for thirties women: Gender and generation in a study of early women psychoanalysts. In *Feminism and psychoanalytic theory* (pp. 199–218). Cambridge, UK: Polity Press.

———. (1994). *Femininities, masculinities, sexualities: Freud and beyond*. Lexington: University Press of Kentucky.

———. (1999). *The power of feelings: Personal meaning in psychoanalysis, gender, and culture*. New Haven, CT: Yale University Press.

———. (2000). *Foreword to three essays on the theory of sexuality, Sigmund Freud*. New York, NY: Basic Books.

———. (2012). *Individualizing gender and sexuality: Theory and practice*. New York, NY: Routledge.

Chodorow, N., & Contratto, S. (1982). The fantasy of the perfect mother. In B. Thorne & M. Yalom (Ed.), *Rethinking the family: Some feminist questions* (pp. 54–57). New York, NY: Longman.

Paul, R. (1990). What does anyone want?: Desire, purpose and the acting subject in the study of culture. *Cultural Anthropology, 5*(4), 431–451.

CHOMSKY, NOAM

Avram Noam Chomsky (1928–) is an American linguist, anarchist, political theorist and activist, a leading thinker of our times, and, according to the *New York Times*, arguably the most important intellectual alive. Chomsky's approach to linguistics has become known as the Chomskyan revolution and has earned him the title of "father of modern linguistics." Chomsky attracts both passionate disciples and antagonists. He bridges disciplines, yet some consider him extremely divisive. There is no doubt that the academic world has never been quite the same since Chomsky first published the now famous sentence "Colorless green ideas sleep furiously." This entry will focus on Chomsky's contribution to linguistics, which has exerted a strong influence in other disciplines including anthropology.

Biography and Scholarship

Noam Chomsky was born in Philadelphia, Pennsylvania, on December 7, 1928. He was the first of the two children of William Chomsky and Elsie Simonofsky, Lithuanian and Russian émigrés, respectively. The Chomskys were Hebrew teachers. They were scholarly and politically active, involving their children in their passions, including the revival of Jewish language, cultural activities, and Zionism. Chomsky grew up to become a public intellectual and activist.

In 1945, Chomsky enrolled in the general studies program at the University of Pennsylvania as an undergraduate. Most accounts of Chomsky's life note his aversion to institutional structures, especially instructional adherence to standardized and structured curricula, which he believes stifles creativity and independent thinking. His scholarship and politics would eventually be dedicated to advocacy for creativity and freedom. In 1947, Chomsky met Zellig Harris, a linguistics professor at the University of Pennsylvania, who inspired him professionally and politically. According to Chomsky, Harris introduced him to linguistics by giving him the page proofs of his work *Methods in Structural Linguistics* to read. Subsequently, he enrolled in linguistics, studying with Harris while also studying philosophy and mathematics. Through Professor Harris, Chomsky joined a student organization called Avuka, which consisted of young Zionists who identified with Kibbutzniks.

In 1949, Chomsky received his BA degree in linguistics, philosophy, and logic, and he married Carol Schatz, with whom he later had two daughters and a son. In 1951, Chomsky received his MA in linguistics and began conducting research for his PhD at Harvard, where he became a junior fellow of the Harvard University Society of Fellows. With this prestigious position, Chomsky became financially secure, joined the intellectual elites of the time, and was able to completely devote himself to research. In 1955, Chomsky received his doctorate from the University of Pennsylvania, after submitting only one chapter of his dissertation, titled *Transformational Grammar*. This work, eventually published in 1975 as *The Logical Structure of Linguistic Theory*, was to mark irrevocably his break with the existing views and to revolutionize linguistics. In 1955, Chomsky became an assistant professor of foreign languages and linguistics at the Massachusetts Institute of Technology. In 1958, he became associate professor. Together with Morris Halle, Chomsky established a graduate program in linguistics at Massachusetts Institute of Technology, and in 1962, he was promoted to full professor. In 1976, he was appointed Institute Professor. He is currently emeritus professor of the Department of Linguistics and Philosophy.

Chomsky's Linguistic Revolution

The three dominant and cooperative theories during Chomsky's student days were structuralism in linguistics, behaviorism in psychology, and positivism/empiricism in philosophy. Chomsky was to challenge the basic tenets of these theories. Linguistic structuralism, led by Leonard Bloomfield, assumes that human behavior, including language, is a self-contained system of interrelated signs that can be analyzed by resolving the logical structures of its parts. By knowing and classifying these parts, the whole could be understood. To perform a structural linguistic analysis, utterances are collected, and the sound system (phonemes), the most basic element of the language, is delineated. Phonemes combine to form the smallest meaningful unit of speech: a morpheme. For instance, the word *cat* is a morpheme; it consists of three distinctive phonemes [k-æ-t]. *Cats* consists of two morphemes, [k-æ-t] + [s] (plural morpheme). Morphemes form the building block for the next level, such as phrases and invariably different sentences. Linguistic structuralism was bolstered by the philosophical perspectives of positivism and empiricism, championed in part by Franz Boas and Bronisław Malinowski, and artfully implemented by adherents through fieldwork and documentation of different languages. Language learning during this era was explained using behaviorism, the leading exponent of which was B. F. Skinner. Skinner's theory was derived from the stimulus-response process of conditioning animals used in the lab. It considered the human mind a blank slate and argued that behaviors—including language, that is, verbal behavior—result entirely from training and reinforcement from the environment. This view, relying on empiricism, rejects any appeal to mental and other unobservable spheres through either introspection or conjecture.

Through a series of arguments and carefully chosen examples, Chomsky argued successfully against these theories. First, he objected to the goal, focus, and method of linguistic structuralism by showing that it only explains morphology but not syntax, which he considers the crux of language. He argued that the structural approach had no way to account for the infinite number of sentences in a language or the internal relations in a sentence, nor could it resolve syntactic ambiguities. He suggested that all languages are far more overwhelmingly similar than they are different; as such, there was no value in the endless collection of data, which he compared to the collection of butterflies. He believed that no amount of collected data can reveal the underlying principles involved in language, its acquisition, or its use. With this, he rejected empiricism, and in its place he proposed innateness, preferring to pry into the mind rather than rely on field observations. Consequently, he separated *competence* (internalized knowledge, assumed to be uniform among speakers) from *performance* (the actual use of language). He suggested a focus on the (internalized) knowledge of language, which makes it possible for speakers to create and understand new sentences, rather than on its overt manifestations. Furthermore, Chomsky strongly refuted the behaviorist theory of language acquisition in a now famous critique of Skinner in 1959. He suggested that it is impossible to link behavior to its immediate antecedent, because doing so consigns human behaviors to "conditioned responses," which negates the creativity, freedom, and complex consciousness of the human mind. For instance, he envisaged the response of a person looking at a painting. This person might say, "Dutch, I thought you liked abstract painting," "Hanging too low," "Remember our camping trip," "Hideous," or any number of things. A stimulus can incite multiple, and even conflicting, responses. Chomsky's *Syntactical Structures* (1957) followed by *Aspects of the Theory of Syntax* (1965) heralded his "revolution" in linguistics.

Critical Contributions to Linguistics

Chomsky has made vast irreversible and seminal contributions to the sciences and humanities in general, and particularly to linguistics, psychology, and philosophy. His theories have been an unremitting presence in the field of linguistics concerning the nature of language, its acquisition, and the method for studying it.

The Nature of Language

Departing from behaviorists' and structuralists' view of language as behavior, Chomsky concludes that language is a form of knowledge, a cognitive capacity, uniquely and equally shared by humans as part of their biological endowment. He terms this the *language faculty*, which is an autonomous area of the mind primarily devoted to language knowledge. Chomsky in 1976 referred to it as a mental organ. Thus, Chomsky understands the mind as compartmentalized into separate modules, such as vision, logic, or language. To Chomsky, language

cannot consist of observable responses to stimuli as its use differs remarkably from all other means of communication in terms of its creativity and productivity. Speakers of any language are able to understand novel grammatical utterances and can recognize them as such even when they appear meaningless (e.g., *Colorless green ideas sleep furiously*). Chomsky developed a nativist theory of language, shifting attention to the nature of linguistic knowledge, how it is acquired, and how the mind works. Over the years, Chomsky has introduced several research concepts, such as the *universal grammar (UG)*, a theory of the language faculty; *competence and performance*; *deep structure* versus *surface structure*; *initial state* versus *final state* of the language faculty; *internal language (I-language)* versus *external language (E-language)*; and *Principles and Parameters*, all in an effort to distinguish the knowledge of language from its use or manifestations, characterize the properties of linguistic knowledge, and articulate a theory of the mind that is biologically endowed to derive the grammar of a language from brief exposure and use the derived grammar creatively to generate an infinity of expressions.

Language Acquisition

How do children become speaking beings? How do they progress from an initial state, in which they have no language, to a final or steady state, in which they are avid users of their language? Consider that children live in different cultures with different child-rearing practices. Some people speak to their infants, while others don't; yet all healthy children become competent language users. Children "learn" language rapidly; they make systematic errors that they could not have derived from the things they hear from adults (e.g., a 3-year-old who says "Mommy *drived* to the store" instead of "Mommy *drove* to the store"), yet they end up with abilities that remarkably transcend the limited experience of language that they received; all children go through the same processes and similar stages of language acquisition. Underscoring further the uniqueness of this process to humans, Chomsky observed that both children and kittens or puppies are capable of induction. However, when they are exposed to the same sets of linguistic data, children end up acquiring language, but kittens and puppies do not. Consequently, he concluded that there must be an innate mechanism that makes it possible for children to acquire language and be able to comprehend and produce novel utterances. Chomsky distinguished language acquisition from language learning. Language grows in the mind. It is not a function of training and practice; rather, it unfolds along predetermined lines. Chomsky argued that every child is endowed with a UG that is aided by an innate ability, which he called the "language acquisition device," that makes it possible for children to use the cues from the language of their environment to construct its relevant grammar. In the 1980s, he introduced Principles and Parameters to further explain UG. He argued that UG is the innate principles that underlie languages, whereas the differences between languages are parameters set by the brain. Language acquisition involves a child acquiring lexical items from his or her linguistic environment and setting the relevant parameters so that he or she speaks Yoruba, Igbo, German, English, or some other language. In the 1990s, Chomsky refined this approach with the Minimalist Program. The aim was to devise more optimal grammatical rules toward the generation of infinite speech.

The UG, according to Chomsky, is fundamental to all languages and specific to humans. What is not clear, however, is how the UG could have been evolutionarily selected for in humans. In response to the problem of the biological origin of language and its diversity, Chomsky has often suggested that questions on the function of language be separated from those on the computations that underlie the system.

Study of Language

For Chomsky, the language faculty is an innate, biological endowment that underlies the productivity and creativity of language. Linguistics, he believes, should focus on making sense of this unique faculty; it should formulate abstract grammatical rules that reflect this state of the mind. To do this, Chomsky makes use of native speakers' intuition to study how language works and to gain insight into the mind. Using physics as a model for scientific inquiry, Chomsky proposed three levels of adequacy for linguistic research: (1) observational adequacy (focus on data from adult users), (2) descriptive adequacy (focus on speakers' competence), and (3) explanatory adequacy (explanation for why linguistic competence is as observed). Thus, he seeks explanation

rather than description or a catalog of examples. He relies on abstraction and construction of models rather than depending on mere observations. For instance, his earliest approach was to develop sets of rules that can generate all possible utterances from limited linguistic forms. Using these rules, he hoped to model speakers' knowledge of language, its productivity, and its creativity. Chomsky's method distinguished between deep structure (speaker's intent) and surface structure (utterance). These two grammatical levels are mediated by a process of transformation through which the surface structure is derived from the deep structure.

In 1986, Chomsky proposed a distinction between I-language and E-language (analogous to his deep structure and surface structure and, perhaps, his competence and performance distinctions). I-language (knowledge of language) is in the brain and should be the object of investigation. E-language is a socially informed object. Chomsky has continued to revise the tenets of his theory: The transformational generative grammar of the 1960s was replaced with Principles and Parameters, later rephrased as Government and Binding Theory in the 1980s. He introduced the Minimalist Program in 1995.

Chomsky's theories have been dynamic; they have received inputs from diverse collaborators and have led to vigorous cross-disciplinary debates on language, its nature, the nature of humanity, and scientific processes in general. While there are serious challenges to his views, their historical and contemporary roles in advancing linguistics cannot be overstated.

Augustine Agwuele

See also Bloomfield, Leonard; Dundes, Alan; Ethnography of Speaking; Generative Grammar; Greenberg, Joseph; Hymes, Dell; Labov, William; Sociolinguistics; Sperber, Dan; Structuralism

Further Readings

Barsky, R. (1997). *Noam Chomsky: A life of dissent.* Cambridge, MA: MIT Press.

Cook, V. J., & Newson, M. (1995). *Chomsky's universal grammar: An introduction* (2nd ed.). Oxford, UK: Blackwell.

Coswell, D., & Gordon, P. (Illustrator). (1996). *Chomsky for beginners.* Danbury, CT: Writers & Readers.

George, A. L. (1990). *Reflections on Chomsky*. New York, NY: Wiley Blackwell.

Harman, G. (1974). *On Noam Chomsky: Critical essays*. New York, NY: Anchor.

Lyons, J. (1991). *Chomsky*. London, UK: Fontana.

Mayer, J., & Groves, J. (2004). *Introducing Chomsky*. London, UK: Icon Books.

Otero, C. (Ed.). (1994). *Noam Chomsky: Critical assessment* (4 vols.). New York, NY: Routledge.

Pinker, S. (1994). *The language instinct: How the mind creates language*. New York, NY: Harper Perennial Modern Classics.

Searle, J. R. (1972, June 29). Chomsky's revolution in linguistics. *New York Review of Books, 18*(12), 16–24.

Website

The Noam Chomsky website: http://www.chomsky.info/

CLIFFORD, JAMES

James Clifford (1945–) was educated at Haverford College (BA, 1967), Stanford University (MA, 1969), and Harvard University, where he earned his PhD (1977) in European intellectual and social history. In 1978, he joined the faculty of the History of Consciousness Program at the University of California, Santa Cruz, where he has remained till date. His work has been recognized in history, literature, cultural studies, and museum studies, as well as in anthropology, where he has been an important theoretical influence since the 1980s.

Throughout his career, Clifford has been engaged with, and by, the crisis of cultural representation that marked anthropology and related disciplines in the late 20th century. That crisis concerned both the identity of cultures, depicted as coherent objects by and in the science of anthropology, and the identities (political, personal, and scientific) of anthropologists, whose careers required them to produce cultural objects (which represented colonized peoples) out of difficult colonial and postcolonial situations. Those situations were anything but settled in terms of the possibilities for identity and representation they offered to the "natives" and the Westerners (and others) engaged within them.

"Representation" here refers to both political and aesthetic-scientific processes. That ethnographic writing is largely bound by certain generic conventions dictating what professional anthropologists can and *cannot* say, especially about the processes of field research, was an unsettling proposition when Clifford and George Marcus brought it to the attention of their colleagues in an important edited volume, *Writing Culture: The Poetics and Politics of Ethnography* (1986). And the control of cultural representation has become increasingly contested as anthropologists have lost the right they once had (guaranteed by the colonial order) to describe other people's culture without first obtaining their explicit permission. The moments and movements in which once colonized peoples have regained their voices, and a public right to protect, preserve, and re-create their cultures, are a central focus of Clifford's work.

Influential Works

Clifford's first book, *Person and Myth: Maurice Leenhardt in the Melanesian World* (1982), offered a template for the intellectual project he would develop over the next 30 years. Leenhardt went to New Caledonia as a Protestant missionary in 1902, where he stayed until 1920. What was unique about Leenhardt, as Clifford shows, was his commitment to translation as a two-way process, one in which, Leenhardt learned, Melanesian concepts taught him new understandings of his own beliefs. He held what today would be seen as advanced views about the dignity of indigenous culture (in the face of colonialist violence) and the importance of indigenous control over processes of cultural adaptation; early in his career, he came to realize that the New Caledonians, to whom he was ministering, "needed to find *new* ways *not* to be white" (Clifford, 1982, p. 45). Clifford's subsequent work, brought together in three volumes of essays, has been animated by a similar problematic. How, he has asked, can indigenous peoples around the world maintain or renew their cultural vitality even as they participate fully in the life of the nation-states of which they are citizens?

The Predicament of Culture (1988) included seminal essays on the relationship between anthropology and modern art, both treated as modernist modes of representing otherness. Clifford analyzed the literary construction of modern "ethnographic authority" as it was initially codified in Bronisław Malinowski's report from the Trobriand Islands, *Argonauts of the Western Pacific* (1922). Before Malinowski, anthropological field research had been carried out as part of the work of scientific teams or by "amateurs" such as colonial officers and missionaries. In the late 19th century, professional anthropologists were "armchair scholars" responsible for the theoretical synthesis of data that came to them from both scientific expeditions and amateurs who were long-term residents among "primitive" people. Field-workers such as missionaries often had years of experience, but they were not credentialed as anthropologists. The Malinowskian model brought together the armchair scholar and field-worker in the same person, by privileging the theoretically informed research of scientifically trained anthropologists, whose experience in the field guaranteed the authority of their writings. Ironically, as Clifford showed, the anthropologist-writer's authority was grounded on the assertion of having "been there," among the people studied; but in classic modernist ethnographies, little was said about the details of being there—that is, the political and social dynamics of the research process. As in modernist fiction, the narrator became an omniscient observer, while the people of the study became at best the author's characters and at worst scientific objects to be analyzed but not engaged.

In the last quarter of the 20th century, after decolonization and with renewed efforts worldwide by indigenous peoples to assert themselves politically, the omniscient anthropologist became suspect, both as a literary persona and as a real person carrying out research. Clifford documented, and influenced, various kinds of "experimental" anthropological writing that attempted to turn anthropological objects into speaking subjects. Such "dialogical" narration had its own difficulties, as it is one thing for anthropologists to stage a dialogue in texts they control and quite another to cede control over the final product to the people they are studying among, or at least share it with them. But in general, the "reflexive" turn in Anglo-American ethnographic writing of this period, in which anthropologists considered both the politics of fieldwork and the epistemological implications of their literary conventions, converged on the issue of cultural representation. Anthropologists questioned the right they had come to presuppose of representing others' cultures (without their permission, in most cases). And they analyzed the relationship between their theory of culture (in which the world is imagined to be made up of distinct cultural groups, clearly delineated) and the literary tropes they used to write such worlds into existence.

In his analysis of anthropological modernism as it developed over the course of the 20th century, Clifford brings to light the discipline's ambivalence concerning the kind of playful cultural deconstruction it had sometimes inspired in modernist painters and writers. Anthropology was, or at least wished to be, a science, and as such, it disciplined itself to present its results as serious, scientific objects—that is, as cultural wholes, scientifically described. While doing so buttressed anthropology's scientific status, there was also a price to be paid, as the final essay of the volume, the influential piece titled "Identity in Mashpee," suggests. In the late 1970s, in a land claims case on Cape Cod, the Mashpee Wampanoag Tribal Council was unable to convince a court of law of its continuous existence as an authentic Indian tribe. Courts of law, Clifford shows, can understand scientific descriptions of bounded cultures and identities, but they cannot give standing to what they saw (in this case) as the deeply compromised (polluted, diluted) Indian identity of the claimants. Anthropological expert witnesses were willing to testify on behalf of the Indians, but anthropology's traditional culture concept won the day; hence, the culture concept had become, for Clifford and many anthropologists at the end of the century, a "predicament."

Routes: Travel and Translation in the Late Twentieth Century (1997) turned our attention to pathways through and between cultures—to the ways in which people from different cultures travel to and engage or make contact with people from other cultures, and to the ways in which cultural materials travel between locations and peoples. Continuing his historical critique of anthropological practices, Clifford argued that modernist ethnographies erased travel, focusing instead on "dwelling." Professional anthropologists derived their scientific authority from being there, in "the field," which was "defined as a site of displaced dwelling and productive work" (p. 22). The field site was treated as the home of the people being studied, and such natives were imagined as purely local people. Given such assumptions, fixed by the conventions of ethnographic writing, natives were not depicted as travelers, and the anthropologist's travels—to and from the metropole, the university, the colonial capital, or the missionary's station—were left out of the picture. One result of these modernist conventions was the erasure of colonialism as an intrusive force in the ostensibly out-of-the-way places where anthropologists worked. Native cultures were depicted as temporal and spatial isolates, despite the easily observed facts of cultural contact, borrowing, and adaptation, not to mention the constant travel of local people to work at colonial plantations, mines, and homesteads.

Clifford then turned his attention from the travels of people to those of things: cultural objects and artifacts. In four essays on museums as "contact zones," Clifford began the analysis of an emergent trend in the world of "cultural property," as nation-states, responding to newly galvanized indigenous groups, began revising the laws governing the ownership of heritage objects. The ethnographic collections of metropolitan museums and archives came to be seen as the result of several centuries of looting: a process in which explorers, colonial officials, missionaries, art dealers, and anthropologists had illicitly acquired a people's material heritage. Museums in particular acquired a new burden—to negotiate the ownership and control of ethnographic objects now being reclaimed by indigenous people around the world. Ethnographic collections were "repatriated," often with provisos stipulating that returned objects be placed in local museums. Clifford's essays explored the ways in which a hegemonic cultural institution, the museum, could be bent to new purposes, specifically the cultural-political needs of native peoples who had traditionally been the objects, but not the authors, of ethnology and museology. These essays have been as influential in anthropology, museum studies, and art history as "Identity in Mashpee" has been to scholars who study the politics of cultural identity.

In *Returns: Becoming Indigenous in the Twenty-First Century* (2013), the term *returns* has several implications. On the one hand, the essays discuss the return of indigenous peoples in the Pacific, in California, and in Alaska to openly avowed native identities they can now construct with a renewed degree of political-cultural power that could not have been imagined 50 years ago. These returns are in one sense renewals, the return to a "traditional" identity, but in another sense, these returns are alternative routes through modernity. Here, the term *routes* implies more continuity through history than terms like *the invention of tradition* have allowed. Clifford (2013) articulates what he calls a "realist" history that takes account of the continuing presence

of indigenous peoples in settler and colonial societies—peoples who were supposed to disappear or assimilate but who remain culturally alive and who see their own histories as ongoing and continuous. As he puts it,

indigenous ways of being "historical" presume complex temporalities of transformation and conservation, looking back while moving ahead. It will be necessary to imagine looping paths, detours and pauses rather than direct lines of development—historical paths that turn and return, going somewhere neither past nor future. (p. 14)

At the center of *Returns* is "Ishi's Story," an extended analysis of cultural continuity in relationship to the politics of cultural representation in 20th-century California. Ishi was a Yahi Indian of California who came to public attention at the beginning, middle, and end of the 20th century. After Ishi's "discovery" in 1911, his life as a semi-public person, resident at the anthropology museum of the University of California at Berkeley, and his death of tuberculosis in 1916, "the last wild Indian in North America," was brought to the attention of a new public by the 1961 publication of *Ishi in Two Worlds*, written by Theodora Kroeber, widow of the anthropologist Alfred Kroeber, who had been Ishi's patron in the museum. Daring for its time was the book's depiction of the extermination of California Indians by Anglo-Californians. More typical of its time was its romanticized presentation of California Indians as authentic cultures that were doomed to disappear. But for Clifford, the book is the central document for an analysis of contested cultural representation. Ishi's people didn't disappear, and with the "return" to the assertion of Indian identities, they demanded and won the right, at the turn of the 21st century, to repatriate and properly bury his remains. Thus, Clifford recontextualizes Theodora Kroeber's famous midcentury statement as part of a different political story, the story of persistence, return, and regeneration, not that of assimilation and death.

Conclusion

The work of James Clifford has at once documented the changing trends in ethnographic writing and culture theory and influenced anthropologists struggling with those changes. Clifford's unique contribution has been to make explicit the deep historical connections between anthropology, art, and literature in several national and regional contexts. Through his scholarship, anthropologists have acquired new ways to understand their discipline as a culturally contingent set of practices and ideas.

Richard Handler

See also Barthes, Roland; Marcus, George; Modernism; Native Anthropology, Native Anthropologist; Postmodernism; Tyler, Stephen A.; Visual Anthropology

Further Readings

Clifford, J. (1982). *Person and myth: Maurice Leenhardt in the Melanesian world.* Berkeley: University of California Press.

———. (1988). *The predicament of culture: Twentieth-century ethnography, literature, and art.* Cambridge, MA: Harvard University Press.

———. (1997). *Routes: Travel and translation in the late twentieth century.* Cambridge, MA: Harvard University Press.

———. (2013). *Returns: Becoming indigenous in the twenty-first century.* Cambridge, MA: Harvard University Press.

Clifford, J., & Marcus, G. (Eds.). (1986). *Writing culture: The poetics and politics of ethnography.* Berkeley: University of California Press.

COGNITIVE ANTHROPOLOGY

Cognitive anthropology is a relatively new subfield, not only in cultural anthropology but also within the social sciences more generally. It represents a turn away from the earlier interest of anthropologists in the cross-cultural study of social structure, and a still older anthropological preoccupation with material culture, to a new emphasis on the way shared practices and cultural institutions and made objects are conceptualized and organized in the minds of those who use them, live them, and reproduce them. This new emphasis did not come out of nowhere: It was sparked by the cognitive revolution that emerged from the brain sciences and had a profound effect on several disciplines at mid-20th century.

This new subfield was initially known as *ethno-science*. As it evolved, it tried on successive names, reflecting the growing pains of a new intellectual

venture. By the end of the 1960s, however, the field marked its maturity by positioning itself in parallel to other related fields such as cognitive psychology and cognitive linguistics, and that label, *cognitive anthropology*, has stuck.

The Influence of Linguistics

In theory, the new field of cognitive anthropology was to be about all kinds of cultural knowledge—about all the knowledge, it was said, necessary to behave in a way expected and appropriate for a member of a given culture. However, for the first several decades after that expansive goal was enunciated in the 1950s, actual efforts were narrowly delimited to describing and ordering knowledge of kinship systems, ethnobotanical systems, and other systems of classification such as those for color or spatial orientation—that is, how these things were categorized and how such systems of categorization varied cross-culturally. This narrower project of the cross-cultural study of objects and their categorization reflected the particular formal methods at hand, which were drawn from the linguistics of the day.

The Model From Phonology

The linguistic theory responsible for the way cognitive anthropologists initially thought about cultural knowledge was drawn from the study of phonology in linguistics in what is known as the Prague school. Phonology is the study of the sounds that the human voice can produce, only a subset of which, called *phonemes*, are meaningful in any given language. Thus, for an example, in English, the phonemes *b* and *d* contrast with *p* and *t*, the first two being voiced, while the second two are not. At the same time, *p* and *b* contrast with *d* and *t* along a second dimension, the first two phonemes being pronounced with what is called a bilabial stop and the second two with an alveolar stop—that is, the air is stopped either by closing the lips or by placing the tongue behind the upper teeth (against what is called the alveolar ridge). The four phonemes can be said, then, to form a *contrast set* made up of four sounds intersected by the two dimensions, voiced/voiceless and bilabial/alveolar. An explanation for why phonemes evolve to capitalize on such binary oppositions is that in this way contrasts between sounds are accentuated, so they will be as unambiguous as possible to the ear.

Linguists extended this theory to word meaning. Thus, to take one famous example, a *bachelor* was defined as an unmarried man, one of four terms defined by the intersecting dimensions male/female (contrasting with *spinster*) and married/unmarried (*bachelor* and *spinster* contrasting with *married man* and *married woman*, respectively). Anthropologists found this approach especially handy for analyzing small, bounded lexical sets such as pronoun sets or kin term systems. The study of kinship, of course, had a very long tradition as a subject of anthropological inquiry. Kin term systems were found to be composed of crosscutting dimensions such as generation, elder/younger, male/female, and lineal/collateral. This kind of analysis came to be called *componential analysis*, and the products of such analyses, *paradigms*. Other terminological systems, notably ethnobiological terms, were also of interest to cognitive anthropologists, growing out of American anthropology's earlier interest in recording everything that native people knew about their natural worlds (hence the initial label, ethnoscience). Native or folk systems of ethnobiological terms were found to be differently organized than kin terms, being structured by *taxonomies*, trees hierarchically organized by successive relations of inclusion—X is a kind of Y.

Such analyses made possible cross-cultural comparison of terminological systems. Perhaps, the most stunning findings to emerge from this approach to word meaning were cross-culturally universal features of ethnobiological taxonomies and of color terms. Folk ethnobiological taxonomies were shown to be typically limited to five levels: (1) unique beginner (e.g., plant), (2) life-form (e.g., tree), (3) genera (e.g., cherry), (4) species (e.g., flowering cherry), and (5) variety (e.g., Japanese flowering cherry). One theory is that this five-level maximum has to do with the limit of human working memory to a small number of items, since every added taxonomic level adds another feature dimension and a taxonomy with more than five or six levels would require remembering, at the lowest level, more than five or six distinguishing features. Also important to systems of categorization such as folk taxonomies is the apparently innate human pattern-recognition ability that makes some configurations of features particularly salient and hence readily classifiable.

In the domain of color, it was shown that basic color terms (which are monolexemic, not included in any other term, and adhering to several further criteria) evolved in a nearly universal sequence: Two-term systems have basic names for *light-warm and dark-cool*; three-term systems split off *red* from *light-warm*, leaving *white*; four- and five-term systems split off *green-blue*, leaving *black*, and split *red* into *red* and *yellow*, in one or the other order; systems with six terms further distinguish *blue* from *green*; with more complex systems making further distinctions. To date, the fullest explanation for this universal sequence has been the irregularity of the color space, which is not perfectly spherical but has an unusual shape, with a number of "bumps" and "indentations" making certain "focal" colors visually more salient to the human eye.

In the end, however, these analyses of kin, ethnobiological, and color terms were analyses of language and, specifically, of how lexical (word) systems were structured and had evolved. They captured only a sliver of what people in any society had to know in order to behave in an expected, appropriate way. This limitation became obvious when some analysts began to argue about which of the alternative componential analyses of kin terms were more psychologically "real." It was not even clear what psychological reality would mean when applied to a componential analysis of kin terms. Systems of linguistic terms, however they had evolved, were external to the brain, structures that scaffolded and constrained thinking but did not hold the key to *how* people thought.

Beyond Paradigms and Taxonomies

During the 1970s, more and more cognitive anthropologists tried to move beyond mere words for things, and the relations of opposition or inclusion that grouped them together linguistically, to describe larger understandings involving, for instance, relations of function, causality, logic, or convention, which underpinned knowledge and the use of these words. Some cognitive anthropologists described routine events such as those structuring ceremonies or everyday conversational exchanges. These various efforts were all signs of frustration with a linguistic model so exclusively concerned with words, the objects that the words named, and the paradigmatic and taxonomic relations among sets of these words.

In the 1970s, too, a new way of thinking about categories from the field of psychology, prototype theory, overtook cognitive anthropology. In this theory, categories were more than members of contrast sets; they were internally structured by prototypical instances. Prototype theory was a step toward weaning cognitive anthropologists away from their older linguistic models. Yet this theoretical development was still focused on the structure of objects.

The Influence of Cognitive Science

It took the arrival from cognitive science of an altogether new way of thinking about the organization of knowledge to redirect cognitive anthropology. This emerging new paradigm generated a flurry of new terms such as *frames*, *scenes*, *scenarios*, *scripts*, and *plans*. These terms reflected a general, cross-disciplinary recognition in the fields touched by the cognitive revolution that some such conceptual entity was needed to capture the way human knowledge was organized. The cognitive sciences of the day, especially artificial intelligence and cognitive psychology, were rife with such concepts and with efforts to work out their theoretical implications.

These related fields eventually settled on the term *schema* (pluralized either with an English -*s* or a Greek -*ta*) to designate the units into which knowledge was thought to be organized. A schema is an abstract representation of regularities in the world, built up over recurring experience of these patterns. It includes cultural and natural regularities in the world external to the person; labeling and other features of language describing these regularities; knowledge conveyed secondhand, linguistically or otherwise, by other people; and all the inner felt experience, such as bodily sensations, emotions, and motivations, that ordinarily accompanies any experience. Schemas can and do change over time to reflect changing experience, but they have a good deal of resilience, too, owing to how they frame new experience in terms already given by prior experience, filling in missing information on the basis of already existing schematic knowledge.

Linguists taken with this new concept began to see a problem with defining a word by merely contrasting it with other words in the same lexical set. The word *bachelor* illustrated the problem. Defining a bachelor as an unmarried man left out a great deal of what gave this word its meaning. (Characterizing

a bachelor simply as an unmarried man, cognitive linguists pointed out, failed to explain why it did not sound right to call the pope a bachelor, for one anomaly.) Instead, word meaning was said to depend on the "scene" or "simplified world" (or, in newer parlance, the schema) that formed the assumed background for a given word (in the case of bachelor and spinster, a very different world from today's, which is why we don't hear these terms, especially *spinster*, used very much anymore). A bachelor, in this simplified world, was a man who had exceeded the typical age for getting married without doing so. He could be, if not too far along in age, an "eligible bachelor" or, if older, a "confirmed bachelor" (or, euphemistically in a day when homosexuality was not spoken of outright, a gay man).

Cultural Models/Schemas

For linguists, reconceptualizing the meaning of words in this new way settled the matter of word definition with which they were concerned. For cognitive anthropologists, it was just a start, opening the question of how such simplified worlds themselves were organized and could be described. This was a radical move beyond how objects were categorized. To take one then current example, one could compile a list of all the diseases that Americans knew, and all the properties of these illnesses, and (because these properties across these illnesses were more complex than either a taxonomy or a paradigm could capture) use cluster analysis to show what diseases and what disease properties went together. But, still, one did not know how Americans *understood* illness— what schema or schemas they invoked when they thought about given diseases so that, for example, they could answer novel questions about them.

In cognitive anthropology, the recognition was that many, many schemas were shared, or cultural. The term of choice on which these anthropologists settled was *cultural models*. Indeed, the idea of cultural models, if not always its cognitive basis, has been widely adopted in cultural anthropology, especially since it has found use in applied fields such as medical and ecological anthropology. Secondarily, and increasingly over time, cultural models also came to be called cultural schemas. (Some cognitive anthropologists prefer to reserve the term *cultural models* for larger clusters of interrelated cultural schemas.)

Cultural Schemas and the Brain

A subsequent turn in cognitive anthropology has been an interest in how cultural models/schemas might be represented in the brain. This new theoretical concern was motivated by the advent of connectionist modeling in artificial intelligence. While earlier ways of thinking about the organization of knowledge were more computer inspired, conceptualizing this organization in terms of propositions and rules, connectionism models knowledge as networks of associations (and for this reason is also called parallel distributed processing). Although early connectionist modelers refrained from explicit claims of this sort, it has become clear that this associationist way of thinking about knowledge organization is quite faithful to a very general neural process known as synaptic plasticity, described as early as the mid-20th century but better understood as neuroscience has advanced. By this process, more or less strong clusters of synapses in a person's brain come to fire together, representing what has co-occurred in that person's experience. Cognitive schemas are simply relatively strong clusters of such associated synapses. The deceptively simple but strikingly novel translation of connectionism into cultural terms by cognitive anthropologists has been to recognize that to the degree two or more individuals share the same or similar experience, they end up with the same or similar schemas in their brains. In this way of thinking, "culture" is shared only to the extent that the experience that led to given associations has been shared, and only by those who have shared this experience. Culture conceptualized in this way is not sharply bounded or homogeneous or unchanging, nor is it a reified something outside of individuals—all difficulties with older conceptions of culture.

Contemporary Trends

This theoretical borrowing from cognitive science has fostered, in cognitive anthropology, a continuing alertness to new approaches from the young fields of cognitive and developmental neuroscience. Such advances promise to shed light on questions such as how cultural schemas might be organized to take advantage of the way the brain works, how the brain's design to make sense and coherence of experience might explain both universals and cross-cultural variation in cultural notions of the self, or how cultural defense mechanisms might be understood in neural terms.

In the wake of cultural schema theory, too, cognitive anthropology has pursued a number of efforts, initiated by largely separate schools of thought, that reflect the new theoretical questions and methodological challenges provoked by this broader conception of cultural knowledge. One issue is how such shared knowledge is distributed. For example, one new endeavor, known under the label of distributed cognition, explores how much scaffolding of individual task performance is provided by the external world, and especially by the tandem efforts of teams of individuals, each possessing only a part of the knowledge needed to perform a given task. Practitioners of another new subfield called consensus analysis explore the cultural competence or expertise of individual members of a group, as reflected in how much cultural knowledge of a given domain each possesses. Another new question about the distribution of knowledge is how individuals come to assemble just some attitudes and opinions out of a vaster pool of available cultural materials and how they manage the inevitable conflicts among the attitudes and opinions that they do hold.

Cognitive anthropologists are also developing a variety of methods for pursuing such questions. Some examples are formal methods for the measurement of cultural consensus; reconstruction of widely shared cultural models and exploration of their variability through analysis of discourse such as interviews and narratives; scalar analysis of the clustering of beliefs, allowing for a much less time-consuming reconstruction of cultural knowledge than does discourse analysis; and simulation of complex interactions among the cultural knowledge on which individual decisions are based, and the external constraints on these decisions, to evaluate how well the simulation model reproduces the observed cultural patterns.

Finally, a renewed interest in the internalization of culture—in how cultural schemas are learned and become motivating—has led some cognitive anthropologists to the work of other psychological anthropologists—those who conduct child development studies cross-culturally and those who study psychodynamic processes. This convergence of interests might be said to represent the revival of an older endeavor, culture and personality, which distinguished American anthropology in the 1930s and 1940s. Cognitive anthropologists have come to recognize that cultural schemas learned in infancy and earliest childhood are highly motivating and lifelong, shaping the culturally distinctive kind of adult person that results. This has led these researchers to an interest in parental ethnotheories of child rearing, the cultural models of the virtuous person (the person that parents are trying to raise their children to be) that these embody, and the psychodynamic processes, such as intrapsychic autonomy and culturally constituted defenses, that are implicated in them. The result has been a cognitively grounded reconceptualization of the relation, originally posed by culture and personality studies, between cultural patterns of child rearing and culturally distinctive adult personality traits.

Naomi Quinn

See also Culture and Personality; Ethnoscience/New Ethnography; Prague School of Linguistics; Psychological Anthropology

Further Readings

Berlin, B. O., & Kay, P. D. (1969). *Basic color terms: Their universality and evolution.* Berkeley: University of California Press.

Casson, R. W. (Ed.). (1981). *Language, culture, and cognition: Anthropological perspectives.* New York, NY: Macmillan.

D'Andrade, R. G. (1995). *The development of cognitive anthropology.* Cambridge, UK: Cambridge University Press.

D'Andrade, R. G., & Strauss, C. (Eds.). (1992). *Human motives and cultural models.* Cambridge, UK: Cambridge University Press.

Dougherty, J. W. D. (Ed.). (1985). *Directions in cognitive anthropology.* Urbana: University of Illinois Press.

Fillmore, C. (1975). An alternative to checklist theories of meaning. In C. Cogen, H. Thompson, G. Thurgood, K. Whistler, & J. Wright (Eds.), *Proceedings of first annual meeting of the Berkeley Linguistics Society* (pp. 123–131). Berkeley: University of California Press.

Holland, D., & Quinn, N. (Eds.). (1987). *Cultural models in language and thought.* Cambridge, UK: Cambridge University Press.

Quinn, N. (Ed.). (2005). *Finding culture in talk: A collection of methods.* New York, NY: Palgrave Macmillan.

Strauss, C., & Quinn, N. (1997). *A cognitive theory of cultural meaning.* Cambridge, UK: Cambridge University Press.

Tyler, S. A. (Ed.). (1969). *Cognitive anthropology.* New York, NY: Holt, Rinehart, & Winston.

COLUMBIA UNIVERSITY

Franz Boas established anthropology at Columbia University at the turn of the 20th century, and his many PhD students carried his principles and teachings to other universities and colleges in the United States. They set the agenda and the tone for the developing field for much of that century.

Anthropology During Boas's Tenure

The appointment of Franz Boas to the Faculty of Philosophy at Columbia University was emblematic of the attempt of Columbia's leaders to build a graduate school based on the style of doctoral education in Germany. Boas brought to Columbia his broad and deep training in the sciences and his vision of a new science of anthropology, uniting cultural anthropology, physical anthropology, and linguistics, with due respect for archaeology. Boas began teaching anthropology as a lecturer in 1896; he was named professor of anthropology in 1899, and in 1902, anthropology became an independent department. There seem to have been only two faculty members at that time, Boas himself and Livingston Farrand, a physician turned psychologist turned anthropologist and, soon after, the university president (the University of Colorado and then Cornell).

Little is known about the undergraduate program that Boas established beyond the fact that he hoped to offer one that stressed "what is valuable in foreign cultures" and "those elements in our own civilization that are common to all mankind" (Stocking, 1974, p. 291). The first Columbia doctorate in anthropology was awarded in 1901 to Alfred L. Kroeber, who then went west to found the Department of Anthropology at the University of California, Berkeley. The second recipient, in 1904, was William Jones, a member of the Mesquakie Fox tribe, whose dissertation was a linguistic study of Algonquian. (Tragically, he was killed in 1909 while doing fieldwork in the Philippines.) The next notable anthropologist, Robert H. Lowie, got his PhD in 1908, followed by Edward Sapir (1909), whose impact on linguistic anthropology was incalculable. Sapir also played a role in the development of the departments at the University of Chicago (as did another Boas student, Fay-Cooper Cole [1915]) and at Yale. Alexander Goldenweiser (1910) and Paul

Radin (1911) were important figures in the development of anthropological theory, and Leslie Spier (1920) established anthropology at the University of New Mexico. In 1914, Laura Benedict was the first of many women to earn a PhD under the tutelage of Franz Boas, for her research among the Bagobo of Mindanao.

In addition to students who received Columbia doctorates, Boas played a significant role in the advanced education of other important early anthropologists who got their degrees elsewhere. These include Frank Speck (University of Pennsylvania) and John R. Swanton, Alfred Tozzer, and Roland B. Dixon, all from Harvard. He was instrumental in the conversion of two psychologists (Livingston Farrand and Clark Wissler) and one sociologist (Elsie Clews Parsons) to anthropology. Manuel Gamio, who played a central role in the development of anthropology in Mexico, received his PhD from Columbia in 1922. Boas was responsible for training 30 of the 54 anthropologists with doctorates in the United States in 1932.

A major concern during the first 2 decades of anthropology at Columbia was the problem of cultural evolutionism, the long-reigning perspective on human culture at the turn of the century. The Boasian answer to the conjectural basis of evolutionism was to attempt to reconstruct actual histories of peoples and elements of culture. During that period, the stalwarts of evolutionism (e.g., J. Wesley Powell and Daniel G. Brinton) insisted that independent invention was the key to culture history and rejected diffusion as an explanation. On the other hand, the "diffusionists" of the Austrian-German and British school, represented by Fritz Graebner and G. Elliot Smith, respectively, insisted that diffusion alone was the key to culture history. The Columbia (and Berkeley) anthropologists carried out distributional studies of art forms, mythologies, rituals, and other aspects of culture, and their results undermined and discredited evolutionism. At the same time that they produced critiques of "diffusionism," they tried to understand the dynamic processes involved in the all-important phenomenon of diffusion—as well as independent invention. Edward Sapir's publication *Time Perspective in Aboriginal American Culture, A Study in Method* (1916) was a key document for those days, presenting methods for a cultural anthropology that the Boasians saw as a "historical science." But underlying the worldview that

Boas imparted to his students was what Robert Lowie wrote in his 1956 essay "Reminiscences of Anthropological Currents in America Half a Century Ago" was "the necessity of seeing the native from within" and the "anachronistic naivete" of "moral judgments of aboriginal culture." And, of course, they all had contempt for the racial determinism and "Nordic superiority" notion then rampant in the United States.

Boas trained his graduate students in physical as well as cultural anthropology, and many of his early students were recruited to the task of describing and analyzing the rapidly disappearing Indian languages. Although most of his students carried out ethnographic research, a good deal of their work depended on "memory culture," carried out almost exclusively among North American Indian groups. Their primary concern in the early years was to record as much as possible of the languages, mythologies, arts, and customs of these groups before they disappeared. During their careers, however, Kroeber, Lowie, Radin, Sapir, and Goldenweiser contributed to the growing field in various ways, building on the Boasian basis and moving far beyond questions of diffusion and evolution to deal with many aspects of theory and substance in ethnography and linguistics.

Boas didn't consider historical reconstruction to be the ultimate aim of their work but was concerned with problems of culture and psychology and the relation of the individual to his or her culture. By the 1920s, he increasingly stressed problems of cultural change and the role of individuals, with their varying experiences and personalities, in processes of change. His students turned to studies of acculturation and to work stressing the individual in culture. Leading students from the 1920s, whose influence continued well into the 1960s, were Gladys Reichard (who taught at Barnard), Ruth Benedict, Margaret Mead, whose work pioneered the "personality and culture" approach, and Melville J. Herskovits, the moving force behind studies of Africa and African American culture in American anthropology. Another significant figure from the 1920s was Otto Klineberg, a psychologist who under Boas's influence became the leading critic of intelligence tests and the attempt to use them to compare "racial" other groups.

Ruth Benedict became Boas's informal assistant in the late 1920s, and he finally succeeded in having her appointed assistant professor in 1931. She was important in the administration of the department and as an advisor to students, as well as being a teacher and a writer. The department continued to produce PhDs from the Boas-Benedict department through the early 1940s—over half of them women. These included Ruth Bunzel, Reo Fortune, Alexander Lesser, Gene Weltfish, Melville Jacobs, Frederica de Laguna, Jules Henry, Ashley Montagu, Ruth Underhill, Ruth Landes, Marian W. Smith, Irving Goldman, E. A. Hoebel, Charles Wagley, Oscar Lewis, and Gordon Willey.

From Boas's Retirement Until 1968

When Nicholas Murray Butler, the president of Columbia, who had hired Boas in 1896, forced him to retire in 1936, Columbia hired Ralph Linton to head the department—over the head of Ruth Benedict and despite the objections of Boas. There, he joined Benedict, George Herzog (a linguist and ethnomusicologist), and W. Duncan Strong (an archaeologist). Harry L. Shapiro began teaching physical anthropology in 1938. Columbia at that time, and for many years more, was devoted to the four-field approach, and students were required to be examined in them all. Margaret Mead's primary appointment was at the American Museum of Natural History, but she frequently taught courses and directed students at Columbia. Three more Columbia PhDs joined the department in the early 1940s: Charles Wagley (a pioneer in the anthropological study of Brazil, who would remain at Columbia until he retired), Gene Weltfish (denied tenure by Columbia because of her leftist political activities), and Marian W. Smith.

Through the 1940s, those who completed dissertations at Columbia were generally in the broader tradition of Boas and his students. Some were more historically oriented, while others studied change and acculturation, often with a stress on economics and political change. The politics of many of the graduate students in the 1930s were also in the Boasian tradition—from liberal to distinctly left, and this showed in many of their works. (Boas himself became increasingly politically active in the 1930s and until his death, fighting racism, Nazism in Germany, America-first chauvinism, limitations on free speech, and economic injustice.) The intellectually left perspective at Columbia was continued after World War II, in 1946, with the entry into the department of a group of veterans, mostly New

Yorkers who had grown up with the deprivations of the Great Depression. A number of these ex-GIs met periodically to discuss the ideas of Karl Marx, and when Julian H. Steward came to Columbia in 1946—replacing Ralph Linton (who had left for Yale)—the meeting of Steward and those students produced the closest approximation to a "school" that Columbia anthropology had seen since the early days of the century.

Julian Steward (PhD, University of California, Berkeley, 1929) had been developing a view of the evolution of complex societies based on his research in the "Greater Southwest Culture Sphere," which emphasized the resources in a people's environment, the technology available to them, and the work necessary to exploit those resources. He referred to his method as "cultural ecology" and was working toward a materialist approach to cultural dynamics that would produce "laws" of development. The 6 years of Steward's tenure at Columbia had far-ranging consequences for the field because it matched the concerns and inclinations of the group of students prepared to work to develop these ideas together. These students included Robert A. Manners, Sidney Mintz, Elena Padilla, Eric R. Wolf, Pedro Carrasco, Stanley Diamond, Morton Fried, Elman R. Service, Betty Meggers, Robert F. Murphy (a slightly later addition), and John Murra (enrolled at the University of Chicago). Later, Marshall Sahlins and Marvin Harris were influenced by Steward's work but were not his students.

Manners, Mintz, Padilla, and Wolf were recruited by Steward for his "People of Puerto Rico" study. This was pioneering research in cultural ecology and involved a controlled comparison of four different regions of the island, each with a distinctive combination of environment, crops, and institutional arrangements. It was a study of a complex society embedded in the modern "world system."

This group of anthropologists had a considerable impact during the 1950s and 1960s, and Columbia and the University of Michigan (home of Leslie White and, for a while, Service, Sahlins, and Wolf) were associated with their approach. But by no means did every student or faculty member at Columbia subscribe to the complex of materialism, neo-evolutionism, and cultural ecology that emerged from their early work. On the contrary, Columbians demonstrated a wide range of interests and approaches. Although Morton Fried and

Marvin Harris carried the flag for the materialist-evolutionist-ecological perspective, the range of interests and research at Columbia in this era was broad and varied. It was actually quite eclectic, despite Marvin Harris's ringing condemnations of eclecticism as "effete bourgeois mystification."

Julian Steward left Columbia in 1952 for a position as research professor at the University of Illinois and was replaced by Conrad Arensberg, a sophisticated scholar of considerable learning and original ideas and a leading theorist of community studies, who guided many students to their PhD degrees. The Columbia department enjoyed a brief era of relative stability in the 1950s (despite the death of Duncan Strong and the loss of Joseph H. Greenberg to Stanford and Harold C. Conklin to Yale) and then a period of great growth. American academia was expanding from the late 1950s, and Columbia anthropology, including Barnard College and Teachers College, expanded with it. In 1962, there were approximately 10 regular faculty members and 4 adjuncts (including Margaret Mead and Harry Shapiro), but by 1969, the department had grown to 26 full-time staff, plus the 4 part-time adjuncts. Columbia continued to stress the four-field approach and remained a major producer of PhD degrees, the graduate students working under a number of different advisors. Columbia's undergraduate programs, including Barnard College, continued to recruit students to graduate schools of anthropology.

In general, the prevailing underlying attitude at Columbia, at least through the 1980s, was more likely to emphasize the "praxis of everyday life," the material and down-to-earth rather than the symbolic, structural, interpretive, or literary side of the field. Columbia's anthropology students and faculty tended to be politically aware and, above all, ready to criticize biological determinism in its various forms (notions of racial inferiority, eugenics, and the cruder versions of sociobiology) whenever they arose. Leaders in this enterprise throughout the decades included Boas himself, Otto Klineberg, Ruth Benedict, Ashley Montagu, Morton Fried, Marshall Sahlins, and Marvin Harris.

1968 and After

Columbia anthropology underwent two crises after 1968. During the campus rebellions of the late 1960s and early 1970s, anthropology students and several faculty members found themselves on the frontline of political battles, placing a great strain on the community of scholars and sometimes incurring the wrath of the administration. By the end of the decade, there were a series of resignations, retirements, illnesses, and death, which hit the department hard and led to a difficult period with considerable turnover of personnel.

Despite the many changes in individuals, theories, fashions, and times, the Department of Anthropology at Columbia University maintained a remarkable continuity of tradition and tone throughout its first 90 years or so. (Robert Murphy called it an "essential style and aroma.") This was true even in the 1950s and 1960s, when Franz Boas was generally considered worse than old-fashioned and to have been an impediment to the development of "true science." The department was remarkably inbred, from the earliest days until the late 1960s. In 1962, 11 of 14 full- and part-time faculty had Columbia PhDs! (The count was only down to 13 of 26 by 1969.) But the whole field of anthropology has undergone revolutionary transformations since the 1970s, and by now that continuity has been broken. In 2011, only 3 of the 37 full-time faculty members in the department had doctorates from Columbia. In the 21st century, the Columbia Department of Anthropology evinces considerable political concern, but that would seem to be the only connection to the earlier tradition. In 1991, Robert Murphy had written, "Boas is much more than a dead ancestor, an ancient giver of now defunct laws. To the contrary, he has always been, and still is, a very live Pied Piper." This is no longer the case.

Herbert S. Lewis

See also Benedict, Ruth F.; Boas, Franz; Cultural Ecology; Diffusionism, Hyperdiffusionism, *Kulturkreise*; Harris, Marvin; Kroeber, Alfred L.; Radin, Paul; Sapir, Edward; Steward, Julian

Further Readings

Lewis, H. S. (2009). The radical transformation of anthropology: History seen through the annual meetings of the American Anthropological Association, 1955–2005. *Histories of Anthropology Annual, 5*, 200–228.

Lowie, R. H. (1956). Reminiscences of anthropological currents in America half a century ago. *American Anthropologist, 58*, 995–1016.

Mead, M. (1959). Apprenticeship under Boas. In
W. Goldschmidt (Ed.), *The anthropology of Franz Boas*
(Memoir No. 89). Menasha, WI: American
Anthropological Association.

Murphy, R. F. (1981). Julian Steward. In S. Silverman (Ed.),
*Totems and teachers: Perspectives on the history of
anthropology* (pp. 171–204). New York, NY: Columbia
University.

———. (1991). Anthropology at Columbia: A
reminiscence. *Dialectical Anthropology, 16*, 65–81.

Stocking, G. (Ed.). (1974). *The shaping of American
anthropology, 1863–1911: A Franz Boas reader.* New
York, NY: Basic Books.

COMMUNITAS

As outlined in essays published in *The Ritual Process*
(1969) and *Dramas, Fields, and Metaphors* (1974),
communitas was a core concept in Victor Turner's
anthropology of ritual and religion. The term was
borrowed from Paul and Percival Goodman's 1947
book *Communitas: Means of Livelihood and Ways
of Life.* For Turner, communitas signifies "a relatively undifferentiated community, or even com-
munion of equal individuals"; designates a feeling
of immediate community and synchronicity; and
may involve the sharing of special knowledge and
understanding. Critical to Turner's theory of religion, communitas was thoroughly grounded in
experience, receiving its most effusive application
in the study of Catholic pilgrimage based on fieldwork conducted in the 1970s with his wife, Edith,
in Mexico and Ireland. While retaining general
use in studies of religion, the concept has attracted
considerable controversy.

Turner proposed three forms of communitas:
spontaneous, ideological, and *normative.* In *spontaneous communitas,* individuals, often strangers
to one another, interrelate relatively free of any
expectations associated with role, status, reputation, class, caste, or gender, and other sociocultural
expectations and structures. Turner defined it as an
"I-thou" relationship of the kind identified by the
theologian Martin Buber. This interaction, characterized by personal honesty, openness, and unpre-
tentiousness, occurs between members of fixed
social categories (under specific ritual conditions),
among those on the edges of structured social life
(in marginality), and among those at the bottom

of the social structure. The concept was developed
metaphorically to cover themes such as the relationship between those undergoing ritual transition,
the "religions of humility" (e.g., members of the
Franciscan order in Catholicism), institutionalized poverty (such as that taught by the Buddha
or Mohandas K. Gandhi) and other monastic and
mendicant states, the middle-class countercultural
movements of the 1960s and 1970s, the status of
autochthonous people, and Christian pilgrimage.
In *normative communitas,* resources are mobilized
and rules and judicial structures are established to
organize communitas into a perduring social system (e.g., a religious order like the Dominicans, the
Puritan settlement in New England, or hippie com-
munes). Finally, *ideological communitas* is a refor-
mative process and is applied to a host of utopian
models inspired by spontaneous communitas (e.g.,
Marxian communism).

As a social experience, communitas has a 1960s
countercultural bearing to it, and it can be regarded
as liberation from conformity, norms, and rules.
Turner argued that normal structural activity
becomes "arid" and a source of conflict if people
are not periodically immersed in the "regenerative
abyss of communitas." However, this leads to communitas becoming prescriptive, institutionalized,
or "normative," replicating the aridity it seeks to
transcend. When this happens, detractors within
organizing bodies (i.e., churches, sects) often seek
to revive the original spontaneity, starting the cycle
anew. It was also observed by Turner that pathological manifestations of communitas "outside or
against the law" (e.g., rebellion) can transpire if
structure (institutionalism, repression, etc.) is exaggerated. And, if communitas is itself exaggerated, in,
for instance, religious or political movements, there
may ensue despotism, over-bureaucratization, and
other modes of structural rigidity, like that found in
totalitarianism.

The origins of Turner's idea of communitas can
be found not only in his fieldwork (1950–1954)
among cults of the Ndembu tribe in Northern
Rhodesia (now Zambia), in the impact of the
American counterculture of the 1960s, and in later
Catholic pilgrimage research, but also in Turner's
literary and poetic background, the camaraderie
he experienced in the Royal Engineers defusing
unexploded bombs with fellow conscientious objec-
tors during World War II, and the life experiences

he shared with Edith Turner. It is clear from interviews with Edith conducted by Matthew Engelke (2004) that the long and intimate dialogue between the Turners (who shared a marriage, parenthood, fieldwork, and a religion) was indispensable to the forging of theory.

Communitas has had a troubled existence. Critics have held that spontaneous communitas seemed more a utopic description of being than a heuristic device. Echoing Mikhail Bakhtin's utopianism, social liminality acquired a transcendent value, but in this case one that was influenced by the Turners' Roman Catholic faith, fueling their approach to Christian pilgrimage. According to critics, the Turners' analysis of the communitas of Christian pilgrimage emphasized an ideal and homogeneous experience at the expense of complexity and power contestations. According to John Eade and Michael Sallnow's influential approach in *Contesting the Sacred* (1991), a pilgrimage may accentuate prior distinctions between pilgrims as much as it dissolves differences, an approach developed in subsequent research on pilgrimage and festivals, such as that taken up by St John in a 2001 article published in *The Australian Journal of Anthropology*.

Others, notably Don Handelman in a 1993 article in *Journal of Ritual Studies*, expressed reservations about the "ontological implications" of communitas, the potential dark side of which (e.g., Nazism) he thought frightened Turner, who "avoided confronting" such implications. In a 1995 article in *American Quarterly*, Donald Weber pointed out that the potency and ambiguity of the "border" (and those subalterns occupying it) has, within American studies at least, made the transcendent and apolitical social liminality of communitas controversial. Indeed, the elective marginality implicit in Turner's later digressions became ill suited to perspectives on colonial history and gender politics. Yet, while the transcendence of the social was unsuited for those concerned with identity politics, communitas continues to provide a highly pertinent conceptual framework for illuminating rock concerts, folk and countercultural gatherings, rave and other electronic dance music events, and other extraordinary social experiences.

Graham St John

See also Bakhtin, Mikhail M.; Manchester School; Religion; Symbolic and Interpretive Anthropology; Turner, Victor W.

Further Readings

Coleman, S. (2002). Do you believe in pilgrimage? Communitas, contestation, and beyond. *Anthropological Theory, 2*(3), 355–368.

Eade, J., & Sallnow, M. (1991). "Introduction." In J. Eade & M. Sallnow (Eds.), *Contesting the sacred: The anthropology of Christian pilgrimage* (pp. 1–29). London, UK: Routledge.

Engelke, M. (2004). "The Endless Conversation": Fieldwork, writing, and the marriage of Victor and Edith Turner. In R. Handler (Ed.), *History of anthropology: Vol. 10. Significant others. Essays on professional and interpersonal relationships in anthropology.* (pp. 6–50). Madison: University of Wisconsin Press.

Goodman, P., & Goodman, P. (1947). *Communitas: Means of livelihood and ways of life.* New York, NY: Vintage Books.

Handelman, D. (1993). Is Victor Turner receiving his intellectual due? *Journal of Ritual Studies, 7,* 117–124.

Jencson, L. (2001). Disastrous rites: Liminality and communitas in a flood crisis. *Anthropology and Humanism, 26*(1), 46–58.

Maxwell, I. (2008). The ritualisation of performance (studies). In G. St John (Ed.), *Victor Turner and cultural performance* (pp. 59–75). New York, NY: Berghahn.

Sallnow, M. (1981). Communitas reconsidered: The sociology of Andean pilgrimage. *Man, 16,* 163–182.

St John, G. (2001). Alternative cultural heterotopia and the liminoid body: Beyond Turner at ConFest. *Australian Journal of Anthropology, 12*(1), 47–66.

Turner, V. (1969). *The ritual process: Structure and anti-structure.* Chicago, IL: Aldine.

———. (1973). The center out there: Pilgrim's goal. *History of Religions, 12*(1), 191–230.

———. (1974). *Dramas, fields, and metaphors: Symbolic action in human society.* Ithaca, NY: Cornell University Press.

Turner, V., & Turner, E. (1978). *Image and pilgrimage in Christian culture: Anthropological perspectives.* New York, NY: Columbia University Press.

Weber, D. (1995). From limen to border: A meditation on the legacy of Victor Turner for American cultural studies. *American Quarterly, 47*(3), 525–536.

COMPARATIVE LINGUISTICS

Approximately, 6,000 languages are currently spoken. One approach to studying them is to compare them for similarities and differences. This can yield insights into the history of the people who speak the languages and into the nature of the human language faculty. Linguists recognize three major structural components of language: (1) phonology (the sounds of language), (2) grammar (the formation of words from sounds and sentences from words), and (3) lexicon/semantics (words and their meanings). Some languages are more similar to one another than to other languages with respect to some or all of these features. Four possible explanations for the observed similarities are recognized: (1) genetic relationship, (2) borrowing, (3) universal tendencies, and (4) chance.

Genetic Relationship

Languages are genetically related when at least some similarities among them are due to inheritance of those features from a common ancestral or parent language (protolanguage). For example, languages of the Romance family, such as modern French, Italian, Spanish, and Romanian, all developed from Vulgar Latin, the spoken language of the Roman Empire. As a consequence, these languages show various similarities inherited from Latin, involving sounds, grammar, and words. For most of its history, the field of historical/comparative linguistics has primarily focused on similarities due to genetic relationship. This emphasis has been largely motivated by the very early recognition by comparative linguists that the sounds of related languages typically correspond in a highly regular manner.

Two sound segments correspond when they occur in cognate words of genetically related languages. Cognates of two or more languages are words similar in sound and meaning due to their development from the same word of a common protolanguage. For example, the K'iche' *raš* ("green") and the Huastec *yaš* ("green") are cognate words since both are descendant forms of a word for "green" in their common ancestor, Proto-Mayan (Mesoamerica). Corresponding sounds in this example are *r:y*, *a:a*, and *š:š*. Sound correspondences always occur in at least two cognate sets for genetically related languages, typically in far more than two. For example, *r:y* is also apparent in the K'iche' *war* ("sleep"):Huastec *way* ("sleep") and in the K'iche' *ra:h* ("spicy"):Huastec *yah-* ("spicy"). Because of recurrence, such matches are dubbed *regular* sound correspondences, typically shortened to just sound correspondences. Sound correspondences are the products of the ways in which the sounds of languages change over time. For example, the *r:y* correspondence recognized for K'iche' and Huastec is the result of a Proto-Mayan sound segment *r*, which developed in different ways in the two daughter languages: maintained as *r* in K'iche' and shifted to *y* in Huastec.

The existence of sound correspondences in two or more languages is a strong, if not definitive, indication that the languages are genetically related and, hence, that they form a language family. Languages of a family can be subgrouped according to the number of shared correspondences, those languages sharing more correspondences being more closely genetically related within the family than those sharing fewer. Recognition of sound correspondences allows identification of cognate words and the possibility of using them to reconstruct vocabularies of protolanguages that typically, unlike Latin, are prehistoric and unrecorded. For example, Proto-Mayan was last spoken in Mesoamerica more than 2,000 years ago, considerably before the development of hieroglyphic writing in the area. Nevertheless, identification of cognate words for the 30 or so modern Mayan languages permits recovery of at least part of the vocabulary of Proto-Mayan. Based on the sound correspondences described above and other information, scholars reconstruct *ra'š* ("green"), *war* ("sleep"), and *ra'h* ("spicy"), and many other words as well, for the Proto-Mayan vocabulary.

Borrowing

When compared languages are not genetically related but, nonetheless, show similarities, the most likely explanation is that resemblances are due to language contact and borrowing, especially when the languages are not too distantly removed from one another geographically. When the genetic relatedness of two or more compared languages is unclear, it is sometimes difficult to distinguish words similar in sound and meaning due to borrowing (loan words) from cognates. If the similar words do not participate in regular sound correspondences, then they are probably loans rather than cognates. Sometimes, loans are readily identified. For example, many Native American Indian languages have words for the nonnative things, such as apple, clock, and Saturday, introduced by the intrusive Europeans.

In Tzotzil, a Mayan language of Mexico, the names for these items are *mantsana*, *reloho*, and *savaro*, respectively. These words are unambiguously loaned into Tzotzil from the Spanish language, in which the words for these items are *manzana*, *reloj*, and *sábado*, respectively.

Comparative linguists have focused on borrowing in the study of the phenomenon of *Sprachbund*, or linguistic area. This is apparent when geographically contiguous languages, some of which are not genetically related to one another, share linguistic features, and also when feature sharing is largely explained by areal diffusion (i.e., borrowing) rather than by factors such as inheritance from a common ancestor, universal tendencies, or coincidence. A number of linguistic areas have been identified, including the Balkans, the Indian subcontinent, Mainland Southeast Asia, Mesoamerica, and others. A possible explanation for most, if not all, recognized linguistic areas is that diffusion was strongly influenced by the past use of a lingua franca or lingua francas in these regions. A lingua franca is a language used, typically in trading or other economic settings, by people who do not share a mother tongue. The most widespread modern lingua franca is English.

Reconstruction and Protolanguages

Identification of language similarities due to genetic relationship and borrowing can contribute substantially to historical interpretation. The reconstruction of words of a prehistoric protolanguage is a clue to the location of the homeland of a language (where it was spoken) and what items were of importance to its speakers. For example, reconstructed words for flora and fauna can help pinpoint a protolanguage's homeland since different biological species are usually fairly circumscribed in geographic distribution. Thus, if a word for orangutan were to reconstruct for a protolanguage, it would be very likely that the ancestral language was spoken in Southeast Asia, a region to which the hominoid in question has been restricted in occurrence since prehistoric times. While a single biological reconstruction can be helpful in locating the general region of a prehistoric homeland, a suite of reconstructed names for plants and animals can narrow homeland areas down to very specific regions. For example, based on reconstructed terms for several crops (avocado, cacao, common bean, cotton, maize, squash, and sweet potato) and other information, the homeland of the New World's oldest noncontroversial protolanguage, Proto-Otomanguean, is determined to have been a relatively small area located in or near the Tehuacán Valley of central Mexico.

The social interaction of prehistoric peoples can be recovered through attention to loan words. The sharing of many words by borrowing between languages is indicative of intense past contact among different groups. Often the degree of intimacy of a contact situation can be determined by the nature of the words borrowed. For example, languages sharing loans for kinship relationships such as uncle, aunt, and grandchild were likely used by peoples speaking different languages that intermarried to a significant extent. Even more specificity can be contributed to historical analysis when comparative study can determine the direction of word borrowing, such as in the Tzotzil/Spanish example mentioned above.

Universal Tendencies

While language similarities resulting from universal tendencies may contribute little if nothing to historical understanding, they can be important guides to the nature of the human cognitive faculty underlying language. A universal tendency is apparent when a linguistic feature occurs across languages that cannot be explained by genetic relationship, language contact (borrowing), or chance. A well-known grammatical example involves word order in the main clause of declarative transitive sentences. All languages have a preferred word order for subject (S), verb (V), and object (O). In English, for example, the normal order is SVO, as in "The dog bit the cat" or "Paul loves Mary." Of the six logically possible word-order types, the patterns SVO, VSO, and SOV, where S precedes O, are found most frequently across the languages of the world. On the other hand, OVS, OSV, and VOS—where O precedes S— are extremely rare. If some kind of human cognitive constraint on basic word order did not exist, each of the six possible types would statistically be expected to occur at about the same frequency. Comparative study brings such constraints to the forefront for scientific explanation.

Examples of universal tendencies occur in phonology and the lexicon as well. One phonological tendency involves nasal consonants. The most common of the latter in the world's languages are n (alveolar nasal), m (bilabial nasal), ñ (palatal nasal), and ŋ (velar nasal). Some languages possess only one of these sound segments, some two, some three, and some all of them. However, if a language has only one nasal, it is always n; if two, always n and m; and if three or four, always n, m, ñ, and/or ŋ.

The lexicon provides some striking examples of universal tendencies. Languages that are neither genetically related nor affiliated through contact often show names concocted for certain objects in very similar ways and at frequencies not compatible with random variation. Figurative labels for body parts are illustrative of this phenomenon. Globally distributed, unrelated languages show the use of complex labels for pupil of the eye, thumb, and limb muscle that literally translate as "baby of the eye," "mother of the hand," and "mouse of the arm/leg," respectively, or very similar expressions. Each of these figurative labels occurs in at least one fifth of the world's languages. Recurring polysemy, where the same two referents are noted by the same word, is also common, for example, eye/face, fruit/seed, hand/arm, finger/hand, sun/day, sun/moon, and wood/tree. These reoccurring nomenclatural associations suggest that humans everywhere perceive some aspects of their environments in very similar ways. Also fitting into the category of universal tendencies is onomatopoeia, that is, the naming of objects through the use of words that phonologically resemble sounds associated with the objects. For example, the nasal sounds mentioned in the above paragraph tend to be found in languages as constituents of words for the body part nose far more frequently than can be expected by chance.

Chance

Some similarities revealed through comparative analysis are indeed coincidental, since they are not explained by genetic relationship, language contact, or universal tendencies. Such chance resemblances while very rare are nonetheless often surprising when encountered. For example, English and Spanish words meaning "much" are *much* and *mucho*, respectively. Since these two languages are both members of the Indo-European family, the obvious similarity of the words might be presumed to result from a common development from a word in their common ancestor, Proto-Indo-European,

but no such prehistoric word existed in the language. Another possibility is that the word has diffused, either from English to Spanish or vice versa, but such a transfer is not documented. However, it has been documented that the developmental histories of these two words are totally independent. The English *much* has developed from the Old English *micel* ("big"), and the Spanish *mucho* has developed from the Latin *multus*, both cases involving well-understood sound changes for these languages. It is purely coincidental that the modern words came to resemble one another.

Automated Aids to Language Comparison

With the advent of computer applications, some comparative linguists have sought to automate their methods. This is understandable since comparative possibilities involving 6,000 contemporary languages are enormous and, furthermore, the number of scholars currently researching such analytical possibilities is, unfortunately, not at all large. Typically, computer approaches have focused on the comparison of languages of individual families such as Indo-European, Austronesian, and Bantu, and are usually designed to automate cognate identification or language-family subgroup recognition. A comprehensive approach has recently been developed by the Automated Similarity Judgment Program, an international consortium of scholars whose goal is to develop a database consisting of computer-readable word lists from all the world's recorded languages. This permits the possibility of comparing all possible pairs of languages. The database has been used thus far to produce, through automation, the dates at which protolanguages ancestral to all the world's language families were last spoken, the geographic coordinates for the location of homelands of most protolanguages, an inventory of most of the sound correspondences with their frequencies found for genetically related languages of the world, and a worldwide survey of sound symbolism tendencies.

Cecil H. Brown

Further Readings

Brown, C. H. (1981). Figurative language in a universalist perspective. *American Ethnologist, 8,* 596–615.
———. (1999). *Lexical acculturation in Native American languages.* New York, NY: Oxford University Press.

Campbell, L. (1999). *Historical linguistics: An introduction.* Cambridge, MA: MIT Press.

Haspelmath, M., Dryer, M. S., Gil, D., & Comrie, B. (Eds.). (2005). *The world atlas of language structures.* Oxford, UK: Oxford University Press.

Haspelmath, M., & Tadmor, U. (Eds.). (2009). *Loanwords in the world's languages: A comparative handbook.* The Hague, Netherlands: De Gruyter Mouton.

Holman, E. W., Brown, C. H., Wichmann, S., Müller, A., Velupillai, V., Hammarström, H., . . . Egorov, D. (2011). Automated dating of the world's language families based on lexical similarity. *Current Anthropology, 52,* 841–875.

Wichmann, S., Holman, E. W., & Brown, C. H. (2010). Sound symbolism in basic vocabulary. *Entropy, 12,* 844–858.

Wichmann, S., Müller, A., & Velupillai, V. (2010). Homelands of the world's language families: A quantitative approach. *Diachronica, 27*(2), 247–276.

COMPARATIVE METHOD

The comparative method was a research practice used by 19th-century evolutionists who focused on the evolution of human society. It was based on the notions of psychic unity and unilineal evolution. The anthropologists who used this method saw many customs and practices from different societies as similar to the point of being identical. They concluded that the existence of identical customs in different societies expressed the working of the uniform laws governing the human mind, an idea often called psychic unity. (This idea seems similar to the modern-day theory known as evolutionary psychology, an approach seen by many to be as flawed as the comparative method.) They then argued that because all human minds were governed by uniform laws, all human societies must traverse the same evolutionary trajectory. Differences between human societies resulted from their different positions on this trajectory. Customs could thus be traced from their origins to the present. The comparative method was used by 19th-century theorists such as Lewis Henry Morgan and Edward Burnett Tylor in their attempts to reconstruct the evolutionary stages of human society. Ethnographic information on indigenous societies was central to these reconstructions because evolutionists believed that non-Western indigenous peoples were living fossils representing earlier stages of human evolution. Although the evolutionary theorists of the 19th century were often critical of their own society, they uniformly believed that the northern European and North American societies they came from were the most evolved human societies and that, in the future, all societies, including their own, would progress further.

In England, Tylor published *Primitive Culture* in 1871. On the basis of comparative data from around the world, he arranged religious beliefs and practices in a unilinear sequence. Tylor argued that *animism* lay at the origins of religion and that religion evolved through a developmental sequence that went from polytheism to monotheism, and then to rationalism. For Tylor, the comparative method was critical since it provided the assurance that the evolutionary history of human society could be determined through the study of "survivals." These were cultural practices that were remnants of past customs and beliefs that no longer had apparent utility. However, their existence provided clues to a society's past and its location on the evolutionary scale. According to Tylor, one could study survivals in the same way a paleontologist studies fossils.

One of the best known practitioners of the comparative method was the American Lewis H. Morgan (1818–1881). In *Ancient Society* (1877), Morgan proposed an evolutionary sequence that went from savagery through barbarism to civilization. Morgan argued that subsistence, technology, and marriage and kinship practices could be used to locate the evolutionary stage of each society. Morgan's use of the comparative method focused particularly on family and property. He understood these as progressing from broader to more restrictive forms. In *Ancient Society*, he attempted to set out his comparative scheme ranking societies from around the world.

The arrangement of artifacts in museum exhibits of the 19th century both reflected and promoted the comparative method. In the early 19th century, Christian Jürgensen Thomsen arranged artifacts in the Danish National Museum according to the "three-age" typology of Stone Age, Bronze Age, and Iron Age. In the years that followed, artifacts were most often grouped by type and function, to demonstrate a supposed evolutionary progression. The Crystal Palace Exhibition of 1851 in London is one of the great examples of the comparative method in the 19th century.

The comparative method was named, analyzed, and interpreted by one of the main critics of the approach, Franz Boas. In a paper read at the 1896 meeting of the American Association for the Advancement of Science at Buffalo, Boas set forth what he called "The Limitations of the Comparative Method of Anthropology." Boas criticized Morgan, Tylor, and others who used the comparative method for tautological reasoning, charging that their methods of data collection and argumentation assumed their conclusions and made disproof impossible. He argued that many factors could explain the presence of similar social forms and artifacts in widely separated societies and that these could not be arranged into a single evolutionary sequence. Boas instead proposed what he referred to as the "historical method" and argued that cultural traits could be understood only within their specific historical and ethnographic context. A particular target of Boas was the arrangement of ethnographic artifacts at the U.S. National Museum, done under the direction of the curator of ethnology, Otis T. Mason. Following accepted practice, Mason had arranged artifacts of particular types, such as cooking pots or weapons from different regions of the world and different cultures, in evolutionary sequences based on their use or function. Boas challenged this notion, arguing that such developmental sequences were unproven and that artifacts from the same culture should be arranged together, not torn from their cultural context.

The comparative method, as described thus far in this essay, included both a powerful ethnocentrism and a belief that, for reasons that were ultimately biological, every human society would evolve in the same way. Thus, because all human minds grew in the same fashion and solved problems in the same ways at the same points in their evolutionary growth, all societies would follow precisely the same stages and produce almost exactly the same material artifacts at these stages. For example, given the right conditions for growth, Australian Aborigines would eventually, and inevitably, acquire the social forms and aesthetic tastes of Victorian Englishmen. These beliefs did not survive the Boasian critique or the data brought back by anthropologists in the early 20th century. However, both the idea of cross-cultural comparison and the idea of evolution remain part of anthropology to this day.

Although Boas rejected the comparative method, he and his students were very much engaged in cultural comparison. Many of their studies involved diffusion, cultural borrowing, and innovation, and these necessarily required a comparison of cultures. This was particularly evident in the culture area approach of Boas's students Clark Wissler and A. L. Kroeber. Furthermore, much, perhaps most, of the work of Boasians held the customs of other cultures up for comparison with those of White, Protestant Europeans and Americans for implicit comparison and cultural critique.

Although almost all of Boas's students rejected the very idea of cultural evolution, by the 1930s, it reemerged with great vigor in the work of Julian Steward and Leslie White. Both cross-cultural comparison and evolutionism were strong elements in the work of George Peter Murdock and other scholars involved with the Human Relations Area Files project at Yale. Murdock in particular used techniques similar to those of Tylor, comparing a large sample of societies and seeking correlations between cultural traits. Murdock even argued that "cultural lag" resulted in the presence of "survivals" from previous forms of organization in most social systems.

In 1962, Elman Service's *Primitive Social Organization: An Evolutionary Perspective* established the "band, tribe, chiefdom, state" model of social development that has been deeply influential and is taught in one form or another in many introductory anthropology courses today. Although the evolutionary aspects of this typology are perhaps rarely stressed by anthropologists, Service clearly understood bands as evolving into tribes, then chiefdoms, and then states. More recently, Keith Otterbein has used Service's types to classify cultures but has never linked a particular band with a particular tribe. In his 2004 *How War Began*, he created a seven-step sequence that applied to the four primary states of Mesopotamia, north China, the Zapotec of Mexico, and the Moche of Peru and argued that these states follow the same trajectories and that their "processes of growth" are identical.

Keith F. Otterbein

See also Boas, Franz; Evolutionary Anthropology; Historical Particularism; Morgan, Lewis Henry; Murdock, George Peter; Neo-Boasianism; Nineteenth-Century Evolutionary Anthropology; Service, Elman R.; Spencer, Herbert; Tylor, Edward Burnett

Further Readings

Boas, F. (1940). The limitations of the comparative method in anthropology. In *Race, Language, and Culture* (pp. 240–280). New York, NY: Macmillan. (Original work published 1896)

Fuller, D. Q. (2010). An emerging paradigm shift in the origins of agriculture. *General Anthropology, 17*(2), 1, 8–10.

Otterbein, K. F. (1972). A typology of evolutionary theories. *Behavior Science Notes, 7,* 237–242.

———. (2004). *How war began.* College Station: Texas A & M Press.

———. (2009). *The anthropology of war.* Long Grove, IL: Waveland Press.

Tylor, E. B. (1888). On a method of investigating the development of institutions: Applied to the rules of marriage and descent. *Journal of the Royal Anthropological Institute of Great Britain and Ireland, 18,* 245–270.

COMPONENTIAL ANALYSIS

See Ethnoscience/New Ethnography

COMTE, AUGUSTE

Auguste Comte (1798–1857) was a French philosopher who gave *sociology*, a term coined by Bishop Sieyès in the 1780s, its definition among other human sciences. After his studies at the École Polytechnique in Paris, he worked as a secretary for Count Saint-Simon. He then gave a philosophy course for scientists, the *Cours de Philosophie Positive*, starting in 1826 and published between 1830 and 1842. After several personal crises (he spent 8 months at a psychiatric hospital in 1826) and a passionate engagement in the 1848 Revolution, he founded a "religion of humanity," described in his *Système de Politique Positive*, published between 1851 and 1854.

Reorganizing Society: Positivism as a Basis for Social Order

Comte's main problem was the reorganization of French society after the revolution. He rejected the liberal position that modern societies should be founded on individual rights and the laws of the market. He held the conservative view of society as a specific order, but he did not want to go back to the social order prior to the revolution. He referred to the new sciences, particularly biology and medicine (as he was close to the Medical School of Montpellier), to argue that the social order must be based on scientific conceptions, not on theological abstractions.

For Comte, sociology was to follow the model of biology as a science based on specific laws. His first law was the law of the three stages, according to which every society passes from a theological stage (when humans think through divinities, as in fetishism, polytheism, and monotheism), to a metaphysical stage (when humans think through abstractions, e.g., individual rights or natural finality), to a positive stage (when humans think through laws based on observations).

For Comte, the French Revolution of 1789 was the moment of crisis during which European societies passed from the metaphysical stage to the positive stage. As he saw it, the role of sociology was to accelerate this change by extending positivism not only to scientific thought but also to politics. Comte believed that this gave French society a position in the avant-garde of humanity, as it experimented on itself this extension of positivism to every thought and action before bringing it to the rest of the world.

Positivism is defined by Comte as a method to make ideas clear, precise, and accurate. It involves observing phenomena to draw relations between them, instead of speculating on confused abstractions. Positivism is relational: "Il n'y a que du positif, voilà le seul principe absolu" (Since relations are the only things that can be observed, it is useless to look for an absolute term behind them). Hence, Comte's rejection of the psychology of consciousness that was developed by Maine de Biran and followed by the philosophical trend called "spiritualism." It was impossible, for Comte, to find in one's own mind an idea on which to base the relations observed in the world. For Comte, what we call "mind" is the way humanity relates to its environment by observing it in order to act on it.

Comte classified the sciences to show how positivism has progressed from one science to others. For him, astronomy was the first domain where observations became positive: It replaced astrolatry, the worship of heavenly bodies. Instead of conceiving of stars and planets as divinities endowed with intentions, men started observing the relations between them. Mathematics came out of this observation, as a science of relations for themselves. This resulted in the birth of property and agriculture, when the relations observed in the sky were applied on earth. Then came physics and chemistry, when mathematical relations were applied to surrounding objects at different levels of visibility. This was followed by biology and sociology, when living beings took themselves as objects of observation.

The progress of the observation of relations in all other sciences was necessary to create sociology as a science. It was the last science to become positive because humans spontaneously think of society as a collective will. Sociology is a reflexive science because society, being in relation to the rest of the world, is itself made of relations. Thus, society, first conceived of as a will or an intention, and then projected onto the world, could only be the object of the final science, a science of relations between relations.

Comte defined society by the notion of consensus. He used the model of the biological organism: Every part of society found its meaning only in relation to the whole. But Comte approached this social totality from two perspectives, the static and the dynamic, modeled on the distinction between anatomy and physiology. Static sociology analyzes the levels of organization of society, starting from the family and proceeding to industrial relations and government. Comte did not believe that the individual was an element of society, and he rejected the idea that organisms were made of cells: He thought that they were made of tissues that relate to each other without closing on themselves. It was then the task of dynamic sociology to show how society developed through time. The law of the three stages was therefore the first law of dynamic sociology. For Comte, it was only when society was analyzed as an organism that its historical development using the law of the three stages could be properly described. Progress through these three stages is what Comte called the "march of humanity."

Comte's perspective makes a distinction between society and humanity. Society is a being determined by its relations with the outside world and within itself. But humanity is the development of these relations through historical temporality. Humanity is constituted, therefore, by the pressure of one generation on the other: "L'humanité est faite de plus de morts que de vivants" (Humanity is made up of the dead more than the living). For Comte, this historical pressure produces a memory that does not determine societies' historical development but, on the contrary, allows for variations. The more humanity develops itself through time, says Comte, the more it becomes modifiable. The great political question for Comte then becomes this: How can humanity be modified without triggering crises?

The French Revolution of 1789 was interpreted by Comte as a modification that went too fast: All the relations were modified at the same time by juridical abstractions, whereas positive observation allows us to see which relations can vary, to what extent, and at which speed. Positivism is not a deterministic view of the world: It enables a politics of variations. If humanity is conceived of as a relation of relations, then it becomes possible to foresee which relations can be modified and to act on them. Human sciences are thus techniques of government because they allow people to act on a reality made up of social relations. "Science d'où prévoyance, prévoyance d'où action" (Science gives prevention, prevention gives action): This motto coined by Comte became the phrase for French reformism.

Yet for Comte, it would be impossible to act on relations if there was not a point in society where they are concentrated. This is the place of the subject or, in other terms, of affectivity. When Comte built his "religion of Humanity" in his *Système de Politique Positive*, he proposed that action should occur where relations are most densely expressed. This is the family, and even more the woman, who acts as a guardian of family, not because she produces children but because she expresses love. Love is defined by Comte as the principle of humanity, in the sense that without love it is impossible to conceive of order and progress, which are the two components, static and dynamic, of humanity. *"L'amour pour principe et l'ordre pour base; le progrès pour but"* ("Love as a principle and order as the basis; progress as the goal.") is the last motto of positivism. By stressing the role of affects in mental life, Comte thus opened the way for a description of moral subjectivities, particularly as they appear in primitive religions. This is the object of his final work, titled *Synthèse Subjective* (1856).

Comte's Legacy

Comte's philosophy has profoundly influenced the development of social sciences and politics, especially in France. Among his early readers, Emile Littré and John Stuart Mill wanted to distinguish between Comte's scientific method and his religion of humanity—as many positivist sects were developing in France, England, and Brazil, and with them many eccentricities and divisions. Littré played a role in setting Comte's "law of the three stages" as one of the dogmas of the Third Republic. When Jules Ferry imposed compulsory education as a way for schoolchildren to learn about the progress of humanity, it seemed that France had reached the positive stage of equilibrium after a century of revolutions. But Littré also read Comte's positivism as a justification for French colonialism, whereas Comte had criticized the conquest of Algeria and defended the "affinities between fetishists and positivists." Mill was instrumental in developing the positive method in the British "moral sciences" at the time when Herbert Spencer was using Comte's notion of "static and dynamic sociology." But Mill rejected what he perceived as Comte's authoritarian politics, and he developed his own psychology and logic on liberal bases that were counter to Comte's principles.

The first thinker who read Comte's work in its totality was Lucien Lévy-Bruhl. He stressed that no clear-cut separation could be traced between Comte's scientific method and his religion of humanity, because both derived from his idea of reorganization after the revolution. But reorganization appears as a contradictory idea: It supposes that society is organized, which means that it is determined, but that it can be changed since it has been disorganized. Lévy-Bruhl thus showed the proximity between Comte and Immanuel Kant: Both of them had constituted humanity as a subject that is both empirical and transcendental, that can observe itself and act on itself (this was later stressed by Georges Canguilhem in his reading of Michel Foucault's *Order of Things* in 1966). Lévy-Bruhl's work on "primitive mentality" is deeply influenced by Comte's idea that humanity's self-reflection can be expressed as a "logic of affects."

Lévy-Bruhl wrote that Émile Durkheim was the most eminent representative of Comte's sociology. However, Durkheim was often critical of Comte: He wanted to give sociology a method that would define clear-cut facts, whereas for Comte it was more a philosophy of history. Durkheim criticized the notion of humanity as too abstract and proposed to analyze "collective representations" as they are expressed in law and religion.

Comte's work largely fell into disfavor in the 1930s, as it was read by nationalist thinkers. However, Claude Lévi-Strauss taught Comte's *Cours de Philosophie Positive* in Brazil in 1935 and praised his views on totemism in the *Savage Mind* (1962). In the 1990s, he discovered Comte's *Système de Politique Positive*, and rewrote the pages on Comte for the edition of *Savage Mind* in the Bibliothèque de la Pléiade, praising Comte's description of fetishism as anticipation of his interest in the "first arts."

In North America, Comte's influence was diminished by that of logical positivism, an understanding of philosophy that started from entirely different assumptions and only shared with Comte his criticism of metaphysics. A new appraisal of Comte has been made possible by the recent revival of pragmatism. The most promising domain is the connection between Comte's view of the social sciences and a theory of action.

Frédéric Keck

See also Durkheim, Émile; Lévi-Strauss, Claude; Lévy-Bruhl, Lucien; McLennan, John; Structural Functionalism

Further Readings

Canguilhem, G. (1994). *Etudes d'histoire et de philosophie des sciences* [Studies of the history and philosophy of science]. Paris, France: Vrin.

Charlton, D. G. (1959). *Positivist thought in France during the Second Empire, 1852–1870*. Oxford, UK: Clarendon Press.

Delvolvé, J. (1932). *Réflexions sur la pensée comtienne* [Reflections on Comtian thought]. Paris, France: Alcan.

Gouhier, H. (1997). *La vie d'Auguste Comte* [The life of Auguste Comte]. Paris, France: Vrin. (Original work published 1931)

Karsenti, B. (2006). *Politique de l'esprit. Auguste Comte et la naissance de la science sociale* [Politics of spirit: Auguste Comte and the birth of social science]. Paris, France: Hermann.

Keck, F. (2011). *La Pensée sauvage* aujourd'hui: D'Auguste Comte à Claude Lévi-Strauss [*La Pensée Sauvage* today: Of Auguste Comte and Claude Lévi-Strauss]. In P. Maniglier (Ed.), *Le moment philosophique des années 1960 en France* [The philosophical moment of the 1960s in France] (pp. 113–124). Paris, France: Presses Universitaires de France.

Lévi-Strauss, C. (2008). *La pensée sauvage* [The savage mind]. Paris, France: Gallimard. (Original work published 1962)

Lévy-Bruhl, L. (1900). *La philosophie d'Auguste Comte* [The philosophy of Auguste Comte]. Paris, France: Alcan.

Littré, E. (1862). *Auguste Comte et la philosophie positive* [Auguste Comte and the positive philosophy]. Paris, France: Hachette.

Macherey, P. (1989). *Comte: La philosophie et les sciences* [Comte: Philosophy and the sciences]. Paris, France: Presses Universitaires de France.

Pickering, M. (1993). *Auguste Comte: An intellectual biography* (2 vols.). Cambridge, UK: Cambridge University Press.

Scharff, R. C. (1995). *Comte after positivism.* Cambridge, UK: Cambridge University Press.

Stuart Mill, J. (1865). *Auguste Comte and positivism.* London, UK: Trübner.

CONDORCET, JEAN-ANTOINE NICOLAS DE CARITAT

Jean-Antoine Nicolas de Caritat, Marquis of Condorcet (1743–1794), was born in Ribemont in northern France. As an adolescent, he demonstrated a remarkable and precocious talent in mathematics. By the age of 20, he moved to Paris to pursue his mathematical studies and began to publish in that discipline. His friendship with the prominent *philosophe* Jean-Baptiste le Rond D'Alembert introduced him to many of the leading figures of the French Enlightenment, notably the economist Anne-Robert-Jacques Turgot. When Turgot took over the finances of France in 1774, Condorcet was named inspector of the Mint. In 1776, he was elected perpetual secretary of the Academy of Sciences, and when Turgot was dismissed the following year, Condorcet gave up his political career for the time being and devoted himself more fully to mathematics and science, though he continued to write on social issues, as well as editing the complete works of Voltaire. When the French Revolution broke out in 1789, he participated actively, writing pamphlets before being elected in 1791 to the Legislative Assembly, where he was an ardent republican, though he did not vote for the execution of Louis XVI. In 1793, he was denounced as an enemy of the revolution, and a warrant was issued for his arrest. While he was in hiding, he wrote his most famous work, the *Sketch for a Historical Picture of the Progress of the Human Mind.* Arrested in 1794, he died in prison the following day, either from illness or by committing suicide.

The *Sketch*, a remarkable tribute to optimism, written in what could only have been his darkest hour, was published posthumously in 1795.

The *Sketch for a Historical Picture of the Progress of the Human Mind* is a testament to Condorcet's unwavering faith in the triumph of human progress. Condorcet identified 10 epochs or stages in the course of human development. The first, situated in the remote past, was when individual families of hunters united to form peoples. The second stage was characterized by the development of pastoralism and the third, by agriculture. All subsequent stages were exclusively European: Greece until the division of the sciences around the time of Alexander; Greece and Rome until the decline of scientific knowledge, the Dark Ages until the Crusades, the beginnings of the renewal of knowledge up to the invention of printing, from printing to the triumph of science and philosophy under Descartes, and, finally, from Descartes until the French Revolution. The 10th stage was reserved for the future progress of the human mind.

Condorcet's scheme is as idealist as it is idealistic, a narrative of the struggle of reason (generally science) against obscurantism (generally religion). He conceded to Rousseau that, at least in the short run, the progress of the mind was not invariably accompanied by moral progress. Even so, he saw counterexamples as temporary setbacks—that is, momentary triumphs of obscurantism over reason—which would ultimately give way to moral as well as intellectual improvement. His scenario is also wildly Eurocentric, far more so than that of Voltaire, whom he had visited at Ferney and whose writings he edited. After the stages of hunting, pastoralism, and agriculture, the entire course of progress of the human mind takes place in Europe. The first three stages were not Condorcet's original contribution but had been sketched out much earlier by his mentor, Turgot, as well as by Scottish thinkers such as Adam Smith and Adam Ferguson. Unlike the Scots, Condorcet's account of the earliest stages was entirely untainted by the inclusion of any ethnographic detail or evidence whatever.

Theoretically, Condorcet's elaboration of the stages of human progress is far less nuanced and theoretically interesting than the slightly earlier work of Smith and Ferguson. However, its unabashed optimism, its diehard faith in the ultimate triumph of moral as well as intellectual progress, set an important precedent for evolutionary thought in the latter half of the 19th century.

Robert Launay

See also Ferguson, Adam; Rousseau, Jean-Jacques; Smith, Adam; Voltaire

Further Reading

Condorcet, J. A. N. (1955). *Sketch for a historical picture of the progress of the human mind* (J. Barraclough, Trans.). London, UK: Widenfeld & Nicolson.

CRITICAL THEORY

Since its professional inception as an academic field during the latter part of the 19th century, anthropology has been influenced by a progressivist tendency to understand and defend the integrity, significance, and viability of human cultures in alternative world areas. Though crosscut by competing influences, orientations, and historical conditions, the anthropological impetus to vouchsafe the value of cultures and of cultural diversity has continued to the present.

During the first decades of the 20th century, anthropologists such as Franz Boas, Bronisław Malinowski, and Margaret Mead were critical of a common tendency by Western scholars to theorize individuals, society, and their relationship in terms heavily based in, and uncritically biased by, Western frames of reference. During the 20th century, anthropologists intertwined this sensibility increasingly with explicit developments in anthropological theory. In a weaker form, which has been common in much of cultural anthropology, *critical theory* may be taken to indicate theorizations of cultural and social relativity that throw into question the naturalness (or the correctness) of Western orientations. In a stronger form, *critical theory* can be taken to refer more specifically to the theorization of how cultural, social, and status differences are created and developed to generate, reinforce, and maintain relations of dominance, inequality, or disenfranchisement—either within societies and cultures or between them.

Emergence and Early Development

This latter sense of *critical theory* is reflexively historical and is itself best described in a historical context. The term *critical theory* itself derives from the so-called Frankfurt school, which included erudite German scholars strongly influenced by Marxism but disillusioned by the way Karl Marx's ideas had been narrowly applied, politically twisted, and made dogmatic, including via the spread of communism, during the early decades of the 20th century. As against this, they wanted the deeper potentials of Marx's own thought, and of social and cultural theory generally, to work against approaches that tended to justify, maintain, and reinforce social and political inequality. The Frankfurt Institute for Social Research, inaugurated in 1923, was the first Marxist-oriented research center at a major German university. With the rise of German nationalist socialism and Nazism, the institute fled to Geneva and then in 1935 moved to New York City, where it associated with Columbia University. The institute remained in the United States until the end of World War II and finally reestablished itself at Frankfurt, Germany, in 1953. Though the members of the Frankfurt school were not anthropologists, they tended to be brilliant interdisciplinary scholars and theorists influenced by the intellectual sensibilities of Marx and with wide-ranging interests that spanned—and interconnected—history, culture, philosophy, art, sociology, and psychology.

In 1937, the head of the institute, Max Horkheimer, published an article titled "Traditional and Critical Theory," which effectively coined the latter term. On Horkheimer's characterization, critical theory was designed to galvanize, crosscut, and integrate the social sciences by critically going beyond, and against, theories that assumed the propriety and functional value of Western structures of politics, economy, and social organization. In the work of Horkheimer and his colleagues, such as Theodor Adorno, culture was not ancillary but central to inequality. This was the case since cultural ideologies, including modern ideologies promoted through vehicles such as propaganda and advertising, easily skew social, political, and economic organization to promote the interests of elites. Non-elites are penalized but are not in a position either objectively or in their subjective orientation to effectively oppose or resist inequality or disempowerment.

As against this, critical theory was critically reflective or "reflexive" in considering the historically bequeathed workings of power and domination in the casting of ideas and of theories themselves.

In opposition to "pure" theory in an academic sense, critical theory in the Frankfurt school was intended, following Marx, to provide understandings that could ultimately change conditions in the world for the better—and not simply to understand or justify them on existing terms. Finally, critical theory according to Horkheimer was against the academic detachment of topical specialization, in which diverse social phenomena were considered separately; instead, it viewed these amid larger or totalizing patterns and structures of domination or inequity.

Drawing variously on the preceding philosophy and social theory of Immanuel Kant, Georg Hegel, and Max Weber—in addition to Marx—Horkheimer argued that ideas and subjectivity in general, including Western culture, had to be continually pushed by critical theorization to provide for the material and social betterment of all in society and in the world. As such, critical theory was concerned with material forces and factors in relation to subjective understanding, and it employed conceptual and theoretical rigor—often at a high or abstract level—to provide intellectual tools that could expose and in principle be used to ameliorate or abolish social injustice.

Putting this formulation in a larger context, critical theory in its stronger form can be seen to connect Marx's notion of historical materialism with current conceptualizations of culture that have been highly germane to anthropologists. Marx's materialism tended to posit that the tensions and, ultimately, contradictions between forces of material production and relations of inequality provide conditions for social transformation—and the potential for disempowered peoples and classes to recast society for the benefit of all. Since Marx's work in the mid-19th century, however, leftist political revolutions in France, Russia, and other countries seldom produced such optimistic results. Increasingly, then, the intellectual Marxists of the 1920s, 1930s, and since have considered how culture and ideology operate amid political and economic inequality to reinforce class and status inequity through dominating systems of belief despite social upheaval and change. The 1930s and onward also saw the publication and dissemination of Marx's early writings of the 1840s, which explored in greater depth issues of human subjectivity and consciousness.

Critical Theory in the Latter Half of the 20th Century

These issues remained largely refractory to and outside of anthropology until the mid-20th century, though they have affected the discipline strongly since that time. In Anglo-American and French anthropology from the late 19th through the mid-20th century, critical theory in its strong form was typically absent. During this period, anthropologists' pragmatic concerns to appreciate, vouchsafe, or appreciatively support alternative ways of cultural life were seldom able to be explicitly addressed or theorized in professional academic terms. Instead, the desire was to make anthropology objectively scientific and for it to be perceived as free of predisposing values. These tendencies became merged with the strong Western stigma against communism, Marxism, and associated theories of inequity in order to keep the theorization of disempowerment—including the domination of Western imperialism and colonialism—largely out of anthropology through the early 1950s.

During the 1960s and the 1970s, however, more explicit awareness of critical theorization, drawing on the writings of Marx, increasingly influenced a range of anthropological concerns. American, English, and French anthropology were significantly influenced during this period by activist social movements, including the civil rights movement and political opposition to the U.S. war in Vietnam and to Western imperialism generally. Social and cultural awareness was heightened by the civil rights movement, feminism and the women's movement, the Watergate scandal, and the increasing awareness of issues such as environmental pollution, the growth of urban ghettos, racism, and wealth and health disparities between the rich and the poor. In the mix, students and faculty of anthropology, especially in the United States, increased greatly in numbers, and many new departments of anthropology were established at American colleges and universities.

During the 1960s and 1970s, intellectual figures such as Marx and Weber began to be central to anthropology's sense of its own theoretical ancestry—though these thinkers had not themselves been anthropologists. As evident in the work of prominent anthropologists such as Eric Wolf, anthropologists since the 1960s have taken significant interest in critically and explicitly theorizing the relationship between material, economic, and political inequality, and culture. More recently, the early writings of Marx—and of Marxist critical cultural theorists from the first half of the 20th century, such as Antonio Gramsci, Walter Benjamin, Georg Lukács, Mikhail Bakhtin, and others—have exerted significant influence among professional anthropologists.

Sometimes associated with designations such as "political economy" or "culture/history/theory," explicitly critical theorizations in anthropology have given rise to large bodies of literature since the 1970s and 1980s. These have prominently and variously addressed issues of class inequality, gender domination, racial inequality, colonialism, sexual inequity and discrimination, and regional or global patterns of political and economic imperialism, both historically and in the present. Critical theorizations have also addressed issues such as disparities of health and medical care, education, environmental quality, and employment or employability. These interests in anthropology have been diversely influenced and broadened by international and interdisciplinary influences that are likewise theoretically "critical" but developed by scholars who are not necessarily anthropologists. Prominent exemplars during the 1960s through 1980s include the work of critical theorists such as Immanuel Wallerstein in the area of world economic development and underdevelopment, Pierre Bourdieu concerning the politics and culture of everyday practices, and Michel Foucault with respect to large-scale and intimate regimes of Western knowledge, power, and subjectivity. More generally, critical theories in anthropology have been strongly influenced by interdisciplinary trends of the 1970s, 1980s, and 1990s that have been variously developed through poststructuralism, cultural studies, postcolonial studies, subaltern studies, feminism, Black cultural criticism, post-Marxism, and practice theory, among others (see overviews vis-à-vis anthropology in Knauft, 1996).

Amid these myriad developments, what counts or may be designated as "critical theory" has become diffuse rather than well defined, including within anthropology. So, too, in a number of humanities fields, less explicit forms of critical theorization have intertwined with literary or hermeneutic orientations concerned with literature and the problems of

critical discourse. More poignantly, transdisciplinary critiques beginning especially during the 1970s and 1980s have criticized the idea of "theory" in general, including in anthropology. These critiques suggest that theory harbors a general tendency to overgeneralize and essentialize its own terms—and that it is uncritical of its own conceptual rigidity and pretense to scholarly authority. Along with a critique of so-called master narratives within Western scholarship generally, critiques of "high theory" or modernist theory have been strongly evident in so-called postmodern orientations, including in anthropology, since the 1980s and 1990s. At the same time, as described and analyzed by the critical theorist David Harvey in 1990, the postmodern condition can itself be seen in significant part as a cultural product of the political, material, and economic conditions and crises of inequality bequeathed by Western capitalism. In this view, postmodernity is itself a manifestation or symptom of Western political economy during the late 20th century—that is, its inequities, excesses, and failure of self-justification.

Recent Trends and Future Directions

In the wake of these developments, theoretically and otherwise, anthropology since the 1990s has continued to be informed by many aspects of critical theory, including as originally set forth by Horkheimer and as more generally informed by Marxist-influenced forms of critical analysis. At the same time, *critical theory*—like other theoretical designations in social and cultural anthropology—is less often used as an explicit label to categorize a particular school of contemporary anthropological thought or scholarship. This is consistent with a general tendency in social and cultural anthropology in recent years to use less grandiose or "middle-level" terms and topics of designation, rather than "high theory" labels, to describe its orientations and fields of study (see the discussions in Knauft, 2006, 2013).

More recently, since about 2000, the legacy of critical theory has informed an increasing and increasingly explicit emphasis in anthropology on what is alternatively called *engaged anthropology*, *practicing anthropology*, *activist anthropology*, or *public anthropology*. While these terms and their respective approaches and practitioners admit of various definitions and distinctions, they emphasize in different ways the link between the scholarly work of anthropologists and the exposition, understanding, critique, and amelioration of human inequity, discrimination, domination, and disempowerment. This trend and its sensibilities are in significant ways consistent with strains that have been evident in anthropology since its professional inception during the 19th century. Since that time, the ability of anthropologists to openly describe and conceptualize the linkage between their scholarship, their activism, and their theorization of inequality has grown, including in relation to our own cultural and conceptual suppositions. The degree to which these developments are explicitly linked to *critical theory* is variable. But the sensibilities of critical theorization that inform them arguably continue to be important, including the refusal, as Horkheimer emphasized, to let the important power of conceptual thinking and theoretical formulation become detached from our awareness of social injustice and our commitment to expose and help alleviate it.

Amid its key and continuing contributions, activist or applied anthropology faces difficulties that critical theorization helps identify and resist or counteract. This includes the risk of practical anthropology becoming influenced or co-opted by organizational or commercial interests, with vested interests that take precedence over those of the people who are being studied or ostensibly served. As such, practical initiatives by anthropologists and others benefit from the critical conceptualization and theoretical analysis of the larger context of political economy and cultural influence within which the effects of this practice are located. In this sense, intellectual independence of academic thought and critical theorization help make contemporary anthropological engagement more effectively reflexive, as well as exposing how culture and power—even when well intentioned—easily work to the detriment of disempowered peoples. Arguably these strands of anthropology—the critically theoretical and the engaged or activist—are best served by being linked together rather than separated or divorced from each other. In this and other respects, the past and present legacy of critical theory has a key practical as well as conceptual role to play in anthropology and, more generally, in engaging problems of human inequity and social injustice in the 21st century.

Bruce M. Knauft

See also Benjamin, Walter; Bourdieu, Pierre; Foucault, Michel; Frankfurt School; Harvey, David; Marxist Anthropology

Further Readings

Harvey, D. (1990). *The condition of postmodernity: An enquiry into the origins of culture.* Cambridge, UK: Blackwell.

Horkheimer, M. (1975). Traditional and critical theory. In *Critical theory: Selected essays* (pp. 188–243). New York, NY: Continuum International. (Original work published 1937)

Horkheimer, M., & Adorno, T. (1969). *Dialectic of Enlightenment.* New York, NY: Continuum International. (Original work published 1944, revised 1947)

Knauft, B. M. (1996). *Genealogies for the present in cultural anthropology.* New York, NY: Routledge.

_____. (2006). Anthropology in the middle. *Anthropological Theory, 6,* 407–430.

_____. (2013). Issues in sociocultural anthropology since the sixties. In J. Carrier & D. Gewertz (Eds.), *Handbook of sociocultural anthropology* (pp. 229–238). London, UK: Bloomsbury.

McClelland, D. (Ed.). (2000). *Karl Marx: Selected writings.* Oxford, UK: Oxford University Press.

Wolf, E. R. (1959). *Sons of the shaking earth.* Chicago, IL: University of Chicago Press.

_____. (1982). *Europe and the people without history.* Berkeley: University of California Press.

CULTURAL ECOLOGY

Cultural ecology is a theoretical approach that seeks to explain cultural similarity and diversity as resulting from technological and social adaptations to environmental challenges. It is the predecessor to most current approaches in ecological anthropology. The U.S. anthropologist Julian H. Steward developed cultural ecology between the 1930s and 1950s as a way to explain the similarity and diversity in the subsistence behaviors and social organization of hunter-gatherers, horticulturalists, farmers, and industrialized nations. Before Steward's time, scholars explained cultural differences using either unilinear evolutionary schemes that proved to be ethnocentric and inaccurate or Boasian historical particularism and diffusionism, which asserted that culture was only influenced by other cultures rather than by outside forces. Cultural ecology is significant because it offers a *causal* explanation for cultural diversity and uniformity based on adaptation; it argues that we should expect similar cultural solutions to similar environmental challenges in different parts of the world. Steward was wary of determinisms (theories employing singular causes, e.g., environment or biology). His cultural ecology tempered environmental causation with culture history and a multilinear view of social evolution, and he avoided biological determinism by divorcing cultural ecology from Darwinian principles. The principles of cultural ecology live on in allied approaches, including human behavioral ecology, political ecology, the ecosystems approach, ethnoecology, and cross-cultural comparison. This entry continues with a brief history, followed by a description of the key concepts, some case studies, and critiques. It concludes with a summary of how cultural ecology is practiced in allied approaches today.

Historical Context

Among the central missions of cultural anthropology is to describe and explain cultural diversity. Why, for example, are some people on earth hunter-gatherers, while others are farmers? Throughout the 19th century, the major explanation was progress: Hunter-gatherers were thought to be less evolved than farmers or industrialists. Franz Boas and his students created modern American anthropology by their efforts to demonstrate that unilinear evolution was both scientifically inaccurate and politically motivated. Boas and students such as Alfred Kroeber and Robert Lowie argued instead that anthropologists should understand cultural differences as resulting from dissimilar cultural histories. Some people are hunter-gatherers because they were born into hunter-gatherer cultural traditions, while others were born into traditions that include agriculture.

When Steward pursued his PhD under Kroeber and Lowie at the University of California, Berkeley, anthropologists were mapping the distribution of cultural traits among Native North Americans and classifying these distributions into "culture areas." They explained regional similarities as being due to diffusion: the spread of culture as small populations share information with each other. Steward, who had a background in biology and geology, noticed that these "culture areas" often corresponded to environmental features. He became dissatisfied with historical particularism and diffusionism and what he saw as circular reasoning that culture is caused by culture. In 1938, he published a data-rich work titled *Basin-Plateau Aboriginal Sociopolitical Groups*, in which he concluded that Native Americans living throughout the Great Basin (an area stretching from Idaho to southern California and including most of Nevada and Utah) shared similar cultural traits such as mobility and nuclear family organization because they were adapted to environments that were similarly characterized by widely dispersed resources.

Steward's cultural ecology was not the first theory to posit that human behavior varies in response to the environment. Scholars like Ellsworth Huntington proposed that climate determined cultural traits such as ingenuity and industriousness, inspiring ambition and civilization in residents of temperate climates and sloth among tropical peoples. This perspective is appropriately labeled today as environmental determinism. One of Steward's instructors at Berkeley, the geographer Carl O. Sauer, founded an approach analogous to cultural ecology called cultural geography, which examined cultural influences on landscape in prehistory and today. Contemporary with Steward were "social ecologists" like August B. Holingshead and Amos Henry Hawley, who considered human communities among those of other animals and plants in a local ecology but who, from Steward's perspective, underplayed the significance of culture in human adaptation.

Steward's Cultural Ecology

Steward offered cultural ecology as both a problem and a method. The problem is to determine under what conditions human societies tend to make similar behavioral "adjustments" or "adaptations" to similar environments. Whereas his predecessors thought that the environment had a limiting or permissive effect on the cultural behaviors a population could practice, Steward argued that adaptation is a "creative process" that generates cultural features. To Steward, it was culture rather than individuals who adapted to environments, where culture is assumed to be superorganic (greater than the thoughts of singular individuals) and to have history.

Because culture is very complex, Steward did not think that all elements of culture were equally likely to be influenced by the environment. This led him to propose the concept of the "cultural core." The first step in Steward's method is to examine the relationship between the natural resources a human population needs to survive and their technology for exploiting these resources. The second step is to investigate the behaviors associated with these exploitive technologies, including labor processes and the organization of labor. The third step is to examine whether the subsistence behaviors influence other aspects of culture, including social institutions and beliefs. The term *cultural core* refers to those aspects of culture that are most directly associated with subsistence, including technology, environmental knowledge, labor, and family organization. Steward argues that the core aspects of culture are most likely to respond to changes in the environment. Beyond the core are secondary aspects of culture, including social institutions and religious beliefs, which are less likely to have adaptive significance and more likely to vary according to culture history.

Steward proposed that cultural change may be described as multilinear evolution (in contrast to the unilinear approaches of the 19th century). As subsistence challenges change, due to either natural or human causes, people will adjust their tools and behaviors in step. Because subsistence challenges do not always change in predictable ways, cultural evolution does not follow a single direction; dissimilar cultures may become similar if exposed to a similar change in the natural or human-influenced environment.

While Steward applied cultural ecology primarily to hunter-gatherers, horticulturalists, and farmers, he insisted that it could also be applied to industrial societies, although he posited that the cultural core of adaptive behaviors would be less significant in societies with a more complex social organization and greater control over the natural environment.

Cultural Ecology Case Studies

In the aforementioned work, *Basin-Plateau Aboriginal Sociopolitical Groups*, Steward describes in great detail the climate, topography, and distribution of natural resources throughout the vast and heterogeneous region of the Great Basin, as well as the subsistence behaviors, movements, and aggregations of the Shoshoni, Ute, and Paiute Native Americans living there. The most important natural resources for these hunter-gatherers were wild grains, roots, and berries, collected by women, and small game, hunted by men. Most of these resources were highly dispersed across the landscape. Steward demonstrated that the most efficient way to harvest these resources was by solitary individual foragers. As a result, the Native Americans of the Great Basin tended to live in dispersed nuclear families. Nuclear families joined together in somewhat larger groups occasionally for brief periods when resources could be more efficiently harvested by cooperative groups—including antelope hunts, jackrabbit drives, and harvesting pine nuts. With high mobility and flexible band membership, no formal leadership positions developed.

In a comparative study of hunter-gatherers from the Great Basin, Kalahari, Central African rainforests, and the Western Desert of Australia, Steward argued that many hunter-gatherer societies shared a patrilocal, patrilineal, and territorial cultural adaptation to the hunting of dispersed, nonmigratory animals. In all of these societies, hunting was the work of men. Hunting required detailed knowledge of the terrain, which hunters learned as boys. Thus, it was more efficient for boys to remain in their home region after marriage and for women, who gathered stable, predictable, plant resources, to leave their natal villages to live with their husband's family (patrilocality). Because wild game populations were prone to overexploitation, related men cooperated to exclude outsiders from hunting territories. The activity of defending territories unified men into socially cohesive groups, encouraging the formation of patrilineal clans.

Steward and Robert Murphy's comparative study of Montagnais fur trappers in northeastern North America and Mundurucú rubber tappers of Amazonian Brazil exemplifies multilinear evolution and adaptation to human-made environments, particularly new export markets. Before they were dependent on trade, Montagnais and Mundurucú practiced very different cultural patterns, but they converged on a similar cultural pattern when faced with the similar challenges of market production. Before the fur trade, Montagnais hunted mobile herds of caribou in winter and exploited fish and small, stationary game in summer. Because caribou were hunted cooperatively by a small team of men, Montagnais lived in multifamily groups in winter. They assembled in larger groups for fishing in summer. There was no formal ownership of territory or formal leadership. The fur trade changed the structure of the resource base. Multifamily groups dissolved into autonomous nuclear families, which relocated to be close to the most important stationary resource, the company store, where they purchased much of their food. As demand for fur-bearing mammals increased and their wild populations diminished, men claimed ownership of private hunting territories. Among the horticultural Mundurucú before the rubber boom, men practiced solitary hunting of small game and cooperated to clear fields and make war, while women worked together to cultivate manioc. The result was a matrilocal family structure (organized around cooperative-farming women) and a patrilineal political structure (organized around cooperative male warriors) headed by a traditional village chief, and a village structure consisting of one large house for men and many smaller houses for women and children. As rubber tapping replaced hunting and gardening, the social structure dissolved into nuclear families. Men defended private lines of rubber trees that they worked alone, while families became more dependent on purchased foods.

A somewhat more recent application of Stewardian cultural ecology is the so-called wild tuber debate started by the anthropologists Thomas Headland, Robert Bailey, and Nadine Peacock in the 1980s. They argued that it is unlikely that hunter-gatherers have ever lived in tropical rainforests without access to cultivated foods. As with Steward's studies, the argument begins with the structure of the environment. The edible biomass of tropical rainforests is low. Most of what humans can eat in the forest comes in the form of meat from wild animals. This meat tends to be very lean, for without a prolonged cold or dry season, animals do not experience seasonal fat deposition. The major source of edible calories is wild tubers. Because rainforest tubers have many natural predators, they tend to be highly toxic and cannot be consumed by humans unless processed. In short, the rainforest does not offer enough food to support a full-time forager. They note that nearly all ethnographically described rainforest foragers exchange wild foods for farmed staples like grain and domesticated tubers with

lower toxicity. Detractors argued that not all tropical rainforests are alike. Some are more calorie rich, with resources like freshwater fish and palm starch.

Critiques

The ecological anthropologists Andew P. Vayda and Roy A. Rappaport, in an essay published in 1968, criticized Steward's cultural ecology on the following grounds. First, while Steward argued that there exist regular correlations between environmental challenges and cultural solutions, his analyses involve case studies chosen specifically because they demonstrate these correlations. Thus, it is not clear how frequently the same environment triggers different cultural adjustments or the same cultural adjustment results from a different environment. Because Steward does not test hypothetical correlations with a large, statistically valid sample of human populations, it is difficult to tell how general these correlations are and if they really exist. Second, the cultural core model implies a causal chain that links resources, tools, labor, and social organization, in that order. Yet it is not clear whether causality proceeds in this singular trajectory or whether there are causal feedbacks. Third, Vayda and Rappaport criticize the cultural core model's assumption that religion and other "secondary components" of culture are generally not adaptive. They cite several case studies where religious rituals appear to have adaptive significance, including from their own research on ritual functioning to regulate pig and human populations in highland New Guinea. Fourth, they accuse Steward of conflating biology with genetics and, on the basis of a fear of genetic determinism, rejecting the possibility of biological adaptations. Throughout their essay, they argue that Steward's attention to ecology was limited to the availability of natural resources and ignored the greater subject matter of ecology (which at the time was dominated by the ecosystems approach). Since Vayda and Rappaport's essay, other researchers have criticized cultural ecology for taking a limited view of the role of political structures in the limits of human adaptation.

New Directions

Interestingly, Steward wrote about evolution and adaptation, yet he denied the influence of Darwinian forces. He described what could be called means of production and social relations of production, yet he denied any similarities of his approach to Marxian perspectives. His research focused on environment, but only to the limited degree that nature supplies resources to human populations. And he considered culture to be superorganic but avoided discussions of cognition. Ecological anthropology since Steward's time has expanded cultural ecology along these multiple lines.

Human behavioral ecology applies Darwinian theory to cultural ecology's mission of explaining behavioral diversity and employs Steward's method of starting analysis with the structure of the environment. This is perhaps most obvious in optimal foraging theory research. Environmental variables such as the patchiness of resources, travel time to prey and patches, prey size and abundance, and probability of encounter are used to predict foraging strategies, sexual division of labor, food sharing, and prestige-enhancing activities. Unlike cultural ecology, behavioral ecologists assume that natural selection has honed human decision-making skills over time, so that individuals rather than populations adapt by using near-optimal decision-making skills rather than by using culture. Concepts from sociobiology, like reciprocal altruism and kin selection, are used to explain cooperation. Increasingly, human behavioral ecologists are adopting concepts from gene-culture coevolution theory, particularly social learning of cultural information, which may be reintroducing a concept of culture that Steward, Kroeber, and Lowie would have recognized.

The cultural core model bears resemblance to Marx's mode-of-production model, in which resources are transformed into commodities by labor processes, including human labor power, the means of production (tools), and the social relations of production (rules and social institutions). Marvin Harris claims in his book *The Rise of Anthropological Theory* that his cultural materialism approach is a descendant of Steward's cultural ecology, which makes more explicit the material objects that connect humans with the environment.

A more orthodox application of mode of production is employed by Eric Wolf, a student of Steward's, in *Europe and the People Without History*. Wolf presents a history of the world economy in which different populations exploit and manage resources through kin-based rules, tributary rules, or capitalist rules. These populations interact through conquest and domination to create the system of global inequalities that we have in the world today. Wolf's political economy approach starts with cultural adaptation to the environment but adds to it the history of political subjugation and structured inequality. More recently, political ecologists have examined human-environment interactions within the lens of political power differences.

Among Vayda and Rappaport's main criticisms of cultural ecology was that it employed a very limited concept of ecology. They urged anthropologists to embrace the work of ecologists, which at the time was largely focused on ecosystems. The 1960s version of the ecosystem concept held that interactions among plant and animal populations and abiotic resources functioned to maintain biotic populations in a stable equilibrium. Rappaport argued that culture could function as a homeostatic mechanism to regulate this equilibrium. Using ecological data from highland New Guinea, he argued that Mae Enga people practice a *kaiko* ritual roughly once per decade when warring communities declare peace and feast on a large portion of the pig population. The decadal cycle of war and pig slaughter prevents either humans or pigs from surpassing the region's carrying capacity. His method is essentially Steward's, but the adaptive behavior, the *kaiko* ritual, is not within the cultural core as Steward conceived it.

Ethnoecology attempts to understand the cognitive components of cultural adaptation to the environment. Culture is superorganic, but it plays out in the thoughts, words, and actions of individuals. Ethnoecologists study the relationships among linguistic categories (words) for plants and animals and the resource management choices people make.

Finally, while not strictly an ecological approach, the cross-cultural studies that began with George Murdock's *Ethnographic Atlas* and continue today with statistical analyses of the Standard Cross Cultural Sample and Human Area Relations Files owe a debt to Steward's cultural ecology, for they test hypotheses about adaptive similarities using representative data sets of world populations.

Bram Tucker

See also Cultural Materialism; Diffusionism, Hyperdiffusionism, *Kulturkreise*; Harris, Marvin; Historical Particularism; Human Behavioral Ecology; Kroeber, Alfred L.; Murdock, George Peter; Rappaport, Roy; Steward, Julian; Vayda, Andrew P.

Further Readings

Bailey, R. C., & Headland, T. N. (1991). The tropical rain forest: Is it a productive environment for human foragers? *Human Ecology, 19*(2), 261–285.

Helms, M. W. (1978). On Julian Steward and the nature of culture. *American Ethnologist, 5*, 170–183.

Murphy, R. F. (1977). Introduction: The anthropological theories of Julian H. Steward. In J. C. Steward & R. F. Murphy (Eds.), *Evolution and ecology: Essays on social transformation by Julian H. Steward* (pp. 1–39). Urbana: University of Illinois Press.

Steward, J. H. (1936). *The economic and social basis of primitive bands.* Berkeley: University of California Press.

———. (1938). *Basin-plateau aboriginal sociopolitical groups.* Washington, DC: Bureau of American Ethnology.

———. (1955). *The theory of culture change.* Urbana: University of Illinois Press.

Steward, J. H., & Murphy, R. F. (1956). Tappers and trappers: Parallel processes in acculturation. *Economic Development and Culture Change, 4*, 335–355.

———. (Eds). (1977). *Evolution and ecology: Essays on social transformation by Julian H. Steward.* Urbana: University of Illinois Press.

Vayda, A. P., & Rappaport, R. A. (1968). Ecology, cultural and noncultural. In J. A. Clifton (Ed.), *Introduction to cultural anthropology* (pp. 477–497). New York, NY: McGraw-Hill.

CULTURAL MATERIALISM

The term *cultural materialism*, a major theoretical model and research strategy in anthropology, was coined by Marvin Harris and first introduced in his book *The Rise of Anthropological Theory* in 1968. This paradigm awaited its full elaboration in *Cultural Materialism: The Struggle for a Science of Culture* in 1979. The term *cultural* denoted the association with anthropology, and *materialism* indicated the priority accorded to the material conditions of human existence. As a research paradigm, cultural materialism provides a framework for analyzing the organization of societies both past and present. It also provides a guide for understanding contemporary social life.

A commitment to scientific principles is intrinsic to cultural materialism. It is a generalizing research strategy dedicated to the explanation of sociocultural differences and similarities around the world. Its ultimate goal, then, is to *explain*, not merely describe, cultural variations in the way people live. Or, as Harris (1979) succinctly wrote, "Cultural materialism is based on the simple premise that human social life is a response to the practical problems of earthly existence" (p. ix).

Basic Tenets

Cultural materialism rejects the timeworn adage that "ideas change the world." Instead, a basic tenet of cultural materialism is *infrastructural determinism*, which assumes that explanations for cultural similarities and differences ultimately lie in the material conditions of human life. In other words, the essence of this approach is that the infrastructure is, in almost all circumstances, the most significant force behind the evolution of a culture.

To operationalize this research paradigm and provide a method for studying societies around the world, cultural materialism proposes that all social systems consist of three levels: (1) infrastructure, (2) structure, and (3) superstructure. The *infrastructure* is viewed as the foundation or base of society for within it lie the material conditions of human existence. The infrastructure of a society is its system of production and reproduction, which is determined by a mix of ecological, technological, environmental, and demographic variables. In sum, the study of a society's infrastructure investigates how people acquire food and shelter, how a population maintains itself in a given environment, and how basic human biological needs and drives are satisfied.

The second level is a society's *structure*, which comprises its domestic economy; its social organization; its kinship system, including marriage patterns; its division of labor; and its political economy, political institutions, and class and other social hierarchies. A society's *superstructure* consists of the ideological and symbolic areas of culture: its religious, symbolic, intellectual, and artistic efforts.

Cultural materialism hypothesizes that all three levels are functionally related, with predictable and significant associations between them. It also suggests that changes in a society's infrastructure—its material base—are mainly the result of shifts in a human population's relationship to its environment. This paradigm further posits that over time and in the long run changes in a society's infrastructure will lead to functionally compatible changes in its social and political institutions (its structure) and in its religious and secular ideologies (its superstructure), all of which enhance the continuity and stability of the system as a whole. To Harris, the study of infrastructure should be a strategic priority because it is the main interface between nature and culture. If the goal of science is to establish lawlike generalizations, then one should begin by studying those aspects of sociocultural systems under the most direct restraints from the givens of nature.

It is crucial to point out that cultural materialism does not suggest a simplistic, mechanistic correspondence between material conditions and structural and ideological phenomena. Structure and superstructure are not considered unimportant, epiphenomenal reactions to infrastructural forces. The structure and the symbolic or ideational aspects of a culture act as regulating mechanisms within the system as a whole. Nor does cultural materialism posit that *every* change in the system under *all* circumstances arises from shifts in infrastructure. In fact, it suggests that there may be a time lag before social and political institutions and ideologies evolve that are compatible with changed material conditions. It proposes a probabilistic relationship between these three levels of society, while also insisting that the primary sources of change are found in the material conditions of human life. As such, when changes are noted in a society's structure or superstructure, we must *first* look to its infrastructure as the likely source of these changes. Then, too, though its critics say otherwise, cultural materialism does *not* claim that structure and superstructure are simply passive entities that have no impact on a society's material base. Still, if structural or superstructural changes are not compatible with the existing modes of production and reproduction, they are not likely to spread and be amplified.

Value of the Model

This paradigm has practical value as well as scientific value. Cultural materialism can be a vehicle for understanding, even solving, contemporary social problems, including poverty, racism, sexism, and oppression of many kinds. After all, before such problems can be solved, they must be understood. If anthropology can struggle against the mystification of the causes and consequences of inequality and exploitation, it is well that anthropology does so.

American society following World War II illustrates how this model can help illuminate societal change. It also provides an example of time lag between shifts in material base and ideology. The "feminine mystique," an ideology celebrating the joys of domesticity, was said to characterize the United States during the 1950s. American women, especially married women, according to the feminine mystique, were said to be content with hearth and home, raising healthy children, and shunning paid employment. But during the same decade, record numbers of married women were, in fact, leaving home to take up jobs. Because of this, the ideology of the feminine mystique did not mesh with what was actually happening in American society. But it was not until a decade later that the infrastructural change of women's large-scale employment resulted in the rise of feminist ideology. Thus, from the perspective of cultural materialism, the rebirth of feminism and the growth of the women's liberation movement were ultimately the *results* rather than the *cause* of women's massive entry into the labor market. Women did not take up jobs because a feminist ideology "liberated" them to do so. Rather, the reason why so many married women sought jobs lay in changes in material conditions in the postwar period in the United States, including a specific demand for *female* labor and inflation, which put a premium on a second family income to maintain a middle-class standard of living, a standard of living that now included a suburban house, two cars, and myriad appliances.

A related social issue that a cultural materialist analysis can shed light on is about reproductive patterns and practices in contemporary American society. While some argue that the rising rates of abortion and contraception point to a failure of moral values and a concomitant weakening of the American family, cultural materialists look to a changing material base as an explanation for the increased use of techniques that led to a decline in fertility over the course of the 20th century. As the United States shifted from a primarily agrarian society, in which having a large number of children was advantageous, to one based on an industrial and service economy, not only did the need for many children decrease, but having a large number of children actually became a drain on a family's economic well-being. Here, cultural materialism suggests that ideal family size is an ideological construct that waxes and wanes with the material costs and benefits of raising children.

Cultural materialism has, in fact, been used to illuminate several riddles of culture, cultural practices that on the surface seem irrational or downright counterproductive. These include materialist explanations for the sacredness of the cow in India as well as other puzzling cultural phenomena such as religious dietary restrictions, including the Jewish and Muslim prohibitions against eating pork. From a materialist perspective, such food taboos can be best understood by seeing animals first as nourishment for the body rather than for their symbolic or ideational value.

Cultural materialism also provides a guide for the ways anthropologists collect and organize data. It distinguishes emic and etic approaches to the study of cultural institutions. In an *emic* approach, the observer attempts to learn the rules and categories of a culture from the native's perspective. As such, emic analyses depend on informants' explanations, and if informants agree on a description or interpretation of data, the data are considered accurate. In contrast, in an *etic* approach, the observer does not use native rules or categories but, rather, those derived from independent observers using agreed-on scientific measures. Quantifiable measurements such as fertility rates, caloric intake, or average rainfall are employed to develop general theories of culture without regard to whether those measurements mean anything to the native populations themselves. Cultural materialists insist that a science of society cannot be based solely on informants' interpretation of their own behavior. Emic and etic analyses can be used to study both thought and behavior, and both are important for an understanding of cultural phenomena.

Cultural materialism evolved from and was influenced by a number of theoretical currents, including evolutionary theory, cultural ecology, and Marxist materialism, and Harris acknowledges his debt to all of them, most especially the latter. Thus, much as in earlier Marxist thought, material changes are seen as largely determining patterns of social and political organization and ideology. However, while acknowledging the debt owed to the economic theories of Karl Marx and Frederick Engels, cultural materialists seek to improve Marx's original strategy by rejecting the Hegelian idea that all systems evolve through a dialectic of contradictory negations. This new paradigm also adds reproductive pressure and ecological variables to the conjunction of material conditions studied by Marx and Engels. Harris himself emphatically separates his own model from *dialectical* materialism as well as from the program for political action that is so closely associated with Marxist materialism.

Cultural materialism as a research paradigm is not limited to cultural anthropology. Strongly convergent research strategies began developing in anthropological archaeology during the 1960s under the rubric "The New Archaeology." The principle of infrastructural determinism serves as a grounding for modern archaeology, especially North American archaeology. Moreover, about half of all practicing American archaeologists consider themselves to be, at least to some degree, cultural materialists. Today, despite a surge of anti-scientism in the guise of "postmodern" and "interpretationist" approaches, cultural materialism is a flourishing research strategy for anthropology and contemporary social science in general.

Maxine L. Margolis

See also Carneiro, Robert L.; Cultural Ecology; Harris, Marvin; Marx, Karl; Marxist Anthropology; Material Production, Theories of; Vayda, Andrew P.

Further Readings

Harris, M. (1974). *Cows, pigs, wars, and witches.* New York, NY: Random House.

———. (1977). *Cannibals and kings.* New York, NY: Random House.

———. (1979). *Cultural materialism: The struggle for a science of culture.* New York, NY: Random House.

———. (1981). *America now: Why nothing works.* New York, NY: Simon & Schuster.

———. (1985). *Good to eat.* New York, NY: Simon & Schuster.

———. (2001). *The rise of anthropological theory.* Walnut Creek, CA: AltaMira Press. (Original work published 1968)

Headland, T., Pike, K., & Harris, M. (1990). *Emics and etics: The insider-outsider debate.* Newbury Park, CA: Sage.

Murphy, M., & Margolis, M. L. (Eds.). (1995). *Science, materialism and the study of culture: Readings in cultural materialism.* Gainesville: University Press of Florida.

Cultural Relativism

Cultural relativism is the doctrine that the standards that ground knowledge and morality are cultural in nature and vary between different societies.

Absolute standards for judging the institutions of one culture as superior to those of another are lacking, and ideas, beliefs, and ethical judgments should be understood in terms of the culture in which they are found. Cultural relativism is the antithesis of ethnocentrism: the practice of understanding and evaluating the beliefs and values of other cultures against the standards of one's own culture.

Relativism has two prongs. Epistemological relativism holds that human knowledge—about nature, religion, society, or anything else—is conditioned by (relative to) the cultural context within which that knowledge is developed. Moral or ethical relativism claims that convictions about what is good or evil, proper or gauche, are likewise conditioned by their cultural contexts.

Relativism in Anthropology

Relativist ideas have been in the air at least since Herodotus and were articulated subsequently in various ways by Michel de Montaigne, Montesquieu, and the pragmatists William James and John Dewey, to name just a few. Anthropological relativism, developed most notably in the early and mid-20th century by Franz Boas's students Margaret Mead, Ruth Benedict, and Melville Herskovits, is one of the discipline's signature concepts. One reason why many anthropologists are attracted to it is their research method of fieldwork by participant observation. Anthropologists live for extended periods in the societies they study, striving to grasp alien ways of thinking and behaving by sharing in their lifeways as much as they can. This is often an unforgettable experience in an anthropologist's life. Empathy and appreciation for the people and their culture are almost inevitable as the field-worker comes to value them as friends and finds their way of life to be a viable and rewarding way to be human. This intimate and powerful experience is far more conducive to a relativist attitude of appreciative understanding than to a detached and judgmental one.

The Dangers of Relativism

Outside anthropology, relativism is often seen as a threat that must be resolutely resisted. Defenders of religious absolutes are seriously offended by relativism. Pope John Paul II decreed in his encyclical *Fides et Ratio* (1998), "Every truth—if it really is truth—presents itself as universal, even if it is not the whole truth. If something is true, then it must be true for all people and at all times" (para 27). Protestants, particularly those of a fundamentalist stripe, are of the same mind.

The secular world contributes its share of virulent critics of relativism. In his post-9/11 tirade *Why We Fight* (2002), William Bennett excoriates the efforts of relativism and its evil twin postmodernism to keep our children from being taught "the superior goodness of the American way of life" (p. 47). In his 1996 book *Slouching Towards Gomorrah: Modern Liberalism and American Decline*, Robert Bork scorns relativism for combining the radical individualist notion that there should be no restraint on personal gratification with a radical egalitarianism that looks to equality of outcomes rather than equality of opportunity and treats everyone the same regardless of merit.

What really bothers most people about relativism is its implication that if there are no objective standards of truth and knowledge, or of moral right and wrong, then one proposition or ethical judgment is as true or good as another and one is free to believe and do whatever one likes. This, they argue, leads to hedonism, libertinism, and nihilism, all of which are destructive to the possibility of an ordered society.

Developments within anthropology over the past 3 decades or so have rendered cultural relativism less palatable than it previously was. Relativism's basic premises that beliefs and values are products of culture and that they vary between cultures are most perfectly realized when different societies are isolated from each other and when the members of each uniformly hold the beliefs and values of their culture. Neither of these conditions has ever existed, but it was much easier to imagine them in the early days of anthropology than it is now.

Whatever validity the assumption of cultural isolation ever had was already being eroded by Marco Polo and the voyages of discovery of the 15th through 18th centuries, and it has been completely set to rest by contemporary globalization. And anthropologists have come to realize that human cultures are not homogeneous. Stemming from the theoretical claims of Karl Marx, and abetted by Antonio Gramsci and Michel Foucault, the interests of many anthropologists have shifted from what people in single societies have in common to what divides them. It is now generally recognized that far from enjoying consensus, society is a field of conflict and domination.

The news of all this reached anthropology fairly late because of its traditional focus on small-scale, exotic cultures. But by the 1960s, we were running out of those, and anthropologists turned to studies of communities embedded in or influenced by large-scale nation-states. Scholars such as Eric Wolf and Sidney Mintz employed Immanuel Wallerstein's world-systems theory to demonstrate how even the smallest and most remote societies were affected by events taking place half a world away. The 1960s also produced a generation of anthropologists whose experience made it natural to extend Marx's ideas about the exploitation of one class by another to a much wider range of conflicts: between races, as in the civil rights movement; the repression of women and gays as addressed by feminism and sexuality studies; and the view that there could be an ideological counterculture within, and opposed to, a dominant culture.

Not content with just documenting internal diversity and conflict, many anthropologists have been moved by a moral imperative to take sides, making common cause with those who were being dominated and exploited. This is perhaps especially true of feminist anthropologists, for many of whom empowering the women with whom they work is at least as important as framing a social scientific analysis.

Even if weakened, however, relativism is far from dead, and the issues it poses remain critically important to doing anthropology and, indeed, to living in general. If the choice is between pure absolutism and pure relativism, neither one is acceptable. One recoils at the sheer hubris of claiming that one has the absolute truth about everything and that everyone with a different opinion is at best wrong and at worst downright stupid or depraved. But the potential libertinism and nihilism springing from the notion that any practice or any idea is as good as any other is scarcely a viable alternative. A more moderate view is methodological relativism. As depicted by Michael Brown and Elvin Hatch, this counsels withholding judgment about beliefs and practices until their full context is known. That does not give a blank check to all alien beliefs and practices, some of which may still be judged intolerable or irrational.

Methodological relativism is a promising approach, but saying only that much arms it with little more than a recommendation for tolerance and open-mindedness. It does not provide explicit justification for judging which practices in other cultures are tolerable and which are not, nor does it explain just what might be good reasons for rejecting some concepts and beliefs as false or irrational. Therefore, it is important to probe more deeply into how methodological relativism might address the ethical and epistemological problems that vex the whole idea of relativism.

Ethics

The basic issue posed by ethical relativism is this: If morality is grounded only in culture, is it necessary to approve or disapprove of behaviors in other societies on the basis of their own standards? Must we judge Aztec human sacrifice by Aztec standards and therefore conclude that it is morally justified? The issue is well posed by Richard Shweder, probably the most thoroughgoing ethical relativist in anthropology today. In a 2006 article, he tells the story of a "tough-minded" anthropologist who achieved such a degree of acceptance in the African community he was studying that the headman invited him to act as one of the three judges in a trial of a man accused of murder by witchcraft. The anthropologist accepted. By the local standards of what witches do and how they are identified, the evidence against the defendant was overwhelming. Although the anthropologist was uncomfortable and did not really believe that the death was caused by witchcraft, he concurred with the other two judges and voted for a verdict of guilty. Going beyond just evaluating the behavior in question by local standards, he also took an active role in applying those standards.

Presumably, Shweder has no problem with what the anthropologist did, for in an earlier article, he argued that one is under no moral obligation to refrain from this type of activity. If you lived in 19th-century China, for example, there would be no moral obligation to prevent you, if you could bring yourself to do it, from eating with chopsticks, binding your young daughter's feet, and wearing Chinese clothes. But what would happen if, after a period of some years in China, you returned to the United States? By the same reasoning, there would be no moral obligation to prevent you from replacing the chopsticks with knife and fork, unbinding your daughter's feet, and wearing Western clothes.

Most people from our culture would see no moral problem with the food and the clothes but would find the foot binding morally repugnant or offensive. They would judge people who do not bind their daughter's feet before moving to China, bind them while living in China, and then unbind them on return to the United States as moral hypocrites who are doing their own daughter serious harm. Something similar might be said of an anthropologist, no matter how tough minded, who agrees to be a judge in a witchcraft trial and concurs in a guilty verdict when he does not believe in witchcraft.

Why does foot binding appear to Americans as immoral? Clearly, there is nothing in the practice itself that is intrinsically repugnant or offends universal moral principles, for millions of Chinese routinely engaged in it. Perhaps it is immoral by some absolute standard. It would then be necessary to identify the source of that absolute standard, and no candidate seems to be forthcoming other than God. If one is not prepared to concede that, the only remaining possibility is culture: the conventions that define proper and improper behavior in a human community.

If that is the case, however, why didn't 19th-century Americans routinely bind their daughters' feet when they would go to China, leaving the zone of American morality and entering that of the Chinese? Because moral codes are inscribed not in geography but in human beings. Moral persons do not cease observing the standards in which they have been enculturated simply by moving away.

The upshot of all this is captured by the simple proposition that understanding does not entail agreeing. It is entirely possible to know what the moral code of another culture is, to understand the relation between its principles and its practices, and, often, to appreciate it as a means of achieving a socially viable and individually fulfilling strategy for living. But that does not oblige one to agree with practices that one finds repugnant and offensive or with those that strike one as entirely benign, no matter how consistent with cultural presuppositions they may be. In many cases, one might refrain from evaluating behaviors in alien communities at all, but in some cases (Aztec human sacrifice, Chinese foot binding, Polynesian fostering of needy children), it is difficult not to make judgments, be they positive or negative. The crucial point is that such judgments are inevitably based on a moral code derived from one's own culture, often with modifications from personal associations and experience. After all, it cannot be *my* evaluation unless it is based on my standards.

This position is deeply disturbing to those who believe that the only reason to adhere to any moral standard is that it is absolute. The relativist would reply that there simply is no such absolute. Anything more than a cultural basis for morality is lacking. This does not mean that the moral standards held by each culture are unique. Many are widely shared among different cultures, and some may even be universal. But one thing it does mean is that people's commitment to their own moral standards is in no way weakened by the fact that they are rooted in culture rather than in the absolute. And another is that the methodological relativist defers evaluation of alien practices until careful study has been conducted to ascertain the meaning of the belief or behavior in the larger context of its moral code and culture in general. Often this process produces a very different conclusion from the ethnocentrist's rush to judgment.

Epistemology

Epistemological relativism has to do with truth and knowledge. It's necessary, then, to know what we mean by those terms. A statement is true if it is an accurate description of some state of affairs. "That's a pear tree" is true if it is in fact a pear tree and false if it is some other kind of tree or not a tree at all. Knowledge refers not to states of affairs themselves but to a person's relation to them. "She knows that's a pear tree" means she is in possession of true information about the tree.

The truth of propositions made in different cultural contexts and the knowledge of those who propose them depends on the theory of truth one applies. The correspondence theory holds that true propositions correspond to the actual state of affairs in the world and that we can know them only through direct observation. This means that there can be one and only one true statement about any particular state of affairs in the world. Proponents of this theory of truth typically insist that the best available method of observation is that of Western science. This view is often called positivism.

Another candidate is the coherence theory of truth. This holds that statements are true when they are logically entailed by some specified set of general presuppositions. Under the coherence theory, different sets of assumptions can generate different truths about the same state of affairs in the world. Thus, in the context of one set of presuppositions, it is true that there are no witches, but it is also true in the context of another set that there are witches. This theory suits the pure version of relativism.

From the point of view of anthropologists interested in cross-cultural studies, neither of these theories of truth is satisfactory. The correspondence theory is highly ethnocentric. To apply it would amount to the dreary task of cataloguing the vast number of errors that have been made in most cultures throughout most of human history. The coherence theory does encourage understanding and appreciating alien beliefs and practices in their own cultural contexts, but it removes truth from any connection with external reality. A proposition is true because people say it is, with no need for further evidence. With no tether in the empirical world, different cultural epistemologies might be incompatible. In that event, if the very concept of understanding is radically different, there could be no meaningful communication between members of such cultures. They would live in different worlds. Among other things, this would render anthropology itself pointless. But this view is clearly absurd, because people from different cultures communicate with and understand each other all the time.

A way out of the dilemma is to recognize that both correspondence and coherence are single-contingency theories of truth. Truth in the correspondence theory rests on facts alone, while in the coherence theory, it depends exclusively on prior general assumptions. But truth is better understood as doubly contingent, resting on both the object of knowledge and the knowing subject. This perspective has a distinguished pedigree, beginning with Immanuel Kant's view that knowledge of the world consists of sense impressions as these are conditioned or ordered by certain a priori categories such as cause and effect. The a priori categories are not given in sensory experience but are products of the mind.

Kant assumed the a priori categories to be identical for all humans, but later philosophers such as C. I. Lewis argued that they were variable. As Arthur Danto summarized it in his 1968 book *Analytical Philosophy of Knowledge*, truth refers neither to the world alone nor to the prior assumptions that we have about the world. Rather, it concerns the *relation between* the world and those assumptions. If one recognizes that the assumptions are cultural in origin, it is possible to affirm that statements about

the world made in the context of a body of culturally grounded assumptions may be true, while different statements made about the same element of reality in the context of other bodies of assumptions may also be true. Again, consider witchcraft. Certain objective events in the world—blighted crops, the illness of children, getting killed by a wild animal, or an accident—are understood by people on the basis of certain cultural assumptions. The objective events are the same, but they are interpreted according to different assumptions. On the basis of one set of assumptions, it is true that the cause of the event is witchcraft, while on the basis of another set of assumptions, that conclusion is false.

This way of construing things gets one away from the narrowness of the correspondence theory of truth. But what of the corollary of the coherence theory that reality does not exist independently but only in what people think about it? That too is avoided because the theory of truth discussed here is doubly contingent, concerned with the relation between the world and how people think about the world. Events in the world—snow, the phases of the moon, an uttered prayer, a scientific paper, or a philosophical treatise—are what they are regardless of what anyone may think about them. They are objects of knowledge available for public inspection. But the knowledge people acquire of them—that is, their interpretations—depends also on their prior assumptions. As an analogy, humans, flies, and octopi have differently structured eyes. They look at the same thing, but what they see is radically different. Those differences have nothing to do with the viewed object and everything to do with the optical apparatus.

This does not mean that the anthropologist is bound to affirm that every statement about the world is true simply because someone says it is. We do not extend this luxury to others in our own society, and we do not owe it to members of other societies. Every cultural mode of discourse has its criteria for determining if a statement is true or false. These criteria vary from one mode to another, and therefore, what makes a statement true or false also varies between them. Assessing the truth of a statement amounts to our own determination as to whether the criteria of that mode of discourse have been correctly applied to the relevant facts. To make such assessments, within one's own culture or mode of discourse or with reference to any other, requires a clear understanding of the assumptions that prevail and the criteria for determining truth and falsity in that setting. That one can do this successfully is strong evidence that ways of knowing in that culture have been accurately understood. Achieving such understanding is the ultimate goal of methodological relativism and the anthropologists who practice it.

F. Allan Hanson

See also Benedict, Ruth F.; Boas, Franz; Herskovits, Melville; Human Universals; Mintz, Sidney; Postmodernism; Wallerstein, Immanuel; Wolf, Eric

Further Readings

Benedict, R. (1934). *Patterns of culture.* Boston, MA: Houghton Mifflin.

Brown, M. F. (2008). Cultural relativism 2.0. *Current Anthropology, 40*(3), 363–383.

Gairdner, W. D. (2008). *The book of absolutes: A critique of relativism and a defence of universals.* Montreal, Quebec, Canada: McGill-Queen's University Press.

Hanson, F. A. (1975). *Meaning in culture.* London, UK: Routledge & Kegan Paul.

Hatch, E. (1983). *Culture and morality: The relativity of values in anthropology.* New York, NY: Columbia University Press.

Herskovits, M. (1972). *Cultural relativism: Perspectives in cultural pluralism.* New York, NY: Random House.

John Paul II (Pope). (1998). *Fides et ratio* [Faith and reason; Encyclical]. Vatican City: Libreria Editrice Vaticana.

Perusek, D. (2007). Grounding cultural relativism. *Anthropological Quarterly, 80,* 821–836.

Renteln, A. D. (1988). Relativism and the search for human rights. *American Anthropologist, 90,* 56–72.

Shweder, R. A. (2006). John Searle on a witch hunt: A commentary on John R. Searle's essay "Social Ontology: Some Basic Principles." *Anthropological Theory, 6*(1), 89–111.

Ulin, R. C. (2007). Revisiting cultural relativism: Old prospects for a new cultural critique. *Anthropological Quarterly, 80,* 803–820.

Wilson, R. A. (1997). *Human rights, culture and context: Anthropological perspectives.* London, UK: Pluto Press.

CULTURAL TRANSMISSION

Cultural transmission is a broad term meaning not only the passing of cultural information from one generation to the next but also our conveying it to one another within a generation. It is what allows the perpetuation of culture over time, such that the French traveler Alexis de Tocqueville's insights into American culture remain startlingly apt today, though he visited during the first half of the 19th century. We will first have to untangle whether this term refers to a unitary process, as in electrical transmission, or whether it is fundamentally more complex. In this essay, we consider cultural transmission through the prism of a simple question: Are the new mass media subverting cultural transmission in ways we should worry about?

When Grandparents Were Wise

Grandparents used to be the go-to people in times of trouble, the respected sources of valuable, practical knowledge. For most of human history, parents could reasonably assume that their children would want to be like them, or at least like some other members of the local community. Change did happen: Wars and plagues and famines at times made for major dislocation, but in general, the pace of social cultural change was sedate. For most of the 20th century, anthropologists studying the cultures of the smaller scale societies of the world took continuity to be the norm. Often ignoring current events, they would write in what was termed the *ethnographic present*, the present tense suggesting an unchanging timelessness. Anthropologists today are very much aware of the rapid cultural change to which we are all witnesses, and so they no longer do this. Indeed, nowadays it is more often the change than the continuity that we take for granted.

Our contemporary stereotype is of the young teaching their seniors how to navigate a world of new media, new music, and new vocabulary. Ours, after all, is a time of worldwide movement from rural to urban areas, a period in which languages spoken by small populations are frequently in danger of extinction, an age in which technological innovation is rapid and training to earn a livelihood is almost always sought outside the home. But if parents are now learning from their children rather than the other way around, does this mean that the long chain of cultural transmission from parents to children has been broken?

Are the Mass Media Subverting Cultural Transmission?

Cultural transmission requires learning from members of our own community, especially from those older than ourselves. Travelers and immigrants have always been agents of change from whom the young could learn new ideas, new ways of doing things, and perhaps even new languages. Relationships with these strangers have also, however, always been much less common than relationships with those we live our lives alongside. This probably remains true even today, when modern transportation makes such contact more common. But the influence of actual people entering our communities is probably very small compared with the impact of the mass media and, increasingly, the new, electronic interactive media.

We tend to learn primarily from those with whom we have social relationships. The mass media create a special form of relationship: *parasocial* or one-way relationships. We often think of the figure on the screen as a friend, a rival, a mentor, or a sex object. We exchange gossip about celebrities much as we do about relatives and people with whom we work. We may even gossip about and follow the lives of entirely fictional characters, such as those whom we meet in drama series or soap operas. Whether these individuals are corporeal or not, our relationships with them are parasocial because we know everything about them and they, even when we follow them on Twitter, know nothing about us. We can learn from these people just as we would from those we meet face-to-face, and they may serve as our role models or as sources of new ideas, values, styles, or goals. Justin Bieber or James Bond, Madonna or Wonder Woman, Kanye West or Conan, for example, are alternatives that may profoundly influence our behavior and aspirations. Thus, it is that talented and ambitious people from Kansas to Kazakhstan write rap songs and dream of achieving fame and wealth by becoming celebrities as professional entertainers, that is, "stars." That their parents may be farmers or goat herders or factory workers may seem irrelevant to them. Media and Internet celebrities can displace not just parents but also influential locals as sources of cultural information. Should we fear this process breaking the chain of cultural transmission, because learning from media figures may replace learning from our own elders? The current state of theory and research on cultural transmission leaves this argument more a possibility, illustrated by plausible examples, than a well-established phenomenon solidly supported by research findings.

Can We Theorize Change Without Theorizing Continuity?

The very rapid pace of contemporary cultural change challenges older social science theories. A major problem is that while some theories seek to explain cultural continuity, others focus on change: Few have dealt with both. The theories of social cultural change most frequently met with emphasize technology as the driver, as in the case of ideas of the influential sociologist William F. Ogburn. Ogburn, however, had little interest in societies in which cultural change is slow. Those who are interested in the apparently slow (or no) cultural change case tend to invoke the vague processes of "enculturation" and "socialization" to account for cultural continuity. These labels have been used in the past (and continue to be used) by thinkers who implicitly assume that cultural transmission ordinarily is unproblematic, except for those aspects of culture that are expressly taught to the child by parents or others. While some anthropologists associated with the fields of psychological anthropology and culture and personality, such as Robert A. LeVine, Margaret Mead, Abram Kardiner, and Ruth and Robert Munroe, have indeed paid attention to the socialization process, their emphasis has been on how psychological traits, personality traits, and values, in particular, are stable from generation to generation. They have not been primarily interested in the transmission of the information pool of which a culture is composed. Current theorists of cultural transmission believe that no theory that fails to encompass both change and continuity can be complete: A single theory that encompasses both is needed.

Gene-Culture Coevolution Theory: Transmission Theorists

An important present-day approach to cultural transmission is represented by the *gene-culture coevolution*, or "dual inheritance," school of thought. This approach involves the construction of mathematical models that simultaneously track both genetic and cultural transmission. All models are meant to be simplified representations of more complex realities, and in cultural transmission models, it is human cognition and social learning that are stripped down. For example, the effect of the choices of others on our own decisions becomes a "frequency-dependent" mathematical bias, and the influence of the relative standing of a possible role model becomes a "prestige bias." The mathematical models generally do not specify what kind of information is being transmitted or by whom; nevertheless, it is likely that these issues are of considerable importance. Except for physical objects, a culture can usefully be thought of as a pool of information, and cultural transmission, therefore, requires the acquisition of informational items from others. The types of information are myriad. Presumably, different kinds of information are acquired through different cognitive processes: It is doubtful that we learn religious values, language, cooking skills, etiquette, or subsistence techniques all in the same way. Quite possibly, different domains of knowledge are learned in different ways, ways that may alter throughout the lifespan. Young children do not learn languages in the way adults do, and the acquisition of core values and the process of moral development have their own trajectory. There may also be both gender and cultural differences in the various culture acquisition processes. That is, part of a culture's information pool may involve rules for who should be learning which information items from whom. Thus, a mathematical model of cultural transmission raises the question of what informational domains the model is relevant to, and to which ages, genders, and cultural groups. An additional complication arises from the fact that a participant in a culture is always a member of a society, and different social classes and other societal segments may have differential exposure to the informational components of the culture. Some groups are deliberately resistant to borrowing practices and values from neighboring cultures (e.g., the Amish). Dual-inheritance theorists are mindful of these challenges, and perhaps we will eventually see different models for different informational domains and social structures.

In the meantime, there is no need to wait for transmission theorists to develop better mathematical models. One of their most powerful ideas—that of the *prestige bias*—both antecedes their mathematical models and lends potential insight into entirely verbal theories of cultural transmission.

Michael Chance's Argument That Primates Preferentially Learn From the High in Rank

It was the ethologist and primatologist Michael Chance and his collaborators who first observed that primates (both human and nonhuman) learn

preferentially from those to whom they pay attention and that they pay attention to those who are high in relative standing. Chance believed that there were two modes of attention to the high in status, each associated with a different kind of learning. Agonistic attention is fear-based attention and is associated with constricted learning, as in rote memory. Hedonic attention is a relaxed mode in which a broad range of learning is possible. Though Chance presented his two modes as distinct, it is more likely that they represent the end points of a continuum. The "prestige bias" of the transmission theorists is in effect a simplified version of Chance's approach in that it lacks the agonistic component. Chance's theory may help us understand much of human behavior, including our tendency to pay scant attention to those less fortunate than ourselves, while being captivated by the activities of those with wealth, power, or celebrity. It is also compatible with the anthropological inference that pride in one's own culture, as with the Tewa or the Amish, appears to confer resistance to acculturation (borrowing from the cultures of neighboring peoples). Presumably, resistant societies are those in which young people in each generation are convinced that prominent members of their own community are more worthy of respect than are outsiders. In the present context, his ideas may help us understand why the mass media are associated with apparent discontinuities in cultural transmission.

How the Mass Media May Be Debasing the Coin of Local Prestige

Earlier, we discussed how, everywhere, people often seem to be learning from media figures rather than from those in their own communities or even in their own families. Chance explains how we learn preferentially from those to whom we pay attention, the high in status in particular. In a world of modern media, who has more prestige, the local business success or the international billionaire? Who gains more attention, the high school athlete or the Olympic gold medal winner? Who is more attractive, your parents or Hollywood and Bollywood celebrities? Who is more frightening, an anthropology professor or Count Dracula? The apparent prestige, power, attractiveness, and even fearsomeness of local figures are devalued by those presented to us by the media and with whom we form parasocial relationships. But it is the local figures who participate in our local culture: If we learn from media figures rather than from those actually around us, then we may learn the almost random informational items associated with these individuals, at the expense of the cultural information of our grandparents. This may be why a young person may wish to seek an identity totally unfamiliar to an older generation by becoming a rap singer or a warlord rather than, say, a respected farmer or factory worker or clan elder: The coins of status and attention have been debased. Worse, by paying attention to local figures, we can learn the cultural steps toward achieving their success, but when we emulate media figures, we do not know how to get there, and we may therefore experience frustration or perhaps even resort to violence. Economics further complicates the picture because many (though perhaps not all) cultures give prestige to the wealthy, and the media figures have more apparent wealth than local figures. In some cases, however, attention to media figures may lead young people to forsake economic pursuits in order to join social, political, or religious movements. This reasoning is no doubt more applicable to some cultural informational domains and age-groups than to others, and it omits the effects of direct tuition in, for example, both secular and religious schools (e.g., madrassas). Nevertheless, debasement of the coin of local prestige and attention is likely to be playing at least some role in the current rapidity of cultural change.

Cultural Transmission Requires a Multilevel Approach

If the term *cultural transmission* were not so well established, there would be a good argument for discarding it. Our understanding of the transmission of electricity is quite complete, and even the complex operations of genetic transmission are well known. In contrast, cultural "transmission" may be more of a metaphor than a clearly analyzed process: By using the term, we risk bringing along an undeserved connotational aura of comprehension. It has been suggested that the terms *cultural acquisition* and *editing* are better tropes than the transmission metaphor because they carry less baggage.

No one type of analysis or even academic discipline will ever account for the complexities of cultural transmission. Different models may be needed for different kinds of information and also for people of different ages and genders. As in the case of the

Amish, it is likely that there are cultural differences in readiness to accept new knowledge (or at least role models). Economic circumstances and social disorganization no doubt influence an individual's readiness to forsake the older practices, values, and religion. Planned communities, totalitarian societies, and deliberate religious and ideological proselytizing all involve purposeful attempts to control cultural transmission. But marked cultural continuities may be present even in areas of great social disruption. Language, dress, food, music, religion, kinship systems, and values can be remarkably persistent. For the social and behavioral scientist, multilevel accounts of cultural transmission are clearly necessary: Sociological, economic, technological, and environmental factors all impinge on the individual, affecting the cognitive processes involved in acquiring and editing cultural information. While we are far from fully understanding the various processes of cultural transmission, much interdisciplinary research and collaboration is in progress.

*Jerome H. Barkow, Rick O'Gorman,
and Luke Rendell*

Authors' note: This work was sponsored by the Air Force Office of Scientific Research, Air Force Material Command, USAF, under grant numbers FA8655-10-1-3012 and FA8655-09-1-5067. The U.S. government is authorized to reproduce and distribute reprints for governmental purposes, notwithstanding any copyright notation thereon. During the preparation of this article, Barkow was visiting professor at the Department of OTANES, University of South Africa. Barkow thanks Peter M. Hejl for his contribution to the development of the core ideas that ultimately led to this article.

See also Culture and Personality; Gene-Culture Coevolution; Kardiner, Abram; Psychological Anthropology

Further Readings

Barkow, J. H. (1989). *Darwin, sex, and status: Biological approaches to mind and culture.* Toronto, Ontario, Canada: University of Toronto Press.

Barkow, J. H., O'Gorman, R., & Rendell, L. (2012). Are the new mass media subverting cultural transmission? *Review of General Psychology, 16*(2), 121–133. doi:10.1037/a0027907

Boyd, R., & Richerson, P. J. (1985). *Culture and the evolutionary process.* Chicago, IL: University of Chicago Press.

Chance, M. R. A., & Larsen, R. R. (Eds.). (1976). *The social structure of attention.* London: Wiley.

Ogburn, W. F. (1964). *Culture and social change: Selected papers.* Chicago, IL: University of Chicago Press.

Richerson, P. J., & Boyd, R. (2005). *Not by genes alone: How culture transformed human evolution.* Chicago, IL: University of Chicago Press.

Tocqueville, A. de, Crăiutu, A., & Jennings, J. (2009). *Tocqueville on America after 1840: Letters and other writings.* Cambridge, UK: Cambridge University Press.

CULTURE AND PERSONALITY

"Culture and personality" was a movement within American anthropology that sought to understand the relationship of individuals to culture. The culture and personality movement broadly spanned the first half of the 20th century and had a lasting impact on subsequent developments in cultural anthropology. This was not an organized movement with leaders, central theoretical propositions, and scholarly training institutions. This entry describes the basic ideas involved in the culture and personality approach to anthropology, discusses the impetus for its emergence, highlights key scholarly developments within the field, presents the standard criticisms of the approach, and outlines the impact of the movement on subsequent developments in anthropology.

Culture and personality scholars hold that the institutions, meanings, values, and practices of a culture are learned by individuals, which then come to shape the way in which such individuals perceive the world. In turn, persons thus socialized produce particular cultural practices, including religious and ritual practices, art, theories, and institutions that bear the imprint of their upbringing in a specific culture. Similar to how it had been claimed that language structures individuals' understanding of their world (the Sapir-Whorf hypothesis), it was argued that early infant and child socialization provided a template for individual behaviors, personal agency, social practices, science, and religion. Scholars who are now grouped together under the rubric of "culture and personality" were interested in developing a set of claims linking the individual to society. They believed that "cultural patterns" undergird all adult behavior in society and that practices related to infant care and child socialization were included in

these cultural patterns, ensuring the transmission of the unconscious and conscious aspects of culture to the next generation.

Culture and personality studies emphasized culture as a system of beliefs, ideas, behaviors, practices, values, and material artifacts that are related to each other. Culture is patterned, as opposed to being a collection of unrelated separate elements; elements are linked in relationships with each other to form a gestalt: a whole. The set of symbols, meanings, and practices in a given culture are consistent—they form an integrated set. So, for example, an early culture and personality scholar, Ruth Benedict, argued that beliefs and practices pertaining to gardening among the Dobuan Islanders displayed the same paranoid *ethos* (emotional style) as practices surrounding marriage. Ideas about whether or not divinity is approachable and merciful may be related to cultural expectations regarding human authority. Patterns of behavior forced on infants and children (e.g., rigid infant feeding schedules or swaddling) may be correlated with patterned behaviors among adults.

Development of Culture and Personality

The group of scholars associated with culture and personality were among the first Americans to regard themselves as anthropologists by discipline—namely, Edward Sapir, Ruth Benedict, Margaret Mead, and A. Irving Hallowell. The first three scholars (Sapir, Benedict, and Mead) were students of Franz Boas at Columbia University. Boas emphasized careful, lengthy fieldwork in the society under investigation, the development of relationships with informants in the field, and a process of rigorous collection of ethnographic data, which set the professional standards for subsequent anthropological work. Boas also vigorously argued against the racism of the anthropological work of his day. At the time he was trained, all societies were thought to exist on a continuum from savage to civilized. The job of the anthropologist was to specify where on the continuum the culture in question fell. Boas, instead, argued that the histories of societies were not a universal narrative of progress toward Western democracy and industrialization. He laid the groundwork for the cultural relativism of his students. In addition to Boas, other crucial influences on the development of culture and personality included psychoanalysis, especially the work of Sigmund Freud and Carl Gustav Jung on the relation of the individual to society, and the work of Bronisław Malinowski, the British-trained Polish New Guineaist, whose ethnographic monograph *Argonauts of the Western Pacific* involved understanding the motivation, emotional conflicts, and values of his Melanesian interlocutors.

Key Scholarly Contributions

Cultural Holism

Sapir's work on language, spanning the early 1920s to the late 1940s, developed the argument that the categories and concepts implicit in language determine the kinds of concepts that speakers hold. Speakers internalize a language, which then shapes the kinds of thoughts they may have. Likewise with culture, argued Benedict. Benedict's most influential book on the emerging discipline of anthropology, *Patterns of Culture*, published in 1934, made two related arguments. First, culture is internally coherent, meaning that all aspects of life—moral values, beliefs, kinship, practices related to work, political structures—are related. The only way to understand religious beliefs, for example, is against the background of other, more mundane practices and values of the society. Second, Benedict argued that culture functions like a personality; culture produces behavior, values, and ideas that bear its particular cultural stamp.

Mead's contribution to the field was to be the first by an anthropologist to investigate how culturally specific parenting and socialization practices in infancy and childhood relate to the development of adult personalities, practices, motivations, and values. Mead's most well-known book, *Coming of Age in Samoa*, published first in 1928, was based on her investigation of the impact of cultural patterns of child socialization on adolescent and adult development among rural Samoans subsisting through fishing and gardening, who had yet to be successfully converted to Christianity. The book described the characteristics of Samoan child rearing, including the practice of having elder siblings care for younger children and preferences for avoiding strong expressions of affect. She persuasively argued that child socialization practices related to attachment and affect were related to the absence of adolescent angst and crisis in Samoan society. Her main contribution to culture and personality was to posit that what

children learn unconsciously and nonverbally from their caretakers distinctively shapes their adult behavior and preferences.

Child Socialization and Personality

In the 1930s and 1940s, scholars associated with the culture and personality movement, namely Abram Kardiner, Ralph Linton, Cora DuBois, and, subsequently, John W. M. Whiting, became interested in demonstrating causality between infant and child-rearing practices and the development of adult personality. Kardiner developed the concept of the basic personality structure (BPS), which he postulated as representative of most, if not all, individuals of a culture. Primary institutions, defined as the practices and ideas related to child rearing (e.g., nursing habits, ideas about authority and discipline, expectations for sibling relationships, etc.), determined adult personality. Adult personality, in turn, determined the types of secondary institutions present in the culture, such as beliefs about divinity, spirits, sin, taboos, moral transgressions, law, politics, exchange, and ideas about personal deportment and conduct.

Subsequent modifications to, and developments of, Kardiner's schema sought to eliminate some of the circularity of the argument (i.e., primary institutions lead to the formation of secondary institutions mediated by BPS) and the arbitrariness of the distinction between primary and secondary cultural institutions. Whiting, working in the 1950s, proposed distinguishing "maintenance systems," such as political and economic systems, and also environmental and geographical factors, such as temperature, soil quality, and vegetation, from child socialization practices. Whiting argued that temperature, for example, might affect infant-parent sleeping practices, which then will have an influence on adult personality. What is significant about both Kardiner and Whiting's contributions to culture and personality studies is that they sought to operationalize and empirically test the central tenets of the culture and personality approach that link child-rearing practices to adult behavior and personality.

DuBois's 1944 *The People of Alor* put forth the concept of the modal personality, a modification of Kardiner's BPS. DuBois's fieldwork in the Dutch East Indies (now Indonesia) among the Alorese involved careful collection of biographies from eight key informants and projective psychological test data, most notably the Rorschach. DuBois's work represented the demand for empirical rigor within anthropology; she presented ample psychological test data, recorded dreams, and autobiographical accounts for each individual described in her book. The plentiful material she had available made it clear to her that she could not defend the concept of a BPS underlying each Alor case. Instead, DuBois argued that there is a type of Alor personality that is the "most frequent" type (modal), yet this "modal" type may not represent the majority of Alorese personalities.

National Character Studies

The beginning of World War II enlisted anthropologists in preparing research for government policy purposes and for the purpose of morale building among Americans. Ruth Benedict, Margaret Mead, Geoffrey Gorer, Gregory Bateson, Erich Fromm, Walter C. Langer, and others produced monographs and articles arguing that members of nations (Nazi Germany, interwar Japan, Britain, and the United States were the nations of interest) have particular psychological and emotional styles in common with their fellow citizens. Benedict's 1946 *The Chrysanthemum and the Sword*, a study of Japanese culture as reported to her by Japanese Americans, is representative of the genre of national character studies. Benedict and others were struck by the behavior of Japanese prisoners of war, who appeared to eagerly change allegiance from Japan to the United States and who had little interest, once captured, in communicating with their families and communities. Benedict's work sought to explain how these phenomena were related and the logics, ethics, and commitments that underlay these astonishing (from the U.S. perspective) behaviors. With *The Chrysanthemum and the Sword*, Benedict began enduring conversations within anthropology of shame versus guilt cultures, situational versus absolute ethics, and collective versus individualistic societies.

Criticism

A primary criticism of work emerging from the Culture-and-Personality school was that not all individuals who identify as participating in a particular nation, culture, or society exhibit the psycho-emotional style that the theorists associated with it. Members of the movement themselves recognized and accounted for this. For example, Benedict argued that for reasons of temperament or idiosyncratic personal history, some individuals will exhibit personality characteristics that are not suited to unproblematic existence in their society. She suggested that these individuals will constitute a subset of individuals with mental disorders in the culture.

Another issue had to do with the difficulty in empirically demonstrating the link between culture and personality. Beginning in the late 1940s and into the 1970s, much effort went into quantitatively demonstrating culture and personality theories, such as the integration of social institutions and personality variables. Other problems with work emerging from the culture and personality movement had to do with the extent to which some monographs could be read as pathologizing the society under investigation.

Some of the less rigorous and careful work spawned by the culture and personality movement ignored important circumstances and events that had a far-reaching impact on the society under study, such as poverty, war, famine, colonialism, and forms of inequality. Such work was rightly criticized as focusing on practices related to child rearing, kinship, religion, and ritual while remaining blind to the tremendous impact of macrolevel events and structures on life within the society under study. Hence, a widespread criticism of culture and personality scholarship is that it is insensitive to the larger sociopolitical and economic influences on society.

Impact on the Discipline

The culture and personality movement was formed in reaction to the racist implications of American evolutionary anthropology of the early 20th century, which sought to position all cultures on a continuum, with Western societies representing the pinnacle of achievement. As such, its practitioners inaugurated an era of cultural relativism in anthropology, which has made a lasting impact on the practice of the discipline. Fieldwork methods, under the tutelage of scholars such as Boas and, later, Kardiner and Whiting, were elaborated and expanded to include long periods of fieldwork on site, intense and prolonged communication with research subjects, reflexive attention to the impact of the ethnographer on the anthropological project, and rigorous qualitative and quantitative methodologies. Contemporary anthropologists interested in psychological phenomena refer to themselves as psychological anthropologists, to distinguish themselves from the culture and personality movement. However, contemporary anthropological works dealing with moral values, aspirations, psychiatry, human behavior, emotion, and mental health and mental illness are heir to the precedents set by the culture and personality movement.

Jocelyn Marrow

See also Benedict, Ruth F.; Kardiner, Abram; Mead, Margaret; Psychological Anthropology; Sapir-Whorf Hypothesis and Neo-Whorfianism

Further Readings

Benedict, R. (2005). *Patterns of culture*. New York, NY: Houghton Mifflin. (Original work published 1934)

Bock, P. K. (1999). *Rethinking psychological anthropology: Continuity and change in the study of human action*. Prospect Heights, IL: Waveland.

DuBois, C. A. (1960). *The people of Alor: A social-psychological study of an East Indian Island*. Cambridge, MA: Harvard University Press. (Original work published 1944)

LeVine, R. A., (Ed.). (2010). *Psychological anthropology: A reader on self in culture*. Malden, MA: Wiley-Blackwell.

Mead, M. (2001). *Coming of age in Samoa: A psychological study of primitive youth for Western civilization*. New York, NY: First Perennial Classics. (Original work published 1928)

Stocking, G. W. (Ed.). (1986). *Malinowski, Rivers, Benedict and others: Essays on culture and personality*. Madison: University of Wisconsin Press.

———. (Ed.). (2003). *American anthropology, 1921–1945: Papers from the American anthropologist*. Lincoln: University of Nebraska Press.

CULTURE AREA APPROACH

A culture area is defined as a more or less contiguous ethnogeographic area inhabited by peoples who share cultural traits to an extent that distinguish them significantly from other societies. Some scholars distinguish a culture area by mapping the distribution of a single cultural trait, whereas others group societies together into more complex clusters sharing a number of cultural traits. The concept was developed in the early 20th century, with particular reference to Native American peoples. Although often criticized, the culture area approach is still frequently used in the comparative study of cultures.

Early Steps Toward Conceptualizing Culture Areas

The idea of distinguishing regions according to how people live in different environments is perhaps as old as humankind itself. It can, at least, be traced to the philosophers of antiquity, who described the "barbarians" of western Europe as different from the Greeks and Romans. However, as an anthropological concept, *culture area* has to be understood against the background of the rise of anthropology in the 19th century.

Many archaeologists and social scientists during the 19th century had the goal of grouping local societies into higher units of classification, applying the typological perspectives of Linnaean taxonomy—that is, every society more or less perfectly exemplified an essence, a certain "type." A tenacious Linnaean legacy was to apply the typological concept in mapping the world according to "race." Whereas the Swedish naturalist Carl Linnaeus (1707–1778) had classified all human "varieties" (he never used the word *race*) as belonging to the same species, it was also evident that they originally occurred in different regions of the world. In the first edition of his *Systema Naturae* (Systematic Nature, 1735), he listed four human varieties, each representing the then known continents: *Europaeus, Americanus, Asiaticus*, and *Africanus*.

Throughout the 18th century and well into the 20th, the concepts of *race* and *culture* were intertwined. For example, in 1832, the French explorer Dumont d'Urville (1790–1840) proposed that the Pacific Islands, or Oceania, consisted of three major areas: *Polynesia* ("many islands"), *Melanesia* ("black islands"), and *Micronesia* ("small islands"). At the beginning, these terms had more to do with racial characteristics and geographical proximity than with culture, but they have often come to refer to culture areas, even though each one of them (especially Melanesia) is quite diverse culturally and at the same time has a lot in common with the others.

An important step to apply the typological concept within cultural analysis was taken by a Danish archaeologist, Christian Jürgensen Thomsen (1788–1865), who in 1818 introduced the terms *Stone Age*, *Bronze Age*, and *Iron Age* for prehistoric Nordic material, thereby connecting typology, time, and geographic area. His chronology was soon used by other scholars for linking cultures not with reference to cultural borrowing or common origins but to the stage of technological development.

It was, however, not until the typological cultural/racial concept and perceived laws of cultural evolution merged with geography that further steps were taken toward the culture area approach.

After Darwin published *On the Origin of Species* in 1859, the typological concept was coupled with an aim to define general laws of cultural evolution as parallel to those of organic evolution. All societies, or cultures, it was often argued, would eventually go through the same evolutionary transformation, following a general pattern from simple to more advanced levels.

In Germany, the geographer and anthropologist Friedrich Ratzel (1844–1904) founded an anthropo-geographical school, where he elaborated his ideas about human migration, cultural borrowing, and the relationship between humans and their physical environments. He is perhaps most of all remembered for coining the concept *Lebensraum*, or "living space," which was used for relating groups of people to their spatial units.

Ratzel argued that people were strongly attached to their traditions and were only seldom able to invent something radically new. Similarities were therefore the result not of a more or less determined development but of cultural contact and borrowing. His fellow countryman Adolf Bastian (1826–1905) became the most influential proponent of the German-Austrian so-called *Kulturkreise* ("cultural circle") school, a continental European version of the diffusionist school, by attempting to reconstruct how cultural traits had spread from a limited number of cultural clusters.

A *Kulturkreise* was not necessarily a geographically contiguous cultural area, because migration and other prehistoric processes could have separated groups of people. The Central African Pygmies, the Andaman Islanders, the Semang and Senoi of Malacca, the Negritos in the Philippines, and the Vedda of Sri Lanka were dispersed over a large, noncontiguous area but nevertheless exemplified the "exogamous, monogamous *Kulturkreise*."

Ahistoric and Historic Culture Area Approaches

By the end of the 19th century, anthropologists had increasingly come to realize that there was a need for a historical approach to explain why certain ideas associated with cultural development—for example, the wheel, metallurgy, or monotheism—were distributed unevenly in time and space. Biologists had shown that species that were not closely related but were separated by time or space could develop similar adaptations under similar environmental conditions. The implication of this for cultural studies was that the notion of a general, linear evolutionary pattern was no longer tenable.

So far, evolutionary approaches to cultural similarities and differences had been both ethnocentric and ahistoric. In the 1880s, however, Otis T. Mason (1838–1908), at the Smithsonian Institution (who was probably the first one to use the term *culture area*), argued that a new taxonomic approach was needed that would make it possible to ascertain, without any reference to the environment and culture at large, whether a certain cultural trait had spread through processes of diffusion or originated independently. According to him, cultures evolved stepwise, and technology was a marker of a culture's stage of development. For this, he was strongly criticized by Franz Boas (1858–1942), who held the view that cultures should be described, not ranked or seen as exemplifying a stage in an evolution. They were all products of particular historic events, hence the term *historic particularism*.

At this time, Boas and his students, as well as other scholars working in North America, had already collected a lot of data about what they perceived as disappearing native cultures. Obviously, a theoretical framework was needed for the information assembled.

Boas's former assistant at the American Museum of Natural History, Clark Wissler (1870–1947), a specialist on Native American cultures of the Plains, took the stance that the emphasis on culture as something unique to a society was ascientific and did not help researchers uncover more general principles, or "laws." One had to define *culture* so that the term could be used comparatively, thereby ensuring anthropology its rightful place among the sciences. He also found *culture area* to be a useful concept and redefined it to use it analytically. It was not to be understood simply as an area inhabited by a certain "race" that exemplified a stage in evolution but as a well-defined geographical area within which one found cultures that shared many features.

By focusing on environment, resources, population size, and other variables through which culture was conditioned, systematic comparisons could now be made. He also applied statistics—more precisely, the Pearson correlation coefficient formula—for testing the correlation of certain artifacts with specific sites.

In *The American Indian* (1917), Wissler based his description of Native American culture areas on 13 major categories, from food and domesticated animals to arts, social organization, mythology, language, and even physiology. In North America, he distinguished 7 culture areas: (1) woodsmen of the east, (2) hunters of the plains, (3) Navaho shepherds, (4) Pueblo farmers, (5) desert dwellers, (6) seed gatherers, and (7) northern fishermen. Altogether, there were 15 culture areas throughout the Americas.

The question of how culture traits spread and why certain ones were more likely than others to do so fascinated Wissler. He concluded that novel ideas were quite likely to spread to groups that had the same "culture pattern" and were less likely to be adopted by people who were more different in cultural respects. Barriers were not only cultural, however, because environmental factors could also be of crucial importance. Bison hunters and salmon fishers were, for example, inhabiting the bordering areas, but the Rocky Mountains were a barrier to the animals on which their subsistence was based.

A major problem in culture area studies was the difficulty in dating archaeological material and ascertaining the age of a certain element of the material culture. Wissler suggested an approach that became known as the "age-area hypothesis." Since innovations were historically particular and had a potential to radiate in all directions from their point of origin, those that had the widest distribution were most likely the oldest. If that was true, one could argue, for instance, that a Coca-Cola bottle must be one of the world's oldest artifacts. Consequently, Wissler's age-area hypothesis was taken as a logical fallacy and never gained high popularity among scholars. However, even Boas promoted the culture

area approach, not the least, perhaps, because he was an authority on the Northwest coast, which remains one of the most classic examples in anthropology of a culture area.

Later Development of the Culture Area Approach

By the 1930s, American anthropology—including archaeology—was relying heavily on the culture area approach. Alfred L. Kroeber (1876–1960), a prominent disciple of Boas, now developed Wissler's culture area approach further. As Wissler had previously noted, two problems were involved in the culture area concept: one was ecological, and the other was about how the people in question functioned in the area.

Kroeber stressed the importance of understanding the ecological correlates and technologies of culture areas along a time axis, an important step toward a human ecological paradigm. The culture area approach was also taken up within other disciplines, most notably perhaps by the geographer Carl Sauer (1889–1975).

Together with their students, several of whom became influential, Kroeber and Sauer continued for many years to apply the concept of culture area to the ever-growing body of ethnographic and archaeological data worldwide. Julian Steward (1902–1972), for example, at one time a student of Kroeber's, edited the volumes of *Handbook of South American Indians* (1940–1947) systematically along the lines of the culture area approach.

Subsequent anthropologists have, however, often criticized the culture area approach for its tendency to portray people in a static and environmentally deterministic way and for being ethnocentric and founded on an essentialist conception of culture. Another point of critique has been that scholars who apply a culture area approach have not only ignored factors such as human creativity and local variation but also been so selective about which and how many traits they focus on (sometimes only one) that the classification has become entirely arbitrary. Contesting its essentialism, recent research in Amazonia suggests that ethnolinguistic identities and boundaries there have been continuously generated and transformed by shifting conditional factors, including economic specialization, trade routes, warfare, political alliances, and demography.

Despite such criticism, however, *culture area* has proven to be a practical concept that is almost as useful in ordering ethnographic variation as the Linnaean system in ordering organisms. It is often used in museum exhibitions, in systematic geography, for setting themes at conferences, and for discussing relationships between neighbor societies. Whereas the concept tends to divide anthropologists theoretically, it may thus also unite them for practical reasons.

Thomas Malm

See also Diffusionism, Hyperdiffusionism, *Kulturkreise*; Historical Particularism; Kroeber, Alfred L.; Morgan, Lewis Henry; Race

Further Readings

Buckley, T. (1988). Kroeber's theory of culture areas and the ethnology of northwestern California. *Anthropological Quarterly, 61,* 15–26.

Hornborg, A., & Hill, J. (Eds.). (2011). *Ethnicity in ancient Amazonia: Reconstructing past identities from archaeology, linguistics, and ethnohistory.* Boulder: University Press of Colorado.

Kroeber, A. L. (1939). *Cultural and natural areas of native North America.* Berkeley: University of California Press.

Murphy, A. B., Jordan-Bychov, T. G., & Jordan, B. B. (2008). *The European culture area: A systematic geography* (5th ed.). Lanham, MD: Rowman & Littlefield.

Sauer, C. O. (1952). *Agricultural origins and dispersals.* New York, NY: American Geographical Society.

Thomas, N. (1989). The force of ethnology: Origins and significance of the Melanesia/Polynesia division. *Current Anthropology, 30,* 211–213.

Wissler, C. (1927). The culture-area approach in social anthropology. *American Journal of Sociology, 32,* 881–891.

Darwin, Charles

Charles Robert Darwin (1809–1882), the British naturalist, is the founder of modern evolutionary biology theory. His influence is not limited to biological anthropology; anthropologists in areas such as cognitive anthropology and evolutionary psychology also find inspiration in his work. The notion of a naturalistic explanation for the origin of all species, including humans, and the clarity and depth of his presentation transformed our view of ourselves and continue to provide the basis of modern studies of human evolution.

Biography and Major Works

Early Years and Education

Darwin was born in Shrewsbury, England, on February 12, 1809, into a wealthy and influential family. His father, Robert Waring Darwin, was a well-known physician, and his mother, Susannah, who died when Darwin was 8 years old, was a member of the famous Wedgwood pottery family. His grandfather, Erasmus Darwin, was an influential physician and poet whose work *Zoonomia* (1794–1796) presented an early, if naive, version of evolution. Charles was the fifth of six children. Following a classical education at Shrewsbury School, Darwin followed his elder brother Erasmus Alvery to Edinburgh to study medicine. Medical studies did not suit Darwin; he famously could not stomach the surgical theater and the screams of the unanesthetized patients, and he spent his time collecting beetles and learning taxidermy from a freed slave rather than attending classes. Unable to continue in the family medical tradition, Darwin was directed by his father into studies to become a country parson (one of the few other respectable choices for an English gentleman) at Christ's College, Cambridge; he completed his bachelor of arts degree in 1831.

The Voyage of the HMS Beagle

While at Cambridge, Darwin impressed several of his professors with his acumen for natural history and his keen powers of observation. He assisted Adam Sedgwick on a geological survey in Wales and was mentored by the botanist John Stevens Henslow. Following Darwin's graduation in 1831, Henslow recommended Darwin to be the gentleman companion of Captain Robert FitzRoy, who had been ordered to take HMS *Beagle* on a voyage to survey the South American coastline and set up weather stations in the South Pacific. Although Darwin had a difficult time convincing his father that the experience would be worthwhile, his time on the *Beagle* and the naturalistic observations he made over the course of the 5-year voyage became the basis of his greatest achievements in the natural sciences. Frequently seasick during the journey, Darwin took up the unofficial role of ship's naturalist. Darwin spent as much time as possible on land, where he managed to collect huge numbers of specimens of animals and fossils, identify and describe new species, and make geological observations, including experiencing a major earthquake in Chile. His now famous observations on the Galapagos Islands of finches and other fauna have become the standard example of adaptive radiation and evolution by natural selection in modern textbooks. Darwin's specimens were distributed to experts, whose work he collected and edited into the *Zoology of the Voyage of the HMS Beagle* (1838–1843). He further published, and was brought considerable fame by, his *Journal and Remarks* (1839), also known as *The Voyage of the Beagle*. Containing both travel log and scientific observations, the *Journal* was widely read and bought Darwin a reputation as one of England's premier naturalists.

The Origin of Species

Based on his observations during his time on the *Beagle*, Darwin began to formulate his theory of evolution by natural selection. In South America, he had found fossils of extinct animals that closely resembled modern species, had seen closely related species adapted to individual niches on island archipelagos, and had noted the variation of individuals within a single species. To Darwin, these observations pointed toward a naturalistic, rather than divine, explanation for the origin of species through descent with modification. He was heavily influenced in this regard by reading Charles Lyell's *Principles of Geology* (1830–1833). Lyell, a Scottish lawyer and geologist, was a proponent of uniformitarianism, the idea that the geological processes that shaped the earth are the same as those observable in modern times. Those processes acted slowly and thus required the earth to be incredibly old. This, of course, contradicted the biblical interpretation of the age of the earth but provided sufficient time for species to change by natural causes. During the formulation of his ideas, Darwin also read Thomas Malthus's *An Essay on the Principles of Population* (1798). From Malthus, Darwin took the idea that population growth would always outstrip resources, leading to a struggle for existence. Because the individuals of a species varied and more offspring would be produced than could survive, individuals more suited to survive in their environment would be "selected." Over geological time, members of a species with traits better suited to their environment would increase in numbers, and the process would inevitably lead to the transmutation of species.

Darwin began to record these ideas in his journals shortly after returning from the journey of the *Beagle* but was hesitant to air them publicly because of the obvious implications for the widely held religious beliefs of the time. He continued to gather evidence for 20 years, performing experiments at home and communicating with scientists and animal breeders across Europe. Darwin was not idle during these years, publishing major works on topics as varied as volcanoes, the formation of coral reefs, and barnacles. He was finally goaded into publication when he received a manuscript for review from the naturalist Alfred Russel Wallace in 1858, 21 years after his earliest notes on the transmutation of species. Wallace had independently developed a theory nearly identical to Darwin's based on his experiences as an explorer and naturalist in the Amazon basin and Malay Archipelago. Shocked by Wallace's letter, Darwin was afraid that he would be accused of stealing Wallace's work; however, Darwin's friends Lyell and the botanist Joseph Dalton Hooker arranged for Darwin's and Wallace's papers to be read jointly before the Linnean Society and established the primacy of Darwin's work.

Darwin then went quickly to work preparing an "abstract" of his ideas, which was published in 1859 as *On the Origin of Species by Means of Natural Selection, or the Preservation of Favoured Races in the Struggle for Life*. In the *Origin of Species*, Darwin combined evidence from embryology, his own observations of animal variation and the inheritance of traits, artificial selection by animal breeders, and the fossil record to build a convincing argument for the transmutation of species by natural selection. Darwin was not the first to propose a naturalistic explanation for the origin of species. His grandfather Erasmus, Jean-Baptiste Lamarck (*Philosophie Zoologique*, 1809), Robert Chambers (*Vestiges of the Natural History of Creation*, 1844), and Wallace had all put forth theories, but none had gone the lengths Darwin had. He had gathered vast amounts of data, had an established reputation built on the prestige of his previous works, and had developed an argument too convincing for the scientific community to dismiss. For the remainder of his life, Darwin mainly relied on others, including Thomas Henry Huxley and Ernst Haeckel, to fight the public fights that his controversial ideas generated. Secluded in his country estate in Downe, Kent, Darwin continued his researches, wrote revised editions of the *Origin of Species* to answer the criticism of his detractors, and published his first works that broached the subject of human evolution.

The Descent of Man *and Later Life*

As evidenced by his hesitation to publish his ideas on the transmutation of species, Darwin was timid. He had avoided addressing the notion of human evolution in the *Origin of Species* nearly completely, saying only that based on his ideas, "light will be shed on the origin of man, and his history." Darwin's supporter, Thomas Henry Huxley, was brasher, and in 1868, he published *Evidence as to Man's Place in Nature*, where he laid bare the anatomical similarities of humans and other apes and the obvious implications. Darwin did not weigh in on the subject of human evolution until 1871. In *The Descent of Man, and Selection in Relation to Sex*, Darwin made his case for a naturalistic origin of humans from preexisting forms. In doing so, he used embryological evidence to demonstrate the relation of humans and apes, identified Africa as the likely geographical birthplace of humans, discussed the evolution of human mental faculties, made cogent arguments about racial differences, and developed his idea of sexual selection based on what appeared to be nonadaptive traits. Darwin followed this with *The Expression of the Emotions in Man and Animals* (1872), where he dealt more directly with adaptive explanations of behavioral traits.

Outside his scientific work, Darwin lived the privileged life of an English gentleman at Down House. He married his cousin Emma Wedgwood in 1839 and was reportedly a devoted husband and father. Emma was a deeply devout Christian, and although Charles had been raised in the Anglican Church, his work and the deaths of 3 of his 10 children caused him to lose his faith. This caused a rift between them that was deeply distressing to them both, but Darwin was always conscientious of Emma's beliefs and relied on her to read early drafts of his manuscripts. Additionally, Darwin was frequently ill after his return from the voyage of the *Beagle* and unsuccessfully sought treatment most of his adult life. There has been much speculation regarding the cause of his symptoms, ranging from nerves to a mysterious tropical disease. He died on April 19, 1882, and although he wished to be buried in the village churchyard at Downe, his stature in English science was so great that he was buried at Westminster Abbey.

Critical Contributions to Anthropology

Darwin's contributions to physical or biological anthropology are obvious and incredibly important.

Modern understanding of human evolution relies directly on Darwin's seminal research. Darwin's ideas have also been adopted into realms other than biology. Here, his contributions to anthropology are less direct, but understanding them is equally important.

Human Evolution

The modern study of human evolution by biological anthropologists looks at several lines of evidence. Anthropologists compare humans with our primate relations both anatomically and behaviorally. They look to fossil remains of human ancestors both within and outside Africa. They study embryonic development to search for clues to when, where, and how traits evolved. They study human variation and our relationship to other species. They follow the inheritance of traits through pedigrees. They examine population dynamics through studies of birth, death, and migration. Amazingly, although the technology has changed (the structure of DNA, the cellular mechanism of heredity, was not described until 1953, long after Darwin's death), all these methods were also used by Darwin in formulating his arguments to demonstrate the process of evolution through natural selection. All modern biological anthropologists are Darwinians, and Darwin himself may be considered the first modern biological anthropologist.

Having focused on Darwin's impact, there is also a negative aspect to the power of Darwin's ideas. For example, it is all too easy to ascribe value judgments to differences both between and within species. There is also a tendency among evolutionary biologists and biological anthropologists to ascribe adaptive value to any and all traits. It is important to keep in mind that demonstrating adaptations requires a huge burden of proof. Because something exists today does not necessarily mean that it is adaptive now or even that it was in the past.

Social "Darwinism"

The idea of natural selection is so simple and so powerful that it has been applied to fields as divergent as quantum physics, computation, art, music, and the cosmos. It is no surprise then that many have applied Darwin's ideas to social issues. The term *Social Darwinism* describes the ideology that societies change over time through much the same processes as species do. In fact, the term is something of a misnomer. These ideas existed before Darwin; Herbert Spencer described such a process in his *Progress: Its Law and Cause* (1857), 2 years prior to the publication of the *Origin of Species*. It was Spencer who coined the phrase "survival of the fittest" (Darwin adopted the term as a synonym for natural selection in later editions of the *Origin of Species*). Unfortunately, this notion was used as a justification for social inequalities and as an argument against social reform. According to this formulation, social progress is achieved through elimination of the unfit and serves mainly to maintain the status quo of social stratification. Mainly a 19th-century phenomenon, social Darwinism has not disappeared and is not likely to do so. Although Darwin certainly held the paternalistic views of an upper-class Englishman at the height of colonial expansion (he was repulsed, however, by the idea of slavery), any appropriation of his ideas into social issues cannot be pinned on Darwin himself.

Darwin's Legacy

Darwin's name is synonymous with evolution, and despite the rocketing advances in the field since the publication more than 150 years ago of the *Origin of Species*, his work remains relevant. Although many of the details were wrong (he was unable to solve the problem of the mechanism of inheritance), his basic notion of descent with modification remains the modern paradigm and has been confirmed again and again with multiple lines of evidence. No fossils of human ancestors existed in Darwin's time, yet his predictions of both the relation of humans to other apes and the location of the cradle of human existence in Africa proved accurate. Modern DNA evidence supports and reaffirms this. The fact that his name has surpassed many of his contemporaries, including Wallace, is a testament to his clear thought and presentation, and the persistence with which he championed his ideas. The *Origin of Species* and many of his other works continue to be published and are considered required reading for anyone interested in the life sciences. His influence on modern evolutionary biological theory can hardly be overstated. In fact, the only negative may be that his ideas are sometimes held in too high esteem. Darwin has reached the status of a deity among scientists, and questioning his

ideas is often seen as blasphemous. This of course is no fault of Darwin's and would be anathema to his scientific character. Nonetheless, Darwin will always have a central place in the history of evolutionary thought and our understanding of our own evolution.

Samuel J. Sholtis

See also Evolutionary Anthropology; Evolutionary Psychology; Gene-Culture Coevolution; Malthus, Thomas R.; Nineteenth-Century Evolutionary Anthropology; Spencer, Herbert; Wallace, Alfred R.

Further Readings

Berra, T. M. (2009). *Charles Darwin: The concise story of an extraordinary man.* Baltimore, MD: Johns Hopkins University Press.

Browne, J. (1995). *Charles Darwin: A biography.* New York, NY: Knopf.

Darwin, C. (1958). *The autobiography of Charles Darwin.* New York, NY: W. W. Norton.

———. (1859). *On the origin of species by means of natural selection.* London, UK: Murray.

———. (1871). *The descent of man and selection in relation to sex.* London, UK: Murray.

DAWKINS, RICHARD

Richard Dawkins (1941–), the British evolutionary zoologist, ethologist, atheist, and author, is one of the leading evolutionary theorists of the late 20th and early 21st centuries; he is also a staunch supporter of science and reason and a persistent critic of religion and irrationality.

Biography

Dawkins spent his early childhood in Africa. His father, Clinton Dawkins (1915–2010), was a British agricultural officer working in what is now Malawi (then called Nyasaland). Dawkins was born in Kenya in 1941, where his father was temporarily stationed during World War II. The family returned to Nyasaland in 1943 and remained there until Dawkins was 8 years old; at that point, they moved to England to live on a farm in Oxfordshire that had been in the Dawkins family since 1726.

Dawkins received his undergraduate and graduate degrees from Balliol College at Oxford University, earning his doctorate in zoology under the direction of the Nobel Prize–winning ethologist Niko Tinbergen (1907–1988). After a brief stint as assistant professor at the University of California at Berkeley from 1967 to 1969, Dawkins returned to England to take the first of several academic positions at Oxford. In 1995, he was appointed the first Charles Simonyi Professor for the Public Understanding of Science at Oxford University, an endowed chair that was created expressly for him. Dawkins retired from that position in 2008.

Since his retirement, Dawkins has devoted much of his time to running the Richard Dawkins Foundation for Reason and Science, a nonprofit scientific and educational organization dedicated to supporting critical thinking and to opposing religious fundamentalism, superstition, and intolerance (the Foundation maintains a website at www.richarddawkins.net).

Dawkins has enjoyed a remarkably successful career. His books have sold millions of copies and have been translated into more than 30 languages, and he has garnered a long list of prestigious honors, including election in 2001 as a fellow of the Royal Society.

With regard to his personal life, Dawkins's first two marriages, to Marian Stamp and Eve Barham, respectively, ended in divorce (Dawkins and Barham had a daughter together, Juliet Dawkins, born in 1984). In 1992, Dawkins married his third wife, the British actress and artist Lalla Ward (1951–).

Principal Works

Dawkins's 11 major books can be divided into two somewhat overlapping categories: (1) those that deal with evolution and (2) those that deal with science, skepticism, and religion.

Evolution

Theodosius Dobzhansky famously observed that nothing in biology makes sense except in light of evolution. Dawkins would certainly agree. He has acknowledged that many of his books return again and again to the theme of evolution, but he is unapologetic about the continuity, saying that he considers Darwinian evolution to be a large enough subject for a lifetime's work.

The Selfish Gene (1976)

This was Dawkins's first book, and it remains his most important and influential work (subsequent editions with additional material appeared in 1989 and 2006). Beginning in the 1960s, a number of scientists on both sides of the Atlantic developed revolutionary new ideas that constituted a breakthrough in the modern understanding of evolutionary processes. Prominent among these innovative theorists were the British biologists William D. Hamilton (1936–2000) and John Maynard Smith (1920–2004) and the American scientists George Williams (1926–2010) and Robert Trivers (1943–). The new concepts they introduced included kin selection, inclusive fitness, reciprocal altruism, and the application of game theory to evolutionary analyses. Collectively, these ideas provided a corrective to the notion of "group selection" that was common at the time (i.e., the notion that a species may survive at the expense of rival groups if the individuals within that species behave altruistically toward each other). The new theorists maintained that natural selection is a matter of differential survival and reproduction of *individuals*, not groups, populations, or species, and therefore, altruistic behavior could be explained at the individual level in terms of kinship (i.e., since individuals and their close kin share many of the same genes, individuals who sacrifice themselves for the sake of their relatives can still propagate their genes if those relatives survive and reproduce as a consequence).

The concepts of kin selection, inclusive fitness, and reciprocal altruism all entailed or implied a *gene-centered* view of evolution. Dawkins synthesized these ideas in *The Selfish Gene* and conveyed them in lucid, eloquent language using original and compelling metaphors (e.g., he described the body as a mortal throwaway receptacle for the immortal genes). Today, the gene-centered view of evolution dominates biology, and Dawkins is primarily responsible for having given the idea wide currency among other scientists (as well as the general public).

The Extended Phenotype (1982)

This book, which is addressed primarily to professional biologists, is essentially a sequel to *The Selfish Gene*. It explores the logical implications of the gene-centered view of evolution: If some genes are favored over others because of their phenotypic effects, those effects would include not just their consequences for the physical attributes of individual organisms but also their consequences for all their extended effects on the world (e.g., things such as beaver dams and termite mounds, which alter the ecosystem for other species).

The Blind Watchmaker (1986)

The title of this book alludes to a famous argument for the existence of God by the 18th-century theologian William Paley, who offered an analogy between a watch and living organisms. Paley argued that just as the intricate complexity of a timepiece allows us to infer that it must have been deliberately and consciously designed, so too the complexity of the living world necessarily implies a designer. Dawkins counters that Paley's argument, despite its eloquence and popularity, is utterly wrong. Natural selection is responsible for the illusion of design that we observe in the living world, and natural selection is a blind, automatic process with no conscious awareness or forethought. This book, like most of Dawkins's later work, is aimed primarily at a popular audience. The book's subtitle summarizes its theme: *Why the Evidence of Evolution Reveals a Universe Without Design.*

River Out of Eden (1995)

The five chapters in this short book describe life on earth as a river of DNA flowing through geological time (of particular interest to anthropological readers will be Dawkins's discussion of the African Eve hypothesis). Dawkins explains that nature is neither cruel nor kind but only pitilessly indifferent, and he speculates about the probable similarity of potential evolutionary processes in other planetary systems.

Climbing Mount Improbable (1996)

This book is devoted to the topic of evolutionary design (it is, in essence, a continuation of *The Blind Watchmaker*). *Climbing Mount Improbable* explains phenomena such as the origins of flight and the evolution of various forms of eyes in the animal kingdom. Like *River Out of Eden*, *Climbing Mount Improbable* is illustrated by Dawkins's wife, Lalla Ward.

The Ancestor's Tale (2004)

This book is a comprehensive history of life on earth; Dawkins described it as the largest and most demanding writing project of his career. *The Ancestor's Tale* is written in emulation of Chaucer's *Canterbury Tales*, with each individual traveler on the journey having a particular tale to tell—but in this case, each individual traveler is a single species, and the tale it has to tell is the story of its evolution.

The Greatest Show on Earth (2009)

The publication of this book was deliberately timed to coincide with the 200th anniversary of Charles Darwin's birth and the 150th anniversary of Darwin's 1859 book, *On the Origin of Species*. Just as Darwin had done in his magnum opus, Dawkins lays out the evidence for the *fact* of evolution; in the process, he covers much the same ground that Darwin had previously explored, including plant and animal domestication, comparative embryology, the geographic distribution of species, skeletal homologies, and vestigial organs.

Science, Skepticism, and Religion

Dawkins has remarked that his interest in debunking the supernatural claims of religion is not as detached from his scientific career as many people might imagine. For Dawkins, the scientific principles of evidential reasoning that illuminate the evolution of life on earth can be applied equally well to questions such as the existence of God; furthermore, Dawkins believes that there are compelling intellectual and moral reasons to subject religious claims to scientific scrutiny. In addition, as an evolutionary theorist, Dawkins is committed to refuting the pseudoscience of creationism (also known as intelligent design) and other similar forms of nonempirical beliefs.

Unweaving the Rainbow (1998)

Subtitled *Science, Delusion and the Appetite for Wonder*, this book addresses a number of paranormal claims, including astrology, telepathy, precognition, and the Loch Ness monster. The book's primary title comes from Keats, who believed that Isaac Newton had destroyed the poetry of the rainbow by explaining its optics. Dawkins argues in rebuttal that science is or ought to be the *inspiration* for great poetry, not its enemy, because science adds to our sense of wonder and awe at the beauty and majesty of the universe.

A Devil's Chaplain (2003)

This book is a compilation of essays most of which had been previously published elsewhere over the preceding 25 years. *A Devil's Chaplain* touches on a wide range of issues, including science, evolution, religion, morality, and justice. Some of the book, Dawkins admits, is passionate and angry—but, he maintains, there is a lot to be passionate about.

The God Delusion (2006)

This compelling book established Dawkins as one of the preeminent atheists of his time (it has sold well over 1 million copies worldwide). Dawkins argues that religious belief is both thoroughly irrational and inherently dangerous. He reviews the traditional arguments for the existence of God, exposing their myriad fallacies, and catalogs the many ways in which religion inspires violence, instills bigotry, and abuses children. Dawkins also elucidates the intellectual and moral advantages of atheism for both the individual and society.

The Magic of Reality (2011)

This book is intended primarily for young people, with lavish illustrations on every page. In relatively simple language, Dawkins explains the fundamental epistemology of science (hence the subtitle, *How We Know What's Really True*) and then offers scientific explanations for various natural phenomena. The word *magic* in the book's title refers not to *supernatural* magic or *stage* magic but to *poetic* magic, the deeply moving, exhilarating sense of awe and wonder that we experience when we encounter great works of art or sublime scenes of natural beauty.

Influence on Anthropology

For the majority of anthropologists, it is probably fair to say that the influence of Dawkins has been fairly minimal (this is certainly true if measured by the quantity of references to Dawkins in the overall anthropological literature). A recent survey of introductory textbooks, for example, reveals that Dawkins is cited only infrequently in works on biological anthropology, and he is almost never mentioned in works on cultural anthropology. Among anthropologists who are interested in the application of evolutionary theory to the analysis of human nature and human behavior, however, the situation is strikingly different: In works dealing with evolutionary psychology, for instance, references to Dawkins are virtually ubiquitous. The past couple of decades have seen an enhanced interest in evolutionary theory within anthropology, as illustrated by the recent formation of the Evolutionary Anthropology Society, a section of the American Anthropological Association devoted to promoting the application of modern evolutionary theory to the analysis of human behavior and culture. If that trend continues, it is reasonable to presume that the work of Dawkins will become more widely appreciated within anthropology.

James W. Lett

See also Darwin, Charles; Ethology, Human; Evolutionary Anthropology; Evolutionary Psychology; Religion

Further Readings

Barkow, J. H., Cosmides, L., & Tooby, J. (1992). *The adapted mind: Evolutionary psychology and the generation of culture.* New York, NY: Oxford University Press.

Boyer, P. (2001). *Religion explained: The evolutionary origins of religious thought.* New York, NY: Basic Books.

Buss, D. M. (1999). *Evolutionary psychology: The new science of the mind.* Boston, MA: Allyn & Bacon.

Coyne, J. A. (2009). *Why evolution is true.* New York, NY: Viking.

Dennett, D. C. (1995). *Darwin's dangerous idea: Evolution and the meanings of life.* New York, NY: Touchstone.

———. (2006). *Breaking the spell: Religion as a natural phenomenon.* New York, NY: Viking.

Grafen, A., & Ridley, M. (Eds.). (2006). *Richard Dawkins: How a scientist changed the way we think.* Oxford, UK: Oxford University Press.

Pinker, S. (2002). *The blank slate: The modern denial of human nature.* New York, NY: Viking.

Stenger, V. J. (2007). *God, the failed hypothesis: How science shows that God does not exist.* Amherst, NY: Prometheus Books.

DECONSTRUCTION

Deconstruction is a term that represents a particular approach to analysis in contemporary theory in the humanities and social sciences. Developed in the writing of the philosopher Jacques Derrida in the mid-1960s, deconstruction is among the most influential cultural movements of the past half-century. Tracing its roots back in literature to Laurence Sterne, James Joyce, and, more recently, Thomas Pynchon and its philosophical roots to Georg W. F. Hegel, Friedrich Nietzsche, and Martin Heidegger, the deconstruction movement began in France in the 1960s amid deep social questioning of traditional institutions, and it enjoyed its greatest popularity in the 1970s and 1980s. The term became associated with (and sometimes was used interchangeably with) poststructuralism, a development that Derrida never accepted.

Theory of Deconstruction

In general, deconstruction involves the process of unraveling meaning in texts. Deconstructionists argue that the meaning of language employed in texts is constantly changing and the meaning that readers derive from a text is outside the control of the author. Thus, the process of deconstruction entails a double movement, the rigorous engagement with a text involving the simultaneous engagement with and undoing of its meaning. Derrida developed the notion of *différance* to accommodate the numerous features that govern the production of such textual meaning. *Différance*, a term Derrida created, is a homophone with the word *différence*, and it implies both "to defer" and "to differ." His intent with this wordplay was to show that words never fully represent what they mean. Consequently, according to Derrida, meaning is forever deferred. Derrida had a mistrust of the metaphysical language commonly associated with phenomenology but decided to work within the language itself to dismantle its entire conceptual structure. Thus, his deconstructive reading of a text conveys a shifting of meanings that have been attached to signs and what they are intended to signify in language and thought. The term *différance* represents the possibility of a void or absence appearing in the very core of a text.

In the traditional Kantian sense of the philosophical term *synthesis*, deconstruction and its antistructuralist approach to the semiotics of texts stands for a movement characterized by the conditions for the possibility of experiencing the absence or presence implicit in the signified and in the act of signification itself. Derrida finds that Western metaphysics attempts to reduce to speech the free play of language found in writing, and he argues that speech is

no better than writing in that it suffers from the same inherent flaws. Derrida's strategy of deconstruction in *Of Grammatology* (1967) is to show that writing has emerged within the discourse of language and the dissemination of texts that intend to sustain and replicate stability of meaning. In its perpetual deferment and postponement of textual meaning, the strategy of deconstruction in effect serves as the vindicator of a repressed but already intelligible discourse of writing. As Derrida argues throughout *Of Grammatology*, especially in his essay on the Enlightenment philosopher Jean-Jacques Rousseau, "There is nothing outside the text."

What Deconstruction Is Not: Derrida's Negative Definitions of the Term

Derrida's core writings reject any philosophical analysis that proceeds from fixed, nonspontaneous concepts that are discursive in the traditional Kantian sense of ability to confirm stable conclusions. Derrida downplays any suggestion that deconstruction is the general name for an intellectual practice or technique. He does not accept the idea that deconstruction names an essence or a procedure, much less a particular method. In fact, Derrida constantly asserts that deconstruction is not to be understood as a philosophical method because he believes that there is no one correct, systematic way to perform deconstruction.

Derrida also does not intend deconstruction to represent or form an intellectual niche. Derrida believes that deconstruction cannot be truly named or signified. For Derrida, concepts, including the concept of the sign itself, can only be understood within texts and then with reference to specific contexts. Deconstruction of a text in this way is both an action and a process. It is the transcendental source of our conceptuality. In this sense, Derrida emphasizes that deconstruction is inescapable and necessary.

The Role of Husserl's Phenomenology in the Development of Deconstruction

In Derrida's early writings, deconstruction marked a break from phenomenology. Derrida's philosophical orientation begins in an argument with Edmund Husserl's phenomenology. In terms of philosophical lineage, deconstruction has its precedent in *Destruktion*, a term coined by Husserl's student

Heidegger. Heidegger's use of *Destruktion* presupposed that metaphysics was not simply the esoteric concern of philosophers far removed from the world but rather that it gave shape and grounded the historical epoch in which we live. Heidegger used the term to indicate taking apart in a way that reveals something's essential structure. Disassembling the metaphysical tradition in this way is a way of overcoming it, but for Heidegger, *Destruktion* also has a positive role: It displays the materials we have from our heritage with which we can build a new beginning. It is the primordial source of all possible meaning.

Derrida's deconstruction is intellectually indebted to Husserl's phenomenology. Derrida portrays himself as developing deconstruction to go beyond phenomenology, which he sees as a philosophical system trapped in a commitment to self-identical truths, true by virtue of the logical operations that produce them. Derrida argues that phenomenology was originally intended to serve as a criticism of traditional metaphysics and that it aimed to reawaken and restore metaphysics to its most authentic and original purpose. In the typical deconstructive sense, Derrida's intellectual debt to phenomenology takes the form of a subversive rewriting of Husserl's and phenomenology's premises. His deconstruction of phenomenology primarily rests on Husserl's treatment of language in relation to thought.

The first of Derrida's full-length philosophical studies, *Speech and Phenomena*, published in 1967, was devoted to Husserl's phenomenology and its theory of signs. In this early application of deconstruction, Derrida attempted to deconstruct Husserl's "pure" philosophical theories of being. Once he did so, Derrida believed that he had liberated any notion of fixed or stable meaning entailed in these theories. For Derrida, this signaled that he had made an intellectual advance that had gone beyond the tradition of phenomenology.

Contextualizing Deconstruction's Departure From Structuralism

Deconstruction arose in the context of the structuralism of Claude Lévi-Strauss and Ferdinand de Saussure. However, Derrida soon broke with this structuralism. Saussure and Lévi-Strauss created systems of binary analysis in speech, linguistics, and culture. Derrida reinterpreted these and ultimately moved beyond them. For instance, in *The Savage*

Mind (1962), Lévi-Strauss used the term *bricolage* to characterize a process of thinking. In his employment of the term, Lévi-Strauss is referring to the process of myth making and mythological thinking. In "Structure, Sign, and Play in the Discourse of the Human Sciences," Derrida deconstructs Lévi-Strauss and expands the usage of *bricolage*, suggesting that it is not only relevant to mythological thinking but is in fact related to all thinking and all text. Derrida's radical argument in the strategy of deconstruction involves the idea that even detailed knowledge of context cannot decide the multiple meanings of the language found in texts. This is so because Derrida holds that context is itself no more stable than the things it ostensibly frames. Context is also "textual."

Deconstruction represents a fundamental departure from structuralism. Where structuralism was built around identifying oppositions and keeping them separate, a priority of deconstruction is to show how oppositions complement each other in a subversive sense where meanings of text are overridden and transformed. Derrida's mission is to demonstrate that there are no pure meanings written in texts. In this sense, Derrida argued in "Structure, Sign, and Play in the Discourse of the Human Sciences" that deconstruction is the rigorous pursuit of a tension embedded deep in the structure of a text that leads to the text's unraveling.

Of Grammatology's Deconstructive Readings of Saussure, Rousseau, and Lévi-Strauss

In *Of Grammatology*, Derrida deconstructs readings of the linguist Ferdinand de Saussure, the Enlightenment philosopher Jean-Jacques Rousseau, and the anthropologist Claude Lévi-Strauss.

In his deconstructive reading of Saussure's posthumously published *Course in General Linguistics*, Derrida demonstrates that Saussure treats writing as a merely derivative form of linguistic notation, secondary and always dependent on the primary reality of speech and the sense of a speaker's presence behind his words. Derrida finds a dislocating tension here. He refuses to accept the paradox of language and speech as part of a larger, encompassing project of semiology (the study and language of signs). He believes that semiology is not able to identify a stable, consistent meaning in speech and writing. Derrida finds that there is a primary blindness in Saussure's text: the failure to think through the problems engendered by Saussure's own mode of discourse resting on the idea of language as a signifying system. For Derrida, Saussure's text contains an argument built around the binary opposition of speech and language, one with a form that intrinsically lent itself to a deconstructive reading. Derrida argued that once this identification had been made via a rigorous reading of the text's premises, the text deconstructed itself.

In Derrida's deconstruction of Rousseau's "Essay on the Origins of Languages," he demonstrates that Rousseau contradicts himself at various points, to the extent that far from proving speech to be the origin of languages and writing merely linked by contagion, Rousseau's text confirms the priority of writing and the illusory character of all such myths of origin.

In Derrida's deconstruction of Rousseau's text, writing rather than speech emerges to represent the center of all intelligible discourse and comes to define its very nature and condition. Derrida shows that Rousseau's essay submits to this reversal of the roles of speech and writing, even as Rousseau condemns the subversive influence he attributes to writing. Derrida's strict, deconstructive reading of Rousseau demonstrates that Rousseau cannot possibly mean what he says, or say what he means. Derrida perceives such discrepancies at every turn of Rousseau's argument. Wherever the primacy of nature (represented by speech) is opposed to the debasements of culture (embodied in writing), an aberrant logic emerges, inverting the opposition and cutting away the very ground of its meaning.

Derrida extends this deconstructive reading to Lévi-Strauss, where he finds the same issues of nature and culture that he found in Rousseau. Derrida sees Lévi-Strauss as employing a metaphor loaded with contradictions and antagonisms of the same magnitude as the one Rousseau employed in writing about the speculative science of the early-modern period. Derrida shows that the nature/culture opposition deconstructs itself even as Lévi-Strauss claims to achieve Rousseau's dream of studying the language and culture of a tribal community untouched by the evils of civilization. For Lévi-Strauss, the themes of exploitation and writing go naturally together, as do those of writing and violence. Derrida's critique of Lévi-Strauss follows

much the same path as his deconstructive readings of Rousseau and Saussure.

Deconstruction Besides Derrida and Anthropological/Cultural Applications

Clifford Geertz is generally acknowledged to have started the move toward understanding culture as text. Once culture was understood as a kind of text, deconstruction was increasingly used by anthropologists, and this paved the way for its becoming a critical aspect of the literary turn/postmodernism in anthropology in the 1980s and 1990s. In 1977, Paul Rabinow published *Reflections on Fieldwork in Morocco*, which examined the experience of ethnography through a deconstructive lens. In 1978, Edward Said published *Orientalism*, which applied deconstruction to Western understandings of the Middle East. In 1986, James Clifford and George Marcus published *Writing Culture*, which was a series of examples of the use of deconstruction in various aspects of anthropology. Together, these were among the most influential books in anthropology in the late 1970s and early 1980s, and they had a profound effect on anthropology in the 1980s and 1990s. In this era, the vast majority of work published in anthropology had at least some aspect of deconstruction.

In addition to Derrida, the literary critics of the Yale school, including Paul de Man, Geoffrey Hartman, and J. Hillis Miller, were key practitioners of deconstruction. Miller later moved to the University of California, Irvine, with Hartman a frequent guest in seminars devoted to deconstruction there. The postcolonial theorist Homi Bhabha at Harvard University studied social subordination and the location of culture through the lens of deconstruction. Gayatri Chakravorty Spivak of Columbia University, the translator of Derrida's *Of Grammatology*, is the most prominent postcolonial theorist to apply deconstruction to subaltern studies. Judith Butler has employed deconstructive themes in her theory construction, encompassing a number of cultural issues.

Although they have had a huge impact on anthropology in the past quarter-century, postmodernism in general and deconstruction in particular have created a strong backlash. Philosophers including John Searle took aim at deconstruction. In 1992, when Cambridge moved to award an honorary degree to Derrida, 18 prominent philosophers wrote a letter of protest calling Derrida's work a semi-intelligible attack on truth, reason, and scholarship. Anthropologists including Marvin Harris, James Lett, Roy D'Andrade, and many others argued, sometimes polemically, against deconstruction. In anthropology, conflicts between postmodernists located largely in cultural anthropology and scholars doing what they believed to be positivist science in archaeology and biological anthropology led to the breakup of major departments and the creation of separate departments of cultural anthropology in many important universities around the United States.

Dustin Bradley Garlitz

See also Butler, Judith; Clifford, James; Derrida, Jacques; Geertz, Clifford; Husserl, Edmund; Lévi-Strauss, Claude; Marcus, George; Phenomenology; Postcolonial Theory; Postmodernism; Poststructuralism; Rabinow, Paul; Rousseau, Jean-Jacques; Said, Edward; Saussure, Ferdinand de; Structuralism

Further Readings

Culler, J. (1982). *On deconstruction: Theory and criticism after structuralism*. Ithaca, NY: Cornell University Press.

Derrida, J. (1978). Structure, sign, and play in the discourse of the human sciences. In *Writing and difference* (pp. 278–293; A. Bass, Trans.). Chicago, IL: University of Chicago Press.

———. (1981). *Positions* (A. Bass, Trans.). Chicago, IL: University of Chicago Press.

———. (1998). *Of grammatology* (Corrected Ed.); G. C. Spivak, Trans.). Baltimore, MD: John Hopkins University Press.

Leitch, V. B. (1983). *Deconstructive criticism: An advanced introduction*. New York, NY: Columbia University Press.

Moran, D. (2000). Jacques Derrida: From phenomenology to deconstruction. In *Introduction to phenomenology* (pp. 435–471). London, UK: Routledge.

Norris, C. (1991). *Deconstruction: Theory and practice* (Rev. ed.). London, UK: Routledge.

DELEUZE, GILLES, AND FÉLIX GUATTARI

The work of Gilles Deleuze (1925–1995) and Félix Guattari (1930–1992) has influenced virtually every field in the humanities and social sciences. This is reflected in the secondary literature on their work,

which is extensive, stretching to more than 300 monographs as well as a journal and literally thousands of articles and book chapters. Two things are striking about the reception of Deleuze and Guattari's work: First, it is interdisciplinary, encompassing both practice-based disciplines like architecture and design and the more abstract and formal disciplines like philosophy, with room in between for the practically oriented disciplines like anthropology and sociology, including variants like health promotion; second, there is relatively little agreement as to what the basic terms created by Deleuze and Guattari actually mean. This fluidity in their concepts has undoubtedly been an enabling factor in the interdisciplinary spread of their readership.

The Partnership

Deleuze and Guattari's backgrounds could not have been more different. Yet somehow it was that very difference that made their working relationship so fruitful. Borrowing one of their own images, Deleuze and Guattari's partnership has often been described as being like that of the wasp and the orchid—two very different species that nonetheless need each other to thrive.

Deleuze's background was solidly philosophical (he studied at the Sorbonne and the University of Lyon), but he forged his own path through the history of philosophy by focusing on figures his teachers had either discounted as antiquated (David Hume, Baruch Spinoza) or, worse, treated with outright suspicion (Henri Bergson, Friedrich Nietzsche). He also wrote about literary figures (Lewis Carroll, Marcel Proust, Leopold von Sacher-Masoch), which further clouded the issue as far as his philosophical peers were concerned. While Deleuze was completing his doctoral work at the University of Lyon in the late 1960s, he became interested in schizophrenia as a particular kind of creativity or production of sense. Alongside the two works he was required to submit for his Doctorat d'État—*Différence et Répétition* (1968; *Difference and Repetition*, 1994), and *Spinoza et le Problème de l'Expression* (1968; *Expressionism in Philosophy: Spinoza*, 1990)—Deleuze also wrote *Logique du Sens* (1969; *The Logic of Sense*, 1990), which tackled the difficult problem of the distinction between sense and nonsense, paying particular attention to the poetic works of Lewis Carroll and Antonin Artaud. It was this "minor" project that was to have the greatest effect on his life and career because it brought him into contact with Guattari and sparked one of the most productive collaborations of the 20th century.

In contrast to Deleuze, Guattari's background was eclectic. He did not hold a university post. He was a hospital administrator and a psychotherapist. His formal university training was as a pharmacist, but he also received training in psychotherapy from Jacques Lacan, France's leading interpreter of psychoanalysis. Guattari attained the status of *analyste membre* (member analyst) in Lacan's school, the École Freudienne de Paris, licensing him as a pyschotherapist. Guattari's relationship to Lacan and Lacanian psychoanalysis was, however, at best ambivalent. Guattari's notebooks, *The Anti-Oedipus Papers* (2006), make it clear just how strained relations were between them, especially after the publication of *Anti-Oedipus*. Guattari wanted to work with Deleuze precisely because he thought Deleuze could help him resolve a number of theoretical impasses he encountered in Lacan's work. In particular, Guattari rejected the idea that the unconscious is structured like a language, which is the cornerstone of Lacan's structuralist reinterpretation of Sigmund Freud. This is why Deleuze's book *The Logic of Sense* interested him so much; it offered a much richer account of the relationship between language and the unconscious than Lacan's work did.

Deleuze and Guattari were introduced by Deleuze's former student from the University of Lyon, Jean-Pierre Muyard, a psychiatrist at the private psychiatric clinic La Borde, about 120 miles southwest of Paris, where Guattari also worked. Deleuze was in touch with Muyard because he was interested in following up on the theoretical speculations he'd made about how schizophrenics use language in *The Logic of Sense*, and as fate would have it, Guattari had recently given a lecture on that topic (later published as "Machine and Structure"), drawing on Deleuze's *Difference and Repetition* and *The Logic of Sense*. Both men were at turning points in their lives—Guattari was restless and dissatisfied with psychoanalysis, while Deleuze was casting about for his next project. In their different ways, both felt that psychoanalysis had made a fundamentally wrong turn when Freud "discovered" Oedipus.

Their Work

Together, Deleuze and Guattari wrote four books in a period of just over a decade: *L'Anti-Oedipe* (1972;

Anti-Oedipus, 1977), *Kafka: Pour une Literature Mineure* (1975; *Kafka: Towards a Minor Literature*, 1986), *Mille Plateaux* (1980; *A Thousand Plateaus*, 1987), and *Qu'est-ce que la Philosophie?* (1991; *What Is Philosophy?* 1994). As the already established professor of philosophy, Deleuze is generally credited with the "senior" role in their collaboration, with Guattari consigned to a junior, helpmeet role when not ignored altogether. That the truth was very different from this is not hard to see if one simply reads their work attentively.

After their first meeting, Deleuze and Guattari agreed to work together, and over the next several months, they met and shared ideas and developed a work that was simultaneously a critique and a rethinking of both Karl Marx and Freud (particularly the Lacanian interpretation of the latter) and a synthesis of a new methodology they proposed to call "schizoanalysis." In developing schizoanalysis, which was intended to be a whole new theory of social and cultural behavior, Deleuze and Guattari drew extensively on anthropology. In their first book, there is a very long chapter titled "Savages, Barbarians, and Civilized Men," which attempts to reconstruct the history of the capture of desire through the formation of different types of government. By scouring the anthropology of so-called primitive peoples, Deleuze and Guattari wanted to demonstrate that the "Oedipus complex" was a historical phenomenon of quite recent origin. In writing this section, Deleuze and Guattari worked closely with the psychoanalytically trained anthropologists Alfred Adler, Michel Cartry, and Andras Zempléni. Under their guidance, Deleuze and Guattari read Gregory Bateson, Marcel Griaule, Meyer Fortes, Pierre Clastres, and Victor Turner, among many others. They spliced this with archaeology, history, philosophy, and several other disciplines, so the resulting synthesis doesn't necessarily resemble anthropology as it is traditionally understood.

It is difficult to summarize the synthesis of theories Deleuze and Guattari called schizoanalysis. Deleuze and Guattari wanted to reengineer psychoanalysis, not depart from it. This entailed jettisoning the idea that the "Oedipus complex" can be used to explain all social and cultural behavior. But in reality, the changes Deleuze and Guattari wanted to make to psychoanalysis were far more complex than that. First of all, Deleuze and Guattari reject Freud's economic model of desire, which holds that the ultimate goal in life is to minimize unpleasure by limiting stimulation. What Deleuze and Guattari reject is the idea that desire is a kind of undifferentiated energy buzzing through our body and prompting us to act. The most basic form of this idea is the notion of the instinct as an unignorable internal force driving us to eat, sleep, procreate, and so on. Deleuze and Guattari instead frame desire as a creative force that gives rise to ideas, thoughts, concepts, dreams, and fantasies. Its ultimate creation is, of course, the human subject, the self. In *Anti-Oedipus*, they refer to this creative force as "desiring-production"; in subsequent work, they would simply call it "desire."

There are a lot of what might be called received misunderstandings of Deleuze and Guattari's work—that is, misunderstandings that have become so entrenched that they are no longer perceived as misunderstandings. One such received misunderstanding is the notion that Deleuze and Guattari reject the idea of the subject or the self. This is false. But one can see how this misunderstanding arises. In the opening chapter of *Anti-Oedipus*, Deleuze and Guattari provide what effectively amounts to a phenomenology of the experience of schizophrenia. They speculate that for the schizophrenic in the full flight of his or her deliria, the self is relatively unimportant; it basically gets crowded off stage by a range of agents and entities that consume the psyche's attention. When the schizophrenic ceases fighting to maintain the central position of the self, there ensues a kind of relief, a feeling of freedom, which many of Deleuze and Guattari's readers have interpreted as a positive affect. But this interpretation forgets that this relief is pathological; it amounts to a kind of surrender whereby the self agrees to and acknowledges its redundancy. Elsewhere in their work, Deleuze and Guattari discuss the different ways by which this self might be restored.

Probably of the greatest interest to anthropology is Deleuze and Guattari's concept of the assemblage, which should be understood as a kind of psychic accommodation a subject makes with his or her environment. This creates a vocabulary for analyzing the intersection of desire in both its conscious and its unconscious forms relative to the context in which a particular subject finds himself or herself. Here, Deleuze and Guattari revive and expand Freud's topography of the psyche. Many of the concepts invented in the course of their collaboration can be understood in this way—they provide a map of the psyche. Not surprisingly then, many of their concepts are spatial in origin: plane of immanence, smooth and striated, deterritorialized and reterritorialized, to name just a few.

The field of anthropology has been relatively slow to embrace Deleuze and Guattari's work, but it has not ignored it. Monographs influenced by their work are starting to appear, and it is clear that Deleuze and Guattari have something to offer even to field anthropologists not particularly interested in theory. Some examples of anthropological works incorporating this perspective are Arun Saldhanha's *Psychaedelic White: Goa Trance and the Viscosity of Race* (2007), Julia Mahler's *Lived Temporalities: Exploring Duration in Guatemala* (2008), and Konstantinos Retsikas's *Becoming: An Anthropological Approach to Understandings of the Person in Java* (2012). Probably the fullest assessment of Deleuze and Guattari's work from an anthropological perspective is the long essay in *Current Anthropology* by João Biehl and Peter Locke, "Deleuze and the Anthropology of Becoming" (2010). It is not without its flaws or misunderstandings, but it nevertheless offers a comprehensive account of Deleuze and Guattari's thought and seems likely in time to prove something of a touchstone for the field.

Ian Buchanan

See also Bateson, Gregory; Fortes, Meyer; Freud, Sigmund; Griaule, Marcel; Lacan, Jacques; Marx, Karl; Turner, Victor W.

Further Readings

Biehl, J., & Locke, P. (2012). Deleuze and the anthropology of becoming. *Current Anthropology, 51*(3), 317–351.

Buchanan, I. (2008). *Deleuze and Guattari's Anti-Oedipus*. London, UK: Continuum.

Colebrook, C. (2002). *Gilles Deleuze*. London, UK: Routledge.

Deleuze, G. (1995). *Negotiations* (M. Joughin, Trans.). New York, NY: Columbia University Press.

Dosse, F. (2010). *Gilles Deleuze and Félix Guattari: Intersecting lives* (D. Glassman, Trans.). New York, NY: Columbia University Press.

Guattari, F. (1984). *Molecular revolutions: Psychiatry and politics* (R. Sheed, Trans.). London, UK: Peregrine Books.

Hughes, J. (2012). *Philosophy after Deleuze*. London, UK: Continuum.

Watson, J. (2009). *Guattari's diagrammatic thought*. London, UK: Continuum.

DEPENDENCY THEORY

Dependency theory was an approach to understanding economic development in terms of historical and economic relations between the developed, industrial countries of the North and the poorer, developing countries of the South. It argued that poverty in the countries of the Third World, or the South (Africa, Asia, and Latin America), was due to their exploitation by the colonial and neocolonial powers (European countries, the United States) for their natural resources and cheap labor, which had created these countries' dependence on the North for manufactured goods. Dependency theorists argued that the wealth of the capitalist powers derived from the "underdevelopment" of the developing countries, and they recommended that Third World countries cut off ties with the industrialized nations and become economically independent by developing their own industries and controlling their surplus production. Several dependency theorists, including Andre Gunder Frank, promoted socialistic revolution as a solution to Third World poverty, pointing to Castro's Cuba as a model to emulate.

Dependency theory offered a counterargument to modernization theory, which held that the poverty in the developing world was due to intrinsic factors, including a conservative traditionalism and lack of entrepreneurial spirit, and that these countries needed to emulate the economic behavior and values of the developed countries. Where modernization theory corresponded with the mainstream and, later, neoliberal policies of the Northern, capitalist countries, dependency theory offered a radical and revolutionary alternative explanation of development. While many anthropologists agreed with the premise of global inequality, they were as a whole reluctant to accept either modernization or dependency theory's holistic and externally driven framework, preferring to focus on the particular social relations and human agency observed in the communities they studied.

The Development of Dependency Theory

Dependency theory developed in the late 1950s following the writings of the liberal economist Raúl Prebisch, who was the director of the United Nations Economic Commission on Latin America. Prebisch and his colleagues suggested that poverty in the developing world was not due to intrinsic conditions of those particular countries but resulted from the rich countries' benefiting from the unequal terms of trade. Poor countries purchased manufactured goods, which had high profit margins, from the developed countries in exchange for exports of raw materials, including agricultural and mineral products, such as coffee and copper, respectively, which had low profit margins. He advocated import substitution, which is the manufacture of goods by the developing countries themselves, and urged these countries to continue to export raw materials but not to use their foreign earnings to purchase manufactured goods from the North.

Building on Prebisch, Marxist writers described dependency as the product of the expansion of capitalism to capture producers and markets in the developing world. This theory was based on Lenin's *Imperialism: The Highest Stage of Capitalism*, which posited that the superprofits acquired in the colonies allowed the capitalist countries to improve wages for their own working class and postpone the inevitable socialist revolution predicted by Karl Marx. Writings in the 1950s and 1960s, including Paul A. Baron's *The Political Economy of Growth*, Andre Gunder Frank's *Capitalism and Underdevelopment in Latin America*, and Walter Rodney's *How Europe Underdeveloped Africa*, described the unequal relationship between the industrial North and the undeveloped South as "underdevelopment," pointing to an impoverishment of the Southern countries in terms of minerals, forestry, and agricultural crops that benefited the North. They also argued that the structures of dependency were repeated internally in the developing world, where local elites exploited their own poor and took profits out of the country for their personal gain.

Dependency theory stood in stark opposition to modernization theory, which held that poverty in the less developed countries resulted from economic institutions that were constrained by "traditional beliefs and irrational practices." Modernization theory, proposed in Walt W. Rostow's 1960 essay "The Stages of Economic Growth: A Non-Communist Manifesto," described development as a series of stages through which a poor country could progress from a "traditional" to a highly industrialized, "mass-consuming" society. It advocated the adoption of Western values of individual entrepreneurship and capitalist investment, which would drive the transition from a traditional to a modern society. Modernization theory was the product of the Cold War, wherein the United States sought to prevent the poor countries of the developing world from engaging in communist-led revolutions that would, as in the case of Cuba or Vietnam, lead them into the Soviet Union's sphere of influence. Modernization sought instead to capture these developing countries into the capitalist economy of the United States and other Western industrialized countries. In contrast, dependency theorists sought to disengage the developing world from the grasp of the core capitalist producers and promote their self-reliance and independence.

Dependency theory was further modified by world-systems theory, proposed by Immanuel Wallerstein in *The Modern World System*. Where dependency theory saw history as the unfolding of relationships between nations and their colonies, world-systems theory argued that the rise of European capitalism in the 17th century had created an integrated international economy through a complex hierarchy of the world's countries into core, semiperiphery, and periphery. This theory was influential in later discussions of globalization characterized by the movement of capital, technology, and migration of people in an integrated but unequal world economy.

Although there were different schools of dependency theory, the concept of dependency was broadly used to understand an international system comprising states in dyadic relationships variously described as core-periphery, dominant-dependent, or metropolitan-satellites. Moreover, dependency theory assumed that the external forces—multinational corporations, international markets, foreign aid—were the main determinant of the economic activities within the dependent states. Dependency theories converged around the idea that relations between dominant and dependent states were an ongoing process of exploitation that continues into the present era.

Criticism of dependency theory came from both the conservative right and the progressive left. From the right, critics argued that dependency was a circular argument—that dependent economies were not autonomous because they were dependent. Some, including World Bank proponents, argued that

modernization led not to exploitation but to growth of infrastructure, education, and healthcare, all beneficial to a developing country. Others asked that if the relationships between the core and the periphery were static, how did one explain the industrial growth of formerly poor countries such as Mexico, Brazil, or Taiwan? Neoliberal critics argued that participation in the global economy, even if unequal, would lead to economic growth for all. Dependency theorists counterargued that the semiperipheral countries were still dependent on multinational corporations, had strong autocratic governments, repressed labor unions, lacked environmental safeguards, and were still dominated by a small elite.

Orthodox Marxists criticized dependency theory for ignoring the positive aspects of capitalism that would create a wage-earning working class that could mature and overthrow their own capitalist elite. French structural Marxists argued against the rigidity of the dependency framework, pointing out that precapitalist subsistence modes of production remained viable and continued to resist capitalist penetration. Non-Marxists argued that it was not just capitalism that exploited developing countries but also the formerly socialist Soviet Union with its own satellites, including Cuba and Eastern Europe.

Anthropologists and Dependency Theory

Anthropologists have long recognized the existence of global poverty and inequality because the societies that cultural anthropologists studied were typically small scale, rural, and poor while situated in larger state systems. Following World War II, anthropologists increasingly looked at issues of social change and inequality in the less developed countries where they researched. British anthropologists who had conducted research for colonial offices in Africa and South Asia developed critical perspectives and looked at contemporary issues of urbanization, migrant labor, and social change. Dependency theory was popularized by the anthropologist Peter Worseley's *The Third World*, which introduced the term to a wider audience. Eric Wolf's *Europe and the People Without History* examined the impact of European commerce and colonization on Africa, Asia, and the New World, but unlike the dependency theorists, it showed the unevenness and particularity with which these relations were carried out by different powers (e.g., Spain, Holland,

England) on populations who reacted in a variety of ways, some with great resistance.

Many cultural anthropologists were reluctant to embrace dependency theory wholeheartedly. While acknowledging the economic and political domination of the Northern industrial countries on the less developed countries, anthropologists were less likely to focus on the role of external forces and looked more closely at social relations and agency in the local communities they studied. James Ferguson's *Anti-Politics Machine* examined how international development efforts in Lesotho failed because donors characterized the country as a traditional, subsistence-based society, ignoring local conditions, attitudes, and a long history of migrant labor to South Africa. Rather than improve agricultural production or alleviate poverty, these development programs reinforced and expanded the bureaucratic Lesotho state, suppressing active politics in the country. Jean Comaroff's *Body of Power, Spirit of Resistance* sought to understand the complexity of responses by the Tshidi of Botswana to modern life but found no single theory adequate for the task. She found little use for dependency theorists who regarded world capitalist penetration as the driving force of a country but ignored the "material, ideological and moral relations" of these local societies.

Medical anthropologists utilized dependency theory during the 1980s, arguing that capitalism's primary goal of profit was incongruent with the goal of health in the developing and developed worlds. Paul Farmer's *Pathologies of Power* and Nancy Scheper-Hughes's *Death Without Weeping* spoke of the "structural violence" of poverty that resulted in malnutrition, high risk of infectious disease, and poor healthcare. Several medical anthropologists, including Scheper-Hughes, rejected the dominance of political-economic explanations for neglecting the subjective content of illness, suffering, and healing as lived events and experiences.

Applied anthropologists who engaged directly in development projects found little help in dependency theory to solve practical problems. Where dependency theory saw socialist revolution and independence from the West as the only solution to poverty, it offered little material for programs combating HIV/AIDS, improving agricultural production, or working toward women's rights issues. Applied anthropologists found themselves struggling with policymakers while simultaneously consulting with and representing the interests of the target beneficiaries. James Ferguson's essay "Anthropology and Its Evil Twin" pointed to the substantial differences in approaches between "development anthropology," which engaged in development projects, and the "anthropology of development," which presented critical approaches to applied anthropology and the practice of development.

Postmodernist approaches emerging in the 1980s and 1990s rejected both dependency and modernization theories as ethnocentric paradigms promoting Western ideals of progress, scientific thinking, and power. Arturo Escobar's *Encountering Development: The Making and Unmaking of the Third World* described the development process as a Western discourse aimed at managing the Third World by imposing a strong bias for urban, industrial, and World Bank financial policies.

Rather than give way to Western frameworks, Escobar called for more "endogenous discourses." Other postdevelopment writers, including Vandana Shiva and Frederique Marglin, promoted alternative development that privileged local and grassroots autonomy rather than a larger, globalized economy. Nevertheless, several postmodernist and postdevelopment arguments accepted the dependency theory premise that the former colonial powers sought to keep developing countries poor and dependent, as Escobar acknowledged.

Conclusion

Dependency theory offered an explanation for the development and underdevelopment of countries in the context of the rise of capitalism as a world system. It demonstrated that poverty and underdevelopment are rooted in history and political economy, where powerful nation-states and multinational corporations came to dominate and exploit less powerful nations and where the local elite in those underdeveloped countries profited from the exploitation of their own country's people. Anthropologists, while critical of the external, hierarchical, and universalistic framework of both modernization and dependency theories, continue to utilize some of their insights in understanding social relations and processes in the local communities they study. Dependency theory continues to guide understandings of development and global poverty, including issues of sweat shop and child labor practices, the resistance by African farmers to subsidized production in the North preventing fair competition, and peasant rebellions in Mexico and India against the impoverishment caused by global capitalism.

Elliot Fratkin

See also Marxist Anthropology; Postmodernism; Scheper-Hughes, Nancy; Wallerstein, Immanuel; Wolf, Eric; World-Systems Theory

Further Readings

Amin, S. (1976). *Unequal development: An essay on the social formations of peripheral capitalism.* New York, NY: Monthly Review Press.

Cardoso, F. H., & Faletto, E. (1979). *Dependency and development in Latin America.* Berkeley: University of California Press.

Ferraro, V. (2008). Dependency theory: An introduction. In G. Secondi (Ed.), *The development economics reader* (pp. 58–64). London, UK: Routledge.

Frank, A. G. (1967). *Capitalism and underdevelopment in Latin America: Historical studies of Chile and Brazil.* New York, NY: Monthly Review Press.

Friedmann, H., & Wayne, J. (1977). Dependency theory: A critique. *Canadian Journal of Sociology, 2*(4), 399–416.

Gardner, K., & Lewis, D. (1996). *Anthropology, development, and the post-modern challenge.* London, UK: Pluto Press.

Morgan, L. M. (1987). Dependency theory in the political economy of health: An anthropological critique. *Medical Anthropology Quarterly, 1*(2), 131–154.

Rostow, W. W. (1960). *The stages of economic growth, a non-communist manifesto.* Cambridge, UK: Cambridge University Press.

Scheper-Hughes, N., & Lock, M. (1987). The mindful body: A prolegomenon to future work in medical anthropology. *Medical Anthropology Quarterly, 1*(1), 6–41.

DERRIDA, JACQUES

Jacques Derrida (1930–2004), the Algerian-born French philosopher and literary theorist, is among the most influential—and controversial—thinkers of the 20th century. Although his work drew most of its concepts from philosophy, its impact on the humanities, including social theory and anthropology, has been profound.

Biography and Major Works

Derrida was born on July 15, 1930, in El-Biar, Algeria, into a Sephardic Jewish family. At the age of 19, he left for France and then, in 1952, entered the École Normale Supérieure in Paris. Here, he focused on the work of G. W. F. Hegel, Martin Heidegger, and Edmund Husserl. The influence of the last of these in Derrida's development is worth stressing; as appreciative as he was, Derrida came to see certain problems in the phenomenological approach—problems that, although they were represented differently in different eras and traditions, were deeply woven into philosophical history.

In his first published work, "'Genesis and Structure' and Phenomenology" (1959), Derrida takes up a detailed discussion of certain aspects of Husserl philosophy. Husserl advanced the idea that what we call "experience" is not simply given to consciousness, awaiting discovery by the human mind. He contends, rather, that things appear to the human mind by virtue of a definable horizon of perceptual expectations and conceptual matrices. Husserl specifies two tasks that need to be undertaken in order to provide an understanding of how human experience is constituted: first, that we provide an account of experiential phenomena in objective, structural terms and, second, that we explicate our experience of the phenomena with reference to the shifting horizon of our consciousness (through which the phenomena appear). Derrida points to a constitutive paradox in Husserl's schema, where the rigid distinction between the objective manifestations of phenomena and the shifting horizons of constitution cannot, in the final case, be upheld. Derrida contends, very simply, that every shift in horizon will alter the ostensible "objective" description of the constituted phenomenon, thereby rendering the distinction between objective and subjective markers of the constituted object unsustainable.

In 1962, Derrida translated and wrote an introduction to Husserl's 1939 text *The Origin of Geometry.* Just as Husserl took geometry as paradigmatic of Western conceptuality, an ideal of knowledge, Derrida saw Husserl's text as *itself* paradigmatic of certain oversights that constituted Western knowledge from the ancient Greeks onward.

Unlike other contemporary French philosophers like Michel Foucault, Derrida possessed as such no "methodology" that could be specified in advance. His analyses are invariably predicated on meticulous readings of the texts under consideration rather than examining them by reference to external criteria; he proceeds via a strict, albeit provisional, adherence to the concepts and logic of a host text to excavate what the text excludes (historically and conceptually) in order to constitute itself. That, in a nutshell, is what is called "deconstruction." Deconstruction is a kind of critique that is simultaneously immanent and transcendental: It is *immanent* in the sense that it draws its analytic resources largely from the text under consideration; it is *transcendental* in the Kantian sense of being a kind of analysis that attempts to show the conditions under which a certain form of thought or conceptuality is made possible in the first instance.

Deconstructive readings typically begin by rendering explicit conceptual oppositions on which a particular text is predicated; they move on to show a kind of precedence—*temporal* or *ontological*—where one term is supposedly prior. These oppositions are then shown to be fundamentally confused in some way—that what first looked like metaphysically grounded opposites end up being nothing of the sort. Derrida works to draw out *aporiae* (Greek for "impasses"), where concepts cannot be figured in terms of stable binary oppositions. So a text that repudiates a particular notion is "always already" unraveling; the axes of any analysis demand that an ostensibly repudiated term be thematized, and as soon as this is done, the repudiation is tacitly withdrawn.

Critical Contributions to Anthropology (Social Thought)

Although Derrida's disciplinary training and orientation was philosophical, his work has not been without significance for anthropology and sociocultural theory more generally. It is worth stressing that from his first series of publications, Derrida was preoccupied with anthropological literature and concepts, and many of his major texts reflect that fact—from a consideration of Claude Lévi-Strauss's conception of language and orality (in *Of Grammatology*) and ideas of kinship and genealogy (in *Glas*) to the idea of "the gift" (in *The Gift of Death* and *Given Time*).

In *Of Grammatology*, Derrida engages with a number of issues that have traditionally been within the disciplinary ambit of anthropology: issues of nature and culture, the relationship between language and prohibition, ethnocentrism, and the question of oral and literate cultures. Most apposite here was his influential discussion of Lévi-Strauss's account of the Nambikwara, an Indigenous people of Brazil. In *Tristes Tropiques*, Lévi-Strauss's self-declared Rousseauism leads him to a lamentation about the ruinous consequences of Western culture—perhaps even culture per se—on Indigenous peoples, whose natural existence has been corrupted by the imposition of alien forms of life and conceptuality, including that introduced by Lévi-Strauss himself. The anthropologist's elaboration of his own discomfort focuses on the issue of writing, and the implication of writing *itself* in colonial exploitation. While Derrida is careful to give credence to Lévi-Strauss's claims about the relationship of culture and writing to the exercise of violence, he detects in the anthropologist's musings itself a form of unwitting ethnocentrism that requires further examination: In his efforts to vindicate his subjects, Lévi-Strauss figures the Nambikwara as an absolute "Other." Furthermore, Lévi-Strauss's opposition between oral and literate culture—on which much of his analysis hangs—is constitutionally unstable: All of the features that he describes as being essential to writing (reproducibility, symbolism, etc.) are present in Nambikwara culture, including their *speech*. In this sense, Derrida contends, they are as possessed of "writing" as the culture that produced the printing press.

Later, in *Given Time: 1. Counterfeit Money*, Derrida took up an issue that had been central to anthropology, at least since the time of Marcel Mauss: the question of the gift. For Derrida, perhaps predictably, the gift becomes the sign under which certain analyses of *aporiae* appear; the gift here becomes a figure of the impossible. The essence of what we call a "gift" is that which is given without desire or expectation of reciprocation. That is, the gift is that which excepts or exempts itself from the economy of exchange, the logic of quid pro quo. Derrida maintains that although the idea of the gift animates the act of giving, the gift per se can only ever exist as a potential. The gift, as such, cannot exist but only ever assume the role of a kind of promise, as something *to be*. As soon as the gift is given and appreciation is expressed or pleasure taken, it is inscribed in an economy of exchange. In "real time," Derrida argues, the gift "annuls itself." The gift is characteristic of a more general pattern of analysis and thematization that Derrida often undertook: It is one of those ideas that functions to actualize things without itself ever becoming actual—it animates something that it cannot, in principle, ever bring into existence.

Of course, these two areas of focus—writing and the gift—are not the only ones apposite to a consideration of the relevance of Derrida's work to social theory in anthropology. He has written, in various places, on racism, on the role of the humanities and philosophy, on forgiveness and cosmopolitanism, and on ideas of political sovereignty and animality. However, it is not just in these directly sociocultural and political areas that his work is or should be of interest to cultural theorists. Derrida's exhaustive and ongoing engagements with structuralism, phenomenology, and empiricism are highly relevant. In one form or another, anthropology and cultural theory have been—and continue to be—predicated on epistemologies that take one or more of these intellectual orientations as fundamental. And to the extent that this is the case, his work has relevance to sociocultural theory.

Derrida's Legacy

As should be expected, Derrida's early interventions were heavily shaped by the climate of French intellectual life in the 1960s. This was a time when structuralism was beginning to establish itself as a new paradigm of thought, a viable successor to phenomenology. Where phenomenology had tied knowledge to experience, structuralism had claimed that what we call "experience" is always mediated by the conceptual structures that precede it. In this sense, structuralism asserted that structure was prior to (experiential) phenomena. Derrida's sympathies with structuralism were real but were invariably tempered with a conceptual inheritance and mindset that owed much to Husserl and Heidegger, both of whom still accorded experience a primary place in their philosophical systems.

Given this imperative, one interpretation of Derrida's work is preeminently negative—he is conceived of as a undoer of ideas rather than as a maker of them. This is a complex issue that cannot be properly considered here; suffice it to say

that part of how one sees the nature of Derrida's work depends on a cultural and intellectual context. Where in France he was seen as a philosopher writing in the phenomenological tradition, his work was picked up in the United States and became a key influence on the so-called Yale school of literary criticism in the late 1970s and early 1980s. The form of deconstruction in the United States was centered on questions of textual interpretation and not on either his phenomenological investigations or the explicitly ethical and political questions that came to characterize Derrida's thought from the 1980s onward. At the same time, another uptake of his work occurred in the United States. Gayatri Chakravorti Spivak, who had translated Derrida's *Of Grammatology*, wrote a foundational essay titled "Can the Subaltern Speak?" in 1988, which was deeply indebted to deconstructive themes and became foundational to postcolonial theory.

Derrida's legacy is one that is heavily contested and has been subject to fierce debate, sometimes even in the popular press. This seems unusual for a thinker whose writings demand a high degree of philosophical training—and undoubtedly patience—to follow. This, perhaps, has been itself one of the sources of controversy. The notorious conceptual density of his work, a digressive style, and a propensity to utilize forms of wordplay such as puns has polarized the intellectual community and, to some extent, the media.

For better or worse, Derrida's name has become synonymous with the noun *deconstruction*. Although there are worse metonyms, the reduction of a highly complex body of work to a single term is, in the case of Derrida, both ironic and unfortunate. By the time of his death, he had written well over 30 books. Furthermore, seminars of his are now in the process of translation. The legacy of his thought is very much an open question, as reliant on fluctuations in intellectual fashion as on any scale of inherent merit. Consistent with the tenor of his thought, there is good reason to believe that, about his own work at least, Derrida himself will not have the last word.

Chris Fleming

See also Foucault, Michel; Gift Exchange; Hegel, George W. F.; Husserl, Edmund; Lévi-Strauss, Claude; Mauss, Marcel; Phenomenology; Structuralism

Further Readings

Derrida, J. (1973). Speech and Phenomena *and other essays on Husserl's theory of signs* (D. Allison, Trans.). Evanston, IL: Northwestern University Press.

———. (1976). *Of grammatology* (G. C. Spivak, Trans.). Baltimore, MD: Johns Hopkins University Press.

———. (1978). *Edmund Husserl's "Origin of Geometry": An introduction* (J. P. Leavey Jr., Trans.). Pittsburgh, PA: Duquesne University Press. (Original work published 1962)

———. (1978). *Writing and difference* (A. Bass, Trans.). Chicago, IL: University of Chicago Press.

———. (1981). *Dissemination* (B. Johnson, Trans.). Chicago, IL: University of Chicago Press.

———. (1986). *Glas* (J. P. Leavey Jr. & R. Rand, Trans.). Lincoln: University of Nebraska Press.

———. (1992). *Given time: 1. Counterfeit money* (P. Kamuf, Trans.). Chicago, IL: University of Chicago.

———. (1995). *The gift of death* (D. Wills, Trans.). Chicago, IL: University of Chicago Press.

Fleming, C., & O'Carroll, J. (2005). In memoriam: Jacques Derrida (1930–2004). *Anthropological Quarterly, 78*(1), 137–150.

Morris, R. C. (2007). Legacies of Derrida: Anthropology. *Annual Review of Anthropology, 36,* 355–389.

DESCENT THEORY

See Alliance-Descent Debate

DESCRIPTIVE LINGUISTICS

Descriptive linguistics (henceforth DL) is the scientific endeavor to systematically describe the languages of the world in their diversity, based on the empirical observation of regular patterns in natural speech.

Definitions

The core principle of DL is that each language constitutes an autonomous system, which must be described in its own terms. Modern descriptive linguists carry out detailed empirical surveys on a language. After collecting language samples from speakers, they analyze the data so as to identify the components of the system and the principles that underlie its organization. Through its commitment to the empirical description of speakers' actual practices and to the diversity of languages as creations of linguistic communities, DL is closely allied with the social sciences.

The research agenda of DL can be contrasted with a number of related yet distinct approaches to language. *Anthropological linguistics* and *sociolinguistics* study, each in its own way, the interaction between cultural or social factors and language use; by contrast, DL focuses on the structural properties of the languages themselves. *Historical linguistics* studies the diachronic processes of language change, whereas DL focuses on the synchronic forms taken by a particular language at a given point in its development. The endeavor to compare individual languages, and the search for potential universals, is known as *linguistic typology*. DL may be understood as the preliminary step in the typological effort, the stage during which the facts of each individual language are established, before comparison can take place.

These subdisciplines of linguistics differ in their scientific goals, yet they essentially share with DL the same fundamental principles, including the emphasis on a bottom-up, empirical approach: All these approaches are complementary components of a single scientific agenda. By contrast, the principles of DL conflict more frontally with those of *formal linguistics*. Formal linguists—particularly proponents of generative grammar—claim that the facts of language are best explained by resorting to an apparatus of theoretical principles that are defined a priori, independently of the facts of particular languages. Descriptivists reject these aprioristic assumptions and require that all results be derived from the observable structures of the languages themselves.

History

A Long History of Language Description

The earliest known attempts to describe a language in a systematic way originated in ancient northwestern India, where the desire for a faithful transmission of the sacred scriptures known as the Vedas brought about the need to describe Sanskrit. The best known member of that grammatical tradition, commonly dated 5th century BCE, is Pānini—arguably the first descriptive linguist. Similar grammatical traditions were later established in other civilizations and gave birth to the first grammars of Greek, Latin, Tamil, Chinese, Hebrew, and Arabic.

Due to the dominance of Latin in medieval Europe, most modern languages had to wait until the Renaissance to be described for the first time—for example, Spanish in 1492, French in 1532, and English in 1586—whether in the form of grammars or lexicons. At the same time, the languages spoken in the newly discovered Americas also became objects of description—often as a result of missionaries' religious agendas. Nahuatl, the language of the Aztecs, had its first grammar written in 1547 and Quechua, the language of the Inca Empire, in 1560.

While the discovery of new languages should have raised awareness of the world's linguistic diversity, such a realization was hampered by the persistent tendency to base grammatical descriptions on the categories that had been established for languages then deemed more prestigious. A good example is Diego Collado's explicit attempt in 1632 to describe Japanese, following the linguistic categories of Latin. Well into the 19th century, many languages were described using the terminology and grammatical concepts of European languages. As more and more languages of the world were explored and as the new discipline of linguistics started to develop in the mid-19th century—following the groundbreaking work of Alexander von Humboldt and the Brothers Grimm—a new approach to language description became necessary.

The Structuralist Revolution and the Theorization of Descriptive Linguistics

The main turning point in the history of DL was the structuralist revolution. During the first decade of the 20th century, the Swiss linguist Ferdinand de Saussure articulated a theory whereby a language is essentially a system of meaningful oppositions. Contrasts between forms (*signifiants*) are paired with contrasts between meanings (*signifiés*). For instance, "I feed my cat" and "I feed my dog" differ by the segments "cat" and "dog"; this contrast in form corresponds to differences in meaning. In English, the meanings of *cat* and *dog* are also defined by the set of words they compare with: *Cat* differs from *dog* but also from *tiger, lion, kitten*, and so on. Each segment gains meaning by virtue of its contrasts with other elements within the system of the particular language. Saussure's insights inspired the new methodological principle of DL: that each language be described on its own terms, based on the empirical observation of contrasts—or "structures"—internal to its system, rather than on categories imported from other languages.

During the same decade, anthropologists developed a sustainable interest in languages and their descriptions. The American Franz Boas placed the description of local languages at the core of his research on American peoples, initiating a long-lasting tradition in which linguistic description forms an integral part of ethnographic description. Boas also articulated a question about language that linguists had not raised: that of the relation between language and culture. Similar issues were later tackled by Boas's student Edward Sapir, who formulated the famous "linguistic relativity hypothesis," later consolidated by Benjamin Whorf. The Sapir-Whorf hypothesis, which concerns mutual influences between language, thought, and culture, still constitutes a significant domain of research.

It took a little longer before linguists followed ethnographers in their interest for human diversity. Saussure's theories had freed linguistic description from the mould of Indo-European patterns, yet Saussure himself worked on Indo-European languages. In the wake of Boas and Sapir, the attention to language diversity became central to another prominent figure of linguistic structuralism, the American Leonard Bloomfield. While Bloomfield became famous for fully developing structuralist theories, he also dedicated his work to American languages, particularly Ojibwe and the Algonquian family, based on firsthand data collected in the field.

Equipped with the appropriate theories and methods, increasingly aware of the scientific and human heritage embedded in linguistic diversity, descriptivists undertook to study as many languages as possible, across all continents. With about 6,000 languages in the world today and only a fraction of them adequately described, the task is colossal—but urgent. Colonization and globalization have already sealed the fate of thousands of languages, and it is estimated that half of today's languages will disappear in the 21st century. In response to this threat, some linguists have developed thorough techniques of language documentation. They emphasize the need for extensive corpora and high-quality sound and video recordings, so as to keep a sound print of each threatened language. The *documentation* of languages does not, however, replace the scientific insight provided by their *description*.

Principles and Methods of Linguistic Description

The first step toward describing a language is data collection. Most descriptive linguists carry out field-work in a linguistic community and record samples of speech from different speakers, embodied in different speech genres: narratives, daily conversation, poetry, and so on. Although spontaneous, naturalistic speech is the ideal, in practice, linguists also carry out *elicitation*, by asking speakers for translations, testing specific sentences, and checking pronunciation or grammar rules.

This patient process can span several years and results in the creation of a corpus, a body of reference materials, against which hypotheses can be tested. Eventually, this analysis results in a published grammar, which spells out most of the rules of the language. Following the "Boasian trilogy," a complete language description includes a grammar, a dictionary, and a collection of texts.

In line with the structuralist agenda, the linguist analyzes the corpus in such a way that the language's own structures emerge from a system-internal analysis rather than being imported from another language or imposed via theoretical assumptions. These internal structures define *emic* categories: categories whose identification is based on the internal properties of a particular system. The terms *etic* and *emic*, whose contrast is central to structural linguistics and to structuralism in general, originate in the study of phonology; they allude to its central contrast between *phonetic* and *phonemic*. While phonetics deals with sounds and how they are produced, phonology deals with the way sounds are grouped together as meaningful, contrastive units (phonemes) in a given language.

Thus, consider the three different sounds noted, [t], [ɾ], [ʔ], in the International Phonetic Alphabet. In English, these sounds are three dialectal variants of a single consonant spelled *t*. Thus, in the word *better*, British Received Pronunciation has a sound [t], [bɛtə]; but American and Australian dialects typically pronounce this word with a "flap," [bɛɾə]; and the modern dialect of London has a "glottal stop" (the sound in *uh-oh*), [bɛʔə]. In spite of their phonetic difference, in English, these three sounds constitute variants of a single phoneme, which linguists will represent as /t/. The phonetic variation between [t], [ɾ], and [ʔ] does not affect the meaning of the word *better*; all three pronunciations can be subsumed under a single underlying form, /bɛtə/. In other terms, even though they differ from the (*phon*)*etic* point of view, these three sounds all instantiate a single (*phon*)*emic* category in the system of this particular language.

Crucially, while this analysis is correct for English, it may not hold for another language. For example, Tahitian contrasts the meanings of *pata* [pata] "sling," *para* [paɾa] "yellowed," and *pa'a* [paʔa] "carapace"; these oppositions are evidence that within the Tahitian system, the three *etic* units (sounds) [t], [ɾ], and [ʔ] reflect three separate *emic* units (phonemes), /t/, /ɾ/, and /ʔ/, each endowed with its own contrastive value. Every system cuts up the phonetic space differently: Where English has a single category, Tahitian has three.

A similar approach governs the exploration of semantic categories. Every word in a lexicon constitutes an *emic* category—that is, a set of potential referents—and this category is language specific. This is well exemplified by kin terms. In English, *father* refers to F alone, while *uncle* groups together FB (father's brother) and MB (mother's brother). But in Dalabon, an Australian language, *bulu* groups together F and FB, while *kardak* refers to MB. Similar observations would apply to other words in the lexicon; words cut up the semantic space in different ways across languages. The structural analysis of the lexicon parallels the one illustrated above in phonology.

Finally, the same structuralist method applies in the realm of grammar. To take a brief example, one must not take it for granted that all languages distribute their words into the same syntactic categories or "word classes"—such as nouns, verbs, and adjectives. In Teanu, a language of the Solomon Islands, the word meaning "beautiful" is an adjective, but "clever" is a verb, despite its English translation, because it behaves like other verbs of the system. Some languages do not even have a separate "adjective" class, because in their systems, the equivalent of English adjectives consistently behaves like verbs (e.g., Northern Iroquoian languages) or like nouns (e.g., Warlpiri, central Australia). While some languages have three major word classes, others may have fewer or more. Languages cut up the "grammatical space," as it were, along different lines.

Just like the units of phonology or of the lexicon, the categories of grammar can only be described accurately by observing how they behave within their own system. The same principles and methods apply throughout language description, whether to establish the units of the system (the categories) or their behavior (the rules).

Conclusion

Every language embodies a different way to perceive and categorize reality. The aim of DL, as a discipline, is to capture that linguistic diversity before it can be explained and interpreted. Of course, this diversity is in turn balanced by a number of properties that are shared by many or even all languages. Based on the description of individual languages, it is then the task of *linguistic typology* to gauge empirically how similar and diverse our languages can be.

Alex François and Maïa Ponsonnet

See also Bloomfield, Leonard; Boas, Franz; Comparative Method; Generative Grammar; Sapir, Edward; Saussure, Ferdinand de; Sociolinguistics; Whorf, Benjamin Lee

Further reading

Ameka, F. K., Dench, A., & Evans, N. (Eds.). (2006). *Catching language: The standing challenge of grammar writing* (Trends in linguistics: Studies and monographs). Berlin, Germany: Walter de Gruyter.

Diffusionism, Hyperdiffusionism, *Kulturkreise*

The term *diffusionism* normally is used to characterize a paradigm within anthropology and the social sciences that aims at writing a history of (early) mankind by reference to similarities between the present cultures of different regions. This approach rests on the assumption that cultural innovations have been rare in the past and their occurrence in distant regions normally is caused by culture contact and associated processes of diffusion that bridge even long distances. Diffusionists thus deny that parallel evolution or independent invention took place

to any great extent throughout history. The term *hyperdiffusionism* designates an even more radical position characterized by the idea that all cultures originated only from a single culture. Furthermore, the adherents to the "culture circle" theory (*Kulturkreislehre*) of German ethnology assumed that the complex cultural picture of the present is the result of the continuous intermixture of a small number of "primary cultures."

The relevance of this complex of theories for the present debates, for reasons that are discussed below, is rather limited. By World War I, diffusionism had been challenged by the newly emerging functionalist school of thought of Bronisław Malinowski (1884–1942) and Alfred R. Radcliffe-Brown (1881–1955). In the 1890s, Franz Boas (1858–1942) rejected the great narratives of both evolutionists and diffusionists. He argued that cultural change had been influenced by many different sources. The critique of Boas and his followers was compelling enough so that most of these concepts lost credibility and ultimately were abandoned. Nevertheless, at least in the German tradition of ethnological research, certain elements of this kind of thinking have survived until the present. And with the more recent "spatial turn" and globalization studies during the past 2 decades, at least some of the elements of this paradigm have been revived.

Diffusion and Diffusionism

Hardly any other theory in anthropology and in the social sciences has such a bad reputation as *diffusionism*. Indeed, the term is used in a pejorative sense by many scholars. This comes as a surprise since diffusion itself, which means the transfer of ideas (technologies, languages, religions) and objects between different places and cultures, is a process familiar to all societies, ancient and modern, and as such is largely uncontroversial. In cultural anthropology, (trans) cultural diffusion was conceptualized by Alfred L. Kroeber, among others, as a process involving three successive phases: (1) the presentation of a new element, (2) its acceptance, and (3) its integration into the new culture, which may be combined with a modification of that element. Diffusion in this sense, which may be caused by exchange/trade, war, or other forms of intercultural contact, is opposed to *migration*, which means the transfer not only of ideas and objects but also of people themselves. In a broader sense, the term *diffusion* sometimes also is used to include migration as well. Migration is the main process in what L. Cavalli-Sforza has called "demic diffusion."

The problem started with the shift from diffusion to diffusionism. The diffusionists among the early anthropologists claimed to be able to reconstruct the history of mankind mainly by reference to the processes of diffusion. They held that innovations of all kinds normally were made only once (or at least only at a small number of different places) and that these innovations later on were transferred to other places and cultures. In this way, starting from the study of the modern spatial distribution of culture traits, it should be possible to reconstruct human history—that is, to write a history even for those periods for which written sources were not available. The basic idea behind this concept was that cultures permanently influence each other and the amount of similarities between them can be taken as a measure for the intensity of the contact. The direction of the influences thereby has often been regarded as a function of the complexity of the cultures involved: More developed cultures influence and ultimately transform less developed cultures.

Diffusionism's bad reputation stems from the fact that its proponents today are regarded as armchair anthropologists, who spent most of their lifetime at home studying travel reports and museum objects collected by others. This is not true in all cases, but there is no doubt that the kind of anthropology that was practiced in the late 19th and early 20th centuries was, on the one hand, strongly object oriented and, on the other, with regard to the value judgments communicated, at least implicitly racist. With regard to the subsequent developments within anthropology, which were characterized by a shift toward contextual analyses of rather small groups that were based on long and intensive field studies, this kind of anthropology quickly came to look rather old-fashioned.

Historical Ethnology in Germany

One other important point about diffusionism worth mentioning is that no other theory in anthropology is so strongly connected to Germany and the German-speaking countries. It is mainly the product of a school of historical ethnology that developed around the turn of the 19th century in Germany. It

was scholars such as Friedrich Ratzel (1844–1904), Leo Frobenius (1873–1938), and Fritz Graebner (1877–1934) who developed the terminology and the methodical principles of the approach, which later became known as *Kulturkreislehre* (culture circle theory).

By challenging the dominant evolutionary thinking of their time, these scholars ultimately aimed at a universal history. Older research focused on a "natural history" of man, which included the search for universals. This was replaced by a new kind of historicism. This has to do with the fact that "historiography" in Germany during the 19th century had become a leading academic discipline that exercised an important influence on the academic debates even in other fields. But the subjects in this new kind of historical enquiry were not important rulers and dynasties, as in the work of Leopold von Ranke (1795–1886), for example, but "cultures" and "culture circles," understood as specific historical combinations of a number of culture traits. Furthermore, despite a critical distance from evolutionist ideas, some of the elements of evolutionary thinking were retained, such as the postulate of growing complexity and the existence of cultural strata.

An early proponent of this kind of thinking was Friedrich Ratzel (1844–1904), who was trained as a zoologist and a geographer before he entered the field of anthropology. With his *Anthropogeographie* (Anthropogeography, two volumes, 1882 and 1891), he aimed at creating a science dealing with the conditional nature of man. Influenced both by Charles Darwin's (1809–1882) theory of evolution and by Ernst Haeckel's (1834–1919) ecology, he was interested in explaining cultural constellations from the perspective of their natural and geographical conditions. He regarded mankind similarly to plants and animals as dependent on adaptation to the environment.

At the same time, Ratzel was interested in cultural processes on a global scale, with special reference to spatial processes like migration and diffusion. Therefore, he looked for regularities ("laws") in the culture process and thus became the founder of "geopolitics" (*geopolitik*). He looked at world history as a process of the development and displacement of centers and peripheries and thereby anticipated ideas quite similar to those expressed in the world-systems theory of the American sociologist Immanuel Wallerstein in the 1970s. Furthermore, given his basic idea that one could read time (history) in the spatial distributions of cultural elements, Ratzel anticipated a central idea of the later *Kulturkreislehre* school of diffusionism. However, culture circle scholars ignored Ratzel's ecological ideas insofar as its members regarded "culture" as something independent from the natural world.

Inspired by Ratzel, the German ethnologist Leo Frobenius (1873–1938), who was involved in extensive research in Africa in 1897–1898, delineated several *Kulturkreise* (culture areas) exhibiting similar traits. These traits he supposed to have been spread by diffusion or invasion. Frobenius saw cultures as living organisms and tried to reconstruct their worldview, which he saw as primarily determined by economic factors.

November 19, 1904, is often regarded as the birthday of the *Kulturkreislehre*. On this day, Fritz Graebner (1877–1934) and Bernhard Ankermann (1859–1943) presented two related papers, "Kulturkreise und Kulturschichten in Ozeanien" (Culture Circles and Culture Layers in Oceania) and "Kulturkreise und Kulturschichten in Afrika" (Culture Circles and Culture Layers in Africa), at a meeting of the Berliner Gesellschaft für Anthropologie, Ethnologie, und Urgeschichte (Berlin Society for Physical Anthropology, Ethnology, and Prehistory), in which they demonstrated the principles of what later became known as the "culture historical method." In the following years, it was especially Graebner, trained as a historian, who tried to refine the methodological principles of this new paradigm. In his influential 1911 book *Methode der Ethnologie* (Method of Ethnology), he formulated the central principles of the so-called culture historical method. Three criteria were central to Graebner's method to determine the historic-genetic relationship between distinct cultures:

1. *The criterion of form (Formkriterium)*: The occurrence of the same forms of objects in different regions points to a common origin of the respective cultures.

2. *The criterion of quantity (Quantitätskriterium)*: The more formal the correspondences between two cultures, the stronger is their historic-genetic connection.

3. *The criterion of continuity (Kontinuitätskriterium)*: A historical connection between two distant cultures with a number of similarities is even more probable if the cultural elements characteristic of them are also found in the spaces between both cultures, as if a *Kulturbrücke* (culture bridge) existed.

From Ethnology to Prehistoric Archaeology

Larger syntheses of universal history that depended on these methodological principles were published by Fathers Wilhelm Schmidt (1868–1954) and Wilhelm Koppers (1886–1961), the main representatives of the so-called Vienna school. Both were members of the Catholic monastic order Societas Verbi Divini (Divine Word Missionaries). Because the Societas Verbi Divini had representatives all over the world, Schmidt and Koppers were able to use cross-cultural data collected by members of their order. Their ideas were carried on by the prehistorian Oswald Menghin (1888–1973), who in his *Weltgeschichte der Steinzeit* (World History of the Stone Age), from 1931, aimed to prove the validity of the historical reconstructions of Schmidt and Koppers by reference to archaeology. He connected special complexes of prehistoric material with special culture circles on a worldwide scale.

Methodologically, Menghin relied on the work of the German prehistorian Gustaf Kossinna (1858–1931), who parallel to and independently of Graebner had developed a concept of archaeological culture areas (*Kulturprovinzen*). For Kossinna, spatially delimited "archaeological cultures" represented ancient peoples, like the Germans or Celts.

Despite the strong nationalistic and even racist undertones in his writing, Kossinna's ideas were later introduced to the Anglophone world by the prehistorian V. Gordon Childe (1892–1957), who in his syntheses of Old World archaeology combined elements of diffusionistic and evolutionistic thinking. Contrary to Kossinna, Childe promoted the idea of *ex oriente lux* ("light from the East"). He believed that the early civilizations of Western Asia and Egypt had a deep influence on the prehistoric cultures of Europe. The central motive in his book *The Dawn of European Civilization* (1925) is the inspiration of European barbarism by Oriental civilization. But, contrary to other diffusionists, Childe always emphasized the creative way in which innovations had been adapted in new contexts.

For Childe, no contradiction exists between evolution and diffusion. Diffusion is not an automatic process comparable to the spread of infectious disease. Instead, he thought of diffusion as possible only when the receiving society has reached a comparable stage of development as the giving society, a point that was made by some of the 19th-century founders of evolutionism, such as Lewis Henry Morgan (1818–1881) and E. B. Tylor (1832–1917).

From "Culture History" to "Ethnohistory"

Unlike archaeologists such as Kossinna, German ethnologists even under the influence of the "volkisch movement" did not adopt the search for ethnic individualities. Instead, their focus of interest rested mainly on "culture" as a reality by itself. The immediate causes of cultural phenomena were thought to be other cultural phenomena. Convergent developments in different cultures were regarded as theoretically possible, but in practice, scholars remained cautious. In case of doubt, they were inclined to think that the relevant historical connections responsible for formal correspondences had not yet been detected.

After 1930—apart from Schmidt and Koppers—most German ethnologists abandoned the ideas of the *Kulturkreislehre*, but they retained a general historical-diffusionist orientation. Thus, "ethnology" continued to be regarded as that part of history that focused on primitive people. In practice, however, scholars were more cautious and avoided larger syntheses. Instead, the focus shifted to smaller regions with good ethnographic documentation. Methodology and source criticism were refined. Consequently, attempts at writing a universal history were replaced by a so-called ethnohistorical approach (*Ethnohistorie*). By reference to literary sources, pictures, oral traditions, as well as objects, ethnohistorians aim to reconstruct cultural change on a local or regional basis.

Hyperdiffusionism

"Hyperdiffusionism" is represented mainly by the work of Grafton Elliot Smith (1871–1937) and that of his pupil William James Perry (1869–1949). Neither were anthropologists or archaeologists. Smith was an anatomist who in 1900 took the Chair of Anatomy at the Government Medical School at Cairo, where he extensively studied prehistoric and historic skeletal materials. Later, he returned to England, where he held chairs at Manchester and at University College London. Two things most interested Smith: (1) mummification and (2) megalithic monuments. Smith became obsessed with the idea that the pyramids and mastabas of ancient Egypt were the prototypes of the megalithic monuments found all over the world. He could not believe that mummification and megalithic architecture could have been invented more than once. So he concluded that both practices had diffused from ancient Egypt all over the world. Perry, professor of comparative religion at the University of Manchester, used ethnographic data to elaborate these ideas. Thus, Smith and Perry saw small groups of people setting out, mainly by sea, from Egypt and colonizing and civilizing the world. Unlike the German diffusionists, the hyperdiffusionists did not care very much about method but tried to make all the historical facts fit their theory.

Today, scholars agree that, since human minds tend to work in a similar manner regardless of context, many cultural innovations, such as agriculture, monumental architecture, and writing, probably developed independently in various parts of the world. To amateur archaeologists all over the world, on the other hand, hyperdiffusionism still remains attractive mainly due to the simple explanations it offers for cultural change. For example, the Norwegian adventurer Thor Heyerdahl (1914–2002) gained huge popular and commercial success by sailing from Peru to Easter Island on an Inca-style raft to prove that Polynesia could have been settled from South America and by crossing the Atlantic Ocean on an Egyptian-style raft to prove the Egyptian origins of a pre-Columbian civilization.

Diffusionism in America

Diffusionism in America was centered on the "culture area" concept. The term refers to relatively small geographical regions containing the contiguous distribution of similar cultural elements. It was first used by O. T. Mason, who identified 18 American culture areas. His ideas were elaborated by scholars such as Alfred Kroeber, Robert Lowie, and Clark Wissler (1870–1947). In *The American Indian* (1917), Wissler explored the regional clustering of cultural traits and the relation between culture and the physical environment. As a curator at the American Museum of Natural History in New York City, Wissler arranged collections and exhibits according to this spatial classification.

An important difference with the German diffusionists is that in Wissler's culture area concept the distribution of cultural traits is primarily seen as the result of an adaptation to environmental conditions. This idea became important to much subsequent anthropological and archaeological research in America, especially the New Archaeology founded in the 1960s by Lewis Binford (1931–2011). At the same time, Binford and his school criticized diffusionists for their atomistic view of culture—the idea of diffusion was replaced in European archaeology by systems thinking as represented, for example, in Colin Renfrew's "culture process model." Despite an interest in spatial patterns, the emphasis of the culture process model was on local evolution in explaining cultural change. In the 1990s, scholars like Andrew Sherratt (1946–2006) developed the idea of "punctuation," or rapid, revolutionary change, and the associated notion of "centricity," a concept that includes the idea of diffusion. More recently, the poststructuralist rediscovery of the significance of materiality and interculturality has opened up new perspectives for dealing with such issues, without repeating the earlier mistakes.

The flaws of the diffusionist approaches consisted, above all, in the object-like approach toward culture, an obsession with origins, and the concentration on abstract "influences" and "flows" of cultural traits. But combined with the more recent concepts of agency and of practice, these flaws may be overcome. They may help direct our interest to the actual contextualization of cultural forms and to possible shifts of meaning.

Ulrich Veit

See also Binford, Lewis R.; Cultural Transmission; Culture Area Approach; Ethnohistory; Frobenius, Leo; Graebner, Fritz; Historical Particularism; Kroeber, Alfred L.; Lowie, Robert; Smith, Grafton Elliot; Wallerstein, Immanuel

Further Readings

Ankermann, B. (1905). Kulturkreise und kulturschichten in Afrika [Culture circles and culture strata in Africa]. *Zeitschrift für Ethnologie, 37*, 54–90.

Binford, L. R., & Binford, S. R. (1968). *New perspectives in archaeology*. Chicago, IL: Aldine.

Childe, V. G. (1957). *The dawn of European civilization* (6th ed.). London, UK: Routledge & Kegan Paul. (Original work published 1925)

Daniel, G. (1964). *The idea of prehistory*. Harmondsworth, UK: Penguin Books.

Graebner, F. (1905). Kulturkreise und kulturschichten in Ozeanien [Culture circles and culture strata in Oceania]. *Zeitschrift für Ethnologie, 37*, 28–53.

———. (1911). *Methode der ethnologie* [The method of ethnology] (Kulturgeschichtliche Bibliothek, Series 1, Vol. 1). Heidelberg, Germany: Winter.

Kroeber, A. L. (1940). Stimulus diffusion. *American Anthropologist, 42*(1), 1–20.

Menghin, O. (1931). *Weltgeschichte der steinzeit* [World history of the stone age]. Vienna, Austria: Schroll.

Schmidt, W., & Koppers, W. (1937). *Handbuch der methode der kulturhistorischen ethnologie* [Handbook on the method of the culture-historical ethnology]. Münster, Germany: Aschendorff.

Sherratt, A. G. (1997). Climatic cycles and behavioral revolutions: The emergence of modern humans and the beginning of farming. *Antiquity, 71*, 271–287.

Wissler, C. (1917). *The American Indian: An introduction to the anthropology of the New World*. New York, NY: Oxford University Press.

DISCOURSE THEORY

Discourse theory denotes broadly the study of aspects of language and communication distinct from linguistic structure. Most theories of discourse nonetheless examine the relation of language to structure. In fact, during the 20th century, many debates in anthropology, and the social and human sciences more generally, centered on the relation between the discursive and structural aspects of social life. Through these debates, and especially through the scholarship that critiqued structural anthropology and linguistics, poststructural approaches to discourse have taken root in anthropological theory and methodology. Poststructuralist approaches continue to influence the trajectories of anthropological thinking about discourse. This entry first describes the structuralist account of signs, associated especially with Ferdinand de Saussure, and then recaps some poststructuralist critiques. The critiques reviewed are from influential French theorists, and then from the linguistic anthropological tradition that maintains closer ties to linguistic structuralism.

Discourse in Structural Linguistic Theory

Until the 1980s, the term *discourse* was used in anthropology with the same meaning common in structural linguistic analysis. Linguistic theory takes the sentence as the limit of grammatical relations and, in contrast, uses discourse to denote the manner in which words, expressions, and sentences are put to use in a particular context to produce meaningful communicative behavior. "Sentences" here are understood as abstracted from their context, while the use of linguistic units in context is generally called an "utterance." The utterance can be a single word or a sentence long, or a very long, complex communicative form, like a whole book. Discourse utterances are understood to have principles of coherence that are distinct from the grammatical coherence of sentences. Understanding how an utterance coheres involves considering how the parts of an utterance relate to each other and the context. In linguistics, the terms *discourse analysis* or *discourse function* are generally used for these issues.

The distinction between grammatical sentence and discourse utterance is based on the highly influential work of the Swiss linguist Ferdinand de Saussure. Saussure's final courses were published posthumously by his students in 1916 as the *Cours de linguistique générale* (*Course in General Linguistics*). These lectures are still considered essential for understanding language as an abstract structure (*langue* in French), including the symbolic quality of producing meaning. Saussure distinguished the study of linguistic structure from speaking in context that uses the signs of language (*parole* in French). The theoretical dualism of *langue* and *parole* (or structure and use) is one of many dualisms that were then incorporated into anthropology's interpretation of structuralism. Another of Saussure's important dualisms is the idea that, when abstracted from contexts of use, a language can be described as a stable and closed system, a state that exists at a single point in time or "synchrony." Synchrony is opposed to "diachrony"—that is, the changes that happen to that language between different synchronic states. For Saussure, modeling a language's structure as a synchronic system is an analytic construct. He characterized this construct as "virtual," meaning this state does not exist in sociohistorical reality, where change and variation are constant.

A final important dualism for Saussure was that linguistic structure is a bipartite system of differences, with basic units he called signs. Each sign involves a form, or signifier, and a related concept, or signified. The English phonic form *tree* is an example of a signifier, while its signified is found by seeing how this form functions in sentences (not in utterances). In linguistic analysis, the signified is very different from a dictionary definition of a word. In fact, in this abstract analysis, the signified is discovered by finding the difference marked by the sign, in its ability to combine with other forms. For instance, the signified of "tree" might be roughly expressed as "common noun, count noun, inanimate," and so on. Saussure was interested in debunking various theories that posited that signifiers were somehow naturally related or determined by what they signified, which led him to emphasize that the relation between signifier and signified is "arbitrary." By "arbitrary," he meant that the system of differences between signifier and signified is entirely a social convention, one that works because there is a group of speakers that continue to use it in their daily discourse. Due to the complexity of the system, Saussure doubted that the group of speakers could actually gain awareness of it in such a way as to change it intentionally. In his analytical construct, human intentionality and agency, like concrete events of interaction (*parole*), remained outside the description of linguistic structure proper. This way of constructing the object of linguistics meant that discourse remained a residual or external phenomenon.

In anthropology, the question has been whether these dualistic assumptions for modeling a synchronic structure can be applied to the study of other salient cultural patterns, including discursive ones. Saussure himself thought that his theory of abstract *langue* could be a model for studying utterances. Most famously, in the mid-20th century, Claude Lévi-Strauss applied some of Saussure's methodology to analyze myth (as well as to analyze kinship). With myth, Lévi-Strauss recognized that he was dealing with an object distinct from *langue*, and yet he sought to set out the basic units of myth as a system of differences. Such studies became a touchstone for structural anthropology. An early critic of this structural anthropology was Clifford Geertz, who sought to consider "symbols" and their signification within a thicker description of action in context. Although Geertz did not explicitly theorize "discourse," in a famous article on the Balinese cockfight, he argued for interpreting cultural performances like scholars view a text (like a work of literature). This symbolic anthropology came just as the poststructural notion of discourse was to introduce a wholesale critique of how structuralism posited the relation between *langue* and *parole*. Geertz's arguments about symbols were themselves critiqued by others using French poststructural theories of discourse, notably Talal Asad, for insufficient attention to power and for circumscribing the symbolic realm of culture to a limited set of phenomena. Geertz's approach to text was also critiqued by linguistic anthropologists, notably in a book called *Natural Histories of Discourse* (1996), for ignoring cultural notions of how texts are constituted and how such notions are related to discursive interaction and language.

Poststructuralist Approaches to Discourse

Part of the goal of poststructuralist critiques and the turn to writing about "discourse" instead of "language" (as a structure) is to develop an approach to communicative practice that does not assume that the speaker, or speaking subject, is autonomous and self-constituting. In discourse theory, attributing many voices to social groups and even individuals, and arguing that these voices are constituted socially, seeks to replace the premise that speakers have an interior self from which they draw their intentions, and that this self is fully constituted prior to the act of communication. This premise is often traced back to philosophical traditions associated with René Descartes and Immanuel Kant, among others. In such philosophies, language could provide a model of the rationality (or logos) that distinguishes humanity from other beings.

Structuralism, including its linguistic and anthropological versions, already moved away from some of these assumptions by suggesting that communication is shaped by a social rather than an individual phenomenon, namely, the system of *langue*. However, structuralism also reiterates other assumptions, by treating an abstract system as the key rationality to understanding the discursive production of meaning. Furthermore, structuralism tends to depict this abstract system as homogeneous across the social or cultural group under study.

In the 20th century, several critiques of these structuralist assumptions took root. Poststructuralist critiques generally question what allows sign systems to exist, and emphasize a greater degree of heterogeneity in how meaning is produced. They promote a view of speakers or participants not solely as initiators but also as the results of discourse. Such a change in analytic perspective has led to new theories of power and polity, as well as to new discussions of how various social categories, like gender, sexuality, race, ethnicity, and class, become palpable in and through discourse. In anthropology, French poststructuralism and linguistic anthropology have both been used to tap into such changes in the study of discourse.

Perhaps the scholar with the greatest influence on anthropological theories of discourse is the French poststructuralist philosopher and historian Michel Foucault. Foucault's work explores how discourse is embedded in sites of knowledge production and helps produce subjects. He argues against conceiving of the history of knowledge-production as a result of the actions of scientists and scholars. He insists instead that subjects are an effect of discourse and that they are produced in a set of historically coalescing sites, or discursive formations. This approach underlies Foucault's concept of power. He moves away from stating that power is in the hands of a sociological group (e.g., economic or political elites) or a social organization (e.g., the police). Instead, he understands power as diffuse, stabilized through the discursive formation of knowing subjects and their known objects. Probably his most famous example is the confession, a discursive practice where a person must tell all his or her transgressions to a confessor; both confessor and confessing subject are formed in the act of giving the confession. The confession as a type of communicative act is very important to Foucault's theory of contemporary sexuality. Although the confession started as a religious institution, according to Foucault, it was dispersed, and now versions are found in psychological and medical institutions, as well as at other powerful sites. This dispersion creates ever more situations where speakers must produce such knowledge of themselves. Foucault posited that the increasing discourse about sexuality in the 19th century was part of this process of disseminating the confession as a way of knowing ourselves as sexual subjects.

The confession is an example of what Foucault calls, in *The Archaeology of Knowledge* (*L'Archéologie du Savoir*, 1969, in French), a "statement." In explaining the statement, Foucault shows that his concept of discourse is developed under a structuralist influence. Just as Saussure sought to produce the concept of *langue* by setting out certain methodological premises (like the abstraction from context and synchrony), Foucault also seeks to describe discourse as an analytic construct. Roughly, a statement is a repeated kind of act that relates subjects and objects, and it can be detected (not unlike *langue*) by looking for regularities in discourse across multiple kinds of powerful institutions. In *The Order of Things* (*Les Mots et les Choses: Une Archéologie des Sciences Humaines*, 1966, in French), for example, he finds such regularities in the way three fields of knowledge—(1) grammar, (2) natural history, and (3) political economy—describe and classify their objects in the emergence of the human sciences. Even though these fields of knowledge do not necessarily refer to each other explicitly, the forms of the statements made within them are comparable. Foucault is then interested to show the rules that allow for the formation of a statement—that is, what can be said, what cannot be said, who can and cannot do the saying, and so forth. Eschewing narrating history as cause and effect, his description produces the effect of making his object seem outside specific events, in ways that are analogous to the description of *langue*.

Another influential French poststructuralist, whose impact on anthropology is more muted, is the philosopher Jacques Derrida. He critiques Saussure's structuralism by questioning the stability of the meaning of a sign, given that it is always available for use in another event of communication. Derrida calls the signifier's unstable quality *iterability*, by which he refers to the impossibility of establishing what is both unique about a singular use of a sign and the potential for its repetition. His methodology for producing an analysis of the inherent instability of signs is called deconstruction, and it is widely influential in arguments about why a text can never achieve a truly stable meaning. Derrida is also influential in debates about *performativity*—that is, the theory associated with the philosopher John Austin that an utterance does not simply reflect a preexisting world but actually helps create social worlds.

A final influential French poststructuralist is the anthropologist and sociologist Pierre Bourdieu. He famously critiqued the structuralist emphasis on communicative behavior that can be described by formal rules, which he felt gave way to a misrecognition of the social fields that regulate discursive practice. Preferring to speak of embodied dispositions rather than rules, Bourdieu emphasized the social process by which a standard language arises, conferring legitimacy on the actors who can speak it, while excluding others. Despite this social process of producing legitimacy, Bourdieu described how many powerful social institutions, and especially educational institutions, misrecognize the standard as the "correct" or "efficient" way of speaking rather than a variety of speaking that is associated with powerful speakers.

The work of Foucault, Derrida, and Bourdieu—and others of their time—has affected the work of many anthropologists interested in discourse. This work helps anchor anthropological approaches to discursive phenomena and enables an examination of shifting and complex signifiers in their fields of communicative practice.

Another tradition of studying discourse in anthropology is linguistic anthropology, which generally maintains a much closer dialogue with linguistic structuralism. Sometimes also engaging with French theories, linguistic anthropology has produced its own version of poststructuralism, attempting to both integrate and question the assumptions of Saussure's theory of *langue*. Much of this critique has been developed through a careful reinterpretation of the writings of the Russian literary critic and philosopher Mikhail Bakhtin, as well as a reevaluation of sign relations in light of the work of the American philosopher Charles S. Peirce.

Prior to the Second World War, in American cultural anthropology, linguistics was seen as a key but separate area of the study of humanity. The program for the study of language was initiated by Franz Boas and his students, who developed ideas about structure similar to Saussure's. Boas's students were generally occupied with the description of lesser studied languages, especially those of the Indigenous peoples of the Americas. In these investigations, the Boasians also contributed to the question of how linguistic structure can bias perception of the world. Such a bias was linked to what Boas called "secondary rationalizations"—that is, native explanations that are insufficient to account for linguistic (or other) facts. Apart from this, they attended to discourse mostly through producing collections of texts, such as myths.

After World War II, criticism of the basic assumptions of linguistics led to new directions within linguistic anthropology. Quantitative sociolinguistics, associated especially with William Labov, an American linguist, studied the demographic variation in speaking across populations, especially in industrialized and postindustrialized societies. This school continues to challenge the idea of a unified grammar within a "language," by showing the complex heterogeneity of social and regional dialects that direct structural change. At the border of sociology and anthropology, Erving Goffman helped initiate the study of the small-scale dynamics of interpersonal interaction. His work explores how participants produce particular social identities, and even shift between identities, as they interact with one another. From within anthropology, Dell Hymes and John Gumperz spearheaded a cross-cultural examination of how utterances are shaped by rules different from those of grammar, a project that focused attention on the relation of discourse to its context. In this vein, Michael Silverstein introduced the tripartite sign theory of Peirce as the basis for the study of language, which folds into it insights developed under Saussure's bipartite theory of signs, which points or shows contiguity to its object. This theory has been enormously influential in reframing the study of how signifiers relate to one another and to their context. The study initiated by these postwar figures has led to a careful analysis of transcripts of discursive interaction, both everyday and ritual, as a means to deepening our understanding of how signs function.

These traditions point to the difficulty of theorizing discourse due to the variation found in language use, and in the social and cultural conditions that inform context. Once linguistic structure or analogous theories are shown to be insufficient to account for the "structures" found in the empirical analysis of discourse, the questions that emerge are what stabilizes the sign relation and how to account for the social variation in the use of signs. Two significant trends in linguistic anthropology seek to answer these questions and undermine basic structuralist dualisms. First, linguistic anthropologists consider how rationalizations about language,

called language ideologies, constitute one means by which conscious, directed social projects affect sign relations. No group of speakers is without ideologies about how they and others speak, and these ideas mediate social relations that are crystallized and transformed through language use. This reflexive attention to signs can lead to attempts by powerful organizations to control the parameters of meaning, as (to draw on the above example from Bourdieu) in the dissemination of a prestigious linguistic standard through schooling. Linguistic anthropological studies of nationalism, gender, race, and other social categories consistently show the importance of language ideologies in the functioning of institutions. Structuralist dualisms like *langue* and *parole*, or language structure and use, are thus shown to be in relation with a third dimension, ideology. These studies also challenge Saussure's notion that structure remains out of the realm of conscious social action. Many have shown, for example, that grammatical elements of languages—although imperfectly understood by speakers—have nonetheless changed along grooves that are shaped by consciousness. A brief example is the elimination of the informal "thou"/formal "ye" distinction for singular referents that once was found in England, which functioned in parallel ways to the French *tu/vous* or, to a lesser extent, the Spanish *tú/Usted*. As Silverstein discusses, this distinction was ended in part due to 17th-century religious movements that emphasized equality, including in forms of address. The leaders of these movements argued that using the plural form "ye" for a single referent was a category mistake. This argument can be shown to be a language ideology that misinterprets the grammatical categories of person as well as person address in discourse. Yet partially under influence of this ideology, and the shifts in practices undertaken by its adherents, the distinction was eliminated.

A second trend in linguistic anthropology is the broadening use of Bakhtin's framework for studying sociolinguistic variation, interdiscursive relations between utterances, and the social qualities of discursive coherence (or textuality). Bakhtin criticizes Saussure for starting the analysis of language with the abstract sentence rather than with the concrete event of interaction, the utterance. By reversing this starting point, Bakhtin moves toward a social analysis of form and function. For Bakhtin, what enables an utterance to appear coherent is not only the structural aspect (as with grammar) but also the way in which the utterance brings together participants in an activity. A second important contribution from Bakhtin is that participants never only speak as a single unique self; rather, they always draw on, invoke, and position their discourse in terms of sociolinguistic variation. For example, to speak in highly formal English (using "big words") in the middle of a casual conversation with friends might be construed as being pretentious, because the varieties of formal English bring to mind the stuffy contexts where that register is typically used (e.g., in the university or in law courts). Participants perceive and respond to discourse as signaling certain types of people from the sociolinguistic world of "voices" with which they are familiar, and this allows them to make sense of the discourse. This approach frames current research on register, style, genre, and textuality.

The past 100 years have seen a decided shift in anthropological theories of language and communication, from frameworks that produce a formal analysis of linguistic structure to an emphasis on social analysis of the participants or subjects that are constituted through discourse. Many of the insights generated in this shift are a product of the wide-ranging critique about the extent to which structuralist models could account for the regular patterns or norms of discourse in social life. Debates still continue on how best to integrate structuralist insights, if at all, and how best to describe the many ways discourse can index and thus produce the categories of subjects and objects that make up our shifting social worlds.

Alejandro I. Paz

See also Bakhtin, Mikhail M.; Bourdieu, Pierre; Derrida, Jacques; Foucault, Michel; Goffman, Erving; Gumperz, John J.; Hymes, Dell; Labov, William; Lévi-Strauss, Claude; Poststructuralism; Saussure, Ferdinand de; Structuralism

Further Readings

Dreyfus, H. L., & Rabinow, P. (1982). *Michel Foucault: Beyond structuralism and hermeneutics*. Brighton, UK: Harvester.

Hanks, W. F. (1989). Text and textuality. *Annual Review of Anthropology, 18*, 95–127.

Morris, R. C. (2007). Legacies of Derrida: Anthropology. *Annual Review of Anthropology, 36*, 355–389.

Schieffelin, B., Woolard, K. A., & Kroskrity, P. V. (Eds.). (1998). *Language ideologies: Practice and theory.* New York, NY: Oxford University Press.

Silverstein, M., & Urban, G. (Eds.). (1996). *Natural histories of discourse*. Chicago, IL: University of Chicago Press.

Todorov, T. (1984). *Mikhail Bakhtin: The dialogical principle* (W. Godzich, Trans.). Minneapolis: University of Minnesota Press.

DOUGLAS, MARY

Mary Tew Douglas (1921–2007), the well-known British social anthropologist, contributed widely to 20th-century anthropology, the social sciences, and the humanities, including African ethnology, the anthropology of diverse social/religious rituals, symbols and food taboos, and social-moral solidarity–oriented critiques of modern economics, politics, and risk-blame issues in mass societies. While her "cultural theory" tackled such concerns, Douglas also offered distinct anthropological interpretations of Old Testament texts.

Early Influences and Education

Margaret Mary Tew at birth, Douglas was born on March 25, 1921, in San Remo, Italy, as the first child of Phyllis Margaret Twomey and Gilbert Charles Tew, employed in the Indian Civil Service in Burma. Closer to her mother and maternal grandfather, Douglas, an English Catholic of part-Irish descent, attended the Sacred Heart Convent in Roehampton (southwest London) for secondary education as a boarder on scholarship. Douglas was an outstanding student, and her Catholic convent girlhood was to have a deep, lifelong influence on the anthropologist's intellectual convictions and scholarly trajectories. The convent life, hierarchical, committed, and closely rule governed, had awarded the teenage girl a sense of belonging and security, albeit within a secluded women's world. Familiar with both the quick rewards and the censures from the church authorities in a minutely ordered daily life, Douglas grew up mostly protected from the harsher surrounding world.

After leaving the convent at her grandmother's suggestion, Douglas spent 6 months in Paris getting a *Diplôme de civilization française* at the Sorbonne in 1938. On return, she passed her Oxford entrance examinations to study for her BSc in philosophy, economics, and politics and rendered war service during 1943–1947 in the British Colonial Office. She had come in contact there with anthropologists. Intrigued, she returned to Oxford in 1946, and after completing a conversion course, she registered for a doctorate in anthropology in 1949. Impressed by its leading light, E. E. Evans-Pritchard, and thus Émile Durkheim, Douglas took to the dominant intellectual ethos of diverse Oxford anthropologists of the 1940s, including Franz Steiner and M. N. Srinivas. Though Douglas remained largely silent about her early struggles to reconcile Catholicism with anthropology, she nevertheless remained anchored lifelong in her Catholic upbringing as surely as she was intellectually rooted in anthropology.

As a doctoral student, Douglas conducted her first extended anthropological fieldwork (1949–1951, and 1953) among the Lele in Belgian Congo (now the Democratic Republic of Congo) and was awarded her DPhil in 1952 on the monograph *A Study of Social Organization of the Lele of Kasai* (published in 1963). She married James A. T. Douglas, a Catholic and a policy researcher for the Conservative Party, in 1951.

Academic Profile

Douglas taught anthropology at the University College, London, from 1951 to 1977 and was made professor of anthropology in 1971. She moved to the United States to work at the Russell Sage Foundation in New York (1977–1981), was at Northwestern University as Avalon Professor of Humanities and Religious Studies during 1981–1985, and was a visiting professor at Princeton University from 1985 to 1989. She returned to London in 1989 and had a distinguished fellowship at the University College in 1994. Though professional honors had come to her late in life, she was elected fellow of the British Academy in 1989, became a Companion of the Order of the British Empire in 1992, and was made a Dame Commander of the Order of the British Empire in 2007.

Douglas's theoretical approach remained firmly grounded in different formations of socioreligious cohesion and in the knowledge, action, and identity "the social" à la Durkheim produces. Evans-Pritchard's important works on Africa, on social structure, religion, and moral accountability, were her early inspiration. An agile, curious mind and a wide-ranging analyst, she pursued her cultural theory by showing how social-moral interconnectivity appeared across all manners of nonmodern, modern, and intramodern human differences, conditions, and issues. Since all thought, for her, was social, her explanations had no room for solipsist self-locations or related philosophical speculations.

The 1950s were the time of Douglas's Africanist phase. While raising her three children (a daughter and two sons) in north London, she published her first paper, "A Form of Polyandry Among the Lele of Kasai," in 1950 and her first ethnographic monograph, *The Lele of Kasai,* in 1963. She accounted for the Lele's lack of hierarchy and authority in terms of their economic backwardness as well as major historical changes in Africa. Notably, Douglas's anthropology had already begun tackling classifications amid the exotic, the anomalous, and the mundane (e.g., raffia cloth being akin to ration coupons) in social symbolic terms.

Major Publications and Contributions

Douglas's most widely known publication is *Purity and Danger: An Analysis of Pollution and Taboo* (1966). Imbibing the Oxford anthropological ethos of the time, especially the influence of the French *Année Sociologique*, it vigorously tackled cultural classifications and their anomalies, illustrating them centrally with the well-known Jewish dietary prohibitions and behavioral norms (as given in Leviticus). This study has long instigated distinct anthropological and comparative religious research initiatives, applications, and critical debates. Exploring comparative social/religious ritual classificatory schemes of purity, pollution and taboos, and related anomalies, Douglas compared the status of pigs for the Jews and of pangolin for the Lele, not only illustrating a cogent anthropological research problem and explanation but also arguing how such a study communicates *across* the us versus them (or the modern and nonmodern) divide. Inspired by Robertson Smith's and Evans-Pritchard's approaches to the study of the religious, she sought to explicate the deeply embedded religious symbolic classificatory schemes and anomalies in terms of the surrounding socially systemic, culturally deeply symbolic, and ritually routinely evident issues.

The esoteric, the anomalous, and even the most mundane were thus rendered socially meaningful. Even dirt carried its social framing; it is not an isolated event but rather a part of a cultural system. Douglas incorporated this distinct approach, one way or another, in all her subsequent major research studies, rendering major religious, ritual, cultural, and modern economic, philosophical, and political problems in their crucial *social* forms, forces, and explanations. This was so whether it was a risk-and-blame issue or the deciphering of borders, fences, and boundaries between, for example, dirt and holiness; favored and tabooed foods; impurity, hygiene, and purity; and economic-rational and social ritual consumption patterns.

Douglas's next major publication, *Natural Symbols* (two editions, 1970 and 1973), launched the signature grid and group comparative sociological method for constructing her cultural theory, influenced by the work of Basil Bernstein, a sociologist of education: *grid* stood for the rules that relate one person to others in an ego-centered basis, and *group* drew on a bounded social unit. Her book passionately argued for the importance of ritual to social life, underscoring the larger deductive cultural axiom that rendered man into a ritual animal. Douglas did so with an implied allusion to the Bog Irish labor class in London. She did so to show how social cohesion required both modality (local community) and sodality (specialized, nonlocal associations). Similarly, if the book dealt comparatively with relevant African (often her Lele) materials, it also took on the modern Western socioreligious debates of the 1960s, arguing distinctly against the antiritual, individualistic trends. Douglas argued that modern anthropology must address the condition of humans in common. In doing so, she perhaps also reflected her Catholic inspiration. Widely read and reviewed, if often critically by anthropologists, *Natural Symbols* raised lasting major issues. They were taken up again in *How Institutions Think* (1986), for showing better how indexes of social cohesion and institutional accountability interrelated in social life (see below).

Douglas as an engaging essayist was in evidence in *Implicit Meanings: Essays in Anthropology* (1975). Here, she argued not only that knowledge was a product of social behavior but also that meanings closely depended on interpreting social contexts and sociological classifications. Widening her circle of readers, she tackled diverse cultural classifications, showing how they were not as much about arid logic as about culturally and religiously constituted classificatory categories, groups (e.g., the Israelites) and their meaning-making rituals, boundaries, and relationships. Illustratively, whether it was the animals of the land, air, or water or food in distinctly well-knit groups, a congruent ritual-religious-symbolic "calculus" appeared to regulate the borders, the boundaries, and the outside. For Levites in the Promised Land, such a social ritual calculus ran through the livestock, foods, meals, and people.

Douglas moved to the United States around this time. As noted earlier, she was at the Russell Sage Foundation, New York, during 1977–1981 and in the United States until 1989. She published prolifically, beginning with establishing a social basis for consumption theory in economics and simultaneously writing on foods, meal structures, food ways and habits, and food problems. She occasionally commented on food policy–related issues and participated in activities of the emerging anthropology of food subspecialty. Although food was not her full-time research topic, her related publications had an impact, whether it was her 1972 "Deciphering a Meal" or 1974 "Taking the Biscuit: The Structure of British Meals" (with Michael Nicod), or her 1984 studies of "high or low culinary complexity" in American communities.

Douglas's *The World of Goods: Towards an Anthropology of Consumption* (1978), written in collaboration with Baron Isherwood, an econometrician, explicated what buying, and buying and sharing meant to people in widely different economic systems. An anthropological critique of neoclassical economics, it also criticized anthropology's blinders and biases against mainstream economics. The book, representing economic anthropology for many, showed how goods socially rank, include, or exclude people; how they identify; and how they, consciously or not, always socially communicate, interrelating different social groups, near and distant. To understand consumption in this social way is to open up the rational decision-making individual of neoclassical economics. It is also to get into the black box of economics—how human social values and tastes influence/control consumption and how people consuming goods enter a ritual process of connecting with other people through things. Here, spending, sharing, and saving appeared against needs, wants, and wishes, expanding on the social ritual cultural contexts, tastes, and meanings the goods forge as they course through families and communities. The consumption rituals, she argued, required wider sharing even in industrial societies, including the poor, emphasizing once again her Catholic, collective we.

Risk and Culture (1982) concerned a research project on American environmental and cultural issues, done in collaboration with Aaron Wildavsky, an American political scientist. Tackling cultural perceptions of environmental risk amid American environmental politics, Douglas explicitly expanded on her cultural theory, employing her style of both analyses and syntheses around identified exemplary social forms. She argued that risk perception in any society turned on some basic social forms and closely related institutions. In American culture, for example, social "hierarchy, frontiers and individualism" identified environmental risks and controlled their dynamics for most Americans. Thus, the prevalent American cultural notions of pollution and danger explained risks far more than did the technical probabilistic chance theory of risk analysts.

Dangers and risks always entail cultural biases, while the social blame and accountability issues are framed by a society's self-image, and its center, borders, and peripheries. Risks reveal not simply the roles of certain and uncertain knowledge but also how the forces of strengthening social cohesion and its hierarchies (e.g., bureaucracies) intersect with the individualist options (e.g., markets) and related contestations. Engaging such social, economic, and political classifiers, Douglas developed a "cultural theory" showing how culture is a way of social thinking that draws "the social environment systematically into the picture of individual choices." She continued her risk and culture studies in *Risk Acceptability According to the Social Sciences* (1985) and *Risk and Blame: Essays in Cultural Theory* (1992). Her sparkling essays in *Risk and Blame*, whether on witchcraft, stigmas, the historical Jesus, a credible biosphere, women priests, or even the Swedish and British trade unions, creatively argued how social institutions, groups, symbolic statements, and individual positions meaningfully intersected, explicating the mundane, anomalous, and profound.

Douglas's *How Institutions Think* (1986), while refining the operation of the strong/weak grid group control markers of *Natural Symbols*, examined modern Western institutions for their social assumptions, debates, and problems, alongside the implied Judeo-Christian values and worldview. The ambiguities were better identified, diagrammed, and visualized against the gradation of social coherence, especially with a socially inclusive and morally sharper focus. Thus, for instance, Douglas specifically addressed the ideas and issues of justice, solidarity, and collective provision for individual needs in modern societies, which were very often critical of social control.

Still, as Clifford Geertz (1987) remarked, Douglas vacillated "between hard and soft versions of Durkheimian sociologism" particularly as individuals, social conditions, thoughts, and institutions interpenetrate the mass societies (p. 36). A similar question was at the center in *Missing Persons* (1998), a book Douglas wrote with Steven Ney on the sociological critique of economic personhood, or *Homo economicus*, in modern economics. Criticizing the solipsist self and any objectivity framing such a person, Douglas had argued for reinstating the social person in economic rationality by letting cultural bias and open political dissent play their due roles, notwithstanding the sway of modern economic rationality centered on the individual.

On the Biblical Studies

A focused interest in an anthropological reading and explication of selected biblical texts distinctly engaged Douglas during her last decade. Started in *Purity and Danger*, she returned to the study of the Old Testament. Her three main studies of the Old Testament were (1) *In the Wilderness: The Doctrine of Defilement in the Book of Numbers* (1993), (2) *Leviticus as Literature* (1999), and (3) *Jacobs Tears: The Priestley Work of Reconciliation* (2004). Approaching anthropologically, she explicated the selected biblical texts for what was often textually indecipherable and taxonomically anomalous or redundant to biblical scholars. Douglas's cultural theory helped explicate the "meaning structures" hidden in the texts behind the several anomalous classifications and reclassifications, while also deciphering some exclusive or inclusive liberal moral meanings and messages. Her first two biblical publications attracted wide attention in the biblical study circles.

In *In the Wilderness*, for instance, Douglas showed how the poet of *The Book of Numbers* attempted to explain through ring composition how a local community (modality) must cohere with specialized, nonlocal social forms (sodality), even in Jerusalem ca. 500 BCE. The book in its modern rendering underscored not only a liberal theology of the biblical texts but also a commentary on today's world split by steep inequalities, religious fanaticism, and fragile nation-states. A similar inclusive, timely message emerged in Douglas's interpretation of *Jacob's Tears*, showing how a political and religious protest against Judah's exclusionary politics was integral to the editors of Pentateuch, stressing the inclusion of all the descendants of Jacob, including the sons of Joseph. As *Leviticus as Literature* identified the literary merits; it uncovered structural plots of the religious text, corresponding to the three parts of the desert tabernacle. Such a new, inclusive reading transformed not only the reading of purity-impurity laws but also the message that all God's creatures command the same respect, emphasizing justice and compassion.

Douglas's last publication, *Thinking in Circles: An Essay on Ring Composition* (2007), focused on figuring out the ancient, antique texts written in a circular rather than a linear pattern, putting the central meaning in the middle of the text. Found not only in the Bible but also in texts from Egypt, China, Greece, and Russia, she asked, does this style of writing derive from the way the human brain works?

Legacy: Centering the Social-Moral for Modernist Anthropology

Douglas occupies a distinct position in 20th-century anthropology. Creatively pursuing Durkheim and her Oxford guru Evans-Pritchard, she viewed undiminished foundational roles of the social, moral, and religious in all human, including modern, life. She repeatedly expanded and refined her cultural theory to be morally inclusive of and politically and economically responsive to the diverse, unequal, restive world. In such a pursuit, her Catholic upbringing and conservative modernist Western self-location mutually extended each other. Her studies examined modern structures of self, society, economics, risks, and politics, showing how different forms of knowledge arose from—and returned to—distinct "archetypical forms" of religious moral reasoning and sociality, enriching them in the process. For her, there was no cognition, context, agency, meaning, or knowledge system totally independent of foundational sociality. Her anthropological modernism and humanism thus rested on inclusive moral, religious, and sociological imagination. Her writings, particularly the essays, showed how a dazzling, challenging intellect was at work.

Douglas's legacy is distinct in 20th-century anthropology for showing how a woman anthropologist vigorously intertwined her early religious influences into diverse scholarly trajectories. If this seed was firmly planted in *Purity and Danger*—expanding the scope of the anthropological—then there was also no looking back after *Natural Symbols*. All the subsequent modern moral, economic, and political studies, issues, and problems tackled by Douglas had to have her anthropological imprint. Whether she was recognized or not by other anthropologists, even the British, did not detain her. She went about transforming and re-etching in her way the direction and scope of sociocultural anthropological methods, research issues, and interpretations. Thus, a fuller intellectual impact might yet emerge. Douglas, along with Victor Turner, today exerts worldwide influence on anthropological research and teaching, especially when comparative religious/social ritual structures and symbolism are juxtaposed with the modern mind, rationality, and material-technological forces. In addition, Douglas today commands a vigorous and expanding following in comparative religious and in biblical studies.

R. S. Khare

See also Durkheim, Émile; Evans-Pritchard, E. E.; Geertz, Clifford; Oxford University; Symbolic and Interpretive Anthropology; Turner, Victor W.

Further Readings

Douglas, M. (1978). *Purity and danger: An analysis of concepts of pollution and taboo.* London, UK: Routledge. (Original work published 1966)

———. (1986). *How institutions think* (Frank W. Abrams Lectures). London, UK: Routledge.

———. (1994). *Risk and blame: Essays in cultural theory.* London, UK: Routledge.

Fardon, R. (1999). *Mary Douglas: An intellectual biography.* London, UK: Routledge.

Geertz, C. (1987, May 25). The anthropologist at large. *The New Republic*, pp. 36–37.

Richards, P. (2008). Mary Tew Douglas (1921–2007). *American Anthropologist, 110*(3), 404–407.

Du Bois, W. E. B.

William Edward Burghardt (W. E. B.) Du Bois (1868–1963) was one of the most prominent scholar-activists of the 20th century. Born in Great Barrington, Massachusetts, Du Bois became the first African American to receive a PhD from Harvard University. As a scholar, he published numerous influential works and gave lectures around the United States and the world on issues of race and the Black experience. He was also one of the founders of urban sociology, and he had an impact on early anthropologists of color and urban anthropology.

In the seminal book published in 1903, *The Souls of Black Folk*, Du Bois stated that the "problem of the twentieth century is the problem of the color line." More than 100 years later, scholars are still raising questions about the color line—exploring issues of race, lived experience, and social inequality within and across national boundaries. The color line has taken on new meanings in a globalized world, but for Du Bois, the color line represented a Black/White dichotomy of varied experiences of inclusion and exclusion understood by his lived experience and research. His scholarship and activism gave voice to these experiences, with a rallying call for justice and social change.

Du Bois lived during a time when there was a struggle for justice surrounding opportunities, access to resources, and full citizenship. Born in the North, he experienced different racialized laws and realities when he attended college at Fisk University in Nashville, Tennessee. Unlike New England, Fisk represented a new, "Negro world." It was during this time, and later when he was a teacher in Nashville, that Du Bois began to have a fuller understanding of the Southern Black experience. He was not only able to reflect on his early experiences of growing up in integrated schools, where he was in the minority and excelled, but also on the experiences of people around him who were less fortunate. In Tennessee, he witnessed the circumstances that many Black people faced postemancipation. As a teacher, he began to understand firsthand the oppression of Black people and the lingering detrimental effects of slavery.

Much of Du Bois's scholarly work centered on the Black experience, in terms of researching and documenting the lives of Black people in the North and the South based on what he had witnessed and experienced in both contexts. In *The Souls of Black Folk*, Du Bois advanced the idea of African Americans having a double consciousness in the United States—a "twoness"—being an American and a Negro. The idea of double consciousness has been applied cross-culturally to represent being "both/ and" or "bi" in different situations (binational, bicultural, etc.). For Du Bois, the notion of twoness captured the experience of Black people who were coming out of slavery and the Reconstruction and had to navigate different racial terrains.

Du Bois, the "Talented Tenth," and Racial Uplift

Du Bois was part of the Black elite that sought to bring about change—on the intellectual and activist fronts. He was a scholar-activist who called on the "talented tenth" to give voice to the experiences of Black folks and to help bring about radical change in American society. The talented tenth represented a segment of the Black community—of highly educated professional people—who would become leaders in the community. The idea was that these leaders could help "lift" the majority by paving the way, by providing opportunities, and by example. Mary Church Terrell, one of Du Bois's contemporaries, who also helped establish the National Association for the Advancement of Colored People (NAACP), embodied the idea of the talented tenth in her community outreach and work. Terrell was president of the National Association of Colored Women, whose motto was "Lifting as We Climb." The main idea is that everyone could not climb at the same time but those who made it and were successful could give a hand and help lift others to the top. For Du Bois and Terrell, this was necessary to "lift the race." However, Du Bois was criticized by some of his other contemporaries with respect to his idea of using the talented tenth and other positions to "lift the race." Booker T. Washington, for example, became one of Du Bois's most outspoken critics.

While Du Bois and Washington were working to bring about change, they differed in their approaches for racial uplift. Both of their positions seemed to come out of self-reflexivity, with a simultaneous connection to the community. Both men proposed change that grew out of their own personal experiences (Du Bois promoting education and Washington supporting agriculture/trades). In many ways, their experiences set them apart as visionaries and leaders. Both men were "mulatto," or biracial (both of their fathers were White), but their experiences were different. Du Bois was often the only student of color in his classes in New England, but he received tremendous support from his teachers during his school years. Du Bois was born in the North and was never enslaved, while Washington was born into slavery in the South. Washington's autobiography, *Up From Slavery*, examines his life and path to leadership. Over time, Du Bois became associated with the Black elite, and Washington was associated with the masses.

While an undergraduate student at Fisk, Du Bois encountered the Jim Crow laws and came into contact with Black men, women, and children not too far removed from slavery. This was part of a racial awakening for him as he witnessed tremendous social inequality and racism, especially exemplified by lynchings. At the same time, there was the idea of promise (the hope that things would be better) as well as calls for civil rights and change. Based on what he saw and experienced, Du Bois set out to challenge the Jim Crow laws and push forward with a radical agenda for change, including cofounding the NAACP. On the other hand, Washington, the founder of Tuskegee Normal and Industrial Institute (now known as Tuskegee University), suggested that Black people could build on their strengths in agriculture and trade skills. In his Atlanta Compromise speech in 1895, Washington called on Black people to "cast down your buckets where you are." In other words, his vision was based on knowing and understanding the skills that Black people had acquired during slavery. Du Bois charged the talented tenth with helping to bring about change (education, professional jobs, organizations, etc.), while Washington charged people to "go with what they knew" and build from there. Du Bois wanted radical change, and he often critiqued Washington for what he considered to be his accommodation of segregation. The critiques went back and forth. One of Washington's critiques of Du Bois was that he was elitist. It is clear from their speeches and publications that Du Bois and Washington disagreed about the path for Black people in the United States. Both men were highly respected public figures and intellectuals—each with his own "camp" and legacy.

Du Bois: Pan-Africanism, Anthropology, and His Legacy

Over his lifetime, Du Bois was at the forefront of Pan-Africanism, supporting African liberation movements and helping organize several Pan-African Congresses. He was also a member of Alpha Phi Alpha Fraternity, Incorporated (a public service fraternity established at Cornell University in 1906). It was the first intercollegiate Greek-letter organization established for African Americans. While at the NAACP, Du Bois served as editor of *The Crisis* magazine, which gave him a platform to challenge prevalent ideas and to have critical and engaged conversations not only about issues of race but also about other pressing issues of the day.

In addition to *The Souls of Black Folk*, some of his most influential books include *The Philadelphia Negro* (1899), still heralded as one of the first most comprehensive sociological studies of Black people in an urban setting, and *Black Reconstruction in America: 1860–1880* (1935), which provides an in-depth account of the role that Black people played during the Reconstruction following the Civil War. In the book, he discusses relationships, social class and race, societal structures, and some of the challenges of the Reconstruction. Numerous volumes have been published from his essays. Du Bois's scholarship and activism have had an impact on social scientists and historians alike. Faye Harrison (1992) discusses the Du Boisian legacy in anthropology by pointing to vindicationist anthropology and Du Bois's attempt to shed light on and highlight the contributions of Black people in various situations and contexts. Vindicationist scholars work to correct distorted interpretations of the African and African American past and often develop counterpositions. Harrison considers Du Bois to be in that tradition and also considers his work in *The Crisis* as anthropological texts in which he communicates his position not only to a community of scholars but also to the community at large. Much of Du Bois's work is anthropological in scope, and he influenced a number of anthropologists. Harrison identifies the following anthropologists as part of the Du Boisian legacy in African American anthropology: Caroline Bond Day, Irene Diggs, Allison Davis, and St. Clair Drake. Along these same lines, another impact that Du Bois had on anthropology is that of activist anthropology.

In 1906, at the invitation of Du Bois, Franz Boas gave a commencement address at Atlanta University. Du Bois was teaching history there at the time. In *Black Folk Then and Now*, Du Bois reflects on Boas's speech and the awakening he had as a result of what Boas discussed. Boas told the graduates that they did not have to be ashamed of their African past. He then went on to talk about Africa and its history. That speech left a lasting impression on Du Bois. Boas became involved in the NAACP in its early years, and in 1910, he wrote "The Real Race Problem" (published in *The Crisis*). Over the course of his life and career, Boas encouraged the study of African and African American culture and corresponded with many Black intellectuals, including Booker T. Washington, Carter G. Woodson, Alain L. Locke, and Zora Neale Hurston, as well as W. E. B. Du Bois, about the study and importance of African American history and culture.

Du Bois was one of the most preeminent scholars and activists of the 20th century. His work is still relevant today, and many anthropologists and other scholars cite his groundbreaking work on the Black experience, social inequality, and social change. Later in life, Du Bois returned to Africa—to Accra, Ghana—where he died while working on an encyclopedia on the African diaspora experience. He is buried in Accra on the grounds of a memorial center named in his honor—The Du Bois Memorial Center for Pan-African Culture.

Kimberly Eison Simmons

See also Boas, Franz; Hurston, Zora Neale

Further Readings

Baker, L. D. (1998). *From savage to Negro: Anthropology and the construction of race, 1986–1954*. Berkeley: University of California Press.

Du Bois, W. E. B. (1899). *The Philadelphia Negro*. Philadelphia: University of Pennsylvania Press.

_____. (1965). *Souls of Black folk: Essays and sketches*. New York, NY: Fawcett. (Original work published 1903)

Harrison, F. V. (1992). The Du Boisian legacy in anthropology. *Critique of Anthropology, 12*(3), 239–260.

Harrison, F. V., & Nonini, D. (1992). Introduction to W. E. B. Du Bois and anthropology. *Critique of Anthropology, 12*(3), 229–237.

Harrison, I. E., & Harrison, F. V. (1998). *African American pioneers in anthropology*. Champaign: University of Illinois Press.

Lewis, D. L. (1994). *W. E. B. Du Bois, 1868–1919: Biography of a race*. New York, NY: Macmillan.

_____. (Ed.). (1995). *W. E. B. Du Bois: A reader*. New York, NY: Macmillan.

_____. (2001). *W. E. B. Du Bois, 1919–1963: The fight for equality and the American century*. New York, NY: Macmillan.

_____. (2009). *W. E. B. Du Bois: A biography*. New York, NY: Henry Holt.

DuBois, Cora

Cora DuBois (1903–1997) became a leading figure in early culture and personality studies and allied fields over a long and rather adventurous career. She also received several awards for her applied work during World War II.

Biography and Major Works

DuBois was born in New York City to the Swiss immigrants Mattie and Jean DuBois. The family then moved to New Jersey, where Jean obtained employment in a chemical company in Perth Amboy. In 1921, DuBois graduated from public high school in Perth Amboy. Interestingly, her first academic attraction appears to have been library science, which she studied at The New York Public Library from 1922 to 1923, before taking a degree in history from Barnard College in 1927. The concern with organization and detail that characterizes library science was to appear in her most important professional contribution.

There was little initial evidence that DuBois would become a major figure in anthropology, as her concentration in history, first a BA at Barnard and then an MA at Columbia, focused on Hellenistic Greece. Not until her senior year at Barnard did she elect a course in anthropology. Franz Boas and Ruth Benedict, two of the major figures in the field, taught that impactive course. Benedict's presence as a prominent woman in this field may have encouraged DuBois to move to California, where she began postgraduate studies in anthropology under Alfred L. Kroeber and Robert Lowie.

Under Kroeber's mentorship, DuBois carried out fieldwork among the Wintu in northern California. She published several articles on the Wintu and two books, *The Feather Cult of the Middle Columbia* (1938) and *The 1870 Ghost Dance* (1939). She received her PhD in cultural anthropology from Berkeley in 1932. Due to the scarcity of academic positions, DuBois remained at Berkeley for 3 years as a research associate. During this period, she appears to have developed an interest in psychoanalysis, which, in 1935, led her to spend 6 months at the Boston Psychopathic Hospital, gaining clinical training and investigating the possibilities of employing a psychoanalytic approach to anthropological materials. These interests led her to the New York School of Psychoanalysis, where, in 1935, she co-taught a course on psychoanalysis and culture with Abram Kardiner. With Kardiner's support and encouragement, and funding from Columbia's Social Science Research Council, DuBois traveled to the island of Alor in the Netherlands East Indies (now Indonesia), to carry out 18 months of fieldwork.

From 1938 through much of 1939, DuBois undertook what can only be regarded as very demanding fieldwork. In addition to withstanding the rigors of a tropical climate, and having little contact with the outside world, DuBois had to learn a language that had never been studied and had no written form. She termed the language *Abui* and mastered it well enough to translate song lyrics, interview a range of informants, and compile several autobiographies. The purpose of her research, in addition to doing ethnography of Alor, was to collect life histories and employ projective materials such as the Rorschach tests, Porteus Maze Test, Draw-a-Person Test, and other devices designed to gain insights into the Alorese personality.

DuBois analyzed these materials, as did Kardiner and Emil Oberholzer, two significant figures in Freudian psychology. The latter was particularly important, as his analysis of the Rorschach material was done blind, while Kardiner dealt with the life histories containing a good deal of cultural information. The result of these efforts was a classic contribution to anthropology and to culture and personality studies, *The People of Alor: A Social-Psychological Study of an East Indian Island*, originally published in 1944 in two volumes comprising more than 600 pages. While some of DuBois's assertions about Alorese parenting have been called into question, the general reception of the book has been quite positive.

Prior to her fieldwork and with the support of Benedict, Kardiner, and others, DuBois obtained a teaching position at Hunter College (1936), where she taught courses in Southeast Asia and cultural anthropology. On her return from fieldwork, she received a teaching position at Sarah Lawrence College (1939–1942). Her teaching duties were interrupted by other involvements during the war. Like many other anthropologists, she was recruited by the Office of Strategic Services, where she joined the Research and Analysis Branch as chief of the Indonesia section.

Later, in 1944, while traveling to Ceylon, she met other Office of Strategic Services employees, including Julia McWilliams, later Julia Child. Child was initially put off by DuBois's perceived lesbianism, but they went on to become lifelong friends. In Ceylon, DuBois headed the Southeast Asia Command, where she directed and assisted resistance movements in Southeast Asian countries under Japanese occupation. For these efforts and others, the army awarded DuBois the Exceptional Civilian Award in 1945. Shortly afterward, she was awarded the Order of the Crown of Thailand for her work with the Free Thai underground movement through the Office of Strategic Services.

Following the war, DuBois continued her applied anthropology interests and worked for the State Department, where she headed their Southeast Asia research section until 1950. She then spent a year working for the World Health Organization. At the World Health Organization, she once again focused on Southeast Asia, doing research on educational and health needs in the area.

During this busy period, DuBois continued to publish articles and, in 1949, published *Social Forces in Southeast Asia*, a collection of three essays she had delivered 2 years before at Smith College. This thin, 78-page volume was very well accepted and has been remarkably durable. It is still available, with the most recent printing occurring in 2009. The book gives a short but trenchant overview of Southeast Asia and briefly discusses the European colonial and Japanese impacts on the area. It also describes the traditional class structure characteristic of several of the countries.

In 1954, Cora DuBois left the employ of the State Department to accept an endowed chair at Harvard, with a joint appointment to Radcliffe. Her courses focused on Southeast Asia and India, with seminars on social change. In 1961, on leave from Harvard, she traveled to India to study value confrontations, comparing a traditional town with a nearby modern one. She worked on this project on and off for 6 years. She also introduced some of her graduate students to her Orissa field sites, so that they might carry out dissertation research.

DuBois remained at Harvard until her retirement in 1969. Later, she was honored as Professor-at-Large at Cornell University, to which she was lured by its excellent Southeast Asia Program and its Echols Collection, an unparalleled library of Southeast Asian source materials, many in the original languages. Adding to her store of honors, DuBois received two honorary doctorates, one from Mills College and one from Wheaton College in Massachusetts. Among the prominent positions she held, DuBois was president of the American Anthropological Association in 1968–1969 and president of the Association for Asian Studies in 1969–1970.

During her many years of teaching, publishing, and accruing honors, there was only one significant negative development. The late 1940s, 1950s, and early 1960s were characterized by a national paranoia about communism, most manifest in the efforts of Senator Joseph McCarthy and the House Un-American Activities Committee. J. Edgar Hoover and the Federal Bureau of Investigation observed and investigated many U.S. citizens who they thought to be subversive. Many of the most prominent anthropologists, ranging from Oscar Lewis to Margaret Mead and a host of others, including Cora DuBois, found their classrooms infiltrated by students trained to record "subversive" utterances. The most common link among these anthropologists was that they were deemed subversive social activists, largely because they had written and/or spoken out on behalf of racial equality. While DuBois suffered no ill consequences at Harvard or at Cornell, in 1949 she did have to decline a faculty position at Berkeley because she refused to sign the California Loyalty Oath. The concerns about DuBois and several other anthropologists are particularly ironic as she and others were conspicuous for their service to this country during and after World War II.

In her later years, between the ages of 72 and 78, she encountered serious health problems, necessitating three operations. Despites these difficulties, she remained, with her long-term companion, Jeanne Taylor, socially and professionally active. As late as 1976, DuBois participated in a major conference that reviewed the past and present condition of anthropology in the United States. She died in Brookline, Massachusetts, in 1991 at the age of 88. Most of DuBois's collected papers and field notes are at Harvard's Tozzer Library, and some are at the University of Chicago's Regenstein Library.

Critical Contributions to Anthropology

Fieldwork Methodology

Cora DuBois compiled a detailed ethnography of the Alorese, describing elements that range from residence rules, quarrels, wealth contests, and sex to mythology and religion. The strong organization of the book and the meticulous attention to ethnographic detail may well be a reflection of her early interest in library science, or both may simply be a reflection of her nature. This information was collected in 1938–1939, before the Japanese occupation of the island and before subsequent modernization greatly affected the traditional culture. Consequently, her work remains relevant to anyone who hopes to work in or understand the history of the area.

The approach that DuBois developed for her study was to significantly advance the role of psychological anthropology in fieldwork. Not since W. H. Rivers and Alfred C. Haddon's expedition to New Guinea's Torres Straits had an anthropologist employed psychological methods in an ethnographic setting as thoroughly as did DuBois. Her use of psychoanalytic projective methods, such as the Rorschach tests, while not unprecedented, did include an important advance: the blind analyses of her results by an external authority. This safeguard has since been adopted in the great majority of psychological anthropological research.

Theory Advances

DuBois is best known and most respected for the theoretical advance she made in her book on Alor. Classical Freudian approaches to culture always displayed the same shortcoming: Symbolic interpretations allowed Freudians to find the same pattern no matter how seemingly different cultures might be. Kardiner, a major figure in the field of culture and personality, labored with Ralph Linton and others to make the classical Freudian "instinctive" model of personality subject to cultural variation. The resulting instrument was called the Basic Personality Structure, and it held that a culture's shared childhood-training practices (primary institutions) created a distinctive personality formation, differing from culture to culture. Utilizing Freudian assumptions, it was argued that the personality type then projected itself into distinctive cultural content (secondary institutions).

DuBois presented an important modification of Kardiner's Basic Personality Structure, the chief shortcoming of which was that it allowed for little personality difference among the cultural populace. It tended to stereotype culture participants, leaving little room for variation. Thus, to engage in hyperbole, all Italians were emotionally expressive, Germans punctual, and French passionate. DuBois's research among the Alorese impressed her with the strength and individuality of many of the people with whom she dealt, from some of whom she collected autobiographies. Her experiences with the Alorese persuaded her that childhood institutions did affect personality formation but that there could still be significant variation among members of the adult population. Thus, she recommended replacing the rather rigid Basic Personality Structure with a more statistical approach, the Modal Personality Structure, emphasizing the most common personality structure rather than making sweeping generalizations about a populace. This refinement gave room for individual differences, without weakening the argument that each culture can produce a distinctive personality type. Her contribution was well received by most scholars of the Culture-and-Personality school, including Kardiner. It was to have an impact on later studies of child rearing by researchers such as Beatrice and John Whiting and on studies of national character by Margaret Mead.

Douglas Raybeck

See also Benedict, Ruth F.; Culture and Personality; Freud, Sigmund; Kardiner, Abram; Kroeber, Alfred L.; Linton, Ralph; Mead, Margaret; Psychological Anthropology

Further Readings

DuBois, C. A. (1932). Tolowa notes. *American Anthropologist, 34*(2), 248–262.

———. (1970). Studies in an Indian town. In P. Golde (Ed.), *Women in the field: Anthropological experiences* (pp. 221–236). Chicago, IL: Aldine.

LeVine, R. A. (2007). Ethnographic studies of childhood: A historical overview. *American Anthropologist, 109*(2), 247–260.

Price, D. H. (2004). *Threatening anthropology: McCarthyism and the FBI's surveillance of activist anthropologists*. Durham, NC: Duke University Press.

Tozzer Library, Harvard College Library. (2004). *Cora Alice DuBois papers* [Online] (Vol. SPEC.COLL. ETHG. D 852 c). Retrieved from http://oasis.lib .harvard.edu/oasis/deliver/~toz00001

Dumont, Louis

Louis Dumont (1911–1998) was a French anthropologist who specialized in the study of systems of social morphology and ideology, particularly in India and Europe. Born in Thessaloniki, Greece; educated in Paris and later a student of Marcel Mauss and Louis Renou; politically engaged during the Front Populaire; prisoner of war in Germany between 1940 and 1945; assistant at the Musée de l'Homme; lecturer at Oxford; and directeur d'études at the École Pratique des Hautes Études VIth section, Dumont also held many visiting fellowships and professorships in the United States and Germany.

The sociological humanism of the works of Dumont ultimately defends and illustrates the results from 50 years of an enduring and inductive attention. Dumont's considerable achievement renewed ethnographical and theoretical approaches to society. Well placed within a French heritage and anthropological tradition, the descriptive and comparative method he designed is deeply indebted to Mauss, who believed that the study of ideas was inseparable from that of institutions. Implicitly inspired by a Tocquevillian spirit of comparison, Dumont also benefited, while in Oxford, from a close association with E. E. Evans-Pritchard, from whom he derived an appreciation for the challenge of translation that ethnography entails and the need to take history into account.

The result of Dumont's formative years and initial experiences in the field led to two critical notions he pursued throughout his career: (1) *holism* and (2) *hierarchy*. He first noted them while observing and collecting data, before he used them as the referent concepts to articulate an attempt at a critical and comparative analysis as well as a highly original epistemology. In Dumont's view, comparison entails a strict methodological dualism, an attitude that implies the necessity of separating the observer from those he or she observes. The picture thus delivered is always a picture seen by someone, but by someone who has internalized the cultural terms and categories of his or her own upbringing. The matter here is not so much to see and understand others through one's own grid and ourselves through their own as it is to combine them both by keeping them joined and contrasted in comparative perspective. Seeking what corresponds on the observed side to what is considered from an internal view, the observer thus strives to construct comparable facts through a higher level of abstraction. Enlarging the scope of comparison, the venture would in the end imply a critical return.

Successively maneuvering across different disciplinary fields and cultural areas, Dumont's sturdy and resolute positionings, at times strongly challenged by their respective experts, never actually departed from their socio-anthropological priority. This disposition led him to a theoretical engagement that questioned the various answers cultures mobilize when confronted and interacting with a dominant ideology.

Dumont conducted several extended periods of fieldwork. He began with a scrupulous description of a regional religious and urban festival in Provençal France. This was followed by a highly detailed monograph of a rural South Indian subcaste. Both case studies described the presence of complementary, interdependent, and unequal forms of ordered relationships. Taken together, the two works challenged the analytical tools, as well as the individualistic premises, that observers bring to the field and use in their interpretations. Dumont's work made it clear that theoretical principles were implicit in descriptions of culture and should be made explicit.

Dumont's own approach to structuralism left a lasting impression on the theory of kinship and particularly on the understanding of the Dravidian and Australian systems of affinity. In these works, he proposed an original structural conception of symbolic systems grounded in the idea of a *distinctive* opposition (as between the complementary terms in a couple) and a *hierarchical* opposition (between a whole and its parts).

Homo hierarchicus and Homo aequalis

With *Homo hierarchicus*—a synthetic and provocative study of the caste system of India—Dumont established himself as a leading authority. By virtue of its encompassing attempt to fit a number of classical and contemporary works into a consistent scheme, the book marked a break in Indian studies, departing from Orientalist creeds and blending textual erudition with field experience and expertise. Controversial at its publication, *Homo hierarchicus* established itself as a classic and continues to be discussed today.

In his own words, Dumont, in a series of articles published in *Contributions to Indian Sociology*, an academic journal he founded and coedited with David Pocock, positioned his work at the "confluence of Indology and sociology." This positioning ultimately allowed him to simultaneously apprehend the ritual nature and implications of a shared morphological order of status groups interrelated through relative purities. Dumont argued that in India a hierarchical disjunction between authority and power subordinates the logics of power and politics to a superior and encompassing set of religious values.

From the mid-1960s, Dumont undertook to reverse perspectives, attempting to describe the main features of modern Western society in contrast to those discovered in the Indian case. The three volumes devoted to the study of *Homo aequalis* articulated, first, the long historical process of differentiation that characterizes modernity—where political domains and territorial sovereignty have become emancipated from the values of religion—and, second, how the economic domain gained its autonomy from the political, which had previously controlled it. Dumont's ambition was to put modern ideology, individualism, and equality in anthropological perspective using the Indian hierarchy as a tool for a critical reappraisal of Western society itself. This approach was intended to distance scholarship from the implicit way our scientific modes of thought and ideas blind us to the exceptional character of the mental universe from which they sprang. Dumont's *Essays on Individualism* and *German Ideology* further refine this analysis by recapturing the historical and ideological stages that shaped Christian and European modernities, their specific nationalist and identitary logics, and their sometimes totalitarian outcomes.

Conceptually, Dumont based his theoretical understanding of human beings around social variation and differentiation (regional configurations, national variants, cultural loyalties). He argued that society invariably entails some form of hierarchy even when ideology denied its presence and silenced its understanding.

Dumont increasingly sought a means to redirect and complement an approach that ultimately relied on differentiation and comparison. He aimed to reveal the significant and constitutive distinctions within an ultimately unified humanity, rather than focusing on collecting distinct and separate units that fragmented and relativized it both empirically and theoretically. Far from ever relativizing, Dumont's central idea remained grounded by the conviction that each civilization, each society, if properly considered, delivers in its own right some conclusion of general use. His overall approach thus celebrates diversity and enforces a human and/or humanistic design that, while distinct and plural, precisely demonstrates the unity of humanity because of its different and indefinite social manifestations and not despite them.

Holism and Hierarchy

The concepts of *holism* and *hierarchy* chart Dumont's entire agenda. One should briefly recapture what both precisely reflect in Dumont's undertakings, as they should not be mistaken for or conflated with Weberian axioms or ideal types. As a principle, *holism* constitutes, enfolds, unfolds, and defines the relative and relational position an element occupies in a given set as well as the priority the set commands over such an element in its encompassing framework. Yet from within the set, the ordered relations between elements could be inverted, even allowing some to appear to challenge the overall ordering, though still by reference to it. No sociological fact in this view ever exists or stands apart from a reference to the entirety of society to which it belongs. Here, the whole encompasses the individual rather than the other way around. Therefore, inquiries that lack reference to a social whole stumble and err. Besides, a holistic system attaches its referent values to the social as a totality rather than to the individual we commonsensically conceive as the only meaningful agent.

While holism expresses and justifies the existing society by reference to its encompassing values, individualism claims to posit its own independently of society as it finds it. However, holism and individualism, as opposed as they might appear, never correspond to either a system closed in on itself (in the case of holism) or a system of universal and exclusive relevance (in the case of individualism).

Dumont's argument further explores the continual interaction of holism and individualism. Not only has individualism been shown historically to be unable to substitute for holism wholesale and rule everywhere in society, but it was actually never able to function (or operate) without an unperceived contribution to holism. A similar statement equally validates the interrelated presence of the two, when within its own cultural singularity the figure of the ascetic-renouncer in the Indian case reveals individualist features.

Strictly respecting the etymological definition of *hierarchy* (a mode of ordering whose meaning depends on the relationship it has to the sacred), Dumont first applied the term to the irreducible presence of difference in the Indian paradigm, making of it a specific cultural principle. But he was later to promote the notion of hierarchy and expand it as a more general, if not universal, scheme that he would use as one of the constitutive dimensions of his comparative theory.

Within a holistic universe, hierarchy implies an outside and superior order through which internal social relations are arranged. Any differentiation implies a distinction between a superior and an inferior level. If any form manifests selectivity, any function thus implies hierarchy.

Dumont argued that a series of logical operations allowed contextual or situational potentialities to overturn any specific hierarchical order without challenging the principle behind it.

Hierarchy is for Dumont at the heart of the "unthought" of modern ideology. The word commands profound aversion in our present world of immanence, economic rationality, and exclusive logics of power. It is wrongly equated with social stratification, inequality, and discrimination. By contrast, Indian society seemed to have best exemplified Dumont's approach to hierarchy and teaches us to recognize it in vivo in all its connections and applications.

Dumont's use of hierarchy has been criticized, often without understanding what it actually aimed to accomplish. Often judged as a too formalist, essentialist, conservative, or even reactionary figure in his formalized translation of the Indian stage, where he discovered the concept, Dumont has frequently been interpreted as voicing literary and Brahmanical views, if not denounced for his propensity to favor Gallic forms of abstractions.

There remains for Dumont the conviction that, when analyzing society, one can never neglect the presence of a transcendental dimension that hierarchy precisely displays. Institutions, in his view, always refer the authority or legitimacy they claim to something beyond themselves. Society, like any other logical system, can never find within itself the rule from which it operates (something that Kurt Gödel demonstrated for all systems of logic). Any society thus depends on a principle necessarily external to it. Every human order derives its meaning from what it conceptualizes as beyond, above, or even in a future state. Likewise, modern society, branded by immanent, individualist, and egalitarian values, nonetheless continues to operate under implicit schemes of holism and hierarchy.

In Dumont's approach, modern civilization is at the same time a culture like any other and a sort of metaculture imposing itself everywhere as such. Still, to the extent that the individual values of Western postindustrial society are now spreading worldwide, they locally undergo modifications and engender new forms. These new modified forms, in their turn, can pass back into the dominant culture and operate there in their own right. The contemporary ideological world is like a fabric woven by the continuing interaction of cultures. Under the impact of modern civilization, a given culture may disappear or conversely reject contact with others and close in on itself. Most often it adapts to the dominant culture, and in so doing, it justifies itself in relation to the dominant culture by constructing ad hoc representations that are often more adaptable and even stronger through their associations. The new hybrid representations, compared with the notions from which they proceed, appear as intensified and hardened forms.

In its own dramatic way and from within the world of modernity itself, totalitarianism illustrates the presence of such interactive ideological processes by combining an all-powerful individualism, on the one hand, and, on the other, one that is perpetually and irremediably haunted by its opposite, aspiring to a totality that only reveals a pseudoholism.

Dumont thus invites social scientists to confront and analyze these more or less hybrid representations and institutions, following the course from which they sprang and that of their subsequent destiny. And he compels us to study the history of ideology in intercultural perspective.

A Reflexive Epistemology

Dumont regularly came back to the evidence that the social creature does not like society to be understood and that there is more in the culture or society than the ideology tells. Therefore, to avoid misleading and alternative explanations that would involve the role of a conscious will, of mere happenstance, or even of a subjective or psychic unconscious of the kind resorted to by Sigmund Freud or Claude Lévi-Strauss, Dumont suggested that we acknowledge the matter as an invariant illustration of a "social inarticulate."

Thus, for Dumont, the issue is not to study the cohesive integration of different groups within society—as the functionalists previously wished and as a current empiricist sociology continues to emphasize—but rather to apprehend in an almost Hegelian fashion the coherent conditions of the integration of ideas in the mind (l'esprit).

The legacy Dumont has left us is the knowledge that the social history of the categories of the human mind still remains the order of the day, only that it now seems more multiplex than it originally did for the Durkheimian enthusiasts of the early 20th century. Yet the program he designed was one that involved both personal and professional commitments, and he believed that these could not be separated. Consistently pursuing the daunting task of understanding more fully the momentous and at times tragic events of his century always remained for Dumont a matter of social commitment and ethical obligation. His resolute attempts at understanding and his austere style of teaching never ceased to articulate deep existential and phenomenological concerns.

Widely acknowledged among English-speaking anthropologists such as Clifford Geertz, Marshall Sahlins, and Bruce Kapferer, and still considered a reference landmark for South Asian specialists, Dumont's legacy remains significantly influential within the French-speaking milieux of historians, political philosophers, and specialists on social thought, such as François Furet, Pierre Rozanvallon, Claude Lefort, Marcel Gauchet, Giorgo Agamben, Vincent Descombes, Jean-François Billeter, and François Jullien.

Jean-Claude Galey

See also Evans-Pritchard, E. E.; Geertz, Clifford; Mauss, Marcel; Musée de l'Homme; Oxford University; Sahlins, Marshall

Further Readings

Descombes, V. (1996). *Les institutions du sens* [Institutions of meaning]. Paris, France: Minuit.

Dumont, L. (1951). *La tarasque* (The tarascan). Paris, France: Gallimard.

———. (1957). *A South Indian sub-caste: Social organization and religion of the Pramalai Kallar.* New York, NY: Oxford University Press.

———. (1962). *La civilisation indienne et nous* [Indian civilization and us]. Paris, France: Armand Colin.

———. (1970). *Homo hierarchicus: The caste system and its implications.* Chicago, IL: University of Chicago Press.

———. (1971). *On putative hierarchy and some allergies to it* (Contributions to Indian Sociology, New Series, No. 5; pp. 58–81). Noida, India: Vikas.

———. (1975). On the comparative understanding of non-modern civilizations. *Daedalus, 104*(2), 153–172.

———. (1978). *From Mandeville to Marx: Genesis and triumph of economic ideology.* Chicago, IL: University of Chicago Press.

———. (1983). *Affinity as a value.* Chicago, IL: University of Chicago Press.

———. (1991). *Essays on individualism.* Chicago, IL: University of Chicago Press.

———. (1994). *German ideology: From France to Germany and back.* Chicago, IL: University of Chicago Press.

Galey, J. C. (1991). Louis Dumont. In P. Bonte & M. Izard (Eds.), *Dictionnaire de l'ethnologie et de l'anthropologie* [Dictionary of ethnology and anthropology] (pp. 204–206). Paris, France: Presses Universitaires de France.

———. (2005). Louis Dumont. In M. Borlandi (Ed.), *Dictionnaire de la pensée Sociologique* [Dictionary of sociological thought] (pp. 441–443). Paris, France: Presses Universitaires de France.

———. (2010). Louis Dumont et la religion [Louis Dumont and religion]. In D. Hervieu-Léver (Ed.), *Dictionnaire des faits religieux* [Dictionary of religious facts]. Paris, France: Presses Universitaires de France.

Ortigues, E. (1962). *Le discours et le symbole* [Discourse and symbol]. Paris, France: Beauchesnes.

DUNDES, ALAN

The American folklorist Alan Dundes (1934–2005) was a major figure in shaping the discipline of folkloristics and made significant theoretical contributions to structural, comparative, and psychological approaches to culture.

Biography and Major Works

Dundes was born on September 8, 1934, in New York City to the lawyer Maurice Dundes and the musician Helen Rothschild. While he was still an infant, the couple moved the family to Patterson, New York. The family had Central and Eastern European Jewish roots, but the children (his sister Marna was born in 1936) were raised in a secular environment. Dundes entered Yale University in 1951, majored in English, and joined the Naval Reserve Officers Training Corps. After serving military duty for 2 years, he returned to Yale in 1957 to complete his Management Aptitude Test in English. After marrying a fellow Yale student Carolyn Browne in 1958 and spending a year in France teaching conversational English, Dundes entered the doctoral program in folklore at Indiana University, which he completed in 1962, with a groundbreaking dissertation applying a structural analysis to North American Indian folktales.

Dundes's experience in France resulted in his first publication, a linguistic study of French tongue twisters collected from children in his class, in the *French Review* (1960). The publication set the stage for a lifelong interest in folk speech, humor, and children's folklore. He followed this research with a string of influential journal articles on the structural definitions of folkloristic genres (superstitions, riddles, games, folktales, and proverbs), psychological analyses of cultural practices and forms (ritual fasting, wishing wells, earth-diver myths, and elephant jokes), and a group-based rather than a class-based modernistic method and theory of folklore. Dundes was a prolific author, publishing eight volumes of essays and five thematic books. He edited numerous book series and textbooks.

Dundes's first college teaching position was in the English department at the University of Kansas in 1962. In 1963, he joined the anthropology department at the University of California, Berkeley, as an assistant professor, and as a result of his productivity and rising influence, he was promoted quickly to full professor in 1968. He additionally became the founding director of a master's degree program in folklore in 1965 and stayed in the post until his death in 2005. Among his accolades were receiving the Giuseppe Pitrè Prize for lifetime achievement in folklore; a distinguished teaching award from the University of California, Berkeley; election to the American Academy of Arts and Sciences; election to the Fellows of the American Folklore Society; and fellowships from the Guggenheim Foundation and the National Endowment for the Humanities.

Critical Contributions to Anthropology

Dundes's ideas on the pivotal role of folklore in modern everyday life and the symbolic content of folklore as a projection of anxieties are among his most lasting contributions. These concepts can be organized under the following headings: "Grouping Interpretation," "Deep Meaning," and "Merging Psychoanalysis and Structuralism."

Grouping Interpretation: The Definition and Significance of Folklore

Dundes operationally defined folklore as *expressive material that repeats and varies*. This characterization allowed for visual humor produced by photocopiers and, later, word processors to be viewed as folklore, along with other nonoral forms. In an expansive definition proposed by Dundes (1965), a folk group was *any group of people whatsoever who share at least one common factor* (p. 2). This modern, elastic definition of "folk" differed from prior European-driven concepts of a lower or peasant stratum of society. Taking away a connection to the land or a lack of learning emphasized that all people by the nature of their social interaction use folklore as an instrumental, communicative device. It can therefore emerge anew or adapt old forms with different social associations, whether in conventional ethnic, occupational, and regional categories; among a temporary group of friends; or in an organization. Dundes implied agency in the groups' production of folklore, rather than the groups passively following or blindly receiving tradition, which he criticized as a "superorganic" model of culture.

Dundes was also influential in codifying the method of folkloristic research as *identification and interpretation*. The terms came from the folklorist Archer Taylor's comparison of mid-20th-century literary and folkloristic methods, but Dundes did not limit interpretation, as Taylor did, to literal readings, using historical and formalistic background as the source of meaning. Interpreted meaning, according to Dundes (1992), involved "plumbing the depths to explore the latent (as opposed to the manifest) content of folklore" (p. xxii).

Deep Meaning: The Projection and Symbolism of Folklore

Dundes cited Sigmund Freud's idea of projection as the cognitive transposition of repression in the statement "I hate him" to "He hates me." Dundes argued that the label "projective inversion" for transposition is more appropriate since desires are not only inverted but also externalized. In a Dundesian perspective, Freud's projection can be read as symbolizing "I hate him" with slurs or stories in which the object of hate is victimized. Dundes (2007) defined projective inversion this way: "a psychological process in which A accuses B of carrying out an action which A really wishes to carry out him or herself" (p. 395). Dundes distinguished this kind of transposition from the transference of feelings onto an external object, which he called projection. Dundes often presented examples of projection in jokes and rituals, such as "dead baby jokes," which expressed anxiety over abortion; "light bulb jokes," which showed the importance of social organization through the double entendre of technology and sex, expressed by "screwing in a light bulb"; Jewish American Princess jokes, which projected unease over the independence of women generally through the stereotype of the self-centered Jewish daughter; and "Bloody Mary rituals," expressing fear of menstruation among preadolescent girls in rituals with representations of blood in the name of the girl and the act of drawing blood.

Dundes found that projective inversion is especially prevalent in folktales and legends, suggesting that their narrative elaboration relates a heightened level of taboo. Examples include the themes of incest and infanticide evident in a classic Oedipal plot in which a father-king attempts to kill his newborn son, a projective inversion of the son's wish to kill his father. Dundes proclaimed that early Freudians were mistaken in assuming that this merely reflected a father's wish to marry his own daughter. He asserted instead that the daughter would like to marry her own father.

Another of Dundes's provocative reinterpretations used projective inversion to analyze the "blood libel" or "ritual murder" legend, a source of European anti-Semitism. In the legend, a Christian child is killed to furnish blood for consumption during Jewish rites. The story has been recognized as one of the most persistent anti-Semitic narratives among European Christians since the 12th century. As a legend, it is frequently told as a true event, in spite of its implausibility, since consumption of blood by humans is forbidden in Jewish law (Genesis 9:4; Leviticus 3:17, 17:12). Dundes purports to solve this puzzle by noting its context in the Easter-Passover season, and pointing out the *projection* of guilt to another group through the *projective inversion* of Christians committing murder.

Taking a cue from the dualism between manifest and latent meanings in "depth" psychology, Dundesian analysis uncovers "deep" meaning in the sense of something being about something that turns out to be something else. The way to get to the "underlying" structure, the "hidden" meaning, or the "unstated" reason is through the identification and comparison of ciphers. Rather than being revealed in observable behavior (what Dundes called "descriptive data") in the field, symbolic meaning is discerned "beneath" the surface and traced to the mind.

Merging Structuralism and Psychoanalysis

In Dundes's view, deriving the meaning of folklore requires more than a literal reading of the text; it calls for contextualizing the expression in behavioral and social conditions. He emphasized this by referring to folklore as a form of sublimation: "Folklore offers a socially sanctioned outlet for the expression of taboo and anxiety-provoking behavior. One can do or say in folkloric form things otherwise interdicted in everyday life" (Dundes, 2005, p. 359). To grasp why folklore is needed as an expressive outlet, one therefore needs to know the cultural values, taboos, anxieties, and beliefs of the society in which individual tradition bearers operate in everyday life.

By analyzing folklore, Dundes wrote, the scholar discovers "general patterns of culture" and raises "levels of consciousness." The assumption in this statement is not just that folklore can be ordered according to form but also that it is cognitively patterned (e.g., through linear, circular, or binary thinking). Another presupposition is the existence of an unconscious—a part of the mind containing repressed instincts and their representative wishes, ideas, and images, which are not accessible to direct examination.

Folklore is especially important in making the unconscious conscious, Dundes affirmed, because it appears to be a "safe" fictive or ritual space in which to symbolize, and thereby control, anxiety or ambiguity, but if the realistic basis of the symbolism is exposed, repression recurs in another form. This transformation accounts for Dundes emphasizing the observer's "analytical" rather than native posture in assessing meaning, although he urged analysts to collect "metafolklore," tradition bearers' comments on their own traditions. These comments are in themselves part of belief, he observed, or else rationalizations for the need for expression. The analyst is essential in the Dundesian process of deriving meaning; an outside eye is necessary to discern the inside, or hidden codes of meaning. Some observers, Dundes understood, would have the tradition bearers' explanation of an event to be sufficient, viewing the role of the folklorist as facilitating self-reflection by natives. But in a Dundesian perspective, the analyst needs to maintain a detached vantage point rather than a position of advocacy, precisely because folk material involves personal and societal anxieties that are repressed or avoided and, when expressed, typically disguised. For example, in a 1978 book with Pagter that discussed humor, full of scatological and sexual references, Dundes argued that humor was the concealed expression of many major problems facing contemporary American society. Dundes linked dualism, particularly the importance of "double meaning," in psychoanalysis with the binary basis of structuralism. The pivotal structuralist approaches of Vladimir Propp (syntagmatic, relating to a sequential pattern of plot functions) and Claude Lévi-Strauss (paradigmatic, relating to a thematic set of contrasting relations) are unified by Dundes to reveal the mental processes underlying the structural patterns of fantastical expressions. The point is that binary structure is basic, whether as the basis of a story (something missing for something found), as a method (identification and interpretation), as the formation of a group (requiring at least two persons), as the authenticity of an item (confirmed by two or more versions), or indeed in the concept of folklore (uniting the social "folk" and the expressive "lore"). The binary is significant in this perspective not just as a framework but also as a representation of the way the mind works—as a psychological concept—and also as the social basis of transmitting, or sharing, folklore.

Aware of the criticism that symbolist interpretations of texts are difficult to empirically verify, Dundes responded with the concept of "symbolic equivalence," using units of analysis he called *allomotifs* and *motifemes*. These terms refer to the actions, or "functions," of a story arranged within a structural system that could replace the prevalent literary or nonstructural classification of motifs as minimal units in a narrative. Applying a linguistic analogy, Dundes offered that allomotifs are to motifemes in narrative as speech allophones (any of various acoustically different forms of the same phoneme) are to phonemes (speech sounds designated by speakers of a particular language) and allomorphs (variant phonological representations of a morpheme) are to morphemes (minimal meaningful language units).

Dundes asserted that an ethnographic goal of folklore research is geared toward situated communication or context. Separating himself from other contextualists, however, Dundes warned against confusing surface *use* and disguised *meaning*. He inferred meaning from symbolic clues that might be outside the awareness of the speaker and not apparent from the context. Use is observed or collected from natives, while the interpretation, he insisted, is inevitably made from the analyst's viewpoint.

Dundes's Legacy

Dundesian analysis identifies basic patterns or concepts and consequently arrives at interpretations of their associations through symbolic equivalences (allomotifs) and social outlooks (worldviews). Dundes's goals were to centralize folklore studies as

an academic discipline and disrupt the social hierarchy of "modern/elite and folk" by conceptualizing tradition as a human necessity.

Dundes's most sweeping influence into the 21st century has been in his definitions of folk group and genres of folklore. They have been instrumental in the formation of a modern, flexible concept of folklore as evidence of and commentaries on culture. Dundes's demonstration of structural analysis as a prelude to content interpretation has been important, along with his introduction of the terminology of allomotif and motifeme, which is still applied in anthropological scholarship. His methodological suggestion of emphasizing identification and interpretation, with attention to texture (performance, practice, or style) and context, is standard in anthropological approaches to folklore. His psychoanalytical perspectives have been less pervasive among performance-oriented folklorists, although his ideas on the projection of anxiety in folklore are essential to interpretative strategies in psychological ethnology and questions of cultural cognition and the rationale for cultural practice.

Simon J. Bronner

See also Freud, Sigmund; Lévi-Strauss, Claude; Pike, Kenneth; Saussure, Ferdinand de; University of California, Berkeley

Further Readings

Bronner, S. J. (Ed.). (2007). *The meaning of folklore: The analytical essays of Alan Dundes*. Logan: Utah State University Press.

Dundes, A. (1965). What is folklore? In A. Dundes (Ed.), *The study of folklore*. Englewood Cliffs, NJ: Prentice Hall.

———. (1975). *Analytic essays in folklore*. The Hague, Netherlands: Mouton.

———. (1980). *The interpretation of folklore*. Bloomington: Indiana University Press.

———. (1987). *Parsing through customs: Essays by a Freudian folklorist*. Madison: University of Wisconsin Press.

———. (1989). *Folklore matters*. Knoxville: University of Tennessee Press.

———. (Ed.). (1992). Introduction. In G. Róheim, *Fire in the dragon and other psychoanalytic essays on folklore* (pp. ix–xxvi). Princeton, NJ: Princeton University Press.

———. (1997). *From game to war, and other psychoanalytic essays on folklore*. Lexington: University Press of Kentucky.

———. (2002). *Bloody Mary in the mirror: Essays in psychoanalytic folkloristics.* Jackson: University Press of Mississippi.

———. (2005). Afterword: Many manly traditions—a folkloristic maelstrom. In S. J. Bronner (Ed.), *Manly traditions: The folk roots of American masculinities* (pp. 351–364). Bloomington: Indiana University Press.

———. (2007). The ritual murder or blood libel legend: A study of anti-Semitic victimization through projective inversion. In S. J. Bronner (Ed.), *The meaning of folklore* (pp. 382–409). Logan: Utah State University Press.

Dundes, A., & Pagter, C. R. (1978). *Work hard and you shall be rewarded: Urban folklore from the paperwork empire.* Bloomington: Indiana University Press.

DURKHEIM, ÉMILE

David Émile Durkheim (1858–1917), the French philosopher, and founder of the French school of sociology and of the journal *L'Année Sociologique*, made significant contributions to the anthropology of religion and developed the structural-functional approach to society.

Biography and Major Works

Durkheim was born in Eastern France, the youngest of four children. His father was a rabbi, as was his paternal grandfather. The young Émile appeared destined to follow this family tradition but had a change of heart while still a schoolboy and abandoned all religious belief by the time he left his home town of Épinal to prepare for the entrance exam to the École Normale in Paris.

By the time he passed his *agrégation* (the examination required one to be eligible to teach in state secondary schools), Durkheim had decided that the topic of his doctoral dissertation in philosophy would be the relations between individualism and socialism. The problem he was concerned with was the development and maintenance of social cohesion in the face of the conflicting demand of modern life toward increasing specialization and individualization. This concern with the glue that held society together was a driving issue for Durkheim and stemmed in part from the social situation of France in the 19th century, a period rife with recurrent political crises. He refined his conception of this work throughout 1884–1886, during which period he visited Germany and studied with the pioneering psychologist Wilhelm Wundt, among others. Durkheim's interest at this point was clearly directed toward the creation of a science of ethics, which was to be part of sociology.

On his return from Germany, Durkheim wrote several articles on social science in Germany, which attracted the attention of Louis Liard, the director of Higher Education at the Ministry of Public Education, and in 1887, he was appointed *chargé de cours* (junior lecturer) of social science and pedagogy, a post especially created for him, at the Faculty of Letters of Bordeaux. It was under this guise that sociology first entered the French university system.

Durkheim's Bordeaux period (1887–1902) was extremely productive. He completed his doctorate and published his two doctoral theses, *La Division du travail social* (1893; translated as *The Division of Labor in Society*) and a Latin dissertation on Montesquieu (1892). He further published *Les Règles de la Méthode Sociologique* (1895; translated as *The Rules of Sociological Method*), *Le Suicide* (1897; translated as *Suicide*), and articles studying specialized social phenomena including social solidarity, family and kinship, incest, totemism, suicide, crime, religion, and law. In 1898, he founded the journal *L'Année Sociologique* around which gathered, over time, an impressive team of collaborators, including Durkheim's nephew, Marcel Mauss, and Henri Hubert, Robert Hertz, Célestin Bouglé, and Maurice Halbwachs. This journal provided an annual survey of the field of social sciences and related fields and published a series of original monographs, allowing Durkheim and his collaborators to exercise considerable influence.

In 1887, Durkheim married Louise Dreyfus, the daughter of a successful businessman, whose family was originally from the Alsace region. According to all accounts, theirs was a happy marriage, and Durkheim's wife made possible his intense work both by removing domestic cares and by taking on administrative and editorial work on his behalf. They had two children, Marie and André.

The Division of Labor

Durkheim, wishing to establish social science on a scientific footing, argued in *The Division of Labor* that it was time to leave behind philosophical systems such as those of Auguste Comte and

Herbert Spencer and to engage in specialized studies of particular social phenomena from the point of view of their functions, asking how and to what extent they perform them. When reviewing German works of social science in the 1880s, Durkheim had praised them for their concreteness and contrasted them to the "French" tendency to deal in generalities. Durkheim shared many of the concerns of the Germans he reviewed: He also wanted to establish the reality of society, its complexity, the fact that it was a natural entity, and the possibility of its scientific study. He made free use of the organic analogy in his early works, although he sometimes emphasized that he did not advocate the identity of society and organism but simply found the analogy useful. It was fundamental, in his view, that people realize the impossibility of altering society at will, its power of constraint over the individual, and its existence apart from individuals—in short, what he called its sui generis nature. He also emphasized the determinism of social phenomena, a determinism that he believed was necessary for sociology to be a science. Durkheim believed in the methodological unity of the social and the natural sciences.

The Division of Labor argued that the real social function of the division of labor was not economic but moral. Its true function was to create the feeling of solidarity among individuals. Because the division of labor obviously increased the productive force of the worker and was thus the necessary condition for the material and intellectual development of societies, it had been assumed that this was its function. But, Durkheim argued, there was nothing obligatory in furthering the economic development of society: If that were the only result of the division of labor, it would have no moral character. Social solidarity, however, was the fabric of society itself as it ensured the cohesion of its members.

Mechanical solidarity was characteristic of simpler, "segmental" societies, where all social units operated similarly—that is, individuals held the same beliefs and performed the same actions. The individual conscience was not very differentiated; it contained the same beliefs, mores, and customs as that of other members of the society. Organic solidarity, on the other hand, was developed by the division of labor and left room for individuality—or rather, made individuality possible in society. As the "collective conscience" decreased in breadth and intensity, it was the division of labor that took over

its role and kept together the higher forms of social aggregates. It thus had a moral importance that the economists and utilitarian philosophers had never realized.

Durkheim introduced here his conception of the essentially double nature of human beings: *Homo duplex*. Humans have two *consciences*, one that they share with their entire group, which, in consequence, is society living and acting within them, and the other, which, on the contrary, represents only that which is personal and distinctive to each, which makes them individuals. For Durkheim, the development of the individual personality and the division of labor are inextricably linked and not in opposition to each other. It was the division of labor, with the new kind of solidarity it created, that allowed for the emergence of individuals.

Although normally the division of labor produced solidarity, there were abnormal cases in which this did not occur. In the third part of *The Division of Labor*, Durkheim first introduced his influential conception of *anomie*, a conception he would further develop in *Suicide* (1897). Anomie was to be found in industrial or commercial crises and in the conflict between labor and capital. It was due to the lack of a body of rules governing the relations between social functions. The lack of rules was, in its turn, due to the absence of sufficiently frequent interactions between the members of society. The sets of rules or laws developed as a "crystallization" of social interaction when these interactions had become solidified by their repetition over time. This process was akin to that of habit formation in the individual. If for some reason, this process of repeated contact did not take place, an anomic form of the division of labor arose.

Durkheim saw social facts as forming a continuum that went from morphological, or structural, social phenomena to "free currents of social life" that were not yet solidified into any particular form. Between one end of the spectrum and the other, there was only a difference in the degree of consolidation of the phenomena, not a difference in nature. In *The Division of Labor*, Durkheim had given structural phenomena the most significant explanatory role. This was qualified in the *Rules* (1895), and in later works, structural facts would be given less importance in relation to the more fluid *collective representations*.

In *The Division of Labor*, Durkheim had explained that the *collective consciousness* included the judicial, governmental, scientific, industrial, and other special functions, which consisted of systems of representations. Although the notion of collective representations can be traced to Durkheim's earliest works, it only gained a central role in his sociology after *Suicide* (1897). Durkheim concurrently scaled down the use of the concept of collective conscience.

Rules of Sociological Method and Suicide

The methodological principles presented in the *Rules of Sociological Method* were, Durkheim wrote, the practical results of his sociology course at Bordeaux and were implicitly contained in *The Division of Labor*. The book opened with a definition of "social fact," possibly its most controversial content. Offering definitions of the subject one wished to treat was standard practice in academic philosophy textbooks, with which it is certain Durkheim was thoroughly familiar. Thus, Durkheim was conforming to standard philosophical practice and could reasonably expect that philosophers would appreciate his logical rigor. Social facts were ways of acting, thinking, and feeling exterior to the individual and imbued with the power to impose themselves on him or her. Durkheim's point was to offer a definition that clearly set social facts apart from both organic and psychological facts, giving sociology a kind of "fact" of its own to work with, thereby guaranteeing its autonomy from other sciences.

The first and most fundamental methodological rule that Durkheim advanced was to consider social facts as things. He criticized various predecessors in sociology (Auguste Comte, John Stuart Mill, and Herbert Spencer) for having dealt with concepts rather than with objective realities. What made social facts "things" was that they were the *data* of sociology. A thing, he specified, was anything that offers itself to observation. This rule derived directly from one of the characteristics of social facts as defined by Durkheim: their "exteriority" to the individual. These rules were controversial even at the time Durkheim proposed them. They are sometimes seen as establishing Durkheim's social realism. It is certainly true that Durkheim always held that society was a part of nature and that he was critical of views that did not consider society as resistant to change as material conditions are. The notion that individual will or reason could in any direct way alter social institutions seemed clearly untrue to him.

Durkheim's emphasis on "things" was directly connected to a less studied aspect of his work, his concern with the reconstruction of a secular, scientific morality for the French republic and its diffusion through education. As Robert Jones and others have shown, Durkheim's desire to communicate the reality of the social realm was due to his belief that individuals needed to find their place in society and that their self-fulfillment depended on recognizing a force greater than themselves that gave meaning to their actions. One could not expect individuals to sacrifice for a mere idea rather than a concrete reality. In *Suicide*, Durkheim had shown the nefarious consequences of unlimited desires and of the lack of social rules on individuals. Only society, in his opinion, could offer satisfying goals and limits to an individual's ambition, while making possible individuality itself through the division of labor.

The Elementary Forms of the Religious Life

Durkheim described his intellectual development as marked by the realization, in 1895, of the foundational role played by religion in social life. He attributes this insight to reading the works of British anthropologists and British and American ethnographers, especially those of Robertson Smith and his school. This led to the publication of a number of articles in the *Année* dealing with various aspects of primitive religion—most notably "Primitive Classification," with Mauss—and eventually culminated in the publication of *The Elementary Forms of Religious Life* in 1912. Three propositions are put forth in this work: (1) that religion is society becoming aware of itself, although in a symbolically altered form; (2) that the representations created in religion are thus the initial source out of which all later forms of human thought have become differentiated; and (3) that as creations of that superior being which is society, religious symbols are "sacred"—that is, they are treated with a special respect or veneration denied to the profane world. The definition of religion offered at the beginning of *The Elementary Forms* presents it as a set of symbolic beliefs relative to sacred things. But religion is not just belief, it is also *practice*: There is no religion without ritual, without a community.

Individuals derive their religious beliefs from the way in which the sacred force is created in rituals. The sentiment of the divine is produced in collective ceremonies during which, as a result of the intense emotionality and interconnection generated, the individual feels overcome by an entity superior to himself. Durkheim called such moments "collective effervescence." The force emanates from the collective assembly, and thus, the individual feels it to be both immanent within him and transcendent over him. Rites play a fundamental role in generating and rekindling periodically the feeling of the sacred.

In a manner reminiscent of Kant's distinction between the sensible and intelligible worlds, Durkheim argues that the individual gets from society the best part of himself or herself, all intellectual and moral culture, and all that makes him or her truly human (in contrast to purely animal). On the other hand, society exists and lives only through individuals. If individuals did not hold social beliefs, traditions, and so on, in their individual minds, society would die. As Durkheim puts it, the gods cannot do without their worshippers any more than they can do without their gods. It is in this dynamic sense that the equation between society and god must be understood: The divine power is the symbolic representation of the creative capacity of the collectivity, a capacity rekindled through social rituals and practices.

The Elementary Forms investigates the origins of the categories or fundamental notions that dominate our entire intellectual life. These categories of understanding were like solid frames that confine thought: They were the notions of time, space, number, cause, substance, and personality (not the Kantian categories but those taken from Aristotle). These categories, Durkheim concluded, were embedded in religious thought, which itself was a social phenomenon. Religious representations were collective representations that expressed collective realities, and so already contained the principal categories. The categories were born in and from religion; they were a product of religious thought. But if they were of religious origin, the categories must share what was common to all religion: They must be social things, products of collective thought. In general, *concepts* were completely social things: One only emerged from the domain of fleeting individual impressions and sensations when human association resulted in the creation of a defined set of categories, which were fixed because they were shared. Even the

notion of contradiction emerged from social conditions, since its predominance varied according to the societies and the times. The principle of identity (one of the fundamental laws of logic, which states that for all propositions p, it is impossible for both p and not p to be true) dominates current scientific thought, but there were vast systems of representations, namely mythologies, where it played a minor role. Another indicator that the categories were of social origin was their necessity; that is, the set of elementary categories was invested with an authority that one could not avoid at will.

The Social Life and the Universalization of Concepts

Durkheim believed that science brought our system of representations into a growing harmony with nature through the social process of verification. Collective representations undergo tests that are repeated indefinitely. Logical thought progressively purges itself of the subjective elements that it had from its origin. This was due to the development of a new kind of social life, of the internationalization of social life, which produced the universalization of concepts. As a consequence of this internationalization, Durkheim believed that things can no longer fit within the social frames in which they were originally classified; they must be organized with principles of their own; logical organization thus differentiates itself from social organization and becomes autonomous. Thought that is truly and peculiarly human is not a given, therefore, but a product of history; it is an ideal limit to which we come ever closer but in all probability will never attain. There is a continuous growth of the fit between knowledge and the world. Durkheim considered categories as not arbitrary because the social was part of the natural and the natural yielded to the human mind, over time, a natural classification—that is, one based on reality. Durkheim believed that science was a necessarily collective enterprise, and the *Année Sociologique* group's work can be fruitfully understood through this lens.

Later Years

In 1902, Durkheim successfully applied for an appointment as *chargé de cours* (junior lecturer) to the chair in the Science of Education at the Sorbonne, and he was made professor 4 years later. In 1913, the chair was renamed "Science of Education and

Sociology." Durkheim was required to lecture on the theory, history, and practice of education throughout his career. While Mauss has presented this required teaching as a burden, there were significant relations between Durkheim's pedagogical enterprise and his sociological interests, especially regarding the development of moral education.

On August 1914, Germany invaded Belgium and northern France, starting the first Great War. Durkheim became involved in the war effort, writing patriotic pamphlets to counter German propaganda and devoting himself to the cause of national defense. In 1916, Durkheim suffered a great blow: His son, a linguist and a member of the younger *Année* circle, was killed in the war. Durkheim was devastated by the death of his son and suffered a stroke from overwork and grief. He recovered sufficiently to take up his work on his final book, *La Morale* (*Ethics*), but in November 15, 1917, he died at the age of 59.

Daniela S. Barberis

See also Aristotle; Hertz, Robert; *L'Année Sociologique*; Mauss, Marcel; Neo-Kantianism; Smith, William Robertson; Spencer, Herbert; Structural Functionalism; Wundt, Wilhelm

Further Readings

Barberis, D. S. (2002). Moral education for the elite of democracy: The classe de philosophie between sociology and philosophy. *Journal of History of the Behavioral Sciences, 38,* 355–369.

Besnard, P. (Ed.). (1983). *The sociological domain: The Durkheimians and the founding of French sociology.* Cambridge, UK: Cambridge University Press.

Borlandi, M., & Vogt, P. (Eds.). (1993). *Durkheim et de la division du travail social* [Durkheim and *The Division of Labor in Society*]. Paris, France: Presses Universitaires de France.

Brooks, J. I., III. (1990). Analogy and argumentation in an interdisciplinary context: Durkheim's "individual and collective representations." *History of the Human Sciences, 4,* 223–259.

Clark, T. N. (1968). The structure and functions of a research institute: The *Année Sociologique. European Journal of Sociology, 9,* 72–91.

Jones, R. A. (1999). *The development of Durkheim's social realism.* Cambridge, UK: Cambridge University Press.

———. (2005). *The secret of the totem: Religion and society from McLennan to Freud.* New York, NY: Columbia University Press.

Lukes, S. (1973). *Émile Durkheim: His life and work, a historical and critical study.* Stanford, CA: Stanford University Press.

Pickering, W. S. F. (2009). *Durkheim's sociology of religion: Themes and theories.* Cambridge, UK: Lutterworth Press.

Pickering, W. S. F., & Martins, H. (Eds.). (1994). *Debating Durkheim.* London, UK: Routledge.

Schmaus, W. (1994). *Durkheim's philosophy of science and the sociology of knowledge: Creating an intellectual niche.* Chicago, IL: University of Chicago Press.

ECONOMIC ANTHROPOLOGY

Economic anthropology is a distinctive field at the interface between anthropology and economics. It achieved a measure of success in the 3 decades after World War II but has been less prominent since then. Free market orthodoxy lent some unity to the past 3 decades, a period now framed in retrospect by the global economic crisis since 2008. Economic anthropology was dominated in the 20th century by fieldwork-based ethnography, but now it should open up once more to world history and to a more critical perspective on economy.

Three Phases of Economic Anthropology's Formation

The development of economic anthropology may be divided into three stages. From the 1870s to the 1940s, most anthropologists were interested in whether the economic behavior of "savages" manifested the same "rationality" that was taken to motivate Western actors. They assembled compendious accounts of world history conceived of as an evolutionary process. After World War I, the practice of fieldwork became more dominant, and ethnographers sought to engage the propositions of "neoclassical" economics with their findings about "primitive societies." They failed, mainly because they misunderstood the economists' epistemological premises.

The purpose of economic anthropology in the 19th century was to ask whether the world economic order must be founded on the principles that underpinned Western industrial society. The search was on for alternatives that might support a more just economy, whether liberal, socialist, anarchist, or communist. Since society was understood to have not yet reached its final form, there was a great interest in origins and evolution. Anthropology was thus the most inclusive way of thinking about economic possibilities. The universities expanded in the 20th century, and knowledge was compartmentalized into many impersonal disciplines modeled on the natural sciences. Anthropology found itself pigeonholed as the study of those parts of humanity that the other disciplines could not reach. The profession became fixed in a cultural-relativist paradigm, by definition opposed to the universalism of economics.

From 1945 to 1975, economic anthropologists argued among themselves about the theories and methods needed to study their special preserve, which now included peasants as well as tribesmen. "Formalists" held that the tools of mainstream economics were adequate to this task, while "substantivists" claimed that institutional approaches were more appropriate. By this, they meant that economic life in societies lacking impersonal markets was always "embedded" in other social institutions, ranging from the household to government and religion. Karl Polanyi was the principal source for the substantivist approach, first in his antimarket polemic, *The Great Transformation*, and later when he inspired a team of ethnographers, archaeologists, and historians to investigate nonindustrial societies. This debate ended in a stalemate, opening the way for Marxists and feminists to dominate for a while, but they too mainly drew on the traditional subject matter of exotic ethnography.

The third stage takes us from the watershed of the 1970s through 3 decades of neoliberal globalization. Anthropologists now expanded their inquiries to address the full range of human economic organization. The question remains, "Do capitalist markets rest on universal human principles or not?" The focus of this entry is mainly on this last period. While a rapidly urbanizing world was consumed by war and economic disaster in the 20th century, anthropologists published monographs on remote peoples presented as living outside of modern history. The period after World War II saw the rise of economics to the public prominence it enjoys today. The neoliberal era was not kind to economic anthropology, which became fragmented and incoherent. We all now live in a world driven by capitalism, so anthropologists have studied it. There has been a marked shift back to the Western heartlands, but the palpable sense of a shrinking world encouraged anthropologists to develop new ways of studying "globalization" everywhere.

Between the Cultural Turn and Hard Science

By the 1980s, many anthropologists had abandoned economics to its own entropy. Marshall Sahlins, after publishing *Stone Age Economics*, denied the value of a comparative "anthropological economics," since material life everywhere was structured by local symbolic orders, of which bourgeois economics was one. This "cultural turn" has both subverted and invigorated economic anthropology in recent decades. Arjun Appadurai drew attention to the complex "biographies" of consumer goods. Such goods might acquire a commodity form but might then leave that sphere to become heirlooms or community sacra. The bourgeois separation of persons (subjects) and things (objects) was deconstructed by new work on personhood, led by Marilyn Strathern. But these approaches often led away from economic anthropology's central concerns.

The substantivist division between industrial and nonindustrial economies lives on in an opposition between "commodities" and "gifts," which represents a contrast between the capitalist West and the rest of the world. Marcel Mauss wrote his classic essay "The Gift" to refute the bourgeois opposition of individual commercial self-interest to the altruism of the gift. Market contracts and gifts, according to him, could both be shown to combine self-interest with social obligation as part of a universal logic of exchange; neither could be said to be "free." Yet a strong opposition between them was later projected onto Mauss's text as a basis for contrasting whole economies, the West versus the rest. Unlike the substantivists, proponents of the gift/commodity pair write about both types of economy, while generally keeping the same moral distance from "capitalism."

Stephen Gudeman's cultural approach to the economy stands out as a good example of this approach. He began by applying a "local models" perspective to some aspects of Western economics as well as to the peasant economies of the non-Western world. He challenges anthropologists to combine fieldwork with serious exposure to the history of economic ideas. His recent overviews build on an opposition between "community" and "market," the former focusing on activities performed and valued for their own sake, primarily within households, and the latter on means-ends relations, typically found in trade. This dialectical framework in principle could be applied anywhere.

Anthropologists who follow the new institutional economics do not always see themselves as "formalists," but they share a commitment to "hard science" and predictive models. Whereas Polanyi regarded markets as one kind of economic institution among several, they view all economic institutions as markets. They incorporate institutions into formal models through an underlying logic of rational choice consistent with neoclassical economics. The new institutional economics approach defines institutions as "the rules of the game." Their favorite example is property, which is often taken to provide the incentive structure for all economies. For example, Jean Ensminger's study of northern Kenyan pastoralists showed how markets transformed local lives, mainly for the better. New institutions emerged to reduce uncertainty and actors' transaction costs. Considerable benefits accrued to individuals following the breakdown of collective land tenure.

The Informal Economy

Ethnographic study of Third World cities generated the principal contribution made by anthropologists to economics. Clifford Geertz wrote about development questions in Indonesia during the 1950s.

He found that the majority of a Javanese town's inhabitants were occupied in a street economy that he labeled "bazaar-type." The "firm-type" economy consisted largely of Western corporations that benefited from the protection of state law. These had *form* in Max Weber's sense of "rational enterprise," being based on calculation and the avoidance of risk. National bureaucracy lent these firms a measure of protection from competition, thereby allowing the systematic accumulation of capital. The "bazaar," on the other hand, was individualistic and competitive, so that accumulation was impossible. Geertz pointed out that modern economics uses the bazaar model to study the decisions of individuals in competitive markets, while treating as anomalous the dominant monopolies protected by the state bureaucracy.

The global crisis of the early 1970s raised fears concerning urban unemployment in the developing countries. Cities were growing rapidly but without a comparable growth in "jobs" conceived of as regular employment by government and corporations. The question was "How are 'we' (the bureaucracy and its academic advisors) going to provide the people with the jobs, health, and housing they need?" The specter of urban riots and even revolution raised its head. This story didn't square with Keith Hart's fieldwork experience in Accra, Ghana, so he tried to persuade economists to abandon the "unemployment" model and consider hitherto invisible aspects of the grassroots economy.

The conceptual pair "formal/informal" grew out of analyzing migration to cities whose markets were only weakly organized by industrial capitalism. The two sides are linked, since "informality" is entailed in the institutional effort to organize society along formal lines. "Form" is *the rule*, an idea of what ought to be universal in social life; and for most of the 20th century, the dominant forms have been those of national bureaucracy. "The informal sector or economy" became a keyword in the development industry, referring as it did to all the economic activities that avoid regulation by the state.

A mania for deregulation of the "free market" from the 1980s led national economies and even the world economy itself to become progressively informal. Not only did money management go offshore, but corporations outsourced, downsized, and casualized their labor forces; public functions were privatized, often corruptly; the drugs and illicit arms trades took off; the global war over "intellectual property" assumed central place in the drive for profits; and whole countries abandoned any pretense of formality in their economic affairs. It has consequently become hard to tell the legal and illegal forms of capitalism apart.

One-World Capitalism

The shift of industrial production to countries with cheap labor has been a consistent feature of recent decades. At home, the political power of labor was undercut, and the Western masses now participated in capitalism, primarily as consumers rather than as producers. Anthropologists have flocked to the study of consumption, often with a perspective drawn from "material culture" rather than economic anthropology. Historians and ethnographers traditionally studied the artifacts of local peasantries that were made by hand. This approach could not easily be applied to the city, since urban domestic interiors are often furnished with artifacts of similar function with only minor formal differences. French sociologists and the anthropologist Mary Douglas took an oversocialized view of consumption, claiming that consumers could not express a distinctive identity through mass-produced commodities. It was assumed that every individual shares the same abstract code of meaning for these object-signs and that this is imposed from the outside. A later generation of anthropologists showed that consumers of mass-produced objects build up a universe that has personal meaning and expresses their social identity. The Hegelian concept of "appropriation" seeks to capture how commodities are made inalienable property as part of a home universe unique to their owner. Daniel Miller has taken this approach to shopping, the Internet, mobile phones, and clothing, from blue jeans to saris.

The process of getting people to spend money—the art or science of marketing—is also a rapidly expanding field of anthropological investigation. Kalman Applbaum argues that modern marketing has absorbed moral criticism into its own quasi-religious system. Whereas an earlier generation of ethnographers highlighted the devastating consequences of capitalist development for local cultures, he shifts the culture contact model to one more suited to the globalizing present. The emergence of consensual meanings and goals in economy is due to corporations' success in controlling every aspect of the social life of the commodities they sell.

The basic capitalist institution is the firm. Small businesses often remain important, but they have long been overshadowed by organizations with a global reach. Of the 100 largest economic entities on earth, corporations now outnumber nations by more than 2 to 1. They are extremely flexible and overlap with governments. Alexandra Ouroussoff shows that the distribution of wealth between shareholders and managers of corporations is contentious. Since the 1980s, the rating agencies have supervised what they take to be investment risk on shareholders' behalf. They imagine that they can calculate and minimize future losses. Corporate executives tend to consider profit and loss to be subject to unpredictable contingency. They have muted their public criticism of the agencies because of their need for investment capital, and they modify their reports of company activities accordingly. An economic collapse was the inevitable result. Yet academicians, politicians, and journalists attribute the crisis to personal moral failure rather than institutional contradiction.

We still think of private property as belonging to living persons and oppose private and public spheres on that basis. This possessive individualism also allows abstract entities like governments and corporations to hold exclusive rights in something against the world. At the same time, corporations have retained their legal privileges, such as limited liability for bad debts. The focus has also shifted from "real" to "intellectual" property, from material objects to knowledge. The digital revolution in communication has allowed for the reproduction and transmission of information services to become increasingly costless, exerting a downward pressure on prices. The social effort needed to maintain high prices in a world where "information wants to be free" is the principal source of economic conflict today.

Money and Financial Crisis

The anthropology of money has enjoyed a revival of late. Anthropologists have long rejected the impersonal approach to money and markets offered by mainstream economics. Ethnographers have found that non-Western peoples tend to take modern money in their stride, turning it to their own social purposes. Money has acquired in Western economies a social force all of its own, but it has not elsewhere.

Money is the principal means for us all to bridge the gap between everyday personal experience and a society whose wider reaches are unknowable. As a token of society, it must be impersonal to connect individuals to the universe of their relations. But people make everything personal, including their relations with society. This two-sided relationship is universal, but its incidence is highly variable. Money is both the principal source of our vulnerability in society and the main practical symbol allowing each of us to make an impersonal world meaningful.

Hart identified two strands of Western economic theory that explained money either as a *token* of authority issued by states or as a *commodity* made by markets. The coin is a metaphor for these two sides of money. One carries the virtual authority of the state (*heads*). The other treats the money medium as a *commodity* (*tails*). Rather than acknowledge the interdependence of "heads *and* tails," economic policy swings wildly between the two extremes.

The modern money system provides a wide repertoire of instruments to help people keep track of their exchanges with the world and to calculate the current balance of their worth in the community. So the chief function of money is *remembering*. If personal credit today points toward greater humanism in the economy, it also entails increased dependence on impersonal governments and corporations, on impersonal abstraction of the sort associated with computing operations, and on impersonal guarantees for contractual exchange. We may become less weighed down by money as an objective force, more open to it as a way of keeping track of the complex social networks that we each generate. It is not enough for anthropologists to emphasize the personal controls that people already impose on money in practice. That occurs in the everyday world as most of us know it. We also need ways of reaching the parts of the macroeconomy that we don't know, if we wish to avert the ruin it could bring down on us.

The failure of the New York investment bank Lehman Brothers in September 2008 triggered a financial collapse, the ramifications of which are with us still. One victim of the crisis has been free market economics. It is hard to assert now that economies will prosper only if markets are freed from political bondage. The conditions for proposing alternative approaches to the economy are now more favorable. This may help explain the runaway success of David Graeber's historical and comparative synthesis *Debt: The First 5,000 Years.*

Future Prospects

The early ethnographers did not understand the economists' aims and methods and settled for a straw man, *Homo economicus* (Economic Man). Then, for a time, the formalist-substantivist debate drew the attention to some fundamental questions of method. But this argument went unnoticed by economists, and it did not leave behind a robust intellectual community of economic anthropologists. Echoes of the debate may be seen in the positions taken by neo-institutional and cultural anthropologists. Economists, policymakers, and the media have found it easy to ignore what anthropologists have to say.

The global crisis has opened up a new space for critical approaches to the economy. We cannot afford to neglect world history. Attempts to match the findings of exotic ethnography to a narrow utilitarian creed are bound to fail; both anthropology and economics were inadequate to our common human purposes.

There is much to recommend a renewed engagement with Mauss and Polanyi. Mauss's key modification of Émile Durkheim's legacy was to conceive of society as a historical project of humanity whose limits were extended to become ever more inclusive. Society cannot be taken for granted as a preexistent form. It must be made and remade, sometimes from scratch. Heroic gift exchange is designed to push the limits of society outward. No society is ever economically self-sufficient. So to the need for establishing local limits on social action must always be added the means of extending a community's reach abroad. This is why markets and money in some form are universal, and any attempt to abolish them must fail.

Polanyi drew attention to a plurality of distribution mechanisms that, in the modern world, affect the lives of millions of people who have no measure of control over them. He highlighted the inequality they created, as they swing between the poles of society's external and internal relations, market and state. The immediate reaction to the financial collapse was to flip the coin from tails to heads. Polanyi's call for a return to social solidarity, drawing on the voluntary reciprocity of associations, reminds us that people must be mobilized to contribute their energies to the renewal of society. It is not enough to rely on impersonal states and markets.

The cultural turn of the neoliberal era has buried the economy from view or allowed it to appear only as consumption or exchange. In addition to marginalizing the many concrete ways ordinary people make economic life their own, economists' focus on individual private property has obscured the role of governments and corporations. Any attempt to build society exclusively on private or common property is doomed, since human beings must combine self-reliance with belonging to each other in society. Ethnographers have shown this over and over again, but our myopic preoccupation with local complexity has prevented our engagement with larger questions of world history.

Markets are indispensable to a viable economy, but as critics have pointed out, unlimited markets threaten democracy itself. Economists disagree among themselves on how far to extend market principles. Some might now take an interest in what anthropologists have discovered. Mauss and Polanyi, by providing the missing link between everyday life and the world at large, offer continuing inspiration for the renewal of economic anthropology as a field.

Keith Hart

Author's note: This entry draws heavily on the author's collaborative work with Chris Hann.

See also Appadurai, Arjun; Douglas, Mary; Geertz, Clifford; Mauss, Marcel; Polanyi, Karl; Sahlins, Marshall; Strathern, Marilyn; Weber, Max

Further Readings

Applbaum, K. (2004). *The marketing era: From professional practice to global provisioning.* London, UK: Routledge.

Geertz, C. (1963). *Peddlers and princes: Social development and economic change in two Indonesian towns.* Chicago, IL: University of Chicago Press.

Graeber, D. (2011). *Debt: The first 5,000 years.* New York, NY: Melville House.

Gudeman, S. (2008). *Economy's tension: The dialectics of community and market.* Oxford, UK: Berghahn Books.

Hann, C., & Hart, K. (2011). *Economic anthropology: History, ethnography, critique.* Cambridge, UK: Polity Press.

Hart, K. (1986). Heads or tails? Two sides of the coin. *Man, 21*(3), 637–656.

———. (2005). *The hit man's dilemma: Or business, personal and impersonal.* Chicago, IL: Prickly Paradigm.

Hart, K., Laville, J., & Cattani, A. D. (Eds.). (2010). *The human economy: A citizen's guide.* Cambridge, UK: Polity Press.

Mauss, M. (1990). *The gift: Form and reason of exchange in archaic societies.* London, UK: Routledge. (Original work published 1925)

Ouroussoff, A. (2010). *Wall Street at war.* Cambridge, UK: Polity Press.

Polanyi, K. (2001). *The great transformation: The political and economic origins of our times.* Boston, MA: Beacon Press. (Original work published 1944)

EMICS AND ETICS

See American Anthropological Association; Cultural Materialism; Pike, Kenneth

ETHNOGRAPHY OF SPEAKING

The ethnography of speaking and the related ethnography of communication embody the dance between anthropology and linguistics that has existed since the two were established as academic disciplines in the United States. At its core, the ethnography of speaking is the attempt to grapple with the relationship between language and culture in a systematic way through a focus on language use in context. To meet this challenge, the approach has interwoven theory and methodology from multiple disciplines, most notably anthropology, linguistics, sociology, and, to a lesser degree, psychology. Many of the foundational ideas of the ethnography of speaking provide the basis for the ways in which linguistic anthropology is practiced in the United States today, and only a consideration of the ethnography of speaking within the context of the development of the disciplines of linguistics and anthropology reveals the ways in which it has been innovative as well as the ways in which it has been contested.

Precursors to the Ethnography of Speaking

Initially, the study of linguistics and the study of anthropology were joined in the United States in the work of Franz Boas. Boas viewed language as a necessary part of the study of culture because grammars and lexicons could give insight into native systems of classification and serve as a window on culture, even if language and culture could not be directly correlated. The field of anthropology included the practice of descriptive linguistics, which provided a means of studying social practices that had a fundamental concern with the relationship between language and culture. However, as linguists sought to define their discipline as independent of anthropology, the form that the study of the relationship between language and culture should take became a question, and the ethnography of speaking arose as an attempt to answer that question.

Early Development of the Approach

Although it has roots in the work of Boas, the start of the ethnography of speaking as a distinct approach is attributed to a 1962 essay by Dell Hymes, written during a period when the disciplines of both linguistics and anthropology were searching for more scientific paradigms. Noam Chomsky had introduced generative grammar as a way to control for factors seen to be external to the grammatical system of a language, thus further distancing linguistics from anthropology as a separate discipline. This approach was a radical turn away from the anthropological beginnings of linguistics, as variation and performance were factored out in favor of a focus on the notion of an "ideal speaker" and on native speaker intuitions about meaning, grammaticality, and usage. Meanwhile, Hymes saw that much of the work in anthropology was focused on the comparative study of cultural themes such as kinship and religion, while language was either ignored or studied only as an instrument, without careful attention to its own patterning. Hymes proposed that ethnographies of speaking should include what had been excluded from grammars and ethnographies— a close examination of language in its sociocultural context. Rather than trying to control for variation, ethnographers of speaking were to make the variation that exists both within and among communities of speakers the focus of study. They would study the act of speaking as a cultural system, thereby providing a theoretical framework that could account for variation and linguistic coherence simultaneously. This understanding could not be accomplished through additive means, that is, by adding social context to a grammatical description of a language or by considering language within contexts of social analysis. It required ethnographic study of language use as a social act with its own internal patterning. Bronisław Malinowski had developed ethnography as a methodology in anthropology and had underscored the importance of language in context. Now Hymes, inspired by Malinowski, detailed the framework within which in-depth ethnographies of the patterns of speaking in different societies could be written and eventually compared to generate a body of theory.

Hymes, by himself and then in collaboration with John Gumperz, laid out guidelines for how the ethnography of speaking would be practiced. In the future, as their independent and collaborative work continued, Hymes would primarily influence the development of linguistic anthropology as a subdiscipline of anthropology, while Gumperz's work would lay the groundwork for sociolinguistics as a subdiscipline of linguistics. In their work together, Gumperz and Hymes emphasized looking for commonality with other disciplines, maintaining the community of use rather than the language as code as the point of departure. Nonetheless, they urged a mutual focus on both the means and the ends of communication. Hymes formulated the notion of the speech economy of a community as the area of focus of study. The speech economy is composed of speech events—the native designations of activities that are defined through the use of speech. In identifying the important components of speech events, Hymes initially drew heavily on the work of Roman Jakobson, to whom he dedicated the original 1962 essay outlining the ethnography of speaking. After several years of work within this paradigm, Hymes summarized the heuristic for investigating the speech event, also referred to as the communicative event, with what became the well-known mnemonic—SPEAKING: Setting, or Scene; Participants, or Personnel; Ends (both goals/purposes and outcomes); Act Characteristics (both the form and the content of what is said); Key (the tone, manner, or spirit in which an act is done); Instrumentalities (channel and code); Norms of Interaction and of Interpretation; and Genres (categories or types of speech act and speech event). Hymes proposed that these components of speech events, always defined by native categories, were the elements that ethnographers should be attuned to.

Within sociology, Erving Goffman and Harold Garfinkel also contributed to the methodology of ethnography of speaking in their work to examine how we use language to make sense of the world

we live in, especially in face-to-face interaction. Garfinkel pointed out that indexical language and actions are continuously established through everyday activities. Garfinkel's work also inspired later, more detailed work on social interaction within the field of conversation analysis, most directly influencing the work of Harvey Sacks and Emanuel Schegloff. This work, though, differed from the ethnography of speaking in its approach to context. Conversation analysts limited context to that which was directly evoked by participants within the text of a conversation. Ethnographers of speaking took an ethnographic approach that defined context more broadly as situated within participants' social and cultural environments.

The Ethnography of Speaking Today

By the 1980s, the ethnography of speaking had begun to produce a substantial body of empirical work to push the approach forward. The volume *Explorations in the Ethnography of Communication* by Richard Bauman and Joel Sherzer and *Explorations in the Ethnography of Speaking* by the same authors brought together analyses of communicative events across a range of cultures and speech communities. In 1983, Joel Sherzer, a student of Dell Hymes, published the first full-length ethnography of speaking, *Kuna Ways of Speaking: An Ethnographic Perspective*, followed by *Verbal Art in San Blas: Kuna Culture Through Its Discourse*, a book that reflected the importance given to verbal art in the ethnography of speaking. At the same time, the anthropological orientation of the ethnography of speaking gained strength as linguistic anthropology once again became more firmly established as one of the four subdisciplines of anthropology. In 1983, Hymes became the president of the American Anthropological Association, and the association was reorganized into separate sections, resulting in the creation of the Society for Linguistic Anthropology.

As a result of these developments, much of the approach to studying language and culture in linguistic anthropology today can be traced to the theoretical interventions of the ethnography of speaking or ethnography of communication. Underlying much of the current work in linguistic anthropology are the core principles of the ethnography of speaking, which are that language is both constitutive and reflective of social realities, that speaking has a patterning of its own, and that ethnography is a necessary methodology for discovering that patterning. However, the degree to which contemporary work exemplifies these principles in the spirit of the ethnography of speaking varies.

Some of the works in which this influence is most clearly identified focus on communicative situations that have immediate social consequences. From its inception, the application of the ethnography of speaking was envisioned as a way to analyze inequality, particularly in institutional settings. In his seminal 1962 essay, Hymes cites applications to studies of the socialization of children, the identification of subcultures, and the recognition of internal stratification within a group. Hymes conducted research in the field of education in addition to his more broadly theoretical expositions, but work on the linguistic socialization of children was given prominence by Bambi Schieffelin and Elinor Ochs. Shirley Brice Heath gave particular attention to the language of socialization and issues of inequality in public schools. Recently, much work in the ethnography of speaking has focused on issues of racial and economic inequality and how relevant categories are constructed and reflected through language use.

Although it has been argued that much work in linguistic anthropology has moved away from the Boasian tradition of linguistic description, much contemporary work in the ethnography of speaking continues to include grammatical description of a language while discussing how linguistic resources are brought to bear in areas of interest in social anthropology. This line of research has had a particularly strong influence on literature about the Indigenous people of the Americas. Inspired by Boas's work on North American Indian languages, Hymes's own work on Chinook led him to a more discourse-centered approach. Since then, work on Native American poetics and work on Latin American verbal art have been inspired by the ethnography of speaking. Much work in the Americas also engages the ethnography-of-speaking approach, as developed primarily by Richard Bauman's work on performance, which was also influenced by studies of folklore in anthropology.

Ethnographies of speaking and communication have focused on a broad range of topic areas. In the face of criticisms that the field of ethnography of speaking had no unifying thread, those who worked to develop the approach argue that it is united

around the principle that both society and culture are constituted through communication, most especially through the use of language. For these reasons, they do not see the ethnography of speaking as a separate subdiscipline within linguistic anthropology but rather as an approach that considers an understanding of the linguistic resources available to a speaker to be important to the understanding of any given interaction. These resources and, therefore, each interaction are viewed as being fully situated in a larger social context. It is in this way that the ethnography of speaking offers a theoretical and methodological framework for the relationship between language and culture within the discipline of anthropology.

María Luz García

See also Boas, Franz; Chomsky, Noam; Discourse Theory; Goffman, Erving; Gumperz, John J.; Hymes, Dell; Jakobson, Roman O.; Malinowski, Bronisław

Further Readings

Basso, K. (1979). *Portraits of the Whiteman: Linguistic play and cultural symbols among the Western Apache.* Cambridge, UK: Cambridge University Press.

Bauman, R., & Sherzer, J. (1989). *Explorations in the ethnography of speaking.* Cambridge, UK: Cambridge University Press.

Gumperz, J., & Hymes, D. (1964). The ethnography of communication [Special issue]. *American Anthropologist, 66*(6, Pt. 2).

Heath, S. (1983). *Ways with words: Language, life and work in communities and classrooms.* Cambridge, UK: Cambridge University Press.

Hill, J. (2011). *The everyday language of White racism.* New York, NY: Wiley.

Hymes, D. (1962). The ethnography of speaking. In T. Gladwin & W. Sturtevant (Eds.), *Anthropology and human behavior* (pp. 15–53). Washington, DC: Anthropological Society of Washington.

———. (1972). Toward ethnographies of communication. In P. P. Giglioli (Ed.), *Language and social context* (pp. 21–44). Harmondsworth, UK: Penguin Books.

Paredes, A., & Bauman, R. (Eds.). (1972). *Toward new perspectives in folklore.* Austin: University of Texas Press.

Schieffelin, B., & Ochs, E. (1987). *Language socialization across cultures.* Cambridge, UK: Cambridge University Press.

Sherzer, J. (1983). *Kuna ways of speaking: An ethnographic perspective.* Austin: University of Texas Press.

Sherzer, J., & Urban, G. (1986). *Native South American discourse*. Berlin, Germany: Mouton de Gruyter.

Webster, A. (2009). *Explorations in Navajo poetry and poetics*. Albuquerque: University of New Mexico Press.

ETHNOHISTORY

In its most general sense, *ethnohistory* refers to a body of scholarship that attempts to bridge the disciplines of anthropology and history—a domain also terminologically covered by other phrases, including historical anthropology and anthropological history—and is often understood as the history of peoples more typically studied by anthropologists than by historians. While this broad sense is still encountered, it is problematic, in part due to the diversification of those disciplines. A more specific and increasingly formalized sense is one that developed initially through Indian rights work in North America and one that is related to theoretical movements referred to as ethnomethodologies or ethnoscience: ethnohistory as a mode of writing histories that respects and reflects the historical perspectives and consciences of the people involved. In this framework, it is not sufficient to simply write a history of an "Other"; rather, one must grapple with the often disparate understandings of historical processes that pertain in situations where different cultures come into contact.

Western scholars have written histories and other accounts of different ethnic groups from the dawn of history, from Greek accounts of barbarians, to European explorers' seeking to understand the origins of the different peoples they encountered and sometimes subjugated, to modern ethnographic and historical studies of particular ethnic groups and of processes of cultural interaction. Ethnohistory, however, is a relatively recent development. The term was perhaps coined by the anthropologist Clark Wissler in 1909, referring to the documentary sources on indigenous groups, which might be used together with archaeological data to understand the pasts of the American Indians being studied ethnographically by anthropologists. The more specific sense emphasized here also derives from American Indian scholarship, but in this case, it derives from the legal cases heard under the Indian Claims Commission beginning after the Second World War, in which scholars testified as to the underlying facts of cases involving land rights of indigenous people. These cases often turned on questions of interpretation, both of specific documents and of more ephemeral matters, like whether a particular group was properly identifiable as descendant from historical treaty signatories. A variety of forms of evidence—some of them new to Western courts and others requiring defense, challenge, and interpretation—became relevant, including archaeological evidence and oral traditions. The classic anthropological subject of kinship took on a significant role in determining meaningful and valid lines of descent. Linguistic interpretation was involved, but other dimensions of culture also needed to be explicated for the courts. Perhaps most critical was unpacking the documentary record as depicting only one of the two (or more) perspectives in situations of cultural interaction, typically representing the Western view to the detriment of understanding the positions of others.

In the mid-1950s, many of the scholars involved in this legal scholarship, and others interested in "Indian history," began to come together for scholarly conferences, particularly the American Indian Ethnohistoric Conference and the Ohio Valley Historic Indian Conference. Those conferences developed into the American Society for Ethnohistory (ASE), which began the publication of its flagship journal *Ethnohistory* in 1954. The ASE also sponsors an annual conference, typically drawing several hundred scholars; its membership includes primarily individuals trained in the larger, more traditional disciplines of anthropology and history, but there are also art historians, geographers, linguists, and others—reflecting the interstitial or liminal disciplinary position that still characterizes ethnohistory. Indeed, a shared sense of marginality has contributed to the camaraderie of the ASE from its inception.

In the 1980s, the scholarship of French historians such as Marc Bloch, Fernand Braudel, Lucien Febvre, François Furet, and Paul Ricoeur, began to be more widely influential in the United States, particularly among anthropologists who were interested in thinking about historical processes in colonial situations. Bernard Cohn, Greg Dening, Nicholas Dirks, William Roseberry, Marshall Sahlins, Eric Wolf, and others worked toward what Cohn referred to as a rapprochement between history and anthropology, and while most would question whether that was truly achieved—and while most of these individuals never identified strongly as ethnohistorians—there at least developed a disciplinary climate that was more hospitable toward ethnohistory.

While American Indian studies had provided the main force in the development of ethnohistory, works examining other parts of the world were a part of the discourse from the very beginning. The 1990s saw an explicit move by the leaders of the ASE and the editors of *Ethnohistory* to institutionalize this greater breadth with outreach to scholars working in other areas and increased non–North American content in the journal, notably including special issues on Papua New Guinea (2000), Madagascar (2001), and Latin America (1995, 2000, 2001) and a special issue on violence and warfare (1999) that drew on cases from around the world. This pattern, a strong core focused on Native American studies with increasing participation from other parts of the world, continues to develop and characterize the field, and works in ethnohistory are often published in other venues as well, particularly in journals of regional or "area studies" focus.

The usual product of ethnohistorical scholarship is a narrative history; while quantitative data, sociocultural theory, textual analysis, and other methodologies and data sets often figure in its production, most practitioners find that the narrative structure best accommodates the felt need to fairly represent different cultural perspectives. Within that genre, there is considerable variety. Some studies seek to depict a particular event or series of events from the various perspectives of participants. Some explore the historiography, or historical consciousness, of a particular group. Typically, documents and other materials are read "against the grain," seeking to see through the constraints of those who produced the records to hidden or unrecognized perspectives of others who did not produce a record in their own voices. Scholars often use "upstreaming"—taking the more recently observed practices that are better documented to understand past practices—and also "downstreaming"—for example, using archaeological findings to interpret later periods. These kinds of interpretive reconstructions have been criticized for not necessarily reflecting the reality of a given moment but are seen by many as valuable tools for fleshing out incomplete records. Comparative cases may also be employed, raising questions of just how comparable, or how different, the examples may be.

In recent years, as increasing numbers of indigenous people have themselves pursued higher education and entered into academic discourse, they have often criticized the fact that Westerners are still constructing and disseminating the histories of indigenous peoples. Indigenous scholars such as Devon Mihesuah and Linda Tuhiwai Smith have sought to "decolonize" historical methods, to formulate "indigenous methodologies," and to raise the awareness of these issues among nonindigenous scholars. Although some might argue that it is not possible to "know" another, others see the attempts to bridge difference as important, even if perhaps inevitably flawed. While occasionally confrontational in nature, for the most part this process has fostered a discursive relationship, with greater awareness of the challenges and differences involved in writing histories, resulting in the production of more interesting and more accurately and fully representative histories.

Frederic W. Gleach

See also Bloch, Maurice; Ethnomethodology; Ethnoscience/New Ethnography; Sahlins, Marshall; Wolf, Eric

Further Readings

Galloway, P. (2006). *Practicing ethnohistory: Mining archives, hearing testimony, constructing narrative.* Lincoln: University of Nebraska Press.

Gleach, F. W. (2003). Controlled speculation and constructed myths: The saga of Pocahontas and Captain John Smith. In J. S. H. Brown & E. Vibert (Eds.), *Reading beyond words: Contexts for native history* (2nd ed., pp. 40–42). Peterborough, Ontario, Canada: Broadview Press.

Harkin, M. (2010). Ethnohistory's ethnohistory: Creating a discipline from the ground up. *Social Science History, 34*(2), 113–128.

Hill, J. D. (Ed.). (1988). *Rethinking history and myth: Indigenous South American perspectives on the past.* Urbana: University of Illinois Press.

Krech, S., III. (1991). The state of ethnohistory. *Annual Reviews of Anthropology, 20,* 345–375.

Mihesuah, D. A. (Ed.). (1998). *Natives and academics: Researching and writing about American Indians.* Lincoln: University of Nebraska Press.

Tuhiwai Smith, L. (1999). *Decolonizing methodologies: Research and indigenous peoples.* London, UK: Zed Books.

Wilson, S. M. (1999). *The emperor's giraffe, and other stories of cultures in contact.* Boulder, CO: Westview Press.

ETHNOLOGICAL SOCIETY OF LONDON

See Royal Anthropological Institute

ETHNOMETHODOLOGY

Ethnomethodology is one of the more recently developed fields in social science. Founded in the 1960s as an alternative to the positivist and functionalist approaches that dominated North American sociology, ethnomethodology draws on phenomenology and the philosophy of ordinary language and focuses intensively on practical action and social interaction in everyday settings. Together with the spin-off program of conversation analysis, ethnomethodology has become a familiar perspective in several fields besides sociology, including anthropology, linguistic pragmatics, communication and information studies, science and technology studies, education studies, and workplace studies. Although ethnomethodologists sometimes investigate everyday and professional quantitative practices (including those in the social sciences), with few exceptions they pursue an observational and descriptive approach to the activities they study.

Origin and Meaning of the Term

The term *ethnomethodology* was coined in the 1950s by Harold Garfinkel (1917–2011) to describe a distinctive orientation to the production of social order, although it was not until the 1967 publication of Garfinkel's *Studies in Ethnomethodology* that the word became familiar in the social sciences. The word is now in the *Oxford English Dictionary*, although its meaning continues to be a source of confusion and consternation. The word is a compound of the Greek *ethnos*, meaning "people," and the neo-Latin term *methodologia*, meaning the general study of disciplinary principles or procedures (methods). Garfinkel linked the term to previously established "ethnoscience" fields in anthropology,

such as ethnobotany, ethnomathematics, and ethnomedicine, which investigated and recorded native classifications, methods of reckoning with numbers, and healing practices. The domain of ethnomethodology is much broader than those of ethnobotany, ethnomathematics, and the other ethnosciences as its scope includes methods in any organized practice. Moreover, with some notable exceptions, ethnomethodologists focus on practices in the same societies in which they live. Sometimes they investigate specialized activities in law courts, scientific laboratories, and other settings, but often they study ordinary conversations and routine practical actions that rarely are graced by the term *methods* but nevertheless exhibit methodic organization.

Endogenous and Academic Methodologies

Compared with other social sciences, ethnomethodology takes an unusual stance toward methodology. As usually defined, a methodology is a *system* of rules, postulates, and general principles for regulating the procedures of a discipline. In a more general sense, methodology is the *analysis* of the extant principles and procedures of a discipline. In the philosophy of science, the analysis of methodology covers all of science and not only the technical methods of a single discipline. The most ambitious analyses of method prescribe criteria—such as Sir Karl Popper's falsifiability—for demarcating science from nonscience. In the social sciences, methodology is important both for establishing disciplinary techniques and as a basis for claiming scientific legitimacy.

Émile Durkheim's *The Rules of Sociological Method* (originally published in 1895) is an especially clear example of a classical sociological text that treats abstract rules and principles as the fundamental grounds for securing sociology's status as a science. In the *Rules*, Durkheim presents a positivistic vision of society as an objective reality constituted by social facts. For Durkheim, social facts are systematic organizations of actions. Although produced by individuals, social actions are reproduced throughout a coherent society and across generations. In Durkheim's view, societal members whose actions produce orderly arrangements rarely attain a comprehensive understanding of the causal regularities that govern and shape those actions; hence, sociological methods are required for observing and describing those regularities. Durkheim's 1897 study

Suicide exemplifies this distinction between ordinary social action and professional sociological analysis. Durkheim explicitly turns away from biographical reasons for specific suicides, as expressed, for example, in suicide notes, and turns instead to statistical rates of suicide. The rates are his social facts, and he explains them causally by reference to variations in nationality, religious affiliation, and social integration. Although Durkheim makes it clear that social facts are methodically produced, he insists that a comprehensive scientific analysis of those facts can only be attained through a detached analysis that adheres to a scientific methodology. Simply put, for Durkheim, ordinary members of a society collectively produce social order by acting *methodically*, but the structured causal relations that govern those actions remain implicit and unknown until the sociologist deploys the appropriate scientific *methodology*.

In many of his ethnomethodological writings, Garfinkel invokes Durkheim's *Rules*, but he argues that actors are not "cultural dopes" who act without comprehending the methodical grounds of their actions. This does not mean that ordinary social actors have a scientific understanding of the social world. Instead, it means that their understandings—regardless of how they are attained and regardless of how adequate or inadequate they appear to be from a detached observer's point of view—are *endogenous* to the practices sociologists study and thus cannot be contained within the precepts and principles of an abstract social science methodology. Garfinkel thus collapses the difference between members' methods and sociological methodology, which is fundamental to Durkheim's program. For Garfinkel and ethnomethodology, both the production of particular actions and the analytical investigation of the systematic organization of such actions constitute the field that sociologists study. This conception of the social field leaves unsettled what ethnomethodology's own "methodology" could possibly be and how it relates to the many varied methods and methodologies at large in society.

In many of the natural and social sciences, methodology is an explicit and fundamental aspect of the discipline's pedagogy, organization, and public presentation. Although they are not usually called "methodologies," the pedagogies and techniques in many legal, clinical, and artistic specialties also include explicit analyses, rules, principles, and examples. In both scientific and nonscientific domains of practice, it is widely recognized that practical mastery requires the development of tacit knowledge or practical know-how, not just formal prescriptions. For some specialties, accredited mastery can be gained only after years of practice under the guidance of experienced practitioners. The mastery of a natural language, driving in traffic, and many other commonplace practices also involve formal and informal pedagogies, analyses, rules, tests of competency, and know-how gained through practice. The balance between formal methodology and tacit know-how varies from practice to practice, but even the most formal disciplines require improvisation and situated practice, while the most commonplace practices have their pedagogies, rules of thumb, and maxims. Given the assumption that rules and other formal prescriptions do not, and cannot, give adequate sociological descriptions of the practices through which they are used, ethnomethodologists closely examine singular situations of practice in great detail, using participant observation and often audio and video recordings to gain firsthand access to those situations.

Ethnomethodology's treatment of methods as phenomena makes no exception for social scientific methods. Instead, ethnomethodologists treat social surveys, statistical techniques, interviews, ethnographic observations, and even their own procedures as *topics* of investigation rather than *resources* for securing reliable scientific knowledge. Some of Garfinkel's earliest studies delve into social science research practices such as coding interview responses and analyzing official records. These studies demonstrate that ad hoc judgments grounded in commonsense knowledge of the social world are crucial for constituting data points, assigning instances to nominal categories, and interpretatively relating observational data to relevant social contexts. Such a treatment of methods as topics does not mean that ethnomethodologists themselves eschew all established methods for collecting, organizing, and analyzing social phenomena but that they are attuned to the necessity of adapting methods to specific social situations and are indifferent to the special truth status assigned to results derived from any particular formal methodology, regardless of its scientific pedigree.

Conversation Analysis

In the late 1960s and early 1970s, Harvey Sacks (1935–1975), along with Emanuel Schegloff

(b. 1938) and Gail Jefferson (1938–2008) developed a distinctive line of ethnomethodological research, which came to be known as conversation analysis (CA).

CA has become a robust mode of analysis in its own right. Consistent with ethnomethodology's treatment of methodology as being reflexively part of the production of social order, as opposed to being an exclusive resource for professional investigators, CA identifies a *phenomenon* of interest. The idea is that the participants in a conversation "analyze" an ongoing conversation while producing it. Accordingly, an utterance placed in a conversational sequence displays an "analysis" of the interactional situation—a situation that importantly includes prior utterances by other speakers—and provides a relevant contribution to that situation as well as a condition for any actions that follow. Even an expression as simple as a beeping automobile horn provides an occasion for drivers and pedestrians in the vicinity to engage in an instant analysis of the immediate situation to determine whether the beeping horn is marking an offense, warning of a hazard, or expressing a greeting. Such "analysis" is displayed in responsive actions and nonactions in the unfolding scene.

In the 1970s, CA began to acquire an identity of its own, distinct from that of ethnomethodology. Leading figures in CA deliberately pursued a technical direction, elaborating on specific sequential and interactional organizations of talk and gesture in "ordinary" conversations and in specific institutional settings, such as courtroom tribunals, clinical diagnoses, classroom lessons, political debates, and survey interviews. One of the valuable lessons from such studies is that interaction in institutional settings is largely made up of "ordinary" interactional exchanges. This focus on the ubiquity of "ordinary" interactional routines in specialized activities has much to recommend it, but it does not delve very deeply into the many and varied repertoires that distinguish specific cultivated practices from one another.

Studies of Work

Starting in the 1970s, Garfinkel and some of his students turned their attention to the work accomplished in various arts, professions, and sciences. Although such work included paid employment in organizations, Garfinkel used it more broadly as a term for the achievement of specialized activities of all kinds. These studies made significant contributions to social studies of science, particularly ethnographies of scientific laboratories that began to be published at the end of the 1970s. They also contributed to the development, starting in the 1980s, of ethnographic research programs of technology design, use, and management, which became known as "workplace studies" or "computer-supported cooperative work."

Ethnomethodological studies of work in the professions and sciences often employ audio recordings of instances of activity, but the main task and challenge is to come to terms with distinctive competencies for playing music, constructing mathematical proofs, conducting litigation, or demonstrating scientific lessons. Depending on the case, it may be necessary to *become* a mathematician, lawyer, or musician and to use the skills and materials of the relevant practice to display and analyze its social organization.

Ethnomethodology's Status as a Theory or Method

Ethnomethodology is not a social scientific theory or method, as such. Because methods of all kinds make up its subject matter, it is necessary for ethnomethodologists to learn the methods studied as a precondition for analyzing them. However, ethnomethodologists also make use of some common research practices, and the field has developed a distinctive set of analytical themes and terms. The primary reason for employing such practices and terms is to elucidate how various plans, rules, algorithms, recipes, maps, guidelines, maxims, protocols, proverbs, and so on, are used in actual conduct. Ethnomethodological methods are thus subordinated to the task of disclosing other methods (and methodologies). For the most part, they are procedures for gaining insight into taken-for-granted organizations of practice, rather than verifying or falsifying scientific inferences about the social world.

Michael E. Lynch

See also Durkheim, Émile; Ethnoscience/New Ethnography; Phenomenology; Popper, Karl; Sociolinguistics; Wittgenstein, Ludwig

Further Readings

Button, G. (Ed.). (1991). *Ethnomethodology and the human sciences*. Cambridge, UK: Cambridge University Press.

Garfinkel, H. (1967). *Studies in ethnomethodology*. Englewood Cliffs, NJ: Prentice Hall.

———. (2002). *Ethnomethodology's program: Working out Durkheim's aphorism*. Lanham, MD: Rowman & Littlefield.

Heritage, J. (1984). *Garfinkel and ethnomethodology*. Cambridge, UK: Polity Press.

Livingston, E. (1987). *Ethnographies of reason*. Aldershot, UK: Ashgate.

Lynch, M. (1993). *Scientific practice and ordinary action: Ethnomethodology and social studies of science*. New York, NY: Cambridge University Press.

Sacks, H. (1992). *Lectures on conversation* (2 vols.). Oxford, UK: Blackwell.

Sacks, H., Schegloff, E. A., & Jefforson, G. (1974). A simplest systematics for the organization of turn-taking in conversation. *Language, 50*(4).

Suchman, L. (2007). *Human-machine reconfigurations: Plans and situated actions*. Cambridge, UK: Cambridge University Press. (Original work published 1987)

Sudnow, D. (1991). *Ways of the hand*. Cambridge, MA: MIT Press. (Original work published 1978)

ETHNOSCIENCE/NEW ETHNOGRAPHY

Ethnoscience was a method of data collection by which anthropologists hoped to document how the people they studied thought about and organized their worlds. Because of a strong linguistic influence, those who practiced ethnoscience conceptualized culture as a mental model and, in this way, turned dramatically away from the evolutionary and material theories of culture that were popular at that time. Although anthropologists since Bronisław Malinowski and Franz Boas claimed that their work should reproduce native reality, the ethnoscientists were the first to outline a concrete method by which they hoped to accomplish this goal.

Beginning in the mid-1950s, some American anthropologists began to critique the discipline's previous methods of conducting ethnographic research. These critics argued that ethnographic studies were idiosyncratic, unscientific, and produced data that were not comparable with the data from other ethnographic research. They further claimed that earlier ethnographic studies distorted their data by forcing them into Western conceptual categories. The answer to these issues, the critics claimed, was to conduct ethnographic research in a new way. They called this new method ethnoscience, or the new ethnography. The followers of ethnoscience argued that to make ethnographic research more accurate, anthropologists should follow a specific methodology, taking what the linguist Kenneth Pike called an *emic* approach. That is, they should attempt to reproduce cultural reality as it was perceived and lived by the members of the societies they studied.

For ethnoscientists, culture consisted of all of a given society's conceptual categories; thus, they argued that ethnographies should describe the folk classifications of native thought. The ideal ethnography in this view would include all the principles that natives must know to think and act appropriately in the social situations within their cultures. Consequently, practitioners of this type of ethnography should be able to think like a native. Furthermore, ethnoscientists believed that research and writing conducted in this manner were scientific in that the validity of one's data was testable (you could ask a native if your work was correct) and that different ethnographers following the prescribed research methods should, in principle, get the same results.

Ethnoscience and Linguistics

Ethnoscientists assumed that native understandings and systems of classification were embedded in language. This idea was in part a result of the popularity of a linguistic theory called the Sapir-Whorf hypothesis, named after the linguists Edward Sapir and Benjamin L. Whorf. Sapir and Whorf were interested in the relationship between language and thought, and in the 1930s, they proposed that language shaped people's perceptions of the world. Whorf especially tried to illustrate this linguistic determinism in his analysis of the conceptual world of the Hopi as illustrated by their language. This emphasis on the influence of language on thought led ethnoscientists to see a close connection between language and culture. They reasoned that replicating the classification system of a language would give an ethnographer the ability to understand the world in the same way as did native speakers of that language.

The method by which one conducted an ethnoscientific analysis was based on insights derived from the study of phonology by members of the Prague school of linguistics. Phonology is the study of the sounds used in language. The particular perspective of the Prague school of linguists was that the sounds of a language, called *phonemes*, were identifiable only when contrasted with other sounds. For example, the phonemes /b/ and /v/ are separate phonemes in English but variations of the same phoneme in Spanish. These can be identified by contrasting words where the only change is in the one sound. In English, /b/at and /v/at are different words. In Spanish, /v/oy and /b/oy mean "to go." The two phonemes thus form a contrast set in English but not in Spanish, and in this way, linguists identified the phonemes and re-created the emic use of the two sounds.

The particular insight of the ethnoscientists was to extend this linguistic theory to cultural patterns of meaning. To elicit native mental models, practitioners of the new ethnography depended heavily on eliciting information through highly structured interviews, using sets of contrasting items that were designed to highlight the essential features of conceptual categories such as kinship, illness, plants, color, or animals. For example, to try to better understand the Lacandon Maya ethnic identity, Jon McGee once presented a series of Lacandon Maya men and women with a set of physical and cultural contrasts he thought would be significant in determining "Lacandoness." This included features such as light or dark hair, light or dark skin, speaking Maya or not speaking Maya, and numerous other contrasts. He discovered that the primary marker of Lacandon identity among the people he questioned was having a Lacandon father. In ethnoscientific terms, McGee replicated the conceptual model of Lacandon ethnic identity.

Basic Principles of Ethnoscience

The fundamental principles of ethnoscience were outlined by Ward Goodenough in his 1956 article "Componential Analysis and the Study of Meaning" and William Sturtevant in his 1964 article "Studies in Ethnoscience." According to these works, the key instrument in fieldwork was a highly structured interview designed to elicit native conceptual categories, which ethnoscientists called *domains*. Once a domain had been identified, the researcher then tried to identify the objects that populated that domain, which they called *lexemes* or *paradigms*. For example, the domain of animal contains classes of objects such as dogs and cats. However, anthropologists should not assume that they understand how or if natives conceptualize the differences between dogs and cats. Both dogs and cats are furry, four-legged animals and have tails. Following the Prague-school linguistic model, ethnoscientists used a technique called *componential analysis* to identify contrast sets. They maintained that by conducting a componential analysis, using a box diagram such as the one in Table 1, a researcher could identify the specific characteristics that a native used to distinguish one object from another. In this instance, having four legs and a tail are not characteristics that distinguish dogs from cats among American pet owners, but having long whiskers, purring, and having retractable claws are components of the conceptual model of cats that separate them from dogs. In theory, data collection in this manner is more systematic and replicable and thus, followers claimed, more scientific. Furthermore, ethnoscientists of the 1950s and 1960s claimed that once a researcher understood a people's conceptual categories, he or she could think like a native member of that culture.

Table I A Componential Analysis of Dogs and Cats

Items of Contrast	Fur	Four Legs	Tail	Retractable Claws	Long Whiskers	Purrs
Dogs	Yes	Yes	Yes	No	No	No
Cats	Yes	Yes	Yes	Yes	Yes	Yes

Early attempts at this form of research picked discrete phenomena for analysis, such as Floyd Glenn Lounsbury's analysis of Pawnee kinship or Harold Conklin's 1955 study of Hanunóo color categories. However, ethnoscientific methods are easily applicable to other topics, and researchers have applied them to a wide variety of situations, including J. P. Spradley's 1971 analysis "Beating the Drunk Charge"; Brent Berlin, Dennis Breedlove, and Peter Raven's 1974 analysis of Tzeltal Maya plant classifications; and Dorothy Holland and Debra Skinner's 1987 study of the cultural models behind American gender terms.

Although claiming to be a scientific method for conducting ethnography, ethnoscience required a level of cultural relativism that made cross-cultural comparison virtually impossible. After all, if each culture has a unique way of conceptualizing the world and could only be described in its own terms, how could cultures be compared? Furthermore, critics argued that it was impossible for ethnographers to get inside another's head and replicate their thought processes. A researcher had to rely on what people said, and much of human behavior is nonlinguistic. A further problem concerned variation within society. When ethnoscientists said that they were trying to re-create a native's cultural reality, an obvious question was "Which native?" Ethnoscientists typically dealt with phenomena in which there was a high degree of consensus, such as kinship terms or names of plants where identification was fairly simple (as in the example of dogs and cats above). However, the total ethnoscientific analysis of a culture would be unbelievably complex. In fact, such a thing was never attempted. Because of these difficulties, the early promises of ethnoscience were never fully realized. However, following developments in psychology and linguistics over the past several decades, ethnoscience led to the development of the field of cognitive anthropology, which has a much stronger emphasis on brain function and neurology.

R. Jon McGee

See also Boas, Franz; Cognitive Anthropology; Ethnomethodology; Goodenough, Ward H.; Lounsbury, Floyd; Malinowski, Bronisław; Pike, Kenneth; Prague School of Linguistics; Sapir, Edward; Sapir-Whorf Hypothesis and Neo-Whorfianism; Whorf, Benjamin Lee

Further Readings

Berlin, B. O., Breedlove, D., & Raven, P. (1974). *Principles of Tzeltal plant classification*. New York, NY: Academic Press.

Conklin, H. C. (1955). Hanunóo color categories. *Southwestern Journal of Anthropology, 11*(4), 339–344.

Frake, C. O. (1961). The diagnosis of disease among the Subanun of Mindanao. *American Anthropologist, 63*(1), 113–132.

———. (1962). The ethnographic study of cognitive systems. In J. P. Spradley (Ed.), *Culture and cognition: Rules, maps, and plans* (pp. 191–205). Long Grove, IL: Waveland Press.

Goodenough, W. H. (1967). Componential analysis and the study of meaning. *Language, 32*(2), 195–216.

Holland, D., & Skinner, D. (1987). Prestige and intimacy, the cultural models behind Americans' talk about gender types. In D. Holland & N. Quinn (Eds.), *Cultural models in language and thought* (pp. 78–111). New York, NY: Cambridge University Press.

Sturtevant, W. C. (1964). Studies in ethnoscience. *American Anthropologist, 66*(2), 99–131.

Whorf, B. L. (1941). The relation of habitual thought and behavior in language. In L. Spier, A. I. Hallowell, & S. S. Newman (Eds.), *Language, culture, and personality: Essays in memory of Edward Sapir* (pp. 75–93). Menasha, WI: Sapir Memorial Fund.

ETHOLOGY, HUMAN

Follow the duck, not the theory of the duck!

—William C. Charlesworth

Human ethology is the study of human behavior from an evolutionary perspective. It is a comparably young scientific discipline dating back to the 1960s. While Konrad Lorenz and even Charles Darwin already had some thoughts about the origins of human behavior, the systematic research of evolved behavioral patterns in humans gained momentum through the works of William Charlesworth, Irenäus Eibl-Eibesfeldt, and Detlev Ploog. The background of those three—developmental psychology, biology, and psychiatry—is an early indicator of the multidisciplinary nature of this research field. The idea of applying evolutionary ideas to human behavior was a novel one and inspired many new questions among scientists from different backgrounds.

Today, scholars with different scientific backgrounds continue to contribute to the understanding of the manifold aspects of human behavior from an evolutionary viewpoint. Evolutionary theory unifies them and thus creates a metadiscipline. The strength of this discipline is at the same time its greatest weakness: Evolution creates a common ground and forms a theoretical basis on which to build a research field, but at the same time, the multitude of disciplines that engage in ethological research have different histories and often use different methodological approaches. For example, evolutionary psychology and ethology base their research on evolutionary theory; both investigate human behavior in a broad sense. But in the European tradition, human ethology descended from ethology as a biological discipline, while in the United States the psychological disciplines were the first to apply evolutionary theory to behavior-related questions. In human ethology, observing behavior is central. In evolutionary psychology, the emphasis lies more on using questionnaires to conduct research.

Additionally, these approaches may alienate scholars who are not open to evolutionary ideas. This is especially true when the research topic is humans and even more so where human behavior is concerned. Bill Charlesworth wrote that his biological approach to the study of children was not welcomed warmly by his colleagues, while the use of animal models was state of the art.

Origins and Methods

Human ethology draws its inspiration from ethology, both in methodological and in theoretical respects. The great ethologist Nikolaas Tinbergen developed four questions that guide ethological research today. These questions illustrate a fundamental perspective of ethology, that is, it integrates evolutionary knowledge with interspecific comparisons, endocrinology, and neurology as well as developmental biology to create a whole picture of behavior. Tinbergen asked the following questions:

- What is the evolutionary function of a behavior, that is, its adaptive value?
- How did this behavior evolve in phylogeny?
- What are the proximate causes for the behavior, that is, the underlying brain functions, hormones, and so on?

- How does this behavior develop during ontogeny, that is, how do genes interact with the environment to manifest it in the organism?

Tinbergen's demand that all four questions be addressed emphasizes the need for ethologists to work in a multidisciplinary context.

Human ethology approaches behavior from three complementary angles: observations of behavior in real-life settings, experiments, and behavior simulation. Observation of behavior in real-life settings is the most basic method, with the advantage that the behavior occurs unencumbered by experimental devices or experimenter and observer effects. The great shortcoming of this approach is that in natural settings the number of intervening variables is large and cannot be controlled. The only way to circumvent this problem is having large data sets, which it is difficult and time-consuming to collect. In the early days of human ethology, in the search for universals in human behavior, observation in natural settings was the method of choice. Early ethologists, such as Rudolf Pöch or Irenäus Eibl-Eibesfeldt, employed special cameras to film behavior without their subjects being aware of it. Certainly, data collected this way do not meet the ethical standards for working with humans delineated in the Helsinki protocol. Nowadays, cameras have become much smaller and almost noiseless, so hiding them is not a great issue, but subjects have to provide informed consent before they can be filmed.

Behavioral observations—whether carried out in natural or experimental settings—are not an easy task, especially when the subjects are of the same species as the observer. It comes naturally to us to assign emotions and intentions to the behaviors of others. While this is adaptive in real life, it poses a problem for the scientist. Therefore, behavioral observation has to follow a number of rules to create a database that is as unbiased as possible. The human ethogram (i.e., the repertoire of all behaviors of humans) is by far larger than that of other animals, like the greylag geese made famous by the pioneering studies of Lorenz. Therefore, scientists have to limit their observations to behaviors relevant to their research question. These behaviors have to be described as behavior categories that are unambiguous and objective. The development of reliable behavior catalogs is tedious but necessary to ensure the quality of the research. Behavior annotation is time-consuming and challenging, but the insights promised through this approach can be far more valuable than mere questionnaire data. Asking direct questions might be easy, but the answers you get this way might not hit the core of your question.

In their attempt to create unbiased categories and achieve detailed description of behavior, behavior categories tend to atomize human behavior into its parts. The development of behavior catalogs for facial expressions, namely, the Facial Action Coding System, by Paul Ekman and Wallace Friesen (1978) and the Bernese System for annotation of body postures by Frey and Pool (1976) are examples of detailed descriptions of very low levels of behavior. The large number of codes necessary to describe a single facial expression or posture guarantees the objectiveness of the system but at the cost of highly time-consuming annotation.

The experimental approach offers the advantage that intervening variables can be controlled but at the cost of making the observations under lab conditions, which might be quite different from natural surroundings. Because the experimental approach usually requires less money and time to carry out experimental studies, it has become more and more popular in current research.

Recent developments in computer science have opened new ways of conducting ethological analysis. Behavior simulation makes use of the aforementioned behavior catalogs for the implementation of behaviors in avatars. Then behaviors, for example, facial expressions or postures, can be generated in the avatar, and the parameters of the behaviors can be modulated. The stimuli thus generated can be evaluated by subjects for their communicative meaning. This allows isolating the meaning of single behaviors from other intervening factors. This approach is also called reverse engineering, which is generating understanding of behavior from the bottom up. The needs of the game industry and man-machine interfaces have created a demand for in-depth understanding of communicative behavior so that these behaviors can be simulated in avatars and virtual agents. This has opened a new field of research in human ethology, which is strongly applied but in itself contributes to the understanding of communicative behavior.

Computer vision methodologies make behaviors accessible to research that are not measurable with traditional methods. For example, Wolfgang Schleidt proposes in his tonic communication model that signals may be sent repeatedly at a level below the perception threshold. These signals are likely motion quality, sounds, and odors. Computer vision is a useful tool for measuring motion quality. Indeed, the interplay between ethology and computer vision creates new research possibilities. While computer vision researchers have made use of guidance from ethology, which helps interpret their findings and guide their research, ethology itself might profit at some point from this synergy; algorithms developed based on video analytics could help ethologists automatize at least parts of their annotation tasks.

Conclusion

The theoretical framework of human ethology is framed by evolutionary theory and biological constraints. Human behavior is thus not arbitrary but shaped by evolutionary history. When a behavior is said to have evolved, this does not equal genetic determinism. All behaviors, like physical features in the phenotype, develop in complex gene-environment interactions. Genes alone never suffice to create a phenotype, while the environment needs a substrate to work with. While human ethology makes use of evolutionary theory to explain the origins of behavior tendencies, and to understand the reasons why this is so, it does not justify behavior in any way. There might be behaviors that make perfect sense in biological terms (furthering the individual fitness) but violate legal, ethical, or social rules. It is not the goal of ethology to make biological usefulness the norm for our ethics. Humans are biological organisms, but they are also sociocultural beings. Therefore, biology and ethology can contribute to an understanding but can never completely decode human behavior.

Elisabeth Oberzaucher

See also Darwin, Charles; Human Behavioral Ecology

Further Readings

Charlesworth, W. R. (1986). Darwin and developmental psychology: 100 years later. *Human Development, 29,* 1–35.

Eibl-Eibesfeldt, I. (1967). Concepts of ethology and their significance in the study of human behavior. In H. Stevenson, E. H. Hess, & H. Rheingold (Eds.), *Early behavior: Comparative and developmental approaches* (pp. 127–146). New York, NY: Wiley.

Ekman, P., & Friesen, W. (1978). *Investigator's guide: Facial action coding system.* Palo Alto, CA: Consulting Psychologists Press.

Frey, S., & Pool, J. (1976). *A new approach to the analyses of visible behavior* (Research Reports of the Psychological Institute). Bern, Switzerland: University of Bern.

Grammer, K., & Oberzaucher, E. (2006). The reconstruction of facial expressions in embodied systems: New approaches to an old problem. *ZIF Mitteilungen, 2,* 14–31.

Lehner, P. N. (1998). *Handbook of ethological methods* (2nd ed.). Cambridge, UK: Cambridge University Press.

Ploog, D. (1964). Verhaltensforschung und Psychiatrie [Psychiatry and behavioral science]. In H. W. Gruhle, R. Jung, W. Mayer-Gross, & M. Mueller (Eds.), *Psychiatrie der Gegenwart* [Psychiatry at the present]. Berlin, Germany: Springer-Verlag.

Schleidt, W. M. (1973). Tonic communication: Continuous effects of discrete signs in animal communication systems. *Journal of Theoretical Biology, 42,* 369–386.

Voland, E., & Grammer, K. (Eds.). (2003). *Evolutionary aesthetics.* New York, NY: Springer.

EVANS-PRITCHARD, E. E.

Edward E. Evans-Pritchard (1902–1973) was one of the outstanding anthropologists of the 20th century. Known best for his field studies in northeastern Africa, especially among the Azande and Nuer of southern Sudan (now Republic of South Sudan), he also wrote extensively on the history of anthropology and its philosophical background. He held the Chair of Social Anthropology at Oxford from 1946 to 1970, becoming a key architect of British social anthropology and developing fruitful links with neighboring disciplines.

Biography

Evans-Pritchard was born in Sussex in 1902. His father, an Anglican clergyman, was from Caernarvon and spoke Welsh; his mother's family was from Liverpool. In 1939, he married Ioma Heaton Nicholls. Knighted in 1971, he eventually died in Oxford in 1973 and is survived by three sons and two daughters.

After Winchester School, the young Evans-Pritchard read history at Exeter College, Oxford, where R. R. Marett had already established a focus on anthropology, mostly devoted to armchair theories of "primitive" society and religion. Evans-Pritchard was tired of the standard kings-and-battles type of history he had to study, and though interested in Marett's lectures, he was curious to meet anthropologists who actually did fieldwork. On graduating in 1924, he moved to the London School of Economics to study with C. G. Seligman and Bronisław Malinowski. From there he proceeded to the Sudan in Seligman's footsteps. After initial research in the southern Funj region of the Blue Nile in 1926, he settled for the first time in the centralized kingdom of the Azande of southwestern Sudan in 1927, completing a London PhD on the Azande later that year. The next 3 years were spent mainly in Zande country, though, at the request of the Anglo-Egyptian Government of the Sudan, he embarked on a series of visits to the cattle-herding Nuer of the Upper Nile. He then taught anthropology from 1932 to 1934 at Cairo University before returning to the Sudan, supplementing his research among the Nuer and beginning fieldwork among the Anuak. Further plans to extend his fieldwork to western Ethiopia were ruled out because of the Italian occupation, but by 1940, he had begun military duties and was soon operating with Anuak irregulars on the frontier. During the Second World War, Evans-Pritchard also saw service in Syria and in post-Italian Libya, particularly in Cyrenaica, which provided an opportunity for further fieldwork.

After a brief postwar appointment in Cambridge, Evans-Pritchard became professor of social anthropology at Oxford and a fellow of All Souls College in 1946. From this base, until his retirement in 1970, he extended a network of worldwide contacts, particularly through graduate students (in which the Oxford Institute of Social Anthropology specialized) and visiting scholars. He himself spent various periods of leave as a distinguished visitor at the University of Chicago, at the Center for Advanced Study in the Behavioral Sciences at Stanford, California, and as an educational advisor to the Government of Ghana.

Influence

Evans-Pritchard's scholarly achievements were both deeply personal and of his time, in the relatively liberal climate for fieldwork in the middle years of

British imperial rule in Africa. He bridged the gulf between an older anthropology, which concerned itself almost exclusively with objectifying "the primitive" and a newer version, which extended its horizons to all humanity, thus capturing the attention of scholars in neighboring disciplines. From the 1950s onward, he devoted much of his energy to excavating anthropological themes from writings in European history and philosophy (an interest in his predecessors was evident even from his teaching days in Cairo). He was keen to reach a wide audience; he took on a variety of public speaking roles and accepted invitations from the BBC to deliver radio lectures. He established good connections with journals such as *The Listener* and the *Times Literary Supplement*, both of which carried regular articles and reviews concerning anthropology during his time. He served as president of the Royal Anthropological Institute (1949–1951) and was a founder, with Meyer Fortes, of the Association of Social Anthropologists (1946).

Evans-Pritchard gave encouragement to many younger scholars who were taking forward the project of developing social anthropology as a rich interdisciplinary field of academic study. Their contribution is now reflected in the range of *festschriften* and other tributes, such as editions of his unpublished lectures, articles, and books about his work, ethnographic films about peoples such as the Azande and the Shilluk, and online presentations of his photographs and material culture collections (through Oxford's Pitt Rivers Museum). There is also a very substantial body of literature commenting on, critically engaging with, and building on his ethnography, particularly about Azande rationality and about Nuer political order and religion.

A Humanities Approach

It is sometimes said that Evans-Pritchard moved away from previous conceptions of anthropology as a natural science (specifically Radcliffe-Brown's vision) toward a view of its place among the humanities. But it would be more accurate to see the marks of the humanities scholar from the start: an acceptance of human intellectual and aesthetic agency behind things that are said and done in the making of history and a view of social life as arising from culturally patterned forms of communication and interaction between people. Malinowski had

spoken of individuals and the way they were shaped by custom and culture, but "functionalism" was an abstraction partly fashioned by its critics. The same could be said of Radcliffe-Brown's notions of social form and structure, which, while derived from the Durkheimian school, scarcely had the same depth. "Structural-functionalism" emerged more or less as a target for criticism at a later date, with the advent of fashions for Claude Lévi-Strauss's linguistics-derived structuralism, for neo-Marxist analysis, and for phenomenology. Evans-Pritchard refrained on the whole from criticisms of the work of his immediate predecessors in anthropology. But it is worth noting that in a very early article on Zande dance (1928), he focused not only on the art, music, and enjoyment of dancing but also on its rivalries and divisive politics—as a way of ridiculing Radcliffe-Brown's portrait of dance among the Andaman Islanders as bringing individuals together in a simple, bodily, expression of social solidarity.

The ways in which Evans-Pritchard incorporated the methods of humanities research into his ethnographic projects are easily summarized. His collections of material culture and photographs are quite substantial. He recorded Zande music on wax cylinders. He took down or had written for him texts and stories, songs, and proverbs, mainly in the Zande language (though this kind of work was much more difficult in the restricted circumstances of his Nuer research). He collected, translated, and published Zande language materials throughout his life. His understanding of their idioms led to subtle observations on the veiled, irony-laden, allusive ways of communicating of the Zande, which the people called *sanza*; and from there, he went on to discuss their views on the inner self-consciousness of the human person. In 1964, he founded, with Wilfred Whiteley and Godfrey Lienhardt, the Oxford Library of African Literature, which produced 26 volumes of linguistic, literary, and artistic significance, including several by African authors.

Evans-Pritchard was one of the first English-language anthropologists to extend the scope of anthropology to those regions of the world where historians had long acknowledged sophisticated civilization. In this, he was following the lead of the Durkheimian school. While Durkheim himself remains famous for his library-based work on the aboriginal peoples of Australia, a good proportion of the reviews and essays published in the journal

L'Année Sociologique from 1898 onward were concerned with the Indian subcontinent, China, the ancient worlds of Greece and Rome, and the Middle East, including the Judaic heritage. It is well-known that he arranged for the translation of many essays from this journal, personally introducing several of these. Evans-Pritchard himself was particularly interested in Islam; following his 2 years of teaching Egyptian students at Cairo, he had a working knowledge of Arabic and was attracted to Sufi poetry. His posting to Libya in the 1940s gave him the opportunity to produce the first modern anthropological study of a Muslim, Arabic-speaking society in the context of its political and religious history.

A Historian With a Philosophical Bent

Evans-Pritchard was never trained as an anthropologist in any formulaic way, and he was not equipped (as today's students often are) with ready-made notions of social structure, culture, ethnicity, or identity. But, as a historian with a philosophical bent, he did come ready to take up some older and very general questions about the remoter regions of the world and their peoples, who had scarcely entered the existing historical record. In his later years, Evans-Pritchard devoted much time to the systematic excavation of post-Enlightenment sources for ideas about the place of what were seen as key achievements of civilization—such as the exercise of reason—in the longer history of human life and society. Ernest Gellner provided a guide to this project in introducing Evans-Pritchard's posthumous collection, *A History of Anthropological Thought*. Here, we see the direction of his quest for predecessors who had pondered such general questions about human history; not that any of them called themselves "social anthropologists," but from Aristotle through Montesquieu to Adam Ferguson, he shows their curiosity to have foreshadowed his own. We might group these recurring questions under three main heads: the place of reason in human life, the place of the state, and the place of religion.

Reason

Perhaps the book Evans-Pritchard is best remembered for is his *Witchcraft, Oracles, and Magic Among the Azande* (1937, later abridged). Written against the background of both popular stereotypes and academic theories concerning the mentality of primitive peoples, swayed as they were supposed to be by impulse and emotion, this whole book points to the doggedly rational way in which the Azande diagnose the presence of *mangu* ("witchcraft substance") in people's bodies and deal with its ill effects on others. The argument is so thoroughly documented for the Azande that no people since has been assumed to lack an ability to reason. And more recently, of course, plenty of doubt has been thrown on the extent to which "our own" behavior is dictated by reason (especially in the domain of illness and misfortune).

Evans-Pritchard's early articles on the Nuer, too, emphasize the strings of reasoning behind their migration with the cattle to seek new pastures as the floods recede and retreat to patches of dry land for cultivation as the rains come on again. He was the first to use the term *oecology* for such an analysis of what we might today call the "rationality of indigenous knowledge."

The State

Under this head, too, we need to start with the Azande. The royal houses and elite of the Zande constituted an imperial system on their own terms in precolonial times, and even today, their political legacy is found across Zande-speaking regions spanning South Sudan, the Democratic Republic of Congo, and the Central African Republic. Evans-Pritchard wrote extensively on the Zande State, on Zande political institutions and history, on Zande warfare and the rise of their political elite largely through conquest, and on the rise of "secret societies" and other changes during the colonial era. He also contributed a late volume of essays on *Man and Woman Among the Azande*—refreshingly not just a standard study of kinship but closer in spirit, perhaps, to questions raised by modern gender studies. He also gave detailed attention to the forms of political organization among the Anuak, including the kingship, and based his Frazer Lecture of 1948 on the divine kingship of the Shilluk.

The main concern of Evans-Pritchard's first book on the Nuer (1940) is to identify—in this context apparently lacking a political center or traditional government—the nature of what political order did indeed exist. Over the wide Nuer-speaking areas, there were mutually understood principles of political agreement. Communities separated during the floods would regularly meet up during the dry season and compete for pastures, and exchanges of cattle were organized according to widespread convention, crucially in cases of marriage transfer or in the settlement of feuds. On marriage, women joined their husband's group; these communities defined themselves around a core of male patrikin but often included other individuals, such as sisters' children, adopted refugees, or conquered assimilees. Relations between such lineage-based groups were represented according to their relative position within a patrilineal genealogy, branching out from early times to include all. Extended forms of this model were used to explain and justify wider conflicts between brotherly groupings, who could nevertheless find a common cause at the appropriate segmentary level and a mediator from the special lineages of leopard-skin chiefs.

There were also outstanding individuals remembered as prophetic leaders, who were potential peacemakers capable of bringing sections and tribal groups together, even non-Nuer peoples. Evans-Pritchard was asked to start work in Nuerland at a difficult time; a British-led military patrol had recently been on a punitive campaign, publicly hanging a son of the key 19th-century prophet Ngundeng. But his ethnographic analysis was far from being simply an intelligence report useful to the government. Overall, his account of Nuer politics, while it became a type case of the "stateless society," remains an astonishing portrait of the resilience of forms of political cooperation that have over time proved their effectiveness against easy co-option by any state or empire.

An important point to note is Evans-Pritchard's insistence on a distinction between patrilineal descent as the essentially *political* idiom of Nuer conflict and reconciliation, on the one hand, and the *personal networks* of kinship created through marriage and the rearing of children, on the other. His second book on the Nuer (first published 1951, though written as early as 1942) makes this clear and was intended to be read in conjunction with the first. His later analysis of the social history of Cyrenaica (1949) owes much to the insights of his earlier work on the Nuer, drawing attention as it does to the unifying potential of the religious order of the Sanusiya among the dispersed clans of the Bedouin, especially in the context of Italian colonial rule.

Religion

Evans-Pritchard's concern with the presence and place of religion among the peoples he had studied emerged a little while after his fieldworking days and his conversion to Roman Catholicism in 1944. It became explicit only with his book *Nuer Religion* (1956). His younger colleague Godfrey Lienhardt, who had by this time carried out his own research on Dinka religion, encouraged him, supplying a number of insights into commonly held notions among the Nilotic-speaking peoples. Broadly, Evans-Pritchard starts with an acceptance that when the Nuer speak of *kwoth* in the most general way, pray to this presence in the Above, and offer sacrifices, the translation "God" can be used. In the circumstances of local peacemaking, where specific lineages or clans hold ceremonies, various species that are held to have helped the parties in the past—such as giraffes—may be named and appealed to. However, what are here still called "totems" are presented as "refractions" of the particular relationship that God might have with a given group. Interestingly, Evans-Pritchard did not find—or perhaps did not look for—much evidence of formal religious cosmology and ritual among the Azande or the Anuak; but then, the Old Testament parallels with the cattle-herding Nilotes are very striking and positively invite theological analysis.

A New Genealogy for Anthropology

In the course of his later writings on social anthropology and theories of "primitive religion," Evans-Pritchard linked his own position very clearly with the school of the *Année Sociologique*. He also acknowledged sympathy with the ideas of the fieldworking archaeologist and philosopher R. G. Collingwood (who himself was independently developing an interest in anthropology by the late 1930s). Like Collingwood, Evans-Pritchard was conscious of the long genealogy behind the way scholars had tackled their own place in the human story. But one had to venture beyond the standard texts and explore outside the library. Direct encounter and engagement was called for; the study of savages (those who could not reason) or barbarians (those outside the state) or Pagan nonbelievers (those as yet unreached by the world religions) was recorded only in caricature form in most of the early sources.

Fieldwork had already been pioneered as *the* mode of anthropological research by Boas in America and Malinowski in Britain, but it was Evans-Pritchard who introduced into field research itself some of the perennially important historical and philosophical questions about the long-term nature of human reason, the sources of political agreement, and the central standing of religion, ritual, and ceremony in human life. Current research in evolutionary psychology and on the beginnings of language and social organization is taking up these old questions once again, though from a complementary perspective on what many today would agree is a coherent field of anthropological study.

Wendy James

See also Durkheim, Émile; Fortes, Meyer; *L'Année Sociologique*; Lienhardt, Godfrey; London School of Economics; Malinowski, Bronisław; Oxford University; Royal Anthropological Institute; Seligman, Charles Gabriel

Further Readings

Beattie, J. H. M., & Lienhardt, G. (Eds.). (1975). *Studies in social anthropology: Essays in memory of E. E. Evans-Pritchard by his former Oxford colleagues*. Oxford, UK: Clarendon Press.

Beidelman, T. (Ed.). (1971). *The translation of culture: Essays to E. E. Evans-Pritchard*. London, UK: Tavistock.

———. (1974). *A bibliography of the writings of E. E. Evans-Pritchard*. London, UK: Tavistock.

Burton, J. W. (1992). *An introduction to Evans-Pritchard* (Studia Instituti Anthropos, Vol. 45). Fribourg, Switzerland: Fribourg University Press.

Cunnison, I., & James, W. (Eds.). (1972). *Essays in Sudan ethnography: Presented to Sir Edward Evans-Pritchard*. London, UK: Hurst.

Douglas, M. (1980). *Edward Evans-Pritchard*. Brighton, UK: Harvester Press.

James, W. (2007). "A feeling for form and pattern, and a touch of genius": E-P's vision and the Institute, 1946–72. In P. G. Rivière (Ed.), *A history of Oxford anthropology* (pp. 98–118). Oxford, UK: Berghahn Books.

Johnson, D. (1982). Evans-Pritchard, the Nuer, and the Sudan political service. *African Affairs, 81*, 231–246.

Kenny, M. (1987). Trickster and mystic: The anthropological persona of E. E. Evans-Pritchard. *Anthropology and Humanism, 12*, 9–15.

Lienhardt, R. G. (1974). E-P: A personal view. *Man (n.s.), 9*, 299–304.

Morton, C. (2009). The initiation of Kamanga: Visuality and textuality in Evans-Pritchard's Zande ethnography. In C. Morton & E. Edwards (Eds.), *Photography, anthropology and history: Expanding the frame* (pp. 119–142). Farnham, UK: Ashgate.

Singer, A., & Street, B. (Eds.). (1972). *Zande themes: Essays presented to Sir Edward Evans-Pritchard*. Oxford, UK: Blackwell.

Evolutionary Anthropology

Evolutionary perspectives have been part of anthropology since its beginnings, but their content and prominence have shifted dramatically. In contemporary anthropology, evolution plays a much more prominent role in biological anthropology, and even in archaeology, than in sociocultural anthropology. However, there is an active set of researchers applying modern evolutionary theory to many facets of human social behavior; this research is the focus here. This entry begins by delineating different approaches or paradigms in evolutionary anthropology: behavioral ecology, cultural evolution, and evolutionary psychology. It then turns to an outline of key topics and research findings.

In contrast to classical evolutionary approaches in anthropology, current research draws much more explicitly on evolutionary biology for both substantive and methodological elements. This creates tension with mainstream views in cultural anthropology, where "biological determinism" is seen as misguided and dangerous, as discussed briefly in the final section on controversies.

Paradigms

Contemporary evolutionary behavioral anthropology clusters around three distinct but overlapping perspectives or paradigms: behavioral ecology, cultural evolution, and evolutionary psychology. Each of these is treated elsewhere in this encyclopedia, but a summary and comparison are warranted here.

Human Behavioral Ecology

Human behavioral ecology (HBE) draws directly on the methods and theory in evolutionary biology that analyze behavior as adaptive responses to natural and social elements of the environment. In essence, behavioral ecology posits that individuals make decisions that maximize fitness-correlated outcomes, given the ecological constraints and opportunities they encounter. These decisions need not be conscious ones (although with humans that may be more likely), and behavioral ecology tends to be quite agnostic about the actual mechanisms (genetic, cognitive, cultural, etc.) underlying adaptive choices. The overall research strategy involves developing mathematical models that provide a deductive basis for hypotheses about adaptive behavioral variation. Under what conditions will monogamy be more adaptive than polygyny? When should a forager seek prey alone versus cooperating in group foraging? Under what conditions will political hierarchy emerge in an egalitarian group? The models attempt to capture the most important variables that affect the costs and benefits of alternative strategies, and empirical applications then evaluate how accurate the derived predictions are, using quantitative data. For example, if wealth (e.g., land or livestock) is a primary factor that brides (or their families) use in choosing grooms, then polygyny will be more likely when wealth is unequally distributed. More precisely, this "polygyny threshold" model predicts that brides will be willing to be a second or third wife if their share of the groom's wealth exceeds that which they can get by marrying monogamously; as a result, wealthy men will end up with more wives, and many poor men with none.

HBE studies began to appear in the late 1970s and initially focused primarily on hunter-gatherer resource choice and land use (foraging strategies), an interest that remains strong in archaeology. In the 1980s, evolutionary studies of human reproductive behavior and social organization became much more prominent and continue to do so today. Most HBE research has focused on "small-scale societies"—hunter-gatherers, horticulturalists, and pastoralists—but recently, a growing number of studies have examined the behavioral ecology of large-scale agrarian or industrialized societies.

Cultural Evolution

Cultural evolution (CE) research (sometimes called "dual transmission" research, as it posits inheritance and evolution in both genetic and cultural channels) also began in the late 1970s, most prominently with the writings of Robert Boyd and Peter Richerson. Unlike the classic evolutionism of Leslie White, this paradigm is explicitly neo-Darwinian and relies on formal mathematical models (mostly drawn from population genetics but adapted to fit cultural transmission). Unlike genetic inheritance, cultural transmission is not limited to inheritance from mother and father, and can involve horizontal transmission (from peers), one-to-many transmission (from teachers or religious leaders), conformist transmission (adopt local norms and practices), and prestige-based transmission (imitate the successful). The resultant models are diverse, and the predicted outcomes myriad. In many cases, CE models predict that CE can diverge from what would be genetically adaptive and that group benefits (in competition with other groups) can override the interests of individuals or kin groups.

Although CE offers intriguing links to long-standing interests in sociocultural anthropology, it has had difficulty attracting followers within anthropology. This is partly because of the complexity of the theory and because, until recently, there were very few empirical applications. Recent work has begun to remedy the latter problem, with empirical analyses of food taboos, ethnic boundaries, cultural complexity, religious belief systems, and even large-scale social evolution. In addition, CE researchers regularly conduct experimental evaluations, usually in computerized lab settings but sometimes in the field.

Evolutionary Psychology

Evolutionary psychology (EP) is the most well-known (some would say notorious) of the three paradigms. EP analyzes psychological mechanisms as "Darwinian algorithms" or evolved cognitive modules. Although primarily based in psychology, EP has a prominent set of anthropological practitioners, including John Tooby, Donald Symons, and Jerome Barkow. A key tenet of most EP researchers is that human decision making is guided by distinct, domain-specific cognitive modules rather than by more general mechanisms that work across multiple domains. In contrast with HBE, EP practitioners tend to favor the view that adaptive strategies are less opportunistic and flexible; many argue that modern environments will produce much maladaptive behavior, since conditions are so radically different from the "environment of evolutionary adaptedness" in which our species evolved. In essence, EP posits that we are adapted to the past and that we should not expect fitness-maximizing strategies in modern contexts.

The bulk of EP work has focused on mate preferences, but a body of work with more anthropological relevance concerns the psychology of cooperation, coalitions, and conflict. The great bulk of EP research takes place in experimental contexts, generally in industrial societies (often with college students), but various researchers have applied the paradigm in field settings, including small-scale societies.

In sum, the three paradigms differ in origins, assumptions, methods, and practice. However, these distinctions are not hard and fast, and recently the boundaries between the paradigms are becoming less defined, with some researchers adopting quite pluralistic approaches.

Key Topics

This section summarizes some key topics and research findings in evolutionary anthropology.

Resource Ecology and Land Use

Anthropologists have long studied the variation in how people make their livelihoods and how this variation tracks ecological conditions. Evolutionary perspectives link this variation to evolved preferences and decision rules, on the one hand, and to consequences for survival and reproduction, on the other.

Hunter-gatherer foraging strategies were an early focus in modern evolutionary anthropology and link it to Julian Steward's cultural ecology. Prey choice models predict the animal and plant species that foragers will choose to harvest, out of the set of available prey; similar models apply to patch (resource area) choice and time allocation. The currency in these models is usually return rate (food harvested per unit foraging time, often measured in calories per hour). When prey types with high return rates are abundant, foragers are predicted to specialize in these and ignore lower-return types, but they have to broaden their choices when high-ranked types are less available. Given the careful measures of time and energy, very precise predictions can be made about variation in prey choice as a function of seasonal (or shorter or longer) changes in prey

abundance, changes in technology (which can alter the return rates and encounter rates of different prey), or individual abilities. Tests in a wide variety of environments with foragers from diverse cultural backgrounds have generally found rather close agreement with these predictions. Similar models have been developed to predict production decisions in pastoral and agricultural economies. People everywhere seem to be quite sensitive to variation in the efficiency with which their labor produces food, even in cultures that lack systems of counting, let alone concepts like caloric value or precise gradations of time.

But research has also revealed some complexities. For example, men and women often engage in very different subsistence tasks or make systematically different choices even when engaged in the same general task; for example, women rarely hunt large, mobile game, and men often pass up productive plant resources while foraging. Researchers disagree about why this occurs. Some argue that this results from child care constraints, especially nursing, and is an efficient division of labor given those constraints. Others argue that men are motivated to take more risks in production (even in contexts where child care is not constraining) and that this differential risk preference is due to the greater potential gains in status and mating success available to males. Much current research and debate focus on these issues.

Another complexity concerns resource depletion. Efficient foraging in the short run, or even over a person's lifetime, does not guarantee that resources will be conserved; similar concerns apply to pasture among pastoralists or forests among swidden ("slash-and-burn") farmers. In these cases, it may not be individually rewarding to safeguard resources for future generations if they are open access (available to all members of a population) or even communally owned—the infamous "tragedy of the commons." Again, researchers disagree about the solution to this problem. Some point to ways in which efficient production can yield sustainable harvests as a byproduct; for example, switching to more productive "patches" when the current one becomes less productive will not only increase labor efficiency but also allow depleted areas to recover—something observed in foraging, pastoral, and swidden systems alike. Other researchers argue that local norms and institutions are designed to prevent overharvesting; these vary from informal understandings to formal rules with strict enforcement. Evidence indicates that such regulations frequently exist but often increase harvest amounts or efficiency, making their rationale unclear. In any case, habitat degradation and extinction of prey have occurred repeatedly in human history, particularly in newly occupied regions.

One solution to conservation dilemmas is land ownership, so that the benefits of conservation fall on those who conserve (or on their immediate descendants). Models of the conditions favoring ownership (often termed *territoriality*) predict that resources must be sufficiently dense and predictable to offset the costs of defending property claims. This "economic defensibility" model has been successfully applied to a variety of foraging, pastoral, and agricultural societies and can explain the variation in land ownership between societies, the historical shifts over time, and even the microvariation within societies (family vs. communal ownership, why some areas are open access while others are owned, etc.).

Reproductive Strategies

Natural selection is driven by differential survival and fertility linked to heritable variation. This makes the study of reproductive strategies central to evolutionary anthropology, and research over the past 3 decades demonstrates this. Reproductive strategies can be subdivided into mating effort (attracting and retaining mates) and parental effort (providing offspring with the resources and care to ensure their own reproductive success). For humans, we must distinguish between mating systems and marriage systems, though these overlap greatly. Furthermore, human parental investment continues long past the weaning or even sexual maturity of offspring, often extending beyond the life of the parent via wealth inheritance. These facts offer opportunities and challenges for research in evolutionary anthropology.

Humans are mammals, and mammalian reproductive biology creates some important constraints. In preindustrial conditions, only women can be certain that a child is their own (no DNA testing for paternity), women cannot produce offspring more often than about once a year, and only mothers can safely and successfully feed nursing infants. As a result, men can potentially benefit more than women from mate guarding as well as from multiple mates (through polygyny, extramarital affairs, serial monogamy, and concubinage). Accordingly,

evolutionary models predict greater investment in mating effort, lower parental investment, and higher variance in reproductive success among men than among women. Mating effort takes many forms, from direct competition with other men, to resource accrual to attract more mates, and even arguably to striving for status, political power, and ritual renown.

Evolutionary models of mating systems generally differentiate between resource-defense polygyny (using control of resources to attract more mates) and mate-defense polygyny (coercing women into marrying or mating with a man and threatening anyone who challenges this). Evidence for resource-defense polygyny is quite detailed, including cases such as East African pastoralists who acquire additional wives with bride price paid in livestock. Evolutionary arguments for coercive mating effort are less carefully documented and raise many political objections (see the "Controversies" section), yet it is hard to deny that raiding for mates, coercive mate guarding, and rape occur (though they are not necessarily condoned) in a wide variety of cultures and are perpetrated almost exclusively by men.

On the other hand, women may also benefit from multiple mates. Polyandry can ensure more male labor to support offspring, and data from Tibetan-speaking areas indicate that women with multiple husbands do have higher reproductive success (surviving offspring) than monogamously married women. As Sarah Hrdy suggested, women can also use ambiguous paternity to convince multiple men to provide some resources in the hope that a child is theirs. Evidence from some South American Indian groups supports this hypothesis up to a point. Finally, in situations where male income is highly unstable, women can increase resource access by shifting between mates according to their current income; this appears characteristic of the urban poor, as documented by many sociologists as well as anthropologists.

Once mating (through marriage or otherwise) has produced offspring, they must be raised. Human children are highly dependent, and researchers have documented that they do not "pay their own way" (in food production) until late adolescence. This creates various adaptive dilemmas: how often to produce a new child, how to feed and care for multiple young ones, how much to invest in offspring based on their quality or gender, and when to cease producing offspring. Much research by evolutionary anthropologists focuses on these questions.

Cooperation, Collective Action, and Hierarchy

The evolution of cooperation is a central focus of modern evolutionary thought. Humans are unique in the degree to which they cooperate in large groups with low relatedness and solve collective action problems that thwart other species. Much research in evolutionary anthropology is concerned with applying evolutionary models of reciprocity, kin selection, group selection, and costly signaling to explain cooperation.

The basic logic of reciprocity is that of mutual aid: Help me when I'm in need, and I'll reciprocate when conditions reverse; we will then both benefit. The problem is that free riders who accept help but don't return the favor can benefit even more. Indirect reciprocity adds reputation to the mix, allowing third parties to shun free riders without being suckered; human language (gossip) is invaluable here, as various theoretical and empirical studies have shown.

The logic of kin selection is expressed in Hamilton's rule: Help relatives as long as the benefit they gain, devalued by degree of genealogical closeness, exceeds the cost to the helper. This is commonly misunderstood as a rule to always help close relatives; but the benefits and costs are critical and vary according to ecological and social factors, independently of relatedness. In fact, close relatives can be one's closest competitors, and Hamilton's rule can readily predict when evolution favors being nasty toward relatives.

But what about large groups with low relatedness? Direct reciprocity fails if one can't exclude free riders from public goods (such as defense against enemy attack). Furthermore, experimental economic games reveal that people often contribute to public goods or punish free riders, even when behaving selfishly would yield higher gains. Some researchers propose that group selection (cultural or genetic) is responsible for such phenomena and that culturally transmitted norms reduce within-group variation in payoffs and increase the differences between groups enough to drive this evolutionary process. Others argue that such costly group cooperation represents misfiring of the cognitive mechanisms that evolved in the past, when small, intimate groups meant that reputations for free riding were impossible to hide.

Still others suggest that mechanisms such as indirect reciprocity or costly signaling (indicating one's superior abilities or commitment by freely contributing to collective action, thereby gaining alliances or mating opportunities) can solve this problem. This debate is currently unresolved.

Two important topics in the evolution of human cooperation are ritual and religion, and the emergence of political hierarchy and economic inequality. All of the explanations just outlined are actively employed by anthropologists analyzing these phenomena. Again, consensus on the main forces shaping them is yet to be achieved.

Controversies

Many sociocultural anthropologists are hostile to evolutionary explanations of human social behavior, believing that these are misguided and dangerous. One concern is that such explanations entail biological or genetic determinism, which are inflexible patterns of behavior that deny agency or cultural meaning. However, most current evolutionary anthropologists are well aware of the pitfalls of simple determinisms and provide ample room for the agency (intentionality), cognition, and cultural variation characteristic of our species. As noted above, most explanations advanced in this research focus on decisions—hardly a form of simple genetic determinism.

Another concern is that evolutionary explanations provide justifications for the status quo and, in particular, for oppressive phenomena, such as racism, sexism, or ethnocentrism. Researchers usually respond to such critiques by noting that attempts to understand phenomena do not entail attempts to morally or politically justify them; furthermore, correct understanding should actually aid attempts to counteract pernicious social phenomena. This does not usually mollify critics who view evolutionary accounts as ideology masquerading as science, and indeed, nothing can mollify such critics, not even evidence recently published that demonstrates that evolutionary anthropologists have liberal social views indistinguishable from those of other anthropologists. In any case, such critiques of evolutionary research seem to be declining in anthropology and the other social sciences as the theory becomes more nuanced and the empirical confirmation more extensive.

Eric Alden Smith

See also Cultural Transmission; Evolutionary Psychology; Gene-Culture Coevolution; Human Behavioral Ecology

Further Readings

Barkow, J. H., Tooby, J., & Cosmides, L. (Eds.). (1992). *The adapted mind: Evolutionary psychology and the generation of culture.* Oxford, UK: Oxford University Press.

Barrett, L., Dunbar, R., & Lycett, J. (2002). *Human evolutionary psychology.* Princeton, NJ: Princeton University Press.

Cronk, L., Chagnon, N., & Irons, W. G. (Eds.). (2000). *Adaptation and human behavior: An anthropological perspective.* Hawthorne, NY: Aldine de Gruyter.

Gangestad, S. W., & Simpson, J. (Eds.). (2007). *Evolution of mind: Fundamental questions and controversies.* New York, NY: Guilford Press.

Laland, K. N., & Brown, G. (2002). *Sense and nonsense: Evolutionary perspectives on human behavior.* Oxford, UK: Oxford University Press.

Mace, R., Holden, C., & Shennan, S. (Eds.). (2005). *The evolution of cultural diversity: A phylogenetic approach.* London, UK: University College London Press.

Richerson, P. J., & Boyd, R. (2005). *Not by genes alone: How culture transformed human evolution.* Chicago, IL: University of Chicago Press.

Shennan, S. (Ed.). (2009). *Pattern and process in cultural evolution.* Berkeley: University of California Press.

Smith, E. A., & Winterhalder, B. (Eds.). (1992). *Evolutionary ecology and human behavior.* Hawthorne, NY: Aldine de Gruyter.

Summers, K. (2005). The evolutionary ecology of despotism. *Evolution and Human Behavior, 26,* 106–135.

Voland, E. (1998). Evolutionary ecology of human reproduction. *Annual Review of Anthropology, 27,* 347–374.

Winterhalder, B., & Smith, E. A. (2000). Analyzing adaptive strategies: Human behavioral ecology at twenty-five. *Evolutionary Anthropology, 9,* 51–72.

EVOLUTIONARY PSYCHOLOGY

Evolutionary psychology integrates principles from a wide range of fields to study the evolved psychological architecture of the human mind. Rather than functioning as a subfield within psychology, evolutionary psychology is an *approach* that can be applied to any area of psychology: developmental, cognitive, social, clinical, and so on. At its core, evolutionary psychology is based on a simple principle: The human brain, like every other organ in the body, evolved over millions of years of natural selection; to understand the functional design of the mind/brain, as with other organs, one must consider the recurring sets of selection pressures that existed over the course of human evolution. Each recurring selection pressure, that is, each feature of the world that influenced survival and reproduction (e.g., disease-causing organisms and predators), created an adaptive problem (e.g., avoiding contact with contaminated substances and avoiding predators, respectively). Evolutionary psychology considers the adaptive problems humans likely faced and generates models of the possible mechanisms that evolved to solve them. So, for instance, research and theorizing on disgust suggest that this emotion is a panhuman system that evolved in response to the selection pressures posed by disease-causing organisms and motivates the withdrawal from substances possessing cues to contamination.

Importantly, evolutionary psychology entails descriptions at multiple levels of analysis, most notably, ultimate and proximate levels of analysis. An ultimate level of analysis explains why a particular system exists—that is, how it would have promoted survival and/or reproduction in ancestral environments. For instance, an ultimate explanation for the disgust system is that it promoted survival by motivating the withdrawal from substances associated with disease-causing organisms. By contrast, a proximate level of analysis details how the system operates and executes its function in an individual. With respect to disgust, a recent proximate model suggests that cues associated with bodily fluids, feces, and rotting meats and fruits are taken as input to generate an index of pathogen presence, which then motivates withdrawal. Additional proximate explanations include neuroscientific analyses of where the system is located and development analyses that specify how the system is calibrated over the life span.

Advancements in many disciplines, including evolutionary biology, cognitive science, and anthropology, have helped establish the field of evolutionary psychology. Evolutionary biologists have a long history of talking about the functional features of nonhuman organisms. Specifically, biologists use the term *adaptation* to refer to structures or behaviors that evolved to perform a specific function in response to a recurring selection pressure. Evidence that a particular feature is an adaptation comes from examining its structure and operation—the more the feature shows evidence of functional specialization and complex organization and possesses properties that are unlikely to have arisen by chance alone, the greater the likelihood that the feature is an adaptation to a particular aspect of the social, biological, or physical world. In addition to the theory of natural selection and the concept of adaptation, evolutionary biology also has developed the principles of kin selection, sexual selection, and parental investment—all foundational theories that constitute the field of evolutionary psychology.

Cognitive science is another important pillar within evolutionary psychology, and it is what distinguishes evolutionary psychology from sociobiology. The cognitive revolution of the 1960s developed a new language for describing mental phenomena. By introducing the concept of computation, this discipline paved the way for a richer description of internal, unobservable psychological processes. One main goal of evolutionary psychology is to provide, in rich information-processing language, the set of computational systems that generate human behavior and that constitute our evolved psychology. Cognitive science also opened discussions of modularity. Evolutionary psychologists maintain that for many of the adaptive problems humans faced, natural selection has led to the evolution of specialized systems tailored to solving specific problems. This has led to heated debate regarding whether the mind is composed of many functionally specialized systems (i.e., it is massively modular) or a few more general-purpose systems. Basic engineering principles suggest that, to solve multiple problems, one device rarely outperforms multiple, functionally specialized devices. However, whether natural selection engineered our psychological architecture using this principle is certainly an empirical matter.

Anthropology has also made invaluable contributions to evolutionary psychology, particularly as a result of ethnographies of the remaining hunter-gatherer groups. Because a fundamental aspect of the evolutionary analysis of human psychology is the environment—physical, social, and otherwise—in which humans evolved, modern hunter-gatherer groups can provide us with clues to the types of selection pressures that might have been relevant over the course of human evolutionary history. Additionally, because evolutionary psychologists

propose that psychological adaptations are human universals, cross-cultural research in anthropology has been instrumental in the investigation of the consistency of this proposal.

Evolutionary Psychology: An Empirical Science

The application of evolutionary principles to the study of cognitive mechanisms provides a powerful two-pronged approach of hypothesis generation and hypothesis testing to uncover the functional architecture of the human brain. The first, which can be considered a reverse-engineering approach, examines known psychological processes and their resulting behaviors or tendencies and applies evolutionary reasoning to generate predictions regarding their functional structure: Were they adaptations to specific adaptive problems? For example, the known sex differences in sexual promiscuity and features deemed attractive have led to a very fruitful body of research that has incorporated principles of parental investment and sexual selection to shed light on many intricacies of mate choice and of sexual and emotional jealousy and to establish them as cross-culturally consistent. The second approach, which can be considered prospective, starts from reasoning about likely adaptive problems to derive novel predictions about psychological adaptations. For example, navigating the social realm to find trustworthy exchange partners has undoubtedly been a recurrent adaptive problem over the course of human evolution. From this starting point, evolutionary psychologists have discovered that humans are remarkably good at detecting cheaters in social interactions and have shown that the mechanism(s) involved in this detection are very sophisticated: They do not apply to general logic problems that take the same structure (i.e., they are specific to social interactions), and they account for intentionality (i.e., accidental "cheaters" are not flagged as such), and the resulting behavior is the avoidance of poor social exchange partners. Thus, the application of evolutionary principles to psychology helps both to elucidate the functions of known phenomena as well as to discover novel ones.

Evolutionary Psychological Approaches to Culture

Most accounts of evolutionary psychology usually describe the field as antithetical to cultural explanations. Yet, one of evolutionary psychology's founding works, *The Adapted Mind*, by Jerome Barkow, Leda Cosmides, and John Tooby, represents the first full-fledged introduction of the field of evolutionary psychology and has as its subtitle *Evolutionary Psychology and the Generation of Culture*! From day one, evolutionary psychologists have been interested in how culture arises and how individuals are influenced by and act within those cultures. Rather than viewing culture as an amorphous, external force that magically organizes the human brain, evolutionary psychologists argue vehemently that culture is a product of the human mind and that the human mind consists of many psychological adaptations that evolved to perform tasks that aided in survival and reproduction. On this account, cultural elements can be linked to specific psychological systems.

Evolutionary psychology maintains that there is a universal human nature but that within-group similarities and between-group differences can emerge. One way differences can emerge is if psychological adaptations develop in different ways in different environments. A thought experiment, known as the "jukebox metaphor," illustrates how this could work. Imagine that, instead of humans, the world is populated by jukeboxes: Every jukebox in the world is constructed in exactly the same manner and contains (a) the same musical tracks, (b) a Global Positioning System device that detects latitude and longitude, and (c) a clock. Furthermore, the mechanism that selects which song to play does so based on the time, date, and location of the jukebox. Thus, jukeboxes in Las Vegas would all be playing the same song, which would be different from the song played by all jukeboxes in Barcelona, and so on. As a result, there would be between-group differences and within-group similarities in the songs played simultaneously by jukeboxes, as with the differences and similarities we observe among cultures. Furthermore, because the mechanism that decides what song to play incorporates the time and date, the song played in any one area would change over time, akin to the way cultures change over time. Additionally, if a jukebox were moved from one "culture" to another, it would play the same song as every other jukebox in its new location, since the mechanism choosing the song does so based on the time, date, and location, which the jukebox now shares with the others in the new area—it has adopted the local "culture." While obviously simplified, this metaphor makes an important point: Jukeboxes (or humans), while sharing an identical underlying architecture can nonetheless express different characteristics in response to the local environment. Thus, the mere presence of between-group differences and within-group similarities does not imply that the underlying species-typical psychological architecture is different. The jukebox metaphor illustrates what evolutionary psychologists refer to as *evoked* culture, which results from the interaction of species-typical psychological mechanisms and the local environment. Evolutionary psychologists distinguish evoked culture from *transmitted* culture, or social learning. Ultimately, both evoked and transmitted cultures arise by virtue of the collection of human psychological adaptations, and one goal of evolutionary psychology is to describe and explain cultural phenomena in terms of their underlying psychological mechanisms.

Areas of Study Within Evolutionary Psychology

Evolutionary psychologists have been investigating a range of phenomena. Here, we provide a small sampling of areas of inquiry within evolutionary psychology.

Attention: To what extent does human attention reflect adaptive design? Are evolutionarily relevant dangers attended to more quickly and efficiently than evolutionarily novel ones? Are there differences in facial recognition based on group membership?

Coalitional psychology: How should in-group and out-group members be treated relative to each other? Are there adaptations for categorizing people by coalitional membership? Are out-group members avoided for reasons of pathogen avoidance?

Cooperation: With whom should one cooperate and direct benefits to? Who should be avoided or punished? How does cooperation in dyads differ from that in groups?

Emotion: What are the evolved functions of the various emotions? Do some psychopathologies have roots in the adaptive functions of some emotions?

Mate choice: What constitutes an attractive mate? Are the criteria different for men and women?

How do asymmetries in parental investment affect mate choice preferences?

Morality: What is the evolutionary basis for morality? Do expressed moral beliefs help one's own reproductive success by restricting that of others?

Social status: To what extent do physical attractiveness and formidability lead to increased social status? Does social status influence reproductive success?

Kinship: How do humans categorize others according to genetic relatedness? Does degree of relatedness affect altruistic behavior? Does degree of relatedness affect sexual attraction?

A Case Study: Incest Avoidance and the Incest Taboo

One area of study within evolutionary psychology has been on inbreeding avoidance. There are sound biological reasons why humans, like many other species, avoid mating with close genetic relatives. Specifically, the effects of deleterious recessive mutations and complications associated with pathogen transmission render the offspring of close genetic relatives less healthy than the offspring of unrelated individuals. This has led to multiple mechanisms across a variety of taxa for detecting close genetic relatives and avoiding them as sexual partners. But how do humans figure out who counts as a close genetic relative, and how does a sexual aversion develop? These questions have sparked a long-lived controversy, but today we are learning more about how human inbreeding avoidance works and its relationship to the cultural incest taboo.

At the end of the 19th century, Edward Westermarck, a Finnish social scientist, proposed an explanation for the commonplace observation that family members rarely find one another sexually appealing. Having noted the injurious effects of inbreeding in many species, Westermarck hypothesized that early-childhood association, which typically occurs among genetic relatives, serves as an inbreeding avoidance mechanism by triggering the development of a sexual aversion that becomes manifest later during adulthood. This has come to be known as the Westermarck hypothesis.

In addition to proposing a specialized mechanism that reduces the probability of choosing a close

genetic relative as a sexual partner, Westermarck also proposed an explanation for the origin of the incest taboo. He claimed that the biological systems responsible for the development of sexual aversions between close kin were also responsible for the culturally expressed incest taboo. That is, the explicit cultural prohibitions regarding incest were hypothesized to be an expression of the natural sexual disinclination that develops between near relatives. Westermarck's explanation of the incest taboo differed drastically from the reigning social learning theories of his day, which privileged the cultural incest taboo as the *origin*, not the consequence, of sexual avoidance behaviors.

Though initially well received, the Westermarck hypothesis and Westermarck's explanation of the incest taboo gradually fell into disfavor, mainly due to arguments posed by popular social scientists of the day (e.g., Sigmund Freud, Leslie White, and Claude Lévi-Strauss). However, in the past decade, evolutionary psychologists have started to uncover the mechanisms responsible for generating sexual aversions toward close genetic relatives, and it appears that Westermarck was correct.

To avoid incest, two basic systems are needed: one that detects kin—that is, estimates the probability that another is kin—and one that uses this probability to regulate sexual avoidance. Regarding sexual avoidance, researchers have identified disgust as the emotion that functions to avoid biologically costly sexual partners, such as close genetic relatives. But how does kin detection operate? Kin detection requires learning which individuals—of all the people in one's social environment—have a high probability of being a close genetic relative. At first, acquiring this information might seem to require no special systems because throughout childhood the people around us use language that implies relatedness (e.g., "Share your cookie with your brother," "Don't tease your sister"). Why did natural selection not simply use the kinship inferences that these sentences make possible as the primary input for sibling recognition? One reason is that linguistic information might not be the most reliable way to learn about relatedness. Kin terms are commonly used to refer to individuals who are not blood relatives, thus blurring genetic boundaries. For instance, "aunt" can refer to a parent's brother's wife (a nongenetic relative), and "brother" can refer to an unrelated coalition member. Furthermore, nonhuman species without the capacity for language also categorize individuals according to relatedness, suggesting that more primitive mechanisms exist. It is unlikely that evolution would have jettisoned prior functional mechanisms in favor of less reliable cultural and linguistic information.

Instead, similar to many nonhuman animals, humans likely rely on ecologically valid cues that correlated with genetic relatedness in human ancestral environments. To the extent that different cues correlated with an individual being a particular type of relative (e.g., a parent vs. a child vs. a sibling), different detection mechanisms might exist. Researchers have identified a short list of candidate cues that might govern the detection of siblings. Specifically, recent findings indicate that different cues are used to detect younger versus older siblings. For instance, seeing one's own mother caring for (e.g., breast-feeding) a newborn is a reliable cue to siblingship. However, as potent a cue as this might be, it is available only to older siblings; younger siblings must rely on other cues to identify probable older siblings.

One solution is for younger siblings to track parenting effort. Because parents are motivated to differentially invest in their own genetic offspring, monitoring which children regularly receive care from one's own parents would reliably identify probable older siblings. For instance, observing one's parents feeding or protecting another child provides evidence that this child might be a sibling. Moreover, the longer the duration of care observed, the more likely it is that the individual in question would have been a sibling under ancestral conditions. This cue—duration of shared parental care—is what Westermarck meant by coresidence duration.

Various anthropological and psychological investigations provide evidence that the human mind uses these cues in the development of sibling-directed sexual aversions. The first investigations were on the "natural experiments," social arrangements created by cultural institutions that caused genetically *unrelated* children to be raised together throughout childhood. One natural experiment was created by the communal practices of Israeli kibbutzim; another was the Taiwanese custom of minor marriage. These investigations found that when unrelated individuals coreside throughout childhood, there are lower marriage rates, as in the case of the kibbutzim; and in the case of the Taiwanese minor marriage, in which the coreared teens are forced to marry, there are decreased rates of fertility and increased rates of divorce and extramarital affairs.

In modern-day families, researchers have found that coresidence duration and observations of infant-directed care (e.g., breast-feeding) continue to operate as cues to siblingship and predict the intensity of sexual aversions. Additional research has investigated whether the strength of personal inbreeding aversions shape moral views regarding incest. Indeed, the strength of one's personal sexual aversions toward one's own opposite-sex siblings influences the strength of moral opposition to third-party sibling incest. These findings suggest that cultural phenomena relating to incest might be governed by systems that evolved to regulate personal decisions regarding the avoidance of close genetic relatives as sexual partners.

In closing, human inbreeding avoidance is one area of research within evolutionary psychology that serves as a good example of how evolutionary psychologists start with selection pressures and from there posit information-processing systems that would have enabled an adaptive solution. The topic of inbreeding avoidance also illustrates how evolutionary psychology can be used to understand cultural phenomena.

Eric J. Pedersen, Adam Smith,
and Debra Lieberman

See also Evolutionary Anthropology; Westermarck, Edward

Further Readings

Barrett, H. C., & Kurzban, R. (2006). Modularity in cognition: Framing the debate. *Psychological Review, 113*(3), 628–647.

Cosmides, L., Tooby, J., & Barkow, J. (1992). Introduction: Evolutionary psychology and conceptual integration. In J. Barkow, L. Cosmides, & J. Tooby (Eds.), *The adapted mind: Evolutionary psychology and the generation of culture* (pp. 3–18). New York, NY: Oxford University Press.

Tooby, J., & Cosmides, L. (1992). The psychological foundations of culture. In J. Barkow, L. Cosmides, & J. Tooby (Eds.), *The adapted mind: Evolutionary psychology and the generation of culture* (pp. 19–136). New York, NY: Oxford University Press.

FACE-TO-FACE INTERACTION

Though rarely discussed explicitly in anthropology, face-to-face interaction (FFI) is a primordial site of social and cultural life. Consider that human infants are treated as possible co-interactionalists from birth (indeed, in some cases, before birth!), and there is evidence, in various forms, that they are capable of intentionally contributing to such interactions within the first few months (and perhaps the first hours) of life. Moreover, everywhere we look, society "on the ground" is, in large part, constituted through the coordinated activities of individuals and groups in direct FFI. Inuit song duels, Wolof greetings, and Iatmul Naven are just a few of the anthropologically more famous forms that human social interaction takes. When seen in comparison with more familiar forms such as those found in English courtrooms, American presidential press conferences, and French family dinners, we may be impressed by the apparently limitless diversity. However, underlying such diversity is a robust, universal, generic infrastructure that exploits a range of species-specific cognitive abilities and prosocial motivations. It is this infrastructure that will be briefly sketched here.

Significant contributions to current thinking about FFI have come from a variety of sources, including linguistic pragmatics, the semiotics of Charles Sanders Peirce, as well as studies in anthropology, psychology, and other disciplines. This brief sketch, however, focuses on an approach to FFI that emerged in the work of Harvey Sacks, Emanuel Schegloff, and Gail Jefferson and has come to be known as

conversation analysis. Both Sacks and Schegloff were students of Erving Goffman—a transdisciplinary scholar who, though trained as a sociologist, had a major impact on, and indeed was himself strongly inspired by, anthropology. Goffman was perhaps the first and certainly the most eloquent defender of the view that FFI constituted its own phenomenon—that it had properties that were sui generis and not reducible to individual psychology or broader social processes. Sacks, Schegloff, and Jefferson incorporated this idea, and it may be understood as the first pillar of conversation analysis.

While Sacks and Schegloff were studying with Goffman at Berkeley, they were influenced by the highly original studies of Harold Garfinkel and the approach he developed known as *ethnomethodology*. The goal of Garfinkel's early studies was to uncover the underlying practices of reasoning that members of a society use in accomplishing everyday activities and that make society possible. A major part of Garfinkel's investigations was taken up with the question of how one person makes sense of another's conduct, including their talk. This concern was incorporated into conversation analysis, the second pillar of which is the idea that participants in social interaction engage in practical reasoning both to produce their own talk and to understand the talk of others. Both Goffman and Garfinkel thus provided inspiration for a new and distinctive approach to the study of ordinary social interaction. Sacks, Schegloff, and Jefferson were left though with the task of inventing a method by which it might be systematically studied.

Sacks, Schegloff, and Jefferson began their study of social interaction by looking at audio recordings of telephone calls as well as copresent interaction and found there to be a locus of intricate order. Early studies showed that any given interaction could be broken down into parts and that these parts consisted of orderly practices of speaking that issue in orderly consequences and that together form orderly sequences of action in interaction. Moreover, this order is not the product of statistical regularities or of categorical imperatives but rather of a persistent and pervasive orientation by the participants to a set of structures or norms. Like any set of norms or rules in this sense, those that organize social interaction do not determine conduct but rather provide a framework through which it is intelligible. That is, participants in interaction can be seen by others as following a rule, deviating from it, attempting but failing to follow it, or simply violating it flat out—these various alternatives generating further informative inferences about what a participant "means" by behaving in a particular way. The orderliness of interaction then is a product of a member's methods that is brought off by participants in interaction in each and every one of its local instantiations through the application of regular practices of reasoning.

The structures or norms of FFI—the largely universal and generic underlying infrastructure alluded to earlier—are organized into partially independent or semiautonomous domains or systems. Three of these domains can be briefly sketched here.

Domains of FFI

Turn Taking

First, there is an organization of turn taking that provides for the orderly distribution of opportunities to participate in talk-in-interaction. Sacks, Schegloff, and Jefferson described a system having two components: (1) a *turn constructional component*, which defines the units out of which a possible turn can be constructed and, by extension, allows participants in interaction to anticipate the possible/probable extent and shape of any actual unit and thus to project its completion, and (2) a *turn allocation component*, which specifies an organized set of practices by which transition from the current speaker to the next speaker is managed. Together, these two components and the rules that organize their relation provide for the detailed orderliness of turn taking in interaction. It can be seen, for instance, that overwhelmingly self-selecting next speakers target possible unit completion points as places at which to start their own talk. In Figure 1, it can be observed that Parky twice attempts to begin his turn "That changed it," before it is eventually produced at line 06. Note the split-second timing evidenced here, with Parky attempting to come in at just those points where Old Man has reached possible (though obviously not actual) completion of his current turn. Clearly, to come in at just these points, Parky must have anticipated where Old Man would reach possible completion of his current turn. Examples are presented using the transcription conventions originally developed by Jefferson. For present purposes, the most important symbols are the period ("."), which indicates falling and final intonation; the question mark ("?"), indicating rising intonation; and brackets ("[ ]"), marking the onset and resolution of overlapping talk between two speakers. Equal signs, which come in pairs—one at the end of a line and another at the start of the next line or one shortly thereafter—are used to indicate that the second line followed the first, with no discernible silence between them; in other words, it was "latched" to it. Numbers in parentheses (e.g. "(0.5)") indicate silence, represented in 10ths of a second. Finally, colons are used to indicate prolongation or stretching of the sound preceding them. The more the colons, the longer is the stretching.

An important and widely underappreciated point is that this turn-taking system operates independently of whatever actions are being accomplished in and through the talk it organizes—that is, whether persons are requesting, inviting, questioning, answering,

```
01 Tourist: Has the park cha:nged much,
02 Parky:   Oh:: ye:s,
03          (1.0)
04 Old man: Th'Funfair changed it'n [ahful lot [didn'i·
05 Parky:                           [Th-        [That-
06 Parky:   That changed it,
```

Figure I Parky

Source: From Sacks, Schegloff, & Jefferson, 1974.

agreeing, disagreeing, complaining, excusing, insulting, or whatever else, they do it in turns at talk constructed and distributed through an orientation to the turn-taking system.

Arrangement of Actions into Sequences

The arrangement of actions into sequences represents a second domain of organization in interaction. A very basic observation is that many—though not all—actions in talk in interaction come in pairs, for example, request and granting (or rejection), invitation and acceptance (or refusal), complaint and excuse (or denial), and so on. These pairs are linked together by a relation of conditional relevance whereby, to paraphrase Schegloff, given a first action (such as a request, invitation, or complaint), a second is made expectable. On the occurrence of a second, it can be seen to be a second item to the first (rather than an independent turn), and on its nonoccurrence, it can be seen to be absent (where an infinite number of other things did not occur but were not "absent" in the same way). Conditional relevance thus establishes a relation between a first and a second action that has both a prospective and a retrospective dimension. The prospective dimension ensures that the doing of a first action will activate a norm, making the doing of the second action relevant and noticeably absent if not produced. The retrospective dimension allows the speaker of the first action to see if and how she was understood—for example, the production of a turn recognizable as an excuse in response will reveal to the first speaker that she was heard to be complaining or accusing, whether that was her intention or not. Thus, the production of actions within sequences constitutes an "architecture of intersubjectivity" by which understandings are publicly displayed and ratified incarnately, en passant in the course of whatever business the talk is occupied with.

Repair

The third and final domain of organization to be described here is the system of repair. Troubles of speaking, hearing, and understanding are endemic to all forms of human interaction. The organized set of practices of repair constitute a natural, interactive system by which such troubles may be addressed at or near their point of production (or manifestation) and potentially resolved more or less immediately. The practices that make up the domain of repair are described in terms of *personnel* (self = *speaker of trouble source*, other = *any other participant*), *component* (trouble source vs. initiation vs. repair proper, etc.), and *position* (same turn, transition space between turns, next turn, third turn, third position). Consider, for instance, the case in Figure 2 excerpted from a talk show in which Ellen Degeneres is interviewing Rashida Jones.

```
01 El:        Al:right tell people about this hilarious
02            show. It's Parks and Recreation an' you
03      A->   an' Amy Poehler how- How great is that.=
04 Ra: B->    =It's pretty great=
05 El:        =mm mh[m.
06 Ra:             [It's- uhm- it- I just mean it- ek-
07            experientially for me it's pr(h)etty
08            [gr(h)ea(h)t(h) [heh heh ha (    )
09 El: C->    [yeah.          [no. an' but I mean it's
10      C->   a- I ah- know what you mea[nt. But I: say
11 Ra:                                  [hih huh ha hah ƚ
12            [huh huh .hh hah
13 El: C->    [it's really great. The two of you.=
14 Ra:        nyeah.
15 El:        yeah. [an' it's about,
16 Ra:              [(it is)
```

Figure 2 Rashida Jones on *Ellen*, April 2009

Where this fragment begins, DeGeneres is raising the topic of Jones's new television show with the comedian Amy Poehler, *Parks and Recreation*. DeGeneres initiates the topic by inviting Jones to tell the audience about the show. She then gives the title, before concluding the turn with "an' you an' Amy Poehler how—How great is that." Note then that this final part of the turn can be heard as a real information question—a request for Jones to specify how great "that" is. At the same time, the construction "How X is that?" is a familiar, idiomatic expression that, by virtue of the presupposition it carries, conveys that "it's X" or, in this case, "it's great." So here the talk at line 03 (the A arrow) takes the form of a wh question ("How great is that"), and Rashida Jones treats it as one by answering, "It's pretty great" (at the B arrow). This response, by treating "How great is that=" as an information-requesting question, reveals a problematic understanding, which Ellen subsequently goes on to repair in lines 09–10 and 13 (the C arrows). By saying, "I: say it's really great," Ellen indicates that "How great is that=" was not in fact meant as a question but rather as an assertion (or, more specifically, an assessment). We call this repair in third position for the following reason. A first-position utterance ("How great is that") has been produced, and the response to it, in second position, "It's pretty great," reveals a problematic understanding of it. This problematic understanding is then repaired in third position by the speaker of the first-position utterance when she clarifies that she was asserting or assessing and not asking.

Note that we can distinguish such cases from instances of third-*turn* repair, as exemplified in Rashida Jones's talk at lines 04–08. Here, the speaker originally produces the turn "It's pretty great," and this is treated as a trouble source when she repairs it by inserting the phrase "experientially for me," resulting in the repaired utterance "I just mean experientially for me it's pretty great." In this case, the repair might have been produced in the transition space between turns but has been "pushed" into third turn by Ellen's "=mm mh[m." at line 05. In contrast to the instance of third-position repair we just considered from this same fragment, here Ellen's "=mm mh[m." does not reveal a problematic understanding of what the prior speaker has just said and thus does not prompt the repair that is eventually produced.

A very important initial step in developing a rigorous account of interaction involves determining the different systems or domains out of which talk-in-interaction is composed. Though obviously interrelated in multiple ways, these domains have their own distinctive properties and operate to some extent independently of one another—so, for instance, it may have been noted that the turn-taking system underlies all the practices of repair just described but does so indiscriminately, irrespective of whether it is a repair or something else that is being done.

Language and the Structure of Interaction

Recent work from an anthropological and crosslinguistic perspective has begun to ask whether the particular language being spoken has consequences for the organization of interaction as described here. That study is still in its infancy, but initial results suggest that the underlying, generic structures of interaction may be inflected or torqued by the particular semiotic structures through which it is accomplished as well as the local circumstances within which it operates.

Jack Sidnell

See also Ethnomethodology

Further Readings

Enfield, N. J., & Levinson, S. C. (2006). Introduction: Human sociality as a new interdisciplinary field. In N. J. Enfield & S. C. Levinson (Eds.), *Roots of human sociality: Culture, cognition and interaction* (pp. 1–35). Oxford, UK: Berg.

Levinson, S. C. (2006). On the human "interaction engine." In N. J. Enfield & S. C. Levinson (Eds.), *Roots of human sociality: Culture, cognition, and interaction* (pp. 39–69). Oxford, UK: Berg.

Sacks, H., Schegloff, E. A., & Jefferson, G. (1974). A simplest systematics for the organization of turn-taking for conversation. *Language, 50*(4), 696–735.

Schegloff, E. A. (1968). Sequencing in conversational openings. *American Anthropologist, 70*(6), 1075–1095.

———. (2006). Interaction: The infrastructure for social institutions, the natural ecological niche for language, and the arena in which culture is enacted. In N. J. Enfield & S. C. Levinson (Eds.), *Roots of human sociality: Culture, cognition, and interaction* (pp. 70–96). Oxford, UK: Berg.

Sidnell, J. (2009). *Conversation analysis: Comparative perspectives*. Cambridge, UK: Cambridge University Press.

———. (2010). *Conversation analysis: An introduction*. Oxford, UK: Wiley-Blackwell.

Tomasello, M. (2008). *Origins of human communication*. Cambridge, MA: MIT Press.

FANON, FRANTZ

Frantz Omar Fanon (1925–1961) was a Martinique-born, French-trained activist, philosopher, and psychiatrist whose theorization of the psychosocial elements of the colonial encounter in metropolitan France and colonial Algeria shaped late-20th-century critical anthropology in Europe and North America.

Biography and Major Works

Born in the city of Fort-de-France, Martinique, a French territorial possession in the Caribbean, Fanon and his brother were raised in relative middle-class comfort. In the lycée (secondary school), he was taught for a time and was befriended by the anticolonial poet-activist Aimé Césaire (known for his endorsement of *negritude*), which contributed significantly to his awareness of racial and colonial inequalities. In the midst of World War II, he opposed the Vichy French government in several French-administered Caribbean islands, before joining the anti-Nazi resistance in France. Despite being decorated for his wartime efforts, the direct encounter with metropolitan racism deeply affected Fanon.

Not long after the war, he was awarded a scholarship to study psychiatry, a field still dominated by psychoanalytic techniques at the time. While obtaining his degree, he met, and came to marry in 1952, Josie Dublé, a French woman who shared similar moral and political attitudes to issues of race and colonialism. This was also the year he published *Black Skin, White Masks* (1952), his first sustained examination of the effects of racism and colonialism on the colonized. The book also included numerous reflections on growing up in Martinique.

The postwar intellectual climate in France tolerated open discussion of leftist ideas in a manner not as possible elsewhere in the West during the Cold War. It was an environment of cross-pollination in theory and practice. Fanon participated in dialogues occurring between and among Marxian-influenced activists and progressive thinkers from Africa and France, existential and phenomenological philosophers such as Jean-Paul Sartre, and psychoanalysts, like Jacques Lacan, refashioning their practice under the influence of structural linguistics. These ideas supported his ever-growing conviction to contest colonialism and racism. In 1953, he enthusiastically accepted a job managing the psychiatry unit of the Blida-Joinville Hospital in Algiers.

Fanon's clinical practice at the hospital was directed toward reform of the institution's policy and practices, leading some to refer to him as the Phillipe Pinel of Algeria, in reference to the reformist physician who, in the wake of the French Revolution, unchained patients in asylums. In particular, Fanon aimed to be culturally and religiously sensitive to those in his care. The political climate in the colony at this time was tense, and in 1954, the National Liberation Front (Front de Libération Nationale, FLN) began its guerrilla campaign to establish Algeria's independence from France. The number of patients increased in the psychiatric unit, many suffering from the effects of sustained interrogations, harassment, and physical and mental torture. Several cases appear in *The Wretched of the Earth* (1961), in the chapter "Colonial War and Mental Disorders." By 1955, Fanon had joined the FLN while continuing to work at the hospital. He began to travel widely throughout Algeria, partly in an effort to extend his understanding of the social and psychic life of rural Algerians and partly to conduct covert activity for the FLN.

Fanon resigned his post in 1956 to distance himself from the French government and to protest the manner in which the war was being conducted by the French troops. The letter of resignation is reprinted in *Toward the African Revolution* (1964). From that period onward, he no longer defined himself as French or Martiniquan, but as Algerian. Expelled from Algeria by the French authorities in 1957, Fanon made his way to Tunis, Tunisia, where he continued his activities with the FLN.

The brief period in Algeria, spanning 1953–1957, provided the experiences and observations that formed the essays collected in *A Dying Colonialism* (1959) and *The Wretched of the Earth* (1961). *Toward the African Revolution*, published posthumously in 1964, consists of a few brief essays written in the 1950s and primarily short pieces written for the FLN broadsheet *El Moudjahid.*

Reception in Anthropology of Fanon's Major Works

Although not formally trained in ethnographic techniques, Fanon's ethnographic sensibilities and empathy for marginalized others made him a sensitive observer of social relations of inequality in context. The three major works he published in his lifetime have had rather different receptions within anthropology. This is partly a consequence of the different intellectual traditions and inflections that inform his works (Marxian anticolonialism, existentialism and phenomenology, and psychoanalysis) and partly a consequence of the social, political, and intellectual milieu in which English-speaking anthropologists adopted his writings. Generally speaking, Anglophone anthropology focused especially on *The Wretched of the Earth* from the mid-1960s into the 1970s and *Black Skin, White Masks* from the mid-1980s into the 1990s, leaving *A Dying Colonialism* less well incorporated, though not altogether neglected.

The Wretched of the Earth

Although this was the last book he published in his native French, released just weeks before his death from leukemia in 1961, it was the first to be translated into English in 1963. In the context of the uneven but steady wave of formal political decolonization globally and the growing civil rights movement in the United States, *The Wretched of the Earth* found a ready audience. This was a period when many anthropologists more openly expressed their support of the colonized populations they studied. In the wake of a receding McCarthyism, this book, among the works of other colonial intellectuals, enjoined anthropologists to take account of the colonial and neocolonial situation, in contrast to the common ahistorical treatises of the day seeking to describe pure and distinct cultures.

Fanon's writing served as an inspiration to many anthropologists of the time, but among the Marxian "New Left" both inside and outside of anthropology it was also considered too simplistic in its Manichean alternatives. This simplicity, however, has also been argued to be a consequence of a translation lacking the nuances expressed in the

original French. Contentious too was Fanon's call for colonized people to respond to colonial violence with counterviolence as a means to overcome colonially generated feelings of inferiority and redefine personal and group identity positively.

Nonetheless, Fanon's text made a substantial contribution to anthropology as the discipline grappled with how to "reinvent" itself in a manner that more directly considered how the "colonial encounter" shaped fieldwork and disciplinary ethics. Despite the charge of oversimplified Manichean racial categories, his call to pay closer attention to (Marxian inspired) class dynamics among colonized and colonizers alike promoted a complexity and fragmentation of the social dynamics most anthropologists faced. The previous bounded and integrationist approaches in ethnography excluded the variety of colonials and their conflicting interests in shaping the sociocultural context. These functionalist ethnographies also paid insufficient attention to the dialectics of inter- and intra-ethnic social relations among colonized groups. In the 1960s and 1970s, *The Wretched of the Earth* was also a source of inspiration for intellectuals and academics, including anthropologists, from Western minority groups in metropolitan centers and in new or emergent postcolonial states, where their critiques of previous representations of colonial life reshaped the direction of Anglophone anthropology.

Black Skin, White Masks

Of Fanon's three major works, this was the first written but the last to be translated into English, in 1967. With its greater theoretical emphasis on existential, phenomenological, and psychoanalytic themes, this work was not as strongly taken up initially by an anthropology rethinking and reinserting historical materialism into its analyses in the 1960s and 1970s. As the discipline's focus shifted to the politics of representation, discourse theories, and identity politics, *Black Skin, White Masks* drew more attention. This was partly in response to a reexamination of the book in feminist, cultural, and postcolonial studies.

Written initially under the title "Essay on the Disalienation of the Black," the analytic focus on the construction of a racially inflected identity always had a practical and clinical goal of achieving psychosocial health for those labeled racially inferior.

As such, Fanon was broadly attuned to cultural context. Methodologically, the work has characteristics similar to what has come to be known as autoethnography, in that many elements of his personal experiences in Martinique and France, such as a White child's automatic fear of his black body, are taken as indicative of racialized colonial situations. Such processes of racial alienation are historical constructions that are specific to time and place. Disalienation, he concludes, requires recognizing that the "Other" of the (black) "Other" is not the (white) "Self."

Because of his style of writing, Fanon's analysis has been criticized on the grounds of overgeneralization. Even though his insights on colonial identity formation were recognized in anthropology at the time, there was also criticism of his not being able to substantially address the dynamics of identity formation among women of color or homosexuals, even as he incorporated them within his schema.

As Foucauldian conceptions of discourse became more widespread in anthropology, the psychoanalytic currents within Fanon were increasingly disregarded as a form of essentialism and reductionism, even though his use was far from orthodox or mechanical. A theme more resonant within the anthropology of the 1980s, and the intellectual climate broadly, was his concern to reestablish the study of bodies and corporeality in analysis in order to disrupt what many considered the undue privileging of the Cartesian ego, or mind over body, in the ethnographic writing of culture. The consolidation of a historical anthropology of colonialism as a subfield during this period also selectively drew inspiration from Fanon's publications.

A Dying Colonialism

The five essays that make up *A Dying Colonialism* are arguably Fanon's most ethnographic writings. It is perhaps because of this that this work has not been as closely scrutinized in anthropology. Unlike the overtly geopolitical and nationalist concerns of *The Wretched of the Earth*, these essays span a variety of different topics loosely threaded around a theme of changes in social and cultural institutions in an anticolonial war of independence. Based on his 4 years of observations in Algeria as a clandestine operative for the FLN, the essays all consider an element of society undergoing redefinition. In doing

so, he challenged the assumption, frequent among Euro-Americans, of tradition and custom being static and repetitive practices rather than dynamic ones. Nonetheless, since this is not fieldwork in any usual ethnographic sense, the essays have an idealistic, and sometimes superficial, character.

The opening essay uses the redefinition of the meanings associated with veils and veiling practices to challenge both colonial assertions of unchanging tradition and women's inferiority. The following essay considers the adoption of the radio by Algerians and generally serves Fanon as a metaphoric instrument to suggest that non-indigenous technologies are adopted or rejected according to the social, political, and economic context. The essay on the family in a situation of anticolonial war traces redefinitions in social relations of age and generation toward greater egalitarianism and personal independence as a result of resisting French colonialism. "Medicine and Colonialism" parallels, in the realm of knowledge and epistemology, what the radio stood for in terms of the adoption of technology according to circumstance. Last, Fanon addresses the political and economic heterogeneity of Algeria's Jewish and European minorities, emphasizing that further stereotypes should not be the response to colonial stereotypes.

An issue Fanon could not address, due to his early death, was the extent to which the transformations he observed in the context of war mostly did not become embedded and normalized in the postcolonial independence period. Fanon's attention to changes in meaning and practice in the revolutionary period prefigures the theme of violence re-creating identity, found in *The Wretched of the Earth*.

Fanon's Influence on Anthropology

Engaging two generations of anthropological thinking, the reception of Fanon's works has always been shaped by the larger political milieu within which anthropology operates and also by the major theoretical and methodological concerns predominating any given moment in the discipline. His appeal over time is connected to his political and ethical commitment toward undoing colonialism and racial oppression as well as his early use of intellectual currents that later became widespread in Anglophone anthropology. Fanon's version of historical materialism in colonial contexts was considered, if not always fully adopted, by anthropologists such as Eric Wolf and Bernard Magubane in the 1960s and 1970s. As the discipline shifted to postcolonial approaches to racism, culture, and identity, his works were critically engaged by Stephan Feuchtwang and Ann Stoler, for example, in the 1980s and 1990s. Despite their not always being directly named, Fanon's works have exerted a pressure within anthropology to pay attention to the psychocultural effects of cross-cultural encounters marked by economic and racial inequalities.

Udo Krautwurst

See also Postcolonial Theory

Further Readings

Fanon, F. (2008). Foreward to the 2008 edition by Ziauddin Sardar. In *Black skin, white masks* (pp. vi–xx). London, UK: Pluto Press.

Feuchtwang, S. (1985). Fanon's politics of culture: The colonial situation and its extension. *Economy and Society, 14*(4), 451–473.

Fuss, D. (1994). Interior colonies: Frantz Fanon and the politics of identification. *Diacritics, 24*(2–3), 20–42.

Geismar, P. (1971). *Fanon.* New York, NY: Dial Books.

Julien, I. (Director). (1996). *Frantz Fanon: Black skin, white mask* (70 minutes). UK: Normal Films.

Read, A. (Ed.). (1996). *The fact of blackness: Frantz Fanon and visual representation.* Seattle, WA: Bay Press.

FEMINIST ANTHROPOLOGY

Feminist anthropology takes as its subject women, men, and gender as a social relationship that is generally marked by inequality and difference or, in short, by power. Feminist anthropologists direct attention to all manner of research questions, but what they have in common is that they bring knowledge of the history of such power relations to bear on their scientific and interpretive work. While feminist anthropology embraces all the traditional subfields of anthropology (sociocultural, linguistic, and biological anthropology, as well as archaeology), this entry will be limited to the largest domain in the discipline, sociocultural anthropology. Moreover, the focus will be on developments in American anthropology, as a discussion of feminist anthropology in Europe and elsewhere in the world would require considerably more space than this entry allows.

Precursors to what we today call feminist anthropology date back to the late 19th century, and some analysts would include among them towering figures in anthropological history such as Lewis Henry Morgan, who revolutionized the understanding of kinship and social organization. Most of the discussion of feminist anthropology, however, begins with early-20th-century pioneering women in the discipline who, often based on their own experience in challenging gender norms, inquired into social relations marked by gender in ways few of their male counterparts had done. Several students of the acclaimed father figure in U.S. anthropology, Franz Boas, were among these now heralded women: Elsie Clews Parsons, Ruth Benedict, Margaret Mead, and Zora Neale Hurston, to name several of the best known. In their day, these women rarely held full-time academic positions—and Hurston never completed a graduate degree—despite their marked intelligence and exceptional talents in research and writing. The social climate of the early 20th century offered little support for women scholars, who might become celebrated authors without becoming established members of the professoriate in anthropology.

Notwithstanding such obstacles to women's entry into the profession, Mead and Benedict were to become widely known as public intellectuals, their writings reaching beyond academia to a large number of readers. Hurston, who faced greater challenges as a woman of color, achieved greater fame only after her own lifetime and is more often recognized as a folklorist and writer than as an anthropologist. As a group, these and other female anthropologists in the early to mid-20th century were notable for recognizing women as protagonists in their own lives, whereas in the past, male scholars frequently overlooked women or relegated them to the sidelines of culture and history. These pioneering women moreover contributed significantly to schools of thought such as historical particularism, culture and personality, and race and identity-based anthropology.

By the late 1960s and early 1970s, the second wave of the women's movement in the United States had inspired a new generation to look to anthropology to answer enduring questions regarding women's status and the origins of women's subordination across societies. Feminist activists hoped that anthropology might explain how women came to be the second sex, carrying the main responsibility for family and household, and earning less than men in the workplace. Activist anthropologists responded by developing research that documented or questioned the universality of women's secondary status. Some argued that it came about historically with the rise of social classes in state societies, when men gained ascendency as property owners, seeking to pass on their wealth to male heirs. Women thus provided the support services for men in the home and in the workplace, and this came to be seen as part of the natural order of things. By the mid-1970s, the "anthropology of women" was born as academic feminists laid claim to a new paradigm that would fundamentally challenge male-centered, or androcentric, anthropology for its flawed conceptualization of culture and society.

The Anthropology of Women

Two landmark edited volumes appeared at this time, Michelle Rosaldo and Louise Lamphere's *Woman, Culture, and Society* (1974) and Rayna Rapp Reiter's *Toward an Anthropology of Women* (1975). While the former tilted toward a more symbolic perspective on the asymmetrical gender relations found in nearly all societies, the latter emphasized the historical emergence of gender inequality in what had been more egalitarian societies of the past. Taken together, the two collections had considerable impact on the thinking in anthropology and beyond, as they made a compelling case that gender arrangements are diverse in form and are not set in stone. Instead, they showed that cultures and societies are malleable and are always undergoing construction—in fact, the evidence suggested that gender itself was socially constructed. Contributors to these volumes and several others around this time upheld the feminist position that anatomy is not destiny and that difference need not always mean inequality. One frequently quoted essay by Gayle Rubin was hailed as a brilliant retheorization of the ideas of Karl Marx, Sigmund Freud, and Claude Lévi-Strauss to account for the remarkably diverse ways in which a "sex/gender system" pervades cultures and creates different expectations for women and men in society.

Scholars of this generation called on anthropology as a discipline to bring women into the picture and not view them simply as pale reflections of their male counterparts. Indeed, they claimed that properly understanding women as occupying central

roles across cultures could shake the foundation of anthropology and transform the field. Some set out to show that while "man, the hunter" was lingering to find food in foraging societies, "woman, the gatherer" was providing the bulk of band societies' diets and also meeting other family needs. The new evidence prompted many in the discipline to revise their understanding, and this was reflected in new and more accurate language to describe both hunting *and* gathering in foraging societies. Such revisionist work lent credence to those who posited that just as present-day foraging societies depend mightily on women's work and value their contributions, so too were women in earlier periods of human history and prehistory likely to have held more prominent positions than had heretofore been understood.

The same attention to reexamining the gender division of labor and gender ideologies in foraging societies was taken to agrarian peasant societies, where it was found that women's labor and household contributions were widely underestimated. Just as anthropologists were considering the inputs of women in rural societies and their decision-making participation there, other scholars too were advancing critiques of Western notions of gender and development. These analysts converged in their discovery that women often played more substantial roles than had been previously documented by researchers. New data collection spurred new theorization about women's agency, or active participation, in agricultural and herding societies and called on development agencies to cease the colonialist practice of favoring men for "modernization" and undermining women's "traditional" roles in supporting families and households. At the same time, others pointed to the ways in which some Western-oriented programs overlooked the superexploitation of women who carried both traditional responsibilities and new burdens of structural adjustment in contemporary neoliberal contexts.

The Anthropology of Gender

By the early 1980s, there was a shift from a central focus on women to a more dynamic attention to gender relations in society, with a recognition that feminist analysis is needed to understand not only women's role in society but also men's and that ultimately the objective is to more fully account for the constitution of gender as a social process always in flux. This decade was also shaped by a broad critique by women of color in the feminist movement and in feminist scholarship, calling for recognition of the intersectionality of gender in relation to race as well as class, sexuality, and other social vectors. Feminist anthropologists who had long studied women of diverse cultural backgrounds nonetheless needed to contend with their own blind spots relating to the profound inequalities among the peoples with whom they conducted research. A more complex and robust anthropology emerged from such critical discussion. It was far from sufficient to "add women and stir" to bring about a transformed anthropology, but rather it would be necessary to decolonize knowledge by recognizing the unearned privileges of certain groups in society—including many women—and the exclusion of others for whom the multiple subjectivity of race, class, and nationality produces positions of subalternity.

An increasingly vibrant feminist anthropology emerged to embrace work that examined masculinity, femininity, and persistent social inequalities at the same time that it recognized the need for research on forms of political resistance, cultural expression, and economic resilience that successfully sustained communities and populations. The 1990s saw collections by Micaela di Leonardo (1991) and Louise Lamphere, Helena Ragoné, and Patricia Zavella (1997) and essays by Sherry Ortner (1996) that brought together critical approaches to gender, culture, and political economy, and sought to situate and deepen our understanding of the contingencies that shape complex lives. The questions they addressed ranged from conceptions of the body to reconceived family forms, from symbolic structures of dominance to the gendered politics of violence in times of economic crisis and national conflict.

An influential collection by Ruth Behar and Deborah A. Gordon (1995) also appeared during this time in response to the postmodern cultural turn in anthropology, whose advocates had often failed to acknowledge the contributions of women writers and theorists. Their work delved into anthropological history to uncover innovative yet nearly forgotten scholars of the past, some of them women of color, calling for a challenge to the canon that favors those with gender and racial privilege. The anthology incorporated fiction and other forms as well as more conventional essays to make a case for new means of conveying new knowledge. A few years

later, a collection on Black feminist anthropology edited by Irma McClaurin (2001) made its mark on the field, offering a rich account of the often obscured Black feminist tradition in anthropology along with exemplary contemporary research. This work inspired feminist anthropologists to reexamine "official" histories and received wisdom in order to be better scholars and produce more adequate and just frameworks of analysis.

Feminist Anthropology

The past decade has witnessed a continued trajectory from an anthropology of women and gender toward a still broader feminist anthropology. It would be incorrect to suggest that there has been an inevitable movement toward an ever more liberated practice in the field, and one could certainly point to setbacks, yet feminist anthropology has become quite firmly established in the field. Some might justifiably claim that the passion that fueled feminist analysts in the past is more muted now that feminist anthropology appears to be here to stay. They would be right to caution scholars about complacently resting on laurels when the wider society shows signs of pulling back on the gains women have made over the past decades. Even so, it is safe to say that anthropology today looks substantially different from the way it looked 40 years ago thanks in no small part to the feminists who challenged the discipline to become more inclusive and to better represent all members of societies, women and men alike. Here, let us consider some of the most productive areas of current debate and discussion in feminist anthropology.

Just as feminist anthropologists have sought to understand the diverse part played by women and men across societies, they have also sought to consider the positionality of researchers themselves in the field. They have suggested that men and women in the field may have different degrees of access to the subjects of their research: While men may have privileged access to those (often men) holding power and authority, women may often have the confidence of women and others who are in less central social positions. Moreover, feminist anthropologists today tend to be mindful of the differences among women, whether cultural, racial, or by social class or sexuality, and the implications these differences may have for their research and their analysis. This is not to say that researchers should only study those who are like themselves, but rather that a recognition of one's own position in relation to those one studies may enrich and deepen understanding of world cultures and societies. In the case of anthropologists who are members of the cultures they study, we may expect somewhat different "insider" perspectives, which complement and enhance the perspectives offered by "outsider" anthropologists.

Relatedly, feminist anthropologists have been among the scholars who bring to their written work significant attention to modes of representation of their research. Thus, they are often particularly attuned to the politics of language, the nuance of description, and the importance of giving voice to the subjects of research, so that those studied do not come across as passive victims, no matter how subordinated they may seem, but as active agents in their own lives. While feminist writers are not the only ones to experiment with form and genre, they have in some cases written autoethnography, collaborative works, fiction, or poetry as alternative means to convey ethnographic insights. This commitment to represent others fairly and accurately is guided by the abiding concern of many feminist anthropologists not only to do no harm but also to reciprocate with their research communities. Sharing knowledge, making work available in the languages of their areas of research, and leaving behind archives for local scholars are all ways in which they may seek to give back to those they study. Engaged anthropologists, feminists among them, have also contributed royalties from their publications, helped establish libraries and clinics, and in other ways tried to leave more than they have taken away. Some would consider themselves "public anthropologists" who are committed not only to the pursuit of knowledge but also to the broad circulation of their findings to inform a wider public on issues such as gender and reproductive health, double standards in paid employment, and race and sexual orientation in identity formation.

The Future of Feminist Anthropology

From feminist anthropology's past as a "squeaky wheel" that called on the discipline to include women more prominently in its analysis, it is fair to say that it has now succeeded in transforming thinking in the field. A gendered perspective is widely considered essential to a comprehensive understanding of human history and contemporary social processes. Today, those who overlook the significance of gender may do so at the risk of being criticized for generating flawed scholarship. Feminist inquiries into areas including gender and the body, identity, sexuality, and materiality are now considered part of the anthropological canon. This has not come easily, and it has taken several decades to achieve the gains that have been made to date. The Association for Feminist Anthropology, a section of the American Anthropological Association, was formed in 1987 to address the underrepresentation of women and gender in scholarly analysis, and it gave support to a broad curriculum development project to transform the discipline. Since then, the Association for Feminist Anthropology has published the journal *Voices*, supported feminist scholarship, and established an archive of the first 20 years of the association's history, now housed in Washington, D.C., in the National Anthropology Archives. A great number of universities in the United States (and elsewhere) offer courses in feminist anthropology, and the wide literature in the field includes many books, journal articles, and films. One recent survey of anthropology courses taught in U.S. colleges showed that courses on gender topped the lists, signaling the desire of a new generation of anthropologists to take women and gender seriously.

A vibrant feminist anthropology now under construction seeks to advance theory and practice in the service of academics and activism, to create more inclusive societies and a more just world. Critiques within feminist anthropology as well as anthropology more generally are sparking efforts by both women and men to further decolonize anthropology, encouraging greater attention to difference and inequality by race, class, sexuality, and nation along with gender in the present era of increasing globalization. Sociocultural anthropologists often work collaboratively with their colleagues in the other subfields of anthropology as well as in related disciplines to better respond to new research questions as they emerge and to generate rich new knowledge for the future in feminist anthropology.

Florence E. Babb

See also Benedict, Ruth F.; Butler, Judith; Chodorow, Nancy; Gender and Anthropology; Hurston, Zora Neale; Lamphere, Louise; Leacock, Eleanor; Mead, Margaret; Modernism; Nash, June; Ortner, Sherry;

Parsons, Elsie C.; Postmodernism; Rosaldo, Michelle Zimbalist; Sanday, Peggy Reeves

Further Readings

Babb, F. E. (Ed.). (2007, April–November). Engendering anthropology. *Anthropology News.*

Behar, R., & Gordon, D. (Eds.). (1995). *Women writing culture.* Berkeley: University of California Press.

Brettell, C. B., & Sargent, C. F. (Eds.). (2001). *Gender in cross-cultural perspective.* Upper Saddle River, NJ: Prentice Hall.

Di Leonardo, M., (Ed.). (1991). *Gender at the crossroads of knowledge: Feminist anthropology in the postmodern era.* Berkeley: University of California Press.

Lamphere, L., Ragoné, H., & Zavella, P. (Eds.). (1997). *Situated lives: Gender and culture in everyday life.* New York, NY: Routledge.

Lewin, E. (Ed.). (2006). *Feminist anthropology: A reader.* Malden, MA: Blackwell.

Lugo, A., & Maurer, B. (Eds.). (2000). *Gender matters: Rereading Michelle Z. Rosaldo.* Ann Arbor: University of Michigan Press.

McClaurin, I. (Ed.). (2001). *Black feminist anthropology: Theory, politics, praxis, and poetics.* New Brunswick, NJ: Rutgers University Press.

Morgen, S. (1990). *Gender and anthropology: Critical reviews for research and teaching.* Washington DC: American Anthropological Association.

Ortner, S. B. (1996). *Making gender: The politics and erotics of culture.* Boston, MA: Beacon Press.

Reiter, R. R. (Ed.). (1975). *Toward an anthropology of women.* New York, NY: Monthly Review Press.

Rosaldo, M. Z., & Lamphere, L. (Eds.). (1974). *Woman, culture, and society.* Stanford, CA: Stanford University Press.

FERGUSON, ADAM

Adam Ferguson (1723–1816) was a prominent member of a circle of Scottish Enlightenment thinkers that included David Hume and Adam Smith. Born in the village of Logeirat, Perthshire, on the fringes of the Scottish highlands, he was the only highlander in the group. Son of a Presbyterian minister, he initially followed his father into the church, serving as chaplain to the Black Watch regiment. He resigned from the ministry and from the army in 1754 and was appointed to a chair at the University of Edinburgh in 1759. He was the author of several books and pamphlets, including a relatively undistinguished history of the rise and fall of the Roman Republic, but his major contribution was *An Essay of the History of Civil Society* (1767). The *Essay* is primarily known as one of the earliest expositions of the stage theory of human progress from "savagery" through "barbarism" to "civilization," very roughly corresponding to different means of subsistence—hunting, pastoralism, agriculture, and commerce. Ferguson's writings directly or indirectly influenced major 19th-century evolutionary thinkers, most notably Karl Marx and Lewis Henry Morgan.

The stage theory of progress had already been formulated slightly earlier by Smith in his unpublished lectures on jurisprudence at the University of Glasgow in 1762 and 1763. Both Smith and Ferguson based their accounts of "savages" on descriptions of the Iroquois by French Jesuit missionaries, the ethnographer Joseph-François Lafitau, and the historian Pierre de Charlevoix. Smith was particularly concerned with the ways in which changes in the means of subsistence affected deep changes in legal notions of property as well as in systems of government. Unlike hunting, he argued, herding allowed the development of relatively permanent forms of inequality, a gap, however moderate, between those who owned a few animals and those who owned many. Moreover, because ownership was transmitted from one generation to another, these inequalities became hereditary and spilled over into the political domain. Such inequalities, only nascent in pastoral societies, grew with the development of agriculture and commerce.

Ferguson's *Essay*, presenting the stage theory in great detail and in published form, is generally regarded as a landmark in European theories of human progress. In fact, Ferguson was by no means guilty of unbridled optimism. Much of the book is devoted to a consideration of decline and decay. Like Smith, he was preoccupied with the moral, social, and political implications of progress that rested on the growth of the division of labor. He was less concerned than Smith with the origins of inequality in pastoralism than with the contrast between humanity in the states of "savagery" and "civilization."

Ferguson's paradigm of "savagery" was Iroquois society as depicted by Lafitau and Charlevoix. He was well aware that Iroquois subsistence was not restricted to hunting but also included horticulture. Rather, their "savagery" depended on the relatively restricted development of property rights. They were highly egalitarian, with no division into rich and poor. This had important consequences for their system of government, which centered on councils where all adult men, and often women, had a voice and a stake. Their conduct of warfare demonstrated that, conversely, the group was concerned with the fate of each individual. The death of even a few warriors in a campaign was considered a calamity given that such small groups could ill afford any losses at all. The Iroquois closely resembled Comte de Montesquieu's paradigm of republican government, which depended on "civic virtue," the close involvement of the individual in the affairs of the whole.

Like Montesquieu, Ferguson was also afraid of the prospect of the decline of European societies into systems of authoritarian rule. The very engine of progress, the division of labor, was also the mechanism that posed the greatest threat to individual liberty. In the first place, the development of specialization radically narrows the scope of the intellectual, not to mention the economic and political interests of the average citizen. Second, inequalities of wealth and power give some individuals a much greater stake, not to mention influence, in the affairs of the state as a whole. Finally, the very progress that develops the minds and capacities of the few actually impoverishes the development of the majority. The officer may have a sophisticated understanding of military matters; however, the common soldier is cannon fodder, whose only responsibility is to obey orders mindlessly. By contrast, the ordinary Iroquois warrior has a far superior grasp of any campaign. In a passage approvingly cited by Marx, Ferguson compares the industrial workshop to a vast machine whose parts are human beings.

Without sharing Jean-Jacques Rousseau's deep pessimism, Ferguson still shows a deep ambivalence toward human progress and a real respect for the qualities of "savages" like the Iroquois, as individuals and as a society. His hope rested in the cultivation of civic engagement, in each citizen's concern for the well-being of society as a whole.

Ferguson's stage theory of progress had a deep impact on 19th-century evolutionary theorists, in particular Morgan, whose personal library reflected his deep interest in the thinkers of the Scottish Enlightenment, not to mention Marx, who admired both Ferguson and Morgan. His vision of civil society has also found contemporary admirers, notably Ernest Gellner.

Robert Launay

See also Condorcet, Jean-Antoine Nicolas de Caritat; Lafitau, Joseph-François; Marx, Karl; Montesquieu, Comte de; Morgan, Lewis Henry; Rousseau, Jean-Jacques

Further Readings

Ferguson, A. (1995). *An essay of the history of civil society* (Fania Oz-Salszburger, Ed.). Cambridge, UK: Cambridge University Press. (Original work published 1767)

Gellner, E. (1996). *Conditions of liberty: Civil society and its rivals.* Harmondsworth, UK: Penguin Books.

Meek, R. L. (1976). *Social science and the ignoble savage.* Cambridge, UK: Cambridge University Press.

FIRTH, RAYMOND

Raymond (later Sir Raymond) Firth was an important contributor to the British school of social anthropology in the early 20th century. His exemplary fieldwork in Polynesia, as well as later work in Malaya and London, provides useful ethnographic records that are supplemented by his more theoretical works.

Biography

Firth was born in south Auckland, New Zealand, in 1901. As a schoolboy, he became interested in the Maori, the indigenous inhabitants of New Zealand. Some of his childhood friends were Maori, but his interest also came from reading Frederick Maning's *Old New Zealand* (1863), an account of an Englishman's relationship with Maori in the early years of colonization. While still a schoolboy, Firth discovered the *Journal of the Polynesian Society* and became a regular reader and, later, a contributor. This laid the basis for his interest in the Polynesian peoples of the Pacific and their languages and customs.

For his undergraduate degree at Auckland University College, Firth studied economics. His master's thesis was based on the economics of the local kauri gum industry. Finding no statistics on earnings in the industry, he went to the north of

New Zealand, where the industry was based, and interviewed kauri gum miners, many of whom were Maori, about their lives, working conditions, and earnings. This was an unusual approach in economics at the time, but it was also, in effect, his first fieldwork and foreshadowed his later theoretical stance about the importance of multiple individual actions contributing to social organization. In 1924, he went to the London School of Economics (LSE) to work toward a doctorate on the economics of the frozen meat industry in New Zealand. However, he came under the influence of the distinguished anthropologist Bronisław Malinowski, which changed the direction of his work. His doctoral thesis, *Primitive Economics of the New Zealand Maori*, was published in 1929. This thesis was largely historical, based on the writings of earlier anthropologists such as Elsdon Best and Peter Buck. In this thesis, his sympathy for the Maori was evident: He showed that he was aware of the effect of colonization on the Maori and the immorality of the expropriation of their land. He also showed how the loss of their forest and land had limited their economic choices.

Firth was raised as a Methodist but later experienced a crisis of faith and became a humanist. He defined his humanistic rationalism as recognizing that human society exists and that people must take account of those by whom they live, which leads to a morality in which the supernatural is not required. After his anthropological fieldwork in Tikopia, a Polynesian outlier in the Solomon Islands, he wrote that he regretted the proselytization of the Tikopians by Christian missionaries, asking what justification there could be in breaking down the customs of a people simply because their gods differed from those of the missionaries.

These elements—the formal training in economics, a recognition of the interrelationship between individual and collective knowledge, and humanistic rationalism—provided a basis for his development as an anthropologist.

Intellectual Journeys and Fieldwork

Anthropology in Britain in the first few decades of the 20th century was moving away from the evolutionist and diffusionist approaches of earlier decades. Under Malinowski, the functionalist perspective became the dominant paradigm, and its emphases included extensive fieldwork. During the 1920s and 1930s, many distinguished anthropologists were trained by Malinowski at LSE, Firth among them. This period could be seen as one that defined modern *British* anthropology, especially as distinct from Boasian anthropology in the United States.

Firth's fieldwork in Tikopia took place in 1928–1929. Malinowski hoped that Firth would write a full and straightforward account of Tikopian culture: It was important to Malinowski that his student present the theoretical point of view, which, by then, was being labeled *functional*. Essentially, this meant that customs should be presented as having a purpose; they are the means by which people fulfill their needs. Firth's grasp of the Tikopian language (cognate with Maori) was very good, and he collected rich and detailed descriptions of Tikopian life. His first book about the island, *We, the Tikopia* (1936), can be seen as Malinowskian in perspective, concentrating on family life through an economic functionalist lens. The word *function* occurs often in this ethnography, as in statements such as "In Tikopia the function of each of these elements [of marriage exchanges] can be clearly seen" (572–573). Firth believed that it was important for the anthropologist to throw light on the natives' fundamental beliefs behind their economic behavior. Here, Firth was looking at the "calculating man," to use Gregory Bateson's phrase. His interest, based on the pre-Keynsian economics he had studied, was on individual choice making, a perspective Malinowski would have contested, holding that individuals were mainly of interest as members of society, not as individuals per se.

By the late 1930s, Firth and others of his generation explicitly recognized the weaknesses of the purely functional approach, asking if everything is related to everything else, where then does description stop? Members of this group were reworking their theoretical perspectives in Britain, with some, though not Firth, later flirting with the French structuralism of Lévi-Strauss. Their marked divergence from American cultural anthropology had become evident. The American anthropologist G. P. Murdock criticized the British school of anthropology for its concentration on kinship and British colonial dependencies. He suggested that British anthropologists were not interested in the theoretical writings of their colleagues elsewhere, or in history, culture change, or psychology. In fact, he suggested that they had become old-fashioned sociologists. Firth accepted Murdock's critique but said that the British had limited resources and therefore were concentrating on a limited set of issues with some success. In effect, the debate, and the divergence, was between British social anthropology and American cultural anthropology and its four-field approach.

Firth and other anthropologists, many of them not British although trained in England, were developing alternative paradigms to that of their teacher, Malinowski. Although the Malinowskian emphasis on participant observation remained a hallmark of British anthropology, Firth had been moving away from the purely functionalist approach for some time. He believed that to concentrate on structure alone obscured the role of the individual, that individual divergences and social change were more interesting than narrow descriptions of collective behavior and culture. His humanism, his warm understanding of the people of Tikopia, and his obvious affection for some of them, made his ethnography unusual at a time when much of British anthropology aspired to a generalized scientific detachment. It was said of Firth that he made his exotic informants both human and comprehensible and that 5 centuries of European colonial condescension were expunged in Firth's insistence on Polynesian rationality.

The importance Firth placed on individuals and social change was the reason for his interest in social organization rather than social structure. In his 1954 article "Social Organization and Social Change," he defined the two fields. He saw social structure as the major patterns of existing social relations that constrained the possibilities of future interactions. Social organization, by contrast, was the constant process of responses to fresh situations by adopting appropriate strategies. The study of social organization reveals how people make decisions or accept the responsibility expected of them by virtue of their position in the social system. This emphasis on the patterns *of* observable human behavior rather than the underlying patterns *for* behavior was paradigmatically the difference between British social anthropology and American cultural anthropology and the basis of Murdock's charge of old-fashioned sociology.

Firth's fieldwork in Tikopia in 1928–1929 and his subsequent visits in 1952 and 1966 produced a corpus of work that is probably unrivaled as an ethnographic record of a society. In addition to *We, the Tikopia*, his major works about the island include discussions of spiritual beliefs and practices in *The Work of the Gods in Tikopia* (1940/1967), *Tikopia Ritual and Belief* (1967), and *Rank and Religion in Tikopia* (1970); change in *Social Change in Tikopia* (1959); language in *Taranga fakatikopia ma Taranga Fakainglisi* (Tikopia-English Dictionary, 1985); and songs and stories in *History and Traditions of Tikopia* (1961) and *Tikopia Songs* (1991). He also wrote numerous articles about material culture, kinship, dreams, and authority structures as well as economic analyses of everyday life (notably in the monograph *Primitive Polynesian Economy*). His book *Human Types* (1938), in which he sets out the main principles of social anthropology, can perhaps be seen as the first textbook on anthropology.

Firth and the Wider Discipline of Anthropology

After his first period of fieldwork in Tikopia, Firth became acting professor at Sydney University 1930–1932, after which he returned to LSE where he became a lecturer (1932–1935), a reader in 1935, and a professor in 1944, inheriting Malinowski's position. He remained there with brief interruptions until his retirement in 1968. Social anthropology was not recognized as a separate discipline in the earlier part of the 20th century, and Firth worked to change this perception as one of the founding members of the Association of Social Anthropologists, inaugurated in 1946. He was also associated with a distinguished group of anthropologists who trained at LSE in the years before and after World War II: Edward Evans-Pritchard, Meyer Fortes, Edmund Leach, Audrey Richards, and Jomo Kenyatta. Under Firth's aegis, important research projects were carried out in East Africa, South America, Oceania, southern Europe, Malaysia, and Japan. He also trained people from related disciplines, for example, Ernest Gellner and Percy Cohen.

Firth's own field research had continued in 1939 and 1940 when he and his wife, Rosemary, also an anthropologist, worked in what was then Malaya on the economy of a fishing village. Firth said he chose this topic because he wanted to do some quantitative work on systematic trading in the fishing industry. This resulted in his book *Malay Fishermen: Their Peasant Economy* (1946). During the war years, Firth served with the Naval Intelligence Division at the Admiralty, writing handbooks about the Pacific Islands, until 1944. In the following year, he was involved in setting up the Colonial Social Science Research Council and in the establishment of the Australian National University. Firth later went on to show the value of the anthropological approach in studying the kinship patterns of both the working and middle classes in London.

By the 1970s, there was a crisis in anthropology, to use Adam Kuper's term—feminist and Marxist critiques and the postcolonial world required a new anthropology. Firth by this time had retired, but he continued to write and contributed to seminars in many parts of the world. Students recalled that Firth rejected and continued to eschew sloppily constructed arguments, thoughtless use of terms and catch phrases, analogical thinking, and speculative generalizations that had no evidential underpinning. The core of his practice and belief as an anthropologist—that the variation in individual knowledge is central to both social organization and social change—remained undiminished to the end, and his pragmatic humanism diffused everything he did.

Firth's influence on British social anthropology has been immense both through his writings and in the effect he had on his many students. His contributions were recognized in a knighthood bestowed in 1973 and in his appointment as a Companion of the New Zealand Order of Merit in 2001. In 2002, the British Academy announced that it was awarding him the first Leverhulme medal to be given to scholars of exceptional distinction, in recognition of his outstanding and internationally acknowledged contributions to 20th-century anthropology. Firth died in 2002, a month before his 101st birthday.

Judith Macdonald

See also Barth, Fredrik; Bateson, Gregory; Biography/Life Writing; Bohannan, Paul; London School of Economics; Mair, Lucy; Malinowski, Bronisław; Murdock, George Peter; Radcliffe-Brown, A. R.; Symbolic and Interpretive Anthropology

Further Readings

Firth, R. (1936). *We, the Tikopia*. London, UK: Allen & Unwin.

———. (1954). Social organisation and social change. *Journal of the Royal Anthropological Institute of Great Britain and Ireland, 84*(1–2), 1–20.

Kuper, A. (1973). *Anthropologists and anthropology: The British school 1922–1972*. London, UK: Penguin Books.

FISCHER, MICHAEL

Michael M. J. Fischer (1946–) is the coauthor of *Anthropology as Cultural Critique* and a contributor to *Writing Culture*, seminal works that set a new path for the discipline of anthropology in the mid-1980s. In the postcolonial condition where anthropological authority is challenged as the gaze of the empire, these works set out to bring the work of anthropology back home as cultural critique. Anthropological authority thus becomes an emergent form of knowledge that depends on dialogical formation processes composed of multiple voices and experiences.

Fischer first studied geography at Johns Hopkins University. He continued his studies in social anthropology at the London School of Economics and earned a PhD in cultural anthropology from the University of Chicago. His early work focused on social change and religion, first in Jamaica and then in Iran (*Zoroastrian Iran Between Myth and Praxis*, 1973). Fischer's ethnographic studies of Zoroastrians, Jews, and Baha'is in the city of Yazd in Iran (and in western India), in the context of the developmental discourses of the time, hinted a decade early at the Iranian revolution of 1979. He also conducted comparative work on religious communities (Muslims, Baha'is, Zoroastrians, and Jews) as well as merchant communities in both Iran and India (Jains and Parsis). Fischer first taught at Harvard and then at Rice University, where he became an active member of an intellectual circle whose work had a significant impact on the field of anthropology in the 1980s. In the 1990s, he began teaching at Massachusetts Institute of Technology, with a new research focus on science, technology, and medicine.

Two discursive formations emerged out of anthropology after World War II. First, there were the discourses of development. In anthropology, these generated debates about language and culture in the context of emerging "new nations." Second, there were comparative fieldwork practices that were set up by universities and foundations to understand and measure the ways in which development models were received by and affected the lives of people. In the 1960s and 1970s, Fischer was part of a larger group of American anthropologists who began a new era of empirical studies in linguistics, comparative religions, folklore, and urban anthropology. There were two countries in the Middle East that attracted in-depth work in this period, Iran and Morocco. Fischer and several colleagues from the University of Chicago focused on Iran. This undertaking was especially significant because their anthropological method provided a grounded understanding of language and culture that countered the existing body of work done by Orientalists.

Studies of Social Transformation in Pre- and Postrevolutionary Iran

Fischer, along with his cohort, was engaged in comparative studies of cultural and economic transformations in Iran in the face of the development projects of the 1960s and 1970s. These projects often involved displacements of local cultural ways of life. For example, the construction of dams displaced villagers along their basins, and the application of agribusiness models to older agrarian communities displaced impoverished farmers, stimulating migration to the rapidly growing urban areas. The growing numbers of displaced populations as a result of these large development projects fueled the social and economic discontent that led to the revolution of 1979. Fischer interprets the revolution in *Iran: From Religious Dispute to Revolution* by pursuing a central question of the time: the relationship between the economic and the cultural causes of the revolution.

The Iranian revolution caught most scholars by surprise. While scholars were looking for social and structural changes to usher Iran from a patrimonial agrarian country into a developing modern one, an emergent social movement reframed the political stage. Ayatollah Ruholla Khomeini led religious leaders to gain power in this social movement. Islam no longer remained at the margins of the society. Rather, it became central to politics, culture, knowledge production, and civic life. Fischer's work traced these changes in urban politics.

Fischer's next book on Iran shifts from a focus on how religion was used to mobilize and achieve the revolution to the construction of a new religious identity in the midst of various possible religious interpretations. Coauthored with Mehdi Abedi, *Debating Muslims: Cultural Dialogues in Postmodernity and Tradition* followed the work that Fischer started in small-town Iran to major

cosmopolitan areas in the United States. Published 2 decades after the revolution of 1979, this work provides detailed autobiographical accounts of actors in the revolution and the formation of their religious discourses, contextualizing them in a multisited global context.

There are perhaps three important arenas of cultural analysis for Fischer in his post–*Anthropology as Cultural Critique* work: (1) the working of posttraumatic society, (2) the role of media subjectivities, and (3) anthropological understandings of science, technology, and medicine. These arenas of analysis are vital for understanding contemporary culture in a global context.

In the early 1990s, with the fall of the Soviet bloc, new and emerging nations had to cope with the loss of a "socialist" identity and remake new forms of national identities. By then, Iranian society had been going through a similar posttraumatic experience for a decade. For Fischer, the work of posttraumatic society was hinted at in Iranian films and other forms of popular culture since the 1980s. For example, he pointed at the ways in which Iranian writers progressively adopted Western-style modern novels in the 20th century and how this genre in turn was adopted by filmmakers in both the pre- and the postrevolution era. The works of posttraumatic society depend on hybrid forms of culture making.

Fischer's work on Iranian cinema is both about visual culture and about media/mediation, in that he explores how Iranian oral traditions and modern genres borrowed from the West are reframed in new technological possibilities. *Mute Dreams, Blind Owls, and Dispersed Knowledges: Persian Poesis in the Transnational Circuitry* was published in 2004, but the work had begun more than 20 years earlier. Fischer asserts that the Islamic world may be a key place where, in the context of a globalized Euro-American cultural onslaught, the work of critical commentary is still possible. He suggests that Iranian films have been produced through the creative reckoning of cultural memory, contemporary politics, and global processes and have offered spaces for alternative commentary.

If the pathbreaking work of *Anthropology as Cultural Critique* in the 1980s tried to find a place for anthropology in the postcolonial world, in the 2000s, Fischer redefines this position in relation to biotechnologies, information technologies, and environmental concerns. These important instances of technoscience will define the future of life and are therefore posing domains of new ethical challenges to the contemporary condition, such as emergent biological sciences' definition of what constitutes a human. He calls these challenges *ethical plateaus*. The anthropological voice, he argues, is best suited to engage in empirical work to elucidate new understandings of such ethical plateaus and to facilitate public engagement in these emergent forms of life.

The Complexity of the Social and the Redefinition of Culture

The anthropological voice, in this moment of Fischer's career, is performed in a "third space" where differences are mediated and translated. The anthropological voice makes these differences and mediations or translations visible. In a multicultural world, they appear both as specific experiences and as multiple epistemologies generating alternative knowledge systems. The critique of modernity as a metanarrative of the contemporary, in *Anthropology as Cultural Critique*, was precisely about the details, conflicts, and alternative perspectives that the metanarrative leaves out. Fischer, in *Emergent Forms of Life and Anthropological Voice*, argues that the ethnographic and anthropological voice in the 21st century is about the complexity of the social. Social classes, gender differences, and the inequity in the formation of capital do not disappear, but they interact in the multilayered space of the contemporary in much more complex ways than can be represented by traditional ethnography. Therefore, the work of the anthropological voice is not a once-for-all description but an ongoing resource and method for social repair and for the growing of flexible and robust institutions for the changing times. Because there are multiple models originating in many disciplines, such as law and the sciences, that have claims over understanding and defining life, complexities and multiple claims over the definition of the good life (*bios* and *polis*) have serious consequences for social and political actions. It has become much harder to ground these understandings for the ground has become more fleeting. This is where Fischer calls for an ethics that unfolds in third spaces beyond older simple dichotomies such as individual and society or medical ethics and biopolitics.

Fischer gives a more complex meaning of culture in his recent book, *Anthropological Futures*. He suggests that emerging scientific knowledge on nature, culture, and body is shifting the anthropological understanding of culture. Emerging forms of knowledge such as molecular biology, environmental studies, and computer science define the meaning of culture in a way that engenders anthropological understanding. The definition of culture in anthropology has gone through several historical changes in meanings. Culture was first a complex interrelated whole, next it was something that was mediated through power and symbols, and then it was conceived as phenomena whose symbols can be shifted by alternative positions of the participant or observer. Symbols that were once maintained through negotiated acts are currently being reworked through emergent technosicences, media, and biotechnical relations, once again redefining culture. Fischer anticipates that this shifting terrain will continue and that it will frame the work of anthropology to come, or anthropological futures.

Mazyar Lotfalian

See also Marcus, George; Postmodernism

Further Readings

Clifford, J., & Marcus, G. E. (Eds.). (1986). *Writing culture: The poetics and politics of ethnography.* Berkeley: University of California Press.

Fischer, M. M. J. (1973). *Zoroastrian Iran from myth to praxis.* Doctoral dissertation, University of Chicago, Illinois.

———. (1974). Value assertion and stratification: Religion and marriage in rural Jamaica. *Caribbean Studies, 14*(1–2).

———. (1980). *Iran: From religious dispute to revolution.* Cambridge, MA: Harvard University Press.

———. (2003). *Emergent forms of life and the anthropological voice.* Durham, NC: Duke University Press.

———. (2004). *Mute dreams, blind owls, and dispersed knowledges: Persian poesis in the transnational circuitry.* Durham, NC: Duke University Press.

———. (2009). *Anthropological futures.* Durham, NC: Duke University Press.

Fischer, M. M. J., & Abedi, M. (1990). *Debating Muslims: Cultural dialogues in postmodernity and tradition.* Madison: University of Wisconsin Press.

Good, B. J., Fischer, M. M. J., Willen, S., & DelVecchio Good, M.-J. (Eds.). (2010). *A reader in medical anthropology: Theoretical trajectories and emergent realities*. Malden, MA: Wiley-Blackwell.

Marcus, G. E., & Fischer, M. M. J. (1986). *Anthropology as cultural critique: An experimental moment in the human sciences*. Chicago, IL: University of Chicago Press.

FORMALISM/SUBSTANTIVISM

During the 1960s, the formalist/substantivist debate, often referred to as the "Great Debate," shaped the subdiscipline of economic anthropology. The principal contributors to the debate were categorized by their willingness to accept either Karl Polanyi's substantive definition of economics or, alternatively, the neoclassical choice-theoretical model. By the close of the 1960s and the beginning of the 1970s, the formalist/substantivist debate passed unresolved.

The anthropologist Keith Hart has argued that the issue for anthropology is to discover the principles that might animate economic organization at every level. Practitioners of Hart's perspective are often classified as economic anthropologists.

Throughout its history, the study of economic anthropology has maintained a process of continuous evolution. During its infancy, economic anthropologists tended to perceive culture as the primary lens from which the choices and actions of human beings could be understood. Anthropologists such as Bronisław Malinowksi often concluded that much of human activity, including economic activity, is a social phenomenon. The introduction of a formal, neoclassical economic theory to the study of economic anthropology caused a theoretical metamorphosis. An early example of an anthropologist applying traditional neoclassical economic-theoretical tools to anthropological analysis is that of Raymond Firth. As the use of formal economic techniques infiltrated anthropological studies, the theoretical understandings of human behavior changed. The differences between those anthropologists who used anthropological techniques synonymous with inductive analysis and those anthropologists and economists who used more formal deductive economic techniques caused a rift. The epistemological conflict elicited the formation of two unique theoretical camps, the formalists and the substantivists.

Karl Polanyi, Conrad Arensberg, and Harry Pearson, incorporating many of Malinowski's ideas, generated the initial thrust of the substantivist analysis. Polanyi, Arensberg, and Pearson argued that self-regulating markets are a relatively recent phenomenon, therefore it is not plausible to apply the same techniques used in the study of capitalist economies to the study of economic behavior in noncapitalist societies. From the substantivist perspective, directing the tools used in describing capitalism toward the description of noncapitalist social relationships was akin to using the concepts embedded in Christianity to study the religions of indigenous peoples.

The basis for the substantive argument originated in the substantive definition of economics as proposed by Polanyi. From Polanyi's perspective, the meaning of economics is derived from the human being's dependence for his living on nature and other human beings. Substantivists viewed their definition as providing a universally applicable point of departure. All societies must in some way provide for their material well-being. At the same time, different societies will employ different techniques for fulfilling material well-being. Therefore, every economic system must also be understood within its own specific terms. From the substantivist perspective, the formal neoclassical definition of economics was too narrow because it refers only to a definite situation of choice in which economic agents always confront scarcity. As such, the tools of formal economics were specifically oriented toward the study of capitalism and were unsuitable for analyzing noncapitalist economies.

Chronologically, joining Polanyi, Arensberg, and Pearson as main contributors to the substantivist argument were Marshall Sahlins and George Dalton. Providing a more anthropologically advanced analysis, Sahlins built on Polanyi's depictions of reciprocity, redistribution, and market exchange. Sahlins argues that exchange ultimately depends on the type of social relations that exist between trading partners and that those social relations are strongly influenced by the distance between the actors: The greater the distance between economic agents, the more impersonal and self-serving the exchange relationship will be. Consistent with the substantive theme, Sahlins argued that the human-economic interaction, as well as the meaning of the term *economic*, may be different depending on social, cultural, and institutional structures.

George Dalton focused on the limits of formalism. He maintained that there are two definitions of the term *economic*, formal and substantive, and he focused on the limits of formalism. Dalton posits that the only way the formal definition of economics may be applicable within a society is after the institutional conditions that incentivize maximization and minimization have been established.

The formalists were unconvinced. For the formalists, the substantive definition unnecessarily submerges the individual beneath social structures. As a result, the central proponents of the formalist argument, Robbins Burling, Edward LeClair Jr., Scott Cook, and Frank Cancian, advocate the use of the neoclassical choice-theoretical model as a means of elevating the role of the individual in anthropological theory, a view previously minimized in anthropology. The application of neoclassical theory alters the starting point of analysis within anthropology. By assuming the universality of maximization, neoclassical economic theory makes the (isolated) individual its primary catalyst of action.

As is typical of a heated controversy, the debate triggered a large influx of contributions into a field that had previously languished in relative obscurity. Despite this energy, the formalist-substantivist debate became the equivalent of a shooting star. In the 1970s, the debate quickly faded without resolution as both sides remained uncompromising and unable to reach a consensus on methodology. In the immediate aftermath, Marxists came to dominate the field of economic anthropology, and several prominent formalists and substantivists began to identify with Marxist positions. Over the longer term, given the unresolved nature of the debate, points of disagreement that were evident during the original debate occasionally reignite.

Justin A. Elardo

See also Economic Anthropology; Firth, Raymond; Malinowski, Bronisław; Marx, Karl; Marxist Anthropology; Polanyi, Karl; Rational Choice Theory; Sahlins, Marshall

Further Readings

Dale, G. (2010). *Karl Polanyi*. Cambridge, UK: Polity.

Hann, C., & Hart, K. (2011). *Economic anthropology: History, ethnography, critique*. Cambridge, UK: Polity.

Hart, K. (2000). Comment on Pearson's "homo economicus goes native." *History of Political Economy, 20*, 1017–1025.

Isaac, B. L. (1993). Retrospective on the formalist-substantivist debate. In B. L. Isaac (Ed.), *Research in economic anthropology* (pp. 213–233). Greenwich, CT: JAI Press.

Polanyi, K. (1968). The economy as an instituted process. In E. E. LeClair Jr. & H. K. Schneider (Eds.), *Economic anthropology: Readings in theory and analysis* (pp. 122–143). New York, NY: Holt, Rinehart & Winston.

Wilk, R. R. (1996). *Economies and cultures: Foundations of economic anthropology*. Boulder, CO: Westview Press.

FORTES, MEYER

Meyer Fortes (1906–1983) was one of the pioneering generation of scholars who established the discipline of social anthropology in Great Britain. Fortes received his PhD degree in psychology from University College, London, in 1930. He then worked at the Emanuel Miller Child Guidance Clinic, sponsored by the Jewish Health Organization, in London's East End. From 1931, he attended the seminar organized by Bronisław Malinowski at the London School of Economics; he also counted among his teachers Charles Seligman, Raymond Firth, and, most important, A. R. Radcliffe-Brown. His close friendship with E. E. Evans Pritchard, established at this time, was extremely important to both men. Fortes's work among the agricultural Tallensi, in what is now northern Ghana (between 1934 and 1937), developed aspects of Evans-Pritchard's earlier work with the pastoral Nuer of the Sudan. After his return to London in 1937, he lectured part-time at the London School of Economics and became a reader in anthropology at Oxford in 1946. From 1950 to 1973, he was William Wyse Professor of Social Anthropology at Cambridge University and a fellow of Kings College Cambridge. Fortes became a fellow of the British Academy in 1967 and an honorary foreign member of the American Academy of Science; he received honorary degrees from Chicago, Belfast, London School of Economics, and Kings College Cambridge. He died in 1983.

Born in 1906 in rural South Africa, Fortes grew up speaking Yiddish, English, and Afrikaans and no doubt was familiar with the African language spoken by his neighbors. He studied psychology and English at Cape Town University; he arrived in London at the age of 20, supported by a scholarship, and registered for a PhD degree in psychology. He hoped his research would lead to the creation of an intelligence test, free of cultural influences. Though his work was eventually used to produce the Raven Matrices IQ test, Fortes became convinced that a culture-free test could not be constructed. His psychological research was grounded in statistical data, and simple statistics are crucially important in some of his later kinship studies. However, in most of his anthropological research, the qualitative results of intensive fieldwork predominate.

Fortes always emphasized the paramount importance of knowing and using the local language in research. His field notes are a superb blend of careful observation, precise description, records of conversation, and interaction with the people of the communities in which he lived and worked. Many of his notes are in the Tallensi language. Fortes also recorded his own emotional reaction to the events he witnessed and participated in.

Fortes is probably best known for his study of kinship systems and the family. However, his concern with kinship in the context of diverse patterns of political and religious organization, as well as his interest in the psychological aspects of explicitly social behavior, give his work a much wider relevance. At the level of psychological data, his work contrasts with the orientation of research in the United States. While American anthropologists usually presented the relationship between culture and psychology using the individual life cycle as a framework, Fortes was concerned with understanding behavior and emotion without an exclusive focus on the individual. His analysis of the individual's role in kinship, politics, religious belief, and the world of economics examined norms of behavior and customary practice as derived from social structure and explored the interdependency of social structure, behavior, and emotion.

The study of kinship among the Tallensi people provided the basic evidence Fortes used in many different contexts and led to a theory of a particular form of kinship structure: the *unilineal descent group*. Fortes found groups of Tallensi households linked to one another through kinship ties traced among men who were patrilineal descendants of common ancestors. Within the households,

constituent families were similarly related so that both the widest and the smallest social groupings depended on the recognition of patrilineal kinship ties. It also emerged that no overarching political or judicial system existed to regulate the relationships among households or wider neighborhoods. Fortes drew a distinction between kinship in the "domestic domain" and its function in the "politico-jural domain." All human societies, Fortes argued, have kinship systems that regulate marriage, procreation, child rearing, death, and the resulting processes of inheritance and the succession of generations. In the Tallensi case, where no centralizing polity existed, the patrilineal kinship system also provided a framework for peaceful coexistence and collaboration in a range of social, ritual, and economic activities.

Fortes's later fieldwork with the matrilineal Ashanti people of what was then The Gold Coast provided a major contrast to the patrilineal Tallensi. Unlike the Tallensi, the Ashanti had an elaborate political system involving kingship and royal courts. Fortes pursued the problems that emerged from the contrast of matrilineal and patrilineal descent systems but also developed the concepts that emerged originally from the Tallensi data.

Important among these was the treatment of the temporal aspect of kin group organization. The "developmental cycle" is mentioned in his Tallensi work, where he notes that a varying composition of household units occurs due to the changes through time as children mature, reproduce, and replace their parents. Among the matrilineal Ashanti, Fortes deals with these repetitive, cyclical processes of change, using statistical data on age, residence, and kinship connections for men and women. He constructs a model that shows how recognition of the unifying principal of matrilineal descent underlies the apparent diversity in Ashanti forms of residence.

Fortes's later work deals often with identity, selfhood, and religious belief. Contrasting Tallensi concepts of fate and ancestorhood are presented as parallel to the relationship of Oedipus to fate and of Job to God. The Tallensi concept of fate is similar to the notion of fate presented in Oedipus. Destiny is a predetermined series of events, essentially amoral and unaffected by the fated person's chosen behavior. By contrast, Tallensi ancestors are similar to the Judeo-Christian God and, depending on the choices made by individuals, may intervene to support moral behavior and authority.

Fortes was much concerned with the bearing of anthropological knowledge on race discrimination, which he considered to be as distinctive an invention of Western civilization as the atom bomb—disastrous for millions and based on absolutely no shred of anthropological evidence. He felt that anthropology had a duty to confront the assumptions on which racial discrimination is based.

Though he considered the study of simpler, (i.e., small, nonindustrialized, and, usually, nonliterate) societies to be ideal for the holistic methods of anthropology, he regarded the results of empirical field research as demonstrating that every human society, no matter where it is located or how peculiar it is, is a paradigm for all human society. Anthropologists, he argued, now know enough to know that they recognize themselves in every human society.

Susan Drucker-Brown

See also Alliance-Descent Debate; Bloch, Maurice; Deleuze, Gilles, and Félix Guattari; Evans-Pritchard, E. E.; Firth, Raymond; Goody, Jack; Leach, Edmond; London School of Economics; Maine, Henry James; Mair, Lucy; Malinowski, Bronisław; Oxford University; Radcliffe-Brown, A. R.; Seligman, Charles Gabriel; Structural Functionalism

Further Readings

Fortes, M. (1949). *The web of kinship among the Tallensi*. London, UK: Oxford University Press.

———. (1959). *Oedipus and Job in West African religion*. Cambridge, UK: Cambridge University Press.

———. (1969). *Kinship and the social order: The legacy of Lewis Henry Morgan*. Chicago, IL: Aldine.

———. (1970). *Time and social structure and other essays*. London, UK: Athlone Press.

FORTUNE, REO

Reo Franklin Fortune (1903–1979) was a brilliant and iconoclastic ethnographer whose major works of the 1930s made a lasting contribution to Melanesian linguistics and anthropology.

Fortune grew up in the New Zealand countryside, the son of a farmer who had left the clergy. Despite financial hardship, Fortune managed to attend Victoria University College in Wellington. His outstanding academic performance and research on the psychology of dreaming earned him the opportunity to continue his studies at the University of Cambridge in 1926, and in 1927, he published his first book, *The Mind in Sleep*. Using his own dreams as data, and writing in dialogue with the psychoanalytic theories of Sigmund Freud and W. H. R. Rivers, Fortune proposed that dreams express ideas or feelings that the waking person has repressed or rejected, especially when the individual's personal commitments are at odds with those prevailing in society. The problems created for individuals in such situations, or when different expectations of society are in conflict, is a theme that recurs throughout Fortune's work.

Fortune is often recalled in relation to his first wife, the American anthropologist and icon Margaret Mead. Fortune met Mead on board the ship he took to study in England, and due in part to her influence, his attention soon turned from psychology to anthropology. In 1927–1928, he conducted fieldwork on Dobu and the surrounding Melanesian islands. The product of this field trip was *Sorcerers of Dobu* (1931), the classic ethnographic description of Dobuan culture for which he is probably best known. A selection from this work served as Fortune's PhD thesis at Columbia, where he had developed good relations with Franz Boas and Ruth Benedict and where he ultimately received his degree. Benedict adapted *Sorcerers* for presentation as one of three case studies in her book *Patterns of Culture* (1934), thereby popularizing (though in Fortune's eyes regrettably oversimplifying) the image of "paranoid" Dobuans as dour sorcerers living in suspicion even of their close kin.

Fortune and Mead married in 1928, and the couple immediately set off for the first of three field trips they undertook together over the next 5 years: Manus, Omaha, and the Sepik district of New Guinea. Fortune wrote one book based on each of these field trips. Two were ethnographies, *Manus Religion* (1935) and *Omaha Secret Societies* (1932); the third, *Arapesh* (published in 1942 but compiled in the mid-1930s), was a masterful grammar of the Arapesh language complemented by a collection of glossed texts. In 1933, Mead separated from Fortune to pursue a relationship with the anthropologist Gregory Bateson, whom she and Fortune had met in the Sepik. Fortune spent the next year in London applying unsuccessfully for academic positions; he then returned to New Guinea for an exceedingly difficult period of fieldwork among the warring Kamano people in the Eastern Highlands. There followed a series of short-term teaching positions in Canton, China; Toledo, Ohio; and Toronto, Canada. These were interspersed with further periods of frontier fieldwork, first in southwestern China and later in Burma. The harrowing violence, harsh conditions, and severe illnesses that Fortune endured during these field trips left him permanently scarred. Fortune's second marriage, to Eileen Pope, was a long and happy one, and he finally received a permanent lectureship at Cambridge in 1948. But by the end of the 1930s, Fortune's real scholarly production had ceased. The few minor publications of his later years are eccentric, convoluted, and ponderous.

It is thus his major works of the 1930s that constitute Fortune's lasting contribution to anthropology. Focusing on culturally defined social roles and the emotions they evoke at various stages of the life cycle, Fortune dramatized the characteristic predicaments created by contradictory features of the society he aimed to describe. In his analysis of Dobuan social organization, the central tension is that felt by the nuclear family in light of the cultural prominence of the property-owning matriline. A Dobuan man finds himself torn between his affection for his own children and his duty to favor his sister's children; similarly, once the period of mourning has passed, a widower is barred from entering his deceased wife's, and hence his children's, village, while his children are reciprocally barred from entering his village as it belongs to another matriline. The consequences of marriage in matrilineal kinship systems was also the subject of Fortune's 1933 article "A Note on Some Forms of Kinship Structure," which explored the asymmetrical implications of prescriptive marriage rules for kin groups of different types. The abstract method of modeling social structure that Fortune developed in this article was groundbreaking, prefiguring Claude Lévi-Strauss's *Elementary Structures of Kinship* (1969).

In part because his writings reflect the influence of A. R. Radcliffe-Brown and Bronisław Malinowski, Fortune is sometimes characterized as a functionalist in his theoretical orientation. To a limited extent, this is correct: He was interested in the way social customs play out in the working of a society. But Fortune was strongly averse to reductionism of any kind, and he occasionally rejected others' generalizations outright, most notably in the work of Malinowski and in efforts by Mead and Benedict to treat culture as "personality writ large." Fortune's inclination was to take a historically situated and particularistic view of each culture he studied. This approach, closely associated with Boas, was in decline by the 1930s, as other styles of anthropology came to be seen as more scientific. Paradoxically, the enduring value of Fortune's work derives in part from his particularistic commitment to understanding each culture on its own terms.

Fortune was an outstanding language learner, developing considerable skill in the local vernacular wherever his research took him. His ethnographic descriptions reflect this, giving prominent voice to local modes of speech and frequently presenting data in the form of texts. His approach to participant observation emphasized an empathetic identification with the people he was studying; this gives his ethnographic descriptions an intimate, emic quality, with his own perspective and basis for knowledge integrated into the finished account. In *Sorcerers*, for example, he describes gardening with an immediacy that derives from his own experience of making a garden (at a time when it was highly unusual for an ethnographer to grow his own food according to native custom). Fortune also experimented in his approach to ethnographic writing. In *Manus Religion*, which centers on the use by the living of the spirits of the deceased, his observations are organized in the form of a "diary of events," illustrating the religious system in action in the villagers' daily lives and his own experience.

The last substantial piece Fortune wrote was the article "Arapesh Warfare" (1939), which took issue with the way Mead represented Arapesh culture in her famous book *Sex and Temperament in Three Primitive Societies* (1935). Based on direct native accounts, Fortune argued that Arapesh men were not gentle, cooperative, and "feminine," as Mead had described them, but before pacification had engaged in woman stealing and warfare. Many of Fortune's obscure later writings can be seen as attempting to discredit the psychologistic terms in which *Sex and Temperament* was couched. Fortune's exasperation with what he saw as an inappropriate "bending" of ethnography to theoretical ends goes some way toward explaining why the insightful and hardworking ethnographer wrote so little in his later years.

Ira Bashkow and Lise M. Dobrin

See also Godelier, Maurice; Historical Particularism; Mead, Margaret; Structural Functionalism

Further Readings

Dobrin, L. M., & Bashkow, I. (2006). "Pigs for dance songs": Reo Fortune's empathetic ethnography of the Arapesh roads. In R. Darnell & F. Gleach (Eds.), *Histories of anthropology annual* (Vol. 2, pp. 123–154). Lincoln: University of Nebraska Press.

———. (2010). "The truth in anthropology does not travel first class": Reo Fortune's fateful encounter with Margaret Mead. In R. Darnell & F. Gleach (Eds.), *Histories of anthropology annual* (Vol. 6, pp. 66–128). Lincoln: University of Nebraska Press.

Lohmann, R. I. (2009). Dreams of fortune: Reo Fortune's psychological theory of cultural ambivalence. *Pacific Studies, 32*(2–3), 273–298.

McLean, A. (1992). In the footprints of Reo Fortune. In T. E. Hays (Ed.), *Ethnographic presents: Pioneering anthropologists in the Papua New Guinea highlands* (pp. 37–67). Berkeley: University of California Press.

FOSTER, GEORGE M.

George McClelland Foster was one of the leading social cultural anthropologists of the second half of the 20th century and remains one of the most cited scholars of his generation. He was committed to the highest standards of ethnography and became a pioneer in long-term research in a single community. He spent more than half a century doing research in Tzintzuntzan, Mexico, where he gathered data that led to important contributions to the study of peasant societies; the role of pottery and technology in traditional societies; the relationship between economy, personality, and social structure; and changing ideas about health and illness. In addition to his fundamental contributions to anthropology theory, especially his well-known ideas about the "dyadic contract" and "limited good," Foster also was active as an applied anthropologist. He was invited to Latin America, Asia, and Africa on consulting assignments for the World Health Organization and other international agencies. Foster's career is a

model of intellectual accomplishment blended with a strong sense of service to the academy, the profession, the Berkeley community, and the wider world.

Biographical Data

Born in Sioux Falls, South Dakota, on October 9, 1913, Foster died on May 18, 2006, at his home in the hills above the campus of the University of California, Berkeley. Foster arrived in Berkeley in mid-August 1935 to begin his graduate studies, received his PhD there in 1941, and taught there as a professor from 1953 until his retirement in 1979, when he was awarded the title of professor emeritus. His years at and beyond Berkeley are well documented in the autobiographical volume *An Anthropologist's Life in the Twentieth Century: Theory and Practice at UC Berkeley, the Smithsonian, in Mexico, and With the World Health Organization.* Assembled from an oral history conducted in 1998 and 1999 by Suzanne B. Reiss of the Regional Oral History Office of the Bancroft Library at University of California, Berkeley, this 413-page volume is remarkable for the candor, modesty, and detail with which Foster tells the story of his personal life and professional career.

Training in American Historical Anthropology

After an undergraduate career studying with Melville Herskovits at Northwestern University, Foster entered the University of California at Berkeley in the depths of the Depression in 1935. He took classes primarily from A. L. Kroeber, Robert Lowie, and Edward Gifford. After a summer trip in 1936, Foster already had become interested in Mexico and made plans to do his dissertation work there. Nonetheless, at Kroeber's suggestion, in the summer of 1937, he did his first fieldwork—among the Yuki Indians living in Round Valley in northern California. He and his wife (Mary LeCron Foster, whom he married in 1938) went to Mexico City in 1940, where they remained from January to May, before traveling to Veracruz, where, at the suggestion of Roberto Weitlaner, they studied the Sierra Popoluca from November to May 1941. The Fosters returned to Berkeley, where, during the summer of 1941, George wrote his dissertation on the Sierra Popoluca, published as an American Ethnological Society monograph in 1942.

Moving From the University to Government Service

In 1941, it was difficult for anyone to find academic work. After a 1-year stint at Syracuse University and the following academic year at University of California, Los Angeles, Foster was called to Washington, D.C. In the process, he went from being an ethnographer in the tradition of Kroeber, Lowie, and Gifford to becoming an analyst and interpreter of culture and behavior in contemporary societies, especially Mexico and Latin America.

This transformation did not occur intentionally but through serendipity. After being declared ineligible for the military draft (because of allergies), Foster was the first anthropologist hired by Julian Steward (whom Foster knew because both had been at Berkeley in the 1930s) to go to Latin America as a representative of the new Institute of Social Anthropology (ISA), created in 1942 within the Smithsonian Institution with special responsibilities for Latin America. Sent to Mexico City to train students at the Escuela Nacional de Antropología e Historia, in 1945 Foster took a group of students to the Tarascan region in the State of Michoacán. After a bumpy start, Foster, his assistant Gabriel Ospina, and several students embarked on their field project in the small town of Tzintzuntzan. At that time, in 1945–1946, Foster had no idea that his long-term ethnographic work would enhance Tzintzuntzan's fame or that Tzintzuntzan would provide him with the source of some of his best ideas.

Doing Field Research in Spain

In 1949–1950, Foster took a leave of absence from the ISA and, with funds from a Guggenheim Fellowship, went to Spain to carry out a detailed study of acculturation. This field research served as the basis of his well-known book *Culture and Conquest: America's Spanish Heritage*, published in 1960, in which he elaborated the important concepts of "conquest culture" and "cultural crystallization." In Spain, he also developed his long-term interest in tracing the impact of Hippocratic medical theories from the Old World to Latin America, which he elaborated in his 1994 book *Hippocrates' Latin American Legacy: Humoral Medicine in the New World*.

Returning to Washington: A New Focus on Public Health

When Foster returned to Washington, he realized that congressional funding for the ISA was no longer a national priority. In response, he refocused the research being done in Mexico, Guatemala, Colombia, Peru, and Brazil from traditional ethnology to the study of health systems. In 1951, Foster assembled a 104-page mimeographed report titled "A Cross-Cultural Anthropological Analysis of a Technical Aid Program." Subsequently, in June 1952, Foster presented the ISA research results. In his autobiographical memoir, he recalled the occasion as one of the great days of his life. In reconfiguring the ISA, Foster transformed his own vision of the world. Always the ethnographer, he saw how bureaucracies had their own cultures and, what later he would call, their own "implicit premises."

Moving to Berkeley

Foster returned to Berkeley in 1953 as a visiting lecturer, hoping to land a permanent job—designed to be split one third and two thirds between public health and anthropology, respectively—but the arrangement never came to fruition. Fortunately, it happened that Gifford retired soon after Foster's arrival and there was a need for a new director of the Museum of Anthropology. As a result, Foster was appointed to Gifford's position. After a 3-year stint as acting director at the museum, Foster moved into the Department of Anthropology on a full-time tenured appointment in 1955.

Returning to Tzintzuntzan, Mexico

With a large grant from the National Science Foundation, in 1958, Foster returned to Tzintzuntzan, where he initiated an innovative long-term study of sociocultural change, economics, personality, and health. This research resulted in many important contributions to the understanding of peasant life, including his oft cited and controversial works on "the Image of Limited Good," "the dyadic contract," and "hot-cold" theories of illness. Foster's goal was to develop models to explain how villagers' traditional worldviews (emphasizing balance, harmony, and reciprocity) were being transformed as the national and international political-economic system increasingly influenced local culture.

Building Medical Anthropology

Apart from restarting his field research in Tzintzuntzan, Foster also took advantage of the opportunity to develop a major grant with the NIGMS (National Institute for General Medical Sciences). Over a period of 15 years, from 1965 to 1979, the grant brought in some $3,000,000 to support about 100 students in the Berkeley doctoral program. Eager to institutionalize training in medical anthropology, Foster established and directed the joint PhD University of California, Berkeley/University of California, San Francisco, program from 1972 until his retirement in 1979. In 1978, Foster coauthored (with Barbara Gallatin Anderson) *Medical Anthropology*, the first textbook in the field.

Applying Anthropology

Although Foster said that he was trained by Kroeber and Lowie to "despise" applied anthropology, Foster's experience in the ISA and with other government assignments led him to recognize the importance of understanding how traditional cultures respond to technological change. Between 1951 and 1983, Foster accepted 36 international consulting assignments related to public health and community health. Through his travels to Latin America, Africa, Asia, and Europe, Foster came to appreciate the importance of the "interaction setting" between "innovating organizations" and "target groups" in determining the success or failure of development projects. His consulting experiences informed his most successful (more than 100,000 copies sold) textbook, *Traditional Cultures and the Impact of Technological Change* (1962; reissued as *Traditional Societies and Technological Change*, 1973), and *Applied Anthropology* (1969), the first textbook in the field.

Summing Up a Career

On June 16, 1979, Foster was presented with a Festschrift volume titled *From Tzintzuntzan to the "Image of Limited Good": Essays in Honor of George M. Foster*, which contained congratulatory letters from numerous colleagues and former students, a dozen articles written by former students, and a comprehensive bibliography of Foster's publications from 1939 to mid-1979. The most important piece in the *Festschrift* has proven to be an essay by Eugene Hammel and Laura Nader, titled "Will the Real George Foster Please Stand Up? A Brief Intellectual History." In their appreciation of Foster's work, they argued that Foster's career is a challenge to anthropologists who believe that specialization is incompatible with breadth, that scientific and applied work cannot be linked, and that long-term fieldwork in the same community and region tends to narrow our comparative vision.

Foster's contributions to anthropological theory and practice still challenge us. In more than 300 publications, he wrote about acculturation, long-term fieldwork, peasant economies, pottery making, public health, social structure, symbolic systems, technological change, theories of illness and wellness, and worldview. The quantity, quality, and long-term value of his scholarly work was extraordinary; virtually all of his major publications have been reprinted and/or translated.

During his long career, Foster's accomplishments were recognized with many honors and awards. He was elected to the National Academy of Sciences and the American Academy of Arts and Sciences, served as President of the American Anthropological Association during the Vietnam years of 1969–1970, and was awarded the Association's Distinguished Service Award (1980). He received the Malinowski Award from the Society for Applied Anthropology in 1982 and an honorary Doctor of Humane Letters degree from Southern Methodist University in 1990. In 1997, the Berkeley Anthropology Library was renamed in honor of the Fosters. Finally, in 2005, Foster was awarded the Society for Medical Anthropology's first Lifetime Achievement Award (renamed in his honor in 2006).

Robert V. Kemper

See also Kroeber, Alfred L.; Lowie, Robert; Nader, Laura; Steward, Julian; University of California, Berkeley

Further Readings

Foster, G. M. (1942). *A primitive Mexican economy* (Monographs of the American Ethnological Society, V). New York, NY: J. J. Agustin.

———. (1948). *Empire's children: The people of Tzintzuntzan* (Institute of Social Anthropology Publication, No. 6). Washington, DC: Smithsonian Institution.

———. (1960). *Culture and conquest: America's Spanish heritage* (Viking Fund Publications in Anthropology, No. 27). New York, NY: Wenner-Gren Foundation for Anthropological Research.

———. (1962). *Traditional cultures, and the impact of technological change*. New York, NY: Harper.

———. (1967). *Tzintzuntzan: Mexican peasants in a changing world*. Boston, MA: Little, Brown.

———. (1969). *Applied anthropology*. Boston, MA: Little, Brown.

———. (1973). *Traditional societies and technological change*. New York, NY: Harper & Row.

———. (1994). *Hippocrates' Latin American legacy: Humoral medicine in the new world*. Langhorne, PA.: Gordon & Breach Science.

———. (2000). *An anthropologist's life in the twentieth century: Theory and practice at UC Berkeley, the Smithsonian, in Mexico, and with the World Health Organization* (An oral history conducted in 1998 and 1999 by Suzanne B. Riess). Berkeley, CA: University of California, Regional Oral History Office, Bancroft Library. Retrieved from http://content.cdlib.org/xtf/view?docId=kt7s2005ng&brand=calisphere

Foster, G. M., & Anderson, B. G. (1978). *Medical anthropology*. New York, NY: Wiley.

Foster, G. M., & Kemper, R. V. (Eds.). (1974). *Anthropologists in cities*. Boston, MA: Little, Brown.

Foster, G. M., Scudder, T., Colson, E., & Kemper, R. V. (1979). *Long-term field research in social anthropology*. New York, NY: Academic Press.

Kemper, R. V., & Brandes, S. (2007). George McClelland Foster Jr. (1913–2006). *American Anthropologist, 109,* 427–433.

Foucault, Michel

Paul-Michel Foucault (1926–1984), French philosopher and historian, was one of the most original and dynamic thinkers of the post–World War II period. He established powerful approaches to the analysis of discourse and opened up paths of critical historical inquiry into the politics and ethics of truth.

Biography and Major Works

Born into a medical family in Poitiers, Foucault's upbringing was highly cultured and bourgeois. Sent from the provinces to Paris in his late teens, he began his intellectual preparations for France's most prestigious institution of tertiary education, the École Normale Supérieure (ENS). At the ENS, he shone scholastically; however, attempts at suicide clearly indicated that he was also struggling with existential problems. Foucault's emerging capacity to analyze the experiences that concerned him, through historical research conducted in archives, was to become characteristic of his work. He graduated from the ENS in 1952 in both philosophy and psychology.

Between graduating and defending his doctoral dissertation at ENS in 1961, he taught at the University of Lille and spent several years in cultural diplomatic positions in Uppsala, Warsaw, and Hamburg. He defended his dissertation, *Folie et déraison: Histoire de la folie à l'âge classique* (*Madness and Unreason: A History of Madness in the Classical Age*), in 1961. According to the unsurpassed biography by Didier Eribon, his passage into the history of madness began in the course of a sleepless night at the *Maison de France* in Uppsala, an institutional setting where he had access to a veritable trove of archival material, offering him a historical substrate for his philosophical vigor. About the thesis, an examiner's report noted several of the elements that would become signatures of Foucault's studied manner of work: the interplay of extensive and painstaking archival documentation and works of doctrine, ignited by the spark of a philosophical problem. The examiner, Georges Canguilhem, an important historian and philosopher of biology, would become a key intellectual interlocutor for the young Foucault. The thesis was not guided by the desire for a reconstituted history of an idea; rather, it was a historical analysis and philosophically oriented synthesis of the concrete practices of "reason," which determined "madness" as a specific object of thought and intervention in what Foucault would call the Classical Age—the period extending from the end of the 16th century to the beginning of the 19th century.

During his tenure at the University of Claremont-Ferrond (1960–1966), he produced three major works: (1) *Naissance de la clinique: Une archéologie du regard medical* (*Birth of the Clinic: An Archeology of the Medical Gaze*, 1963), which continued his historical-philosophical analysis of medicine; (2) *Raymond Roussel* (*Death and the Labyrinth: The World of Raymond Roussel*, 1963), which explored the thresholds of thought in life; and (3) *Les Mots et les choses: Une archéologie des sciences humaines* (*The Order of Things: An Archaeology of the Human Sciences*, 1966), which catalyzed his reputation and was his most synthetic work, bringing together his multiple inquiries into the human sciences.

The Order of Things revisited concerns first introduced in his "minor" thesis, which was a translation from German to French of Kant's *Anthropology From a Pragmatic Point of View*, with an extended critical essay, "Introduction à l' Anthropologie de Kant," published in English as "Introduction to Kant's Anthropology" in 2008.

Foucault relocated to Tunisia during 1966–1968, teaching at the University of Tunis. While observing the protests of May 1968 in France from afar, he had firsthand experience and was affected by the risk men and women in Tunisia took to protest and demonstrate against the forms of power they experienced in daily life. In 1969, he published *The Archaeology of Knowledge* (*L'Archéologie du savoir*) and returned to serve as director of the philosophy department at the experimental University of Paris, Vincennes, created in the wake of the May 1968 uprisings.

In 1970, he was awarded a chair at the Collège de France, which he named the History of Systems of Thought. This was a position Foucault had campaigned energetically to achieve. It was, however, constraining as an institution. He had no formal students, and there was a ritualized performance of weekly public lectures, with little possibility for intellectual exchange. He characterized the experience as that of an acrobat performing in solitude before a stunned audience. Foucault traveled frequently during this period, arguably to escape the burden of his growing reputation and to find a different way of work and life. He cultivated working relationships in the United States, especially at the University of California, Berkeley.

In the period 1970–1984, Foucault published four major works: *Surveiller et punir: Naissance de la prison* (*Discipline and Punish: The Birth of the Prison*, 1975), a monograph on the emergence of forms of incarceration and discipline, and three volumes of *Histoire de la sexualité* (*The History of Sexuality*). He wrote numerous essays and articles and published many interviews during this time, as ways of experimenting with genres and avenues of thinking. He died in 1984 from a septicemia characteristic of AIDS.

Critical Contributions to Anthropology

Foucault's contribution to contemporary anthropology can be divided between his archaeological inquiry into the human sciences, his genealogical inquiry into the emergence of discipline and biopower, and his problematization of truth and subjectivity.

Archaeology of the Human Sciences

In his *Introduction to Kant's Anthropology*, Foucault reworked this neglected text to investigate the relations of psychology and anthropology to Kant's critical philosophy. The problem Foucault begins to articulate is how it is possible to engage in an empirical analysis of the multiple forms of the human being on the basis of an object of knowledge, "Man." Such an object was fundamental for the human sciences that emerged in the Classical Age. Foucault showed that this object has a highly problematic double status: "Man" is supposed to be simultaneously a natural creature conditioned by physical forces and a subject capable of "freedom" through self-knowledge and intervention in the conditions of this subject's being.

This core problem was extended and catalyzed in *The Order of Things*, whose subtitle is *An Archaeology of the Human Sciences*. An archaeology of knowledge was the manner in which Foucault excavated the forms, conditions, and practices through which the possibility of this paradoxical double was constituted: a subject of knowledge becoming the object of knowledge. His analysis is of the epistemic conditions and changes necessary to make possible sciences of life, language, and labor in the 19th century, in the form of economics, biology, and linguistics. Foucault analyzed how discursive regimes gave rise to a corpus of knowledge having the status and effects of a science.

One effect of his archaeology of knowledge was to show how the emergence of this figure of "Man" made possible novel forms of intervention through the creation of new social institutions; he had worked already on studies of the asylum and the clinic and would carry on this work by analyzing penal institutions.

Genealogy of Discipline and Biopower

In the 1970s, Foucault forged a genealogical transformation of his archaeology-of-knowledge research into the substrata of the forms of knowledge in the human sciences. Genealogy, in Foucault's hands, became a means of modifying his work on the systematic formation and productivity of discourse. It was a way of intensifying the problematic interconnection among and between historical artifacts so as to destroy the mystifying primacy of origins and of claims to unchanging truths. Foucault calls this genealogical strategy a way of writing a "history of the present." Such history begins with a diagnostic question: How did we get to a situation in the present where a specific mechanism of power functions the way it does? Genealogy works by isolating the components of political technologies and tracing the conditions of their historical emergence.

Discipline and Punish shows how the institutionalization of disciplinary reforms, including the emergence of imprisonment as a form of punishment in the 18th and 19th centuries, took on a self-evident character. Foucault showed at the level of practices, visible in their banality, how such a solution first had to be constituted by a problem of deviance from both a normal and a normative figure of the productive human being. The space of confinement was rendered as a productive space through discipline—forms of enclosure and exercise rendering the persons enclosed visible, knowable, and transformable. His insight was to show, with respect to the transformation in the exercise of confinement, how power requires a field of knowledge to operate. Furthermore, and internal to this field, knowledge requires a subject and object of knowledge, which involves a relation of power.

If discipline operates on the deviance of the maladapted individual, Foucault crafted a further concept—biopower—to show how the specific techniques of discipline were part of a much larger general reconfiguration of power relations since the end of the Classical Age. Until approximately the beginning of the 19th century, power was exercised by and for a sovereign, either in the person of the ruler or diffused into the state. Foucault shows how a new relationship between the individual body and the population of which it is a part becomes the object of intervention for the techniques and strategies of those who are able to exercise power. These interventions have as their aim the vitality of bodies and populations, visible in the emergence of diverse domains of governance and knowledge, such as public health. The concept of biopower, introduced in *The History of Sexuality*, Volume 1, enlarged the range and scope of his analyses of the rationalities through which power over life could be exercised and administered.

Subjectivity and Truth

In the late 1970s and 1980s, Foucault turned with regularity to the theme of ethics, the subject and truth, and in October 1980, he gave the Howison lectures at Berkeley under the title "Truth and Subjectivity." One can see by the distance and change from his Tanner lectures at Stanford in the previous year (an investigation of pastoral power and modern political reason) a movement toward a different problematization of knowledge, ethics, and power. During this period, and especially in the last 3 years of lectures at the Collège de France (1981–1984) and the last two volumes of *The History of Sexuality*, Foucault concentrated on two terms: (1) the neglected ancient Greek maxim *epimeleia heatou*, care of the self, which he took up within the broader problem of the way in which persons govern themselves and others, and (2) the ancient Greek practice of *parrhēsia*, which means "to say all," or freely and frankly speaking the truth. Foucault was thus beginning a line of inquiry into ethics, understood as how a subject becomes a subject capable of claiming to speak the truth. Furthermore, he was asking what difference such speech makes to the situation in which subjects govern themselves and others by way of their claims to truth. Foucault's working sessions with Paul Rabinow and Hubert Dreyfus in Berkeley, published as *On the Genealogy of Ethics*, indicate that the object of the general ancient Greek problem of ethics was not primarily the self, or subject, but rather *technē tou biou*, or "arts of living"; Foucault's entrance into the genealogy of ethics asked how the question of how to live came gradually to be subsumed within techniques and practices of the self.

Foucault's Legacy

Foucault is sometimes referred to as a "theorist," offering a relativist "theory" of knowledge, with antihumanist consequences. As he explains in several of his essays, rather than theory his objective was to write critical histories of the ways through which human beings are made subjects. His relation to the dominant philosophical schools of the 20th century was an abutting one. With respect to Marxism and phenomenology, he showed the historical conditions for knowledge about particular subjects and their histories at the level of concrete practices. By so doing he undermined theoretical pretense to universal knowledge of a subject of history, which was foundational to these theoretical traditions. With respect to structuralism, he showed how the positing of a relation of a subject to an object of knowledge is not only a matter of defining the formal conditions of a relationship, it is also a matter of how a subject becomes a legitimate subject of a type of knowledge. When analyzed at the level of practice, such research opens up diverse modes of (what he called) *subjectivation*.

Foucault's archaeological and genealogical manners of inquiry, as well as his attention to the force fields of power-knowledge, have become cornerstones of research, where science, ethics, and politics intersect. His nascent explorations of truth and subjectivation opened up a vast terrain of problems for further inquiry, which were cut short by his untimely death.

Anthony Stavrianakis

See also Abu-Lughod, Lila; Althusser, Louis; Asad, Talal; Critical Theory; Derrida, Jacques; Discourse Theory; Lévi-Strauss, Claude; Marxist Anthropology; Neo-Kantianism; Postcolonial Theory; Postmodernism; Poststructuralism; Queer Theory; Rabinow, Paul; Race; Structuralism; Subaltern Studies

Further Readings

Burchell, G., Gordon, C., & Miller, P. (Eds.). (1991). *The Foucault effect: Studies in governmentality*. Chicago, IL: University of Chicago Press.

Dreyfus, H., & Rabinow, P. (1983). *Michel Foucault, beyond structuralism and hermeneutics*. Chicago, IL: University of Chicago Press.

Eribon, D. (1991). *Michel Foucault* (B. Wing, Trans.). Cambridge, MA: Harvard University Press.

Faubion, J. D. (1998). Introduction. In J. D. Faubion (Ed.), *Essential works of Foucault (1954–1984): Vol. 2. Aesthetics, method, and epistemology* (pp. xii–xliv). New York, NY: New Press.

Foucault, M. (1976–1984). *The history of sexuality* (Vols. 1–3). New York, NY: Vintage Books.

Gros, F. (2005). Course context. In M. Foucault (Ed.), *The hermeneutics of the subject: Lectures at the Collège de France 1981–1982* (G. Burchell, Trans.; F. Gros, Ed.). New York, NY: Palgrave Macmillan.

Rabinow, P. (1994). Introduction: The history of systems of thought. In P. Rabinow (Ed.), *Essential works of Foucault (1954–1984): Vol. 1. Ethics* (pp. xi–xlii). New York, NY: New Press.

Frankfurt School

Founded in 1923 by Felix Weil and his students Max Horkheimer and Friedrich Pollock, the Institut für Sozialforschung (Institute for Social Research) in Frankfurt am Main was a network of intellectuals whose studies of political economy, cultural analysis, and critical sociology generated some of the 20th century's most influential interventions into Western capitalist society.

With their personal origins in the crises of the Weimar Republic, its primary members—Theodor Adorno, Erich Fromm, Horkheimer, Leo Lowenthal, Herbert Marcuse, Franz Neumann, and Pollack—were raised in assimilated Jewish families and educated in rigorous philosophical traditions. This philosophical training extended from Plato and Aristotle's antiquity through the Enlightenment epoch, culminating in the modern era, as exemplified in the writings of G. W. F. Hegel. Despite this pedigree, members identified themselves as outsiders within the German bourgeoisie, due in part to rampant anti-Semitism in the 1930s. As a result, the institute became an unflinching critical voice in the decades that were to follow. The unimaginable catastrophe, subsequent collective trauma, and attempted political reparations following World War II—events without precedent in German history—were among the foremost problems grappled with by this prodigious group of researchers.

Critical Theory

The enduring relevance of the institute resides, however, in their genesis of "critical theory." The term was coined by Horkheimer in a 1937 article, "Traditional and Critical Theory." Faced with this unique mix of influences and problems, its members engaged in precise studies of their cultural past and economic realities, leading them to examine the meaning of *intellectual praxis*. The division between "traditional" and "critical" theory was based on whether intellectual activity reproduced status quo social relations or subverted them. Although the institute emerged at a time of growing national conservatism, it nonetheless became most productive from 1930 onward, when Horkheimer became its director. Horkheimer maintained an ambitious plan for the institute: to create a shared engagement with the fundamental myths and invidious structures that shaped contemporary Europe. Whereas many theorists in the 1930s were content to specialize and narrow the scope of their investigations, institute members consistently defied the insularity of provincial academic scholarship to instead enlarge the scale and complexity of what constituted thought. For example, in 1944, Adorno and Horkheimer published *The Dialectic of the Enlightenment* (written during the war and circulated furtively beforehand). A seminal text representative of the institute's challenge to the illusions of modern rationality, the authors drew from *The Odyssey*, Hebrew scripture, modern philosophy, and popular culture to question how the practice of modern science and industry promised to liberate people from ignorance, disease, and exploitation and yet catalyzed a culture in which people adhered to fascist ideology and xenophobia, killed one another on a large scale, and practiced mass deception in the face of lived reality. If one of the promises of the Enlightenment was to foster independent thought and intellectual maturation, Adorno and Horkheimer argued that the myths implicit in various technological advancements had, in fact, renewed Western civilization's barbaric and regressive traits.

In its early formation, the institute showed an affinity for thinkers who contested the legitimacy of the European Enlightenment. This is not to say that the institute outright rejected the epoch's tenets. Instead, their interest in Enlightenment critique raised urgent questions that were left unaddressed by their religious cosmologies and philosophical training. These questions concern a broad swath of detailed topics: the nature of freedom and necessity, the dialectical tension between rationality and irrationality, the meaning of a "disenchanted" natural history, and the politics of critical thinking threatened by the modern calamity of calculation, profit, and pleasurable immediacy. Predicated by the complex sociological shifts occurring after Weimar, members employed techniques of critique developed by a series of thinkers who defy simple categorization.

These included Sigmund Freud, Georg Lukács, Karl Marx, Friedrich Nietzsche, and Max Weber.

Influences

From Freud, members became attuned to unconscious aspects of the self—its repressions and dreams, the gendered antagonisms of familial life (often envisioned archetypally), the stultifying norms of bourgeois conduct, and a largely tragic view of social life. In particular, Marcuse and Fromm saw psychoanalysis as a demystifying mode of sociology. Freud, they thought, was willing to employ innovative hypotheses and narratives against the commonly held belief that humans are rational actors and have control over their own destiny. Psychoanalytic theory thus proved to be an invaluable counter to the epistemologically limited and empirically based psychologies and cognitive theories (e.g., Jean Piaget, B. F. Skinner) that grew within the postwar academy.

From Lukács, especially his late work *History and Class Consciousness* (1923), the institute grasped how commodification, the effects of mass production in cultural realms, came to mediate a subject's consciousness and unwittingly acclimatize one to the struggles of socioeconomic disparity. "Reification," the reduction of human relations to relations between things, became a hallmark concept for the group, and it signaled their contention with the subject's estrangement from the past and from his or her community. Although Lukács was never associated with the institute, both he and the Frankfurt school are credited with the rise of "Western Marxism." This term is associated with scholars who include cultural phenomena in their interpretation of and struggle within the political economy. Unlike Lukács, the Frankfurt school dissociated its leftist politics from the German Social Democratic Party and from the German and Soviet Communist party's rigidly deterministic policies.

Similar to Lukács, Marx's work on the capitalist political economy gained an axiomatic place in the institute's understanding of historical events. For many of the institute's contemporaries, capitalism was deemed a natural or merely incidental part of social problems. For the Frankfurt school, the reproduction of capitalist social relations through decades of needless poverty, capitalism's power to shape large-scale populations, and its crisis-prone contradictions provided fecund material for the members' critiques. The ideological dimension of culture, whose influence was often difficult to imagine in purportedly "freethinking societies," gained greater intelligibility and force with texts such as Marcuse's *Reason and Revolution* (1940) and *One Dimensional Man* (1964). Marcuse argues here and in the essay "The Affirmative Character of Culture" (1937) that the objects of critical social theory are the seemingly innocent "tolerant" or "positive" attitudes that reproduce larger structures of domination, such as class, ethnic, and gender inequalities.

Nietzsche's fragmented and aphoristic writing style and his genealogical studies of Judeo-Christian morality were taken up as modes of expression and itineraries for the group's readily secular interpretations of contemporary life. No idol was too sacred for scrutiny, and much like Nietzsche's meditations on interpersonal hostility, the institute's members learned from Nietzsche the psychosocial scapegoating inherent to struggles for power. Nietzsche's influence also led to a reckoning with Martin Heidegger and existentialist strains of thought circulating prominently throughout interwar Europe. Adorno's *The Jargon of Authenticity* (1964) is a polemic opposing the nativist and mystifying tendencies in Heidegger's thought.

Finally, Weber's deft account of the rational mechanization of social institutions—that is, the management and structure of bureaucracies—is expanded by Adorno and Horkheimer in texts such as *The Dialectic of Enlightenment* and Adorno's collaborative empirical study *The Authoritarian Personality* (1950). Neumann's *Behemoth: The Structure and Practice of National Socialism* (1941) stands as the work from the institute that is most indebted to Weberian sociology. This study made a great impact on the thought of the sociologist C. Wright Mills.

Walter Benjamin was the most influential fellow traveler of the institute. After rescinding his application to teach aesthetics at Goethe University in 1924, Benjamin worked as an independent literary critic for nearly a decade thereafter and was funded intermittently by the institute until his death in 1940. Renowned for his 1936 essay "The Work of Art in the Age of Technological Reproducibility," Benjamin's focus on aesthetic perception, formed by the changing conditions of mass-produced art forms (i.e., film and photography), fascism, and urbanization, had a lasting influence on Adorno, Horkheimer, and Marcuse. A revealing correspondence between Adorno and Benjamin remains one of the most instructive documents of intellectual discourse in the institute's history—especially their discussion of the relevance of Marx for their work.

In contrast to the practice of philosophy, then, "critical theory" became the name associated with the institute's integrated engagement with a constellation of intellectual resources (not to mention their extensive studies of film, classical and popular music, literature, advertising, etc.). The initial generation of research associated with "critical theory" represents an instructive overturning of the usual ways rationality, freedom, culture, power, and the material necessities of thinking and action are interpreted and represented. Although Horkheimer proposed an entirely new mode of intellectual practice, tracing its antecedents is essential for a grasp of its thought.

Exile

The institute became known as "The Frankfurt school" only after its members fled the Third Reich in 1936 and regrouped in New York City at Columbia University. Surprised that the German proletariat were unwilling to oppose the Nazi party, members learned firsthand how fascism was an extension (and not anomalous) of industrial parliamentary political culture. This prolonged exile splintered the group as some remained in the United States after the war, but the relocation failed to temper the members' incisive work. Adorno, in particular, became a prolific writer on everything from phenomenology to jazz. He contributed to Paul Lazarsfeld's Princeton University Radio Research Project, continued to publish the institute's writings in *Zeitschrift fur Sozialforschung* (*Journal for Social Research*, which produced eight volumes between 1922 and 1939), and wrote innumerable essays. The Frankfurt school's transition to North America also saw many of the members change their research focus to class issues and the "culture industry," with many of their examples drawn from the United States.

In 1941, Adorno and Horkheimer moved to Los Angeles to join other émigrés, including Bertolt Brecht and Thomas Mann. Adorno published one of the most severe indictments of Western culture ever written, *Minima Moralia: Reflections From Damaged Life*, in 1951. Consisting of hundreds of essayistic fragments (a form borrowed from Benjamin), the text is a prime example of his synthetic interest in literature, classical music, and other facets of German culture. Despite the increased circulation of his and other member's texts after their move to the United States, Adorno's work would not attract substantial attention in North America for almost 20 years. The translation of ideas, problems, and methods between Germany and the United States is one of the most interesting issues facing Frankfurt school scholars today.

Continued Relevance

A second generation of the school emerged in the mid- to late 1950s when the institute officially reopened in Frankfurt (in 1950), and Adorno became director in 1958. Jürgen Habermas is associated with the reformation of the Frankfurt school after Adorno's death in 1969. Mentored in the tradition of German philosophy and sociology, Habermas's habilitation, *The Structural Transformation of the Public Sphere: An Inquiry Into a Category of Bourgeois Society* (1962), is a landmark account of the historical shifts in the notion of the public sphere, from the Renaissance in western Europe to the revolutionary United States. Habermas thus shifted the school's stance on a number of core methods of inquiry. Perhaps the most significant is his reconciliation with positivist sociology (e.g., those advocated by August Comte and Talcott Parsons), pragmatist political science (his most lucid writings concern the 1990 German reunification process), and discourse ethics (see his theory of "communicative action"). Horkheimer would have deemed these methods "traditional theory." Nevertheless, Habermas has claimed fidelity to the projects of the Enlightenment and of modernity, calling both "unfinished projects" and insisting on opposition to "postmodern" and "antimodern" philosophies.

The operations of the institute continue today, and its legacy of critical engagement with a sociological focus is evident in the work of Karl Löwith, Oskar Negt, and Axel Honneth. The school's work has been translated into numerous languages and is taught in universities worldwide. Today, many of the most influential "critical theorists" have no direct affiliation with the school but instead examine its vast archive for lessons on contemporary theoretical and sociological problems. In the United States, Susan Buck-Morss, Fredric Jameson, and Martin Jay (among many) employ the school's teachings

and have undertaken landmark studies of Benjamin, Adorno, and the history of the school (until 1950), respectively; in Brazil, Roberto Schwarz and Paolo Freire (d. 1997) engage with contemporary culture, with a focus on culture industries, literature, and pedagogy; in Sweden and England, Göran Therborn and Terry Eagleton are two of the school's most astute interlocutors; and in Slovenia, Slavoj Žižek's dialectical investigations into topics both popular and specialist have gained wide reception. In this sense, the practice of "critical theory" lives on beyond the Frankfurt school.

Tim Kaposy

See also Benjamin, Walter; Critical Theory; Habermas, Jürgen; Hegel, Georg W. F.; Jameson, Fredric; Marx, Karl; Weber, Max

Further Readings

Buck-Morss, S. (1977). *The origin of negative dialectics: Theodor W. Adorno, Walter Benjamin, and the Frankfurt Institute.* Cambridge, MA: MIT Press.

Eagleton, T. (2000). *The idea of culture.* London, UK: Wiley-Blackwell.

Honneth, A. (1996). *The struggle for recognition: The moral grammar of social conflicts.* Cambridge, MA: MIT Press.

Jameson, F. (1990). *Late Marxism: Adorno, or, the persistence of the dialectic.* London, UK: Verso.

Jay, M. (1973). *The dialectical imagination: A history of the Frankfurt school and the Institute of Social Research, 1923–1950.* Berkeley: California University Press.

Therborn, G. (1970). The Frankfurt school. *New Left Review, 63,* 75–96.

Wiggershaus, R. (1995). *The Frankfurt school: Its history, theories, and political significance.* Cambridge, MA: MIT Press.

FRAZER, JAMES G.

James George Frazer, classicist, anthropologist, and trained lawyer, helped found British anthropology in the 19th century.

Biography and Major Works

Frazer was born in Glasgow on January 1, 1854. Frazer was one of four children. He grew up in Helensburgh, a small town on the west side of

Scotland, located at the mouth of the Gare Loch. Frazer's father, Daniel, and his mother, Katherine, had moved the family there to avoid the industrialization in Glasgow. The Frazers lived a middle-class Presbyterian existence, devoting themselves to the Free Kirk movement—an evangelical and puritanical religious movement that rebuffed efforts by the state to interfere in the governance of the Church of Scotland. The Free Kirk movement attracted lower-middle-class merchants who espoused the value of individualism. As a pharmacist (known in Scotland as a "chemist"), Daniel represented the Free Kirk's base of support. Katherine was also a devout Presbyterian, who ensured that her children never left the house on Sunday other than to attend church twice.

Daniel was keen to advance his children's scope of learning. He chose their schools with care. Frazer attended Larchfield Academy, a Presbyterian school for nonconformist, middle-class families. Under the tutelage of his headmaster, Alexander Mackenzie, Frazer studied the classics. When his ability became evident, he was sent to the University of Glasgow to complete an undergraduate liberal arts degree. Frazer studied classics and Latin under George Gulbert Ramsay, professor of humanity; history, philosophy, and literature under John Veitch, professor of logic and metaphysics; and physics under William Thomson (later Lord Kelvin), professor of natural philosophy. By the time he graduated, Frazer had adopted the belief that through science humanity can discover the universal causes of physical and social phenomena.

Frazer attended the University of Cambridge, which had gained a reputation for matriculating Scottish (Free Kirk) Presbyterians and other dissenters (i.e., Quakers, Unitarians, and Methodists), as well as Roman Catholics and Jews. By the time Frazer arrived at Cambridge in 1873, he had already read the classics, including Plato, Euripides, and Pindar, and he had studied a long lineage of Scottish philosophers, including Thomas Reid and William Hamilton. Frazer finished with first class in 1875, 1876, and 1877 and graduated second in his class in the 1878 Classics Tripos examination. In 1879, Frazer submitted a dissertation titled *The Growth of Plato's Ideal Theory* for a fellowship application to Trinity College. Frazer argued that Plato had misunderstood Socrates in interpreting the latter's theory of knowledge (i.e., epistemology) as a theory of

being (i.e., ontology). Frazer received the fellowship, which was later renewed for life.

Frazer's reading list at Cambridge included books by scientific naturalists and social evolutionists, such as Herbert Spencer. Scientific naturalists had argued that there was no place for the supernatural in the explanation of physical and social phenomena. In this view, science is preferred to intuition as it offers objective accounts of cause and effect. Likewise, social science ought to avoid appealing to intuitions for causal explanations and should focus instead on empirical evidence that demonstrates the evolution of society. Frazer adopted this scientific naturalist philosophy and began to interpret changes in rituals and religious customs as the outcome of immutable and universal evolutionary progress.

Taking a break from his academic studies, Frazer sought to please his father by getting admitted to one of the Inns of Court in London, where he studied law and passed the exams set by the Council of Legal Education. He was called to the bar in 1882, but he never practiced, choosing instead to return to academic life in Cambridge.

Frazer first became interested in anthropology after reading E. B. Tylor's *Primitive Culture* (1871). In 1884, Frazer befriended William Robertson Smith, who had recently lost his academic post at the Free Church College at Aberdeen due to his unconventional (some claimed "heretical") views of the Bible's authoritativeness. At the time, Smith was serving as assistant editor of the *Encyclopedia Britannica* (he became editor in 1887). Smith asked Frazer to write articles on taboo and totemism for the encyclopedia. The research Frazer carried out to complete the articles whetted his appetite for historical and comparative treatments of ritual and myth. In 1885, Frazer delivered his first lecture to the Anthropological Institute in London on the topic of burial customs and primitive theories of the soul. Motivated by his research on totems and taboos, he began to amass a large repository of anthropological material, including letters from missionaries, archaeologists, and other colonialists who had traveled abroad and encountered new societies and customs.

Frazer's first anthropological manuscript was an extension of his encyclopedia entry "Totemism." Published as an 87-page book, *Totemism* (1887) was one of the smallest books Frazer ever produced. He later expanded it to a 2,000-page, 4-volume series titled *Totemism and Exogamy* (1910). Frazer also used his repository of anthropological notes and correspondences to forge his most famous book, *The Golden Bough*. First published in 1890 in 2 volumes, the book was republished in 3 volumes in 1900 and reissued in 12 volumes between 1911 and 1915, with a 13th volume, *Aftermath*, added in 1936. Meanwhile, *Immortality and the Worship of the Dead* (1913) and *Folklore in the Old Testament* (1918), for which Frazer learned to read and speak Hebrew, both courted controversy, although they also gained him a reputation in comparative anthropology.

Frazer contributed to classical studies as well. His most extensive contribution was a translation and annotation of *Pausanias's Description of Greece* (1898), which still serves as a leading source of knowledge about ancient Greece. Frazer's edition of Ovid's *Fasti* (published in five volumes in 1929) made a hefty contribution to classical studies as well.

Despite the seemingly steady stream of publications, Frazer's finances were rarely constant. Frazer avoided lecturing at Cambridge, choosing instead to live on his fellowship salary and the small amount of money he received annually from his father's business. Once Frazer married, his bills became untenable, and he had to appeal for occasional grants from the Literary Fund to pay his debts. Although Frazer had developed a friendly relationship with the publisher George Macmillan, he was inclined to expand his works without concern for the needs of the publishing industry or Macmillan's profitability. Books that were originally meant to be 1 volume, such as *The Golden Bough*, grew to 2, then 3, and then (eventually) 13 volumes. By the turn of the century, Macmillan had come to know Frazer's style well—lengthy, elaborate, and always overdue. Despite strong reviews of both *The Golden Bough* and *Pausanias*, Frazer's early works failed to produce much by way of profits for Macmillan or the author.

Frazer's second edition of *The Golden Bough* was a stronger sell, and his third edition became so popular that by 1922 more than 36,000 copies of all 12 volumes had been sold. Later in his career, Frazer was able to live comfortably from his royalties. He also delivered a set of 20 paid Gifford Lectures on the topic of immortality at Scottish universities between 1911 and 1912 (later published as *The Belief in Immortality*, 1913). Meanwhile,

Frazer's wife, Elizabeth Grove Frazer, published children's books and worked as a French translator during World War I to supplement the household income.

Frazer's marriage had caught his friends and family by surprise. In 1894, Frazer was introduced to Elisabeth Grove (née de Boys Adelsdorfer). Grove had traveled the world and raised two children with her late husband, the mariner Charles Baylee Grove. Following her husband's death, she took up writing to pay the bills. Grove was commissioned to write an article on "primitive dancing" for the Badminton Library's survey of dancing traditions when she met Frazer in Cambridge. The couple married in 1896, when both Frazer and Grove were in their 40s (having been born in the same year). Lilly, as she was known, moved to Cambridge to join Frazer with her teenage children.

By all accounts, Lilly managed her husband's financial affairs. She disliked the quiet, rural life of Cambridge and often pressured Frazer to move to London or travel to France. In 1908, Frazer was offered the position of professor of social anthropology at the University of Liverpool, the first professorship of its kind in the world. Lilly encouraged the move to Liverpool for both financial and personal reasons (she had lived in that city with her previous husband and was more comfortable in the bustling industrial town). Five months after arriving in Liverpool, however, Frazer promptly quit his position and headed back to Cambridge, citing his misery amid the industrial development as a reason for his return. The move was costly and encumbered the couple with a debt that lasted years.

Despite financial hardship, Frazer was ultimately rewarded for his long and arduous publications. In 1914, he was knighted, becoming Sir James Frazer. In 1920, the Royal Society made him a fellow, and the University of Cambridge honored him with a DLitt degree. In 1921, colleagues and supporters made donations to a fund for the Frazer Lectureship on Social Anthropology, hosted at Oxford, Cambridge, Glasgow, and Liverpool. In 1925, Frazer's name was added to the Order of Merit, an honor shared by only a handful of people in Britain.

Frazer went blind in the 1930s. Subsequently, he relied on aides who would read for him and take dictation. His wife monitored the aides tightly, even though she herself had long suffered from deafness. R. Angus Downie was one of the people to aid Frazer at this time. While authoring Frazer's biography, *Frazer and the Golden Bough* (1941), Downie recollects Lilly redacting every portion of the book. Not surprisingly, the manuscript presents Frazer as an unassailably studious and prolific academic; it fails to mention any serious criticism or controversy his work caused. As a result of Lilly's insistent lobbying, Macmillan printed a series of small books by Frazer after his reputation and marketability had waned. Those books included *Creation and Evolution in Primitive Cosmologies and Other Pieces* (1935), *Aftermath* (1936), and *Totemica* (1937). Frazer died on May 7, 1941, in Cambridge. Lilly died a few hours later. They were buried together at St Giles's cemetery in Cambridge.

Critical Contributions to Anthropology

Frazer's primary contributions to anthropology took the form of comparative studies of folklore and mythology.

Taboo and Totemism

Frazer's first significant contribution to the emerging field of anthropology appeared as two articles on taboo and totemism, published in the *Encyclopedia Britannica*. In those articles, Frazer argues that taboos are sets of religious prohibitions generated to maintain order in primitive tribes, while totemism involves a relationship between a group of kindred people and a species of natural or artificial objects. Over the course of his life, Frazer proposed multiple theories of totemism by linking them to taboo. He proposed that totems serve a religious purpose as repositories of the external soul (i.e., of the person or animal). Tribe members gain union with the sacred and divine by envisioning the totem as the physical embodiment of the soul they worship. Frazer also proposed that totems serve a social purpose. They ensure sharing and trade among tribe members by virtue of taboo. Because it is taboo in a totemic tribe to kill or eat one's own totem plant or animal, members of the tribe must engage in sharing and trade to survive (since hunters can eat the totem animals of other hunters). In *Totemism and Exogamy*, Frazer further relates totems and taboos to fertility and reproduction. Frazer hypothesizes that members of the totem clan believe that conception occurs when the spirit of the totem plant or animal impregnates a woman. Thus, it becomes taboo to kill or eat the

plant or animal that constitutes a physical representation of one's spiritual self.

The "Dying King" and The Golden Bough

Frazer is perhaps best known for the concept of the "dying king." The story of the priest-king who is slaughtered by a member of his own tribe and is then reborn in the shape of the slaughterer serves as the foundation for Frazer's three editions of *The Golden Bough*. The book starts with the ancient myth of the King of the Wood, Diana's priest at Nemi. A runaway slave breaks a golden bough from the sacred tree in the wood and uses it to kill the priest-king. The killer then takes the king's place. From the point of view of the tribe, the priest-king is killed and reborn in the form of the younger slave.

Frazer argues that the ritual of the dying king relates to the tribe's desire to encourage fecundity and fruitfulness in nature. The King of the Wood is intimately connected to Diana, Queen and Goddess of the Wood and Trees. The priest-king's aging and degradation over the years implies a corresponding decay of the sacred spirit that maintains the natural world. As the king ages, his death and renewal (through the ascendancy of a younger surrogate) become necessary. The evils of society are transferred to the king. Through his death, evil spirits are extinguished and the tribe is saved.

Starting with the myth from Nemi, Frazer expands his work to include a massive archive of examples from around the world and antiquity. Frazer contends that there are many myths in which kings are slain and reborn or scapegoats are slain in their stead. In some tribes, he notes, festivals take place to reenact the proverbial death and rebirth of the king.

Frazer's comparative method assumes that social rituals between societies develop along similar evolutionary paths. As a result, Frazer strings together disparate gods and kings to develop theories as to why similar priest-king myths emerge in different societies. In the first edition of the *Golden Bough*, Frazer starts from a historical standpoint, hypothesizing that stories about the gods are based on real people. Myths about dying kings are accounts of actual people who have lived and who had been killed as leaders or priest-kings in the past. Frazer believes that his theory demonstrates that religion is nothing but a set of false claims pertaining to human priest-kings and the gods they claim to represent.

However, in his second edition of *The Golden Bough* (1900), for which Frazer changed the subtitle from *A Study in Comparative Religion* to *A Study in Magic and Religion*, Frazer defends a different theory of myth based on cognitivism. Here, myths are failed attempts to rationalize natural phenomena through proto-scientific accounts. Proto-scientific myths evolve over time from primitive magical beliefs to sophisticated religious worship to progressive scientific theories. Societies are first observed to express awe at nature. Tribes perform magical rituals in attempts to avoid catastrophes and destruction. When magic fails, the tribe evolves further as elite members convince the group to make religious sacrifices. This is evident in the worship of the priest-king. Because the priest-king personifies the gods of nature, reviving the king through a sacrifice (or surrogate sacrifice) is believed to revive nature itself. This religious stage in social evolution involves building a sacred relationship with the gods to encourage the gods to do as the tribe bids. When religious worship and sacrifice fail to produce the desired results, highly evolved individuals then attempt a new means of controlling nature—namely, science. Frazer contends that the advent of science hearkens a new era in belief, one in which humans attempt to force nature to do as they bid through technology and scientific practice.

In the third edition of *The Golden Bough*, Frazer returns to his earlier historical theory of myth, using three gods—Adonis, the god of beauty and desire; Attis, the god of death and resurrection; and Osiris, the god of the afterlife—to argue that myths originate from real-life events. Frazer compares Adonis, Attis, and Osiris with the myths of Jesus, Buddha, and the Ugandan king Kibuka, for whom Frazer believed there was physical evidence of existence. Frazer contends that the latter three gods existed as living priest-kings within their respective communities at some point. Their deaths were the result of superstitious religious worship, and their godliness was abstracted from a belief in the necessary renewal of the priest-king.

Although Frazer's theories evidently changed over time, his methodology did not. He held unswervingly to the *comparative method* as the best means of discovering universal truths about the evolutionary development of human societies. Frazer's comparative methodology caused him to clash with Andrew Lang, an anthropologist who defended an orthodox interpretation of monotheism. Lang contended that primitive tribes and early humans had partaken in divine revelation. They had all started from a monotheistic belief structure rather than from the polytheistic worship of various gods of nature. Lang used evidence from Australian aboriginal tribes to defend his argument. Frazer countered Lang's evidence, arguing that it was nothing other than Christian ideology masquerading as anthropology. Frazer deemed Lang's work an unscientific attempt to promote Christianity through the misinterpretation of comparative anthropological data.

Frazer's Legacy

While Frazer was a central figure in anthropology in the late 19th and early 20th centuries, his influence waned significantly in the post–World War II era. Frazer's works were revivified in the 1960s to justify the theories of the Cambridge Ritualists, including Jane Ellen Harrison, Gilbert Murray, F. M. Cornford, and A. B. Cook, who believed that all myth was preceded by rituals whose meaning had been lost (a view that Frazer had held briefly and that he later rejected). Frazer's legacy was bolstered in the first half of the 20th century by the recognition Bronisław Malinowski accredited him in citing *The Golden Bough* as an original inspiration to study anthropology (Frazer later wrote the preface to Malinowski's *Argonauts of the Western Pacific*, published in 1922).

However, anthropologists and historians today reject Frazer's evidence, his theories, and his methodology, viewing him as the quintessential armchair anthropologist—a researcher who never generated raw data and who relied on ethnocentric accounts provided to him by colonial observers, missionaries, archaeologists, and explorers. Although Frazer traveled to Greece to collect archaeological data for his translation of *Pausanias*, he never traveled elsewhere for anthropological purposes, and he never sought to observe rituals directly.

Frazer is remembered in anthropology, literature, and classical studies as one of the last remaining rationalists of the 19th century—one whose explicit goal it was to relegate the Church to a peripheral position in society.

Josipa G. Petrunic

See also Bastian, Adolf; Comparative Method; Freud, Sigmund; McLennan, John; Modernism; Smith, William Robertson; Spencer, Herbert; Tylor, Edward Burnett

Further Readings

Ackerman, R. (1987). *J. G. Frazer: His life and work.* Cambridge, UK: Cambridge University Press.

Besterman, T. (1934). *A bibliography of Sir James George Frazer and a note by Sir J. G. Frazer.* London, UK: Macmillan.

Downie, R. A. (1940). *James George Frazer: The portrait of a scholar.* London, UK: C. A. Watts.

———. (1970). *Frazer and the golden bough.* London, UK: Gollancz.

FREUD, SIGMUND

Sigmund Freud (1856–1939) was an Austrian physician and the founder of psychoanalysis. His discoveries about the mind and his clinical investigations shaped how Western peoples conceive of human beings, their personal and collective histories, and their role in the universe. According to Freud, no matter how mature or sophisticated persons are, their infancy and childhood experiences undergird their adult lives. Poets had long noted that the "child is father to the man." Through brilliant clinical reports and a lifetime of writing, Freud showed how this was true. After him came generations of child psychiatrists, psychologists, counselors, teachers, and others who charted the subtle ways in which developmental histories shape adult character. Because each culture tells its members how to raise children, how to control sexuality, and how to become an adult, Freud's discoveries intrigued anthropologists who had long studied these features of culture. For these reasons, Freud influenced the past 100 years of anthropology. While contemporary anthropologists cite him less frequently than did their counterparts from the 1930s to the 1980s, Freud remains an essential figure in the history of anthropology.

Freud's Psychoanalytic Theory

Trained as a neurologist in Vienna, Austria (then the center of the medical world), Freud took up the study of mental illness around 1890. Treating upper- and middle-class Viennese men and women (mainly Jewish, like himself), Freud initially studied what the physicians of the time labeled "hysteria." Patients had problems like sudden fainting, loss of speech, or paralysis, which were not caused by identifiable medical conditions. In the language of 19th-century medicine, their problems were not caused by lesions—visible scars or damage—in their brains or their bodies.

If these problems were not caused by brain lesions, Freud and other physicians deduced that they must be caused by "mental lesions"—that is, by conflicts in their patients' minds. From around 1890 to around 1980, psychiatrists and psychologists studied hysteria and other maladies (like drug and alcohol addictions, sexual problems, obsessional actions, and numerous other disorders) as manifest behaviors whose latent causes were to be found in the early-childhood experiences of their patients. Therapists tried to discover patterns between these symptomatic actions and their patients' early experiences. For example, do women who manifest hysteria around sexual matters have developmental histories in which sexual contact between them and older people occurred? Do men who stutter and are afraid to speak in public have problems controlling their private sexual lives, especially the urge to masturbate? Do religious and ethical strictures on adolescent sexuality, a dominant theme of late-19th-century European and American education, cause what Freud called "modern nervous illness"?

Jean Charcot, an influential French physician, had shown that not only were psychiatric symptoms "lesion-less"—that is, not caused by anomalies in the brain—but that they could be induced or produced in normal subjects. Using hypnosis, Charcot demonstrated that otherwise healthy people would manifest hysterical blindness or paralysis if he suggested these behaviors to them. This meant that mere "ideas" could produce physical maladies. Charcot asked, "How did this leap from the psychical to the physical occur?" If mere ideas could cause hysterical symptoms in normal people, did similar, unconscious ideas cause hysterical symptoms in his clinical patients? Freud assumed that if psychiatric symptoms could be produced in normal subjects—who had neither physical lesions nor traumatic histories—then perhaps the patients who came to him had a psychological basis for their symptoms. In other words, perhaps persons diagnosed as "hysterical" suffered real pain but their pain was based on memory or other psychological processes. In Freud's terms, hysterics suffer from ideas (or more accurately, fantasies). How was this possible?

Freud's answer was that the mechanisms that produced hypnotic phenomena and hysterical symptoms were unconscious and not controlled by conscious reasoning. Joining philosophers like Friedrich Nietzsche and Karl von Hartmann, Freud reasoned that a large part—perhaps the largest part—of the human mind was unconscious, shaped by preverbal experience, and could be known only by its emanations. Because normal subjects could manifest the same (or similar) behaviors seen in his neurotic patients, he held that everyone had a similar psychological structure—that we are as a species united in our psychological organization.

Nineteenth-Century Social Thought and Dreams

Freud's notion that all humans had a similar psychological structure was in line with the cultural anthropology of his day. Freud considered himself an "archaeologist of the mind," and he was familiar with the work of prominent evolutionists such as E. B. Tylor and L. H. Morgan, whose unilineal theories of evolution were based on the doctrine of psychic unity.

The Interpretation of Dreams (1900) was Freud's most important book. In it, he extended clinical models generated in his work with psychiatric patients to study dreaming. In *Dreams*, Freud published a 15-page interpretation of one of his own dreams that he called "Analysis of a Specimen Dream" (pp. 106–121). The promise and limitations of Freud's theory originate in this notion of *specimen*. Specimens are things, like fossils or tissue samples or pottery shards, with material histories and more or less fixed structures. If we find specimens of bone, teeth, and tools, we can deduce a great deal about the lives of people who came before us. Similarly, Freud saw dreams as artifacts from peoples' earlier lives. The dreams in Freud's 1900 book are illustrations of how he (and his patients) talked and thought about behavior we call "dreaming." As clusters of behavior, dreams are products of an individual's body, mind, culture, and unknown random elements. Freud created brilliant ways to "read" dreams as the products of mental mechanisms he called the "dream work." This is

the set of devices the mind uses to create the dream; among them are condensation, displacement, and symbolization. If I dream about my father as a policeman who looks like the U.S. president, I am *condensing* my thoughts and feelings about all three men into this one image. If I dream about the smell of gasoline and through associations come to feelings about my father (who worked on gasoline engines), I am *displacing* my complex story and feelings about him onto this simpler item. If I dream about a huge bison about to run me over and my associations take me to images and feelings of my father as a "force of nature," I am *symbolizing* my father and my feelings about him. Thus, for Freud, dreams demonstrated an essential kinship between moderns and primitives and between normal people and psychiatric patients. In this sense, dreams are specimens of a universal human psychology. Mid-20th-century anthropologists such as A. L. Kroeber, who rejected Freud's attempts to reconstruct actual human history, found value in Freudian concepts such as repression, regression, and the centrality of childhood experience, dream symbolism, and similar clinical generalizations.

Freud's brilliance as a writer and his ability to give scientists and humanists new ways to read old texts, current dreams, and neurotic patients' actions, and to discover their hidden meanings, excited generations of intellectuals. Freud led the way by interleaving his works with illustrations taken from European classics, especially the Greeks, Shakespeare, the Bible, and folklore, because in his view these illustrated earlier stages of human psychology and psychological development.

In these literatures, he found support for his clinical theory that sexuality in its various modes, ranging from intense "libidinal" sucking in newborns to adult sexual intercourse, provided a motive force for culture, and at the same time, culture—represented by paternal, religious, and governmental authorities—sought to control it. This dialectic seemed revelatory to people who read him in the early part of the 20th century. In many ways, Freud and his followers championed the possibility of a new kind of freedom of sexual life and sexual honesty. He contributed to the modern view that sexuality is not inherently evil, dangerous, or to be controlled at all costs.

From these clinical observations, Freud derived the psychoanalytic technique. Deformations of memory weaken the ego; it loses sovereign access to each of its domains. Once the ego is weakened, patients live a divided life. Rather than know their wishes and make conscious, mindful choices, patients act them out. The technique provides methods with which we help patients repair the rent in their memory. By studying the manifest effects of unconscious processes, we help them discover, name, and confront their actual wishes with increased self-knowledge and deliberation.

Freud and Anthropology

Anthropology plays at least three roles in Freud's thought. First, anthropology and its affiliated discipline, archaeology, gave Freud a model for investigating the prehistory of his patients. Just as archaeologists uncovered evidence of past civilizations and groups, so too did psychoanalysts investigate the origins of their patients' lives in hidden, what Freud called "repressed," fantasies. Second, anthropologists' findings about nontechnological peoples (whom 19th-century authors called "primitives") offered to Freud and other psychoanalysts test cases against which they could compare clinical discoveries made with European and American patients. In this regard, Freud was particularly interested in indigenous religions. Third, Freud felt that his hard-won insights into childhood and its aftermath pertained to children of all groups and all cultures.

Psychoanalysis as Archaeology of the Mind

Educated people were fascinated when Heinrich Schliemann (1822–1890), an amateur archaeologist, uncovered convincing evidence that Troy, the ancient city described in the Homeric epics, the *Iliad* and the *Odyssey*, was real, not merely a legend. These discoveries, much commented on by breathless reporters in the 1870s, excited Freud when he read about them as a boy. Thirty years later, when he began to probe his patients' memories for their "buried past," Freud felt that he was repeating, in a way, Schliemann's great adventure. This analogy became more than a metaphor. By the late 1890s, and ever afterward, Freud wrote extensively about psychoanalysis as an archaeological investigation.

In more technical terms, Freud used archaeology as a model. It helped him describe both his subject matter (repressed, long-buried personal secrets) and his method (the slow digging, recovery, and reconstruction of personal narratives and memories.)

By 1889, he was describing his work with patients as analogous to Schliemann's discovery of Troy. Because he hoped to make psychoanalysis a general psychology, and not merely a method of medical treatment, Freud needed to show its applicability to anthropology, literature, theater, and religion. The latter became especially important. In Freud's words, religion alone was the great antagonist to psychoanalysis. Religious authorities that dominated European history, shaped its politics, and sought absolute control of human sexuality were squarely opposed to Freud's discipline and his philosophy.

Freud and Indigenous Religion

From 1907 onward, Freud expended a great deal of his intellectual capital investigating religion in so-called primitive groups and in its contemporary instances. The first appeared in *Totem and Taboo*, a set of articles that Freud published in 1912 and 1913. Its subtitle declares Freud's thesis: "Some Points of Agreement Between the Mental Lives of Savages and Neurotics." In brilliant, often persuasive accounts, Freud shows surprising parallels between the beliefs and actions of his Viennese patients and those reported by anthropologists working in various contexts. Freud's terms, such as *savages*, offends modern ears because it evokes for us the horrific facts of European crimes against indigenous peoples. However, Freud was no fan of war or crimes against defenseless peoples. On the contrary, his more radical thesis is the psychic unity of human beings—that the sophisticated European is not "higher" or superior to persons and groups dominated by European armies and navies. The refined German banker, for example, had aggressive and sexual wishes that so-called savages enacted, or at least were said to enact according to Western anthropologists.

Freud also examined contemporary religious institutions, such as the German Catholic and Lutheran churches, as organizations designed to "sublimate"—that is, channel—an individual's aggressive and sexual forces, what Freud called the libido. He called this an "economic" tax that civilizations extract from their subjects. Like income tax, this libidinal tax must be paid to fund the efforts and ambitions of the modern state. However, it can be burdensome and so onerous for some that it results in neuroses, as he argued in *Civilization and Its Discontents* (1930).

In his last major work, *Moses and Monotheism* (1939), Freud summarized his clinical and anthropological theories by seeking to uncover the long-buried truth of Moses, who legend said rescued his fellow Hebrews from the Egyptians, crossed the Red Sea, and led them to the Promised Land. Using an assortment of texts drawn from highly selected histories of Egypt as well as the Hebrew Bible, Freud argued that the latter was like a manifest dream about a traumatic and long-denied past. While he noted that his efforts to discover this supposed trauma were novelistic, he did not waiver. Few professional historians and Egyptologists agreed: Like Kroeber, they found Freud's "reconstructions" of what might have happened to Moses unscientific poetry. Alongside these faults, Freud's stubborn, brilliant, and courageous virtues as investigator and observer appear in this last great book.

Conclusion

Freud was prominent in anthropology from the 1920s until finally losing favor with the national character studies of the 1950s. However, during that period, anthropologists at Harvard, Yale, the University of Chicago, and similar American research universities used versions of psychoanalytic theory to study how child-rearing techniques produced "modal personalities." For example, Erik Erikson, at Harvard, studied how one American Indian group produced warriors while another group produced quiet farmers. Other anthropologists, like Margaret Mead at the American Museum of Natural History and Columbia University, examined Pacific Island groups that produced adolescents and young adults whose notions of sexuality and ethics differed markedly from those of middle-class, midcentury Americans. Similarly, Mead's colleague Ruth Benedict examined the personality characteristics of the Japanese during the Second World War.

Some anthropologists became clinicians and did psychotherapy with their subjects. Going the reverse direction, some argued that native cultures had their own versions of psychoanalysis. Claude Lévi-Strauss, for example, argued that the shamans of South American cultures were structural equivalents to New York City psychoanalysts. Freud would have affirmed Lévi-Strauss's claim. He believed that his insights into the ubiquity of repression, sublimation, and other unconscious devices pertained to each of these domains: societal, group, and personal. He generalized his clinical model of the mind to the study of groups—historical and prehistorical

societies—and so-called higher civilizations, like those of 20th-century Germany and the United States.

Looking at Freud 100 years later, this may seem commonplace. We live in a world saturated with sexual jokes, movies, TV shows, and a nearly infinite supply of pornographic narratives and images. Freud became world famous because he forced medical experts and lay persons alike to see more clearly that sexuality is central to human development, to culture, to ethical discourse, and especially to religious instruction. Complex historical events, such as the rise of industry, urbanization, increasing freedom for women, mass communication, the demise of traditional powers, and World War I, among others, created a context in which Freud's ideas were exciting, revolutionary, and persuasive. By the 1920s, anyone with claims to intellectual sophistication, whether in Europe or the United States, talked about Freud and his creation, psychoanalysis.

Volney P. Gay

See also Bachofen, Johann J.; Benedict, Ruth F.; Chodorow, Nancy; Culture and Personality; DuBois, Cora; Dundes, Alan; Frankfurt School; Frazer, James G.; Hall, Edward T.; Kardiner, Abram; Kroeber, Alfred L.; Lévi-Strauss, Claude; Lyotard, Jean-François; McLennan, John; Mead, Margaret; Myth, Theories of; Psychological Anthropology; Sacrifice; Smith, William Robertson; Spencer, Walter Baldwin, and Francis James Gillen; Spiro, Melford; Symbolic and Interpretive Anthropology

Further Readings

Erikson, E. (1963). *Childhood and society* (2nd ed.). New York, NY: W. W. Norton.

Frank, J. (1991). *Persuasion and healing: A comparative study of psychotherapy* (3rd ed.). Baltimore, MD: Johns Hopkins University Press.

Freud, S. (1953–1974). *The standard edition of the complete psychological works of Sigmund Freud* (J. Strachey, Trans. & Ed.). London, UK: Hogarth Press/ Institute of Psychoanalysis. (Original work published 1886–1939)

———. (1900). The interpretation of dreams. In J. Strachey, Trans. & Ed., *The standard edition of the complete psychological works of Sigmund Freud* (Vols. 4–5, pp. 1–628). London, UK: Hogarth Press/Institute of Psychoanalysis. (Original work published 1886–1939)

———. (1913). Totem and taboo: Some points of agreement between the mental lives of savages and neurotics. In J.

Strachey, Trans. & Ed., *The standard edition of the complete psychological works of Sigmund Freud* (Vol. 13, pp. 1–164). London, UK: Hogarth Press/Institute of Psychoanalysis. (Original work published 1886–1939)

———. (1930). Civilization and its discontents. In J. Strachey, Trans. & Ed., *The standard edition of the complete psychological works of Sigmund Freud* (Vol. 21, pp. 59–148). London, UK: Hogarth Press/Institute of Psychoanalysis. (Original work published 1886–1939)

———. (1939). Moses and monotheism: Three essays. In J. Strachey, Trans. & Ed., *The standard edition of the complete psychological works of Sigmund Freud* (Vol. 23, pp. 3–140). London, UK: Hogarth Press/Institute of Psychoanalysis. (Original work published 1886–1939)

Mead, M. (1928). *Coming of age in Samoa*. New York, NY: William Morrow.

FRIED, MORTON

Morton Herbert ("Mort") Fried (1923–1986) was a central member of the cohort of students of Julian H. Steward at Columbia University in the years after World War II and an important contributor to the neo-evolutionary and materialist theory of the 1950s and 1960s.

Biography and Major Works

Fried was a quintessential New Yorker (even though he lived across the Hudson River in Leonia, New Jersey, with many of his Columbia colleagues). Born in the Bronx, and coming of age during the Great Depression, he was educated at The City College of New York and Columbia University and spent almost his whole career teaching at the latter institution. He began graduate study at Columbia in 1946 after serving in the U.S. Army during World War II, and there he found a number of like-minded fellow students from similar backgrounds. Among these were Stanley Diamond, Robert A. Manners, Sidney Mintz, Elman R. Service, Eric R. Wolf, and John Murra (a student at the University of Chicago). This group of friends, who called themselves the Mundial Upheaval Society, studied the literature of political economy and Marxism; in various ways, this experience would color their subsequent work and was the basis for one of the major trends in American anthropology in the following decades.

The major faculty influence on Fried and his fellow students was Steward, who arrived to teach at Columbia in 1946. There was a synergistic outcome, as Steward and the students mutually educated each other, resulting in the complex of ideas and studies that characterized the Stewardian version of neo-evolutionism, materialist-based approaches to anthropology, and cultural ecology. Another significant influence on Fried was the work of Karl Wittfogel, the Sinologist, whose study of the Hsiung-nu Empire (Liao Dynasty) and "hydraulic theory," as presented in *Oriental Despotism*, played an important role in Fried's teaching and writings on the state.

Fried studied the Chinese language while he was in the army, and although he ranged widely in his scholarship, Chinese cultures and history was his special area. He used his language skill for his dissertation research and first book, *Fabric of Chinese Society*. Fried carried out the research in 1947–1948 under difficult conditions, in the aftermath of China's war with Japan and until Mao Zedong and the communists took power. He carried out a community study in a complex society in which kinship (still) played a major role but was superseded by a variety of nonkin and "civil" actions. *The Fabric of Chinese Society* deals with kinship and other behaviors, in families and in clans, in both agricultural and urban contexts, and among farmers, merchants, artisans, and the gentry. It was the first of his works centered on the problem of the evolution of political institutions—his lifelong interest.

Most of Fried's publications in political anthropology derived from his concern for Jean-Jacques Rousseau's statement "Man was born free and everywhere he is in chains." Stimulated by the writings of Lewis Henry Morgan, Karl Marx, and Friedrich Engels, but not satisfied with their ethnography, ethnocentrism, and solutions to major questions, he devoted major efforts to problems related to the growth of economic stratification, class, political power, and the origin of states—or, borrowing from Morgan, "political society." Fried wanted to understand the processes that led from kin-based egalitarian societies—as he presumed all of them must once have been—to ranked societies, then stratified ones, and, finally, "the state." And once the state exists, how does it deal with challenges to its sovereignty and authority, and what is its impact on its neighbors? Toward this end, he joined like-minded colleagues writing about the evolutionary paradigm of band-tribe-chiefdom-state (e.g., Elman Service, Marshall Sahlins, Lawrence Krader). He was particularly exercised by what he called "the notion of tribe," the idea that there were discrete, organized, political units before the development of states. He argued, on the contrary, that what anthropologists (and others) call tribes are secondary formations produced by the actions of states and colonialism. This idea gained some currency, especially with respect to Amazonian ethnography.

Fried taught at Columbia from 1950 until his death in 1986. He was an engaging and witty lecturer and was devoted to teaching. He twice published volumes of readings in anthropology noted for their sophistication. His *The Study of Anthropology* is an unusual work intended to give the student both an overview of the field and a guide to studying anthropology at the undergraduate and graduate levels and to choosing it as an occupation. Fried also took seriously the Boasian-Columbian tradition of speaking out to counter racial determinism when it arises—as it did a number of times during his career.

Herbert S. Lewis

See also Columbia University; Harris, Marvin; Marx, Karl; Material Production, Theories of; Mintz, Sidney; Morgan, Lewis Henry; Rappaport, Roy; Sahlins, Marshall; Service, Elman R.; Steward, Julian

Further Readings

Fried, M. H. (1953). *Fabric of Chinese society: A study of the social life of a Chinese county seat.* New York, NY: Praeger.

———. (1957). The classification of corporate unilineal descent groups. *Journal of the Royal Anthropological Institute of Great Britain and Ireland, 87,* 1–29.

———. (1967). *The evolution of political society: An essay in political anthropology.* New York, NY: Random House.

———. (1972). *The study of anthropology.* New York, NY: Crowell Press.

———. (1975). *The notion of tribe.* Menlo Park, CA: Cummings.

Service, E. R. (1988). Morton Herbert Fried (1923–1986). *American Anthropologist, 90,* 148–152.

Wittfogel, K. (1957). *Oriental despotism: A comparative study of total power.* New Haven, CT: Yale University Press.

FROBENIUS, LEO

Paradoxically, one of the most important figures for the process of anthropology's becoming a science proper in the German-speaking countries at the turn of the past century was an academically marginalized figure who failed to get a doctoral degree and hardly ever conformed to scientific etiquette, Leo Frobenius (1873–1938). In spite of these particularities, Frobenius was widely acknowledged as an outstanding personality who efficiently promoted ethnology in Germany. Although he was one of the most controversial anthropologists of his time, he is also the most frequently quoted Germanophone ethnologist.

Life and Intellectual Roots

Born in Berlin, Frobenius spent his youth in different garrison towns in Germany, where his father, a Prussian army officer, was assigned. Soon after graduating from high school, he developed an interest in ethnographic studies and travel reports. As it was not possible to study anthropology at a German university at that time, he sought museum employment and managed to get different short-term contracts at the Bremer Überseemuseum. This allowed him to expand his studies, and he published several short articles on masks and secret societies in Africa and Oceania. In 1898, he published his first theoretically oriented article titled "The West African Culture Circle." It was well received and much debated among his fellow museum anthropologists.

"The West African Culture Circle" is simultaneously an expansion of the theories of Adolf Bastian and a long-term research agenda for German anthropologists. The central argument refers to the methodology of culture history. It is best described through the example of one of the cultures under consideration, the "malayo-nigritic" culture. Frobenius was convinced that there was no common origin of African cultures. He argued that the different cultures in Africa are heirs to quite different influences from the various continents. Contemporary cultures that show congruent cultural influences are defined by Frobenius as "culture circles" (*Kulturkreise*). A culture circle does not so much reflect actual cultural relations among the cultures subsumed under its label as it refers to a historically antecedent diffusion of cultures. For example, Frobenius argued that the West African culture circle is an outcome of the diffusion of the so-called malayo-nigritic culture.

By using the term *culture circle*, Frobenius adopted a concept that had been used some years earlier by Friedrich Ratzel in a much looser, more commonsensical manner. For Ratzel, culture circles were simply areas with similar cultures. By narrowing the definition, Frobenius assigned a much more specific historical meaning to the term. Culture circles, according to Frobenius, originate from much older, currently invisible cultures, and it is the task of the trained ethnologist to identify these ancient cultures by documenting so-called cultural complexes. Cultural complexes consist of a number of unrelated yet concurrent cultural phenomena. These can be objects of material culture, principles of ornament, myths, or forms of social organization.

The idea of seeking shared roots in extinct basic cultures comes from Adolf Bastian, one of the founders of anthropology in Germany. Bastian distinguished between the visible phenomena of culture, which he called "flowers of culture" (*Kulturblüten*), and culture's more fundamental traits, assumed to represent a hidden cultural level that can only be identified by ethnologists.

Defining the Agenda of Cultural-Historical Anthropology

By presenting this theory, Frobenius suggested a scientific agenda for the discipline in the moment of its birth. His concepts of culture circles and culture complexes contain a theoretically grounded objective and a far-reaching research question about the identification of ancient cultures. Frobenius also proposed a method: a close examination of museum collections, which should lead to the identification of culture complexes as indicators of ancient cultures. He had himself presented the first example of such an analysis: the history and diffusion of the West African culture circle and its origin, through the diffusion of the malayo-nigritic culture.

In Frobenius's view, the key to understanding culture circles lay in the hypothetical reconstruction of the diffusion of culture complexes. However, the precise historical reconstruction only plays a minor role. History was not so much a sequence of dates and events as a question of identifying the essence or the nucleus of an actual culture.

Frobenius is representative of diffusionist anthropology and is among the many anthropologists of his time who supported this view. However, additional elements in his approach should also be highlighted. His key terms have a particular relation to the idea of fertility of cultures. According to Frobenius, cultures have the potential to generate other cultures. Not only did he attribute this particular capacity to cultures, he also insisted that cultures must be understood in their historical and geographical context. In an obituary, the Austrian anthropologist Robert Heine-Geldern praised Frobenius for overcoming the "anxiety of space." Frobenius transformed the romanticist and idealistic ideas about cultures as unchangeable (as per Bastian) into a pragmatic research program. He was interested in the origins of culture, which he sought in remote historical eras.

A shortcoming of Frobenius's approach is that even a brief glance at a world map raises some doubts about the formation and diffusion of culture complexes. How is it possible to trace the diffusion of the malayo-nigritic culture, composed of particular wooden drums, knives, bodily adornments, and other elements from Malaysia, to both West Africa and Papa New Guinea? Frobenius did not appear to be preoccupied with documenting the diffusion of such traits. He acknowledged that in his time such diffusion would hardly be possible. But he assumed that at the time of the original diffusion, there must have been several intermediate cultures (e.g., in southern India), which have since disappeared.

Culture, Essence, and a Culture's Soul

By delineating such huge cultural units, Frobenius sketched a global anthropology long before the advent of globalization. In his time, the idea of huge cultural units quickly found many adherents. Two of them were Fritz Graebner and Bernhard Ankermann, who presented an outline of the culture circles in Oceania in 1904. Frobenius was present at the oral communication, on the occasion of the annual meeting of the anthropological society of Berlin. At the same meeting, he argued against the concept of culture circle and the methodology of using dominantly museum objects, which he himself had presented only 6 years earlier, criticizing the methodology as too "mechanistic." Renouncing his own approach, he urged the anthropologists present at the meeting to include mythology and tales into their consideration of cultural relations. He criticized the objective of identifying patterns of diffusion as too narrow and mechanistic. As Frobenius said, a proper understanding of "the essence" of a culture (*das Wesen*) and of its "soul" (*die Seele*) is more important than identifying its origins. To identify these aspects, he started to organize "Africa Expeditions" and thus proceeded to fieldwork. Between 1904 and 1934, he undertook no fewer than 20 expeditions, some lasting more than 12 months.

As Frobenius did not hold any academic position and had no support from any university, he organized his own fund-raising. The archives of his institute contain many of his letters in which Frobenius pressed his sponsors to provide financial means for his travels. Among his most important donors were ethnographical museums in Germany. Some of them prepared a general agreement that identified a fixed price for any ethnographic object he could collect. Some museums, like the one in Hamburg, ran into serious economic trouble when Frobenius delivered an unexpectedly high number of artifacts from Africa.

Meanwhile, Frobenius created a private "Africa Archive" in Munich. In 1925, he managed to sell this archive to the city of Frankfurt and to establish at the university an institute of the morphology of cultures. In 1932, he finally was appointed honorary professor at the university and thereby gained the right to teach there. Of even greater importance were his connections to powerful individuals in the realm of politics. As early as 1912, he had an audience with the German emperor. It marked the beginning of an ongoing relationship that was to intensify after World War I. The emperor's interest in Frobenius and his work was related to his enthusiasm for culture history and his empathy with the idea of the cyclic development of cultures. Wilhelm, by then no longer the emperor, and living in exile in the Netherlands, perceived his own destiny as an outcome of a period of decline within the logic of a cyclic evolution of cultures.

Influence and Followers

To the present day, the idea of a culture circle is still the most popular aspect of Frobenius's oeuvre. However, by the 1920s, he had become less interested in this term, and during his Frankfurt period, he dedicated his scientific work to what he called a "look at the people's soul" (*Seelenschau der Völker*). In his polemical manner, which included self-irony, Frobenius claimed to have found a way to recognize the "thou" (personal address) of cultures. He intended to understand cultures by intuitive observation of their articulations. He competed with Oswalt Spengler, the author of the monumental study *Der Untergang des Abendlandes* (The decline of the West), for the honor of having coined the metaphors of adolescence, adulthood, and old age as distinguishing stages of vitality of cultures. Frobenius's demand that culture not be described in a mechanical way and his delineation of cultures' stages according to age outline the contours of his own approach to cultures as living beings.

Frobenius used the new metaphors to describe the different levels of creativity of African cultures. For example, he identified several cultures in Africa that he considered very old and identifiable only as fragments. Frobenius explicitly claimed that an objective of his work was to return to Africans what is their possession, namely the reconstruction of old cultures. He considered that ethnologists had the exclusive capacity to identify such cultures in spite of their fragmentation.

Frobenius's analysis of such cultures, including the *paideuma* (the creative mental nucleus), can be perceived as a criticism of other social theories of his time. Frobenius rejected scientific approaches that referred only to empirical and statistical data. He defended his approach by underlining the moral superiority and authenticity of African societies. He thereby joined the widespread criticism made by intellectuals of his time such as Georg Simmel. For them, Africa was not just an ethnographic field but an antidote to the decline of European cultures. The latter were part of his model, as he explained the antagonism between French and German cultures as an outcome of different cultural souls.

Frobenius's ideas about the vitality of cultures at different moments in the time depth of history, which were metaphorically expressed through age differences, and the idea that cultures act like living beings according to their own logic, found some resonance in France, particularly in the context of Henri Bergson's vitalist philosophy. Furthermore, in the 1930s, African intellectuals studying in Paris became fascinated by Frobenius's idea of the creativity and age of African cultures. The most famous of them was Leopold Senghor, who later became the president of independent Senegal. They referred to Frobenius's work to stress the cultural autonomy of African societies and argue for the independence of African nations. Frobenius himself did not consider colonialism to be relevant, because he did not believe that the vitality of cultures could be deeply influenced through such ephemeral phenomena. For the young African elite, however, the encounter with Frobenius constituted an important support for the African peoples' political struggles.

Another feature of Frobenius's theory is the idea that every culture is the outcome of a configuration. Cultures are autonomous, at least in the sense that they represent a mixture of different influences of ancient cultures. Like Ruth Benedict, Frobenius conceived of cultures as having a specific "gestalt." Recognizing the gestalt of present-day cultures as an outcome of diffusion and the influences of ancient cultures was a way of historicizing anthropology. It therefore can be considered as an attempt to rescue the approach of culture history after the notion of culture circles had lost its initial appeal in anthropology.

Antimodernism, vitalism, and the idea of the gestalt of cultures may be considered as key elements in Frobenius's culture theory, after he had articulated his critique of culture circles. Each of these terms may have little plausibility from today's perspective. However, against the background of the anthropology of his time, they indicate the originality and insightfulness of Leo Frobenius.

Hans Peter Hahn

See also Bastian, Adolf; Diffusionism, Hyperdiffusionism, *Kulturkreise*; Graebner, Fritz; Simmel, Georg

Further Readings

Fox, D. C. (1936, September 3–October 25). Frobenius' Paideuma: A philosophy of culture. *The New English Weekly*, pp. 1–7.

Frobenius, L. (1933): *Kulturgeschichte Afrikas: Prolegomena zu einer historischen Gestaltlehre* [Cultural history of Africa: Prolegomena to a doctrine of historical form]. Zurich, Switzerland: Phaidon Press.

Haberland, E. (Ed.). (1973). *Leo Frobenius 1873–1973: An anthology.* Wiesbaden, Germany: Steiner.

Hahn, H. P. (2010). Leo Frobenius in West Africa: Some remarks on the history of anthropology. In R. Kuba & M. Hambolu (Eds.), *Nigeria 100 years ago: Through the eyes of Leo Frobenius and his expedition team* (pp. S27–S32). Frankfurt, Germany: Frobenius Institut.

Heinrichs, H.-J. (1998). *Die fremde Welt, das bin ich. Leo Frobenius: Ethnologe, Forschungsreisender, Abenteurer* [The alien world that I am. Leo Frobenius: Anthropologist, explorer, adventurer]. Wuppertal, Germany: Hammer.

Jahn, J. (1974). *Leo Frobenius, the demonic child* (Occasional publication, 8). Austin: University of Texas, African and Afro-American Studies and Research Center.

Kalous, M. (1968): Review article: Frobenius, Willett and Ife. *Journal of African History, 9,* 659–663.

Marchand, S. (1997). Leo Frobenius and the revolt against the West. *Journal of Contemporary History, 32*(2), 153–170.

Streck, B. (1989). *Kultur als Mysterium? Zum Trauma der deutschen Völkerkunde* [Culture as a mystery? The trauma of German ethnology]. In H. Berking & R. Faber (Eds.), *Kultursoziologie: Symptom des Zeitgeistes?* [Cultural sociology: Symptom of the Zeitgeist?] (pp. S89–S115). Würzburg, Germany: Königshausen & Neumann.

Zwernemann, J. (1969). *Leo Frobenius et la recherche scientifique sur les civilisations africaines* [Leo Frobenius and the scientific research of African civilizations]. *Notes et Documents Voltaïques, 2,* 27–42.

GADAMER, HANS-GEORG

Hans-Georg Gadamer was a long-lived (1900–2002) German philosopher, best known as a student of Martin Heidegger. He developed an account of philosophical hermeneutics in his magnum opus *Truth and Method.*

Biography and Major Works

Gadamer was born in Breslau in 1900, the son of a chemist, Johannes Gadamer. The elder Gadamer was prominent in Breslau, where he served as an academic researcher and administrator as well as a chemist in Germany's rapidly industrializing chemical industry. As a child, Gadamer resisted his father's strict discipline and insistence on a career in science and became interested instead in philosophy and the classics.

Gadamer's interest in philosophy led him to Marburg, where he wrote a dissertation on Plato under the direction of Paul Natorp, a leading exponent of the Marburg school of neo-Kantian philosophy. This school was noted for its Kantian approach to the philosophy of science, as well as for work on epistemology and logic. In particular, Marburg philosophy acknowledged the power of modern experimental science but resisted the idea that it was the epitome of all knowledge, arguing instead for the continued relevance of the humanities. The Marburg school produced many influential students, such as the philosopher Ernst Cassirer.

The decisive event in Gadamer's intellectual life, however, was not his dissertation in 1922 but his postgraduate studies. Introduced to phenomenology by Natorp, Gadamer moved to Freiburg in 1922 to study under Heidegger, and he followed him back to Marburg when Heidegger received an appointment there. As a result, Gadamer participated in a remarkable intellectual period when Heidegger trained a cadre of young scholars, including Karl Lowith, Leo Strauss, and Hannah Arendt. The lectures Heidegger gave at the time led to the publication of his *Being and Time* in 1928, which would become recognized as one of the most important philosophical works of the 20th century.

This period was decisive for Gadamer in two ways. First, Heidegger's existential phenomenology, not Neo-Kantianism, became the fundamental framework for Gadamer's thought. Second, during this time, Gadamer began in-depth philological training with Paul Friedländer. The result of both these influences was Gadamer's 1928 habilitation, later published as *Plato's Dialectical Ethics.* In this work, Gadamer proved himself to be a specialist in classics even as he maintained a broad philosophical viewpoint and avoided the narrow focus that sometimes accompanies philological work.

The next few decades were tumultuous for Germany but remarkably quiet for Gadamer. In 1929, he received an appointment at Marburg, and he then went on to teach at other German universities—first Kiel in 1934 and then Leipzig in 1939.

During this period, German academics approached Nazism in a variety of ways, ranging from collaboration to resistance to emigration. Heidegger, famously, was receptive to Nazism, but Gadamer was not. His extremely erudite focus on ancient philosophy removed him from politics and life outside the academy, and after the fall of the Reich, the Allied occupation considered him uncontaminated by Nazism. As a result, he was appointed rector at Leipzig, where he became active in rebuilding the university there.

During the late 1980s and 1990s, revisionist historians discovered that many academics had been more sympathetic to Nazism than was previously realized: Prior to 1987, for instance, it was not widely known that Heidegger had embraced Nazism. Although one author has attempted to demonstrate that Gadamer's interpretation of Plato implicitly supported Nazi policies, few have found this view compelling, and the bulk of scholarly opinion concurs that Gadamer was free from the taint of Nazism. Communism also had little appeal for him, and as the Iron Curtain closed over Leipzig, Gadamer moved west, eventually taking a position at Heidelberg. Finally, in 1960, Gadamer published *Truth and Method*, the book that would come to define his career.

In the 3 decades prior to the publication of *Truth and Method*, Gadamer lectured regularly and gave public speeches, but he had not published extensively. *Truth and Method*, then, represented the first and main statement of Gadamer's thought. Published when he was 60 years old, it seems likely that Gadamer imagined this to be the summation of his career. As it happened, he would continue to live and publish for another 4 decades.

The critics lauded *Truth and Method*, and Gadamer soon became an internationally known philosopher. His work on hermeneutics appeared at a time when continental philosophy was read and taken up in the United States among not only humanists but social scientists as well. As a result, Gadamer became very influential, and he published many books of interviews, essays, and speeches after *Truth and Method* appeared. In addition to these secondary works, which grew out of, amplified, and explained *Truth and Method*, Gadamer was engaged in several other scholarly activities in the second half of the 20th century.

First, *Truth and Method* dealt with ethics, aesthetics, and interpretation in the context of the Western canon. After its publication, Gadamer turned his focus to modernism and modernist writing, in particular to the works of the poet Paul Celan. The slim volume by Gadamer on Celan is a central intellectual

contribution to Gadamer's project because it extends the range of his hermeneutic work beyond its narrow focus on "classic" texts.

Second, Gadamer engaged in a series of well-known debates with other intellectuals that touched on central issues in the interdisciplinary realm known as "theory," which developed in the 1970s, 1980s, and 1990s. His most famous debate occurred with Jürgen Habermas, in which the two argued about the possibility of objective knowledge—Habermas arguing that such a thing was possible and Gadamer arguing for the situatedness of all understanding. Gadamer was also well-known for his encounters with Jacques Derrida. Although Derrida and Gadamer had many similarities, their different approaches and personalities meant that their debates, published as *Dialogue and Deconstruction*, would be widely read even though the two authors often talked past one another.

Finally, Gadamer engaged in a series of smaller projects—on the concept of health and aging, autobiographical writings about his own career, as well as that of Martin Heidegger, and on his relationship with Nazism.

Overall, Gadamer was a remarkable figure of extraordinary longevity who witnessed the most important events of the century and became one of the world's most prominent intellectuals. And yet Gadamer personally lived a quiet, even primitive, existence. He was late for his dissertation defense, for instance, because his overcoat had frozen to the door of his unheated house. During a trip to the United States, he watched the American election results on television, fascinated by the democratic system he had heard so much about, but he was unable to turn off the television because he had never used a remote control before. His impressive intellectual accomplishments were counterbalanced by a quiet, mundane family existence despite the remarkable times he lived through.

Critical Contributions to Anthropology

The Limitations of Science

Throughout his career, Gadamer argued against the idea that modern experimental science ought to be taken as the purest, most primary, or most important form of knowledge. Today, such positions are often associated with "postmodernism" and skepticism regarding the claims of science and reason. Gadamer, in contrast, came of age in the first half of the 20th century, when industrialization was still occurring in Germany, and *Truth and Method* was written in the postwar period, when technocratic confidence was at its peak. His critique, rooted in his classical training, was a conservative one: Gadamer opposed the idea that science could provide us with ethical guidance, was skeptical about narrowing the definition of truth to include merely instrumental knowledge, and decried the narrow education of technical specialists. He attempted to demonstrate the fundamental legitimacy of philosophy, literature, aesthetics, and religion, even as modern science was slowly becoming the sole form of modern knowledge. In contrast to a postmodern position skeptical of the possibility of transcendent truth, Gadamer argued consistently for truth in its traditional mode, and rooted its claims to adequacy in prescientific forms of knowledge.

The Universality of the Hermeneutic Problem

Hermeneutics is the art of interpreting messages. Typically, it concerns deciphering difficult, obscure, or ancient texts. Traditionally, interpretation of texts was the central activity of the university and in the pursuit of knowledge more generally. In *Truth and Method*, Gadamer takes the process of hermeneutics and elevates it to the level of a universal problem. That is, Gadamer argues that our existence and understanding of the world operate on the same principles as those of textual interpretation.

Thus, while some would argue that science is true knowledge and aesthetic judgment is subjective, Gadamer argues that the scientific method is just one subset of human understanding encompassed by our more general experience of reality. For Gadamer, life itself is a process of interpretation within which methodical science is an important but limited source of knowledge whose value should not be overestimated. In sum, Gadamer argues that truth is opposed to method and that we as humans experience the world through an interpretive process. For this reason, he felt that "objectivity" was a goal that is both impossible and undesirable.

Practical Knowledge and the Rehabilitation of Prejudice

The process of arriving at truth is a very general one that follows the course of a *hermeneutic circle*: Initial presumptions are tested against the world and then revised in light of what one encounters. For this reason, Gadamer believed that it is possible to speak about the correct interpretation of meaning without relying on a scientific method of interpreting texts or on notions of objectivity.

Central to his argument is the *rehabilitation of prejudice*. In English, the term *prejudice* has a negative connotation because it implies that one is not free to judge a case on its own merit. But for Gadamer, prejudice is not an impediment to objectivity but an inevitable and essential part of understanding. Gadamer believed that it is only by bringing our prejudices to light, becoming aware of them, and using them as the initial departure point for an act of interpretation that we can truly understand the world.

Historically Effected Consciousness

One of Gadamer's best known concepts is *wirkungsgeschichtlichess Bewußtein*, a term that is perhaps best translated into English as "consciousness affected by history." Gadamer argues that prejudice is a result of our consciousness and the way it has been affected by history.

People often speak of a difference between the "human sciences" or "social sciences," on the one hand, and the natural sciences, on the other. On this account, the human sciences deal with the realm of meaning and intention and involve interpretation, while the natural sciences deal with natural facts and do not attend to meaning. This distinction can be traced back to Wilhelm Dilthey, who argued that understanding a text involved understanding the intention of the author who wrote it and imaginatively participating in the lived experience of the author. How one can be objectively empathetic is something Dilthey never definitively solved, and this issue remains a contentious topic in the philosophy of social science to the present.

Gadamer attempts to solve the problem by breaking from this tradition altogether. He argues that Dilthey's concept of "lived experience" (*erlebnis*) assumes a primacy of experience unmediated by culture and tradition. Following Heidegger, Gadamer argues that human beings are, in contrast, fundamentally linguistic beings, shaped to their very core by the tradition and culture into which they are born. They have, in other words, a consciousness that is affected by the history of the traditions and culture they inherit. Gadamer thus argues for the primacy of *erfahrung*, experience interpreted through a cultural lens, and against *erlebnis*, or a fundamentally raw, unprocessed, and acultural experience.

Gadamer thus argues that understanding in the social science does not involve recovering the intention of the author. Rather, it means realizing the history of the effect that the text has had on one's consciousness, a process that Gadamer calls the "fusing of horizons between one's own work and the original." Understanding a text, according to Gadamer, means understanding how the text has, in some small way, become part of the social and historical context in which the reader lives. It is a process of self-understanding in which we recognize the way in which we ourselves are shaped by the world that the text helped create.

Aesthetic Truth

It is in this light that we can understand Gadamer's defense of aesthetics. For him, art has a "truth" as important as (or more important than) scientific truth. Again, context is important: Gadamer wrote at a time when people believed judgments of beauty to be completely subjective and when the classical tradition of fine arts was challenged by avant-garde and modernist forms. While Gadamer's greatest concern is with the truth revealed in poetry, theater and the experience of play are central to his aesthetic theory. Just as we lose ourselves in the moment of a drama or in the flow of playing a game, so too, Gadamer argues, artistic truth reveals itself to us as we experience ourselves merging, or perhaps dissolving, into it. Thus, for Gadamer, artistic truth is derived from our deeper involvement in communities and traditions of meaning of which we are only a part—not from a subjective sense of the beautiful.

The Dialogue That Is Ourselves

Overall then, Gadamer viewed people as always engaged in dialogical relations with others. Indeed, as beings born and socialized into a world not of our own making, we are ourselves a sort of dialogue: a location through which broader forces of history and tradition move. Understanding is self-understanding, and truth the recognition of this fact. In this light, it is easy to understand why Gadamer was not convinced by claims that humans can, or

ought to, be guided by disinterested, objective scientific reason.

Gadamer's Legacy

Despite his importance in the tradition of continental philosophy, Gadamer has not had a great impact on anthropological thought. The reception of Gadamer's work in anthropology began in the late 1960s and early 1970s with the rise of interpretive or symbolic approaches, such as the work of Clifford Geertz. These authors were more theoretically sophisticated and interdisciplinary than the previous generation, and they drew on a wide variety of thinkers outside of anthropology for inspiration, such as Paul Ricoeur and Ludwig Wittgenstein. Gadamer was one of the thinkers cited by these early authors.

In the 1980s, the next generation of anthropological theorists extended this tradition. Some, such as Paul Rabinow, had deeper and more thorough engagements with continental philosophy as they articulated the philosophical grounding of interpretive social science. Others sought to radicalize interpretive anthropology's concern with rhetoric as they sought to experiment with anthropological genres. The flurry of "dialogical anthropology" produced in the 1980s by authors such as Kevin Dwyer and Barbara and Dennis Tedlock often cited Gadamer—a major theorist of dialogue—as an inspiration. The "Writing Culture" group also included him on their theoretical horizon. In the late 1980s, James Peacock also pondered, only somewhat successfully, the potential influence of Gadamer on ethnographic practice.

None of these streams of thought, however, engaged deeply with Gadamer's work. While thinkers such as Michel Foucault and Pierre Bourdieu became the topic of intense scrutiny, Gadamer (like Ricoeur) remained on the periphery of these projects, cited but never truly used to build anthropological theory.

There are many reasons for this: Anthropology came to "theory" in the course of its increasing politicization, and Gadamer was not a political thinker. Gadamer's work is highly technical and often takes the form of commentary on other thinkers. As a result, it requires deep immersion in Western philosophical traditions, which is not necessarily a requirement of anthropological training. Even those who do have a background in philosophy are more familiar with the French traditions rather than the German ones that influenced Gadamer.

Indeed, in many ways, Gadamer lacks elective affinity with anthropological theory: His commitment to Heidegger makes him an opponent of the neo-Kantian traditions in which he was initially trained—the same traditions that informed Franz Boas and the first generation of American anthropologists. A conservative, he uses Heidegger to ground and validate the Western canon. In contrast, most anthropologists read French "poststructuralism," where Heidegerian thought is put in the service of politically leftist and progressive causes that seek to question the legitimacy of inherited notions of truth, reason, and beauty.

Finally, because Gadamer's work is a purely philosophical clarification of the grounds of understanding, it does not provide concrete analytic tools for anthropology but merely claims to describe what all human beings already do. Although Gadamer's work has serious implications for anthropology, they must be drawn out, and unfortunately, few have attempted to do so to date.

Alex Golub

See also Boas, Franz; Derrida, Jacques; Geertz, Clifford; Habermas, Jürgen; Hermeneutics; Rabinow, Paul; Tedlock, Barbara and Dennis; Wittgenstein, Ludwig

Further Readings

Gadamer, H.-G. (1976). *Philosophical hermeneutics.* Berkeley: University of California Press.

———. (1999). *Truth and method.* New York, NY: Continuum.

Grondin, J., & Plant, K. (2003). *The philosophy of Gadamer.* Montreal, Quebec, Canada: McGill-Queen's University Press.

Grondin, J., & Weinsheimer, J. (2003). *Hans-Georg Gadamer: A biography.* New Haven, CT: Yale University Press.

Hoy, D. C. (1978). *The critical circle: Literature, history, and philosophical hermeneutics.* Berkeley: University of California Press.

GAME THEORY

In much of social life, the best course of action depends on what others do. For example, choosing to commute by car rather than by train depends on traffic, and traffic depends on how many other commuters choose to drive. Finding a spouse depends on what you want and how attractive you are, and how attractive you are depends on what your potential spouses want. Game theory provides a powerful language to model social phenomena like these, in which people respond to the choices of others.

The game theorist builds simple mathematical models to understand the complex dynamics linking individual choices and group-level properties, dynamics difficult to predict without mathematics. Consider residential patterns. Do segregated neighborhoods imply that people are racist? Perhaps. But, as Thomas C. Schelling has noted, segregation can also emerge even if people want to live in integrated neighborhoods, as long as they slightly prefer being in the majority. The problem is that everyone can't simultaneously live in integrated neighborhoods and be in the majority. As individuals move to relatively integrated neighborhoods in which they are in the majority, neighborhoods can become more and more segregated. It's hard to predict this kind of dynamic without building a model.

There are two traditions in game theory: classical and evolutionary. Classical game theorists assume that people are "rational" in the sense that choices maximize "utility," which might be anything from money to leisure. After setting up the model, the game theorist seeks the *Nash equilibrium:* a set of strategies, each of which is a best response to the other strategies. At the equilibrium, no one can improve by acting differently. For example, when neighborhoods become totally segregated in the residential choice model, no one can do better by moving.

Fredrik Barth's 1959 study of competition between Pathan tribesmen in the Swat Valley of northern Pakistan represents a well-known anthropological application of classical game theory. Barth examined competition between lineage segments over land using the concepts of zero sum games and positive sum games outlined in John von Neumann and Oscar Morgenstern's 1944 *Theory of Games and Economic Behavior.* In a positive sum game, winnings can be increased by cooperation, whereas in a zero sum game, the reward is fixed and thus leads to competition between players over how the winnings are distributed. In Barth's view, relations in the Swat Valley were best explained as a zero sum game because Pathan lineage mates were competing for control of a fixed amount of land. The result was fierce competition between members of the same lineage segments. Today, game theory in anthropology is applied to a variety of areas including economics, politics, hunting, and the evolution of social behavior.

Evolutionary game theorists assume that individuals follow a specific "strategy," a behavioral prescription that doesn't imply that individuals strategize in a rational manner or that they strategize at all. The modeler also specifies the pattern of interaction. The simplest assumption is *random interaction,* meaning that an individual's strategy doesn't influence the kinds of opponents she or he encounters. Interactions can also be *assortative* (i.e., interactions are nonrandom with respect to strategy). Evolutionary forces, be they natural selection or cultural processes, change the frequencies of different strategies, favoring those with higher "fitness," which might be the genetic or cultural contribution to future generations. The game theorist seeks the *evolutionarily stable strategy* (ESS), a strategy that, when common, has higher fitness than any other strategy occurring at low frequency.

Evolutionary game theory originated in biology and is now popular in the social sciences. Classical game theory is a "static" framework in the sense that individuals are assumed to consider all possibilities, including others' deliberations, resulting in everyone simultaneously playing his or her best response. One problem is that games often have *multiple equilibria.* Societies can, for example, be organized in either an egalitarian or a hierarchical manner. The static framework of classical game theory cannot explain how and why societies transition from one arrangement to another. Evolutionary game theory provides a *dynamic* framework, explaining not only best responses ("equilibria") but also how social institutions change ("equilibrium selection").

The *Hawk-Dove* model provides an introduction to evolutionary game theory that illustrates the way game theorists approach problems and offers insight into the logic of conflict. In the 1960s, biologists puzzled over animals engaging in low-cost, ritualized contests over resources. Such ritualized contests contradict the caricature of natural selection as a "survival of the fittest" in which the strong triumph over the weak. Many biologists championed *group selection*, arguing that groups in which animals fought to the death would go extinct, leaving behind only groups that resolve conflict through ritual. The problem is that natural selection usually acts at the level of individuals, not groups. The Hawk-Dove model provided conceptual clarity, showing how ritualized contest can result from *individual selection*.

The model assumes that pairs of individuals meet at random and allocate some resource. There are two strategies: "Hawk" always contests the resource and "Dove" shares with another Dove but concedes to a Hawk. Since a Hawk always beats a Dove, it's tempting to predict that Hawks will replace Doves in the population. But the outcome is not that simple. If the resource benefit exceeds the fighting cost, Hawks will indeed replace Doves. But if the resource cost exceeds its benefit, the population settles down to a mix of Hawks and Doves. When Doves are common, Hawks mostly meet Doves and do well. However, as the population of Doves decreases, Hawks increasingly meet other Hawks and engage in costly contests. Doves do better by avoiding costly fights.

At the "mixed equilibrium," fights erupt whenever two Hawks meet. Even though everyone would be better off if everyone played Dove, selection acting on individuals favors a mix of Hawks and Doves. This illustrates an important lesson. Self-interested behavior can lead to collectively bad outcomes. Such "social dilemmas" characterize many of our pressing problems, like corruption, overharvesting of natural resources, and pollution. The *Prisoner's Dilemma* is the canonical game to model social dilemmas. The outcome of these dilemmas depends on the pattern of interaction. With assortative interaction (e.g., Doves selectively interacting with Doves), group benefit can trump self-interest because cooperation is channeled to cooperators and denied to free riders. Assortment, which can be generated through kin-biased interaction (i.e., *kin selection*) or behavior-biased interaction (e.g., *reciprocity*), is the key to understanding the evolution of cooperation.

Returning to conflict, game theory models assume that some individuals fight and others do not. But resource conflicts seem to be resolved by ritualized contest. When a model's predictions match reality, the hypothesized process may explain the pattern observed in the real world. However, when the predictions are way off, something important has been left out of the model. The Hawk-Dove game, for example, assumes symmetry between players. However, if individuals vary in fighting ability, then the "Assessor" strategy is an ESS. Assessors size up their opponents and fight only when they are sure to win. Fighting ability, an asymmetry correlated with contest outcomes, provides a convention that efficiently allocates resources with few fights. The Assessor, arising through individual selection, achieves a higher average payoff than a mixture of Hawks and Doves.

A convention that privileges bullies isn't the only possibility. Ownership, an asymmetry uncorrelated with contest outcomes, is another. The "Bourgeois" strategy plays Hawk when finding the resource first and Dove when second. Like the Assessor, the Bourgeois is an ESS that efficiently allocates resources without fighting. This result may explain the origin of informal property rights and some forms of cooperation. But the model has another ESS, one in which individuals play Dove when owner and Hawk when intruder! According to the model, this anti-Bourgeois strategy is as likely an outcome as the Bourgeois strategy. In nature, the Bourgeois strategy seems common; the alternative convention does not. What might be missing from the model?

Karthik Panchanathan

See also Barth, Fredrik; Economic Anthropology; Evolutionary Anthropology; Gene-Culture Coevolution; Human Behavioral Ecology; Rational Choice Theory

Further Readings

Gintis, H. (2009). *Game theory evolving: A problem-centered introduction to modeling strategic interaction* (2nd ed.). Princeton, NJ: Princeton University Press.

McElreath, R., & Boyd, R. (2007). *Mathematical models of social evolution: A guide to the perplexed.* Chicago, IL: University of Chicago Press.

Neumann, J. von, & Morgenstern, O. (1944). *Theory of Games and Economic Behavior.* Princeton, NJ: Princeton University Press.

Schelling, T. C. (2006). *Micromotives and macrobehavior.* (Rev. ed.). New York, NY: W. W. Norton.

Skyrms, B. (1996). *Evolution of the social contract.* Cambridge, UK: Cambridge University Press.

Sugden, R. (1986). *The economics of rights, cooperation and welfare.* Oxford, UK: Blackwell.

GEERTZ, CLIFFORD

Clifford Geertz (1926–2006) was easily the best known American cultural anthropologist of his generation, both greatly admired and a lightning rod for criticism. He resisted being identified with any particular school of anthropology, insisting, "I don't do systems," yet many anthropologists of his generation came to identify themselves as Geertzian. In *Available Light* (2001), his last book, he describes himself as an ethnographer who investigated the role played by ideas in human behavior, the meaning of meaning, and the judgment of judgment. In a career that spanned half a century, he spent almost 3 years doing fieldwork in Java, 1 year in Bali, and nearly 3 years in Morocco; he authored or coauthored 10 books stemming from his ethnographic research, observing that fieldwork did more to nourish his soul than the academy ever did. Intertwined with these ethnographies, Geertz regularly produced what he once described as "cliff-hanging" essays on the concept of culture.

Biography

Geertz opens his final book, a collection of essays titled *Available Light*, with an intellectual autobiography. After serving in the navy in the Second World War, he studied philosophy at Antioch College. On graduation, he took the advice of a philosophy professor who advised him to try anthropology because philosophy had fallen into the hands of Thomists and technicians. Encouraged by a serendipitous encounter with Margaret Mead, in 1950, Geertz began graduate studies in the new, interdisciplinary Department of Social Relations at Harvard, where Talcott Parsons presided over a vigorous effort to construct a common language for the social sciences (Geertz recalls that someone helpfully suggested English). Parsons launched the Social Relations program to embody his vision of an integrated social science, where psychologists would study individuals and sociologists, the functioning of social systems, leaving culture to the anthropologists.

This division of academic labor put Parsons in conflict with the dominant Boasian school of American anthropology, the issue turning on the meaning of culture. The issue came into sharp focus with the publication of Parson's *The Social System* in 1951. Parsons argued that to become an analytical empirical science, anthropology needed to take as its subject a restricted view of culture that was independent of both sociology and psychology. The same year, two leading anthropologists, Alfred Kroeber and Clyde Kluckhohn, expressed their dissatisfaction with the idea that social systems could be separated from culture. Kluckhohn argued that social structure is a part of the cultural map and that social systems are built on a framework of explicit and implicit culture. To this, Kroeber and Kluckhohn soon added an evolutionary postscript, arguing that culture originated with early man's facultative abilities to use symbols, generalize, and make imaginative substitutions.

At Harvard, Geertz was assigned to study and comment on the draft of Kluckhohn's and Kroeber's *Culture: A Critical Review of Concepts and Definitions*, which aimed at a definitive compilation of all the prevailing definitions of culture. Geertz seized on this question and pursued it for more than 50 years. When he was a beginning professor at Chicago in the 1970s, his students recall, the reading list for his signature course on "Theories of Culture" included 277 items, drawing from philosophy, literature, religion, and psychology, as well as anthropology. In *Available Light*, Geertz reflected that in the history of the concept of culture—its drift toward and away from clarity and popularity over the next half century—could be seen both his own intellectual biography and that of anthropology itself.

But in 1951, resolving—or at least working through—these conflicting ideas about culture still lay in Geertz's future. In 1952, Clifford and Hildred Geertz began doctoral fieldwork in a small town in east Java, joining a team that Geertz described as the very stamp and image of the Social Relations idea as conceived by Parsons: a long-term, well-financed, multidisciplinary field project focused not on a small tribal culture but on a 2,000-year-old civilization in the midst of revolutionary change. Geertz's task in the team was to study Javanese religion. His approach was to try out a Weberian hypothesis, that the strongly Muslim sector of Javanese society would be functionally equivalent to Reformation Protestants, spearheading a comprehensive social transformation. In 1956, Geertz received his PhD with a 700-page doctoral dissertation, published in 1960 as *The Religion of Java*: an account of the everyday religious practices of Javanese Muslims, in which the informants spoke for themselves in indented excerpts from field notes.

After completing their fieldwork in Java, the Geertzes made their way to Bali, where they lived in the village of Tihingan for most of a year and investigated kinship, calendars, laws, states, villages, and cockfights. Returning from Indonesia, they spent 1958 at the Center for Advanced Study in the Behavioral Sciences in Palo Alto, followed by a year at the University of California, Berkeley. In 1960, they moved to the University of Chicago, where Geertz directed another multidisciplinary center, the Committee for the Comparative Study of New Nations. Soon thereafter, Geertz began his third major fieldwork project, this time in an ancient walled town in the Moroccan Middle Atlas Mountains, studying bazaars, mosques, olive growing, and oral poetry. In 1970, Geertz was invited to found a new School of Social Science at the Institute for Advanced Study in Princeton, where he remained for the rest of his career, seeking (as he later wrote) to advance a conception of research centered on the analysis of the significance of social actions for those who carry them out and the beliefs and institutions that lend significance to those actions.

Geertz's First Ethnographies

Between 1960 and 1966, Geertz published five monographs based on his Indonesian fieldwork: *The Religion of Java*, *Agricultural Involution*, *Peddlers and Princes*, *The Social History of an Indonesian Town*, and *Person, Time and Conduct in Bali*. The most widely cited of these books was *Agricultural Involution*, a study of social change in rural Java that caught the interest of American social scientists and quickly became an indispensable text for courses on modernization and development. As Geertz later recalled, he danced for rain and got a flood.

Geertz borrowed the term *involution* from the American anthropologist Alexander Goldenweiser to describe a peasant society in which endless small-scale innovations in agriculture failed to trigger economic growth. Dutch colonial policies had produced "shared poverty," in which the economic pie was divided into ever smaller fragments. Involution occurred as a result of incremental changes to labor and land tenure arrangements, and virtuosity in rice cultivation techniques using human and animal labor. These productive arrangements were mirrored in social and religious systems, *pace* Max Weber. Intensified cultivation of rice paddies was matched by a similar involution in rural family life, social stratification, political organization, and even religious practice: the "folk culture" value system in terms of which shared poverty was normatively regulated and ethically justified.

Geertz's thesis was exhaustively analyzed and critiqued; in his review of *Economic Change in Southeast Asia, c. 1830–1980*, Colin Brown described it as a brilliant hypothesis brought down by available evidence. Geertz was further criticized by Wim F. Wertheim for a "sociological blindness" that paralleled the blind spots of colonial and post-colonial elites, whose vision of the harmonious and peaceful village community, characterized by solidarity and mutual aid, was derived from and promoted by the village elite themselves. Another Dutch historian, Ernst Utrecht, similarly argued that Geertz had turned a blind eye to class distinctions and class struggle. In 1965, Geertz published *The Social History of an Indonesian Town*, in which he argued that one of Java's greatest needs was for a virile yeomanry. But 1965 was the year of the Indonesian massacres, an anticommunist coup in which hundreds of thousands of people died, mostly in rural Java and Bali. The killings were especially savage in east Java, where Geertz had done his fieldwork. Although the army organized the first death squads, most of the villagers died at the hands of their neighbors, and the consensus of subsequent research on the causes of violence emphasized tensions in rural society stemming from class and religion.

Geertz's first four ethnographies focused on rural Java and were not specifically aimed at anthropologists but rather at the wider social science community interested in modernization and development. If Parsons and Weber proved to be imperfect guides to counterrevolutionary Java, arguably more successful, if less well-known, are Geertz's first publications about Bali, notably *Person, Time and Conduct* and a 1959 article, "Form and Variation in Balinese Village Structure." In these works, Geertz set aside both the methods and the questions of Parsonian development theory in favor of an open-ended phenomenology of everyday life in Bali. To explain this departure from Parsonian orthodoxy, he argued that while conventional sociological analysis can ferret out the functional implications for a society of a particular system of "person-categories," and at times even predict how such a system might change under certain social processes, the success of the analysis depends on whether the social system—the categories, their meanings, and their logical relationships—can be taken as already known. This approach revived some of the themes

Margaret Mead and Gregory Bateson had developed in their studies of Bali in the 1930s, which explored the interplay of culture and personality. But where Mead and Bateson had focused on child rearing, dreams, and visual art, Geertz was interested in the social world.

Bali, like Java, had been extensively studied by several generations of Dutch colonial ethnographers, for whom scholarly publications in ethnology were the key to professional advancement in the colonial civil service. In particular, the intricacies of *adat*—local custom and law—were considered to be vital to the mission of the colonial government, and civil servants competed to produce lucid descriptions of local variation in *adat*. Geertz wondered how the pieces might fit together. The Balinese make extensive use of both a lunisolar and a permutational calendar, which in combination depict time as unfolding in intricate patterns of embedded cycles. Geertz explored the ways in which this "wheels within wheels" view of time shapes Balinese concepts of the self as reflected in the progression of personal names encoded by generational kinship terminology and teknonymy. Later on, he extended this analysis to encompass interlocking cycles in the organization of irrigation. Here, Parsons was nudged aside in favor of the phenomenological perspective of Alfred Schutz—in particular Schutz's concept of the "lifeworld," which relates concepts of the self to the social universe. The social system was not sui generis (as in the Parsonian scheme) but rather built up from more fundamental ideas, like time. Geertz concluded that the variation in Balinese village structure observed by colonial scholars was not accidental but intrinsically meaningful.

The Interpretation of Cultures

In 1973, Geertz published what was to become his most influential book, a compendium of essays titled *The Interpretation of Cultures*. In one of them, "The Growth of Culture and the Evolution of Mind," originally published in 1962, he endorsed Kroeber and Kluckhohn's view that the development of culture profoundly affected the evolution of the brain. Rather oddly, he cited Parsons in a footnote to support the idea that culture should be defined as a learned pattern of the meaning of signals and signs. But Parsons was soon to drop out of Geertz's footnotes, because for Geertz, psychology and the social system (the other two legs of the Parsonian triad) could not be separated from culture. In the most frequently cited passage in the book, Geertz offered his own definition of culture, derived from Max Weber's view that man is an animal suspended in webs of significance that he himself has spun. Culture, wrote Geertz, is equivalent to those webs. Consequently, cultural analysis is not an experimental science in search of laws but an interpretive one in search of meaning. Two later chapters differentiated Geertz's views from those of Claude Lévi-Strauss and offered a model for a Geertzian style of cultural analysis.

In *The Interpretation of Cultures*, the question is how subjects create meaning, not (as Lévi-Strauss would have it) how meanings create subjects. Exactly how meaning is to be read from the ethnographer's up-close observations was explored in the final chapter, "Deep Play: Notes on the Balinese Cockfight" (1972), the most cited of Geertz's essays. As the historian Natalie Zemon Davis recalls, Geertz's techniques for observing, understanding, and writing about Indonesia and Morocco burst like fireworks on the horizon of historians back in the 1970s. From an intensely significant and observable local event, like the Balinese cockfight, could be teased a world of meaning and an enduring style of life. "Deep Play" is a close reading of an ordinary cockfight witnessed by Geertz in 1958, 10 days after arriving in the Balinese village of Tihingan. The cocks are surrogates for the owner's personalities; the cockfight a simulation of a social matrix in which status and prestige are the driving forces. To read the meaning of events like cockfights as if they were plays, Geertz concluded, opens up the possibility of an analysis that attends to their substance rather than to reductive formulas professing to account for them.

At Princeton, Geertz joined a seminar taught by the historian Robert Darnton. Like his Princeton colleague Zemon Davis, Darnton credits "Deep Play" as the inspiration for a new style of microhistorical analysis, exemplified by Darnton's analysis of the slaughter of cats by a printer's apprentice in Paris in 1730, *The Great Cat Massacre* (1984). In the era of incredulity toward metanarratives, when structuralists like Louis Althusser were questioning whether the modern concept of history is more than an artifact of the 18th-century struggle of the revolutionary bourgeoisie against feudalism, "Deep Play" showed what historians and ethnographers could decipher from primary texts and up-close observations.

Later Works

In 1980, Geertz published a book-length study of 19th-century Balinese kingdoms. *Negara: The Theatre State in Nineteenth Century Bali* offered the provocative thesis that displays of status and prestige were as important to the princes of Bali as to the cockfighters (often the same individuals) and that Balinese rulers competed to produce grand spectacles in which power served pomp, rather than the reverse. This argument was met with bafflement; critics felt that Geertz had upended the relationship between ideology and the material foundation of the state, and his thesis was regarded as so provocative that reviewers seldom attended to the evidence Geertz offered in its support. Geertz had simply lost interest in sociological issues, in the view of Adam Kuper.

Yet as Geertz showed, Balinese rulers competed not for land but for manpower and expended their fortunes on spectacular rites of world renewal. The constantly changing borders of their tiny kingdoms could usually be traversed in less than a day, and they shared power with acrobat's pyramids of princelings, whose signatures were generally required to execute the business of the state, such as making a treaty or concluding a peace. Geertz mined the colonial archives to discover how it all worked: the intricate webs of *adat* relationships between lords and subjects, the organization of irrigation, taxation, trade, and warfare. Whatever intelligence Bali may have to offer us about the nature of politics, Geertz concluded, it can hardly be that big fish eat little fish or that the rags of virtue mask the engines of privilege.

After *Negara*, Geertz returned to essays, his favorite genre, and from time to time scooped up a collection of them to publish as books. In the 1988 book *Works and Lives: The Anthropologist as Author*, Geertz confronted the criticism that attention to ethnographic writing calls into question the whole project of ethnology, by celebrating the struggles of four anthropologists to "get texts exact and translations veridical . . . getting them sufficiently on the page that someone can obtain some comprehension of what they might be" (pp. 145–146). *After the Fact: Two Countries, Four Decades, One Anthropologist* (1995) gives us Geertz on Geertz. A complete bibliography through 1999 was published by Fred Inglis as an appendix to his monograph *Clifford Geertz: Culture, Custom and Ethics*. In his last book *Available Light*, Geertz offers reflections on philosophical topics. If all we wanted was home truths, he tells us, we should have stayed at home.

J. Stephen Lansing and Thérèse A. de Vet

See also Althusser, Louis; Goldenweiser, Alexander A.; Kluckhohn, Clyde; Kroeber, Alfred L.; Lyotard, Jean-François; Parsons, Talcott; Weber, Max

Further Readings

Geertz, C. (1963). *Agricultural involution: The processes of ecological change in Indonesia.* Berkeley: University of California Press.

———. (1973). *The interpretation of cultures.* New York, NY: Basic Books.

———. (1980). *Negara: The theatre state in nineteenth-century Bali.* Princeton, NJ: Princeton University Press.

———. (1995). *After the fact: Two countries, four decades, one anthropologist.* Boston, MA: Harvard University Press.

———. (2001). *Available light: Anthropological reflections on philosophical topics.* Princeton, NJ: Princeton University Press.

Geertz, C., Geertz, H., & Rosen, L. (1979). *Meaning and order in Moroccan society: Three essays in cultural analysis.* Cambridge, UK: Cambridge University Press.

Inglis, F. (2000). *Clifford Geertz: Culture custom and ethics.* Cambridge, UK: Polity Press.

———. (Ed.). (2010). *Life among the Anthros and other essays by Clifford Geertz.* Princeton, NJ: Princeton University Press.

Kroeber, A. L., & Kluckhohn, C. (1952). *Culture: A critical review of concepts and definitions* (Papers of the Peabody Museum, Harvard University, Vol. 47, No. 1). Cambridge, MA: Harvard University.

Kuper, A. (2000). *Culture: The anthropologist's account.* Boston, MA: Harvard University Press.

Shweder, R. A., & Good, G. (Eds.). (2005). *Clifford Geertz by his colleagues.* Chicago, IL: University of Chicago Press.

White, B. (2007). Clifford Geertz: Singular genius of interpretive anthropology. *Development and Change, 38*(6), 1187–1208.

GEFFRAY, CHRISTIAN

After studying philosophy, then anthropology, Christian Geffray (1954–2001) published four books between 1991 and his death in 2001. These make him one of the most remarkable anthropologists of his generation.

Extending the work of Claude Meillassoux in *Ni père, ni mère: Critique de la parenté chez les Makhuwa* (Neither Father nor Mother: Critique of Kinship Among Makhuwa, 1991), Geffray, basing his approach on an examination of reproduction, dismantles the logic of kinship and domestic economy of the Makhuwa societies of Mozambique. Geffray shows in particular that the power of women in this matrilineal and matrilocal society vanishes if one moves from the domestic unit to the realm of marriages. Although in the domestic unit men and junior women work under the control of elder women, men accede to power by controlling marriages. Men marry their sons (over whom they exercise little other control) to their sisters' daughters and further strengthen the control this provides by marrying their granddaughters of the maternal line of their wife to the sons issued from these unions. It is on the basis of social relations of production that Geffray reconstructed the logic of Makhuwa kinship.

But Mozambique was at war, and with the agreement of the authorities, Geffray investigated this subject. *La cause des armes au Mozambique* (The Cause of War in Mozambique, 1990) is a pioneering book in the anthropology of war. Geffray tackled taboo subjects such as the collusion between revolutionary intellectuals and members of the state bureaucracy and the scorn these persons had for traditional village leaders. He showed that the forced relocation of isolated village communities helped support the guerrillas and the ways in which war had become a life project for the peasantry.

Geffray's next project, done under the auspices of the National Institute of Research and Development, concerned various locales on the edge of the Brazilian rain forest and resulted in *Chroniques de la servitude en Amazonie brésilienne* (Chronicles of Servitude in the Brazilian Amazon, 1995). In this work, he questions the power of paternalism as a paradigm and begins to propose an anthropology that connects the forms of social ties to the process of identification of individual subjects. The specificity of the paternalistic exploitation Geffray found in Brazil is based on the absence of monetary relationships. The boss (*patrão*) has a monopoly on the movement of goods that come to him (latex, lumber, gold, etc.) and on the commercial products he provides. The market value of the products of the labor of his customers is always greater than that of the goods necessary for his subsistence; however, a continual increase in the value of tools and necessities engages the community in a cycle of dependency and a voluntary servitude based on an imaginary debt (one that has been repaid many times over).

The issue of this debt led Geffray to write *Le Nom du maître: Contribution à l'anthropologie analytique* (The Name of the Master: Contribution to Analytical Anthropology, 1997), where, drawing on the theory of the psychoanalyst Jacques Lacan, Geffray theorizes about the identificatory alienation of individual subjects and their collective alienation to a "We," tackling questions about the relationship between individual subjectivities and larger social collectives. These reflections continue with *Trésors: Anthropologie analytique de la valeur* (Treasure: Analytical Anthropology of Value, 2001). Drawing from the worlds of the ancient Greeks, the Yanomami, the Trobriand Islanders, and the Cheyenne, Geffray reflects on what determines value in social life. His answer is that the circulation of death (including the willingness to engage in transactions that put one's life at stake), of gifts, and of commodities makes life meaningful. Geffray then shows the recurrence of an opposition between, on the one hand, faith, the oath of loyalty, and the dignity of men and, on the other, the calculations that determine the relative value of commodities but are indifferent to honor. With goods, the belief in the truth of the subject's speech are no longer at stake, and it is instead the measurable value of the object.

Geffray also co-led an international research program on cocaine, conducting research in prisons in Mexico, Bolivia, and Brazil. With Frederic Letang, he codirected a film, *La terre de la pein* (Land of Suffering, 1997), shot in the Amazon state of Para, that shows the pure violence regulating social relations. The movie shows *fazendeiros* ("land-owning farmers") sure of their rights after having cleared the jungle, building roads and cities, announcing, "If they continue, they will die," speaking about the exploited people who occupy their land.

During his short career, Geffray's work was published in *Politique Africaine, les Cahiers d'Etudes Africaines, International Social Science Journal, Lusothopie, Cahiers de sciences humaines, Autrepart, Revista Internacional de Estudos Áfricanos*, and *Trabalhos de Arqueologia e Antropologia*. Although there are Portugese translations of his work, none have yet appeared in English.

Gérald Gaillard

See also Lacan, Jacques; Meillassoux, Claude

Further Readings

Copans, J., & Dozon, J.-P. (2001). Christian Geffray, 1954–2001. *Cahiers d'études africaines, 41*(162), 239–242.

Goudineau, Y. (2001). Christian Geffray, 1954–2001. De la valeur des choses à la valeur de l'homme [On the value of things and the value of people]. *Autrepart, 3*(19), 5–10.

———. (2001). La valeur des biens contre les hommes de valeur: Sur l'anthropologie analytique de Christian Geffray [The value of goods versus men of value: On the analytical anthropology of Christian Geffray]. *Anthropologie et Sociétés, 25*(3), 123–136.

Guillaud, Y., & Letang, F. (Eds.). (2009). *Du Social hors la loi: L'anthropologie analytique de Christian Geffray* [The social outside the law: The analytic anthropology of Christian Geffray]. Paris, France: IRD-Orstom.

Héritier, F. (2001). Christian Geffray, 1954–2001. *L'Homme, 160*, 7–10.

Meillassoux, C. (2001). Hommage à Christian Geffray. *Journal des anthropologues, 87*, 219–221.

Simoney, D. (2001). Christian Geffray, 1954–2001. *La Clinique lacanienne, 5*, 198–201.

GENDER AND ANTHROPOLOGY

It might fairly be said (to paraphrase the poet Philip Larkin's claim that sexual intercourse began in 1963) that "gender" in anthropology began in 1975 with the publication of Gayle Rubin's article "The Traffic in Women." In her article, Rubin argued that social practices such as marriage exchanges established a "sex/gender system" that divided humans into at least two genders and established borders between them. "Women" and "men" were thus cultural categories, as exchangers and objects for exchange. The article was both an appreciation and a critique of Claude Lévi-Strauss. Rubin credited Lévi-Strauss with placing the exchange of women at the center of social life. She criticized him for not taking the opening offered by his theory on the arbitrariness of boundaries but rather building that theory on the assumption that the male/female boundary was a part of nature that men might use as a reference point for culturally imposed divisions such as those between brothers and brothers-in-law, creditors and debtors, and even nature and culture. It was central to Lévi-Strauss's argument that the difference between two *kinds* of women, sisters and wives, be seen as culturally imposed (and therefore arbitrary). This artificial division was the basis of the incest taboo, which in turn was the basis for the complex systems of exchange that, as Marcel Mauss had argued in *The Gift*, constituted social life in preindustrial societies. Neither Lévi-Strauss nor Mauss, however, felt it necessary to ask why men exchanged women and not the reverse.

Because the boundaries between sisters and wives were artificial, according to Lévi-Strauss, they needed defending, and in his study of totemism, he argued that this arbitrary division was propped up by naturalizing the divisions between the unilineal clans that exchanged wives, so that they were equated with the divisions between plant and animal species. The consequences that might ensue if "men" and "women" were themselves seen as arbitrary categories did not enter into the arguments of these two magisterial works. Ironically, in 1949, the same year that Lévi-Strauss published *The Elementary Structures of Kinship*, Simone de Beauvoir, his classmate, argued in *The Second Sex* that "Woman" was made, not born, citing him in her introduction as someone whose general line of thinking had influenced her argument. It took until the mid-1970s for de Beauvoir's work to exert a worldwide influence in anthropology through Sherry Ortner's 1972 essay "Is Female to Male as Nature Is to Culture," in which the author argued, citing both de Beauvoir and Lévi-Strauss, that the ability to give birth made women convenient symbols for the "natural" (and therefore less human) aspects of social life, establishing the basis of what she believed to be universal female subordination.

This entry examines some key work in ethnography and theory to see what insights anthropology offered before and after this turning point in the 1970s toward understanding the production and workings of "sex/gender" systems, emphasizing analysis rather than a comprehensive survey. *Gender* in this discussion will be understood to mean the social categories developed around, but by no means determined by, the biological facts of sexual difference, while *sex* and *sexuality* refer to erotic desires and behaviors as these are defined, permitted, mandated, or prohibited in sociocultural contexts. The notion of a "sex/gender system" was premised on the belief that the regimes of "sex" and "gender" were defined in interconnecting ways and that scholars (and activists wishing to change the rules) needed to approach them with these interconnections in mind.

Significant Developments in Gender Studies

Sexuality and the status of women were interconnected themes in some classic 19th-century writings on cultural evolution. Lewis Henry Morgan and Friedrich Engels (who borrowed heavily from Morgan) argued that early human groups had been both promiscuous and matriarchal. With the development of technology and human knowledge, the desire of males to pass their property to their own offspring was said to have led to the development of patriarchy. Polygamy, prostitution, and ultimately a form of monogamy, in which fathers headed families, replaced both the imagined "primitive promiscuity" and group marriage of the early hunter-gatherers and the matriarchal clans linked by "pairing" marriages, said to have characterized early village life. Although for Engels and Morgan, promiscuity and matriarchy were linked to the most primitive states of humankind, both looked forward to a more egalitarian regime for women in the future. Work of this type put sexuality, gender roles, and the regimes of kinship and marriage that were linked to them at the core of anthropological theory; later, they were to become uncoupled and relatively marginalized, at least until the later 20th century.

In the 1920s, Bronisław Malinowski published a series of works based on his fieldwork during World War I in the Trobriand Islands off the coast of New Guinea. According to Malinowski, the Trobrianders traced clan membership through women and encouraged sexual experimentation among adolescents. Malinowski wrote extensively about these matters but stressed repeatedly that premarital sex was followed by stable marriages and that matriliny did not mean matriarchy. His work on the relationship between kinship and exchange provided an important impetus for Mauss. Malinowski stressed the social importance of fatherhood in a society in which, he alleged, people were unaware of the facts of physiological paternity. To some degree, he saw the Trobrianders as typical of primitive societies, and therefore as an appropriate vehicle for rejecting the matriarchal theorists. Malinowski rejected Freud's ideas about the Oedipus complex, arguing that family dynamics varied in cultures with differing regimes of kinship and marriage, but he mainly relied on a single example, the Trobrianders, in his critique of Freud. An important trend in the mid-20th century, the period that followed Malinowski's work, was that "kinship," "marriage," "sex," and "women's roles" became to some degree independent topics in the anthropological literature, coupled with the assumption that each was subject to a wide range of variation.

Margaret Mead, whose first book, *Coming of Age in Samoa*, was published in 1928, the same year as Malinowski's *The Sexual Life of Savages in Northwestern Melanesia*, wrote several works that dealt with sexuality, gender roles, and particularly child socialization. She described a series of societies in Polynesia and Melanesia in which rules about sexuality, marriage, and gender roles differed greatly, and during the 1930s, her main stress was on these differences. She argued against universal theories of sex and gender, seeing cultures as setting their own rules in accord with broadly defined "values" such as competitiveness or cooperation. In 1949 (the same year as *The Second Sex* and *The Elementary Structures of Kinship*), Mead published *Male and Female*, a comparative study of gender role development in seven different cultures. While Mead did not reject the idea of variability of men's and women's roles, she argued that women were unlikely to be happy in societies that did not make provision for and place a high value on child rearing. One could, therefore, argue that this book had an essentialist dimension, presuming rather than seeking to explain women's nurturing role. *Male and Female* was singled out for criticism by Betty Friedan in *The Feminine Mystique*, a foundational work of second-wave feminism. Friedan alleges that Mead had given up her stance on the relativity of gender norms to argue for a normative femininity centered on motherhood. The book was one of many writings of the Culture-and-Personality school and its

descendants, continuing to the present in works like those of Nancy Scheper-Hughes, which discuss gender largely through the lens of motherhood.

British anthropology after Malinowski had relatively little to say about gender. Functionalism had a theoretical bias in favor of coherence rather than disjuncture in its presentation of individual societies; thus, studies of kinship and marriage discussed marriage arrangements in terms of social stability but did not question the basic assumptions of natural gender differences. Some functionalist ethnographies included brief remarks about the status of women in various societies, usually arguing that women supported the status quo, regarding matters such as polygamy, wife beating, and female circumcision. Anthropologists outside Britain as well have frequently defended the people they studied against stereotyping by playing down the effects of gender inequality. Within the functionalist tradition, Audrey Richards and Phyllis Kaberry wrote book-length treatments of women's roles in the communities they studied but did not examine gender as such.

Some data potentially critical of a naturalized view of sex/gender did emerge from functionalist accounts, notably E. E. Evans-Pritchard's account of woman-woman marriage among the Nuer, a custom that contributed to Rubin's notion of a sex/gender system, despite Evans-Pritchard's insistence that female husbands (and perhaps more significantly female fathers) were a legal fiction to allow for the inheritance of cattle in the absence of a suitable male heir. In this discussion, as well as in his accounts of marriages of women to the ghosts of dead men and the treatment of Nuer children born of adultery, Evans-Pritchard reiterated the distinction between biological and social paternity, a notion somewhat canonical in British functionalism, though, it must be emphasized, without interrogating the notion of gender itself. Many years later, Evans-Pritchard published an article on marriages between adolescent boys and young men among the Azande, which were succeeded by heterosexual marriages at the appropriate stage of life. Though Evans-Pritchard did not draw the conclusion that gender might be a fluid category, even within an individual lifetime, this article was cited by later scholars, such as Gilbert Herdt, in support of such arguments.

In the 1980s, scholars began to examine gender as a social construct. One very important early work in this area was Herdt's 1981 study *The Guardians of the Flutes.* Herdt described male initiation in a New Guinea society in which masculinity was believed to be a gradually acquired and precarious status, dependent on the ingestion of semen by boys, on rituals of nose bleeding and the consumption of certain tree saps by adults, as well as the avoidance of female pollution. According to Herdt, Sambia culture suggested that both gender identity and sexual orientation might best be considered as processes rather than statuses.

Work such as Herdt's had an impact on feminist thinking both inside and outside the academy. In 1982, in a conference paper titled "Thinking Sex," Rubin revised her earlier suggestion that, insofar as they were mutually constructed, sex and gender norms could be concurrently addressed by the feminist movement, both intellectually and in the realm of practical politics. In "Thinking Sex," Rubin argued that feminists had not been a force for the dismantling of restrictive sexual norms and had, in fact, allied with sexual conservatives on key issues such as pornography. The conference at which "Thinking Sex" was presented was picketed by feminists opposed to pornography, and Rubin herself was singled out for attack because she had engaged in research and advocacy with groups in San Francisco supportive of consensual sadomasochistic practices. The conference proceedings were ultimately published in *Pleasure and Danger: Exploring Female Sexuality* (1984), edited by the anthropologist Carole Vance, who had been one of the leading organizers of the conference. Despite this collaboration, feminist anthropology and the anthropology of sexuality have remained largely separate during the past 30 years.

Feminist studies in anthropology, which have often claimed to be about "gender," have been concerned with diverse issues—among them women's strategies for empowerment; women's work; women's health and reproductive issues; the intersection of gender, race, and class; and a reevaluation of the treatment of gender in the study of human evolution and primatology. Traditional "kinship" studies were reinvented so that families could be studied as a site of gender construction and contestation. For example, Lila Abu Lughod challenged traditional anthropological notions of culture to portray Bedouin life as a set of multiple voices, male, female, old, and young, rather than as a unified system of values and statuses.

All of these studies might fairly be said to have stressed the "gender" side of sex/gender, though certainly "sex" made up a significant part of some of the studies, particularly in connection with topics such as HIV, AIDS, birth control, and sex work. Indeed, an important part of the argument of many works was that discourses about "sex" (e.g., discussions of prostitution) were ultimately discourses about gender and power relations.

Heterosexuality and Homosexuality

Since the 1970s, a large body of writing has emerged that does stress sexuality, particularly same-sex sexuality, and in some cases integrates it with discussions of gender, particularly in works about gender categories other than "male" and "female." Esther Newton's influential work on drag queens analyzed their performances as a challenge to the prevailing norms of sex and gender in the United States. Earlier anthropological and archival literature on so-called berdaches (from the French *bardache*, for "catamite")—socially recognized cross-dressing, cross-gender, or "third gender" individuals in many Native North American cultures—was reexamined. These studies had often seen these customs in terms of homosexuality, with varying attitudes on the part of the anthropologists; some anthropologists in the first half of the 20th century had treated them as ritualized cross-dressing and had denied a sexual component. New fieldwork showed that these institutions had either fallen into disuse or greatly changed their meaning.

Studies in the 1980s and 1990s varied in the degree to which they saw such phenomena as forms of "homosexuality," a discussion made more complex by the identification of some contemporary gay Native Americans with these traditional forms, once called "berdache" and since the1990s increasingly called "two-spirit," to include the religious dimension that such institutions had in many traditions. Harriet Whitehead wrote a much cited article in which she stressed the performance of work and the kinship roles usually assigned to the opposite sex as the key parameters in such institutions—rather than erotic desire. Others, such as Walter Williams, argued that anthropologists should not neglect the erotic when discussing the multiple aspects of institutionalized transgender behavior in Native North America. The many other anthropological studies of gender-crossing institutions in North America, Polynesia, Siberia, India, Brazil, and elsewhere that have been published during the past 30 years have stressed that gender categories, erotic desire and behavior, and many other aspects of life, religious and secular, may be interconnected in local understandings of figures such as the two-spirit, the Tahitian *mahu*, the Polynesian *fa'afafine*, the Brazilian *travesti*, the Indian *hijra*, and the Albanian sworn virgin. Some of these figures were accepted in their cultures, some were stigmatized, but all were recognized as distinct categories of human beings.

Contemporary literature has pointed to a rethinking of gender and sexuality, indeed of personhood itself, that rejected essences in favor of varying bundles of characteristics that constitute local understandings of *gender* and *sexuality*. These writings challenged Eurocentric notions of "homosexuality" as well as of "gender," since the components of the institutions described varied from place to place. Two such challenges are worth noting: Deborah Elliston criticized Herdt for using the word *homosexual* to describe the Sambia practice of inseminating initiates by means of fellatio because Sambia understandings of what they were doing were not congruent with English speakers' understandings of "homosexual" behavior; Herdt, in fact, dropped the word in later publications. Another discussion where anthropologists' understandings of the malleability of gender boundaries and same-sex relationships coincide concerns woman-woman couples in which one partner adopts a "masculine" role and the other a more "feminine" one. In lesbian communities in the United States, such "butch-femme" roles had been rejected by feminists as reifications of the gender norms of the dominant culture. However, anthropologists like Evelyn Blackwood, Saskia Wieringa, and Megan Sinnott found that roles of this type were recognized in a variety of cultures, while Elizabeth Kennedy and Madelyn Davis argued in *Boots of Leather, Slippers of Gold* that their historical role in the United States challenged the sex/gender system at a time when lesbians were highly stigmatized.

It has become clear to scholars in many fields that categories such as "homosexual," "heterosexual," and "masculine" and "feminine" are highly contingent, and they are now often discussed in the plural: sexualities, homosexualities, and femininities and masculinities. Anthropology has played a leading role in questioning these taken-for-granted but misleading understandings.

Harriet D. Lyons

See also Abu-Lughod, Lila; Evans-Pritchard, E. E.; Freud, Sigmund; Lévi-Strauss, Claude; Malinowski, Bronisław; Mauss, Marcel; Mead, Margaret; Morgan, Lewis Henry; Ortner, Sherry; Richards, Audrey

Further Readings

Abu Lughod, L. (1986). *Veiled sentiments: Honor and poetry in a Bedouin society*. Berkeley: University of California Press.

Blackwood, E., & Wieringa, S. E. (Eds.). (1999). *Same-sex relations and female desires: Transgender practices across cultures*. New York, NY: Columbia University Press.

Engels, F. (1986). *The origin of the family, private property and the state*. London, UK: Penguin Books. (Original work published 1884)

Evans-Pritchard, E. E. (1970). Sexual inversion among the Azande. *American Anthropologist, 72*(6), 1428–1434.

Herdt, G. (1981). *Guardians of the flutes: Idioms of masculinity*. New York, NY: McGraw-Hill.

Jacobs, S.-E., Thomas, W., & Lang, S. (Eds.). (1997). *Two-spirit people: Native American gender identity, sexuality, and spirituality*. Urbana: University of Illinois Press.

Kulick, D. (1998). *Travesti: Sex, gender and culture among Brazilian transgendered prostitutes*. Chicago, IL: University of Chicago Press.

Nanda, S. (1990). *Neither man nor woman: The hijras of India*. Belmont, CA: Wadsworth.

Newton, E. (1972). *Mother camp: Female impersonators in America*. Englewood Cliffs, NJ: Prentice Hall.

Ortner, S. B. (1972). Is female to male as nature is to culture? In M. Z. Rosaldo & L. Lamphere (Eds.), *Woman, culture and society* (pp. 67–88). Stanford, CA: Stanford University Press.

Rubin, G. (2011). *Deviations: A Gayle Rubin reader*. Durham, NC: Duke University Press. (Contains the articles mentioned above and a selection of Rubin's other work)

Whitehead, H. (1982). The bow and the burden strap: A new look at institutionalized homosexuality in Native North America. In S. B. Ortner & H. Whitehead (Eds.), *Sexual meanings: The cultural construction of gender and sexuality* (pp. 80–115). Cambridge, UK: Cambridge University Press.

GENDER DIVERSITY

Gender diversity, sometimes called sex/gender diversity, is related to, but different from, *sex*, the biologically differentiated status of male or female; *gender*, the social, cultural, and psychological constructions imposed on sexual differences; and *sexuality*, which refers to erotic desires, sexual practices, or sexual orientation. There is no simple, universal, or inevitable correspondence between sex, gender, sexuality, and gender diversity, which is today primarily understood as a cultural construction.

Roles transcending the sex/gender binaries of male and female, man and woman, exist in societies at all levels of cultural complexity and in all parts of the world. Sex/gender diversity is variably associated with sexual orientation, sexual practice, cross-dressing, occupation, or a range of biologically rooted intersex conditions. Sex- or gender-variant individuals are culturally often distinguished from both men and women, understood as a "mixture" of masculine and feminine qualities, which may be expressed in dress, behavior, or occupation.

Various theories and perspectives attempt to explain the occurrence and specific forms of sex/gender diversity. Until the mid-20th century, biological factors and medical perspectives dominated, but in the past 50 years, the view that both gender and sex are cultural constructions has become perhaps equally important. While traditional cultural factors are important in explaining specific forms of sex/gender diversity, these forms have also been influenced by colonialism, modernization, and contemporary globalization.

The common Euro-American identification of sex/gender diversity with homosexuality and the essentialized identity of "the homosexual" is *not* universal. It has frequently been misapplied in other cultures, where homosexual desire and practice are not viewed either as permanent or even as important components in the definition of gender. In Brazil, a male who takes the masculine role in same-sex relations is not considered sexually deviant or even marginal, while in Thailand and Indonesia, same-sex relationships are defined not by sex but rather as relationships embodying the complementary gender roles of masculine and feminine. These relationships are differentiated from the Western concept "gay," which has diffused globally but takes on various meanings in different cultures.

Most recorded alternative gender roles are associated with males rather than with females, perhaps because of the more contingent nature of the development of masculinity, perhaps because of male power dominance in most societies, or even perhaps because of male bias in ethnographic research. Alternative female gender roles are, however, found in many cultures, such as the "sworn virgin" of the Balkans, the *sadhin* of India, the Mohave *hwame*, or the contemporary *tombois* of Indonesia. The gender-diverse roles of the Hawaiian *mahu*, the Thai *kathoey*, or the Indonesian *bissu* traditionally applied to either males or females, though under the impact of patriarchal colonial cultures, they now refer mainly to feminine males.

While in contemporary societies, fear, ridicule, and even legal sanctions may attach to alternative gender roles, traditionally, gender-variant individuals were accepted and sometimes even highly valued. Native American *two-spirit* persons, for example, were often healers and shamans, and the Indian *hijras* and Brazilian *pasivos* are also associated with powerful ritual roles and magical powers.

In precontact Hawaii, the *mahu* (literally, hermaphrodite) were valued caregivers for children and the elderly, were considered highly skilled in the traditional arts of hula and chanting, and were keepers of cultural tradition. Under the impact of American colonialism, *mahu* became a derogatory term applied to effeminate males or male-to-female transgendered individuals, but with the contemporary renaissance of Hawaiian culture, the role is taking on its older, more positive meanings.

In Thailand and the Philippines, the adoption of Western psycho-medical theories of sexuality and sexual orientation resulted in gender diversity being treated as a mental illness, an important departure from its traditionally accepted status. In addition, the contemporary association of gender-variant males with sex work has degraded their popular image. In some Muslim nations like Malaysia, gender diversity is considered incompatible with the current religious emphasis on marriage and "family values."

Simultaneously, however, due partly to the global spread of a human rights ideology and the high status associated with "modernization," integrating gender-variant persons into civil society has become an issue of national debate in many societies, including Muslim societies like Pakistan. In Thailand, Tonga, and the Philippines, the widespread participation of gender-diverse males in transgender beauty contests connects them to a modern, glamorous persona, which is viewed as a source of national prestige. In Indonesia, the gender-variant *waria* have gained popular respect and even state support through their expertise in creating a wedding industry that valorizes a "true Indonesian image" and encourages national unity.

Various theories may help explain gender diversity in a particular society, though none is conclusive. One of these theories is gender differentiation—that is, the extent to which gender roles are well-defined, specialized, and hierarchical as opposed to fluid, overlapping, and egalitarian. But India, for example, has high gender differentiation yet also contains several gender-variant roles, while many Native American cultures, which have relatively low gender differentiation, also have a high degree of sex/gender diversity.

Another important factor is the culturally variable idea of the person. Hinduism, which explicitly recognizes that humans achieve their ultimate goals by following many different paths of life, affords the individual temperament wide latitude in behavior, including gender transformations, thus providing psychic space for the expression of *hijra* transgenderism. In Oman, also, where the social philosophy accepts that people are created with dissimilar natures and are imperfect, like the world itself, a social space is permitted for the mixed-gender role of the *xanith*. *Xanith* status is not considered permanent: If a *xanith* marries and proves his male sexual potency on the wedding night, he will be reclassified as a man. Native American ideologies also give wide scope to individual differences, institutionalizing them in social roles rather than driving them underground. In these and other societies, sexual and gender transformations over a lifetime may be viewed as natural, a perspective that inhibits negative moral evaluations, punishment, or even pressures to conform. Unlike in the West, many societies, for example, in Polynesia, are little concerned with *why* individuals become the way they are or why they change from one role to another.

In addition, the Western emphasis on cultural binaries—nature/culture, male/female, man/woman, and homosexual/heterosexual—is not significant in many cultures. In the West, this ideology has been imposed not only on gender roles and gender identities but on sexual anomalies as well. Thus,

transsexuality became the major category of sex/gender diversity since the 1950s, when individuals who experienced their bodies as incongruent with their gender identity could take advantage of the development of sex reassignment surgery and become members of the *opposite* sex, a form of gender diversity that has gradually been integrated into Western cultures.

Today, however, both *transgenderism* and *intersexuality* are challenging the dominance of transsexualism. These terms cover many different subjective experiences, physical/biological conditions, and outward expressions of gender. Both the transgender and the intersexuality movements reject the hold that psychological and medical professionals have had in defining and "curing" sex/gender diversity. They claim that, among other things, such control violates the predominant American cultural value that enshrines the individual as the autonomous unit of decision making. This view, supported by a human rights agenda, is now going global, appearing, for example, in the expansion of transgender and intersex websites accessible to people throughout the world.

In comparison with transsexualism, transgenderism and intersexuality raise theoretical questions about the influence of culture not just on gender but also on sex—that is, our understanding of what is biological and "natural." The transgender and intersex movements have been empowered by knowledge about sex/gender diversity throughout the world. This increasing knowledge of the "other" has led to a closer look at the constructed nature and assumptions of our own sex/gender system and has resulted in more accommodation for sex/gender diversity.

Serena Nanda

See also Gender and Anthropology

Further Readings

Boelstorff, T. (2005). *The gay archipelago: Sexuality and nation in Indonesia.* Princeton, NJ: Princeton University Press.

Herdt, G. (1996). *Third sex third gender: Beyond sexual dimorphism in culture and history.* New York, NY: Zone Books.

Jackson, P. (1999). *Lady boys, tom boys, rentboys: Male and female homosexualities in contemporary Thailand.* Binghamton, NY: Haworth Press.

Karkazis, K. (2008). *Fixing sex: Intersex, medical authority, and lived experience*. Durham, NC: Duke University Press.

Matzner, A. (2001). *'O au no keia: Voices from Hawai'i's Mahu and transgender community*. Philadelphia, PA: XLibris.

Nanda, S. (2000). *Gender diversity: Crosscultural variations*. Prospect Heights, IL: Waveland Press.

Peletz, M. (2009). *Gender pluralism: Southeast Asia since early modern times*. New York, NY: Routledge.

Reddy, G. (2005). *With respect to sex: Negotiating hijra identity in South India*. Chicago, IL: University of Chicago Press.

Valentine, D. (2007). *Imagining transgender: An ethnography of a category*. Durham, NC: Duke University Press.

Winter, S. (2006). *Transphobia: A price worth paying for gender identity disorder?* Retrieved from Transgender Asia: http://www.transgenderasia.org/

GENE-CULTURE COEVOLUTION

Coevolution refers to a process where two or more different inherited traits affect selection on one another. Some of the most famous cases relate to coevolution between predators and prey or between host-defense mechanisms and parasite virulence. In these examples, both traits are typically expressed as a result of genetic inheritance. By contrast, a prerequisite for gene-culture coevolution is that there are two different tracks of inheritance; one for genetically transmitted information and the other for culturally transmitted information. Gene-culture coevolutionary theory examines the interactions between traits that are derived from these two inheritance systems.

How Genetic and Cultural Inheritance Systems Interact

Many animals can learn from one other. However, learned behavior that is socially transmitted across many generations can in some cases constitute a consistent environment that affects genetic selection. Gene-culture coevolution ensues if there is a statistical association between the differential fitness of genetically inherited variants and culturally inherited variants. For these occasions, either a purely genetic or a purely cultural model underspecifies the evolution of phenotypic variation. Thus, the most parsimonious unit of selection is the combination of each genetic variant and cultural variant, sometimes referred to as the *phenogenotype*.

Necessarily, gene-culture coevolution describes systems where the phenotypic variation under investigation is highly unlikely to be explained only by genetic variation. For instance, while the genetic makeup of humans may contribute to their intelligence, it would be ridiculous to suggest that variation in particular types of farming methods can be explained by genetic variation across human farming populations. Yet different farming technologies can be stably transmitted across generations, and thus modeled as an evolutionary process that is subject to descent with modification.

A gene-culture coevolutionary model is developed by explicitly accounting for (1) the transmission of genetic and cultural variants between generations, accounting for phenogenotype mating probabilities and biases in the pathways of cultural transmission, and (2) the differential fitness of the phenogenotypes per generation. For diploid organisms, genetic information is commonly transmitted vertically, from parents to offspring. Cultural information, however, is often recognized to be transmitted vertically, obliquely (between generations but not from parents to offspring), horizontally (within a generation), or some combination thereof. Gene-culture coevolution requires the stable transmission of cultural variants across generations and thus, typically, is assumed to rely on vertical transmission, oblique transmission, or a mechanism whereby individuals conform to commonly held views or beliefs.

By accounting for both patterns of transmission and fitness, the relative frequency of phenogenotypes can be traced across generations. Initially, gene-culture coevolutionary models were developed by modifying population genetic theory to account for culturally specific forms of inheritance. For instance, the two-locus model can be modified to consider the coevolution of a genetic trait and a cultural trait, in place of two genetic traits at separate loci.

These relatively simple systems were tractable for mathematical analysis and yet yielded a rich set of dynamics that provided predictions distinct from those of equivalent genetic models. This is because the cultural-trait dynamics often behave differently than genetic-trait dynamics. Cultural variants can spread much faster than genetic variants and can alter the rate of genetic evolution. For instance, the effect of farming on available diet is likely to have increased the rate of genetic evolution, affecting physiology and disease resistance. Alternatively, the swift cultural evolution of health interventions can potentially buffer or shield otherwise deleterious genetic variants from selection. Furthermore, patterns of cultural transmission can be biased in ways that are distinct from genetic transmission, altering evolutionary trajectories by modulating the statistical association between the cultural and genetic variants.

Comparisons With Other Approaches

Gene-culture coevolutionary theory has been contrasted with a number of other approaches to explain the evolution of human behavior. The school of human behavioral ecology typically assumes that behavior is adaptive and evolves to maximize lifetime reproductive success, while evolutionary psychologists often assume that psychological predispositions are adaptations to past environments during human evolution. By contrast, gene-culture coevolutionary models are typically minimalist in this regard, as they do not require either assumption to hold.

A second difference from the approaches of these other schools is the explicit distinction between genetic and cultural transmission systems. While many human behavioral ecologists and evolutionary psychologists would not deny that cultural transmission occurs, gene-culture coevolutionary theorists emphasize that some patterns of behavior and psychology are affected by the interactions between genes and culture over evolutionary time.

Cultural Niche Construction and Rapid Genetic Selection of Traits

Since the sequencing of the human genome, a substantial number of genes have been identified as having been subject to rapid and recent selection. Many of these genes have putative functions whose fitness may have been affected by a culturally modified environment, sometimes referred to as *cultural niche construction*, and thus are prime candidates for gene-culture coevolution. The functional domains for these genes include the capacity for learning, forms of intelligence, and the facility for language (e.g., FOXP2). It is easy to envisage that a selective advantage for the capacity for innovation and social learning of adaptive information could coevolve with cumulative adaptive knowledge.

The cultural evolution of some innovations is likely to have affected the recent and rapid genetic evolution of anatomical, physiological, and immune-related traits. For instance, the cultural transmission of cooking techniques and the production of new diets may have affected the selection of genes relating to reduced jaw musculature and metabolism, respectively. Furthermore, it is highly plausible that farming practices and domestication in the Neolithic provoked strong selection in disease susceptibility genes through exposure to infectious and nutritional disease.

Other genes that appear to have been subject to recent, rapid selection contribute to external physical characteristics such as hair, eye, and skin color. These traits may have been subject to selection induced by cultural influences on patterns of human migration, affecting survival in particular physical environments, such as the effect of low–ultra violet rays outside the tropics on selection for skin depigmentation to enhance vitamin D biosynthesis. Also, external features can be subject to sexual selection, coevolving with culturally transmitted mating preferences.

The best known case of gene-culture coevolution is perhaps that of dairy farming and lactase persistence. Following weaning, most mammals, including most humans, cannot digest the sugar lactose, found in unprocessed milk, as they cease production of the enzyme lactase, which helps break down the sugar. However, a small number of independently evolved genetic variants originating in European, African, and Middle Eastern populations allow the persistence of lactose absorption after weaning through continued high production of lactase. For instance, most Europeans are lactose tolerant as a result of a single nucleotide base substitution in a region of the genome that promotes lactase gene activity.

It is now well established that the European genetic variant for lactase persistence spread as a consequence of dairy farming in the Neolithic, approximately 7,500 years ago. Gene-culture coevolutionary models showed that for lactase persistence to spread it was important that there was a high probability of cultural transmission for using dairy products between generations, which would facilitate a statistical association between dairy farming and the genetic variant over evolutionary time.

The coevolutionary explanation was supported further by evidence that dairy farming originated prior to the evolution of lactase-persistent alleles and thus provided the selective environment for the genetic evolution of lactase persistence, and not the other way around. Among dairy farmers, those individuals who exhibit the lactase-persistent variant would be at a selective advantage, benefiting from the consumption of milk—a regular, nutrient-rich, and high-calorie dietary supplement. Thus, the genetic trait and the cultural practice coevolved.

An interesting example of gene-culture coevolution relating farming and disease resistance is found in West African, Kwa-speaking populations of yam cultivators, who cut clearings in forests to grow crops, with a cascade of consequences. The clearings increase the amount of standing water, which provides a better breeding ground for mosquitoes and increases the prevalence of malaria. One consequence of the culturally transmitted farming practice was to provoke genetic selection for malarial resistance in these yam-cultivating populations.

In most human populations, the sickle-cell allele, HbS (sickle hemoglobin), is rare as it results in sickle-cell anemia in its recessive homozygous form (expressed when both gene copies are of type HbS). However, in the heterozygous form (i.e., where only one copy is of type HbS) the sickle-cell allele confers protection against malaria, with only mild sickling of the red blood cells. This heterozygous form is more prevalent in the West African yam-cultivating populations than in neighboring non-yam-cultivating populations, indicating that the cultural practice has coevolved with malarial resistance. Interestingly, the relatively high frequency of sickle cell may actually encourage further yam cultivation, as these crops appear to have medicinal properties circumventing the sickling effects.

The gene-culture coevolutionary system can also apply across species. A classic case is the coevolution of human antibiotic use and bacterial antibiotic-resistant strains. This is effectively a special case of a host-parasite coevolutionary system, where the host behavior, antibiotic use, is culturally derived. Cultural transmission of antibiotic use favors selection of resistant bacterial strains, which in turn can result in cultural selection for the avoidance of antibiotic use. Thus, culturally transmitted host behavior can maintain bacterial strain polymorphism where it would not otherwise be expected.

Possible Derivation of Prosocial Behaviors

Aspects of prosocial behavior, characteristically exhibited in humans more than in other primates, may have been derived through gene-culture coevolution. This argument has been made to explain a number of prosocial features, including a propensity for conformity to norm adherence; strong reciprocity, where the cooperative activity of others is rewarded while norm violators are punished at a cost to the punisher; and parochial altruism, where altruism is only directed within a culturally defined group. These prosocial predispositions can encourage the cultural evolution of symbolic group markers, assortative mating, and low genetic mixing between groups. Genetic selection may then occur on prosocial predispositions across groups. For instance, within-group cooperative behavior can enhance food productivity and also success in between-group conflict. These prosocial predispositions evolve if their benefits, accrued as a consequence of group structure, outweigh their within-group costs. Gene-culture coevolution of prosociality occurs if the fitness advantage of the prosocial genetic predispositions is reliant on the stable cultural inheritance of normative variants that are not themselves prescribed by genetic makeup.

Sex Ratios and Gene-Culture Coevolution

A final example of gene-culture coevolution pertains to the genetic evolution of sex ratio distorter genes and the cultural evolution of preference for sons, manifest, for example, through the neglect of female offspring, sex-selective abortion, or direct (female) infanticide. Sex ratio distorter genes can affect the sex at conception, for instance, by altering the proportion or viability of sperm carrying an X or Y chromosome. The primary sex ratio, that is the fraction of male offspring from a mating prior to any sex-specific mortality, can differ from the adult sex ratio, measured at reproductive age. Gene-culture coevolutionary models have shown that a female-biased primary sex ratio can evolve if parents always increase their proportion of sons by a fixed amount, compensating for loss of daughters by having more children. In this case, the mating success of an excess of sons is less than that of daughters, resulting in an increase in the frequency of female bias distorter genes. Eventually, the strength of parental bias for sons over daughters matches the female-biased primary sex ratio, resulting in an unbiased adult sex ratio (recovering a standard result in sex ratio theory). In contrast, if parents attempt to bring their offspring's sex ratio closer to their ideal preference but without compensating for offspring loss, models predict that the primary sex ratio can become biased until it matches the male-biased preference exhibited in the adult sex ratio. Thereafter, there would be no further sex ratio adjustment by parents as the primary sex ratio matches their ideal preference.

The Future

The future of gene-culture coevolutionary studies lies in examining the possible interactions between culturally transmitted practices and specific genes that have undergone rapid and recent selection. This is a complex, interdisciplinary task, often requiring geneticists, psychologists, archaeologists, anthropologists, demographers, mathematicians, and computer scientists. Cross-population studies are required to identify signatures of genetic selection, and often, complex gene functions need to be established. Meanwhile, archaeological and anthropological data are needed to infer rates of cultural change based on particular patterns of cultural transmission, cognitive biases, and demographic change. Mathematical models and computer simulation studies can then rederive the most likely patterns of genetic and cultural evolution, testing for interactions that suggest gene-culture coevolution.

Jeremy R. Kendal

See also Evolutionary Anthropology; Evolutionary Psychology; Human Behavioral Ecology

Further Readings

Feldman, M. W., & Laland, K. N. (1996). Gene-culture coevolution theory. *Trends in Ecology & Evolution, 11,* 453–457.

Gerbault, P., Liebert, A., Itan, Y., Powell, A., Currat, M., Burge, J., . . . Thomas, M. G. (2011). Evolution of lactase persistence: An example of human niche construction. *Philosophical Transactions of the Royal Society B: Biological Sciences, 366,* 863–877.

Laland, K. N., Kumm, J., & Feldman, M. W. (1995). Gene-culture coevolutionary theory: A test case. *Current Anthropology, 36,* 131–156. (This article describes the sex ratio model)

Laland, K. N., Odling-Smee, J., & Myles, S. (2010). How culture shaped the human genome: Bringing genetics and the human sciences together. *Nature Reviews Genetics, 11,* 137–149.

Perry, G. H., Dominy, N. J., Claw, K. G., Lee, A. S., Fiegler, H., Redon, R., . . . Stone, A. C. (2007). Diet and the evolution of human amylase gene copy number variation. *Nature Genetics, 39,* 1256–1260.

Richerson, P. J., Boyd, R., & Henrich, J. (2010). Gene-culture coevolution in the age of genomics. *Proceedings of the National Academy of Sciences USA, 107,* 8985–8992.

Generative Grammar

As a theory and description of human language, generative grammar (also known as transformational or transformational-generative grammar) conceives of a language as an infinite set of well-formed sentences defined—or "generated" in a mathematical sense—by a series of rules that, collectively, provide for each sentence a multifaceted structural description that includes both the sounds the sentence contains and the meaning that it conveys. On this account, a grammar is to the set of well-formed sentences in a language what the Pythagorean theorem is to the set of well-formed right triangles in a two-dimensional space. Every well-formed right triangle will satisfy the "rule" $x^2 + y^2 = z^2$: The sum of the squares of the lengths of the two sides at right angle to each other (x and y) is equal to the square of the length of the side opposite the right angle (z, which is called the hypotenuse). And every well-formed sentence in a language will satisfy the rules that constitute the generative grammar of that language.

First put forward in 1957 by Noam Chomsky, employing concepts and methods drawn from symbolic logic and mathematics, this formal, set-theoretic approach to language gave rise to numerous revisions and variants in the field of linguistics, but work in social and cultural anthropology has drawn primarily on the fundamental analytical and theoretical principles of generative grammar, described in Chomsky's *Aspects of the Theory of Syntax* (1965) as "a branch of cognitive psychology." In *Aspects,* and virtually all subsequent versions of generative grammar, Phrase Structure Rules specify the internal structure of the words and phrases of a language's sentences without initial reference to their sound or meaning. For example, one type of sentence in

English consists simply of a noun phrase (e.g., *the dog*) followed by a verb phrase (e.g., *ate the food*). A generative grammar can capture this generalization by means of the rule S → NP + VP. To begin generating, or "deriving," a sentence, the grammar applies this rule to "expand" an input symbol S into a three-part syntactic structure that can be graphically presented as a node labeled S (for sentence) dominating two nodes labeled NP (for noun phrase) and VP (for verb phrase):

```
        S
       / \
     NP   VP
```

Other rules can then expand each of the lower nodes in this structure to specify the internal components of the verb phrase (VP → V [for verb] + NP) and the two noun phrases (NP → Det [for determiner] + N [for noun]), to result in the following derivational "tree":

```
        S
       / \
     NP   VP
    /\   /\
  Det N V NP
          /\
        Det N
```

At this point, Lexical Insertion Rules can apply to each of the five bottom-most nodes, to result in the following deep structure:

```
        S
       / \
     NP   VP
    /\   /\
  Det N V NP
  | | |  /\
  | | | Det N
  | | | | |
```

The dog ate the food

Although each of the lexical items appearing in the bottom line of such a structure has semantic (meaning specifying) and phonological (sound specifying) content, additional rules must apply to a deep structure to derive a semantic interpretation or a phonological realization of the sentence. Notice, moreover, that the input to the Phrase Structure Rules—the impetus that triggers the sequential application of the rules of the grammar to derive a well-formed sentence—is *not* a meaning to be expressed, or a string of words to be construed, but rather and simply the abstract symbol S. Once triggered, the rules, if they are correct, generate all and only the well-formed sentences of a language, but they do so in an essentially non-predetermined manner. For example, when the first lexical insertion rule applies in the example above, there is nothing in the derivation at that point to force the insertion of *the* as opposed to *a* or *this* or *that*, or any of a number of other lexical items in the category Det. Similarly, when the next node is reached, any item in the category N might be selected. The grammar in no way provides a basis for generating, when needed, a particular sentence to express an intended meaning, to say nothing of providing, when needed, an analysis or interpretation of a particular input sequence of lexical items.

The term *transformational* or *transformational generative* came to be applied to generative grammars because deep structures typically describe the structural relations among elements in sentences in ways that also describe the identical relations among those elements that occur in sentences with different word orders and word structures. For example, the deep structures of the sentences "The dog ate the food." and "Did the dog eat the food?" might be identical except for the presence of a question marker. Before specifying the phonological forms of the bottom-most nodes in the deep structure of the latter sentence, Transformational Rules would derive, because of the presence of the question marker, a surface structure in which the past tense marking on the verb *ate* is extracted, leaving the verb *eat*, and then moved to first position in the sentence, where it becomes *did*, and then a rising pitch is added to the final word of the sentence to mark it as a yes/no question rather than a statement.

Chomsky carefully and repeatedly explains that a generative grammar does not produce (or understand) utterances. Although Chomsky does not use the analogy to right triangles in a two-dimensional space, he would agree that a grammar generates a language—that is, specifies the membership of the set of sentences in a language—in much the same sense that the Pythagorean theorem generates right triangles. Furthermore, just as the Pythagorean theorem does not pretend to describe how to recognize or draw actual (approximations of) right triangles, so a generative grammar describes neither how to go about achieving an understanding of a particular string of input words nor how to go about expressing a specific intended meaning as a string of words. The rules of a grammar describe, one sentence at a time and in a totally undirected manner, what sounds, words, phrases, and meanings occur in each of the sentences it generates, but not one of these sentences is available on demand. Likewise, the formula $x^2 + y^2 = z^2$ cannot be used to produce or recognize a triangle with the dimensions 3 inches by 4 inches by 5 inches, or any other particular dimensions. Grammars express truths about the sounds, structures, and meanings of a language, but they do not in themselves explain how people manage to say what they mean or to understand what they hear.

Having made this point very clearly, however, Chomsky does go on to posit that (1) linguistic "performance"—the actual production and comprehension of utterances in a language—draws on speakers' and hearers' (tacit) knowledge of the generative grammar of their language, which he calls their linguistic "competence," even though the grammar on its own can only generate sentences in an essentially random manner. He also claims that (2) the grammars of all languages share fundamental structural features, a universal grammar (or UG) innate to the human mind, on which children build the specifics of the generative grammar that underlies a particular language to which the children are exposed.

These two claims—of the psychological reality (as opposed to merely the descriptive truth) of generative grammar and of the innateness of UG—have provoked continued controversy both within linguistics and throughout the biobehavioral and social sciences, and even in the humanities. However, most anthropologists' criticism of the Chomskyan paradigm, as exemplified by the early reactions of John Gumperz and Dell Hymes, has objected less to its psychological and genetic claims than to its arid focus on *structural* norms ("all and only the well-formed sentences of a language"). In its place,

many anthropologists have preferred a richer, more *functional* focus on the rough-and-tumble reality of social discourse and the ethnographic variety of language use, which require, in Hymes's terms, "communicative" as opposed to merely linguistic "competence."

H. Stephen Straight

See also Chomsky, Noam; Gumperz, John J.; Hymes, Dell; Structural Functionalism; Structuralism

Further Readings

Chomsky, N. (1957). *Syntactic structures* (Janua Linguarum, Series Minor, 4). The Hague, Netherlands: Mouton.

———. (1965). *Aspects of the theory of syntax.* Cambridge, MA: MIT Press.

Gumperz, J. J. (1982). *Discourse strategies.* Cambridge, UK: Cambridge University Press.

Hymes, D. H. (1974). *Foundations in sociolinguistics: An ethnographic approach.* Philadelphia: University of Pennsylvania Press.

GENNEP, ARNOLD VAN

Arnold van Gennep (1873–1957), the French ethnographer and folklorist, was a great scholar in the classical sense, a founding figure of both anthropology and folklore studies, in spite of a blocked academic career.

Biography

Van Gennep was born in Württemberg, southwestern Germany, into a Dutch-French family. He was 6 years old when his parents separated, after which he lived in Lyons, where his mother remarried. Such dislocations had a definite impact on van Gennep's character and abilities. Speaking four languages, French, German, English, and Spanish, in childhood, he ended up mastering 18, including Arabic, Finnish, and several Slavic languages. He also became extremely independent, and difficult in school—winning prizes but poor in conduct; he broke away from his family when they opposed his marriage to a beautiful girl without dowry. Independence also marked his academic career, contributing to his marginalization by the followers of Émile Durkheim but helping him persist and produce, without an academic position, some of the most significant studies of his day.

Van Gennep's academic education was atypical by contemporary standards. He graduated in 1896 from the Paris School of Oriental Languages, also having a passion for prehistory, a field that was just emerging at that time, and for numismatics. He came into contact with Antoine Meillet, the great linguist and a member of Durkheim's circle. His familiarity with languages offered him a unique methodological perspective in ethnography, suggesting a practical immersion in sounds and attention paid to roots. This led him to the more general conclusion that knowledge consists in the study of living reality, through understanding the animating forces.

At university, he studied with Léon Marillier, finding his vocation in the study of religious phenomena. This happened at the same time as Durkheim's interest turned to the anthropology of religion, and Marcel Mauss and Henri Hubert both became his university acquaintances. Mauss even became van Gennep's mentor after Marillier died in 1901.

Van Gennep's first book was *Taboo and Totemism in Madagascar* (1904), taken from the first part of his doctoral thesis. It was a thorough study (with more than 360 pages) of the then available ethnographic evidence. Its preface, dated April 1903, ended with warm words of thanks to his friend Mauss, who not only gave him useful advice but even read the proofs. Van Gennep repeatedly cautioned against the imposition of an alien, Western-theoretical perspective on the material. He was particularly critical of the ideas of James G. Frazer, whom he knew personally, visiting him in London and translating his book on totemism (which appeared in 1898), and also of the Scottish Orientalist William Robertson Smith. As Durkheim, Mauss, and Hubert relied much on the works of Frazer and Smith, van Gennep occasionally voiced critical remarks about them as well, in particular concerning the presumed universality of their system of classification, assuming that this would be taken in the spirit of normal scientific practice. He was to be severely disappointed.

Van Gennep's next book, *Myths and Legends of Australia* (1906), consisted of two parts, a substantial (more than 100 pages) introduction followed by translations. Van Gennep argued that in Australia links between myths and rituals are particularly tight, comparable only with Vedic India and Northern America. He also voiced critical remarks concerning the scholarly debate over the primacy of myths or rituals. As Australia was central to the interests of Durkheim and his followers, van Gennep's criticisms multiplied. Beyond finding problematic a number of Durkheim's ideas, such as male-female affiliation or the problem of incest, van Gennep was particularly unhappy about Durkheim's preoccupation with integration, which he considered a modern concept, not presenting difficulties for Australian Aborigines. Other shortcomings van Gennep found in Durkheim's work, going beyond the general problems of Frazer's approach, was that Durkheim was searching for excessive systematicity, imposing a priori categories on the evidence, which prevented understanding, while his emphasis on the "needs" of society, by assigning agency to an abstract category, was transmogrifying the social into a metaphysical object. Such an attack on Durkheimian orthodoxy could not be left unanswered, and Mauss wrote a long and quite critical, though still measured, review of van Gennep's book. In particular, he reasserted the Durkheimian position concerning the classification of myths, legends, and fables, and the nature of Australian totemism.

The conflict escalated into open warfare in the next few years, when both van Gennep and Durkheim published their magnum opuses. Van Gennep's *Rites of Passage* (1909) was a new and original synthesis based on his familiarity with ethnographic material collected throughout the world. The work was also the product of an inner illumination: He had suddenly recognized the ordering principle inherent in the various rites accompanying the individual life cycle and the periodicity of seasons. Durkheim's *Elementary Forms of Religious Life* (1912), on the other hand, was a monumental effort to confirm his theoretical hypotheses, including the idea that Australian Aborigines represent a "laboratory" for the earliest stages of human evolution. Much of the empirical analysis in *Elementary Forms* was entrusted to Mauss, whose in-depth contribution was recognized by close associates.

Rites of Passage received a hostile review from Mauss, who interpreted van Gennep's failure to follow Durkheimian principles as an absence of theoretical work, resulting in a mere amassing of a huge amount of facts. Consequently, Durkheim's 1912 work ignored van Gennep's milestone book. On its publication, *Elementary Forms* also received a large amount of criticism, the most consistent and authoritative being van Gennep's dismissal of the book as a mere theoretical construct, a castle of sand built on shaky facts and further misinterpretation of the evidence.

In 1908, van Gennep founded his own journal, *La Revue des Études Ethnographiques et Sociologiques*, and in 1912, he became chair for ethnography at the University of Neuchâtel. There he threw himself into work, organizing a major conference for the summer of 1914. More than 600 social scientists showed up from around Europe, with Mauss leading the French delegation and delivering a paper. Durkheim was absent, just as—for a different reason—were all British scholars. However, van Gennep was again sorely disappointed: The conference all but coincided with the outbreak of World War I, and—as he protested the Swiss partiality to Germany in the war—in 1915, he was deprived of his chair and expelled from Switzerland. Through Mauss, he appealed to Durkheim, the unchallenged ruler of relevant French academic appointments, for help finding an academic position, but van Gennep had offended Durkheim and would never hold a university position in France.

The direction of van Gennep's work was significantly altered in the mid-1920s. He gave up interest in comparative ethnography, even burning his notes, and devoted all his efforts to collecting and studying French folklore. This work resulted in the monumental multivolume *Manual of Contemporary French Folklore*, widely considered a milestone of 20th-century French social science. Van Gennep published two volumes of reference material in 1937–1938, and was hoping to finish the work in two further volumes, on life cycle and periodical rites. Instead, he ended up publishing two volumes on the cycles of human life itself, in 1943 and 1946, with further volumes about the seasonal calendar coming out in 1947, 1949, 1951, and 1953. Van Gennep managed to proofread the seventh volume, which was published posthumously in 1958, while an eighth volume based on his notes came out in 1988. The entire work, together with a series of precious unpublished notes and a comprehensive bibliography, was republished in 1999.

Major Works

Van Gennep emphasized the fundamental unity of humankind, opposing the dichotomization of nature and society and considering the division between ethnography and folklore as artificial. Still, partly due to the necessity of specialization and partly due to his problems with academic life, his lifework came to be divided into two main periods: The central concern of the first was comparative ethnography, culminating in *Rites of Passage*, while the second was fully devoted to French folklore, resulting in the *Manual*.

Rites of Passage

While van Gennep's book is not theoretical in the neo-Kantian and neopositivist sense, it has philosophical depth, revealing an ontology embedded in the rites. Social life consists of a plethora of autonomous social groups and spheres of existence. Passage between them poses problems, whose handling requires ceremonies to assist and mediate. Passages can take place in space, such as by travel between different villages and countries. Rites of passage can also take place in time, whether related to the individual life cycle, from birth through childhood, adolescence, and marriage up to old age and death, or the periodicity of nature, with its seasons, where rites of passage gain cosmic connotation. All such rites have a sequential structure, consisting of separation, then a temporary, transitory existence on the limit or margin, and then reintegration. This sequential structure was van Gennep's central theoretical innovation; but far from proclaiming originality, he acknowledged that Robert Hertz had developed the idea before him.

The central part of rites of passage is the time spent on the limit. The acts of crossing the limit and being on the limit are both symbolic and material: Crossing a threshold transforms one's mode of existence, implying something mysterious and involving a deep symbolic meaning. Yet, at the same time, it is very material, a real and concrete passing through, with time spent on the borderline. The limit is usually a zone, not just a line, though the breadth of such limit zones and the amount of time spent there varies according to rites and cultures. Crossing limits is a sacred activity, but the location of the sacred varies according to one's place within the rite. This is why the figure of the "stranger" takes up such a prominent place in rites of passage, closely associated with the sacred.

Most of the book is a meticulous study of various rites of passage, focusing on the individual life cycle.

Of particular interest is the study of funerary rites; the dead and mourners belong to a special, transitory mode of existence, in between life and death, being preoccupied with the eventuality that a dead individual not properly accompanied to the other world might be stuck in his or her condition, becoming revengeful and threatening to the living. Such sequentiality and cyclicality of human life, as van Gennep makes it evident both at the start and at the end of the work, has cosmic significance. Passages between social groups and across human life imitate and reflect the great cosmic rhythms of existence. Not accidentally, the last word of the book is *universe*, which in his own copy he eventually capitalized.

Manual of French Folklore

Preoccupation with the cosmic nature of rites of passage is evident in the *Manual*, which is more than a simple collection of material. Periodical rites predominate, a fact commented on both in the text and in a series of posthumous notes, intended for a conclusion that was never completed. Folklore is different from history; it rather reflects the living spirit of a particular culture, the vital dynamism of a people that even events like the French Revolution could not alter. Its inherent perspective and sensitivity is aesthetic rather than scientific, being oriented toward beauty, integrity, and gracefulness—not utilitarian, functionalist, or technologically efficient; yet it contains and reflects an entire philosophy of existence that is in harmony with the great rhythms of cosmic cycles; thus, it is more lasting and real than modern artificial constructs. Toward the end of his life, van Gennep increasingly became interested in the dramatic character of rites, arguing that they reveal the deep dramatic instinct of the French people, and tentatively compared this with those of various other European nations.

Van Gennep's Legacy

Van Gennep and his writings were shunned by many in Durkheim's circle, in spite of his close affinity and mutual respect with several members (Mauss, Meillet, and Lucien Lévy-Bruhl). His influence in anthropology started after the English translation of *Rites of Passage* (1960), owing to the efforts of Solon Kimball and also thanks to E. E. Evans-Pritchard and Rodney Needham. Victor Turner also

played a central role when he chanced on the book in 1963 and suddenly recognized that it held the key to the anthropology he was searching for. Through Turner's notion of *liminality*, an ingenious translation of van Gennep's term *marge*, van Gennep's perspective has been increasingly used in a range of social and human sciences, though its broader philosophical implications have rarely been explored.

Arpad Szakolczai

See also Durkheim, Émile; Frazer, James G.; Hertz, Robert; Lévy-Bruhl, Lucien; Mauss, Marcel; *Rites de Passage*; Smith, William Robertson; Turner, Victor W.

Further Readings

Belmont, N. (1974). *Arnold van Gennep: Créateur de l'ethnographie française* [Foundations in sociolinguistics: An ethnographic approach]. Paris, France: Payot.

Thomassen, B. (2009). The uses and meanings of liminality. *International Political Anthropology, 2*(1), 5–28.

———. (2012). Émile Durkheim between Gabriel Tarde and Arnold van Gennep: Founding moments of sociology and anthropology. *Social Anthropology, 20*(3), 231–249.

Zumwalt, R. L. (1982). Arnold van Gennep: The hermit of Bourg-la-Reine. *American Anthropologist, 84*, 299–313.

———. (1988). *The enigma of Arnold van Gennep (1873–1957): Master of French folklore and hermit of Bourg-la-Reine*. Helsinki, Finland: Suomalainen Tiedeakatemia.

GIFT EXCHANGE

Few assumptions have a more powerful hold on both the Western academic and the public imagination than a vision of human nature based on the norms of market economic exchange. Consequently, it is unsurprising that questioning the universality of this model of exchange has been a major theme for a discipline like anthropology, in which the critique of such assumptions has always been important.

Early Theorists of Gift Exchange: Malinowski and Mauss

The first major development in a theory of gift exchange was Bronisław Malinowski's *Argonauts of the Western Pacific*. At its heart is a lengthy description of a network of exchange of shells known as the *kula*, which linked many of the Trobriand Islands of eastern New Guinea. Rather than aiming to maximize the shells in their possession, *kula* traders gained respect by passing items along the circuit. This may have seemed irrational from the perspective of economic individualism, but according to Malinowski, it was entirely rational in a context where authority and respect depended on the number of trading relationships that one could enter into.

This perspective was developed in Marcel Mauss's essay *The Gift*, which brought together Malinowski's description of the *kula* and accounts of other gift exchange networks. In *The Gift*, Mauss outlined three obligations that he claimed characterize the exchange of gifts: (1) the obligation to give, (2) the obligation to receive, and (3) the obligation to return. These obligations are morally charged, creating ongoing enduring bonds of interdependence between those engaged in their circulation.

Elements of Mauss's essay seemed to suggest that he saw gift exchange, and the bonds of enduring reciprocal interdependence that it established, as a fundamental element in establishing the social solidarity that was so important to his uncle and collaborator, the sociologist Émile Durkheim. As Marshall Sahlins was later to observe, a major part of Mauss's aim was to tackle the problem of how people could live together with a degree of harmony and mutual obligation in the absence of the kind of strong repressive state championed in Western political theory from Hobbes onward. As a consequence, much of the anthropological development of gift theory after Mauss had a tendency to describe how gift exchange produced self-contained and self-reproducing social systems. The *kula*, at least as Malinowski had described it, seemed to provide a template for this conception, with its fixed and bounded circuits of exchange through which men who were separated by vast distances were still bound together in ties that ideally could never be broken.

Structuralism and Gift Exchange

The Gift was as important to Claude Lévi-Strauss's structuralist anthropology as the Saussurian model of linguistics from which he took the model of underlying structural grammars. For Lévi-Strauss, Maussian reciprocity was one of the fundamental structuring principles of the human mind, shaping consciousness and culture. In particular, kinship systems, which were viewed by most anthropologists as the basis of social organization in "non-Western" societies, were analyzed by Lévi-Strauss as the most important manifestation of this cognitive structure. In Lévi-Strauss's model, systems of "bride exchange" in which women acted as the "supreme gift" moved the focus of kinship studies away from "descent" toward an analysis of how ongoing "alliances" created between groups through marriage exchange formed the basis of social solidarity.

Lévi-Strauss's reading made Maussian reciprocity as fundamental to a universal human nature as the free market individual had been to the neoclassical economic theory that Malinowski had set out to critique in *Argonauts*. However, it was a fundamental drive that varied depending on cultural context. Lévi-Strauss detailed the ways in which different kinds of marriage rules dictated different kinds of social structures, while Mauss's student Louis Dumont developed Lévi-Strauss's analysis of exchange marriage into a cornerstone of his analysis of the Indian caste system. Other notable anthropologists, such as Mary Douglas and Marshall Sahlins, made gift exchange into a cornerstone of analyses of social structures that could be contrasted with the individualism of Western society, as Dumont had done in his contrast between Indian "holism" and Western "individualism."

During the heyday of structuralism in the 1960s and 1970s, there were other anthropologists who focused more on the interplay between different spheres of exchange that coexisted in the same social situation. Most noteworthy was Paul Bohannan's analysis of different spheres of exchange among the Tiv people of West Africa. Bohannan claimed that the Tiv had three distinct spheres of exchange: (1) everyday items, (2) wealth items, and (3) marriageable female relatives. Different moralities of exchange governed each sphere, and conversion of wealth between spheres was difficult. Although it was possible to present this kind of division of social life into different spheres as building a stable, self-replicating structure, changes in the wider political economic context carried the possibility of altering or dissolving the boundaries between spheres. Bohannan argued that this had occurred among the Tiv with the introduction of Western money, which broke down the barriers between the three spheres of exchange owing to money's nature as a universal medium of exchange. Other anthropologists in this period, most notably Fredrik Barth, also focused on the importance of borders and the conversion of value between different spheres of exchange.

The Poststructural Era

As structuralism fell out of favor in the 1970s and 1980s, other analyses of exchange came to the fore. Pierre Bourdieu's focus on the timing of return gifts was an attempt to overcome the potential deterministic pitfalls of structuralism by showing the artistry and gamesmanship that go into making gifts socially effective. Chris Gregory observed that Marx's description of commodity exchanges as transitory and impersonal transactions conducted between persons in a state of independence from each other could easily be contrasted with the Maussian gift's tendency to create ongoing ties of personal interdependence. Gregory's work drew attention to the way in which gifts and commodities coexisted and indeed could be converted into each other, so that an item that was traded as a commodity in one context could be exchanged as a gift in another. Like Bohannan's model, Gregory's model sought to explain social change, but Gregory stressed the ways in which Western-produced commodities had been incorporated into Melanesian gift exchange systems. Maurice Bloch and Jonathan Parry subsequently continued this challenge to Bohannan's assumption of the unidirectional transformative power of money and Western commodities.

Gregory's reading of Mauss hit a nerve at a time when the emphasis in anthropological theory was increasingly on models that sought to explain social change in a globally interconnected world. But almost immediately it was reinterpreted in ways that its author would not have recognized, both by its critics and by those who sought to build on its theoretical architecture. The 1980s saw the rise to prominence of postcolonial and poststructuralist approaches in anthropology, and from this perspective, any attempt to construct theoretical models on the basis of opposed categories, such as gift and commodity, seemed redolent of an old-fashioned structuralism that was best abandoned. Arjun Appadurai's introduction to *The Social Life of Things* led the intellectual attack on the gift/commodity distinction. For Appadurai, this had become an oversimplified conceptual division that

both romanticized "small-scale" societies and overlooked the fact that Western societies operated in part according to "cultural" norms and not just economic rationality. For Appadurai, it was better to characterize all forms of exchange as varieties of commodity exchange, instead of relying on what were now seen as outdated opposed categories. Appadurai's critics were quick to point out that belief in the universality of commodity exchange could be seen as a return to faith in the universality of economic rationalism. In addition, it left him arguing that some commodities were more "commodified" than others, which to his critics appeared to be a fundamental logical inconsistency.

Others took Gregory's gift/commodity distinction in the opposite direction, using it as the basis for precisely the kind of distinction between Western and non-Western cultures that Appadurai had found so problematic. Marilyn Strathern used it to draw a comparison between Western and Melanesian societies. In the former, the predominance of commodity exchange was tied to the predominance of a conception of the person as a self-contained discrete individual whose existence was prior to the relations that he or she entered into, while in the latter, the predominance of gift exchange was linked to a conception of the person made up of the relations of ongoing reciprocal obligation within which he or she was entangled. Whereas Bohannan had assumed the culturally transformative power of money, Strathern's followers seemed to take the opposing transformation of the power of Melanesian customary ritual to transform commodities into gifts as their starting point, leading to an expectation of underlying cultural continuity.

Strathern was adamant that her model was not a description of how all Melanesians (or indeed all Westerners) thought in all contexts but rather an ideal-type contrast. Nonetheless, it seemed to be taken as a return to a Dumontian-style contrast between two different societies—both by supporters, for whom it proved the continued fruitfulness of this kind of anthropology, and by detractors, for whom it was an example of the kind of Orientalism that anthropology urgently needed to transcend. Meanwhile, for Gregory and those committed to a historical political economy, there was an equal sense of confusion that their approach seemed to have been read as the basis for an ahistorical contrast of cultures by opponents and followers alike.

Conclusion

The debates around how to analyze exchange that characterized 20th-century anthropology carry on into attempts to make sense of the pressing concerns of the 21st century, such as the role of financial markets in public life. Some anthropologists point out that the ways in which even Wall Street operates according to cultural codes mean that we should be wary of dividing the world into commodity and noncommodity spheres of exchange. Others argue that if there is one thing that characterizes popular anxieties about contemporary neoliberalism, it is concern about where the limits of market rationality are drawn. This might suggest that understanding the ways in which exchange practices are shaped by the ways in which those participating in them morally evaluate them is key to anthropological analysis. In particular, the ways in which participants to exchanges themselves evaluate those exchanges as ideally belonging in separate categories remains important. From this perspective, the distinction between gift and commodity is partially dependent on social perspective and is the outcome of ongoing social contest rather than the expression of a fixed cultural order. This focus can be traced back to Mauss, for whom getting the right balance between the logic of the gift and the logic of the market was a political battle of immense importance. It can even be found among Malinowski's *kula* traders, who would dispute among themselves whether a man was really conducting *kula* or was in fact conducting *gimwali*: a less prestigious form of barter carried out for material gain that looked a lot more like commodity exchange.

Perspectives that stress the ways in which sharply divergent moral evaluations of exchange practices shape those very practices seem to be gaining purchase in contemporary anthropological debates, perhaps as a consequence of the current economic crisis, which has brought these issues back to the forefront of public attention. It remains to be seen how strong and long lasting this trend is, but it is clear that the long-running fascination with exchange and the debates concerning its nature, which have characterized much of the most important anthropological theory of the past 100 years, still have some way left to run.

Keir Martin

See also Appadurai, Arjun; Barth, Fredrik; Bloch, Maurice; Bohannan, Paul; Bourdieu, Pierre; Douglas, Mary; Dumont, Louis; Durkheim, Émile; Economic Anthropology; Lévi-Strauss, Claude; Malinowski, Bronisław; Mauss, Marcel; Sahlins, Marshall; Strathern, Marilyn

Further Readings

Appadurai, A. (Ed.). (1986). *The social life of things.* Cambridge, UK: Cambridge University Press.

Bohannan, P., & Bohannan, L. (1968). *Tiv economy.* Evanston, IL: Northwestern University Press.

Gregory, C. (1982). *Gifts and commodities.* London, UK: Academic Press.

Lévi-Strauss, C. (1969). *The elementary structures of kinship.* London, UK: Eyre & Spottiswoode.

Malinowski, B. (1922). *Argonauts of the western Pacific.* London, UK: Routledge.

Mauss, M. (1954). *The gift.* London, UK: Cohen & West.

GILLEN, FRANCIS JAMES

See Spencer, Walter Baldwin, and Francis James Gillen

GIRARD, RENÉ

René Girard, the French literary and cultural theorist, is one of the most influential thinkers of the 20th century. He has had a marked and lasting impact on cultural and literary theory, an influence that shows few signs of abating.

Biography and Major Works

Girard was born on December 25, 1923, in Avignon, France. After obtaining his baccalaureate in philosophy at the Lycée of Avignon, he attended the École des Chartes in Paris, graduating as an *archiviste-paléographe* (medievalist) in 1947. Girard then moved to the United States and, in 1950, received his PhD in modern history from Indiana University. While at Indiana, Girard was asked—on account of his nationality—to teach courses on French literature. Such was his fascination with the novels that he was asked to teach that a decade later he would make his mark as a literary critic. In his debut theoretical work, *Deceit, Desire and the Novel* (1961), Girard argued that in certain works of literature—works he termed "novelistic"—there existed a conception of human desire that had more lucidity than most properly theoretical accounts of desire. Girard's contention is that novelistic works reveal a desire to be "mimetic"—that is, fundamentally imitative. Rather than desire emanating from the preferences or appetites of a sovereign, individual will, humans take their cues as to what to desire from others who model that desire for them. This, however, raises the possibility that our desires will lead us into conflict as subjects converge on the same object.

The next stage of Girard's work occurred just over 10 years later, with the publication of *Violence in the Sacred* in 1972. Here, Girard shifted his thinking into the anthropological domain. In his literary analyses, Girard indicated the ways in which intensifications of conflictual desire lead toward a certain kind of "doubling" of adversaries: As antagonists intensify their conflicts, they come more and more to resemble each other. In *Violence and the Sacred*, this analysis of doubling and dedifferentiation is extended to the cultural domain: That is, what may begin as a conflict between a small number of adversaries may soon extend to incorporate whole communities. Girard contended that what eventually arrests this slide into unanimous violence and antagonism is a nonconscious polarization around a victim—or group of victims—who is thought to be responsible for the disorder afflicting the community. A mimesis of *appropriation* is replaced, in other words, by a mimesis of *accusation*. The lynching or expulsion of a scapegoat has the effect of reconciling the community and generating an *esprit de corps* that, post hoc, justifies the lynching in the mob's eyes. Girard argues that many of the signal features of culture—perhaps even culture itself—is the result of this "surrogate victimage mechanism."

The last stage in Girard's work involves his consideration of the Judeo-Christian scriptures. In *Things Hidden Since the Foundation of the World* (1978)—a dialogue between Girard and two psychiatrists, Jean-Michel Oughourlian and Guy Lefort—Girard sets out his work to date, including a new theory about the role of the Judeo-Christian scriptures in culture. Girard's contention is that, despite the highly ambivalent historical legacy of institutional Christianity, the Judeo-Christian texts work to expose and undermine surrogate victimage. In a

thesis that parallels aspects of Friedrich Nietzsche's in *The Genealogy of Morals*, Girard argues that the Bible is preeminently a victim literature: Unlike the culture that they displaced, biblical texts narrate cultural violence from the viewpoint of the *victims* of that violence rather than the perpetrators. Despite their impact, the historical import of the Judeo-Christian texts has, Girard suggests, very often gone unnoticed—or been entirely misunderstood.

Critical Contributions to Anthropology (Social Thought)

From the appearance of *Violence and the Sacred*, Girard began to be known as a broadly "anthropological" theorist. His engagement with anthropology has been extended and extensive, and he has framed his analyses of culture in terms of three central anthropological categories: (1) myth, (2) ritual (primarily identified with sacrifice), and (3) prohibition. Like Émile Durkheim, Girard insists on the coevalness of the social and religious domains. Girard argues that the sacred is the primary expression of social order rather than something that is added to the social as a sort of "supplement" or epiphenomenon.

One of Girard's key interlocutors has been Claude Lévi-Strauss. Girard has expressed appreciation of structuralist anthropology's thesis that there are generative structures that exist independently of individual human will and that mythology is, in an important sense, "differential thought." However, he has questioned both Lévi-Strauss and Durkheim for their refusal to countenance how the sacred or differential thought is generated in the first place. If the sacred is a transcendent expression of social order or a privileged plan of differential thought, Girard wants to raise the possibility of giving a morphogenetic account of culture—to understand the mechanism by which the sacred and differential thoughts arise in the first place. He does this through his theory of surrogate victimage, which is not merely an attempt to explain the signal features of culture but an account of hominization—of the emergence of the human from animal in the natural history of the species.

As a hermeneutic or heuristic device in empirical anthropology, Girard's theories have yet to be fully tested, although there are marked exceptions. Perhaps most notable here is Simon Simonse's fieldwork in the Sudan.

Girard's Legacy

Since the publication of *Things Hidden Since the Foundation of the World*, all of Girard's work has been a tracing out, an elaboration, of the three lines of his work: (1) mimetic desire, (2) surrogate victimage, and (3) the Judeo-Christian scriptures. This is not to say, however, that his intellectual labors have involved a simple restatement of earlier hypotheses. Recent work of Girard's has, for instance, involved a detailed reading of Carl von Clausewitz's *On War* (in *Battling to the End*) and a novel interpretation of the role of victimage and sacrifice in the Vedas (in *Sacrifice*).

Girard's work has had an impact on a wide variety of disciplines and interdisciplinary work. In a significant series of publications, Eric Gans, for instance, has elaborated a comprehensive theory of the origin of language and culture. Another line of thought has been taken up by Jean-Pierre Dupuy and colleagues at Stanford and the Centre de Recherche Epistémologie Appliquée in Paris; they have utilized Girard's work in their theories on self-organizing systems. Michel Aglietta and André Orléan have applied Girard's work to economics and financial markets. Oughourlian has applied Girard's work in psychiatry and theories of psychopathology. In addition, there have been extended forays in disciplines across the humanities: theology (Raymund Schwager and James Alison), philosophy (Michel Serres and Gianni Vattimo), and literary criticism (Sandor Goodhart, Cesáreo Bandera, and Andrew McKenna). Girard's seminal contribution to the humanities was recognized in 2005 with his election as an "immortal" to the Académie Française.

Chris Fleming

See also Durkheim, Émile; Lévi-Strauss, Claude; Sacrifice; Structuralism

Further Readings

Cowdell, S., Fleming, C., & Hodge, J. (Eds.). (2012). *Violence, desire, and the sacred: Girard's mimetic theory across the disciplines*. New York, NY: Continuum.

Fleming, C. (2004). *René Girard: Violence and mimesis*. Cambridge, UK: Polity Press.

Gans, E. (1997). *Signs of paradox: Irony, resentment, and other mimetic structures*. Stanford, CA: Stanford University Press.

Girard, R. (1966). *Deceit, desire and the novel* (Y. Freccero, Trans.). Baltimore, MD: Johns Hopkins University Press.

———. (1977). *Violence and the sacred* (P. Gregory, Trans.). Baltimore, MD: Johns Hopkins University Press.

———. (with Oughourlian, J.-M., & Lefort, G.). (1987). *Things hidden since the foundation of the world* (S. Bann & M. Metteer, Trans.). Stanford, CA: Stanford University Press.

———. (2010). *Battling to the end: Conversations with Benoît Chantre* (M. Baker, Trans.). East Lansing: Michigan State University Press.

———. (2011). *Sacrifice* (M. Pattillo & D. Dawson, Trans.). East Lansing: Michigan State University Press.

Goodhart, S. (1996). *Sacrificing commentary: Reading the end of literature*. Baltimore, MD: Johns Hopkins University Press.

Oughourlian, J.-M. (2010). *The genesis of desire* (E. Webb, Trans.). East Lansing: Michigan State University Press.

Schwager, R. (1987). *Must there be scapegoats? Violence and redemption in the Bible* (M. L. Assad, Trans.). San Fransisco, CA: Harper & Row.

Simonse, S. (1992). *Kings of disaster: Dualism, centralism and the scapegoat king in the southeastern Sudan*. Leiden, Netherlands: E. J. Brill.

GLOBALIZATION THEORY

There are two quite different approaches to the understanding of the global. The first, dating to the work of Fernand Braudel, is based on a systemic perspective in which globalization is a particular historical phase linked to the decline of hegemonic centers and the rise of new hegemonies financed by the export of wealth from the declining areas. The second tends to see globalization as a historical era understood in evolutionary terms, in which the entire world is united in a complex of cultural flows, the latter referring to the diffusion of dominant ideas, technology, identities, and so forth, and their mixture in a quasi-evolutionary moment of change.

The popularity of globalization as a topic is clearly a social fact, but it is not clear that its intellectual content warrants such popularity. This uncertainty is the starting point for the following discussion, in which the popularity of the term is dealt with as a social phenomenon, its content is analyzed in terms of its intellectual shortcomings, and a larger framework of analysis is suggested to comprehend both of these issues. This reflection begins with relatively early work, both within anthropology and elsewhere, that considers things that we can call "global." Next is a presentation of important aspects of the more contemporary uses of globalization, primarily in anthropology but also in adjacent disciplines. This presentation will suggest that much of the key work on globalization is not empirical and analytical but clearly normative, which is expressive of the distinctive social location of some of the authors of important writings about globalization and at least an identification with a particular cosmopolitan discourse. Finally, the entry will consider the conceptual confusion that exists in those writings; this discussion will draw on a different way of approaching the global, one that springs from some of the ideas described in the following section, the prehistory of the concept.

Foundations

The idea of the global was imported into anthropology from outside the discipline. It was a concept that had acquired its meaning in part as a reflection of a number of approaches that were circulating among various sets of people who shared a broad orientation toward political economy. These included dependency theory, imperialism theory, the new world division of labor, world-systems theory, and various related debates that took place primarily among Marxist economists.

These approaches differed in significant ways. However, they had in common a growing attention to the idea that society, the focus of social theory generally, could not be approached adequately if the connections between societies were ignored. Social scientists had not, of course, ignored those connections. The now largely forgotten school of diffusionism was built on a presumption of such connections, and Bronisław Malinowski's (1922) *Argonauts of the Western Pacific* placed Kiriwina firmly in its regional context. At the same time, it is true that attention to these connections varied over time and was particularly low in the 1940s and 1950s, when both functionalism and neo-evolutionism assumed society as the explanatory totality. Against this background, the stress on the connections between societies found in dependency theory and its fellows was novel and salutary.

In the 1970s, these sorts of approaches began to have a visible impact in anthropology, mostly under the name of world-systems theory. It marked the development of those older approaches as well as the incorporation of the French *Annales* school, primarily the work of Braudel. This approach appears in the work of sociologists such as Immanuel Wallerstein, Stuart Hall, and Christopher Chase-Dunn and economists such as Andre Gunder Frank. It appears as well in the work of some anthropologists, such as Eric Wolf, Kajsa Ekholm, and Jonathan Friedman, who saw the existence of global systems as historically more significant than the recent history of Western capitalism. For the latter, global systems were the basis of ancient as well as modern civilizations, and the global approach was one in which local populations were understood as constituted loci within larger reproductive processes rather than autonomous actors that forged *external* relations, after the fact.

The 1980s marked the decline of formerly dominant materialist as well as modernist approaches in the social sciences. The more salient forms of imperialism theory (dependency, center-periphery as fixed relationships) declined sharply even as historically oriented global-systemic approaches were taking root. At about the same time, we can see the beginnings of the approach that is concerned with what is now called "globalization." This emerged from a number of sources but generally was not an extension of the older world-systems approach, with its broadly Marxist political economy. Rather, much of it reflects the work of liberal business economists, especially Keniche Ohmae. It was an expression of a real change in the configuration of the world, but an expression that was far less critical than the older approaches. That change in the world was the product of a huge wave of capital export from the old centers in the United States and Europe to other parts of the world, especially to East and South Asia. The processes that underlay this change were understood in fairly evolutionary terms; what was construed as a world of enclosed nation-states was seen as being supplanted by what was construed as an open world.

As the term caught on in the media, it seemed to make sense to many academics. For instance, in economic and cultural geography, a number of works appeared in the 1980s concerned with globalization. Some geographers, such as David Harvey, continued the older Marxist analysis. However, others moved in a more liberal direction (e.g., Nigel Thrift), and some of them appear to have adopted an evolutionary local-to-global perspective. Such an approach appeared fairly justified if one looks at the changes that had occurred since World War II, but it was less secure if one took account of longer term trends.

The growing scholarly attention to these changes in the world took other forms in other fields. In the 1970s, the concept of cultural imperialism attracted attention, linked to the dominance of the United States in the larger world. In cultural sociology in the 1980s, this merged into a number of debates surrounding George Ritzer's so-called McDonaldization thesis, of the emergence of a single, homogenized world. From the end of the 1980s, sociologists concerned with these issues were influential, including Roland Robertson and his work on cultural globalization and, later, Manuel Castells, with his encyclopedic and more holistic sociological work on the emergence of "network society," a post-Fordist world that is no longer vertically organized but is horizontal and fragmented. The decay of the older order was given important expression in the work of Saskia Sassen on global cities. She discerned a world moving away from large-scale central and peripheral regions. Instead, center and periphery increasingly were to be found in specific urban zones throughout the world. Cities replace the nation-state as the new global actor, and the Third World is no longer "out there"; rather, it is next door (a notion that had also been embraced by Braudel for early-modern Europe).

More influential in anthropology was the development of cultural studies, especially postcolonial cultural studies. Writers in this emerging field claimed that the more conventional approaches in the humanities and social sciences were distorted by the influence of the nation-state, especially in its Western form. In their assertions, these writers promoted a vocabulary of globalization, relegating what they saw as expressions of essentialism, homogeneity, ethnic absolutism, and national bias to the dustbin, to be replaced by new terms, more suited to the world that was emerging: the globalized world, in the form of the transnational and postnational, the hybrid, the creole, border crossing, and so on.

The Discourse of Globalization

In anthropology, a discourse on globalization emerged in the 1980s and 1990s, associated especially with

the work of Arjun Appadurai and Ulf Hannerz and with the journal *Public Culture*. These and subsequent anthropologists take globalization to be a new phenomenon that has occurred in their own lifetimes, and what they describe is often a direct expression of their personal experience of a changing world. They argue that we are entering a new era in which the world is, finally, a single place. People, information, money, and technology all flow around the globe in disjunctive circuits that bring us all together in a *hybrid* if somewhat fragmented world culture.

The primary characteristics of this approach to emerging globalization can be listed as follows:

- The world was once organized into separate cultural units.
- As a result of globalization, these units, whether ethnic groups or nations, mix with one another in new creole or hybrid forms, both of people and of their cultures.
- The relations between different locations has become so intense that the world has come to consist of networks of relations that link substate actors in a new world of transnational populations and cultures.
- This is an evolutionary movement from a former mosaic of localized places to a world of intermixture. Although not always clearly stated, the main cause is changes in technology, especially the effects of new information technologies.
- The increasing transnational "flows" weaken the nation-state. For some writers, this transcendence of the homogeneous nation-state by the new global hybridity is morally progressive.
- Anthropology must be refashioned to study the new flows and processes that transcend the old nation-state.

Predicaments of Globalization Discourse

It is important to understand the emergence of discourses of globalization in terms of their social context, especially where they take the form "globalism," the embrace and advocacy of globalization and its fruits (e.g., cosmopolitanism). This embrace of the transnational, border crossing, and the postnational is more a classificatory or interpretative device used by intellectuals than it is a product of research into the realities of the global-local arena. For instance, globalist writers have virtually nothing to say about how borders and boundaries are constituted, a silence that is significant given that one cannot cross boundaries unless they already exist.

There is also an evolutionary assumption within this emerging model of globalization that seems to have become doxa for many scholars writing about globalism. This is the notion that the move from the local to the global marks a move to a higher stage of world history. Just as with the older notion of civilization, those who belong to the global are truly *évolué* (a term used by the French to refer to the more educated and assimilated members of their subject populations). Such people have left the parochial masses behind and have entered the new world of the cosmopolitan, in which all the familiar values of humanism, democracy, and human rights have been modified so that they fit a new cosmopolitan position. For those in that position, the most serious problems faced by modern societies are found in their own, downwardly mobile, national populations. Echoing the older notion of *dangerous classes*, those populations are becoming too local, even xenophobic. The discourse of globalism thus has a strong ideological component, what Friedman called a "global vulgate," which contains definitions of reality that, it appears, are assumed to be obvious and unassailable, not subject to debate, much less research.

The globalist vulgate, then, has an individualist orientation that sees boundaries and borders as denials of uniformitarian collectivity and its presumed benefits. As critique, that vulgate rejects those boundaries and borders by celebrating what crosses them (let us call it the Trans-X): the translocal, the transcultural, and the transnational. This rhetoric of rejection can be traced down to the human body and its transgressions. Trans-X discourse deconstructs supposedly pure or homogeneous categories to reveal their artificial nature, and in this, it entails a logical relation between the trans-X and the hybrid or creole. That is because the hybrid and the creole result from the movement of culture throughout the world, trans-X-wise. Because the vulgate misperceives the idea of the nation-state as referring to a homogeneous entity, for globalists that homogeneity denies the real heterogeneity. Two models explain how this emerging trans-X uniformity comes about. One, partially suggested by Homi Bhabha

and Mahmoud Mamdani, is that hybridity existed before the Western, modernist, colonial imposition of national uniformity. With the decline of colonialism, the true hybridity of the world is returning. The other model is the "leaky mosaic" proposed by Friedman in 1994. Both of these models portray the world as having changed profoundly. Our old categories of place, locality, culture, and even society have been displaced by hybridity, translocality, movement, and, to use Deleuze and Guattari's terminology, rhizomes. However, this globalist assertion might well be, as suggested above, an expression of the experiential world of cultural elites and other traveling intellectuals, an experience that is presaged and reinforced by the representations of internationalized media and international networks of media managers, politicians, diplomats, and global organizations. If this is so, globalism can be understood as a socially positioned discourse, that of certain elites whose relation to the earth is one of consumerist distance and objectification. Theirs is the bird's-eye view of the multiethnic bazaar or ethnic neighborhood, and they marvel at the fabulous jumble of cultural differences that they see. Hybridity is, thus, the sensual, and especially the visual, appropriation of a space of cultural difference, a space that may be quite different for those who inhabit that space.

The political, ideological aspect of globalism is apparent in the writing of its adherents, such as Appadurai's statement in 1993 that "we need to think ourselves beyond the nation." John Kelly elaborates on this in the context of an article in *Public Culture* in 1995, in which he takes both native Fijians and Hawaiians to task for their wrongheaded, romantic assertions that they are a people linked to a place.

Lisa Malkki is another adherent of this globalist ideology. In her 1992 monograph on Burundian refugees in Tanzania, published in *Current Anthropology*, she presents a dichotomy between those who stay in the camp and cultivate their Hutu nationalism, on the one hand, and those who abandon their Hutu identity and head to town, on the other. They are described as leaving their essentialized Hutu identities to become creolized and rhizomatic. Although she cites no ethnographic evidence for her dichotomization, her thrust is clear. Camp refugees are dangerous nationalists: Their rooted identity as Hutu can only lead to violence. On the other hand, those who have given up that identity to become "broad people" point the way for the rest of us, toward a lively cosmopolitan hybridity. This is an extraordinary statement of a simple ideological scheme: good guys versus bad guys—essentialist, nationalist refugees longing for their imagined homeland versus hybrid cosmopolitans adeptly adapting to their current circumstances. In this metaphoric space, the evil is easy to spot.

Some of Malkki's ire is directed at those who associate native people and ecological sensitivity, and her expression of that ire includes her own celebration of cosmopolitanism. The association that excites her anger conflates, she says, "culture and people," "nation and nature." "Natives are thought to be ideally adapted to their environments." These are understandings that entail, in Appadurai's (1988) words, that natives "are somehow *incarcerated*, or confined, in those places" (p. S37). But is this really the case? Is it not obvious that people move, that the history of global systems has been one of massive displacement as well as the emergence of dominant global elites? Is it not also obvious that people adapt to their environments? Is it not equally obvious that they are likely to develop social and cultural worlds around specific places, worlds that Malkki sees as conflations of culture and people, nation and nature? Is it not reasonable that people maintain practical relations to their territories and that they develop a spiritual relationship to them as well?

It might be difficult to discern the problem here. There is, however, a real conflict for these new globalizers. If the Kalahari Bushmen have a long history of integration and marginalization within the Western world system, does this eliminate their identification with their territories? One senses a distinct disenchantment with what was perhaps an assumed anthropological authenticity, just as many have taken to criticizing "natives" for having invented traditions for political reasons.

Anthropological Versions of Jihad and McWorld

Work in this vein that has appeared more recently pits global flows against local, essentialized identity. For instance, in *Globalization and Identity: Dialectics of Flow and Closure* (1999), Brigit Meyer and Peter Geschiere argue that sociocultural closure is a reaction to the experienced, if not real, loss of control over conditions of existence that comes from

global flows. This is not a new idea, and it is clearly stated by the political theorist Benjamin Barber as the Jihad versus McWorld thesis—that is, fundamentalism as a reaction to Western-based globalization. While this more recent work accepts the new globalized world as a fact of nature, it is less optimistic than earlier writing, as illustrated in the dire situation described in a 1999 essay by John and Jean Comaroff in *American Ethnologist*, in which poverty and magical practices are interpreted as reactions to globalization in South Africa.

Unfortunately, these globalist writers understand globalization as a thing in itself, an evolutionary reality composed of intensifying flows. The older, global-systemic perspective would allow for such flows. However, it would see them as generated by specific conditions of capital accumulation, as it would see their forms and consequences as shaped by specific articulations between local conditions and global relations. Put more simply, the globalists can describe disaster and social disintegration in much of Africa but cannot explain why the same rising tide of globalization has seen East Asia become increasingly integrated in conditions of rapid growth.

It is, paradoxically, the limited character of the globalist approach, obsessed with the closure of the local, that leads its practitioners to criticize those who talk of bounding and territorialization, since such terms are thought to be old fashioned, even reactionary. However, in seeking to explain everything from the New Right to African witchcraft in terms echoing the Jihad-McWorld thesis, as a reaction to globalization, globalists ignore an important possibility, namely, that the local is not a mere response but a historical and complex reality in its own right no matter how transformed within the global context. And since the global is much more than globalization, the collapse of an economic and social order is not due to globalization but to systemic contradictions that globalists do not even address.

It is worth considering this spirited attack on the local. It is true that there have been tendencies in anthropology to treat societies as closed units. As noted above, this was especially the case during the heyday of structural functionalism. It is also true, however, that anthropologists have long attended to the place of the people, which they studied in terms of larger contexts. The idea that people make their world where they are and with the people who are a part of their lives does not, after all, contradict the idea that those people and that place are integrated into a larger system of relationships.

Marshall Sahlins has made similar points in his criticism of what he called "afterology." Just where, he asks, are the classical anthropologists who maintained a view of culture as bounded and homogeneous, as essentialized? Sahlins argues, on the contrary, that those classical anthropologists could even speak of "the fallacy of separation": the mistaken idea that because cultures are distinctive they are closed. This is hardly the sort of thing one would expect of people who see cultures as bounded and self-contained. Equally, those classic writers said things that one would not expect of those who see cultures as essentialized and homogeneous. Thus, Sahlins describes how the cultural relativists stressed that cultures were constantly undergoing change, and he refers to Melville J. Herskovits himself on the complexity of cultural patterns. To echo a point made earlier, the globalist discourse needs to be situated if we are to make sense of what has been described as its distinctive view of the world and of the discipline. That discourse is the product of a particular historical conjuncture, one of real globalization, in which globalists participate and with which they identify. The discourse is not new in itself, but it tends to become salient in periods when declining hegemony, increasing class polarization, mass migration and ethnicization, and the globalization of capital coincide and produce a confrontation between indigenizing, downwardly mobile classes and new cosmopolitanizing elites. In a 2000 essay in *New Left Review*, Slavoj Žižek noted that the emerging elites identify with the world rather than with their nation-states, which are cast as dangerously racist, and they espouse a discourse that supports global control, global governance, and a new centrism of respectability pitted against the national *classes dangereuses*.

Global Systems, Globalization, and Anthropological Theory

The balance of this entry presents an argument that many of the problems so far identified in globalism in anthropology do not only reflect a set of social processes at work among anthropologists. In addition,

they reflect some basic flaws in the globalist approach. Interestingly, those flaws reflect the very thing that the globalist vulgate seeks to reject, a fixation on and valorization of phenomena other than the flows and relations in which they exist. Most obviously, the vulgate's fascination with the multicultural, hybrid, and creole directs attention to the things that exhibit these thinglike properties, whether individuals, neighborhoods, cities, or countries. In doing so, it deflects attention from the systemic conditions in which flows and relations emerge and are reproduced.

An approach concerned with such conditions is global-systemic anthropology. Its emergence in the mid-1970s was marked by the publication in 1974 of Wallerstein's first volume of *The Modern World System* and, in anthropology, by several works by Ekholm Friedman and Jonathan Friedman (Ekholm, 1976; Ekholm Friedman & Jonathan Friedman, 2008a, 2008b) and by Eric Wolf's major work, *Europe and the People Without History*. Wallerstein and Wolf were concerned primarily with the 15th century onward and tended to cast the world system as a phenomenon of the modern era. Ekholm Friedman, Friedman, and, later, Frank, however, claimed that the past 5,000 years could be characterized in terms of a single system or closely related set of world systems.

This systemic approach considers societies in terms of social reproduction rather than in terms of institutional arrangement or cultural practices. To consider a society in terms of social reproduction means attending to how it is constituted within processes of production, distribution, and consumption, through which the population reproduces itself over time. It is important to note that this approach does not see material factors as determinant. Those factors can constrain, and may contradict, the dominant strategies of social life, but this is different from asserting that they cause those strategies. In fact, the primary constraints at a particular historical moment are the product of the historical operation of the social system itself.

With this groundwork laid, the question of global systems becomes, at least in principle, fairly straightforward. One need simply ask whether the population in question reproduces itself based on its own territorial resources or whether its reproduction is part of a larger regional or even wider set of circuits and flows.

This global-systems approach differs in important ways from the orientation of much of anthropology of globalization, which is concerned with the visible movement of people and things, diasporas, the Internet, and the like. In the global-systems approach, the global is the social arena within which social life is reproduced, an arena whose structural properties constitute local institutional forms and identities, as well as economic and political cycles of expansion and contraction. For the globalist, movement generates relations, and migration creates transnational networks, while in global-systemic terms, transnational relations are produced by intentional practices of transnationality. The latter are specific to specific historical contexts and contrast with periods in which migration leads to rapid assimilation.

To say that the local is part of the global does not mean that it is produced by the global. Rather, the global is an emergent property of interactions among different local social units and actors. Thus, global systems are not observable phenomena as such, since "global" refers to the underlying properties of the structure and dynamics of such larger social spaces. This implies that the globalization that most anthropologists describe is a phenomenon that occurs within already existing global systems that constitute, as they are constituted by, localities and their interrelationships (see Friedman & Ekholm, 2008a, 2008b). From this perspective, neither the global nor globalization is new, and the isolated societies of anthropological mythology are not leftovers untouched by the larger world. Rather, they are historical products of larger processes, as indicated by a body of scholarship in historical anthropology and archaeology that includes Robert Gordon's *The Bushman Myth*, Matthew Spriggs's "Ethnographic Parallels and the denial of History," and Ed Wilmsen's *Land Filled With Flies*.

It is clear, then, that studies of global systems are about something different from studies of globalization; or, rather, though each is concerned with *the global*, they construe the word in very different ways. From the global-systems perspective, "the global" refers to the invisible logics or properties of interlocal relations, which can generate phenomena such as globalization, the export of wealth, the diffusion of culture, mass migration, and the inversion of hegemonic ideology, whereas from the perspective of globalization discourse the former is an empirical novelty expressing the birth of a new world of open-ended connections. From the perspective of global systems, any approach that assumes that the global is an empirical field in its own right, different from the local, is a victim of misplaced concreteness. Even doing fieldwork on airplanes is local, and transnational fieldwork is likewise always about relations between localities. Much of the globalization literature, however, sees the global as somehow postnational or transnational, and compounds that with its own evolutionary bias: Once we were local, but now we are global; we have gone beyond all that, finally.

The fundamental difference between these two approaches is not new to the discipline. It echoes the difference between the structural functionalists and structuralists, and that difference is worth attention because it helps illustrate the difference between globalization and global systems. For the structural functionalists, the primary analytical object is the descent group or residential group. When relations are established between such groups, new levels of sociocultural integration emerge, a process that repeats and builds until we get to the global. For the structural functionalists, then, relations are links between already constituted entities, which, by definition, exist prior to the relations in which they are involved. For the structuralists, on the other hand, larger structures and smaller ones constitute each other. So, where structural functionalism saw descent groups as logically prior to the alliances that they formed, for structuralists alliance and descent form a single reproductive process in which the exchange relation is dominant.

The logic of global-systemic analysis lies at the core of Claude Lévi-Strauss's concept of the atom of kinship. His argument against the nuclearity of A. R. Radcliffe-Brown's nuclear family was based on his argument that the group, as an exogamous unit, could only reproduce itself through social relations with other groups, so that the wife giver (or husband giver) is a necessary part of the elementary structure of kinship. In more general terms, structuralism holds that relations are not something added on to already existing units. Rather, the unit is an aspect constituted within the larger set of relations. A lineage is an aspect of a larger structure of reproduction organized along kinship lines; a factory is an aspect of a larger structure of reproduction organized along commercial lines.

From the global-systemic perspective, then, local political units, such as nation-states, are constituted in larger relations within the global. The global, on the other hand, is that structured field of larger relations. It is not an entity in its own right. Not being an entity in itself, the global cannot generate the local. It is rather the field whose processes are necessary and sufficient for understanding the formation of the local. It should be clear, then, that locality is not a common global product that is spread by diffusion or generated from "above," in the way Roland Robertson and Appadurai seem to see it. Localization may be a global process, but the local is always an articulation between a specific set of historical and cultural and localized practices and the larger social field within which they are maintained, reproduced, and transformed. The structuralist critique of structural functionalism resides in the latter's empiricism—structure as observable interaction, as opposed to the explicit hypothetical approach of structuralism. The properties that account for physical phenomena such as falling objects are not identical to the falling objects themselves and are linked to more hypothetical-abstract relations between physical objects in general, namely, gravity, which is not an observable "phenomenon." Similarly, elementary structures of kinship are hypothetical models rather than empirical abstractions, and global systems are of the same order.

If globalization is an essential and new reality of flows and connections, and if there is no accounting for the way in which the phenomenon is generated, then the focus of analysis can easily be reduced to simple diffusionism. If anthropologists and others busy themselves with discovering where things come from and with showing how they get all mixed up in particular urban or other localities—that is, as hybrid or creolized cultures—that busying need not have anything to do with social lives other than their own. If such is the case, then we are dealing not with the nature of the world but instead with the identity of the collectors themselves, observing a reified world of objects from above rather than trying to grasp the emics of people's lives. This classification and hierarchization resembles that of the older colonial administrators—academics who were concerned with identifying hybrids and creoles in their empires. Like those older colonials, writers concerned with globalization have missed the point that "phenomena" like hybridity and creolization

are largely products of the global gaze—they are part of the emic world of the observer unless otherwise demonstrated. That is because they are ways of identifying the experience of multiplicity at a distance. The issue of *real-existing hybridity* is one of self-identification. But it is important not to confuse etic and emic identifications, as has been common in the literature.

The globalists, then—that is, those who adopt the globalist vulgate—have failed to recognize that globalization is a process within global systems that depends on the prior existence of such systems. This failure leads to a range of errors. These include the assumption of evolution from local to global, the renaissance of diffusionism, and the focus on strange combinations that become a new kind of exoticism—hybrid cultures of Coca-Cola, *Dallas*, and "traditional" rituals and objects. This new diffusionism has a clear ideological component, identified as the unquestionably positive evaluation of cosmopolitanism or transnationalism in the vulgate: "Diffusionism, whatever its defects and in whatever guise, has at least the virtue of allowing everyone the possibility of exposure to a world larger than their current locale" (Appadurai, 1988, p. S39). Is this a new project of "enlightenment"?

To focus on diffusion, no matter what its virtues, is not to have a theory. Rather, it is to be preoccupied with the genealogy of objects, instead of attending to their integration into the social context in which they exist. This looks like a step backward, a forgetting of what we already knew. The celebrated archaeologist Gordon Childe understood that diffusion is embedded in larger systems of exchange. American cultural anthropology has long been concerned not with the origins of cultural elements but with the ways in which they are part of larger schemes of life. It is people's ability to produce coherent, structured local life from the cultural materials at hand that these new diffusionists quite absurdly deny.

Conclusion

Notions of globalization surfaced early in the 1980s in a number of disciplines in which a sudden awareness or experience that the world had changed became salient. The global perspective is not new, and aspects of globalist work are continuations of previous scholarly concerns. However, the globalization literature was relatively novel in its stress on the evolutionary character of the current situation and its discontinuity with the past, not the least in its propositions concerning the end of the nation-state and the growth of a diasporic and postnational world.

It is useful to expand our frame, to look beyond the single society or nation-state, a desire shared by both globalist and global-systemic approaches. The focus on transnational relations, global networks, and multiculturalism has brought much to anthropological debate. However, globalization "theorizers" have too often assumed that the world had once been more local and was now entering a new age, and they have done so in a way that indicates evolutionist and normative biases that merit critical reflection. This entry has pursued that reflection by placing globalization in the context of global systems. Doing so encourages us to ask where and when globalization occurs and whether it is a long-term trend or a cyclical phenomenon. Similarly, it encourages us to avoid a trap that, as suggested earlier, globalists have failed to avoid, the trap of assuming that their personal experiences represent the world that they describe, rather than their distinctive locations within it.

Jonathan Friedman

See also Appadurai, Arjun; Dependency Theory; Diffusionism, Hyperdiffusionism, *Kulturkreise*; Harvey, David; Herskovits, Melville; Lévi-Strauss, Claude; Marxist Anthropology; Sahlins, Marshall; Structural Functionalism; Structuralism; Wallerstein, Immanuel; Wolf, Eric; World-Systems Theory

Further Readings

Appadurai, A. (1988). Putting hierarchy in its place. *Cultural Anthropology, 3*, S36–S49.

———. (1996). *Modernity at large: Cultural dimensions of globalization*. Minneapolis: University of Minnesota Press.

———. (2006). *Fear of small numbers: An essay on the geography of anger*. Durham, NC: Duke University Press.

Calhoun, C. (2003). The class consciousness of frequent travelers: Toward a critique of actually existing cosmopolitanism. *South Atlantic Quarterly, 101*(4), 869–897.

Clifford, J. (1997). *Routes*. Cambridge, MA: Harvard University Press.

Ekholm, K. (1976). Om studiet av det globala systemets dynamik [On the study of global system dynamics]. *Antropologiska Studier, 14*, 15–23.

Friedman, J. (1994). *Cultural identity and global process*. London, UK: Sage.

———. (2002). From roots to routes: Tropes for trekkers. *Anthropological Theory, 2*, 21–36.

Friedman, J., & Friedman, K. E. (2008a). *The anthropology of global systems: Vol. 1. Historical transformations*. Lanham, MD: Altamira Press.

———. (2008b). *The anthropology of global systems: Vol. 2. Modernities, class, and the contradictions of globalization*. Lanham, MD: Altamira Press.

Hannerz, U. (1996). *Transnational connections: Culture, people, places*. London, UK: Routledge.

Wallerstein, I. (2004). *World system analysis: An introduction*. Durham, NC: Duke University Press.

Gluckman, Max

Max Gluckman (1911–1975) was a distinguished social anthropologist who did pioneering studies of African legal systems and maintained an abiding interest in the dynamics of local conflict and its resolution.

Biography

The second of four children, Herman Max Gluckman was born in Johannesburg, South Africa, in 1911 to Jewish immigrant parents. He excelled in academics and sports at King Edward VII School, a school modeled after British public schools, emphasizing public service and personal character. He entered the University of the Witwatersrand in 1928, intending to pursue a legal career, a professional path his father and two brothers were to pursue. However, on a whim, he and his school friend Hilda Kuper decided to do a course in social anthropology with Agnes Winifred Hoernle. During the second-year anthropology course, Hoernle took a sabbatical, with Isaac Schapera taking her place. Schapera took Gluckman, Kuper, Eileen Krige, and Ellen Hellman on a field trip to Botswana, an experience that was to play a major role in Gluckman's eventual decision to pursue a career in anthropology. After graduating with first classes in both social anthropology and logic in 1930, Gluckman concentrated on his legal studies and student politics. In his third year, however, he switched to the BA Honors degree in social anthropology, which he completed in the first class in 1934. Gluckman's thesis focused on Zulu chiefs, who were, as he claimed, "a sort of clearing house for economic energy—to and from [whom] . . . flowed the constant stimulus of social energy"—a model of how he was later to run seminars at Manchester University.

Gluckman's extracurricular activities while a student at Witwatersrand also played a formative role in shaping the direction his later anthropological studies would take. He was a member of the student government and almost single-handedly ran the student newspaper, an experience that helped Gluckman hone his lucid expository writing style. He also played a leading role in the National Union of South African Students (NUSAS), serving as secretary for the Bantu Studies Department. In the NUSAS Student Parliament, he was leader of the Liberals (undoubtedly inspired by his teachers, the Hoernles, both leading Liberals) and was instrumental in proposing that Fort Hare, a Black college, be admitted to NUSAS. This action eventually led the Afrikaans universities to secede from NUSAS and create their own apartheid-oriented student organization.

Awarded a Rhodes scholarship, Gluckman enrolled in Exeter College in 1934 and, studying with Robert Marrett, obtained in 1936 the first anthropology doctorate awarded at Oxford. Gluckman's dissertation, *Realm of the Supernatural Among the South-Eastern Bantu*, was based on library research rather than ethnographic fieldwork. While a student at Exeter, Gluckman also regularly attended Bronisław Malinowski's famous seminar in London and formed a close intellectual relationship with E. E. Evans-Pritchard and Myer Fortes.

In 1936, courtesy of Carnegie funding, Gluckman undertook fieldwork in Zululand. While in the field, he pushed the notion of "participant observation" to a level well beyond that practiced by Malinowski. Having studied the Zulu language (isiZulu) for 2 years at Witwatersrand, Gluckman rapidly gained fluency, but his adoption of local customs, including the wearing of traditional costume and living in a traditional hut, upset the local authorities. Fortunately, several of Gluckman's "old school chums" were technical officers in Zululand, who intervened on his behalf. Through this personal network and experience, Gluckman developed many of the insights that were incorporated into his most

famous article, published in 1940, "'The Bridge': Analysis of a Social Situation in Zululand"—commonly referred to as "The Bridge."

Following this fieldwork, Gluckman returned to Oxford for his third year as a Rhodes Scholar, tutoring under the newly appointed A. R. Radcliffe-Brown. It was at this time that he married Mary Brignoli, the daughter of a prominent Italian communist. He finally managed, as the fourth choice, to secure a position in 1939 at the newly established Rhodes-Livingstone Institute (RLI) in northern Rhodesia. Apparently, rampant anti-Semitism and Gluckman's alleged communist sympathies were key factors in hindering his appointment.

Two years later, following the death of Godfrey Wilson, Gluckman was appointed director of the institute, a position he was to hold until 1947. During this time, he astutely managed to balance fieldwork in Barotseland with administrative and fund-raising chores and developed a largely successful 7-year plan, which he conceived in terms not of anthropology but as comparative sociology, encompassing both traditional and industrial life. His plan sought to analyze the region as a single social system including Whites and Blacks. In Barotseland, he initially concentrated on economic issues, but his most famous fieldwork entailed his pioneering ethnographies of law and jurisprudence. Gluckman had a knack for attracting a coterie of impressive young fieldworkers who were later to make their own major contributions to anthropology, including J. Clyde Mitchell, J. A. Barnes, Victor Turner, Elizabeth Colson, J. H. Holleman, William Watson, Max Marwick, A. L. Epstein, Ian Cunnison, Norman Long, and Jaap van Velsen.

Leaving the RLI in 1948, Gluckman lectured for 2 years at the Institute of Social Anthropology at Oxford before leaving to take the Foundation Chair at the Victoria University of Manchester. Over the following decade, a distinct "Manchester school" approach emerged. The unique direction anthropology and sociology were to take at Manchester was in part not only due to Gluckman adopting the role of a Zulu chief in his management of departmental affairs (including an expectation that all department members should attend Manchester United football games) but also due to his deep commitment to interdisciplinary studies. Gluckman worked closely with other Manchester academics, in particular the professor of government W. J. M. MacKenzie and the economist Ely Devons. Interdisciplinary dialogue was a hallmark of Gluckman's approach, epitomized in the 1964 edited volume *Closed Systems and Open Minds: The Limits of Naïveté*. Skillfully deploying Simon Visiting Fellowships, Gluckman attracted both well-established and promising young scholars to Manchester, including Erving Goffman, George Homans, Leo and Hilda Kuper, and apartheid exiles like Jack Simons.

Gluckman also managed to maintain productive links with the RLI, bringing RLI fieldworkers to Manchester to complete their dissertations and to study the British equivalents of their African research. Those gravitating to Manchester, apart from the original RLI nucleus, included Peter Worsley, F. G. Bailey, Ronald Frankenberg, Bruce Kapferer, Richard Werbner, and the sociologists Tom Lupton and Norman Long. Under Gluckman's leadership, these prominent British community studies specialists are said to have launched "modern British sociology" as several of the Manchester acolytes, such as Mitchell, Barnes, and Worsley, obtained chairs in sociology at major universities.

Convinced of the importance of popularizing anthropology since his days as a student and his early experience at the RLI, Gluckman wrote a large number of articles for the popular press and made presentations on the BBC. Gluckman also sought to show how anthropological perspectives could provide insights into contemporary society, writing on topics ranging from English football crowds, to the application of Azande notions of witchcraft, to understanding Nazi hatred of the Jews. By contemporary standards, Gluckman would be seen as a true public intellectual.

A long-term and ardent public critic of colonialism, who was regularly accused of being a "negrophiliac" and a "communist" by settlers and bureaucrats, Gluckman was denied a visa to visit Papua New Guinea and was declared as a Prohibited Immigrant to Northern Rhodesia. Eventually, the ties to Zambia loosened, and disillusioned with the developments there, Gluckman started developing an academic interest in Israel. His interest in Israel and secular Zionism was both long-standing and complex. His mother was a leading Zionist in South Africa, and Gluckman's parental family followed his elder brother in immigrating to Israel after World War II. So strongly did he feel about Israel that he volunteered for the Israeli Defense Force after the

Six-Day War. In 1963, Gluckman launched a unique concentrated effort by a team of anthropologists to explore the industrialized state. Funded by the Manchester-based Bernstein Foundation, he supervised a number of dissertations on different aspects of Israeli society and saw them through to publication. He also trained a number of prominent Israeli anthropologists, including Don Handelman, Moshe Shokeid, Emmanuel Marx, and Shlomo Deshen, who were to establish anthropology as an academic discipline in Israel. This project can also be seen as an intellectual riposte to a generational conflict that developed at Manchester, resulting in a rather acrimonious splitting of the sociology department, led by Worsley and Mitchell, who believed that with decolonization, anthropology was destined for extinction. After retirement, Gluckman spent most of his time in Israel as the Lady Davis Professor at the Hebrew University of Jerusalem. He died of a heart attack in 1974, leaving his widow, three sons, and a listed probate at just under £2,000.

Contributions to Anthropology

Unlike the present vogue in the social sciences, Gluckman did not produce an explicit theoretical exegesis. Instead, the theoretical perspectives he employed are embedded within the very fabric of his ethnographic work. This intimate link between theory and practice is one of the hallmarks of Gluckman's approach to anthropology and of his own personal commitment to political action. Gluckman thus approached his African field research, his participation in radical British politics, and his chairmanship of the Department of Anthropology and Sociology at Manchester University as critical anthropological projects.

Gluckman's theoretical perspectives were built on selected elements of the views expressed by Evans-Pritchard, Radcliffe-Brown, and Durkheim. However, rather than merely recapitulating their theoretical views, Gluckman's anthropological genius was revealed in the ways in which he built on their concerns with social structure in several distinctive ways. Unlike the earlier structural functionalists, Gluckman did not view social structure as monolithic or homeostatic, but instead he saw the pervasive presence of conflict within all social institutions and relationships. Borrowing heavily from Marxian views, Gluckman believed that conflict permeated every aspect of social life. However, rather than seeing these conflicts perpetually ripping asunder the nature of social life, Gluckman saw the crosscutting ties of kinship, ethnicity, politics, and economics acting to ensure that these conflicts did not undermine the existing social structure but instead reinforced it. For Gluckman, such conflicts *frequently* led to revolts but *rarely* to revolutions, the critical distinction being that revolts focus on the removal of a particular office holder but not on the dissolution of the political office itself or the structural principles it embodied. Thus, Gluckman saw social structure doing its greatest work—and at its most visible—at the very moments when other anthropologists contended that social structure was being actively challenged, altered, or discarded altogether.

Gluckman explored these views through a form of anthropological inquiry that he called the "extended-case" method, inspired most probably from his legal background and his interest in Freudian analysis. This "method" was far more than a mere methodology but represented a critical integrative element in his attempt to examine the expression of social structure in the concrete reality of everyday life. Gluckman was critical of anthropologists (Malinowski in particular) who produced ethnographies that were full of "cases" that illustrated a particular insight into cultural practices but eschewed the integration of these cases into a synthetic examination of the underlying social structure. Gluckman suggested that his extended-case method permitted a deeper understanding of what Malinowski and others dismissed as accidental quarrels and personality conflicts, as evidence of the actual social processes and relations underlying every aspect of social life. These views make Gluckman one of the first social anthropologists in the British tradition to employ an explicitly Hegelo-Marxian dialectical perspective on theory and practice. These views placed Gluckman at the forefront of a turn in anthropological theory, a movement that was to eventually find its fullest expression in Pierre Bourdieu's theory of practice.

The extended-case study can be broken down into two basic types. First, there is the use of what can be termed "situational analysis," where the focus is on a single event proscribed by time and space and the case serves largely as a didactic device to illustrate the workings of a complex social order. The second version, as developed by Gluckman's protégé Jaap van Velsen, is processual rather than morphological and has much greater depth of time and space. Overall, the method of analysis and presentation contrasted sharply with the static morphological and abstracted empiricism of conventional accounts and not only served for illustration but also allowed the reader to scrutinize the interpretation in greater depth.

Gluckman's use of the extended-case study, and its impact, can be traced into three areas of cultural anthropology that were later to become flourishing subdisciplines: (1) legal anthropology, (2) urban anthropology, and (3) the anthropology of colonialism and world systems. Given his long-standing interest in politics and his legal training, it was a good fit for him to study the Barotse judicial process, and his 1955 study became a classic. Following the legal realists, like Hoebel, to find the law through "trouble cases," he famously argued that despite cultural variations, dispute resolution processes were similar in that they employed the concept of "the Reasonable Man." Unlike colleagues such as Paul Bohannan, who argued that each culture was unique and thus needed to be analyzed in its own terms, Gluckman focused on similarities rather than differences across cultures and held that to make generalizations one needed a toolkit of standardized concepts, like that provided by Anglo-Roman law.

Although Gluckman's use of Marxian conflict theory was anticipatory of emerging theories in the social sciences, he actively resisted the growing mid-20th-century tendency of anthropologists to stress the importance of individuals and personal psychological factors over the cultural contexts and social processes he saw structuring and conditioning the individual in the first place. For Gluckman, individuals—including their psychological capacities—were the product of the social structure and were not, as some of his anthropological contemporaries seemed to argue, created in a philosophical vacuum, unaltered by the social structure or social life. Thus, Gluckman stressed the structural nature of social conflict rather than personal or psychological factors. Such views led Gluckman into pitched rhetorical conflict with several of his contemporaries—most famously, Sir Edmund Leach. Given that many of the theoretical currents of the late 20th century were built on philosophies of individuality largely unconcerned with the cultural contexts structuring that individuality, Gluckman's views were prescient.

Although Gluckman did not do any urban fieldwork himself, he actively encouraged it both in Northern Rhodesia and at Manchester. Most famously, in 1961, he asserted that an "African miner is a miner" and should be analyzed first as a miner and then only as an African. While colonial administrators were concerned about "detribalization," Gluckman was asking why "tribalism" persisted. The extended-case study also led to important developments in urban anthropology, largely by his students, in particular A. L. Epstein and J. C. Mitchell, the former pioneering the study of ethnicity and the latter lauded for his role in developing network analysis, a logical development of the extended-case study.

Gluckman's interest in the urban situation stemmed from his Radcliffe-Brownian view that one had to examine the total social situation. By this, he meant that colonial society had to be seen as a single social field that incorporated both urban and rural, colonizer and colonized. The seeds for this view are apparent in his famous "Bridge" paper, first published in 1940, in which he described the opening of a bridge in Zululand and used the event to examine aspects of the South African colonial situation. In his popular broadcasts, he was to return repeatedly to the theme of how societies, with so many contradictions and conflicts, managed to cohere. It was not the machine gun but money, he suggested, that bound these disparate and conflicting groups together—plus the nature of crosscutting ties, which were multiplex rather than simplex. Along with the sociologist Leo Kuper and the Caribbean anthropologist M. G. Smith, he tried to develop a framework for analyzing what became known as plural societies, but with the rise of radical scholarship in the 1970s, this approach fell out of favor.

Gluckman's work was integral to the development of the Manchester school's approach to anthropology, with many of his students and departmental colleagues pushing his theoretical ideas into a variety of productive areas of anthropological inquiry. Despite his considerable impact on the discipline, at present, Gluckman is not seen as having made the same theoretical impact as several of his contemporaries. Perhaps, this oversight is due to Gluckman's inability to consider the question of why social structures found themselves in perpetual conflict rather than simply assuming its presence.

To the end of his life, South Africa remained an important intellectual and ethical lodestar for Gluckman. One of his last essays was *Anthropology and Apartheid*. The task of anthropology was not to translate between different cultures—that is what ethnologists were doing, and it sustained apartheid. Rather, for Gluckman, the anthropologist had to take a wider perspective and had to analyze Black and White as part of a single social system.

Robert Gordon and Cameron Wesson

See also Bourdieu, Pierre; Evans-Pritchard, E. E.; Fortes, Meyer; Goffman, Erving; Kuper, Hilda B.; Malinowski, Bronisław; Manchester School; Oxford University; Radcliffe-Brown, A. R.; Schapera, Isaac; Turner, Victor W.

Further Readings

Evens, T. M. S., & Handelman, D. (Eds.). (2006). *The Manchester school*. New York, NY: Berghahn.

Gluckman, M. (1940). Analysis of a social situation in modern Zululand. *Bantu Studies, 14*, 147–174.

———. (1955). *The judicial process among the Barotse of Northern Rhodesia*. Manchester, UK: Manchester University Press.

———. (1961). Anthropological problems arising from the African industrial revolution. In A. Southall (Ed.), *Social change in modern Africa* (pp. 67–82). New York, NY: Oxford University Press.

———. (1975). Anthropologists and apartheid: The work of South African anthropologists. In M. Fortes & S. Patterson (Eds.), *Studies in African social anthropology* (pp. 21–39). London, UK: Academic.

Hannerz, U. (1980). *Exploring the city*. New York, NY: Columbia University Press.

Kapferer, B. (1987). The anthropology of Max Gluckman. *Social Analysis, 22*, 3–21.

Kuper, L., & Smith, M. G. (Eds.). (1969). *Pluralism in Africa*. Berkeley: University of California Press.

Schumaker, L. (2001). *Africanizing anthropology*. Durham, NC: Duke University Press.

GODELIER, MAURICE

Maurice Godelier (1934–), an oceanist ethnologist, is among the founders of French Marxist anthropology.

A graduate of École Normale Supérieure, with an *agrégation* in philosophy and a double degree in psychology and literature from Sorbonne University, Godelier also trained in economics with Charles

Bettelheim and in history with Fernand Braudel at the École Pratique des Hautes Études. Under the supervision of Claude Lévi-Strauss, who recruited him as his assistant at the Collège de France, he undertook fieldwork in Papua New Guinea between 1967 and 1969. His academic career was spent at the École des Hautes Études en Sciences Sociales, where he inaugurated the chair in economic anthropology in 1975, before creating and leading the Centre for Research and Documentation in Oceania in 1995. He was further involved in the institutional development of French anthropological research: by introducing and putting in perspective the translations of Karl Marx, Reo Fortune, Karl Polanyi, Mary Douglas, Eric Wolf, and Edmund Leach, when he was general editor of the Library of Anthropology from 1970 to 1977, and by becoming the founding director of both the Humanities and Social Sciences department at the National Centre for Scientific Research (Centre national de la recherche scientifique, CNRS) and the Research and Teaching department of the Musée du Quai Branly in 1982 and 2000, respectively. His work was awarded the highest scientific distinctions in Germany (Humboldt Research Award, 1989) and in France (CNRS gold medal, 2001), on the basis of its theoretical project of merging Lévi-Strauss's structuralism into Marx's historical materialism.

Against postmodernism and cultural studies, Godelier has reasserted the reflexive, scientific, and empirical features of anthropological practice as well as its distinctive status among the social sciences. Godelier insists that anthropological knowledge can be objective and cumulative beyond its critical function, so long as it exercises systematic comparison, decenters the ethnographic stance, objectifies the historical and social conditions of participant observation, and keeps deconstructing and reconstructing theories, methods, and empirical data in light of new facts, concepts, and controversies. This is why his publications review the main debates in kinship, religion, economics, and politics, and why his methodological inquiry is based on a deep immersion in people's daily life over the long term (between his original fieldwork and 1988, he returned eight times to Papua New Guinea's Eastern Highlands).

Ethnography of the Baruya

Godelier carried out fieldwork among the Baruya, a recently contacted tribe in Papua New Guinea,

comprising some 2,000 individuals. He conducted a comprehensive survey of clans and genealogies on the basis of a topographical study of 600 garden plots and produced an inventory of kinship relations within horticultural work teams and between first land clearers, freeholders, and beneficiary users. He also undertook an exhaustive monograph dealing with warfare, pig husbandry, shamanism, and the building of houses and irrigation canals. The main result of this work was to bring to light a fundamental, asymmetrical gender relationship in the cross-functional sexual division of labor. Women were excluded from the manufacture, ownership, and use of clearing tools, weapons, musical instruments, and ritual objects. They had restricted access to land, political assemblies, cooperative tasks, and primitive forms of money, which were all under male control. Women were directly exchanged as spouses between brothers or lineage segments; they were socialized into submissive behaviors and were subjected to physical and symbolic violence. This masculine domination was inscribed both in women's real separation from the means of production, destruction, and ritual communication and in the imaginary and symbolic production of gendered bodies and minds through initiation ceremonies. Whereas only 2 weeks was sufficient to ritually transform a pubescent girl into a potential spouse and mother, young boys were separated from their mothers and sisters for 12 years and were obliged to live in the big initiates' house; they had to endure four long ritual cycles before becoming actual men begotten by other men, and therefore able to marry and procreate.

Consent to masculine domination was thus produced through sharing the same cosmology: The sun was the source of living beings and the root of bodily forms and intentional minds; its power of growth was embodied in sperm; and sperm was the human source of vitality and fecundity from which mother's milk and blood were derived. Initiatory revelation consisted for women in learning how to suck breast milk and to regularly swallow their husband's sperm; men's initiatory secret was the obligation for young novices to practice fellatio on their co-initiated elders who were still virgins and whose penises had not yet been contaminated by female bodily fluids. This regular ingestion was supposed to make them grow stronger and more powerful than women during their long period of seclusion. It was this ritual of homosexuality, restricted to the initiates' house, that gave men the power to give social birth to the boys who came out of their mother's womb. Baruya male power and domination were both grounded on the depreciation and denial of women's reproductive role and on the dispossession of female (pro)creative abilities through their ritual transfer and imaginary attribution to initiated men, the only ones who had the legitimacy to act on behalf of the Baruya polity.

Theoretical Contributions to Anthropology

Godelier's main theoretical aim was to compare the basic structures of polities as well as their historical genesis, cultural evolution, and transformational logic. From Marx and Lévi-Strauss, he retains three axiomatic principles: first, the distribution of agency in different kinds of materiality (e.g., brains, symbols, artifacts, social relations, and ecological environments); second, the notion of an underlying logic of social relations, the unintentional properties of which may be contradictory in their synchronic articulation and organization into a hierarchical structure; and third, the analysis of these structuring-structured relations prior to theorizing their change over time on the basis of their interactions, inside and outside the system they form.

The Work of Imagination in Material Agency

Relating to the first point, Godelier goes beyond neoclassical formalism and cultural materialism to theorize a kind of bounded rationality whose available options and optimization devices arise from conceptual schemes associated with the hierarchical complementarity of economic, kinship, and political-religious relations. These conceptual schemes are in part autonomous, owing to the human capacity for imagination and analogical thinking; but they also result from the embodiment of the properties of unequal social relations and their transfiguration into an external, nonhuman source. Thus, while the Baruya attribute restricted agency to women, they conceive of the sun as an ultrapowerful agent. In the same vein, each ethnotheory of procreation postulates that the mating between a woman and a man isn't sufficient to make a child (only a fetus!). The intervention of gods, ancestors, or the State appears necessary to engender a new human being. Kinship is thus conceived as the transmission of forms of interiority and physicality (i.e., soul, mind, substance, and

phenotype) that are essential to the reproduction of life. As a result, incest is defined within each society as sexual unions between people who share these identical original components. For Godelier, Lévi-Strauss's mistake was to neglect this mental dimension of kinship and the fact that what matters most in marriage is for families to perpetuate themselves. The founding principle of exogamy and of women exchange fails to fully account for the prohibition of incest, which is better explained by its function in perpetuating family procreation and the parenting units that emerged following the domestication of fire and the correlative invention of the hearth and the base camp.

Godelier criticizes Marxists for having underestimated the significance of operational chains, skills, taxonomies, or ideas that, within productive forces, justify the distribution of tasks in labor processes. Likewise, he reproaches them for having neglected the rules of possession and of the usage of resources and of energy sources within relations of production. This concern with mental and public representations leads him to identify three universal conceptual schemes that frame the rationality of human activities: (1) the notion of keeping for transmitting (with the preservation of both property and usage rights), (2) the idea of giving for indebting and sharing (maintaining property rights while transferring usage rights), and (3) the principle of exchanging for growing (which concerns both the transfer and the acquisition of property and usage rights). A polity reproduces itself over time because its social relations assume a hierarchy of functions at the same time that they are fueled by these three combined principles.

Primitive forms of money are a case in point. It is not the amount of incorporated work that fixes their value, as Godelier has shown by measuring the length, quantity, and type of labor involved in the different production phases of vegetal salt among the Baruya. The bars of salt are used by the men as if they were commodities and units of accounting within the provincial intertribal exchange system to acquire weapons, foods, and ornaments that are scarce within their own territory. However, salt bars are used as valuables within the tribe, by being given to affines and cross-cousins as compensation for social obligations. And they are considered as an equivalent for sperm in initiations, just as they can serve as a compensation for a homicide, when they become a substitute for sacred objects or human persons. The origin of universal currencies should thus be sought in the commercialization of these valuables along the commodity chains.

The Logic of Social Relations

On the second point related to the internal dynamics of polities, Godelier keeps away from neo-evolutionist and vulgar Marxist approaches. Evolutionary typologies (bands, tribes, chiefdoms, and states) are based on shared features that do not take into account the structural diversity of the relations of production within each category. Thus, the Trobriand, Tikopia, and Hawaii islands are all credited with chiefdoms that are alike in terms of the chief's control over the distribution of the products of work, but they differ in terms of their chief's involvement in the organization of labor processes: Trobriand chiefs remain direct producers, Tikopian chiefs only supervise the farming of sago and collective fishing, and Hawaiian aristocrats do not engage in any form of material production at all. Furthermore, these chiefdoms contrast sharply in terms of their chief's control over the workforce, natural resources, and the technologies used by their descent groups: no control among the Trobrianders, weak in Tikopia, and monopolistic in Hawaii. Elsewhere, Godelier rejects economic determinism by reformulating the infrastructure/superstructure distinction and the dominant historical role played by certain social relations within polities. For a practice—whether ritual, governmental, parental, or productive—and its associated ideas, institutions, and relations to play a major role in the organization and the evolution of a polity, it must endorse—in addition to its explicit finalities—the function of production relation. In other words, it must consist in achieving the appropriation of resources, of the means of production, and of the product itself. This is the case, for instance, of kinship among the Australian Aborigines, of politics in Ancient Greece, of the Hindu religion, or of Western capitalist economy. For Godelier, however, there can be no such a thing as a kin-based, economic-based, or religious-based polity. In the final instance, it is the exercise of a sovereign power on a territory—through the exploitation of its resources and through the governance of the populations involved in this exploitation—that is at the basis of polities and of their imagined representation as interrelated, ordered

totalities. The Baruya case offers a good illustration of this idea. Descent and matrimonial alliances serve as frames for cooperation, for the appropriation of the means of production, and for the sharing of products. But kinship remains nevertheless subordinate to the power relations and hierarchies between men and women that are enacted during male initiations. The organization of initiations requires the gathering of the whole tribe and the reactivation of hierarchies between the autochthonous and conquering clans, the latter being the owners of the sacred objects (*kwaitmanié*) that are necessary for the making of great men (warriors, shamans, and cassowary hunters). During these initiations, an intergenerational male solidarity operates, even greater than the one created within a generation, through the direct exchange of sisters. Indeed, each initiatory grade becomes both the recipient and the bestower of sperm in relation to the preceding and the following initiatory grades, and becomes indebted to the owners of the *kwaitmanié*.

Structural Changes in History

The last point concerns the multilinear evolution of polities from the hunting-gathering bands of the Paleolithic to the revolutions of the Neolithic, the Bronze Age, and the industrial 19th and 20th centuries. Godelier has opened four main avenues of inquiry: (1) the metamorphoses of kinship, (2) the state formation processes, (3) the transition from great- to big-men polities in Melanesia, and (4) the expansion of capitalist economy. In each case, he explores the specific transformational logics at work.

First, Godelier shows how, in kinship, the transfer of the attributes of economic and political-religious relations to the imagined roles and status of parent and child, and of siblings and cousins, is afterward embodied into masculine and feminine genders. For example, the evolution of kinship terminologies has been driven by long-term social and cultural changes. They gradually created equivalences between parallel and cross-cousins. Prescriptive rules of alliance as well as the exchange of sisters disappeared. Dravidian terminologies constitute the origins of several evolutionary lines. Some of them became Australian, Iroquois, Hawaiian, and Sudanese systems. Others developed into Crow-Omaha and Eskimo systems, deriving from Iroquois and Sudanese terminologies, respectively.

Second, Godelier critically applies the Marxist concept of *Asiatic mode of production* to the functioning of early states, as for instance the Inca Empire. He demonstrates the weak significance of this concept, which leaves unspecified the productive forces and the relations of production (multiple and varied within autonomous village and tribal communities) and reduces them to the extraction of tribute and *corvée* labor. Nonetheless, he retains the idea that all early states are based on divine kingship, whose religion organizes certain relations of production and justifies the separation between direct producers and surplus consumers, as well as their endogamy and imagined essentialization. He considers the monopolistic use of ritual and sacred objects to control the imaginary conditions of reproduction of the universe/life and argues that it must have preceded the internal differentiation of social status and the formation of new hierarchies such as orders, castes, or classes. This monopoly of the means of communication with the divine and the occult constitutes an evolutionary step leading to the control of the visible material means of production and distribution.

Third, Godelier goes beyond Marcel Mauss's distinction between antagonistic gift giving (*potlatch*) and nonantagonistic gift exchange (*kula*) by conceptualizing the emergence of the former from the latter. By comparing more than 50 Melanesian societies, he identifies two structural conditions that are necessary for the transition from great-men polities (e.g., Baruya), based on male initiations and endemic warfare, to big-men polities (e.g., Enga), characterized by their intertribal ceremonial exchanges and their female spirit cults. First, marriage must no longer be implemented through the direct exchange of women, and bride wealth should for the most part replace sister exchange. Second, access to nonhereditary positions of power and prestige is now competitive and open to those seeking to dominate through redistribution of their wealth. An important evolutionary step toward commodification, such transformation institutes for the first time the connections between the reproduction of kinship relations and the production and accumulation of wealth. The underlying mental revolution is twofold. On the one hand, the equivalence (wealth = a person) replaces the identity (a person = a person). On the other hand, in the act of giving, the search for nonequivalence rather than equivalence, rivalry

and indebtness rather than solidarity and sharing, becomes the main goal and motivation.

As a result, Godelier develops the Marxian theory of formal and real subordination of labor processes under capital. He establishes the set of possible articulations between different kinds of productive forces and relations of production according to their novelty. He does so by taking into account the fundamental and changing role of cultural representations, kinship, and religious and political relations. This line of reflection is well illustrated through his case study of the colonial impact on the Baruya's way of life, following not only the introduction of wage earning, commodity production, and steel tools but also the loss of their sovereignty, the prohibition of their rituals, and the intertribal schooling of their children by Christian missions.

Laurent Berger

See also Economic Anthropology; Gift Exchange; Lévi-Strauss, Claude; Marx, Karl; Marxist Anthropology; Mauss, Marcel; Structural Marxism; Structuralism

Further Readings

Godelier, M. (1972). *Rationality and irrationality in economics.* New York, NY: Monthly Review Press.
———. (1977). *Perspectives in Marxist anthropology.* Cambridge, UK: Cambridge University Press.
———. (1986). *The making of great men: Male domination and power among the New Guinea Baruya.* Cambridge, UK: Cambridge University Press.
———. (1986). *The mental and the material: Thought, economy, and society.* London, UK: Verso.
———. (1999). *The enigma of the gift.* Chicago, IL: University of Chicago Press.
———. (2009). *In and out of the West: Reconstructing anthropology.* London, UK: Verso.
———. (2012). *The metamorphoses of kinship.* London, UK: Verso.
Goody, J. (2005). The labyrinth of kinship. *New Left Review, 36,* 127–139.

GOFFMAN, ERVING

Erving Goffman (1922–1982) created a framework for examining how people manage the complex interactions of everyday life; by focusing on what he understood as social routines and face-saving practices, he paid attention to the obligations and expectations that govern ordinary interactions, to how obligations and expectations are breached, and to how participants attempt to repair offenses and possible harm to social status. In his 1984 essay "Goffman Reconsidered: Pros and Players," Roger Abrahams called Goffman "the philosopher-poet of modernity in the mid-twentieth century, of mobilized people whose daily lives are less and less affected by home and community" (p. 80).

Works

Forms of Talk

In his 1981 work *Forms of Talk*, Goffman described his work as "the naturalistic study of human foregatherings and comminglings, that is, the forms and occasions of face-to-face interaction" (p. 162). This excerpt, from his subtly argued, densely layered metacommunicative essay "The Lecture," provides a guide for considering an appropriately Goffmanesque encyclopedia entry on his work. Goffman was explicitly critical of the unchallenged use of biographical detail in an entry such as this. Several scholars have valiantly attempted to provide the information that Goffman was reluctant to offer. It is not that Goffman wanted the work to stand on its own but rather that he was profoundly interested in the forms of communication that we take for granted (such as encyclopedia entries and lectures, among many others). In this, he drew on phenomenology and its interest in everyday life, but what often served as anecdotes in phenomenological discussions were topics for scrutiny for Goffman.

Presentation of Self in Everyday Life

Goffman referred to the fundamental forms of interaction as "the interaction order," observable in face-to-face interaction in everyday life. He introduced these ideas in *The Presentation of Self in Everyday Life*, first published in 1956 and revised in 1959, based on his doctoral dissertation fieldwork in the Shetland Islands. As a student of Lloyd Warner, Goffman might have been expected to write about the larger social structure of the community. Instead, he focused on the multiple and complex interactions between locals, tourists, hotel workers, and others to understand how people take up a variety of roles to negotiate different sorts of encounters.

Presentation of Self explores how people manage what they imagine to be the impressions others have of them. Participants define the situations they are in, assess the particular frame of the interaction, and present themselves accordingly.

Through attention to interaction and to face-to-face encounters, Goffman developed a performative approach that led to several key frameworks, including an interactional concept of self and personhood and the notion of frame as a central feature of how people assess the obligations and expectations of particular situations. For Goffman, the presentation of self is produced through interaction. His concept of the self is not an interior psychological state but instead is performed, situated, and relational. Like Judith Butler (more than a decade later), Goffman in his 1979 work *Gender Advertisements* argued, "There is no gender identity. There is only a schedule for the portrayal of gender" (p. 8), in which individuals learn how to read and produce the signs of belonging to a particular gender. His understanding of self is often tied to the concept of face, as in saving face, and the "face-work" of managing relationships. In 1967, Goffman wrote,

> To study face-saving is to study the traffic rules of social interaction; one learns about the code the person adheres to in his movement across the paths and designs of others, but not where he is going, or why he wants to get there. (p. 12)

Goffman undertook extensive observations of how people manage the damage done to their self-image and demonstrated how people manage breaches through remedial interchanges that can acknowledge the departure from expectations, offer a remedy to an offense, or shift the frame.

Asylums

In his 1961 observations of "total institutions" (asylums, mental hospitals, prisons, etc.), Goffman described how "territories of the self are violated; the boundary that the individual places between his being and the environment is invaded and the embodiments of self profaned" (p. 23). He observed that total institutions purport to extend surveillance to every dimension of a person's experience but that they inevitably also, sometimes inadvertently, provide "free spaces" in which surveillance is reduced. These exceptions, seemingly outside both the typical researcher's and the institution's awareness, prove to be central to our understanding of how an institution works; they show the interactions among participants in the institution to be performances, subject to the constraints of the situation rather than an indication of the inmates' abilities, limitations, or character flaws.

Stigma

Goffman's discussion of the concept of stigma further developed his understanding of the situational, interactional relationships attributed to and inscribed on individuals. *Stigma: Notes on the Management of Spoiled Identity* (1963) presaged contemporary discussions of normalcy, especially as a critique of the adequacy of the concept of deviance. The work has been controversial among sociologists who have critiqued Goffman's interactional approach as insufficiently attending to the power relations underlying social inequities. Goffman argued that the interaction order was itself constitutive of, rather than epiphenomenal to, social structure. He rejected any neat mapping of social structure onto interaction rituals and instead suggested that the larger economical, racial, and class-based social structural relationships became relevant to and were observable in particular interaction patterns.

Recently, Goffman's work on stigma has become center stage in disability studies' rethinking of concepts of normalcy and ability. By locating stigma in interaction, rather than in the biological or cultural attributes of persons, Goffman provided observations of how stigmatizing categories are integrally connected to other social systems. Blindness, deafness, or using a wheelchair is only disabling if it discredits a person's warrant to participate in a particular interaction. Goffman's concept of stigma differentiates between the discredited and the discreditable, those already categorized as deviant and those vulnerable to becoming stigmatized. As part of this argument, Goffman explored the concept of the ally (useful, e.g., to describe people who identify as allies of those stigmatized for their sexual preferences); the allies take up the case of those who are stigmatized and then, often, are stigmatized themselves.

Philip Manning has credited Goffman with introducing the concept of "identity politics," but Goffman's 1963 discussion of the politics of identity

actually offers a critique of the kind of essentialized identity later described by this concept. In *Stigma: Notes on the Management of Spoiled Identity*, Goffman pointed out that "phantom acceptance" of "phantom normalcy" in practice provided only a very conditional veneer for performing tolerance.

Interaction Ritual

Goffman offered numerous terms and categories to describe the complexity of interaction. Some of the most significant of these are his concepts of information state, frame, footing, replaying, and front and back stage. Early in his work, he discussed the inadequacy of the familiar dyad of speaker and hearer to understand interaction. Alternatively, he proposed four participant possibilities (animator, author, figure, and principal—who stands behind the position put forth) and differentiations among the participants in an exchange, for example, among hearers, ratified hearers, and unratified hearers.

This work on the participants in an interaction helped replace less precise terms such as *role*. Similarly, Goffman's work on alignment or "footing" affords precise attention to both the social categories people adopt or are ascribed to as well as the ways participants shift among categories. In narrative research, the concept of alignment has proven useful for describing how narrators position themselves and their characters in relation to each other and in relation to listeners.

Frameworks such as these continue to be applied in new ways, beyond the situations Goffman described. His work on participants in an interaction, footing, frame, and replaying (among other concepts) continues to be influential in narrative research.

Frame Analysis

Frame Analysis, which some biographers report to be the work that Goffman expected to be his crowning achievement, complicated his earlier work by adding a dimension of reflexivity, or meta-awareness, to his understanding of interaction. Frames define situations as one kind or another. The problem of frame, building on Gregory Bateson's work, begins with the concept of genre, or the type of communication. Contextualization cues are framing devices. These cues are crucial for understanding how to interpret a particular message. The same information and/or experiences can be "reframed" or repackaged, in other forms (a request can be reframed as a joke, an invitation can be framed as a summons, etc.), significantly changing the import and meaning of the message.

As part of his work on frame, Goffman distinguished between reports of past events and "replayings," which involve "vicariously re-experiencing what took place." Goffman's interactional approach to narrative takes into account questions of reported speech and other forms of repetition, including the conditions for the repeated telling of a story and for the suspenseful recounting of a story, in which a teller might withhold information and the listeners would permit it. For example, he observed that in some situations, tellers are permitted to retell a story as if it is the first telling, as long as there is a listener who has not already heard it.

The concept of frame is part of a larger interactional model that identifies varieties of situations and strategies for negotiating among them. He differentiates among (a) primary frames; (b) keys, which reformulate the primary frame, for example, when something is rekeyed as a rehearsal rather than the actual performance; and (c) fabrications, in which participants try to convince others, through persuasion, playfulness, or duplicity, that something is other than it is, for example, that a con game is a legitimate exchange. Multiple frames can operate at the same time, and participants can change their footing in relation to these frames. In related work, he proposed the concepts of back stage and front stage to offer elaboration of categories such as formal and informal or public and private. In Goffman's work, these are not discreet zones but rather are accounts of the different requirements and expectations demanded by situations.

These observations about narrative interaction are tied to what Goffman called "information states": assessments of others' knowledge and strategies based on those assessments. He defined information state as "the knowledge an individual has of why events have happened as they have, what the current forces are, what the properties and intents of the relevant persons are, and what the outcome is likely to be" (p. 133). In brief, each character at each moment is accorded an orientation, a temporal perspective, a "horizon." For instance, Goffman provides the example of a con operation where the dupe does not know that he is going to happen upon someone who will become his confederate and that they both will in turn meet someone who seems to be a dupe.

Goffman has been criticized for his dramaturgical approach, his use of theater metaphors for exploring interactional encounters. However, in his 1974 work *Frame Analysis*, he specifically insisted that "All the world is not a stage"; and in *Forms of Talk*, he argued that he made no claim that social life was a stage, only that elements of theatricality were deeply incorporated into the nature of talking.

Goffman's Legacy

It is easier to chart the fields that Goffman has influenced than to identify his genealogy. Several disciplines claim him and continue to utilize his concepts of interaction. Although he was trained as a sociologist, particularly influenced by Émile Durkheim and George Herbert Mead, biographers note other disciplinary connections and influences, including his engagement with film studies at the University of Toronto, his work with the game theorist Thomas Schelling, and his dialogues with conversational and discourse analysts, including John Gumperz at the University of California, Berkeley, and Dell Hymes at the University of Pennsylvania, where Goffman also had a profound influence on the field of folklore. In response to the critique of Goffman's work as not addressing the politics of power and hierarchy underlying social interaction, scholars such as Roger Abrahams and Patricia Clough have recognized the subversive dimension of his work. Goffman can be seen as a cultural/social/political critic who demonstrated how subordination works by calling attention both to how subversion is enacted and to how the subordinated are called on to perform their prescribed roles.

A Goffmanesque understanding of an encyclopedia entry would observe that it is an ultimately failed effort to make connections between a scholar's life, work, and influences and that it is meant to offer facts rather than, for example, interpretations or anecdotes. The author of the entry has been selected for some authority, but that is to be assumed rather than claimed—unlike, for example, the preface of a book written by another author who might describe her relationship as a point of entry and connection. Goffman exhorted us to pay attention to these taken-for-granted assumptions about genre and form. Using his own interactional approach, we might observe that Goffman never drew his readers into his own biographical narrative and rarely described his intersections with other scholars. At times, he explicitly differentiated himself from particular schools of thought. His work continues to be central to the study of everyday life.

Amy Shuman

See also Bateson, Gregory; Butler, Judith; Durkheim, Émile; Gumperz, John J.; Hymes, Dell; Mead, George Herbert

Further Readings

Abrahams, R. D. (1984). Goffman reconsidered: Pros and players. *Raritan Review, 3,* 76–94.

Clough, P. T. (1992). Erving Goffman: Writing the end of ethnography. In *The ends of ethnography: From realism to social criticism* (pp. 94–112). London, UK: Sage.

Fine, G. A., & Manning, P. (2003). Erving Goffman. In G. Ritzer (Ed.), *The Blackwell companion to major contemporary theorists* (pp. 34–62). Oxford, MA: Blackwell.

Goffman, E. (1959). *The presentation of self in everyday life.* New York, NY: Doubleday Anchor.

———. (1961). *Asylums: Essays on the social situation of mental patients and other inmates.* New York, NY: Doubleday Anchor.

———. (1963). *Stigma: Notes on the management of spoiled identity.* Englewood Cliffs, NJ: Prentice Hall.

———. (1967). *Interaction ritual: Essays on face-to-face behavior.* New York, NY: Doubleday Anchor.

———. (1974). *Frame analysis: An essay on the organization of experience.* New York, NY: Harper.

———. (1979). *Gender advertisements.* London, UK: Macmillan.

———. (1981). *Forms of talk.* Philadelphia: University of Pennsylvania Press.

Hacking, I. (2004). Between Michel Foucault and Erving Goffman: Between discourse in the abstract and face-to-face interaction. *Economy and Society, 33*(3), 277–302.

GOLDENWEISER, ALEXANDER A.

Alexander Alexandrovich Goldenweiser (1880–1940), who made several important contributions to anthropology in the decades preceding World War II, was born in Kiev (Ukraine, Russian Empire) in 1880 in an educated middle-class family of assimilated Russian Jews, where European high culture was greatly valued. His father, Alexander Solomonovich Goldenweiser (1855–1915), a prominent liberal lawyer, had a major influence on him. In 1900, he brought Alexander and his younger brother Emmanuel to the United States, so that they could escape the discrimination faced by Jewish youngsters trying to get into Russian institutions of higher education. Alexander enrolled in Harvard, where he majored in philosophy, graduating in 1902. He then went to Columbia, where his academic interests shifted to religion and, later, anthropology. He earned his PhD in 1910 under the direction of Franz Boas.

While in New York, Goldenweiser was the center of a small but lively group of young intellectuals, most of them anthropologists or anthropology graduate students like himself (e.g., Robert Lowie, Paul Radin, and Elsie Clews Parsons), who gathered frequently to discuss their discipline as well as broader issues such as the philosophy of the social sciences, psychology, politics, and literature. He was the organizer and the heart and soul of several study "circles" and intellectual groups. Best known among them were The Pearson Circle and The Unicorns. At that time, Goldenweiser was seen by many as Boas's favorite and most promising student. Not surprisingly, his mentor offered him a position as lecturer in his own department. For about a decade, Goldenweiser taught many of the core undergraduate anthropology courses and was widely admired as an effective and charismatic instructor.

Goldenweiser's only ethnographic field research involved several trips to the Six Nations Reserve in Ontario in 1911–1913, where he worked with Iroquois consultants, having been recruited by Edward Sapir, the chief ethnologist of the Division of Anthropology of the Geological Survey of Canada. He published several short articles based on that research, but the full reports on this work were never published because of the division's falling out with the government. Thanks to Margaret Mead, an erroneous notion that Goldenweiser disliked fieldwork became firmly entrenched among American anthropologists. He actually appears to have enjoyed it and managed to collect a good deal of data on social organization, religion and mythology and several other topics. According to William Fenton, to whom Goldenweiser turned over his field notes in the 1930s and who later worked with some of the same consultants, his data were first-rate.

In addition to teaching undergraduate courses at Columbia, Goldenweiser also taught anthropology at the Rand School, affiliated with the Socialist Party between 1915 and 1929, and gave numerous public lectures to earn some badly needed money and also to spread Boasian ideas on race, sex and marriage, and cultural relativism. For the same reasons, he published numerous articles and book reviews in liberal and left-leaning magazines such as *The Nation*, *The New Republic*, and *The Modern Quarterly*. In some of his publications, he used anthropological concepts such as magic and *mana* to make sense of contemporary social issues. As far as Goldenweiser's politics are concerned, he was a leftist but with a strong anarchist bent. He rejected Marxist theory as economic determinism and distrusted American communists because of their authoritarianism and pro-Stalinist position. With his Russian background, he understood the totalitarian nature of the Soviet political system and was never seduced by it the way many left-leaning American intellectuals were.

Boas's efforts to obtain a permanent position for his protégé failed, and in 1919, Columbia let him go. While many of his contemporaries as well as subsequent commentators believed that his Jewishness and his own as well as Boas's leftist politics were the reasons for this, Goldenweiser's "irregular" behavior, including his failure to return university library books and pay personal debts, played a major role in his dismissal. Luckily, 1919 was also the year when a group of distinguished progressive social scientists, Goldenweiser among them, established The New School for Social Research. Here, his courses were pitched at a higher level, and he had a lot more freedom to choose their subject matter. In addition to lecture courses in the social sciences, he taught seminars in which students had to undertake their own field research. For example, in 1924–1925, he offered a seminar titled *Racial Groups in Greater New York*. Among Goldenweiser's anthropology students at the New School were prominent future scholars such as Ruth Benedict, Ruth Landes, Melville Herskovitz, and Leslie White. He had a particular influence on Benedict, whom he persuaded to enroll in Columbia's graduate anthropology program. Goldenweiser's concept of *Gestalt*, developed in the late 1920s, influenced Benedict's own thinking, as articulated in her *Patterns of Culture*. After

the New School decided not to offer him a full-time appointment, Goldenweiser became a member of the editorial board as well as a contributor to the *Encyclopedia of the Social Sciences*, a major, multivolume reference work.

Unable to find any teaching position on the East Coast, Goldenweiser moved to Portland in 1930, where he taught anthropology and sociology at the University of Oregon's Extension between 1930 and 1938; simultaneously, he taught anthropology, sociology, and even social psychology at Reed College as a visiting professor in the department of sociology between 1933 and 1939. While he continued to enjoy a reputation as a great teacher, he viewed Portland as a backwater and made several attempts to obtain a position in larger West Coast cities, such as Seattle and San Francisco. However, except for a 1-year visiting appointment at the University of Wisconsin, Madison, plus occasional summer teaching at Stanford and the University of Washington, none of his efforts came to fruition. Eventually, Goldenweiser's reputation as an iconoclast and a leftist led to some serious conflicts between him and Reed's administration, so that in 1939, the latter decided not to renew his contract. At the same time, in the 1930s, he finally found personal happiness when he married a younger woman by the name of Ethel Cantor. Goldenweiser died suddenly of a heart attack on July 6, 1940.

Critical Contributions to Anthropology

In his PhD dissertation, published in 1910 as *Totemism: An Analytical Study*, Goldenweiser demonstrated that the presumed unity of totemic phenomena was a scholarly invention. In fact, he argued that totemism was a blanket term for a wide variety of practices. He also suggested that it was based on symbolic or mystical relationships, with every society having its own totemic practices. Goldenweiser's work prompted a lively debate among anthropologists and provided one of the theoretical bases for Claude Lévi-Strauss's 1962 *Totemism*.

His other important contribution to anthropological theory in general and the study of cultural dynamics in particular was a 1913 article, "The Principle of Limited Possibilities in the Development of Culture," in which he argued that institutions and objects with a limited number of forms were almost certainly contrived independently by cultures located at a great distance from each other. This idea helps explain those cases in which convergence provides a much better solution than diffusion.

Goldenweiser also developed the important concept of "involution," which he articulated in a brief 1936 essay "Loose Ends of Theory on the Individual, Pattern, and Involution in Primitive Society." According to him, involution described culture patterns that in reaching a definitive form stopped evolving into new patterns but continued developing only in the direction of internal complexities, leading to "progressive complication, a variety within uniformity, virtuosity within monotony." Thirty years later, Clifford Geertz used this concept to study Indonesian agriculture.

In several of his publications, Goldenweiser also argued that when cultures come into contact, there is no automatic assimilation of ideas and practices from one to another, but whether or not any new items will be accepted depends on the receptivity of the culture, which in turn depends on various social and psychological factors. Many areas of the social sciences have found this idea useful.

Generally speaking, Goldenweiser was much more interested in broad theoretical questions than many of his fellow Boasians, especially "strict" ones such as, for example, Lowie. From this perspective, Goldenweiser was much closer to Radin and Sapir, whose work he admired greatly. In fact, he considered Sapir to be the most brilliant anthropologist of his time. He also shared Sapir's and Radin's interest in the role of the individual in "primitive" society and the use of autobiography in anthropological research. Goldenweiser was also one of the first Boasians to pay serious attention to psychology, including psychoanalysis; and his works frequently make references to the key role of psychological motivations in social life and cultural production. Thus, one of his early articles contains an interesting argument about the importance of religious "thrill" in religious experience.

What also distinguished Goldenweiser from many of the other leading figures in American anthropology of the pre–World War II years was his interest in crossing interdisciplinary boundaries and engaging in a dialogue with sociologists, psychologists, historians, and other social scientists. This breadth of his scholarly interests is best illustrated by a collection of essays he coedited with William F. Ogburn, a prominent American sociologist. Titled *The Social Sciences and Their Interrelations* (1927), it contains 34 chapters, each of them devoted to the interrelation between two specific social sciences and written by a leading scholar of the day. A commitment to this dialogue (combined with a perennial search for honoraria) explains Goldenweiser's frequent contribution to various edited volumes dealing with hot contemporary issues such as sex, marriage, and others. While Lowie dismissed Goldenweiser's interdisciplinary activities by calling him the number one among "the liaison officers of the social sciences," they gained him recognition and respect among many leading figures in the social sciences.

Goldenweiser was also the first student of Boas to publish a comprehensive textbook in anthropology. Titled *Early Civilization: An Introduction to Anthropology* (1922), it was based on his lectures at the New School. Fifteen years later, he published another textbook, *Anthropology: An Introduction to Primitive Culture*. In addition, he produced a popular book called *Robots and Gods: An Essay on Craft and Mind* (1931), as well as a collection of essays titled *History, Psychology and Culture* (1933).

As far as his academic career was concerned, Goldenweiser did not accomplish very much, but most of the blame for this must rest with his own difficult personality and erratic behavior. For this reason plus the fact that quite a few of his articles appeared in nonanthropological journals, he receives little attention in many of the histories of anthropology. However, a careful reading of the entire corpus of his work reveals the brilliant mind of a highly erudite scholar.

Sergei Kan

See also Benedict, Ruth F.; Boas, Franz; Herskovits, Melville; Lévi-Strauss, Claude; Lowie, Robert; Parsons, Elsie C.; Radin, Paul; Sapir, Edward; White, Leslie

Further Readings

Benedict, R. (1940). Alexander Goldenweiser. *Modern Quarterly, 6*(Summer), 32–33.

Kan, S. (2009). Alexander Goldenweiser's politics. In R. Darnell & F. Gleach (Eds.), *Histories of anthropology annual* (Vol. 5, pp. 182–199). Lincoln: University of Nebraska Press.

Wallis, W. D. (1941). Alexander A. Goldenweiser. *American Anthropologist, 43*, 250–255.

White, L. (1958). Alexander Goldenweiser. *Dictionary of American Biography, 22*(Suppl. 2), 244–245.

GOODENOUGH, WARD H.

Ward Hunt Goodenough (1919–), American cultural anthropologist, applied anthropologist, and ethnographer of Micronesia and Melanesia, carried out pioneering theoretical studies of kinship, formulated linguistic models of culture and cognition, and sought a comparative anthropology geared toward understanding human nature.

Biography and Major Works

Goodenough was born on May 30, 1919, in Cambridge, Massachusetts. He received a BA in Scandinavian languages and literatures from Cornell University in 1940. His marriage to Ruth A. Gallagher on February 8, 1941, produced four children and eight grandchildren. Shortly after their marriage, he enlisted in the U.S. Army, serving from November 1941 until his discharge with the rank of technical sergeant in December 1945. For the following 8 months, he worked in the Adjutant General's Office of the War Department as a civilian case analyst.

In 1949, Goodenough received his PhD in anthropology from Yale University under the supervision of George Peter Murdock. Murdock's interests in social structure and cross-cultural comparison on a scientific basis would persist in Goodenough's own anthropology throughout his career. In 1940, he was a research assistant in Murdock's Cross-Cultural Survey, which would evolve into the Human Relations Area Files (HRAF). In 1947, Murdock took a team of graduate students, including Goodenough, to Truk (now called Chuuk) in Micronesia for 7 months of fieldwork. His dissertation, *Kin, Property and Community in Truk*, published by Yale in 1951, argued that Trukese kinship could not be understood in isolation from access to land; that is, social structure, economics, and political organization were intermeshed and intelligible only in terms of their mutual embedding. Other significant early influences were Bronisław Malinowski, ethnographer of the Melanesian Trobriand Islands, and the Yale linguist George Trager. Goodenough conducted additional fieldwork in Kiribati in the Gilbert Islands and in Papua New Guinea in 1951 and in Lakalai, New Britain Island, in 1954.

Goodenough taught at the University of Wisconsin in 1948–1949. On completing his dissertation, he took up a position as assistant professor of anthropology at the University of Pennsylvania, where he remained until his retirement in 1989 as University Professor Emeritus. He was promoted to associate professor in 1954, to professor in 1962, and to university professor in 1980. He chaired the department from 1959 to 1961 (acting) and from 1976 to 1982. He also taught at Cornell University, Swarthmore College, Bryn Mawr College, University of Hawaii, University of Wisconsin at Milwaukee, Yale University, and Colorado College. He spent 1957–1958 as a fellow at Stanford's Center for Advanced Study in the Behavioral Sciences. Goodenough delivered the Lewis Henry Morgan Lectures at the University of Rochester in 1968, held a Guggenheim fellowship in 1980, and served as Fulbright lecturer at St. Patrick's College in Ireland in 1989.

Goodenough was elected to the National Academy of Sciences in 1971, the American Philosophical Society in 1973, and the American Academy of Arts and Sciences in 1975. He received the Distinguished Service Award of the American Anthropological Association in 1986 and the Society for Applied Anthropology's Malinowski Award in 1997. He is an honorary fellow of the Society for Social Anthropology in Oceania. He was president of the American Ethnological Society in 1962 and of the Society for Applied Anthropology in 1963. He served as editor of the flagship journal *American Anthropologist* from 1966 to 1970 and on multiple other editorial boards.

In addition to his scholarly work, Goodenough has published a volume of poetry and another volume of piano pieces. Since the death of his wife, Ruth, Goodenough and his partner Joan May reside in Haverford, Pennsylvania.

Critical Contributions to Anthropology

Kinship Studies

Goodenough's early work in kinship moved the study of social organization from a fill-in-the-blanks exercise to a cultural analysis seen through the lens of family and community relationships. Beginning with his dissertation on kin, property, and community, he adapted Malinowski's strategy of focusing successively on overlapping and distinct, at least from the point of view of the analyst, cultural domains. His 1956 article on residence rules challenged the objective character of observed social relations by contrasting his own analysis of the lineal descent system of Trukese kinship with that of his fellow graduate student John Fischer. Based on essentially the same fieldwork and census data, one deemed them patrilineal and the other, matrilineal. Goodenough argued that lineality was not assigned on kinship grounds alone. The Trukese were less worried about mother's family or father's family lines than about activating whatever lineal ties would provide maximal access to arable land; marital households had to choose a family line but did not do so based on kinship in the narrow sense. Goodenough's more general analysis of Malayo-Polynesian kinship in 1955 also emphasized land as the key dimension used when people apply kinship rules to particular life circumstances.

During the 1960s, Goodenough was a leading figure in the emergence of componential analysis as a formal method of ethnographic semantics. In addition to his work in kinship, he explored the domain of Malayo-Polynesian navigation systems and sought evidence on how members of culture organized their experience around normative rules that were broken in interpretable, though not predictable, ways. He famously claimed ethnographic adequacy if he was surprised at the same time as were the Trukese. His theoretical article on componential analysis and the study of meaning, which appeared in *Language* in 1963, has been acknowledged alongside the work of the Yale linguist Floyd Lounsbury as the foundational document of this approach. Goodenough argued that kinship terms consisted of underlying clusters of semantic features combined uniquely in different cultures, even when the particular set of terms was superficially similar to those found elsewhere. Because they were highly structured, such formal semantic domains allowed the analyst to approach the meaning system of the culture as a whole. This method drew on the binary feature analysis pioneered by Roman Jakobson in phonology. Drawing on his linguistic training at Yale, Goodenough enriched the interpretive dimensions of his ethnography by seeking systematic semantic patterns implicit in cultural categories but not normally analyzed by members of culture.

The question of multiple possible analyses of the same kinship system was highlighted in his 1965 analysis of Yankee kinship terminology. David Schneider was prominent among those who disputed Goodenough's definition and ordering of the underlying features of this system. He attributed Goodenough's choices to the idiosyncracies of his personal family tree and considered the analysis nonrepresentative of the kinship system of most Americans. The ensuing somewhat acrimonious debates on American kinship terms attracted a wide audience of self-styled experts applying their own native intuitions. The debate proved Goodenough's point that the reliability and validity of any cultural analysis required constant vigilance to filter out differences among individuals in a culture as well as differences introduced by the standpoint of the anthropologist. Alternative analyses could be explained in terms of these variables.

Linguistic and Cognitive Anthropology

The structural linguistics and sign theory of his training are inseparable from Goodenough's cultural anthropology. A 1957 article on cultural anthropology and linguistics argues that the methodological problems of the two disciplines are fundamentally the same. Goodenough aspires to apply the formal rigor of linguistics to the analysis of cultural phenomena, at the same time broadening the cultural scope of linguistic descriptions. In both cases, explanation was to be grounded in the search to define human nature across languages and cultures.

Goodenough's understanding of the systematic nature of culture draws from the insights of linguistics. He is not so much a linguist, however, as an ethnographer sensitive to the powerful influence of the structure of language on culture-specific meaning and the role of language in everyday interaction. *Culture, Language and Society* appeared in 1971 and was widely adopted as a textbook. In it, Goodenough lays out the title relationships as he understands them. The third term of society, juxtaposed to the traditional American anthropological binary of language and culture, brings the people back into the ethnography.

Goodenough insisted that sophisticated ethnography required knowledge of the local language. He considered his Trukese-English dictionary, published by the American Philosophical Society in 1980 with a supplement in 1990, to be among his most difficult projects. He argued, and illustrated, that a dictionary requires deep ethnographic knowledge to calibrate potentially incommensurable categories and lexical entries. The English speaker must know a great deal about Truk and the Trukese to be able to use the dictionary.

Comparative Anthropology

Goodenough's problematization of ethnographic categories in his kinship studies called into serious question the quality of the data available for systematic cross-cultural comparison. In *Description and Comparison in Cultural Anthropology*, published in 1970, Goodenough reviewed the uncertainties implicit in ethnographic descriptions of kinship, marriage, and family, arguing that cross-cultural comparison required a universal set of categories such as those provided for social structure by his mentor, Murdock. Again, he drew on a linguistic analogy, taken from phonetics, in which the categories of a particular language or culture could be expressed in an analytic language that was, insofar as was possible, independent of any particular ethnographic case. In addition to facilitating comparison across widely different cultures, this method enabled the anthropologist to minimize the effects of his or her own cultural background. Goodenough attempted to apply this method in his own work, but it was left to his successors to pursue the implications. He concluded that the traditional "etic" (ostensibly culture-free) categories of anthropology, for example, kinship, were questionable in their universal applicability.

Goodenough was not prepared to give up on comparison but called for a much more careful assessment of comparability. He went beyond his former teacher Murdock in questioning the adequacy of the cross-cultural data that had been coded for comparison through the HRAF. He believed, however, that judicious use of the HRAF data could ameliorate the problems: The HRAF files included the full texts from which coded categories, such as kinship terms or marriage practices, were extracted, thus allowing the researcher to recover the context of the category to be compared cross-culturally as it applied in a particular case. Because the HRAF files amassed multiple works on the same culture by different investigators writing at different periods

in time, the investigator had to use such contextual information to exercise a degree of control over potential dimensions of unreliability.

Culture Change

Goodenough's commitment to applied anthropology grew out of his wartime experience of small-scale societies that were being catapulted into an unfamiliar and rapidly changing world. The ethnographer of such societies was in a position to ease this transition. When he wrote *Cooperation and Change: An Anthropological Approach to Community* in 1963, Goodenough was consulting for the Peace Corps to train culturally sensitive personnel for work overseas. Development work risked imposing external values and infrastructure on local systems of meaning; the anthropologist could calibrate potential conflicts and help establish effective collaboration between communities and outside entities.

Goodenough was active in the establishment of the Society for Applied Anthropology and insisted that all anthropologists should be committed to using their science for the benefit of those studied. He also remained engaged with Oceania as an ethnographic area. A Festschrift edited by Mac Marshall and John Caughey in 1989 demonstrates his continuing influence among scholars working in the Pacific.

Goodenough's Legacy

Goodenough has long provided an exemplar for an anthropology ranging across the subdisciplines, especially linguistics and cultural anthropology. He combined traditional ethnographic studies of small-scale societies with an applied anthropology directed toward the rapidly changing circumstances of such societies in the post–World War II world. His work models the potential of the anthropologist to move back and forth between rigorous, often quantitative, cross-cultural comparison and respect for the ethnographic integrity of particular cultures. He has been a pioneer in revising the traditional concept of culture to incorporate culture change.

Regna Darnell

See also Cognitive Anthropology; Ethnoscience/New Ethnography; Human Relations Area Files, Cross-Cultural Studies; Jakobson, Roman O.; Lounsbury, Floyd; Malinowski, Bronisław; Murdock, George Peter; Schneider, David M.

Further Readings

Caughey, J. (2004). Goodenough, Ward H. In V. Amit (Ed.), *Biographical dictionary of social and cultural anthropology* (pp. 202–203). London, UK: Routledge.

Kimmel, A. (n.d.). *Ward H. Goodenough.* Retrieved from http://www.indiana.edu/~wanthro/theory_pages/goodenough.htm

Marshall, M., & Caughey, J. (Eds.). (1989). *Culture, kin and cognition: Essays in honor of Ward H. Goodenough.* Washington, DC: American Anthropological Association.

GOODY, JACK

Jack Goody (1919–) became an anthropologist in the context of World War II and the anticolonial revolution it spawned. He carried out fieldwork in Northern Ghana under the direction of Meyer Fortes in Cambridge and has continued to maintain a link between the two places for half a century since. With Fortes, he founded a school of West African ethnography based on meticulous documentation of kinship and marriage practices and especially of "the development cycle in domestic groups." Later, his wife, Esther Goody, was his partner in much of this research.

Ethnography, the aspiration to write about another culture studied intensively through fieldwork, never defined Goody's intellectual horizons. His subject has always been historical comparison and, beyond that, "the development of human culture." He was sympathetic to Africans' drive for independence, and he responded by studying the history of West Africa's precolonial states that were linked to Islamic civilization. From this extension of his approach, he launched the project of global comparison, for which he is best known today. The ultimate historical question is where human civilization is going. For Goody, the answer lies in the similarity and divergence of regions with an agrarian past or present. Beginning with *Production and Reproduction*, he set out over the past 4 decades to compare the preindustrial civilizations of sub-Saharan Africa and Eurasia, with the aim of identifying why Africa is so different, while questioning Western claims to be exceptional.

Early Research

Goody's early research started with kinship and marriage, the domestic relations through which people manage their own reproduction and participate in the wider society. In *Death, Property and the Ancestors*, he concluded that the key to variations in kinship organization lay in the transmission of property, the material link between generations constituted by patterns of inheritance and manifested in religious observances, such as the ancestor cult. The book drew extensively on classical sources of British comparative jurisprudence; but Goody balked at making a systematic comparison of Africa and Europe then. In *Tradition, Technology and the State*, he questioned the habit of transferring categories from European history to the study of precolonial states in Africa. Again, his focus was on property forms. European feudalism was based on private property in land, and this was absent in traditional West Africa. Why? Because land was scarce in western Europe but not in Africa, where the scarce factor was people, and control over them was exercised through monopolies of the "means of destruction" (horses, guns, etc.), not the means of production. Africa's polities were both centralized and decentralized, the former acquiring manpower by force through carrying out slave raids on the latter. Shifting hoe agriculture was the norm, with the bulk of manual labor being performed by women. In both centralized and decentralized societies, women were hoarded as wives by polygamous older men, and their children were recruited to exclusive descent groups. The key to major differences in social organization between Africa and Eurasia thus lay in the conditions of production and specifically in demography, in the ratio of people to the land.

Kinship, Marriage, and Property Transmission

In 1976, Goody took off from this premise about people and land into a global survey of kinship, marriage, and property transmission, using the data compiled in the *Ethnographic Atlas*. Kin groups in the major societies of Eurasia frequently pass on property through both sexes, a process of "diverging devolution" (including bilateral inheritance and women's dowry at marriage) that is virtually absent in sub-Saharan Africa, where inheritance follows the line of one sex only. Especially when women's property includes the means of production, in agricultural societies, attempts will be made to control these heiresses, banning premarital sex and arranging marriages for them, often within the same group and with a strong preference for monogamy. Direct inheritance by women is also associated with the isolation of the nuclear family in kinship terminology, where a distinction is drawn between one's own parents and siblings and other relatives of the same generation, unlike in lineage systems. All of this reflects a class society. Diverging devolution (especially dowry) was the main mechanism by which familial status was maintained in an economically differentiated society.

Goody argued that the agrarian economies of all the major Eurasian civilizations conformed to this pattern. They were organized through large states run by literate elites, whose lifestyle embraced both the city and the countryside. Goody (1976) writes, "In the societies of the late Bronze Age an elaborate bureaucracy, a complex division of labor and a stratified society were made possible by intensive agriculture; and title to landed property was of supreme importance" (p. 24). Africa south of the Sahara apparently missed out on these developments, even though North Africa was one of the first areas to adopt the new institutional package.

Repudiating "Us/Them" and Other Binaries

Jack Goody chose to attack the lingering opposition of "modern" and "primitive" cultures by studying the chief activity of literate elites, of which he was himself a leading example, namely, writing. He argued that contrasted mentalities should be seen as an effect of using different means of communication. The most important of these are speech and writing, orality and literacy. Most African cultures are predominantly oral, whereas the ruling classes of Eurasian civilization have relied from the beginning on literate records. Goody published his most general assault on the habit of opposing us and them, *The Domestication of the Savage Mind*, as a pointed repudiation of Claude Lévi-Strauss, suggesting that the latter's lists linking "hot" and "cold" societies to other pairs, such as history and myth, and science and magic, far from exemplifying universal reason, were a parochial by-product of mental habits induced by writing. This emerged in a specific time and place and became essential to the reproduction of Eurasian civilization, reducing the status of oral communication, which still predominated in African cultures. Literacy was a key feature of the institutional complex that marked the urban revolution.

Jack Goody rejects the notion that modern world history has made a decisive break from what went before. The unequal society of agrarian civilization lives on, but inequality has been amplified by the machine revolution. His anthropological vision offers one indispensable means of contemplating how human culture is to be rescued from the consequences of these developments. Four elements of this vision stand out. First, the key to understanding social forms lies in production, and that now includes the uneven spread of machine production. Second, civilization or human culture is largely a consequence of the means of communication—once writing, now an array of mechanized forms, but always interacting with oral and written media. Third, the site of social struggles is property—for example, are nation-states still an effective instrument for enforcing global contracts? Finally, Goody's focus on reproduction has never been more salient when the aging citizens of rich countries depend on the proliferating mass of young people from elsewhere as migrants. So kinship needs to be reinvented too.

In numerous volumes since *The East in the West*, Goody's focus has been less on what makes Africa different and more on subverting Europe's pretension to superiority over Asia. He has gained credibility from the latter's rise as home to new capitalist powers, first Japan, now China, India, and others. Since the claim for Europe's exceptional status always lay in identifying the distinctive social and cultural conditions for capitalist development, this shift in the economic balance between the West and the rest reinforces a perspective on world history that long predates current evidence for it.

Dismantling Racist Evolutionism

Twentieth-century anthropology retained more of its predecessor's racist evolutionism than its practitioners like to admit. This took the form not only of treating the indigenous inhabitants of Oceania, Africa, and the Americas as "primitives" but also of regarding the civilizations of the East, explicitly or implicitly, as backward and more suitable for comparison with the primitives than with Western societies. This attitude was reproduced by historians who traced the global mastery ensured by industrial capitalism to the Renaissance or Reformation and even to medieval feudalism and Greco-Roman antiquity. Marx's and Weber's theories of capitalist development provided intellectual support for these views.

Goody has sought to dismantle the evolutionist myth of Europe's unique historical path in the following areas: kinship, the family and individualism; urban commerce; the puritan roots of capitalism; and communications technology. His main thesis—following the prehistorian Gordon Childe, whom he read during the Second World War, and, before him, L. H. Morgan—is that the emergence of cities and civilization in the Bronze Age constituted an "urban revolution," in which all of Eurasia participated eventually. The relative standing of its constituent regions has fluctuated over 5,000 years, with western Europe (and its North American offshoots) enjoying some advantage since the Renaissance and especially in the past 2 centuries since the Industrial Revolution. Goody utterly rejects any claim that this advantage has its roots in Western history before then or that non-Western Eurasia was ever structurally inferior. In most respects, Asian civilizations were well ahead of Europe for much of history. The speed with which they have adopted modern capitalism—faster than the Renaissance diffused to northwestern Europe—points to a fundamental similarity between Europe and Asia that helps us understand the reversal in dominance under way now.

Goody thinks that too much has been made of the Industrial Revolution as a decisive break in history, that modern capitalism may not be so radically different from its predecessors, and that attempts to associate recent history exclusively with the achievements of the West are deluded. He obviously feels that the contrast between the Old and New Worlds is exaggerated, since he never contemplates the Americas. This leads him to assert that many of the features taken to be culturally distinctive of particular regions (notably Europe) may be found elsewhere, often in quite well-developed forms. So, rather than classify whole societies according to the presumed presence and absence of cultural traits, it is better to consider the institutional variation between them as a matter of emphasis and combination. In this way, the core grounds for racial superiority are undermined, and economic development might be less readily conceived as a series of radical revolutions.

Sir Jack Goody is rarely explicit that his whole oeuvre is an attack on the fragmented idealism of contemporary cultural anthropology. Like Morgan and Childe before him, he explains cultural difference by technological change. The unequal class structure of agrarian civilization underpins many of the overt cultural differences between Eurasia and Africa, and this was made possible in turn by the intensification of agriculture (the plough and irrigation) and by new means of communication (writing). So Western supremacists are not only mistaken in their pretense of Europe's uniqueness, but they fail to grasp the material conditions that underpin the real differences in world society that they celebrate.

In the 19th century, anthropologists tried to explain how Europeans came to dominate the planet so quickly and easily. Racist binaries (and even triads) were the result. The Whites believed that they succeeded because of intrinsic cultural advantages that had a biological foundation; the empire was justified as an alternative to the permanent inferiority of the colonized. The ethnographic revolution was in part a way of rejecting this evolutionism, but the contrast between Western civilization and its primitive, nonindustrial or non-Western antithesis survived. As a comparative history of preindustrial civilizations, Jack Goody's contribution is enormous; but, like Bruno Latour, he says that we have never been modern. Modern democracy is predicated on the abolition of the unequal society that ruled the Eurasian landmass for 5,000 years. Goody reminds us of the durable inequality of our world and suggests that its causes may be less tractable than we think. The rise of China and India underlines his warning against European complacency.

Keith Hart

See also Fortes, Meyer; Latour, Bruno; Lévi-Strauss, Claude; Morgan, Lewis Henry

Further Readings

Goody, J. (Ed.). (1958). *The development cycle in domestic groups.* Cambridge, UK: Cambridge University Press.

———. (1962). *Death, property and the ancestors: A study of the mortuary customs of the LoDagaa of West Africa.* Stanford, CA: Stanford University Press.

———. (1976). *Production and reproduction: A comparative study of the domestic domain.* Cambridge, UK: Cambridge University Press.

———. (1977). *The domestication of the savage mind.* Cambridge, UK: Cambridge University Press.

———. (1991). Towards a room with a view: A personal account of contributions to local knowledge, theory, and research in fieldwork and comparative studies. *Annual Review of Anthropology, 20,* 1–22.

———. (2007). *The theft of history.* Cambridge, UK: Cambridge University Press.

———. (2010). *The Eurasian miracle.* Cambridge, UK: Polity.

Hart, K. (2011). *Jack Goody's vision of world history and African development today.* Halle-Saale, Germany: Max Planck Institute for Social Anthropology. Retrieved from http://thememorybank.co.uk/2012/01/10/jack-goodys-vision-of-history-and-african-development-today/

Olson, D., & Cole, M. (Eds.). (2006). *Technology, literacy and the evolution of society: Implications of the work of Jack Goody.* Mahwah, NJ: Lawrence Erlbaum.

GRAEBNER, FRITZ

Fritz Graebner (1877–1934) is a representative of the so-called culture historical method, or diffusionist school, which dominated cultural anthropology in the German-speaking countries from its beginning in the late 19th century until the mid-20th century. He fiercely defended the principles of diffusion and the shared origins of societies showing similar cultural traits.

Born in Berlin, Graebner studied history in Marburg and Berlin and received his PhD in 1901. Subsequently, he worked at the anthropological museum in Berlin and became the curator of the anthropological museum in Cologne in 1906. In 1925, he became the director of that museum, and a year later, he was appointed as professor at the University of Cologne. Owing to chronic illness, he retired in 1928.

Graebner's main interest was in the relation between cultures and their historical development. Perhaps due to his background in history, he intended to outline methodological principles for how to identify mutual influences between cultures. During his time, the cultural historical method was in vogue at most anthropological institutions, universities, and museums in the German-speaking countries. Nevertheless, there were internal divisions with regard to the appropriate method by which culture history could be scientifically analyzed.

The 1911 publication of Graebner's book titled *The Method of Ethnology* was a hallmark of the "culture historical method," defining the guiding principles of cultural "kinship." He introduced the so-called *Formkriterium,* referring to crafted objects, as the constituting part of the material culture. Whenever two objects belonging to different cultures have a certain congruity in their formal design, Graebner considered this as an indicator of previous diffusion between the two cultures. Several formal congruities would be proof of a close relation dating back to ancient times. He aimed at defining culture relations, and subsequently cultural strata and cultural circles (*Kulturkreise*). Graebner assumed that all present cultures had developed through the diffusion of traits from a limited number of original cultural centers and that the history of those cultures that do not have written records could be reconstructed by analyzing the material elements of those cultures and by tracing the respective elements to an original cultural center. He distinguished his notion of cultural circles from the Boasian concept of culture areas by the fact that they represent historical links rather than mere geographical proximity. Opponents, like Father Wilhelm Schmidt from Vienna, argued that Graebner's criterion of form was too schematic and that it did not meet the prerequisite of understanding culture. Another ethnographer of the time, Leo Frobenius, was even more critical. He suggested that objects should not be considered as indicators of culture history but the idea of the culture as such. Frobenius blamed Graebner for overestimating the evidence available through museum objects.

Graebner's focus on the diffusion of material culture is also evident in his entry "Ethnologie," published in a volume titled *Anthropology* (1923). The editor allowed 150 pages for Graebner to expand on his perspective on the state of ethnology. Half of the entry describes "culture circles," whereas the other half deals with cultural elements, which are, in Graebner's view, the artifacts and their formal similarities. Besides inspiring discussion over the appropriate methods in culture history, Graebner's major achievement is the idea that no culture exists in complete separation from other cultures. Following Graebner's lead, every culture can be described through a grid of similarities and differences, which also constitute the kinship of that respective culture. Perhaps, it is not an exaggeration to call him a taxonomist of cultures, since he locates cultures' relative position in a larger system of kinship of cultures.

Hans Peter Hahn

See also Bastian, Adolf; Boas, Franz; Culture Area Approach; Diffusionism, Hyperdiffusionism, *Kulturkreise;* Frobenius, Leo

Further Readings

Graebner, F. (1905). Kulturkreise und Kulturschichten in Ozeanien [Culture circles and cultural strata in Oceania]. *Zeitschrift für Ethnologie, 37,* 28–90.
———. (1911). *Methode der Ethnologie* [Method of ethnology]. Heidelberg, Germany: Winter.
———. (1923). Ethnologie. In G. Schwalbe & E. Fischer (Eds.), *Anthropologie: Kultur der Gegenwart* [Anthropology: Contemporary culture] (pp. 435–587). Leipzig, Germany: B. G. Teubner.
———. (1924). *Das Weltbild der Primitiven: Eine Untersuchung der Urformen weltanschaulichen Denkens bei Naturvölkern* [The worldview of the primitives: An examination of the original forms of philosophical thinking among primitive peoples]. Munich, Germany: Ernst Reinhardt.
Leser, P. (1978). On the role of Fritz Graebner in the development of historical ethnology. *Ethnologia Europaea, 10,* 107–113.
Lips, J. E. (1935). Fritz Graebner. *American Anthropologist, 37,* 320–326.

GRAMSCI, ANTONIO

Scholars have mined the works of Antonio Gramsci since 1947 to analyze his novel ideas. Early in his career, Gramsci (1891–1937) was a Marxist thinker, writer, and revolutionary. Later, he became disillusioned over the failure of the Marxist reliance on the power of the economic base to generate a proletariat revolution. Instead, Gramsci developed a project that turned Marxist thinking on its head. He subordinated the Marxist determination of the economic base to the revolutionary power of the ideational superstructure. His project was dedicated to a dialectic intended to explain how political agents might change the culture of the proletariat to challenge their exploitation by bourgeois capitalist governments. Gramsci's ideas and project are sufficiently

distinct from traditional Marxist thinking that they are better identified as "Gramscian." They continue to invigorate thinking about change, revolutionary and otherwise.

Writings

Antonio Gramsci's body of work can be divided between his pre-prison and prison writings. In his pre-prison writings (ca. 1910–1926), Gramsci introduced the ideas on which he would muse more elaborately in his prison writings. In effect, his pre-prison writings provided the frame of reference for the revolutionary ideas he would develop later in prison. Gramsci's ideas were sufficiently threatening to Mussolini's fascist government that he was prosecuted for subversion and sentenced to 20 years in prison.

Gramsci's prison writings (1926–1937) constitute his prison notebooks, or *Quaderni del Carcere.* The *Quaderni* lack coherent integration. He intended to refine them after his release from prison. This never happened. Gramsci, always frail, died shortly after his early release due to ill health.

The *Quaderni* are a compilation of the nearly 3,000 pages of notes Gramsci compiled while he was incarcerated. Quintin Hoare and Geoffrey Nowell edited a fragment of those notes to produce the *Prison Notebooks of Antonio Gramsci.* To what extent the *Prison Notebooks* represents what Gramsci might have preferred is moot. The *Quaderni* were fragmentary, sometimes contradictory, and replete with neologisms and a code to confound prison censors. Still, the *Prison Notebooks* remain sufficiently connotative to allow diverse interpretations of Gramsci's ideas.

Ideas

The *Prison Notebooks* contain Gramsci's seminal ideas from which he developed his revolutionary project to subvert Western capitalist governments. This project relied largely on the relationship between his three central ideas: (1) hegemony, (2) the intellectuals, (3) and culture. The work that became uniquely Gramscian is identified most closely with his idea of hegemony. As a concept and problematic, hegemony has influenced extensive research in the social sciences and humanities.

Lenin defined hegemony as the domination of one state over another. Gramsci redefined hegemony as an intellectual and moral leadership that is materialized in political organizations. Hegemony effectively is synonymous with leaders and leadership in a collective sense, such as a structure, group, apparatus, or political party. Gramsci argued that every man is an intellectual. But some had leadership skills that most lacked. He identified two categories of intellectuals: traditional and organic. Traditional intellectuals, the nobility, lawyers, ecclesiastics, for example, represent the interests of the bourgeoisie. Organic intellectuals extrude from the subaltern classes and represent the interests of the proletariat. The intellectuals represented a dialectic that infused much of Gramsci's thinking.

Before his incarceration, Gramsci was a journalist and a theater critic for various communist publications. The ideas and definitions of culture that he developed at this time pervade Gramsci's writings. Among them was a politically directed idea of culture that was fundamental to his revolutionary project. Gramsci identified culture as the exercise of thought, the acquisition of general ideas, and the habit of connecting cause and effect enlivened by political organization. Culture was personified in, and a political product of, the intellectuals. They were dedicated to persuading those they represented to accept a unified conception of the world and an ideology favorable to their interests—traditional intellectuals/capitalists and organic intellectuals/proletariat. The intellectuals represented the dialectic of hegemonies, which was the keystone of his revolutionary theory.

Revolutionary Theory

Gramsci developed two propositions to explain how a revolution of the proletariat might succeed in subverting the power of the West's bourgeois governments: a war of movement and a war of position (also a passive revolution). The war of movement relied on a strategy presumed to be effective against weak governments that ruled largely through coercion and lacked the support of their citizens. Gramsci argued that an armed insurrection by a hegemonic proletariat probably would be sufficient to overthrow these governments. The entrenched capitalist governments of Europe and North America required a different strategy, however: a war of position.

More than any other Marxist thinker, Gramsci recognized the significance of culture in revolutionary practice. A war of position would be a slow and protracted struggle by organic hegemons for the support of the proletariat. In this war, organic hegemons would confront the traditional hegemons of capitalist governments that had successfully articulated an established culture—ideas and relations of cause and effect—to sustain the support of their populations. Fully aware of the cultural density and depth of false consciousness imposed by capitalist hegemons on their populations, Gramsci argued that the proletariat must exercise leadership before usurping the governmental power of the bourgeoisie. This involved a paradox: A cultural revolution led by organic hegemons would have to precede the final political revolution.

The task the organic intellectuals faced was to replace bourgeois culture and undermine the false consciousness it imposed on the proletariat. This strategy engaged the dialectic of hegemonies. Traditional intellectuals would strive to maintain a culture and false consciousness amendable to capitalism. Organic intellectuals would engage in a counterhegemony to raise the subalterns' consciousness, alter their ideas and habitual relations of cause and effect, marshal their revolutionary energies to subvert capitalist domination, and establish a communist utopia.

Gramsci died before his theories could be tested. But over the years, his ideas, especially hegemony, have been analyzed surgically in a series of critical examinations. Some exegetes, James Scott (*Weapons of the Weak*) for example, reject Gramsci's ideas because of their Marxist taint. Scott argues that hegemony is nothing more than a synonym for the Marxist idea of false consciousness. Most stretch his ideas to apply them to different scenarios, and reinterpretations are abundant. Robert Bocock, David Adamson, and Joseph Femia identify different kinds of hegemony; Ernesto Laclau and Chantal Mouffe reject the role of the intellectuals in social and political change. Some of this variation is due to the complexity of the *Prison Notebooks*.

Exegetes

A vast literature has developed that explores the complex and intertwined implications of Gramsci's ideas, especially in the *Quaderni*, where his ideas are often open to interpretation. Gramsci did not make it easy to interpret his ideas. His notes were not meant for public consumption; they were meant for his own use and for the project he hoped to develop after he was released from prison. Those who decipher his ideas often relate his primary ideas, hegemony, intellectuals, and culture, to his other, secondary ideas.

Gramsci used a rich terminology, often capriciously, to insinuate ideas of hegemony in different contexts. For example, in some contexts, his idea of civil society is an ensemble of social institutions; in others, it is the source of organic intellectuals' hegemonic apparatus. Gramsci's notion of a political society often is equated with the state, an idea around which much of his thinking on hegemony and the work of the intellectuals revolves. The state also is identified with bourgeois oppression and has a negative connotation. In some instances, civil society (social institutions) and political society (state) are separate entities. In others, they are absorbed into the state. Common sense to Gramsci refers to traditional conceptions of the world, while good sense implies a coherent culture that is a desirable product of the work of organic intellectuals. This shifting intertexture of ideas makes the *Quaderni* a challenge to read.

Still, the largest investment in the Gramscian idea industry is related to interpretations of hegemony. Some have explored hegemony as a philosophical problem regarding why different types of hegemonies have developed. Others are dedicated to exploring different types of hegemony and their application by agents and organizations in different circumstances. Still others ponder how organic hegemons obtain consent from subaltern populations. Many locate hegemony in a Marxist epistemology and retain its relationship to the economic base. In these works, hegemony is explored in the context of ideas from other Marxist thinkers, such as Louis Althusser, Laclau, Mouffe, or Karl Marx himself, and often is synonymous with ideology. They overlook the fact that Gramsci rejected the Marxist subordination of the ideational superstructure to the economic base. Some subordinate hegemony to the presumed power of his secondary ideas, such as civil society, political society, or common sense. This suggests a misunderstanding of the power of hegemony and weakens its revolutionary potential. Devout Marxists decry that Gramsci displayed more interest in politics and culture than in the power of the economic base. Yet Femia points out that it is ironic that in Gramsci

Marxists found a true guardian of the empirical epistemology that Marx had used to predict a design in human history that ends with the collapse of capitalism and the victory of the proletariat.

Gramsci rejected the Marxist idea of an a priori dialectic to history. Instead, Gramsci argued that nothing moves people to action except ideas and ideals. Although this argument does not comply with Marx's materialist motivation for history, it does conform to Marx's argument that people make their own history but not necessarily as they please. Femia points out that Gramsci's project is not averse to this latter Marxist proposition, because Gramsci's thinking derives from first-hand experiences with demonstrations and strikes that occurred before, during, and after World War I in Turin—an industrial city that was the center of Italian communism. Because of the variety Gramsci brings to his idea of culture, there is confusion as to whether hegemony shapes culture or is shaped by it, and what exactly the relationship is between the two. Kate Crehan argues that anthropologists could learn much from Gramsci's ideas of culture. But for the most part, anthropologists have muddled his ideas badly.

Anthropologists

Anthropologists have misconstrued Gramsci's ideas because they rely on secondary interpretations of his ideas and not the writings of Gramsci himself. They are inspired primarily by interpretations of hegemony provided by Raymond Williams, an icon in the field of cultural studies. Williams established a relationship between hegemony and culture that attracted anthropologists because of their traditional attachment to the idea of culture. Richard Fox (*Gandhian Utopia*), for example, relies on Williams to develop his idea of a "cultural hegemony" that establishes sets of meanings that enable and constrain resistance to existing social formations.

To what extent Williams read Gramsci is questionable. He never mentions or cites the *Prison Notebooks*. But "culture" loomed large in his work, *Marxism and Literature*. In different contexts, Williams described hegemony as a concept that includes culture, went beyond culture, and was synonymous with culture. The conflation of hegemony and culture precluded the need for anthropologists to engage the density of the *Prison Notebooks* and other writings of Gramsci. In effect, Williams appropriated Gramsci word *hegemony*, welded it to a notion of culture, and established ownership over ideas that had little to do with how Gramsci or his nonanthropological exegetes understood them. He was sufficiently convincing for Sherry Ortner (*High Religion*) to imply that the concept of hegemony originated with Williams. Williams's interpretations of hegemony corrupted almost all anthropological understanding of Gramsci's ideas. Jean and John Comaroff (*Of Revelation and Revolution*) correctly point out that anthropologists often use hegemony as nothing more than a trendy buzz word.

Anthropologists commonly cite Gramsci and then rely on the ideas of his exegetes to address Gramsci's ideas. They also ignore Gramsci's idea of the intellectuals and the dialectic of hegemonies. None seem to understand Gramsci's idea that culture is a product of hegemony. For example, those anthropologists who understand hegemony as a social and political force (James Brow, Martha Kaplan, John Kelly, and Daniel Linger, among others) invert Gramsci's idea of hegemony and use it to explain how elites further their interests by dominating and exploiting native populations. Of the dozen or so anthropologists who used Gramsci's ideas in the 1980s, only Peter Carstens (*The Queen's People*) and, to a lesser extent, Claudio Lomnitz Adler (*Exits From the Labyrinth*) relied on Gramsci's depiction of hegemony in the *Quarderi* as a practice by which subjugated masses develop leadership that helps them resist their exploitation.

The Comaroffs (*Of Revelation and Revolution*) developed one of the best known anthropological interpretations of hegemony. It is also perhaps the most egregious corruption of Gramsci's thinking. After rejecting Gramsci's idea of hegemony, they conflate the ideas of hegemony provided by Williams and Laclau and Mouffe and develop a functionalist model that reduces hegemony to shared traditions and orthodoxies that are devoid of the human agency of the intellectuals. They conclude that, at its most effective, hegemony is mute, an idea that primarily is good to think of and fodder only for ideological discourse. In effect, the Comaroffs strip hegemony of its revolutionary power.

The transmogrifications of Gramsci's idea of hegemony have disseminated widely among anthropologists. These ideas, however, are not authentic Gramsci. And they create a paradox for an anthropology that some of its practitioners have identified as the most subversive of the social sciences. Anthropologists in general have stripped hegemony of its revolutionary significance and theory and muddled Gramsci's ideas. Still, many of these anthropological studies are creative and convey a kind of structuralist, postmodern neo-Gramscian interpolation that represents another tangent of presumed Gramscian thinking.

Donald V. Kurtz

See also Althusser, Louis; Cultural Transmission; Marx, Karl; Marxist Anthropology; Ortner, Sherry; Structural Marxism; Subaltern Studies

Further Readings

Bocock, R. (1986). *Hegemony.* Chichester, UK: Ellis Horwood.

Cavilcanti, P., & Piccone, P. (1975). *History, philosophy and culture in the young Gramsci.* St. Louis, MO: Telos Press.

Crehan, K. (2002). *Gramsci, culture and anthropology.* London, UK: Pluto Press.

Femia, J. V. (1988). *Gramsci's political thought: Hegemony, consciousness and the revolutionary process.* Oxford, UK: Clarendon.

Gramsci, A. (1971). *Selections from the prison notebooks* (Q. Hoare & G. N. Smith, Eds. & Trans.). New York, NY: International Publishers.

Kurtz, D. V. (1996). Hegemony and anthropology: Gramsci, exegeses, reinterpretation. *Critique of Anthropology, 16*(2), 103–135.

Laclau, E., & Mouffe, C. (1985). *Hegemony and socialist strategy: Toward a radical democratic politics.* London, UK: Verso.

Sassoon, A. S. (1980). *Gramsci's politics.* London, UK: Hutchison.

Thomas, P. D. (2009). *The Gramscian moment: Philosophy, hegemony, Marxism.* Leiden, Netherlands: Brill.

GREAT EXHIBITION OF 1851 (CRYSTAL PALACE)

The Great Exhibition held in London in 1851 at the Crystal Palace, a temporary structure created at Hyde Park for the occasion, was a major undertaking that came to be seen as a model of commercial success melded with philanthropically inspired public education. Many exhibition organizers of subsequent fairs harked back to the Great Exhibition's perceived achievements, while at the same time trying to surpass them. As objects of national policy, fairs originated primarily as trade and industrial events in France in the late 18th century. They were relatively brief, most often running for 6 months. By the late 1800s, they had become commercially successful, competitive ventures that were inextricably tied to a range of political, scientific, and technological ideals. With respect to anthropology, the Crystal Palace was most important in fostering an interest in using the fairs to examine human diversity among visitors, displaying a range of ethnological material in the official exhibits, and in setting precedents that were followed by later world fairs.

Visitors

As early as 1851, commentators noted the diverse ethnic backgrounds of the attendees and the curiosity it stirred in those interested in watching the crowds. For instance, the journalist Henry Mayhew's *1851; or, The Adventures of Mr and Mrs Sandboys* (1851) pointed out that almost every London omnibus now carried foreigners among the passengers. The comical account reflected a broader mood as, in the press, Londoners and visitors to the palace were portrayed as interested in seeing the foreign visitors as much as the official exhibits. Much of this press coverage now seems riven with revealing anxieties about race and empire. Yet, in many senses, it was crucial in perpetuating the sense that visitors were available for visual inspection and that they, given their ethnic heterogeneity, would make ideal ethnological exemplars for both the lay and the learned to study human races.

Ethnological Models and Living Performers

From the outset, people's watching of visitors was complemented by the inclusion of human models and other ethnological material among the official exhibits. For example, the Crystal Palace featured life-size models of many foreign peoples, including Native Americans, which had been commercially exhibited in the 1840s by George Catlin. Meanwhile, there was also one living exhibit at Hyde Park: an Arab man who sold sweetmeats in a mock Tunisian bazaar in the courts devoted to the Ottoman Empire. His inclusion in the Crystal Palace echoed the broader practice of commercially exhibiting foreign peoples, or "living curiosities,"

in the theaters, museums, galleries, and zoos of the metropolis in ways designed to showcase their ethnic singularity. After the original Crystal Palace closed, a new "people's palace" opened in Sydenham in 1854. A more nationalist venture than the 1851 exhibition, it featured newly commissioned ethnological models that were used to create a court of natural history. Curated by the leading expert Robert Gordon Latham, the court functioned as an ethnological museum and training ground for budding scholars. The incorporation of such material into both the 1851 and the 1854 Crystal Palace was crucial as it became directly tied to the emergence of new disciplines in the study of race.

Emerging Anthropology and Lasting Legacies

Between the 1840s and 1860s, in Britain, France, and Germany in particular, the human models, cultural artifacts, and displayed peoples on show at world fairs increasingly became tied to the emergence of the new disciplines of ethnology and anthropology. In Britain, for example, the shows were explicitly and routinely advertised as ideal opportunities to see specimens of ethnic diversity; and members of the Ethnological Society of London (founded in 1843) and Anthropological Society of London (founded in 1863) took advantage of the opportunity both to study the displayed peoples and to use them to bolster the credibility of these newly founded institutions. Meanwhile, anthropologists' involvement in later world fairs became extensive. They acted as curators and exhibition organizers and used the fairs to conduct their ongoing research into the nature of human races. In this context, exhibitions and performers became experimental resources used by anthropologists to provide them with access to new resources, train new practitioners, and educate the public about new anthropological theories.

In conjunction, the Crystal Palace displayed objects in numerous national contexts, enabling cross-cultural comparisons of material culture; thus, many visitors interpreted the displays in teleological, developmental, and evolutionary terms. For instance, the exhibits were sometimes read as a progressive ascent from the lowest forms of humanity to the apex of civilization as exemplified by the commercial activities of Victorian Britain. The displays were often interpreted as evidence of human "improvement" or "progress" through the ages. At Sydenham, the temporal development was even more explicit as visitors walked and retraced the pathway from the emergence of dinosaurs from the ground's lake to the beacon of national progress provided by the palace. Historians have speculated that this influenced important anthropologists. For instance, the evolutionary anthropologist E. B. Tylor's family exhibited their wares in 1851, and Tylor kept photographs of the human models at Sydenham in his personal collection. Likewise, A. H. L. F. Pitt Rivers's collections were later exhibited to show the evolutionary development of human material culture.

The use of models and a live performer at the Crystal Palace set an important precedent that was emulated until the mid-20th century. For instance, in 1867, foreign peoples were employed as shopkeepers and servants at the Parisian Exposition Universelle. Later, at the Colonial and Indian Exhibition of 1886 in London, the Exposition Universelle of 1889 in Paris, and Chicago's World Columbian Exposition of 1893, foreign peoples were specifically imported to be exhibited within purpose-built "native villages" on the exhibition grounds. Within this context, living foreign peoples were transformed into professional performers and became tied to new forms of cheap mass entertainment. Such displays reached their peak in terms of scale, commercial success, and public access under the aegis of the international trade of Europe, India, America, Africa, and Australia, which followed in the wake of the Great Exhibition. Traditionally, historians have looked to Paris (1867 and 1889), Chicago (World's Columbian Exposition, 1893), and St. Louis (Louisiana Purchase Exposition, 1904) as the best examples of the use of displayed peoples and the means of discussing and establishing their broader connections to anthropological study. However, the Great Exhibition of 1851 inaugurated the practice of displaying living foreign peoples in international fairs. The 1854 opening of the new Crystal Palace at Sydenham witnessed one of the earliest and most significant attempts to incorporate displayed peoples into ethnological practice for both the lay and the learned. And the 1886 Colonial and Indian Exhibition provides an exemplary case of the diverse ways in which displayed peoples were presented in international fairs and used by anthropologists in late-19th-century Britain. Thus, ultimately, it is the formative role of the Crystal Palace within the broader histories of anthropology that needs to be remembered.

Sadiah Qureshi

See also Nineteenth-Century Evolutionary Anthropology; Pitt Rivers, Augustus Henry Lane Fox; Tylor, Edward Burnett

Further Readings

Auerbach, J. A. (1999). *The Great Exhibition of 1851: A nation on display.* New Haven, CT: Yale University Press.

Greenhalgh, P. (1988). *Ephemeral vistas: The expositions universelles, great exhibitions and world's fairs, 1851–1939.* Manchester, UK: Manchester University Press.

Hoffenberg, P. H. (2001). *An empire on display: English, Indian and Australian exhibitions from the Crystal Palace to the Great War.* Berkeley: University of California Press.

Qureshi, S. (2011). *Peoples on parade: Exhibitions, empire and anthropology in nineteenth-century Britain.* Chicago, IL: University of Chicago Press.

Stocking, G. W., Jr. (1987). *Victorian anthropology.* New York, NY: Free Press.

Tallis, J. (1852). *Tallis's history and description of the Crystal Palace and the exhibition of the world's industry in 1851* (3 vols.). London, UK: Tallis.

GREENBERG, JOSEPH

Joseph Harold Greenberg (1915–2001) was one of the most influential linguists of the second half of the 20th century. He made major contributions to the study of all aspects of language, including grammatical structure, historical linguistics, phonology, psycholinguistics, sociolinguistics, and anthropological linguistics. Greenberg's most important theoretical contributions are to the empirical study of universals of language, known as typology, and to the genetic classification of languages.

Greenberg was trained in the classics, Indo-European comparative linguistics, and anthropology, receiving his PhD from Northwestern University under Melville Herskovits. He published 19 books and more than 200 articles and received many awards, including the Academy of Arts & Sciences' Talcott Parsons Prize for Social Science in 1997.

Genetic Classification of Languages

Greenberg's first major contribution to linguistics was the genetic classification of the languages of Africa in the late 1940s. At that time, the language families of Africa were defined by nonlinguistic traits, such as race, and by structural traits, such as the presence or absence of gender class inflections. Greenberg argued that these traits were irrelevant to the genetic classification of languages. Only the arbitrary pairing of phonetic form and meaning in large numbers of basic vocabulary items and grammatical inflections are accurate guides to genetic classification. Greenberg's classification of African languages into four families based on pairings of form and meaning at first aroused great controversy but then became widely accepted.

Greenberg's method, which he called multilateral comparison, is the large-scale comparison of vocabulary and grammatical inflections in all of the languages in a large area. Greenberg's hypothesis is that the distributional pattern of similarities in meaning and form across a large number of words and inflections and across a large number of languages can reveal genetic families of languages, as well as identifying patterns due to other factors such as borrowing, sound symbolism, and chance.

Greenberg proposed many ancient language families. In Oceania, he proposed that all of the languages in Papua New Guinea and the neighboring islands, excluding the more recent Austronesian family and the aboriginal languages of Australia, form a single family, which he called Indo-Pacific. In the Americas, he proposed that all of the languages in North and South America, with the exception of the Eskimo-Aleut and Na-Dene families in the far north and northwest, belong to a single family, Amerind. At the end of his life, Greenberg published evidence for a large family in northern Eurasia, which he called Eurasiatic, ranging from the Indo-European family in the West to the Eskimo-Aleut family in northern North America.

Greenberg's method did not use regular sound correspondences, the basis of the comparative method used by other historical linguists. Greenberg argued that the comparative method was required to analyze language families only after the genetic unity of the languages being compared has been established, and that multilateral comparison was an explicit means to achieve that first step of the comparative method. Most historical linguists continue to believe that the comparative method is the only way to "prove" the genetic unity of a set of languages, and so Greenberg's proposed ancient language families remain highly controversial. However, Greenberg's proposals and the debate that followed has revived the subfield of genetic linguistics, stimulated connections to research on human migration, and prompted the greater employment of quantitative methods in language classification.

Universals of Language

Greenberg's other major contribution to linguistics is in the area of universals of language structure. Greenberg was the founder of modern typology and universals research. At the time that Greenberg developed this approach, the field of linguistics was dominated by the structuralist view that languages could vary in their structure in unlimited ways. At the same time, Noam Chomsky was developing the theory of generative grammar, in which it is claimed that all languages have the same underlying structure.

Greenberg's research combined a novel theoretical approach to language universals—the implicational universal—with an original empirical discovery, dependencies among word orders. Greenberg's theory falls between the structuralist view that language variation is unlimited and the generative grammar view that all languages have certain structural features in common. Greenberg introduced the implicational universal, in which there is a dependency between two (or more) structural features of a language: The dependency restricts the range of possible language types but does not require all languages to be the same with respect to those structural features. Implicational universals can be illustrated by Greenberg's empirical discovery of dependencies between the word orders of different grammatical constructions. For example, one of Greenberg's word order universals states that if a language has the subject-object-verb order, then it has postpositions (which follow the noun). This universal allows for language variation: It allows for languages with subject-verb-object order (such as English), and these subject-verb-object languages may have prepositions (as English does) or postpositions (as the subject-verb-object language Grebo does). But the cross-linguistic variation is restricted: Languages with the subject-object-verb order and prepositions are expected not to occur, or are extremely rare.

Greenberg's discovery of implicational universals of word order was unprecedented, and his paper on the topic is one of the most cited papers in linguistics. The basic facts of word order dependencies are empirical phenomena that every linguistic theory attempts to explain. Greenberg's seminal paper, which proposes universals of grammatical categories as well as universals of word order, spawned an entire subfield, typology, which explores the cross-linguistic variation of all aspects of language structure and has discovered hundreds of implicational universals. Greenberg developed models to account for language universals, including grammatical hierarchies; the role of frequency of use in language universals; and the explanation of universals of language structure in terms of universal processes of language change. Greenberg's approach has far-reaching consequences for ongoing debates about universals and relativity, which are often still framed in terms of the two extremes of unlimited variation versus complete uniformity in language structure. Nevertheless, Greenberg's typological discoveries and theories about language universals form one of the foundations of contemporary linguistics.

William Croft

See also Chomsky, Noam; Comparative Linguistics; Comparative Method; Descriptive Linguistics; Generative Grammar; Herskovits, Melville; Human Universals

Further Readings

Comrie, B. (1989). *Language universals and linguistic typology* (2nd ed.). Chicago, IL: University of Chicago Press.

Croft, W. (2003). *Typology and universals* (2nd ed.). Cambridge, UK: Cambridge University Press.

Greenberg, J. H. (1963). *The languages of Africa*. The Hague, Netherlands: Mouton.

———. (1966). *Language universals*. The Hague, Netherlands: Mouton.

———. (1987). *Language in the Americas*. Stanford, CA: Stanford University Press.

———. (1990). *On language: Selected writings of Joseph H. Greenberg* (K. Denning & S. Kemmer, Eds.). Stanford, CA: Stanford University Press.

———. (2000–2002). *Indo-European and its closest relatives: The Eurasiatic language family* (Vols. 1–2). Stanford, CA: Stanford University Press.

———. (2005). *Genetic linguistics: Theory and method* (W. Croft, Ed.). Oxford, UK: Oxford University Press.

GRIAULE, MARCEL

Marcel Griaule (1898–1956) made multiple contributions to anthropology. He was the most active founder of the Société des Africanistes (1931) and also inaugurated the first French professorship of ethnography (1942). He contributed to anthropological methodology by opening Africa to French academic research in 1932 and 1933, and in 1937, he was the first to initiate aerial survey research in archaeology and ethnology. He contributed to anthropological theory through his "invention" of the Dogon, creating an approach to fieldwork that continued for half a century.

Born of modest origins, Griaule interrupted his studies to volunteer for military service during World War I. Discharged as a lieutenant of aviation in 1922, he enrolled at the Religious Sciences section of l'École Pratique des Hautes Études with Marcel Mauss and took courses in Amharic at l'Institut des Langues Orientales with Marcel Cohen. In 1927, the Department of Public Instruction and Fine Arts assigned him to an ethnological and linguistic mission in Ethiopia (then called Abyssinia). His work there resulted in the publication of a long essay "Mythes, croyances et coutumes du Begamder" (Myths, Beliefs and Customs in Begamder) in the *Journal Asiatique* (1928, Volume 212, pp. 19–124) and a smaller one in *l'Anthropologie*. Griaule also published in *Documents*, an avant-garde magazine. Recruited in 1929 as Mauss's assistant at the Laboratory of Ethnology of the Vème section of l'Ecole pratique des hautes études (Religious Science section), Griaule translated (with Abbas Jerome) *Le Livre de recettes d'un dabtara abyssin* (*The Spell Book of an Abyssinian Magician*), which was published by the Institute of Ethnology in 1930.

Exoticism was fashionable, and Griaule joined the "stew" of artists, nobility, bourgeoisie, and scholars at the Trocadero Museum (which became the Museum of Man in 1937). With the support of its director Paul Rivet and his deputy Georges-Henri

Rivière, Griaule then organized and directed the first major French expedition to Africa with funding from various sources, including a direct grant from the Chamber of Deputies, and also organized a boxing match, in which the world champion, the Panamanian boxer Al Brown, "proud to help the discovery of his ancestor negroes," defeated a boxer named Simendé.

Arriving in Dakar in May 1931, the expedition left Djibouti for Paris in February 1933 after passing through 15 countries. The spirit of this expedition was much like that of Cambridge University's Torres Straits expedition of 1898. It was faithful to the spirit of Mauss, who wished for extensive surveys rather than in-depth fieldwork at a single location. It was an era of salvage ethnography. "We will prospect for the future," wrote Griaule. Like the Torres Straits expedition, the Dakar-Djibouti expedition included a variety of specialists. At various times, it included a naturalist, a musicologist, a movie camera operator, linguists, interpreters, and an artist, in addition to botanists and ethnographers. The mission brought a wide variety of items back to France, including embryos of several species of mammals, boxes of bones, and a number of live animals, as well as a record of 30 languages, 300 manuscripts, 24 cylinders of sound recording, thousands of feet of film, and 3,500 objects, including Dogon masks and 60 square meters of paintings from one of the oldest Ethiopian churches. There were also 15,000 sheets of ethnographic reporting. Here again, the mission followed Mauss's techniques. These field notes were classified in alphabetical order without mention of the name of the author or the date of writing. All expedition members drew from this collective data as they published their reports. Travelogues were then fashionable, and two were published in the aftermath of this expedition. Michel Leiris published l'Afrique fantôme (Ghost Africa, 1934), a subjective, honest, but provocative diary, and Griaule published Les Flambeurs d'hommes (Burners of Men: Modern Ethiopia, 1934), a report of his Ethiopian mission, in a flamboyant style.

Griaule represented French ethnology at the First Session of the International Congress of Anthropological and Ethnological Sciences, held in London in 1934, and then directed the Sahara-Sudan Mission, leaving on January 7, 1935.

The main objective of this third mission was to study the Dogon of the Bandiagara cliffs, who were considered particularly interesting because they were "authentically wild and archaic." Like the Dakar-Djibouti expedition, this mission involved a wide variety of scholars, including three additional students of Marcel Mauss: Helen Gordon, the Countess de Breteuil (Solange de Ganay), and Denise Paulme. The last two remained in Dogon country between March and September 1935, thus constituting the first instance of long-term fieldwork by French ethnographers.

In this and earlier expeditions, Griaule and his colleagues essentially invented the Dogon. Prior to Griaule, the group now known as the Dogon consisted of village dwellers known as the Habre to the neighboring Fulani people, but without a sense of their own collective identity. Griaule unified various practices and entities under a single name, giving birth to the Dogon as such.

On his return, Griaule popularized ethnography in magazines and fought for the independence of Ethiopia after the Italian aggression of October 1934. After writing a memorandum for the League of Nations, he published La peau de l'ours (The Skin of the Bear, 1936). The book denounced the atrocities of the Italian military campaign and showed the complexity of Ethiopian culture, making arguments that prefigured the relativistic themes of Races and History (Claude Lévi-Strauss, 1952).

Appointed deputy director of the Laboratory of Ethnology of the École Pratique des Hautes Études in 1936, Griaule led a new expedition called Mission Sahara-Cameroon (July 1936 to October 1937). He flew to West Africa in a small plane. At the same time, Solange de Ganay and Germaine Dieterlen arrived in Dakar by ship and remained in the field. Using the plane, Griaule demonstrated the use of aerial photography to "read invisible remains and arrangements of space." Griaule traveled up the Niger River to explore the neighboring populations before turning to the archaeological excavations being undertaken by John Paul Lebeuf, another student of Mauss. In addition to 3,000 photos, this fourth mission returned with 800 ethnographic objects, 150 herbal plants, and a collection of 150 insects. The ethnographic sheet was still the master: The mission brought back 6,000 of them.

In his earlier work, Griaule had addressed "Abyssinian totemism." He returned to this theme in 1935 and in 1937 in his work on the Dogon, with the publication of Masques Dogon (Dogon Masks,

1938b). This work explored the mask societies present in all Dogon villages. The text proposed that Dogon religion reflects the myths and rituals that come from the Old Mande World. Like Herodotus gathering the stories of Greek mythology, Griaule gathered scattered material and assembled this to constitute Dogon cosmogony and cosmology. One can imagine the enthusiasm for this kind of work of a small group of French anthropologists whose imagination was inspired by classical culture (the same thing happened with Frobenius in Germany).

Griaule had written "Abyssinian Games" for *Documents* in 1929, and he turned once again to this subject for his second dissertation for the École Pratique des Haute Études (at the time, candidates for the doctorate had to defend two theses). Although Griaule argued that the games prepared their participants for life, following Mauss, he also wrote that the games were strategic locations to read the survivals of old institutions.

After defending his theses at the Sorbonne in October 1938, Griaule began a fifth mission, which included Ganay, Dieterlen, Lebeuf, Manouka Laroche, a doctor, and Jean Lebaudy, a sugar industry magnate who financed the expedition. Called the Niger–Lake Ir Mission, it traveled the Niger bend, reporting on the Tellem, Kouroumba, Dogon, and Kotoko peoples before being cut short due to the outbreak of World War II.

In September 1939, Griaule joined the French air force and received the Croix de Guerre before his demobilization in July 1940. With the Vichy regime in power, Jews were forbidden to teach, and at the beginning of September 1941, Griaule took over the courses that had been taught by Mauss and Cohen. He also became deputy director for ethnology at the Museum of Man. The Hellenist and anti-Semite Abel Bonnard was appointed minister of education in April 1942. He then created a professorship in ethnography at the Sorbonne, which he intended for Georges Montandon, a deeply anti-Semitic champion of "scientific racism." The Assembly of Teachers showed relative independence by electing Griaule to the professorship instead.

In 1947, Griaule led a sixth mission to again explore the Dogon, Bambara, Bozo, and Kouroumba societies. This last one included Genevieve Calame-Griaule, his 22-year-old daughter, who was responsible for checking the knowledge of the Qur'an of Muslim scholars. This mission would be a turning point. Griaule was no longer interested in collecting material for Museum of Man and abandoned the study of material culture to dedicate himself to oral literature and mythologies. After a "wise old Dogon" (Ogotemmeli) conversed for 34 days with him, Griaule published *Dieu d'eau* (*Conversations With Ogotemmeli: An Introduction to Dogon Religious Ideas*) in 1948. Written for the general public, the book shows the richness of the Dogon mythology.

Griaule developed the conception that by conditioning thought, myths and symbols explain social organization. Thus, unifying the male and female principles, the weaver or the blacksmith reproduces the mythical first events with his work. He explained the joking relationship between Dogon and Bozo by metaphysics, as the rule of twinning is present from the origin of the world. Reality is identified with the metaphysical representation system that operates independently and by refraction reaches the social world. This idea of the suprasocial recalls Durkheim's collective consciousness. This view has often been criticized by noting that Griaule presents no scientific explanation, but confuses this last with data subsumed in a metalanguage, and that his approach assumes that myths represent a homogeneous body of information.

When Griaule died in 1956 after a long illness, the Dogon of Bandiagara preformed a traditional funeral for him. Griaule founded a theoretical school studying the cosmology of the peoples of the Niger bend. Long led by the anthropologist Germaine Dieterlen (1903–1999), the laboratory of Systems of Thought in Black Africa of the Centre National de la Recherche Scientifique extended the study of mythic representations to the entire continent.

Gérald Gaillard

See also Frobenius, Leo; Institut d'Ethnologie (Paris); Mauss, Marcel; Musée de l'Homme; Rivet, Paul; Torres Straits Expedition

Further Readings

Clifford, J. (1983). Power and dialogue in ethnography: Marcel Griaule's initiation. In G. W. Stocking Jr. (Ed.), *Observers observed: Essays on ethnographic fieldwork* (pp. 121–156). Madison: University of Wisconsin Press.

Copans, J. (1973). Comment lire Marcel Griaule? À propos de l'interprétation de Dirk Lettens [How to read Marcel

Griaule? About the interpretation of Dirk Lettens].
Cahiers d'Études africaines, 13(1), 153–157.

Douglas, M. (1975). If the Dogon . . . . In M. Douglas (Ed.), *Implicit meanings: Essays in anthropology* (pp. 124–141). London, UK: Routledge & Kegan Paul.

Fiemeyer, I. (2004). *Marcel Griaule citoyen dogon* [Marcel Griaule, Dogon citizen]. Arles, France: Actes sud.

Forde, D. (1956). Griaule, M. *Africa, 26*, 217–228.

Griaule, M. (1934). *Les Flambeurs d'hommes.* Paris, France: Calman-Lévy. (Reprinted in 1991; translated as *Burners of men: Modern Ethiopia*, Philadelphia, PA: Lippincott, 1935, and *Abyssinian Journey*, London, UK: J. Miles, 1935)

————. (1935). *Jeux et divertissements abyssins* [Abyssinian games and pastimes]. Paris, France: Ernest Leroux.

————. (1938a). *Jeux dogons* [Dogon games]. Paris, France: Institut d'Ethnologie.

————. (1938b). *Masques dogons* [Dogon masks]. Paris, France: Institut d'Ethnologie.

————. (1957). *Méthode de l'ethnographie* [Method of ethnography] (G. Calame-Griaule, Ed.). Paris: Presses universitaires de France.

————. (1965). *Conversations with Ogotemmeli: An introduction to Dogon religious ideas.* London, UK: Oxford University Press. (Original work published 1948 as *Dieu d'Eau*)

Griaule, M., & Dieterlen, G. (1986). *The pale fox.* Chino Valley, AZ: Continuum Foundation. (Original work published 1965 as *Le Renard Pâle*)

Jolly, É. (2001). Marcel Griaule, ethnologue: La construction d'une discipline (1925–1956) [Marcel Griaule, ethnologist: The construction of a discipline]. *Journal des africanistes, 71*(1), 149–190.

GUMPERZ, JOHN J.

John Joseph Gumperz (1922–) is a sociolinguist who was professor of anthropology at the University of California Berkeley and is currently affiliated with the University of California Santa Barbara. He is particularly known for his development of interactional sociolinguistics.

Gumperz was born in Germany and moved to the United States in 1939. He completed a bachelor's degree in science at the University of Ohio, Cincinnati, then, while doing graduate studies in chemistry at the University of Michigan, he became interested in linguistics and changed his field of study. The University of Michigan awarded his PhD degree in German linguistics in 1954. His doctoral research was a study of the German Swabian dialect of a group of third-generation farmers in Michigan.

In the 1950s, it was widely accepted that people are divided into distinct community groups, each with its own language or dialect, and culture. Gumperz spent 2 years (1955–56) doing fieldwork in a caste-stratified North Indian village. He found that linguistic variation did not reflect caste differentiation. In fact, untouchable caste members spent a lot of time working in touchable caste members' households and had limited opportunity to socialize with peers. Nevertheless, they did not adopt their employers' ways of speaking, so frequency of contact also did not explain linguistic variation. What linguistic variation did reflect was normative principles about what is said, when, and by whom. Confirming evidence came in his 1963 study in a small, culturally homogeneous Norwegian town with a strong egalitarian ideology. Income and occupational status were not clearly reflected in talk, but differences in terms of regular and close relationships with speakers outside the town were reflected. In informal discussions, groups whose friendship networks were within the town tended not to switch from the local dialect to standard Norwegian, while groups whose networks extended outside the town did switch when talking about nonlocal topics. Both studies thus showed how social relationships and ideologies are reflected in speech behavior in social groups.

Subsequently, Gumperz took up an academic appointment at the University of California, Berkeley, and in 1965 became professor of anthropology and, later, emeritus professor there. During his time at Berkeley, Gumperz developed a theoretical and methodological framework known as *interactional sociolinguistics*, though that name was not used in the earlier years. In common with some other linguists, sociologists, and philosophers at the time, Gumperz's focus was on the language of everyday interaction. In the 1970s, he did fieldwork in London for a study of how cultural ways of using language could result in discrimination in employment against immigrants from Pakistan, India, and the West Indies. He was interested in miscommunication for reasons to do with both social injustice and making visible, and thus gaining insight into, how language works in interaction.

Gumperz argues that interactional sociolinguistics focuses on communicative practice because we have no other access to experiential reality. He positions interactional sociolinguistics as attempting to bridge the gap between top-down theoretical approaches that privilege macrosocietal conditions in explaining how people communicate and those, such as conversation analysis, that take a bottom-up, social constructivist approach. Interactional sociolinguistics takes a microanalytic approach to interactions, but it also explicitly takes account of the wider sociocultural context in which an interaction occurs. In particular, it pays attention to participants' goals (because participants may have different goals from each other) and the related interpretive processes that underlie utterances.

Gumperz gives an example of an older South Asian student who asked an adult education center lecturer about enrolling in a new course at a community college. The lecturer told him that she had contributed to planning the course but was not part of the selection process. Over several minutes of the interaction, he contradicted her, and she became more and more annoyed. His repeated denials puzzled Gumperz and his two younger South Asian research assistants, until the assistants noted that the student sounded as if he was pleading. This reminded Gumperz of a situation in North India where an older man asked him for help regarding his college student son in the United States. Gumperz explained that he did not have the right connections, but the man replied, "You can do everything"—similar to the stance taken by the South Asian student. Thus, in both cases, taking account of the wider sociocultural context could reveal that the requesters of help believed that people in positions of power could do anything they wanted to, which in turn could explain their linguistic behavior at the microlevel.

Interactional sociolinguistic research methodology involves close observation, often using audio (and in more recent years, video) recording, of interactions. A central concept underlying analysis is the *contextualization cue*. The analysis pays attention not just to *what* is said (the words) but also to *how* it is said (e.g., pitch, intonation, and tone of voice). Contextualization cues relate to contextual presuppositions (tacit awareness of meaningfulness) that allow us to make inferences relevant to the context about how to interpret an utterance. Gumperz points out that speakers make choices at a number of levels, for example, dialect, prosodic features, lexical and syntactic options, and sequencing strategies. Contextualization cues are often culturally specific and speakers tend not to be aware of the presuppositions and meanings that they signal in different cultures. Another step in the methodology can be that key segments of the recordings are played back to participants for their comments, which in turn become data to be analyzed for participant interpretations and insights into the talk and the situation in which it occurred.

Interactional sociolinguistics allows researchers to take account of unstated assumptions and background knowledge that participants in an interaction draw on as part of their interpretive processes. The analysis traces how participants use contextualization cues to frame the intended meanings and, thus, how participants move (or do not move) toward a shared interpretation.

Elaine W. Vine

See also Hymes, Dell; Sociolinguistics; University of California, Berkeley

Further Readings

Eerdmans, S., Prevignano, C., & Thibault, P. J. (Eds.). (2003). *Language and interaction: Discussions with John J. Gumperz.* Amsterdam, Netherlands: John Benjamins.

Gumperz, J. J. (1996). The linguistic and cultural relativity of conversational inference. In S. C. Levinson & J. J. Gumperz (Eds.), *Rethinking linguistic relativity* (pp. 374–406). Cambridge, UK: Cambridge University Press.

———. (1999). On interactional sociolinguistic method. In S. Sarangi & C. Roberts (Eds.), *Talk, work and institutional order: Discourse in medical, mediation and management settings* (pp. 453–471). Berlin, Germany: Mouton De Gruyter.

Sarangi, S. (Ed.). (2011). In honour of John Gumperz [Special issue]. *Text & Talk: An Interdisciplinary Journal of Language, Discourse & Communication Studies, 31*(4).

HABERMAS, JÜRGEN

Jürgen Habermas (1929–) is by far the most influential German philosopher, social theorist, political thinker, and public intellectual of the past several decades. He has contributed decisively to philosophy and the other humanities, the social sciences, the foundations of democracy and law, and the cultural critique of industrial societies. What he has to offer to anthropologists is some of the most relevant insights and approaches from continental European philosophy, which he develops in an—for a thinker from this background—extraordinarily strong interaction with the social sciences and awareness of the problems of modern societies.

Habermas's central question throughout his richly varied career has been this: What is, and what should it be, to be human? He has developed an answer in terms of, first, a critique of reductionist views of agency and a call for reasonable, intersubjective agency and dialogue, in everyday life as well as in law and politics, and, second, an analysis of the threats to which autonomous agency is exposed in contemporary industrial society. In the following, the main lines of his fully fledged position will be sketched, focusing on these two themes and the relevance of his hermeneutic (interpretive) philosophy for anthropology.

Life and Works

Habermas grew up in a Protestant upper-middle-class family in Germany. He studied and subsequently taught philosophy in various universities, including Frankfurt University, where he was influenced by Theodor Adorno and Max Horkheimer. As a professor at Frankfurt University from 1964 to 1971 and from 1983 to 1993, Habermas gave a decisive new impulse to the Frankfurter Schule (Frankfurt school) and its neo-Marxist critical theory of Western society and culture.

Habermas is the author of a series of influential books, starting with *The Structural Transformation of the Public Sphere: An Inquiry Into a Category of Bourgeois Society* (1962), on the constitution of public opinion through reasoned discussion. Here, he shows how the participation of all citizens in public dialogue, intimately connected to the rise of democratic societies, is in permanent danger of degradation to commercialism, consumerism, entertainment, or too much influence of experts—to interactions purely about means, no longer about goals. That analysis foreshadowed key themes of his later work, which culminated and were synthesized in his 1,000-page magnum opus, *The Theory of Communicative Action* (1981), in two volumes, with the telling subtitles *Reason and the Rationalization of Society* and *Lifeworld and System: A Critique of Functionalist Reason*. The book analyzes reasonable interaction in cultural lifeworlds and the democratic and legal systems founded in that interaction, and it shows how it is continually threatened by the systemic constraints of power (politics) and money (economy). *Between Facts and Norms: Contributions to a Discourse Theory of Law and Democracy* (1992), another major work, draws out the political, legal, and institutional implications of the theory of communicative action.

In developing his theory, Habermas has critically synthesized insights from Immanuel Kant, Karl Marx, Max Weber, and Émile Durkheim, and his work has been inspired by phenomenology and hermeneutics, pragmatism, and analytical philosophy. He has been characterized as a Marxist Weber, or a Weberian Marxist. He has engaged in debates and dialogues with, among others, more positivistically minded social scientists such as Niklas Luhmann; with postmodern thinkers such as Jacques Derrida and Richard Rorty; with Cardinal Joseph Ratzinger, who became Pope Benedict XVI; and with determinist neuroscientists. The public debates he contributed to include the struggle to come to terms with the German past, the role of religion as a source of meaning in society, the ethics of eugenics and biotechnology, postnationalism, and the implications of neuroscience for free agency.

Habermas retired in 1993 but has kept publishing, particularly in the context of various public debates, lecturing internationally, not the least in the United States, and receiving some of the highest awards, in Germany and abroad.

Reasonable Dialogue

The key element of *The Theory of Communicative Action* is a hermeneutic microanalysis of everyday linguistic communication, embedded in local cultural lifeworlds. The analysis then broadens to the macro themes law, democracy, and technocracy in modernized societies and a theory of modernization. Habermas analyzes "reasonable" human communication as a process of achieving, sustaining, and reviewing mutual understanding, in a game of give-and-take of good—reasonable and acceptable—reasons, of discussion of the validity of claims that are made. Every speech act in that game has a performative aspect—something is asserted, promised, asked for, and so on—and makes three different validity claims that are equally important, not reducible to one another, and intricately intertwined: (1) theoretical truth (regarding "it," what the facts are), (2) normative rightness (regarding "we," what we think is right), and (3) expressive or subjective truthfulness (regarding "me," what I feel and think).

Reasonable human communication, Habermas argues, is thus oriented to achieving consensus on the basis of intersubjective recognition of criticizable validity claims. In this sense, human agency is responsible—agents have to respond to critical questions, to justify their actions with good arguments, in everyday life, in courts of law, and in parliament. Accountable agency (*verantwortliche Urheberschaft*), in Habermas's formalist, procedural view of interaction, has to do with the form, not the contents, of communication. His political ideal, therefore, is (formal) solidarity among strangers, who respectfully remain strange to one another as to the contents of their beliefs and values. In the background, however, there is always the threat of a narrowing down of the interaction to strategic aspects, to tactical power plays. This happens when the interlocutors stop responding seriously to arguments and resort to purely instrumental rationality instead, such as rhetoric, ruse, or force—in such cases, the reasonable nature of interaction disappears.

This hermeneutic, normative philosophy of dialogue argues against positivistic or scientistic reduction of the I-you, intersubjective participants' perspective, which is so important to anthropology. It objects to a purely third-person perspective of agency, processes of communication, and validity claims. Such claims, in Habermas's view, can never be fully accounted for in terms of purely factual processes. Functionalist approaches in the social sciences reduce the richness of human interaction to its strategic aspect and miss out on its concern, always and everywhere, with reasonableness as a counterfactual regulative principle. With all this, in particular the implied view, and promise, of the universal, trans- and intercultural reasonableness of human interaction in a formal sense, Habermas is one of the most interesting philosophical interlocutors for anthropology as a discipline that tends to conceive of itself as not just a human but also a humane, critically engaged science.

Endangered Lifeworlds

Habermas's analysis of emancipative communicative reason, much indebted to Immanuel Kant and Enlightenment thought, broadens to a political philosophy, and a political economy of neo-Marxist inspiration. Habermas shows how, in the course of the past few centuries, systemic aspects of society have come to threaten the reasonableness of human interactions in local cultural lifeworlds. Bureaucratic power and monetary exchange, both focused on strategic rationality—the "functionalist reason" from the subtitle of the second volume of *The Theory of Communicative Action*—have "colonized" and corrupted the lifeworld and the public sphere. The strategic, instrumental rationality of state and the market now operates on its own terms to a considerable extent, without social grounding. It bypasses consensus-oriented communication and threatens to fully determine what happens in human lives and lifeworlds. In a truly deliberative, parliamentary democracy, it should be the other way around: The legitimacy of the state should result from the will or consent of its people, who are sovereign, the source of all political power.

Habermas criticizes modern, globalized civilization as a technocracy, in which, for example, multinational corporations intrude into the political process and, through control of the market and publicity, into personal lives. Here, they, instead of the people themselves, determine what one should eat and how one should raise one's children, dress, or spend one's leisure time. In processes of commodification and alienation, human and social values become market values. Habermas criticizes Max Weber, Niklas Luhmann, and Talcott Parsons for overstressing functionalist rationality and systemic aspects in their reductionist views of modernization and modernity.

Anthropology and Enlightenment

It is surprising that Habermas's normative philosophy of what it means to be human has not been more influential in anthropology, the comparative study of humankind. This discipline also draws on Marx, Durkheim, and Weber; has strong theoretical interests; uses interpretive methods and dialogues; addresses questions of domination and discrimination; and also engages in cultural critique. Most important, Habermas provides a rationale for the humanist conception of the disciplinary identity of mainstream, in particular North American, cultural anthropology, which tends to conceive of itself as not just a human but also a humane science operating on the assumption that the sciences, in particular the life sciences, are not equipped to fully deal with the human world of language, symbolic meaning, moral responsibility, and culture.

Its humanistic disciplinary identity, its concern with human dignity and bondage, and its constructivist take on cultural lifeworlds show how strongly anthropology is rooted in Enlightenment discourse. Habermas's cosmopolitan theory of reason and cultural anthropology's disciplinary identity converge because they are both, more or less directly, indebted to the Enlightenment philosopher Immanuel Kant, the predominantly neo-Kantian climate of opinion in late 19th- and early 20th-century academia, the closely associated hermeneutic tradition, and Max Weber's sociology. These continental developments influenced North American cultural anthropology through Franz Boas, a German immigrant, and his pupils Alfred Kroeber and Edward Sapir. Max Weber's and the French philosopher Paul Ricoeur's influence on Clifford Geertz's interpretive turn in the 1970s added to that effect. French *ethnologie* and British social anthropology received Kantian input through Émile Durkheim and Claude Lévi-Strauss.

Two Metaphysics

One of the urgent challenges for anthropology presently is the long-standing tension between interpretive (hermeneutic) and explanatory (nomothetic) methodologies. The same goes for philosophy. Two mutually incompatible metaphysical traditions keep feeding into these epistemic stances, one stressing the uniqueness and dignity of human subjectivity, the other stressing the continuity between humans and other animal species. Habermas advocates a dialogue and offers a sophisticated attempt to integrate both approaches in order to overcome the polarization that holds anthropology captive. This is highly relevant for a discipline that has been described as the most scientific of the humanities and the most humanistic of the sciences and still has not sorted out its contested disciplinary identity.

Habermas's sustained argument regarding the possibility, premises, and promise of reasonable dialogue in society and between cultures, founded in the universality of human nature, challenges the tendency of much of anthropology toward cultural relativism with regard to both truth and morality. In particular, it challenges the postmodern, posthumanist tendencies of its "textual turn" of the 1990s, with its repudiation of grand theory. Habermas offers reflection on both epistemic and normative aspects of both humanistic and scientific conceptions of anthropology's disciplinary identity and, while stressing the former view, contributes toward their conciliation and integration.

Conclusion

There is much in anthropology that is relevant for a critical evaluation of Habermas's theory of communicative rationality. He has been criticized for his negative casting of nonliterate societies, for his reconstruction of the cultural evolution of humankind, for underestimating the role of conflict and exclusion, for overstressing the linguistic nature of human nature and lifeworlds, for being unrealistically utopian, and for his Kantian proceduralism—all in all, for being too Eurocentric in various ways. But this only adds to the challenge his grand theory poses to anthropology in its present era of theoretical diversity, fragmentation, and eclecticism. Habermas's thought is a major asset for reflexively scrutinizing the philosophical roots, conceptual assumptions, disciplinary identity, basic values, and ethical issues of anthropology.

Raymond Corbey

See also Boas, Franz; Critical Theory; Durkheim, Émile; Frankfurt School; Hermeneutics; Neo-Kantianism; Phenomenology; Weber, Max

Further Readings

Bernstein, R. J. (Ed.). (1985). *Habermas and modernity.* Cambridge, UK: Polity.

Fultner, B. (Ed.). (2011). *Jürgen Habermas: Key concepts.* Durham, UK: Acumen.

Ungureanu, C., Günther, K., & Joerges, C. (Eds.). (2011). *Jürgen Habermas* (2 vols.). Avebury, UK: Ashgate.

HABITUS

In anthropology, the term *habitus* is primarily associated with the work of the French sociologist/ethnologist Pierre Bourdieu. It is a fundamental element in what is referred to as Bourdieu's theory of practice, or practice theory. According to Bourdieu, each person embodies a habitus—that is, a configuration of linguistic behaviors, bodily postures and ways of moving, and emotions, desires, tastes, beliefs, and values. The habitus is socially produced, acquired in childhood, and shared by those who have a similar social background. Although shared, there are some (albeit limited) individual variations in the ways in which the habitus is lived and embodied.

Historical Overview

The word *habitus* has its origins in Latin and at the most general level refers to both conditions of the body (including disease) and customary practices. Although the concept can be traced back to Aristotle, Bourdieu's notion of habitus builds most directly on the work of Marcel Mauss, Norbert Elias, and Erwin Panofsky. In a short essay first published in 1936, Mauss used the concept of habitus to refer to ways of holding and moving the body, which he called "body techniques."

For Mauss, a "technique" was something traditional or customary, as well as practical or useful. Body techniques were the product of training received in a particular social milieu, and it reflected collective modes of behaviors and values. One of his examples came from his observation that during World War I, armies of different nations marched differently, with their own characteristic movements of the knee, postures, and so on. These constitute different bodily habitus. Mauss also included behaviors associated with caring for the body and dancing as elements of habitus. Body techniques varied by gender and age as well. Norbert Elias, also influential in Bourdieu's conceptual framework, used the concept of habitus in his theory of the "civilizing process"—a process of socialization at the individual level and a metahistorical trend that began in Europe in the court society of the Middle Ages. According to Elias, in the 19th century, the bourgeoisie in France, Germany, and other nations adopted the manners and mannerisms of the earlier "court society" to express a self-image of their superiority and that of their nation as "civilized." Part of this involved increasing levels of self-regulation and self-control of drives and impulses by individuals. For Elias, habitus was a site for the articulation of social and mental structures, so that people internalized social constraints and adopted tastes and habits that were considered "civilized." Habitus for him was a form of embodied social learning and constituted the social makeup and also self-image of individuals. Elias, like Mauss, focused primarily on national identity in his view of habitus, seeing that each nation had its own "we-feelings" and forms of national habitus. Later, Erwin Panofsky (1951) employed habitus to discuss Gothic architectural styles and what he called the "habits of mind" that produced different art styles in different historical periods and settings. Bourdieu followed Panofsky in seeking to eliminate a distinction between forms of individual and collective creativity, shared values, and orientations.

Bourdieu developed the concept of habitus in his early ethnographic studies of peasants in rural France and Algeria during the late 1950s and early 1960s. His first published use of the term appeared in a 1962 article on rural bachelors in Bourdieu's own natal village in southeastern France. Two years later, he used this term in an article, coauthored with Abdelmalek Sayad, about displaced and uprooted Algerian peasants he had interviewed in resettlement camps during the Algerian War of Independence. Bourdieu's emphasis was on bodily habitus in this earlier work, following Mauss, and with it he expressed the uncomfortable condition of feeling displaced and outside of one's familiar milieu, one's taken-for-granted social reality. In rural France, urbanization following World War II had led to changes in the village that caused peasant bachelors, who were unable to find wives, to feel uneasy and awkward, a situation illustrated by Bourdieu through his analysis of their behaviors at a village dance. Although they had stayed in place in the village, they felt out of place. The Algerians had been physically displaced and forced into resettlement camps, where their own sense of uneasiness was the result of not being in the familiar, customary space in which they had acquired their habitus.

Bourdieu further developed his theory of habitus in later work on rural France and Algeria, education, tastes and lifestyles, language, photography, and the economics of real estate. Most of this work used examples from France.

Habitus, Cultural Capital, and Social Space

Practice theory refers in Bourdieu's work both to social practice and to practical (as opposed to theoretical or scholarly) forms of knowledge and behavior that are part of the habitus. With this theoretical framework, Bourdieu attempted to break down the conceptual division between social structure and social practices. For Bourdieu, the habitus is part of everyday life and commonsense understandings

of one's social world and how to behave within it. Therefore, it is not a conscious aspect of identity or action under most circumstances. It is acquired through informal mechanisms of socialization from early childhood and onward. In an early essay on the Kabyle house (in Algeria), Bourdieu wrote about the ways in which children learn gendered values and social roles through the layout, physical orientation, and uses of space within the home. He argued, importantly, that the habitus is acquired through bodily movement and bodily experiences as much as through what is told or observed from the behaviors of others. For Bourdieu, the body is a "memory pad." Bourdieu referred to commonsense understandings of the world as *doxa*. Such taken-for-granted assumptions about social reality vary, however, according to the orientations and dispositions of any particular acquired habitus.

The primary habitus is already present when children first encounter school, although they may acquire a secondary habitus through schooling experiences and other types of life experience that take them outside their original social milieu and its assumptions, values, and so on. Bourdieu himself was an example of this, having been raised in a rural environment in southeastern France but acquiring a "secondary habitus" through his pursuit of higher education at elite schools. The orientations and dispositions of the habitus take on differing amounts of value within the wider social space. Bourdieu referred to these as forms of capital—cultural, symbolic, and social. Depending on one's habitus, a person may have qualities (forms of capital) that are more or less highly valued by the dominant sectors of society. Examples of this are "tastes" in music, art, food, and lifestyle that lead to various forms of distinction among habitus within social space. A child who has lower valued forms of cultural capital (including ways of speaking, familiarity with reading and writing, and knowledge of art and museums) than those forms most highly valued by the school will, according to Bourdieu's theory of education and social reproduction, do less well in school than those children whose forms of capital are recognized by and shared with their middle-class teachers.

Bourdieu also suggested that people can experience an uncomfortable "split habitus" when their life experiences are not in harmony with the primary habitus they acquired in early childhood through family life. This can occur through education, as in

Bourdieu's own case, or through the experience of living through rapid social changes or dramatic disruptions of social life, as in the case of Algerians who were placed in resettlement camps. Even though Bourdieu did not specifically address transnational migration in his own research, this idea can obviously be extended to immigrants.

Bourdieu's theory of habitus refers frequently to spatial positioning, both in physical settings and in social life more generally. Each diverse and stratified nation, such as France, will contain several different types of habitus related to social positions and social positioning within the social space of the nation. For example, people who work in small, family-owned companies have a different position in the social space from executives in large corporations. Bourdieu conceptualized a nation as a social space containing a variety of habitus, each taking a different position and having a different trajectory (moving toward either higher or lower status over time). He also noted that those sharing a particular type of habitus will inhabit differently valued geographical settings, so that the rich will live in more pleasant and favored neighborhoods within cities.

Habitus Beyond Bourdieu

The concept of habitus has been influential throughout the social sciences and humanities, and it is, therefore, impossible to provide a comprehensive overview of the legacy of this term here. Only two examples will be provided. In his book *The Practice of Everyday Life*, Michel de Certeau criticized Bourdieu's theory of practice (and habitus) for being a circular argument about the relationship between structure and practice. According to de Certeau, Bourdieu posited a sort of invisible and stable reality in the social structure that produces the habitus and within which the habitus employs limited forms of improvisation and tactics, which in turn tend to reinforce and reproduce that structure. In his own theory of everyday practices, tactics, ways of operating, and so on, which can be viewed in dialogue with Bourdieu, de Certeau paid more attention to the prevalent forms of "making do," cunning tricks, and other everyday practices in particular types of culture. He also focused on consumption practices and popular culture, with an acknowledgement that these are constrained by structures of power.

A more recent, and perhaps the most thorough, extension and development of the concept of habitus has been the one provided by Barnard Lahire. Lahire has written that habitus is a theory of socialization, a theory of action, and a theory of practice. He takes issue with Bourdieu's emphasis on the early acquisition of the habitus because it implies that a person's current orientations and behaviors depend primarily on past experiences. Moreover, Bourdieu assumed that people will seek situations where there is no disruption of their habitus and where they could experience a sense of harmony between their own dispositions and their social position. In his own notion of the "plural actor," Lahire posits that contextual factors in the present may lead some people to have more than one disposition or habitus and that this may be more common than Bourdieu acknowledged.

Deborah Reed-Danahay

See also Bourdieu, Pierre; Mauss, Marcel; Phenomenology; Poststructuralism; Practice Theory

Further Readings

Bourdieu, P. (1977). *Outline of a theory of practice* (R. Nice, Trans.). Cambridge, UK: Cambridge University Press. (Original work published 1972)

———. (1984). *Distinction: A social critique of the judgment of taste* (R. Nice, Trans.). Cambridge, MA: Harvard University Press. (Original work published 1979)

———. (2008). *The bachelor's ball* (R. Nice, Trans.). Chicago, IL: University of Chicago Press. (Original work published 1962)

Certeau, M. de. (1984). *The practice of everyday life* (S. Randall, Trans.). Berkeley: University of California Press.

Elias, N. (2000). *The civilizing process: Sociogenetic and psychogenetic investigations* (Rev. ed.; E. Jephcott, Trans.). Oxford, UK: Blackwell. (Original work published 1939)

Goodman, J. E., & Silverstein, P. A. (Eds.). (2009). *Bourdieu in Algeria: Colonial politics, ethnographic practices, theoretical developments*. Lincoln: University of Nebraska Press.

Lahire, B. (2011). *The plural actor* (D. Fernbach, Trans.). Cambridge, UK: Polity Press. (Original work published 2001)

Mauss, M. (1979). Body techniques. In *Sociology and psychology: Essays* (pp. 97–123; B. Brewster, Trans.).

London, UK: Routledge & Kegan Paul. (Original work published 1936)

Panofsky, E. (1951). *Gothic architecture and scholasticism.* Latrobe, PA: Archabbey Press.

Reed-Danahay, D. (2005). *Locating Bourdieu.* Bloomington: Indiana University Press.

HADDON, ALFRED C.

Alfred Cort Haddon (1855–1940), British biologist, zoologist, and ethnologist, established anthropology as a professional discipline at the University of Cambridge and had a major impact on the development of anthropology in Britain and beyond.

Biography and Major Works

Haddon was born into a nonconformist London family, the eldest son of Caroline and John Haddon, owner of a London printing firm specializing in missionary tracts. In 1875, he was accepted to read natural sciences at Christ's College in Cambridge, where he took classes in zoology, geology, and embryology and trained under Michael Foster, a protégé of Darwin's apologist Thomas Huxley. A central concern of these biologists was to test evolutionary theories explaining survival through adaptation, with marine populations a key site for investigation. Following the completion of a BSc, Haddon pursued this work at the Naples marine station (1879), as curator of the Cambridge Zoological Museum (1879–1880), as professor of zoology at the Royal College of Science in Dublin (1880–1900), and as assistant naturalist in the Dublin Science and Art Museum (1880–1888).

In 1888, Haddon went to the Torres Straits to study marine biology and became fascinated with the Islanders with whom he lived and worked. Concerned that traditional beliefs and practices were dying out, he resolved to return with an anthropological expedition "before it was too late."

On return to Britain, Haddon resumed his Dublin Chair. In 1892, Haddon advocated an ethnographic survey of the British Isles, which gained the sponsorship of the British Association for the Advancement of Science. He himself contributed research on the Aran Islands in Ireland. The survey's focus on local customs and the racial composition of various populations remained a central goal of Haddon's far-flung research, while its limited success highlighted the need for trained observers in the collection and analysis of ethnographic data. From 1893, he also worked part-time in the Anatomy Department at Cambridge as a freelance lecturer in anthropology and comparative anatomy. He was awarded an ScD in 1897.

Within a paradigm of salvage ethnography and encompassing a broad multidisciplinary vision of anthropology, Haddon led the 1898 Cambridge Anthropological Expedition to the Torres Straits. The expedition members—William McDougall, Charles Myers, Sydney Ray, Charles Seligman, William Rivers, and Anthony Wilkin—included scholars in the fields of medicine, physiology, experimental psychology, and linguistics, with expertise in art, music, and photography. With the assistance of named Islanders, the expedition generated an enormous amount of ethnographic data, compiled in the six volumes of the expedition's *Reports* (1901–1935), and made an extensive collection of objects, photographs, drawings, and film and audio recordings.

Following the success of the Torres Straits expedition and with much lobbying by James Frazer and others in Cambridge, Haddon was appointed the first University Lecturer in Ethnology in 1900, a fellow of Christ's College in 1901, and a reader in 1909, a position he held until his retirement in 1926. He was instrumental in setting up the Board of Anthropological Studies at Cambridge in 1904.

Haddon also campaigned for the colonial government to recognize the importance of anthropological training, arguing that it was crucial to a more humane and efficient colonial service. In 1908, a Diploma in Anthropology was established in Cambridge, which bolstered the profile and funding for anthropology within the university and provided training for members of the Indian Civil Service as well as colonial administrators and anthropologists in Melanesia and Africa.

Throughout his career, Haddon retained an active role in various scholarly associations, serving as president of the British Association for the Advancement of Science Section H, the (Royal) Anthropological Institute, and the Folklore Society; he was also a fellow of the Royal Society. He published extensively for more than 50 years on various areas of anthropology and received numerous professional accolades.

Critical Contributions to Anthropology

Haddon's main contributions were methodological and as a tireless promoter of the professionalization of the discipline and its wide-ranging public value. The 1898 Torres Straits Expedition was noted for the integration of field research and scholarly interpretation, for Rivers's development of the "genealogical method," and for the use of state-of-the-art recording devices. Credited with being the first person to apply the term *fieldwork* to anthropology, as leader of the Cambridge school with Rivers, Myers, and Seligman, Haddon promoted the "intensive study of limited areas." Their methodology was consolidated in the 1912 edition of *Notes and Queries on Anthropology*. Although their own field research was within the survey mode, they taught the first generation of professionally trained students, including Alfred Radcliffe-Brown, John Layard, Bronisław Malinowski, and Gregory Bateson, who established intensive fieldwork by a lone participant observer as the core methodology for a modern social anthropology.

Haddon's Darwinian approach focused on the distribution of forms within a particular region, rather than constructing a universal sequence of development. He worked to illuminate the diversity and complexity of racial and cultural groups, based on a comparative study of the distribution of physical characteristics, languages, sociocultural traits, and material culture. Haddon's research interests overlapped with diffusionism, although he was critical of later hyperdiffusionistic models. Despite his underlying concern with racial difference, Haddon rejected racial determinism. The Torres Straits research indicated that the Islanders had the same range of capacities as the British test subjects. By the 1930s, Haddon was strongly critical of the "pseudoscience of racial biology" and cautioned against its use by political forces.

Haddon was a keen advocate of museums for research and public education. In addition to his own work at the Cambridge Museum of Archaeology and Anthropology and as advisory curator to the Horniman Museum in London, he encouraged his students to make well-documented field collections of objects and photographs, many of which are now housed at the museum. He was also founder of the Haddon library for Archaeology and Anthropology in Cambridge. The extensive results of his Torres Straits research remain foundational for researchers in the region and are of particular importance to Torres Straits Islanders today.

Anita Herle

See also Cambridge University; Diffusionism, Hyperdiffusionism, *Kulturkreise*; Rivers, W. H. R.; Royal Anthropological Institute; Seligman, Charles Gabriel; Torres Straits Expedition

Further Readings

Herle, A. C., & Rouse, S. (Eds). (1998). *Cambridge and the Torres Strait: Centenary essays on the 1898 expedition.* Cambridge, UK: Cambridge University Press.

Stocking, G. W., Jr. (1995). *After Tylor: British social anthropology 1888–1951.* Madison, WI: Athalone.

Urry, J. (1993). *Before social anthropology: Essays on the history of British anthropology.* Chur, Switzerland: Harwood Academic.

HALL, EDWARD T.

Edward Twitchell Hall (1914–2009) was an American anthropologist, a researcher specializing in cross-cultural studies, and is considered one of the founders of the study of nonverbal behavior and intercultural communication.

Biography and Major Works

Born in 1914 in Webster Groves, Missouri, Hall spent his early years in New Mexico. In 1936, he earned his BA in anthropology from the University of Denver; in 1938, his MA in anthropology from the University of Arizona; and in 1942, his PhD from Columbia University. In 1942–1945, he served in World War II in Europe and in the Philippines. In 1946, Hall married Mildred Ellis Reed and started postdoctoral research at Columbia University. Later, he worked at the University of Denver, Washington School of Psychiatry, Illinois Institute of Technology, and Northwestern University, among others. He did extensive fieldwork studying intercultural relations with the Navajo, Hopi, Spanish Americans, and Trukese. He belonged to the American Anthropological Association, the Society for Applied Anthropology, and the Building Research Advisory Board of the National Academy of Sciences. After retiring in 1977, he lived in Santa Fe, New Mexico, till his death in 2009.

Hall is the author of many books devoted to cultural studies and anthropology. In *The Silent Language* (1959), Hall discussed how people communicate without the use of words, stressing the importance of space and time in sending and receiving messages. The issue of temporal dimensions was also researched in his 1983 book *The Dance of Life*, to show how time determines intercultural contacts. *The Hidden Dimension*, published in 1966, focused on discussing space and its role in personal, organizational, and societal life. In *Beyond Culture* (1976), Hall stressed the importance of the cultural environment in one's life, focusing on high- and low-context cultures. Due to common experience and tradition, high-context cultures provide information not only verbally but also by using context-related features. On the other hand, low-context cultures, which are less homogeneous than the high-context ones, rely mainly on verbal messages in communication. The book titled *Hidden Differences: Doing Business With the Japanese* (1987), coauthored with his wife, Mildred Reed Hall, was devoted to describing business relations between Americans and Japanese. The issue of cultural differences between French, Germans, and Americans was discussed in the book titled *Understanding Cultural Differences: Germans, French and Americans* (1990), also coauthored with Mildred Reed Hall. The authors studied the characteristics of German, French, and American culture, taking into account notions such as stereotypes, the attitude to time and space, communication styles, and cultural values. In *The Fourth Dimension in Architecture: The Impact of Building on Behavior* (1975), Hall and his wife researched the role of the architecture of buildings and offices in the performance of workers. Hall also wrote two autobiographical works: *An Anthropology of Everyday Life* (1992) and *West of the Thirties: Discoveries Among the Navajo and Hopi* (1995). The first book covered the first 50 years of his life, and the second work was devoted to his experience acquired working with Navajo, Hopi, and Hispanic peoples.

Critical Contributions to Anthropology

Hall's contributions to anthropology were wide-ranging and important. His research findings offer a new perspective on the relations between humans, taking into account the role of culture in shaping one's behavior. Thus, Hall is the author whose theories and concepts set the foundation for anthropological research in nonverbal communication and the use of space.

For example, Hall is the author of concepts such as *proxemics*, *adumbration*, *monochronic* and *polychronic cultures*, as well as *high-* and *low-context cultures*. *Proxemics* is related to the role of space in human contacts. Hall distinguished various levels of distance—intimate distance, personal distance, social distance, and public distance—depending on the relation between the speakers and the culture they represent. *Adumbrations* are understood as the signals preceding or accompanying formal communication that provide information to the interlocutors and enhance mutual understanding. Hall also argued that cultures could be classified by the ways in which their members understood time. Members of *monochronic cultures* experience time in a linear way and perform one action at a time. They do not like interruptions and perceive time as a tangible object that can be wasted, saved, or spent. On the contrary, members of *polychronic cultures* favor the simultaneous occurrence of activities, and they are not against interruptions. They value contacts with people more than time-related obligations. The other division of cultures proposed by Hall is that of low-context and high-context cultures. In *low-context cultures*, information does not flow freely since it is controlled and compartmentalized. On the other hand, *high-context cultures* favor unrestricted information flow and interpersonal contacts.

Hall's Legacy

Hall's work was noteworthy for its interdisciplinary nature. Among those whose work was influential in Hall's thinking were Franz Boas, Ruth Benedict, Edward Sapir, Benjamin Lee Whorf, Sigmund Freud, Harry Stack Sullivan, Margaret Mead, David Riesman, Buckminster Fuller, Melville J. Herskovitz, and Erich Fromm. Moreover, Hall cooperated with the linguist George L. Trager on the notion of cultural events and their performance on three levels: formal, informal, and technical. Apart from linguistics, Hall was also interested in media studies. In the period between 1962 and 1976, he exchanged more than 130 letters with Marshall McLuhan, the Canadian specialist on topics such as the media, media technological determinism, and the relation between the media and the people. This correspondence influenced some of McLuhan's scientific writing.

Since his research concerned issues pertinent to anthropology, linguistics, ethology, and Freudian psychoanalytic theory, Hall's insights about culture and anthropology continue to exert an influence on various fields of studies. His scientific legacy is visible, among others, in intercultural communication, sociology, linguistics, management, and anthropology. For example, looking closer at organizational studies, his anthropological research on the classification of cultures and the study of the role of space and time is of interest not only to scholars but also to business practitioners. Notions of social space, socialization, and identity rely on Hall's proxemic studies, and Hall's typology of culture to study cultural variations in various groups and societies is used in cultural anthropology.

Magdalena Bielenia-Grajewska

See also Boas, Franz; Columbia University; Sapir, Edward

Further Readings

Hall, E. T. (1963). A system for the notation of proxemic behavior. *American Anthropologist, 65*(5), 1003–1026.

———. (1964). Adumbration as a feature of intercultural communication. *American Anthropologist, 66*(6), 154–163.

———. (1990). *The silent language.* New York, NY: Anchor Books.

Hall, E. T., & Hall, M. R. (1990). *Understanding cultural differences: Germans, French and Americans.* Yarmouth, UK: Intercultural Press.

Rogers, E. M. (2000). The extensions of men: The correspondence of Marshall McLuhan and Edward T. Hall. *Mass Communication and Society, 3*(1), 117–135.

Rogers, E. M., Hart, W. B., & Miike, Y. (2002). Edward T. Hall and the history of intercultural communication: The United States and Japan. *Keio Communication Review, 24,* 3–26.

Website

Edward T. Hall: http://www.edwardthall.com/

HALLOWELL, A. IRVING

Alfred Irving Hallowell (1892–1974) was an influential American anthropologist who studied and then taught for most of his academic career at the University of Pennsylvania. His professional reputation and personal identity were based on his research among Native North American peoples, especially the Ojibwa of Canada. The subjects to which Hallowell made original contributions included kinship and social organization, psychological anthropology, folklore, worldview, religion, sociolinguistics, cultural ecology, acculturation, transculturalization, dreams and dreaming, and the history of anthropology. During his professional career, he became a member of the Permanent Council of the International Congress of Anthropological and Ethnological Sciences and served as president of the American Anthropological Association and the American Folklore Society. Among his many honors and awards were a Guggenheim Fellowship, the Viking Medal and Award for outstanding achievement in anthropology, and election to the National Academy of Sciences.

Hallowell came to anthropology indirectly by way of graduate courses in sociology and a job as a social worker in his native Philadelphia; he eventually went to New York City to work with Franz Boas and Ruth Benedict. Finally, he decided to study intensively for his PhD degree with Frank Speck at the University of Pennsylvania. He received his doctorate in 1924 for his study "Bear Ceremonialism in the Northern Hemisphere," which turned out to be the last of the comparative cross-cultural distributional studies within the Boasian tradition. It was published in 1926 as a 175-page essay in the *American Anthropologist.* From 1927 through 1963, he worked as a professor of anthropology at the University of Pennsylvania, where he became known for his training of a cohort of prominent graduate students, including Melford Spiro, Anthony F. C. Wallace, Raymond Fogelson, George W. Stocking, Regna Darnell, James Van Stone, and Marie-Françoise Gúedon.

Hallowell's initial fieldwork centered on learning indigenous languages, gathering kinship terminologies, and collecting folktales from the St. Francis Abenaki of Quebec and the Lac du Flambeau Band of Lake Superior Chippewa in Wisconsin. During the 1930s and 1940s, he made repeated summer visits to the Montagnais-Naskapi (Innu) in Quebec, as well as the Oji-Cree of northern Ontario and the Berens River Saulteaux of Lake Winnipeg, Manitoba.

Thanks to his long-term relationship with William Berens, an Ojibwa treaty chief on the

Berens River, Hallowell was able to make engaging and memorable contributions to the anthropological literature. Many years before the "writing culture" and the "collaborative" movements in ethnography, Hallowell and Berens became close friends and mutual interlocutors, sharing experiences, autobiographical narratives, and dreams. From their conversations, for example, Hallowell learned that the Ojibwa people interpret the manifest content of their dreams as experiences of their selves, which are continuous in time and space with those of their waking lives. For nonindigenous peoples, however, while dream images may be recognized as self-related, they are only rarely included in their memoirs or autobiographies.

Known to their friends as "Pete" Hallowell and "Willy" Berens, these men worked together using various narrative genres and rhetorical tropes to convey and enliven the Native point of view. In an early field encounter, Hallowell asked Berens a naive question, to which Willy gave a sharp response. In his 1972 autobiography *On Being an Anthropologist*, Hallowell sketched the scene in which he hesitatingly asked his mentor whether a man could marry a woman who was his cross-cousin. Berens replied immediately, "Who the hell else would he marry?" In this exchange, we see a timid student learning a key lesson in Ojibwa marriage practices from an experienced, worldly mentor. By recording and presenting this type of field dialogue, Hallowell portrayed himself as a student within an ongoing active learning context.

In a classic essay "Ojibwa Ontology, Behavior, and World View," Hallowell told of his experience of strolling down the road with Berens one summer day soon after he learned that stones are grammatically animate in the Ojibwa language. He took the opportunity to ask his mentor if all the stones around them were alive. Willy reflected for a time and replied, "No! But *some* are." On another occasion, Berens told Hallowell that he saw a large stone move during a Midewiwin, or Grand Medicine Society, ceremony led by his father, a famous Midé conjurer. His father walked around the lodge twice; then, when he returned to his original place, he began to sing; at this point, the stone rolled over and over itself, following his trail around the lodge.

Hallowell summed up this teaching story saying that the movement of the stone was not a voluntary act initiated by the stone but a demonstration of the magical power of the Midé leader. By means of these and other anecdotes, we learn that some stones, indeed, have the capacity to connect human persons to other than human persons in the world of the spirits. In Grand Medicine Society ceremonies, other than human persons manifest themselves audibly for the audience in different voices. Sometimes they named themselves or sang songs. The Ojibwa name by which Hallowell is remembered in Canada to this day is Midewigimaa, meaning "master of Midé ceremonies," indicating that he was extremely knowledgeable about these ceremonies.

At the age of 72, Hallowell completed his only full-length monograph centering on his ethnographic work with the Ojibwa of Manitoba. In 1962, he began writing it for the series of undergraduate books known as *Case Studies in Cultural Anthropology*, edited by George and Louise Spindler of Stanford University. In 1967, when Railway Express reported to Holt, Rinehart and Winston that they had lost his copyedited manuscript, Hallowell was in very poor health. He searched, to no avail, for another copy of his manuscript until he died on October 10, 1974. Several years later, when Jennifer S. H. Brown, now a historian at the University of Winnipeg, took over the project, she found a copy of an early version of his manuscript at the American Philosophical Society in Philadelphia, edited it, and added a preface and an afterword. In this way, she helped Hallowell and Berens to speak together once more from their graves.

Barbara Tedlock

See also Benedict, Ruth F.; Boas, Franz; Spiro, Melford; Wallace, Anthony F. C.

Further Readings

Hallowell, A. I. (1942). *The role of conjuring in Saulteaux society*. Philadelphia: University of Pennsylvania Press.

———. (1963). Papers in honor of Melville J. Herskovits: American Indians, White and Black: The phenomenon of transculturalization. *Current Anthropology, 4*(5), 519–531.

———. (1966). The role of dreams in Ojibwa culture. In G. E. Von Grunebaum & R. Caillois (Eds.), *The dream and human societies* (pp. 267–292). Berkeley: University of California Press.

———. (1972). On being an anthropologist. In *Contributions to Ojibwe studies: Essays, 1934–1972* (J. S. H. Brown & S. E. Gray, Eds.; pp. 1–15). Lincoln: University of Nebraska Press.

———. (1975). Ojibwa ontology, behavior, and world view. In D. Tedlock & B. Tedlock (Eds.), *Teachings from the American earth: Indian religion and philosophy* (pp. 141–178). New York, NY: Liveright. (Reprinted from *Culture in history: Essays in honor of Paul Radin*, pp. 19–52; by S. Diamond, Ed., 1960, New York, NY: Columbia University Press)

Hallowell, A. I., & Brown, J. S. H. (1992). *The Ojibwa of Berens River, Manitoba: Ethnography into history*. Fort Worth, TX: Harcourt Brace.

Lassiter, L. E. (2000). Authoritative texts, collaborative ethnography, and Native American studies. *American Indian Quarterly, 24*(4), 601–614.

Harris, Marvin

The American anthropologist Marvin Harris (1927–2001) was the creator and proponent of the theory of cultural materialism. Many of his writings sought to popularize anthropology for the general public, producing years of columns for *Natural History* magazine and several books—such as *Cows, Pigs, Wars, and Witches* (1974) and *Cannibals and Kings* (1977)—written for general readers, while other works were directed for more exclusively academic audiences, most notably *The Rise of Anthropological Theory* (*The RAT*, 1968) and *Cultural Materialism* (1979).

Marvin Harris was born in Brooklyn, New York, on August 18, 1927. He grew up in the working-class poverty of the Great Depression. During the Second World War, he served in the U.S. Army Transportation Corps (1945–1947); like many scholars of his generation, he later entered college on the G. I. Bill. Anthropology courses at Columbia University with Charles Wagley led to a general interest in anthropology and a specific interest in Brazilian ethnography. At Columbia, he earned his bachelor's degree in anthropology in 1949 and his PhD in 1953. In 1952, he married Madeline Grove, with whom he had two children and to whom he remained married for the rest of his life. Marvin Harris died in Gainesville, Florida, on October 25, 2001, from medical complications following hip surgery.

Harris's Early Career

While other Columbia graduate students of Harris's cohort had an explicit interest in pursuing Marxist theory, Harris had few such theoretical interests at that time. Harris conducted his dissertation fieldwork in 1950–1951 in Rio de Contas, Brazil, producing a descriptive village study of enculturation—later published with little modification as *Town and Country in Brazil* (1958). Harris's early ethnographic writing produced nothing prefiguring his later interest in anthropological theory; instead, this ethnographic work was a Boasian-derived descriptive village study. On defending his dissertation, Harris became an assistant professor at Columbia University in 1953, where he remained a member of the faculty until 1980.

While conducting field research in Mozambique in 1955–1956, Harris became aware of the ways in which the Portuguese colonialism created behavioral regimes of segregation not fully acknowledged in the culture's ideology. Harris switched his fieldwork focus from studying agricultural communities to studying racial segregation and colonial oppression, until he was forced to leave by government officials. He befriended Antonio de Figueiredo and Eduardo Mondlane—a founder of the Mozambique liberation movement; de Figueiredo later described Harris's critique and denunciation of the Portuguese as having "decisively influenced the abolition of the forced labour system" (Burns, 2001). In "Portugal's African 'Wards': A First Hand Report on Labor and Education in Moçambique" (1958), Harris denounced the Portuguese domination of local populations. Harris later recounted that the control exerted on him and his research in Mozambique by his Ford Foundation sponsors soured him on funding research by grant writing and led him to pursue writing trade books for a popular audience as a means of independently funding research.

Harris's experiences in Mozambique and the contradictions he observed between claims of egalitarian treatment for all and the behavioral practices of the system of apartheid spawned his interest in studying the differences between beliefs and behaviors. In an effort to develop a methodology and vocabulary for studying minute elements of human behaviors and beliefs, he wrote *The Nature of Cultural Things* (1964). This early interest in devising ways to directly study human behavior and statements led to a series of research projects using newly available videotape technologies to record the home lives of two African American and two Puerto Rican families living in Harlem. While Harris later abandoned much of the esoteric technical vocabulary and cumbersomely detailed methods of breaking down human behaviors into minimal units of analysis, the basic methods of analyzing what at the time were called the *emic* and *etic* components of culture had their roots in this early research.

In the early 1960s, Harris led student research programs in Ecuador (1960) and Brazil (1962). In 1965, he first wrote about the Hindu ban on killing cows—arguing that Hindu cattle veneration was based on sound ecological practices protecting cattle as milk providers and a source of plow traction. Later, in 1976, he conducted fieldwork in India, studying the behavior and ideology of cattle veneration firsthand. With Charles Wagley, Harris coauthored *Patterns of Race in the Americas* in 1964, a work that demonstrated that racial systems were cultural, not biological, systems of classification. *Patterns of Race* demonstrated the social construction of race, and in this work, Harris analyzed race as an ideological system embedded within a highly stratified political economy.

The Rise of Anthropological Theory

From 1963 to 1966, Harris served as Columbia University's chair of the Department of Anthropology. In this capacity, he gained access to a new technological innovation: the department's photocopy machine, which he used to photocopy key passages from classic social science works, passages that he cut and taped between the critical commentary he wrote responding to these passages, a writing technique he used to construct the manuscript for *The RAT*.

With the 1968 publication of *The RAT*, Harris became a central figure in anthropological theory. *The RAT* filled gaps in American anthropology's disciplinary self-conception, combining a new theoretical-centric approach to studying disciplinary ancestral ties with a critical-theoretical overview of the development of Western social science during the Enlightenment up to 1960s anthropology. Its publication coincided with a period of growth in American anthropology, and *The RAT's* championing of materialist and ecological anthropological approaches helped usher in an era of ecological anthropology and encouraged the primacy of theory

as an anthropological focus. *The RAT* combined an ambitious survey of theoretical developments stretching from Enlightenment thought to the 1960s with a critical-materialist analysis weighing the efficacy of past theoretical efforts—with the end goal of establishing the legitimacy of his own cultural materialism theory. Harris championed select elements of early works such as Henry Lewis Morgan's cultural evolutionism, Karl Marx's historical materialism, and Leslie White and Julian Steward's neo-evolutionism—while criticizing, for example, what he described as Boas's antitheoretical "historical particularism" and a broad range of psychological, or culture and personality approaches to culture, by Herbert Mead, Ruth Benedict, and others, as misguided. With funds earned from the publication of *The RAT*, Harris purchased a large waterfront house on Cranberry Island, Maine, where he and his family summered—and Harris mixed passions for writing and fishing—for the next 30 years.

In *The RAT* (and later works, such as *Cultural Materialism*), Harris championed Marxian principles of the primacy of infrastructure in producing the particulars of social life, while rejecting Marx and Engels's principle of the dialectic. Harris formulated a mechanical analysis of cultural phenomena with the explicitly stated purpose not of necessarily changing the world (as Marx would have it) but of understanding the world, though Harris also allowed for the possibility that designed changes in infrastructure could lead to the desired social changes. Harris's conception of cultural materialism excised Marx's materialist approach to history from Marx's revolutionary political program. Harris maintained that scientific methods necessarily operated independently of political programs, and he rejected applications of Marxist dialectical methods as nonverifiable, dogma based, and unnecessary for materialist analysis. Yet, while rejecting these elements of orthodox Marxism, as an individual, Harris aligned himself with progressive and radical political movements and at times privately referred to his own political orientation as socialistic.

Political Activism

Harris was critical of military or intelligence agencies using anthropology, and in 1965, he joined Harold Conklin, Morton Fried, Dell Hymes, Robert Murphy, and Eric Wolf in producing a handbill circulated among anthropologists across the country condemning anthropologists' involvement in Project Camelot. In the 1960s and 1970s, Harris was active in a variety of political movements opposing the American wars in Southeast Asia. Harris helped found the group Anthropologists for Radical Political Action (satirically taking its name from the Pentagon's Advanced Research Projects Agency), and he was vice chairman of Vietnam Facts, an intercampus organization of university professors opposing the Vietnam War. In 1967, with Morton Fried and Robert Murphy, he organized a seminal session at the American Anthropological Association's annual meetings, later published as *War: The Anthropology of Armed Conflict and Aggression*. During the 1968 student uprisings and campus takeover of Columbia University, Harris was among the handful of faculty who sided with the students as they occupied the campus, and he was one of the four anthropologists who formed a human chain in an effort to protect the students occupying Columbia's Fayerweather Hall from the police.

Cultural Materialism and Theoretical Critiques

Harris conceived of anthropology as a science whose holistic evolutionary perspective and focus on the differences between ideology and behavior could help develop solutions to a variety of social problems. He believed that anthropology as a science would flourish only if anthropologists directly interrogated and challenged anthropological theories and explanations. Harris became well known for holding forth at the annual meetings of the American Anthropological Association, where he would frequently rise from the floor of sessions and interrogate presenters, pressing them to account for what he saw as mistaken forms of analysis in their papers. Harris was a vocal critic of biological determinism, challenging the sociobiological claims of Napoleon Chagnon that Yanomamo males achieved differential reproductive success by engaging in warfare and raiding neighboring groups. He criticized the work of Marshall Sahlins as obscuring the material causes of culture that Sahlins viewed as products of cultural atavism.

With the publication of *Cultural Materialism* in 1979, Harris formalized his theoretical tenets stressing the primacy of infrastructure, which he had developed in *The RAT* (1968) and which guided his analysis in *Cows, Pigs, Wars, and Witches* (1974) and *Cannibals and Kings* (1977). *Cultural*

Materialism presents a selectively Marxist-derived paradigm focusing on the infrastructural forces of demography, technology, economic, and environmental conditions to explain cultural beliefs and practices—regardless of how nonutilitarian these elements of culture seem. Harris argued that cultural-materialist analysis is "based on the simple premise that human social life is a response to the practical problems of earthly existence" (1979, p. xv).

With the death of his son Robert and the increasing infighting within the department at Columbia, Harris left New York and joined the faculty at the University of Florida in 1980, where he was Graduate Research Professor until his retirement in 2000. Harris's appointment had no required teaching obligations, though he regularly taught a graduate-level theory course, often held at his home. During the past 2 decades of his life, he established a disciplined writing routine, where he read and wrote for an 8- or 9-hour period each day, producing a steady stream of articles and books.

In 1987, Harris coauthored with the anthropologist Eric Ross) *Death, Sex, and Fertility*, a work focusing on demographic pressure as what he increasingly came to see as the primary force among infrastructural features. Harris delivered the 1991 annual Distinguished Lecture at the annual meeting of the American Anthropological Association, titled "Anthropology and the Theoretical and Paradigmatic Significance of the Collapse of Soviet and East European Communism." In 1992, he conducted his final field research in Brazil, investigating changes in Brazil's racial classification systems. Harris's last book, published in 1998, *Theories of Culture in Postmodern Times* (originally titled *The Fall of Anthropological Theory*), critiqued the developments in postmodern anthropology and lamented the rejection of positivism, the rise of anthropological analysis rejecting notions of cultural evolution and the possibility of meta-analysis. Harris criticized postmodern anthropology for its lack of empirical analysis, arguing that postmodernism's rejection of positivism weakened anthropology's ability to influence public policy debates.

David H. Price

See also Columbia University; Cultural Materialism; Marx, Karl; Sahlins, Marshall; Steward, Julian; White, Leslie; Wolf, Eric

Further Readings

Fried, M., Harris, M., & Murphy, R. (Eds.). (1968). *War: The anthropology of armed conflict and aggression.* New York, NY: Natural History Press.

Harris, M. (1958). Portugal's African "wards." *Africa Today, 5*(6), 3–36.

———. (1968). *The rise of anthropological theory.* New York, NY: Thomas Y. Crowell.

———. (1971). *Culture, man, nature* (1st ed.). New York, NY: Thomas Y. Crowell. (Published as *Culture, People, Nature* in later editions)

———. (1977). *Cannibals and kings.* New York, NY: Vintage.

———. (1979). *Cultural materialism.* New York, NY: Random House.

———. (1998). *Theories of culture in postmodern times.* Walnut Creek, CA: AltaMira.

Harris, M., & Ross, E. B. (1987). *Death, sex, and fertility.* New York, NY: Columbia University Press.

Wagley, C., & Harris, M. (1964). *Patterns of race in the Americas.* Westport, CT: Greenwood.

HARVEY, DAVID

David Harvey (1935–) is an urban geographer whose influence on anthropology has been both institutional and theoretical. His primary contribution to social scientific thought has hinged on two questions: (1) Why does capitalism need geographical space? and (2) How does it use geographical space in a manner that both facilitates and threatens its own continued existence? These questions form the heart of an intellectual rapprochement that has simultaneously challenged geography to make effective theoretical use of Marxism, and Marxism to make effective theoretical use of geography. Since the late 1960s, Harvey has viewed this dialectic primarily through the lens of urban social theory, examining the ways in which the territorial logic of capital accumulation drives urbanization, and urbanization in its own turn establishes the conditions for further capital accumulation, including geographic barriers that must be surmounted by continued spatial reinvention if capitalism is to reproduce itself at all. These contradictions are most succinctly exemplified in his concept of the "spatial fix," in which capital's tendency to affix itself in particular places generates a crisis of accumulation that can only be resolved through capital's often violent movement across geographical space: a fixture of capitalism's character amounting to something of an addictive fixation. His work has therefore been described as a historical-geographical materialism, grounding the immanent logic of the capitalist mode of production in the development and redevelopment of the built environment under its auspices.

Harvey was born in the town of Gillingham in County Kent, United Kingdom, in 1935. He completed a PhD in geography at Cambridge University in 1961, writing a dissertation on the 19th-century history of hops cultivation in his native Kent. Following a postdoctoral fellowship at the University of Uppsala in Sweden and a subsequent lectureship at Bristol University in southwest England, Harvey moved to the United States in 1969 to take up a position at Johns Hopkins University, where he developed an interest in both Marxism and urbanization, inspired by the political struggles of the late 1960s and the urban decline he witnessed in Baltimore. Harvey found Marx's work to be historically compelling but geographically inadequate, and he began to question why capital behaves in spatial ways, at times congregating in specific places and at specific scales and at times abandoning the former spatial concentrations to bleed away and coagulate in other locations, leaving human immiseration in its wake. He would engage these intellectual problems on three fronts: (1) in his teaching, beginning particularly with his long-standing course "Reading Marx's *Capital*"; (2) in his writing, beginning with the publication of *Social Justice and the City* (1973); and (3) in his more limited supporting role in political activism, beginning with his involvement with the Progressive Action Center in Baltimore in the early 1970s. His influences from this period include not only historical figures from the Marxist canon (Marx, Engels, and Lenin) but also more contemporary urbanists such as Henri Lefebvre, Bertell Ollman, and Manuel Castells. Harvey taught subsequently at Oxford University and the London School of Economics before moving to the City University of New York's Graduate School and University Center, where he accepted a distinguished professorship in the PhD program in anthropology in 2001.

Anthropologists have typically engaged Harvey's canon as a framework for theorizing the condition of the peoples they encounter in the course of ethnographic research. One of the primary ways in which anthropologists (e.g., Matt Ruben and

Jeff Maskovsky) have made ethnographic grist of Harvey's ideas is by embracing his work on neoliberalism, especially in the wake of his 2005 publication, *A Brief History of Neoliberalism.* Anthropologists (e.g., Sharryn Kasmir and Gus Carbonella) have made particular use of Harvey's concept of "accumulation by dispossession," a term he employs to describe the process by which groups of human beings are systematically deprived of their common property and rights by the mechanisms of capitalism, especially in its neoliberal form, and which resonates strongly with the anthropological focus on peoples "othered" by dominant systems of power. Anthropologists (e.g., Setha M. Low, Owen M. Lynch, and Paige West) whose work concerns space, nature, landscape, environmental justice, and the urban condition have critically employed his ideas to understand the othering and dispossession of particular local places through pollution, displacement, capital flight, ghettoization, and other forms of spatial marginalization. One of Harvey's most popular works with anthropologists was the 1989 volume *The Condition of Postmodernity,* which the reviewer Mark Moberg called "an indignant yet bemused ethnography for our time" in his review for *American Ethnologist.* The book constitutes one of Harvey's most accessible attempts to analyze the cultural implications of shifting capitalist configurations, positing postmodernity as a generalized cultural condition (irreducible to postmodernism as a specific theoretical epistemology) arising in part from the destabilization entailed in the dissolution of Fordism and the rise of flexible accumulation in the early 1970s.

Although anthropologists cite Harvey's work with considerable frequency, the discipline has yet to engage systematically with his theoretical pronouncements on space, particularly in any critical manner, perhaps due to anthropology's own often narrow territorial predilections, especially its habitual tendency toward place-based ethnographic research entailing long-term participant observation. Such commitments to the intimate localism of the field-worker sit ill at ease with Harvey's more expansive and theoretical analysis of space. Rather, Harvey's primary critics have come from his own discipline. As with many scholars of magisterial scope, Harvey's critics are legion. They include both those staunchly opposed to his radical vision of an inherently politicized, anti-imperialist geography, as well as more sympathetic interlocutors who concur broadly with his program for a radical geography but take Harvey to task for focusing on class to the exclusion of covalent but nonidentical oppressive institutions. Feminist geographers (e.g., Cindi Katz and Nancy Hartsock), in particular, have pushed Harvey to theorize such institutions (patriarchy, racism, and heteronormativity) not as incidental appendages of identity politics but as structurally fundamental to the way in which capitalism manifests and reproduces itself in the world.

Harvey's ideas have gained increasing public exposure through their expression in digital technologies, including a Royal Society of Arts Animate production of his lecture on the 2008 financial crisis and the online production of his classic course "Reading *Capital,*" and through the translation of his books into more than a dozen languages.

Eliza Jane Darling

See also Critical Theory; Globalization Theory; Marxist Anthropology; Smith, Neil; Urban Studies

Further Readings

Castree, N. (2004). David Harvey. In P. Hubbard, R. Kitchin, & G. Valentine (Eds.), *Key thinkers on space and place* (pp. 181–188). London, UK: Sage.

Castree, N., & Gregory, D. (Eds.). (2006). *David Harvey: A critical reader.* Oxford, UK: Blackwell.

Jones, J. P. (2006). *David Harvey: Live theory.* New York, NY: Continuum.

Merrifield, A. (2002). David Harvey: The geopolitics of urbanization. In A. Merryfield (Ed.), *Metromarxism: A Marxist tale of the city* (pp. 133–155). New York, NY: Routledge.

HEGEL, GEORG W. F.

The German scholar Georg Wilhelm Friedrich Hegel (1770–1831) revolutionized European philosophy, developing a comprehensive system that gathered together the major strands of the speculative tradition, especially Plato, Aristotle, Baruch Spinoza, and Immanuel Kant. His work has continued to exert a profound influence on writers and thinkers in many disciplines down to the present today. In Hegel's system, the term *anthropology* is used in a technically narrow sense as the discipline that makes explicit the way embodiment affects awareness. Nonetheless, considered in a broader sense, anthropology, the study of human existence in its structure and in its history, is its center. In Hegel's view, the goal of the cosmos itself is to create the conditions for comprehending it and for reordering it for human well-being.

Biography

Hegel was born into a family of Lutheran pastors and minor public officials. He attended the theology seminar at Tübingen, where his roommates were the philosopher-to-be Friedrich Schelling and the poet-to-be Friedrich Hölderlin. In honor of the French Revolution, they planted a Freedom Tree; and Hegel annually toasted Bastille Day. His first position was as a private tutor. Through Schelling, he secured a position at the University of Jena, where he taught for 2 years. There, in 1807, he finished his best known work, *The Phenomenology of Spirit*, as Napoleon won the battle of Jena. Hegel said he saw "the World Spirit on horseback" riding triumphantly through the streets of Jena. He then took a 1-year position as editor of a pro-French newspaper, after which, for 8 years, he served as headmaster of a *Gymnasium*. During this time, he wrote two of his most important works, his *System of Logic* and the first draft of his *Encyclopaedia of the Philosophic Sciences*, which covered Logic, Nature, and Spirit/Mind. In 1816, he was appointed professor at Heidelberg. Two years later, he was called to the newly founded University of Berlin, where he served, with a term as rector, until his death. In 1821, he published his political theory in *Elements of the Philosophy of Right*, on which Marx wrote a notable critique. His lectures on the philosophy of history and on art, religion, and the history of philosophy were published posthumously.

Dialectic and the Whole

For Hegel, "The truth is the Whole." What makes *anthropos anthropos* is the notion of Being that points us, albeit emptily, at everything and everything about everything. That is why every people, no matter how "primitive," necessarily develops a *world*view. With the rise of philosophy among the Greeks, those views were subject to critique based on making explicit what is involved but not thought about in all our experience. Aristotle, in particular, following his master, Plato, surveyed the field of experience and laid out the bases for particular forms of inquiry that grew into the sciences. Hegel's thought keeps the Whole in view and heads off the temptation to derive various "isms" by projecting a limited method on the Whole. He claims to rewrite Aristotle in terms of what has developed since Aristotle.

In his *Phenomenology of Spirit* (1807), Hegel arrived at the starting point for his system in following out the various governing forms of consciousness operative in Western culture from the beginning. The examination of those forms showed that each form, more fully developed, led to its own breakdown, which inaugurated new forms, which, in turn, went through the same process. They exhibited what he called *dialectic*. His dialectic traced an *Aufhebung*, a polyvalent, ordinary German word that can mean cancellation, retention, or elevation. As this appears both in the history he traces and in the conceptual generation of his system, it describes the process of development in which conflicting forms of life or conflicting concepts are overcome by canceling their respective limitations, preserving what is legitimate in them, and elevating them to a higher level of compatibility. This dialectic is not Hegel's "method"; it is the process of reality itself and the conceptual system that can be shown to underpin it.

Phenomenology of Spirit

Human beings, according to Hegel, are bipolar. Experience is anchored in two immediately given factors that are abstracted out of concrete experience: (1) *sensory features* (color, sound, etc.) and (2) the notion of Being as an empty reference to the Whole. *Phenomenology of Spirit* begins with the former and ends with the conceptual space governed by the notion of Being that launches the Logic. Phenomenology, in the analysis of *consciousness*, shows the way in which scattered sensory experiences are gathered around the things exhibited in *perception*; it also shows how we can speak about these matters because of the universal forms (color, sound, things, forms, language, etc.) involved in *language*. But consciousness implies *self-consciousness*, first of appetites that reveal the needs of the conscious being. But distinctively, human self-consciousness emerges out of encounter with other human beings, which forms the existential center of Hegel's thought.

Here, we find the famous master/slave dialectic that grounds all development in history. It arises in the situation of encounter between living, self-determining beings. The slave clings to life and thus gives up his freedom to the master, who is unafraid to risk his life and thus secures his self-determination. But the master's self-determination has the character of irrational arbitrariness. The slave, in being forced to work for the master, learns what the self-indulgent master never learns but what every child should learn through obeying commands: that one does not have to follow one's whims but can determine oneself. This is the first stage of rationally free self-determination. The slave through manipulating materials also learns things about nature that one could not know merely by contemplating it and develops skills for reworking nature that would otherwise have lain fallow. History follows the slave in learning more and more about the natural world by endeavoring to develop techniques for shaping it.

The situation is transcended in the recognition by the Stoics that, whether on the throne (Marcus Aurelius) or in chains (Epictetus), through *reason* the human being is essentially free to take up his attitude toward his external condition.

Logic

There are three parts to Hegel's system, (1) Logic, (2) Nature, and (3) Spirit, each exhibiting the dialectic in its own way. Logic is broader than formal logic, though the latter finds its place within the larger Logic. Hegel develops the categories that human beings necessarily employ without making them explicit.

The *Logic* begins with the empty notion of Being and shows how it dialectically transforms itself when we carry out careful analyses. The Logic lays out the categories involved in (a) the sensory encounter with individual things (quality, quantity, and measure), (b) the intelligible apprehension of the universal notions things exhibit to an intellectual being (essence, existence, and actuality), and (c) the human subject together with the formal logical categories employed in intellection (what we may call Formal Logic, Systems Logic, and the Logic of Life). It is the human subject, grounded in life and seeking

the true and the good, who is typically left out of the scientific picture but who is the basis of science and, for Hegel, the purpose of the cosmos.

Spirit/Mind

The Logic is instantiated in *Nature* and in *Geist* (Mind/Spirit). The latter refers to the way human awareness, beyond the sensations and desires that govern animal awareness, transcends the here-and-now by being aware of the Cosmos and its time-encompassing, transcendent Ground mediating the relation between persons. Humans are thus able to pursue the True and the Good in cooperation with other humans. Nature and history display the further conditions that make possible ongoing scientific inquiry and the kind of society grounded in human rights where people can move creatively in all directions compatible with a sense of identity with family, with groups formed around occupations, and with the various levels of the state.

According to Hegel, the state comes into being historically when agriculture and marriage are institutionalized. It expands into empire with the invention of writing. The story of the development of rationality is centered on freedom. In the ancient empires, only one person was free, the emperor; and his freedom was only *formal freedom* or arbitrary will. A further development occurs with the Graeco-Roman period, when citizens, but not slaves, were free. A kind of culmination occurred through Christianity, which affirms the intrinsic dignity of all humans. It required centuries before that could fully penetrate society. Hegel discerned the main lines of that development in the Prussian Reform Movement, which was cut short by monarchical reaction. In the society he envisioned, what was made possible was the choice of rational or *substantial freedom*.

Objective Spirit

Hegel explores the institutional structures within which the free spirit can reach full actuality: the realm of *objective spirit*, residue of the work of those long dead, treated in his "Philosophy of Right." He follows Aristotle in rooting human development in the institution of the family, where one learns what it is to identify with and foster others. As in Aristotle, there is an encompassing level Aristotle called the *polis*, which, historically developed, became the complex of institutions Hegel calls the *State*.

In modernity, two new features appeared: (1) recognition of *abstract right* in the right to property and (2) the inviolability of *conscience*, which together developed into a set of rights inserted between family and state to form *civil society*, the locus of free-entry associations like business enterprises, universities, churches, fine arts societies, and the like. Here, we find freedom of the press, of religion, of enterprise, of inquiry and publicity, and of marriage and occupational choices, and the right to a jury trial. A major function of the state is to preserve such rights, constitutionally structured in a hierarchy of functions and jurisdictions that buffer the individual from unwarranted intrusion from above. The function of administration at the level of civil society is to provide infrastructure, ensure fair trade practices, and provide a safety net for those severely disadvantaged by the otherwise free enterprise system. Nonetheless, poverty and the possibility of an alienated rabble arise through the changing relation between overproduction and the economic capacity for consumption.

The state features an independent judiciary and a legislative assembly comprising the commercial, agricultural, and civil service branches. Members of the latter are to be "educated to universality" of outlook at the University of Berlin. The monarch stands atop the system, constitutionally limited and dependent on a cabinet of trained civil servants. In an ideal organization, like the Queen of England, his function is to sign documents and preside over official functions.

Absolute Spirit

Hegel rejects a world society of lasting peace, which would further support the natural tendency of individuals to limit their horizons to purely private interests, with little or no concern for the Whole. The threat of war between sovereign states makes individuals aware that they need to think in terms of the nation as a whole. The tension that this unsettled relation between states produces leads into the ultimate rational dimension of final reconciliation brought about by religion. Religion provides the highest mission of art, to represent the Absolute in sensory form. Philosophy provides the ultimate interlocking set of categories that completes and rationally grounds religious orientation.

Relation to Marx

Karl Marx was one of the Young Hegelians, who followed the philosopher Ludwig Feuerbach's reduction of religion to anthropology, rejected the grounding of the Whole in Spirit rather than in material forces, focused on the alienation involved in the master/slave relation as that played out in the emerging proletariat, and employed the dialectic for historical analysis. In setting thought back on its feet, reversing Hegel's general position, Marx regarded philosophy as ideology, dependent on and rationalizing the basically formative control of the means of production.

Robert E. Wood

See also Aristotle; Deconstruction; Frankfurt School; Marx, Karl; Marxist Anthropology; Plato

Further Readings

Hegel, G. W. F. (1981). *Hegel's phenomenology of spirit* (A. Miller, Trans.). Oxford, UK: Oxford University Press.

———. (1991). *Elements of the philosophy of right* (H. Nisbet, Trans.). New York, NY: Cambridge University Press.

———. (2007). *Hegel's philosophy of mind* (M. Inwood, Trans.). Oxford, UK: Clarendon Press.

Inwood, M. (2007). *A commentary on Hegel's philosophy of mind*. Oxford, UK: Clarendon Press.

Petry, M. (1977). *Hegel's philosophy of spirit* (3 vols.). New York, NY: Springer.

Pinkard, T. (2000). *Hegel: A biography*. Cambridge, UK: Cambridge University Press.

HERMENEUTICS

Hermeneutics refers to the theory and practice of interpretation. It raises important questions about the possibility of texts, artifacts, and human behavior. The entry provides a brief history of philosophical hermeneutics, followed by a discussion of the use of modern hermeneutics in the social sciences and the debates surrounding it.

History

The word derives from the Greek designation for the wing-footed god Hermes, whose task it was to communicate the word of the gods to the mortals.

For the ancient Greek philosophers, hermeneutics referred to the art of making the unintelligible and the strange familiar. They were concerned with the relationship between words and things and the ability of language to tell us something about the nature of the world. One of the earliest philosophical texts, Aristotle's *Peri hermeneias*, is dedicated to exploring interpretation by exploring the nature of declarative sentences. Rather than about truth itself, Aristotle systematically explored statements about truth and falsehood.

Yet this is not how the term *hermeneutics* is being used today. Modern hermeneutics is associated with the Renaissance and the Reformation. In particular, The Age of Exploration, contact with other cultures, and questions arising from the translation of biblical texts from Latin into vernacular languages were critical factors shaping hermeneutics. Two important issues arising from the translation of scripture were directly related to the formulation of a variety of more general theories of interpretation: first, the awareness of the different conceptual resources provided by vernacular languages vis-à-vis Latin and, second, the impossibility of interpreting a text purely with reference to itself. To achieve a faithful rendering of the author's intention, the interpreter of the text needed a good understanding of context, of the lifeworld of the author. Translation was not passive consumption but a creative act that necessitated an exploration of the original language and the context in which it was used as well as a sympathetic reproduction of the author's "mental state."

Especially in 18th-century Germany, these issues were to be reworked into a number of general theories of language and interpretation, starting with the work of Johann Gottfried Herder (1744–1803) and Friedrich Daniel Ernst Schleiermacher (1768–1834). They argued that language does not have objective referents but that words acquire meaning only in connection with other words. Therefore, human experience is only accessible indirectly, through interpretation. Both attempted to set out a general theory of interpretation that extended to phenomena other than texts, particularly works of art. Their work, sometimes called *romantic hermeneutics*, included an important psychological component of empathy with the objects of investigation, be they artifacts from other cultures or historical periods. Careful interpretation always demanded respect for that which is to be interpreted.

While the German romantics laid the foundations, it is the work of 20th-century authors such as Hans-Georg Gadamer (1900–2002) and Paul Ricoeur (1913–2005) that has been important for the reception of hermeneutics in the social sciences. Gadamer's work stresses the communicative features of understanding. Understanding something is not an act in which the subject imposes meaning onto a foreign object, but rather understanding arises from the interaction of two sets of traditions or horizons of understanding in a process that de-emphasizes human agency. Traditions are not consciously chosen but given to us by "culture," the accumulation of historical experiences and interpretations, and mediated by language. Whereas, Gadamer emphasizes the importance of history and tradition as providing an inescapable predicament for interpretation, Ricoeur's work stresses the possibility of emancipation from these constraints that the text affords. For Ricoeur, a text always transcends the circumstances of its own creation and opens up an infinite variety of interpretations for the reader, for whom the act of reading, rather than merely recreating the authorial intention and context, is itself creative. Hermeneutics can therefore assume a critical and transformative potential for the interpreter.

Hermeneutics and the Social Sciences

Hermeneutics has played an important although often unacknowledged role in the social sciences and especially in debates about whether or not social phenomena can be studied scientifically. Since at least the 19th century, some economists, political scientists, and anthropologists have argued that explaining social phenomena by reference to a small number of general laws is the only way social research can be properly scientific. That is, this way of proceeding allows social scientists to arrive at progressively more general laws, eventually allowing them to predict events. If explanation is the method germane to the study of the social world, hermeneutics, with its emphasis on the individual and the nongeneralizable, has no useful contribution to make to the scientific study of society.

Their opponents, on the other hand, argue that social reality is inherently unstable and therefore unpredictable. In opposition to the natural world, behavior in the social world is self-reflective and therefore meaningful. This is particularly pertinent in a situation where the investigator is not just the external observer vis-à-vis his subject but in a dialogic relationship, in which both parties constantly evaluate their behavior in response to the interaction itself. In such a situation, investigators need to uncover the specific context in which events take place, and the method suitable for social research is the interpretation of meaning.

While philosophical hermeneutics investigates the possibility of understanding in general, its insights have been debated in the context of a number of social sciences. In their attempts to reconstruct "the native point of view" or to be an "interpreter of the native," anthropologists like Clifford Geertz and Bronisław Malinowski have faced issues similar to those confronted by the philosophical hermeneuticists. They have been especially interested in Gadamer's idea of "pre-understanding." The anthropologist undertaking fieldwork, for example, approaches a foreign culture with preconceptions that are given to him by his background and his academic training. He must examine his own pre-understanding and that of his academic community. Anthropologists should also be concerned about the pre-understandings of their interlocutors and the changes they may undergo as the result of interaction with researchers.

While some have accepted these hermeneutical insights, there is disagreement about how to deal with the issue of pre-understanding. Structuralists have maintained that the issue of preconceptions in the understanding of culture can be resolved by developing more sophisticated formal models that accurately reflect "native" meaning, thus reducing the variety of cultural phenomena to a small number of universal patterns amenable to scientific study. Interpretivists have branded these claims as overly optimistic and reductionist. For Clifford Geertz, interpretation means the understanding of inevitable pre-understandings, resulting in what he calls "thick description." Thick description is description not only of events themselves but also of the conditions that make them meaningful. Taking the insights of hermeneutics seriously should mean that, rather than imposing our models and categories of understanding on cultural practices other than our own, we need to make conceptual room for these practices. Hermeneutics suggests that when we use concepts such as "witchcraft" or "magic" to approach a practice, we should critically examine how we arrived at their formulation, instead of postulating models that merely presume, say, the opposition

between science and nonscience, which may not do justice to the context of the practitioner.

Therefore, behind this debate about the relevance of hermeneutics for the study of culture are larger questions about the status of knowledge gained from interpretation. Can anthropological knowledge claim to have validity beyond the specific phenomena it interprets? Can anthropology claim the label of a social "science" if its results are neither cumulative nor generalizable beyond the singular case in question? Those favoring an interpretivist approach to the study of culture, which is most closely associated with hermeneutics, have maintained that comparison between cultures and generalization beyond individual cases is difficult if not impossible. On the other hand, Carl Martin Allwood has suggested that interpretation is not the only method available to anthropologists and that it can also be combined with other methods. Engaging in the study of individual cultural phenomena, texts or artifacts should not automatically preclude generalization. Moreover, the possibility of going beyond individual cases is inherent in hermeneutics, especially through the concept of the hermeneutic circle. This characterizes the problem of interpretation, whether it is a text or human behavior as a dialectical relationship between the whole and its parts, in which none is completely reducible to the other. The researcher is not confronted with subject-independent objects but needs to move back and forth between the parts of a text, the whole of the text, and the text's relationship to its cultural and historical context, in a never-ending process of interpretation.

According to Gadamer, interpreting any phenomenon means engaging in a process that can never be final—it can only enlarge but can never complete one's understanding of its context. An interview with an individual from another culture not only constitutes a dialogue, and hopefully a gradual approaching of horizons, between the interviewer and the interviewee but also elicits a dialogue between the subject and his or her own culture. The very act of establishing the boundaries of the domain under investigation by the interpreter necessitates placing it in a wider context. This is probably what Gadamer himself had in mind when he characterized understanding as a "fusion of horizons" between the interpreter and the object of interpretation. A degree of comparison through a concentric putting-into-context constitutes the very possibility of engaging across cultures. Thus, while it might be impossible to derive universal laws from the application of hermeneutics-inspired methodologies, it would be equally impossible to insist on their strictly idiographic and isolated character. In other words, while ethnographic studies might not be, strictly speaking, cumulative, they can tell us something about larger phenomena.

Critique of Hermeneutics

The hermeneutic enterprise has generated considerable controversy, especially over its use in the social sciences. One criticism has been the charge of hermeneutics embracing a relativist view of truth and objectivity. In other words, how can the interpreter judge any interpretation as superior to any other? A good example for illustrating this is Margaret Mead's and Reo Fortune's very different observations of the Arapesh in Papua New Guinea. Whereas Mead characterized them as largely pacific, gentle, and egalitarian, Fortune depicted them as fierce warriors. Hermeneutics allows for a number of explanations as to why the two accounts differ—the contrasting pre-understandings of the researchers, the differences in their academic background and training, or that one interpretation may have been a reaction to the other—but it will not settle the question as to which is correct.

Many criticisms of hermeneutics relate to the structural inequalities inherent in much of social science research, especially research into foreign cultures, where the idea of a fusion of horizons masks an unequal power relationship. Jürgen Habermas and Andreas Vasilache have argued that more often than not the dialogue between anthropologist and subject is set in a context of conquest and oppression in which the researcher mostly hails from the dominant culture. In this context, Gadamer's emphasis on placing oneself in a tradition as a precondition to understanding opens his hermeneutics to the charge of conservatism. Related to that is the accusation that hermeneutics privileges the written word and therefore has an inherent bias toward literate over oral cultures. Mitchell makes this point in connection with Black preaching—that the transcription of a sermon is not the same as the sermon. The act of transcribing the spoken word deprives speech of its performative aspect and flattens out its effects. None of these critiques invalidate the hermeneutic enterprise at large. They will instead lead to the refinement of methodologies attempting to bridge the gap between the interpretation of individual social phenomena and the need for generalization.

Paul Petzschmann

See also Aristotle; Cultural Relativism; Ethnoscience/ New Ethnography; Gadamer, Hans-Georg; Geertz, Clifford; Malinowski, Bronisław; Structuralism

Further Readings

Allwood, C. M. (1989). Hermeneutics and interpretation in anthropology. *Cultural Dynamics, 2*(3), 304–322.

Forster, M. (2007). Hermeneutics. In M. Rosen & B. Leiter (Eds.), *Oxford companion to continental philosophy.* Oxford, UK: Oxford University Press.

Geertz, C. (1983). *Local knowledge.* New York, NY: Basic Books.

Ricoeur, P. (1981). *Hermeneutics and the human sciences.* Cambridge, UK: Cambridge University Press.

Swearingen, C. J. (1986). Oral hermeneutics during the transition to literacy: The contemporary debate. *Cultural Anthropology, 1*(2), 138–156.

Watson-Franke, M-B., Watson, L. C., Freilich, M., Hanson, F. A., Hayano, D. M., Heinen, H. D., . . . Scholte, B. (1975). Understanding in anthropology: A philosophical reminder [and comments and replies]. *Current Anthropology, 16*(2), 247–262.

HERSKOVITS, MELVILLE

Melville Jean Herskovits (1895–1963), an American ethnologist and educator, was among the founders of African anthropology and African studies in the United States. He was also a pioneer in documenting the importance of African cultural influences on the cultures of the Americas.

Biography and Major Works

Herskovits was born in Bellefontaine, Ohio, in 1895 to Jewish immigrant parents, his father from Hungary and his mother from Germany. He had one sister. Growing up in a Jewish family in predominantly Protestant small towns, Herskovits grappled with questions about his cultural identity and his place in American society, which foreshadowed his interests as a cultural anthropologist. During World War I, Herskovits served in the U.S. Army Medical Corps. After the war, Herskovits earned an undergraduate degree in history at the University of Chicago and an MA in political science at Columbia University in New York, where he met Frances Shapiro (1897–1972), the daughter of Russian Jewish immigrants and an aspiring writer. Shapiro married Herskovits in 1924 in Paris. Although not a university-trained anthropologist, Frances Herskovits collaborated with her husband on his research and coauthored five books and several articles.

In 1920, Herskovits entered the doctoral program in anthropology at Columbia University, where he studied under Franz Boas—the most influential American anthropologist of the early 20th century. Boas taught a new generation of anthropologists, including Herskovits, to embrace the culture concept, which replaced the race concept as an explanation for human behavioral differences. Boas and his students argued that environmental and cultural influences were the primary determinants of human behavior and intelligence. By separating culture from race, Boas and his students debunked the notions of White racial superiority embraced by an earlier generation of Victorian anthropologists and biologists. At Columbia, Herskovits's classmates included the future anthropologists Ruth Benedict and Margaret Mead.

Unlike most American anthropologists of his cohort, who studied Native American cultures, Herskovits focused on African and African American cultures, earning his PhD in 1923 with a dissertation titled "The Cattle Complex in East Africa." In this study, Herskovits marshaled extensive evidence to show that cattle were the central organizing principle behind East African cultures from the Sudan to southern Africa.

From 1923 to 1926, while teaching anthropology at Columbia and at Howard University in Washington, D.C., Herskovits studied the physical anthropology of Black Americans with funding from the National Research Council. This research yielded two books, *The American Negro* (1928), and *The Anthropometry of the Negro* (1930), in which Herskovits challenged the concept of race as a fixed, unchanging category.

Herskovits did not gain a full-time faculty position until 1927, when Northwestern University, in Evanston, Illinois, hired him. Anti-Semitism likely limited Herskovits's teaching opportunities in an era when many American universities hired few, if any, Jewish faculty. At Northwestern, where he taught for 36 years until his death in 1963, Herskovits created and expanded the anthropology department, which emphasized African and African American cultures. Before World War II, he taught most of the American anthropologists who specialized in Africa. During his long career, his students included the anthropologists William Bascom, Joseph Greenberg, Hugh H. Smythe, Alan Merriam, Erika Bourguignon, George Simpson, Simon Ottenberg, Johnnetta B. Cole, and James W. Fernandez; the political scientist Ralph Bunche; the dancer and choreographer Katherine Dunham; and the historian Harvey Wish. Under his leadership, Northwestern became the leader in African anthropology in the United States.

From 1928 to 1941, Melville and Frances Herskovits undertook field trips to Dutch Guiana (now Suriname), Dahomey (now Benin), Haiti, Trinidad, and Brazil, marshaling evidence to demonstrate the richness and complexity of African and African American cultures and the influence of African cultures in the Americas. This work yielded several books, notably *Rebel Destiny: Among the Bush Negroes of Dutch Guiana* (1934), *Life in a Haitian Valley* (1937), *Dahomey: An Ancient West African Kingdom* (1938), and *Trinidad Village* (1947).

In the late 1930s and early 1940s, Herskovits participated in the Carnegie Corporation's study of African Americans. The Swedish economist Gunnar Myrdal headed the project and wrote the final report, *An American Dilemma: The Negro Problem and American Democracy* (1944), in which he notably rejected Herskovits's argument in favor of the important African influence on African American culture. Nonetheless, Herskovits's magnum opus, *The Myth of the Negro Past* (1941), the first publication of the Carnegie project, underscored the wide-ranging influence of African cultures in the United States.

As his influence with the philanthropic foundations grew, Herskovits helped promote African and African American studies, often advocating research opportunities for Black scholars. But he also used his institutional influence to limit Blacks' opportunities when they may have challenged his authority. For example, he criticized some activist Black scholars, most notably the historian Carter G. Woodson and the sociologist-historian W. E. B. Du Bois, whom he considered propagandists because of their social reform orientation. In the 1930s, Herskovits sought to discredit the *Encyclopedia of the Negro* project, which was edited by Du Bois. He also opposed the establishment of an African studies program at Fisk University, a Black college in Nashville, Tennessee, during World War II.

In the postwar era, Herskovits played a key role in the development of African studies programs at American universities. American involvement in the Second World War and the Cold War induced policymakers to advocate the creation of area studies programs to provide experts so that the United States could implement policies to serve its global interests. Herskovits successfully lobbied for foundation funding from the Carnegie Corporation to create the first major interdisciplinary African studies program in the United States in 1948, at Northwestern University. In 1957, he played an important role in the founding of the African Studies Association, and served as its first president. In 1961, he was named to the first endowed chair of African studies in the United States. Herskovits's support for African studies helped ensure that Africa would become a legitimate area of academic study.

In the context of Africa's drive for independence, Herskovits moved to the political stage to argue for African autonomy and as a voice for Africans in international affairs. In 1947, he wrote the American Anthropological Association's Statement on Human Rights for the United Nations, advising against an ethnocentric formulation of human rights, to ensure that a statement of human rights based on Western values would not be imposed on developing nations. From 1958 to 1960, Herskovits prepared an extensive report on Africa for the U.S. Senate and testified twice before the Senate Foreign Relations Committee, criticizing America's Africa policy and advocating African self-determination. He challenged the Cold War paradigm whereby American foreign policymakers considered African countries as mere objects in the Soviet-American battle for global hegemony. Herskovits argued that a collaborative process between Americans and Africans would advance U.S.-African relations, serve America's foreign policy interests, and improve life in Africa.

Critical Contributions to Anthropology

Herskovits contributed to anthropology through his studies of African and African American cultures, and through his role in the institutional development of African anthropology and African studies programs in the United States.

Physical Anthropology

Herskovits's physical anthropology research in the 1920s was part of the broader Boasian attack on the race concept, the notion that race determined intelligence, personality, and behavior. Based on the physical measurements and genealogies of African Americans in New York City and Washington, D.C., Herskovits, in *The American Negro* (1928) and *The Anthropometry of the Negro* (1930), demonstrated that most American Blacks were of mixed racial heritage and, consequently, were not really a race at all but a mixed population group. This conclusion demonstrated the fallacy of racist views of mulatto infertility and biological degeneracy and challenged the biological definition of race, steering scholars toward a more modern conception of race as a sociological category.

Economic Anthropology

Herkovits published *The Economic Life of Primitive Peoples* (1940), the first general study of comparative economics of nonliterate cultures, and a revised version of that work, titled *Economic Anthropology: A Study in Comparative Economics* (1952). In these works, Herskovits emphasized the importance of social relationships and cultural values in economic decision making, while acknowledging the role of individual choice.

Ethnographic Work on Diasporic Africans

From the late 1920s to the early 1940s, when most American anthropologists studied Native Americans, Melville and Frances Herskovits conducted fieldwork in Dutch Guiana (now Suriname), Dahomey (now Benin), Haiti, Trinidad, and Brazil to research the cultural connections between Africans and Americans of African descent. Based on that fieldwork, Herskovits rejected the widely held view that African cultures had no impact on Blacks in the Americas. Instead, he argued that African cultures influenced the music, folklore, material culture, social structure, and religious beliefs and practices of African American cultures. In his controversial classic *The Myth of the Negro Past* (1941), Herskovits challenged those who maligned Black cultures and

African cultures, including Black and White liberal scholars who argued that Black American culture was a pathological version of White culture, with little or no African influence. At a time when most White Americans assumed Black Americans to be inferior as a race and culture, Herskovits's establishment of the strength and complexity of African and African-influenced cultures was an important intellectual achievement.

Herskovits's research on Black cultures showed the diverse influences on American culture, helped transform notions of American identity from exclusive and unitary (White Anglo-Saxon Protestant) to inclusive and pluralist, and defined a dynamic view of cultural change that emphasized cultural diversity and cultural pluralism. In his most important post–World War II book, *Man and His Works: The Science of Cultural Anthropology* (1947), Herskovits proclaimed that the most important conceptual contribution of anthropology was cultural relativism, the belief that cultures could not be ranked in a developmental hierarchy. In this connection, Herskovits argued for mutual respect among cultures and attacked ethnocentric evaluations of cultures.

African Anthropology and African Studies

Herskovits pioneered African anthropology and African studies in the United States. In his dissertation, he employed the culture area methodology pioneered by Clark Wissler to argue that East Africa was a distinct culture area shaped by the cultural importance of cattle. Building on his use of the culture area methodology, Herskovits published journal articles that divided Africa into nine culture areas based largely on two broad economic divisions: (1) agricultural cultures and (2) pastoral cultures. In his use of the culture area methodology, Herskovits rejected Wissler's embrace of a cultural hierarchy with northern Europeans at the top. Instead, Herskovits employed Boas's concept of cultural relativism, which rejected cultural hierarchies. Herskovits's work represented a significant step toward a value-free study of world cultures.

In 1931, Herskovits became one of the first American anthropologists to conduct fieldwork in Africa. In the 1930s, Herskovits led the way in developing the subfield of African anthropology and thereby helped move African studies into the mainstream of academia in the United States. Herskovits's work on African culture areas and his two-volume study of Dahomey sought to understand Africans by studying their culture and history. In this way, he refuted the writings of missionaries, travelers, and historians of imperialism, who assumed African inferiority and insisted that the complex aspects of African culture were imported from Europe. Herskovits's approach to the study of African cultures helped steer writers away from a Eurocentric cultural hierarchy and toward a more objective study of world cultures.

Herskovits's Legacy

From the 1920s to the 1960s, the American anthropologist Melville J. Herskovits employed anthropological fieldwork to confront questions about race and culture in innovative and groundbreaking ways, as he undermined the hierarchical ways of thinking about humanity and underscored the value of human diversity. His research in West Africa, the West Indies, and South America documented the far-reaching influence of African cultures in the Americas and showcased the vibrancy of African American cultures. After World War II, he played a key role in the development of African studies programs in the United States, founding the first major interdisciplinary program in African studies at an American university, Northwestern University in Evanston, Illinois. Herskovits's work on Africans and African Americans was inextricably connected by his embrace of cultural relativism and his attack on racial and cultural hierarchy. As an anthropologist, Herskovits underscored the necessity of recognizing the dignity of all cultures; he maintained that marginalized peoples were worthy of study in higher education and worthy of consideration in politics.

Jerry Gershenhorn

See also Boas, Franz; Columbia University; Cultural Relativism; Goldenweiser, Alexander A.; Mead, Margaret; Mintz, Sidney

Further Reading

Baron, R. (2003). Amalgams and mosaics, sycretisms and reinterpretations: Reading Herskovits and contemporary creolists for metaphors of creolization. *Journal of American Folklore, 116,* 88–115.

Frank, G. (2001). Melville J. Herskovits on the African and Jewish diasporas: Race, culture, and modern anthropology. *Identities, 8,* 173–209.

Gershenhorn, J. (2004). *Melville J. Herskovits and the racial politics of knowledge.* Lincoln: University of Nebraska Press.

Jackson, W. A. (1986). Melville J. Herskovits and the search for Afro-American culture. In G. W. Stocking Jr. (Ed.), *Malinowski, Rivers, Benedict and others: Essays on culture and personality* (pp. 95–126). Madison: University of Wisconsin Press.

Yelvington, K. A. (2001). The anthropology of Afro-Latin America and the Caribbean: Diasporic dimensions. *Annual Review of Anthropology, 30,* 227–260.

———. (2011). Constituting paradigms in the study of the African diaspora, 1900–1950. *Black Scholar, 41,* 64–76.

HERTZ, ROBERT

Although he was a French sociologist of religion in his lifetime, Robert Hertz (1881–1915) strikes us now as a martyr as much as a scholar, a figure of truncated promise who sacrificed himself in leading a futile attack on German positions in the First World War in 1915. He had considerable influence on later anthropology through his works on the structure of death ritual and the symbolic polarity of right- and left-handedness. The fragment of his thesis on sin that has come down to us is certainly less well-known, though it is actually more central to his overall intellectual project than either of these better known works. There is also the more ethnographic text on the Catholic cult of Saint Besse, north of Turin, in which Hertz links the various versions of the myth to different social groups (e.g., the local shepherds, the Church, and local folklorists and historians).

Hertz's studies were firmly situated within the wider intellectual project of the school of Émile Durkheim (1858–1917), a leading figure in sociology, which he established firmly as an academic discipline in France. Among other ideas, Durkheim saw society as being of positive benefit to the individual, who can only live an incomplete life without it, and indeed can scarcely exist outside it except as a malefactor. Nonetheless, there are negative aspects to social life, and these are what Hertz concentrated on: death, which tears the social fabric and has to be repaired through ritual; the negativity of the left hand, which stands in symbolic opposition to the positive attributes of the right; and, above all, sin, whereby the individual becomes estranged from God (a metaphor for society here).

The work on sin also illustrates another common Durkheimian method: It takes a topic that might be considered purely a matter for the individual, only to show that it has a social aspect too. Thus, the sinner appears to be alone in the cubicle, apart from the priest who receives his confession. However, the event is actually held in the public space of the church, and the entire structure of the event is socially determined and approved. Similarly, death is not a crisis just for the deceased; it also involves society, and the more so the greater the deceased's status. In the case of the polarity of the hands, Hertz goes even further. This polarity is ostensibly located in the physiology of the brain, the focus being on the individual as a member of a species rather than of a society. However, Hertz claims that the reasons for this polarity are actually social, in that a traditional preference for right-handedness in most societies around the world has, over time, affected the very development of the brain itself.

Hertz's article on the polarity of the hands also exemplifies yet another aspect of this school's writings: its peculiar variant of evolutionism. Although they rejected the highly structured, supposedly progressive but in reality ahistorical phases of British social evolutionists like Herbert Spencer and Edward Tylor, Durkheim and his circle were still concerned with evolutionary questions. But the evolutionary paradigm was different here. Generally, an institution was seen as combining many different aspects in early and also contemporary "primitive" humanity. World history was then an account of the gradual separation of these aspects through the emergence of separate institutions, a process finally accomplished in the modern world. For Hertz in this article, the shift in the modern world toward encouraging ambidexterity in children in effect represents the separation of the original fusion of the symbolic values of the hands and their practical value as instruments. In the modern world, the idea of ambidexterity separates fact and value by denying the different symbolic values of the hands while treating their practical capabilities as equal.

As already noted, it was the fragmentary text on sin that was really central to Hertz's view of his own academic work, from which he saw the now better known, because completed, works on death and handedness as diversions. In fact, these are serious contributions in their own right, which have done the most to establish Hertz's credentials as a scholar to posterity. For Hertz himself, however, academic work in general was ultimately of less value than practical activities for the disadvantaged, which he felt he owed to society because of his relatively wealthy and privileged background and upbringing. In addition, Hertz felt that he owed a debt to France itself because of the refuge and the opportunities it had offered to families of German Jewish origin, like his own (though Hertz himself was French through and through). The ideas that Jews should do a little more than others for France and that the wealthy should lead by example explain what has seemed to some like his sacrificing his own life in the war by leading a hopeless attack against German lines (although in fact he was following orders in doing so), as well as his considering the possibility of joining his wife as an expert in pedagogy had he survived it. We cannot be sure, therefore, that he would have continued with the sort of scholarship that Durkheim wanted him to do and that, Durkheim persuaded him, helped cast light on the social and political problems of the French Third Republic. Hertz responded to this persuasion not only by carrying out purely intellectual work but also by founding and running the Groupe d'Études Socialistes, a left-leaning debating society bringing together like-minded intellectuals and political activists to discuss matters of public policy of urgency in contemporary France (Hertz himself contributed a somewhat chauvinistic pamphlet on the problem of depopulation in France).

Is Hertz, therefore, really a symbol of a life of scholarly promise cruelly cut short by a futile war, or was what we have by him his last word as regards a purely intellectual sociology? There is no clear answer, but his reputation can only be judged by the work he actually left behind him (which also includes numerous reviews, as well as folklore notes taken from his men at the front during the war). That work is pioneering in its focus, vivid in its descriptions, and still stimulating for students and scholars today.

Robert Parkin

See also Durkheim, Émile; Institut d'Ethnologie (Paris); Needham, Rodney

Further Readings

Hertz, R. (1960). A contribution to the study of the collective representation of death. In R. Needham & C. Needham (Eds.), *Death and the right hand*. New York, NY: Free Press.

Parkin, R. (1996). *The dark side of humanity: The work of Robert Hertz and its legacy*. Amsterdam, Netherlands: Harwood Academic.

HISTORICAL PARTICULARISM

Historical particularism is the label most often attached to the body of method and theory developed by Franz Boas and several generations of his students for the study of Native American societies in the first part of the 20th century. Beginning with his appointment at Columbia University and the American Museum of Natural History in New York City in 1897 and continuing to his death in 1942, Boas dominated both the intellectual and the institutional character of American anthropology. Although many Boasian anthropologists have rejected the idea of a "school" of anthropology, and the core group around Boas incorporated considerable internal diversity, there were, nonetheless, widely shared distinctive features. These focused on the historical and symbolic nature of culture and on the importance of language. Historical particularism went out of fashion with the expansion and internationalization of anthropology after World War II. More recently, however, many anthropologists have returned to reassessing the ongoing legacy of historical particularism and the approach to culture that it entailed.

Reconstructing Culture Histories

In "The Study of Geography" (1887), Boas adopted Wilhelm Dilthey's distinction between *Naturwissenschaften* and *Geisteswissenschaften*, the natural and the humane or cultural sciences. Anthropology was to lie with the latter, along with geography and cosmography. Although the natural and humane sciences had different objects of study and different methods, critically for Boas, both were sciences. He believed in the principle that universal laws might someday arise from the comparative study of cultures but did not expect this to happen in his lifetime because the ethnographic database was thoroughly inadequate. Such laws could only be formulated after sufficient factual evidence had been collected, and one could expect no counterexamples from further research. In particular, Boas's critique of cultural evolution as an explanatory theory was based on the evolutionists' assumption that generalizations that accepted Western civilization as the standard for "progress" were premature. These theories did not do justice to the particularities and diversities of known cultures, never mind others that might later come to be known.

Boas turned instead to the histories of particular Native American cultures. In the absence of either written records or useful archaeological dating methods, he was left with two choices for accessing such histories: (1) historical linguistics or (2) the distribution of culture elements. Initially, Boas was enthusiastic about linguistic classification. He proposed several genetic connections among Northwest Coast languages (Tlingit and Haida; Kwakiutl and Nootka) during his survey work there for the Bureau of American Ethnology and the British Association for the Advancement of Science. By 1894, however, he had become skeptical about the analyst's ability to distinguish between the lingering effects of prior historical development within a language family and the similarities arising from more recent borrowing among genetically unrelated languages as a result of culture contact and migration. Boas was self-trained in linguistics as a discovery procedure for fieldwork on unwritten languages and was not well versed in the methods of 19th-century Indo-European philology, with its breakthroughs in historical reconstruction on the basis of systematic sound changes. His principal linguistic student, Edward Sapir, later joined by the Germanicist and Algonquianist Leonard Bloomfield, would pursue the philological route, arguing that linguistic elements—sound change and even grammatical categories—behaved in a much more predictable fashion than other elements of culture, thus allowing their histories to be traced even in unwritten languages. Bias was minimized because speakers of a language were usually not aware of the categories they employed.

Boas, however, chose to pursue time perspective through the diffusion, borrowing, and integration of folklore elements. He was perhaps much influenced in this choice by the character of the area where he chose to do his primary ethnographic work. The Northwest Coast culture area of the United States and Canada contains remarkable linguistic diversity accompanied by cultural convergences across linguistic boundaries. The area's rich marine and maritime resources enabled permanent villages, leisure for cultural elaboration, monumental architecture, and developed art traditions. Boas's year with the Eskimos of Baffin Island in 1883–1884 convinced him that the environment could pose limits on human culture but did not determine expressive capacity or cultural style. The Northwest Coast, then, offered a chance to explore the variety of cultural elaborations possible within a relatively homogeneous geographical and environmental area.

Boas chose to focus most of his historical work on folklore elements. The same stories were told throughout the Northwest Coast culture area, but they differed in form and elaboration in ways that reflected their complexly interwoven sources among neighboring cultures. As early as 1891, Boas was committed to the idea that the dissemination of folklore elements would reveal migrations, trade patterns, and intermarriage as mechanisms through which borrowed elements from unrelated sources were integrated into new cultural contexts that retained traces of their multiplex origins. Boas's student Robert Lowie coined the term *shreds and patches* for this cultural process, but he did not intend to preclude later processes of integration (despite misreadings by his successors). In 1895, Boas denied the "organic growth" of myths but emphasized that "accretion" of borrowed material occurred in alignment with the "genius" of a people. He was drawing here on the German romantic tradition of folklore and linguistics in the vein of Wilhelm von Humboldt, J. G. Herder, Hermann Steinthal, and the brothers Grimm. Boas's denial of wholesale borrowing distinguishes his historical particularism from diffusionist models developed in Europe that postulated the simultaneous co-movement of complexes of culture traits; Father Wilhelm Schmidt's migrating Egyptian pyramids of the sun and a Melanesian bow culture exemplify what Boas doubtless considered another form of premature generalization, based on speculation without empirical evidence.

By 1914, Boas was prepared to argue that no culture's myths were entirely local in their origins, certainly not on the Northwest Coast. He seems to have assumed that all culture areas would illustrate processes of diffusion similar to those he had identified on the Northwest Coast. The original form of a particular plot could never be recovered, because such forms were always in flux. There is nothing static about the definition of culture underlying this position. Boas saw history as a product of agency in the borrowing and integration of folklore elements or motifs.

The core comparative method of historical particularism could not be formulated from the point of view of the members of any particular culture, however, because they did not have access to the range of versions of traditional tales and motifs that would allow the analyst to undertake comparisons of motifs and their integration. Members of a culture had stories about their own history, to be sure, but these were likely to be biased because they understandably justified the identity and significance of the tellers. Boas considered this to be "secondary rationalization" rather than a source of reliable historical inference. The myths and stories were critical for understanding the psychological reality of individuals in a particular cultural context, but that was another matter and required a psychological rather than a historical methodology.

The analyst, in contrast, could stand apart from particular folklore texts and attend deductively to their distribution and its historical interpretation. This is why it was so important to assemble a detailed and accurate database from which historical inference might proceed.

The historical and the psychological, then, were the two sides of the particularist coin. Indeed, the historical approach led naturally to questions of psychological integration that would be reflected in the stories narrators recorded from their particular cultural locations. The classic descriptions of distribution of culture complexes over wide culture areas provided the data necessary to generalize about how borrowing took place. The exemplars include Ruth Benedict on the Plains vision quest, A. Irving Hallowell on circumpolar bear ceremonialism, and Leslie Spier on the Plains sun dance. The distribution of elements in different tribes proved far from random. Something very like Boas's "genius" of the particular people was at work. Adopting the terminology of Herder and von Humboldt's *Volkerpsychologie*, Boas argued that each culture developed its own unique integration of elements from diverse sources and was thereby distinguished from its neighbors.

Language, Culture, and Psychology

Conventional evaluations of historical particularism have emphasized only the historical side of the program and failed to note Boas's theoretical commitment to moving between questions of history and psychology, using in alternation the methods appropriate to each. George W. Stocking Jr. suggests that Boas's theoretical ideas were so thoroughly incorporated into American anthropological practice that they were no longer attributed to him or considered theoretical. These theoretical premises include the inseparability of race, language, and culture and the equal validity and expressive capacity of all human cultures due to the character of what Boas called "the mind of primitive man," the title of his 1911 paradigm statement for anthropology as a science encompassing culture, biology, and environment.

Regna Darnell has enumerated the shared positions of historical particularism in its heyday during the first half of the 20th century. The most basic premise is that culture is a set of ideas or symbols held in common by a group of people who see themselves as a social group: Culture is not a thing, and it is always changing in response to the circumstances of the group's history. Language is key to assessing the symbolic world of a particular people. Thought is only possible through language, and each language structures reality, the nature of the world, uniquely. Although history in the sense of reconstructed cultural history is not the direct focus of Boas's insistence on the inseparability of language, thought, and reality, the strictures of speaking a particular language, itself a product of a particular history, give a group its cohesion and sense of identity. Boas edited the *Handbook of American Indian Languages* for the Bureau of American Ethnology in 1911, with a second volume coming out in 1922. Each of the grammatical sketches included in these two volumes was intended to provide a model for producing grammars of other "psychological types" (i.e., different language families) that used the categories of those languages rather than importing ill-fitting analytic distinctions from Latin or Greek. Boas's introduction to the *Handbook* was a passionate defense of particularism, implicitly as the binary opposite of unilinear cultural evolution. Societies at every scale of development or complexity had their own integrity based on categories of language and symbolic thought developed under particular historical circumstances in relation to their environment and experience.

Boas argued that the only way to get at the "native point of view" in the absence of a written history and philosophy was through language, not as an abstract structure or even as a grammar but through texts recorded from the spontaneous speech of fluent speakers. Such texts were a necessary adjunct to an adequate grammar. A dictionary was the third prong of the historical particularist approach to language, alongside grammar and texts. Calibration of different worldviews and categories of thought required extensive cultural information to make them intelligible when words for the same concept did not exist in the analyst's language. Boas considered such texts to instantiate a crucial part of the record of all human culture. It was an urgent task to ensure that no more such thought-worlds would be lost. The task of recording and preserving "traditional" Native American understandings of the world was much more interesting to historical particularists than the contemporary situation of Native American tribes, although many of them supported the positions of Native activists and intervened with government and church authorities on behalf of the peoples they studied. Only in the 1930s, however, did ethnographic interest in acculturation become significant; the proponents were second-generation Boasians, whose interests in culture and psychology required attention to contemporary circumstances.

Boas's psychology leads to a view of the initial incommensurability of different cultural worlds that has serious implications for the task of the ethnographer as a fieldworker. This meant that it would take a long time for anthropologists to establish trust, to learn the language, to learn to think with the categories locally employed. Indeed, the move from "informants" to "collaborators" begins with the linguistics and the texts' mandate. Because each culture reasons from its own standpoint, externally imposed policies and programs are often ill suited to local needs. The Boasian attention to Native points of view and particular histories, especially in recent decades, has supported recognition of Native American communities' claims to exerting control over research and their own futures.

The Legacy of Historical Particularism

American anthropology shifted dramatically in the years following World War II. University programs expanded, with returning veterans on the G.I. Bill drawn to anthropology by their military experience overseas. American isolationism was challenged on multiple fronts both before and after the war, and policymakers turned to anthropologists as advisors in dealing with unfamiliar cultural differences. The stage for this sea shift was set by Boasian anthropologists: Margaret Mead and Rhoda Metraux's Culture at a Distance project during the war (later, this became the Columbia University Cultures at a Distance Project) and Ruth Benedict's postwar book *The Chrysanthemum and the Sword* (1946), an analysis of Japanese culture aimed at postwar reconstruction, were particularly influential. Mead was an active public supporter of the United Nations. However, the cultural relativism that made sense for studying isolated American Indian tribes seemed increasingly naive in the face of postwar political realities. At the end of her life, Benedict, the single most important theorist of cultural relativism, was talking about the "synergy" that emerged "beyond relativism" in a complex and increasingly interdependent world. Boas himself was an activist intellectual who spoke out on behalf of Jews in Hitler's Europe and Blacks in the American South. The particularist respect for the value and integrity of each culture did not preclude moral judgment about the relations between cultures. Sapir wrote "Culture, Genuine and Spurious" and about the predicament of the individual's self-realization in different cultural contexts.

The new postwar generation of anthropologists chose fieldwork sites in places far distant from American Indian reservations. Many returned to the Pacific, where they had been stationed during the war. Others went to Africa, Asia, and Latin America. Meanwhile, American academic life was reorganizing itself around a geopolitical understanding of cultural diversity. Interdisciplinary programs in area studies proliferated, and anthropologists found themselves working with colleagues from other social sciences who did not share the Americanist socialization of prewar anthropology.

Moreover, Boas's control over the American discipline began to wane after his retirement from Columbia in 1936. Those who had felt stifled by the shared program of their Boas-trained elders rejected the historical particularist paradigm in favor of new theoretical positions. The neo-evolutionary models posed by Leslie White and Julian Steward seemed to many particularly well suited to the new complexity of anthropology. White was particularly virulent in his critique of historical particularism, arguing that Boas's position was atheoretical and had set anthropology back by at least half a century. Although acknowledging that Boas's critique of social evolution in its judgmental Victorian form provided a needed corrective at the end of the 19th century, White insisted that this exercise had been entirely negative and that its time was over. He castigated Boas and his coterie for the "memory culture" tenor of their so-called salvage ethnography. Indeed, many of the Boasians had worked with the last generation of fluent speakers of traditional Native American languages, who were also the last generation to have lived in anything like a traditional manner. These ethnographers worked hard to record, at a time of rapid social change, what was remembered by this generation. In many cases, elders and ritual specialists failed to find successors within their own communities and chose to talk to the anthropologists as a last chance to ensure that their knowledge would not be lost. As cultural revitalization gained momentum in the 1960s and 1970s, moreover, younger Indians came forward to preserve the knowledge of their elders.

The simultaneous switch of anthropology to evolution, ecology, more quantitative and purportedly objective methodologies, and the study of complex communities, especially peasants, brought the everyday social life of ethnographic subjects and their response to the rapid social change around the world to center stage in a way that seemed to render the Americanist ethnographic tradition passé. The proponents of these new approaches emphasized discontinuity rather than continuity or rapprochement. Across the social sciences, positivism was in ascendancy, and historical particularism retreated to a theory adhered to primarily by anthropologists and linguists who continued to work in Native American communities.

The development of the Culture-and-Personality school of anthropology, almost exclusively a North American phenomenon, retained more of the qualitative ethnographic character of prewar Boasian anthropology. This work had its roots in Boas's insistence that problems of psychology or the native point of view were just as significant as the historical problems that had preoccupied him during the early part of his career, because he considered them descriptively and methodologically prior to ultimate psychological questions. Margaret Mead suggested that the change from history to psychology could be dated around 1910, although the emphasis shifted gradually during the interwar years. The psychological turn, however, tallied well with the national character emphasis pioneered by Benedict and Mead during and after World War II. By the 1960s, another sea change was under way, toward interpretivist and meaning-oriented ethnography that rejected or at least marginalized questions of positivist science and deductive generalization.

One might have expected this paradigm shift to produce renewed attention to historical particularism and the balance between history and psychology advocated by Boas. This was not the case, however. Anthropologists for the most part accepted at face value the revisionist dismissal of Boasian theoretical positions by postwar critics. Marvin Harris, in *The Rise of Anthropological Theory* (1968), exemplified the trend, both in his rejection of Boasian work and in the absence of interest in disciplinary historicism or reflexivity. For Harris, the history of anthropology was unilinear, to be valued only insofar as it led to the "techno-environmental determinism" that he favored. More recent scholarly work (see "Neo-Boasianism," this encyclopedia) has corrected the historic record and made reassessment possible, in correlation with a larger turn to history across the social sciences.

Regna Darnell

See also Benedict, Ruth F.; Bloomfield, Leonard; Boas, Franz; Cultural Ecology; Cultural Materialism; Cultural Relativism; Mead, Margaret; Sapir, Edward; Steward, Julian; White, Leslie

Further Readings

Bennett, J. (1998). *Classic anthropology: Critical essays 1944–96.* New Brunswick, NJ: Transaction.

Darnell, R. (1998). *And along came Boas: Continuity and revolution in Americanist anthropology.* Amsterdam, Netherlands: John Benjamins.

———. (2001). *Invisible genealogies: A history of American anthropology.* Lincoln: University of Nebraska Press.

Harris, M. (1968). *The rise of anthropological theory.* New York, NY: Thomas Crowell.

Stocking, G. W., Jr. (1974). *The shaping of American anthropology, 1880–1911: A Franz Boas reader.* New York, NY: Free Press.

HOBBES, THOMAS

Thomas Hobbes (1588–1679), English philosopher, was one of the early Enlightenment theorists in British social anthropology.

Biography and Major Works

Hobbes was born on April 15, 1588, near Malmesbury in England. His mother's family lived in Brokenborough, where his father was a curate. Very little is known about his family life as a child growing up, except that he had two brothers. Although his father was an uneducated clergyman, several of his uncles were prosperous in business matters. Hobbes was raised by one of his uncles, Francis, who paid for his education at Magdalen College, Oxford. After leaving Oxford, Hobbes was recommended to be a tutor to William Cavendish. He maintained a lifelong affiliation with the Cavendish family, from which his intellectual career benefited a great deal. He was able to travel abroad, afforded direct contact with intellectual circles that included scientists, and provided access to the library at Hardwick Hall. All of these were especially important for Hobbes's intellectual development after leaving Oxford. In his vita, Hobbes expressed dissatisfaction with the large amount of Aristotle's philosophy that he was required to learn. Despite his professed disdain for scholasticism, in several important respects, his earlier study of Aristotle influenced the scientific account of human nature he would later develop.

Francis Bacon, an acquaintance of Cavendish, employed Hobbes as an amanuensis and included among his duties the translation of Bacon's *Essays* into Latin. Although Bacon shared Hobbes's anti-scholastic disposition, his influence on Hobbes was mitigated by Hobbes's preference for Euclid's deductive method rather than the inductive method Bacon touted. Nevertheless, Bacon, like Hobbes, advocated the idea of grounding ethics and civil philosophy on a scientific account of human nature.

Hobbes's close association with William and Charles Cavendish during the 1630s facilitated his study of science. He obtained for William a copy of Galileo's *Dialogues* and soon after began writing on physics and psychology. On a continental trip in 1634, Hobbes was introduced to Marin Mersenne, who had formed an intellectual circle that included René Descartes. Hobbes's earliest scientific work was a manuscript on optics that provided a mechanistic account of perception. Unfortunately, it closely resembled the account already published in Descartes's *Dioptrics*. Influenced by Galileo, both had attempted independently to apply his physics to sense perception. Hobbes had planned to incorporate his work on optics into a trilogy devoted to physics, psychology, and politics. His aim was to derive an account of natural right from a scientific account of physiology, psychology, and physics. *Elements of Law* (1640) was an early manuscript in which Hobbes spells out the basic rudiments of the view of human nature and politics he later presents in *De Cive* (1642) and *Leviathan* (1652). Some of his work on physics and psychology from this period appeared later in *De Corpore* (1650) and *De Homine* (1658).

Toward the end of the 1630s, Hobbes's work on physics and psychology was interrupted by political events. His royalist ties required him to seek exile, along with Charles II, for 11 years in France. The prior completion of *De Cive* draws in question whether his politics was deduced from the physics and psychology he presented in *De Corpore* and *De Homine*. In *Leviathan*, Hobbes even suggests that this deduction is unnecessary. He allows his definitions of psychological terms to be confirmed by each individual through introspection rather than by deduction from physics.

Contributions to Anthropology

Hobbes was the first modern philosopher to present a scientific account of natural right and political obligation. His main contribution to anthropology was an egoistic theory of human nature derived from physiological psychology. He employed this theory to explain an earlier transition from a state of nature to civil society.

Animal Motion and Psychological Egoism

In the materialist view Hobbes assumes throughout his writings, everything can be understood in terms of matter and motions. He viewed introspection, and all modes of consciousness such as imagination, memory, dreams, and sense perception, to be nothing more than motions in the brain. Perception occurs when tiny motions from objects cause a reaction of tiny motions from the sense organ, the interaction of which produces appearances. Hobbes couples his *reduction* of psychological phenomena to motions in the brain with an *extension* of the term *endeavor* or *conatus* from its original application to the motions of inanimate objects in physics to apply as well to the purposeful behavior of living creatures. The invisible "small beginnings" of motions in the body, as well as the visible actions they constitute, are equally referred to as "endeavors."

Animals and humans have innate "vital motions" that function without cognition, such as those involved in breathing. They also have a capacity for voluntary motions that augment vital motions. "Animal motion" begins with perception and results in bodily movement either toward or away from objects that appear beneficial or harmful. Hobbes maintained that the aim of all voluntary acts is to obtain some apparent benefit for the agent. He derived this egoistic psychology from his physiological explanation of behavior in terms of appetites and aversions—which he defined as animal motion toward or away from what appears beneficial or harmful.

State of Nature

Hobbes is well known for his bold statement in *Leviathan* of a pessimistic view of human life in a state of nature. He characterized this "natural condition" as involving anarchy and war. Unlike the work of later thinkers such as John Locke and Jean-Jacques Rousseau, in which a precivil society model is the focus of their discussion of the state of nature, Hobbes was also concerned with civil war and international relations, and he includes these two examples to illustrate the idea.

War was, for Hobbes, a rational outcome of human interaction in the state of nature, due mainly to the role passions play in human motivation. He believed that, with few exceptions, fear of death is the strongest passion. Indeed, it is because all living creatures are constructed physiologically to avoid death that they have a natural right of defense. Using a metaphor drawn from physics, Hobbes pointed out, with regard to this natural inclination, that just as a stone falls downward, as a matter of physiological constitution, humans "cannot do otherwise" (*De Cive*).

What leads to war in the state of nature is not so much competition for resources as the "diffidence," or anxiety, engendered by an inherent insecurity against invaders, who aim to dispossess others. Under such circumstances, Hobbes argues that by natural right an agent is allowed to secure his possessions through anticipation and a policy of preemption. When Hobbes attributes to all humans a restless desire for power that ceases only in death, he meant that even those willing to live moderately have this desire, which is simply a desire for assurance that their present power to live well will continue. Because of the few who will invade for glory, those who are content to live within modest means must consider, as necessary for their defense, invading a neighbor to increase their power in order to ensure their future security. Despite the rationality of a first-strike policy as a defensive measure, when everyone is known to have adopted it, the result is a general disposition to engage in violence.

Hobbes presents the tendency toward war in the state of nature as a natural outcome of everyone having a desire for self-preservation and a natural right to ensure this with a rational calculation of available options. Hence, human nature is not to be condemned as evil for fostering this outcome. In the absence of the protection of a sovereign with sufficient power to enforce the law, preemptive measures are rational for the modest majority in anticipation of the vainglorious few. The problem is that, when everyone has a first-strike policy, life under these conditions is "solitary, nasty, brutish, and short" (*Leviathan*, Chapter 13). Hobbes cites fear of death and hope for a more "commodious life" as passions that motivate agents in a state of nature to seek the security and benefits of a civil society.

Origin of Civil Society

For Hobbes, the purpose of government is to provide security. The social contract authorizes a sovereign to carry out this function. A social contract can be entered into through the process of instituting a sovereign or through conquest and domination. Hobbes claims that the latter has been far more common throughout history. To illustrate a covenant of mutual trust, he uses a case of ransom involving an extorted promise. This example illustrates the role of coercion in sovereignty by conquest. When comparing the coerced promise of the vanquished under a conqueror with the uncoerced agreement that subjects enter into under institution, Hobbes points out that both are based on fear (of a conqueror or of each other, respectively) and that, because of this, both are voluntary. As he insisted in the ransom case, coerced agreements motivated by fear are no less valid, and the terms must be fulfilled, just as in the case of uncoerced agreements.

Locke criticized Hobbes's account of the state of nature as lacking social and moral norms. He maintained that even without a formal government there would be a social structure with moral norms that most people follow. When Hobbes speaks of "the savages in America," he has a notion of a contemporary precivil society in mind. He operates with a scheme of earlier and later stages of social development when he uses the term *savages* to refer also to the ancient Germans. Locke was right to criticize Hobbes's notion that Native Americans lived without society and morality, but only to the extent that Hobbes relies on this example. Given that the advent of the English civil war had prompted Hobbes to complete his political theory earlier than planned, it is not difficult to understand his inclusion of a dissolution model along with a precivil society model of the state of nature.

Rousseau criticized Hobbes and Locke for their inaccurate portrayals of life in the state of nature. He charged them with describing civilized humans, not "natural man," in their state-of-nature theories. Hobbes's account of sovereignty by acquisition emphasizes later stages by focusing on conquest as a natural historical process that explains the origin, growth, and development of society from small families to large kingdoms. A version of the social contract that establishes civil society first occurs within the household to establish the authority of the father, husband, and master over his children, wife, and servants and slaves, respectively. Hobbes insists that this patriarchical social arrangement is not natural, as Aristotle believed, and cites Amazon women as a case in which it is contested (*Leviathan*, Chapter 20).

A master's authority is based on his ability to provide protection from invaders. When a master is conquered by another head of a household, all of the members of the conquered household are obligated to the conqueror or enslaved if they refuse to submit. Hobbes maintained that slaves, unlike servants, have no obligation to their masters. By refusing to enter into a social contract, they remain in a state of nature and are still at war. He explains the growth of commonwealths as a sociohistorical process of combining households through conquest and acquisition.

Hobbes believed that rebellion and civil war loom in the background of every civil society. His state-of-nature theory functions as a reminder of this constant threat. He was more keen on the idea that civilized people will behave "savagely" toward each other when political authority is removed than he was on the savagery of primitive people. He presents the civil war case as evidence of an atavistic tendency to lapse into behavior characteristic of a precivil society stage of human development. He held that an absolute sovereign was required to prevent the conditions under which this relapse would occur.

In his discussion of relations between commonwealths, Hobbes's view of human nature is no less pessimistic. Yet, unlike the dissolution case involving conquest, rebellion, or civil war, Hobbes did not argue for a social contract between commonwealths that would establish an absolute sovereign at the global level to provide international security. Instead, he marshaled these potential threats to the commonwealth to bolster his case for a sufficiently powerful absolute sovereign at the domestic level.

Hobbes's Legacy

Hobbes was a major influence on important philosophers such as Baruch Spinoza, G. W. Leibniz, John Locke, David Hume, Friedrich Engels, Karl Marx, and John Rawls. In science and social anthropology, he presaged Charles Darwin, Herbert Spencer, Lewis H. Morgan, John B. Watson, B. F. Skinner, Clark L. Hull, and Edward O. Wilson. His account of the state of nature as an antecedent stage of cultural development and his reconstruction of the origin of the social contract represent an early evolutionary development theory favored by many social scientists. The utilitarianism of Jeremy Bentham and John Stuart Mill, with its focus on self-interest, as well as the emphasis on materialism and economics in Karl Marx's political writings were heavily influenced by Hobbes's views. Hobbes's endorsement of mother right, which is rather unique in 17th-century thought, accommodates many contemporary feminist concerns regarding the origin of patriarchy. His account of the role honor plays in the mutual behavior of sovereigns continues to loom large in the field of international relations.

Tommy Lee Lott

See also Darwin, Charles; Marx, Karl; Morgan, Lewis Henry; Sahlins, Marshall; Spencer, Herbert

Further Readings

Kavka, G. (1987). *Moral paradoxes of nuclear deterrence.* New York, NY: Cambridge University Press.

Macpherson, C. B. (1962). *The political theory of possessive individualism: Hobbes to Locke.* Oxford, UK: Oxford University Press.

Peters, R. S. (Ed.). (1962). *Brett's history of psychology.* New York, NY: Macmillan.

Rogow, A. A. (1986). *Thomas Hobbes: Radical in the service of reaction.* New York, NY: Norton.

Wright, J. H. (2002). Going against the grain: Hobbes's case for original maternal dominion. *Journal of Women's History, 14*(1), 123–155.

HOCART, ARTHUR M.

Arthur Maurice Hocart was born on April 26, 1883, at Eeterbeck in Belgium. His early education was at Elizabeth College in Guernsey, in the Channel Islands. He then went on to Oxford, where he obtained his first degree with honors at Exeter College in 1906, receiving training in Greek, Latin, ancient history, and philosophy. He did further studies in Germany at the University of Berlin, delving into psychology and phenomenology. Hocart's most important career change was when he was recruited by William Halse Rivers Rivers for the Percy Sladen Trust Expedition to the Solomon Islands in 1908, which was to be the first instance of modern-style anthropological fieldwork involving prolonged residence among the people studied. Hocart spent 6 months with Rivers on the small island of Simbo in the New Georgia group of the Solomon Islands, researching themes such as kinship, social organization, religion, and myth through firsthand field observations and conversations with key informants in the Melanesian Pidgin of the day. This on-site training under Rivers left a lasting impact on the young scholar, as seen in his continued fieldwork in other parts of the Pacific. The two scholars kept in contact even after Rivers drifted into other areas of interest, culminating in his very different work as a military psychiatrist during World War I.

After the Solomon Islands expedition, Hocart settled at Lakeba in Fiji, where he had obtained a position as a school headmaster. He continued a long record of anthropological fieldwork in Fiji during his career there and also worked farther east in Polynesia, in Wallis, Rotuma, Tonga, and Samoa. Although he returned briefly to Oxford in 1914 to do postgraduate studies, World War I interrupted his plans as he soon found himself on military service in France. After the war, Hocart studied Sanskrit, having obtained the position of Archaeological Commissioner of Ceylon. In the period 1921–1929, he managed and followed up a long series of excavations, of which the most famous may be the groundbreaking fieldwork at the Singhalese Buddhist Temple of the Tooth at Kandy. He returned finally to England in 1929 in poor health. In 1930, Hocart married Elizabeth G. Hearn, who had been his nurse during his prolonged illness. Hocart made continued attempts at acquiring a permanent position in conventional academia throughout his career, but he failed to secure such a position until the latter part of his life, when in 1934 he was appointed to the chair of sociology at the University of Cairo. He died in Cairo in 1939 at the age of 56.

Hocart's contributions to academia can be said to be representative of theoretical trends at the time, and he was strongly occupied with evolutionary theory and the origins of social customs and institutions. This may have hampered his career when he applied for positions in England, since the theoretical fashion of the time was strongly antievolutionary. Nonetheless, Hocart's ideas were original and strongly founded in empirical materials. His interest in themes such as leadership and social origins was to be carried further in his contributions to a general theory of kingship. Indeed, Hocart is one of the very few who have tackled the comparative concept in the manner represented by his book *Kingship.* In that treatise, he drew on sources from ancient history and contemporary ethnography, again revealing the influence that his own firsthand anthropological fieldwork had on him throughout his scholarly life. Importantly, Hocart's ideas on caste and hierarchy were carried further by Louis Dumont, who acknowledged his debt to Hocart in his volume on caste.

Hocart's now somewhat outdated theoretical points aside, his ethnographic materials were of the highest quality. This is particularly evident in the ethnographic materials stemming from his fieldwork with Rivers in the Solomon Islands and his own subsequent work in Fiji, resulting in a series of scholarly articles from 1922 onward. The material from Simbo (in the Solomon Islands) had originally been planned to be brought out as a monograph based on joint fieldwork, which would have been the very first of its kind from Melanesia, but apparently Rivers was unable to do his part. Hocart admits in the foreword to his article "The Cult of the Dead" that his intention was to rescue the ethnographic material by publishing it as a series of descriptive articles in the *Journal of the Royal Anthropological Institute of Great Britain and Ireland*. The fieldwork he carried out jointly with Rivers predated Bronisław Malinowski's iconic fieldwork in the Trobriand Islands of New Guinea by 6 years and was of very high quality. Hocart's published articles, unpublished field notes, and other texts kept in archives continue to be a valuable source of materials for contemporary scholars of Oceania. His attention to both history and social institutions was undoubtedly the result of his wide education in several academic disciplines and of his training under a formidable scholar such as Rivers, but it also undoubtedly was founded in Hocart's own academic curiosity and intellectual keenness. Thus, A. M. Hocart remains one of the true pioneers in the anthropology of Oceania, which is remarkable given his very diverse training and background.

Cato Berg

See also Dumont, Louis; Needham, Rodney; Rivers, W. H. R.

Further Readings

Hocart, A. M. (1922). The cult of the dead in Eddystone of the Solomons: Part I. *Journal of the Royal Anthropological Institute of Great Britain and Ireland, 52,* 71–112.

———. (1922). The cult of the dead in Eddystone of the Solomons: Part II. *Journal of the Royal Anthropological Institute of Great Britain and Ireland, 52,* 259–305.

———. (1925). Medicine and witchcraft in Eddystone of the Solomons. *Journal of the Royal Anthropological Institute of Great Britain and Ireland, 55,* 229–270.

———. (1929). *Lau Islands, Fiji* (Bulletin 62). Hololulu, HI: Bernice P. Bishop Museum.

———. (1931). Warfare in Eddystone of the Solomon Islands. *Journal of the Royal Anthropological Institute of Great Britain and Ireland, 61,* 301–324.

———. (1936). *Kings and councillors. An essay in comparative anatomy of human society.* Cairo, Egypt: Printing Office Paul Barbey. (Republished 1970, with an introduction by R. Needham (Ed.) and a foreword by E. E. Evans-Pritchard, Chicago, IL: University of Chicago Press)

———. (1954). *Social origins.* London, UK: Watts.

———. (1969). *Kingship.* Oxford, UK: Oxford University Press.

HUMAN BEHAVIORAL ECOLOGY

Behavioral ecology is the application of evolutionary biological theory to the study of animal behavior. Human behavioral ecology is the part of behavioral ecology that studies human behavior. Most human behavioral ecologists are anthropologists. Human behavioral ecology has made important contributions to theories in social and cultural anthropology. This article describes the development of the approach, how it compares and contrasts with related approaches, its core concepts, its methods, its topical foci, and its institutional manifestations.

The development of human behavioral ecology was fostered by a series of theoretical advances in the 1960s and the 1970s, most notably William D. Hamilton's development of inclusive fitness theory, John Maynard Smith and George Williams's critiques of group selection, Robert MacArthur and Eric Pianka's use of optimization models in the study of animal behavior, and Richard Alexander's pioneering applications of evolutionary biological theory to the ethnographic record.

Human behavioral ecology is also related to the ecological tradition in anthropology. However, because evolutionary theory predicts that group-level selection will usually be weak, human behavioral ecology differs from earlier types of ecological anthropology in focusing on how behavior is shaped by selection at the levels of the gene and individual rather than the group. Human behavioral ecology also differs from the 19th-century approaches to cultural and societal evolution. While the 19th-century evolutionists relied on pre-Darwinian notions such as developmentalism and predetermination, human behavioral ecology is grounded in Darwinian principles such as variation, differential reproduction, selection, and adaptation.

Recognizing that humans are biologically similar and that human behavior is extraordinarily plastic, human behavioral ecologists base their explanations of human behavioral and cultural diversity on the ways in which our shared, evolved nature interacts with different physical, social, and cultural environments to produce our widely varying behavioral phenotypes. Because we usually know little about how specific genes influence specific behaviors and because in the long run selection is expected to favor high-quality phenotypes regardless of the genes responsible for them, human behavioral ecologists focus on phenotypes. This is known as the "phenotypic gambit."

Explanations of behavior and other biological phenomena vary in terms of the causal distance of interest to the researcher. Functional biologists, for example, produce "proximate" explanations that focus on mechanistic, causally immediate factors. Human behavioral ecologists focus on explanations in terms of adaptations designed through the Darwinian process of variation and differential reproduction. Such explanations are usually referred to as "ultimate" or, for a better contrast with proximate, "distal." Explanations at different levels complement rather than compete with one another.

Because evolution is driven by differential reproduction, human behavioral ecologists often focus on behaviors that have clear impacts on reproductive rates. Because most theories used by human behavioral ecologists were developed to explain the behavior of nonhumans, they have also tended to focus on behaviors that humans and nonhumans have in common, such as foraging, mating, parenting, and cooperation. Human behavioral ecologists collect most of their data through fieldwork, often among people living in subsistence economies. In addition to interviews, surveys, and participant observation, human behavioral ecologists make quantitative observations of behavior and perform experiments, and they occasionally make use of historical demographic and archaeological data.

A hallmark of the early human behavioral ecology of the 1970s and the 1980s was the application of optimal foraging theory to data from hunting-and-gathering societies. Optimal foraging models have been used to examine aspects of foraging such as diet breadth and patch choice. Human behavioral ecology's use of optimization models makes it unusual in cultural anthropology to embrace rather than eschew rational choice models of human behavior. Human behavioral ecologists see such models as useful not because they believe human behavior to be fully rational or optimal but rather because they make predictions about behavior that are clear and falsifiable. In addition to foraging, human behavioral ecologists have focused a great deal of attention on reproductive and social behaviors, shedding light on issues such as mate preferences, systems of mating and marriage (e.g., monogamy, polygyny, and polyandry), the sexual division of labor, sex biases in parental behavior, male parental behavior, enculturation, inheritance patterns, altruism among both kin and nonkin, coalitional behavior, conflict, food sharing, reciprocity, and risk pooling.

The culture concept played little role in early human behavioral ecology, but this has changed considerably over the past 20 years or so. This is primarily due to three factors: (1) culture's incorporation into animal behavior studies, (2) the development of cultural transmission theory, and (3) the use of animal signaling theory to study cultural phenomena. Human behavioral ecologists have also made important contributions to the study of the demographic transition, wildlife conservation, human life history theory, and the study of religion.

Human behavioral ecology is often seen as one of three main approaches to the evolutionary study of human behavior, the others being evolutionary psychology, and cultural transmission or dual inheritance theory. The division of labor among these three approaches is similar to that found in the behavioral sciences more generally. Evolutionary psychologists and cultural transmission theorists focus on causal forces that are internal and external to the individual, respectively. Human behavioral ecologists, in contrast, use simple models to bring both kinds of causal factors to bear on questions regarding human behavior, adding complexity to those models as needed to increase their explanatory power. Human behavioral ecology also has close ties to related areas in biological anthropology, such as reproductive ecology and nutritional ecology.

Organizations supporting human behavioral ecology include the Human Behavior and Evolution Society, the Evolutionary Anthropology Society (a section of the American Anthropological Association), and the International Society for Human Ethology. In addition to general science, anthropology, and animal behavior journals, human behavioral ecologists routinely publish their findings in specialized journals such as *Evolution and Human Behavior* and *Human Nature*.

Lee Cronk

See also Cultural Ecology; Evolutionary Anthropology; Evolutionary Psychology; Game Theory; Gene-Culture Coevolution; Human Universals

Further Readings

Dunbar, R., & Barrett, L. (2007). *The Oxford handbook of evolutionary psychology.* Oxford, UK: Oxford University Press.

Gangestad, S. W., & Simpson, J. A. (Eds.). (2007). *The evolution of mind: Fundamental questions and controversies.* New York, NY: Guilford Press.

Laland, K. N., & Brown, G. R. (2011). *Sense and nonsense: Evolutionary perspectives on human behaviour* (2nd ed.). Oxford, UK: Oxford University Press.

HUMAN RELATIONS AREA FILES, CROSS-CULTURAL STUDIES

The Human Relations Area Files, Inc. (HRAF, pronounced *her-aff* or sometimes *H-raff*) is a non-profit membership corporation located at Yale University. Its mission is to facilitate the cross-cultural study of human culture, society, and behavior in the past and present. The unique feature of its two main databases, eHRAF World Cultures and eHRAF Archaeology, is that full-text materials (primarily ethnographies and archaeological reports) are subject indexed by anthropologists at the paragraph level to facilitate research across cultures and archaeological traditions.

Background and History

The HRAF was incorporated in 1949 as an inter-university consortium designed to foster cross-cultural studies. The name was derived from Yale University's Institute of Human Relations, which housed the Cross-Cultural Survey, a precursor to HRAF. A group of social scientists at Yale created the Cross-Cultural Survey in 1937 to systematically catalog cross-cultural variation. Influenced by the cultural evolutionary theories of Herbert Spencer, Yale's first sociologist, William Graham Sumner, began collecting information on a wide variety of societies and organizing that information to allow for the systematic exploration of cultural evolutionary patterns. Sumner's student, Alfred Galloway Keller, and Keller's student, George Peter Murdock,

expanded on Sumner's initial efforts in developing the Cross-Cultural Survey. The underlying idea of the Cross-Cultural Survey was that any generalizable explanation for human behavior should hold true across a variety of cultures and that the Cross-Cultural Survey would provide the data for testing such explanations. The HRAF collection of ethnography (often referred to as "the HRAF files") was an extension of that basic idea—providing a large, easily searchable source of cultural information for cross-cultural studies.

The initial members of the HRAF consortium were Harvard University, the University of Oklahoma, the University of Pennsylvania, the University of Washington, and Yale University, joined shortly thereafter by the University of Chicago, the University of North Carolina, and the University of Southern California. Each member institution received an annual installment consisting of several thousand 5- by 8-inch pages of text copied from primary ethnographic sources. The text on each page was subject indexed in the margin for the information it contained, using an indexing system developed by the anthropologist George Peter Murdock and his colleagues, called the *Outline of Cultural Materials* (first published in 1938). The text pages were grouped by the indexed items, so that a page containing information on five different indexed topics would be found five times in the annual installment—once in each of the indexed groupings for the information the text contained. A researcher at one of the member institutions could then go to the HRAF collection and pull out information on an indexed topic from many ethnographic sources without having to consult each source individually. This greatly simplified the process of cross-cultural research.

In 1958, HRAF began to produce the annual installments on microfiche as well as paper. Member institutions continued to receive paper installments (although paper installments stopped being produced in the mid-1980s), but any institution could gain access to the microfiche by becoming an "associate" member of the HRAF consortium. Soon many libraries were able to provide access to HRAF. Opening access to HRAF was intended to expand cross-cultural studies, and it appears to have worked: In 1958, there were fewer than 100 published cross-cultural studies; in 1997, when HRAF switched to a completely online format, there were more than 1000 published studies based on the HRAF collection. In 1994, HRAF began offering the annual installment on CD-ROM, and in 1997, the collection was converted to online access. At the time of this writing (2011), there were roughly 400 members of the HRAF consortium located in 25 countries.

Research Collections

Since 1999, HRAF has produced two collections of indexed primary-source documents. The Collection of Ethnography is a continuation of the original HRAF collection begun in 1949. As of this writing, the Collection of Ethnography contains more than 1.3 million pages of information on more than 400 cultures (although not all have yet been converted to electronic format) and indexed by more than 700 categories. The new online version of HRAF (eHRAF World Cultures), with 260 cultures as of this date, allows searching by keyword in addition to the indexed categories. The online version of HRAF also maintains each page of text in its original context, so that a researcher can read forward and backward from the page that contains the information of interest to those preceding and following it. This allows the information to be understood within the broader context of the document—something not possible with the old paper or microfiche files.

In 1999, HRAF launched the eHRAF Collection of Archaeology (now called eHRAF Archaeology) to provide indexed primary-source documents on archaeological sites and traditions. As of this writing, the eHRAF Archaeology contains more than 125,000 pages of indexed primary-source documents on 85 archaeological traditions. The purpose of the eHRAF Archaeology is to allow for the diachronic testing of explanations. In typical cross-cultural research, explanations that hold true for a large number of cultures are thought to probably reflect true causal relationships. But testing causal relationships across cultures does not allow one to test whether presumed causes or causal conditions actually preceded the presumed effects. The information in the eHRAF Archaeology allows researchers to directly test causal relationships.

It is a common misunderstanding that the HRAF collections provide precoded, numerical data on ethnographic cultures or archaeological traditions; they do not. What both provide are primary-source documents that have been carefully indexed at the paragraph level to allow for rapid retrieval of information. While indexers have made decisions about the content of each page in each document, the researchers decide what that content means within the context of their research and how to code it for use in cross-cultural studies. With the advent of online collections, researchers also have the option of retrieving information by keyword rather than indexed content.

Publications

In addition to the collections of indexed primary-source documents, HRAF has also published a wide range of monographs, data sets, bibliographies, and encyclopedias. Between the mid-1960s and mid-1970s, HRAF Press published several hundred scholarly monographs, in addition to more general works for government and business that provided readily accessible information on foreign cultures. HRAF also published bibliographies of ethnographic works into the 1990s, with its massive *Bibliography of Native North America* being perhaps the most well-known. During the 1980s and 1990s, HRAF Press also published collected works of cross-cultural findings and a series of data sets on time allocation and cultural variation. In recent years, HRAF has focused its publishing efforts on encyclopedias, compiling encyclopedias on world cultures, national cultures, immigrant cultures, urban cultures, and prehistoric cultures, as well as encyclopedias of sex and gender, cultural anthropology, medical anthropology, and diasporas. HRAF has also sponsored the journal *Cross-Cultural Research* (formerly *Behavior Science Notes* until 1974 and *Behavior Science Research* until 1993) since 1966. The journal has been a key publication outlet for cross-cultural studies since its inception.

Influence

Cross-cultural studies have been controversial in anthropology from the very beginning of the discipline. Many anthropologists feel that cross-cultural studies are flawed because they take information out of the broader context of the culture in which it exists and, thus, end up comparing things that may not actually be alike. For example, a researcher interested in adolescent sexual behavior might not be able to take into account the subtleties with which individual cultures deal with sexuality. Cross-cultural researchers counter that while they may not be able to explain the unique features of individual cultures, they can explain dimensions of cross-cultural variation in such behaviors. Some researchers argue that ethnographic information is so subjective that comparing materials derived from work by different ethnographers, even on the same culture, is futile, as each ethnographer's description is purely idiosyncratic. Cross-cultural researchers counter that if this were the case, no patterns of behavior could ever be discerned, and yet they are. Finally, there are some researchers who argue that cultures are such poor units of analysis that any statistical relationships discovered through cross-cultural studies should be suspect. While there are many sampling and data quality challenges that must be addressed when conducting cross-cultural research, most cross-cultural researchers employ methods (many disseminated through HRAF publications) that minimize the risk of generating spurious results.

HRAF has had a major influence in countering the general antipathy toward cross-cultural studies found in anthropology by providing researchers with the information, methodology, and publishing outlets to counter many of the arguments made against cross-cultural research. For example, both collections contain some kind of representative sample. The Collection of Ethnography contains the Probability Samples Files (which has one well-described society from each of 60 culture areas), and the eHRAF Archaeology provides a random sample of cases drawn from a larger population to provide researchers with statistically valid samples for cross-cultural research. HRAF has published a number of methodological guides to cross-cultural research and, recently, ideas and exercises for using cross-cultural methods and findings in anthropology courses. By demonstrating the value of cross-cultural research to students and providing methodological guidance to researchers, HRAF is ensuring that cross-cultural studies will have an enduring presence in social science.

Peter N. Peregrine

See also Comparative Method; Goodenough, Ward H.; Murdock, George Peter

Further Readings

Ember, C. R. (2011). Human relations area files. In W. S. Bainbridge (Ed.), *Leadership in science and technology* (pp. 619–627). Thousand Oaks, CA: Sage.

Ember, C. R., & Ember, M. (2009). *Cross-cultural research methods*. Lanham, MD: AltaMira.

Ember, M. (1997). Evolution of the human relations area files. *Cross-cultural research, 31*, 3–15.

Levinson, D., Malone, M. J., & Brown, C. H. (1980). *Toward explaining human culture: A critical review of the findings of worldwide cross-cultural research*. New Haven, CT: HRAF Press.

Murdock, G. P., Ford, C. S., & Hudson, A. E. (2006). *Outline of cultural materials* (6th ed.). New Haven, CT: HRAF Press.

Human Universals

Human universals comprise those features of culture, society, language, behavior, and psyche that, so far as the record is clear, are found in all ethnographically or historically recorded human societies. Theoretically, as acknowledged in anthropological textbooks, human universals are half of anthropology's concerns, the others comprising the differences among humans. However, although the theoretical significance and implications of human universals are relatively straightforward, the research concerns of anthropologists have largely emphasized the differences. The reasons for this emphasis must be addressed to understand the current place of human universals in anthropological theory.

During much of the past century, a series of assumptions and conditions within anthropology limited the theoretical significance of human universals (hereafter, "universals" for short). Particularly important were assumptions about culture in relation to human nature. Twentieth-century anthropologists developed or largely agreed with a layer-cake concept of reality, in which culture was an autonomous, sui generis level of reality lying over biology, which in turn lay above the realms of chemistry and physics. Culture had its own dynamics and could not be reduced to the lower levels. This view of culture led to a considerable skepticism about the existence of universals, which were often presumed to have their roots or explanation in human nature, that is, in the lower level of biology.

In their attempt to warn against and illustrate ethnocentric fallacies and socially conservative appeals to human nature, some anthropologists published or accepted seemingly scientific refutations of what was considered natural in their own culture. Margaret

Mead, for example, famously showed that adolescent stress did not occur among Samoans and that sex roles were largely reversed among the Tchambuli (or Chambri) of Papua New Guinea. Benjamin Lee Whorf's claim that the Hopi had no concept of time analogous to those in the West was widely accepted in anthropology. In light of what such studies purported to show, some anthropologists doubted that there was any such thing as a human nature beyond what culture dictated from one society to another.

The racist thinking that reduced aspects of culture and behavior to biological inheritance, as in some forms of eugenics and in Nazism, produced among anthropologists and others a profound moral and scientific rejection or suspicion of biological reductionism in general.

Throughout much of the 20th century, but presently diminishing, there was a powerful and legitimate concern to emphasize ethnography, to capture its richness and variations before all melded into a modern, heavily Westernized world culture. In this frame of mind, a great many theoretical issues were subordinated. It was not uncommon to hear dismissals of causal or evolutionary concerns as armchair theorizing, insufficiently empirical. At present, many cultural anthropologists, at least in the West, still reflect those attitudes.

Beyond the confines of anthropology were and are yet other factors. One is that the human mind is much concerned with differences: the pitch and volume of sounds; sizes, colors, shapes, and movements; hardness, softness, roughness, and smoothness; sweet, refreshing, and foul smells; young and old; male and female; and so forth. Accordingly, in the very earliest ethnographic descriptions—by the Chinese, Greeks, Romans, and Arabs—differences are explicit; the vast range of similarities among humans is largely taken for granted.

Another factor, to loosely paraphrase a Confucian scholar, is that some individuals notice change and think that nothing is constant; others note constants and think that nothing ever changes. Western thought near its foundations polarized similarly around the Heraclitan notion of all being in flux and the Platonic notion of eternal forms. Variants of these polarities, weighting toward the particularistic Heraclitan, are strong in anthropology to the present.

The cumulative effect of these factors was a minor and sporadic explicit interest in universals in general,

even doubts that they could be of substantial interest. In the 1960s, the anthropologist Clifford Geertz summed up much of this view, while acknowledging the reasonable assumption that if universals do exist they might well have biopsychological foundations.

The extent, detail, and clarity revealed by recent decades of research into those biopsychological foundations figure largely now in a much expanded interest in universals. Whatever credibility the layer-cake view of reality ever had in biology, chemistry, and physics has vanished. Interdisciplinary studies of all sorts are now taken for granted. Stunningly successful drug therapies, among other considerations, made psychology as reductionist as the other sciences. At the same time, the ever-increasing sophistication of experimental psychology elucidated human (and animal) nature and offered new means of testing hypotheses about the human nature that may underlie universals of behavior and psyche.

Darwinian thinking—as in sociobiology and evolutionary psychology—coupled with breakthroughs and inventions that allowed the burgeoning study of DNA, the study of molecular structures and the detailed functions of the endocrine system, the discovery of highly specific mental modularity, the imaging of brain activity, and the discovery of numerous close analogs of human behaviors in other species all opened routes for tracing connections between our biology and our behavior—cultural or otherwise. Game theory and computer modeling provided further means of understanding human behavior.

At the same time, restudies that refuted the aforementioned works by Whorf and Mead were published, with implications that were widely noted. The dwindling number of "pristine" or "traditional" societies to study before they disappeared allowed a thorough reprioritization of aims and funding in ethnology. Thus, under present conditions, the anthropological rationale for the study of universals is much clearer.

The grand theory of universals is that in combination they constitute the building blocks or armature of the human condition; subsets of them are equally the building blocks and armature of human nature. As such, universals are both constraining and generative. On his website, the anthropologist Doug Jones formulates the goal of research on the generative aspect of universals as "understanding how a limited stock of innate ideas can be recombined and customized to generate the kaleidoscopic variety of human cultures." In a personal communication, he gives as an example the semanticist Anna Wierzbicka, whose work he summarizes as follows:

> She's a linguist who thinks there is a stock of about 50–60 innate abstract ideas lexicalized in pretty much every language (BECAUSE, THING/SOMETHING, PERSON/SOMEONE, DO, THINK, KIND, etc., etc.) that can be combined to generate culture-specific concepts, which an empiricist stuck with perceptual categories (SQUARE, RED, HIGH-PITCHED, etc.) would have a hard time doing.

For Jones, Wierzbicka has shown that a small number of innate abstract ideas are generative of a universe of different cultural forms.

Turning the grand theory into working propositions requires clarifying and extending the very idea of universals, identifying and classifying them, describing each universal with precision, finding ways around the methodological limitations on verifying universality, and then explaining the universals.

In addition to the hundreds of "absolute" universals, there are also some variant forms. One variant is the "near" universal, such as possession of the domestic dog. Linguists, who pioneered much of the conceptual framework for universals, add another important variant, the "conditional" (or "implicational") universal, which can be described as an if-then universal: If a certain condition A obtains, then the conditional universal B will obtain. For example, if one hand is culturally given a positive evaluation, then it will be the right hand, as in the Western practice of using the right hand to greet or take an oath. In cases such as these, neither A nor B is universal, but some universal underlying situation or mechanism(s) must be at work. In this case, it is the universal preponderance of physical right-handedness.

A "statistical" universal may fall far short of near universality and yet occur in unrelated societies with a frequency well above chance, which raises the question of whether mere chance cultural convergences are at play. Thus, in a surprising number of languages, a term indicating a little person designates the pupil of the eye. The reasonably proposed explanation for this is that people everywhere looking into another person's eye see a small person there—the reflection of themselves. In this case, a universal or near-universal experience is the apparent explanation.

Near, conditional, and statistical universals are among the formal variants of universality. For various purposes, others may be added. It may be useful, for example, to refer to something like "new universals," such as the use of metal or plastic objects, which are surely very nearly if not entirely universal among extant peoples.

As indicated earlier, universals may also be classified according to whether they are cultural, societal, linguistic, behavioral, psychological, and so on. The phenomenal realm within which they occur has an important bearing on how each is to be explained—what its ultimate origin is and how it is reliably reproduced in the individual or society.

Some cultural universals—such as the use of fire and the specific use of fire for cooking—presumably spread to all peoples in the distant past because of their great utility. The same is presumably true of near universals such as the domestic dog. Most universals are almost certainly not cultural. As was long assumed, many universals are components of human nature or very closely reflect human nature. These universals raise questions such as the following: When did they emerge in our evolutionary past—in the evolution of our species or farther back in the hominid line or even more distantly? What functions were they designed to serve? What is their ontogeny in the individual? Are they sex or age linked? Are they maladaptive in some circumstances? What roles do they play in human affairs?

Every claim of universality is just that: a claim. It could not be otherwise, since we do not have accurate reporting on all relevant topics for a great many societies that have been known to history and ethnography. Whole ranges of societies have disappeared or have become very few—preliterate hunter-gathering societies, for example. Even where their remnants exist, they are nearly always sufficiently contacted by the larger world to raise questions about whether they truly represent their noncontacted forms. This has placed a premium on developing methods that to one degree or another give greater confidence to claims of universality. Studying the few preliterate societies very minimally affected by the outside world has been especially important. Finding analogs in other species, particularly in the hominid line, has also been useful in identifying universals of mind and behavior—even of culture, which for decades was mistakenly considered to be virtually exclusively human.

Whether discovering universals, seeking to explain them, or tracing their ramified consequences in human affairs, the anthropological four-field approach—the combination of cultural and physical anthropology with linguistics and archaeology—is almost mandatory. Moreover, the study of universals must often extend beyond the four fields as conventionally defined. On the other hand, the idea of universals and the consideration of particular ones can be and are exploited outside anthropology. There is, for example, considerable activity in literary studies, focused on universal themes and structures in both folktales and the classics of literature.

Given the present assumptions and conditions impinging on and shaping anthropological theory, the study of human universals is assuming a larger role than was possible during much of the last century. That role extends well beyond anthropology yet remains centrally dependent on anthropologists' ethnographic reporting.

Donald E. Brown

See also Cultural Relativism; Evolutionary Anthropology; Evolutionary Psychology; Gene-Culture Coevolution; Greenberg, Joseph; Whorf, Benjamin Lee

Further Readings

Antweiler, C. (2007). *Was ist den Menschen gemeinsam? Über Kultur und Kulturen* [What is human universality? About culture and cultures]. Darmstadt, Germany: Wissenschaftliche Buchgesellschaft.

Brown, D. E. (1991). *Human universals*. New York, NY: McGraw-Hill.

———. (2000). Human universals and their implications. In N. Roughley (Ed.), *Being humans: Anthropological universality and particularity in transdisciplinary perspectives* (pp. 156–174). Berlin, Germany: Walter de Gruyter.

———. (2004). Human universals, human nature and human culture. *Daedalus, Fall*, 47–54.

Jones, D. (1999). Evolutionary psychology. *Annual Review of Anthropology, 28*, 553–575.

Wierzbicka, A. (2005). Empirical universals of language as a basis for the study of other human universals and as a tool for exploring cross-cultural differences. *Ethos, 23*(2), 256–291.

HUMANISTIC ANTHROPOLOGY

Humanistic anthropology is an approach that focuses on values and meanings, their construction and deployment, in a holistic vision of humanity that encompasses the physical and cultural dimensions of human societies along with the environments in which these societies exist. Humanistic anthropology includes a range of practices and interests. It may engage the creative and philosophical traditions of the humanities as both subject of study and method of expression, and thus it participates in creative, poetic, and dramatic writing and other artistic expression, in addition to the production of more traditionally academic ethnographic writing. Humanistic anthropology recognizes the dynamic, relational, and processual nature of our world, and thus the consequences of our work in the world at large. It hopes to bring about improvements in the world and in people's lives, through better understanding of the diverse, increasingly multicultural, semantically polyvalent, and socially constructed nature of reality.

Many of the concerns of humanistic anthropology trace back to the development of humanistic philosophy, long before anthropology came to exist as a discipline. Jean-Jacques Rousseau's *Discourse on the Origin and Foundation of Inequality* (1755) is often taken as a foundational work because it argues the importance of studying human diversity to better understand ourselves. A humanist focus was found in much of the earliest anthropological work, from Thomas Jefferson's excavations and other questions surrounding the "Moundbuilders" of North American prehistory through Lewis Henry Morgan and Edward Burnett Tylor's efforts to understand the diversity of human practices and values, and even Émile Durkheim's investigations of religion. While these precedents are most often cited for their contributions to making the study of humanity scientific, that science was founded on humanistic concerns.

In the 1960s, as scientific rhetoric and methods were prioritized in anthropology as in other social sciences, a sense arose among some that this balance between science and the humanities was being lost—specifically, that particular constructions of science were displacing the human dimensions in the social sciences. Many of the most dominant theoretical frameworks developed through the later 19th and 20th centuries—evolutionary models, functionalism, and structuralism—sought to develop understandings that their proponents believed were more rigorous and scientific, more testable, defensible, and rational than humanistic understandings developed through evocative description. Humanistic scholarship did not disappear, but it is no coincidence that psychology, sociology, and anthropology all institutionalized societies for humanistic approaches in the early 1970s. The scholars who organized these societies were openly insistent: They were not against science but against a scientization of the study of human societies that left no room for humanism in its constructs.

The Society for Humanistic Anthropology was established in 1974 as a section of the American Anthropological Association, with *Anthropology and Humanism Quarterly* (now *Anthropology and Humanism*) begun as its journal in 1976. In addition to publishing work in humanistic anthropology, the Society for Humanistic Anthropology provides venues at the annual meeting for presenting and participating in workshops on creative and ethnographic writing and other modes of expression. The society also presents annual awards for ethnographic fiction and poetry, along with the Victor Turner Prize for Ethnographic Writing, one of the discipline's premier awards; Turner was a founder of the Society for Humanistic Anthropology, and he and his work are seen by many as one of the models for doing humanistic anthropology.

Although interest in humanistic anthropology is global, as a formal subdiscipline, it has been largely an American development. Franz Boas himself, and several of his students, exemplified an approach that insisted on keeping humanistic concerns at the forefront of the developing science of humanity. Before Boas, Frank Hamilton Cushing's experiential approach to understanding American Indians is noteworthy (as is the too easy dismissal he still sometimes receives in the discipline). Humanistic interests can be seen in the work of mainstream Boasian anthropologists, like Margaret Mead and Clyde Kluckhohn, and in more idiosyncratic Boasians like

Jaime de Angulo and Paul Radin. One area in which many anthropologists expressed their humanist side, even before "humanistic anthropology" became formalized, was in taking on "modern" or "Western" life, in works including Boas's *Anthropology and Modern Life* (1928), Robert Lowie's *Are We Civilized?* (1929), Kluckhohn's *Mirror for Man* (1949), and Jules Henry's *Culture Against Man* (1963)—works that sought to construct understandings through interpretive and comparative readings of modernity and to write clearly and accessibly for a general audience. Margaret Mead built such a strong reputation through her newspaper, magazine, and television contributions that she remains for many the most visible face of anthropology, even decades after her death. These sorts of works, encouraging not just scholars but the general public to think anthropologically about everyday life and the changing world, exemplify humanistic concerns even among those pursuing a scientific anthropology. The Americanist focus on "culture"—behavior, beliefs, and values shared and learned by individuals within societies—and its "four-fields" approach articulated particularly well with humanistic concerns, but humanist strands can be found in other world traditions as well. R. R. Marrett's moral philosophy was influential for E. E. Evans-Pritchard, for example, and Claude Lévi-Strauss's interest in art—and his personal engagement with artists—can be seen particularly in his later works and also in concepts such as bricolage.

Prompted by civil rights movements, global decolonization efforts, the Vietnam War, and other aspects of the dynamic social milieu of the mid-20th century, the late 1960s and early 1970s saw dramatic conflicts within anthropology over its place in the world. The development of an institutionalized humanistic anthropology was only one response to the many calls for reinventing the discipline. Even when not overtly connected, though, other disciplinary responses often had humanistic dimensions, and they can be seen in the developing humanistic anthropology. The "interpretive turn" credited to Clifford Geertz, for example, and Marshall Sahlins's rethinking of the "original affluent society" were not framed as humanistic approaches but nevertheless have that dimension, and they were influential for those who were thinking in terms of a humanistic anthropology. Victor Turner's work on ritual and performance and his influence in developing a symbolic anthropology are more closely associated, but the linguistic turn of the mid-1960s toward an ethnography of communication is also part of the development of humanistic anthropology.

The 1980s and 1990s saw shifting emphases in the broader discipline that in some cases articulated with humanistic anthropology's concerns, and these largely continue to the present. The so-called reflexive turn, for example, that called for anthropologists to explicitly consider positioning as shaping the anthropological project and the focus on the process of writing and constructing narratives highlighted questions that had long interested humanists. Fieldwork sites beyond traditional kinds of locations, including studies of humanistic domains like art and performance, media and music, and contemporary sites of interaction like tourism, became increasingly acceptable. Ethnographic poetry and fiction are regularly featured in *Anthropology and Humanism*, along with articles discussing the genres as anthropological domains. Life histories and memoirs, long a staple of humanistic scholarship, have become more common; and the production of dramatic works, and even art and music events have become acceptable enough to be included in venues like the annual meeting of the American Anthropological Association and in some cases are even included in tenure and promotion dossiers.

This is not to suggest that humanistic anthropology has become the mainstream; many of these sorts of projects are still considered beyond the pale by many scholars. Humanistic anthropologists continue to seek an expansive, holistic vision of humanity, trying to push the boundaries of what can be considered proper and professional anthropology, willing to experiment and play with forms but not always taken seriously in their attempt to better represent human realities.

Frederic W. Gleach

See also Boas, Franz; Kluckhohn, Clyde; Lévi-Strauss, Claude; Mead, Margaret; Radin, Paul; Rousseau, Jean-Jacques; Turner, Victor W.

Further Readings

Glass, J. F., & Staude, J. R. (Eds.). (1972). *Humanistic society: Today's challenge to sociology*. Pacific Palisades, CA: Goodyear.

Grinker, R. R. (2007). *Unstrange minds: Remapping the world of autism*. New York, NY: Basic Books.

Jackson, M. (1986). *Barawa and the ways birds fly in the sky: An ethnographic novel*. Washington, DC: Smithsonian Institution Press.

Narayan, K. (2007). *My family and other saints*. Chicago, IL: University of Chicago Press.

Richardson, M. (1975). Anthropologist: The myth teller. *American Ethnologist, 2*(3), 517–533.

Society for Humanistic Anthropology. (1994). The place of humanism in anthropology today [Special issue]. *Anthropology and humanism, 19*(1).

Vargas-Cetina, G. (Ed.). (2013). *Anthropology and the politics of representation*. Tuscaloosa: University of Alabama Press.

Wilk, S. (1991). *Humanistic anthropology*. Knoxville: University of Tennessee Press.

HURSTON, ZORA NEALE

Zora Neale Hurston (1891–1960) is well known as an African American author who was part of the Harlem Renaissance. Her skills as a writer were fashioned at Howard University and then honed through her study of the theories of anthropology at Barnard College and Columbia University. Hurston's books and articles, once all but forgotten, were rediscovered and celebrated by the writer Alice Walker, who wrote an essay about her in *Ms.* magazine in 1975.

Hurston's contributions to anthropology have received comparatively less attention due to the force and impact of her novels, but she has an important place within several theoretical perspectives. Her theoretical perspectives reflect the times of her life, but these contributions remain central to the social sciences today. Hurston focused on language as the bridge between individual creativity and initiative and structural and historical patterns. Her descriptions of one of the surviving towns incorporated by African Americans freed from slavery add to our understanding of race and class in small-town America. Finally, her keen awareness of the African Diaspora in the circum-Caribbean contributed not only to area studies but to Caribbean and Creole studies as well.

Hurston was the first African American woman to be admitted to Barnard College, and like her contemporaries, she was intrigued by the new discipline of anthropology. She took classes at Columbia University, taught by the physicist-turned-anthropologist Franz Boas. There, Hurston found other writers in her classes, including Ruth Benedict, who likewise combined a passion for literature with an equal passion for anthropology. Boas's radical view that race, language, and culture were independent from one another led Hurston to an interest in the anthropology of language in rural Florida, and his focus on immigration no doubt complemented her interest in the migrations and movements of African Americans throughout Florida and the Caribbean. Huston began her PhD work at Columbia in 1935, but she had been studying anthropology since 1925. The strong fieldwork ethic of the Colombia program led her to preliminary fieldwork in Harlem and then to substantial studies in her hometown, Eatonville, Florida, as well as in Haiti, Jamaica, and New Orleans. Like other students of Boas, such as Margaret Mead, Hurston took pride in questioning assumptions that human nature was the same everywhere, that societies could be compared on some sort of evolutionary scale, and that people of the African Diaspora were without history or culture.

Eatonville, Florida, where Hurston grew up, is a town now almost completely engulfed by the city of Orlando. It was one of a dozen towns incorporated by African Americans after emancipation and remains today as the only survivor of this historic initiative. As such, Eatonville was and is a place where African American residents have confidence, political experience, and great initiative. Community ethnography of the small towns of the United States was a new theoretical direction, which took hold in the 1930s and 1940s. Doing anthropology of small-town America became popular. Among those studies was Robert and Helen Lynd's Marxist-inspired study of social class formation in a small Midwestern town undergoing industrialization, referred to as "Middletown." Racial segregation and a caste social structure were documented in the famous book, "Deep South." These critical community studies made a refreshing theoretical context for Hurston as she began her U.S.-based research. She described and analyzed Eatonville as having an African American Diaspora culture as it flourished without the constant oppression of White society. Hurston's *Mules and Men* (1935) focuses on the language, public performance, and folklore of Eatonville. As such, it is a dramatic break from

the socio-structural approaches of other community studies. Boas recognized Hurston's skills in understanding expressive culture, and he wrote a glowing introduction to the book.

Hurston's transcription of African American English is inconsistent from one page of her work to the next, and today it seems archaic and even comical. Although Hurston had undergone linguistic training in her graduate career, she chose a "free" rather than phonetic transcription of the language of Eatonville. In 1939, she became part of the Federal Writers Project alongside Alan Lomax Jr., Stetson Kennedy, and others who adopted recording equipment to accurately document talk, stories, and songs throughout Florida. Hurston was a leader in adopting recording equipment, and used motion pictures in her methodological repertoire as early as the 1920s. Her films showed children playing, men working, a woman walking out of her home, baptisms, and life in a turpentine camp in Polk County, Florida. That footage shows the tension between her aesthetic and academic interests, a tension that continues in the field of visual anthropology today.

Hurston also did one of the first anthropological studies of farmworkers. Her book *Their Eyes Were Watching God* (1937) is in part a portrayal of African American migrant workers at the time the citrus industry was beginning to flourish in south-central Florida. It is also a book about sexuality, abuse, and the deep poverty in the African American communities of Florida during the Great Depression. Her focus on gender and sexuality in this and other works is reflected today in feminist anthropology.

Hurston advanced anthropological theory as well through linking the African Diaspora communities in the Caribbean and in the Gulf states of Florida, Alabama, Mississippi, and Louisiana. Hurston was an anthropologist of transnational cultures, and her work included multisited ethnographies in Florida, the Bahamas, Haiti, Jamaica, and New Orleans. While Florida was and is often thought of as the southern United States, Hurston saw it as the northern Caribbean. Migration to and from the Caribbean islands and across the Gulf Coast of the United States was common in Hurston's time. Her work shows that she was the first anthropologist to see Florida not just in the context of the United States but in a Caribbean context. Hurston focused on expressive culture—religion, trance, and small-group events as well—in her Caribbean ethnographies. Her contemporary and fellow Columbia University classmate Melville Herskovits focused on African vestiges and customs that still were practiced in Haiti and the Caribbean, a concern that still influences a segment of Caribbean studies. Hurston's remarkable contribution was to describe and celebrate the Caribbean's expressive and linguistic culture in the United States, and in that way she foresaw what later became known as a Creole culture approach in Caribbean anthropology. Representative of this theme is the article "Hoodoo in America" (1931) and the book *Go Tell My Horse* (1938).

Zora Neale Hurston continued to lead a dual career as an anthropologist and a writer, but her success in that field overshadowed the contributions she made to anthropological theory. She never sought a position in an anthropology program, and like Dorothy Lee, Edward Hall, and Benjamin Lee Whorf, she worked outside the academic world, using her writing skills to bring the insights of anthropology to a public, nonacademic audience. Hurston's literary and professional career slowed down during the 1950s. She wrote essays in favor of segregation at the time when the Supreme Court ruled against it in *Brown vs. Topeka Board of Education*. She fell into controversy over an unsupported claim that she had engaged in child abuse, which limited her ability to win writing contracts, and the royalties from her books were few and far between. She became a domestic worker in Tampa and died there in 1960 after experiencing a stroke.

Allan Burns

See also Autoethnography; Benedict, Ruth F.; Boas, Franz; Columbia University; Du Bois, W. E. B.; Feminist Anthropology

Further Readings

Boyd, V. (2003). Zora Neale Hurston: The Howard University years. *Journal of Blacks in Higher Education, 39*, 104–108.

Charnov, E. (1998). The performative visual anthropology films of Zora Neale Hurston. *Film Criticism, 23*, 1–10.

Hemenway, R. (1977). *Zora Neale Hurston: A literary biography.* Champaign-Urbana: University of Illinois Press.

Hurston, Z. N. (1931). Hoodoo in America. *Journal of American Folklore, 44*(174), 317–417.

————. (1935). *Mules and men.* Philadelphia, PA: J.B. Lippincott.

————. (1938). *Go tell my horse.* Philadephia, PA: J.B. Lippincott.

————. (1942). *Dust tracks on a road.* Champaign-Urbana: University of Illinois Press.

Walker, A. (1975, March). In search of Zora Neale Hurston. *Ms. Magazine*, pp. 74–79, 84–89.

HUSSERL, EDMUND

Edmund Husserl (1859–1938) was an influential German philosopher and the principal founder of transcendental phenomenology

Biography

Husserl was born in Prossnitz, Moravia, in 1859, into an assimilated Jewish family, which gave him a liberal view of religion (in 1886, he was baptized as a Lutheran and remained religious but nonconfessional for the rest of his life). Husserl did not excel in high school but eventually developed an interest in astronomy, which he pursued at the University of Leipzig, and mathematics, which he studied in Berlin and then in Vienna, where in 1882 he received a PhD with a dissertation on the calculus of variation. Husserl found particular inspiration in the teachings of two remarkable scholars: the mathematician Karl Weierstrass (1815–1897) at the University of Berlin and the philosopher Franz Brentano (1838–1917) at the University of Vienna. Husserl's writings have been said to combine Weierstrass's rigorous scientific thinking and Brentano's insights into human psychology. Husserl borrowed Brentano's use of the Scholastic notion of "intention" as the property of human mental activity to be about or directed toward something, whether or not that something exists. Over time, an increasingly complex notion of intentionality became for Husserl the foundation of his transcendental phenomenology.

Following Brentano's suggestion, in 1886, Husserl went to Halle to study with Carl Stumpf (1848–1936), a mathematician and philosopher who had become interested in the perception of space and sound. His *Habilitation* thesis *Über den Begriff der Zahl* ("On the Concept of Number"), written under Stumpf's supervision, became the basis for Husserl's first book, *Philosophie der Arithmetik* (Philosophy of Arithmetic), published in 1891. In 1887, Husserl married Malvine Steinschneider, who was also from a Prossnitz Jewish family with a similar background (before the wedding, Malvine decided to follow Husserl's example and be baptized). Their three children—Elizabeth (known as "Elli"), Gerhart, and Wolfgang—were born between 1892 and 1895 in Halle.

Husserl's second book (which he dedicated to Stumpf) came out as two separate volumes with one main title *Logische Untersuchungen* (Logical Investigations) and two subtitles. The first volume (Prolegomena to Pure Logic), published in 1900, defines logic as the foundation of all theories and argues that it cannot be reduced to or explained through human psychology (the antipsychological argument). The second volume (Investigations on Phenomenology and the Theory of Knowledge) appeared in 1901 and is a comprehensive discussion of meaning-conferring acts (meaning-intentions) aimed at accounting for the ideal identity of meanings across contexts and speakers. Husserl's position is that when we understand an expression like *the Queen of England*, there is one essential content (the "meaning-intention") that we all share regardless of the kind of image or memory that such a linguistic expression might evoke in each of us. Throughout the book, in addition to proposing a formal ontology (a theory of the relation between a whole and its parts) and comparing traditional views of logic with his own, Husserl offers his own analysis of intentional experiences, from the act of wanting or liking something to the feeling of pain provoked by contact with extreme heat. Whether or not one agrees with his specific distinctions, these phenomenological analyses give us an appreciation of the analytical power of Husserl's approach.

Thanks to the interest generated by his *Logical Investigations*, in 1901, Husserl accepted a position at the University of Göttingen, where he refined his views on the special role of philosophy in providing the foundations of epistemological inquiry, including any kind of science. A major accomplishment during this period was the publication in 1913 of a new treatise titled *Ideen zu einer reinen Phänomenologie und phänomenologischen Philosophie* (Ideas for a Pure Phenomenology), now commonly known as *Ideen I*, or *Ideas* (Volume 1), because it was meant to be followed by two more volumes that never materialized during Husserl's lifetime. *Ideas* refined and expanded the theory first introduced in *Logical Investigations* and now called "pure phenomenology." Here, Husserl introduces the notion of "the natural standpoint" or "the natural attitude" (*die natürliche Einstellung*), the phenomenological reduction (made possible by the *époché*, i.e., "suspension" or "bracketing" of the natural attitude), the discovery (made possible by the phenomenological reduction) of the transcendental Ego, and the more nuanced exploration of meaning-making acts through the notions of *noesis* (the process of knowing broadly conceived) and *noema* (plural *noemata*; the object of knowledge as such).

While at Göttingen, Husserl attracted a number of brilliant students and followers, including Adolf Reinach (1883–1917), who developed a theory of social acts in the domain of civil law that is a precursor of speech act theory, and Edith Stein (1892–1942), who in 1916 completed a dissertation about empathy (*Einfühlung*), published in 1917 as a book, which draws heavily on Husserl's views on the subject.

Husserl's efforts were finally fully recognized in 1916 with a chair in philosophy at the University of Freiburg. Unfortunately, this appointment came under the most difficult personal circumstances. In 1914, his two sons had been sent to war. The youngest, Wolfgang, was killed at Verdun in 1916. Gerhart was wounded a year later. Husserl himself fell ill from nicotine poisoning. Six months after Husserl delivered his inaugural lecture at Freiburg on "pure phenomenology" (May 1917), there was another tragic loss: The talented Adolf Reinach was killed in a battle in Flanders. In the meantime, Edith Stein had followed Husserl to Freiburg to transcribe and organize some of his stenographic lecture notes and manuscripts. After 2 years of hard and often frustrating work, she succeeded in producing what became Husserl's book on the consciousness of time, published in 1928 with little recognition of her contribution.

Husserl retired from Freiburg University in March 1928, after helping his former teaching assistant Martin Heidegger to succeed him. In a short time, however, the relationship between the two philosophers deteriorated for philosophical and political reasons, including Heidegger's support—publicly announced during his inaugural speech as rector of the university in 1933—for national socialism and its leader, Adolf Hitler.

Despite some health problems, including periods of profound depression, after his retirement Husserl remained intellectually active and had a strong desire to continue to write and refine his theory. In 1929, he went to Paris to deliver the lectures that became the *Cartesian Meditations* (first published in French in 1931), where he argued against a solipsistic view of his phenomenology and laid out the argument in favor of transcendental intersubjectivity. In 1935, he was invited to Vienna and Prague to deliver lectures, which were later included in the posthumous volume *Crisis of the European Sciences and Transcendental Phenomenology*, where he introduced the concept of *Lebenswelt* ("lifeworld") to characterize the pregiven, taken-for-granted world of both sense experience and thinking, that is, the world we inhabit when we are in what he had called "the natural attitude" in *Ideas*. More important, however, in *Crisis*, Husserl raises the issue of the limitations of the sciences in addressing the meaning of human existence. Anticipating later studies of laboratory work and scientific discovery, Husserl promoted the importance of going beyond what scientists consider *facts* to reveal what makes them into facts. He wrote, "Merely fact-minded sciences make merely fact-minded people" (*Crisis*, p. 6). For Husserl, then, toward the end of his life, transcendental phenomenology represented more than a theory of knowledge. It was his proposal for rescuing European civilization from irrationality gone violent and repressive.

The increasingly oppressive German racial laws eventually stripped Husserl not only of his right to teach but of his German citizenship as well. Without a passport, he was not allowed to travel freely, and, given his views on the universal properties of human consciousness, which did not square with Nazi claims of the superiority of the German race, he was also forbidden from publishing in Germany. He became ill in 1936 while revising his *Crisis* manuscript, was bedridden in 1937 due to a fall, and never fully recovered. He died on April 27, 1938, at the age of 79.

Husserl's wife Malvine and his assistant Eugen Fink succeeded in saving from the Nazis some 40,000 pages of shorthand lecture notes and unpublished manuscripts, plus about 10,000 pages of typewritten transcriptions that had been made during Husserl's lifetime by his assistants. With the help of the Franciscan priest Hermann Van Breda, those documents were sent to the Catholic University of Leuven, where the Husserl Archive was established in 1939. Since 1973, the hard work of dedicated scholars has produced more than 40 volumes of Husserl's works (in the *Husserliana* series). The translation of some of those volumes into English, French, Italian, and other languages has helped make Husserl's work known to an increasingly wider audience of humanists and social scientists. Husserl's finished and unfinished manuscripts demonstrate that he had something interesting and profound to say about a vast range of fundamental human activities, including knowing, thinking, theorizing, imagining, remembering, reflecting, empathizing, evaluating, and paying attention.

Husserl's Phenomenology

Even though the term *phenomenology* had been used by earlier writers, Husserl gave it a particular meaning, which he kept refining throughout his whole career. To engage in *a phenomenology of our being in the world* for Husserl meant to study how objects—broadly defined—are *given to us*. This means that we need to attend to what appears to us (the phenomena), their essential properties, and the role of our consciousness in recognizing them and making them into what they are—that is, constituting them. To engage in such an investigation, Husserl proposed to ignore the issue of whether or not something exists in the world and to focus instead on our experience of its essential qualities. By engaging in the phenomenological reduction, we are able to "bracket" our taken-for-granted world of the "natural attitude" so that we can examine in detail and without prejudice what is distinctive about a given entity "out there" (a tree in the garden, a friend's voice on the phone) or in our mind (the memory of a face, an excuse we are prepared to use) or about the ways in which we relate to such an entity (e.g., by having beliefs, wishes, preferences, feelings, and fantasies). To engage in phenomenological analysis of the kind proposed by Husserl, then, means to be able to identify the essential qualities of each experience in order to account for its distinctiveness. What makes remembering a trip among friends different from imagining it? What makes being tired after shoveling snow in front of our own house different from shoveling snow as a job? How is the anticipation of the feeling in my mouth while I am about to bite into a sandwich suddenly affected and changed if I become aware of a homeless person watching me? Since observationally, in each of these cases, I might not be able to "see" what is different—a problem for the strictly "observational" sciences—I need to focus on the role played by my consciousness in providing an interpretation in response to or sometimes despite the sense data that are available to me. Through intentional acts of different levels of complexity (e.g., listening to a song, remembering someone's name, looking for a street name, feeling sorry for someone, etc.), we play an active role in assigning interpretations to perceived, sensuous data (*hyle*) as well as in interpreting culturally rich information. When we read from a text, we are exposed to sensuous data, but our natural attitude is to see those marks as *words* and not as lines or dots against a white or lighter background (in fact, we need to suspend our ordinary way of looking at a familiar script in order to attend to it as an aesthetic object). Similarly, when we hear people speak a familiar language, we do not hear "mere sounds." Instead, we hear *what they are saying*. Even when we do not understand the words (because we are too far or because people are speaking a foreign language we do not understand), we still know that a language (as opposed to gibberish) is being spoken. Husserl conceived phenomenology as a descriptive science that should allow people to distill out the essence of each of these lived experiences. The ultimate goal, however, is not the identification of one's *own* personal, subjective experience but a general, universal science of lived experiences *as such*.

In pursuing the *essential specific characteristics* of human experiences, Husserl identified a *transcendental ego*—the a priori constituting (pure) subject of all experiences—that partakes in a flow of consciousness. This is a stream, which Husserl discussed in his lectures on time consciousness as the "living" (*Lebende*) and later (in his lectures later published in *Analysis Concerning Passive and Active Synthesis*) as the "living present" (*lebendige Gegenwart*). Husserl's genetic method consists in the uncovering of the origins of our special way of being in the living present and attending to the surrounding world, often in a pre-predicative, pre-reflective, and perceptual mode—which he calls "passive." The living present is occupied by other human beings who participate in a simultaneous fashion (in a "pairing") in one's lifeworld.

Even though we cannot enter into another person's consciousness and have a first-person experience of what he or she is thinking or perceiving, in our everyday life we are able to have an intuitive sense of other people's goals, motivations, and even feelings. This is made possible through empathy (*Einfühlung*), a concept that Husserl borrowed from Theodor Lipps (1851–1914). Empathic apperception makes it possible to see another person not simply as a physical body (*Körper*) that has a certain weight, size, and shape but also and crucially as a lived body (*Leib*), which moves, reacts, and anticipates its surroundings in the ways in which our lived body would. When I see another person moving a hand to grasp a cup, I have an immediate, embodied, intuitive understanding of that action as something that I myself might do were I in the same position. This is where the concept of intersubjectivity comes in as the foundation of both objectivity and human sociality. The world is "objectified" not by the simultaneous occupation of the same viewpoint—that is, you and I do not need to be in the same place at the same time to know that the world is the same for the two of us—or by the complete matching of our perceptions, beliefs, or feelings but by the possibility of "trading places" (*Platzwechsel*). My lifeworld by definition presupposes the lifeworld of others. I can assume that the cup I am seeing from my point of view has another side that is visible to another person standing *over there* and that were that person to stand where I am, he or she would see it as I do. This is *transcendental intersubjectivity*, the condition for a shared objective world and for interdependence among humans. I am an alter ego for someone else and, vice versa, he or she is my alter ego. Intersubjectivity is implicated in everything we do and everything we touch, see, hear, smell, grasp, or read, including this text, which assumes a community of readers invested in approximating each other's stream of thought through analogy and a shared world of texts, authors, ideas, and interests.

Husserl's Legacy

Husserl's ideas spread into the social sciences in the United States, thanks to Alfred Schütz (1899–1959) and Aron Gurwitsch (1901–1973), who, with other European scholars who had escaped Nazi-dominated Western Europe, taught at the New School for Social Research in New York during and immediately after World War Two. It was partly thanks to interactions with Schütz and Gurwitsch that Harold Garfinkel (1917–2011) developed the field of ethnomethodology, which adopted some of Husserl's key concepts, such as the lifeworld and the method of bracketing. Over the past 2 decades, a number of anthropologists, including Michael Jackson, Robert Desjarlais, and C. Jason Throop, have adopted or revised some of Husserl's key concepts to analyze culture-specific expressions of pain, suffering, illness, and loss. These and other authors have suggested that some of Husserl's concepts offer themselves for an immediate translation into anthropological discourse. The notion of "natural attitude," for example, can easily be recast as the "cultural attitude," namely, the taken-for-granted way of being in the world that ethnographers try to capture in their writing. An exploration of Husserl's writings on intersubjectivity can help us describe the tension between autonomy and sociality, or between individual resilience and interrelatedness, that has been documented in so many societies around the world. It can also illuminate contemporary discussions of the phylogenetic and ontogenetic roots of human sociality. Husserl's writings about temporality and a sense of a shared objective world can help ethnographers grappling with how individuals and social groups establish continuity while recognizing change through birth rites, marriages, funerals, and other public events. Just like an otherwise lifeless ink mark on a piece of paper acquires meaning through an intentional act produced by someone who "sees" it as a "word," so does a gathering of people around a newborn, a young couple, or a dead body *constitute* the newborn, the couple, or the dead, respectively, into a being(s) of a certain kind and the moment as one within a series of moments that make up the "whole" of the human cycle and, on a grander scale, the history of the community and its tradition. Husserl's writings provide myriad insights into the unfolding interplay of subjectivity and intersubjectivity in the constitution of self and society.

Alessandro Duranti

See also Benjamin, Deconstruction; Derrida, Jacques; Walter; Phenomenology

Further Readings

Desjarlais, R., & Throop, C. J. (2011). Phenomenological approaches in anthropology. *Annual Review of Anthropology, 40*, 87–102.

Donohoe, J. (2004). *Husserl on ethics and intersubjectivity. From static to genetic phenomenology.* Amherst, NY: Humanity Books.

Duranti, A. (2010). Husserl, intersubjectivity and anthropology. *Anthropological Theory, 10*(1), 1–20.

Husserl, E. (1960). *Cartesian meditations: An introduction to phenomenology* (D. Cairns, Trans.). The Hague, Netherlands: Martinus Nijhoff.

———. (1970). *The crisis of European sciences and transcendental phenomenology* (with an introduction by D. Carr, Trans.). Evanston, IL: Northwestern University Press.

———. (1991). *On the phenomenology of the consciousness of internal time (1893–1917)* (J. B. Brough, Trans.). Dordrecht, Netherlands: Kluwer Academic.

Jackson, M. (1998). *Minima ethnographica: Intersubjectivity and the anthropological project.* Chicago, IL: The University of Chicago Press.

Moran, D. (2005). *Edmund Husserl: Founder of phenomenology.* Cambridge, UK: Polity.

Moran, D., & Cohen, J. (2012). *The Husserl dictionary.* London, UK: Continuum.

Throop, C. J., & Murphy, K. M. (2002). Bourdieu and phenomenology. *Anthropological Theory, 2*, 185–207.

Zahavi, D. (2001). *Husserl and transcendental intersubjectivity* (E. A. Behnke, Trans.). Athens: Ohio University Press.

HYMES, DELL

Dell Hathaway Hymes (1927–2009), a linguistic anthropologist, folklorist, and educational administrator, was a key figure in the historical development of linguistic anthropology as a distinct subfield of anthropology.

Biography

Hymes was born in Portland, Oregon, in 1927 to a family that, like many during the period, endured the hardship of the Depression. After attending public schools there and graduating high school at the age of 17, Hymes attended Reed College. However, his studies there were interrupted after only 1 year for 2 years of military service in (South) Korea. When he returned in 1947, he resumed his studies while supported by the G.I. Bill and eventually earned his BA in 1950. His Reed experience provided a foundation for his later academic work since it allowed him to combine his emerging interests in anthropology and English. Also significantly, he began a long association with his mentor, David H. French (1918–1994), an anthropologist who introduced the young Hymes to the Kiksht—a Chinookan-speaking people who resided on the Warm Springs Reservation in central Oregon.

Hymes went to Indiana University to pursue a PhD in anthropology and folklore. At this point in time, Indiana University was a virtual mecca for various innovative approaches to the study of language and communication well beyond the American structuralism of the linguist Leonard Bloomfield. Faculty appointments of C. F. Voegelin and, later, Thomas Sebeok and others helped focus and develop academic interests in anthropological linguistics, psycholinguistics, sociolinguistics, and semiotics. Indiana University hosted major national and international conferences on psycholinguistics, sociolinguistics, and linguistic style, as well as several summer institutes of the Linguistic Society of America. Thus, at Indiana, Hymes was immersed in the flow of many emerging currents in the study of language and met influential figures such as the anthropologist Claude Lévi-Strauss, the poet and critic Kenneth Burke, and the linguist Roman Jakobson. Hymes completed his doctoral dissertation, *The Language of the Kathlamet Chinook*, in 1955, while working as a postdoctoral fellow with Harry Hoijer, a leading linguistic anthropologist of Athabascan languages and a founder of the Department of Anthropology of the University of California, Los Angeles. From there, Hymes traveled to Harvard to serve as an instructor and assistant professor from 1955 to 1960. These new experiences further positioned Hymes on the cutting edge of emerging and converging interests in anthropology, folklore, and linguistics and provided appropriate resources for him to craft his first major book-length publication, the edited volume *Language in Culture and Society: A Reader in Linguistics and Anthropology* (1964). This massive volume (exceeding 750 pages) is often regarded as the first reader in the developing field of linguistic anthropology. Hymes's editorial goal was to demonstrate the often unacknowledged relevance of language and the many ways in which the study of language "intersects almost every concern of the anthropologist . . . and to show that the field has a noteworthy history, a lively present, and a future of promise" (p. xxii). Though many of the nearly 70 chapters were written by nonanthropologists, the volume is clearly a clarion call for a socioculturally centered view of language at a time when the influential linguist Noam Chomsky was constructing an asocial linguistics preoccupied not with actual speech communities but with idealized, perfectly homogeneous speech communities, which displayed none of the complexities and limitations of actual speakers.

From 1960 to 1965, Hymes joined the anthropology department at the University of California, Berkeley, as an associate professor and later as a full professor. Berkeley provided an especially appropriate environment of language and communication for scholars across departments, including Erving Goffman, John Gumperz, Susan Ervin-Tripp, and John Searle. This type of interdisciplinary array of scholars from anthropology, education, folklore, linguistics, philosophy, psychology, and sociology provided the basis for the foundational symposium "The Ethnography of Communication" at the American Anthropological Association Meetings in 1963 and for later publications. During this period, Hymes was the tireless author of many programmatic articles that created a sense of unity and organization in an emerging science of the study of language usage. In a manner both eloquent and persistent, Hymes argued for the importance of and the need for such inquiry at a time when Chomsky's emphasis on nativism and formal universals seemed to restrict linguistic investigations to concerns about the nature of a speaker's innate grammatical "competence."

In 1965, Hymes began a 22-year career at the University of Pennsylvania, where he was a full professor in the Department of Anthropology and later in the Departments of Folklore, Linguistics, and Sociology, before accepting the position of dean of the Graduate School of Education. At the University of Pennsylvania, his intellectual interests further developed in interaction with colleagues such as Erving Goffman, Ward Goodenough, and William Labov. During this period, Hymes's mentoring efforts helped develop a distinguished cohort of younger scholars who would further develop the ethnography of communication and the other fields that he had so steadfastly promoted. During this period, Hymes's disciplinary influence was recognized in his election as president of four academic societies: the American Folklore Society (1973–1974), the

Linguistic Society of America (1982), the American Anthropological Association (1983), and the Society for Applied Linguistics (1986–1987).

Completing his service as dean, Hymes moved to the University of Virginia, where he served as a professor of anthropology. There, he renewed and fortified earlier interests in Native American verbal art, verse analysis of narrative discourse, and related areas in a field of inquiry he variously called anthropological philology or ethnopoetics. These interests preoccupied him into retirement in 1998. He died at the age of 83 as Commonwealth Professor Emeritus of Anthropology at the University of Virginia.

Range of Research and Major Works

Hymes deserves much of the credit for shaping linguistic anthropology in the United States during the second half of the 20th century. His efforts were crucial in the transformation of linguistic anthropology from a "service" subfield that provided the necessary linguistic expertise to archaeologists and biological and cultural anthropologists to a field of linguistic inquiry that was guided by anthropological theories and concerns. His mentor at Indiana University, C. F. Voegelin, had in an influential 1949 article critiqued both a linguistics "without meaning" and an anthropological study of culture "without words." Voegelin's essay deftly analyzed the deficiencies of Bloomfieldian linguistics, in which meaning was ignored in favor of the formal rigor possible in phonological and morphological analysis. It illuminated the lack of a linguistic emphasis in the British social anthropology–influenced American anthropology of the 1940s and 1950s. However, the essay neither mobilized scholars nor demonstrated the potential of greater linguistic emphasis for anthropologists. But Hymes wrote voluminously to make the case for a socioculturally based linguistics and an anthropology that properly recognized the many functions provided by language—as a medium of data collection, as a theoretical model, and as a cultural practice—in anthropological projects. In addition to his field-nucleating reader in linguistic anthropology, *Language in Culture and Society*, Hymes wrote extensively and influentially in three main areas—the ethnography of communication, ethnopoetics, and education and communication.

Hymes's pioneering efforts in creating a field of inquiry, which he named the ethnography of speaking

(later generalized to the more inclusive focus on communication), began with his recognition of how the study of language use had been neglected in both linguistics and anthropology. Linguistic grammars specified what was structurally possible but not what was actually said and by whom, to whom, and under what contexts. Anthropologists, on the other hand, demonstrated the cultural relativity of technology, kinship, and religion but somehow neglected communication. Anthropologists by the mid-20th century had become familiar with the Sapir-Whorf hypothesis, also known as "linguistic relativity," but Hymes deftly demonstrated that recognition of the relativity of linguistic structure needed to be supplemented by appreciating the cultural relativity of language usage. He argued persuasively for recognizing the importance of the social, contextual, and cultural criteria that members used in producing and evaluating culturally appropriate speech. At a time when Chomskyan linguistics focused exclusively on grammatical order, Hymes encouraged anthropologists to understand that cultural concerns mattered critically in determining what counted as appropriate communication. In 1964, Hymes and his colleague John Gumperz coedited a landmark collection of articles from the first major conference on the ethnography of communication as a special issue of the *American Anthropologist*. In a fortified and expanded version, a similar collection was developed by these coeditors in 1972 as *Directions in Sociolinguistics: The Ethnography of Communication*. This collection included work by social anthropologists (Barth), sociologists (Fishman, Garfinkel), conversational analysts (Sacks, Schegloff), sociolinguists (Labov), educational researchers (Bernstein), ethnographers (Frake), psychologists (Ervin-Tripp), and folklorists (Dundes), in an effort to present a clear, socioculturally centered alternative to Chomsky's asocial emphasis on the formal universals of language. These collections and the movement they represented did much to allow linguistic anthropology to shed its image as a "service" subfield, as Hymes and other scholars succeeded in an educational campaign to more fully recognize and confront the many roles of language and linguistic analysis in anthropological research.

Another key area in Hymes's research was "ethnopoetics"—the use of linguistic and anthropological analysis in the understanding and interpretation of narrative and other verbal art. Hymes's interest in this area was represented early in his research with the 1959 publication of "Myth and Tale Titles of the Lower Chinook," and it continued throughout his life, most visibly in the two major collections of essays on this topic—*"In Vain I Tried to Tell You": Essays in Native American Ethnopoetics* (1981) and *"Now I Only Know So Far": Essays in Ethnopoetics* (2003). A major accomplishment in Hymes's work in this area was his recognition of what he called "measured verse"—linguistic patterning other than by rhyme and meter, which often involved patterns of repetition of discourse features and forms of linguistic parallelism. Preferring to work on materials indigenous to his primary research area, Hymes often studied previously documented narratives from Chinookan and other North Pacific communities. His detailed analysis and careful translation of narratives like "Seal and Her Younger Brother Lived There" revealed how attention to linguistic and cultural detail could provide a basis for a more ethnographically relevant reading of these texts—a reading that took into account the identities of the performers and their audiences.

A third area of sustained research, one that represents the intersection of Hymes's abiding interest in oral narrative with his service to the field of education, may be termed "narrative inequality." In *Ethnography, Linguistics, Narrative Inequality: Toward an Understanding of Voice* (1996), he examines written and oral narratives of Native Americans and African Americans and explores how many educational institutions enforce ideals based on literacy and social class, which reproduce class differences. Attempting to provide alternative goals, Hymes develops an ethnopoetic notion of voice as the individual's preferred languages and styles for the narrative construction of self and society.

In addition to these main areas of sustained research, Hymes also made significant contributions as a researcher, programmatic writer, and book and journal editor, including work on topics such as the history of linguistics and linguistic anthropology—*Studies in the History of Linguistics* (1974) and *Essays in the History of Linguistic Anthropology* (1983)—and studies of language contact and creolization—*Pidginization and Creolization of Languages* (1971), an edited volume. In work such as *The Use of Computers in Anthropology* (1965) and the edited volume *Reinventing Anthropology* (1972), he foreshadowed contemporary interests. In the latter work, he and other authors asked the radical question "If anthropology ceased to exist, would it have to be reinvented?" The volume explores the uses of activist anthropology in advocacy for the people anthropologists study and as a more general basis for a socially engaged anthropology. As in other aspects of Hymes's oeuvre, he displays here what has been described as his career-long linkage of "ethnography and democracy."

Paul V. Kroskrity

See also Humanistic Anthropology; Phenomology; Sociolinguistics; Tedlock, Barbara and Dennis; Whorf, Benjamin Lee

Further Readings

Blommaert, J. (2009). Ethnography and democracy: Hymes's political theory of language. *Text & Talk, 29*, 257–276.

Silverstein, M. (2010). Dell Hathaway Hymes. *Language, 86*, 933–939.

Institut d'Ethnologie (Paris)

Between its foundation in 1925 and the 1960s, the Institute of Ethnology of the University of Paris was the only place where French anthropologists received training. With the notable exception of Claude Lévi-Strauss, every single French anthropologist received a certificate from it.

Background

Until the birth of the Institute of Ethnology, elements of a proto-discipline of anthropology were scattered in places that had specific traditions: The National Institute of Living Oriental Languages and Civilizations (1795), The Chair of Anthropology of the Natural History Museum (1856), The Paul Broca Paris School of Anthropology (1876), The Colonial School (1884), and the religious studies of the École Pratique des Hautes Études (1885).

The university hegemony of Durkheim and his followers of the French school of sociology changed this situation. Until World War II, 45% of their journal *l'Année Sociologique* was concerned with anthropological themes (the first issue opened with Durkheim's article on the origin of the incest taboo) or with reports on exotic countries (under the name of "primitive sociology"). Contributors included Henri Hubert, Robert Hertz, Marcel Granet, Célestin Bouglé, and Marcel Mauss.

The creation of the Institute of Ethnology originated with three men: Marcel Mauss, Durkheim's nephew, who was director of the Study of Religions of Uncivilized Peoples at l'École Pratique des Hautes Études; Lucien Lévy-Bruhl, professor at the Sorbonne, who intended "to define mental types including archaic types"; and Paul Rivet, a physician, naturalist, and linguist, assigned by the army to the National Museum of Natural History.

Mauss, Lévy-Bruhl, and Rivet were socialists who opposed the monarchist and antirepublican scholars of the Ethnographic Society of Paris (publishers of the journal *l'Ethnographie*) and the rightist republicans at the Anthropological Society of Paris (who published the journal *l'Anthropologie*). Unlike these latter, Mauss, Lévy-Bruhl, and Rivet were profoundly antiracist but still favored strong colonial engagement based on their idea of the universality of the Revolution of 1789.

Early Years

The victory of a left-wing coalition government in the elections of 1924 opened the way for the three to organize the Institute of Ethnology, which opened in 1925. Funded by the French colonial office and housed at the Institute of Geography of the University of Paris, the institute was responsible for coordinating the teaching of ethnological studies, research, and publication. In 1926, the collection of *Travaux et Mémoires de l'Institut d'Ethnologie* (Works and Reports of the Institute of Ethnology) published its first titles. Around a hundred titles followed, and the series continues today.

The Institute of Ethnology began granting a "certificate in ethnography" in 1927, to which was added in 1928 a "certificate of anthropology." Certificates were granted for the successful completion of a yearlong series of courses and exams. The institute aimed primarily to educate colonial civil servants, but there were none in its first classes. Instead, the classes were filled with interested amateurs. Of the 26 students who registered, only 3 took the end-of-course examinations and received certificates. However, the institute's fortunes improved during succeeding years. The ability to issue certificates led to its success against its rival, the School of Anthropology of Paris. This being a private institution was unable to issue certificates that could be part of a degree recognized by the state. The eminent position of the Institute of Ethnology was ensured after the election of Rivet to the Chair of Anthropology at the Museum of Natural History in 1928. This allowed him to create a formal linkage between the institute and the Museum of Ethnography of the Trocadéro. Rivet's election was followed in February 1931 by the election of Mauss to the Collège de France, the most prestigious French institution. The enrollment at the institute grew from an initial class of 21 in 1926 to 256 by the start of World War II. Although most of these students did not take the examinations and receive the certificate, all of the future French anthropologists did.

Providing certification in ethnography and anthropology cost the state little, since the institute merely coordinated courses already existing at other institutions. At the start of 1927, the program included courses from Mauss (ethnography); Marcel Cohen (linguistics); Maurice Delafosse (Africa), replaced after his death by Henri Labouret (African ethnography) and Mlle. L. Homburger (African languages); and Jean Przyluski (Asia Pacific), a student of Mauss, and optional lectures by Arnold van Gennep (folklore) and Rene Maunier (colonial law). In 1928, the anthropology certificate added courses from Rivet (physical anthropology), Paul William (psychophysiology of man and anthropoids), Étienne Rabaud (biological anthropology and zoology), and Léonce Joleaud (geology of human paleontology and Quaternary time). In 1929, the institute offered a seminar given by Abbot Henri Breuil on "exotic prehistory" and courses by Alain Demangeon (human geography) and Jacques Millot (comparative physiology of the human races).

These scholars were the pillars of the teaching program of the institute until World War II. The list of students during the same period included Paul Mus, Jacques Faublée, Michel Leiris, André Schaeffner, Denise Paulme, Deborah Lifshitz, George Soustelle, Georgette Soustelle, Louis Dumont, André Leroi-Gourhan, Robert Gessain, Germaine Tillion, Jean-Pierre Vernant, Paul-Emile Victor, André Haudricourt, George Devereux, Germaine Dieterlen, Renee Maupoil, Leopold Senghor Segar, Jean Paul Lebeuf, Paul Levy, Roger Caillois, Pierre Métais, and many others (but not Lévi-Strauss). In most cases, students from law, philosophy, literature, or medicine were drawn to the institute because they were interested in a certificate that was exotic and supposedly easy to get. They were recruited to work as volunteers at the Museum of the Trocadéro. After obtaining their *licence* (equivalent to the U.S. bachelor's degree), students would enroll for a PhD (there was no master's degree at the time). Mauss and Rivet used their connections both in the French government and with the Rockefeller Foundation to find funding for students to do fieldwork. Fieldwork conducted by the institute's students was highly variable. There were fieldwork teams (e.g., the Griaule or Victor missions), others worked as married couples (e.g., Lévi-Strauss and Leroi-Gourhan), and occasionally, some worked as individuals. Some fieldwork lasted only a few days and some several years. Despite this diversity, all aimed to collect objects for the Ethnographic Museum and gather information for writing doctoral theses. Between 1926 and 1939, there were 104 missions. The first was undertaken in 1926, by M. Gromand (a student of Mauss), who traveled to Morocco to study the Berber. The fieldwork missions of this era fit into three broad categories: (1) missions carried out by colonial personnel, (2) missions carried out by students who studied with Mauss before the birth of the institute, and (3) missions carried out by the first generation of institute students. One of the most spectacular of these was the extravagant yacht mission sponsored by Count Étienne and Monique de Ganay. Between 1934 and 1936, the yacht crossed Oceania from Solomon Islands to New Guinea, bringing back to France thousands of objects that were deposited in the Trocadéro Museum.

In 1935, Rivet was elected deputy for Paris's 5th arrondissement. He was the first candidate to be supported by both communist and socialist voters. This combination of parties on the Left enabled the formation of the Popular Front government in 1936. Already chairman of the Anti-Fascist Committee, Rivet's political activism was intense. His deputy,

Georges River, took care of the Museum, and Mauss took care of the institute, which after 1938 was subsidized by the Ministry of Education. The objects brought back by the various missions were presented in numerous exhibitions at the Trocadéro Museum, which became the Museum of Man in 1938.

World War II and After

After the German defeat and occupation of France in 1940, many of the scholars associated with the institute went into exile: Rivet to Columbia, the Soustelles to London, and Alfred Metraux and Lévi-Strauss to the United States. Some joined the resistance and died in the war. When anti-Semitic laws were promulgated in 1941, Mauss was banned from teaching and was replaced first by Marcel Griaule and then later by Rev. Maurice Leenhart. Henri Vallois was appointed to replace Rivet as director of the Museum of Man in 1942. He, in turn, appointed Léon Pales as deputy director for physical anthropology and Griaule as secretary general of the Institute of Ethnology. Students of this era included Gilbert Rouget (b. 1916), Georges Balandier (b. 1920), Georges Condominas (b. 1920), Jean Poirier (b. 1921), Jean Guiart (b. 1925), and Jean Rouch (1917–2004).

On December 17, 1941, the Board of the Institute of Ethnology requested the establishment of a Chair of Anthropology in the Faculty of Arts at the Sorbonne. Griaule was elected to this position and thus became director of the institute. Reports of this era show that the institute had about 80 students each year. Most of these were French, but other nationalities were also represented. The French community of anthropologists, including physical anthropologists and prehistorians, had fewer than 50 people before the war. Many of these were still present after the war. However, Lévy-Bruhl died in 1939, and Mauss, although he survived until 1950, had become senile around 1943. Thus, of the institute's founders, only Rivet remained after the Liberation. He not only returned to his positions at the institute and the Museum of Man, but he also became very active in politics. Elected to Parliament in 1945, he held positions including vice president of the Foreign Affairs Committee of the National Assembly, chairman of the radio broadcasting committee, and vice president of the League of Human Rights. He was involved in the founding of the United Nations Educational, Scientific, and Cultural

Organization as well as the reorganization of the National Center for Scientific Research. Thus, he had little time for the institute.

In 1949 and 1950, the institute had a teaching staff of 13, including Lévi-Strauss, Denise Paulme, Marcel Maget, Paul Mus, and Leroi-Gourhan. In 1945, an associate professorship of colonial ethnology had been created in the Geography Faculty of Lyon for André Leroi-Gourhan. Leroi-Gourhan was a student of Mauss who was decorated for the role he had played in the Resistance. Leroi-Gourhan focused on prehistory, often bringing his students to archaeological sites. However, his most important impact was on anthropological education. In 1946, he created the Centre de Formation a la Recherche en Ethnologie (CFRE; the Center for Training in Ethnological Research), a joint program with the Museum of Man, and the Office of Overseas Scientific and Technical Research. Students interested in the discipline during their *licence*, had now to complete their training, with two more years of study, before working on a thesis. The CFRE was in fact an extension of the teaching of the institute without being officially a part of it. The core of the teaching staff included Leroi-Gourhan himself, Jean Poirier, René Granai, Raoul Hartweg, Pierre Métais, and André Haudricourt. The program covered museology, human geography, anthropology, and ethnology, and included writing a thesis based on fieldwork in France. In 1946–1947, 15 students enrolled in CFRE, but only 9 passed the tests for the degree. By 1947–1948, applications had grown to 30. Eighteen students were admitted, but again relatively few of them passed the examinations and received degrees.

Twice, in 1926 and 1932, Mauss had unsuccessfully proposed the creation of a Section of Economics and Social Sciences in the École Pratique des Hautes Études. Anxious to develop the social sciences in France, the Rockefeller Foundation created it in 1947; and finally, the Ministry of Education gave its financial support in 1951. The initial faculty consisted mainly of historians (including Lucien Febvre and Fernand Braudel), who were joined by social scientists, including the anthropologists Lévi-Strauss, Roger Bastide, and Jacques Soustelle (who soon joined the government as Minister of Information). In 1950, Lévi-Strauss succeeded Leenhard, becoming director of the center for the Study of Religions of People without writing at the École Practique des Haute Études. Lévi-Strauss became politically powerful in the new Economics and Social Sciences section, which was directed by Braudel, who, like Lévi-Strauss, had spent time in Brazil. Between 1953 and 1960, a generation of new young scholars, including Balandier, Paulme, and Condominas, were hired. The establishment created laboratories whose research missions were subsidized by the Rockefeller Foundation, and later by the Ford Foundation, and it offered an alternative education to that of the Institute of Ethnology and the CFRE of Leroi-Gourhan. When Griaule died in 1956, his Sorbonne chair was taken over by Leroi-Gourhan, and a second chair of ethnology was inaugurated by Roger Bastide in 1958. Pierre Jean Servier and Pierre Métais then received associate professorships in the University of Bordeaux (1953) and Nice (1965), and positions were created in Strasbourg, Lille, Montpellier, and other locations throughout France.

At that time, Leroi-Gourhan and Lévi-Strauss (elected to the Collège de France in 1959), codirected the Institute of Ethnology, but the discipline was already fragmented, and by the time of Rivet's death in 1958, the institute had lost power in the discipline. If it had lost hegemony over the organization of teaching and research, the institute had also lost its monopoly on publications as several collections of books and professional journals had appeared. In 1965, the CFRE was administratively attached to the Institute of Ethnology, but from 1966 to 1967, the Department of Sociology and Anthropology, led by Eric De Dampierre at Paris X Nanterre (now Paris West University Nanterre La Défense), and the Department of Ethnology at the Jussieu campus (now Pierre and Marie Curie University, Paris VI), led by Robert Jaulin (both ex-students of Lévi-Strauss), also offer licences in ethnology. This division of the field was further established after the May 1968 movement, and the Higher Education Reform Act reorganized teaching and research in independent units. These developments led Leroi-Gourhan to question the ability of the institute to operate in the new framework, and to Lévi-Strauss's resignation as codirector. Henri Raulin, Jean Guiart, and Claude Tardits were successive secretaries general of the institute, which was now reduced to its publications. In 1973, the now defunct institute left the University of Paris to become part of the National Museum of Natural History.

Gérald Gaillard

See also Durkheim, Émile; Griaule, Marcel; Lévy-Bruhl, Lucien; Mauss, Marcel; Musée de l'Homme; Rivet, Paul; Rouch, Jean

Further Readings

Blumenson, M. (1977). *The Vildé affair: Beginnings of the French Resistance*. Boston, MA: Houghton Mifflin.

Gaillard, G. (1989). Chronique de la recherche ethnologique dans son rapport au Centre National de la Recherche Scientifique 1925–1980 [Chronicle of anthropological research in its report to the National Center for Scientific Research 1925–1980]. *Cahiers pour l'Histoire du C.N.R.S.* (éditions du C.N.R.S), No. 3, 85–126.

———. (1990). *Répertoire de l'ethnologie Française, 1950–1970: Cadres institutionnels et activités de l'ethnologie Française entre 1950 et 1970* [Directory of French ethnology, 1950–1970: Institutional frameworks and the activities of French ethnology between 1950 and 1970] (2 vols.). Paris, France: Edition du Centre national de la Recherche scientifique. Retrieved from http://www.univ-lille1.fr/bustl-grisemine/pdf/rapports/G2003-27.pdf

Griaule, M. (1942). Rapport sur l'activité de l'Institut pendant l'année scolaire 1940–1941 [Report on the activities of the institute during the academic year 1940–1941]. *Annales de l'université de Paris, 17*, 318–319.

Karady, V. (1981). French ethnology and the Durkheimian breakthrough. *Journal of the Anthropological Society of Oxford, 12*, 165–176.

Leroi-Gourhan, A. (1951). *Rapport 1949–1950 sur le centre de formation à la recherche en ethnologie* [1949–1950 Report on the training centre for research in ethnology] (5 pp.). Paris, France: Musée de l'Homme.

Lévy-Bruhl, L. (1925). L'institut d'ethnologie de Paris [The Institute of Ethnology in Paris]. *Revue d'Ethnographie et de tradition populaire, 23–24*, 233–236.

———. (1927). L'institut d'ethnologie pendant l'année scolaire, 1925–1926 [The Institute of Ethnology during the academic year 1925–1926]. *Annales de l'Université de Paris, 2*(2), 90–95.

———. (1939). L'institut d'ethnologie pendant l'année scolaire, 1936–1937 [The Institute of Ethnology during the academic year 1936–1937]. *Annales de l'Université de Paris, 14*(1), 52–59.

Mazon, B. (1988). *Aux origines de l'Ephess: Le rôle du mécénat américain (1920–1960)* [The origins of Ephess: The role of American philanthropy (1920–1960)]. Paris, France: le Cerf. (Preface by P. Bourdieu)

Rivet, P. (1940). L'ethnologie en France [Ethnology in France]. *Bulletin du Muséeum national d'Histoire naturelle, 12*, 38–52.

Jakobson, Roman O.

Roman Osipovich Jakobson (1896–1982) was a Russian-born linguist, literary theoretician, and semiotician.

Biography and Major Works

Jakobson was born on October 11, 1896, in Moscow and died on July 18, 1982, in Cambridge, Massachusetts. As an undergraduate at the philological faculty of Moscow University, he focused on Slavic studies and graduated, in 1918, with a master's degree for his work on Russian dialectology. Linguistics at that time was dominated by neogrammarians, who advocated a strictly genetic and historical approach that ignored the fact that the parts of language, in particular the sound system, form an internally cohesive system that regulates sound shifts or linguistic borrowing while being simultaneously tied to its use, to communication. On the other hand, Jakobson appreciated a model of language that treated it as an object of analysis as well as a creative tool rather than just a conduit of preexisting thoughts or a transparent window onto the object world. By the time Jakobson completed his undergraduate studies, he and his friends had become exposed to several key developments in the arts and sciences. But it was the new approaches to the study of language, in particular the work of the Swiss linguist Ferdinand de Saussure, that drew attention to the internal structure of language and provided a systematic, conceptual framework to describe it. Jakobson is often credited with being the first, in 1929, to use the term *structuralism*.

In 1915, Jakobson, together with his friends, established the Moscow Linguistics Circle and shortly thereafter, in Saint Petersburg, the Society for the Study of Poetic Language. Together known as Russian Formalism, these organizations promoted a programmatic approach to language and, in particular, verbal art. They brought together linguists, folklorists, literary scholars, and writers who emphasized the analysis of the intrinsic properties of literature and poetry as autonomous modes of expression that engage language in ways distinct from language's other uses. Jakobson, himself a poet, would train his analytical skills on the language of poetry, and it can be safely argued that it was from this vantage point that so much of his contributions to linguistics derive.

From 1920 until 1939, Jakobson lived in Czechoslovakia. He became fluent in Czech (he was already bilingual in Russian and French) and a close friend of avant-garde artists, poets, and playwrights. In 1926, he helped found the Prague Linguistic Circle, considered by many as one of the pivotal moments in 20th-century linguistics and aesthetics and the cradle of structuralism. In 1930, he received his doctorate from Prague University and, from 1933 to 1939, taught at Masaryk University in Brno. Many of Jakobson's groundbreaking studies in Slavic linguistics and poetics and his initial forays into general linguistics date from this period. Among them is his groundbreaking work with his colleague Nikolai S. Trubetzkoy in phonology, which first defined phonemes in terms of their distinctive features that are both relationally invariant and yet work in consort with other units of sound, with which they form binary sets.

In 1939, Jakobson fled Nazi-occupied Prague together with his second wife, Svatava Pírková-Jakobson (a Czech folklorist), first to Copenhagen and Oslo, where he lectured and met with the Danish linguist Louis Hjelmslev, and then, in 1941, to Uppsala (Sweden). His pioneering work on child language acquisition and aphasia dates from these years. Both topics would reveal the intrinsic relationship between the brain's cognitive functions, the developmental logic of phonology's distinctive features, and the language of poetry. Jakobson asserted that the key figures of speech, metaphor and metonymy are present in all modes of language and thought and that they form part of the brain's cognitive and linguistic functions, a point widely accepted today.

After a brief stay in Sweden, Jakobson arrived in New York in 1941, where he taught at the École Libre des Hautes Études and later at Columbia University. A refuge for many exiled European artists and scholars, New York was a fertile crossroads of ideas and friendships that would define an era. Jakobson met Franz Boas and Benjamin Lee Whorf, who would introduce him to linguistic anthropology, in particular to the work of Edward Sapir. It was also while teaching at the École Libre that he first met Claude Lévi-Strauss, 12 years his junior, who attended his lectures on sound and meaning. The fundamentally holistic model of the American anthropologists dovetailed nicely with Jakobson's own, hierarchical understanding of language as a total phenomenon, as did their investigation into the relationship between language, thought, and culture. The close relationship between the two is not coincidental. Both schools of thought share the same historical source, namely, the German tradition associated with Alexander von Humboldt and Immanuel Kant.

Jakobson moved to Cambridge, Massachusetts, in 1949, where he was offered a professorship at Harvard in Slavic and general linguistics and where he would make his home with Svatava-Pírková and, later, his third wife, Krystýna Pomorská, herself a distinguished Slavicist. In 1957, he also joined the MIT faculty as head of the Center of Communication Science. Among the many publications that appeared during the postwar years,

several stand out as pivotal to the development of a general theory of signs (semiotics), to the study of verbal art, and, in particular, to the development of linguistic and cultural anthropology. *Fundamentals of Language*, with Morris Hale (1956), marks the culmination of his long interest in the distinctive features that constitute the phonology of a given language. Instead of phonetic description, which focuses on the points of articulation (their human physiology), Jakobson, the student of verbal art, was drawn to the acoustic quality of the sound itself, noting that individual phonemes are distinguished from each other by the presence or absence of a feature (such as pitch), together forming a multidimensional grid of binary oppositions that define a language's phonological system and that, additionally, have a distinct semantic aspect (e.g., the *i* in "high" is pitched high, whereas the *o* in "low" has a low pitch).

His discovery of the American pragmatist philosopher and logician Charles Sanders Peirce's sign typology—symbol, index, and icon—allowed Jakobson to expand on de Saussure's distinction between the signifier (the sound) and the signified (the sense). The indexical sign operates by using a part of the signified (the sense) as the signifier, the form of the sign. In this relationship of contiguity (whether physical, special, or temporal), a part stands for a whole; for example, smoke is an indexical sign of fire. On the other hand, an iconic sign works through the similarity or likeness between the two parts of the sign, as, for example, a portrait painting stands in for the person depicted. Two important features about this expanded typology reinforce Jakobson's view of language. First, the underlying mechanisms of the index and icon correspond to the two fundamental figures of speech, metonymy and metaphor, respectively. Second, the relationship between the signifier and the signified is motivated and not arbitrary. Where this relationship could be thought of as given and natural, it is established by habit and is culturally relative. In fact, as Jakobson never tires of emphasizing, the two sides of the linguistic sign (symbol in Peirce's terminology) are also formed by habit and are culturally relative. Contrary to de Saussure, Jakobson argues that the very phonological makeup of a language can operate at the level of syntax and meaning in a nonarbitrary, relatively motivated way. And while this is best realized in poetry, Jakobson shows that it is present in nonpoetic language as well. For example, the word *long* sounds long in contrast to *short*, which has a clipped, short sound to it. Once again, where the poetic function of speech dominates in verbal art, it proves, for Jakobson, to be the analytical gateway to the fundamentals of language.

In a landmark article, *Shifters, Verbal Categories and the Russian Verb* (1957), Jakobson drew attention to the manner in which the speech act is grammatically encoded; its intended meaning depends on referencing contextual information. Known as *deictic shifters*, personal pronouns, grammatical tense, place markers, mood (e.g., imperative, subjunctive, etc), and the evidential (e.g., whether the event reported is presented as witnessed, quoted, or remembered) are typical examples of indexical symbols (in Peirce's sense). These indexical symbols work to continuously position and reposition the participants in discourse vis-à-vis each other and the topic.

The conception of language as practice received its full elaboration in *Linguistics and Poetics* (1960). Inspired by the recent developments of communication theory, Jakobson's model of discourse consists of six factors and their corresponding functions. Typically, (1) an addresser sends (2) a message to (3) an addressee, but three additional components must be in place for the transaction to be successful: (4) a shared context (the referent), (5) the code (language) shared by both sides, and, finally, (6) contact, the physical, psychological, and social channel enabling the exchange. Most communication is focused on making claims by referring to objects outside of the speech act itself; that is, its function is cognitive (4). Traditionally, linguistics and the philosophy of language had been, in Jakobson's view, absurdly reductionist, because their attention was focused primarily on this function. But an act of speech may be oriented toward any one of the factors. The psychologist Karl Bühler had already shown that an explicative draws attention to the sender (emotive function), while a declarative and vocative phrase draws attention to the recipient (conative). It was Jakobson's attention to the message (2), the language itself (5), and also the channel through which the message was sent (6) that was groundbreaking and helped redraw the boundaries of linguistics research. Orientation toward the contact (6) dominates when the purpose of an utterance is primarily social (*phatic*, a term first suggested by Bronisław Malinowski). For instance, the greeting "Good day" is a social act of recognition, not a

statement about the weather. Orientation on the code (5) as in "Can you repeat that?" elicits the metalinguistic function. Finally (2), when the message refers to itself (self-referential), it engages the poetic function of language. Rhythm, rhyme, elements of style, or ornamentation all work by selecting identical or similar units (from sound to meaning) and stringing them along contiguously. Jakobson devoted his life to analyzing the subliminal patterning of verbal art and highlighting the key place the poetic function or parallelism occupied in all discourse. This topic received its fullest elaboration in his landmark study *Poetry of Grammar and the Grammar of Poetry* (1961).

Contributions to Anthropology

Roman Jakobson was a prolific scholar; a selection of his works fills seven hefty volumes. His contribution to research in any one of the fields of inquiry he turned his attention to was always notable and, more often than not, pathbreaking. From his lifelong interest in verbal art through his analysis of the internal organization of language (phonology, morphology, syntax, and semantic) and the underlying logic of communicative practices (pragmatics) to child language acquisition, to his study of aphasia (a class of language disorders) and his work in general linguistics, semiotics (the study of a broad range of phenomena centered on the use of signs and signifying practices), and the history of linguistics, his presence is felt in a wide range of disciplines in addition to linguistics proper. Among these Slavic studies, comparative literature and literary theory, aesthetics, medieval studies, and the study of folklore can certainly lay claim to him. And, of course, so can anthropology. In fact, his broad take on language as both an object of investigation and a process implicated in all social and cultural practices arguably identifies Roman Jakobson as an important figure in the development of modern anthropology.

Claude Lévi-Strauss, Jakobson's lifelong friend, was undoubtedly his best known protégé. Of his mentor's many ideas, the following were pivotal to Lévi-Strauss: (a) the theory of distinctive features as sets of differences, (b) the identification of figurative language as generalizable linguistic forms and thought-governing rules, and (c) the conviction that both of these principles, among others, are universal and part of human makeup. Both Jakobson and Lévi-Strauss found further inspiration (and confirmation) in the new developments in cybernetics, game theory, and, of course, genetics. All three place emphasis on information and on the underlying, rule-governing structures operating on a dualistic logic: the binary code.

The distinctive-feature model had a significant influence on the study of kinship (Lévi-Strauss, Rodney Needham), cognitive anthropology (Ward Goodenough), and mythology. In addition to the cross-cultural study of phonology, morphology, and grammatical semantics, Jakobson had an important impact on the linguistic and cultural analysis of deixis (the role of context in determining the meaning of speech), metalinguistics (the study of language in relation to culture and society), and metapragmatics (the functions of speech in discourse; William Hanks, Michael Silverstein); the ethnography of communication (Dell Hymes, James J. Fox); ethnopoetics (Steven Caton, Paul Friedrich); and, generally speaking, symbolic anthropology (James W. Fernandez).

Andrew Lass

See also Ethnography of Speaking; Goodenough, Ward H.; Lacan, Jacques; Lévi-Strauss, Claude; Prague School of Linguistics; Saussure, Ferdinand de; Semiotics; Structuralism

Further Readings

Caton, S. C. (1987). Contributions of Roman Jakobson. *Annual Review of Anthropology, 16,* 223–260.

Holenstein, E. (1976). *Roman Jakobson's Approach to Language.* Bloomington, Indiana University Press.

Jakobson, R. (1976). *Six lessons on sound and meaning.* Cambridge, MA: MIT Press.

Jakobson, R., & Pomorska, K. (1983). *Dialogues.* Cambridge, MA: MIT Press.

Lass, A. (2006). Poetry and reality: Roman O. Jakobson and Claude Lévi-Strauss. In C. Benfey & K. Remmler (Eds.), *Artists, intellectuals, and World War II: The Pontigny encounters at Mount Holyoke College, 1942–1944* (pp. 173–184). Amherst: University of Massachusetts Press.

JAMESON, FREDRIC

Although he was born in Cleveland, Ohio, Jameson (1934–) spent most of his early life in New Jersey. He was educated at Haverford College and Yale University, studying French. He taught at Harvard University while completing his PhD dissertation on Jean-Paul Sartre, which was published in 1961 as *Sartre: The Origins of a Style.* When Harvard denied him tenure, Jameson moved to the University of California, San Diego, where he remained for more than a decade. He returned to Yale in 1982, joining the French Department, which had by this time become internationally renowned as the home of deconstruction. In 1985, he was recruited by Duke University to head up a new program in literature, and he has remained there ever since. Jameson is the author of more than 20 books as well as a great many articles and book chapters. There is virtually no 20th-century critic or theorist of consequence he has not engaged in dialogue.

Jameson's career cannot really be broken into stages as there are no major shifts of perspective or changes of focus. If an image is needed, then there may be no better way to envisage his career than to picture a stone dropping into a large pond. The ripples that spread wider and wider from that initial impact would represent Jameson's incredible appetite and capacity to absorb and process new ideas, new languages, new theories, and new kinds of media (his work embraces everything cultural, from poetry to opera to computer games). He began his career in French, but then spent the next 10 years or so mastering the leading lights of 20th-century German critical theory (Theodor Adorno, Walter Benjamin, Ernst Bloch, Georg Lukács, and Herbert Marcuse). This work yielded the magisterial *Marxism and Form* (1971) and the equally impressive companion volume, *The Prison-House of Language* (1972).

In the long essay concluding *Marxism and Form,* "Towards a Dialectical Criticism," Jameson plotted his basic hypothesis, which he has expanded and revised but never really altered in the 40 odd years since. His central idea is that all texts, be they literary, philosophical, theoretical, or even filmic, are produced in dialogue with history understood as an ineffable real. His next major work, *The Political Unconscious: Narrative as a Socially Symbolic Act* (1981), would give methodological substance to this idea. Jameson argues there that we cannot but historicize because it is as historicizing machines that cultural works are intelligible to us. Every work of art, every film, and every piece of music or literature communicates to us, at a minimum, the message that the time of this work is now, that in no other period in history before or since would it be possible. This is why, as Gilles Deleuze argues (after Nietzsche), all great works feel untimely to us; they always arrive too soon. If they did not, they would seem neither new nor interesting, as our boredom with extinct forms attests.

The Political Unconscious transformed literary and cultural studies by offering a persuasive thesis explaining the relation between texts and history in anthropological terms as social and cultural purpose. For Jameson, history is an inexorable force; it is the outer limit, the necessary "beyond" or "horizon" of all human activity. He describes history as that which hurts, by which he means to say that history is a set of empirical facts (events unfolding across time), but goes on to add that it is only knowable as textual traces. His conception of history is, in this respect, something of an uneasy compromise between the skeptical viewpoint of poststructuralism and the absolutist position of Marxism. It accepts that history is not knowable to us in any complete way—we can never really know what the Romans thought or felt about their gods on an individual level, for example—but nevertheless insists that history is a constant force whose effects are to be seen everywhere. Culture is in this respect both a product of history and an active agent shaping history.

Borrowing from Claude Lévi-Strauss's interpretation of Caduveo face painting, Jameson argues that cultural texts manage (in a symbolic way) the multiple and various antinomies and contradictions that history throws at us. In brief, Lévi-Strauss's claim is that the Caduveo face paintings enact symbolic solutions to real social contradictions that cannot otherwise be resolved. For example, the various and complex power relations within the Caduveo tribe, and more especially in its relations with its neighbors, the Guana and Bororo, are "worked through" (in the psychoanalytic sense of resolving psychic tension by giving it expression) in a formal and aesthetic manner. In subsequent work, Jameson enlarged on this thesis to account for the cultural logic of contemporary late capitalism.

In the case of postmodernism, the subject of Jameson's next and probably most influential work, *Postmodernism, or, the Cultural Logic of Late Capitalism* (1991), it was the gloomy sense that somehow everything had ended: In art, in the wake of modernism, there was nothing new left to do; in politics, it was the end of the idea that government should be the engine of change; in capitalism

itself, it was the end of the idea that the function of corporations was something other than sheer moneymaking; globally, it was the end of the idea of the nation as a discrete entity. Culturally, postmodernism responded to these forces by celebrating what remained—it made a virtue of pastiche, repetition, plagiarism, and unoriginality; it advocated an individualist approach to politics that made the resilient individual worker, who neither needed nor looked for security of tenure, the new hero of the age; it separated the idea and practice of creativity from the actuality of creating things, and in the process, it brought about a massive global realignment whereby design and sales is a First World activity, while manufacturing is exclusively a Third World activity. Although some critics suggest that postmodernism is over as a movement, it is clear that we are still in thrall to these forces.

For Jameson, the postmodern period is characterized by two major transformations: the shift from nature to culture as the key resource for capitalist growth and expansion, and the resulting penetration and colonization of the unconscious. Jameson's point is that, for the First World at least, the growth of capitalism depends on the exploitation of ideas, tastes, feelings, desires, and emotions, rather than the physical resources central to late-19th-century and early-20th-century capitalism. This does not mean that manufacturing is unimportant, but it does mean that in the first world it is no longer seen as a source of growth. In the 3 decades since Jameson made this claim, his thesis has certainly been borne out. These days, some of the largest corporations in the world, among them Google and Facebook, do not make anything at all. Their wealth derives from focusing and repackaging, and on selling our attention. As many commentators have pointed out, from the perspective of capitalism, we are not Facebook's consumers, we are its product: We use it, but it sells us (and all the information it gathers about us) to other corporations, which in turn try to sell us things. Insofar as it is meaningful to talk about manufacturing in postmodernity, it is noteworthy that the richest manufacturing corporation in the world, Apple, makes devices that absorb and indeed package our attention too. Jameson's basic point, then, is that the most valuable resource of our era is *attention* (and all that it entails), not coal, steel, oil, or any other extracted resource.

Inasmuch as *postmodernism* is an attempt to historicize an entire era, it is perhaps not surprising that it demanded several further installments to round out, if not complete, the global pen portrait Jameson wanted to sketch. This rounding-out process has been pursued in three distinct directions. First, there has been a straightforward expansion of the original material—*The Geopolitical Aesthetic* (1992), *The Seeds of Time* (1994), *The Cultural Turn* (1998), and *A Singular Modernity* (2002) all fall into this category. Second, Jameson has expanded on the theoretical underpinnings of his diagnosis—*Late Marxism* (1990), which describes Adorno's work as a joyous countertoxin to postmodernism, and *Brecht and Method* (1998) can be listed here. Third, he has produced a monumental work on modernism, the product of 30 years of musing on the subject, *The Modernist Papers* (2007), against which his account of postmodernism should be situated. In recent work, Jameson has tended to use the term *globalization* rather than postmodernism, but the thesis remains the same: He is interested in the cultural expressions of this most recent stage of capitalism.

If every great theorist must have an abiding passion or interest, then for Jameson it is the concept of the dialectic. It underpins all his writing and thinking but only infrequently receives direct or extended treatment. This changed with the publication of *Valences of the Dialectic* (2009), which also brings in full circle Jameson's earlier thoughts on history, particularly in *The Political Unconscious*.

In addition, Jameson has also published two further works that can but be read as pendants: *The Hegel Variations: On the Phenomenology of Spirit* (2010) and *Representing Capital: A Reading of Volume One* (2011). Alongside these books, he frequently publishes new essays in *Critical Inquiry*, *New Left Review*, and the *London Review of Books*, his three favored journals. In 2008, Jameson was awarded the Holberg Prize in recognition of his enormous contribution to 20th- and 21st-century letters.

Ian Buchanan

See also Bloch, Maurice; Frankfurt School; Lacan, Jacques

Further Readings

Buchanan, I. (2006). *Fredric Jameson: Live theory*. London, UK: Continuum.

Helmling, S. (2000). *The success and failure of Fredric Jameson: Writing, the sublime, and the dialectic of critique*. New York: State University of New York Press.

Homer, S. (1998). *Fredric Jameson: Marxism, hermeneutics, postmodernism*. London, UK: Polity.

Irr, C., & Buchanan, I. (2006). *On Jameson: From postmodernism to globalism*. New York, NY: State University of New York Press.

Jameson, F. (2007). *Jameson on Jameson: Conversations on cultural Marxism*. Durham, NC: Duke University Press.

Kellner, D., & Homer, S. (2004). *Fredric Jameson*. London, UK: Palgrave.

Roberts, A. (2000). *Fredric Jameson*. London, UK: Routledge.

KARDINER, ABRAM

Although little read today, Abram Kardiner (1891–1981) was one of the founding figures of the Culture-and-Personality school of anthropology. His concept of *basic personality structure* provided a theoretical integration of social anthropology and psychoanalytic theory by showing that social structure and character formation inform and constrain each other. Kardiner was one of the founders in 1930 of the New York Psychoanalytic Institute, the first psychoanalytic institute in the United States. Not an anthropologist himself, Kardiner drew on the ethnographic research of Ralph Linton, Carl Withers, and Cora DuBois. In 1939, he published *The Individual and His Society* and in 1945, *The Psychological Frontiers of Society*. Both books consist largely of analyses by others, most prominently Ralph Linton and Cora DuBois. In the 1950s, Kardiner was a professor of psychiatry at Columbia University and, from 1955 to 1957, director of the Psychoanalytic Clinic. There he attended patients until just a few weeks before his death. His other books included *The Traumatic Neuroses and War* (1941), *Sex and Morality* (1954), *Mark of Oppression: Explorations in the Personality of the American Negro* (with Lionel Ovesey, 1951), *They Studied Man* (with Edward Preble, 1961), and *My Analysis With Freud: Reminiscences* (1977). Kardiner's influence on the emerging field of psychological anthropology is recognizable in the work of John and Beatrice Whiting, Clyde and Florence Kluckhohn, Weston LaBarre, Anthony F. C. Wallace, Melford Spiro, Gananath Obeyesekere, and Howard Stein.

Biography and Major Works

Abram Kardiner was born in New York on August 17, 1891, and graduated from the City College of New York. In 1917, he received his medical degree from Cornell and interned at Mount Sinai Hospital for 2 years. Kardiner had just completed his psychiatric residency when he was accepted as a patient by Sigmund Freud in Vienna. Freud set two conditions for Kardiner's analysis: that it last only 6 months (1921–1922) and that he be paid $10 a session in American dollars. He was proud of the fact that Freud acknowledged him as a *Menschenkenner* (knower of people). Kardiner ended up departing from Freud in placing less emphasis on the instincts and their vicissitudes. Instead, he developed an enduring interest in the ego and its adaptive mediation of biological drives and institutional disciplines. Soon he came to see culture as a set of environmental and social structural exigencies and the basic problem of individual development as the culturally specific means available for the adaptation of the ego to these exigencies. His key insight was that cultural values derive from, and provide compensation for, institutionalized constraints—constraints shaped in relation to the social and economic environment.

In the 1930s, Kardiner joined with several anthropologists to study the processes by which culture is transmitted from one generation to the next, and it was at this time, working with anthropologists such as Ruth Benedict and Cora DuBois, that he formed his concept of the basic personality structure. The structure is a configuration shared by most of a society's members as a result of the experiences they have in common. It does not correspond to the total personality of the individual but to the value-attitude systems that are basic to the individual's personality configuration. The concept was meant to integrate patterns of child care and training with social institutions, values, and roles. The ego is the site of this integration, in keeping with the view associated with psychoanalytic theory that the basic disciplines of infant and child care play a significant role in the formation of personality. According to Kardiner, the basic personality structure was formed by primary institutions. Primary institutions (subsistence methods and family organization) establish structures for the formation of the individual ego, and the ego, in adapting to these structures, generates secondary institutions that include symbolic systems such as folklore, myth, and ritual. Secondary institutions in turn shape child-rearing practices and personality structure.

Kardiner hypothesized that the structure of the ego derives from culture-specific problems of psychological adaptation. He was not interested in the Oedipus complex or in other classic Freudian dimensions of the id and the superego, although he accepted the reality of instinctual drives. Kardiner did not reduce cultural formations to the development of psychosexual states or the renunciation of libidinal desires. In fact, he argued that describing a culture in Freudian terms such as anal or erotic was useless. Kardiner instead focused on the ego as an *adaptive* mechanism that mediated biological drives and institutionalized disciplines. The ego adapts to its environmental and social conditions, and this adaptation, in turn, shapes the formation of cultural institutions that exist to defend against and provide substitute satisfaction for the frustrations established by these socially and historically contingent disciplines.

Kardiner tended to avoid notions of causality—the "chicken or the egg" problem—by stressing that primary and secondary institutions can only be analyzed in reciprocal interaction with each other. Still, he accepted to some degree the Freudian view that the basic disciplines (of infant and child care) constrain the formation of "basic" personality—that is, the personality structure that is common to

all members of the social group who are similarly conditioned by the same practices. He argued, for example, that premature sphincter discipline in Tanala child training created the template for obedience to authority in adulthood—a defensive adaptation that was reinforced in the relation of father and son, with its constant relationship between obedience and security, loyalty and protection.

In his 1939 magnum opus *The Individual and His Society*, Kardiner drew on the fieldwork of Ralph Linton (his coauthor in all but name) among the peoples of the Marquesas Islands and the Tanala of Madagascar. Simpler societies were preferred because the authors assumed that small-scale, tribal societies possess relatively uniform institutions conditioning basic ego constellations. In the Marquesas, widespread and regular famine led to female infanticide and a skewed adult sex ratio, with men outnumbering women more than 2 to 1. This, Kardiner said, gave rise to polyandry as a primary institution and also to a cultural emphasis among women on maintaining erotic attractiveness; after all, they had several husbands, not just one, to keep happy. Kardiner found a corresponding de-emphasis of the relationship between women and their children, and he asserted that this led to a neglect of breast-feeding. In the Marquesas, this led to frustrations and an unfilled longing for dependency. Dissatisfactions of this sort became the elements of Marquesan myth, a secondary institution that both represents and attempts to resolve the underlying anxieties of early childhood.

Among the Tanala of Madagascar, Kardiner found that the ancestral spirits—a secondary institution—projectively recapitulated the relationship between father and son. Sons were trained to be obedient to their fathers, following the expectation that they would later inherit the fathers' land. But the recent shift to wet rice cultivation and the increasing economic insecurity—the result of the decline of the joint family and its replacement by a complex caste system—meant that sons could no longer expect the same benefits, no matter how well they ingratiated themselves with their fathers. Primary institutions, in other words, inhibited successful ego adaptation and led to beliefs about malevolent ancestral spirits. The construct of "spirit" is the Tanala symbolic representation, or projection, of the hostility to fathers.

Projection is a form of ideational representation whereby a person attributes his or her feelings or psychology to an external person or object. Among the Marquesans, for example, a belief in supernatural *vehini-hia*—"wild women" feared by children as cannibalistic—is a projective manifestation of unsatisfied and inverted desires centered on the mother. Fantasies and fears about food and about eating/being eaten are reinforced by the material circumstances of Marquesan society, especially the tendency for famine.

Kardiner recognized that in the absence of better empirical data he could not make strong testable claims about culture and personality. When the anthropologist Cora DuBois returned from the Indonesian island of Alor in 1939, Kardiner thought the moment had come, since DuBois had collected detailed autobiographies and projective test results. Kardiner inferred from this information that precarious material circumstances led mothers to neglect the regular feeding of their children and to provide inconsistent disciplines of rewards and punishments. Children's "unsatisfied orality" and fear of abandonment gave rise to a pervasive sense of distrust and suspicion, which impeded the formation of strong social bonds. Alorese religious beliefs—a secondary institution—mirrored their early upbringing, with ancestor spirits considered by the people of Alor as at best fickle and more likely to do harm than good. Not surprisingly, Kardiner noted, Alorese myths and legends were suffused with fantasies of revenge—a feature no doubt motivated, he said, by the child's wish to visit retribution on his emotionally detached and unreliable mother.

The study of Alor appeared in Kardiner's second famous book, *The Psychological Frontiers of Society*, published in 1945, which also included chapters on the Comanche (by Linton) and white Americans in "Plainville," a small town of 175 inhabitants in the American state of Missouri (based on fieldwork by "James West," the nom de plume of Carl Withers). Unlike the Alorese, Kardiner concluded, the mothers of Plainville did not convey mixed messages to their children, and in fact, most children grew up idealizing their mothers. Fathers, on the other hand, could not provide sufficient rewards for submission to their authority, and their arbitrary punitive acts led children (especially sons) to leave home early. Kardiner believed that the Protestant deity worshiped in Plainville's churches represented transplantations of the father in the household and of the conditions under which he loves and forgives or reinstates. In Plainville, Kardiner saw the United States—indeed,

the Western world—in microcosm, and he even went so far as to state that his conclusions applied just as well to Sophocles and Shakespeare.

Frequently overlooked in discussion of Kardiner's approach is his work on American race relations, "war neuroses" (now called posttraumatic stress disorder), and unemployment during the Depression. In the case histories that constituted *The Mark of Oppression* (1951), Kardiner and his collaborator Lionel Ovesey studied the external sources of prejudice in relation to the internal sources of self-hatred in African Americans living in Harlem. Although a pioneering work, the study has been criticized for assuming that there is no Black culture independent of its construction by oppression. On the traumatic neurosis of war, he came to see that the defensive maneuver to ward off the trauma sometimes destroyed the individual's adaptive capacity. The traumatic neurosis of war, he claimed, was the result of an adaptive failure, not a conflictual illness. Finally, with reference to Depression-era unemployment, Kardiner warned that economically insecure people are prone to masochism and become fodder for ruthless demagogues who promise relief from aggression directed toward the self. Government-sponsored work relief can help—Kardiner's nod to the New Deal—but he worried that the lowered expectation of competition cannot lead to permanent security in the workforce.

Critique of Kardiner's Approach

The difficulties with Kardiner's approach, as noted at the time, are that it says little about the development of real personalities in the cultures under discussion; the distributions of personality types within cultures; the dynamics of the personality-culture interaction, especially in the context of social change; and the relevance of the basic-personality approach to complex societies. Anthropologists criticized Kardiner for attempting to reconstruct the basic personality of a culture without data on specific individuals and without testable hypotheses. Margaret Mead even considered it arrogant. Meanwhile, psychoanalysts criticized Kardiner for minimizing or omitting the Oedipus complex and the tripartite structure of the psyche. In fact, Kardiner disputed the universality of the Oedipus complex and believed that it only emerged when cultural proscriptions of sexual behavior result in the fusion of sexual and dependency needs toward the mother. This was the case, he said, in Plainville, and by extension in most of Western culture.

Concluding Remarks

Abram Kardiner attempted a synthesis of cultural and Freudian analysis, and while the concept of "basic personality" as the structure that mediates "primary" and "second" institutions has been dropped, the interest in cultural systems as projective systems remains. Psychoanalytic anthropologists (e.g., Spiro, Stein, and LaBarre) continued to relate concepts of morality and the religious to the exigencies of early childhood, and even today there is still a lively debate on the universality of the Oedipus complex. The eclipse of the Kardinerian approach, in fact, has less to do with the rejection of psychocultural synthesis than with the general retreat from encompassing social theory in the field of anthropology as a whole. Kardiner hearkens back to an earlier phase in the development of the discipline, to a time when it was considered possible (even necessary) to connect biological, political/economic, cultural, and psychological dynamics.

Charles W. Nuckolls

See also Culture and Personality; DuBois, Cora; Freud, Sigmund; Kluckhohn, Clyde; LeVine, Robert; Linton, Ralph; Psychological Anthropology; Wallace, Anthony F. C.

Further Readings

Kardiner, A. (1939). *The individual and his society: The psychodynamics of primitive social organization.* New York, NY: Columbia University Press.

———. (with Linton, R., Du Bois, C., & West, J.). (1945). *The psychological frontiers of society.* New York, NY: Columbia University Press.

Mead, M. (n.d.). "Plan for Kardiner review," Container I-20, The Papers of Margaret Mead, Manuscript Division, Library of Congress. (quoted in Manson, William, The Psychodynamics of Culture: Abram Kardiner and Neo-Freudian Anthropology. New York: Greenwood Press, 59–60)

KLUCKHOHN, CLYDE

Clyde Kay Maben Kluckhohn (1905–1960) made three significant contributions to the discipline of anthropology—(1) his pioneering ethnography, (2) his innovative approach to cultural theory, and (3) his long-term service to the profession. His field studies of the Navaho Indians of New Mexico are still unsurpassed, and he was one of the founders of the subdiscipline known as culture and personality, or psychological anthropology. As an organizer and administrator, he was a major figure in the development of cultural anthropology from 1936 until his untimely death in 1960, and he spent most of his academic life at Harvard University as a student and a professor. He was a central figure in creating institutional bonds among anthropologists at different universities, and between them and agencies of the federal government. During World War II, Kluckhohn served with the U.S. Office of War Information, analyzing the problems of morale in the Japanese population. After the war, he was the first director of the Russian Research Center at Harvard, founded in 1947 with a Carnegie grant. He served as chair of the anthropology department from 1957 until his death and was also at various times director of Harvard's Institute of Ethnic Affairs and a consultant to the U.S. Indian Service.

Biography

Born in Iowa, Kluckhohn received his undergraduate education at Princeton and the University of Wisconsin, before attending Oxford University on a Rhodes scholarship, graduating in 1931 with a master's degree in social anthropology. At Oxford, he was exposed to the "culture-circle" ethnohistorical theories of Wilhelm Schmidt at the University of Vienna, before returning to the United States to take his doctorate in anthropology from Harvard University in 1936. His major intellectual influences at Harvard were the sociologist Talcott Parsons and the social psychologist Gordon Allport, as well as the linguist Edward Sapir, who was then at Yale University. Immediately on finishing his doctoral studies, Kluckhohn joined the Harvard faculty. His doctoral dissertation was largely a composite of then current anthropological theories, titled simply *Some Aspects of Contemporary Theory in Cultural Anthropology*. It has not been published.

Kluckhohn's 1936 dissertation reflected his academic training up to that time. It was a survey, one might say a hodgepodge, of ideas from the Boasians, from structural functionalism, from the culture circle, and from recent psychology, with Kluckhohn taking the role of synthesizer of these various topics and themes. This was a pattern that continued throughout his career: Kluckhohn was an eclectic synthesizer, never developing a tight theoretical scheme of his own.

Kluckhohn had become acquainted with the Navaho Indians when, as a 17-year-old, he was sent to the Southwest to recover from a serious disease, probably tuberculosis. Kluckhohn stayed with a mother's cousin on a sheep ranch bordering the Navaho Reservation. Over the next few years, Kluckhohn not only recovered from his illness but also became an expert horseman, traveling about the Reservation and learning to speak Navaho. He wrote two travel books on these experiences, *To the Foot of the Rainbow* (1927) and *Beyond the Rainbow* (1933).

Kluckhohn and Anthropological Theory

Perhaps Kluckhohn's theoretical posture as he graduated from Harvard in 1936 can be best understood if we picture him with a wealth of diverse theoretical training in his background, from social anthropology to psychiatry, returning to the Navahos for professional ethnographic work after a long absence. Like other intellectuals of his generation who went on to become the founders of culture and personality studies, Kluckhohn was in a marvelous position to create a novel theoretical perspective as he undertook the integration of the various schools of theory he had studied. This position was enhanced during the next decade by the increasing possibilities of global fieldwork made possible in the wake of World War II, because of global political changes and the increase in available funding.

Although Kluckhohn continually published ethnographic works over the next 2 decades, they were not necessarily coordinated among themselves or congruent with the theoretical work he published in the same period. Talcott Parsons and Evon Vogt observed that Kluckhohn's failure to publish a full-scale ethnography of the Navaho often drew criticism from his colleagues. The most thorough and best structured of Kluckhohn's ethnographic works is undoubtedly *Navaho Witchcraft* (1944), which comprises 242 pages of first-person narrative based on fieldwork conducted in the 1930s. Strangely for ethnographic books of the day, it is not richly illustrated and contains but one tiny drawing (p. 187) and no other diagrams or maps. But the book is cogent and well written, and it attracted a large nonprofessional audience as well as the admiration of colleagues and students.

Ten additional previously published pieces of Navaho ethnography are collected in Kluckhohn's Festschrift, published in 1962 as *Culture and Behavior*, edited by his son Richard Kluckhohn. They address ethnographic topics such as women's songs, ceremonial patterns, dreams, socialization, and personality formation. But altogether, these published works do not constitute a complete ethnography. Missing, for example, are quantitative examinations of major topics such as demography and Navaho techniques of farming and stock raising.

Values Orientation Method

Historians and critics of the field of culture and personality usually place Kluckhohn among the founders, alongside Ruth Benedict, Erik Erikson, Ralph Linton, Margaret Mead, Edward Sapir, and Benjamin Whorf, although some observers have assigned him to a secondary echelon of theorists, along with Cora DuBois and Abram Kardiner, perhaps because of his eclecticism. In any event, Kluckhohn's particular theoretical contributions to the field became known as the Values Orientation Method, or sometimes "The Harvard Study of Values," an approach that is probably best known from *Variations in Value Orientations*, written by his wife, Florence Kluckhohn, and the University of Chicago psychologist Fred Strodtbeck, published a year after Clyde Kluckhohn's death. In general, the principal themes of the Values Orientation Method spread among Kluckhohn's many books and articles can be summarized as follows:

1. *The importance of psychoanalysis in uncovering cultural attitudes:* Kluckhohn not only believed that authentic but masked attitudes could be uncovered from native subjects but also suggested that ethnocentric biases among anthropology students, which might impede their success in the field, could be detected and resolved by their own psychoanalysis, which he recommended for aspiring fieldworkers. He asserted that psychoanalysis was "scientific."

2. *How cultural attitudes affect international politics*, especially war making, by reference not only to his own research but also to the swaddling and toilet-training hypotheses developed by psychological anthropologists including Ruth Benedict and Geoffrey Gorer during and immediately following

World War II: These blossomed into the "National Character Studies," which played an important role in anthropology in the 1940s and early 1950s. However, such studies invited harsh criticism largely because they were based on literary sources and the memories of expatriates, rather than fieldwork. Kluckhohn observed and participated in a subsequent debate about the utility of such studies, largely through his role in the Russian Research Center.

3. *The beneficial effects of "culture crossing":* Far from being a racial or a cultural chauvinist, at least in his early years, the young Kluckhohn saw the social and intellectual benefits that accrued to persons of "mixed" ancestry; mostly he meant mixed European ancestry. Later in his life, he was sometimes ambivalent about the effects of Black-White "miscegenation" on personal behavior. Especially in Chapter 5 of *Mirror for Man*, titled "Race: A Modern Myth," Kluckhohn seems to hedge against a strictly egalitarian position concerning racial differences, suggesting that "temperament," "mental capacity," and musical ability might be unequally distributed among the "races."

4. *Making anthropology more "scientific":* Although Kluckhohn continually used the word appreciatively, it is not clear what he meant by "science." Perhaps he meant only "logic" or "clear thinking." He does not seem to have believed that science required defining variables, hypothesizing the consequences of the interactions among variables and testing the hypotheses by experiments that are replicable. Rather, Kluckhohn tended to use the term *science* rather loosely. Although he admired statistical work, his own research was not quantitative.

5. *Values Orientation Theory:* This was spun off Kluckhohn's ideas about national character and explicitly comprised analysis of the following topics as treated in different cultures: (1) Human Nature, (2) the Man-Nature Relationship (developed with his wife, Florence Kluckhohn), (3) Time, (4) Activity, and (5) Social Relations. This formulation of a research agenda has probably attracted more negative attention than any other of Kluckhohn's theoretical constructions. All the social sciences seems to be embodied in number 5, while number 3, Time, seems to be more a philosophical than a social science category. Carried forward by Florence

Kluckhohn and Fred Strodtbeck after Clyde Kluckhohn's death, Values Orientation Theory stimulated a generation of social psychology students in the 1960s.

6. *The importance of language:* As an ethnographer, Kluckhohn was especially attentive to native language, and was probably at his best when describing the language used in Navaho ceremonies. In the narrative portion of *Navaho Witchcraft*, he provided 130 pages of description, which admirably employed the social anthropology he learned at Oxford. This material is preceded by a phonetic guide and followed by rich, substantial appendices totaling 85 pages, concerning details of language, the context of language use, and symbolism. He was especially careful in noting semantic variation in the terms he recorded.

Key Later Works

Kluckhohn's early theoretical contribution *Personality in Nature, Culture and Society* (1948), coedited with Henry Murray, was intended as a textbook for culture and personality. It incorporated contributions from a number of distinguished anthropologists—Benedict, A. Irving Hallowell, Jules Henry, Mead, Hortense Powdermaker, and John Whiting—and articles from psychologically oriented scholars such as Allport, J. S. Bruner, John Dollard, Erich Fromm, and David Levy. Contributions from the sociologists Robert Merton and Talcott Parsons were also included. For many scholars of culture and personality, this became the standard textbook and reference in the field. For their part, Kluckhohn and Murray essentially defined the field in this volume in two coauthored articles titled "Outline of a Conception of Personality" and "Personality Formation: The Determinants."

The next year, Kluckhohn published *Mirror for Man* (1949), which by 1971 had gone through 17 printings. It was written, as Kluckhohn put it in his preface, "for the layman, not for the carping professional." It became a standard introductory textbook for anthropology in many colleges and universities in the 1950s and 1960s. It not only covers the four traditional fields of anthropology—biological, archaeology, social cultural, and linguistic anthropology—but also, not surprisingly, contains a full chapter on culture and personality.

Another side of Kluckhohn's character and intellect is also exhibited in *Mirror for Man*: his American patriotism or national chauvinism. Especially in view of Kluckhohn's statements regarding the need for psychoanalysis to purge ethnocentrism from the thinking of potential fieldworkers, certain statements in the book seem out of place. In Chapter 9, for example, Kluckhohn claims that no people moralize as much as Americans and that American mothers offer love to their children based on their meeting certain performance standards, as if this kind of behavior provides contrasts with normal or ideal behavior in other cultures. But no concrete evidence is offered. Kluckhohn tried to correct this methodological deficiency in an article published in *Daedalus* in 1958, explicitly endorsing a "conservative" political perspective, based on colorful interviews of 69 young men in the Boston area, sponsored by the Russian Research Center. As director of the center, Kluckhohn repeatedly criticized Soviet values and politics, while in *Mirror for Man* and the *Daedalus* article, he embraced the parallel but allegedly opposite moral precepts of his native country.

For many people, especially colleagues and graduate students in anthropology, Kluckhohn's most useful and enduring book is *Culture: A Critical Review of Concepts and Definitions*, coauthored with Alfred L. Kroeber and first published in 1952. It begins with a 70-page history of the word *culture* and then moves on to an equally lengthy list of specific uses and definitions of it, divided into the categories of Descriptive, Historical, Normative, Psychological, Structural, Genetic, and Incomplete. This is followed by a section of comments and criticisms by philosophers and scientists of the past, and a final section where Kroeber and Kluckhohn try to make sense of it all. As professors and students have discovered over the past half-century, the value of the book is that Kluckhohn and Kroeber have raised these issues in such an interesting and entertaining manner. The basic idea and pedagogy of this book, as well as his careful work in Navaho ethnography, probably constitute the heart of Kluckhohn's intellectual legacy.

John H. Moore

See also Benedict, Ruth F.; Cognitive Anthropology; Culture and Personality; Diffusionism,

Hyperdiffusionism, *Kulturkreise*; DuBois, Cora; Kardiner, Abram; Linton, Ralph; Mead, Margaret; Parsons, Talcott; Psychological Anthropology; Sapir, Edward; Whorf, Benjamin Lee

Further Readings

Kluckhohn, C. (1949). *Mirror for man*. New York, NY: Fawcett.

———. (1958). The evolution of contemporary American values. *Daedalus, 87*(2), 78–109.

———. (1962). *Culture and behavior*. New York, NY: Free Press.

———. (1963). *Navaho witchcraft*. Boston, MA: Beacon Press.

Kluckhohn, C., & Leighton, D. (1974). *The Navaho*. Cambridge, MA: Harvard University Press.

Lindesmith, A. R., & Strauss, A. L. (1950). A critique of culture-personality writings. *American Sociological Review, 15*(5), 587–600.

Parsons, T., & Vogt, E. Z. (1962). Clyde Kay Maben Kluckhohn 1905–1960. *American Anthropologist, 64*, 140–161.

KROEBER, ALFRED L.

Alfred Louis Kroeber (1876–1960) was the leading American anthropologist of his generation. Widely regarded as the successor to his mentor, Franz Boas, he dominated the discipline during the first half of the 20th century.

Biography and Major Works

Alfred Kroeber was born in Hoboken, New Jersey, and grew up in New York City. His German immigrant father was an upper-middle-class importer. As a child, Alfred was bilingual, speaking German at home. The broadly humanistic culture of German immigrants was a decisive influence on his intellectual formation; the study of natural history was also fundamental to his development. He was educated at Columbia University, earning bachelor's (1896) and master's degrees (1897) in English literature.

In 1896, Kroeber was introduced to Franz Boas and anthropology. His earliest anthropology research was with a group of Inuit (Eskimo), then living in the city. For his doctoral dissertation on Arapaho Indian decorative symbolism, Kroeber did fieldwork in Wyoming and Oklahoma (1898–1899), sponsored by the American Museum of Natural History, where Boas served as a curator. His 1901 doctorate was the first to be awarded by Columbia for anthropology.

Kroeber first came to California in 1900 for a curatorial position at the California Academy of Sciences, San Francisco, but he soon left when it became clear that there would be little provision for field research. In the fall of 1901, Kroeber was hired by the University of California, which had just initiated a department and museum of anthropology, founded by the regent, Phoebe A. Hearst. With periods of sabbatical and leave, Kroeber spent the rest of his professional life at the university, serving as instructor (1901), assistant professor (1906), associate professor (1911), and professor (1919), retiring in 1946 as professor emeritus. In the University of California's Museum of Anthropology, he served as curator and director. Although he effectively held these positions from 1901 and 1909, respectively, the titles were not formally given until 1909 and 1925.

Most of Kroeber's fieldwork was in California, especially between the years 1901 and 1911. In 1903, he began a systematic survey of California Indian cultures, including his own fieldwork and that of his students and colleagues. Between 1911 and 1916, Kroeber worked with Ishi, the last Yahi, who lived at the museum, then in San Francisco. Today this ethnographic relationship is probably the thing for which Kroeber is most famous, at least in the mind of the general public. With his publication of the summary *Handbook of the Indians of California* in 1925, Kroeber effectively founded the scholarly study of California Indians.

During the 1910s, Kroeber spent several summers in Zuni, New Mexico, sponsored by the American Museum of Natural History. During the first 6 months of 1918, he focused on the museum's Philippines collection, curating an exhibition and writing an excellent handbook, despite his lack of any fieldwork in the country.

By the late 1910s, following the deaths of his wife, Henrietta, and of Ishi, Kroeber underwent a personal and professional crisis. He became interested in psychoanalysis and developed a private practice in the field (1918–1923) before returning full-time to anthropology.

Although Kroeber had not been interested in archaeology during his early career, after 1920, he turned increasingly to the field, as he worked with

the ancient Peruvian collections at the university museum. His study of Max Uhle's collections with the graduate students William Duncan Strong, Anna Gayton, and Lila O'Neale led to his excavations in Peru (1925, 1926, and 1942), the first two trips sponsored by the Field Museum in Chicago. For the rest of his life, Kroeber continued to study the chronological development of Nasca pottery designs.

Kroeber's lifelong interest in geography, encouraged by his Berkeley colleague Carl Sauer, culminated in his 1939 monograph on *Cultural and Natural Areas of Native North America*. Leading up to this study was a second survey of California Indians, the Culture Element Distribution Survey, carried out by his students.

Kroeber's last major work was *Configurations of Culture Growth* (1944), an ambitious comparison of civilizations, focusing on the development of artistic styles. He extended these ideas in a series of late lectures, published as *Style and Civilizations* (1957).

As a noted teacher, Kroeber mentored at least two generations of students, from Samuel Barrett, the department's first doctorate in 1908, through a cohort of important students in the late 1920s and 1930s, including William Duncan Strong, Julian Steward, Cora DuBois, Ralph Beals, George Foster, and Robert F. Heizer. With his fellow Boasian Robert H. Lowie and his protégé Edward W. Gifford, Kroeber made the department the largest and most important, as well as the oldest, in the American West. With his student Thomas T. Waterman, Kroeber wrote the first—and for many years, the only—textbook in the field: *Anthropology* (1923; revised edition, 1948).

Alfred Kroeber played a dominant role in the institutional organization of the discipline of anthropology: as one of the founders of the American Anthropological Association in 1902 and as its president (1917–1918). He was also president of the American Folklore Society (1906) and a founder of the Linguistic Society of America (president in 1940).

He helped organize displays of anthropology and Native American culture for the Golden Gate International Exposition, San Francisco (1939–1940); during World War II, he was the director of an Army Special Training Program at Berkeley on the cultures and languages of East Asia (1943–1945).

After his retirement, Kroeber continued to teach, travel, and write. During these years, he focused on issues of style and comparative civilizations.

His stature in the discipline was indicated by the comprehensive conference he organized in 1952, whose proceedings he edited as *Anthropology Today: An Encyclopedic Inventory* (1953). In the 1950s, Kroeber offered testimony on aboriginal occupancy of territory for the U.S. Indian Claims Commission, arguing against his former student Julian Steward. Although a social and political liberal, he believed that these personal values should be kept separate from his professional efforts. He also spent much time going over old research, preparing manuscripts for publication.

Kroeber was married twice: first to Henrietta Rothschild in 1906, who died in 1913, and for the second time, in 1926, to Theodora Kracaw Brown, who later became famous for her writings on Ishi. Along with his two stepsons, Theodore and Clifton, Kroeber had two children with her: Karl and Ursula (later LeGuin, the science fiction author).

Alfred Kroeber died in Paris, shortly after attending a conference in Austria. Over his lifetime, he was awarded numerous prizes and honorary doctorates, and the anthropology building at the University of California, Berkeley, was named after him in the year of his death. Kroeber's personal papers were given to The Bancroft Library, University of California, Berkeley.

Critical Contributions to Anthropology

Alfred Kroeber considered himself first of all an ethnologist, but given his wide-ranging interests and long life, he was able to make contributions to many areas of anthropology, including archaeology and linguistics as well as sociocultural anthropology. Virtually all of Kroeber's anthropology can be traced to his conception of culture and its patterning in space and time.

Culture Theory

Alfred Kroeber generally integrated his theoretical discussions with descriptive presentations. However, in his late anthology *The Nature of Culture* (1952), he explicitly summarized his cultural theory. Here, he restated his position that culture was a coherent and separate phenomenon that gave the discipline of anthropology its scholarly autonomy.

In his general orientation, Kroeber's anthropology was based on a unique combination of empirically rooted disciplines: natural history and the humanities; he fought against the grouping of anthropology as part of the social sciences. Despite his earlier background in natural history and his later foray into statistics during the Culture Element Distribution Survey, in the end, he shunned predicative models of causality and denied that anthropology was a science. In a famous debate with Boas in the 1930s, he accused his teacher of being more interested in causal explanation and the discovery of general laws.

Kroeber's most famous contribution to anthropological theory was his concept of the "superorganic," published first as an article in the *American Anthropologist* (1917). In opposition to Edward Sapir and many of his colleagues, he de-emphasized the role of the individual in culture. For Kroeber, culture applied only to a collective level, a world of meaning, norms, and values, and as such could not be explained by relating it to psychological or biological phenomena. With Clyde Kluckhohn and Talcott Parsons, he later distinguished between culture, viewed as a pattern of meaning, and society, which he applied to the behavior of individuals and groups.

Kroeber shared his basic theory of culture as patterning with Boas and many of his students. Employing a set of related terms to characterize cultural wholes—patterns, complexes, and configurations—he emphatically avoided analyses of structure and function. He felt that a comparison of these holistically conceived cultural types could reveal the processes of their historical productions. Kroeber expanded these perceptions, first worked out among tribal societies, to the styles of entire civilizations. This kind of metahistory was similar to the work of Herbert Spencer, Oswald Spengler, and Arnold Toynbee.

Kroeber's cultural relativism was basically Boasian, although, unlike Boas, there was a stronger residue of Victorian evolutionism and cultural ranking (derived from E. B. Tylor and Spencer).

Ethnography and Geographical Orientations

As a student of Franz Boas, Kroeber made important contributions to ethnography, most notably in California but also in the American Southwest, Plains, and Arctic. Among this work was important intensive study of particular peoples, advocated by his mentor: especially the Yurok and Mojave. Like

Boas, Kroeber never wrote a single, comprehensive ethnography of any particular culture. Yet, unlike Boas, throughout his life, Kroeber stressed survey and cultural comparison. Along with Otis T. Mason and Clark Wissler, Kroeber was one of the prime formulators of the concept of culture areas. His concerns with cultural boundaries and mapping led to the definition of culture regions of Native North America. He extended this comparative approach in his work on civilizations.

Like most ethnographers of his generation, Kroeber's conception of ethnography was not what we would call participant observation. Instead, it was essentially the collection of memory culture, based on collecting data and interviews. Taking these sources, his ethnographic work is characterized by a focus on the "ethnographic present," not the tracing of historical developments in the postcontact period. His interest in cultural reconstruction was embodied most thoroughly in his California handbook, published in 1925. Despite his knowledge to the contrary, he did not want to take into account the massive genocide and culture change under which these populations had suffered. This approach was most notable in his writings on Ishi. Also like his mentor, Kroeber never taught ethnographic methodology, expecting his students to pick up the necessary skills on their own.

Temporal Styles and the Comparative Study of Civilizations

Another aspect in which Kroeber went beyond his mentor was his greater emphasis on temporal patterns. He famously explored this topic in several essays (1919 and 1940) on historical trends in European women's dress styles, especially hem lengths, which he correlated with periods of political instability. Kroeber was one of the pioneers in developing the archaeological method of seriation: a system of relative dating based on design sequences or the changing frequency of styles. He first applied this perspective in 1916 to the design styles of Zuni potsherds and later to the pottery styles of Nasca, Peru.

Between 1934 and 1938, Kroeber sent 13 students to 254 tribes or bands in the American West to determine the presence or absence of hundreds of ethnographic traits in these societies. The results of this work were published in 25 reports. This tracing of the distribution of discrete and narrowly defined cultural "elements" was almost the opposite of his earlier, and later, work on cultural patterning and integration.

Partly as a result of his belief that this atomistic methodology had failed to explain cultural processes, Kroeber turned increasingly to so-called "configurational" approaches. Not recognizing any substantive differences between tribal societies and states—only methodological ones—for him it was more a question of finding the suitable historical documentation for his analyses. In his later work on cultural creativity, he related the production of individually creative works to evolving collective traditions. Nevertheless, he maintained a cultural determinism, allowing relatively little room for personal creativity. This collectivist orientation also underlay his general antipathy to the Culture-and-Personality school of the 1930s (despite his sympathy for Benedict's concept of patterning).

Kinship and Social Organization

Although kinship study was not one of his major theoretical areas, Kroeber did make an important contribution to the field. In his 1909 essay "Classificatory Systems of Relationship," he argued that kin terms should not be regarded as direct reflections of social systems but more as linguistic or conceptual categories. This position, the basis of his "Zuni Kin and Clan" (1917), was challenged by most British social anthropologists, particularly W. H. R. Rivers and A. R. Radcliffe-Brown.

Language and Linguistics

Compared with some Boasian ethnographers, Kroeber contributed relatively little to linguistics. Yet he did field research on more than 2 dozen Californian languages, in many cases writing the first grammatical descriptions of these languages. Even more fundamental was his work on language classification in mapping and comprehending the relations of Native Californians. Between 1903 and 1919, Kroeber worked with Harvard's Roland B. Dixon to reduce the number of language families in the region, anticipating the continental classificatory work of Edward Sapir. Kroeber and Dixon were the first, in 1913, to identify the Hokan and Penutian families.

In his work on the speech of Zuni children and Yurok ritual oratory, Kroeber was an innovator in the anthropological study of speech, as opposed to language. Toward the end of his life, he became interested in animal communication. Methodologically, Kroeber was an innovator in the ethnographic use of the wax cylinder machine to record speech and music, especially in using multiple cylinders to record lengthy narratives.

Kroeber's Legacy

Author of more than 500 publications, Alfred Kroeber dominated the field during the first half of the 20th century. As the last great generalist in American anthropology, he made important contributions to all aspects of the field except physical anthropology. In addition to his substantial theoretical and ethnographic contributions, he helped formulate the primary institutional structures of American anthropology.

In many ways, however, Alfred Kroeber is largely forgotten today. Although he is rarely cited by contemporary anthropologists, he has continued to influence anthropology in recent decades.

Kroeber's legacy in Native California was immense but controversial. As an ethnographer and generalist, his contribution to the study of California Indians is foundational. Yet he has been criticized for his perceived colonialist relationship with Ishi, his declaration that groups such as the Costanoan (Ohlone) and Gabrielino (Tongva) were extinct, his stress on the salience of wealth over religion among the Yurok, and his avoidance of genocide and culture change as historical factors. Yet one must note that this shift in his reputation is due to more general changes in intellectual and cultural climates, which were largely the result of his own work.

With Clark Wissler, Kroeber helped codify the culture area approach. Through his student Julian Steward, his concern with issues of the environment and regional patterning led to the development of cultural ecology.

In archaeology, his pioneering work in seriation is a foundation of the field in North America; his analyses of the pottery styles of Nasca, Peru, were later developed by his Berkeley colleague John H. Rowe and his students. In linguistics, beyond his formative contributions to Native California studies, his work on speech made him a forerunner of the ethnography of speaking developed by Dell Hymes. Kroeber's interest in historical questions

and statistical methods made him a developer of the fields of glottochronology or lexicostatistics, which he had first explored in a 1907 paper on the Yokuts language.

Kroeber's work on comparative civilizations was an inspiration for the work of Robert Redfield and the development of area studies in academia. His work on cultural configurations influenced the art historian George Kubler's *The Shapes of Time* (1962). More recently, it has attracted attention among anthropologists and historians, most notably Eric Wolf's *Europe and the People Without History* (1982).

Kroeber's concept of the superorganic has been widely criticized as reification, and many regard his "descriptive integration" of concrete phenomena as overly particularist. In many ways, however, Kroeber was a forerunner of the recent development of cultural studies. Through his work on cultural theory with Clyde Kluckhohn, Kroeber was an inspiration for the interpretative anthropology of Clifford Geertz. His rooting of kinship in the development of language made him a precursor of what would become componential analysis and ethnosemantics. His kinship theory influenced David Schneider, and through him many modern students in gender studies.

Whatever the vicissitudes of historical reputations, Alfred Kroeber's leading role in the anthropology of his day will ensure his relevance to future generations.

Ira Jacknis

See also Boas, Franz; Culture Area Approach; Historical Particularism; Steward, Julian; University of California, Berkeley

Further Readings

Darnell, R. (2001). *Invisible genealogies: A history of Americanist anthropology*. Lincoln: University of Nebraska Press.

Gilkerson, J. S. (2010). *Anthropologists and the rediscovery of America, 1886–1965*. New York, NY: Cambridge University Press.

Kroeber, A. L. (1925). *Handbook of the Indians of California* (Bureau of American Ethnology, Bulletin No. 78). Washington, DC: Smithsonian Institution.

———. (1939). *Cultural and natural areas of Native North America* (University of California Publications in

American Archaeology and Ethnology, Vol. 38).
Berkeley: University of California.

———. (1944). *Configurations of culture growth.* Berkeley: University of California Press.

———. (1952). *The nature of culture.* Chicago, IL: University of Chicago Press.

———. (1957). *Style and civilizations.* Ithaca, NY: Cornell University Press.

Kroeber, A. L., & Kluckhohn, C. (1952). *Culture: A critical review of concepts and definitions* (Papers of the Peabody Museum of American Archaeology and Ethnology, Vol. 47, no. 1). Cambridge, MA: Harvard University.

Kroeber, A. L., & Kroeber, C. (Eds.). (2003). *Ishi in three centuries.* Lincoln: University of Nebraska Press.

Kroeber, T. (1970). *Alfred Kroeber: A personal configuration.* Berkeley: University of California Press.

Steward, J. H. (1961). Alfred Louis Kroeber, 1876–1960. *American Anthropologist, 63,* 1038–1060.

Thoresen, T. H. H. (1971). *A. L. Kroeber's theory of culture: The early years* (Doctoral dissertation). American Civilization, University of Iowa, IA.

Kuper, Hilda B.

Hilda Kuper (née Beemer; 1911–1982), Swazi ethnographer par excellence, critical colonial analyst, littérateur, and liberal political activist, belonged to a remarkable cohort of South African anthropologists that included Max Gluckman, Ellen Hellman, and Eileen Jensen Krige, who, inspired by Agnes Winifred Hoernle (affectionately known as the "mother of South African social anthropology"), all studied social anthropology at the same time at the University of the Witwatersrand.

Kuper was born to Jewish immigrants on August 23, 1911, in the Southern Rhodesian town of Bulawayo. The family moved to Johannesburg when her father died and Hilda, the youngest of five siblings, was six. Lack of financial resources was to be a major obstacle during her early career. She entered the University of the Witwatersrand in 1927, where, on a whim and encouraged by her school friend Max Gluckman, she enrolled in a yearlong social anthropology course taught by Hoernle, one of the leading liberals in South Africa. Hoernle had a profound effect on Kuper in how she interpreted the causes and effects of injustice, inequality, and cruelty. While Hoernle had worked closely with Radcliffe-Brown, she also grounded her students in European and American diffusionist approaches. The result was that Kuper was to see them as complementary to her own.

In the second and final year of the undergraduate social anthropology major, Hoernle went on a sabbatical and was replaced by Isaac Schapera, who took the class on a monthlong field trip to Botswana. After graduating in 1930, Kuper worked at the South African Institute of Race Relations, where she did a pioneering urban anthropological study examining the impact of the liquor prohibition on Africans and how women coped by developing voluntary organizations. Using a small inheritance, Kuper made her way to London, where from 1932 to 1934 she was a participant in Bronisław Malinowski's famous seminar at the London School of Economics and served as Malinowski's research assistant. Later, when she successfully applied for funds from the International Africa Institute to undertake fieldwork for her doctorate, one of her referees, Schapera, wrote that she "was extremely bright although temperamentally rather romantic." He thought so highly of her that he was encouraging her to study the "woman side of things" among the Tswana and had even proposed marriage to her to ensure this research. Although they didn't marry, this "romantic temperament" was to lead to one of Kuper's unique and pioneering contributions to anthropology, her experimenting with alternative ways of presenting data and insights.

Serendipitously, while in South Africa to address an international educational conference, Malinowski met the King of Swaziland, Sobhuza II, who invited him to visit his kingdom after the conference. Malinowski and his research assistant, Kuper, then spent 2 weeks there, regaled by the commissioner and the king, and the result was a lifelong commitment to the Swazi people stretching from 1934 to 1984. Sobhuza, who ruled Swaziland from 1921 to 1983, was Kuper's personal friend and confidante, and he appointed her his official biographer and awarded her Swazi citizenship.

Her 1936 marriage to the lawyer Leo Kuper (uncle to the anthropologist Adam Kuper) precipitated a crisis of sorts as her grant did not allow for married female researchers. Fortunately, the matter was resolved, and she completed her fieldwork and took a position as a senior lecturer at Wits University in Johannesburg from 1940 to 1947. During this time, she managed to write up her dissertation, which was published in two volumes in 1947, *The Swazi: An African Aristocracy* and *The Uniform of Colour*. While the first volume was almost vintage Malinowskian, in the second volume Kuper broke away from the discipline's emphasis on "social control" and "culture contact" by combining an analysis of changing institutions with an implied critique of society. Her analysis of Swazi militarism, internal politics, the colonial state, and surrogate colonialism was revolutionary. It exposed the hypocrisy of the ruling White colonial elite, who owned more than two thirds of the land in the Swaziland Protectorate and who had tried to have her expelled from the Protectorate because of her liberal political views.

After the Second World War, a demobilized Leo Kuper decided to become a sociologist, and Hilda accompanied him to North Carolina and Birmingham (United Kingdom) for his studies before Leo accepted the Chair of Sociology at the University of Natal. Unable to secure a position in the anthropology department, Kuper obtained funding to do some 4 years' fieldwork on the Indian community in Natal, working with Sidney Kark, the pioneering community health exponent. The result was a landmark study, *Indian People in Natal* (1960), on immigrant communities. The Kupers became actively involved in the Gandhian passive resistance movement against apartheid in Durban and in the formation of the Liberal Party and courageously stood up to various forms of government intimidation and harassment.

Eventually, both Kupers accepted positions at the University of California, Los Angeles, where Hilda taught from 1963 until her retirement in 1977. There she made three major contributions to anthropology. She pioneered the study of biography in anthropology with her authorized biography of Sobhuza. More important, with Leo and her colleague M. G. Smith, she developed the intellectual underpinnings of the Plural Society approach to understanding complex and colonial societies. She also explored alternative ways of presenting ethnographic data and understanding through fiction. Her novel *The Bite of Hunger* (1965) and her play *A Witch in My Heart* (1970) are exemplars of intuitive communication of deep meanings that complement the knowledge of another culture gained by discursive scholarship.

Perhaps most intriguing about Kuper's legacy is her later realization that rather than the anthropologist exploiting colonial subjects, in her case, the Swazi elite skillfully used her and other progressive South Africans to adroitly and constantly invent myths and traditions in the interests of the hegemony of the Swazi royalty.

Robert Gordon

See also Gluckman, Max; Malinowski, Bronisław; Schapera, Isaac

Further Readings

Kuper, H. (1947). *An African aristocracy: Rank among the Swazi*. London, UK: Oxford University Press.

———. (1947). *The uniform of colour: A study of White-Black relationships in Swaziland*. Johannesburg, South Africa: Witwatersrand University Press.

———. (1960). *Indian people in Natal*. Pietermaritzberg, South Africa: Natal University Press.

———. (1965). *The bite of hunger*. New York, NY: Harcourt, Brace.

———. (1970). *A witch in my heart*. Oxford, UK: Oxford University Press.

———. (1978). *Sobhuza II*. London, UK: Duckworth.

LABOV, WILLIAM

William Labov (1927–) is an American linguist best known for his central role in the foundation of modern sociolinguistics, and more specifically for an approach to the investigation of language in its social context known as *variationist sociolinguistics*. He rose to prominence in the 1960s as part of a broad movement in the social sciences to focus attention on language as a social phenomenon in fields like linguistics, anthropology, sociology, and philosophy of language. As such, Labov's work stands in dialogue with prominent anthropologists from that period, including Dell Hymes and John Gumperz, who share a focus on the complex relationship between language and society. What sets Labov apart is his end goal of developing a socially informed linguistic theory and his methods, which focus on the quantification of variables as a means to describing social stratification and linguistic change. He is currently one of America's most distinguished linguists, with a body of work spanning 50 years.

Labov grew up in Rutherford and then Fort Lee, New Jersey. Educated at Harvard (BA in 1948), he worked as an industrial chemist at the Union Ink Company (1949–1960), before returning to academia at Columbia (MA in 1963, PhD in 1964). There, he worked under the direction of Uriel Weinreich, a pioneer in the field of language contact and a scholar of Yiddish. Labov stayed on to teach at Columbia from 1964 to 1970. Since 1971, Labov has been a professor of linguistics at the University of Pennsylvania in Philadelphia, a city that has served as a laboratory for much of his research.

Diachronic Studies of Linguistic Behavior and Social Patterning

Labov broke from linguistic tradition, which in the 1960s was more and more dominated by Noam Chomsky and generative grammar, by rejecting the *idiolect* (the variety of language unique to an individual) as the primary object of study. Generative linguists considered language a property of the individual and thus relied on individual speaker data, often in the form of intuitions or grammaticality judgments. In direct contrast, Labov argued that language is a community property and that individuals' speech can only be understood relative to that of the *speech communities* they belong to. Speech communities are considered to share linguistic norms and to be the level at which linguistic patterning can be most clearly observed. Labov also called for a combination of the *synchronic* (studies of language at one point in time) and the *diachronic* (studies of change over time). This was in response to the emphasis on synchrony made by both the newer generative and the earlier structuralist traditions (the latter being well known in anthropology due to the influence of Claude Lévi-Strauss). Labov's suggestion was to move away from the exclusively synchronic study of abstract idiolects to consider the variation in communities of speakers and how these patterns of variation provide information about community change over time. In this, he updated traditions in dialectology, which had combined synchrony and diachrony by collecting data in the field to answer largely historical questions. While European in origin, dialectology was compatible with an earlier American tradition of descriptive, anthropologically influenced linguistics, deriving from Edward Sapir and Franz Boas, who were well aware of the extent of linguistic diversity, if not necessarily of intracommunity variation.

Synchronically, Labov set out to demonstrate that linguistic behavior varies systematically according to the social patterning found in speech communities. His first study found that local attitudes toward island life on Martha's Vineyard (Massachusetts) were correlated with the pronunciation of certain vowels. He then demonstrated the social stratification of several features of the New York City dialect. In the famous Department Store Study, Labov visited three stores of differing social status (Klein's, Macy's, and Saks), and he found that the sales clerks had corresponding differences in their production of the *r*s in the phrase *fourth floor*. The main part of Labov's dissertation study was on the Lower East Side of Manhattan, where he recorded interviews with a random, socially stratified sample of the population. Published in 1966 (revised edition, 2006) as *The Social Stratification of English in New York City*, this work was more rigorous than dialectologists' previous attempts to observe variation in American English. It demonstrated that several features of pronunciation varied systematically with the social class of the speakers and also with the style of their speech, along a continuum from casual to formal. At the same time, Lower East Siders of all class backgrounds agreed in their negative evaluation of the local dialect. Labov argued that this was evidence that New Yorkers formed a single speech community, sharing norms for linguistic use as well as socially stratified patterns of production.

The variation present synchronically in New York City was further important, Labov argued, in that it related to diachronic change. For example, he found that for the upper middle class, the younger the speaker, the more likely the person was to pronounce the *r* after a vowel. Dismissing the alternative possibility of *age grading*—that is, that speakers use less postvocalic (*r*) as they age—Labov called this pattern *change in apparent time*: The synchronic variation between age-groups is a snapshot of a change in progress in the community. In addition,

patterns showing individual speakers using more postvocalic (*r*) in more formal styles (where more attention would be paid to speech) and middle class speakers leading in their use of postvocalic (*r*) were both indicative of what Labov calls *change from above* (above the level of conscious awareness). In this case, the change from above involved the adoption of an external prestige standard where coda (*r*) was pronounced. The framework also includes *change from below*, which for Labov is a language- and community-internal process, involving changes that speakers are not consciously aware of. Change from below was exemplified in New York City by the raising of the vowel in *bad* toward *ey* (or even *ee*) and the vowel in *bought* toward *oo*.

Much of Labov's recent work pursues diachronic questions, including the three-volume *Principles of Linguistic Change* (1994, 2001, 2010), which acts as a compendium of variationist sociolinguistic work (including Labov's own studies of Philadelphia English), orienting it within the larger body of work seeking to understand the principles underlying language change.

Another major recent publication (with Sharon Ash and Charles Boberg) is the *Atlas of North American English* (2006), which presents an acoustic analysis of the dialects of the United States and Canada, delineating the boundaries of the major dialect regions and characterizing broad patterns of phonological change. Based on telephone fieldwork, this was the first dialect atlas to cover such a large region and to be based on instrumental measurements.

Labov aligns with the fields of dialectology and anthropology in his methodological contributions. He focuses on gathering naturalistic data, trying to observe the type of speech people use when unobserved. The most valuable speech to elicit for analysis he terms the *vernacular*, which refers to the most casual and systematic of an individual's speech styles. Labov pioneered a methodology known as the *sociolinguistic interview*, a face-to-face recorded session designed to elicit variation across contextual styles (from the vernacular to the very formal) in long stretches of naturalistic speech. The sociolinguistic interview provides the individual data that, when aggregated, is the primary evidence used in sociolinguistic analysis. Today, it is often used in combination with ethnographic observation, allowing researchers to bring both qualitative and quantitative linguistic observations to bear on their research questions.

A Quantitative Approach to Data Analysis

Labov adopts a quantitative approach to data analysis. His concept of the *linguistic variable* refers broadly to a set of referentially equivalent variants (ways of "saying the same thing"). Defining the linguistic variable allows for variants to be systematically tracked and counted across stretches of speech. Labov's earliest work used tables and graphs to compare the percentages of use of variants such as the presence or absence of *r* in phrases like *fourth floor*, aggregated over stylistic contexts and/or social classes. The regular patterns revealed in such displays constituted the evidence for *orderly heterogeneity* and the social stratification of the speech community, revealing intricate order in place of what had been dismissed as chaotic *free variation* by structuralist and generative linguists.

Later developments by Labov and others enabled a more sophisticated approach to the quantitative analysis of language. Computer programs called *variable rule programs* (VARBRUL) were developed to estimate the social and linguistic contextual effects on many types of linguistic alternations "coded" from naturalistic data. For example, researchers could use a single data set to show that a variable like *t/d* deletion (e.g., saying "wes' coast" instead of "west coast") is favored by particular social groups (e.g., by men more than by women) as well as in particular linguistic environments (e.g., before a consonant, as in *lef' hand*, more than before a vowel, as in *lef' out*). Over the next decades, practitioners would rely on this type of quantitative estimation to compare and contrast VARBRUL parameters between different varieties of a language as well as for studying individual varieties. Although statistical tools other than VARBRUL are now used, sociolinguists build on Labov's early demonstrations that linguistic variation is not random but is governed by orderly quantitative principles.

Nonstandard Language Varieties: Beyond the Deficit Model

Labov has also had a major impact through his focus on the description and legitimization of nonstandard language varieties, most notably the variety currently known as African American English (AAE).

In Harlem in the late 1960s, Labov directed a team of field-workers who conducted ethnographically informed group interviews with African American youth. In his 1972 book *Language in the Inner City*, Labov described the speech of his participants as linguistically structured and sociolinguistically patterned, reiterating his stance on the orderly heterogeneity of all linguistic systems. In the case of AAE, demonstrating its systematicity was crucial at the time, when popular theories like the *deficit hypothesis* posited that linguistic, cultural, or even genetic differences accounted for the poor performance of African American children in schools. The work of the sociologist Basil Bernstein on *restricted and elaborated codes* also contributed to the popular view—one that still holds today—that AAE is a poor or incomplete version of English and reflects a broader cultural deficit for African Americans. Labov has remained an activist throughout his career, working to bring insights from sociolinguistics to a broader audience, both academic and popular. He testified as an expert during the 1979 Ann Arbor trial, which established the precedent that the home language of Black children should be taken into account in public education. More recently, he has worked to develop tools for educators that draw on linguistic knowledge about nonstandard varieties like AAE and Latino English to improve the teaching of reading to minority students. Furthermore, his work has sparked a massive subdiscipline devoted to the study of AAE, large enough to be considered almost a separate branch of sociolinguistics.

Sociolinguistics remains heavily influenced by the variationist paradigm. While some approaches, including many qualitative subdisciplines like discourse analysis and interactional sociolinguistics, critique variationism's reliance on quantifiable data and its use of fixed macro-sociological categories, variationist sociolinguistics remains in dialogue with the broader field. The so-called third wave of variationist studies (developed by Penelope Eckert, herself a student of Labov's) proposes to extend and refine early variationism by retaining its use of empirical and quantifiable data while calling for a renewed focus on the individual, critiquing Labov's assertion that individuals are worthy of study only in the aggregate of speech communities. Eckert's focus on individual practice, style construction, and social meaning also differs from Labov's variationism in drawing on theoretical models from anthropology and social theory, including indexicality (from Charles Sanders Peirce and more recently revived by Michael Silverstein), enregisterment (Asif Agha), and language ideologies (Paul Kroskrity, Bambi Schieffelin).

Labov's own focus on the social life of language is primarily intended to inform linguistic theory. Nevertheless, his work has had a major impact on, and retains substantial relevance for, those who work at the intersections of language use and social behavior, across many disciplines.

Daniel Ezra Johnson and Kara Becker

See also Chomsky, Noam; Gumperz, John J.; Hymes, Dell; Sociolinguistics

Further Readings

Gordon, M. J. (2006). Interview with William Labov. *Journal of English Linguistics, 34*(4), 332–351.

———. (2013). *Labov: A guide for the perplexed.* London, UK: Continuum.

Hazen, K. (2010). Labov: Language variation and change. In W. Ruth, B. Johnstone, & P. E. Kerswill (Eds.), *The SAGE handbook of sociolinguistics* (pp. 24–39). London, UK: Sage.

Labov, W. (1963). The social motivation of a sound change. *Word, 19,* 273–309.

———. (1969). The logic of non-standard English. In J. Alatis (Ed.), *Linguistics and the teaching of standard English to speakers of other languages and dialects* (pp. 1–44). Washington, DC: Georgetown University Press.

———. (1972). *Language in the inner city: Studies in the Black English vernacular.* Philadelphia: University of Pennsylvania Press.

———. (1972). *Sociolinguistic patterns.* Philadelphia: University of Pennsylvania Press.

———. (1994). *Principles of linguistic change: Vol. 1. Internal factors.* Oxford, UK: Blackwell.

———. (2001). *Principles of linguistic change: Vol. 2. Social factors.* Oxford, UK: Blackwell.

———. (2006). *The social stratification of English in New York City* (2nd ed.). New York, NY: Cambridge University Press. (Original work published 1966)

———. (2010). *Principles of linguistic change: Vol. 3. Cognitive and cultural factors.* Oxford, UK: Blackwell.

Labov, W., Ash, S., & Boberg, C. (2006). *The atlas of North American English: Phonetics, phonology, and sound change.* New York, NY: Mouton de Gruyter.

Weinreich, U., Labov, W., & Herzog, M. (1968). Empirical foundations for a theory of language change. In W. Lehmann & Y. Malkiel (Eds.), *Directions for historical linguistics* (pp. 95–198). Austin: University of Texas Press.

LACAN, JACQUES

Jacques Lacan (1901–1981) was a French psychiatrist and psychoanalyst who had a deep influence on philosophy, literary theory, and anthropology. One way to describe the work of Lacan is as an anthropology—a theory of what it means to be human. According to Lacan, Sigmund Freud's greatest contribution was the invention of the unconscious and the emphasis he placed on sexuality, both of which were specific to humans. Unlike animals, governed by instincts, nature, and biology, humans were defined by desire and language, by their ability to symbolize. Human subjectivity was thus always a form of intersubjectivity in which the encounters with the social and the "Other" were key in the construction of the self.

Lacan's thought presents a number of intrinsic difficulties. On a historical level, Lacan insisted again and again on the fact that he was simply reading Freud, that all of his concepts were anchored in Freud's texts. Such a claim is problematic in light of the fundamentally divergent interpretations of Freud throughout the 20th century. If Lacan's writings found little echo in the United States or in Great Britain, they nonetheless radically shaped the field of French psychoanalysis. Whether one argued with or against him, Lacan became a necessary reference within the French context. Lacan's work is also extremely complex on a theoretical level. His notoriously dense prose, his opaque references, his frequent digressions, and his general refusal of any systematic presentation have led many scholars to misconstrue or to simply dismiss his thought. The difficulty of Lacan's style, however, must be understood within his larger philosophical enterprise, as an attempt to *perform* his theory, to put it into practice. How does one write when language is inherently unstable, when meanings shift constantly, when the signifiers and signified are simply connected by an arbitrary relation, and, most important, when the self who writes, the author, is never an autonomous, centered self?

Born in 1901 in a Parisian bourgeois Catholic family, Lacan studied medicine before choosing to specialize in psychiatry in 1927. His interest in the question of madness and the psyche drew him toward surrealism, toward André Breton, Georges Bataille, and Salvador Dalí, who were some of the earliest readers of Freud in France. During those years, he decided to undergo analysis with Rudolph Loewenstein, one of the original founders of the Société Psychanalytique de Paris, which Lacan joined in 1934. In 1932, he defended his doctoral thesis, *On Paranoid Psychosis and Its Relations to the Personality*, in which he maintained that psychosis was not the outcome of a specific malfunctioning of the brain as many neuroscientists believed but rather the product of biological and cultural factors. The subject, he argued, was never isolated as many psychiatrists assumed. He or she was neither the autonomous reflexive Cartesian self nor the transcendental Kantian actor. Rather, Lacan's understanding of the self was closest to G. W. F. Hegel's.

Theory of the Mirror Stage

Lacan became particularly engaged with Hegel's thought through Alexandre Kojève's seminar on the *Phenomenology of the Spirit*, which he attended in the 1930s. Kojève's reading of Hegel emphasized the constitutive role of desire and of the "Other," who is both desired and the agent of desire and, consequently, of recognition. Hegel offered a way to bypass the divide between the individual and the social by suggesting that the two were neither autonomous nor overdetermined by one or the other but, rather, were mutually constitutive. Hegel's influence was particularly palpable in Lacan's theory of the "mirror stage," which he first presented at an International Psychoanalytic Association (IPA) congress in 1936 and which he reworked throughout his career. The mirror stage describes the reaction of a baby from 6 to 18 months, who, despite his lack of physical coordination, recognizes himself in a mirror. Although the child experiences his body as fragmented, the image he perceives is whole, integrated, and contained. This contrast produces a feeling of conflict and aggressiveness, which the child attempts to overcome by identifying with the image, which in itself leads to a sense of jubilation. For Lacan, the mirror stage describes the structure of subjectivity more generally: The unconscious, self-defined by the free play of the drives, identifies with an ideal I, the ego, the social self. This constitutive ambiguity in identity formation, this fundamental alienation, is absolutely central to Lacan's work: Identifications are based on self-recognitions that are always already misrecognitions. The mirror stage, as Lacan will later argue, also marks the subject's entry into language. There is an imaginary dimension to this double process of language acquisition and identity formation, resulting from the sense of mastery, autonomy, and wholeness. There is also, however, a symbolic element as the child looks up to the adult carrying him, the "Other," to confirm his identity.

Lacan reworked his concepts of the Imaginary, the Symbolic, and the Real in his 1953 IPA paper "The Function and Field of Speech and Language in Psychoanalysis," also known as the Rome Discourse. A few months before this presentation, Lacan had—along with other French psychoanalysts—resigned from the Société Psychanalytique de Paris to found the Société Française de Psychanalyse. The relationship between Lacan and the IPA had been contentious for a several years, particularly because of his practice of variable-length sessions, which could last from a few minutes to several hours. Lacan's Rome Discourse emerged in this context as a sort of theoretical manifesto for a new psychoanalysis, a new practice and a new theory, one increasingly influenced by structuralism. Language was the starting point of Lacan's "return to Freud," because language, the patient's word, or rather *parole*, was the only medium available to psychoanalysis. Lacan opposed his notion of language to that of the ego-psychologists or the behaviorist school interested in establishing "communication" with the patient. Psychoanalysis, he argued, ought to focus on the gaps in language, silences, paradoxes, symptoms, and dreams, even if they did not appear to communicate anything. The idea behind the variable-length sessions was precisely to revive the "talking cure" along Freud's guidelines, to provide a forum in which the unconscious, as opposed to the ego, could speak.

Theory of Language

According to Lacan, contemporary psychoanalysts had overlooked Freud's two most important innovations: (1) the unconscious and (2) sexuality. Both of these, he argued, had a linguistic expression and could only be studied in relation to language. Lacan's theory of language was indebted to structural linguistics and particularly to the work of Ferdinand de Saussure and Roman Jakobson, who conceived of language as a system of differences. The second greatest influence for the Rome Discourse was the work of Claude Lévi-Strauss. From *The Elementary Structures of Kinship*, Lacan borrowed Lévi-Strauss's system of structural equivalence between subjectivity, the social, and language, all of which were mediated by the prohibition of incest. Indeed, according to Lévi-Strauss, the law or prohibition was productive rather than restrictive in the sense that it forced men to marry outside their clan, to establish new social relations, and to mediate this process through language. Lacan's notion of castration operated similarly: No object could ever fully satisfy desire, not even the mother or the child, but other "small objects" (*objets petit a* as opposed to the big "Other") could come into being. Although these *objets a* generate desire, they also remain unobtainable. The structural lack of the object—the impossibility of having the full thing, *das Ding*—was once again analogous to the structural inability to ever have a full, transparent, immediate language. Just as Lévi-Strauss suggested that man could never return to a state of nature—which was by definition always already foreclosed—Lacan indicated that man would never lead a purely instinctual existence.

Imaginary, Symbolic, and Real

The Imaginary, the Symbolic, and the Real—the three orders that Lacan would eventually represent in a Borromean knot to illustrate the mutual implication of the terms—were also defined in relation to castration and to language. The Imaginary, illustrated in the mirror stage, describes the identification of the ego and the specular image. As such, the Imaginary is the realm not only of synthesis, plenitude, duality, and autonomy but also of alienation and illusion. The Symbolic is always already implicated in the Imaginary as the image of the parent holding the child suggests. If the Imaginary is the realm of the signified, the Symbolic is the realm of the signifier, of the "Other," and of radical alterity. The law that regulates desire in the Oedipus complex or that mandates the prohibition of incest is also located in the Symbolic. In this context, Lacan also developed the notion of the *nom-du-père* ("name of the father"), based on the homophony *nom* as "name" and *non* as "no," to expand the role of the biological father in the Oedipus complex—as the one who breaks the dual identificatory relation between mother and child—to larger structures of authority (other people but also institutions such as the school, the army, and the law). Finally, the Real designates what escapes from both the Imaginary and the Symbolic, the undifferentiated, the traumatic, the impossible, that which cannot be expressed in language but always returns.

Later Work

In 1963, the Société Française de Psychanalyse finally received from the IPA the official recognition that it had sought for years, but under the condition of Lacan's exclusion. Following his "excommunication" from the IPA and the Société Française de Psychanalyse, Lacan founded the École Freudienne de Paris, where he continued to imagine new, unorthodox practices to prevent the reification of the psychoanalytic theory and experience. One of these was "the pass," in which analysts-in-training testified to their experiences of analysis before being allowed to practice themselves.

In 1966, Lacan published his only collection of written texts, *Écrits* (Writings). His main teaching during those years was oral, in the form of his seminar, first held at the Sainte Anne Hospital from 1953 to 1964, then at the École Normale Supérieure from 1964 to 1969, and finally at the Faculté de Droit until his death. It was at the École Normale Supérieure that Lacan acquired some of his most loyal disciples, many of whom were students of Louis Althusser and Maoist sympathizers. Among these was Jacques-Alain Miller, who eventually married Lacan's daughter, Judith, and was responsible for the posthumous publication of the seminars. After 1968, the University of Vincennes (Paris VIII) instituted the first official department of psychoanalysis, where many of Lacan's students taught and propagated his ideas. After the 1970s, Lacan was increasingly attracted to mathematics, logic, and formalization as a way to represent certain psychoanalytic concepts differently and to avoid impasses of the written word. In 1980, he singlehandedly dissolved the École Freudienne de Paris and constituted the École de la Cause Freudienne, over which he presided for a few months until his death in 1981.

Among other themes, Lacan continued to explore neurosis, perversion, and psychosis. While

Freud conceived of these categories phenomenologically, Lacan treated them as *structures* in which symptoms and behaviors may or may not be present. Furthermore, he defined all three around the modalities of avoiding or refusing castration: What does it mean to live as decentered subjects, with lack of objects for one's desire and with a language that always already fails? In neurosis, the solution to this dilemma takes the form of seduction. Perversion is the "demonstration" or repetitive staging of a scenario directed toward the production of a specific *jouissance*, an unbearable pleasure. In psychosis, it takes the form of delusion. Lacan was particularly interested in the structure of psychosis, which resulted, he argued, from the foreclosure of the signifier—a "hole" in the Symbolic due to the absence of the *nom-du-père*. The psychotic was unable to function in the social just as he or she was unable to "signify" linguistically or be understood.

Another important theme in Lacan's later work was the problem of sexual difference. As a psychic structure, sexual difference was reducible neither to sex (biological) or to gender (social). It escaped representation. Lacan, for instance, devised the concept of the phallus, a symbol of desire that was discursive rather than anatomical, as was the penis in Freud's work. Similarly, he devoted a seminar to feminine sexuality (Seminar XX: *Encore*) in which he made famous (and famously misunderstood) declarations such as "Woman does not exist" and "She is not-whole." These statements point once again to the structural impossibility of having or of being a complete object of someone's desire. Throughout his career, Lacan worked and reworked this anthropology, a theory of the decentered self.

Camille Robcis

See also Freud, Sigmund; Lévi-Strauss, Claude

Further Readings

Evans, D. (1996). *An introductory dictionary of Lacanian psychoanalysis*. New York, NY: Routledge.

Fink, B. (1995). *The Lacanian subject: Between language and jouissance*. Princeton, NJ: Princeton University Press.

———. (1997). *A clinical introduction to Lacanian psychoanalysis: Theory and technique*. Cambridge, MA: Harvard University Press.

Marini, M. (1992). *Jacques Lacan: The French context*. New Brunswick, NJ: Rutgers University Press.

Roudinesco, E. (1997). *Jacques Lacan*. New York, NY: Columbia University Press.

Silverman, K. (1983). The subject. In *The subject of semiotics* (pp.126–193). New York, NY: Oxford University Press.

Turkle, S. (1992). *Psychoanalytic politics: Jacques Lacan and Freud's French Revolution*. New York, NY: Guilford Press.

LAFITAU, JOSEPH-FRANÇOIS

Father Joseph-François Lafitau (1681–1746) was a Jesuit missionary in Quebec from 1712 to 1717. Most of this time was spent in a settlement of Iroquois converts to Christianity at Sault St. Louis, near modern Montreal. Here, he conducted the methodical and meticulous ethnographic observations that were to form the core of his voluminous two-volume treatise *Customs of the American Savages Compared to the Customs of the Earliest Times* (1724). More than a century before Lewis Henry Morgan, he used his own detailed observation of the Iroquois along with comparable descriptions by other missionaries and secular travelers as well as the corpus of classical antiquity to elaborate an ambitious scheme of universal history. His ethnography, however impressive, was hardly unique, but the comparative scope of his inquiry was truly remarkable, foreshadowing anthropological thought in the following century.

For Lafitau, the "earliest times" referred to classical antiquity and the Bible. He accepted biblical chronology as a given—in his day an uncontroversial stance. His theology also committed him to a monogenetic vision of human origins, and consequently an explanation for the peopling of the New World. He seized on the fact that, like the Iroquois, the Lycians of Asia Minor, as described by Herodotus, were matrilineal, a condition he labeled "gynococracy." On these grounds, he conjectured that the Iroquois and other Native American peoples were descendants of Lycian migrants who had migrated across Asia and crossed over to the New World from Siberia.

Lafitau's theologically inspired vision of world history posited that, originally, all humanity had been granted divine instructions for living a proper life but that only the "chosen people" had kept these intact. Nevertheless, the institutions of other peoples—especially religion, marriage and the family, and government—reflected, however imperfectly, the divine mandate. In his chapter on religion, the longest in the book, he attempts to reconstruct a sort of primal paganism by amalgamating features of Greek and Roman religion and accounts of Native American practices, not only of the Iroquois and their neighbors but also from accounts of Virginia, Brazil, and the Antilles. His portrayal was by no means unsympathetic. For example, he depicted pagan "mysteries"—initiation rites—as techniques for inculcating the practice of asceticism as a means of accessing the sacred, imperfect refractions of the divine spark. This section on religion is the one where he makes the least use of Iroquois ethnography.

The chapter on marriage is a far more straightforward account of Iroquois kinship. Here, Lafitau takes great pains to argue that Iroquois mores are in most respects consistent with Christian morality, lavishing praise on their marital fidelity and their systematic avoidance of marriages between relatives and only deploring the ease of divorce. Here and elsewhere, Lafitau saw no inconsistency between matrilineal kinship and the divine plan. This chapter contains an accurate explanation of Iroquois kinship terminology, earning the admiration of A. R. Radcliffe-Brown and Sol Tax, among others.

Other sections of the book leave theological concerns aside, providing a highly detailed account of Iroquois government, male and female occupations, warfare, foreign policy, trade, hunting and fishing, games, sickness and medicine, and burial and mourning, interspersed from time to time with comparisons with practices from classical antiquity.

Lafitau's work had virtually no impact on contemporary French secular Enlightenment thinkers, who had no interest in his theology and little patience with his pedantic style, especially in his discussions of classical antiquity. Voltaire lampooned his diffusionist account of the peopling of the New World. Just because the Greeks hunted, told myths, and danced on holidays and the Iroquois did likewise was hardly, he ironized, a compelling argument. Voltaire conveniently, if unfairly, omitted all reference to matrilineal descent, a far more striking coincidence. In fact, Lafitau's diffusionism, however erroneous, was hardly as careless as Voltaire suggested. Notably, Lafitau carefully considered and

rejected on evidentiary grounds speculation that Native Americans were the long-lost Israelites.

Ultimately, Lafitau left a deeper mark on Scottish than on French Enlightenment thinkers. Adam Smith and Adam Ferguson relied on Lafitau, along with another Jesuit, Pierre de Charlevoix, a historian of New France, for their construct of "savagery" as the earliest stage of human progress. The Scots were particularly interested in Lafitau's descriptions of government and warfare, especially his analysis of how the Iroquois managed to maintain order, wage war, and engage in highly successful foreign diplomacy in the absence of a monarchy and indeed any central authority. Although, because of his description of Iroquois kinship, he has been retrospectively hailed as a precursor, his analysis of Iroquois government is arguably his most enduring contribution.

Robert Launay

See also Ferguson, Adam; Morgan, Lewis Henry; Voltaire

Further Readings

Lafitau, J.-F. (1974). *Customs of the American Indians compared with the customs of primitive times* (W. N. Fenton & E. L. Moore, Trans.; 2 vols.). Toronto, Ontario, Canada: Champlain Society.

Launay, R. (2010). Lafitau revisited: American "savages" and universal history. *Anthropologica, 52,* 337–343.

LAMPHERE, LOUISE

Louise Lamphere (1940–) is considered one of the "founding mothers" of feminist anthropology. Her career has encompassed Navajo studies, urban and workplace ethnography, family and kinship studies, U.S. immigration and ethnic group formation, and U.S. healthcare policy. She was among the first women to be hired for a permanent faculty position at Brown University but was denied tenure there in 1975. Always combining scholarship with activism and political engagement, she instituted a gender discrimination lawsuit, which was settled (in her favor) out of court and which had wide-ranging implications for women in higher education. She has served as president of the American Anthropological Association, the American Ethnological Society, and the Association for Feminist Anthropology, among many other positions, and has received many honors and awards.

Since receiving her PhD from Harvard in 1968, Lamphere's scholarship has been characterized by a consistent emphasis on how subordinated individuals and groups construct strategies of resistance within specific, local political economies. Her theoretical contributions avoid the dichotomous thinking (between nature and culture, e.g., or structure and agency) so common in the social sciences, in favor of an emphasis on how practice emerges from structural conditions. Her body of work is often closely related to public policy initiatives and collapses the distinctions between applied, practicing, and public anthropology. Many of her research projects were conducted with interdisciplinary teams and employed the methodologies of historians and sociologists as well as anthropology.

Lamphere became nationally known as coeditor of a volume that helped define the field of feminist anthropology, *Woman, Culture, and Society*, published in 1974. Influenced by second-wave feminism and by the contributors' own experiences as women within the academy, the book originated with graduate students at Stanford in 1971. Lamphere was a young assistant professor at the time, and she undertook the organizing and editing duties with Michelle Zimblast Rosaldo. They explicitly defined their project as "a first generation's attempt to integrate an interest in women into a general theory of society and culture." Among the questions addressed by the contributors, and by the editors in their introduction were the following: Are women everywhere, as Simone de Beauvoir posited, the "second sex"? If so, can this universal secondary status be explained by biological factors? If not, and if gender hierarchies are historical constructs, how can they be changed? How is gender asymmetry related to other forms of stratification and domination? The ethnographic literature at the time relegated descriptive information on women largely to the topics of kinship and marriage, but there were suggestions that domestic tensions could have larger political implications. The contributors to *Women, Culture, and Society* were simultaneously trying to read an existing literature in new ways, supply ethnographic evidence that had gone previously unreported, and stretch the boundaries of existing theory, including Marxist historical materialism, British structural functionalism, and

the emerging transactional political anthropology of authors such as Fredrik Barth and F. G. Bailey. Taken together, the essays represent an ambitious attempt to explain both variation and continuities in women's lives across time and space.

Within this collection, Lamphere's own contribution prefigures much of her later writing. Lamphere used her own ethnographic study of Navajo families, in dialogue with material from a range of other societies, to develop the idea that women's domestic strategies were shaped by very different sets of interests, even within the same household. At a time when evolutionary theories held that women were "naturally" competitive with each other (to attract and hold on to a male provider), Lamphere demonstrated that in situations where men and women share domestic authority, as among the Navajo, it was in women's interest to work together across kin groups and generations. Where women's household standing depended on their ability to covertly influence men, on the other hand, significant intrahousehold conflict was often generated between cowives or between the mother-in-law and daughter-in-law. The resulting domestic dramas were an outcome of social structure, not of women's "intrinsic" nature.

Lamphere explored similar themes in her dissertation fieldwork with Navajo communities in northern New Mexico in 1965–1966. Classic Navajo studies by Clyde Kluckhohn and George Collier had emphasized the negative psychological aspects of witchcraft and other beliefs; Lamphere was interested in mutual aid, cooperation, and reciprocity. Living with several different families in dispersed seasonal groups, she documented the overlapping networks through which religious ceremonies, family events, and other activities were organized and resources and labor were mobilized. Navajo conceptions of personal autonomy were often in tension with equally strong values placed on generosity and cooperation. Choices about whom to ask for help and decisions to grant or withhold assistance led Lamphere to important insights about Navajo kinship, the "loose" structure of which had defied analysis through the structural-functionalist models of the day.

Beginning in the mid-1970s, Lamphere undertook a series of large, multidisciplinary projects tracking the changing political economy of the United States, with a focus on how families made decisions about deploying labor within and outside the home. In *From Working Daughters to Working Mothers* (1987), she traced the rise and fall of the New England textile industry, into which successive waves of immigrants sent first their unmarried daughters and later their wives and mothers, over the course of the 20th century. *Sunbelt Working Mothers*, published in 1993, examined the same process as American companies relocated from the northeast to the southwest, sparking significant changes in the household division of labor between husbands and wives, as fairly well-paid factory jobs for women became briefly available (before moving offshore by the end of the 20th century). The importance of ethnicity and immigration in both sites was further explored in two edited volumes, *Structuring Diversity: Ethnographic Perspectives on the New Immigration* (1992) and *Newcomers in the Workplace: Immigrants and the Restructuring of the U.S. Economy* (1994). As feminist anthropology developed into a vibrant and theoretically rich subfield within the discipline, Lamphere contributed another "state-of-the-art" edited volume, *Situated Lives: Gender and Culture in Everyday Life* (1997). Her commitment to documenting the ways working families adapt to the changing economic environment led her to medical anthropology and a major project on Medicaid managed-care initiatives in New Mexico, resulting in a special issue of *Medical Anthropology Quarterly* in 2005.

In 2007, Lamphere published a work bringing together her scholarly and personal history across 40 years, *Weaving Women's Lives: Three Generations in a Navajo Family*, in which she shares authorship with Eva Price, Carole Cadman, and Valerie Darwin, a grandmother, a mother, and a daughter of one of the families Lamphere lived with during her 1965–1966 doctoral fieldwork. The book traces the transformation in Navajo women's experience across the 20th century and incorporates Lamphere's own biography as a Westerner of a very different class and ethnic status. *Weaving Women's Lives* literally brings Lamphere full circle, drawing together her years of scholarship on questions of gender, ethnic identity, and economic change and their relationship to work in the United States.

Mary H. Moran

See also Barth, Fredrik; Economic Anthropology; Feminist Anthropology; Gender and Anthropology; Kluckhohn, Clyde; Rosaldo, Michelle Zimbalist

Further Readings

Lamphere, L. (1977). *To run after them: Culture and social bases of cooperation in a Navajo community.* Tucson: University of Arizona Press.

———. (1987). *From working daughters to working mothers: Immigrant women in a New England industrial community.* Ithaca, NY: Cornell University Press.

———. (2007). *Weaving women's lives: Three generations in a Navajo family.* Albuquerque: University of New Mexico Press.

Rosaldo, M. Z., & Lamphere, L. (1974). *Woman, culture and society.* Stanford, CA: Stanford University Press.

L'ANNÉE SOCIOLOGIQUE

L'Année Sociologique is a journal published annually in Paris: first from 1898 to 1907 and then at various intervals (see below) until the present day. The title followed a current fashion when it was founded: "The Year in (the area of knowledge)." The 1890s was a decade of rapid expansion of such journals in France, so in choosing this title, the founders were stating the arrival of their new discipline in the scientific world of the time. The current editors describe it as "the oldest scientific journal devoted to the social sciences."

The Group

The name is also applied to the group of French scholars who founded it and worked together on it in the early years, under the direction of Émile Durkheim, who is considered to be one of the three great founders of sociology (with Karl Marx and Max Weber). At that time, Durkheim was only 40 years old. He had already published three major works, *The Division of Labor in Society* (1893), *The Rules of Sociological Method* (1895), and *Suicide* (1897), and had visited scholars in Germany, notably the social psychologist Wilhelm Wundt. His masterwork *The Elementary Forms of Religious Life* was published much later, in 1912, so it was written with the benefit of many years of ongoing study, reflection, and engagement with the group and with the vast emerging new scholarship that they were reviewing for the journal and drawing on to define their own distinctive approach.

The efforts of Durkheim and his followers bore remarkable fruit, in part due to the brilliance of the work itself and in part due to the commitment of the members. Those mentioned on the face page in 1898 were Durkheim and 12 others, of whom 3 were at other universities. A whole new generation of young people are mentioned by name for Volume 7, and there was another surge in growth in 1912. By Volume 10, there were 20 members. For Volume 12, there were 29, from 10 universities. This growth was perhaps due to Durkheim's move from Bordeaux to Paris, where he gained an appointment in 1902. By the time of Volume 12, he was established in Paris and was a major intellectual figure in the capital. Membership in the group was markedly consistent over this time. Besides Durkheim, 7 of the first participants were listed for all 12 prewar volumes: Celestin Bouglé, Emmanuel Lévy, Paul Fauconnet, Henri Hubert, Marcel Mauss, Dominique Parodi, and François Simiand.

Durkheim's nephew Mauss was the other universally recognized scholar who belonged to the group from the beginning. He contributed disproportionately to the review essays and revived the journal in the 1920s, after Durkheim's death and the losses of the First World War. Mauss summarized and characterized their work in his moving eulogy in the edition of 1923–1924. Through what he referred to as a "true sharing of work," the collaboration of the *Année Sociologique* scholars not only provided the foundation for an entire school of the new discipline of sociology, with its own links throughout European scholarship, but also fostered what he referred to as a "flowering" of the varied individual work of its members.

The Journal Format

For the first 10 issues, the journal comprised two sections: (1) original memoirs and (2) review articles. The memoirs established the most notable themes of what became known as the "French school": religious practices in society (systems of classification, sacrifice, magic, caste, and representations of death); the division of labor, law, penal practices, and property; and general theoretical issues of social reproduction and comparative analysis. The original memoirs of the first edition were by Durkheim and Georg Simmel. Durkheim had essays of his own in 5 of the first 12 editions (up to 1912); Mauss authored

or coauthored 4 editions, and Robert Hertz and Hubert authored or coauthored 1 each. The pervasive theme was society as a moral order.

The reviews were composed individually or in small teams, and the scholarship addressed in the reviews was wide-ranging and voluminous. In Volume 6 (1901–1902) alone, the 15 group members reviewed about 250 works, in more than 50 titled review sections, covering French-, English-, German-, and Italian-language scholarship. An example is one 16-page section titled Philosophical Sociology, where Mauss reviewed works by 15 anthropologists, written in French, English, and German, on religious and totemic systems all over the world, most especially in Melanesia, Central Africa, and Native America. This would be the basis for the seminal essay by Durkheim and Mauss on "primitive classification" published in 1903 (see later). Also included in this one issue were books and articles by famous scholars including Gabriel Tarde, Franz Boas, Benedetto Croce, Georges Sorel, Werner Sombart, James G. Frazer, A. L. Kroeber, and others.

For Volume 11, Durkheim decided to change strategy, to publish the memoirs more fully as a separate series, so that the members could devote more time to their individual research. The journal was then devoted only to review articles, and its frequency was reduced from the annual issue to one edition every 3 years, without, however, changing the name. Only two issues—Volumes 11 and 12—were published in this form, before the First World War brought everything to a halt. The war had a devastating effect. Several young members of the *Année Sociologique* group were killed, including Durkheim's only son, André. Durkheim died 2 years after his son's death, in 1917. The journal and the group were relaunched only in 1925 (edition for 1923–1924), under the leadership of Mauss, whose famous "Essai sur le Don: Forme et Raison de l'Échange dans les Sociétés Archaïques" (Essay on the Gift: The Form and Reason of Exchange in Archaic Societies) was the original research paper for that issue. The turbulence and loss in membership was much more marked than any variability of theory and vision in the group.

Mauss picked up "the task" left by "our dead," although the journal never regained the international stature it had achieved when Durkheim was alive. This would be impossible, since the first 10 volumes are identified as groundbreaking in the history of the social sciences.

Theory and Method

The memoirs of the first 12 volumes indicate the theoretical and methodological innovations that the group proposed and that have become identified with the thrust of their enormous influence. Some of those titles are the following:

Durkheim: "The Prohibition of Incest and Its Origins"

Simmel: "How Social Forms Maintain Themselves"

Durkheim: "On the Definition of Religious Phenomena"

Hubert and Mauss: "Essay on the Nature and Function of Sacrifice"

Durkheim and Mauss: "On Some Primitive Forms of Classification: Contribution to the Study of Collective Representations"

Bouglé: "General Review of Recent Theories of the Division of Labor"

Hubert and Mauss: "Outline of a General Theory of Magic"

Paul Huvelin: "Magic and Individual Right"

Hertz: "Contribution to the Collective Representation of Death"

Bouglé: "Note on Law and Caste in India"

These titles convey the theoretical themes and the favored method of the school. The themes center on religion and meaning, on the one hand, and on what they called "social morphology" and law, on the other. The method is rigorously empirical. Case studies and ethnography figure prominently, and they cover the world: Australia, India, France, Native America, and the Arctic. The review section covers an even wider geographical world. Integrating the two themes, several articles aim toward a "general theory" of, or at least an approach to, specific phenomena such as magic, death, religion, words, and collective representations. They insert a characteristic method of comparison here: the detailed study of signal cases, elementary forms, or specific instances of general phenomena in which the qualities they see as central are particularly evident.

Although they sometimes refer to these elementary forms as "primitive," they do not embed the argument in evolutionary theory. Rather, the adjective *primitive* refers at once to a condensed, generative "first" (as in "basic") as well as "ancient." Mauss, in particular, was deeply opposed to speculative history and in favor of identifying consonances and overlaps among phenomena from all places and eras of history, to elucidate their commonalities. This is his method in the most celebrated of all the memoirs published in the journal, the "Essay on the Gift" (1925), where he starts at two ends of the world, with the Icelandic Edda epic and the Maori *hau* ("spirit of the gift"), and ends with the civic life of his own time in postwar Europe, by way of Melanesia, Ancient Rome, and India, and stretching to include institutions such as sacrifice, which broadens the very definition of "gift."

The early theoretical articles make the links explicit between the two broad themes of religion and society and draw on the ethnographic sources to make the case. Over the years, the headings for the review sections reflect the growing breadth of their reach and the focus of their analysis. Each group of reviews is broken down into subthemes as well, where the specialist reader may pick up threads across the years. By Volume 6 (1901–1902), the major headings are as follows: General Sociology, Religious Sociology, Moral and Juridical Sociology, Sociology of Crime and Moral Statistics, Economic Sociology, Social Morphology, and, finally, Diverse, which included Art and Socialism.

From the early years, out of all the general theoretical papers, the one by Durkheim and Mauss together, originally published in Volume 6 of *Année Sociologique* as *De quelques formes primitives de classification* (1903) and translated into English as *Primitive Classification* (1963), best exemplifies their method and showcases their most inspired contributions. Here, the authors argue clearly for holding aside psychology and philosophy from the study of "mental operations," in favor of a rigorous, empirically based linking of the categories of classification of the world to the classifications of human society. In "Primitive Classification" (1963), Durkheim and Mauss focus on the signal case of totemism, the widespread practice of identifying a social group with a natural species with which they maintain an active relationship of some sort (avoid eating, wear as a talisman, perform in ritual, etc.).

The social groupings of our social past and "distant present" are still "the very cadre of all classification . . . the ensemble of mental habits by virtue of which we conceive things and facts in the form of coordinated or hierarchized groups" (p. 88). Durkheim and Mauss conclude that phenomena such as totemism demonstrate how sociology can shed light on the beginning and functions of logical operations. These are arguments taken up by a long genealogy of intellectual heirs, including Claude Lévi-Strauss in his magnum opus, his four-volume work on the logic of myth.

Although the work of *L'Année Sociologique* is sometimes represented in a schematic way, as positing the social foundations of cognitive categories and moral thought, the school's propositions emerged from a matrix of vast study, ongoing interchange, and the interweaving of individual, collaborative, and team work by more than a dozen scholars over a dozen issues of a journal, each of which ran to more than 600 pages. Collectively, they created a profoundly researched, empirically supported, and philosophically sophisticated body of work, encompassing societies ancient and modern, across the world. By encompassing all societies, they created a basis for general theory, comparative sociology, and a bridge between the two disciplines of anthropology and sociology that did not exist for those who divided the social world into industrial and preindustrial societies, East and West, literate and nonliterate.

Translation

It is largely through British social anthropology that the journal's essays moved into wide circulation in English-speaking scholarship. Translations were organized by E. E. Evans-Pritchard, professor of anthropology at Oxford, who met Mauss before he died in 1950. In the 1950s and 1960s, several of Mauss's authored and coauthored memoirs from the journal were published in English as short books: *The General Theory of Magic* (1950), *The Essay on the Gift* (1954), *Death and the Right Hand* (Hertz, 1960), *Primitive Classification* (Durkheim & Mauss, 1963), and *Sacrifice* (Hubert & Mauss, 1964). These works are still widely studied, as Mauss's work gains in influence: through the compelling relevance of the ideas, through the continuation of the journal, and through the Paris-based network that bears his name

as an acronym, Le Mouvement Anti-Utilitariste dans les Sciences Sociales (MAUSS).

Jane I. Guyer

See also Boas, Franz; Durkheim, Émile; Frazer, James G.; Hertz, Robert; Kroeber, Alfred L.; Mauss, Marcel; Simmel, Georg; Wundt, Wilhelm

Further Readings

Durkheim, E., & Mauss, M. (1963). *Primitive classification* (R. Needham, Trans.). Chicago, IL: University of Chicago Press.

Fournier, M. (2006). *Marcel Mauss: A biography.* Princeton, NJ: Princeton University Press.

————. (2007). *Émile Durkheim (1858–1917).* Paris, France: Fayard.

LATOUR, BRUNO

Bruno Latour (1947–) is a French sociologist, philosopher, Bible scholar, anthropologist, and scientist; one of the founders of actor-network theory; and among the most unconventional thinkers of the past century. With his creative approaches to the collective production of knowledge, technology, metaphysics, and ecology, his work not only transcended the boundary between social and natural sciences but also provided a defining impulse to the discourse on the interaction of society, knowledge, and time in a world that, in his view, was never "modern." Latour is one of the most cited authors in the social sciences.

Biography and Major Works

Latour was born on June 22, 1947, in Beaune (Burgundy, France), into a wine-growing family steeped in tradition. His ideas stem from a classical Jesuit education and a comprehensive philosophical training. Even though he is now widely seen as a historian of science and a sociologist of technology, his early influences came from ancient mythologies and his enthusiasm for Friedrich Nietzsche. He felt highly attracted to the well-grounded epistemic attempts to grasp the essence of "Being."

Following his studies in philosophy, biblical exegesis, and anthropology in Dijon, Latour completed his voluntary military service (1973–1975) with the Office de la Recherche Scientifique et Technique

Outre-Mer in Abidjan, Côte d'Ivoire, where he wrote an ethnographic study on the ideology of "competence" in industrial relations and associated racist discourses. In 1975, he undertook doctorate studies at the Tours University.

Anthropology Beyond the Tropes: Laboratory Life, Science Studies, and Actor-Network Theory

In the late 1970s, Latour shifted from his anthropological research to focus on studying highly sophisticated scientific laboratories. He spent 2 years (1975–1977) in the Salk Institute for Biological Studies in San Diego, California, in the neuroendocrinology research lab of Roger Guillemin (who was later awarded the Nobel Prize), where he pioneered an ethnographic study of the scientific community, focusing on the processes of scientific discovery. The product of this fieldwork was *Laboratory Life: The Social Construction of Scientific Facts*, published in 1979, coauthored with the British sociologist Steve Woolgar. Through this work, Latour and Woolgar attempted to illuminate the roles of rhetorical strategies, technical artifacts, and discipline-specific research procedures in the construction of scientific "facts." For Latour, knowledge, be it technical skills, scientific theories, worldviews, or anything else, has no absolute certainty. Rather, it is merely a specific kind of familiarity in interaction with certain people, things, places, or events.

After his fieldwork in Côte d'Ivoire and California, Latour participated in a scientific-historical research project on the significance of Louis Pasteur for medicine and for French society (1978–1981). A summary of his findings was published in 1984 as *Les Microbes: Guerre et Paix: Suivi de Irréductions* (*The Pasteurization of France*, 1988). In 1987, he obtained his postdoctoral degree (*habilitation*) from École des Hautes Études en Sciences Sociales and published *Science in Action: How to Follow Scientists and Engineers Through Society*.

Nous n'avons jamais été modernes, or "we have never been modern," is perhaps Latour's most eye-catching aphorism. Latour revealed the dichotomy between nature and society, and object and subject, as useless, replacing them with concepts like "collective" or "human and non-human actors and actants." Latour shows how even the smallest (e.g., microbes) and seemingly unimportant, placid, and presumably lifeless things, such as keys or automobile safety belts, possess their own personal expressivity and action potentials and thus actively influence human lives. Within this reality-constitutive interplay of the most diverse forces, he presented the concept of "labor" as the quintessential social *topos*.

As a participant in numerous projects in political science and in research management, Latour has peered carefully over the shoulders of scientists and engineers. He developed all his epistemological thoughts and hypotheses on the basis of empirical studies (as exemplified in *Laboratory Life: The Social Construction of Scientific Facts* and *Aramis, ou l'Amour des Technique* [*Aramis, or the Love of Technology*]), through which he provided the crucial momentum for the development of new international and interdisciplinary research subjects, for instance, science and technology studies (STS or, in short, science studies), dedicated to the examination of the history of science and technological research.

Within the scope of science studies, he first employed poststructuralist, postmodern ideas to show that the knowledge produced by the sciences is not objective. Such knowledge is socioculturally constructed—that is, influenced by the prevailing cultural assumptions, ideologies, and power structures. But additionally, he criticized poststructural thinkers such as Roland Barthes, Jean Baudrillard, Jacques Derrida, Jacques Lacan, and Jean-François Lyotard. Jürgen Habermas and Pierre Bourdieu are also among his intellectual antagonists. Latour transcends social constructivism by arguing that reality is not mainly constructed but is set up by all the interacting and interrelated human and nonhuman protagonists at large. Latour assumes that technology, matter, nature, culture, and the social do not influence one another one-sidedly in their diverse features and domains. Rather, they are mutually dependent and interfused. In *La Clef du Berlin* (The Berlin Key, 1993), Latour used the "Berlin key" as an analogy to show that the artificial separation between society and technology is not sustainable.

In collaboration with other sociologists, specifically Michel Callon and John Law, he developed actor-network theory, a bundle of theoretical conceptions and qualitative methodologies for the examination of the processes of knowledge building in science, laboratory studies, and technology (*Reassembling the Social, an Introduction to Actor-Network-Theory*, 2005).

Latour and the Science Wars

In the 1990s, Latour became involved in the burning dispute between the humanities and natural sciences, popularly known as the Science Wars. The impetus for the scientific wars was a growing trend in the humanities to make use of physics or mathematical terms and formulas to clarify their arguments. The natural sciences raised a defense against this "infringement," and it came to an indignant cross-border fight between scientific warriors strongly tethered to their respective disciplines. In 1996, the physicist Alan Sokal parodied postmodernism by submitting a carefully crafted essay that he considered nonsense to the journal *Social Text*, which published it. Sokal critiqued the logic of postmodernists including Lacan, Baudrillard, Gilles Deleuze, Julia Kristeva, and Louis Althusser, and he attacked Latour, accusing him of irrationalism and philosophical mystification of his own social scientific approach in exploring the scientific procedures employed by the natural sciences. After Sokal and the physicist Jean Bricmont published *Impostures Intellectuelles* (Intellectual Impostures) in 1997, Latour reacted with his collected essays, *Pandora's Hope: Essays on the Reality of Science Studies* (1999), in which he addressed anew the consequences of scientific wars and renewed his antimodernistic credo, calling for flexibility, dynamism, and openness to cooperation across different scientific disciplines.

Willful Things, Politics-Capable Ecology, and the Power of Images

With *Politiques de la Nature: Comment Faire Entrer les Sciences en Démocratie* (*Politics of Nature: How to Bring the Sciences Into Democracy*), Latour, in 2004, broke new ground and not only delivered a stimulating analysis of the political philosophy of ecological movements but also renewed his call for a politically competent ecology. He provided an examination of the concepts of politics, ecology, and nature and decoupled each from the others. He separated ecology from nature, and to avoid conflict, he differentiated between ecology and economics. He proposed that nature should have a political representation consisting of humans and all other living things, such as animals and other presumably "dead" things. The new Parliament of Things that should legislate over the ecological economy, as Latour both playfully and earnestly

referred to it, must first produce a new constitution that will resolve the remaining dichotomy between democracy and science. Latour, together with Peter Weibel, co-curated the 2002 international exhibition: *Iconoclash: Beyond the Image Wars in Science, Religion, and Art.* In 2005, they curated *Making Things Public. The Atmospheres of Democracy* at the Center for Art and Media Technology in Karlsruhe, Germany, and coauthored the accompanying catalog. Through *Iconoclash*, Weibel and Latour displayed a very prominent ambivalence visible in contemporary religion, science, and art: the ambivalence between iconoclastic and iconophilic attitudes, between the condemnation and admiration of the omnipresence of images—two positions that fight against one another but nevertheless need each other to exist through reciprocal opposition.

Gaia, Factish Gods, and Different Modes of Existence

In addition to his comprehensive publication and lectures on the interaction of society, science, and technology, Latour also examined the consequences of the passive presence of technology to our belief systems and religious expressions (*Jubiler ou les Tourments de la Parole Religieuse* [Glee or the Torments of Religious Speech], 2002, and *On the Modern Cult of the Factish Gods*, 2010).

In 2013, Latour delivered the Gifford lectures in Edinburgh. His lectures focused on the concept of Gaia, a complex mixture of mythical, spiritual, and scientific ideas about the nature of our planet Earth, as well as on "natural religion," a concept that in itself already consists of two highly disputed terms: nature and religion. Latour advances a secularized examination of nature, the sciences, religion, and related collective healing rituals. And he proposes a well-grounded inquiry into the supernatural.

Since 2011, Latour has been working with AIME (An Inquiry Into Modes of Existence), a project of the European Union, examining the metaphysics of different forms of existence. In the context of this project, he has developed a full-scale collaborative digital platform.

To date, Latour has written 15 monographs (translated into many languages), produced collected works (together with Callon and Pierre Lemonnier, among others), created sensitive portraits of thinkers such as Michel Serres and François Ewald based on extensive interviews with them, and written numerous essays in scientific journals and many short texts, such as reviews and newspaper articles. In 1998, he published with Emilie Hermant a photo-essay on the technical and social aspects of the city of Paris. He has created performances, written theater pieces, and curated exhibitions. He has provided responses to numerous in-depth interviews, and his own works and thoughts have been the subjects of many other monographs.

Teaching

From 1982 to 2006, Latour taught at the Centre de Sociologie de l'Innovation and the École Nationale Supérieure des Mines in Paris and was a visiting professor at the University of California in San Diego, the London School of Economics, and the History of Science department, Harvard University. Since 2007, Bruno has been a professor at Sciences Po (Institut d'Études Politiques de Paris), where until 2012 he directed scientific research. He set up a media lab at Sciences Po to experimentally explore the opportunities offered to social theory through the spread of digital methods, and with Valrie Pihet, he created a new experimental program in art and politics.

Awards

Since 1992, Bruno has continued to be recognized with numerous prizes, honors, and honorary doctorate degrees (University of Lund, Sweden; University of Lausanne, Switzerland; University of Montreal, Quebec, Canada; University of Goteborg, Sweden; and University of Warwick, United Kingdom). In 2008, he received the Siegfried-Unseld Prize for scientific and literary accomplishments. He was the 2010 recipient of the *Kulturpreis* (Culture Prize) from the Society of the University of Munich.

Critical Contributions Within the Scientific Landscape

Latour is known as a lateral and pioneering thinker. The world that he envisages is one with its own will—one that has not really allowed itself to be tamed by the determining grip of a seemingly modern and rationally guided humanity. It is a world that emanates from the interaction of the temporarily controlled knowledge and experiences of actors and actants, be they artifacts, gods, humans, stars, electrons, technology, labor, market, mythologies, ideas, norms, things, or events. According to Latour, reality is not absolute, less so is its synonym, truth. Latour contends that even when the result of the interactions among humans and instruments cannot be calculated, the processes involved are completely empirically observable and can be closely grasped in a sort of "thick description" from a social scientific perspective. With the expansion of his examinations into areas of interest previously excluded from academic fields, Latour reveals historical totalizations and shortages in the sciences. By this, he opens our view to a new realism, one that is not naturalistic but that investigates the vitality of perceptible and tangible things—a vitality that is unconventionally independent and dynamic.

Latour's thinking and methodology connect him with those of Deleuze, Peter Sloterdijk, and Tarde; with Martin Heidegger's phenomenology; and with the philosophy of American pragmatism in the style of John Dewey, William James, and Richard Rorty.

Expansion instead of reduction, acceptance of many perspectives in place of totalization, and inclusion instead of exclusion, these are the themes that run prominently throughout Latour's works. The goal of a modern science, from Latour's perspective, can be neither the taming of nature or society nor the persistence of orthodox epistemologies. In contrast, it must derive from collaboration with the environment and public discourses and must be continuously renewed by the sparks emanating from this interaction. Modern science must fit contemporary needs to prove the relevance of its content and not appear like a mechanical toy that performs the same routine endlessly, while all that surrounds it has long since changed. This is Latour's unmistakable demand and hope. The hope for the success of a transformed science that is conscious of the complex interdependence of knowledge, politics, the public, technology, economic necessity, an endless labyrinth of intermediaries (social networks), and the urgency of interdisciplinary convergence.

Sina Lucia Kottmann

Editor's note: The editors wish to express their appreciation to Augustine Agwuele for translating this article from the German.

See also Althusser, Louis; Barthes, Roland; Baudrillard, Jean; Bourdieu, Pierre; Deleuze, Gilles, and Félix Guattari; Derrida, Jacques; Habermas, Jürgen; Lacan,

Jacques; Lyotard, Jean-François; Network Theory/ Social Network Analysis; Postmodernism; Poststructuralism; Social Constructionism; Social Studies of Science

Further Readings

Blok, A., & Jensen, T. E. (2011). *Bruno Latour: Hybrid thoughts in a hybrid world.* (Series: Key Sociologists). New York, NY: Routledge.

Harman, G. (2009). *Prince of networks: Bruno Latour and metaphysics* (Anamnesis Series). Melbourne, Victoria, Australia: re.press.

Kneer, G., Schroer, M., & Schüttpelz, E. (Eds.). (2007). *Bruno Latours kollektive: Kontroversen zur entgrenzung des sozialen* [Bruno Latour's collective: Controversies on the delimitations of the social]. Frankfurt, Germany: Suhrkamp.

Schmidgen, H. (2011). *Bruno Latour zur einführung* [An introduction to Bruno Latour]. Berlin, Germany: Junius Verlag.

Wieser, M. (2012). *Das netzwerk von Bruno Latour: Die akteur-netzwerk-theorie zwischen science und technology studies und poststrukturalistischer Soziologie* [The network of Bruno Latour: Actor-network theory between science and technology studies and poststructuralist sociology]. Bielefeld, Germany: Transcript.

Website

Bruno Latour: http://bruno-latour.fr/

LEACH, EDMUND

Edmund Ronald Leach (1910–1989) was one of the most emphatic and colorful figures in modern social anthropology. He spent much of his time writing for and speaking to lay audiences and so became perhaps the most widely known British anthropologist of his generation. Writing on an improbably vast range of topics, between 1937 and 1988, Leach published nine books, four edited volumes, more than 50 scholarly articles, and hundreds of shorter pieces. Although he is remembered primarily as the Anglophone purveyor of Claude Lévi-Strauss's structuralism, his intellectual achievement does not align with any one theory. He founded no "school," constructed no theoretical systems, and was impatient with theoretical assertions. Leach's assaults on established theories provoked charges of

inconsistency from his colleagues, but his intellectual restlessness was far from the petulant belligerence of which he was often accused. Rather, it expressed a steady vision of social anthropology, which he maintained throughout his life. For Leach, unsettling old dogmas was not a matter of settling into new ones but of challenging intellectual habits. He saw anthropology's subject matter not as a set of theoretical edifices but as other worlds of human action and thought, there to be understood.

Early Life and Introduction to Anthropology

Leach was born on November 7, 1910, in Sidmouth, a town in Devon, into a large and densely intermarried family of Lancashire mill owners, to William Edmund Leach and his wife Mildred (née Brierley). At the time he was born, the family fortunes came from a sugar plantation and a sugar-refining factory in northern Argentina. Leach grew up in Rochdale; studied at Marlborough College, a public school, which he entered as the twenty-first Leach; and was later admitted to Clare College, Cambridge. Like most anthropologists of his generation, he had no initial training in the discipline, and at Cambridge, he read mathematics and engineering. On graduating with a first class BA in 1932, he joined a British trading firm, John Swire and Sons (later Butterfield and Swire), with operations in East Asia, and was posted to China. He spent more than 3 years living in Hong Kong, Shanghai, Chunking, Tsingtao, and Beijing, all the while traveling a great deal. In China, Leach was struck by an extraordinary fact: Here was a great, ancient, and wholly viable civilization in which everything was, as Leach liked to say, "back to front." Chinese religion, architecture, clothing, ritual, cuisine, and art offered solutions to universal human problems and seemed to invert comprehensively the ways things were thought of and done in the West. While traveling all over China, Leach wrote swathes of letters and detailed notes on the local customs, religion, and (especially) technology.

By 1936, he had grown weary of commerce. Instead of renewing his contract, he followed a spur of the moment call by an expatriate American psychiatrist, former Mormon missionary, and amateur anthropologist, Kilton Stewart (whom Leach had met in Beijing), to visit "Bottle the Bugger"—that is, the island of Botel Tobago (now Langu) off the coast of Taiwan. Having spent 8 weeks on the island, he wrote voluminously about his observations, drew sketches, and took many photographs of the native Yami, the first "real primitives" he encountered close-up. On his return to England, Leach was introduced by a childhood friend, Rosemary Upcott, to her husband, the anthropologist Raymond Firth, and through him to Bronisław Malinowski, the leading grandee in British social anthropology at the time. Malinowski was a big, forceful, and tremendously charismatic man, who presided unchallenged from his chair at the London School of Economics over the entire discipline in Britain. Malinowski was a pioneer of extended fieldwork as anthropology's central method and of "functionalism" as its theoretical stance, which was maintained in British anthropology well into the 1950s. When Leach went to the London School of Economics as a student of anthropology, he joined Malinoswki's legendary seminars, which he ran between 1924 and 1938. These salon-like meetings, which brought together a motley gathering of anthropologists, psychologists, sociologists, philosophers, missionaries, and colonial administrators from around the world, were the nursery for much of that generation of British anthropology. Participants included the anthropologists Isaac Schapera, Audrey Richards, S. F. Nadel, Meyer Fortes, M. N. Srinivas, and E. E. Evans-Pritchard, as well as Leach's mentor and immediate teacher, Raymond Firth. Here, Leach met Noël Stevenson, a colonial administrator in Burma, through whom he came to do fieldwork in the Kachin Hills of northeastern Burma (following an abortive spell among the Rowanduz Kurds in Pakistan in 1938).

Contributions to Anthropology

During the 6 years (1939–1945) Leach spent in Burma, he conducted extensive fieldwork, served in the Burmese Rifles (reaching the rank of Major), raised a force of Kachin irregulars, got married (to Celia Buckmaster), and had his first child, Louisa. On the basis of his researches, he published his first professional monograph, *The Political Systems of Highland Burma* (1954), which is now widely regarded as his most enduring book and a momentous contribution to political anthropology. His key breakaway assertion was that the notion of a bounded "tribe" with its own language and culture was useless for understanding the Burmese highlands. Instead, he argued,

the social landscape of the Kachin Hills comprised a shared system of social and political relations, in which clans segmented and allied themselves to one another via marriage and identity codes such as dialect and dress. This "system" was neither stable nor closed, as people constantly entered, left, and shifted their position within it. The changes were made possible by three ideal political models that actors had at their disposal: (1) the hierarchical *gumsa*, (2) the anarchic egalitarian *gumlao*, and (3) the Shan state system of the neighboring valleys. Ambitious persons seeking political and economic advantage employed these models strategically to justify their actions, and the accumulated weight of their decisions tilted polities this way or that, shifting the whole structure of local society over time.

This was trailblazing work, far ahead of its time. By dissolving the old ethnographic notion of tribe as an isolated totality, Leach dissented from the persistent habit in anthropology of treating village, tribal, national, or any other communities as islands unto themselves, rather than as constituents of broader relational schemes. This insight informed, for instance, his student Fredrik Barth's celebrated thesis (1969) that ethnic groups were not cultural isolates but relational entities defined vis-à-vis one another. Leach's stress on a broad regional approach also anticipated work done by anthropologists in the 1970s under the rubric of "political economy." His emphasis on the flux inherent in social systems and on changes in societies over time was radical in the age of functionalism, in which anthropologists generally described societies as existing in a state of static, ahistorical equilibrium. His insistence that societies were made and unmade by human action and interaction also prefigured criticisms of social stasis leveled at functionalist-structural anthropology by "practice theorists" from the late 1970s.

Leach pursued the two concerns central to *Political Systems*—the relationship between social structure and individual agency (Malinowski's legacy) and between ideology and the material conditions of life—through much of the rest of his career. One set of responses to these concerns appeared in *Pul Eliya, a Village in Ceylon* (1961), his next monograph based on fieldwork conducted in Ceylon (Sri Lanka) in 1954. Here, he argued that kinship was "not a thing in itself," a concrete organization for anthropologists to study, but an idiom for speaking about property relations, used to pursue the pragmatic, material goals of political actors. *Pul Eliya* has been criticized for Leach's unquestioning adoption of the economically motivated, self-maximizing individual and for the reduction of culture to a residual consequence of paddy cultivation. The monograph, nevertheless, developed the theoretical coup that Leach launched in *Political Systems* and for which he is still mainly remembered today. One of the book's central assertions is that the local "sub-castes" (*vaigas*) were not discrete groups bound by blood and descent; divisions between them were important not because they formed social enclosures but because they constituted the basis for conflictual or cooperative affinity. The implications of this, seemingly minor, ethnographic quibble were pivotal. As in *Political Systems*, here Leach was challenging the prevailing functionalist picture of societies as separate, self-sufficiently functioning organisms to be labeled and typologized by anthropologists, an exercise he derided as "butterfly collecting."

The year 1961, when *Pul Eliya* was published, was a watershed year in Leach's career. This was when he issued a collection of essays, *Rethinking Anthropology*, in which he departed drastically from his teachers' functionalism, urging anthropologists to abandon their taxonomies of cultural systems in favor of organizing the ideas that underlie patterns of action and thought in societies. This turn was accelerated by two felicitous encounters, one with the polymath-anthropologist Gregory Bateson and the other with the linguist Roman Jakobson, both of whom he met while working at the Center for Advanced Studies in the Behavioral Sciences at Palo Alto, California (1960/1961). Bateson and Jakobson were developing, in their own different ways, the means to understand systems of relations. Leach was particularly struck by the work of Jakobson, one of the most important linguists of the 20th century and a pioneer of structural linguistics. Jakobson's analysis of sound systems hinged on the pivotal proposition that meaningful sound units (phonemes) in a language did not exist in isolation but were necessarily defined relative to one another. The sounds /t/ and /d/, for instance, are separate phonemes in the English language because its speakers perceive the difference undetectable to speakers of Korean, in which they together constitute a single phoneme. So the smallest units of language could be identified only in contrast to others and were not freestanding but were fundamentally relational

entities. Jakobson went on to analyze syntax, morphology, and even poetry, music, and cinema just as he analyzed sounds, by identifying elements in a system through relational opposing pairs. His work was the primary inspiration for the anthropologist Claude Lévi-Strauss, considered the father of "structuralism" in anthropology.

Leach remembered that when he first encountered Jakobson's ideas, his reaction was as follows: "Ah! I have been there before!" By 1961, he had been grappling with relational systems for at least a decade, and Jakobson's method offered robust analytical tools. That year, he also published two essays—"Golden Bough or Gilded Twig?" and "Lévi-Strauss in the Garden of Eden: An Examination of Some Recent Developments in the Analysis of Myth"—which signaled his fascination with Lévi-Strauss and the shift of interest from kinship and politics to narrative, art, and myth. From then on, Leach wrote prolifically on art, ritual, architecture, mythology, communication, biblical narrative, humanism, masquerades, computing, time, and the meaning of hair, among other topics. For at least a decade, he brandished Lévi-Strauss's name in his attacks on functionalism, acquiring the reputation of an advocate. But he never took on Lévi-Strauss's structuralism in its entirety and in fact rejected much of it, especially as it later began to crystallize into a metatheory of cognitive universals. Leach described himself, in a characteristically defiant manner, as both a "functionalist" interested in how things "worked" and a "structuralist" who strove to understand the required cognitive machinery. But he never fully subscribed to either theory. Although Leach was driven by the desire to grasp general patterns, and even provocatively claimed that he was "bored by the facts," his loyalties remained with ethnographic detail, never to be trumped by theory.

Legacy

Leach's painstaking attention to and admiration for ethnography came out in his excitement about the work of his students, to whom he devoted tremendous amounts of energy and time. As in his own work, he insisted on independent thinking and welcomed challenges to his own assertions, in fact scolding students for failing to disagree with him. The resulting major achievement was a generation of leading anthropologists—including Ray Abrahams,

Fredrik Barth, Jean La Fontaine, Chris Fuller, Stephen Gudeman, Alfred Gell, Stephen Hugh-Jones, Caroline Humphrey, Adam Kuper, Jonathan Parry, Marilyn Strathern, and Nur Yalman, among many others—whose regional foci, subject matter, and theoretical attitudes have been as wide-ranging as his own.

Leach remained a maverick, intellectually as well as institutionally. Although he became a lecturer in social anthropology at the London School of Economics in 1946, moved to Cambridge in 1953, became Provost of King's College, Cambridge (1966–1979), was president of the Royal Anthropological Institute (1971–1975), was elected fellow of the British Academy (from 1972), and was knighted in 1975, Leach remains the most prominent British anthropologist never to become a professorial head of department. His persistent dissent from intellectual orthodoxies was strategic. What was surprising was that what first drew him to anthropology in China, and his continued fascination with the "exotic," did not amount to unfocused reflections on the "Other" but to a real intellectual method. Leach constantly sought out contrasts between "us" and "them" to offer new insights into the lives of others, and in the process into ourselves. He saw theoretical statements as intellectually deadening if they became mental objects in their own right instead of aids to better understanding. Theory had to follow empirical observation, not the other way around, a message that remains as pertinent to anthropology now as in Leach's own day.

Anastasia Piliavsky

See also Barth, Fredrik; Bateson, Gregory; Evans-Pritchard, E. E.; Firth, Raymond; Fortes, Meyer; Jakobson, Roman O.; Lévi-Strauss, Claude; Malinowski, Bronisław; Richards, Audrey; Schapera, Isaac; Srinivas, M. N.; Strathern, Marilyn

Further Readings

Edmund Leach: An interview with Frank Kermode. (1982). Retrieved from http://www.alanmacfarlane.com/ancestors/Leach.html

Edmund Leach [Special issue]. (1989/1990). *Cambridge Anthropology, 13*(3).

Fuller, C., & Parry, J. (1989). "Petulant inconsistency?" The intellectual achievement of Edmund Leach. *Anthropology Today, 5*(3), 11–14.

Kuper, A. (1983). *Anthropology and anthropologists: The modern British school*. London, UK: Routledge & Kegan Paul.

———. (1986). An interview with Edmund Leach. *Current Anthropology, 27*(4), 375–382.

Leach, E. (1967, December 17). *A runaway world?* London, UK: BBC Radio.

———. (1984). Glimpses of the unmentionable in the history of British social anthropology. *Annual Review of Anthropology, 13*, 1–23.

Royal Anthropological Institute of Great Britain and Ireland. (1990). *Edmund Leach: A bibliography* (Occasional Paper, No. 42). London, UK: Author.

Tambiah, S. J. (2002). *Edmund Leach: An anthropological life*. Cambridge, UK: Cambridge University Press.

LEACOCK, ELEANOR

Eleanor Burke Leacock (1922–1987), known to friends and colleagues as "Happy," had an extraordinarily active and productive career as a Marxist-feminist anthropologist. Leacock was admired for her politically committed scholarship, and she was always outspoken against injustices and exploitation. The daughter of the well-known literary critic Kenneth Burke, she was also remarkable for her ability to combine being a mother of four, a wife (she was married twice), chair of the anthropology department at City College, City University of New York for 9 years, and a political activist. Despite her multiple involvements, she was always available as a loyal friend, supportive colleague, and encouraging teacher who fought forcefully to assist minority students and to promote the careers of Third World and female colleagues.

Leacock died in Honolulu on April 2, 1987, of a stroke suffered a few weeks after returning to Samoa to complete the fieldwork that she had begun in 1985 on the problems of urban youth. This last field project, in keeping with her previous work, was undertaken to gather detailed ethnographic material with which to challenge analyses that she regarded as theoretically unsound and politically pernicious—in this case, Derek Freeman's claim that suicide and rape among contemporary Samoan youth reveal the "darker side" and "grim realities" of an unchanging Samoan culture earlier described by Margaret Mead.

As a leading U.S. Marxist-feminist anthropologist, Leacock carried out fieldwork in four major world regions—the United States and Canada, Europe, Africa, and the Pacific—addressing a wide range of topics, including hunting-and-gathering societies, ethnohistory, urban anthropology, anthropology of education, cross-cultural studies of women, and Marxist anthropology. In all, she published 81 articles and 10 books (some edited). She is best known for her historical and ethnographic analysis of egalitarian societies and gender relations, with a focus on the transformations that produced or intensified inequalities of class, race, and gender. This work constituted a major contribution to the development of Marxist historical/evolutionary theory. Her other body of work addressed the contemporary sociocultural reproduction of inequality in U.S. society. Here, she detailed processes by which specific practices and concepts produce and reproduce forms of race, class, and gender inequalities and their intersections. Her ethnographic work attacked previous approaches that assumed the universality of both private property and male dominance.

Leacock's early fieldwork in British Colombia's Fraser Valley with the Harrison Indians during the summer of 1945 was followed by research on child training in Germany, Switzerland, and Italy during 1948–1949. Two periods of field research with the Montagnais-Naskapi (Innu) in Quebec and Labrador in 1950–1951 resulted in her dissertation *The Montagnais "Hunting Territory" and the Fur Trade* (1954), a published work of major theoretical significance. This early Innu research employed detailed ethnohistoric and ethnographic data to show that the so-called individually owned family-hunting territory was a product of the French fur trade and not aboriginal. This challenged the then current antievolutionary, anti-Marxist beliefs concerning the existence of primitive concepts of private property. At the same time, she pioneered the view that non-Western cultures could not be properly understood without examining the harmful effects of colonialism, along with people's forms of cultural resistance to colonial domination.

Like many other woman scholars of her generation, Leacock spent the first decade of her career employed on urban-based research projects—mental health, interracial housing, and city schools. In 1963, she joined the faculty of the Polytechnic Institute of Brooklyn as a full-time member, and in 1972 she accepted the chair of the anthropology department at City College, City University of New York, where

she remained until her death. In 1970–1971, she went to Zambia to study primary schooling in relation to community background, and 14 years later, she began her research on Samoan adolescents.

In the 1960s, Leacock became engaged in three major new projects: (1) American Indian ethnohistory, (2) the rehabilitation of major classics in social evolutionary theory by Lewis Henry Morgan and Friedrich Engels, and (3) coediting with colleagues at Polytechnic a 10-volume series of readings called *Social Science Theory and Method: An Integrated Historical Introduction.* The latter reinforced her interest in developing a unified philosophical and methodological approach to the natural and human sciences, an interest she later returned to in her writings on emergent levels of integration in human evolution.

As a Marxist and an accomplished and critical ethnographer, Leacock was uniquely qualified to reintroduce Morgan's and Engels's work to new generations of readers. The Leacock edition of Engels's *The Origin of the Family, Private Property, and the State* has become the standard one for most anthropologists, a key text in the rebirth of a Marxist-feminist tradition of scholarship. Her combining of evolutionary theory with careful ethnography and ethnohistory also informs a series of coedited volumes on women's experiences historically and cross-culturally.

Leacock retained a lifelong interest in the emergence of and transformations in stratification and gender hierarchies. Her focus was on two kinds of social transformations: (1) those brought about by processes of state formation and (2) those produced by Western colonialism and world capitalism. She synthesized her thinking on these issues in three important articles published in 1975, 1983, and 1986. Her evolutionism always sought to identify concrete processes of conflict and change in specific historical/cultural contexts and to relate these to emerging levels of sociocultural complexity. And as a Marxist anthropologist, Leacock privileged the long-term development of commodity production and exchange as her central analytic concept in evolutionary developments.

Leacock's work on the social reproduction of contemporary forms of inequality employed ethnography to expose the social and ideational processes involved in race and class inequality. Her 1969 *Teaching and Learning in City Schools* became an early model of classroom ethnography in the growing field of the anthropology of education. At the time, she was active in the lively struggles around community control over schooling that took place in New York City. Her 1970 article in *Schools Against Children, the Case for Community Control* and her 1971 edited book *The Culture of Poverty: A Critique*, which criticized Oscar Lewis's "culture of poverty" concept, are excellent illustrations of the way she linked her research to concrete grassroots movements for empowerment. At another level, her *Myths of Male Dominance* (1981) reveals the importance she gave to combating concepts she saw as distorting reality and harmful politically—such as the structuralist notion concerning the exchange of women or the assumption that had plagued early gender research, namely, that male dominance was a universal.

Leacock defended the view that the subordination of women was a product of history and not a transhistorical, universal condition. She criticized attempts to "naturalize" patriarchy by projecting it on all societies at all times. First, she documented the autonomy and power of women in preclass societies and the effects of colonialism and imperialism in undercutting this power. Second, she gave searching scrutiny to the social milieu that gave rise to the ahistorical, essentialist theories of women's subordination and to the interests such theories served. She insisted that gender analysis not be restricted to a separate category of study but become central to all social analysis.

For Leacock, cross-cultural studies were important not only because they challenged what was taken for granted but also because they offered an alternative vision of more egalitarian, people-centered lifeways. By focusing on the social context of theory formation, she encouraged her students to reflect on their positioning in society and on how the questions we ask are shaped by broader issues. For Leacock, reflexivity was not just a theoretical stance; it was a practice that grew out of political engagement. She played a central role in the development of The International Women's Anthropology Congress, an international network of anthropologists and others interested in research on gender that is informed by a cross-cultural perspective and that is global in its concerns. It was this engagement and holism—the unity of theory and practice—that

characterized all of Leacock's life and work. Her work remains relevant today.

Constance R. Sutton

See also Burke, Kenneth; Feminist Anthropology; Gender and Anthropology; Marx, Karl; Morgan, Lewis Henry

Further Readings

Leacock, E. (1954). *The Montagnais "hunting territory" and the fur trade* (Memoirs of the American Anthropological Association, No. 78). Arlington, VA: American Anthropological Association.

———. (1958). Social stratification and evolutionary theory. *Ethnohistory, 5,* 193–199.

———. (1969). *Teaching and learning in city schools: A comparative study.* New York, NY: Basic Books.

———. (Ed.). (1971). *The culture of poverty: A critique.* New York, NY: Simon & Schuster.

———. (1972). Introduction. In F. Engels (Ed.), *Origin of the family, private property, and the state* (pp. 7–64). New York, NY: International.

———. (1975). Class, commodity, and the status of women. In R. Rohrlich-Leavitt (Ed.), *Women cross-culturally: Change and challenge* (pp. 601–618). The Hague, Netherlands: Mouton.

———. (1978). Women's status in egalitarian society: Implications for social evolution. *Current Anthropology, 19,* 247–275.

———. (coedited with Etienne, M.). (1980). *Women and colonialization.* New York, NY: Praeger.

———. (1981). *Myths of male dominance.* New York, NY: Monthly Review.

———. (1983). Interpreting the origins of gender inequality: Conceptional and historical problems. *Dialectical Anthropology, 7,* 263–284.

———. (1986). Postscript: The problems of youth in contemporary Samoa. In L. D. Holmes, *Quest for the REAL Samoa: The Mead/Freman controversy and beyond* (pp. 177–188). South Hadley, MA: Bergin & Garvey.

———. (1986). Women, power and authority. In L. Dube, E. Leacock, & S. Ardener (Eds.), *Visibility and power: Essays on women in society and development* (pp. 107–135). New Delhi, India: Oxford University Press.

Sutton, C. R. (Ed.). (1993). *From Labrador to Samoa: The theory and practice of Eleanor Burke Leacock.* Arlington, VA: American Anthropological Association/ International Women's Anthropology Conference.

LeVine, Robert

Robert Alan LeVine (1932–) is a leading figure in psychological anthropology, having contributed to the field since the late 1950s. LeVine's work is particularly distinctive for its breadth, covering topics in child development research, psychoanalysis, culture theory, education, and demography. In each topical area, LeVine has formulated a conceptual framework designed to synthesize existing knowledge and establish priorities for future research. He has also attempted to unify psychological anthropology in terms of its shared history, theory, concepts, and specific problems of interest.

Biography

LeVine was born on March 27, 1932, in New York City. He entered the University of Chicago in 1949. In his first year, he took David Riesman's culture and personality course, and Riesman became his long-term mentor. He received his BA in 1951, and his master's degree, also from Chicago, in 1953. His advisor, Fred Eggan, arranged for LeVine to work with Clyde Kluckhohn at Harvard. LeVine began doctoral work there in 1953, with David M. Schneider as his adviser.

Once at Harvard, LeVine found that his interests corresponded with those of John and Beatrice Whiting, who were just beginning the Six Cultures Study of child socialization in six diverse cultures. LeVine became research assistant to Beatrice Whiting and later received a Ford Foundation fellowship to go to Kenya to perform child socialization research there. When he got back in 1957, he wrote his dissertation under John Whiting's direction, with Kluckhohn as one of the committee members.

Major Works

LeVine taught first at Northwestern University (1958–1960), then at the University of Chicago (1960–1976), where he continued research on child rearing and development in Africa and undertook training at the Chicago Institute for Psychoanalysis. In Chicago, he was influenced by Clifford Geertz, Heinz Kohut (at the Chicago Institute for Psychoanalysis, where LeVine was a research candidate), Melford E. Spiro, and Donald T. Campbell at Northwestern

(with whom he collaborated on the cross-cultural study of ethnocentrism, in *Ethnocentrism: Theories of Conflict, Ethnic Attitudes, and Group Behavior*, 1972). His orientation shifted toward cultural phenomenology and symbolic analysis while remaining empirically focused on the study of childhood environments. One product of those years was *Culture Behavior and Personality* (1973), LeVine's major attempt to provide a new framework for psychocultural research. Another was his chapter "Cross-Cultural Study in Child Psychology," replacing Margaret Mead's chapter in the third edition of *Carmichael's Manual of Child Psychology*.

LeVine's work from 1973 onward, including his years at Harvard (1976–1998 and beyond), can be divided by topical areas as follows: (a) person-centered ethnography, (b) parenting and early childhood, (c) schooling, and (d) history of psychological anthropology.

Person-Centered Ethnography

In *Culture, Behavior, and Personality*, LeVine considered how to revive the project on culture and personality originally launched by Edward Sapir, Mead, and Ruth Benedict. Influenced especially by the social psychologist Donald T. Campbell, Levine proposed that culture plays adaptive roles in the individual's mental functions and behavioral patterns and that a method based on psychoanalysis was the best way to uncover the emotional dynamics of this psychocultural adaptation. Deviating from orthodox Freudian theory, LeVine advocated the need to investigate culture-specific experiences. In the second edition (1982) of *Culture, Behavior, and Personality*, LeVine proposed a "person-centered ethnography" focused on cultural narratives of the self in several arenas of social communication. More broadly, he argued that most theoretical formulations in psychological anthropology can be recast as proposed relationships between the external world of collective cultural representations and the internal world of individual psychodynamics. Two examples of his own work in this vein are the articles on funerals (1982) and house design (1991) among the Gusii of Kenya.

Parenting and Early Childhood

In the late 1960s and later, LeVine combined quantitative approaches with qualitative approaches in studies of parents and children in different cultures. With his wife, Sarah, he conducted fieldwork on early childhood among the Hausa of Nigeria (1969) and the Gusii of Kenya (1974–1976). The Gusii Infant Study involved naturalistic observations of infants' social environments over a 17-month period. Their findings showed these to be organized by locally formulated standards of child rearing, reflecting not only moral traditions but also on ecological factors that included threats to child survival, high fertility, and the need for children's labor contribution to domestic agriculture. Levine's Gusii work exemplifies his "cultural mediation" synthesis, showing cultural models of parenting everywhere as filtering multiple influences and providing parents with a "moral direction," a "pragmatic design," and "conventional scripts for action" (LeVine et al., 1994).

Schooling: Communicative Resocialization in the Less Developed Countries

In 1976, LeVine moved to the Harvard Graduate School of Education. Concern with the high fertility rates among the Gusii and convinced that women's schooling played an important role in the demographic transition to lower birth and death rates, LeVine decided to investigate the processes by which schooling has an impact on demographic change. With his wife, Sarah, and their students, he conducted studies of maternal literacy in Mexico, Nepal, Venezuela, and Zambia. Their data showed that even rudimentary literacy skills acquired in low-quality schools helped mothers attend to public health messages and services and gave them the cognitive skills to navigate the bureaucratic processes needed to obtain health services for their children. This theory of communicative socialization in school, based on the work of Max Weber, Lev Vygotsky, and Sylvia Scribner and Michael Cole, was presented in the 2012 volume *Literacy and Mothering: How Women's Schooling Changes the Lives of the World's Children*, winner of the American Psychological Association's 2013 Eleanor Maccoby Award.

History of Psychological Anthropology

LeVine always treasured the legacy of the culture and personality movement, which had come into disfavor in anthropology and the social sciences just as he became a graduate student, and he saw himself as continuing its work. His research on child rearing was clearly part of a project initiated by Mead and amplified by the Whitings, and his person-centered ethnography was based on the ideas of A. Irving Hallowell. In his retirement, LeVine traced the historical antecedents further, to Sapir's (1993) visionary teachings and Franz Boas's study of the physical growth of immigrant children. Like Sapir, LeVine embraced the child's acquisition of culture as the central process relating culture to the individual psyche. His *Psychological Anthropology: A Reader on Self and Culture* (2010) presents his recent views on this history and its significance for the field.

LeVine's Legacy

In his research career, LeVine strove to realize the potentialities for scientific understanding he saw in the culture and personality movement. His goal was to transform psychological anthropology into a "population psychology" resembling other population sciences that study distributions of individual characteristics in ecological context. To this end, he developed conceptual syntheses, launched comparative research linking microsocial with macrosocial variables, and explored the history of psychological anthropology to understand where it had come from—the better to determine where it should be going.

Hidetada Shimizu

See also Benedict, Ruth; Culture and Personality; Geertz, Clifford; Hallowell, A. Irving; Kardiner, Abram; Mead, Margaret; Sapir, Edward; Spiro, Melford

Further Readings

LeVine, Robert. (1972). *Ethnocentrism: Theories of conflict, ethnic attitudes, and group behavior.* New York, NY: Wiley.

———. (1982). *Culture, behavior, and personality: An introduction to the comparative study of psychological anthropology* (2nd ed.). New York, NY: Aldine.

———. (Ed.). (2010). *Psychological anthropology: A reader on self in culture.* Malden, MA: Wiley-Blackwell.

LeVine, R., Dixon, S., LeVine, S., Richman, A., Leiderman, P. H., Keefer, C. H., & Brazelton, T. B. (1994). *Childcare and culture: Lessons from Africa.* Cambridge, UK: Cambridge University Press.

LeVine, R., LeVine, S., Schnell-Anzola, B., Rowe, M., & Dexter, E. (2012). *Literacy and mothering: How women's schooling changes the lives of the world's children.* Oxford, UK: Oxford University Press.

LÉVI-STRAUSS, CLAUDE

Claude Lévi-Strauss (1908–2009) was the preeminent French anthropologist of the 20th century and a founder of the theory of structuralism. His prominence reached far beyond France and beyond anthropology. His work was influential in literary studies, philosophy, and the humanities more broadly, as well as in certain areas of information science. He was translated into many languages and was particularly well received in the United States, Canada, the United Kingdom, and Japan. His work covered a wide range of material—Australian kinship, Greek myth, Northwest Coast masks—but was centered on his interpretation of Native American oral literature. This literature—drawn from the Arctic to the tip of South America—provided an infinitely rich source of material for Lévi-Strauss's interpretive devices. He claimed to be able to connect these widely disparate myths in the context of a hemispheric whole.

Early Life

Lévi-Strauss was born in Paris, in a neighborhood (16th arrondisement) where he would spend most of his life. His father was a modestly successful portrait painter, who preferred the older, academic style to the forms of modernism that were popular in the early 20th century. This situation provided the young Lévi-Strauss with a rich visual environment and early training in art, as well as a sense of cultural dynamics and historical change. His maternal grandfather, with whom he lived during the First World War, was chief rabbi in Versailles. From him, Lévi-Strauss developed a sense of the opposition between the world of the sacred and ritual and the secular everyday world that he and his parents inhabited. Such insights would prove relevant in his later anthropological career, especially as he would consider the ability of ritual to create its own reality apart from the everyday world.

Lévi-Strauss attended school at the Lycée Janson de Sailly and the Lycée Condorcet. He studied law and philosophy at the Sorbonne, receiving his *aggrégation* in the latter, despite his dissatisfaction with what he felt to be the pseudo-sophistication and mechanical style of philosophical discourse. He went on to teach in provincial high schools for several years. During this time, he married his first wife, Dina Dreyfus, with whom he would share the beginnings of an anthropological career.

Lévi-Strauss's move toward anthropology was facilitated by a serendipitous opportunity in 1935 to teach sociology in Brazil, at the University of São Paolo. This was part of a French cultural mission that reflected the prestige with which French culture and scholarship were regarded in that country. Although he was promised that there would be Indians in the suburbs of São Paolo, this was patently untrue. What he found instead was a somewhat dowdy colonial town that gave way to rustic suburbs and then to the forested hills of the interior. Eventually, he was able to travel to the north into Amazonia, where he made contact with Indian groups such as the Caduveo, living in two worlds. Finally, at the end of his 4-year stint in Brazil (with trips back to France each year), Lévi-Strauss planned and mounted an expedition to the Mato Grosso and Amazonia, where he encountered the Bororo, the Nambikwara, and the Tupi-Kawahib. This was a true expedition, of the sort last seen around the turn of the century, involving a half a dozen scientists (including Dina Lévi-Strauss and the Brazilian anthropologist Luiz de Castro Faria), numerous support personnel, mules, trucks, and huge amounts of provisions and items for barter. Funded by the Brazilian government, the logistics of this operation impeded the scientific aspects of the project. Additionally, sickness and injury meant the loss of team members (Dina was forced to return to São Paolo for treatment of conjunctivitis). Beyond this, the very design of the expedition, according to an outmoded idea of ethnographic research, meant that Lévi-Strauss and the others would have only weeks with each tribe, never reaching the point of rapport or easy communication. Nonetheless, Lévi-Strauss was able to record material of interest. A keen observer and gifted draftsman and photographer, he brought back important images and insights into material culture, bodily adornment, and kinship. Although not yet a "structuralist," he was beginning to move in that direction by observing societies that organized themselves around the principle of complementary opposition.

Lévi-Strauss returned to Paris in 1939 with a great many material artifacts destined for the new Musée de l'Homme. This material provided the basis of their South American collection, as his later Northwest Coast collection would for that region. (Both are now at the Musée de Quai Branly.) His interest in material culture was shaped by his own early interest in art and aesthetics and reinforced by his mentor Marcel Mauss.

When the Germans crossed the Maginot line in 1940, Lévi-Strauss was called to military service in northern France. This was for a brief period, and he returned to Paris and then moved to Montpelier, in the south of France, where he was given a teaching post. However, the Vichy government soon passed racial laws that ended his employment. He realized almost too late the virulence of the anti-Semitism within France and made an effort to flee. He hoped to return to Brazil and was nearly successful but was denied a final visa stamp. His only option was to take a steamer to Martinique. His fellow refugees included figures such as the surrealist writer André Breton. By various strokes of good fortune (he was under the protection of the ship's captain, who remembered him fondly from previous sailings to Brazil), he made his way to Puerto Rico. There, he was placed under house arrest while his ethnographic papers were examined. Eventually, he was allowed to proceed to New York, where he had an invitation to teach at the New School for Social Research.

Lévi-Strauss in New York

If the period in Brazil was crucial for Lévi-Strauss's understanding of American Indian cultures (it would prove to be his only stint of fieldwork, brief though it was), his time in New York during World War II was a period of phenomenal intellectual dynamism. The assortment of European refugees gathered in Manhattan provided a fertile milieu for developing new ideas. Many were employed at the New School for Social Research, and many were also part of the circle of Franz Boas, who, although in his 80s, made an effort to welcome and encourage these younger scholars and artists. Lévi-Strauss was immediately drawn into that circle, as he had already become enamored of the textual ethnographies produced by the Bureau of American Ethnology, to which Boas contributed many volumes. This was to become the basis of his greatest achievement: the four-volume *Mythologiques*, an analysis of myth and cultural data recorded in these and similar publications.

In 1942, Boas died literally in Lévi-Strauss's arms in the faculty club at Columbia University.

A second key figure in this period was Roman Jakobson. It was he who gave Lévi-Strauss the intellectual underpinnings for what would become structuralist anthropology. Jakobson, a linguist who specialized in phonology, had adapted Saussurian linguistics to an analysis of distinctive features in language, extending beyond phonology to syntax and semantics. The underlying point—that linguistic value and, hence, meaning were constructed in a context of opposition among features, not by any inherent qualities—appealed to Lévi-Strauss because it expressed insights that he had already acquired regarding ethnographic data. Lévi-Strauss would extend this perspective to an analysis of kinship, myth, ritual, and other cultural data.

In New York, one final piece to Lévi-Strauss's professional profile would fall into place: his interest in Northwest Coast culture. Obviously, Boas was influential in this development (as had been Mauss back in Paris). But probably most significant were Boas's displays at the American Museum of Natural History and the availability of Northwest Coast artifacts for sale through Manhattan dealers at prices that even refugee academics could afford. He acquired a considerable collection of masks and other objects while in New York, and would, much later, write a remarkable book, *The Way of the Masks*, on the relation of mask form to ritual function in neighboring Northwest Coast societies.

Beyond his professional development, his time in the United States was a transformative period of his life. His experience of New York and Chicago provided him with a different idea of what a city, and what modern civilization itself, could be, which he had not found in either European cities or their colonial copies, such as São Paolo. Like other exiled French intellectuals, such as Simone de Beauvoir, Lévi-Strauss wrote affectionately of his time in the United States. Indeed, he stayed on for 2 years after the war as a cultural attaché.

Return to Paris

Lévi-Strauss returned to Paris at the end of 1947. Over the next 2 years, he submitted two publications to be considered as qualification for his doctorate in anthropology. These were accepted, and Lévi-Strauss eventually obtained a teaching position.

During the 1950s, Lévi-Strauss both was shaped by and helped shape the institutional and intellectual milieu of postwar France. In 1950, the new organization the United Nations Educational, Scientific, and Cultural Organization, based in Paris, commissioned a work that would become *Race and History*, a significant meditation on an emerging issue of great import. During this period, Lévi-Strauss worked assiduously to carve out an institutional space for anthropology as a "human science," space that necessarily would be taken from humanistic disciplines, given the limited resources available. Unlike the United States, France did not experience rapid growth in the academy during the 1950s. The academic philosophy that he found so stultifying and nationalistic academic history were his main targets. By the end of the decade, Lévi-Strauss had successfully created a home for anthropology in the new Laboratoire d'Anthropologie Sociale affiliated with the Collège de France.

Far from wishing to isolate anthropology from other intellectual currents, Lévi-Strauss engaged in the broader exchange of ideas taking place in the Left Bank cafes of postwar Paris. Lévi-Strauss was close to Jean-Paul Sartre and Simone de Beauvoir, and he exerted a strong influence over a younger generation of philosophers, notably Michel Foucault and Jacques Derrida. His ideas were borrowed by Louis Althusser and Maurice Godelier in their attempt to forge a structural Marxism in the late 1960s. His influence within anthropology was especially pronounced among his English and American colleagues, notably Edmund Leach, Mary Douglas, and Marshall Sahlins. In recognition of his increasingly global reputation, Lévi-Strauss was elected to the Académie Française in 1973 and received a number of honors both in France and internationally in the subsequent 4 decades.

Key Ideas

Alliance Theory and Totemism

In *The Elementary Structures of Kinship*, Lévi-Strauss tackles one of the central themes of English structural functionalism. Within that tradition, as represented by A. R. Radcliffe-Brown, the key issue was descent. Descent and ways of reckoning consanguinity (e.g., matrilineal or patrilineal) defined social identity. Lévi-Strauss, by contrast, emphasized affinity—that is, marriage relations among groups. Following from his early observations of the Bororo in Brazil, Lévi-Strauss saw the "exchange" of women among groups that defined themselves in opposition to their partners as following formal rules that embedded exogamous social groups within multigenerational contexts of exchange and alliance. In this way, two groups mutually constructed themselves, creating a social whole out of two interdependent, incomplete parts. The Australian and Kachin marriage systems he analyzes in *Elementary Structures* are much more complex but can be seen as an elaboration of the underlying principle.

Social identity, like all questions of cultural meaning, is oppositional. It is also, as Ferdinand de Saussure argued for language, arbitrary. Thus, the incest taboo was for these societies not a question of the degree of consanguinity as it was of the demarcation of arbitrary social boundaries. Indeed, in certain societies, such as those of the northern Northwest Coast, the preferred marriage partner may well be a cross-cousin: a much closer relative than almost all members of one's own clan, which constituted the exogamous group. Implicit in these marriage relations was exchange: of material goods and symbolic properties (e.g., names and ritual dances on the Northwest Coast). Building on an insight developed by Émile Durkheim and Mauss, Lévi-Strauss viewed reciprocity as an essential building block of society.

The main mode by which primitive cultures understood the complementary opposition of social groups was the model of the natural world. The essence of totemism is relational, not substantive. As Lévi-Strauss famously quipped, totems are "good to think" (rather than eat). Thus, the opposition between raven and eagle for the Northwest Coast cultures (an opposition approximately as that between Odysseus and Achilles in Homer) provides a template for the opposition between two human groups, the Raven and Eagle clans.

The Structural Study of Myth

Most of Lévi-Strauss's academic writing was on the theme of myth. We learn a great deal by example about his method in *Mythologiques*. However, his most programmatic writing on myth, as well as his most famous, is his reanalysis of Oedipus. Against the background of perhaps the most famous and influential interpretation of myth, Lévi-Strauss argued audaciously against Freud's famous and influential interpretation of the Oedipus myth as a recapitulation of a primordial series of events of universal importance. As the notion of incest is itself subject to very diverse interpretations depending on cultural context, Lévi-Strauss knew that such a global, archetypal reading was not correct. Rather, he analyzes the mythical elements ("mythemes") that arise in the myth itself and arranges them in terms of structured oppositions and mediations. Some of this is fairly straightforward: overvaluation versus undervaluation of kinship ties, while other oppositions (autochthony vs. impeded locomotion) are more recondite. Nevertheless, he demonstrates convincingly that myths must be read both syntagmatically (in the order in which events are told) and paradigmatically (where themes resonate with parallel or opposed themes in other parts of the myth). Here, he employs a theme that runs throughout his work on myth: music and the symphonic structuring of elements by counterpoint, harmony, repetition, and so forth. Like a symphony, a myth must be listened to carefully with a connoisseur's ear. Although his method has been viewed as rather mechanistic, due in part to Lévi-Strauss's own insistence that it is scientifically rigorous, it is in fact a highly aesthetic mode of interpretation.

At the root, Lévi-Strauss claims that myth is about fundamental, existential oppositions, themselves universal but interpreted in highly culturally specific ways. Life and death, culture and nature, male and female are among the most basic of these. Myth thus expresses these universal concerns while resolving them in some way. Oppositions are mediated. Thus, cooked food is contrasted with raw food (nature); but these may be mediated culturally by partially cooked food, viewed culturally as falling between the two.

Mediators may also be agents, in which case they take on the role of tricksters. In North American myths, tricksters are usually Raven or Coyote. They are mediators because they are scavengers, falling between the category of herbivores (who collect rather than hunt their food) and beasts of prey (who eat meat). This invokes larger oppositions between agriculture and hunting, and between life and death. As agents, tricksters are very potent characters, even to the point of bringing the world into being (as Raven does in a Haida myth). They are also figures who provide a comical, photographic negative image of the established social order. Uncontrollable sexuality and other appetites define them. As such they may be seen to mediate between the cosmos and chaos; while they flout all standards of acceptable behavior, they at the same time acknowledge those standards in specifically breaching them.

"Wild Thinking"

This is an alternate translation of the title of Lévi-Strauss's most important single volume, *The Savage Mind*. Here, he sets out to address another central anthropological question: the so-called psychic unity problem. Were all humans equipped with comparable cognitive faculties, a position central to both evolutionary and structural-functionalist anthropologies, or was there such a thing as a "primitive mentality" in Lucien Lévy-Bruhl's phrasing, an idea that has held a certain appeal among Romantic thinkers of all stripes? Lévi-Strauss sides with the unitarians but with a twist: The thought process of "primitive" people is equally impressive as that of we moderns, but they begin from a different epistemological starting place. Unlike the model of modern science, beginning with formal systems of classification and scientific theories from which one can generate hypotheses, the "savage" thinker begins with the data on hand and constructs classifications based on what she or he determines to be the significant features. Thus, local taxonomies of plants or animals are bound to differ from Linnaean ones, but they too are based on empirical data. Thus, the main difference is that the wild thinker is a radical inductivist rather than a deductivist. This is, interestingly, how Lévi-Strauss viewed his own thought process. He immersed himself in all kinds of information: tide charts, star maps, topographical maps, fisheries data, along with all the ethnographic and myth data, when writing about Northwest Coast cultures. This was, as it were, his Boasian side; he certainly possessed a more formal, deductive side as well.

Lévi-Strauss's term for this mode of thought was "science of the concrete." A companion term, which stands in relation to it as engineering does to science in the Western context, is *bricolage*, a common French word meaning something like tinkering: building or repairing things with materials at hand (similar to Heidegger's notion of "building"). That is, one begins not with a master plan but with a critical and creative assessment of the materials at hand, a noticing of the relations (similarity, complementarity, opposition, etc.) that pertain among them and how these elements and their relations may be put to use. This describes not only material building of structures but also the rebuilding and restructuring that is constantly occurring in myths. Myth elements circulate freely across cultural and linguistic boundaries but are transformed as they cross them. Culture is not static, although in many cases (as in "cold" societies), it pretends to be. Rather, it is rebuilt using the principles of bricolage. Again, Lévi-Strauss considered himself a *bricoleur*, which does fairly well describe his method of analyzing myth.

Identity and Alterity

Beginning with some of his earliest writings, Lévi-Strauss was concerned with the relation between alterity and identity. As he describes exogamous, totemic clans in Australia or moiety organization in Amazonia, he forcefully makes the point that difference, although arbitrary, is what constitutes identity, rather than something inherent or essential to the group (although that may well be the ideology of the said group). This applies not only to tribal society but to modern nation states as well. In *Race and History*, Lévi-Strauss identifies the problem of creeping global monoculture, or cultural entropy, as a fundamental threat to human well-being. On one level, this echoes long-standing Gallic complaints about the intrusion of Anglo-Saxon language and culture (a topic with which Lévi-Strauss as a member of the *Académie Française* was intimately familiar). However, for Lévi-Strauss, this was only part of a larger assault on cultural difference.

The problem with global monoculture is not only the loss of cultural distinctiveness but also the loss of the "Other" as a foil to identity. It is a version of what Max Weber called the disenchantment of the world. A world in which everything significant takes place in a space dominated by the monoculture of information technology with English as the lingua franca is culturally much reduced. It is a recapitulation of what Lévi-Strauss observed in Brazil in the 1930s: Tribal cultures were being absorbed into a "sad" relationship of dependency with the global world system. By the end of the 20th century, even large and powerful nation-states were threatened with a similar fate.

Significance

The work of Lévi-Strauss has been extremely influential in anthropology and in related fields. In his later years, he distanced himself from the structuralist paradigm, to the degree that he actually denied being a structuralist. (This obviously was connected entirely with academic politics. Many other structuralists or quasi structuralists, such as Roland Barthes and Pierre Bourdieu, populated the French academic scene.) Like so many before him, it is evident that his genius lay mainly in synthesis rather than in purely original thought. One can trace the genealogy of his major concepts through fairly wide thoroughfares of French and European thought, whether of René Descartes, Jean-Jacques Rousseau, Henri Bergson, Karl Marx, Sigmund Freud, Émile Durkheim, or Ferdinand Saussure. His particular value was in applying these concepts to ethnographic and mythical material, in connecting them with problems of the modern world, and with fashioning a vision of anthropology as a "human science."

Michael E. Harkin

See also Althusser, Louis; Barthes, Roland; Bloch, Maurice; Boas, Franz; Bourdieu, Pierre; Butler, Judith; Derrida, Jacques; Douglas, Mary; Durkheim, Émile; Foucault, Michel; Jakobson, Roman O.; Lacan, Jacques; *L'Année Sociologique*; Leach, Edmund; Lévy-Bruhl, Lucien; Mauss, Marcel; Needham, Rodney; Sahlins, Marshall; Saussure, Ferdinand de; Structuralism

Further Readings

Descola, P. (Ed.). (2012). *Claude Lévi-Strauss: Un parcours dans le siècle* [Claude Lévi-Strauss: A tour through the century]. Paris, France: Odile Jacob.

Hénaff, M. (1998). *Claude Lévi-Strauss and the making of structural anthropology*. Minneapolis: University of Minnesota Press.

Johnson, C. (2003). *Claude Lévi-Strauss: The formative years*. Cambridge, UK: Cambridge University Press.

Wilcken, P. (2010). *Claude Lévi-Strauss: The father of modern anthropology*. New York, NY: Penguin Books.

Wiseman, B. (Ed.). (2009). *The Cambridge companion to Lévi-Strauss*. Cambridge, UK: Cambridge University Press.

LÉVY-BRUHL, LUCIEN

Lucien Lévy-Bruhl (1857–1939) was a French philosopher who became an armchair anthropologist. His first and most important anthropological
work, *How Natives Think*, was originally published in France in 1910 as *Les Functions Mentales
Dans les Sociétés Inférieures* and was translated
into English only in 1926—3 years *after* the translation of his second and next most important
anthropological work, *Primitive Mentality* (1923),
originally published in France as *La Mentalité
Primitive* in 1922.

"Primitive" and Modern Thinking

Lévy-Bruhl never asserts, as is commonly charged,
that "primitive" peoples are inferior to moderns. On
the contrary, he means to defend primitive peoples
against this charge, made above all by the pioneering British anthropologists Edward Burnett Tylor
and James G. Frazer. For Tylor and Frazer, "primitives" think the way moderns do. They just think
less rigorously. For Tylor and Frazer, the difference
between primitive and modern thinking is only of
degree. For Lévy-Bruhl, the difference is of kind. He
maintains that primitive thought is both mystical
and prelogical.

Lévy-Bruhl attributes primitive thinking to culture, not to biology. Like other 20th-century anthropologists, he separates culture from race. What
distinguishes primitives from us is their "collective
representations." By collective representations
(*représentations collectives*), a term taken from the
French sociologist Émile Durkheim, Lévy-Bruhl
means group beliefs, which for him are the same
across all primitive societies. Primitive representations, or *conceptions*, shape *perceptions*, or experiences. According to Lévy-Bruhl, primitive peoples
believe that all phenomena, including humans and
their artifacts, are part of an impersonal sacred, or
"mystic," realm that pervades the natural one. To
take Lévy-Bruhl's most famous example, when the
Bororo of Brazil declare themselves red parakeets,
they mean that they are in all respects outright identical with red parakeets.

Mysticism is only the first of the two key characteristics of primitive mentality. The other characteristic, "prelogicality," builds on the first one but
is more radical: It is the belief that all things are not
only mystically one but somehow also distinct. The
Bororo believe that a human is a parakeet yet still
a human. They do not believe that a human and a
parakeet are, say, identical invisibly while distinct
visibly. That belief would merely be a version of mysticism, itself hardly limited to "primitives." Rather,
primitive peoples believe that humans and parakeets
are simultaneously both identical and separate in the
same respects. Visibly as well as invisibly, humans
and parakeets are at once the same and different.
According to Lévy-Bruhl, that belief violates the law
of noncontradiction—the law that something cannot be both *X* and non-*X* at the same time—and is
uniquely primitive.

Lévy-Bruhl does not conclude, as is conventionally said of him, that primitive peoples cannot
think logically, that they are mentally deficient.
Instead, he concludes that "primitives," ruled as
they are by their collective representations, regularly suspend the practice of logic. Primitive thinking is prelogical, but "prelogical" does not mean
illogical. Still, many readers mistook prelogical for
illogical, so that Lévy-Bruhl seemed to be making
primitive peoples even more hopelessly inferior to
moderns than Tylor and Frazer had made them—
the opposite of his intent. However, in arguing
that primitive thinking differs in nature from modern thinking, Lévy-Bruhl is not arguing that it is
equally true. Primitive thinking does make sense
in light of its premises, but its premises are still
illogical: Something cannot simultaneously be both
itself and something else in the same respects at the
same time. Where for Tylor and to a lesser extent
Frazer primitive thinking is false but still rational,
for Lévy-Bruhl primitive thinking is irrational and
consequently false.

Unlike many other anthropological writers of his
day and ours, Lévy-Bruhl is not a relativist. Like both
Tylor and Frazer, he is an absolutist. There are several varieties of relativism—conceptual, perceptual,
and moral—but none fits Lévy-Bruhl. Conceptual
relativism denies the existence of objective criteria
for assessing the diversity of *beliefs* about the world.
Beliefs can supposedly be evaluated only within a
culture. Lévy-Bruhl is scarcely a conceptual relativist, since he is prepared to judge both mysticism
and prelogicality outright as false beliefs about the
world. Perceptual relativism denies the possibility of
evaluating objectively the diversity of *experiences* of

the world. Where conceptual relativism allows for common experiences that simply get interpreted differently by different cultures, perceptual relativism, which is bolder, maintains that experiences themselves differ. One culture deems real the purported experience of a god. Another culture deems delusory the same experience. There is no way to judge these differing evaluations. Lévy-Bruhl is hardly a perceptual relativist, since he is prepared to judge the experience of oneness as delusory. Moral relativism, which denies that objective criteria exist for evaluating the undeniable diversity of *values* around the world, is not relevant to Lévy-Bruhl, who does not consider morality in his characterization of primitive thinking.

While Lévy-Bruhl takes the concept of collective representations from Durkheim, he stresses the differences rather than, like Durkheim, the similarities between primitive and modern thinking. For Lévy-Bruhl, primitive representations, or beliefs, come between primitives and the world. They determine how primitives experience the world and not merely how they think about the world. They shape perceptions as well as conceptions. Primitive peoples experience, not merely think, everything in the world as at once mystically one and separate. By contrast, modern representations, which do exist, shape only conceptions, and thus convey the world to moderns rather than come between moderns and the world. According to Lévy-Bruhl, modern representations, or beliefs, determine how moderns think about the world but not how moderns experience the world. Moderns experience the world as it actually is.

In a section of *How Natives Think* titled "The Transition to the Higher Mental Types," Lévy-Bruhl writes of "progress" in cognition. Progress requires the filtering out of the emotional elements that distort primitive perceptions. Only modern representations have been subjected to "the test of experience." In fact, for Lévy-Bruhl, it is only "scientific theorizing" that is abstract enough to be free of emotion and therefore free of mystical and prelogical proclivities. The difference between primitives and moderns is not, then, that moderns think wholly logically. It is that primitives think wholly prelogically. For Lévy-Bruhl, the emotional allure of mystical oneness makes its total disappearance unlikely, and he cites example after example of the retention of prelogical thinking among moderns. Conversely, he traces the lessening of mystical ties among primitive peoples themselves. The opposition that he draws is, then, between primitive and modern *thinking*, not between primitives and moderns *themselves*.

Many others no less absolutist than Lévy-Bruhl have been criticized far less severely. The reason is that, despite his undeniably neutral intent, Lévy-Bruhl in fact characterizes primitive mentality much more negatively than even Tylor and Frazer characterize it. Tylor and Frazer take for granted that primitive peoples recognize not only the law of noncontradiction but most "modern" distinctions as well: those between appearance and reality, subjectivity and objectivity, supernatural and natural, human and nonhuman, the living and the dead, the individual and the group, one time and another, and one space and another. True, for Tylor and Frazer, primitives fail to think sufficiently critically and thereby produce religion rather than science, but not because of any missed distinctions. Primitives still think, and think logically and systematically. For Tylor and Frazer, religion no less than science is the product of scientific-like observation, hypothesis, and generalization. It is not the product of primitive perceptions.

To be sure, for Frazer, the efficacy of magic, which for him constitutes a stage prior to that of religion, does presuppose the failure to make two distinctions: (1) that between the literal and the symbolic—for otherwise a voodoo doll would merely symbolize, not affect, a person—and (2) that between a part and the whole—for otherwise a severed strand of hair would merely have once been part of a person, not still affect that person. But Frazer never assumes that in even this stage, primitives are oblivious to the other distinctions that Lévy-Bruhl denies them, such as the distinctions between appearance and reality and between subjectivity and objectivity. And any distinctions missed by primitive peoples are, for Frazer, of conception, not of perception, which he, together with Tylor, considers invariant universally.

For Lévy-Bruhl, primitive peoples do not even have religion. What beliefs they do have come from their collective representations and not from any observations of the world, let alone from any rational responses to observations. Far from thinking rationally, primitive peoples, brainwashed by their mystical and prelogical beliefs, scarcely think at all.

Critique and Response

Lévy-Bruhl was castigated by field-workers who claimed never to have come on any culture with a distinctively primitive mentality. In *Primitive Man as Philosopher* (1927), the American anthropologist Paul Radin gave the classic anthropological rebuttal. Like other anthropological critics, Radin denies that primitive peoples miss the distinctions that Lévy-Bruhl declares them to be bereft of: cause and effect, subject and object, natural and supernatural, nonmystical and mystical, individual and group, and literal and symbolic. Yet Radin, unlike other anthropological critics, divides the members of any society, modern and primitive alike, into "men of action," who may well fail to make some of Lévy-Bruhl's distinctions, and "thinkers," who do not. By contrast, Lévy-Bruhl insists that the "average man" as well as the "cultured, scientific man" differ from primitive man.

Against Lévy-Bruhl, the French structural anthropologist Claude Lévi-Strauss, in *The Savage Mind* (1966) and elsewhere, similarly argues that primitive peoples think no differently than moderns. They merely focus on the observable, qualitative aspects of phenomena rather than, like moderns, on the unobservable, quantitative ones. Colors and sounds, not mass and length, faze them. Far from being prescientific, primitive peoples attain a fully scientific knowledge of the world. Theirs is simply a "science of the concrete" rather than of the abstract. And even if they do not, like moderns, separate abstractions from concrete cases, they do express abstractions through concrete cases. Furthermore, primitive knowledge is for Lévi-Strauss basically taxonomic, so that "primitives" are quite capable of categorizing. In fact, their taxonomies take the form of oppositions, which, as the equivalent, for Lévi-Strauss, of contradictions, make primitives not only aware of contradictions but also intent on resolving them. Myths most of all evince the austere, rigorous, logic-chopping nature of primitive thinking. No view of primitive peoples could be more opposed to Lévy-Bruhl's than Lévi-Strauss's.

The chief defender of Lévy-Bruhl was the English anthropologist E. E. Evans-Pritchard, above all in his *Witchcraft, Oracles and Magic Among the Azande* (1937). Yet even he faults Lévy-Bruhl for deeming primitive thinking prelogical. Where for Lévy-Bruhl primitive magic takes the place of science, for Evans-Pritchard magic and proto-science coexist. To the Azande, the sheer physical features of a tree explain its ordinary, natural "behavior." Witchcraft, Evans-Pritchard's most famous example of supernatural causality, explains only unfortunate events involving the tree: why one day it falls on one person or, to cite his most famous example, why a granary under which Azande are sitting collapses when it does. Witchcraft attributes to malevolent intent what science writes off as bad luck. For Lévy-Bruhl, in contrast, even events as regular and therefore as seemingly natural as birth, disease, and death get attributed to *magic*—a term that he, unlike Evans-Pritchard and others, uses broadly to encompass all supernatural causes. In shifting from the Azande to the Nuer, Evans-Pritchard, in *Nuer Religion* (1956), challenges Lévy-Bruhl's most striking evidence of prelogical mentality: statements, for example, that a cucumber is an ox and that human twins are birds. Lévy-Bruhl maintains that mystical representations override the senses, so that primitive peoples somehow actually perceive, not just conceive, a cucumber as an ox. Evans-Pritchard denies that they do either. The Nuer, he asserts, are speaking only metaphorically. They are saying that a cucumber is sufficiently like an ox to serve as a substitute for it. Similarly, a human twin is like a bird in certain respects but is not therefore a bird.

In his posthumously published notebooks, Lévy-Bruhl abandons his view of primitives as prelogical, though not as mystical. He does not, like Evans-Pritchard, assert that the Bororo, in deeming Trumai tribesmen fish, are merely comparing the Trumai with fish. He is claiming that the Bororo deem the Trumai mystically identical with fish. He does, however, now grant that the Trumai are fish supernaturally, not physically. Their "fishness" complements, not contradicts, their ordinary, physical humanness. Primitives thus recognize at least the distinction between the supernatural and the natural. But overall, primitive thinking remains distinct from modern thinking.

Robert Segal

See also Durkheim, Émile; Evans-Pritchard, E. E.; Frazer, James G.; Lévi-Strauss, Claude; Radin, Paul; Tylor, Edward Burnett

Further Readings

Durkheim, E. (1915). *The elementary forms of the religious life* (J. W. Swain, Trans.). London, UK: Allen & Unwin. (Original work published 1912)

Evans-Pritchard, E. E. (1937). *Witchcraft, oracles and magic among the Azande.* Oxford, UK: Clarendon Press.

———. (1956). *Nuer religion.* Oxford, UK: Clarendon Press.

Lévi-Strauss, C. (1966). *The savage mind.* Chicago, IL: University of Chicago Press. (Original work published 1962)

Lévy-Bruhl, L. (1923). *Primitive mentality* (L. A. Clare, Trans.). London, UK: Allen & Unwin. (Original work published 1922)

———. (1926). *How natives think* (L. A. Clare, Trans.). London, UK: Allen & Unwin. (Original work published 1910)

———. (1938). *L'expérience mystique et les symboles chez les primitives* [The mystical experience and symbols in primitives]. Paris, France: Alcan.

Radin, P. (1927). *Primitive man as philosopher* (1st ed.). New York. NY: Appleton.

LEWIS, OSCAR

In 3 decades of field research, Oscar Lewis (1914–1970) contributed significantly to the shift in American anthropology away from North American Indians to peasant communities and finally to urban studies. Throughout his career, he was committed to the proposition that anthropologists should focus attention on the conditions of poverty. Especially in his writings on individuals and families, Lewis effectively employed the narrative approach to give a voice to the poor so that readers, whether anthropology students or government policymakers, would understand the challenges of living in poverty and the adaptations that people developed to it.

Biographical Data

Born in New York City in 1914 as Yehezkiel Lefkowitz (but also given the Anglicized first name Oscar), Lewis was the son of Jewish immigrants from Poland. For a time, his father practiced as a rabbi in New York City, but poor health forced him to move his family to a small town in upstate New York. There, the family had a farm and eventually constructed a family hotel on their land. The family struggled to succeed, being forced to move back to the city in the winters. Thus, Lewis grew up with firsthand experience of rural and urban poverty.

The first member of his family to attend college, Lewis entered City College of New York in 1930. Although the tuition was free, books and living expenses were a burden. He focused on philosophy and history and read extensively on Marxist approaches to the struggles of the poor. He received his bachelor's degree in social science in 1936 and was accepted into Columbia Teachers College. However, Lewis soon transferred to the anthropology department at Columbia, where he studied with Ruth Benedict and Ralph Linton. He married Ruth Maslow (sister of the psychologist Abraham Maslow) in November 1937 and also thus gained a lifelong research collaborator. The couple went together to the Blackfoot reservation in 1939, when Benedict organized a summer study there. This work led to his library-based dissertation, published by the American Ethnological Society. In 1940, the year in which he received his PhD, he legally changed his surname from Lefkowitz to Lewis.

In 1942, Lewis obtained a position at the Human Relations Area Files. While working there on the Strategic Index for Latin America, he obtained a grant to study Spanish during the summer. His focus on Latin America intensified when he moved on to a short-term appointment in 1943 at the Justice Department's Special War Policies Unit, concerned with propaganda. In August 1943, he was sent to Mexico as a representative of the Department of Interior's National Indian Institute. In this role, he was assigned to coordinate a joint study (known as the Indian Personality Project) with the Interamerican Indian Institute on the impact of government policies on Mexican Indians. The most important product of this work was his decision to begin a field project in the peasant community of Tepoztlán, located in the State of Morelos just south of Mexico City. When his assignment in Mexico was completed, Lewis was transferred to the Bureau of Agricultural Economics in the Department of Agriculture, where he first did a survey of ongoing research projects throughout the central states. Eventually, he did field research in Bell County, in central Texas, resulting in a monograph titled *On the Edge of the Black Waxy: A Cultural Survey of Bell County, Texas* (1948). Along with Walter Goldschmidt's study of a central California agricultural community, this is one of the first social anthropological studies of non-Indian rural America.

Lewis's first full-time academic position came in 1946, when he was hired as an associate professor at Washington University in Saint Louis. After 2 years there, he accepted an appointment at the University of Illinois, where he remained for the rest of his career—apart from a consultancy with the Ford Foundation in northern India during 1952–1954. Besides his administrative duties in India, he was able to conduct research with Indian field-workers and interpreters in the community of Rampur. This led to the publication of his 1958 monograph, *Village Life in Northern India.*

The Tepoztlán Restudy

While in Mexico in 1943, Lewis had initiated a restudy of the community of Tepoztlán, where, in 1926, the anthropologist Robert Redfield had done fieldwork that resulted in his monograph *Tepoztlán: A Mexican Village* (1930). The scope of Lewis's project went well beyond the mandate of the Indian Personality Project, within which it was developed. It became clear to Lewis that he would need to return to Mexico as soon as possible to gather additional data to complete what was collected in 1943–1944. He was finally able to return to Tepoztlán in the summers of 1947 and 1948. During these field trips, he and his wife, Ruth, focused on detailed family studies and individual life histories to complement the survey work that had been carried out earlier. When his monograph *Life in a Mexican Village: Tepoztlán Restudied* appeared in 1951, it set off a controversy among anthropologists concerned with the differences between the idyllic portrait sketched by Redfield for the late 1920s and the conflict-laden community described by Lewis for the late 1940s. The so-called Redfield-Lewis controversy has become the textbook example of the challenges facing anthropologists doing fieldwork and also provides an early example of the value of systematic restudies and long-term research in understanding the processes of community transformation.

The Mexico City Studies

In 1951, Lewis returned to Mexico City to take up the question of how well migrants from Tepoztlán adapt to life in Mexico City. He had first considered this question during his 1944 research but could not pursue it then. With a list of migrant families obtained from his contacts in the village, Lewis and his team of student assistants were able to visit some 100 families spread throughout the city. Just as he had with Redfield's work, Lewis now took on the standard model of "urbanism as a way of life," as proposed in 1938 by the sociologist Louis Wirth. Based on his analysis of the Mexico City data, Lewis wrote an article, "Urbanization Without Breakdown: A Case Study," published in 1952 in the general magazine *The Scientific Monthly.* Although published in an unusual venue for social anthropological research, Lewis's article has been reprinted many times and is considered a classic riposte to the claims by Wirth about the international applicability of a Euro-American model of urbanization.

Subsequently, in 1956, Lewis went to Mexico to carry out a more detailed study of family life. Using a tape recorder, he began to record detailed life histories of persons in Tepoztlán and of residents of Mexico City. The major results of this endeavor were the monographs *The Children of Sánchez* (1961) and *Pedro Martínez: A Mexican Peasant and His Family* (1964). With funding from a Guggenheim Fellowship and awards from the Wenner-Gren Foundation for Anthropological Research and his university, Lewis also began what would become his most famous and most controversial research: the culture of poverty.

The ethnographic base of the research was in two lower class *vecindades* (housing settlements) located in the old central section of Mexico City. These *vecindades* were selected to represent different socioeconomic levels among the poor in Mexico City. Subsequently, to look at the differences among other lower- and middle-class families, Lewis obtained additional funding from the Social Science Research Council (1958) and the National Science Foundation (1959). Thus, what became controversial research on the culture of poverty was supported by the most important funding sources then available to social anthropologists.

The results of his research came out in a 1959 monograph, *Five Families: Case Studies in the Culture of Poverty,* although the 1961 translation carried the more appropriate title *Antropología de la Pobreza: Cinco Familias* (Anthropology of Poverty: Five Families). Much of the controversy that erupted over Lewis's work on poverty focused on whether (or not) there was a culture of poverty, when Lewis originally meant only to elaborate an anthropological approach—emphasizing family case studies—to the socioeconomic conditions associated with poverty in Mexico City. When *Five Families* was issued, Lewis had not yet worked out the characteristics of the culture of poverty. Eventually (in 1966), he published an article with that title in *Scientific American* and followed it with a 1969 article, "The Possessions of the Poor," in the same journal. A close reading of the numerous publications by Lewis during the 1960s on the culture of poverty suggests that for Lewis a comparative, cross-cultural *theory* of a culture of poverty was far less important than a recognition that the poor were always and everywhere with us in contemporary societies and that governments had responsibilities to deal with the situation of the poor. In the end, according to Lewis, being poor was *not* the fault of those who found themselves in poverty but was due to the social, economic, political, and cultural conditions in the society. It was not Lewis himself but other U.S. social scientists and political commentators (especially Daniel Patrick Moynihan, then Assistant Secretary of Labor in the Johnson administration, whose 1965 report *The Negro Family: The Case for National Action* focused on the role of ghetto culture as the key to the increase in single-mother families) who expanded Lewis's ideas about poverty to fuel the so-called War on Poverty during the 1960s and 1970s. Consequently, Lewis was unfairly criticized by numerous scholars for introducing a cultural view of poverty that misrepresented the results of his research in Mexico—and led him to pursue cross-cultural testing of his theory in New York, Puerto Rico, and Cuba.

The New York and Puerto Rico Studies

Always interested in testing ideas cross-culturally, Lewis wanted to go to Cuba after the 1959 revolution. However, after the Bay of Pigs fiasco, it proved impossible to get a visa. Instead, Lewis turned his attention to a comparative analysis of slum families in New York City and Puerto Rico. This study (funded by multiyear grants from the Social Security Administration of the Department of Health, Education, and Welfare) was intended to examine hypotheses about the characteristics and extent of the culture of poverty. Two monographs resulted from the study: *La Vida: A Puerto Rican Family in the Culture of Poverty—San Juan and New York* (1966) and *A Study of Slum Culture: Backgrounds for La Vida* (1968). However, even

though the *La Vida* book was a public success and winner of a National Book Award, numerous anthropologists and other social scientists continued to have serious issues with the notion of a culture of poverty.

The Cuba Study

In 1969, Lewis finally was able to implement a field project in Cuba. There he hoped to test the hypothesis that the culture of poverty would be different (or even absent) in a socialist nation. Unfortunately, he was suffering from heart disease and was unable to see the project through to its completion. His wife, Ruth, carried on with the Living the Revolution project, and in 1977, the University of Illinois published (under the joint authorship of Oscar Lewis, Ruth Lewis, and Susan M. Rigdon) its major results in three volumes: *Four Women*, *Four Men*, and *Neighbors*. In addition, his colleague Douglas Butterworth compiled data for a study titled *The People of Buena Ventura: The Relocation of Slum Dwellers in Postrevolutionary Cuba* (1980).

Conclusion

Just before his untimely death from heart disease in 1970, Lewis collected some of his more important essays, articles, and book chapters into an eponymous volume *Oscar Lewis: Anthropological Essays*. This collection of 24 chapters is divided into six parts: (1) Theory and Method, (2) American Indians, (3) Rural U.S.A., (4) Peasantry, (5) Urban Studies, and (6) Selections From Life Histories. In arranging his own work in this manner, Lewis summed up his contributions to social and cultural anthropology. He challenged orthodox positions about rural and urban life; focused on fieldwork as the principal source of data; developed systematic research methods, especially involving family histories; believed in comparative analysis as cultural anthropology's hallmark; and was committed to social justice for impoverished people, whether living in the countryside or in the city, in the United States or elsewhere.

Robert V. Kemper

See also Benedict, Ruth; Human Relations Area Files, Cross-Cultural Studies; Linton, Ralph; Redfield, Robert; Urban Studies

Further Readings

Leacock, E. B. (Ed.). (1971). *The culture of poverty: A critique*. New York, NY: Simon & Schuster.

Lewis, O. (1970). *Oscar Lewis: Anthropological essays*. New York, NY: Random House.

Rigdon, S. M. (1988). *The culture façade: Art, science, and politics in the work of Oscar Lewis*. Urbana: University of Illinois Press.

Valentine, C. A. (1968). *Culture and poverty, critique and counter-proposals*. Chicago, IL: University of Chicago Press.

LIENHARDT, GODFREY

Ronald Godfrey Lienhardt (1921–1993) was born to a Swiss father and English mother in Bradford, Yorkshire. Both he and his younger brother Peter Arnold Lienhardt studied at Downing College, Cambridge, reading English with F. R. Leavis. While retaining a fond connection with the north of England throughout their lives, both were eventually to become distinguished colleagues of Edward Evans-Pritchard at Oxford's Institute of Social Anthropology.

Godfrey's degree studies began in 1939 but were interrupted by military service during the Second World War, years that included a posting to East Africa. He returned to Cambridge in 1945, met Evans-Pritchard, and transferred to archaeology and anthropology. On graduating in 1947, he embarked on fieldwork among the Dinka people of southern Sudan. Oxford subsequently became his base, first as a postgraduate student, subsequently as a university lecturer, and then as a reader in social anthropology and as a professorial fellow of Wolfson College. He returned to the Sudan several times, extending his studies to the Anuak; he also had visiting positions in Baghdad, Iraq (1955–1956), and Accra, Ghana (1964); he visited Northwestern University, Illinois, for the award of an honorary DLitt in 1983.

Lienhardt's best known work remains his monograph *Divinity and Experience: The Religion of the Dinka* (1961). It is a story told through the reflections of those Dinka people Lienhardt came to know well and whose trust he had won. While dedicated to Evans-Pritchard and acknowledging his 1930s researches on the Nuer, it has a refreshing quality of immediacy and intimacy flowing from

Lienhardt's sensitivity to the subtleties of language as well as his own deeply held, though very liberal, religious views (as a convert to Roman Catholicism). His exploration of Dinka understandings of *nhialic*, or "divinity" (and the various overlapping "divinities" as they manifested themselves in people's lives) begins with the practical activities of cattle herding. It moves on to the less obvious forms of social experience, through their images of patrilineage and clan, themselves dependent for continuing life on the marriage alliances created through transfers of cattle. Birth, illness, and death are part of a cosmology in which the human sphere is intermittently engaged with that of divinity, especially through the flesh, words, and dreams of those born to the priestly lines of "Masters of the Fishing Spear."

Lienhardt's insights into the experiential foundations of shared belief among the Dinka were further developed in lectures and publications. In these, he explored, for example, variable notions of the High God in Africa, the place of internal consciousness in African concepts of the person, and the harder edge of reciprocity. Among a range of Nilotic peoples, popular myths are told about lineage heads or royals demanding their lost or lent possessions back, even former gifts such as beads subsequently swallowed by a cow or a child. If pursued to the end, such a cow or child will have to die. The tale is sometimes told to explain why two lineages separated long ago or to illustrate how only royals could get away with such cruel behavior. One of his most influential papers is devoted to the impact of Catholic missionaries among the western Dinka and the way the meanings of religious terms were artfully shifted, and reimagined, in this new context.

The stories, myths, and conversations Lienhardt reports from his fieldwork are never simple ethnographic data—they are presented as a part of the ongoing life he engaged with among the Dinka. What gives a lasting quality to his writings is not so much an observer's "grand theory" as an approach to ethnography that privileges the *meanings* of human encounter—both within the community being studied and between the ethnographer and his or her informants. *Divinity and Experience* is widely regarded today as an anthropological classic, respected by historians and scholars of comparative religion and theology.

A similar direct approach to the realities of human encounter runs through Lienhardt's modest (but much translated) introductory book of 1964, titled simply *Social Anthropology*. This work appeared at a time of transition, when cynics, at least in Britain, saw the end of empire and forecast the end of anthropology. However, the younger generation was looking to fresh sources for the renewal of the subject: Lévi-Straussian structuralism, Marxism as revived in France, and, sometimes in tandem, a new focus on anthropology "at home." In these various ways, they were seeking to make the subject genuinely universal, emphasizing similarity, and comparability, over difference. Lienhardt in his own way was doing this too. By focusing on how ethnographic research was actually carried out, Lienhardt's very readable account of the intellectual roots of anthropology introduces some memorable scenes of personal encounter. His lens is focused as much on the ethnographers themselves as on the people studied; taking an ironic swipe at Lévy-Bruhl's classic on primitive mentality (*How Natives Think*, 1910), his concluding chapter is ironically titled "How Anthropologists Think." He had little sympathy with casual notions of cultural relativism and was quite outspoken about this toward the end of his life.

Lienhardt was a warm, witty, provocative teacher; while taking a very modest attitude to career advancement, he accepted several invitations to deliver radio talks, and his informal seminars were always exciting events. His home was always open to students and visitors, especially from the Sudan (north and south) and from West Africa. Among the Sudanese scholars, Francis Mading Deng has paid special tribute to Lienhardt's friendship and influence in encouraging his own writings on the songs, poetry, and history of the Dinka. Lienhardt's papers and photographs are preserved at the Pitt Rivers Museum, Oxford.

Wendy James

See also Evans-Pritchard, E. E.; Lévi-Strauss, Claude; Lévy-Bruhl, Lucien; Oxford University; Religion; Structuralism

Further Readings

Al-Shahi, A. (Ed.). (2010). Letters from the field: Godfrey Lienhardt and the Dinka of southern Sudan. A personal view. *Societal Studies, 5*. Khartoum, Sudan: Centre for Society Studies. Available through the system of the Bodleian Library, Oxford, UK.

Al-Shahi, A., & Coote, J. (Eds.). (1997). Special issue in memory of Godfrey Lienhardt (includes a comprehensive bibliography). *Journal of the Anthropological Society of Oxford (JASO), 28*. Retrieved from http://www.isca.ox.ac.uk/fileadmin/ISCA/JASO/JASO_Archive_pdfs/1997_JASO_28.pdf

James, W. (2003). *The ceremonial animal: A new portrait of anthropology* (dedicated to the memory of Godfrey and Peter Lienhardt). Oxford, UK: Oxford University Press.

James, W., & Johnson, D. H. (Eds.). (1988). *Vernacular Christianity: Essays in the social anthropology of religion, presented to Godfrey Lienhardt* (JASO Occasional Papers, No. 7.). Oxford, UK: JASO & Lilian Barber Press. Retrieved from http://www.isca.ox.ac.uk/publications/jaso/archive/jaso-occasional-papers-1982–1993/

LINTON, RALPH

Ralph Linton (1893–1953), an American anthropologist, Curator of Ethnology at the Field Museum of Chicago, and President of the American Anthropological Association, is best known for his contributions to culture and personality theory and for books aimed at both popular and professional audiences.

Biographical Sketch

Several important dimensions of Ralph Linton's early life affected his scholarship in a number of interesting ways. Linton was born to a Quaker family in Pennsylvania in 1893. His father was authoritarian, which was the cause of some tension and bitterness according to Adelin Linton's 1971 account of her husband's childhood. Among other things, Ralph Linton manifested a disdain for anthropologists such as A. R. Radcliffe-Brown and Franz Boas, who were authoritarian in their dealings with students and who tended to attract faithful disciples. Linton was self-consciously more egalitarian in his interactions with students. This (in addition to having spent half of his career outside of universities with anthropology graduate programs) may be one reason why fewer anthropologists trace their direct intellectual lineage to him. It was also the case that Linton claimed no singular influence from any particular formative figure in the discipline. Nevertheless, he had a profound influence at the undergraduate level on many students including Sol Tax, Clyde Kluckhohn, Abraham Maslow, and others, and he left a significant theoretical footprint on the field of anthropology.

Linton was an undergraduate at Swarthmore College from 1911 to 1915, and during that time, he undertook his first archaeological fieldwork in the American Southwest. It was archaeology that drew him to anthropology initially, although he later shifted toward cultural anthropology. He received a Master's degree at the University of Pennsylvania in 1916, after which he transferred to Columbia University to work with Franz Boas. Boas, however, found him to be an unremarkable student. Linton interrupted his studies to enlist in the military during World War I. When he returned from Europe to meet Boas and resume graduate studies, Linton came straight from Fort Dix, still in uniform. This likely annoyed Boas further because of his disagreement with American involvement in World War I, and Boas expressed deep skepticism that Linton could succeed in graduate studies at Columbia. This interaction with Boas led Linton to leave Columbia immediately and enroll at Harvard, where he received his PhD in 1925. This was the beginning of what was to become a long-standing tension between Linton and the Boasians that became progressively entrenched as Linton's career continued, and it was most pronounced when he replaced Boas as the chair of anthropology at Columbia in 1937.

Linton's career can be divided into four phases linked to the institutions where he worked: (1) as the curator of ethnology at The Field Museum of Chicago (1922–1928), (2) as a professor at the University of Wisconsin–Madison (1928–1937), (3) as the chair of the Department of Anthropology at Columbia (1937–1946), and (4) as a Sterling Professor of Anthropology at Yale (1946–1953). In his first position at the Field Museum, Linton became devoted to fieldwork. He spent almost 2 full years (1926–1927) on a museum expedition to collect artifacts and conduct ethnographic research in Madagascar. This resulted in a number of field reports and publications, including his 1933 monograph *The Tanala: A Hill Tribe of Madagascar*. While Linton would have liked to continue curation and fieldwork for the museum, sickness and an alluring offer to institute an anthropological curriculum at the University of Wisconsin–Madison drew him

into academe. He soon became a much sought-after lecturer.

When he moved to Columbia University in 1937, Linton continued to grow in influence. At this point, his 1936 book *The Study of Man* was beginning to have an impact on the field. Linton also participated in the Social Sciences Research Council's Committee on Personality and Culture and on a subcommittee with Robert Redfield and Melville J. Herskovits. They jointly authored the "Memorandum for the Study of Acculturation," which spurred a generation of scholarship on the topic. This was an integral concept in the theoretical synthesis that Linton sought in *The Study of Man* and in his posthumously published *The Tree of Culture*.

Linton was an avid fieldworker, and he considered his success in mastering the cultural practices and gaining status in the institutions of the people he studied among his greatest achievements. It was fieldwork that both drew him into the discipline and inspired his shift from archaeology to cultural anthropology. His broad archaeological and ethnographic fieldwork experience included research in the American Southwest, Marquesas Islands (1920–1922), Madagascar (1926–1927), Ohio, Wisconsin, New Jersey, Guatemala, and work with Native American groups, including the Comanche and the Pawnee.

Key Works and Theoretical Contributions

Linton was an important theoretician and an influential teacher, well-known and respected in his time. Several of his works are of note in the history and development of anthropological theory. One of Linton's early essays made a salient point about the fundamental similarities in the beliefs and practices of "modern" Europeans and Americans and those of the members of "primitive" societies who were the most frequent object of anthropological inquiry. In "Totemism and the A.E.F.," Linton drew on his experience in the Rainbow Division of the American Expeditionary Forces during World War I. He described how the rainbow insignia became a totem for the soldiers in the division, outlining how it took on sacred and supernatural powers. This was an important insight at the time, and a contribution to the more reflexive anthropology that would follow.

Linton attempted to take what he considered the best elements from each competing theoretical school of the time to construct an encompassing and synthetic theoretical approach. He did not position himself in any one school, but rather proclaimed his willingness to accept some, but not all, of the central propositions of each. In *The Study of Man* (his best known single work), he sought to outline this encompassing paradigm and to apprehend the relationship between the psychological functioning of individuals and the suprapersonal dimensions of culture.

The Study of Man was not only a theoretical but also a historical synthesis. The text begins with human origins and seeks a basic explanation of contemporary cultural diversity. In doing so, Linton examined the concept of race, critiqued its popular usage, and showed that it lacked empirical validity. He subsequently moved to explain variations in social organization through a theoretical integration of diffusionist, evolutionary, historical particularist, functionalist, psychological, and humanistic perspectives. One challenging aspect of the text is its near complete lack of citations and footnotes—Linton maintained some unconventional views of such scholarly conventions. Nevertheless, one can see connections between his grand synthesis and the ideas of his contemporaries. Interestingly, he seemed to want to integrate most thoroughly the schools of two contemporaries with whom he had significant personal animosity—Boas and Radcliffe-Brown. Linton proposed a typology of the different forms, meanings, uses, and functions of cultural elements. He believed that this typology could take account of the ultimate functions of cultural elements, while also being sensitive to social and cultural change, and the diffusion of particular practices and tools. He further added to this synthesis what he saw as a more sophisticated treatment of the psychology of individuals, which he argued that key players were ignoring or mistreating in each school.

Status and Role

One chapter in *The Study of Man* has been widely cited in anthropology and sociology for its contribution to our understanding of social systems. In "Status and Role," Linton lays out several important distinctions regarding specialization in society. A status is a particular place or position within a social organization, such as the status of "father" or "neighbor." A role, however, constitutes the attitudes, values, and behaviors that each person occupying a particular status carries out (what Linton termed the *dynamic* aspect of inhabiting a status). While statuses and roles are linked, they are experienced as distinct by individuals. Statuses are experienced as structural placements within a social system, while roles involve what has to be learned by an individual in order to effectively carry out and validate their placement in the social order. The other important distinction that Linton makes here is the difference between achieved status (status based on one's activities) and ascribed status (status based on one's inherent characteristics at birth), and he explicates the varying conditions in which a status may be either achieved or ascribed.

Culture and Personality

Linton is often identified with the "culture and personality school." What is interesting is that the cultural essentialism that modern anthropologists often assume characterizes that the "school" is not inherent in the assumptions or the explicit treatment of individual variation in Linton's writings. Linton's descriptions of ascribed versus achieved status, as well as his subsequent concept of status personalities, seek to take stock of the extensive individual psychological variation within social systems. Robert LeVine describes how the contemporary disciplinary myth about the Culture-and-Personality school incorrectly assumes that these theorists believed the relationship between personality and culture was relatively unproblematic (i.e., personality writ large) and that culture exerted its influence more or less uniformly across the personalities that it shaped. Linton explicitly rejected these ideas, and his writings in the early twentieth century have a strikingly modern feel. He ruminated about the dangers of essentialism (though he does not use this term) and considered the complex philosophical issues at stake in simplistic cultural representation. He wrote about the variety of ways that anthropologists ought to take individual variation into account, arguing that some dimensions of psychological function can indeed be independent from cultural fashioning and that culture surely exerts differential pressures on varying subgroups within each society (male and female, different classes and castes, age groups, etc.).

Disciplinary entrenchment was increasingly important in the academy when Linton began his career. He became an important figure in calling for the transcendence of these boundaries to deal with interesting investigations of the human condition without regard to what he considered superficial divisions. From his time at Wisconsin to his chairmanship at Columbia, he participated in joint seminars and initiatives to promote cross-disciplinary teaching and research. One of the best known of these efforts was the joint seminar that he held with Abram Kardiner. In this seminar, Kardiner would bring psychoanalytic interpretation to ethnographic presentations made by anthropologists. Kardiner's work included analyses of Linton's material on Comanche, Tanala, and Marquesan culture. Other presenters at the seminar included Cora DuBois, Carl Withers, Charles Wagley, and Francis L. K. Hsu.

Kardiner's melding of psychoanalysis and ethnographic material had far-reaching influence, and a number of notable publications came of the seminar, including Linton's 1945 book, *The Cultural Background of Personality*. This work can be seen as Linton's attempt to refine some of the efforts to integrate psychological function with particular cultural patterns that were typical of the seminar, as well as a refining of his own arguments in *The Study of Man*. For example, he proposes the "status personality" as a concept that can integrate a functionalist understanding of social configurations while still accounting for variations from the "basic" or "modal" personality types in a given society. Status personalities are personality configurations specific to the interactions of people in particular positions in the social configuration. This allowed for a diachronic dynamism not inherent in Kardiner's formulation, as well as an understanding of more extensive variation in the types of personalities that were seen as distributed across a cultural group.

Linton's Legacy

Ralph Linton died of a heart attack in 1953. He was actively writing and lecturing at the time of his death, which is evidenced by the posthumous publication of two books, *The Tree of Culture* in 1955 and *Culture and Mental Disorders* in 1956. The former was approximately two thirds completed at the time of his death and was completed by his widow. *The Tree of Culture* included a more comprehensive historical synthesis than *The Study of Man*, which

was more theoretical. *Culture and Mental Disorders* was based on a set of interdisciplinary seminars at Yale and was edited and published by George Devereaux.

Linton's footprint on the discipline of anthropology can be seen in the way that he synthesized important observations from competing schools of thought into a coherent approach, developed a theoretical framework that could account for both macrosocial patterns as well as idiosyncratic psychological factors (the enduring central concern of contemporary psychological anthropology), and in the ways that he communicated these ideas to both popular and specialized audiences through his lectures and writings. He fashioned a more reflexive discipline and drew from a wealth of ethnographic and archaeological experience to push forward a grand synthesis of understanding the human condition for social scientists and the general public alike.

Jacob R. Hickman

See also Boas, Franz; Columbia University; Culture and Personality; DuBois, Cora; Herskovits, Melville; Kardiner, Abram; Kluckhohn, Clyde; LeVine, Robert; Psychological Anthropology; Redfield, Robert; Tax, Sol

Further Readings

LeVine, R. A. (2001). Culture and personality studies, 1918–1960: Myth and history. *Journal of Personality, 69*(6), 803–818.

Linton, A., & Wagley, C. (1971). *Ralph Linton*. New York, NY: Columbia University Press.

Linton, R. (1924). Totemism and the A.E.F. *American Anthropologist, 26*, 296–300.

———. (1936). *The study of man: An introduction*. New York, NY: D. Appleton-Century.

———. (1938). Culture, society, and the individual. *Journal of Abnormal and Social Psychology, 33*(4), 425–436.

———. (1939). The Tanala of Madagascar. In A. Kardiner (Ed.), *The individual and his society* (pp. 251–290). New York, NY: Columbia University Press.

———. (1943). Nativistic movements. *American Anthropologist, 45*, 230–240.

———. (1955). *The tree of culture*. New York, NY: Alfred A. Knopf.

———. (1961). *The cultural background of personality*. East Norwalk, CT: Appleton-Century-Crofts.

Linton, R., & Devereux, G. (Ed.). (1956). *Culture and mental disorders*. Springfield, IL: Thomas.

Manson, W. C. (1986). Abram Kardiner and the Neo-Freudian alternative in culture and personality. In G. W. Stocking (Ed.), *Malinowski, Rivers, Benedict, and others: Essays on culture and personality*. Madison: University of Wisconsin Press.

Robert, R., Linton, R., & Herskovits, M. (1936). Memorandum for the study of acculturation. *American Anthropologist, 38*, 149–152.

LONDON SCHOOL OF ECONOMICS

London School of Economics (LSE), formally known as the London School of Economics and Political Science, is a research institution of higher education in the United Kingdom.

History of the LSE and the Tradition of Anthropology at the School

The LSE specializes in the social sciences, offering graduate programs in all traditional disciplines. Organizationally, it is a school of the University of London. As a distinct entity, the LSE has played a significant role in the institutional development of anthropology in higher education, most notably in Britain. Formative anthropologists, theorists, philosophers, and intellectual figures serving on the faculty of the school, either on a permanent or a visiting basis, full-time or part-time, have included Edward Westermarck, Charles Gabriel Seligman, Bronisław Malinowski, Raymond Firth, Lucy Mair, Audrey Richards, I. Schapera, Sir Karl Popper, Maurice Bloch, and Dan Sperber. Former LSE students who have gone on to make significant contributions to anthropological theory include E. E. Evans-Pritchard, Meyer Fortes, Edmund Leach, Hilda B. Kuper, and Jean and John Comaroff.

The LSE was founded in 1895, having socialist origins as an intellectual endeavor of the Fabian Society. Beginning in 1900, formal courses were offered at the school, with degrees conferred from the year 1902. By 1904, the LSE had fully joined the University of London as one of its schools, at which time degrees were awarded by the university. At that time, the school had an enrollment of more than 1,400. The school's students were instructed by an academic staff of more than 40 lecturers.

As an academic teaching and research area, ethnography and social institutions were historically grouped together at the school, and the director, Lord William Beveridge, expressed interest in prioritizing the expansion of this academic area in these earliest years of the institution's history. Expansion of the area's resources took place under the direction of the Finnish philosopher and sociologist Edward Westermarck and later under the leadership of the pioneering ethnologist Charles Gabriel Seligman. In the early years of the LSE, academic departments did not exist. In fact, for the most part, the school did not have formal academic departments until the 1960s. It has been said that the word *department* was taboo in the early history of the school and that only when enrollment numbers soared did the LSE find it necessary to accommodate students in academic departments. Rather, for a great part of its institutional history, certain subjects were taught for credit as course requirements in the LSE's syllabi of degree programs.

In the 1920s and 1930s, a priority at the school was to keep all the social sciences under one roof. Another institutional goal was to enhance the offerings in the social sciences. To broaden the offerings of the social sciences in the school's degree catalog of syllabi, the senior leadership decided to expand the courses in anthropology. This included the creation of a formal graduate program with significant additional resources.

The Anthropology Faculty and Its Notable Students

Since departments did not exist in the early years of the school, faculty posts were structured around certain courses and subjects in the school's degree syllabi. Westermarck started lecturing in anthropology in 1904. He remained on the faculty at the LSE as a part-time professor until 1930. The year 1913 marked the creation of the first faculty post in ethnology, to which Seligman was appointed. Although this appointment was permanent, it was only part-time. Seligman had already been appointed to a lecturer's post in ethnology in 1910.

By 1927, the school had created its first full-time professorship in anthropology, to be held by Malinowski. Offered a scholarship that was arranged with the help of Seligman's leadership, Malinowski had become a student at the LSE in 1910 and had studied with Seligman and Westermarck. The school awarded him a DSc in 1913, and he began lecturing at the school, taking on students alongside his teachers Westermarck and Seligman. The school formally elected him a social anthropology readership in May 1923, which commenced in 1924.

Malinowski's faculty post in social anthropology at the school was in part made possible by significant funding from the Rockefeller Foundation. The anthropologist Jack Goody has argued that by insisting that the faculty position carry the title of Social Anthropology rather than Cultural Anthropology, Malinowski and the LSE hoped to distance themselves from their institutional neighbor University College London. This gave the school a distinct reputation in British anthropology that was rivaled only by nearby Oxford University. By the end of the 1920s, Malinowski had attracted a group of formidable scholars to the LSE to carry out graduate studies under his direction.

By 1925, Evans-Pritchard and Firth had joined the anthropology graduate program, followed by Schapera a year later. The first of Malinowski's PhD students was Firth, who was awarded his degree in 1927. Evans-Pritchard, Fortes, and Max Gluckman all studied with Malinowski at the LSE prior to transferring to Oxford to study under A. R. Radcliffe-Brown. Firth, Richards, Leach, and Schapera kept LSE their primary academic affiliation in research and fieldwork dating from that time period. Monica Wilson was one of the students attending Malinowski's LSE seminars. Hilda B. Kuper was a full-time PhD student of his at the school.

Structural functionalism had become the mainstay at Oxford with Radcliffe-Brown's commanding presence there. The LSE emerged as its rival institution in British social anthropology, serving in part as Malinowski's mouthpiece for articulating a more implicit form of functionalism, one that was not structural in its theoretical foundations and did not depart as much from early intellectual figures such as Herbert Spencer and Auguste Comte as that promoted by Radcliffe-Brown. Malinowski died in 1942, and in 1944, his chair was given to Firth, thus continuing Malinowski's tradition in anthropology. During Firth's tenure, the school enhanced its theoretical reputation in anthropology. His faculty appointment at the school was followed by teaching posts for Schapera and Mair. This trio of scholars became a fixture in the school's anthropology department in the succeeding years.

The Anthropology Graduate Program and Its Resources

Malinowski had been successful in developing a formal graduate program in anthropology at the LSE in the years following the First World War. The program peaked in the 1930s and then rose to prominence again in the 1950s. The LSE received significant funding from the Rockefeller Foundation from 1923 to 1939. In addition to funding students, the institution also used the money to help finance the expansion of its library, its buildings, professorships, research projects, and overseas travel to the United States for professional purposes. Among the University of London community of schools and colleges, the LSE gained the reputation of preferring additional faculty resources and professorships to the expansion of school buildings. Nevertheless, the LSE soon housed the largest social science research library in Britain. Today, the British Library of Political and Economic Science at the LSE is one of the institutional legacies of funding by the Rockefeller Foundation in the 1920s and 1930s.

Theory at Other Departments of the School and the Next Generation of Anthropology

Shortly after publishing his treatises *The Poverty of Historicism*, which were writings dating from 1930, and *The Open Society and Its Enemies*, the eminent philosopher Sir Karl Popper arrived at the LSE in early 1946. Popper took up a full-time academic position; served as the founding figure of the LSE's Department of Philosophy, Logic, and Scientific Method; and 3 years later was appointed professor of logic and scientific method. He held this faculty post until 1972. Primarily because of Popper's early achievements, the LSE gained a reputation as a leader in the philosophy of the social sciences. Popper's research, teaching, and scholarly influence after arriving at the school were primarily in the philosophy of physics, philosophy of science and methodology, and history of science. The department continues today to attract leading faculty.

Jean and John Comaroff, today editorial affiliates of the highly influential journal *Public Culture*, were both students in the Department of Anthropology's graduate program. John Comaroff earned his PhD from the LSE in 1973, and Jean Comaroff was awarded the same degree the following year. There was a group of South Africans in the school's anthropology department, and they were represented by the Comaroffs. Soon after the Comaroffs departed, the emerging interdisciplinary field of contemporary cultural studies was embraced by the school. The prolific contemporary cultural studies scholar Scott Lash earned his PhD in 1980 from the school's Department of Sociology.

As a faculty member in the Department of Anthropology for the major portion of his career, Maurice Bloch generated theoretical works that stemmed from and engaged structuralism and the French Marxist traditions. The works also had implications for, and relied on, developments in cognitive science. Another notable scholar who had employed cognitive science in his theory construction, Dan Sperber, arrived at the LSE in 1988 as a distinguished visitor. He returned as a visiting professor in the late 1990s through the 2000s, most of the time sponsored by the Department of Anthropology.

The LSE in Recent Years: Contemporary Theorists and Their Contributions

The leading contemporary sociological theorist Anthony Giddens served as director of the school from 1997 to 2003. Under his leadership, the school's Department of Sociology grew to greater prominence. This was especially the case in its theoretical orientation to critical and cultural studies, particularly in contemporary social and political issues. Most visible was his case for advances and dialogues in globalization theory.

The vocal sociologist Ulrich Beck has become a mainstay at the LSE Department of Sociology in recent years. He teaches graduate social theory courses to students enrolled in programs there. His research on the theoretical aspects of modernity received significant attention. His arrival further raised the profile of the school's sociology department.

The field of urban studies has emerged in recent years at the LSE. For the most part, this has been made possible through funding for a research project on cities undertaken by the school's Department of Sociology. The department has welcomed the urban sociologist Saskia Sassen, originator of the term *global city*, as a recurring centennial visiting professor in recent years. It has also housed other leading scholars devoted to urban studies in their theoretical constructs.

The highly respected sociologist Craig Calhoun took over as director of the school in September 2012. A cultural sociologist and theoretician, Calhoun served as founding director of the Institute for Public Knowledge at New York University prior to his arriving at the LSE. He had also been president of the Social Science Research Council. For a number of years, Calhoun had worked with the LSE's eminent sociologist Richard Sennett in the cofounding of a research consortium consisting of New York- and London-based graduate students focusing on incorporating ethnographic, historical, and other qualitative methods into their research in the social sciences. Under Calhoun and Sennett's direction, the students in the consortium brought these methods to light in their work encompassing cultural, social, and political themes, for which the LSE had gained an international reputation in the 1990s and 2000s.

The famed cultural studies figure Paul Gilroy joined the faculty of the LSE Department of Sociology as inaugural Anthony Giddens Professor of Social Theory prior to Calhoun's arrival at the school. A product of the Centre for Contemporary Cultural Studies at the University of Birmingham in Britain in the early 1980s, Gilroy was a PhD student of the formative cultural theorist Stuart Hall. He was a vocal advocate of British cultural studies at the school. This tradition was pervasive in the course offerings at the Department of Sociology and within a number of the school's interdisciplinary research clusters prior to Calhoun's arrival.

Dustin Bradley Garlitz

See also Bloch, Maurice; Evans-Pritchard, E. E.; Firth, Raymond; Fortes, Meyer; Gluckman, Max; Kuper, Hilda B.; Leach, Edmund; Mair, Lucy; Malinowski, Bronisław; Popper, Karl; Richards, Audrey; Rockefeller Foundation; Schapera, Isaac; Seligman, Charles Gabriel; Sperber, Dan; Urban Studies; Westermarck, Edward; Wilson, Monica

Further Readings

Dahrendorf, R. (1995). *LSE: A history of the London School of Economics and Political Science, 1895–1995.* New York, NY: Oxford University Press.

Eriksen, T. H., & Nielsen, F. S. (2001). *A history of anthropology.* London, UK: Pluto Press.

Goody, J. (1995). *The expansive moment: The rise of social anthropology in Britain and Africa 1918–1970.* Cambridge, UK: Cambridge University Press.

Kuklick, H. (Ed.). (2008). *A new history of anthropology.* Malden, MA: Blackwell.

Kuper, A. (1973). *Anthropologists and anthropology: The British school 1922–1972.* New York, NY: Pica Press.

———. (1988). *The invention of primitive society: Transformations of an illusion.* London, UK: Routledge.

LOUNSBURY, FLOYD

Floyd Glenn Lounsbury (1914–1998) was an American linguist and anthropologist known for contributions to the anthropology of kinship relations, ancient Mayan hieroglyphic writing, and the linguistics of Iroquoian languages. Along with Ward Goodenough, Lounsbury was a foundational theorist in the "new ethnography," or "ethnoscience," a formal approach to the analysis of cultural systems from the perspective of native categories, as represented in lexical semantics of language.

Biography

Lounsbury was born in Stevens Point, Wisconsin, on April 25, 1914, to John Glenn Lounsbury and Anna Louise Jorgensen Lounsbury. He completed his undergraduate degree in mathematics at the University of Wisconsin. During that time, he also took courses in anthropology and linguistics from several noted scholars, including Einar Haugen, Morris Swadesh, and Freeman Twadell. Swadesh hired Lounsbury as an assistant in his Oneida language project, funded by the Works Progress Administration, which Lounsbury himself led from 1939 to 1940 after Swadesh moved to Mexico. He completed his research and wrote his master's thesis on Oneida phonology using the data gathered from the project. Like many scholars of the time, Lounsbury's work was interrupted by the outbreak of World War II. After 4 years of military service, Lounsbury formally completed his master's degree at the University of Wisconsin in 1946 and received a Rockefeller grant to carry out his doctoral studies in anthropology at Yale University, where he studied with Bernard Bloch. His dissertation, *Iroquoian Morphology*, was finished in 1949 and published in 1953 as *Oneida Verb Morphology*. On graduating,

Lounsbury took a faculty position in anthropology at Yale, where he remained until retiring in 1979. At the time of his death in 1998, he held the title of Sterling Professor Emeritus of Anthropology at Yale University.

Major Contributions

Lounsbury contributed to several different fields. His most significant contributions, however, have been in Iroquoian linguistics, kinship, and the decipherment of Mayan hieroglyphics.

Iroquoian Linguistics

Much of Lounsbury's later contributions to anthropological theory and to the decipherment of Mayan hieroglyphic writing can be related to his formative training in the rigorous and systematic approaches of mathematics and descriptive linguistics. His master's thesis and doctoral dissertation on Oneida continue to be standard reference material for Iroquoianists today, most of whom were mentored by Lounsbury. In his work on Iroquoian phonology and morphology, Lounsbury developed much of the descriptive framework and terminology for describing Iroquoian languages.

Kinship

Lounsbury is perhaps best known for his application of the methods of componential analysis—pioneered in linguists for the study of the sound systems of language—to kinship. In an influential article published in the journal *Language* in 1956, Lounsbury explained how the terms used in the Caddoan language Pawnee to talk about kinship relations could be systematically analyzed in terms of individual components of meaning to discern the underlying organizing distinctions, the system of kinship. The basic method was to gather a comprehensive list of words used in a language to refer to kin relations and then to define each item in terms of a fairly small but theoretically universal set of contrastive features (parallel to the place and manner of articulation and voicing in phonology). The system of meaningful distinctions for a given language can be inferred from the feature contrasts that are lexicalized (expressed with different words) in the language and those that are not. The method he laid out was rigorous, methodical, and—as he showed in subsequent articles on L. H. Morgan's

"Omaha"- and "Crow"-type kinship systems, and others—readily applicable to any group.

Lounsbury's systematic, empirical approach attracted linguists, who were struggling to investigate language meaning with the same methodological rigor that had been achieved in post-Bloomfield structural linguistics in the realm of phonology and morphology. It also appealed to anthropologists as it seemed to bridge the space between the systematicity of language and other, seemingly less structured cultural patterns and behaviors. Lounsbury's work also complemented the work of fellow Yale graduate Ward H. Goodenough, whose "Componential Analysis and the Study of Meaning" appeared in the same 1956 issue of *Language* as did Lounsbury's study of Pawnee kinship. Both Lounsbury and Goodenough emphasized a systematic, empirical approach to the study of society that sought to define, primarily on the basis of lexicon, the indigenous categories and structures according to which a given society organized the world. Both their methods and their goals have been important in the "new ethnography," ethnoscience, and in cognitive anthropology.

Mayan Hieroglyphics

Lounsbury's characteristic analytical rigor can also be seen in his contributions to ancient Maya hieroglyphics. He was an early proponent of looking to the Mayan languages to understand hieroglyphs and was among the first American scholars to see the value of the work on phoneticism in Mayan hieroglyphics by the Russian Yuriy Knorosov. Lounsbury advocated investigating Mayan hieroglyphs as language rather than as abstract representations of ethereal ideas, and he introduced a new degree of rigor into the methods of decipherment, which at the time were fairly loose and slipshod. Lounsbury became interested in Mayan hieroglyphics in the 1960s, but he was particularly active in efforts to decipher Mayan hieroglyphic writing during the 1970s and 1980s. In addition to contributing specific proposed decipherments and interpretations of texts, especially at Palenque, and introducing more rigorous methods for formulating and testing hypotheses about glyphic readings, Lounsbury also contributed to the understanding of ancient Mayan numeration, mathematics, and astronomy. He published work on the "Venus tables" in the Dresden Codex and addressed and resolved several issues with specific distances numbers and calendric cycles in various inscriptions. He also wrote an important summary of the current state of the art in Mayan numeration and calendrics.

Daniel Law

See also Ethnoscience/New Ethnography; Goodenough, Ward H.; Swadesh, Morris

Further Readings

Conklin, H. C. (2000). Obituary of Floyd Glenn Lounsbury (1914–1998). *American Anthropologist, 102*(4), 860–864.

Lounsbury, F. G. (1953). *Oneida verb morphology* (Yale University Publications in Anthropology, No. 48). New Haven, CT: Yale University Press.

———. (1956). A semantic analysis of Pawnee kinship usage. *Language, 32,* 158–194.

———. (1964). A formal account of the Crow- and Omaha-type kinship terminologies. In W. Goodenough (Ed.), *Explorations in cultural anthropology* (351–393). New York, NY: McGraw-Hill.

———. (1978). Maya numeration, computation, and calendrical astronomy. In C. C. Gillespie (Ed.), *Dictionary of scientific biography* (Vol. 15, Suppl., pp. 759–818). New York, NY: Scribner.

LOWIE, ROBERT

Robert H. Lowie (1883–1957) was born in Vienna to a German-speaking Jewish father born in Hungary and a Viennese Jewish mother. When he was 10, his family immigrated to New York, where he grew up as a bilingual youngster in a middle-class German Jewish intellectual milieu. Lowie retained his bilingualism and his European (and specifically Viennese) cultural tastes and habits for the rest of his life. In 1897, he entered City College, concentrating first on Greek and Latin and later on science. On graduation, Lowie taught in the New York public schools for 3 years and then enrolled in a graduate program in anthropology at Columbia University. His main mentor, Franz Boas, had a major influence on him as a scholar. However, he was just as much a student of Clark Wissler, his supervisor at the American Museum of Natural History, where Lowie worked as a volunteer while still in graduate school. It was Wissler who sent him on his first ethnographic field trip to the Lemhi Shoshoni in 1906. In 1908, on completion of a thesis dealing with comparative mythology, Lowie received his PhD degree and continued working as a curator at the American Museum of Natural History until 1917.

As both an undergraduate and a graduate student, Lowie was very interested in the history and methodology of science and was a particularly devoted follower of the Austrian philosopher Ernst Mach, with whom he corresponded. He shared these interests with several other members of the first cohort of Boas's graduate students, especially Alexander Goldenweiser and Paul Radin. He also shared their literary tastes and political orientation. During his New York years, Lowie espoused socialist ideas and supported various left-wing and liberal causes, including socialism and feminism. His articles and book reviews appeared in publications such as *The Masses, The Freeman, The Liberal Review, The Dial, and The New Republic.* However, once he became older and settled in California, Lowie moderated his political views, while remaining a liberal for the rest of his life.

His move from the East to the West Coast was made possible by A. L. Kroeber, another early student of Boas, who founded the anthropology department of the University of California, Berkeley. After teaching there as a visitor for a few years in the late 1910s, Lowie was promoted to full professor in 1921 and remained on the faculty of that department until 1950. He and Kroeber taught several generations of (mainly graduate) students, taking turns chairing the department, while the more junior faculty members taught the undergraduate courses. Lowie was never considered a charismatic teacher, but his students did receive a thorough grounding in world ethnography and the history of anthropology, while his command of ethnographic literature was considered to be truly encyclopedic. He was also widely admired by students and colleagues for his genuinely courteous manners and generosity of spirit.

Lowie was highly respected in his profession. For 9 years (1923–1931), he was the editor of the *American Anthropologist.* He also served as president of the American Folklore Society in 1916, the American Ethnological Society in 1920, and the American Anthropological Association in 1935 and was elected to the National Academy of Sciences.

After retiring in 1950, Lowie was much in demand as a visiting lecturer in the United States and abroad.

In 1933, Lowie married Luella Cole, who became his closest friend and traveling companion. During World War II, Lowie taught courses on German culture and European ethnography, and this experience plus his own background stimulated his interest in writing a book, *The German People* (1945). After the war, accompanied by his wife, Lowie carried out ethnographic research in Germany, using the data from it for his book *Toward Understanding Germany*, published in 1954. In both of these works, he tried to avoid the superficial theorizing typical of many of the "national character" studies of that era.

Lowie's main ethnographic works dealt with the Crow Indians of the Great Plains, whose culture he studied over many years. He also conducted ethnographic research among the Shoshoni, the Ute, the Hidatsa, the Mandan, the Arikara, the Washo, and the Hopi. In addition, he studied several South American Indian cultures from a distance, using data provided by local ethnographers. Lowie developed good rapport with his Native American consultants, all of them elderly men and women whom he meticulously interviewed about the "old culture" of their own younger days as well as that of their parents and grandparents. Hence, along with most of the other Boasians, he was a strong advocate of *salvage anthropology*, a term some scholars actually attribute to him.

Most scholars agree that Lowie's contributions to anthropological theory were not as significant as those of the more brilliant Boasians such as Edward Sapir, Radin, Goldenweiser, and Kroeber. However, a number of his books and articles did make an impact on the discipline at the time of their publication, and some have continued to do so long after. His general theoretical orientation can be described as "mainstream Boasian." Like his mentor, Lowie emphasized cultural relativism as opposed to Victorian social evolutionism. His books *Primitive Society* (1920) and *Primitive Religion* (1924) established him as the main opponent of evolutionism in American anthropology, while his 1929 brochure *Are We Civilized?* questioned the common assumption that technological and economic progress inevitably lead to moral progress.

Generally speaking, Lowie was a dedicated empiricist and positivist who viewed cultural anthropology as a science—trusted facts—and mistrusted any theorizing that he viewed as unsubstantiated. Many of his specific theoretical positions can be characterized as middle-of-the-road. Thus, for example, on the question of the correlation of semantic categories in kinship terminologies, on the one hand, and social organization and behavior, on the other, he advocated a position in between American historical and British functional ones. Similarly, while he was sympathetic to some of the arguments put forward by the proponents of the theory of cultural diffusion, he rejected their more radical speculations. When it came to the relationship between psychology and anthropology, Lowie argued that the former was a study of the innate behavior, in contrast to the learned behavior, of culture. At the same time, he suggested that mythology and religion have common elements across cultures, which might have been derived from dreams, and that these dreams may have some sort of biological basis (*History of Ethnological Theory*, 1937). He did not trust the Freudian generalizations of the early culture and personality studies.

Not surprisingly, some of Lowie's most original contributions to anthropological method and theory can be found in his studies of specific ethnographic cases rather than in his general works. For example, the historical and comparative summaries at the end of his work on Plains Indian age societies (1916) were praised even by the most empirically oriented Boasians. They are among the best examples of the kind of comparative and historical interpretation produced by that school. It is this work that had a major impact on the American historical tradition of kinship studies spearheaded by Fred Eggan, the British functional approach to kinship and social organization, and even the work of Claude Lévi-Strauss on the same subjects.

Sergei Kan

See also Boas, Franz; Goldenweiser, Alexander A.; Kroeber, Alfred L.; Radin, Paul; Sapir, Edward

Further Readings

Harris, M. (1968). *The rise of anthropological theory.* New York, NY: Columbia University Press.

Lowie, R. H. (1959). *Robert H. Lowie ethnologist.* Berkeley: University of California Press.

Murphy, R. F. (1972). *Robert H. Lowie.* New York, NY: Columbia University Press.

Radin, P. (1958). Robert H. Lowie, 1883–1957. *American Anthropologist, 60*(2), 358–375.

Steward, J. H. (1974). Robert Harry Lowie, 1883–1957. *National Academy of Sciences: Biographical Memoirs, 44,* 175–211.

LUBBOCK, JOHN

Sir John Lubbock (1834–1913), Lord Avebury, an English avocational archaeologist, naturalist, banker, and member of parliament, was a close associate of Charles Darwin and a leading evolutionist of the 19th century. He was the eldest son of a London banker who was also the treasurer of the Royal Society. The Lubbock estate neighbored Downe village in Kent, where Charles Darwin lived, and Darwin encouraged the young aristocrat's interest in natural history. Lubbock's principal scientific work was in entomology under Darwin's direction. He also worked closely with the geologist Charles Lyell and the biologist Thomas Henry Huxley, who promoted his membership in leading English scientific societies. Lubbock was also deeply interested in archaeology and visited the well-known sites of his day with leading prehistorians such as Joseph Prestwich and John Evans. Lubbock's descriptions of these sites in his 1865 book *Pre-Historic Times, as Illustrated by Ancient Remains, and the Manners and Customs of Modern Savages* helped build his reputation as one of the leading proponents of human antiquity in Victorian England.

Lubbock finished his education at Eton at the age of 14 and immediately became active in his family's banking business. In his 30s, he ran for parliament and was elected in 1870. As a member of parliament, his greatest achievements were to legislate banking holidays and shorter working hours, and for protecting archaeological sites through the Ancient Monuments Act of 1882. In 1879, Lubbock was elected first president of the Institute of Bankers, and from 1881 to 1886, he served as president of the Linnean Society. Lubbock also received honorary degrees from Oxford, Cambridge, and the University of Edinburgh, and in 1878, he was made a trustee of the British Museum. In 1900, Lubbock was made a peer and took the title Lord Avebury from the important henge monument he purchased in 1871 to save it from destruction.

In *Pre-Historic Times*, Lubbock attempted to prove human antiquity and create a picture of the lives of Stone Age humans. He did this, as one can tell from the book's full title, using archaeology and the 19th-century theory of the comparative method, especially the notion that modern indigenous people were a window into earlier stages of human society. In addition to archaeological reports, Lubbock made full use of ethnographic descriptions of the "primitive" people of his day, such as Australian aborigines, Native Americans, and the people of Tierra del Fuego. However, rather than starting in the prehistoric past and working forward, Lubbock's book moves backward in time, with a focus on archaeological excavations, starting with the Bronze Age through the Alpine Lake dwelling sites in Switzerland to the Somme River gravel beds excavated by the French archaeologist Boucher de Perthes, where Acheulian hand axes were first discovered. Additionally, in *Prehistoric Times*, Lubbock coined the terms *Neolithic* and *Paleolithic* as subdivisions of Christian Thomsen's three-age system of Stone, Bronze, and Iron Ages.

In 1870, Lubbock published *The Origin of Civilization and the Primitive Condition of Man*. Whereas Lubbock's purpose in *Prehistoric Times* was to study archaeology and the "primitive" people of his day in order to understand more accurately the culture of ancient peoples, *The Origin of Civilization* set out to describe the social and mental condition of "savages." He argued that there were three principles to be emphasized in the study of the "lower races": first, that savage cultures resemble those of our ancestors from long ago; second, that such cultures include customs that no longer have present utility but are rooted in our minds like fossils in soil; and, third, that studying aboriginal peoples shed some light on the future. Following Henry Main's *Ancient Law* (1861) and E. B. Tylor's *Researches Into the Early History of Mankind and the Development of Civilization* (1865), Lubbock's book was strongly evolutionist in tone, tracing the evolutionary history of art, marriage, religion, morality, language, and laws from their first appearance in savagery to their culmination in modern Europe.

In many ways, Lubbock's books, in particular *The Origin of Civilization*, encapsulate the main themes of English evolutionary thought in the mid-19th century so typically associated with Tylor and Lewis Henry Morgan. First, there is the belief in unilineal evolution—that all societies were evolving in the same way. This parallel evolution is driven by psychic unity—a principle first enunciated by Adolf Bastian. Bastian argued that because all humans share biologically similar brains, all will share similar elementary ideas and therefore when confronted with similar problems will solve them in similar ways. The implication of cultural evolution and psychic unity was that cultures were simply at different places in their progress up the evolutionary ladder. Lubbock's ethnographic reporting described the many cultural parallels found in savage societies around the world and the "fossils" of those practices that remained in modern society. His archaeological writings pointed out these parallel developments through time, demonstrating the similarities between the lives of modern savages and the materials revealed in the archaeological excavations of his day.

Lubbock was famous in his day and widely known for his writings on various topics in biology and natural history. *Prehistoric Times* was a popular archaeology text and went through seven editions by the time of Lubbock's death in 1913. Today, however, Lubbock's legacy has been eclipsed by that of Tylor and Morgan. He is primarily remembered today in anthropology as one of the founders of prehistoric archaeology.

R. Jon McGee and Alice Beck Kehoe

See also Comparative Method; Darwin, Charles; Morgan, Lewis Henry; Nineteenth-Century Evolutionary Anthropology; Spencer, Herbert; Tylor, Edward Burnett

Further Readings

Fichman, M. (2002). *Evolutionary theory and Victorian culture.* Amherst, NY: Humanity Books.

Kehoe, A. B. (1998). *The land of prehistory: A critical history of American archaeology.* New York, NY: Routledge.

Lubbock, J. (1865). *Pre-historic times: As illustrated by ancient remains and the manners and customs of modern savages.* London, UK: Williams & Norgate.

———. (1870). *The origin of civilisation and the primitive condition of man: Mental and social condition of savages.* London, UK: Longman, Green.

Murray, T. (2009). Illustrating "savagery": Sir John Lubbock and Ernest Griset. *Antiquity, 83,* 488–499.

Patton, M. (2007). *Science, politics and business in the work of Sir John Lubbock.* Aldershot, UK: Ashgate.

Stocking, G. W., Jr. (1987). *Victorian anthropology.* New York, NY: Free Press.

Trigger, B. G. (2006). *A history of archaeological thought* (2nd ed.). Cambridge, UK: Cambridge University Press.

LYOTARD, JEAN-FRANÇOIS

Jean-François Lyotard (1924–1998) was a French intellectual and philosopher. Although most commonly associated with postmodernism, he was also an important part of the French poststructural movement. He is best known for his critique of modernity and for his view of reality as a fragmented ensemble of complex events that cannot be represented or interpreted accurately. Although Lyotard's work has been extremely influential in social and cultural anthropology, it spans several other realms, including philosophy of language, psychology, ethics, political philosophy, and aesthetics. Mirroring this diversity is Lyotard's engagement with a number of eminent thinkers: Immanuel Kant, G. W. F. Hegel, Karl Marx, Sigmund Freud, Martin Heidegger, Jacques Lacan, Gilles Deleuze, and Jean Baudrillard, to mention a few. This entry offers a brief biography followed by a discussion of some of Lyotard's fundamental ideas and his work *The Postmodern Condition*, concluding with some critiques and comments on his legacy.

Biography and Major Works

Lyotard was born in Vincennes in 1924. After graduating from the Sorbonne in philosophy and literature, he taught philosophy in a number of schools, including one in Constantine, Algeria, where he experienced firsthand the conflict between Algerian workers and the French oligarchy. In 1948, he married Andrée May, with whom he had two children, Corinne and Laurence. In 1993, he married his second wife, Dolorès Djidzek, with whom he had a son, David.

In 1954, Lyotard joined the Marxist Trotskyte group Socialisme ou Barbarie (Socialism or Barbarism) and was a contributor to the journal *Socialisme ou Barbarie*. In 1964, due to internal discord, he joined the splinter group Pouvoir Ouvrier (Workers' Power), until 1966, when he also resigned from his academic post as assistant professor at the Sorbonne. Around that time, he took up a position in the philosophy department of the University of Paris X (Nanterre) and, despite his loss of faith in Marxism, participated in the May 1968 student protests against the government. Eventually, Lyotard's critique of Marxism was outlined in *Libidinal Economy* alongside his critique of capitalism. Arguing that both systems are intertwined with libidinal forces—irrational desires and impulses underlying a multitude of events that are exploited by economic structures—Lyotard concluded that Marxism's "truth" is no better than the "truths" it criticizes, while acknowledging that libidinal forces potentially have the power to destabilize and transform these structures.

Lyotard's academic career reached new heights as a professor of philosophy and languages at various distinguished institutions, including the University of Paris VIII (Vincennes), where in 1978 he became professor emeritus; the University of California; and Emory University. He was a visiting professor at several universities around the world, including the University of Montreal, Quebec, Canada; the University of São Paulo, Brazil; and the University of Siegen, Germany. Between 1968 and 1970, he was in charge of research at the National Centre for Scientific Research in Paris. In 1983, with Jacques Derrida, Gilles Deleuze, and others, he cofounded and was one of the presidents of the International College of Philosophy in Paris. Lyotard died of leukemia in Paris in 1998.

Lyotard's most famous books include *Phenomenology* (1954), *Discourse, Figure* (1971), *Libidinal Economy* (1974), *Au Juste: Conversations* (*Just Gaming*, 1979), *The Postmodern Condition: A Report on Knowledge* (1979), *The Differend: Phrases in Dispute* (1983), *The Inhuman: Reflections on Time* (1988), *Peregrinations: Law, Form, Event* (1988), *Lessons on the Analytic of the Sublime: Kant's Critique of Judgment* (1991), *Political Writings* (1993), and *Postmodern Fables* (1997).

Some Fundamental Ideas

In *Discourse, Figure*, Lyotard critiques structuralism, to which he relates "discourse" (written text), a form of cognitive communication that he juxtaposes with "figure," the potentially subversive product of the senses (phenomenology). These two categories are not simply opposites; they are intertwined. Despite the fact that discourse has historically dominated, it has been inadequate in representing historical events as well as the *sublime*, a concept that Lyotard adopted and modified from Kant to include not only the "transcendentally great" but also anything that we as humans are incapable of representing or fully grasping.

These ideas are tied to Lyotard's important anthropological insights. First, he challenged the notion of the "subject" as the central, rational entity of modernity, suggesting instead that it is as fragmented as reality itself. Second, in later works, for instance, in *The Inhuman*, these ideas gave rise to his notion of humanism, where, influenced by Lacan and Freud, he disputed the idea of human nature as the essence and argued that humans are not born human and that this inherent inhumanness never leaves us completely—in contrast to teleological interpretations that interpret the unhuman as only the initial stage of the life cycle.

Furthermore, as Veronica Vesterling notes, Lyotard's humans are permanently afflicted by high levels of "affectability" or sensitivity to external events, thus remaining finite and vulnerable in the universe, unable to express the sublime. In contrast to Kant, Lyotard does not believe that rationality compensates for the failure of the senses and imagination; moreover, what our imagination cannot grasp should not be suppressed or hidden. The only exception to humanity's inability to express the sublime are subversive and disruptive forms of "avant-garde" art, a realm at the periphery of society sufficiently detached from established language games, hence free of the prejudices and limits imposed by reason and convention. "Good art" is not about faithful representation or about harmony between form and contents as modernity would have us believe. It is not even about new ways to represent. For Lyotard, it is about discovering the limitations of representation and unmasking the unpresentable: Art becomes an important catalyst for social and political revolutionary change.

Failure to adapt to the world is significant not only in the anthropological sense but also politically. Lyotard built on Wittgenstein's theory of language as something complex, multifaceted, and governed by forces that are neither eternal nor universal.

He regards "language games" as phrases or utterances that carry their own rules—by being incommensurable and heterogeneous, they ensure the fragmentation of discourse. They can be descriptive (knowledge) or prescriptive (action). What phrases are chosen and which ones are silenced are political decisions. Mirroring his idea of the social world as fragmented and diverse, Lyotard's language games are individual expressions of conflicting realities, values, and practices from a range of social areas engaged in a power struggle. Just as there is no narrative superior to any other, there is no language that is higher than any other or capable of resolving conflict between the different language games. The important point is that discourses that are incommensurable should not be forced to speak a common homogeneous language, for that would not be just.

Taking this idea further, Lyotard conceptualized injustice in discourse in *The Differend*, argued by many to be Lyotard's most important book. The "differend" is a situation of unresolved language conflict where victims cannot present the wrong they suffered or their side of the story; the inability to negotiate the unpresentable is part of the notion of the sublime. Lyotard believes that the duty of philosophy is to continuously expose the differend or the misappropriation of language games. The matter of how ideas about reality and justice differ is also explored in *Au Juste*. Lyotard argued that a single "rational rule" of judgment cannot be applied to both parties in a dispute. In postmodernity, it is crucial that we build a system of ethics that includes a willingness to allow others to express their own language games. According to Lyotard, justice in modernity is rationalized by descriptive knowledge and universal preexisting criteria. He argued that it should instead be based on indeterminate reflective judgment, using the Kantian constitutive imagination, where the criteria differ in each case according to its own circumstances. This allows the coexistence of incommensurable and irreducible differences, a situation Lyotard refers to as *paganism*.

The Postmodern Condition (1979)

Arguably, *The Postmodern Condition* is Lyotard's most famous book. It was originally a report commissioned by the Council of Universities of the Quebec government on the status of knowledge in developed countries. It is regarded by many as the guiding text of postmodernism, extending its key ideas from the realm of art to that of sociopolitical and cultural theory. Others regard it as a critique of Jürgen Habermas's appeal to discursive coherence in the public sphere. At a basic level, *The Postmodern Condition* is a book about the effects of technological progress on the nature and role of knowledge. According to Lyotard, in modern advanced societies driven by "performativity" or efficient performance, knowledge becomes a commodity, a way to power rather than the means to a better life. Knowledge is linked to both science and language in the sense that there is scientific knowledge and narrative knowledge, the latter taking on a variety of forms or language games.

In *The Postmodern Condition*, Lyotard argues that grand narratives or metanarratives, which underpin modernity, have lost credibility. This is the postmodern condition, one of "incredulity towards metanarratives." Grand narratives are stories that set the rules for other narratives and language games by organizing knowledge in universal terms to justify the way things are or to explain the occurrence of important events, whether theological (e.g., the creation of the world) or political (e.g., capitalism). In modernity, Lyotard identifies two grand narratives: (1) the speculative narrative (knowledge is the basis of the progress of human life in the quest for truth) and (2) the emancipation narrative (which makes knowledge the prerequisite for human freedom in the pursuit of justice).

However, loss of faith means that narratives no longer have unifying power—identity and reason no longer play a legitimizing role in the formation of knowledge, values, and institutions. Knowledge is no longer the means to a better society underpinned by universal values. The world dominated by capitalism runs on efficiency and profitability, and these are the standards by which the nature and status of knowledge are determined. At the same time, societies become fragmented and individuals alienated from the networks and bonds they previously relied on. This moral and ethical disintegration has been identified by countless scholars as a problem. What makes Lyotard different is the fact that he thinks that the grand narratives themselves are the problem; thus, it is not a matter of replacing one narrative with another. In other words, consensus, compromise, and cooperation are not the solution, and neither is the forceful imposition of a single narrative. For Lyotard, the answer is small local narratives (*petit recits*) and the maximization of language games to ensure a difference.

Criticisms and Legacy

Lyotard's work, contentious at the best of times, has been condemned as philosophically and politically self-defeating. Can any political or legal system work without universal values and without a unifying vision or compromise of some sort? Another criticism is that the postmodern rejection of the Enlightenment does not take it into account that the rights of minority and exploited groups owe much to the values that emerged from it. Furthermore, in the anthropological sense, there seems to be little acceptance of human limitations, and the obsessive emphasis on diversity denies that humans, at least those who live in the same societies, do have some similarities. Finally, there is the most obvious trap for postmodernism to consider: Loss of faith in grand narratives is itself a narrative.

Despite these critiques, Lyotard's assault on grand narratives has important anthropological and political implications: He does not simply wish to tinker with the political spectrum, he wishes to change the very way in which we practice politics. Politics as we know it needs to shift beyond representation; furthermore, he is not concerned with political parties or ideologies but with a politics where difference is cherished rather than downsized and where small narratives speak about the unpresentable. Yet respect for diversity is not the only legacy: Lyotard's commitment to a sociopolitical system that is just and ethical rescues him from the emptiness of relativism and inspires those who wish to change the world for the better.

Daniela di Piramo

See also Baudrillard, Jean; Deleuze, Gilles, and Félix Guattari; Derrida, Jacques; Freud, Sigmund; Habermas, Jürgen; Lacan, Jacques; Modernism; Phenomenology; Postmodernism; Poststructuralism; Structuralism; Wittgenstein, Ludwig

Further Readings

Browning, G. K. (2000). *Lyotard and the end of grand narratives*. Cardiff, UK: University of Wales Press.

Dunn, A. (1993). A tyranny of justice: The ethics of Lyotard's differend. *Boundary 2, 20*(1), 92–220.

Malpas, S. (2003). *Jean-François Lyotard*. London, UK: Routledge.

Reading, B. (1991). *Introducing Lyotard: Art and politics*. London, UK: Routledge.

Rojek, C., & Turner, B. S. (Eds.). (1998). *The politics of Jean-Françoise Lyotard*. London, UK: Routledge.

Vasterling, V. (2003). Body and language: Butler, Merleau-Ponty and Lyotard on the speaking embodied subject. *International Journal of Philosophical Studies, 11*(2), 205–223.

Williams, J. (1998). *Lyotard: Towards a postmodern philosophy*. Cambridge, UK: Polity Press/Blackwell.